ANNICE MACLEOD

ANNICE MACLEOD

Marketing

Marketing

Concepts and Strategies

Tenth Edition

William M. Pride
Texas A & M University

O. C. Ferrell
University of Tampa
University of Memphis

Houghton Mifflin Company   Boston   New York

To Nancy, Michael, and Allen Pride

To Linda Ferrell

Sponsoring Editor: *Jennifer B. Speer*
Associate Sponsor: *Joanne M. Dauksewicz*
Senior Project Editor: *Margaret M. Kearney*
Senior Production/Design Coordinator: *Jill Haber*
Senior Manufacturing Coordinator: *Priscilla Bailey*
Marketing Manager: *Michael B. Mercier*
Senior Designer: *Henry Rachlin*

Cover Design: Chroma Design
Cover Image: "Earth in Space," Photri Inc., Virginia

Credits for advertisements and photographs:

Chapter 1 *Page 3:* © BMW of North America, Inc., Fallon McElligott Agency. *Page 5:* Reprinted with permission of MULLEN Agency; Creative Director, Paul Silverman; Copywriter, Paul Silverman; Art Director, Margaret McGovern; Photographer, David Stocklein. *Page 7:* Copyright 1995 Living Books. Dr. Seuss characters, text & images copyright TM 1995 Dr. Seuss Enterprises, L.P. All rights reserved. *Page 8 (left):* Reprinted with permission of Massachusetts Tobacco Control Program. *Page 8 (right):* Florida Department of Citrus. *Page 11:* Courtesy of Panasonic Company. *Page 13:* Great Brands of Europe, Inc. *Page 14:* Courtesy of Guess Home Collection.

(Credits continue on page 639.)

Printed in the U.S.A.

Library of Congress Catalog Card Number: 96-76948

Student Book ISBN: 0-395-78574-X
Examination Copy ISBN: 0-395-83793-6
Library Edition ISBN: 0-395-83684-0
International Edition ISBN: 0-395-85473-3

23456789-VH-00 99 98 97

Brief Contents

v

Contents

Chapter 11　　*Branding and Packaging* 248

Branding 250

Packaging 261

Labeling 266

Chapter 12　　*Services* 272

The Nature and Importance of Services 274

Characteristics of Services 275

Classification of Service Products 280

Chapter 16   *Physical Distribution* 367

Part 5   *Promotion Decisions* 391

Chapter 17   *Promotion: An Overview* 392

Preface

*A*s educators anticipating a new millennium, we are particularly aware of the challenges facing marketers today. The economic and social environment is constantly evolving—and with lightning speed. Technology, the global marketplace, diversity, and communication will no doubt continue to influence marketing decisions and the essential task of recognizing and responding to market opportunities.

This edition of *Marketing: Concepts and Strategies* provides a comprehensive framework for understanding how contemporary realities affect marketing decisions. The text has been thoroughly revised to provide the most up-to-date information about changes occurring in our economic and social systems. At the same time, we have been careful to retain the strengths that have made this one of the most popular introductory marketing texts in the United States and throughout the world.

Like its predecessors, the Tenth Edition explores the depth and breadth of the field, combining comprehensive coverage of marketing concepts and strategies with detailed and highly interesting real-world examples. Our primary goal—as always—is to equip students with the decision-making skills they will need to be successful in today's changing business climate. By focusing on the universal concerns of marketing decision makers, we demonstrate that marketing is a vital and challenging field of study—and a part of our world that influences almost everything we do.

New in the Tenth Edition

*T*o keep pace with developments in the teaching and practice of marketing, several important changes have been made to this edition:

- *A new chapter, Chapter 24, entitled "Marketing and the Internet."* This is a new chapter located on the Internet in the Pride/Ferrell Marketing Learning Center (http://www.hmco.com/college/PridFerr/home.html). This unique chapter explores how marketers are using the Internet in their strategies, their relationships with customers, and their day-to-day work. The Pride/Ferrell Marketing Learning Center is a one-stop guide to the world of online marketing. This site serves as a forum for marketers and students of marketing to discuss how the Internet is changing marketing. In addition to Chapter 24, the Marketing Learning Center also contains: **Internet Exercises** for Chapters 1-23; a **Research Center,** with links to marketing organizations, publications and other information sources; and the **Idea Exchange,** inviting you to share your perspective on marketing and the Internet.

- *Greater emphasis on the concept of relationship marketing.* A crucial aspect of today's market-driven competitive environment is the importance of customer value and customer relationships. This edition provides more complete coverage of this concept.

- *Greater emphasis on the importance of technology.* Many of the changes throughout the text relate to the use of technology in marketing. Topics such as the Internet and online marketing are addressed throughout the text. We also focus on the use of new technologies in marketing research, including database research, electronic bulletin boards, single source data, online information services, and E-mail surveys.

- *Greater emphasis on supply chain management.* The distribution chapters have been revised based on the concept of supply chain management. There is an emphasis placed on long-term partnerships among channel members working together to reduce inefficiencies, costs, and redundancies in order to heighten customer satisfaction.

- *New coverage of brand loyalty and brand equity.* The coverage of brand loyalty has been expanded. The new section on brand equity examines the four major elements that underlie brand equity, including brand name awareness, brand loyalty, perceived brand quality, and brand associations.

- *Expanded coverage of public relations.* The publicity coverage in the previous edition has been broadened into a discussion of public relations. Publicity is treated as a part of public relations in this new edition.

- *New chapter-opening vignettes, boxed features, and cases.* Almost all chapter opening-vignettes and boxed features are new in this edition. About half of all end-of-chapter cases are new.

- A thoroughly revised, contemporary *design* provides greater visual appeal. The *new* $8\frac{1}{2}$ *X 11 page size* takes full advantage of our loose-leaf format, allowing the text to be more easily placed within a binder along with student notes, syllabus, and handouts.

Features of the Book

As with previous editions, we are providing a comprehensive and practical introduction to marketing that is both easy to teach and to learn. The entire text is structured to excite students about the subject and to help them learn completely and efficiently.

- An *organizational model* at the beginning of each part provides a "roadmap" of the text and a visual tool for understanding the connection between concepts.

- *Learning objectives* at the start of each chapter give students concrete expectations about what they are to learn as they read the chapter.

- An *opening vignette* about a particular organization or current market trend introduces the topic for each chapter. Vignettes in the Tenth Edition include interesting anecdotes about the marketing issues surrounding a variety of products and organizations—products ranging from the BMW-Z3 to SnackWell's to Procter & Gamble's Uni Diapers, and organizations as vastly different as Boston Market, the Beverly Hills Hotel, Neiman Marcus, and the King Ranch. Interesting issues are also explored, such as McDonald's hot coffee lawsuit. Through these vignettes, students are exposed to contemporary marketing realities and are better prepared to understand and apply the concepts they will explore in the text.

- *Key term definitions* appear in the margin to help students build their marketing vocabulary.

- Numerous *figures*, *tables*, and *photographs* increase comprehension and stimulate interest.

- Four types of *boxed inserts* reinforce students' awareness of the particular issues affecting marketing and the types of choices and decisions marketers must make.

  The *Technology in Marketing* boxes include discussions about the impact of technological advances on the entertainment and medical industries, as well as information on how technology is currently used in marketing activities such as advertising and warehousing.

  The *Ethical Challenges* boxes raise students' awareness of ethical issues and the type of ethical choices that marketers face every day. Of particular interest to students will be the boxes on R.E.M.'s dispute with Hershey and on Calvin Klein's controversial ad campaigns. In addition, issues such as targeting underprivileged groups for certain products and preserving privacy on the Internet are examined.

The *Global Perspective* boxes examine global issues, such as the challenges of marketing to widely diverse cultures; global organizations, such as Gillette and PepsiCo; and global products, such as snack foods, personal care products, business machines—and even refrigerators!

The *Inside Marketing* boxes focus on recognizable firms and products and extend the text discussion of marketing issues and decisions. Topics of particular interest include the proliferation of the Nickelodeon brand and the use of movie tie-ins to products.

- A complete *chapter summary* reviews the major topics discussed, and the list of *important terms* provides another end-of-chapter study aid to expand students' marketing vocabulary.

- *Discussion and review questions* at the end of each chapter encourage further study and exploration of chapter content, and *application questions* enhance students' comprehension of important concepts.

- Two in-depth *cases* end each chapter to help students understand the application of chapter concepts. One of the end-of-chapter cases is related to a video segment and is identified by an icon. Approximately half of these cases are new to this edition. The new cases discuss marketing issues related to organizations and products such as Schwinn bicycles, Chili's restaurants, Walt Disney Company, and Windows '95.

- A *strategic case* at the end of each part helps students integrate the diverse concepts that have been discussed within the related chapters.

- A comprehensive *glossary* defines more than 625 important marketing terms.

- *Appendixes* discuss marketing career opportunities, explore financial analysis in marketing, and present a comprehensive example of a marketing plan.

- A *name index* and a *subject index* enable students to find topics of interest quickly.

Text Organization

*W*e have organized the seven parts of *Marketing: Concepts and Strategies* to give students a theoretical and practical understanding of marketing decision making. Part 1 presents an overview of marketing and examines marketing environment forces, ethics and social responsibility, and international marketing. Part 2 considers information systems and marketing research, consumer and industrial buying behavior, and target market analysis. Part 3 focuses on the conceptualization, development, management, and branding and packaging of goods and services. Part 4 deals with marketing channels, wholesaling, retailing, and physical distribution. Part 5 covers promotion decisions and methods including advertising, personal selling, sales promotion, and public relations. Part 6 is devoted to pricing decisions. Part 7 discusses strategic market planning, organization, implementation, and control.

A Comprehensive Instructional Resource Package

*F*or instructors, this edition of *Marketing: Concepts and Strategies* includes an exceptionally comprehensive package of teaching materials.

- The *Instructor's Resource Manual* includes a complete set of teaching tools. For each chapter of the text, there is (1) a teaching resources quick reference guide, (2) a purpose and perspective statement, (3) a guide for using the color transparencies, (4) a comprehensive lecture outline, (5) special class exercises, (6) a debate issue, (7) a chapter quiz, (8) answers to discussion and review questions, and (9) comments on the end-of-chapter cases. In addition, the Instructor's Resource Manual includes a video guide, comments on the end-of-part strategic cases, and answers to the questions posed at the end of Appendix B, "Financial Analysis in Marketing."

- *The Power Connection* is a unique classroom presentation program consisting of over 400 PowerPoint® slides relating to the learning objectives for each chapter in the text. The slides, created by Milton Pressley of The University of New Orleans, are completely original representations of the concepts in the book, providing additional insights and examples to reinforce learning. In addition, embedded within the program are lecture notes relating to each of the slides, which instructors can use or adapt as they wish.

- *Test Bank.* The *Test Bank* provides a total of more than 3,000 test items including true/false, multiple-choice, and essay questions for each chapter. Each objective test item comes with the correct answer, a main text page reference, and a key to whether the question tests knowledge, comprehension, or application. The *Test Bank* also provides difficulty and discrimination ratings derived from actual class testing for some of the multiple-choice questions. Lists of author-selected questions have been developed that facilitate quick construction of tests or quizzes. These author-selected lists of multiple-choice questions are representative of chapter content.

- *Computerized Test Generator.* This program is designed for use on IBM and IBM-compatible computers. With this program, the instructor can select questions from the *Test Bank* and produce a test master for easy duplication. The program gives instructors the option of selecting their own questions or having the program select them. It also allows instructors to create new questions and edit existing ones.

- *Call-in Test Service.* This service lets instructors select items from the *Test Bank* and call our toll-free number to order printed tests.

- *Color Transparencies.* A set of 250 color transparencies offers the instructor visual teaching assistance. About half of these are illustrations from the text; the rest are figures, tables, and diagrams that can be used as additional instructional aids.

- *Marketing Videotapes.* This series contains the videos for use with the end-of-chapter video cases. Specific information about each video is given in the Video Guide found in the Instructor's Resource Manual.

A Complete Package of Student Supplements

*O*ne of the most exciting developments related to this revision is the creation of an entire World Wide Web site for students and instructors. The site includes:

- *Chapter 24, entitled "Marketing and the Internet."* This chapter explores the world of online marketing and will be updated at least once every semester to incorporate the latest developments that impact marketing on the Internet.

- *Internet Exercises for Chapters 1-23.* These exercises reinforce chapter concepts by guiding students through specific Web sites and asking them to assess the success of the site and its information from a marketing perspective. Students will be invited to go online with the American Marketing Association, read recent articles in *Business Ethics* magazine, visit Restrac and the "Monster Board," explore American Airlines' NetsAAver fares—even order flowers—all while expanding their knowledge of marketing.

- *Research Center.* This comprehensive list provides links to a variety of marketing information resources and will be continually updated.

- *The Idea Exchange.* The Idea Exchange is a forum where students can share their perspectives about online marketing and the Internet.

In addition, the support package for this text continues to include these excellent learning resources:

- The *Study Guide,* which helps students to review and integrate content.

- *PC Study,* a self-instructional program for personal computers, which reinforces the learning of key marketing concepts.
- A new edition of *Marketer: A Simulation,* which gives student teams working on personal computers valuable decision-making experience.
- If instructors choose, *The Power Connection* slides may be custom published as a print supplement for students. In this custom-published version, printed representations of the slides are provided in a workbook format, with plenty of space next to each slide for note taking. The workbook can then be used by students as a study aid.

Comments and Suggestions Are Valued

*T*hrough the years, professors and students have sent us many helpful suggestions for improving the text and ancillary components. We invite your comments, questions, and criticisms. We want to do our best to provide materials that enhance the teaching and learning of marketing concepts and strategies. Your suggestions will be sincerely appreciated. Please write us, or E-mail us at w_pride@TAMU.EDU(Pride) or OCFerrell@AOL.COM(Ferrell), or call 409-845-5857(Pride) or 813-258-7532(Ferrell).

Acknowledgments

*L*ike most textbooks, this one reflects the ideas of a multitude of academicians and practitioners who have contributed to the development of the marketing discipline. We appreciate the opportunity to present their ideas in this book.

A number of individuals have made many helpful comments and recommendations in their reviews of this or earlier editions. We appreciate the generous help of these reviewers.

Zafar U. Ahmed
Minot State University

Thomas Ainscough
University of Massachusetts—Dartmouth

Joe F. Alexander
University of Northern Colorado

Mark I. Alpert
University of Texas at Austin

Linda K. Anglin
Mankato State University

George Avellano
Central State University

Emin Babakus
University of Memphis

Julie Baker
University of Texas—Arlington

Siva Balasabramanian
Southern Illinois University

Joseph Ballinger
Stephen F. Austin State University

Guy Banville
Creighton University

Joseph Barr
Framingham State College

Thomas E. Barry
Southern Methodist University

Charles A. Bearchell
California State University—Northridge

Richard C. Becherer
Wayne State University

Russell Belk
University of Utah

W. R. Berdine
California State Polytechnic Institute

Stewart W. Bither
Pennsylvania State University

Roger Blackwell
Ohio State University

Peter Bloch
University of Massachusetts—Amherst

Wanda Blockhus
San Jose State University

Paul N. Bloom
University of North Carolina

James P. Boespflug
Arapahoe Community College

Joseph G. Bonnice
Manhattan College

John Boos
Ohio Wesleyan University

James Brock
Montana State University

John R. Brooks, Jr.
Houston Baptist University

Jackie Brown
University of San Diego

William G. Browne
Oregon State University

John Buckley
Orange County Community College

Karen Burger
Pace University

Gul T. Butaney
Bentley College

Pat J. Calabro
University of Texas—Arlington

Linda Calderone
State University of New York College of Technology at Farmingdale

Joseph Cangelosi
University of Central Arkansas

James C. Carroll
University of Central Arkansas

Terry M. Chambers
Westminster College

Lawrence Chase
Tompkins Cortland Community College

Larry Chonko
Baylor University

Barbara Coe
North Texas State University

Ernest F. Cooke
Loyola College—Baltimore

Robert Copley
University of Louisville

John I. Coppett
University of Houston—Clear Lake

Robert Corey
West Virginia University

Deborah L. Cowles
Virginia Commonwealth University

Melvin R. Crask
University of Georgia

William L. Cron
Southern Methodist University

Bernice N. Dandridge
Diablo Valley College

Norman E. Daniel
Arizona State University

Lloyd M. DeBoer
George Mason University

Sally Dibb
University of Warwick

Ralph DiPietro
Montclair State University

Paul Dishman
Idaho State University

Suresh Divakar
Suny—Buffalo

Casey L. Donoho
Northern Arizona University

Peter T. Doukas
Westchester Community College

Lee R. Duffus
University of South Florida

Robert F. Dwyer
University of Cincinnati

Roland Eyears
Central Ohio Technical College

Thomas Falcone
Indiana University of Pennsylvania

Gwen Fontenot
University of Northern Colorado

Charles W. Ford
Arkansas State University

John Fraedrich
Southern Illinois University, Carbondale

David J. Fritzsche
University of Washington

Donald A. Fuller
University of Central Florida

Terry Gable
University of Memphis

Cathy Goodwin
University of Manitoba

Geoffrey L. Gordon
University of Kentucky

Robert Grafton-Small
University of Strathclyde

Harrison Grathwohl
California State University—Chico

Alan A. Greco
Winthrop College

Blaine S. Greenfield
Bucks County Community College

Thomas V. Greer
University of Maryland

Sharon F. Gregg
Middle Tennessee University

Jim L. Grimm
Illinois State University

Charles Gross
University of New Hampshire

Roy R. Grundy
College of DuPage

Joseph Guiltinan
University of Notre Dame

Robert R. Harmon
Portland State University

Mary C. Harrison
Amber University

Michael Hartline
Louisiana State University

Timothy Hartman
Ohio University

Salah S. Hassan
George Washington University

Del I. Hawkins
University of Oregon

Dean Headley
Wichita State University

Esther Headley
Wichita State University

Debbora Heflin-Bullock
California State Polytechnic University—Pomona

Merlin Henry
Rancho Santiago College

Neil Herndon
City Polytechnic of Hong Kong

Lois Herr
Elizabethtown College

Charles L. Hilton
Eastern Kentucky University

Elizabeth C. Hirschman
Rutgers, State University of New Jersey

Robert D. Hisrich
University of Tulsa

George C. Hozier
University of New Mexico

John R. Huser
Illinois Central College

Ron Johnson
Colorado Mountain College

Theodore F. Jula
Stonehill College

Peter F. Kaminski
Northern Illinois University

Yvonne Karsten
Mankato State University

Jerome Katrichis
Temple University

James Kellaris
University of Cincinnati

Alvin Kelly
Florida A&M University

Philip Kemp
DePaul University

Sylvia Keyes
Bridgewater State College

William M. Kincaid, Jr.
Oklahoma State University

Roy Klages
State University of New York at Albany

Douglas Kornemann
Milwaukee Area Technical College

Priscilla LaBarbara
New York University

Patricia Laidler
Massasoit Community College

Bernard LaLonde
Ohio State University

Richard A. Lancioni
Temple University

David M. Landrum
University of Central Oklahoma

Irene Lange
California State University—Fullerton

Geoffrey P. Lantos
Stonehill College

Charles L. Lapp
University of Texas—Dallas

Virginia Larson
San Jose State University

John Lavin
Waukesha County Technical Institute

Hugh E. Law
East Tennessee University

Ron Lennon
Barry University

Richard C. Leventhal
Metropolitan State College

Jay D. Lindquist
Western Michigan University

Terry Loe
Baylor University

Mary Logan
Southwestern Assemblies of God College

Paul Londrigan
Mott Community College

Anthony Lucas
Community College of Allegheny County

George Lucas
University of Memphis

William Lundstrom
Old Dominion University

Rhonda Mack
College of Charleston

Stan Madden
Baylor University

Patricia M. Manninen
North Shore Community College

Gerald L. Manning
Des Moines Area Community College

Allen S. Marber
University of Bridgeport

Gayle J. Marco
Robert Morris College

James McAlexander
Oregon State University

Donald McCartney
University of Wisconsin—Green Bay

Jack McNiff
State University of New York College of Technology at Farmingdale

Lee Meadow
Northern Illinois University

Jeffrey A. Meier
Fox Valley Technical College

James Meszaros
County College of Morris

Brian Meyer
Mankato State University

Martin Meyers
University of Wisconsin/Stevens Point

Stephen J. Miller
Oklahoma State University

William Moller
University of Michigan

Kent B. Monroe
University of Illinois

Carlos W. Moore
Baylor University

Carol Morris-Calder
Loyola Marymount University

David Murphy
Madisonville Community College

Keith Murray
Northeastern University

Sue Ellen Neeley
University of Houston—Clear Lake

Terrence V. O'Brien
Northern Illinois University

Mike O'Neill
California State University—Chico

Allan Palmer
University of North Carolina at Charlotte

Teresa Pavia
University of Utah

John Perrachione
Northeast Missouri State University

Michael Peters
Boston College

Lana Podolak
Community College of Beaver County

Thomas Ponzurick
West Virginia University

William Prescutti
Duquesne University

Kathy Pullins
Columbus State Community College

Victor Quinones
University of Puerto Rico

Daniel Rajaratnam
Baylor University

James D. Reed
Louisiana State University—Shreveport

William Rhey
University of Tampa

Glen Riecken
East Tennessee State University

Winston Ring
University of Wisconsin—Milwaukee

Ed Riordan
Wayne State University

Robert A. Robicheaux
University of Alabama

Robert H. Ross
Wichita State University

Michael L. Rothschild
University of Wisconsin—Madison

Bert Rosenbloom
Drexel University

Kenneth L. Rowe
Arizona State University

Elise Sautter
New Mexico State University

Ronald Schill
Brigham Young University

Bodo Schlegelmilch
American Graduate School of International Management

Edward Schmitt
Villanova University

Donald Sciglimpaglia
San Diego State University

Stanley Scott
University of Alaska—Anchorage

Harold S. Sekiguchi
University of Nevada—Reno

Richard J. Semenik
University of Utah

Beheruz N. Sethna
Lamar University

Steven J. Shaw
University of South Carolina

Terence A. Shimp
University of South Carolina

Carolyn F. Siegel
Eastern Kentucky University

Dean C. Siewers
Rochester Institute of Technology

Lyndon Simkin
University of Warwick

Paul J. Solomon
University of South Florida

Robert Solomon
Stephen F. Austin State University

Sheldon Somerstein
City University of New York

Rosann L. Spiro
Indiana University

William Staples
University of Houston—Clear Lake

Bruce Stern
Portland State University

Claire F. Sullivan
Metropolitan State University

Robert Swerdlow
Lamar University

Hal Teer
James Madison University

Ira Teich
Long Island University—C. W. Post

Debbie Thorne
University of Tampa

Dillard Tinsley
Stephen F. Austin State University

Sharynn Tomlin
Angelo State University

Hale Tongren
George Mason University

James Underwood
University of Southwest Louisiana

Barbara Unger
Western Washington University

Tinus Van Drunen
Universiteit Twente (Netherlands)

Dale Varble
Indiana State University

R. Vish Viswanathan
University of Northern Colorado

Charles Vitaska
Metropolitan State College

Kirk Wakefield
University of Mississippi

Harlan Wallingford
Pace University

James F. Wenthe
Georgia College

Sumner M. White
Massachusetts Bay Community College

Alan R. Wiman
Rider College

Ken Wright
*West Australia College of Advanced
Education—Churchland Campus*

George Wynn
James Madison University

We deeply appreciate the assistance of Barbara Gilmer and Pam Swartz for providing editorial suggestions, technical assistance, and support. Gwyneth M. Vaughn made significant contributions as an editorial consultant. For assistance in completing numerous tasks associated with the text and ancillary components, we express appreciation to Terry Gable, Terry Loe, Heather Bowen, Nina DeRouen, Todd Lybeck, Leonard Sifuentes, Phylis Mansfield, Teresa Franks, and Neva Joyce Walkoviak.

We appreciate Milton Pressley, the University of New Orleans, for developing *The Power Connection.* For creating *Marketer: A Simulation,* we wish to thank Jerald R. Smith, University of Louisville. We also wish to thank Kirk Wakefield, University of Mississippi, for developing the class exercises included in the *Instructor's Resource Manual.* We especially thank Jim L. Grimm, Illinois State University, for drafting the financial analysis appendix.

We express appreciation for the support and encouragement given to us by our colleagues at Texas A & M University, the University of Memphis, and the University of Tampa.

WILLIAM M. PRIDE
O. C. FERRELL

*T*he U.S. market for "roadsters," two-seat convertible sports cars, has shifted into high gear after sputtering in neutral for years. Once dominated by the Germans and British, and now ruled almost solely by Japan's Mazda Miata, the roadster market will soon include a new Corvette, the Porsche Boxster, the Mercedes SLK, and BMW's recently launched Z3.

BMW hopes the Z3 will evoke fond memories of the alluring roadsters of the past. Its broad curves are reminiscent of the BMW 327/8 roadsters of the 1930s, while its side air vents and front bumper guards recall the BMW 507 of the late 1950s. Slightly larger than its chief rival, the Mazda Miata, the Z3 has a similar profile with the "long nose" and "short tail" of the classic roadster. The Z3, which made its U.S. debut at the Detroit auto show in January 1996, is available in two 1.8 liter, 4-cylinder models, with either a 5-speed manual or automatic transmission, and a manual ragtop roof. A 2.8 liter, 6-cylinder model with an automatic roof will soon be introduced. The German-designed roadster is being built at BMW's plant in Spartanburg, South Carolina, which plans to produce 30,000 Z3s a year.

Americans got their first eye-opening look at the Z3 in the latest James Bond thriller, *Golden-*

Eye. Getting the car in[...] feat, one BMW was qu[...] spy known for his hi[...] cars usually drives ultr[...] cles. A special edition[...] replica of the Z3 driv[...] James Bond in the m[...] Neiman Marcus Chr[...] model sports a special[...] telephone; hi-fi stereo[...] high-tech beige leather[...] shift knob, console, an[...] alloy wheels; wind de[...] roadster luggage. Price[...] vehicles initially offered[...] mas catalog sold out in[...] make an additional eig[...] available to Neiman M[...] customer requests as po[...]

BMW priced the re[...] about $28,750 in the Un[...] more than the MX-5 Mia[...] allows BMW to take a hig[...] compete head on with[...] world's best-selling ragto[...] Boxster and the Merced[...] into the U.S. market mor[...] higher—both are priced[...]

Part 1

Marketing and Its Environment

*I*n Part 1 we introduce the field of marketing and offer a broad perspective from which to explore and analyze various components of the marketing discipline. In the first chapter we define marketing and discuss why an understanding of it is useful in many aspects of everyday life, including one's career. We provide an overview of general strategic marketing issues, such as market opportunity analysis, target market selection, and marketing mix development. Marketers should understand how environmental forces can affect customers and their responses to marketing strategies. In Chapter 2 we consider competitive, economic, political, legal and regulatory, technological, and sociocultural forces in the marketing environment. Chapter 3 deals with the role of ethics and social responsibility in marketing decisions. In Chapter 4 the nature, opportunities, and challenges of international marketing are discussed.

Chapter 1

An Overview of Strategic Marketing

- To be able to define marketing
- To understand why a person should study marketing
- To gain insight into the basic elements of the marketing concept and its implementation
- To understand the major components of a marketing strategy
- To gain a sense of general strategic marketing issues, such as market opportunity analysis, target market selection, and marketing mix development
- To understand the purpose and major elements of the marketing plan

BMW
revved-up

4

Will the BMW Z3 overtake the Mazda Miata in the U.S. roadster market? Tying the car to James Bond in consumers' minds will stimulate interest, but only time will tell whether BMW has fashioned a successful strategy for marketing the Z3. The automaker must develop a product that consumers want, communicate useful information about it to excite consumer interest, price it appropriately, and make it available when and where consumers may want to buy it. And even if BMW does these things well, competition from rival car makers, economic conditions, and other factors may affect the Z3's success.

This first chapter introduces the concepts and decisions covered in the text. In this chapter we first develop a definition of marketing and explain each element of the definition. Then we look at some of the reasons why people should study marketing. We introduce the marketing concept and consider several issues associated with implementing it. Next we define and discuss the major tasks associated with marketing strategy: market opportunity analysis, target market selection, marketing mix development, and management of marketing activities. We conclude by discussing the marketing plan.

Marketing Defined

Marketing The process of creating, distributing, promoting, and pricing goods, services, and ideas to facilitate satisfying exchange relationships in a dynamic environment

*I*f you ask several people what *marketing* is, you are likely to hear a variety of descriptions. Marketing encompasses many more activities than most people realize. In this book, we define **marketing** as the process of creating, distributing, promoting, and pricing goods, services, and ideas to facilitate satisfying exchange relationships in a dynamic environment.

In this definition, an **exchange** is the provision or transfer of goods, services, or ideas in return for something of value. Any product may be involved in a marketing exchange. We assume only that individuals and organizations expect to gain a reward in excess of the costs incurred. We now examine selected parts of the definition more closely.

Exchange The provision or transfer of goods, services, or ideas in return for something of value

■ Marketing Deals with Products, Distribution, Promotion, and Pricing

Marketing is more than simply advertising or selling a product; it involves developing and managing a product that will satisfy customer needs. It focuses on making the product available in the right place and at a price that is acceptable to customers. It also requires communicating information that helps customers determine if the product will satisfy their needs.

■ Marketing Focuses on Goods, Services, and Ideas

Product A good, service, or idea

For purposes of discussion in this text, a **product** can be a good, a service, or an idea. A *good* is a physical entity one can touch. A Ford Explorer, a Garth Brooks compact disc, a box of Kellogg's Frosted Flakes, and a kitten in a pet store are examples of goods. A *service* is the application of human and mechanical efforts to people or objects to provide intangible benefits to customers. Air travel, dry cleaning, banking, medical care, and day care are examples of services. *Ideas* include concepts, philosophies, images, and issues. For instance, a marriage counselor, for a fee, gives spouses ideas to help improve their relationship. Other marketers of ideas include political parties, churches, and schools. In Figure 1.1, the North Shore Equestrian Center can be said to be a marketer of ideas as well as services.

■ Marketing Facilitates Satisfying Exchange Relationships

Individuals and organizations engage in marketing to facilitate exchanges. Businesses as well as nonprofit organizations—such as colleges and universities, charitable organizations, hospitals, and conservation groups like the World Wildlife Fund—perform marketing activities. For example, colleges and universities and their students engage in exchanges. To receive instruction, knowledge, a degree, use of facilities, and sometimes room and board, students give up time, money, and perhaps services in the form of labor;

Figure 1.1
Ideas and Services
Marketing
By inspiring people to think about the excitement and adventure of horseback riding, The North Shore Equestrian Center hopes to convince consumers to use its services.

they may also give up opportunities to do other things. Inside Marketing describes how the Texas Parks and Wildlife Department is using marketing to boost revenues and foster exchanges.

For an exchange to take place, four conditions must exist. First, two or more individuals, groups, or organizations must participate. Second, each party must possess something of value that the other party desires. Third, each party must be willing to give up its "something of value" to receive the "something of value" held by the other. For example, if you want to acquire the latest CD by Hootie and the Blowfish, you must be willing to shell out approximately $15 for it at your favorite music store. The objective of a marketing exchange is to receive something that is desired more than what is given up to get it. Fourth, the parties to the exchange must be able to communicate with each other and to make their somethings of value available.[2]

Figure 1.2 illustrates the exchange process. The arrows indicate that the parties communicate that each has something of value available to exchange. An exchange will not necessarily take place just because these four conditions exist, but even if there is no exchange, marketing activities have still occurred. The somethings of value held by the two parties are most often products and/or financial resources, such as money or credit. When an exchange occurs, products are traded for other products or for financial resources.

Marketing activities should attempt to create and maintain satisfying exchange relationships. To maintain an exchange relationship, buyers must be satisfied with the

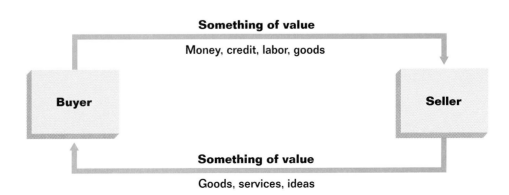

Something of value

Money, credit, labor, goods

Buyer

Seller

Something of value

Goods, services, ideas

Figure 1.2
Exchange Between
Buyer and Seller

INSIDE MARKETING

Texas State Parks Employ Creative Marketing

At the same time that record numbers of people are heading to our state and national parks to enjoy family vacations and to flee workplace stress, those same people, as taxpayers, are demanding more effective and efficient use of government funds. The result? The parks face bigger crowds, but with tighter budgets. Providing value to park users while conserving valuable natural and historic resources has thus become a complex challenge for parks departments in every state.

The Texas Parks and Wildlife Department (TPWD), which oversees 130 state parks as well as numerous wildlife management areas and other sites, is working to meet this challenge by applying basic business and marketing principles to its operations. TPWD has implemented a new program called the "entrepreneurial budget system," through which it hopes to become economically self-sufficient. The program encourages individual park managers to come up with their own fund-raising methods and frees them to allocate their own budgets.

Many TPWD parks have started their own gift shops and now offer special guided bird- or animal-watching, native plant-identification, and other tours.

Brazos Bend State Park created its own logo, an alligator dressed as a forest ranger, for use on souvenirs sold in its gift shop. At Longhorn Cavern State Park, campers can pay $190 for the chance to search underground caverns for treasure purportedly buried by legendary outlaw Sam Bass. Mother Neff State Park guests can rent a converted headquarters building for family reunions and other events.

TPWD also puts out a four-color retail catalog of novelties such as Texas-style Christmas cards, T-shirts and other apparel, books, maps, art, educational toys, and stuffed animals. The agency offers special package tours, including a longhorn cattle drive in Big Bend State Park and trips to Mexico. It has even introduced its own low-interest, no-annual-fee Visa credit card that comes in three pretty nature designs. TPWD gets a half-cent of every dollar consumers spend using the cards.

The new program is definitely paying off. In its first year, park revenue increased 23 percent to nearly $20 million, meaning the parks paid for about 62 percent of their $32 million budget, up from 50 percent the year before.

Sources: Caleb Solomon, "State Parks Hunt for Cash in the Wilds of Capitalism," *Wall Street Journal*, June 7, 1995, p. T1; "Texas Parks and Wildlife Collection," special advertisement supplement appearing in *Texas Monthly*, Nov. 1995; and "Today's Riddle: How Is a Parks Service Like a Bank?" *Wall Street Journal*, Sept. 27, 1995, p. T2.

obtained good, service, or idea, and sellers must be satisfied with the financial reward or something else of value received. A dissatisfied customer often searches for other sellers and new exchange relationships.

Maintaining positive relationships with buyers is an important goal for a seller. Through buyer-seller interaction, a buyer develops expectations about a seller's future behavior. To fulfill these expectations, the seller must deliver on promises made. Over time, a healthy buyer-seller relationship results in interdependencies between the two parties. Dave Thomas, founder of Wendy's, indicates that the success of his business rests on repeat purchases. His customers' expectations include good food, reasonable prices, and clean restaurants staffed by clean, polite people.[3]

■ *Marketing Occurs in a Dynamic Environment*

The marketing environment consists of many changing forces: competition, economic conditions, political pressures, laws, regulations, technological advances, and sociocultural factors. The effects of these forces on customers and marketers can be dramatic and difficult to predict. They can create threats to marketers and also generate opportunities for new products and new methods of reaching customers. Figure 1.3 shows how traditional children's books have altered their format to take advantage of technological advances.

**Figure 1.3
Technology
Generates New
Product Opportunities**
Publishers are taking
advantage of changing
technology by making their
children's books available
on CD-ROM.

Why Study Marketing?

*T*he definition of marketing reveals some of the obvious reasons why the study of marketing is relevant. In this section we discuss several perhaps less obvious reasons why one should study marketing.

■ *Marketing Is Used in Many Organizations*

From 25 to 33 percent of all civilian workers in the United States perform marketing activities. The marketing field offers a variety of interesting and challenging career opportunities, such as personal selling, advertising, packaging, transportation, storage, marketing research, product development, wholesaling, and retailing. In addition, many individuals working for nonbusiness organizations engage in marketing activities to promote political, cultural, church, civic, and charitable activities. Whether a person earns a living through marketing activities or performs them voluntarily for a nonprofit group, marketing knowledge and skills are valuable assets.

■ *Marketing Is Important to Businesses and the Economy*

Businesses must sell products to survive and grow, and marketing activities help sell their products. Financial resources generated from sales can be used to develop innovative products. New products allow a firm to better satisfy customers' changing needs, which in turn enables the firm to generate more profits.

Marketing activities help produce the profits that are essential not only to the survival of individual businesses, but also to the health and ultimate survival of the whole economy. Profits drive economic growth because without them businesses find it difficult, if not impossible, to buy more raw materials, hire more employees, attract more capital, and create additional products that in turn make more profits.

■ *Marketing Knowledge Enhances Consumer Awareness*

Besides contributing to the well-being of our nation, marketing activities help improve the quality of our lives. In Figure 1.4, the Massachusetts Department of Public Health attempts to educate consumers about the hazards of second-hand smoke, and Florida

**Figure 1.4
Marketing
Efforts Can Improve
Quality of Life**
These ads enlighten
consumers about the
hazards of second-hand
smoke and the benefits
of drinking orange juice.

orange juice producers promote the health aspects of drinking orange juice. Studying marketing allows us to weigh costs, benefits, and flaws more effectively. We can determine which marketing efforts need improvement and how to attain that goal. For example, an unsatisfactory experience with a warranty may make you wish for stricter law enforcement so that sellers would fulfill their promises. You may have also wished that you had more accurate information about a product before you purchased it. Understanding marketing enables us to evaluate corrective measures (such as laws, regulations, and industry guidelines) that could stop unfair, damaging, or unethical marketing practices. Consumers today demand that marketing claims accurately reflect the products in question. Figure 1.5 indicates how consumers go about obtaining product information and giving feedback after buying. In the future, online communication through the Internet, especially the World Wide Web, will connect more and more consumers seeking and submitting product information.

■ Marketing Costs Consume a Sizable Portion of Buyers' Dollars

Studying marketing will make you aware that many marketing activities are necessary to provide satisfying goods and services. Obviously, these marketing activities cost money. About one-half of a buyer's dollar goes for marketing costs. If you spend $15.00 on a new

**Figure 1.5
Methods Consumers
Use to Request
Information and
Express Opinion**

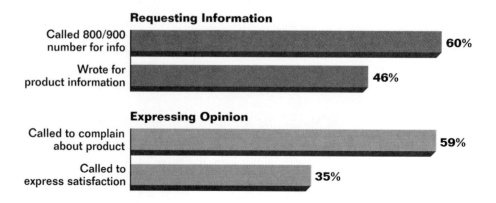

compact disc, about $7.50 goes toward activities related to distribution and the retailer's expenses and profit margin. The production (pressing) of the CD represents about 90 cents, or 6 percent of its price. A family with a monthly income of $3,000 that allocates $600 to taxes and savings spends about $2,400 for goods and services. Of this amount, $1,200 goes for marketing activities. If marketing expenses consume that much of your dollar, you should know how this money is used.

The Marketing Concept

*S*ome firms have sought success by buying land, building a factory, equipping it with people and machines, and then making a product that they believe customers need. However, these firms frequently fail to attract buyers with what they have to offer because they defined their business as "making a product" rather than as "helping potential customers satisfy their needs and wants." Such organizations have failed to implement the marketing concept.

Marketing concept
A managerial philosophy that an organization should try to satisfy customers' needs through a coordinated set of activities that also allows the organization to achieve its goals

According to the **marketing concept,** an organization should try to provide products that satisfy customers' needs through a coordinated set of activities that also allows the organization to achieve its goals. Customer satisfaction is the major focus of the marketing concept. An organization must determine what customers want and use this information to create satisfying products. The organization must also continue to alter, adapt, and develop products to keep pace with customers' changing desires and preferences. Taco Bell, for example, introduced its Border Lights line of reduced-fat menu items to satisfy older adults and families increasingly concerned about trimming the fat from their diet.[4] The marketing concept emphasizes that marketing begins and ends with customers. The Texas Parks and Wildlife Department's fund-raising projects (described in Inside Marketing) demonstrate that nonbusinesses can also apply the marketing concept. By offering parks-related gifts and tours, the agency is educating and entertaining its "customers"—park users—and thereby making the parks experience more satisfying for them, while at the same time helping itself become more economically self-sufficient so that it can provide greater value for both taxpayers and tourists.

The marketing concept is not a second definition of marketing. It is a management philosophy guiding an organization's overall activities. This philosophy affects all organizational activities, not just marketing. Production, finance, accounting, personnel, and marketing departments must work together.

The marketing concept is not a philanthropic philosophy aimed at helping customers at the expense of the organization. A firm that adopts the marketing concept must satisfy not only its customers' objectives, but also its own, or it will not stay in business long. The overall objectives of a business might relate to increasing profits, market share, sales, or a combination of all three. The marketing concept stresses that an organization can best achieve these objectives by providing customer satisfaction. Thus, implementing the marketing concept should benefit the organization as well as its customers.

It is important for marketers to consider not only their current customers' needs, but also the long-term needs of society. Striving to satisfy customers' desires by sacrificing society's long-term welfare is unacceptable. For example, while parents want disposable diapers that are comfortable, absorbent, and safe for their babies, society in general does not want nonbiodegradable disposable diapers, which create tremendous landfill problems now and for the future. Marketers are expected to act in a socially responsible manner, an idea we discuss in more detail in Chapters 2 and 3.

■ *Evolution of the Marketing Concept*

The marketing concept may seem like an obvious approach to running a business. However, businesspeople have not always believed that the best way to make sales and profits is to satisfy customers.

The Production Era During the second half of the nineteenth century, the Industrial Revolution was in full force in the United States. Electricity, rail transportation, division of labor, assembly lines, and mass production made it possible to manufacture products more efficiently. With new technology and new ways of using labor, products poured into the marketplace, where consumer demand for manufactured goods was strong.

The Sales Era   In the 1920s, strong consumer demand for products subsided. Businesses realized that they would have to "sell" products to consumers. From the mid-1920s to the early 1950s, businesses viewed sales as the major means of increasing profits, and this period came to have a sales orientation. Businesspeople believed that the most important marketing activities were personal selling, advertising, and distribution.

The Marketing Era   By the early 1950s, some businesspeople began to recognize that efficient production and extensive promotion did not guarantee that customers would buy products. These businesses, and many others since, found that they must first determine what customers want and then produce it, rather than make products and try to persuade customers that they need what is produced. As more organizations realized the importance of satisfying customers' needs, U.S. businesses entered the marketing era, one of marketing orientation. Today, businesses want to satisfy customers and build meaningful long-term buyer-seller relationships. The term **relationship marketing** refers to "long-term, mutually beneficial arrangements in which both the buyer and seller focus on value enhancement through the creation of more satisfying exchanges."[5] Relationship marketing continually deepens the customer's dependence on the company, and as the customer's confidence grows, this in turn increases the firm's understanding of the customer's needs. Successful companies respond to customer needs and strive to increase value to customers over time. Eventually, this interaction becomes a solid relationship that allows for cooperative problem solving. For example, Netscape Communications Corp. offered cash or prizes to any user who could find serious flaws in the new version of its software for browsing the Internet's World Wide Web.[6]

Relationship marketing
Establishing long-term, mutually satisfying buyer-seller relationships

■ *Implementing the Marketing Concept*

A philosophy may sound reasonable and look good on paper, but that does not mean it can be put into practice easily. To implement the marketing concept, an organization must accept some general conditions and recognize and deal with several problems. Consequently, the marketing concept has yet to be fully accepted by all American businesses.

Management must first establish an information system to discover customers' real needs and use the information to create satisfying products. When M&M Mars asked consumers to choose a new M&M color to replace tan, 10.2 million people cast a candy-color vote by mail, phone, fax, and E-mail. Blue received 54 percent of the vote, with purple, pink, and "no change" losing.[7] Within months, blue joined red, green, yellow, orange and dark brown in the M&M lineup. This example illustrates one method for discovering information about consumers' desires and responding in a way that forges a positive marketing relationship. Because an information system is usually expensive, management must commit money and time for its development and maintenance. Without an adequate information system, an organization cannot be customer-oriented.

To satisfy customers' objectives as well as its own, a company must also coordinate all activities. This may require restructuring the internal operations and overall objectives of one or more departments. If the head of the marketing unit is not a member of the organization's top-level management, he or she should be. Some departments may have to be abolished and new ones created. Implementing the marketing concept demands the support not only of top management, but also of managers and staff at all levels.

Market orientation
An organizationwide commitment to researching and responding to customer needs

Effective implementation of the marketing concept also requires a **market orientation,** the "organizationwide generation of market intelligence pertaining to current and future customer needs, dissemination of the intelligence across departments, and organizationwide responsiveness to it."[8] In Figure 1.6, Technics demonstrates a strong market orientation through the development and promotion of its new musical synthesizer. Research has shown a positive relationship between market orientation and perfor-

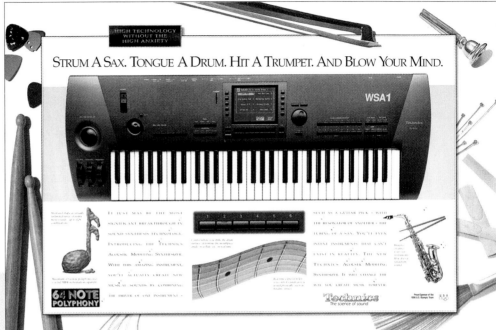

Figure 1.6
Developing a
Market Orientation
Technics directly
responds to consumer
needs by creating and
promoting its break-
through synthesizer for
musicians who want to
explore radically new
musical sounds.

mance.[9] Top management, marketing managers, nonmarketing (production, finance, personnel, and so on) managers, and customers are all important in developing and carrying out a market orientation. Unless marketing managers provide continuous customer-focused leadership with minimal interdepartmental conflict, achieving a market orientation will be difficult. Nonmarketing managers must communicate with marketing managers to share information important to understanding the customer. Finally, a market orientation involves being responsive to ever-changing customer needs and wants. Trying to assess what customers want, difficult to begin with, is further complicated by the speed with which fashions and tastes can change. For example, sales of so-called New Age beverages such as Snapple, Fruitopia, and Clearly Canadian grew rapidly in the early 1990s. Because these products were purchased mainly by trendy young consumers constantly looking for the new and different, sales for this beverage category have declined to one-third of their early 1990 levels.[10]

Achieving the full profit potential of each customer relationship should be the fundamental goal of every marketing strategy. Marketing relationships with customers are the lifeblood of all businesses. At the most basic level, profits can be obtained through relationships in the following ways: (1) by acquiring new customers, (2) by enhancing the profitability of existing customers, and (3) by extending the duration of customer relationships.[11] Implementing the marketing concept means optimizing the exchange relationship, which is the relationship between a company's financial investment in customer relationships and the return generated by customers responding to that investment.[12]

Marketing Strategy

Marketing strategy
A plan of action for developing, distributing, promoting, and pricing products that meet the needs of specific customers

*T*o expedite exchanges and develop beneficial exchange relationships, a firm's marketing managers must develop and manage marketing strategies. A **marketing strategy** is a plan of action for developing, distributing, promoting, and pricing products that meet the needs of specific customers. A marketing strategy articulates the best use of the firm's resources and tactics to meet its objectives. To develop and manage marketing strategies, marketers focus on several tasks: selecting a target market, developing a marketing mix, assessing environmental forces, and managing marketing efforts

Environment and market opportunity analysis

▸ The marketing environment (Chapter 2)
▸ Marketing ethics and social responsibility (Chapter 3)
▸ Global markets and international marketing (Chapter 4)
▸ Information systems and marketing research (Chapter 5)
▸ Consumer markets and buying behavior (Chapter 6)
▸ Organizational markets and buying behavior (Chapter 7)
▸ Target market segmentation and evaluation (Chapter 8)

Marketing mix development

▸ Product decisions (Chapters 9, 10, 11, and 12)
▸ Distribution decisions (Chapters 13, 14, 15, and 16)
▸ Promotion decisions (Chapters 17, 18, and 19)
▸ Price decisions (Chapters 20 and 21)

Marketing management

▸ Strategic market planning (Chapter 22)
▸ Marketing implementation and control (Chapter 23)

Figure 1.7
Marketing Strategy Tasks

effectively. Figure 1.7 shows which chapters of this book discuss each of these tasks. Figure 1.8 presents the components of the marketing mix and the marketing environment.

■ *Marketing Strategy: Target Market Selection*

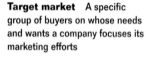
Target market   A specific group of buyers on whose needs and wants a company focuses its marketing efforts

A **target market** is a specific group of buyers on whose needs and wants a company focuses its marketing efforts. (Note, then, that the buyer is at the center of Figure 1.8.) The marketer of Kix cereal, for example, targets its brand at mothers with children under twelve. Evian, in Figure 1.9, promotes the health aspects of its natural spring water,

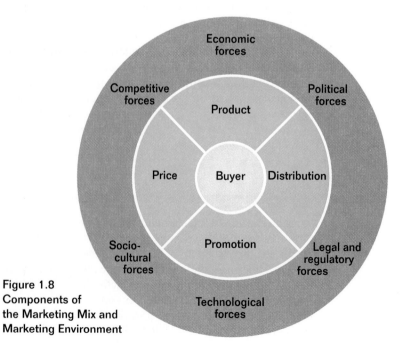

Figure 1.8
Components of
the Marketing Mix and
Marketing Environment

Figure 1.9
Appealing to Target Market Needs
Evian promotes its natural spring water to fitness-conscious consumers.

appealing to the fitness conscious. Marketing managers may define a target market as a vast number of people or as a relatively small group. Rolls-Royce, for example, targets its automobiles at a small, very exclusive market—wealthy people who want the ultimate in prestige in an automobile. Some companies target multiple target markets, with different products, promotion, prices, and distribution systems for each market. Nike uses this strategy, marketing different types of shoes to meet specific needs of cross-trainers, basketball players, aerobics enthusiasts, and athletic shoe buyers.

When choosing a target market, marketing managers try to evaluate possible markets to see how entering them would affect the company's sales, costs, and profits. They assess whether the company has the resources to develop the right mix of product, price, promotion, and distribution to meet the needs of a particular target market. They also determine if satisfying those needs is consistent with the firm's overall objectives. The size and number of competitors already marketing products in possible target markets are of concern as well.

Market opportunity A combination of circumstances and timing that permits an organization to take action to reach a particular target market

A **market opportunity** exists when the right combination of circumstances and timing permit an organization to take action to reach a particular target market. A significant market opportunity for Microsoft, the marketer of the Windows 95 computer operating system, is home computer owners. Although growth of the corporate PC market—Microsoft's traditional strength—is slowing to 10 percent a year, the home market is increasing by 30 percent annually. To capitalize on this opportunity, Microsoft's consumer division developed twenty new consumer software programs and new hardware including a computer track ball for kids called Easy Ball and a precision joy stick for computer games called Sidewinder.[13]

Marketers need to be able to recognize and analyze market opportunities. In fact an organization's very survival depends on developing products that satisfy its target market(s). Few organizations can assume that products popular today will interest buyers in five years, or even next year. To stay competitive a company can choose among several alternatives for continued product development that will achieve its objectives and satisfy buyers: it can modify existing products (for example, Oscar Mayer and Armour have reduced the fat content of some meat products to address increasing health concerns among consumers), introduce new products (such as Microsoft's computer track ball and joy stick), or delete some that customers no longer want (such as the Jeep Wagoneer).

Accurate target market selection is crucial to productive marketing efforts. Products and even companies sometimes fail because marketers do not identify appropriate customer groups at which to aim their efforts. Organizations that try to be all things to all people rarely satisfy the needs of any customer group very well. An organization's management must therefore designate which customer groups the firm is trying to serve and must gather adequate information about these customers. Identification and analysis of a target market provide a foundation on which a marketing mix can be developed.

■ *Marketing Strategy: Marketing Mix Development*

Marketing mix Four marketing activities—product, distribution, promotion, and pricing—that a firm can control to meet customer needs

The **marketing mix** refers to four marketing activities—product, distribution, promotion, and pricing—that the firm can control to meet the needs of customers within its target market. These four activities are called marketing mix decision variables because a marketing manager decides what type of each element to use and in what amounts. A primary goal of a marketing manager is to create and maintain a marketing mix that satisfies consumers' needs for a general product type. Note in Figure 1.8 that the marketing mix is built around the buyer (a principle also stressed by the marketing concept).

Marketing mix variables are often viewed as controllable variables because they can be changed. However, there are limits to how much they can be altered. For example, economic conditions, competitive structure, or government regulations may prevent a manager from adjusting prices frequently or significantly. Making changes in the size, shape, and design of most tangible goods is expensive; therefore, such product features cannot be altered very often. In addition, promotional campaigns and methods used to distribute products ordinarily cannot be rewritten or revamped overnight.

Marketing managers must develop a marketing mix that precisely matches the needs of people in the target market. Before they can do so, they must collect in-depth, up-to-date information about those needs. Such information might include data about the age, income, ethnicity, gender, and educational level of people in the target market; their preferences for product features; their attitudes toward competitors' products; and the frequency with which they use the product. Armed with such data, marketing managers are better able to develop a product, distribution system, promotion program, and prices that appeal to people in the target market.

Let's look more closely at the decisions and activities related to each marketing mix variable.

The Product Variable   The *product variable* is the aspect of the marketing mix that deals with researching customers' product wants and designing a good, service, or idea that satisfies those wants. It also involves creating or modifying packaging and brand names, and may include decisions regarding warranty and repair services. Actual production of tangible goods is not a marketing activity.

**Figure 1.10
Creating Products
That Satisfy Consumer
Needs**
Guess recognizes that its 100 percent cotton towels will satisfy consumers' preferences for natural cotton fabrics.

Product variable decisions and related activities are important because they are involved directly with creating products that meet consumers' needs and wants. In Figure 1.10, Guess promotes its Home Collection of products to satisfy customers' demands for natural 100 percent cotton. To maintain a set of products that helps an organization achieve its goals, marketers must develop new products, modify existing ones, and eliminate those that no longer satisfy enough buyers or yield acceptable profits. Levi's latest product innovation is mass-marketing custom-fit jeans. The jeans fit according to your measurements; laser technology makes the individual tailoring possible.[14]

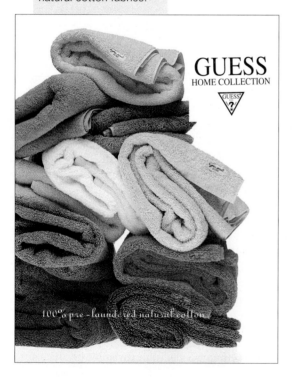

The Distribution Variable   To reach and keep customers, products must be available at the right time and in convenient locations. In dealing with the *distribution variable,* a marketing manager makes products available in the quantities desired to as many target market customers as possible, keeping total inventory, transportation, and storage costs as low as possible. With these objectives in mind, McDonald's is expanding distribution by installing its restaurants in Wal-Mart stores, Amoco and Chevron service stations, and Incredible Universe electronics stores. This practice permits the fast-food giant to share costs with the partner store and to reach more customers when and where hunger strikes.[15] A marketing manager may also select and motivate intermediaries (wholesalers and retailers), establish and maintain inventory control procedures, and develop and manage transportation and storage systems. Wal-Mart has been especially successful at designing an efficient distribution system.

The Promotion Variable   The *promotion variable* relates to activities used to inform individuals or groups about an organization and its products. Promotion can be aimed at increasing public awareness of an organization and of new or existing products. Promotion can also educate consumers about product features or urge people to take a particular stance on a political or social issue.

Promotion can keep interest strong in an established product that has been available for decades. Many companies use promotion to associate themselves or their products with things that make consumers feel good, such as the Super Bowl or the Olympics (see Inside Marketing). More and more companies are setting up "home pages" on the Internet's World Wide Web to communicate information about themselves and their products. Ragu's home page, for example, offers Italian phrases, recipes, and a sweepstakes; Zima's home page features a serialized story whose characters drink the clear alcoholic beverage. Although still in its infancy, this new promotion medium promises to help businesses reach a highly desirable target market—young, college-educated, affluent men.[16]

The Price Variable   The *price variable* relates to decisions and actions associated with establishing pricing objectives and policies and determining product prices. Price is a critical component of the marketing mix because consumers are concerned about the value obtained in an exchange. Price is often used as a competitive tool. McDonald's, Burger King, and other fast-food chains often use price reductions to increase store traffic. For example, 99-cent Whoppers at Burger King and 2 Big Macs for $2 may be offered for a limited time to increase sales, especially among frequent fast-food users. Intense price competition sometimes leads to price wars, but high prices can also be used competitively to establish a product's image. A company's pricing decisions send a message to the market that helps shape the overall marketing strategy.[17]

Developing and maintaining an effective mix of product, distribution, promotion, and price are the key requirements for a strong marketing strategy. Thus, as indicated in Figure 1.7, a large portion of this text (Chapters 9 through 21) focuses on concepts, decisions, and activities associated with the components of the marketing mix.

INSIDE MARKETING

The '96 Olympics: Not Just for Athletes

In the summer of 1996, some 10,000 athletes competed for medals in 271 events at twenty-seven venues at the Olympic games in Atlanta, Georgia. But the athletes were not the only competitors. Major marketing firms also joined the competition for consumer dollars and goodwill by sponsoring the games.

To help raise money to host the Olympic games, the Atlanta Committee for the Olympic Games (ACOG) solicited businesses to ante up as much as $40 million each to be official Olympic sponsors. Many companies did so, including John Hancock Mutual Life Insurance Co., Nationsbank, Anheuser-Busch, McDonald's, Coca-Cola, Home Depot, IBM, Xerox, and AT&T. Coca-Cola's investment, including its $40 million sponsorship fee, hospitality during the games, television advertising, billboards, and a $50-million attraction near Olympic Park, amounted to more than $200 million.

The games also gave several sponsors an opportunity to promote cutting-edge technology and expertise to potential customers. Sensormatic Elec-

tronics Corp., for example, handled security at the games. The Florida firm, which makes plastic garment tags used to deter shoplifters, developed technology to create microchip-embedded badges for athletes and officials that opened doors as wearers approached. Xerox provided facilities to turn out bound volumes of scores and athlete information for judges and journalists within 3 to 24 hours of an event. IBM built the games' complex information infrastructure to connect athletes, visitors, and media worldwide. The system tallied scores and fed them to the global press within seconds and provided officials, athletes, and coaches access to 60 gigabytes of data through kiosks scattered throughout the Olympic Village.

Corporate sponsors are willing to shell out millions to sponsor the Olympics in the hope that the affiliation will generate goodwill, exposure, and sales. Some, like IBM and Sensormatic, also gained new knowledge of how to coordinate a complex enterprise that they can bring to their customers.

Sources: David Greising, "Let the Hype Begin," *Business Week*, Feb. 27, 1995, pp. 114, 118; Nicole Harris, "The Game's Afoot—and It's Marketing," *Business Week*, Jan. 22, 1996, p. 95; and Mark Starr and Karen Springen, "A Piece of the Olympic Action," *Newsweek*, Jan. 15, 1996, pp. 58–59.

Marketing environment
The competitive, economic, political, legal and regulatory, technological, and sociocultural forces that surround the buyer and affect the marketing mix

■ *Marketing Strategy: Influence of the Environment*

The **marketing environment,** consisting of competitive, economic, political, legal and regulatory, technological, and sociocultural forces, surrounds the buyer and the marketing mix (see Figure 1.8). Marketing mix elements—product, distribution, promotion, price—are factors over which an organization has control; the forces of the environment, however, are subject to far less control. But even though marketers know they cannot predict changes in the marketing environment with certainty, they must nevertheless plan for them. Because these environmental forces have such a profound effect on marketing activities, we will explore each of them in considerable depth in Chapter 2.

The forces of the marketing environment affect a marketer's ability to facilitate exchanges in three general ways. First, they influence customers by affecting their lifestyles, standards of living, and preferences and needs for products. Because a marketing manager tries to develop and adjust the marketing mix to satisfy consumers, effects of environmental forces on customers also have an indirect impact on marketing mix components. The evolving development of telecommunications and computer technologies, for example, have given FedEx Corporation a new medium for interacting with customers. FedEx is now accessible via America Online, a national computer information service, and through the Internet World Wide Web, making it possible for subscribers to track packages from their home or office computers and send E-mail feedback to FedEx about its products and service. This technology enables FedEx to gather marketing research information about company services directly from consumers.[18] Second, marketing environment forces help determine whether and how a marketing manager can perform certain marketing activities. Third, environmental forces may affect a marketing manager's decisions and actions by influencing buyers' reactions to the firm's marketing mix.

Marketing environment forces can fluctuate quickly and dramatically, which is one reason why marketing is so interesting and challenging. Because these forces are closely interrelated, changes in one may cause changes in others. For example, after Starkist, a unit of H.J. Heinz, received letters objecting to dolphin slaughter and faced an organized boycott of its canned tuna, the company announced a dolphin-safe policy and stopped buying tuna from fishing vessels that net dolphins. Starkist's response to consumer demands echoed throughout the tuna industry, as other tuna companies quickly adopted dolphin-safe policies to please consumers.

Even though changes in the marketing environment produce uncertainty for marketers and, at times, hurt marketing efforts, they also create opportunities. Marketers who are alert to changes in environmental forces can not only adjust to and influence them, but also capitalize on the opportunities such changes provide. For example, compact disc distributors responded to consumers' concerns about wasteful packaging by eliminating the bulky cardboard containers initially used to package CDs.

■ *Marketing Management*

Marketing management
The process of planning, organizing, implementing, and controlling marketing activities to facilitate exchanges effectively and efficiently

Marketing management is the process of planning, organizing, implementing, and controlling marketing activities to facilitate exchanges effectively and efficiently. Effectiveness and efficiency are important dimensions of this definition. *Effectiveness* is the degree to which an exchange helps achieve an organization's objectives. *Efficiency* refers to minimizing the resources an organization must spend to achieve a specific level of desired exchanges. Thus the overall goal of marketing management is to facilitate highly desirable exchanges and to minimize the costs of doing so.

Planning is a systematic process of assessing opportunities and resources, determining marketing objectives, and developing a marketing strategy and plans for implementation and control. Planning determines when and how marketing activities are performed and who performs them. It forces marketing managers to think ahead, establish objectives, and consider future marketing activities. Effective planning also reduces or eliminates daily crises.

Organizing marketing activities involves developing the internal structure of the marketing unit. The structure is the key to directing marketing activities. The marketing unit can be organized by functions, products, regions, types of customers, or a combination of all four.

Proper implementation of marketing plans hinges on coordination of marketing activities, motivation of marketing personnel, and effective communication within the unit. Marketing managers must motivate marketing personnel, coordinate their activities, and integrate their activities both with those in other areas of the company and with the marketing efforts of personnel in external organizations, such as advertising agencies and research firms. An organization's communication system must allow the marketing manager to stay in contact with high-level management, with managers of other functional areas within the firm, and with personnel involved in marketing activities both inside and outside the organization.

The marketing control process consists of establishing performance standards, comparing actual performance to established standards, and reducing differences between desired and actual performance. An effective control process has four requirements. It should ensure a rate of information flow that allows the marketing manager to detect quickly any differences between actual and planned levels of performance. It must accurately monitor various activities and be flexible enough to accommodate changes. The costs of the control process must be low relative to costs that would arise without controls. Finally, the control process should be designed so that both managers and subordinates can understand it. In Chapters 22 and 23 we examine the planning, organizing, implementing, and controlling of marketing strategies in greater detail.

The Marketing Plan: An Overview

Marketing plan
A written document that specifies an organization's resources, objectives, marketing strategy, and implementation and control efforts planned for use in marketing a specific product or product group

A marketing plan is a written document that specifies an organization's resources, objectives, marketing strategy, and implementation and control efforts planned for use in marketing a specific product or product group. The marketing plan describes the firm's current position or situation, establishes marketing goals or objectives for the product or product group, and specifies how the organization will attempt to achieve these objectives.

Marketing plans vary with respect to the time period involved. Generally, short-range plans are for one year or less and moderate-range plans for two to five years. Both types of plans are usually quite detailed. Long-range plans cover periods of more than five years, perhaps up to fifteen years, and are usually not as specific.

Developing a clear, well-written marketing plan, though time-consuming, is important. The plan is used internally among employees for communication purposes. It covers the assignment of responsibilities, tasks, and schedules for implementation purposes. It presents objectives and specifies how resources are to be allocated in order to achieve these objectives. Finally, it helps marketing managers to monitor and evaluate the performance of a marketing strategy. We discuss marketing plans more fully in Chapter 22.

SUMMARY

Marketing is the process of creating, distributing, promoting, and pricing goods, services, and ideas to facilitate satisfying exchange relationships in a dynamic environment. An exchange is the provision or transfer of goods, services, and ideas in return for something of value. Four conditions must exist for an exchange to occur: (1) two or more individuals, groups, or organizations must participate; (2) each party must have something of value desired by the other; (3) each party must be willing to give up what it has in order to receive the value held by the other; and (4) parties to the exchange must be able to communicate with each other to make their somethings of value available. In an exchange, products are traded either for other products or for

financial resources, such as cash or credit. Products can be goods, services, or ideas.

It is important to study marketing because it permeates our lives. Marketing activities are performed in both business and nonbusiness organizations. Moreover, marketing activities help business organizations generate profits, the lifeblood of a capitalist economy. The study of marketing enhances consumer awareness. Finally, marketing costs absorb about half of each consumer dollar.

The marketing concept is a management philosophy prompting a business organization to try to satisfy customers' needs through a coordinated set of activities that also allows the organization to achieve its goals.

Customer satisfaction is the marketing concept's major objective. The philosophy of the marketing concept emerged in the United States during the 1950s, after the production and sales eras. To make the marketing concept work, top management must accept it as an overall management philosophy. Implementing the marketing concept requires an efficient information system and sometimes restructuring of the organization.

Organizations that develop activities consistent with the marketing concept become market-oriented organizations. Market orientation is generation of market information and coordination and communication of market information across departments. Participation of top management, marketing managers, and nonmarketing managers is important in creating a market-oriented organization. Open exchange of information and relationship-building activities with customers are also important.

A marketing strategy is a plan of action for developing, distributing, promoting, and pricing products that meet the needs of specific customers. Marketing strategy requires that managers focus on four tasks to achieve set objectives: (1) target market selection, (2) marketing mix development, (3) marketing environment analysis, and (4) marketing management.

A target market is a specific group of buyers on whose needs and wants a company focuses its marketing efforts. Marketers should be able to recognize and analyze marketing opportunities, which are circumstances that allow an organization to take action toward reaching a particular target market. An organization's management must designate which customer groups the firm is trying to serve and have some information about them. Identification and analysis of a target market provide a foundation for developing a marketing mix.

The four marketing mix variables are product, distribution, promotion, and price. The product variable is the aspect of the marketing mix dealing with researching consumers' wants and designing a product with the desired characteristics. A marketing manager tries to make products available in quantities desired to as many customers as possible and keep the total costs of inventory, transportation, and storage as low as possible (the distribution variable). The promotion variable relates to activities used to inform one or more groups of people about an organization and its products. The price variable refers to establishing pricing policies and determining product prices.

Marketing management is a process of planning, organizing, implementing, and controlling marketing activities to facilitate effective and efficient exchanges. Planning is a systematic process of assessing opportunities and resources, determining marketing objectives, developing a marketing strategy, and preparing for implementation and control. Organizing marketing activities refers to developing the marketing unit's internal structure. Properly implementing marketing plans depends on coordinating marketing activities, motivating marketing personnel, and effectively communicating within the unit. The marketing control process consists of establishing performance standards, comparing actual performance to established standards, and reducing the difference between desired and actual performance.

A marketing plan is a written document specifying an organization's resources, objectives, marketing strategy, and implementation and control efforts planned for use in marketing products. Marketing plans can be short-, moderate-, or long-range.

IMPORTANT TERMS

Marketing	Relationship marketing	Market opportunity	Marketing management
Exchange	Market orientation	Marketing mix	Marketing plan
Product	Marketing strategy	Marketing environment	
Marketing concept	Target market		

DISCUSSION AND REVIEW QUESTIONS

1. What is marketing? How did you define marketing before you read this chapter?

2. Why should someone study marketing?

3. Discuss the basic elements of the marketing concept. Which businesses in your area use this philosophy? Explain why.

4. Identify several businesses in your area that obviously have *not* adopted the marketing concept. What characteristics of these organizations indicate nonacceptance of the marketing concept?

5. Describe the major components of a marketing strategy. How are the components related?

6. Identify the tasks involved in developing a marketing strategy.

7. Why is the selection of a target market such an important issue?

8. What are the primary issues that marketing managers consider when conducting a market opportunity analysis?

9. Why are the elements of the marketing mix known as variables?

10. What are the variables in the marketing environment? How much control does a marketing manager have over environmental variables?

11. What types of management activities are involved in the marketing management process?

12. Describe the content of a marketing plan. How does a good marketing plan benefit an organization?

APPLICATION QUESTIONS

1. Felicia owns an automobile dealership in her hometown. Her typical day begins with breakfast at a local coffee shop where she usually "bumps into" her customers. Following breakfast today, she contracted to redecorate and redesign the dealership showroom. Afterward, she met with advertising agency personnel to discuss next month's advertising for the dealership. Which of Felicia's actions would be considered marketing and why?

2. Identify possible target markets for the following products:

   a. Kellogg's Corn Flakes
   b. Wilson tennis rackets
   c. Walt Disney World
   d. Diet Pepsi

3. Discuss the variables of the marketing mix (product, price, promotion, and distribution) as they might relate to each of the following:
   a. a trucking company
   b. a men's clothing store
   c. a skating rink
   d. a campus bookstore

Case 1.1   AutoZone: Where the Customer Is Boss

Founded as Auto Shack by grocery wholesaler Malone & Hyde, Memphis-based auto parts retailer AutoZone opened its first stores in 1979. By focusing primarily on expanding its highly customer- and service-oriented operations into smaller markets posing little competition, AutoZone experienced tremendous growth. Following a lawsuit brought against it by home electronics giant Radio Shack, the company changed its name to AutoZone in 1988. That same year, the company posted sales of nearly $440 million, having by then established itself as a force to be reckoned with in the highly competitive do-it-yourself (DIY) auto parts industry.

The early 1990s witnessed continued growth at AutoZone. In 1992, with 678 stores at year's end, sales surpassed the $1 billion level for the first time in the company's relatively short history. AutoZone topped this mark the following year with sales of $1.2 billion, and *Forbes* magazine recognized the company for having the second-highest average annual growth in earnings over the previous five years. In 1995, the company's seventh straight year of growth in net income, AutoZone's 1,143 stores operating in twenty-six states amassed sales of over $1.8 billion, up a full 20 percent from the previous year. By this time, the company was, on average, opening a new store every other day.

The DIY market is expanding as a result of several relevant factors. First, as the price of the average automobile has steadily increased in recent years, so too has the age of the typical vehicle on the American road. In fact, approximately one-third of all cars and light trucks in the United States are over ten years old, well beyond the coverage of automobile warranties. Second, with the average hourly rate of professional mechanics and other auto repair labor hovering around $45, more and more people are choosing to work on their cars themselves to save money. Additionally, there are more cars on the road and people are driving more miles every year. AutoZone believes it has but scratched the surface of its vast growth potential.

AutoZone targets the DIY customer with an extensive selection of automotive replacement parts, maintenance items, and accessories. Everything from lug nuts and antifreeze to floor mats, water pumps, and even complete engines can be found in the company's spacious retail outlets. However, these products can be purchased from many competitors. AutoZone differentiates itself from the competition in a number of ways. Although most of its competitors can also claim that they offer customers high-quality parts and accessories at low prices, AutoZone goes much further in the effort to give customers exactly what they want.

AutoZone stores are conspicuously clean and attractive, dispelling the common perception of auto parts stores as dirty, greasy establishments where only the most knowledgeable mechanics dare tread. More important, AutoZone differentiates itself by providing a premium level of customer service. The company has achieved its phenomenal success by adhering to one simple central premise: put the customer first. At AutoZone, the customer is the boss. Unlike many organizations, AutoZone regards "customer service" as more than a mere catch phrase. For the experienced mechanic, AutoZone offers not only a complete range of parts and accessories at low prices, but the assistance and support of service personnel knowledgeable about the most technical aspects of automotive repair. For the novice, the wide selection and very low prices are also significant. But what matters most is that Auto-Zoners are there to listen and help customers find exactly what they want.

Every store manager's name tag says, "Manager of Customer Satisfaction," and every employee ("Auto-Zoner") goes the extra mile for each and every one of the company's customers, whether a well-trained mechanic or a thrifty driver who wants to change her own oil. AutoZone's absolute commitment to customer service is even embodied in its own unique terminology. "Drop/Stop—30/30" means that AutoZoners drop whatever they are doing to wait on customers before they've been in the store for 30 seconds or stepped 30 feet from the front door. "GOTCHA" is the company's practice of going out to customers' cars to help install items or resolve problems.

To further enhance customer service, AutoZone developed its own in-house information technology system for which it was named one of six finalists for the 1995 *Computerworld* Smithsonian award for business and commerce. The system, which includes a nationwide satellite link, a centralized call center, and a computerized store management system, is called "WITT-JR"—Whatever It Takes To Do the Job Right. The satellite routes calls to the central calling center instead of putting customers on hold. There, "Phone Pros" answer questions, look up prices, and check availability in the ten stores closet to the caller's location. All customer parts warranties are registered on computer, reducing the hassles for customers who misplace their receipts. In-store electronic parts catalogs let customers locate the exact parts and accessories needed quickly and accurately, even identifying where in the store the items are shelved. AutoZone's system also monitors and evaluates product sales and availability at each retail outlet.

AutoZone's commitment to customer service is evidenced as well in its pricing and product assortment policies. Its outlets stock a wide range of automotive parts and accessories based on what customers tell the company they want. In 1995 AutoZone developed "flex-ograms," which tailor the parts inventory at each retail outlet to match the needs of that store's customers based on knowledge of the types of automobiles driven. AutoZone's everyday low prices on these goods often beat the sale prices of competitors. Thus, AutoZone offers the customer savings all the time, a matter of particular importance given the nature of the auto parts industry. For example, when an alternator or water pump fails, it must be replaced immediately; the customer cannot wait for a sale. When it comes to more costly parts under a car's hood, AutoZone's own private label line can save customers even more money.

In considering strategic alternatives for the future, AutoZone executives are seeking innovative ways to increase the company's share of the thriving DIY auto parts market. So far, AutoZone's aggressive growth strategy of continually adding new stores has been highly successful; in 1995, for instance, the chain added 210 new stores. To try to ensure its future growth, the company is considering installing DIY repair bays where customers would install parts and accessories themselves but could get assistance from expert Auto-Zone service personnel. Another option for AutoZone might be to employ mechanics, adding expert parts installation to the range of services it already offers. No matter how the company chooses to pursue future growth, one thing is certain: the customer will always be the ultimate boss at AutoZone.[19]

Questions for Discussion

1. What types of customers make up AutoZone's target market? Speculate as to why the firm has chosen to concentrate on this one segment of customers.
2. How does AutoZone implement the marketing concept?
3. Is AutoZone a market-oriented organization? Explain.

Case 1.2   **Windows 95: Start Me Up**

One of the most hyped marketing events in recent decades occurred on August 24, 1995: the launch of Microsoft's Windows 95. To ensure the success of Windows 95, Microsoft set about to develop a marketing strategy that would not only capitalize on Americans' growing use of computers but also captivate our imaginations. Says Steven A. Ballmer, a Microsoft executive vice president, "This is the biggest marketing thing we've ever done." *Big* may be an understatement.

Windows 95 is an operating system, the set of instructions that controls a computer's basic functions. As such, it replaces both DOS and Windows 3.1.

Microsoft is targeting Win95 at 85 million home and business owners of personal computers. Although more than 80 percent of those users already boot up with Microsoft's DOS and Windows 3.1, Windows 95 faces competition from IBM's OS/2 Warp, Mac OS for Apple's Macintosh computers, various versions of UNIX, as well as Microsoft's own, more advanced, Windows NT operating system. To persuade these users to upgrade to Win95 or switch from other operating systems, Microsoft spent years developing, testing, and refining the Win95 features that make PCs easier to use. In fact, some 400,000 customers "beta-tested" the product to identify bugs. Built-in network connections and administrative software were included for corporate users.

To simplify computer use, Win95 provides a friendly graphical interface that organizes a computer's contents into a desktop-like screen with icons representing programs and files. Users can click on a start button with a mouse to get a series of menus. A task bar—a strip across the bottom of the screen—lets users see what applications are running and switch programs with a click of a mouse button.

Among the most significant features of Win95 is "plug and play," which enables the system to identify and work with most manufacturers' peripheral hardware (hard drives, disk drives, modems, CD-ROM drives, printers, and the like) without the hassle of a complicated installation and configuration process. Win95 also permits users to multitask, or run multiple programs at the same time, so that they can, say, download files from an online service while printing a spreadsheet file. It also allows different programs to share information through OLE (Object Linking and Embedding). Moreover, Win95 permits long file names, so users aren't stuck trying to think of meaningful eight-character names for their files.

To make use of Windows 95, a computer must have at least a 386 processor with 4 megabytes of RAM (random access memory, or temporary storage space) and 60 megabytes of hard disk (or fixed memory) space, but Microsoft "recommends" a 486 processor with 8 megabytes of RAM. For optimal performance, a Pentium chip with 12 megabytes of RAM is preferred. Although Win95 can run applications designed for earlier versions of Windows, programs designed specifically for Windows 95 can best take advantage of the new operating system.

Microsoft set a suggested retail price of $209 for the complete Windows 95 package; $109 for customers upgrading from Windows 3.1. However, many customers were able to obtain the upgrade for as little as $90 through discounts and sales.

Microsoft's distribution strategy for Windows 95 was two-pronged. Consumers could buy the software off the shelves of nearly 20,000 retail stores across the country, including Wal-Mart, Babbage's, Software Etc.,

Computer City, CompUSA, Incredible Universe, and Egghead. Or, they could be patient. Within a few months of Win95's introduction, virtually every new PC on the market had Windows 95 pre-installed as its operating system.

Among the major challenges for Microsoft were exciting interest in the new program, informing consumers of its features, and convincing them to upgrade. To stimulate corporate purchases, Microsoft gave away 10 million demo disks in the six months before the launch and went on a 23-city tour to show off Win95 to 40,000 people. To appeal to home users, Microsoft launched one of the biggest promotion blitzes in recent marketing history. Months before the release, advertising backed by the sounds of the Rolling Stones' "Start Me Up" (to highlight the program's start button feature) aired on television and radio. Some 1.2 million in-store demonstrations were held before the August 24 launch. Many retailers even held "Midnight Madness" sales, opening at midnight on August 23 for 95 minutes to sell the first copies of Win95.

But the biggest hoopla was reserved for August 24 itself when the company held launch parties for 70,000 people in forty cities—from the Las Vegas Luxor Hotel to the Great America theme park in Silicon Valley. In Britain, Microsoft painted fields with giant Win95 logos for aerial viewing. It threw a gala in Paris's Palais des Congrès and unfurled a 300-foot Windows 95 banner down Toronto's tallest building. In Australia, all babies born on August 24 got free copies of the program. At the same time, an elaborate launch party was held online via the Internet.

Microsoft also produced a thirty-minute prime-time network "info show" starring *ER*'s Anthony Edwards and Microsoft chairman Bill Gates which aired on August 27 and 28. It featured Windows users, from students in Appalachia to the Las Vegas Cirque du Soleil. The $5 million tab was shared by Microsoft and sponsors Coca-Cola, Kodak, Compaq, and CompUSA. Bill Gates also appeared on *Good Morning America* and *Larry King Live* to tout the new program. Other promotions included 250,000 point-of-sale displays, special Cracker Jack boxes containing key chains and coupons for free PCs, and discounts on plane tickets with the purchase of the new PC operating software. In all, Microsoft planned to spend $200 million on advertising and marketing expenses for the first year of Windows 95.

The launch of Windows 95 was marred by a Justice Department investigation of Microsoft. Rivals of Microsoft have accused the software giant of using unfair and monopolistic practices to maintain market dominance with Windows. Although the Justice Department has not brought charges against the company to date, it continues to investigate the firm's marketing practices, particularly the bundling of connections to Microsoft's new online service, Microsoft

Network, with Windows 95 and the terms of its contracts with PC makers who will pre-install Win95 on their machines.

Despite these problems, more than 1 million copies of Windows 95 were sold in its first four days; Microsoft expected to sell 30 million copies by Christmas 1995, and 63 million in 1996 (in comparison, 33 million copies of its predecessor Windows 3.1 sold in 1994). Other companies—from PC makers to software firms—hope to ride the Win95 bandwagon to the bank as well. Their hope is that consumers buying Windows 95 will need to upgrade or replace their systems in order to handle the complex software. Makers of disk drives and RAM chips in particular will benefit as consumers boost memory to take advantage of Windows. Software marketers (including Microsoft itself) are also pleased as consumers will need to buy new Windows 95–compatible software to be able to take full advantage of the operating system's features. In fact, the computer industry was expected to spend $1 billion over the final four months of 1995 to promote the new program and tie it to new PCs, peripherals, and compatible software.[20]

Questions for Discussion

1. Describe Microsoft's marketing strategy for Windows 95.
2. What aspects of Microsoft's activities foster relationship marketing?
3. What forces of the marketing environment must Microsoft carefully monitor to ensure success with Windows 95 and its other software products?

Chapter 2

The Marketing Environment

OBJECTIVES

- To recognize the importance of environmental scanning and analysis

- To become familiar with how competitive and economic factors affect organizations' ability to compete and customers' willingness and ability to buy products

- To identify the types of political forces in the marketing environment

- To understand how laws, government regulations, and self-regulatory agencies affect marketing activities

- To explore the effects of new technology on society and on marketing activities

- To be able to analyze sociocultural issues that marketers must deal with as they make decisions

Nabisco offers consumers more of "less."

*T*he surprise inside your Cracker Jacks box these days is more tempting than a lick-and-stick tattoo—it's no fat. And that is welcome news to snack-lovers.

Government health watchdogs inform us that we eat more than we should and too much of the wrong things, but many of us don't need the reminder. Aging baby boomers (born between 1945 and 1965) are recognizing the toll of age and less-than-perfect nutritional habits in the form of increasing pounds. In fact, 27.5 percent of all Americans are overweight (that is, at least 20 percent heavier than what they should weigh). Moreover, Americans consume an average of 165 grams of fat (saturated, monounsaturated, and polyunsaturated) per day, when experts suggest limiting fat intake to just 65 grams of all kinds of fat (assuming the recommended 2,000 calories/day, which most Americans also exceed). With high-fat diets contributing to health concerns such as heart attacks and diabetes, as well as undesirable extra pounds, many Americans are modifying their eating and cooking habits and seeking out foods lower in fat and calories.

Marketers of consumer products, especially foods, typically monitor the marketing environment to detect changes that may create problems for their product line or present opportunities to develop new products. Accordingly, firms like Borden and Nabisco regard consumers' health concerns as an invitation to develop new products to address them. Several companies have catered specifically to dieters' needs by marketing low-calorie foods and snacks for years. But with Americans becoming increasingly concerned about their fat intake, companies are responding by introducing low-fat versions of traditionally popular food and snack products.

Borden, for example, recently unveiled fat-free Cracker Jacks in both original and toffee flavors, along with a new promotional campaign tied to baseball. Competitor Nabisco, Inc. has developed reduced-fat versions of many of its flagship brands, as well as SnackWell's, a line of low-fat or fat-free snacks. Nabisco recently launched Planters Reduced-Fat snacks, including peanuts (with 45 percent less fat than Planters regular peanuts), Cheez Balls, and Cheez Curls. The reduced-fat products are not packaged in Planters familiar blue, but rather in the same green used in SnackWell's packaging. With sales of snack nuts down 5.5 percent, Nabisco executives hope that the Planters Reduced-Fat choices will bring consumers back.[1]

Companies like Borden and Nabisco are modifying products and developing new ones in response to customers' changing desires. Recognizing and addressing such changes in the marketing environment are crucial to marketing success, so we will focus on them in some detail. This chapter explores the competitive, economic, political, legal and regulatory, technological, and sociocultural forces that comprise the marketing environment. First, we define the marketing environment and consider why it is critical to scan and analyze it. Next we discuss the effects of competitive forces and explore the effect of general economic conditions: prosperity, recession, depression, and recovery. We also examine buying power and forces that influence consumers' willingness to spend. Then we discuss the political forces that generate government actions affecting marketing activities and examine the effect of laws and regulatory agencies on these activities. After analyzing the major dimensions of the technological forces in the environment, we consider the impact of sociocultural forces on marketing efforts.

Examining and Responding to the Marketing Environment

*T*he marketing environment consists of external forces that directly or indirectly influence an organization's acquisition of inputs (human, financial, and natural resources and raw materials, and information) and creation of outputs (goods, services, or ideas). As indicated in Chapter 1, the marketing environment includes six such forces: competitive, economic, political, legal and regulatory, technological, and sociocultural.

Whether fluctuating rapidly or slowly, environmental forces are always dynamic. Changes in the marketing environment create uncertainty, threats, and opportunities for marketers. Although the future is not very predictable, marketers try to predict what may happen. We can say with certainty that marketers continue to modify their marketing strategies in response to dynamic environmental forces. Consider, for example, how technological changes have affected the products offered by computer companies and how consumers' growing emphasis on health and fitness has influenced the products of shoe, clothing, food, and health care companies. Marketing managers who fail to recognize changes in environmental forces leave their firms unprepared to capitalize on marketing opportunities or cope with threats created by changes in the environment. Monitoring the environment is crucial to an organization's survival and to the long-term achievement of its goals.

▮ *Environmental Scanning and Analysis*

Environmental scanning
The process of collecting information about forces in the marketing environment

To monitor changes in the marketing environment effectively, marketers engage in environmental scanning and analysis. **Environmental scanning** is the process of collecting information about forces in the marketing environment. Scanning involves observation, secondary sources such as business, trade, government, and general-interest publications, and marketing research. Research suggests that environmental scanning gives companies an edge over competitors in taking advantage of current trends. Of course, simply gathering information about competitors and customers is not enough. Companies must know how to use that information in the strategic planning process.[2] Managers must be careful not to gather so much information that sheer volume makes analysis impossible.

Environmental analysis
The process of assessing and interpreting the information gathered through environmental scanning

Environmental analysis is the process of assessing and interpreting the information gathered through environmental scanning. A manager evaluates the information for accuracy, tries to resolve inconsistencies in the data, and, if it is warranted, assigns significance to the findings. By evaluating this information, managers should be able to identify potential threats and opportunities linked to environmental changes. Understanding the current state of the marketing environment and recognizing threats and opportunities arising from changes within it help marketing managers assess the performance of current marketing efforts and develop future marketing strategies.

■ *Responding to Environmental Forces*

Marketing managers take two general approaches: accepting environmental forces as uncontrollable or influencing and shaping them.[3] An organization that views environmental forces as uncontrollable remains passive and reactive toward the environment. Instead of trying to influence forces in the environment, its marketing managers adjust current marketing strategies to environmental changes. They approach with caution market opportunities discovered through environmental scanning and analysis. On the other hand, marketing managers who believe that environmental forces can be shaped adopt a proactive approach. For example, if a market is blocked by traditional environmental constraints, marketing managers may apply economic, psychological, political, and promotional skills to gain access or operate within it. Once they identify what is blocking a market opportunity, marketers assess the power of the various parties involved and develop strategies to overcome the obstructing environmental forces.

A proactive approach can be constructive and bring desired results. In Figure 2.1, Ford responds proactively to sociocultural environmental forces by manufacturing car bodies that are 100 percent recyclable and therefore safer for the environment. To exert influence on environmental forces, marketing management seeks to create market opportunities or extract greater benefits relative to costs from existing market opportunities. Thus a firm losing sales to competitors with lower-priced products may develop a technology that makes its production processes more efficient; greater efficiency allows it to lower prices of its own products. Political action is another way to affect environmental forces. However, managers must recognize that there are limits on how much environmental forces can be shaped. Although an organization may be able to influence legislation through lobbying, it is unlikely that a single organization can significantly increase the national birthrate or move the economy from recession to prosperity.

We cannot say that either of these approaches to environmental response is better than the other. For some organizations, the passive, reactive approach is most appropriate, but for other firms, the aggressive approach leads to better performance. Selection of a particular approach depends on an organization's managerial philosophies, objectives, financial resources, customers, and human skills, as well as on the environment within which the organization operates.

The remainder of this chapter explores in greater detail each of the six environmental forces—competitive, economic, political, legal and regulatory, technological, and sociocultural.

**Figure 2.1
Responding to
Environmental Forces**
Responding proactively to sociocultural environmental forces, Ford has developed aluminum car bodies that are 100% recyclable and help to conserve fuel.

Competitive Forces

Competition Organizations marketing products that are similar to or can be substituted for a marketer's products in the same geographic area

*F*ew firms, if any, operate free of competition. Broadly speaking, all firms compete with each other for consumers' dollars. More practically, however, a business generally defines **competition** as other firms marketing products that are similar to or can be substituted for its products in the same geographic area. For example, with the increasing popularity of the Internet (a huge network of government, educational, and business computer networks), national online services such as CompuServe, Prodigy, and America Online are facing significant competition from other companies. In addition to small, local Internet service providers, many large firms, including MCI and Microsoft, are developing their own network services that include access to the so-called information superhighway. America Online and similar competitors are fighting back by improving their Internet services and promoting them vigorously. With the Internet access market expected to grow from $123 million currently to more than $4 billion by the year 2000, companies that gain a solid foothold in the market now will have the best chance for survival and success.[4] In this section we consider the types of competitive structures, competitive tools, and the importance of monitoring competitors.

■ *Types of Competitive Structures*

The number of firms that supply a product may affect the strength of competition. When only one or a few firms control supply, competitive factors exert a different sort of influence on marketing activities than when there are many competitors. Four general types of competitive structures are presented in Table 2.1: monopoly, oligopoly, monopolistic competition, and pure competition.

Monopoly A market structure in which an organization offers a product that has no close substitutes, making the organization the sole source of supply

A **monopoly** exists when a firm offers a product that has no close substitutes, making the organization the sole source of supply. Because the organization has no competitors, it controls supply of the product completely and, as a single seller, can erect barriers to potential competitors. In actuality, most monopolies surviving today are local utilities, such as telephone, electricity, and cable companies, which are heavily regulated by local, state, or federal agencies. These monopolies are tolerated because of the tremendous financial resources needed to develop and operate them. For example, few organizations can obtain the resources to mount any competition against a local electricity producer. On the other hand, competition is increasing in the telephone and cable television industries.

Oligopoly A competitive structure in which a few sellers control the supply of a large proportion of a product

An **oligopoly** exists when a few sellers control the supply of a large proportion of a product. In this case each seller considers the reactions of other sellers to changes in marketing activities. Products facing oligopolistic competition may be homogeneous, such as aluminum, or differentiated, such as cereal and automobiles. Usually, barriers of some

Table 2.1 Selected Characteristics of Competitive Structures				
Type of Structure	**Number of Competitors**	**Ease of Entry into Market**	**Product**	**Example**
Monopoly	One	Many barriers	Almost no substitutes	Dayton (Ohio) Power and Light (gas and electricity service)
Oligopoly	Few	Some barriers	Homogeneous or differentiated (with real or perceived differences) products	General Mills (cereal)
Monopolistic competition	Many	Few barriers	Product differentiation, with many substitutes	Levi Strauss (jeans)
Pure competition	Unlimited	No barriers	Homogeneous products	Vegetable farm (sweet corn)

sort make it difficult to enter the market and compete with oligopolies. For example, because of the enormous financial outlay required, few companies or individuals could afford to enter oil-refining or steel-producing industries. Moreover, some industries demand special technical or marketing skills, a qualification that deters the entry of many potential competitors.

Monopolistic competition exists when a firm with many potential competitors attempts to develop a marketing strategy to differentiate its product. For example, Levi Strauss has established an advantage for its blue jeans through a well-known trademark, design, advertising, and a reputation for quality. Although many competing brands of blue jeans are available, this firm has carved out a market niche by emphasizing differences in its products.

Pure competition, if it existed at all, would entail a large number of sellers, not one of which could significantly influence price or supply. Products would be homogeneous, and there would be easy entry into the market. The closest thing to an example of pure competition would be an unregulated agricultural market.

Pure competition is an ideal at one end of the continuum. Monopoly is at the other end. Most marketers function in a competitive environment somewhere between these two extremes.

Monopolistic competition
A market structure in which a firm has many potential competitors and, in order to compete, tries to develop a differential marketing strategy to establish its own market

Pure competition   A market structure characterized by an extremely large number of sellers, none of them strong enough to significantly influence price or supply

■ *Competitive Tools*

Another set of factors affecting competition is the number and types of competitive tools used by competitors. To survive, a firm uses one or more available competitive tools to deal with competitive economic forces. Once a company analyzes its particular competitive environment and decides which factors in that environment it can or must adapt to or influence, it chooses among variables that it can control to strengthen its competitive position in the overall marketplace.

Probably the first competitive tool that most organizations grasp is price. Southwest Airlines has been successful over the past twenty years by offering lower fares than its competition. However, price as a competitive tool poses one major problem: competitors will often match or beat the price. This threat is one of the main reasons for using non-price competitive tools based on markets, product offering, promotion, distribution, or enterprise.[5]

**Figure 2.2
Monitoring the Competition**
Princeton Instruments recognizes that competitive products exist and reminds its customers that its PentaMax camera is still the best.

■ *Monitoring Competition*

Marketers need to be aware of the actions of major competitors. They should determine what specific strategies competitors are using and how those strategies affect their own. Monitoring also guides marketers in developing competitive advantages and aids them in adjusting current marketing strategies and planning new ones.

In monitoring competition, it is not enough to analyze available information; the firm must develop a system for gathering ongoing information about competitors. Understanding the market and what customers want, as well as what the competition is providing, will assist in marketing orientation.[6] Information about competitors allows marketing managers to assess the performance of their own marketing efforts and to recognize the strengths and weaknesses in their own marketing strategies. In Figure 2.2, Princeton Instruments, the makers of PentaMax cameras, demonstrates its awareness of competitive products and its competitive edge in terms of quality and customer satisfaction. Data about market shares, product movement, sales volume, and expenditure levels can be useful. However, accurate information on these matters is often difficult to obtain.

Economic Forces

*E*conomic forces in the marketing environment also influence both marketers' and customers' decisions and activities. In this section we first examine the effects of general economic conditions. We also focus on buying power and willingness to buy.

■ *General Economic Conditions*

The overall state of the economy fluctuates in all countries. Changes in general economic conditions affect (and are affected by) supply and demand, buying power, willingness to spend, consumer expenditure levels, and the intensity of competitive behavior. Therefore, current economic conditions and changes in the economy have a broad impact on the success of organizations' marketing strategies. Fluctuations in the U.S. economy follow a general pattern often referred to as the business cycle. In the traditional view, the business cycle consists of four stages: prosperity, recession, depression, and recovery.

During **prosperity,** unemployment is low and total income is relatively high. Assuming a low inflation rate, this combination causes buying power to be high. If the economic outlook remains prosperous, consumers generally are willing to buy. In the prosperity stage, marketers often expand their product offerings to take advantage of increased buying power. They can sometimes capture a larger market share by intensifying distribution and promotion efforts.

Because unemployment rises during a **recession,** total buying power declines. Pessimism accompanying a recession often stifles both consumer and business spending. As buying power decreases, many consumers become more price- and value-conscious, looking for basic and functional products. During a recession, some firms make the mistake of drastically reducing their marketing efforts, thus damaging their ability to survive. Obviously, marketers should consider some revision of their marketing activities during a recessionary period. Because consumers are more concerned about the functional value of products, a company must focus its marketing research on determining precisely what product functions buyers want and make sure that these functions become part of its products. Promotional efforts should emphasize value and utility.

A **depression** is a period in which unemployment is extremely high, wages are very low, total disposable income is at a minimum, and consumers lack confidence in the economy. The federal government has used both monetary and fiscal policies to offset the effects of recession and depression. Monetary policies control the money supply, which in turn affects spending, saving, and investment by both individuals and businesses. Through fiscal policies, the government influences the amount of savings and expenditures by altering the tax structure and changing the levels of government spending. Some experts believe that effective use of monetary and fiscal policies can eliminate depressions from the business cycle.

Recovery is the stage of the business cycle in which the economy moves from depression or recession to prosperity. During this period, high unemployment begins to decline, total disposable income increases, and the economic gloom that reduced consumers' willingness to buy subsides. Both the ability and willingness to buy rise. Marketers face some problems during recovery—for example, difficulty in ascertaining how quickly and to what level prosperity will return. In this stage, marketers should maintain as much flexibility in their marketing strategies as possible to be able to make needed adjustments as the economy moves from recession to prosperity.

■ *Buying Power*

The strength of a person's **buying power** depends on the size of the resources—money, goods, and services that can be traded in an exchange—that enable the individual to purchase and on the state of the economy. Fluctuations of the business cycle affect buying power because they influence price levels and interest rates. For example, during inflationary periods, when prices are rising, buying power decreases because more

Prosperity A stage of the business cycle characterized by low unemployment and relatively high total income, which together cause buying power to be high (provided the inflation rate stays low)

Recession A stage of the business cycle during which unemployment rises and total buying power declines, stifling both consumer and business spending

Depression A stage of the business cycle when unemployment is extremely high, wages are very low, total disposable income is at a minimum, and consumers lack confidence in the economy

Recovery A state of the business cycle when the economy is moving from recession toward prosperity

Buying power Resources such as money, goods, and services that can be traded in an exchange situation

Table 2.2 A Comparison of 1980 and 1995 Prices for Selected Products

Product	1980	1995
Fast-food meal: McDonald's hamburger, regular fries, and small soft drink	$1.21	$2.39
Opryland, Nashville: adult admission	$8.00	$31.65
L.L. Bean: country corduroy pants	$30.50	$40.00
Round-trip flight: full fare, NY–LA on American Airlines	$570	$1442
Oscar Mayer hot dogs: one pound, all-beef franks	$1.94	$2.99
People magazine: weekly cover price	$.75	$2.95

dollars are required to buy products. Table 2.2 compares 1980 and 1995 prices for selected products.

The major financial sources of buying power are income, credit, and wealth. From an individual's viewpoint, **income** is the amount of money received through wages, rents, investments, pensions, and subsidy payments for a given period, such as a month or a year. Normally, this money is allocated among taxes, spending for goods and services, and savings. The mean annual family income in the United States is approximately $36,812.[7] However, because of differences in people's educational levels, abilities, occupations, and wealth, income is not equally distributed in this country (or in other countries).

Income The amount of money received through wages, rents, investments, pensions, and subsidy payments for a given period

Marketers are most interested in the amount of money left after payment of taxes. After-tax income is called **disposable income** and is used for spending or saving. Because disposable income is a ready source of buying power, the total amount available in a nation is important to marketers. Several factors determine the size of total disposable income. One is the total amount of income, which is affected by wage levels, rate of unemployment, interest rates, and dividend rates. Because disposable income is income left after taxes are paid, the number and amount of taxes directly affect the size of total disposable income. When taxes rise, disposable income declines; when taxes fall, disposable income increases.

Disposable income After-tax income

Disposable income that is available for spending and saving after an individual has purchased the basic necessities of food, clothing, and shelter is called **discretionary income.** People use discretionary income to purchase entertainment, vacations, automobiles, education, pets, furniture, appliances, and so on. Changes in total discretionary income affect sales of these products—especially automobiles, furniture, large appliances, and other costly durable goods. About 65 percent of all U.S. households have discretionary income; the average household discretionary income is around $11,000.[8]

Discretionary income Disposable income available for spending and saving after an individual has purchased the basic necessities of food, clothing, and shelter

Credit enables people to spend future income now or in the near future. However, credit increases current buying power at the expense of future buying power. Several factors determine whether consumers use or forgo credit. First, credit must be available to consumers. Interest rates, too, affect consumers' decisions to use credit, especially for expensive purchases such as homes, appliances, and automobiles. When credit charges are high, consumers are more likely to delay buying expensive items. Use of credit is also affected by credit terms, such as size of the down payment and amount and number of monthly payments.

A person can have a high income and very little wealth. It is also possible, but not likely, for a person to have great wealth but not much income. **Wealth** is the accumulation of past income, natural resources, and financial resources. It may exist in many forms, including cash, securities, savings accounts, jewelry, and real estate. Like income, wealth is unevenly distributed. The significance of wealth to marketers is that as people become wealthier they gain buying power in three ways: they can use their wealth to make current purchases, to generate income, and to acquire large amounts of credit.

Wealth The accumulation of past income, natural resources, and financial resources

Information about buying power is available from government sources, trade associations, and research agencies. One of the most current and comprehensive sources of buying power data is the *Sales & Marketing Management Survey of Buying Power,* published annually by *Sales & Marketing Management* magazine. Table 2.3 shows effective buying income data and the buying power index for specific geographic areas.

The most direct indicators of buying power in the *Survey of Buying Power* are effective buying income and buying power index. **Effective buying income (EBI)** is similar to what

Effective buying income (EBI) Income similar to disposable income, comprising salaries, wages, dividends, interest, profits, and rents—less federal, state, and local taxes

Table 2.3 Example of *Sales & Marketing Management's* **Effective Buying Power and Buying Power Index**

Metro Area	Total Effective Buying Income (EBI) ($000)	Median Household EBI	% of Hslds. by EBI Group (A) $10,000–$19,999 (B) $20,000–$34,999 (C) $35,000–$49,999 (D) $50,000 & Over				Buying Power Index (BPI)
			A	**B**	**C**	**D**	
Albuquerque	10,368,112	$34,696	15.9	23.4	19.3	30.3	.2501
Bernalillo	8,432,384	33,978	16.3	23.9	18.7	29.7	.2108
Albuquerque	6,922,088	34,308	16.6	22.9	19.0	30.1	.1815
Sandoval	1,222,509	42,316	11.6	19.8	22.5	38.4	.0229
Valencia	713,219	31,873	17.4	24.2	20.6	24.8	.0164
SUBURBAN TOTAL	3,446,024	35,487	14.4	24.3	19.9	30.8	.0686
Kokomo	1,650,377	37,817	14.7	20.6	20.8	33.0	.0387
Howard	1,387,590	37,430	14.5	20.4	20.8	32.7	.0333
Kokomo	693,570	31,425	17.5	21.3	21.1	24.2	.0220
Tipton	262,787	38,648	15.7	22.3	21.0	34.2	.0054
SUBURBAN TOTAL	956,867	43,887	11.9	20.3	20.5	41.8	.0167
West Palm Beach–							
Boca Raton	21,289,570	38,187	14.2	22.1	18.9	35.5	.4561
Palm Beach	21,289,570	38,187	14.2	22.1	18.9	35.5	.4561
Boca Raton	2,114,771	49,098	9.9	17.6	17.5	48.9	.0476
Boynton Beach	996,749	33,868	16.6	25.4	20.4	27.8	.0230
Delray Beach	1,217,488	36,794	15.2	21.9	18.1	34.5	.0391
West Palm Beach	1,222,485	31,215	16.6	23.9	18.3	25.9	.0386
SUBURBAN TOTAL	17,952,314	38,024	14.3	22.9	19.1	35.2	.3699

Source: *Sales & Marketing Management*, copyright © 1993, "Survey of Buying Power," 1995, pp. C-38, C-54, C-101. Used with permission.

Buying power index (BPI)
A weighted index consisting of population, effective buying income, and retail sales data

we call disposable income; it includes salaries, wages, dividends, interest, profits, and rents, less federal, state, and local taxes. The **buying power index (BPI)** is a weighted index, consisting of population, effective buying income, and retail sales data.[9] The higher the index number, the greater the buying power. The buying power index is most useful for comparative purposes. Marketers can use buying power indexes for a particular year to compare the buying power of one area with the buying power of another, or they can analyze trends for a particular area by comparing the area's buying power indexes for several years.

Income, wealth, and credit equip consumers with buying power to purchase goods and services. Marketing managers need to be aware of current levels and expected changes in buying power in their own markets because buying power directly affects the types and quantities of goods and services that consumers purchase. Just because consumers have buying power, however, does not mean that they will buy. Consumers must also be willing to use their buying power.

■ *Willingness to Spend*

Willingness to spend
An inclination to buy because of expected satisfaction from a product, influenced by the ability to buy, and numerous psychological and social forces

People's **willingness to spend** (their inclination to buy because of expected satisfaction from a product) is, to some degree, related to their ability to buy. That is, people are sometimes more willing to buy if they have the buying power. However, a number of other elements also influence willingness to spend. Some elements affect specific products; others influence spending in general. A product's absolute price and its price relative to the price

32

Introducing The New, Wider Diameter Solo® Classic®

A writing instrument designed by those who
know fine quality, for those who prefer a little more.

Luxurious proportions are suddenly within your grasp.

Choose from four classic colors and styles,
including ball-point pen or mechanical pencil at $22.50,
rolling ball at $27.50, or fountain pen at $32.50.

CROSS
SINCE 1846

Solo Classic is available at local retailers and features an unconditional lifetime mechanical guarantee.
Prices are manufacturer's suggested retail.

Figure 2.3
Willingness to Spend
Customers are willing to spend more
for Cross pens because of their prestige
and beauty.

of substitute products influence almost all of us. Cross pens, for example, appeal to customers who are willing to spend more for expensive writing instruments, even when lower priced pens are readily available (see Figure 2.3). The amount of satisfaction currently received or expected in the future from a product already owned may also influence consumers' desire to buy other products. Satisfaction depends not only on the quality of the functional performance of the currently owned product, but also on numerous psychological and social forces.

Factors that affect consumers' general willingness to spend are expectations about future employment, income levels, prices, family size, and general economic conditions. If people are unsure whether or how long they will be employed, willingness to buy ordinarily declines. Willingness to spend may increase if people are reasonably certain of higher incomes in the future. Expectations of rising prices in the near future may also increase willingness to spend in the present. For a given level of buying power, the larger the family, the greater the willingness to buy. One of the reasons for this relationship is that as the size of a family increases, more dollars must be spent to provide the basic necessities to sustain family members.

Political Forces

*P*olitical, legal, and regulatory forces of the marketing environment are closely interrelated. Legislation is enacted, legal decisions are interpreted by courts, and regulatory agencies are created and operated, for the most part, by elected or appointed officials. Legislation and regulations (or their lack) reflect the current political outlook. Consequently, the political forces of the marketing environment have the potential to influence marketing decisions and strategies.

Marketing organizations must maintain good relations with elected political officials for several reasons. Political officials well disposed toward particular firms or industries are less likely to create or enforce laws and regulations unfavorable to these companies. For example, political officials who believe that oil companies are making honest efforts to control pollution are unlikely to create and enforce highly restrictive pollution control laws. In addition, governments are big buyers, and political officials can influence how much a government agency purchases and from whom. Finally, political officials can play key roles in helping organizations secure foreign markets.

Many marketers view political forces as beyond their control and simply adjust to conditions arising from those forces. Some firms, however, seek to influence political forces. In some cases, organizations publicly protest the actions of legislative bodies. At times, organizations help to elect to political offices individuals who regard them positively. Much of this help is in the form of campaign contributions. Although laws restrict direct corporate contributions to campaign funds, corporate money may be channeled into campaign funds as corporate executives' or stockholders' personal contributions. Such actions violate the spirit of corporate campaign contribution laws. A sizable contribution to a campaign fund may carry with it an implicit understanding that the elected official will perform political favors for the contributing firm. A corporation may even contribute to the campaign funds of several candidates who seek the same office. Occasionally, some businesses find it so important to ensure favorable treatment that they make illegal corporate contributions to campaign funds.

While laws limit corporate contributions to campaign funds for specific candidates, it is legal for businesses and other organizations to contribute to political parties. Table 2.4 shows selected organizations, their interests, and their contributions to political parties. A number of organizations give to both parties. Note that the labor unions contribute only to the Democratic Party, whereas all the tobacco-related organizations contribute, often substantially, to both parties.

Table 2.4   Contributions to Political Parties

Organization	Major Interests	Dems ($)	GOP ($)
Occidental Petroleum Corp.	Natural gas, crude oil, fertilizers, and agricultural chemicals; also plastics and other industrial chemicals	34,000	140,000
Philip Morris Companies, Inc.	Brand names include Marlboro and Virginia Slims cigarettes, Miller beer, Kraft products, Post cereals, Maxwell House coffee, and Jell-O puddings and gelatins	32,000	279,830
RJR Nabisco, Inc.	Subsidiaries include RJ Reynolds Tobacco and Nabisco Brands	231,850	382,500
Service Employees International Union	Members include custodians in public and private offices, apartment buildings, hotels, and hospitals; lobbies for minimum wage improvements, hospital cost containment, and collective bargaining rights for federal workers	100,250	
Sheet Metal Workers' International Union	Labor union of 150,000 members, including installers of heating and air conditioning ducts	164,350	
Shell Oil Company	Exploration, production, transportation, and marketing of crude oil, natural gas, refined oil, and other chemical products	55,000	66,000
Sunkist Growers Inc.	Cooperative of citrus fruit and vegetable growers that markets approximately 65% of all citrus products consumed in the United States		100,000
Tobacco Institute	Consortium of tobacco product manufacturers; fights increased regulation of tobacco use and favors price supports for tobacco growers	98,175	64,720
United Auto Workers' Political Committee	Labor union lobbying to restrict imports of foreign-made automobiles; supports a comprehensive national health insurance program for workers	115,000	
United States Tobacco Co.	Tobacco products, including Skoal and Copenhagen oral snuff	56,200	308,174
United Steelworkers of America	Labor union representing 600,000 steel workers; favors trade restrictions on imports, assistance for workers who lose jobs to foreign competition, and "Buy American" campaigns	389,000	

Source: Copyright 1992, *USA Today*. Reprinted with permission.

Legal and Regulatory Forces

A number of laws and regulations influence marketing decisions and activities. Our discussion focuses on procompetitive and consumer protection laws and their interpretation. We also examine the effects of federal, state, local, and self-regulatory agencies on organizations' marketing efforts. Then we discuss some of the issues and problems of deregulation.

■ Procompetitive Legislation

Table 2.5 describes fourteen major procompetitive laws—laws designed to preserve competition—most of which were enacted to end various antitrade practices deemed unacceptable by society. Allegations of antitrade activities have brought Ticketmaster, the nation's largest distributor of sports and entertainment tickets, under investigation. Bands, fans, and competitors complain that Ticketmaster, which sold $1.6 billion worth of concert, theater, and event tickets in 1994, has a virtual monopoly over ticket sales, that

Table 2.5   Major Federal Laws Affecting Marketing Decisions

Act	Purposes
Sherman Antitrust Act (1890)	Prohibits contracts, combinations, or conspiracies to restrain trade; establishes as a misdemeanor monopolizing or attempting to monopolize
Clayton Act (1914)	Prohibits specific practices such as price discrimination, exclusive dealer arrangements, and stock acquisitions in which the effect may notably lessen competition or tend to create a monopoly
Federal Trade Commission Act (1914)	Created the Federal Trade Commission; also gives the FTC investigatory powers to be used in preventing unfair methods of competition
Robinson-Patman Act (1936)	Prohibits price discrimination that lessens competition among wholesalers or retailers; prohibits producers from giving disproportionate services or facilities to large buyers
Wheeler-Lea Act (1938)	Prohibits unfair and deceptive acts and practices regardless of whether competition is injured; places advertising of foods and drugs under the jurisdiction of the FTC
Lanham Act (1946)	Provides protection and regulation of brand names, brand marks, trade names, and trademarks
Celler-Kefauver Act (1950)	Prohibits any corporation engaged in commerce from acquiring the whole or any part of the stock or other share of the capital or assets of another corporation when the effect substantially lessens competition or tends to create a monopoly
Fair Packaging and Labeling Act (1966)	Makes illegal the unfair or deceptive packaging or labeling of consumer products
Magnuson-Moss Warranty (Federal Trade Commission) Act (1975)	Provides for minimum disclosure standards for written consumer product warranties; defines minimum content standards for written warranties; allows the FTC to prescribe interpretive rules in policy statements regarding unfair or deceptive practices
Consumer Goods Pricing Act (1975)	Prohibits the use of price maintenance agreements among manufacturers and resellers in interstate commerce
Trademark Counterfeiting Act (1980)	Provides civil and criminal penalties against those who deal in counterfeit consumer goods or any counterfeit goods that can threaten health or safety
Trademark Law Revision Act (1988)	Amends the Lanham Act to allow brands not yet introduced to be protected through registration with the Patent and Trademark Office
Nutrition Labeling and Education Act (1990)	Prohibits exaggerated health claims and requires all processed foods to contain labels with nutritional information
Telephone Consumer Protection Act (1991)	Establishes procedures to avoid unwanted telephone solicitations; prohibits marketers from using an automatic telephone dialing system or an artificial or prerecorded voice to certain telephone lines

it charges inflated service fees that make tickets outrageously expensive, especially for teenage fans, and that it has too much control over access to arenas. These accusations have led several consumers to file lawsuits charging the company with price gouging and antitrust violations, and prompted the U.S. Justice Department and several states' attorney general offices to investigate whether Ticketmaster is in fact engaging in monopolistic, antitrust behavior.[10] Let's take a closer look now at some of the most important procompetitive laws.

Sherman Antitrust Act
Legislation passed in 1890 to prevent businesses from restraining trade and monopolizing markets

The **Sherman Antitrust Act,** passed in 1890 to prevent businesses from restraining trade and monopolizing markets, condemns "every contract, combination, or conspiracy in restraint of trade." For example, a request that a competitor agree to fix prices or divide markets would, if accepted, result in a violation of the Sherman Act.[11] Proof of intent plays an important role in attempted monopolization cases under the Sherman Act.[12] Enforced by the Antitrust Division of the Department of Justice, the Sherman Antitrust Act applies to firms operating in interstate commerce and to U.S. firms operating in foreign commerce. The Sherman Antitrust Act, still highly relevant one hundred years after its passage, is being copied throughout the world as the basis for regulating fair competition.[13]

Clayton Act   A law passed in 1914 that prohibits specific practices, such as price discrimination, exclusive dealer arrangements, and stock acquisitions, that may decrease competition and lead to a monopoly

Because the provisions of the Sherman Antitrust Act were rather vague, courts have not always interpreted it as its creators intended. The Clayton Act was passed in 1914 to limit specific activities that can reduce competition. The **Clayton Act** prohibits price discrimination, tying and exclusive agreements, and the acquisition of stock in another corporation "where the effect may be to substantially lessen competition or tend to create a monopoly." In addition, the act prohibits members of one company's board of directors from holding seats on boards of competing corporations. The Clayton Act also exempts farm cooperatives and labor organizations from antitrust laws.

Federal Trade Commission Act   A 1914 law that established the Federal Trade Commission, which currently regulates the greatest number of marketing practices

The **Federal Trade Commission Act,** also passed in 1914, created the Federal Trade Commission (FTC), which today regulates the greatest number of marketing practices. Like the Clayton Act, the Federal Trade Commission Act was written to strengthen antimonopoly provisions of the Sherman Antitrust Act. Whereas the Clayton Act prohibits specific practices, the Federal Trade Commission Act more broadly prohibits unfair methods of competition. This act also empowers the FTC to work with the Department of Justice to enforce the Clayton Act. Later sections of this chapter discuss the FTC's regulatory activities.

Wheeler-Lea Act   Legislation enacted in 1938 to outlaw unfair and deceptive acts or practices, regardless of whether they injure competition

As in the case of the Sherman Antitrust Act, courts did not always interpret the Federal Trade Commission Act in ways its creators had intended. Hence, in 1938, Congress passed the **Wheeler-Lea Act,** which essentially outlaws unfair and deceptive acts or practices, regardless of whether they injure competition. It specifically prohibits false and misleading advertising of foods, drugs, therapeutic devices, and cosmetics. The Wheeler-Lea Act also provides penalties for violations and procedures for enforcement.

Robinson-Patman Act
A 1936 law prohibiting price discrimination that decreases competition and also prohibiting provision of services or facilities to purchasers on terms not offered equally to all purchasers

The 1936 **Robinson-Patman Act** is significant because it directly influences pricing policies. Its most important provision prohibits price discrimination among different purchasers of goods of similar grade and quality where the effect of such discrimination reduces competition among the purchasers or gives one purchaser a competitive edge. The Robinson-Patman Act did *not* outlaw price differentials, which are legal if they can be justified as cost savings or as meeting competition in good faith. The act also makes it unlawful knowingly to induce or receive discriminatory prices when they are prohibited by the Robinson-Patman Act. Finally, it outlaws providing services or facilities to purchasers on terms not offered equally to all purchasers.

■ *Consumer Protection Legislation*

The second category of regulatory laws, consumer protection legislation, is not a recent development. During the mid-1800s, lawmakers in many states passed laws to prohibit adulteration of food and drugs. However, consumer protection laws at the federal level mushroomed in the mid-1960s and early 1970s. A number of them deal with consumer safety—such as the food and drug acts, designed to protect people from actual and potential physical harm caused by adulteration or mislabeling. Other laws prohibit the sale of various hazardous products, such as flammable fabrics and toys that may injure children. Congress has also passed several laws concerning information disclosure. Some require that information about specific products—such as textiles, furs, cigarettes, and automobiles—be provided on labels. Other laws focus on particular marketing activities—product development and testing, packaging, labeling, advertising, and consumer financing. For example, the 1990 Nutrition Labeling and Education Act attempts to prevent exaggerated health claims on food packages. Products affected by the new law include cereals claiming to reduce heart disease and peanut butter touted as cholesterol free (as a vegetable product, peanut butter by nature does not contain cholesterol to begin with).

■ *Interpreting Laws*

Laws seem to be quite specific because they contain many complex clauses and subclauses, but in reality many laws and regulations are vague. This vagueness forces marketers to rely on legal advice rather than their own understanding and marketing ethics. Some organizations test the limits of certain laws by operating in a legally questionable way to see how far they can get with certain practices before being prosecuted. Other marketers, however, interpret regulations and statutes conservatively and strictly to avoid violating a vague law. When marketers interpret laws in relation to specific marketing practices, they often analyze recent court decisions, both to better understand what the law is intended to do and to predict future court interpretations.

■ *Encouraging Compliance with the Law*

Marketing activities are often at the forefront of organizational misconduct, with fraud and antitrust violations the most frequently sentenced organizational crimes. Legal violations usually begin when marketers "push the envelope" of standards and develop programs that unknowingly or unwittingly overstep the legal bounds. Many marketers lack experience in dealing with complex legal actions and decisions regulated by the Robinson-Patman Act, Sherman Antitrust Act, and the Federal Trade Commission. Consequently, they may not recognize that certain activities may be unacceptable or illegal. Advertising executives at Calvin Klein, for example, did not anticipate that the U.S. Justice Department would investigate their use of youthful models in provocative ads as a potential violation of child pornography laws.[14]

To ensure that marketers comply with the law, the federal government is moving toward greater organizational accountability for misconduct. In 1991 the United States Sentencing Commission (USSC) introduced a detailed set of guidelines to regulate the sentencing of companies convicted of breaking the law. The basic philosophy of the Federal Sentencing Guidelines for Organizations is that companies are responsible for crimes committed by their employees. These guidelines were therefore designed to hold companies accountable for the illegal actions of their employees as well as to streamline the sentencing and fine structures for offenses. (Previously, laws punished only those employees directly responsible for an offense, not the company.) The underlying assumption is that "good citizen corporations" can maintain compliance systems and internal controls to prevent misconduct and to educate employees about questionable activities. Thus, the new guidelines focus on crime prevention and detection by mitigating penalties for firms that have chosen to develop such compliance programs should one of their employees be involved in misconduct.

The bottom line is that unless a marketer works in a company with an effective compliance program that meets the minimum requirements of the U.S. Sentencing Commission's recommendations, both the marketer and the company face severe penalties if the marketer violates the law. Further, the Federal Sentencing Guidelines for individuals often mandate substantial prison sentences even for first-time offenders convicted of a felony, such as antitrust, fraud, import/export violations, or environmental crimes. The minimum requirements for an organizational compliance program are described in Chapter 3.

■ *Federal Regulatory Agencies*

Federal regulatory agencies influence many marketing activities, including product development, pricing, packaging, advertising, personal selling, and distribution. Usually, these bodies have the power to enforce specific laws, such as the Federal Trade

Commission Act, as well as some discretion in establishing operating rules and regulations to guide certain types of industry practices. Because of this discretion and overlapping areas of responsibility, confusion or conflict regarding which agencies have jurisdiction over which marketing activities is common.

Federal Trade Commission (FTC) An agency that regulates a variety of business practices and curbs false advertising, misleading pricing, and deceptive packaging and labeling

Of all the federal regulatory units, the **Federal Trade Commission** (**FTC**) influences marketing activities most. Although the FTC regulates a variety of business practices, it allocates a large portion of resources to curbing false advertising, misleading pricing, and deceptive packaging and labeling. When it receives a complaint or otherwise has reason to believe that a firm is violating a law, the commission issues a complaint stating that the business is in violation. If the company continues the questionable practice, the FTC can issue a cease-and-desist order, which is an order for the business to stop doing whatever caused the complaint. The firm can appeal to the federal courts to have the order rescinded. However, the FTC can seek civil penalties in court, up to a maximum penalty of $10,000 a day for each infraction if a cease-and-desist order is violated. In its battle against unfair pricing, the FTC has issued consent decrees alleging that corporate attempts to engage in price fixing or invitations to competitors to collude are violations even when the competitors in question refuse the invitations. Therefore, enforcement actions that prevent the intent to collude in price fixing serve as an important deterrent to price fixing.[15] The commission can also require companies to run corrective advertising in response to previous ads considered misleading. This mandated corrective advertising is proving to be costly to many companies.[16]

The FTC also assists business in complying with laws. New marketing methods are evaluated every year. When general sets of guidelines are needed to improve business practices in a particular industry, the FTC sometimes encourages firms within that industry to establish a set of trade practices voluntarily. The FTC may even sponsor a conference bringing together industry leaders and consumers for this purpose.

Unlike the Federal Trade Commission, other regulatory units are limited to dealing with specific products, services, or business activities. For example, the Food and Drug Administration (FDA) enforces regulations prohibiting the sale and distribution of adulterated, misbranded, or hazardous food and drug products. The FDA outlawed the sale and distribution of most over-the-counter hair-loss remedies after research indicated that few of the products were effective in restoring hair growth. Ethical Challenges (on the next page) discusses litigation surrounding silicone breast implants, which fall under the jurisdiction of the FDA. Table 2.6 outlines the areas of responsibility of seven federal regulatory agencies.

Table 2.6   Major Federal Regulatory Agencies

Agency	Major Areas of Responsibility
Federal Trade Commission (FTC)	Enforces laws and guidelines regarding business practices; takes action to stop false and deceptive advertising and labeling
Food and Drug Administration (FDA)	Enforces laws and regulations to prevent distribution of adulterated or misbranded foods, drugs, medical devices, cosmetics, veterinary products, and potentially hazardous consumer products
Consumer Product Safety Commission (CPSC)	Ensures compliance with the Consumer Product Safety Act; protects the public from unreasonable risk of injury from any consumer product not covered by other regulatory agencies
Federal Communications Commission (FCC)	Regulates communication by wire, radio, and television in interstate and foreign commerce
Environmental Protection Agency (EPA)	Develops and enforces environmental protection standards and conducts research into the adverse effects of pollution
Federal Power Commission (FPC)	Regulates rates and sales of natural gas producers, thereby affecting the supply and price of gas available to consumers; also regulates wholesale rates for electricity and gas, pipeline construction, and U.S. imports and exports of natural gas and electricity

■ ET**H**I**C**A**L** CHALLENGES ■

Breast Implant Litigation

Our society places an inordinate emphasis on physical attractiveness, and many women feel obligated to go to great lengths to shape up into that "ideal" silhouette. Many have opted to receive silicone-gel breast implants for cosmetic reasons or in reconstructive surgery following mastectomies. Between 1963 and 1992, as many as 2 million women received these implants, which were developed by Dow Corning in 1962.

A number of these women say they have experienced complications and adverse reactions to the silicone gel. In other cases, the sac containing the silicone has ruptured, allowing the gel to stray to other parts of the body, where it can interact with bodily organs and fluids and affect the immune system and connective tissues, possibly causing immune system disorders, arthritis, extreme fatigue, swollen lymph nodes, or lupus. The Food and Drug Administration (FDA) prohibited the use of the silicone implants in 1992, and they were pulled from the market.

As health problems escalated, thousands of women filed lawsuits against Dow Corning and other companies. Realizing that they faced years of court battles and billions of dollars in legal fees and potential losses, these companies joined together in 1994 and agreed to a $4.2 billion package to settle claims from women harmed by the implants.

Within a year, however, some 440,000 women registered to participate in the settlement, with about 70,000 of them qualifying for immediate compensation—far more than the 6,000 expected. Moreover, after spending more than $1 billion defending itself against implant lawsuits, Dow Corning was forced to seek bankruptcy protection in May 1995. As a result, the settlement package seems destined to fall apart. A new deal being negotiated in its place may eventually amount to as much as $7.2 billion (if Dow Corning participates) in settlements to women experiencing health problems as a result of their implants and to women who may face such problems over the next thirty years.

Sources: O. C. Ferrell and John Fraedrich, *Business Ethics: Ethical Decision Making and Cases;* 2nd ed. (Boston: Houghton Mifflin, 1994), pp. 221–224; Linda Himelstein, with John Carey and Keith Naughton, "A Breast-Implant Deal Comes Down to the Wire," *Business Week,* Sept. 4, 1995, pp. 88–92; Reuter's news story (via America Online: Rtr 13:22), Sept. 14, 1995.

■ *State and Local Regulatory Agencies*

All states—as well as many cities and towns—have regulatory agencies that enforce laws and regulations regarding marketing practices within their states or municipalities. State and local regulatory agencies try not to establish regulations that conflict with those of federal regulatory agencies. They generally enforce laws dealing with the production and sale of particular goods and services. Utilities, insurance, financial, and liquor industries are among those commonly regulated by state agencies. Among their targets are misleading pricing. Recent legal actions suggest that states are taking a firmer stance against perceived deceptive pricing practices and are using basic consumer research to define deceptive pricing.[17]

■ *Nongovernmental Regulatory Forces*

In the absence of governmental regulatory forces and in an attempt to prevent government intervention, some businesses try to regulate themselves. A number of trade associations have developed self-regulatory programs. Even though these programs are not a direct outgrowth of laws, many were established to stop or stall the development of laws and governmental regulatory groups that would regulate the associations' marketing practices. Sometimes trade associations establish ethics codes by which their members must abide or risk censure or exclusion from the association. For example, many cigarette manufacturers have agreed, through a code of ethics, not to advertise their products to children and teenagers. SGS International Certification Services, Inc. provides a special

Now there's living proof

As a responsible organization, you will almost certainly have systems in place to minimize the impact of your activities on the environment.

Now there is a way to prove it and ensure that you receive full commercial benefits from such systems - the **Green Dove Award**.

The Green Dove Award is the world's first accredited DIS **ISO 14001** registration for manufacturing and service companies. It is living proof of your commitment to the environment.

To be awarded the Green Dove Award, you must demonstrate the implementation of an environmental management policy which is committed to legislative compliance and continual environmental improvement. In return, you gain strategic advantages in marketing and public relations, reduce your environmental risks, improve your relationships with regulatory agencies and achieve cost reductions through improved resource usage. Everyone associated with your business will applaud these objectives with the knowledge that your decision has helped to improve the environment.

DIS **ISO 14001** certification, incorporating the Green Dove Award, is now available exclusively from SGS International Certification Services.

To find out how to achieve registration call us today at **1-800-747-9047**.

Ask for the living proof.

SGS International Certification Services, Inc.

Raising Industry Standards

Figure 2.4
Nongovernmental Regulatory Forces
SGS recognizes that effective incentives for protecting the environment can raise industry standards and improve the relationships between businesses and governmental regulatory agencies.

"Green Dove Award" to manufacturing and service organizations that show proof of their commitment to the environment (see Figure 2.4).

Self-regulatory programs have several advantages over governmental laws and regulatory agencies. Establishment and implementation are usually less expensive and guidelines are generally more realistic and operational. In addition, effective self-regulatory programs reduce the need to expand government bureaucracy. However, these programs have several limitations. When a trade association creates a set of industry guidelines for its members, nonmember firms do not have to abide by them. Furthermore, many self-regulatory programs lack the tools or authority to enforce guidelines. Finally, guidelines in self-regulatory programs are often less strict than those established by government agencies.

Better Business Bureau
A local, nongovernmental regulatory agency, supported by local businesses, that aids in settling problems between specific business firms and customers

Perhaps the best-known nongovernmental regulatory group, the **Better Business Bureau** is a local regulatory agency supported by local businesses. More than 140 bureaus help settle problems between consumers and specific business firms. Each bureau also acts to preserve good business practices in a locality, although it usually does not have strong enforcement tools for dealing with firms that employ questionable practices. When a firm continues to violate what the Better Business Bureau believes to be good business practices, the bureau warns consumers through local newspapers or broadcast media.

The Council of Better Business Bureaus is a national organization composed of all local Better Business Bureaus. The National Advertising Division (NAD) of the Council of Better Business Bureaus operates a self-regulatory program that investigates claims regarding alleged deceptive advertising. For example, after reviewing a commercial for a Nintendo video game, NAD complained that the advertisement implied that Nintendo was the sole marketer of ice hockey video games, when in fact two other ice hockey games were on the market. Nintendo disagreed with the complaint but agreed to consider NAD's concerns in future advertising campaigns.

National Advertising Review Board (NARB) A self-regulatory unit that considers cases in which an advertiser challenges issues raised by the National Advertising Division (an arm of the Council of Better Business Bureaus) about an advertisement

Another self-regulatory entity, the **National Advertising Review Board (NARB),** considers cases in which an advertiser challenges issues raised by the National Advertising Division about an advertisement. Cases are reviewed by panels drawn from NARB members representing advertisers, agencies, and the public. For example, after an NAD ruling, the NARB upheld the ruling that Colgate-Palmolive should discontinue an advertising claim that calcium in Colgate Great Regular Flavor toothpaste helps Colgate's fluoride penetrate teeth for outstanding cavity prevention. The ruling was based on the fact that both regulatory groups found that Colgate's data supporting the claim were inconclusive. Colgate responded that it had discontinued the campaign before the NARB ruling but would consider the ruling when developing future advertisements.[18]

The NARB, sponsored by the Council of Better Business Bureaus and three advertising trade organizations, has no official enforcement powers. However, if a firm refuses to comply with its decision, the NARB may publicize the questionable practice and file a complaint with the FTC.

Technological Forces

*T*he word *technology* brings to mind scientific advances such as personal computers, compact discs, cordless phones, electronic fuel injection and antilock brakes, fax machines, robots, superconductors, lasers, space shuttles, the Internet, and more. Such developments make it possible for marketers to operate ever more efficiently and to provide an exciting array of products for consumers. However, even though these innovations are outgrowths of technology, none of them *is* technology. **Technology** is the application of knowledge and tools to solve problems and perform tasks more efficiently. Technology grows out of research performed by businesses, universities, government agencies, and nonprofit organizations. More than half of this research is paid for by the federal government, which supports research in such diverse areas as health, defense, agriculture, energy, and pollution.

Technology The application of knowledge and tools to solve problems and perform tasks more efficiently

The rapid technological growth of the last several decades is expected to continue into the twenty-first century. It is transforming the U.S. economy into the most productive in the world and providing Americans with an ever-higher standard of living and tremendous opportunities for sustained business expansion.[19] Technology and technological advancements clearly influence buyers' and marketers' decisions, so let's take a closer look at the impact of technology and its use on the marketplace.

**Figure 2.5
The Impact of Technology**
Newsweek maximizes its visibility to Internet users by placing its magazine online.

■ *Impact of Technology*

Technology determines how we, as members of society, satisfy our physiological needs. In various ways and to varying degrees, eating and drinking habits, sleeping patterns, sexual activities, health care, and work performance are all influenced by both existing technology and changes in technology. Because of the technological revolution in communications, for example, marketers now can reach vast numbers of people more efficiently through a variety of media. Fax machines, voice mail, cellular phones, pagers, and notebook computers help marketers stay in touch with clients, make appointments, and handle last-minute orders or cancellations. Telecommuting—using telecommunications technology to work from home or other nontraditional areas—is becoming an increasingly popular use of computer technology. About 9 million employees telecommute for at least part of their workweek, with marketing a significant telecommuting job.[20]

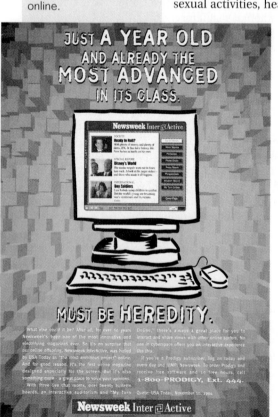

Personal computers are now in 36 percent of all U.S. consumers' homes, and 18 million of them include modems for phone line hook-up. These consumers represent an opportunity for marketers to use online marketing communications,[21] as well as to introduce new products to satisfy customers. In Figure 2.5, *Newsweek* takes advantage of technological advances by making its magazines available online. More and more companies are using the World Wide Web—an Internet program that organizes information into hyperlinked pages with text, pictures, and sound—to sell products. Club Med's page, for example, depicts its resorts, and Fidelity Investments has a Web page with descriptions of its funds, worksheets, and software samples available for downloading.[22] Online stores sell everything from neckties and coffee to books and records, and whole cybermalls invite consumers to browse catalogs and order merchandise. Who shops in cyberspace? At the beginning of 1996, about 37 million people over the age of sixteen in North America had access to the Internet either at home or at work. The average user spends five and a half hours online each week. These numbers lead experts to anticipate that by the year 2000 consumers and companies will buy and sell goods and services worth up to $22 billion over the Internet.[23]

Technology can help marketers become more productive. Many restaurants, for example, are using computers to track customers' eating habits, speed up order taking, and reduce waste and labor in food preparation. At the Stinking Rose in San Francisco, waiters record orders on hand-held computers, and Taco Bell is testing a computer system that would allow customers to place their own orders.[24] Computer technology also helps make warehouse storage and inventory control more efficient and, therefore, less expensive. Often these savings are passed on to consumers in the form of lower prices. Technological advances in transportation enable consumers to travel farther and more often to shop at a larger number of stores. They also improve producers' ability to deliver products to retailers and wholesalers. The ability of today's manufacturers of relatively lightweight products to reach any of their dealers within twenty-four hours (via overnight carriers like UPS and FedEx) would astound their counterparts of fifty years ago.

■ *Adoption and Use of Technology*

Many companies do not stay market leaders because they fail to keep up with technological changes. It is important for firms to determine when a technology is changing the industry and to define the strategic influence of the new technology.[25] For example, through its client/server partnership with IBM, Warner Bros. now has a multimedia system for displaying and selling original cartoon artwork in its Studio Stores (see Figure 2.6).

The extent to which a firm can protect inventions stemming from research also influences its use of technology. How secure a product is from imitation depends on how easily it can be copied by others without violating its patent. If ground-breaking products and processes cannot be protected through patents, a company is less likely to market them and make the benefits of its research available to competitors.

Technology assessment
A procedure for anticipating the effects of new products and processes on a firm's operation, other business organizations, and society

Through a procedure known as **technology assessment,** managers try to foresee the effects of new products and processes on their firm's operation, on other business organizations, and on society in general. With information obtained through a technology assessment, management tries to estimate whether benefits of adopting a specific technology outweigh costs to the firm and to society at large. The degree to which a business is technologically based also influences its management's response to technology.

Figure 2.6
Adopting and Using Technology
IBM has created an OS/2®-based multimedia system that allows a network of Warner Bros. Studio Stores to quickly and efficiently display and sell original cartoon artwork.

Sociocultural Forces

Sociocultural forces
The influences in a society
and its culture(s) that change
people's attitudes, beliefs, norms,
customs, and lifestyles

Sociocultural forces are the influences in a society and its culture(s) that bring about changes in attitudes, beliefs, norms, customs, and lifestyles. Profoundly affecting how people live, these forces help determine what, where, how, and when people buy products. Like the other environmental forces, sociocultural forces present marketers with both challenges and opportunities. For a closer look a sociocultural forces, we examine three major issues: demographic and diversity characteristics, cultural values, and the consumer movement. We further explore the effects of culture and subcultures on buying behavior in Chapter 6.

■ *Demographic and Diversity Characteristics*

Changes in a population's demographic characteristics—such as age, gender, race, ethnicity, marital and parental status, income, and education—have a significant bearing on relationships and individual behavior. These shifts lead to changes in how people live and ultimately in their consumption of products such as food, clothing, housing, transportation, communication, recreation, education, and health services. In this section, we take a look at a few of the changes in demographics and diversity that are affecting marketing activities.

One demographic change affecting the marketplace is the increasing proportion of older consumers. According to the U.S. Census Bureau, the number of people aged sixty-five and older is expected to more than double by the year 2050, reaching 80 million.[26] Consequently, marketers can expect significant increases in the demand for health-care services, recreation, tourism, retirement housing, and selected skin-care products. Del Webb Development Co. is one firm taking advantage of this opportunity by creating several Sun City retirement communities for mature adults. In addition to providing housing, facilities, and activities designed for older residents, Del Webb's newest Sun City is located to take advantage of the scenic beauty and moderate climate of the Texas Hill Country, as well as close proximity to cultural events in nearby Austin. To reach older customers effectively, of course, marketers must understand the diversity within the mature market with respect to geographic location, income, marital status, and mobility and self-care limitations.

The number of singles is also on the rise. Nearly 40 percent of U.S. adults are single and many plan to remain that way. Moreover, single men living alone comprise 10 percent of all households (up from 3.5 percent in 1970), and single women living alone make up 15 percent of all households (up from 7.3 percent in 1970).[27] Single people have quite different spending patterns from couples and families with children. They are less likely to own homes and so buy less furniture and fewer appliances. They spend more heavily on convenience foods, restaurants, travel, entertainment, and recreation. In addition, they tend to prefer smaller packages, whereas families often buy bulk goods and products packaged in multiple servings.

The United States is about to enter another baby boom, with 72 million Americans aged 18 or younger. The new baby boom represents 28 percent of the total population, compared to the original baby boomers, now aged 31 to 49 and comprising 30 percent of the total. The children of the current baby boomers differ from one another radically in terms of race, living arrangements, and socioeconomic class. Thus the newest baby boom is much more diverse than previous generations.[28] Inside Marketing profiles a restaurant chain that targets families.

Another noteworthy population trend is the increasing multicultural nature of U.S. society. The number of immigrants into the United States has steadily risen during the last thirty years. In the 1960s, 3.2 million people immigrated to the United States; in the 1970s, 4.2 million came; and in the 1980s, the U.S. received over 6 million legal immigrants, very few of whom were of European origin. Another reason for the increasing cultural diversification of the United States is that most recent immigrants are relatively young, whereas U.S. citizens of European origin are growing older. These younger immigrants tend to have more children than their older counterparts, further shifting the population balance. By the end of the 1990s, the U.S. population will have shifted from one dominated by whites

INSIDE MARKETING

Rainforest Cafe

To satisfy Americans' desire for unique dining experiences, themed restaurants like Hard Rock Cafe and Planet Hollywood have multiplied in recent years. The newest entry is Rainforest Cafe, a jungle-themed restaurant.

Located in Bloomington, Minnesota's huge Mall of America, the Rainforest Cafe provides a primal dining adventure. Diners of all ages eat amid fancy aquariums, live parrots, fake monkeys, and synthetic banyan trees draped with Tarzan-style vines. Every quarter hour or so, a simulated cloudburst, complete with thunder and lightning, entertains patrons. Rain falls through puffs of fog onto a mossy rock wall. Diners can choose from among menu items such as Eyes of the Ocelot (meat loaf with mushrooms), Jungle Chowder (vegetable soup), and Gorillas in the Mist (banana cheesecake). They can also buy T-shirts, sweatshirts, coffee mugs, glass sculptures, and environmental and animal toys from a shop inside the restaurant.

While other theme restaurants target an 18-to-40-year-old crowd, Rainforest Cafe caters to families. For example, space is set aside for wheelchairs and strollers. The restaurant also hires a professional trainer to take its thirteen parrots to shows at local schools and civic associations, which stimulates interest among local citizens.

The Rainforest Cafe has been wildly successful since its opening in 1994. Diners often wait as long as two hours for tables (most check in, then shop the Mall of America until time to eat). The cafe turns over its 295 seats seven times a day, double the average for comparable restaurants, and its per-seat revenues exceed $2,500 a month. In its first year, it had sales of $35,000 per seat; the norm for entertainment theme restaurants is about $10,000 per seat. Moreover, a third of all diners buy a memento from the retail shop, where margins are a fruitful 50 percent.

In fact, Rainforest Cafe has been so popular that the restaurant plans to expand the concept to eight more stores by the end of 1997. The second, which opened at Woodfield Mall in Schaumberg, Illinois, in 1995, is larger, with 450 seats. A third restaurant was slated to open at Disney World in 1996.

Sources: Christie Brown, "Meat Loaf and Monkeys," *Forbes,* Oct. 23, 1995, pp. 44–45; and Tony Kennedy, 'Rainforest Cafe Expects Profit; Shares Rise $1," *(Minneapolis) Star Tribune,* June 14, 1995, p. 3D.

to one consisting of three large racial and ethnic groups: whites, blacks, and Hispanics. By the year 2005, the U.S. government estimates nearly 38 million blacks, almost 36 million Hispanics, over 14 million Asians, and more than 2 million Native Americans will call the United States home.[29] Table 2.7 illustrates this demographic mix.

Marketers recognize that these profound changes in the U.S. population bring unique problems and opportunities. Ethnic minorities, for example, generate nearly $600 billion in annual buying power.[30] But a diverse population means a more diverse customer base, and marketing practices must be modified—and diversified—to meet its changing needs.

Table 2.7 Projected U.S. Population by Age and Race for the Year 2010				
Age	**White**	**Black**	**Hispanic**	**Other**
0 to 17	14.3%	3.9%	4.5%	1.8%
18 to 34	14.5	3.2	3.6	1.6
35 to 54	19.4	3.3	3.4	1.7
55+	19.5	2.2	2.0	1.1
All ages	67.7%	12.6%	13.5%	6.2%
TOTAL PROJECTED POPULATION = 300,431,000				

Source: U.S. Bureau of the Census, *Statistical Abstract of the United States 1994,* 114th edition (Washington, D.C.: U.S.G.P.O., 1994), pp. 24–25.

■ *Cultural Values*

Changes in values have dramatically influenced people's needs and desires for products. Although cultural values do not shift overnight, they do change at varying speeds. Marketers try to monitor these changes knowing that this information can equip them to predict changes in consumers' needs for products at least in the near future.

Cultural values seem to have veered away from materialism and conspicuous consumption. During the 1980s, the "me" orientation of the 1970s gained a strong materialistic focus, but consumers of the 1990s seem less bent on public display of wealth and its trappings. This change affects not only the types of products consumers desire, but also how these products are branded, priced, promoted, and distributed.

Starting in the late 1980s, issues of health, nutrition, and exercise grew in importance. People today are more concerned about the foods they eat, choosing low-fat, nonfat, and no-cholesterol products. Compared with the previous two decades, Americans are more likely to favor smoke-free environments and reduced consumption of alcohol. They have also altered their sexual behavior to reduce the risk of contracting sexually transmitted diseases. Marketers have responded with a proliferation of foods, beverages, and exercise products that fit this new lifestyle, as well as with programs to help people quit smoking and contraceptives that are safer and more effective.

The major source of cultural values is the family. For years, when asked about the most important aspects of their lives, adults specified family issues and a happy marriage. These days, however, only one out of three marriages will last. Studies suggest that values about the permanence of marriage are changing. Because a happy marriage is prized so much, more people are willing to give up an unhappy one and seek a different marriage partner or opt to remain single.[31] Children remain important, however. Marketers have responded with safer, upscale baby gear and supplies, children's electronics, and family entertainment products. Marketers are also aiming more marketing efforts directly at children because children often play pivotal roles in purchasing decisions.

Today's consumers are more and more concerned about the natural environment. One of society's environmental hurdles is proper disposal of waste, especially of non-

Figure 2.7
Companies Respond to Cultural Values
Phillips Petroleum responds to our cultural concern for environmental safety and conservation.

degradable materials, such as disposable diapers and polystyrene packaging. Companies have responded by developing more environmentally sensitive products and packaging. Procter & Gamble, for example, uses recycled materials in some of its packaging and markets environment-friendly refills. Raytheon has developed a new Amana refrigerator that does not use chlorofluorocarbons (CFCs), which harm the earth's ozone layer. In Figure 2.7, Phillips Petroleum builds customer awareness of its commitment to develop products and programs that conserve natural resources and protect the environment. A number of marketers sponsor recycling programs and encourage their customers to take part in them.

■ *The Consumer Movement*

Consumer movement
Organized efforts by individuals, groups, and organizations seeking to protect consumers' rights

The **consumer movement** is a varied array of independent individuals, groups, and organizations seeking to protect consumers' rights. The movement's major forces are individual consumer advocates, consumer organizations and other interest groups, consumer education, and consumer laws.

To achieve their objectives, consumers and their advocates write letters to companies, lobby government agencies, broadcast public service announcements, and boycott companies whose activities they deem irresponsible. For example, several organizations evaluate children's products for safety, often announcing dangerous products at Christmastime so parents can avoid them. Consumer protests about child-proof medicine containers that seem to be adult-proof as well (especially for older adults with arthritis) led the U.S. Consumer Product Safety Commission to introduce new packaging standards. Under the revised rules, manufacturers must make it possible for adults to open containers designated as child-resistant within five minutes, while children must remain unable to open them.[32] Other actions by the consumer movement have resulted in seat belts and air bags in automobiles, dolphin-safe tuna, the banning of unsafe three-wheeled motorized vehicles, and numerous laws regulating product safety and information.

SUMMARY

The marketing environment consists of external forces that directly or indirectly influence an organization's acquisition of inputs (personnel, financial resources, raw materials, information) and generation of outputs (goods, services, ideas). The marketing environment includes competitive, economic, political, legal and regulatory, technological, and sociocultural forces.

To monitor changes in these forces, marketers practice environmental scanning and analysis. Environmental scanning is the process of collecting information about forces in the marketing environment; environmental analysis is the process of assessing and interpreting information obtained in scanning. This information helps marketing managers predict opportunities and threats associated with environmental fluctuation. Marketing management may assume either a passive, reactive approach or a proactive, aggressive approach in responding to these environmental fluctuations. The choice depends on an organization's structures and needs and on the composition of environmental forces that affect it.

Although all businesses compete for consumers' dollars, a company's direct competitors are usually businesses in its geographic area that market products resembling its own or ones that can be substituted for them. The number of firms controlling the supply of a product may affect the strength of competition. There are four general types of competitive structures: monopoly, oligopoly, monopolistic competition, and pure competition. Marketers monitor what competitors are currently doing and assess changes occurring in the competitive environment.

The economic factors that can strongly influence marketing decisions and activities are general economic conditions, buying power, and willingness to spend. The overall state of the economy fluctuates in a general pattern known as a business cycle. The stages of the business cycle are prosperity, recession, depression, and recovery. Consumers' goods, services, and financial holdings make up their buying power, or ability to purchase. Financial sources of buying power are income, credit, and wealth. After-tax income used for spending or saving is disposable income. Disposable income left after an individual purchases the basic necessities of food, clothes, and shelter is discretionary income. Two measures of buying power are effective buying income (including salaries, wages, dividends, interest, profits, and rents, less federal, state, and local taxes) and the buying power index (a weighted index consisting of population, effective buying income, and retail sales data). Factors affecting consumers' willingness to spend are product price, level of satisfaction obtained from currently used products, family size, and expectations about future employment, income, prices, and general economic conditions.

The political, legal, and regulatory forces of the marketing environment are closely interrelated. Current political outlook is reflected in legislation and regulations or lack of them. The political environment may determine what laws and regulations affecting specific marketers are enacted and how much the government purchases and from which suppliers; it can also be important in helping organizations secure foreign markets.

Federal legislation affecting marketing activities can be divided into procompetitive legislation—laws designed to preserve and encourage competition—and consumer protection laws. The Sherman Antitrust Act sought to prevent monopolies and activities that limit competition; subsequent legislation, such as the Clayton Act, the Federal Trade Commission Act, the Wheeler-Lea Act, and the Robinson-Patman Act, was directed toward more specific practices. Consumer protection laws generally relate to product safety and information disclosure. Actual effects of legislation are determined by how marketers and courts interpret the laws. New federal sentencing guidelines represent an attempt to force marketers to comply with the laws.

Federal regulatory agencies influence most marketing activities. Federal, state, and local regulatory units usually have power to enforce specific laws and some discretion in establishing operating rules and drawing up regulations to guide certain types of industry practices. Industry self-regulation represents another regulatory force; marketers view this type of regulation more favorably than government action because they have more opportunity to take part in creating guidelines. Self-regulation may be less expensive than government regulation, and its guidelines are generally more realistic. However, such regulation generally cannot ensure compliance as effectively as government agencies.

Technology is knowledge of how to accomplish tasks and goals. Consumer demand, product development, packaging, promotion, prices, and distribution systems are all influenced directly by technology.

Sociocultural forces are the influences in a society and its culture that result in changes in attitudes, beliefs, norms, customs, and lifestyles. Major sociocultural issues directly affecting marketers include demographic characteristics and diversity, cultural values, and the consumer movement. Changes in a population's demographic characteristics, such as age, income, race, and ethnicity, can lead to changes in that population's consumption of products. Another sociocultural force is diversity. With blacks and Hispanics representing a growing percentage of the population, the United States is becoming a multicultural society. For marketers, this increasingly diverse population means a more diverse consumer base. Changes in cultural values, such as materialism, the importance of health and nutrition and of marriage and family, and concerns about the natural environment, have had striking effects on people's needs for products and therefore are closely monitored by marketers. The consumer movement includes independent individuals, groups, and organizations trying to protect consumers' rights. Consumer rights organizations inform and organize other consumers, raise issues, help businesses develop consumer-oriented programs, and pressure lawmakers to enact consumer protection laws.

IMPORTANT TERMS

Environmental scanning	Recovery	Sherman Antitrust Act	National Advertising
Environmental analysis	Buying power	Clayton Act	Review Board (NARB)
Competition	Income	Federal Trade Commission	Technology
Monopoly	Disposable income	Act	Technology assessment
Oligopoly	Discretionary income	Wheeler-Lea Act	Sociocultural forces
Monopolistic competition	Wealth	Robinson-Patman Act	Consumer movement
Pure competition	Effective buying income	Federal Trade Commission	
Prosperity	(EBI)	(FTC)	
Recession	Buying power index (BPI)	Better Business Bureau	
Depression	Willingness to spend		

DISCUSSION AND REVIEW QUESTIONS

1. Why are environmental scanning and analysis so important?
2. In what ways can each of the business cycle stages affect consumers' reactions to marketing strategies?
3. What business cycle stage are we experiencing currently? How is this stage affecting business firms in your area?

4. Define income, disposable income, and discretionary income. How does each type of income affect consumer buying power?
5. How is consumer buying power affected by wealth and consumer credit?
6. How is buying power measured? Why should it be evaluated?

7. What factors influence a consumer's willingness to spend?

8. How are political forces related to legal and governmental regulatory forces?

9. Describe marketers' attempts to influence political forces.

10. What types of procompetitive legislation directly affect marketing practices?

11. What was the major objective of most procompetitive laws? Do the laws generally accomplish this objective? Why or why not?

12. What are the major provisions of the Robinson-Patman Act? Which marketing mix decisions are influenced directly by this act?

13. What types of problems do marketers experience as they interpret legislation?

14. What are the goals of the Federal Trade Commission? List the ways in which the FTC affects marketing activities. Do you think a single regulatory agency should have such broad jurisdiction over so many marketing practices? Why or why not?

15. Name several nongovernmental regulatory forces. Do you believe that self-regulation is more or less effective than governmental regulatory agencies? Why?

16. What does the term *technology* mean to you?

17. How does technology affect you as a member of society? Do the benefits of technology outweigh its costs and dangers? Defend your answer.

18. Discuss the impact of technology on marketing activities.

19. What factors determine whether a business organization adopts and uses technology?

20. What is the evidence that cultural diversity is increasing in the United States?

21. In what ways are cultural values changing? How are marketers responding to these changes?

22. Describe the consumer movement. Analyze some active consumer forces in your area.

APPLICATION QUESTIONS

1. Reread the environmental scanning and analysis section in this chapter. Assume you are opening *one* of the retail stores listed below. Identify publications at the library that could provide useful information about the environmental forces likely to affect the store that you choose. Briefly summarize the information that each provides.
   a. convenience store
   b. women's clothing store
   c. grocery store
   d. fast-food restaurant
   e. furniture store

2. Refer to Table 2.3 for this question. Which *city* has the strongest buying power index? Which *metro area* has the weakest effective buying income?

Explain how EBI is determined. How is EBI useful to a marketer?

3. Assume Bryant Pipe and AAA Pipe are the only two manufacturers of steel pipe in the United States. Bryant has negotiated with AAA to purchase 40 percent of AAA. Bryant also has come to an agreement with AAA to purchase some of AAA's small pipes. What law(s) are most likely to influence the interactions between Bryant and AAA (refer to Table 2.5)?

4. Technological advances and sociocultural forces have had a great impact on marketers. Identify at least one technological advancement and one sociocultural change that has affected you as a consumer. Explain the impact of each on your needs as a customer.

Case 2.1 AT&T: Working Toward a Safe and Green Tomorrow

With Alexander Graham Bell's famous call for help—"Mr. Watson. Come here. I want you"—the American Telephone and Telegraph Company (AT&T) was born. The year was 1876, and those, the first words spoken over a telephone, came as Bell was perfecting his invention. The same invention later would propel an entire industry and change the lives of billions of people.

The early history of AT&T was characterized by dynamic growth internally and through acquisition. Once Bell's invention was patented in 1877, Boston-based Bell Telephone was formed. The following year, another company, New England Telephone, was established by the same group. The two organizations were consolidated into National Bell Telephone in 1879. By 1882, AT&T was flourishing and had gained enough size and power to take control of the nation's largest electrical equipment manufacturer, Western Electric, from Western Union, its chief rival in telecommunications.

The company's original patents ran out in the 1890s and it struggled to maintain market position. After relocating its corporate headquarters to New York and changing its name to AT&T, the focus was turned to gaining control of smaller competitors and preventing independent telecommunications operators from accessing Bell System phone lines. Bell Labs, the company's much heralded research and development center, was founded in 1925. By 1949, the company had grown so dominant in the communications industry that the federal government forced it to divest itself of Western Electric. Government intervention also caused AT&T to be stripped of its telephone equipment monopoly, to let competing long-distance service providers hook up to its phone network in the late 1960s.

In the early 1980s, the company was again forced to reorganize. As a result, AT&T became highly diversified, with ventures into financial services, supercomputers, and emergent forms of video and other electronic communications. With 1995 sales of $80 billion and profits of $139 million, AT&T today is not only still the largest telecommunications company in the United States, but also the nation's largest service company of any kind.

Often, large and highly successful companies such as AT&T are viewed by the public as being a burden to the environment. Such perceptions are unwarranted with AT&T, as the company is one of the most environmentally innovative and responsible companies in the world. For example, during a five-year period in the late 1980s and early 1990s, the company lowered air emissions 81 percent and cut disposal of manufactured waste in half. At the same time, AT&T reduced its release of ozone-depleting chlorofluorocarbons (CFCs) by nearly 90 percent. The company was also praised for its efforts to increase recycling of paper and for providing financial incentives to employees for devising ways to improve environmental performance. Also, AT&T produced detailed annual reports documenting the corporation's socially responsible actions. The company was awarded almost 20 environmental awards in just the first three years of the 1990s for its efforts.

Gaining a better understanding of the nature of AT&T's commitment to preserving the environment requires the examination of some of the successful programs enacted at the company's individual production and research facilities, located at every corner of the globe.

For example, the company's consumer products facility in Singapore was AT&T's first CFC-free facility, completely phasing out emissions of the harmful substance fully four years ahead of the corporate deadline in 1990. Quality Improvement Teams (QITs) at the Singapore facility now are focused on improving social responsibility through increased company recycling efforts. Already, some 15 tons of paper, plastics, and other materials are recycled each month, which saves the company about $50,000 per year and helps preserve the environment for future generations.

In the United States, AT&T's socially responsible activities take many forms. At the company's Richmond, Virginia, printed circuit board facility, for example, comprehensive environmental programs have set the standard for the rest of the industry. Great strides have been made toward the elimination of CFCs and the reduction of toxic air emissions. As regards the latter, through development of water-based chemical solutions to replace oil-based solvents formerly used, toxic emissions were cut by 98 percent over a six-year period. This reduction represents a decrease of 4.6 million pounds of pollutants released into the environment per year.

In Atlanta, AT&T has established itself as a leader in recycling technology. Faced with area recycling facilities' refusal to accept the company's massive accumulation of waste paper for recycling, AT&T worked out an arrangement with the Fort Howard Paper company, a local paper products manufacturer, to have the company recycle all of AT&T's waste paper into paper products AT&T would buy again at discount prices. Two tractor trailer loads of waste paper, or around 88,000 pounds, are loaded at the Atlanta facility each week. It is then processed by Fort Howard into tissues, paper towels, and napkins, which are used at AT&T's Atlanta facility. According to AT&T's recycling manager, the programs "close the loop" on what was previously a waste of scarce resources. They are both economically and environmentally sound.

In Phoenix, AT&T has used its telecommunications technology to solve nagging environmental problems caused by high per-capita automobile usage. In response to a mandate by the state legislature to reduce the number of commuter miles driven by 5 percent annually, the company set up a pilot "telecommuting" program with Arizona's largest employer, the state. Through use of AT&T telecommunications technology—fax, modem, and computer—the 134 participants in the initial program were allowed to work from their homes one day a week. In six months, amazing results were realized. The participants drove nearly 100,000 fewer miles, preventing some 1.9 million tons of air pollution, and saving nearly 4,000 hours of work time, which otherwise would have been spent unproductively in transit. Now, several years after completion of the pilot project, AT&T has nearly 450 "telecommuters" in the Phoenix area.

AT&T continues to invest millions of dollars into research aimed at developing products and manufacturing processes which will not harm the environment and prove profitable to the company. The company recently invested some $25 million out of its operations in an attempt to develop an array of technologies designed to eliminate ozone-depleting emissions, for example. As a result, AT&T was able to eliminate all such emissions by early 1993—well over a year ahead of corporate goals. AT&T took into account costs associated with product tracking and labeling production entailing CFC emission and the high taxes levied on such activities, and estimates that the early phase-out saves it approximately $25 million each year. In addition, while some of these technologies were sold to other companies, some were simply given away in a company effort to spread socially responsible production technologies to other firms and industries.

AT&T views socially responsible corporate behavior as environmentally sound and economically practical. The company is active in school recycling and other environmental education programs in many areas in which it has operations, proof that a large company can be successful and still be concerned about the environment and welfare of future generations. All in all, AT&T considers social responsibility an investment in our future and will continue to strive to be at the forefront of environmentally conscious technology.[33]

Questions for Discussion
1. Evaluate the legal and regulatory forces that AT&T must monitor.
2. How do the forces of competition, technology, and economics influence the development of AT&T's marketing strategy?
3. Evaluate AT&T's efforts to improve the environment. How will these efforts foster relationships with customers?

Case 2.2 Legal Issues at Archer Daniels Midland

The Archer Daniels Midland Company (ADM) reaches into so many of the products that consumers around the globe eat and drink that it calls itself the "supermarket to the world." The nearly century-old firm mills flour and processes linseed oil, soybeans, corn, soybean-based vegetable protein, sugar, peanuts, citric acid, and a variety of vitamin products and additives for human and animal consumption. As the largest agricultural commodities processor in the United States, ADM employs nearly 15,000 to operate 200 plants processing 150,000 tons of grain, seed, and vegetable products each day. In 1995, ADM generated profits of $786 million on sales of $12.7 billion.

Although profitable, 1995 was a tumultuous year for ADM. The media and competitors questioned Chairman and CEO Dwayne Andreas's personal relationships with political figures including President Bill Clinton and Senator Bob Dole, as well as the company's history of hefty political contributions to legislators. Allegations surfaced that ADM and some of its larger rivals in the flour-milling industry had become too powerful, perhaps at the expense of consumer choice. There were charges that ADM's board of directors was overgrown, overpaid, and under the thumb of company insiders. While these issues alone raised serious ethical, legal, and performance questions for ADM, the firm's major source of trouble involved accusations of price fixing, or conspiring with competitors to set artificially high prices for a product called lysine.

In 1989, ADM formed a new biochemical products division and hired Dr. Mark Whitacre, a biochemist, to head it. Whitacre's first objective was to get into the production of lysine, an amino acid derived from corn used in swine and poultry feed to promote the growth of lean muscle. ADM invested $150 million in lysine production and marketing and formally entered the market in early 1991. Adopting an aggressive price-cutting strategy, ADM gained market share quickly. A fierce price war soon developed, and the per-pound price of lysine dropped from $1.30 to around $.60. Although ADM swiftly grabbed 30 percent of the global lysine market, it was losing millions of dollars a month on its lysine operations.

Mark Whitacre was asked to begin working with Terry Wilson, the president of ADM's corn-processing division, a fact that Whitacre says made him nervous, as he had heard rumors of Wilson's alleged involvement in price-fixing activities in several of the firm's other divisions. Wilson apparently asked Whitacre to set up a meeting with ADM's chief competitors, the two Japanese companies that dominated the lysine industry, Kyowa Hakko and Ajinomoto. When representatives of Kyowa Hakko and Ajinomoto refused to come to ADM's Decatur, Illinois, headquarters, Wilson and Whitacre flew to Tokyo in April 1992. According to Whitacre, Wilson suggested that the three firms form a cooperative association to promote and expand lysine sales jointly, and Kyowa Hakko and Ajinomoto were receptive to this idea. Additional meetings in Hawaii and Mexico City followed.

ADM continued to lose money on its lysine operations. Production costs were running at roughly twice the market price as a result of contamination problems long since overcome by the Japanese producers, both of whom had sent engineers to inspect ADM facilities in the summer of 1992. During one of many phone calls to technical personnel at Ajinomoto, Whitacre, frustrated by the contamination problem, says he joked, "Hey, you guys don't have a guy out here sabotaging our plant, do you?" The lack of a response made Whitacre wonder if there was indeed a saboteur.

He contacted Michael Andreas, the chairman's son and himself vice chairman, about the issue. Whitacre says Michael Andreas suggested that he offer the Ajinomoto technician a finder's fee for information regarding the problem. When Whitacre made the offer—a perfectly legal practice—the vague, neutral response reinforced his suspicion that the Japanese competitor did have a mole inside ADM's lysine plant. Whitacre claims that Michael Andreas then told him that he should worry less about finding the saboteur and instead learn whether the informant would be willing to divulge inside technological information that could end the contamination problem and even improve ADM's competitive position in other ways. Although Whitacre maintains that he was aware that ADM had gained technical information this way in the past, he also realized that it was risky. Conversations with the technician took place, but no deal was struck.

When Dwayne Andreas learned about the possible sabotage, he called a friend at the FBI. However, according to Whitacre, the younger Andreas was not pleased with his father's action. Whitacre asserts he was then coached by Michael Andreas about what to say—and not to say—to the FBI. Accompanied by ADM head of security Mark Cheviron, Whitacre subsequently met with FBI officials at the FBI's Decatur office to talk about the sabotage issue. As instructed, an uneasy Whitacre lied about the attempted technology purchase. However, when FBI agent Brian Shepard arrived at Whitacre's home that evening to install phone taps, Whitacre told him the truth about everything, including his concerns about possible price fixing.

The FBI began listening in as Whitacre talked from a phone in his home to contacts at Kyowa and Ajinomoto about the proposed lysine association. The FBI also supplied Whitacre with a small wired pocket recorder to tape lysine and other product-type meetings. Over the next three years, Whitacre recorded meetings using a device concealed inside a panel in his briefcase, while the FBI wired hotel rooms where Whitacre tipped them meetings were to take place. Whitacre says, "It's amazing, some of the stuff that came up on the tapes. There were recordings where agreements on world volume were reached, as well as prices." Based on this information, the FBI raided ADM corporate headquarters in search of further evidence regarding alleged price-fixing practices. Mark Whitacre was fired soon after.

ADM denies the price-fixing allegations. In fact, Chairman Dwayne Andreas argues that fixing the price of a commodity such as lysine would be nearly impossible because inflating prices would cause customers to switch to alternative feed additives such as soy meal.

Further, Andreas accused Whitacre of stealing $9 million from ADM, a charge Whitacre emphatically denies. A friend of Whitacre's told *Fortune* that ADM had in fact transferred a large sum of money—$2.5 million—to Whitacre after his firing, but that the funds were an "agreed-upon part" of Whitacre's compensation. Mark Whitacre, despite being shaken by the consequences of his actions, continues to stand firmly behind his allegations that ADM conspired to fix the price of lysine and other products. He believes he was right to expose these practices.

Angry shareholders and other critics pointed fingers at ADM's board of directors. They asserted that the price-fixing allegations, along with other antitrust and compensation-related issues for which the firm is under investigation, were clear evidence of director oversight. These issues, they insisted, should have been detected and dealt with long before they became public. Some have protested that the board's large size, high levels of member compensation, and the fact that ten of the seventeen directors were either retired ADM executives or relatives of senior management contributed to the problem.

These issues were addressed at a tense 1995 annual meeting of ADM shareholders. ADM's board members were barely re-elected, a sign that the composition and nature of the board had to change. In January 1996, ADM's board of directors agreed to implement a reform plan, including cutting the board down to as few as nine members, with the majority being outsiders; trimming management seats from five to three; requiring committees to be composed entirely of outsiders, except for the executive committee; and mandating that outside directors retire at age 70.

The Justice Department and the FBI continue to investigate whether ADM conspired with its competitors to violate antitrust laws by fixing prices on high-fructose corn syrup, citric acid, and lysine. The Securities and Exchange Commission is also looking into whether ADM violated securities laws. However, as of February 1996, no charges have been filed against ADM.[34]

Questions for Discussion

1. What should top management do to prevent price fixing by marketing managers?
2. What do marketing managers need to know about price fixing in developing marketing strategy?
3. How could a compliance program be used to avoid legal problems in the development and implementation of marketing strategy?

Chapter 3

Marketing Ethics and Social Responsibility

OBJECTIVES

- To be able to define and describe the importance of marketing ethics

- To learn about the factors that influence ethical or unethical decisions

- To discover some important ethical issues in marketing

- To become familiar with ways to improve ethical decisions in marketing

- To be able to explain the concept of social responsibility

- To recognize several important issues of social responsibility

Is the coffee too hot for consumers to handle?

52

*I*magine yourself at the drive-through window of your local fast-food restaurant. You order a cup of coffee to fortify yourself for the long drive home from school. As you pull out of the parking lot, you have to hit the brakes suddenly, and the cup topples into your lap. Ouch! Whose fault is it? Is the coffee too hot to be safe?

Stella Liebeck and her attorney, S. Reed Morgan, believe the fault lies with the restaurant—in their case, McDonald's—and that the coffee is indeed too hot. Liebeck sued McDonald's after the hot coffee she spilled in her lap landed her in the hospital with third-degree burns. She won a $2.9 million judgment, a sum later reduced to $640,000. During the trial, burn experts and dermatologists testified that McDonald's could have spared Liebeck the painful burns by reducing the temperature at which it serves its coffee. McDonald's and other fast-food chains, however, argue that they must serve coffee at 180°F to 190°F to ensure the best taste and to prevent a quick cool down.

Although many businesspeople and politicians cite the original $2.9 million judgment in the Liebeck case as evidence that the legal system needs to be reformed, Morgan, Liebeck's lawyer, believes that the huge award was more than justified by the extent of Liebeck's injuries, which required skin grafts. Moreover, he contends that McDonald's has known for years that consumers have been suffering burns from hot drinks. In fact,

Morgan won $27,000 for another client in a case against McDonald's over a spilled hot drink in 1988, and in 1990, the courts awarded a California woman $235,000 in a similar case. And McDonald's is certainly not the only company in court over hot spills: about a dozen such suits are pending against several firms, with more expected to be filed.

Congress is currently debating legislation that would rein in such suits. One provision under consideration would limit punitive damages in product-liability cases like Liebeck's to $250,000. In the meantime, to protect themselves from such lawsuits, fast-food companies are carefully cautioning customers. McDonald's, which has had warning labels on coffee cups since 1991, now posts warning signs at its drive-through windows and coffee-refill stations as well. Burger King, Wendy's, and Hardee's have added warnings on hot-drink cups in the last year, and Wendy's also posts warnings on its chili containers. Starbucks not only prints warnings on its cups, but also has employees remind customers to be careful.[1]

So, is McDonald's coffee too hot? And whose fault is it if a customer suffers burns from a spilled drink? The fact that several customers have filed lawsuits implies that at least some people believe the fault lies with the company. Such incidents illustrate that all marketing activities can be viewed as right or wrong by society, consumers, interest groups, competitors, and others. Although most marketers operate within the limits of the law, some engage in activities that are not deemed acceptable by other marketers, consumers, and society in general. A number of recently publicized incidents in marketing, such as deceptive or objectionable advertising, misleading packaging, questionable selling practices, manipulation, and deceit, have raised questions as to whether specific marketing practices are acceptable to society. The issues of what is acceptable in marketing practices and what obligations marketers owe to society are issues of marketing ethics and social responsibility.

This chapter gives an overview of the role of ethics and social responsibility in marketing decision making. We first define marketing ethics and discuss the factors that influence ethical decision making in marketing. We explore ethical issues in marketing and identify ways to improve ethics in marketing decisions. Then we address the issue of social responsibility and consider the impact of marketing decisions on society. We close the chapter by comparing and contrasting the concepts of marketing ethics and social responsibility and providing an audit of control mechanisms.

Because marketing ethics is so controversial, it is important to state as we begin that it is not the purpose of this chapter to question anyone's ethical beliefs or personal convictions. Nor is it our purpose to examine the behavior of consumers, although consumers, too, may be unethical (engaging, for instance, in coupon fraud, shoplifting, and other abuses). Instead, our goal here is to underscore the importance of resolving ethical issues in marketing and to help you learn about marketing ethics.

The Nature of Marketing Ethics

*E*thics may be one of the most misunderstood and controversial concepts in marketing. Nonetheless, this concept and its application need to be examined in order to support marketing decisions that are acceptable and beneficial to society. Marketing managers may need guidance recognizing and meeting two kinds of ethical challenges: (1) decisions in so-called gray area situations, in which the right decision is debatable; and (2) decisions in which the right course of action is clear, but individual and organizational pressures, as well as contingent circumstances, push well-intended marketing managers in the wrong direction.[2] In this section, we consider the meaning of marketing ethics and its relationship to legal issues.

■ *Marketing Ethics Defined*

Marketing ethics Principles that define acceptable conduct in marketing

The term *ethics* relates to values and choices and focuses on standards, rules, and codes of conduct that govern the behavior of individuals. For our purposes, **marketing ethics** refers to principles that define acceptable conduct in marketing. The most basic ethical issues have been codified as laws and regulations to encourage marketers to conform to society's expectations of conduct. At a minimum, marketers are expected to obey these laws and regulations. However, it is important to realize that marketing ethics goes beyond legal issues; ethical marketing decisions foster trust in marketing relationships.

Some marketers engage in ethical behavior because of enlightened self-interest, or the expectation that "ethics pays." These businesses believe that if they do not act in the public interest, the public and customers will strike back with restrictive regulations and legal action. Sega Enterprises, Ltd., was ready to launch a $200 virtual reality game system based on its popular Genesis machine. But when Sega managers received results from a study that indicated that some users of the game suffered adverse symptoms ranging from nausea to sore eyes, they decided to withhold the product.[3]

Marketers must be aware of ethical standards and acceptable behavior from several viewpoints—company, industry, and society. When marketing activities deviate from accepted standards, the exchange process can break down, resulting in customer dissatisfaction, lack of trust, and lawsuits. In fact, 78 percent of consumers currently say they avoid certain businesses or products because of negative perceptions about them.[4]

Ethical conflict occurs when it is not clear whether to apply one's personal values or the organization's in a decision situation. Research has shown that the values of and examples set by the organization often have more influence on ethical decisions in marketing than a person's own values.[5]

■ *Why Study Marketing Ethics?*

Studying marketing ethics can help you to better recognize, understand, and resolve ethical conflicts. Your interests and values may differ from those of the organization for which you work, and from society's in general. In this text, rather than taking a philosophical perspective on what is right, we provide insights into approaches to resolve ethical issues.

Ethical issues in marketing can include such questions as these: What is deceptive advertising? What constitutes a bribe in a personal selling situation? What constitutes irrelevant or false claims about a product? These and other ethical issues may seem at first glance straightforward and easy to resolve, but in reality most marketers will need experience within a specific industry to understand how to operate in gray areas or handle close calls. For example, when does a salesperson's offer to take a customer on a fishing trip become a bribe rather than a good sales practice? Although there are no easy answers to these questions, studying marketing ethics can help prepare you to participate with confidence in many challenging decisions.

■ *Marketing Ethics and the Role of the Legal System*

Although we often try to draw a boundary between legal and ethical issues, the distinction between the two is often blurred in decision making. Marketers operate in a marketing environment in which overlapping legal and ethical issues color many decisions. To separate legal and ethical decisions, one must assume that marketing managers can instinctively differentiate legal and ethical issues.[6] However, while the legal ramifications of some issues and problems may be obvious, more often, questionable decisions and actions result in disputes that must be resolved through litigation. The legal system therefore provides a formal venue for marketers to resolve ethical disputes as well as legal ones; in fact, many of the examples we cite in this chapter had to be resolved through the courts. One such example is described in Ethical Challenges.

When ethical disputes wind up in court, the costs and distractions associated with litigation can be paralyzing. In addition to compensatory or nominal damages actually incurred, punitive damages may be imposed on an organization judged to have acted improperly in order to punish the firm and to send an intimidating message to others. BMW, for example, lost a suit brought by a person who purchased a "new" BMW and later discovered the car had been damaged and repainted before being sold as new. The court awarded the buyer $4,000 in compensatory damages, as well as $4 million in punitive damages to punish BMW and to deter other companies from engaging in this type of deception.[7] On appeal the U.S. Supreme Court overruled the punitive damages.

Although the virtues of honesty, fairness, and openness are often assumed to be self-evident and universally accepted, marketing strategy decisions involve complex and detailed discussions in which correctness may not be so clear cut. A high level of personal morality may not be sufficient to prevent an individual from violating the law in an organizational context in which even experienced lawyers debate the exact meaning of the law. Because it is impossible to train all the members of an organization as lawyers, the identification of ethical issues and implementation of codes of conduct that incorporate both legal and ethical concerns comprise the best approach to preventing violations and avoiding civil litigation. Codifying ethical standards into meaningful policies that spell out what is and is not acceptable gives marketers an opportunity to reduce the probability of behavior that could create legal problems. Without proper ethical training and guidance, it is impossible for the average marketing manager to understand the exact boundaries for

ETHICAL CHALLENGES

R.E.M. Goes to Court over Dispute

R.E.M., a popular alternative rock band, has a policy of neither endorsing products nor allowing commercial use of its name because band members feel that such commercialism detracts from their artistic integrity. The group has publicized this policy in magazine, radio, and newspaper interviews.

In August 1995, Hershey Foods Corporation used R.E.M.'s name in a contest to promote its Kit Kat candy bar. The promotion included national radio advertising that aired on stations that play R.E.M.'s music and thus represent its target market. The radio ad, using generic rock music as background rather than an R.E.M. song, ran as follows:

> Kit Kat wants to give you a chance to win a trip for two to the September 30th R.E.M. concert at Hershey Park Stadium or one of 25 copies of R.E.M.'s latest CD. Be among the first 10,000 people to call 1-800-xxx-xxxx with your name and complete address and you'll be in the running for the Kit Kat concert trip to Hershey, Pennsylvania.

R.E.M. quickly filed a civil suit against Hershey Foods charging Hershey with blatantly exploiting the R.E.M. name for crass commercial purposes by conducting a Kit Kat/R.E.M. concert sweepstakes. In R.E.M.'s view, the "background music is vastly inferior to R.E.M.'s music, but unfortunately people are likely to believe that R.E.M. is performing, or in some manner associated with, this substandard, watered down, sound-alike accompaniment." R.E.M. also charged that the commercials implied R.E.M.'s involvement, sponsorship, or affiliation with the contest.

On August 31, 1995, the two sides settled their dispute out of court. Hershey's advertising agency, DDB Needham Worldwide Inc., agreed to make a contribution of $50,000 to charities specified by R.E.M. and not to use R.E.M.'s name in connection with any commercial endorsement or promotion without R.E.M.'s prior written approval.

Source: U.S. District Court of Northern District of Georgia, Atlanta, Georgia, R.E.M., plaintiff, v. Hershey Food Corp., defendant, 1995.

illegal behavior in the areas of price fixing, copyright violations, fraud, export/import violations, and on and on. But a corporate focus on ethics helps create a buffer zone on issues that could potentially trigger serious legal complications for the company. In Figure 3.1, Liberty Mutual offers to assist companies in detecting internal fraud and providing support programs to help injured employees.

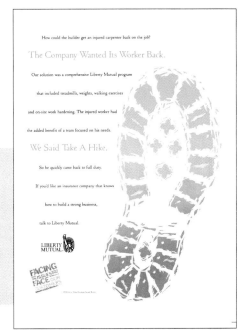

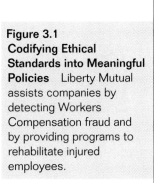
Figure 3.1 Codifying Ethical Standards into Meaningful Policies Liberty Mutual assists companies by detecting Workers Compensation fraud and by providing programs to rehabilitate injured employees.

Understanding the Ethical Decision-Making Process

*T*o grasp the significance of ethics in marketing decision making, you must first examine the factors that influence the ethical decision-making process. Individual factors, organizational relationships, and opportunity are three factors that interact to determine ethical decisions in marketing (see Figure 3.2).

■ *Individual Factors*

Ethical conflict arises when people encounter situations they cannot control or resolve in the privacy of their own lives. In such situations, individuals base their decisions on their own concepts of right or wrong and act accordingly in their daily lives. Moral philosophies—the principles or rules that individuals use to decide what is right or wrong[8]—are often cited to justify decisions or explain behavior. People learn these principles and rules through socialization by family members, social groups, religion, and formal education. It is widely believed that ethical decision making can be enhanced by identifying and improving one's personal moral philosophy.

At least two major types of moral philosophy are associated with marketing decisions, each with its own concept of rightness, or ethicalness, and rules for behavior. *Utilitarianism* is concerned with maximizing the greatest good for the greatest number of people. Utilitarians judge an action or decision by the consequences for all the people affected. In other words, in a situation with an ethical component, utilitarians will compare all possible options and select the one that promises the best results for the most people.

Ethical formalism is a rights- or rule-oriented philosophy that focuses on the intentions associated with a particular behavior and on the rights of the individual. Ethical formalism develops specific standards of behavior by determining whether an action can be taken consistently as a general rule, without considering alternative results.[9] Ethical formalists judge an action or decision on the basis of whether it infringes on individual rights or universal rules. The biblical Golden Rule—do unto others as you would have them do unto you—exemplifies ethical formalism. So does Immanuel Kant's categorical imperative: Every action should be based on reasons that everyone could act on, at least in principle, and that action must be based on reasons that the decision maker would be willing to have others use.[10]

There is no universal agreement on the correct moral philosophy to use in resolving ethical issues. Moreover, research suggests that marketers may use different moral philosophies in different decision situations. Each philosophy could result in a different decision in an ethical dilemma. And, depending on the particular situation, marketers will sometimes change their value structure or moral philosophy when they are making decisions.[11] These changes in individual philosophies are usually based on organizational relationships.

Figure 3.2
Factors That Influence the Ethical Decision-Making Process in Marketing

■ *Organizational Relationships*

Although it is true that individuals can and do make moral choices pertaining to business affairs, it is also true that people do not operate in a vacuum.[12] Ethical choices in marketing are most often made jointly in work groups and committees or in conversations and discussions with coworkers. Marketers learn to resolve ethical issues not only from their individual backgrounds, but also from people with whom they associate in work groups and in the marketing organization. The outcome of this learning process depends on the strength of each individual's personal values, opportunity for unethical behavior, and exposure to others who behave ethically or unethically. **Significant others** include superiors, peers, and subordinates in the organization who influence the ethical decision-making process. Although people outside the organization, such as family members and friends, also influence decision makers, organizational structure and culture operate through significant others to influence ethical decisions. Figure 3.3 advertises a consulting firm that helps managers develop skills in leadership and in dealing with ethical issues.

Organizational, or **corporate, culture** can be defined as a set of values, beliefs, goals, norms, and rituals that members or employees of an organization share. A firm's culture may be expressed formally through codes of conduct, memos, manuals, and ceremonies, but it is also expressed informally through work habits, dress codes, extracurricular activities, and anecdotes. An organization's culture gives its members meaning and suggests rules for how to behave and deal with problems within the organization. In Figure 3.4, the Body Shop demonstrates its strong cultural commitment to ethical behavior through its campaign to stop violence against women.

Most experts agree that the chief executive officer or vice president of marketing sets the ethical tone for the entire organization. Lower-level managers obtain their cues from top managers, but they, too, impose some of their personal values on the company. This interaction between corporate culture and executive leadership helps determine the ethical value system of the firm.

The role of coworkers in influencing ethical choices depends on the person's exposure to unethical behavior in making ethical decisions. Especially in ethical gray areas, the more a person is exposed to unethical activity by others in the organizational environment, the

Significant others Superiors, peers, and subordinates in an organization who influence the ethical decision-making process

Organizational, or corporate, culture A set of values, beliefs, goals, norms, and rituals that members or employees of an organization share

**Figure 3.3
Significant Others
Influence Ethical
Decision Making**
Management consulting firms can assist organizations in developing strong leaders who make positive ethical decisions.

Blow the whistle

on violence against women

Join the Body Shop campaign to stop violence against women

**Figure 3.4
Organizational Culture
Influences Ethical
Behavior** The Body
Shop has a strong
corporate culture that
supports many social
causes. Here, it pro-
motes its campaign to
stop violence against
women.

more likely it is that he or she will behave unethically. Most marketers take their cues or learn from coworkers how to solve problems—including ethical problems.[13]

Organizational pressure plays a key part in creating ethical issues. Nearly all marketers face difficult issues where solutions are not obvious or where organizational objectives and personal ethical values may conflict. For example, a salesperson may be asked by a superior to lie to a customer over the phone about a late product shipment. A survey conducted by the Ethics Resource Center found that almost one-third of those surveyed felt pressure from superiors to violate company policy in order to achieve business objectives. Of the nearly one-third who had witnessed behavior that they viewed as a violation of company policy or the law, fewer than half said they reported the misconduct to their companies.[14] Table 3.1 indicates the percentage of employees who believe specific ethical violations are committed by coworkers.

Because organizational culture, relationships, and pressures influence ethical behavior, it is suggested that the management of marketing ethics should focus on designing and developing organizations for marketers, who, like all human beings, display the normal range of personal ethical variations and the tendency sometimes to take advantage of opportunities. As mentioned at the beginning of this chapter, in some situations it is hard to identify the right or wrong choice, and in other situations individuals may think they know what is right, but competitive or organizational pressures encourage the wrong behavior.

■ *Opportunity*

Another pressure that may shape ethical decisions in marketing is opportunity, a favorable set of conditions that limit barriers or provide rewards. Just as the majority of people who go into retail stores do not try to shoplift at each opportunity, most marketers do not try to take advantage of every opportunity for unethical behavior in their organization. Individual factors as well as organizational culture may influence whether an individual becomes opportunistic and tries to take advantage of situations unethically.

If a marketer takes advantage of an opportunity to act unethically and is rewarded or suffers no penalty, he or she may repeat such acts as other opportunities arise. For example, a salesperson who receives a raise after using a deceptive sales presentation to increase sales is being rewarded and so will probably continue the behavior. Indeed, opportunity to engage in unethical conduct is often a better predictor of unethical activities than are personal values.[15]

Besides rewards and the absence of punishment, other elements in the business environment tend to create opportunities. Professional codes of ethics and ethics-related corporate policy also influence opportunity by prescribing what behaviors are acceptable. The larger the rewards and the milder the punishment for unethical behavior, the greater is the probability that unethical behavior will be practiced.

Table 3.1 Percentage Who Believe These Ethical Infractions Are Committed by Coworkers	
Lying to supervisors	56%
Falsifying records	41%
Sexual harassment	35%
Conflict of interest	31%

Source: Ethics Resource Center survey, reported in *USA Today*, Oct. 18, 1995, p. B1.

Ethical Issues in Marketing

Ethical issue An identifiable problem, situation, or opportunity requiring an individual or organization to choose from among several actions that must be evaluated as right or wrong, ethical or unethical

*D*eveloping awareness of ethical issues is important in understanding and improving marketing ethics. An **ethical issue** is an identifiable problem, situation, or opportunity requiring an individual or organization to choose from among several actions that must be evaluated as right or wrong, ethical or unethical. Basically, anytime an activity causes marketing managers, or consumers in their target market, to feel manipulated or cheated, a marketing ethical issue exists, regardless of the legality of that activity. For example, organizational objectives that call for increased profits or market share may pressure marketers to knowingly bring an unsafe product to market. This activity is an ethical issue.

Regardless of the reasons behind specific ethical issues, once the issues are identified, marketers must decide how to deal with them. Thus it is essential to become familiar with many of the ethical issues that may arise in marketing so that they can be identified and resolved when they occur. A number of ethical issues related to product, promotion, price, and distribution (the marketing mix) are in Table 3.2.

In general, product-related ethical issues arise when marketers fail to disclose risks associated with the product or information regarding the function, value, or use of the product. Pressures can build to substitute inferior materials or product components to reduce costs. For example, Compaq Computer filed suit against Packard Bell, accusing its rival of marketing computers with used parts as new and even altering serial numbers on components to hide their prior use. Although some personal computer manufacturers recycle good parts from returned PCs into new machines, Compaq, IBM, and other major manufacturers do not. Compaq has taken its dispute to court in an effort "to level the playing field and get everyone to play by the same rules," in the words of one research

---

Table 3.2   Typical Marketing Mix Ethical Issues

Product Issue

Product trademark	The prospective appearance of a new Muppet in the movie, *Muppet Treasure Island*, resulted in a lawsuit. Jim Henson Productions, Inc., named the new Muppet, an exotic wild boar, "Spa'am." Hormel Foods Corporation, which manufactures Spam, feared that the use of the Spa'am character would harm sales of Spam and sued Henson. A U.S. district judge ruled that the Spa'am Muppet would be unlikely to harm Hormel's Spam trademark.

Promotion Issue

Advertising	Many local auto dealers advertise deals that are too good to be true. One dealer advertised a $30,000 Mercedes C-class for $18,036. The down payment and other conditions were vague.

Pricing Issue

Price fixing	Archer Daniels Midland, a Decatur, Illinois, company, was accused of fixing prices on key agricultural commodities—high fructose corn syrup, citric acid, and lysine.

Distribution Issue

Distributing counterfeit products	Some record stores offer counterfeit recordings as authentic; in fact one in four record albums is counterfeit. China and Bulgaria distribute $1 billion in pirated CDs each year. Some direct marketing companies have been set up to sell counterfeit products.

Sources: United States District Court, Southern District of New York, Hormel Foods Corporation against Jim Henson Productions, Inc. 95 civ. 5473 (KMW); Earle Eldridge, "Some Offers Too Good To Be True," *USA Today*, Nov. 27, 1995, p. 3B; Robyn Nerdith, "Archer Daniels' Investors Launch Revolt: Price Fixing Investigation Secrecy Cause Stir," *USA Today*, Oct. 20, 1995, p. 1B.

consultant.[16] Certainly some Packard Bell computer buyers will feel deceived if Compaq's allegations are verified in court. Ethical issues also arise when marketers fail to inform customers about changes in product quality; this failure is a form of dishonesty about the nature of the product.

Promotion provides a variety of situations that can create ethical issues—for instance, false and misleading advertising and manipulative or deceptive sales promotions, tactics, or publicity efforts. For example, a study found that numerous issues of *The Weekly Reader*, a newsletter targeted at elementary school children, disseminated pro–tobacco-industry views and positive images of Joe Camel—the cartoon character created to promote Camel cigarettes. The publication is owned by a unit of Kohlberg Kravis Roberts, which until recently was the largest shareholder of RJR Nabisco, the marketer of Camels and other cigarette brands. Children's and health advocates say that *The Weekly Reader's* failure to balance such articles with more information about the hazards of smoking reinforces the tobacco industry's promotion and may encourage kids to smoke.[17] Some may question whether RJR Nabisco has taken unfair advantage of its association with *The Weekly Reader* to promote its product inappropriately to children. Ethical Challenges discusses another recent incident related to ethics in promotion. Many other ethical issues are linked to advertising and personal selling. In addition, the use of bribery

---

■ ETHICAL CHALLENGES

Sex Sells, But Did Calvin Klein Cross the Line?

Advertisers have been using sex to promote products for years, and Calvin Klein, Inc., has been in the vanguard of the sexy ad brigade ever since a fifteen-year-old Brooke Shields cooed in a commercial, "Nothing comes between me and my Calvins." However, many consumers think the designer's recent advertising campaign to sell CK jeans went too far.

Klein's 1995 spots featured young, scantily clad models in provocative poses. The print ads, shot by the same Steven Meisel who photographed Madonna's controversial book, *Sex*, show some models revealing their underwear. In the television commercials, an off-camera adult male asks the models to take off articles of clothing and makes suggestive comments and queries.

Shocked consumers claimed the ads crossed the line into pornography, particularly because many of the models appeared to be under age eighteen. Several religious and children's advocate groups protested and threatened boycotts against Klein and retailers who carried the jeans. The American Family Association, a coalition of church groups that promotes family values, even asked the U.S. Justice Department to investigate, saying the ads "sexually exploit what appear to be children by exhibiting them in a lascivious manner although the models are not

completely nude." Many retailers responded to the protests by asking Klein to pull the ads.

The company refused to reveal the ages of the models appearing in the ads, but agents for some of the models insisted their clients were over eighteen. Nonetheless, the Justice Department and the Federal Bureau of Investigation examined whether the campaign may have violated laws against child pornography.

The public furor and retailer protests apparently worked. Klein announced in a full-page ad in *The New York Times* that the company was halting the "misunderstood" campaign early.

Advertisers will almost certainly continue to use sex to sell products as they have for years. Just turn on the TV or flip through fashion magazines to see barely-dressed celebrities and models in sensual poses hawking everything from cruises to colas. Society's standards about what level of sexual innuendo is permissible in advertising may have relaxed in recent decades, but using children in such situations is clearly taboo.

Sources: Roy H. Campbell, *Philadelphia Enquirer*, Sept. 19, 1995 (via America Online); Michele Ingrassia, with Seema Nayyar, Claudia Kali, Susan Miller, and Marcus Mabry, "Calvin's World," *Newsweek*, Sept. 11, 1995, pp. 60–66; Cyndee Miller, "Sexy Sizzle Backfires: Calvin Klein Advertised Jeans, But Real Message Is for Marketers," *Marketing News*, Sept. 25, 1995, pp. 1, 2; and Nancy Millman, *Chicago Tribune*, Sept. 10, 1995 (via America Online).

in personal selling situations is an ethical issue. Even when a bribe is offered to benefit the organization, it is usually considered unethical. Because it jeopardizes trust and fairness, it hurts the organization in the long run.

In pricing, the typical ethical issues are price fixing, predatory pricing, and failure to disclose the full price associated with a purchase. Pricing laws were discussed in Chapter 2. The emotional and subjective nature of price creates many situations in which misunderstandings between the seller and buyer cause ethical problems. Marketers have the right to price their products so that they earn a reasonable profit, but ethical issues may crop up when a company seeks to earn high profits at the expense of its customers. In the contact lens solution market, a number of manufacturers promote identical products with different prices. Bausch & Lomb, for example, prices its 1-ounce bottle of Sensitive Eyes Drops at about $5.65. That sounds fair until you discover that a 12-ounce bottle of its Sensitive Eyes Saline Solution—same ingredients, same formulation, different label—is priced at $2.79. Other manufacturers do the same thing. You don't need contact lenses to see an ethical issue here. Says consultant Jack Trout, "It's not only a sneaky way to make money, but it's lousy marketing, the type of thing that backfires . . . when it's made public."[18]

Ethical issues in distribution involve relationships among producers and marketing middlemen. Marketing middlemen, or intermediaries (wholesalers and retailers), facilitate the flow of products from the producer to the ultimate consumer. Each intermediary performs a different role and agrees to certain rights, responsibilities, and rewards associated with that role. For example, producers can expect wholesalers and retailers to honor agreements and keep them informed of inventory needs. Manipulating a product's availability for purposes of exploitation and using coercion to force intermediaries to behave in a specific manner are particularly serious ethical issues in the distribution sphere.

Organizational Approaches to Improving Ethical Behavior

*I*t is possible to improve ethical behavior in an organization by eliminating unethical persons and improving the organization's ethical standards. One way to approach improvement of an organization's ethical standards is by considering a "bad apple–bad barrel" analogy. Some people always do things in their own self-interest, regardless of organizational goals or accepted moral standards; they are sometimes called "bad apples." To eliminate unethical behavior, an organization must rid itself of such bad apples through screening techniques and enforcement of the firm's ethical standards.[19] However, organizations sometimes become "bad barrels" not because the individuals within them are bad, but because the pressures to survive and succeed create conditions (opportunities) that reward unethical behavior. A way of resolving the problem of the bad barrel is to redesign the organization's image and culture so that it conforms to industry and societal norms of ethical behavior.[20] Sears, in Figure 3.5, promotes its commitment to business ethics and announces its sponsorship of the 1995 Business Ethics Awards.

If top management develops and enforces programs to encourage ethical decision making, then they become a force to help individuals make better ethical decisions. When marketers understand the policies and requirements for ethical conduct, they can more easily resolve ethical conflicts.

On the other hand, marketers can never fully abdicate their

Figure 3.5 Organizational Commitment to Ethical Behavior Sears promotes its strong commitment to ethical standards with its sponsorship of the Business Ethics Awards.

Table 3.3 A Method to Create Ethical Relationships in Marketing

1. **Listen and learn.**

   Recognize the problem or decision-making opportunity that confronts your company, team, or unit. Don't argue, criticize, or defend yourself—keep listening and reviewing until you are sure you understand others.

2. **Identify the ethical issues.**

   Examine how coworkers and consumers are affected by the situation or decision at hand. Examine how you feel about the situation and understand the viewpoint of those who are involved in the decision or the consequences of the decision.

3. **Create and analyze options.**

   Try to put aside strong feelings such as anger or desire for power and prestige and come up with as many alternatives as possible before developing an analysis. Ask everyone involved for ideas about which options offer the best long-term results for you and the company. Which option will increase your self-respect even if, in the long run, things don't work out the way you hope?

4. **Identify the best option from your point of view.**

   Consider it and test it against some established criteria, such as respect, understanding, caring, fairness, honesty, and openness.

5. **Explain your decision and resolve any differences that arise.**

   This may require neutral arbitration from a trusted manager or taking "time out" to reconsider, consult, or exchange written proposals before a decision is reached.

Source: Tom Rusk with D. Patrick Miller, "Doing the Right Thing," *Sky* (Delta Airlines), Aug. 1993, pp. 18–22. Used by permission.

personal ethical responsibility in making decisions. Claiming to be an agent of the business ("the company told me to do it") is not accepted as a legal excuse and is even less defensible from an ethical perspective.[21]

To promote ethical conduct requires teamwork and initiative, which often result in higher-quality products. This leads to the potential for an ethical advantage: better reputation, sales, market share, and profits. A proactive ethical approach to marketing should consider at least four fundamental values of interpersonal communication: respect, understanding, caring, and fairness.[22] Table 3.3 shows one recommended method for developing ethical relationships and promoting integrity in marketing.

Ethics Compliance Programs

In Chapter 2, we briefly discussed the Federal Sentencing Guidelines for Organizations established by the United States Sentencing Commission to deter corporate misconduct. The guidelines urge organizations to develop ethics and legal compliance programs before infractions occur. If individuals within an organization act illegally, the firm must show that it had implemented reasonable programs for deterring and preventing misconduct to avoid penalties under the new sentencing guidelines. The seven minimum requirements for a compliance program (listed in Table 3.4) are not "a superficial checklist requiring little analysis or thought."[23] Rather, a firm's compliance and ethics program must be capable of reducing the opportunity that employees have to engage in misconduct.

Without compliance programs and uniform standards and policies on conduct, it is hard for employees to determine what behavior is acceptable within a company. In the absence of such programs and standards, employees will generally make decisions based on their observations of how their peers and superiors behave.

Table 3.4   Seven Steps to Ethical Compliance
1. Establish codes of conduct.
2. Appoint or hire high-level compliance manager (ethics officer).
3. Take care in delegating authority.
4. Institute a training program and communication system (ethics training).
5. Monitor and audit for misconduct.
6. Enforce and discipline.
7. Revise program as needed.

Source: U.S.S.C. Federal Sentencing Guidelines for Organizations, 1991.

Codes of conduct
Formalized rules and standards that describe what the company expects of its employees

To improve ethics, many organizations have developed **codes of conduct** (also called codes of ethics), which consist of formalized rules and standards that describe what the company expects of its employees. Most large corporations have a formal code of conduct, and most codes have been revised since 1990.[24] In fact, 94 percent of *Forbes 500* companies responding to a 1994 survey indicated that they had a code of conduct.[25]

Codes of conduct promote ethical behavior by eliminating opportunities for unethical behavior because employees know both what is expected of them and what kind of punishment they face if they violate the rules. Codes help marketers deal with ethical issues or dilemmas that develop in daily operations by prescribing or limiting specific activities.

Codes of conduct do not have to be so detailed that they take into account every situation, but they should provide guidelines for employees that are capable of achieving organizational ethical objectives in an acceptable manner. For example, the American Marketing Association Code of Ethics (reprinted in Table 3.5) does not cover every possible ethical issue, but it *does* provide a useful overview of what marketers believe are sound principles for guiding marketing activities. This code serves as a helpful model for structuring an organization's code of conduct.

Marketing compliance programs must have oversight by high-ranking persons in the organization known to abide by legal and common ethical standards. This person is usually referred to as an ethics officer. About half of the largest U.S. companies have an ethics program and approximately one-third of *Fortune 1000* firms have an ethics officer. The vast majority of these positions have been created within the last five years. Ethics officers are usually responsible for

- Meeting with employees, the board of directors, and top management to discuss or provide advice about ethical issues
- Disseminating a code of ethics
- Creating and maintaining an anonymous, confidential service to answer questions about ethical issues
- Taking action on possible code violations
- Reviewing and modifying the code of conduct[26]

In addition to selecting a high-level compliance officer, companies must take care in delegating authority to ensure that individuals prone to misconduct are not given management positions.

To nurture ethical behavior in marketing, open communication and coaching on ethical issues are essential. This means providing employees with ethics training, clear channels of communication, and follow-up support throughout the organization. Some firms set up ethics hotlines to handle employee questions on ethical issues. For example, NYNEX (with 82,000 employees) set up an ethics hotline that received over 2,700 calls in one year, 10 percent of which dealt with alleged misconduct.[27] About 5 percent of the 32,000 employees at Northrop used its "Open Line" hotline.[28]

Table 3.5 Code of Ethics, American Marketing Association

Members of the American Marketing Association (AMA) are committed to ethical professional conduct. They have joined together in subscribing to this Code of Ethics embracing the following topics:

Responsibilities of the Marketer

Marketers must accept responsibility for the consequences of their activities and make every effort to ensure that their decisions, recommendations, and actions function to identify, serve, and satisfy all relevant publics: consumers, organizations and society. Marketers' professional conduct must be guided by:

1. The basic rule of professional ethics: not knowingly to do harm;
2. The adherence to all applicable laws and regulations;
3. The accurate representation of their education, training and experience; and
4. The active support, practice and promotion of this Code of Ethics.

Honesty and Fairness

Marketers shall uphold and advance the integrity, honor, and dignity of the marketing profession by:

1. Being honest in serving consumers, clients, employees, suppliers, distributors and the public;
2. Not knowingly participating in conflict of interest without prior notice to all parties involved; and
3. Establishing equitable fee schedules including the payment or receipt of usual, customary and/or legal compensation for marketing exchanges

Rights and Duties of Parties

Participants in the marketing exchange process should be able to expect that:

1. Products and services offered are safe and fit for their intended uses;
2. Communications about offered products and services are not deceptive;
3. All parties intend to discharge their obligations, financial and otherwise, in good faith; and
4. Appropriate internal methods exist for equitable adjustment and/or redress of grievances concerning purchases.

It is understood that the above would include, *but is not limited to,* the following responsibilities of the marketer:

In the area of product development management:

Disclosure of all substantial risks associated with product or service usage

Identification of any product component substitution that might materially change the product or impact on the buyer's purchase decision

Identification of extra-cost added features

In the area of promotions:

Avoidance of false and misleading advertising

Rejection of high pressure manipulations, or misleading sales tactics

Avoidance of sales promotions that use deception or manipulation

In the area of distribution:

Not manipulating the availability of a product for purpose of exploitation

Not using coercion in the marketing channel

Not exerting undue influence over the resellers' choice to handle a product

In the area of pricing:

Not engaging in price fixing

Not practicing predatory pricing

Disclosing the full price associated with any purchase

In the area of marketing research:

Prohibiting selling or fund raising under the guise of conducting research

Maintaining research integrity by avoiding misrepresentation and omission of pertinent research data

Treating outside clients and suppliers fairly

Organizational Relationships

Marketers should be aware of how their behavior may influence or impact on the behavior of others in organizational relationships. They should not encourage or apply coercion to obtain unethical behavior in their relationships with others, such as employees, suppliers or customers.

1. Apply confidentiality and anonymity in professional relationships with regard to privileged information.
2. Meet their obligations and responsibilities in contracts and mutual agreements in a timely manner.
3. Avoid taking the work of others, in whole, or in part, and represent this work as their own or directly benefit from it without compensation or consent of the originator or owner.
4. Avoid manipulation to take advantage of situations to maximize personal welfare in a way that unfairly deprives or damages the organization or others.

Any AMA members found to be in violation of any provision of this Code of Ethics may have his or her Association membership suspended or revoked.

Source: Reprinted by permission of the American Marketing Association.

It is important that companies consistently enforce standards and impose penalties or punishment on those who violate codes of conduct. In addition, the company must take reasonable steps in response to violations of standards and, as appropriate, revise the compliance program to diminish the likelihood of future misconduct.

The Nature of Social Responsibility

Social responsibility
An organization's obligation to maximize its positive impact and minimize its negative impact on society

*C*ompared with ethics, social responsibility represents a broader conceptualization. **Social responsibility** in marketing refers to an organization's obligation to maximize its positive impact and minimize its negative impact on society. Whereas ethics relates to doing the right thing in making individual and group choices, social responsibility is achieved by balancing the interests of all stakeholders in an organization.

The four dimensions of social responsibility are generally considered to be economic, legal, ethical, and philanthropic concerns (Figure 3.6). The first two have long been acknowledged, but philanthropic and ethical issues have gained recognition more recently. We have already covered ethics in this chapter because it is essential to social responsibility and is a vital ingredient of trust in both organizational relationships and customer relations. Philanthropic activities are additional responses that may not be required but promote human welfare or goodwill, as do economic, legal, and ethical considerations.

In enlightened companies today, social responsibility is a vital factor in major marketing strategy decisions. There has been ample evidence of how ignoring social responsibility can destroy trust with customers and be a stimulus for government regulations. When marketers deviate from socially acceptable activities, they can be held legally responsible; they can also be damaged in terms of economic success. Social responsibility, then, can be viewed as a contract with society, whereas ethics relates to carefully thought-out rules of moral values that guide individual and group decision making.

RESPONSIBILITIES

Philanthropic
Be a good corporate citizen
▶ Contribute resources to the community; improve quality of life

Ethical
Be ethical
▶ Obligation to do what is right, just, and fair
▶ Avoid harm

Legal
Obey the law
▶ Law is society's codification of right and wrong
▶ Play by the rules of the game

Economic
Be profitable
▶ The foundation upon which all others rest

Figure 3.6
The Pyramid of Corporate Social Responsibility
Source: Reprinted from *Business Horizons*, July/Aug. 1991. Copyright © 1991 by the Foundation for the School of Business at Indiana University. Used with permission.

■ *Impact of Social Responsibility on Marketing*

Marketing managers try to determine what accepted relationships, obligations, and duties exist between the marketing organization and society. Recognition is growing that for a firm's survival and competitive advantage, the long-term value of conducting business in a socially responsible manner far outweighs short-term costs.[29]

In a recent survey of 1000 heads of households, nearly 90 percent said that when quality, service, and price are equal among competitors, they are more likely to buy from the company with the best reputation for social responsibility. Some 48 percent of these consumers who indicated they were boycotting certain products were doing so because of objectionable business practices.[30]

To preserve socially responsible behavior while achieving organizational goals, marketers must monitor changes and trends in society's values. For example, companies around the world are developing and marketing more nutritional and healthier products in response to increasing public concerns about cancer and heart disease. Furthermore, marketers must develop control procedures to ensure that daily decisions do not damage their company's relations with the public. An organization's top management must assume some responsibility for the employees' conduct by establishing and enforcing policies.

Business Ethics magazine acknowledges excellence in the area of corporate social responsibility with a Business Ethics Award. It uses these four criteria for choosing winners:

1. Commitment to ethics and social responsibility over a sustained period and with an ongoing fervor.
2. Sincere and well-developed programs.
3. Programs that must be a part of the company's culture.
4. Visible presence and ability to impact the business community.

Winners for 1995 included Xerox Corporation, for exceptional success with workplace diversity and employee relations; The Home Depot, Inc., for exceptional community involvement at all levels of the company; and Odwalla, Inc., for incorporating outstanding environmentalism in everything it does.[31] Home Depot, for example, was recognized for its donation of $8 million, or about 2 percent of its pretax profits, to community programs; in keeping with the "company's culture," about 45 percent of Home Depot's contribution helped build affordable housing projects.[32] Table 3.6 summarizes a few social responsibility success stories.

Marketers must determine what society wants and then predict the long-run effects of their decisions. Often outside specialists such as doctors, lawyers, and scientists are consulted, but there is sometimes a lack of general agreement within the discipline as to what is an acceptable marketing decision. Forty years ago, for example, tobacco marketers promoted cigarettes as being good for one's health. Now, years after the discovery that cigarette smoking is linked to cancer and other medical problems, society's attitude toward smoking is changing, and marketers are confronted with new social responsibilities, such as providing a smoke-free atmosphere for customers. Most major hotel chains allocate at least some of their rooms for nonsmokers, and most other businesses within the food, travel, and entertainment industries provide smoke-free environments or sections.

Because society is made up of many diverse groups, finding out what society as a whole wants is difficult, if not impossible. In trying to satisfy the desires of one group, marketers may dissatisfy others. In the smoking debate, for example, marketers must balance smokers' desires to continue to smoke cigarettes against nonsmokers' desires for a smoke-free environment.

Fundamentally, there are costs associated with many of society's demands. For example, society wants a cleaner environment and the preservation of wildlife and habitats, but it also wants low-priced products. Thus companies must carefully balance the costs of providing low-priced products against the costs of manufacturing, packaging, and distributing their products in an environmentally responsible manner. *Business Ethics* magazine honored Odwalla with a 1995 Business Ethics Award, in part for converting its

Table 3.6   Social Responsibility Success Stories

Company	Accomplishment
VF Corporation	Manufacturer of Wrangler and Lee jeans; has begun manufacturing clothing from 100 percent organic cotton and nontoxic dyes
Chevron Corporation	Curbed consumption of fresh water by 45 percent in early 1994 by using treated wastewater in refining operations
Export Packers Company of Winnipeg, Canada	Turned more than seven tons of eggshells it produced every day into a protein supplement for chicken feed, resulting in a substantial profit each year
New England Electric System	Teamed with Innoprise, a forest products corporation in Malaysia, to reduce carbon dioxide emissions by using harvesting practices that do not destroy neighboring trees; thus prevented between 80,000 and 160,000 metric tons of stored carbon from being released into the atmosphere each year
Safeway Inc.	Adopted a dolphin-safe policy covering all tuna products, including tuna used in pet foods and store brands
Medical Center Hospital of Vermont	Gives Intervale Foundation, a nonprofit farming and educational organization, about a hundred tons of waste food a year to be used in compost for vegetable farming; then buys vegetables from the organization
Mazda Motor Corporation	Eliminated the use of trichloroethylene, a cleaning solvent that erodes the earth's ozone layer
Merck & Co.	Leads in restraining prices on drugs; supports elementary math and science education; donated $30 million in medical supplies in 1991 to countries in need; donated $1 million to a Costa Rican organization to save the rain forests

Sources: "Trend Watch: And Now from Friends of the Planet Department," *Business Ethics* (Mar/Apr. 1993): 9; and "Earth Watch," *Business Ethics* (July/Aug.1993). Used by permission.

143-truck fleet to compressed natural gas. The company also recycles waste and supports pesticide-free farming.[33]

Balancing society's demands to achieve the satisfaction of all members of society is difficult, if not impossible. Marketers must also evaluate the extent to which members of society are willing to pay for what they want. For instance, consumers may want more information about a product yet be unwilling to pay the costs the firm incurs in providing the data. Marketers who want to make socially responsible decisions may find the task a challenge because ultimately economic survival must be ensured.

■ Social Responsibility Issues

Although social responsibility may seem to be an abstract ideal, managers make decisions related to social responsibility every day. To be successful, a business must determine what customers, government regulators, and competitors, as well as society in general, want or expect in terms of social responsibility. Environmental issues are often a key concern when a company develops a social responsibility program (see Figure 3.7). Table 3.7 summarizes four major categories of social responsibility issues: the consumer movement, community relations, green marketing, and diversity.

Consumer Movement   One of the most significant social responsibility issues in marketing is the consumer movement, which Chapter 2 defined as the efforts of independent individuals, groups, and organizations to protect the rights of consumers. A number of interest groups and individuals have taken actions such as lobbying government officials and agencies, letter-writing campaigns, public service announcements, and boycotts of companies they consider irresponsible.

Ralph Nader, one of the best-known consumer activists, continues to crusade for consumer rights. Consumer activism on the part of Nader and others has resulted in

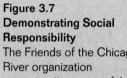

Figure 3.7
Demonstrating Social Responsibility
The Friends of the Chicago River organization promotes its successful clean-up of the Chicago River, a strong incentive for businesses to keep the river clean.

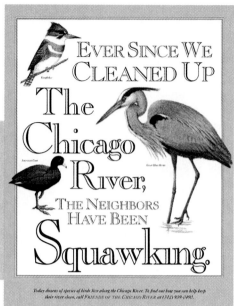

legislation requiring various safety features in cars: seat belts, airbags, padded dashboards, stronger door latches, head restraints, shatter-proof windshields, and collapsible steering columns. Activists' efforts have helped facilitate the passage of several consumer protection laws, such as the Wholesome Meat Act of 1967, the Radiation Control for Health and Safety Act of 1968, the Clean Water Act of 1972, and the Toxic Substance Act of 1976.

Also of great importance to the consumer movement are four basic rights spelled out in a consumer "bill of rights" drafted by President John F. Kennedy. These rights include the right to safety, the right to be informed, the right to choose, and the right to be heard.

Ensuring consumers' right to safety means that marketers have an obligation not to market knowingly a product that could harm consumers. This right can be extended to

Table 3.7 Social Responsibility Issues

Issue	Description	Major Societal Concerns
Consumer Movement	Activities undertaken by independent individuals, groups, and organizations to protect their rights as consumers	The right to safety The right to be informed The right to choose The right to be heard
Community Relations	Society anxious to have marketers contribute to its well-being, wishing to know what businesses do to help solve social problems Communities demanding that firms listen to their grievances and ideas	Equality issues Disadvantaged members of society Safety and health Education and general welfare
Green Marketing	Consumers insisting not only on the quality of life, but also on a healthful environment so that they can maintain a high standard of living during their lifetimes	Conservation Water pollution Air pollution Land pollution
Diversity	Employees and consumers pressing for greater awareness and acknowledgment of demographic and lifestyle diversity issues, which are rising in importance for organizations as diversity in the work force and general population grows	Equal opportunity in employment Integration Appreciation of how differences can contribute to success

imply that all products must be safe for their intended use, must include thorough and explicit instructions for proper and safe use, and must have been tested to ensure reliability and quality.

Consumers' right to be informed means that consumers should have access to and the opportunity to review all relevant information about a product before buying it. Many laws require specific labeling on product packaging to satisfy this right. In addition, labels on alcoholic and tobacco products inform consumers that these products may cause illness and other problems.

The right to choose means that consumers must have access to a variety of products and services at competitive prices; they should also be assured of satisfactory quality and service at a fair price. Activities that reduce competition among businesses in an industry jeopardize this right of consumers.

The right to be heard ensures that consumers' interests will receive full and sympathetic consideration in the formulation of government policy. The right to be heard also promises consumers fair treatment when they complain to marketers about their products. This right benefits marketers, too, because when consumers complain about a product, this information can help the manufacturers modify the product to make it more satisfying.

Community Relations   Social responsibility also extends to marketers' roles as community members. Individual communities expect marketers to make philanthropic contributions to civic projects and institutions. Thus many marketers view social responsibility as including contributions of resources (money, products, time) to community causes such as education, the arts, recreation, disadvantaged members of the community, and others. John Hancock Mutual Life Insurance Co. has made a major donation to Habitat for Humanity of Boston to reduce interest rates on mortgages on local condominiums renovated by Habitat. The families will pay $1 a month for ten years and then $197 a month for the remaining ten years of the mortgage. The homeowners will provide a hundred hours of "sweat" equity on other Habitat for Humanity housing projects. Such efforts, of course, have a positive impact on local communities, but they also indirectly help the contributing organizations in the form of goodwill, publicity, and exposure to potential future customers. Thus, although social responsibility is certainly a positive concept, most organizations do not embrace it without the expectation of some indirect long-term benefit.

Concern about the quality of education in the United States grew after many firms recognized that the current pool of prospective employees lacks the basic reading, writing, and spelling skills necessary to work. Acknowledging that today's students are tomorrow's customers and employees, firms such as The Kroger Co., Campbell Soup Co., Kodak, American Express Company, Apple Computer, Inc., and Coca-Cola Enterprises, Inc. have donated money, equipment, and employee time to help improve local schools. In a job-training program sponsored by Target and coordinated by Goodwill/Easter Seals, students aged fifteen to twenty-two are given an opportunity to broaden their skills and a chance to determine if they are capable of far better jobs. The students learn basic customer skills by working with regular Target employees. Those who have shown promise during the twelve-week program are encouraged to go on in school to study retail management issues.[34] McDonald's Corp. provides scholarship money for college students who work part-time in its restaurants. Although some members of the public fear business involvement in education and other social areas, business participation is necessary in helping to educate the employees and customers of the future.

Green marketing
Development, pricing, promotion, and distribution of products that do not harm the environment

Green Marketing   **Green marketing** refers to the specific development, pricing, promotion, and distribution of products that do not harm the environment. The Alliance for Social Responsibility, an independent coalition of environmentalists, scientists, ethicists, and marketers, is one group involved in evaluating products to determine their environmental impact and marketers' commitment to the environment. Several environmental groups have also joined together to create a seal of approval to distinguish products that are environmentally safe. Companies receiving the green seal can use it in advertising and public information campaigns and on packaging.[35]

Developing a green marketing program is not easy, however. The environmental movement in marketing consists of many different initiatives and values. There is a widespread call to construct economic, legal, and ethical solutions to environmental problems. The aim is to sustain the environment by meeting the objectives listed below.

1. *Eliminate the concept of waste.* Recognizing that pollution and waste usually stem from inefficiency, the question is not what to do with waste but how to make things without waste.

2. *Reinvent the concept of a product.* Products need to be reduced to only three types and eventually just two. The first would be consumables, which are either eaten or, when placed in the ground, turn into soil without harmful side effects. The second type would be durable goods, such as cars, televisions, computers, VCRs, and refrigerators. These products could be made, used, and returned to the manufacturer within a closed loop system. The products would be designed for disassembly and recycling. The third category would be unsalables and include such products as radioactive material, heavy metals, and toxins. These products would always belong to the original makers, who would be responsible for them and their full life-cycle effects.

3. *Make prices reflect the cost.* Every product should reflect or at least approximate its actual cost—not only the direct cost of production, but also the cost of air, water, and soil. For example, the World Resources Institute in Washington, D.C., has estimated that the cost of a gallon of gas, when pollution, waste, disposal, health effects, and defense expenditures like the Persian Gulf War are factored in, is approximately $4.50. A study done by the University of California in San Francisco showed that a pack of cigarettes costs citizens in the state another $3.63 in health care and related costs.

4. *Make environmentalism profitable.* Consumers are beginning to recognize that competition in the marketplace should not be between companies harming the environment and those trying to save it.[36]

A program developed by Xerox Corp. called Asset Recycle Management, which will enable the company to get a jump on competition because of its potential for recyclable copier cartridges, illustrates these four principles. Many photocopiers and photocopier cartridges end up in landfills after outliving their usefulness. Under the new program, Xerox would offer a $24 discount on a new cartridge when a used cartridge is returned. To entice prospective recyclers, Xerox would provide a prepaid mailing envelope. Parts of the used cartridge are identified, reworked, and incorporated into new cartridges for new copiers. Eventually, all new cartridges may be assembled in a way that would allow the casing, as well as the inside parts, to be saved and recycled.[37]

Diversity Issues Diversity in the work environment, as we discussed in Chapter 2, is the integration and utilization of an increasingly diverse work force (see Figure 3.8). Companies that successfully utilize the work force are finding increases in creativity and motivation and reductions in turnover. From a marketing perspective, the more closely the work force matches the population, the better it understands consumer needs and wants. Levi Strauss recruits and manages a very diverse work force: more than half of all its U.S. employees come from minority groups. Fourteen percent of its top

**Figure 3.8
Diversity in the Work Environment**
Con Edison promotes its commitment to diversity in the workplace by reaching outside the workplace as well.

Con Edison industrial engineer Rosanna Jimenez was 12 when her family emigrated from the Dominican Republic. They were poor and spoke no English, but Rosanna grew up to be the first person in her family to graduate from college.

Through the New York City Board of Education's Speaker in the Classroom Program, Rosanna shares her success story with middle and high school students from all over the city. Rosanna's lively, engaging presentation teaches kids to raise their aspirations and grow up to achieve their goals.

Rosanna's work with the Speaker in the Classroom Program is just one of the many volunteer efforts of Con Edison people. When it comes to helping others, our employees are our finest role models.

THE ENERGY TO MAKE THINGS HAPPEN FOR YOU

management is non-Caucasian, and 30 percent is female.[38] Xerox also deserves praise for its outstanding workplace diversity. Of its more than 47,000 employees, 32 percent are women and 26 percent are minorities. Moreover, about one-fourth of the company's corporate officers are women and minorities.[39]

Social Responsibility and Marketing Ethics

*A*lthough the concepts of marketing ethics and social responsibility are often used interchangeably, it is important to remember that ethics relate to individual and group evaluations—judgments about what is right or wrong in a particular decision-making situation. Social responsibility is the obligation of an organization to maximize its positive impact and minimize its negative impact on society. Thus social responsibility deals with the total effect of marketing decisions on society. These two concepts are interrelated because a company that supports socially responsible decisions and adheres to a code of ethics is likely to have a positive impact on society.

One way to evaluate whether a specific behavior is ethical and socially responsible is to ask other persons in an organization if they approve of the behavior. For social responsibility issues, contact with concerned consumer groups and industry or government regulatory groups may be helpful. A check to see if there is a specific company policy about an activity may resolve issues. If other persons in the organization approve of the activity and it is legal and customary within the industry, chances are that the activity is acceptable from both an ethical and a social responsibility perspective. Table 3.8 provides an audit of mechanisms to control ethics and social responsibility in marketing.

A rule of thumb for ethical and social responsibility issues is that if they can withstand open discussion and result in agreements or limited debate, then an acceptable solution may exist. Nevertheless, even after a final decision is reached, different viewpoints on the issue may remain. Openness is not the end-all solution to the ethics problem. However, it does create trust and facilitates learning relationships.[40]

Table 3.8   Organizational Audit of Marketing Ethics and Social Responsibility Control Mechanisms

Answer True or False for each statement.

T   F   1. No mechanism exists for top management to detect social responsibility and ethical issues relating to employees, customers, the community, and society.

T   F   2. There is no formal or informal communication within the organization about procedures and activities that are considered acceptable behavior.

T   F   3. The organization fails to communicate its ethical standards to suppliers, customers, and groups that have a relationship with the organization.

T   F   4. There is an environment of deception, repression, and cover-ups concerning events that could be embarrassing to the company.

T   F   5. Compensation systems are totally dependent on economic performance.

T   F   6. The only concerns about environmental impact are those that are legally required.

T   F   7. Concern for the ethical value systems of the community with regard to the firm's activities is absent.

T   F   8. Products are described in a misleading manner, with no information on negative impact or limitations communicated to customers.

True answers indicate a lack of control mechanisms, which, if implemented, could improve ethics and social responsibility.

Summary

Marketing ethics are principles that define acceptable conduct in marketing. Many marketing decisions can be deemed either ethical or unethical, but others cannot be so clearly categorized. Marketers need assistance with primarily two types of ethical challenges: (1) decisions in gray areas where the "right" decision is debatable and (2) decisions where the right course of action is clear, but individual and organizational pressures, along with situational circumstances, push the marketer in the wrong direction. Though a very important concern in marketing decisions, ethics may be one of the most misunderstood and controversial concepts in marketing.

To grasp the significance of ethics in marketing decision making, one must examine the factors that influence the ethical decision-making process. Three of the important components of ethical decision making are individual factors, organizational relationships, and opportunity. Individual factors are the principles or rules that people use to decide what is right or wrong—in short, their moral philosophy. Two major types of moral philosophies are (1) utilitarianism and (2) ethical formalism. Utilitarian moral philosophies are concerned with maximizing the greatest good for the greatest number of people. Ethical formalism philosophies, on the other hand, focus on general rules for guiding the behavior of individuals. Individual ethical choices are not made in a vacuum, however. Organizational relationships with one's coworkers, employees, or superiors affect these choices and may create potential ethical problems. Organizations often evaluate success in terms of achieving objectives such as increased profits, market share, or product quality. How these objectives are pursued is determined not only by the individual's personal ethical decisions, but also by group influences. Significant others—superiors, peers, and subordinates—also influence the ethical decision-making process. The role of coworkers depends on the person's ratio of exposure to unethical behavior to exposure to ethical behavior. The more one is exposed to unethical activity in an organization, the greater the likelihood that one will behave unethically. Opportunity provides an additional pressure in ethical decisions. Opportunity is a favorable set of conditions that limit barriers or provide rewards. If an individual takes advantage of an opportunity to act unethically and escapes punishment or even gains a reward, that person may repeat such acts when circumstances favor them.

An ethical issue is an identifiable problem, situation, or opportunity requiring an individual or organization to choose from among alternatives that must be evaluated as right or wrong. Ethical issues typically arise because of conflicts between the individual's moral philosophy and the organizational environment in which the individual works. Product-related ethical issues may develop when marketers fail to disclose risks associated with the product or information regarding the function, value, or use of the product. The promotional process provides situations that can result in ethical issues, such as false and misleading advertising and deceptive sales tactics. Sales promotions and publicity that use deception or manipulation also create significant ethical issues. Bribery may be an ethical issue in some selling situations. Price fixing, predatory pricing, and failure to disclose the full price associated with a purchase are typical ethical issues. Ethical issues in distribution relate to conflicts among producers and marketing middlemen.

Organizations can improve the ethical behavior by formalizing what the organization expects of its employees. Codes of conduct are formal statements of rules and standards that describe what the company expects of its employees. Employees thus know what is expected of them and what the punishments could be for violating the rules. It is important to make ethics a part of everyday job responsibility. If managers and coworkers can provide direction and encourage ethical decision making, then they become a force helping individuals make better ethical decisions.

Social responsibility in marketing refers to an organization's obligation to maximize its positive impact and minimize its negative impact on society. The four dimensions of social responsibility are generally considered to be economic, legal, ethical, and philanthropic. Marketing managers try to determine what accepted relationships, obligations, and duties exist between the business organization and society.

To be successful, a business must determine what customers, government regulators, and competitors, as well as society in general, want or expect in terms of social responsibility. Major categories of social responsibility issues include the consumer movement, community relations, green marketing, and diversity. The consumer movement refers to the efforts of independent individuals, groups, and organizations to protect the rights of consumers. Consumers expect to have the right to safety, the right to be informed, the right to choose, and the right to be heard. Social responsibility also extends to marketers' roles as community members. Society expects marketers to contribute to the satisfaction and growth of their communities. Green marketing refers to the specific development, pricing, promotion, and distribution of products that do not harm the environment. Diversity in the workplace is the integration and utilization of a work force that reflects the general population. It also means greater awareness and acceptance of cultural differences.

The concepts of marketing ethics and social responsibility are interrelated because a company that supports socially responsible decisions, as well as individuals and groups that act ethically, is likely to have a positive impact on society. If other persons in the organization approve of an activity and it is legal and customary within the industry, chances are that the activity is acceptable from both an ethical and social responsibility perspective.

IMPORTANT TERMS

Marketing ethics   Organizational, or   Ethical issue   Social responsibility
Significant others   corporate, culture   Codes of conduct   Green marketing

DISCUSSION AND REVIEW QUESTIONS

1. Why is ethics an important consideration in marketing decisions?
2. How do the factors that influence ethical or unethical decisions interact?
3. What ethical conflicts could exist if business employees fly certain airlines just to receive benefits for their personal "frequent flier" program?
4. List the components of the marketing mix and an example of how each can be affected by ethical issues.

5. How can the ethical decisions involved in marketing be improved?
6. How can people with different personal values work together to make ethical decisions in an organization?
7. What is the difference between ethics and social responsibility?
8. What are major social responsibility issues?

APPLICATION QUESTIONS

1. The introduction of Aklaim Entertainment's Mortal Kombat video game into retail stores was met with a great deal of criticism from consumer advocates. Select another product or service that you feel caused ethical conflict between the marketer and a segment or group of society. Discuss why the conflict arose. What was its outcome, if any? If you had been the marketing manager for the company, how would you have resolved the conflict? What would have been a better approach in introducing the product or service?
2. Some organizations have a public image of social responsibility. Often these companies claim that being ethical is good business and that it pays to be a good citizen of the community. Identify a company or organization in your community that has a reputation for being ethical. What activities by the company account for this image? Is the company successful? Why?

3. As an employee, you face situations in your job that cause you to make decisions about what is right or wrong, and then you have to act on these decisions. Describe a recent situation at your workplace in which you had to make such a decision. Without disclosing your actual decision, tell what you based it on. What and whom did you think of when you were considering what to do? Why did you consider these things or these people?
4. Consumers interact with many businesses daily and weekly. Not only do companies in an industry acquire a reputation for being ethical or unethical, but entire industries become known as ethical or unethical. Identify two *types* of businesses with which you or your friends have had the most conflict involving ethical issues. Describe these ethical issues.

Case 3.1   Hershey Foods: Ethics and Social Responsibility

The Hershey Foods Corporation is the number one confectionery in North America. Its Hershey Chocolate U.S.A. division, the nation's largest chocolate producer, makes up approximately 44 percent of the U.S. chocolate industry. Hershey manufactures more than fifty-five brands of confectionery products including the familiar Hershey's Milk Chocolate bar, Hershey's Syrup, Hershey's Cocoa, Almond Joy, Mr. Goodbar, Hershey's Kisses, Kit Kat, and Reese's Peanut Butter Cups. In its Confectionery Division, Hershey sells ready-to-eat puddings in four candy bar flavors. Hershey Pasta group is the second largest pasta producer in the U.S. and manufactures regionally distributed brands of pasta including San Giorgio, Skinner, and Ronzoni. Confectioners Mars and Nestlé are Hershey's major competitors.

Founder Milton Hershey was born in 1857 of Pennsylvania Dutch descent. At 15, he became an apprentice to a candy maker. By age 30, Hershey had begun the Lancaster Caramel Company. From the beginning, Milton Hershey was concerned not only with making superior candy but also with running a superior company. His firm was built to reflect the utmost in integrity, honesty, and respect. Hershey also believed in treating consumers fairly and provided the highest quality mass market product. Everything he did was based on what he believed to be the highest ethical standards. These values influenced Hershey's relationship with customers, employees, and the community.

An example of this entrepreneur's concern for the community was his founding of the Hershey Industrial School, now called the Milton Hershey School, an orphanage, in 1909. Many of the children who attended the school became Hershey employees, and former Hershey chairman William Dearden (1976–1984) was a graduate. Today, the 10,000-acre school houses and educates nearly 1,200 socially disadvantaged children. Although Hershey is a public company, the school is supported by a trust that owns 44 percent of Hershey Foods. This stock ownership provides substantial dividends that offset the school's operating costs. In addition, the Hershey trust owns 77 percent of the Hershey Entertainment and Resort Company, a family-fun theme park developed by Milton Hershey.

The strong value system that was put in place by Milton Hershey is still the guiding philosophy of Hershey Foods today. His system dictates that all employees conduct their business in an ethical manner. While some companies post eloquent codes of ethics on the board room wall—much seen, little observed—Hershey's ethical values are an integral part of the corporate culture. Employees know that their company will support them as long as they focus on quality, integrity, and honesty. All Hershey employees benefit from specific written policies that provide guidance for handling ethical issues. Such policies also exist for relationships with stockholders, suppliers, employees, and customers. The following excerpts give you a taste of Hershey Foods' corporate philosophy:

- Honesty, integrity, fairness, and respect must be key elements in all dealings with our employees, shareholders, suppliers and society in general.
- Our operations will be conducted within regulatory guidelines and in a manner that does not adversely affect our environment.
- Employees will be treated with respect, dignity, and fairness.
- Our ongoing objective is to provide quality products and services of real value at competitive prices that will also insure an adequate return on investment.

Each year, Hershey distributes the "Key Corporate Policies" booklet to all employees. The booklet contains the corporation's statement of corporate philosophy and policies on the use of corporate funds, resources, and conflict of interest, the Antitrust Law Prohibition on price-fixing, trading in Hershey Foods and other related securities, and the personal responsibilities of employees. Employees are asked to review the policies carefully, then sign, date, and return a certification card that states the employee has read, agrees with, and "will adhere to" the guidelines.

Hershey employees with questions concerning proper conduct are instructed to consult their supervisor first, but if the supervisor is deemed a problem, alternatives are available. Antitrust questions are referred to the legal department. Questions about ownership or stock purchases are directed to the corporate secretary's office. The human resources office handles personnel problems. Employees also have the right to go to any corporate or division officer. In addition, employees in a quandary can call an 800 number and hear the following instruction:

> You have reached the Hershey Foods' employee concern line. This forum is provided for Hershey Foods' employees without fear of retribution or reprisal as long as this call is made in good faith. If you choose to remain anonymous, please provide specific and detailed information pertaining to your concern. If you would like your call returned, please leave your name and number and you will be contacted by . . . within 48 hours. If you would feel more comfortable expressing your concern in writing, address your letter to . . . Your concern will be reviewed and if warranted, a confidential investigation will be conducted. Please begin speaking after you hear the tone. You will have three minutes to deliver your message. Thank you for calling the concern line.

Ethics and social responsibility are not just words at Hershey; they are the foundation of the corporate culture, and they shape the way business is conducted on a daily basis. All managers go through ethical training programs that prepare them to deal with the complex issues they are likely to face in operating the company. Employees have a clear understanding of the company's ethical values and know that they will be supported in upholding them. The company continues to be the most profitable company in the confectionery market and has outperformed the stock market over the last ten years.[41]

Questions for Discussion

1. What impact did Milton Hershey's personal values have on today's Hershey corporate philosophy of ethics?
2. How has social responsibility at Hershey helped the company attain success?
3. Identify what you believe is the most significant ethics or social responsibility program at Hershey Foods. Explain your choice.

Case 3.2 Eli Lilly & Co.: Inventing a New Corporate Culture

Eli Lilly and Co. researches, produces, and markets pharmaceuticals, including insulin, antibiotics, and antidepressants, as well as treatments for animal diseases and for improving the efficiency of animal food production. Although many of these drugs have literally been lifesavers for millions around the world, some have generated controversy and become thorny ethical issues for Eli Lilly. As a result, the company is working to instill new ethical and socially responsible values in the 1990s.

Indianapolis-based Eli Lilly and Co. was founded in 1876 by Colonel Eli Lilly, a pharmacist and Union officer in the Civil War. In the years since, Lilly researchers have developed numerous groundbreaking drugs, including insulin in 1923 to treat diabetes, Merthiolate (an antiseptic), Seconal (a sedative), and treatments for anemia and heart disease. In 1952, Lilly researchers isolated the antibiotic erythromycin. The company also produced more than 60 percent of the Salk polio vaccine during the 1950s. In the 1970s, Lilly began to diversify, acquiring Elizabeth Arden (cosmetics), which it sold in 1987, IVAC (medical instruments), and Hybritech (biotechnology). Today, the company, with more than $5 billion in sales, manufactures and markets drugs worldwide.

Despite its role as a developer of lifesaving drugs, Eli Lilly has not escaped a collision with numerous ethical and social responsibility issues. In 1992, its manufacturing facilities were cited by the Environmental Protection Agency as the nation's twenty-fourth largest emitter of carcinogens. And some of its best-known drugs have had unintended side effects, both for patients and for Eli Lilly itself. The firm has been in litigation for decades over DES (diethylstilbestrol), which has not been widely used since 1971 because of concerns that it causes cancer and other problems in children whose mothers took the drug. Some 200 cases related to DES are still pending. In 1983, the firm lost a $6 million suit over a death caused by its arthritis drug Oraflex.

Perhaps no drug has been more controversial for Eli Lilly than Prozac, which the firm introduced in 1988. Prozac is now the most-prescribed antidepressant, with sales of $2 billion in 1995, about 27 percent of Lilly's revenues. Prescribed for depression and obsessive-compulsive disorders, Prozac is taken by more than 16 million patients in more than 80 countries. It works by elevating a patient's level of serotonin, a chemical in the brain that positively affects a person's moods. Prozac has made it possible for millions of victims to live a more normal life. However, some critics charge that Prozac's negative side effects outweigh the benefits of the drug.

On September 14, 1989, Joseph Wesbecker, an out-of-work pressman, walked into the printing plant of his former employer, Standard Gravure, in Louisville, Kentucky, and opened fire with an AK-47. When the shooting stopped, twelve people were wounded, and nine lay dead, including Wesbecker, who shot himself. A month before the shooting, Wesbecker had begun taking Prozac as a treatment for depression. Survivors and families of the victims of the shooting, convinced that Prozac brought on Wesbecker's rampage, sued Eli Lilly for damages. Lilly, however, argued that Wesbecker's attack was carefully planned and not induced by Prozac, and that the plaintiffs' charges lacked scientific merit. The Wesbecker case, which was decided in Lilly's favor, was the first of 160 lawsuits over Prozac to go to trial.

Prozac has generated controversy for Lilly in other ways as well. Among its reported side effects are jitteriness, insomnia, nausea, and loss of sexual function. Because of cases like Wesbecker's, the Church of Scientology began a campaign against the drug, claiming that it triggers psychotic and suicidal reactions in users. The Citizens Commission on Human Rights, a group founded by the Church of Scientology, even petitioned the Food and Drug Administration (FDA) in 1991 to remove Prozac from the market. The FDA denied the petition after finding "no credible evidence" of a link between the drug and violent behavior. In the fifty-six criminal cases brought to trial thus far, defendants who cited Prozac as a defense for their crimes failed to prove their cases. Nonetheless, professional psychologists have expressed concerns that use of the drug may be harmful when doctors prescribe it as a cheap and quick alternative to therapy instead of trying to resolve a patient's underlying psychological problems. The fact that Prozac has been prescribed for gambling, obesity, PMS, fear of public speaking, and other maladies—even though depression is the only condition for which it is approved—adds weight to their concerns.

Moreover, Prozac does not help an estimated 30 percent of patients. In fact, the wife of Eli Lilly's CEO, Randall Tobias, took her own life while being treated with Prozac for depression. Tobias says, "Because it didn't work with my wife, I better understand how incredibly important it is for the millions of people it does help, and how we need to continue working very hard to find products that treat everybody."

Tobias's reaction is representative of the more humanistic direction he wants Eli Lilly to take in the 1990s. As Lilly's chairman and CEO since 1993 and the first outsider ever to head the company, Tobias is taking steps to make Eli Lilly more ethical and responsible. He is trying to create a new corporate culture for Lilly that truly respects all stakeholders, not just customers and suppliers, because he believes that there are both financial and moral payoffs to treating people with respect and dignity in business.

To reap some of these rewards, Eli Lilly determined to slash by 50 percent the amount of chemicals it emits into the atmosphere, particularly methylene chloride and toluene, although it had not been required to do so. To accomplish this, the firm is replacing solvents used in pharmaceutical processing with water-based materials. The company already recovers and reuses about two-thirds of its manufacturing solvents, which lowers overall costs by cutting down the amount of new materials required for production. In fact, Eli Lilly has become a major advocate of recycling. Since 1991, the firm has recycled 900 tons of office paper, 4 million beverage cans, 90 tons of telephone books, nearly 900 tons of cardboard, and 14 tons of glass. By 1997, the firm plans to implement management practices outlined by the Chemical Manufacturers Association's Responsible Care initiative at all of its U.S. operations.

Lilly has tried to develop its new corporate culture even through a painful downsizing effort in 1993 that cut 3,000 jobs. Instead of pink slips, Lilly offered many employees early retirement options. Employees close to retirement age saw two more years added to the number of years served and to their ages. Those who accepted the offer of early retirement also received one year's pay. Out-and-out layoffs would have been less costly for the firm: Lilly's humane actions cost it $535 million before taxes.

Lilly also tries to correct problems quickly. For example, in 1994, the company immediately recalled 4 million bottles of antibiotics after four patients discovered small plastic caps inside the bottles. Although the firm was not asked to recall the drug—and spent $66 million to recover potentially tainted bottles—Lilly executives believed it was the right thing to do.[42]

Questions for Discussion

1. Although the courts have thus far absolved Eli Lilly of any legal responsibility with regard to Prozac, what ethical and social responsibility issues are associated with the antidepressant?
2. What ethical and social responsibility obligations do you think a pharmaceutical company owes to its patients and society?
3. How do Lilly's recent actions illustrate its commitment to be more socially responsible?

Chapter 4

Global Markets and International Marketing

OBJECTIVES

- To become familiar with the nature of global markets and international marketing

- To understand the environmental elements that create global markets

- To analyze the environmental forces affecting international marketing efforts

- To be able to identify several important regional trade alliances, agreements, and markets

- To learn about methods of involvement in international marketing activities

Procter & Gamble cleans up in global consumer markets.

78

Y*ou've* probably heard of Procter & Gamble products such as Tide, Crest, Ivory, Cover Girl, Head & Shoulders, Vick's, and Pampers. Perhaps you even use some of them. What you may not realize is that Procter & Gamble has a phenomenal marketing presence outside the United States. In fact, the 160-year-old company generates more than half of its $34 billion sales of 300 different brands in other countries.

To enhance its worldwide operations, P&G recently reorganized into four regional divisions: North America; Europe, the Middle East and Africa; Asia; and Latin America. The company has also commenced a comprehensive strategy to build consumer value, cut costs, and globalize. To enhance value, P&G is slashing product prices worldwide, improving product quality, and introducing economy-priced brands into markets where consumer purchasing power is most restricted. To reduce costs (which can be passed onto consumers as lower prices), the Cincinnati-based firm has consolidated facilities; improved manufacturing, engineering, and distribution efficiency; and cut 13,000 jobs. Globally, P&G is focusing on expanding proven successful product lines.

In Latin America, all three tactics are paying off. "We are winning consumer loyalty by delivering superior performance with both premium-priced and economy-priced versions of our brands," says Jorge Montoya, executive vice president for the region. For instance, P&G introduced Pampers Phases diapers into Brazil in 1991, followed in 1993 by Pampers Uni, an economy-priced product, which quickly became the market leader. Before the introduction of Pampers Uni, P&G held 13 percent of the Brazilian diaper market; now it commands 38 percent. P&G built on the success of Pampers Uni by expanding them into Asia, Eastern Europe, and the Middle East, as well as other parts of Latin America.

P&G's strategies have helped it build a $2.2 billion business in Latin America, a market that now accounts for 7 percent of P&G's global revenue. It continues to invest heavily in the region—$800 million in the past five years. With a strong investment and sound strategy, P&G expects Latin American sales to double in the next five years to $4 billion.[1]

International marketing activities are performed to compete beyond the domestic market. Procter & Gamble's marketing efforts in Latin America provide a good example of the development of a global market opportunity. In many cases, serving a foreign target market requires more than minor adjustments of marketing strategies.

This chapter looks closely at the unique features of global markets and international marketing. We begin by focusing on involvement in global markets and international marketing. The environmental forces in international markets are discussed to provide an understanding of the reasons for differences in national and regional markets. Then we consider several regional and global trade agreements, alliances, and markets. Finally, we examine the levels of commitment American firms have to international marketing and their degree of involvement in it.

Global Markets and International Marketing

*B*efore picking up an Egg McMuffin at McDonald's, a young woman in Hong Kong this morning could have brightened her smile with Colgate toothpaste and highlighted her eyes with Avon eye shadow. Her brother, while on business that same day in Frankfurt, can cash a $500 check in a local Citicorp branch bank. Elsewhere that day, a Polish office worker, at lunchtime, can enjoy a pizza from Pizza Hut, fried chicken from KFC, or a taco from Taco Bell. An Australian mother shopping for a birthday present in Melbourne can drop in at Daimaru, a Japanese department store, and a New Yorker in Syracuse can find a train set for his two-year-old at The Lost Forest, an Australian toy boutique. By the year 2000, the earth will be populated with around 7 billion people whose lives will be intertwined in one tremendous global marketplace.

Technological advances and rapidly changing political and economic circumstances are making it possible for more and more companies to market their products overseas as well as at home. **International marketing** means developing and performing marketing activities across national boundaries. For example, Wal-Mart, the largest retailer in the United States, is opening new discount stores and supercenters in Argentina, Brazil, Canada, China, and Mexico. The discount chain already operates 128 Canadian Wal-Mart stores and another 119 in Mexico.[2] Blockbuster, the largest video rental chain, earns 15 percent of its revenue from foreign business and expects that figure to double to 30 percent by the year 2000.[3] Another example is Sprint Business, which is utilizing its public data network to gain business in Europe (see Figure 4.1). But don't assume that expanding

International marketing
Developing and performing marketing activities across national boundaries

Figure 4.1
Technological Advances Provide International Opportunities   When Rail Europe needed a way to communicate its huge database of schedule and fare information, Sprint Business provided SprintNet—the world's largest public data network—thus expanding its market in Europe.

Thanks to Sprint Business, Rail Europe increased its speed to 256 kilobits per second.

Table 4.1   The Top Fifteen U.S. Exporters, 1995

	Major Export Products	Annual Export Sales ($ millions)	Percent of Total Revenues
General Motors	motor vehicles and parts, locomotives	$16,127.1	10.4%
Ford Motor Co.	motor vehicles and parts	11,892.0	9.3
Boeing	commercial aircraft	11,844.0	54.0
Chrysler Corp.	motor vehicles and parts	9,400.0	18.0
General Electric	jet engines, turbines, plastics, medical systems, locomotives	8,110.0	12.5
Motorola	communications equipment, semiconductors	7,370.0	33.1
IBM	computers and related equipment	6,336.0	9.9
Philip Morris	tobacco, beer, food products	4,942.0	9.2
Archer Daniels Midland	protein meals, vegetable oils, flour, alcohol, grain	4,675.0	41.1
Hewlett-Packard	measurement, computation, communications products and systems	4,653.0	18.6
Intel	microcomputer components, modules, systems	4,561.0	39.6
Caterpillar	engines, turbines, construction, mining, and agricultural machinery	4,510.0	31.5
McDonnell Douglas	aerospace products, missiles, electronic systems	4,235.0	32.1
E.I. du Pont de Nemours	chemicals, polymers, fibers, specialty products	3,625.0	10.4
United Technologies	jet engines, helicopters, cooling equipment	3,108.0	14.7

Source: James Aley, "New Lift for the U.S. Export Boom," *Fortune*, Nov. 13, 1995, p. 74. © 1995 Time Inc. All rights reserved.

international operations is limited to giant corporations. A recent survey found that 20 percent of U.S. small businesses (companies with fewer than 500 employees) exported goods and services in 1994, up from 11 percent in 1992. For example, StoneHeart Inc., based in Cheney, Washington, has expanded sales of its product—a scooter for people with leg/foot injuries—beyond the United States to Japan and Canada and in 1995, expected such exports to account for 20 percent of its $500,000 annual sales.[4] The proportion of midsize companies marketing overseas reached 56 percent in 1995, up from about 25 percent in 1993.[5]

Many U.S. firms are finding that international markets provide tremendous opportunities for growth. One such firm is profiled in Global Perspective (page 82). The United States exported approximately $800 billion worth of goods and services in 1995, and most experts believe the numbers will reach $1 trillion by 1998.[6] Table 4.1 lists the top fifteen U.S. exporters; General Motors tops the list with $16 billion in export sales.

■ *International Involvement*

Marketers engage in international marketing activities at several levels of involvement that cover a wide spectrum, as Figure 4.2 shows. Domestic marketing involves marketing strategies aimed at markets within the home country; at the other extreme, global mar-

**Figure 4.2
Levels of Involvement in
Global Marketing**

keting means developing marketing strategies for major regions or for the entire world. Many firms with an international presence start as small companies serving local and regional markets and expand to national markets before considering opportunities in foreign markets. Limited exporting may occur when a firm's products are sold in foreign countries with little or no effort to obtain foreign sales. Sometimes such sales take place when foreign buyers seek out the company and/or its products. Or a marketing channel member or distributor may discover the firm's products and export them. Regardless of the level of involvement, marketers must choose either to customize their marketing strategies for different regions of the world or to standardize their marketing strategies for the entire world.

■ *Customization versus Globalization of International Marketing Strategies*

International marketers develop strategies to serve specific target markets. Traditional international marketing strategies customize marketing mixes according to cultural, regional, and national differences. Many soap and detergent manufacturers, for example, adapt their products to local water conditions, washing equipment, and washing habits. Colgate-Palmolive Co. even devised an inexpensive, plastic, hand-powered washing machine for use in households that have no electricity in less-developed countries. From a practical standpoint, in order to standardize the marketing mix, the strategy needs to group countries by social, cultural, technological, political, and economic similarities.

Globalization Developing marketing strategies as though the whole world were a single entity

In contrast, **globalization** of marketing involves developing marketing strategies as though the entire world (or its major regions) were a single entity; a globalized firm markets standardized products in the same way everywhere.[7] Nike and Adidas shoes, for example, are standardized worldwide. Other examples of globalized products include electrical communications equipment, Western American clothing, movies, soft drinks, rock and alternative music CDs, cosmetics, and toothpaste. Sony televisions, Levi jeans, and American cigarette brands post year-to-year gains in the world market. Even take-out food lends itself to globalization: McDonald's, KFC, and Taco Bell restaurants seem to satisfy hungry consumers in every hemisphere.

For many years, organizations have attempted to globalize the marketing mix as much as possible by employing standardized products, promotion campaigns, prices, and distribution channels for all markets. For example, Komatsu provides basically the

GLOBAL PERSPECTIVE

Brother Industries Taps into Foreign Markets

Brother Industries USA Inc. markets typewriters and word processors. In fact, the company makes 40 percent of all word processors and typewriters sold in the United States. Brother wants to double world sales by 2000 but faces huge problems—namely product obsolescence. Typewriters are gathering dust on back shelves, and word processors have been eclipsed by personal computers. The domestic typewriter and word processor market shrank 15 percent in 1994, and analysts expect it to continue to wither at a rate of 10 to 15 percent a year for the rest of the decade. A major rival, Smith Corona, recently filed for bankruptcy, attributing many of its problems to the dying industry.

Brother began making typewriters in 1961, but only about 30 percent of its revenues come from typewriter sales today. To survive, Brother is embarking on an aggressive five-year plan to develop new products. In the last few years, for example, the company has developed a new line of ink-jet word processors and a very successful labeling machine.

A second goal is to expand in and enter new markets overseas so that exports will far exceed the current 10 percent level. The Far East and Latin America represent particularly desirable markets because consumers there are more likely to consider cost and space than the latest technology when shopping for business equipment. Japan's $2 billion word processor market offers Brother room for growth. Mark Thompson, senior vice president at New Jersey–based Brother International Corp., which owns Brother Industries, says of the Japanese, "They like PCs a little, but they like word processors a lot, so it's a different market than the U.S. market." Brother planned to launch a Japanese-character word processor in 1996 and is hard at work developing word processors in other languages. Brother already makes typewriters in Spanish, Portuguese, Vietnamese, and Thai. Typewriters sell very well in Latin American markets, particularly Brazil, the only place Brother typewriters are made outside of the United States. China represents another valuable market if trade tariffs are reduced. Only time will tell whether Brother can capitalize on these market opportunities in a global economy driven increasingly by new, not familiar, technology.

Source: Jan Van Valkenburgh, "Brother Maps Strategy as Typewriter Sales Dip," *The Commercial Appeal,* September 17, 1995, pp. B1, B5. Copyright, 1995, The Commercial Appeal, Memphis, TN. Reprinted by permission.

Think locally. Act globally.

KOMATSU

same products worldwide (see Figure 4.3). The economic and competitive payoffs for globalized marketing strategies are certainly great. Brand name, product characteristics, packaging, and labeling are among the easiest marketing mix variables to standardize; media allocation, retail outlets, and price may be more difficult. In the end, the degree of similarity between the various environmental and market conditions determines the feasibility of globalization.

International marketing demands some strategic planning by the firm to incorporate foreign sales into its overall marketing strategy. International marketing activities confirm the importance of customized marketing mixes in achieving the firm's goals. Globalization requires a total commitment to the world, regions, or multinational areas as an integral part of the firm's markets; world or regional markets become as important as domestic ones.

Figure 4.3
Globalizing the Marketing Mix
Komatsu is an organization that provides standardized products throughout the world.

Environmental Forces in International Markets

*B*efore a company enters a foreign market, it must thoroughly analyze the environment. If a marketing strategy is to be effective across national borders, the complexities of all the environments involved must be understood. In this section we see how differences in the cultural and social, economic, political and legal, and technological forces of the marketing environment in other countries affect marketing activities.

■ Cultural and Social Forces

Culture refers to the concepts, values, and tangible items, such as tools, buildings, and foods, that make up a particular society. Culture is passed on from one generation to another; in a way, it is the blueprint for acceptable behavior in a given society. This notion of culture, or national character, involves the idea that people of a given nation have distinctive patterns of behavior and personality characteristics.[8]

When products are introduced from one nation into another, acceptance is far more likely if there are similarities between the two cultures. For international marketers, these cultural similarities have implications in terms of product development, advertising, packaging, and pricing. For example, cranberries, a holiday favorite of Americans, are virtually unknown outside the United States. Ocean Spray Cranberries, Inc., has therefore had to make adjustments to entice foreign consumers to try cranberry products in hopes of reaching $500 million in foreign sales by the year 2000. In Great Britain, Ocean Spray experienced poor sales until it mixed cranberry juice with black currant juice, which is popular among British children, and started using juice boxes, which are preferred by Britons over the bottles Ocean Spray uses in the United States.[9] Cross-cultural similarities in eating trends are shown in Table 4.2. A new global sensitivity about food has resulted in middle-class U.S. families eating more like their counterparts in Japan or France.

Product adoption and use are also influenced by consumers' perceptions of other countries. When consumers are generally unfamiliar with products from another country, their perceptions of the country itself affect their attitude toward the product and help determine whether they will adopt it. If a country has a reputation for producing quality products and therefore has a positive image in consumers' minds, marketers from that country will want to make the country of origin well known. For example, a generally favorable image of Western computer technology has fueled sales of Compaq and IBM

Table 4.2   Cross-Cultural Similarities in Eating Trends

Country	Past Dietary Trends	Current Dietary Trends
Japan	Home-cooked fish and rice, as well as gourmet foods Generally low-fat and contributing to a longer life span Small dishes of fish and vegetable served with rice and miso soup	Frozen food, take-out and precooked foods Fast-food outlets such as McDonald's and KFC more popular than in the U.S. Microwavable entrees growing in popularity
France	Fat-filled dishes prepared with fresh ingredients from the market Homemade pastries and desserts Warm chicken gizzards, sliced baguettes (bread), paté, and a green salad	Takeout pizzas, hamburgers, Tex-Mex food, and convenience foods very popular Leaner cuts of meat and fewer traditional butter- and cream-loaded dishes
United States	Steak, pork chops, boiled potatoes, french fries, bacon, whole milk, and eggs Traditional meat and potatoes	Pizza, tacos and burritos, bagels, pasta, frozen entrees, rice, instant potatoes, diet soft drinks, bottled water, frozen yogurt, and microwave popcorn

Sources: Kathleen Deveny, "America's Heartland Acquires Global Taste," *The Wall Street Journal*, Oct. 11, 1995, pp. B1, B6; Norihiko Shirouzu, "Home-Cooked Fish, Rice Lose Importance in Japan," *The Wall Street Journal*, Oct. 11, 1995, p. B1; and Gabriella Stern, "French Add Convenience to Customary Cuisine," *The Wall Street Journal*, Oct.11, 1995, pp. B1, B6.

personal computers and Microsoft software in Japan.[10] Conversely, marketers may want to dissociate themselves from a particular country. Because Mexican cars have not been viewed by the world as being quality products, Volkswagen, for example, may not want to advertise that some of the models it sells in the United States are made in Mexico.

Culture may also affect marketing negotiations and decision-making behavior on the part of marketers, industrial buyers, and other executives. Research has shown that when marketers use a problem-solving approach—that is, gain information about a particular client's needs and tailor goods or services to meet those needs—it leads to increased customer satisfaction in marketing negotiations in France, Germany, the United Kingdom, and the United States. However, the attractiveness of the salesperson and his or her similarity to the customer increase the levels of satisfaction only for Americans. Furthermore, marketing negotiations proceed differently in the various cultures, and the role and status of the seller are more important in both the United Kingdom and France.[11] Cultural differences in the emphasis placed on personal relationships, status, decision-making styles, and approaches to bidding have all been shown to complicate business dealings between Americans and Japanese.[12] In the Far East a gift may be considered a necessary introduction before negotiation, but in the United States or Canada a gift may be misconstrued as a bribe.

Marketing activities are primarily social in purpose; therefore they are influenced by the institutions of family, religion, education, health, and recreation. For example, in Greece, where sunbathing is a common form of recreation, U.S. products such as Johnson & Johnson Baby Sunblock have a large target market. In every nation, these social institutions can be identified. By finding major deviations in cultural institutions among countries, marketers can gain insights into the adaptation of a marketing strategy. Because India's Hindu population considers it taboo to eat beef, McDonald's will market beefless burgers there, serving chicken, fish, and vegetable patties instead.[13] Although football is a popular sport in the United States and a major opportunity for many television advertisers, soccer is the most popular television sport in Europe. The role of children in the family and a society's overall view of children also influence marketing activities. For example, the use of cute, cereal-munching children in advertising for Kellogg's is illegal in France. In the Netherlands, children are banned from confectionery advertisements, and candy makers are required to place a little toothbrush symbol at the end of each sweet spot.[14]

■ *Economic Forces*

It is important for international marketers to understand the international trade system. When analyzing global markets, U.S. firms may find that they would face various trade restrictions, such as tariffs. An import tariff is any duty levied by a nation on goods bought outside its borders and brought in. Use of protective tariffs, which raise the price of foreign goods, impedes free trade between nations. Tariffs are designed either to raise revenue for the country or to protect domestic products. For example, the United States has threatened to raise tariffs on certain Chinese products unless China cracks down on the pirating of CDs, movies, books, and computer software: China has twenty-nine CD plants making illegal copies of copyrighted music and exporting them for sale worldwide.[15] Such a tariff would function to protect the marketing of authorized recordings. Nontariff trade barriers include cultural and social rejection of a foreign country's products and restrictive product standards, which prevent another country's products from entering a particular market.

In addition, an exporter to a foreign country may be constrained by a quota, which sets a limit on the amount of goods the importing country will accept for certain product categories in a specific time period. Then there are embargoes: the suspension, by a government, of trade in a particular product or with a given country. Embargoes are generally directed at specific goods or countries and are established for political, health, or religious reasons. For example, the United States forbids the importing of cigars from Cuba for political reasons.

Another reason countries limit imports is to maintain a favorable balance of trade. The balance of trade is the difference in value between a nation's exports and imports. When a nation exports more products than it imports, a favorable balance of trade exists because money is flowing into the country.

Table 4.3   A Comparative Economic Analysis of Germany and the United States

	Germany	United States
Land area (sq. mi.)	137,821	3,536,338
Population (millions)	81.4	260.8
Population density (persons per sq. mi.)	590	73.7
Employed persons (millions)	35	123
GDP, 1994 ($ billion)	$2,046.5	$6,738.4
GDP per capita	$25,140	$25,852

Source: Ekkehard Brose, Betsy Wittleder, and Hans Sturm, eds., "Spotlight on German-American Economic Relations and the Global Economy," Germany Embassy Press Department, Washington, D.C., September 1995, p. 1. Used by permission.

Exchange controls, or restrictions on the amount of a particular currency that can be bought or sold, also affect international marketing strategy. They can force businesspeople to buy and sell foreign products through a central agency, such as a central bank. On the other hand, some countries have joined to form free trade zones, or multinational economic communities that eliminate tariffs and other trade barriers, in order to promote international trade. These economic communities and trade alliances are discussed later in the chapter.

Economic differences dictate many of the adjustments that must be made in marketing abroad. The most prominent adjustments are caused by differences in standards of living, availability of credit, discretionary buying power, income distribution, national resources, and conditions that affect transportation.

Gross domestic product (GDP) Overall measure of a nation's economic standing

In terms of the value of all products produced by a nation, the United States has the largest gross domestic product in the world, $6,738 billion. **Gross domestic product (GDP)** is an overall measure of a nation's economic standing in terms of the market value of the total output of goods and services produced in that nation for a given period of time. However, it does not take into account the concept of GDP in relation to population (GDP per capita). The United States has a GDP per capita of $25,852. Germany is roughly twenty-five times smaller than the United States—about the size of Montana—but its population density is eight times greater than that of the United States. Although Germany's GDP is about one-third the size of the U.S. GDP, its GDP per capita is about the same.[16] Table 4.3 provides a comparative analysis of Germany and the United States. Knowledge about per capita income, credit, and the distribution of income provides general insights into market potential.

Opportunities for international marketers are not limited to countries with the highest incomes. Some nations are progressing at a much faster rate than they were a few years ago, and these countries—especially in Latin America, Africa, Eastern Europe, and the Middle East—have great market potential. However, marketers must understand the political and legal environment before they can convert buying power into actual demand for specific products.

■ *Political and Legal Forces*

A country's political system, national laws, regulatory bodies, special interest groups, and courts all have great impact on international marketing. A government's policies toward public and private enterprise, consumers, and foreign firms influence marketing across national boundaries. Some countries have established import barriers. Many nontariff barriers, such as quotas and minimum price levels set on imports, port-of-entry taxes, and stringent health and safety requirements, still make it difficult for American companies to export their products.[17] Just a few years ago, companies exporting electronic equipment to Japan had to wait for the Japanese government to inspect each item. A

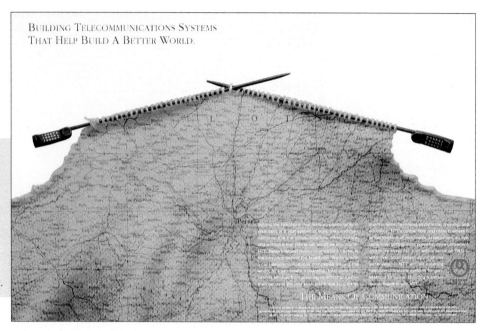

Figure 4.4
Technological Forces
By working with local telecommunications companies throughout the world, NTT has built a communications system that connects remote locations and promotes technological development.

government's attitude toward cooperation with importers has a direct impact on the economic feasibility of exporting to that country.

Differences in political and government ethical standards are illustrated by what the Mexicans call *la mordida,* "the bite." The use of payoffs and bribes is deeply entrenched in many governments. Because U.S. trade and corporate policy, as well as U.S. law, prohibits direct involvement in payoffs and bribes, American companies may have a hard time competing with foreign firms that do engage in these practices. Some U.S. businesses that refuse to make payoffs are forced to hire local consultants, public relations firms, or advertising agencies—which results in indirect payoffs. The ultimate decision about whether to give small tips or gifts where they are customary must be based on a company's code of ethics. However, under the Foreign Corrupt Practices Act of 1977, it is illegal for U.S. firms to attempt to make large payments or bribes to influence policy decisions of foreign governments. The act also subjects all publicly held U.S. corporations to demanding internal control and record-keeping requirements related to their overseas operations.

■ *Technological Forces*

Much of the marketing technology used in North America and other industrialized regions of the world may be ill-suited for developing countries. For example, advertising on television or through direct-mail campaigns may be difficult in countries that lack up-to-date broadcast and postal services. Nonetheless, many countries— particularly China, South Korea, Mexico, and Poland—want to engage in international trade, often through partnerships with American and Japanese firms, so that they can gain valuable industrial and agricultural technology. Helping to make such partnerships possible is NTT, Japan's largest telecommunications carrier (see Figure 4.4). But the export of technology that has strategic importance to the United States may require the approval of the U.S. Department of Defense.

Regional Trade Alliances, Markets, and Agreements

Although some firms are beginning to view the world as one huge marketplace, various regional trade alliances and specific markets affect companies engaging in international marketing—some create opportunities, others impose constraints. This section examines several regional trade alliances, markets, and changing conditions affecting markets, including the North American Free Trade Agreement between the

United States, Canada, and Mexico; the unification of Europe; the General Agreement on Tariffs and Trade (GATT); the Pacific Rim markets; and changing conditions in Eastern Europe and the former Soviet Republics.

■ *The North American Free Trade Agreement (NAFTA)*

North American Free Trade Agreement (NAFTA) An alliance that merges Canada, the United States, and Mexico into a single market

The **North American Free Trade Agreement (NAFTA),** which went into effect on January 1, 1994, effectively merged Canada, Mexico, and the United States into one market of about 374 million consumers. NAFTA will eliminate virtually all tariffs on goods produced and traded between Canada, Mexico, and the United States to create a totally free trade area by 2009. The estimated annual output for this trade alliance is $7 trillion. Obviously, NAFTA has major implications for developing marketing strategies in the United States.

NAFTA makes it easier for U.S. businesses to invest in Mexico and Canada, provides protection for intellectual property (of special interest to high-technology and entertainment industries), expands trade by requiring equal treatment of U.S. firms in both countries, and simplifies country-of-origin rules, hindering Japan's use of Mexico as a staging ground for further penetration into U.S. markets. Although most tariffs on products coming to the U.S. will be lifted, duties on more sensitive products such as household glassware, footware, and some fruits and vegetables will be phased out over a fifteen-year period.

Canada's 29 million consumers are relatively affluent, with a per capita GDP of $15,500.[18] Trade between the United States and Canada reached $260 billion in 1994, up 50 percent from 1988 when the two nations signed a free trade agreement that laid the groundwork for NAFTA. Currently, exports to Canada support approximately 1.5 million U.S. jobs. Canadian investments in U.S. companies are also increasing, and various markets, including air travel, are opening as regulatory barriers dissolve.[19]

Although Mexican consumers are less affluent (per capita GDP is about $3,200), they bought $51 billion worth of U.S. goods in 1994.[20] The Mexican market prefers U.S. goods; for every $1 spent on imports in Mexico, 70 cents purchases U.S. goods. However, a devaluation of the Mexican peso in early 1995 threw Mexico into a financial crisis and resulted in a sharp drop in U.S. exports to Mexico and an increase in products imported from Mexico. Privatization of some government-owned firms and other measures instituted by the Mexican government and businesses have helped alleviate the situation.[21] In Figure 4.5, Amistad encourages foreign industries to locate their businesses in Mexico. Moreover, the increasing trade between the United States and Canada constitutes a strong base of support for the ultimate success of NAFTA. Mexico's membership in NAFTA also links the United States with other Latin American countries, providing additional opportunities for integrating trade among all the nations in the Western Hemisphere. Chile, for example, is expected to become the fourth member of NAFTA, although politics may delay its entry into the agreement for several years.[22]

Figure 4.5
Marketing in Mexico
Amistad Industries encourages foreign businesses to locate in Mexico.

Although NAFTA remains politically controversial, it is expected to be a positive factor for U.S. firms wishing to engage in international marketing. Because licensing requirements have been relaxed under the pact, smaller businesses that previously could not afford to invest in Mexico will be able to do business in that market without having to locate there. NAFTA's long phase-in period provides ample time for adjustment by those firms affected by reduced tariffs on imports. Furthermore, increased competition should lead to a more efficient market, and the long-term prospects of including most of the countries in the Western Hemisphere in the alliance promise additional opportunities for U.S. marketers.

■ *The European Union*

The European Union (EU), also called the European Community or Common Market, was established in 1958 to promote trade among its members, which initially included Belgium, France, Italy, West Germany, Luxembourg, and the Netherlands. In 1991 East and West Germany merged into one nation, and by 1993 the United Kingdom, Spain, Denmark, Greece, Portugal, and Ireland had joined as well. (Eventually, some countries of the former Soviet Union and Eastern Europe may also become members.) Until 1993, each nation functioned as a separate market, but at that time, the twelve officially unified into one of the largest single world markets with nearly 340 million consumers.

To facilitate free trade among members, the EU is working toward the standardization of business regulations and requirements, import duties, and value-added taxes; the elimination of customs checks; and the creation of a standardized currency for use by all members. The long-term goals are to eliminate all barriers for trade within the EU, improve the economic efficiency of the EU nations, stimulate economic growth, and thus make the union economy more competitive in global markets, particularly against Japan, the rest of the Pacific Rim, and North America. However, several disputes and debates still divide the member nations, and many barriers to completely free trade remain. Consequently, it may take many years before the EU is truly one deregulated market.

Although the EU nations are trying to function as one large market and consumers in the EU may become more homogeneous in their needs and wants, marketers must be aware that cultural differences among the twelve nations may require modifications in the marketing mix for consumers in each nation. Differences in taste and preferences in these diverse markets are significant for international marketers. For example, the British prefer front-loading washing machines, whereas the French prefer top-loaders. Consumers in Spain eat far more poultry products than Germans do.[23] Such differences may exist even within the same country, depending on the geographic region. Thus international marketing intelligence efforts are likely to remain very important in determining European consumers' needs and developing marketing mixes that satisfy those needs.

■ *Pacific Rim Nations*

Companies of the Pacific Rim nations—Japan, China, South Korea, Taiwan, Singapore, Hong Kong, the Philippines, Malaysia, Indonesia, Australia, and Indochina—have become increasingly competitive and sophisticated in global business in the last three decades. The Japanese in particular have made tremendous inroads on world consumer markets for automobiles, motorcycles, watches, cameras, and audio and video equipment. Products from Sony, Sanyo, Toyota, Mitsubishi, Canon, Suzuki, and Toshiba are sold all over the world and have set standards of quality by which other products are often judged.

Despite the high volume of trade between the United States and Japan, the two economies are less integrated than the U.S. economy is with Canada's and Western Europe's. To keep economic expansion on track and to maintain job growth, the United States needs to increase exports to Japan.[24] Economists estimate that if Japan imported goods at the same rate as other major nations, the United States would sell $50 billion more annually to Japan.[25] Few U.S. firms have large investments in Japan, and Japanese investment in the U.S. is concentrated in the auto and technology industries. The United States and Japan continually struggle with cultural and political differences and are, in general, at odds over how to do business with each other.[26]

One Japanese market that is opening for U.S. is personal computers. Although the personal computer market in Japan has traditionally been dominated by Japanese companies, PC purchases there have doubled in recent years, and America's Intel makes the chips that run most of the machines Japan now buys.[27] Compaq, Apple, IBM, and other U.S. PC marketers have gained 30 percent of Japan's $9 billion PC market, partly by pricing their products 20 to 30 percent below those of rival Japanese companies. These PC purchases, along with Japan's importation of Japanese autos from U.S. transplant facilities, and an increase in U.S. retailers such as the Gap opening stores in Japan, have helped

GLOBAL PERSPECTIVE

Marketing to Japan

U.S. marketers have long considered Japan a tough market to crack because of formidable trade barriers. While many U.S. firms complain about these barriers, astute marketers see great opportunity in Japan. Companies that focus on satisfying customers' needs are not only getting into Japan, they are succeeding there.

High-tech products are at the forefront of the crusade into Japanese markets. Motorola, for example, commands nearly a quarter of the Japanese market for mobile phones. AT&T has also found success with its model-3600 parallel computers and computer chips that process voice signals and record messages for cordless phones. Japanese sales of Apple personal computers are growing at 30 percent a year, and Apple now holds more than 20 percent of the Japanese market, more than double its share at home.

U.S. sales to Japan are being fueled in part by the rising yen. This trend has reduced the price of imported goods for Japanese customers, while at the same time making Japan's exports more expensive and thus harder to sell. Moreover, Japanese consumers are becoming increasingly fond of American goods, especially clothes, outdoor equipment, collectibles, and CDs. Mail-order merchandise from the United States is often cheaper than comparable Japanese products because of Japan's complex retail distribution system. Japanese customers also get a personal exemption on import tariffs of mail-order goods up to 10,000 yen (about $115).

These factors are helping U.S. catalog retailers such as Patagonia, REI, Eddie Bauer, and California Gold rack up record sales in Japan. Catalog firms are setting up toll-free 24-hour international phone and fax lines, providing fast delivery, and even employing Japanese-speaking telephone operators in the states. L.L. Bean has set up local retail stores in Japan as well as a service center to handle orders, returns, and complaints. It also supplies Japanese-language inserts in its catalogs with information on sizing, tariffs, and ordering. Land's End and Franklin Mint offer full Japanese-language catalogs. Sports Endeavors, a North Carolina sports catalog firm, offers express shipping to get orders to customers within 72 hours, well ahead of the plodding two weeks Japanese firms take.

Sources: Larry Holyoke, with Douglas Harbrecht, "Can AT&T Get Through to Japan?" *Business Week,* May 15, 1995, pp. 112–114; Robert Neff, with Brian Bremner and Edith Updike, "The Japanese Have a New Thirst for Imports," *Business Week,* June 5, 1995, pp. 52, 54; and Edith Hill Updike, with Mary Kuntz, "Japan Is Dialing 1 800 Buyamerica," *Business Week,* June 12, 1995, pp. 61, 64.

reduce the United States' trade deficit with Japan in 1995.[28] Global Perspective describes other firms' efforts to market to Japan.

South Korea has also become remarkably successful in world markets with familiar brand names like Samsung, Daewoo, and Hyundai. But even before those companies became household names, their products prospered under U.S. company labels such as GE, GTE, RCA, and J.C. Penney. Korean companies are now capturing market share away from Japanese companies in the world markets for videocassette recorders, color televisions, and computers, despite the fact that the Korean market for these products is limited. With Europe and Japan blocking entry to some of their markets, Korean firms have decided to go head-to-head with Japanese and domestic firms for a piece of the U.S. market.

The People's Republic of China, a country of 1.2 billion people, has been inching toward economic reform. Per capita annual income is less than $500, but a middle class is slowly developing. The potential of China's consumer market is so vast that it is almost impossible to measure, but there are also many risks associated with doing business in China. Political and economic instability, especially inflation, combined with corruption and erratic policy shifts, undercut businesses that desire to stake a claim in what could become the world's largest market.[29] Moreover, piracy is a major issue and protecting a brand name in China is difficult. Because China denies access to most of its markets, the country is flooded with counterfeit videos, movies, compact disks, and computer software. This piracy costs U.S. companies more than $1 billion a year.[30]

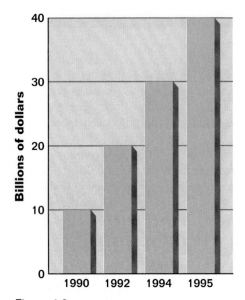

Figure 4.6
China's Increasing Trade Surplus
with the United States

China's trade surplus with the United States reached an estimated $40 billion in 1995. If current trends continue, as illustrated in Figure 4.6, China will surpass Japan's $66 billion U.S. trade surplus before the year 2000.[31] Nike and Adidas shoes have shifted most of their production to China, and more recently, China has become a major producer of compact disc players, cellular phones, portable stereos, and personal computers. It is apparent that the Chinese intend to use American and European investments to accelerate export industries for automobiles, automobile parts, semiconductors, and telecommunications products. Both Ford and General Motors are competing to produce automobiles, vans, and trucks in China for export to other countries.[32]

Less visible Pacific Rim regions, such as Singapore, Taiwan, and Hong Kong, have become major manufacturing and financial centers. Singapore boasts huge world markets for rubber goods and pharmaceuticals. Hong Kong, however, faces an uncertain future after it reverts from British to Chinese control in 1997. Taiwan may have the most promising future of all the Pacific Rim nations. Its strong local economy and low import barriers are drawing increasing imports. Some analysts believe that it may replace Hong Kong as a regional financial power center when Great Britain relinquishes Hong Kong. Firms from Thailand and Malaysia are also blossoming, carving out niches in the world markets for a variety of products, from toys to automobile parts.[33] And, in 1994, the nineteen-year U.S. trade embargo against Vietnam was lifted, opening one of Asia's fastest growing markets to U.S. businesses.

■ *Changing Relations with Eastern Europe and the Former Soviet Union*

The countries of the former Soviet Union and other Eastern European nations are experiencing great political and economic change. Widespread measures instituted to improve the region's economic environment are aimed primarily at making the new nations more responsive to the market forces of supply and demand. Other reforms include replacing the system of state-owned enterprises and farms with independent businesses leased or owned by workers, shareholders, cooperatives, and joint ventures; overhauling the system of centrally determined prices; and allowing free market prices for many products.

While it is hoped that these measures will prove beneficial in the long run, the short-term results have been serious economic distress, including severe food shortages and unemployment. For example, when Russia cut state assistance to aging, uncompetitive factories, many failed. Subsequent unemployment has adversely affected Russia's living standards. In the absence of a stable government and coherent economic strategy, Russia's GDP shrank in the early 1990s. With Russia facing an annual inflation rate that reached as high as 900 percent, many Russians have become ambivalent about reform.[34]

The changing economic conditions in Eastern Europe and the former Soviet Union are creating many marketing opportunities in these countries for American, Western European, and Asian firms. Procter & Gamble, Monsanto, Combustion Engineering, McDonald's, and Pizza Hut are just some of the U.S. companies marketing products in Russia, either through joint ventures with Russian firms or through direct ownership. However, because of the swift and uncontrolled nature of the changes taking place in the former communist bloc, firms considering marketing their products in these countries must carefully monitor events and be aware of the political and economic risks.

■ *General Agreement on Tariffs and Trade (GATT)*

General Agreement on Tariffs and Trade (GATT) International marketing negotiations to reduce worldwide tariffs and increase trade

The **General Agreement on Tariffs and Trade (GATT),** like NAFTA and the European Union, is based on negotiations between member countries to reduce worldwide tariffs and increase international trade. Originally signed by 23 nations in 1947, GATT provides a forum for tariff negotiations and a place where international trade problems can be discussed and resolved. GATT negotiations currently involve some 124 nations and have had far-reaching ramifications for the international marketing strategies of U.S. firms.

GATT sponsors rounds of negotiations aimed at reducing trade restrictions. Seven rounds of GATT negotiations have reduced the average worldwide tariffs on manufactured goods from 45 percent to 5 percent, and negotiators have been able to eliminate or ease nontariff trade restrictions such as import quotas, red tape in customs procedures, and "buy national" agreements.

Dumping Selling products at unfairly low prices

The most recent round, the Uruguay Round (1988–1994), further reduced trade barriers for most products and provided new rules to prevent **dumping,** the selling of products at unfairly low prices. In the United States marketers of large equipment, toys, paper, scientific instruments, aluminum, furniture, steel, liquor, and medical equipment, and apparel retailers will benefit from these tariff reductions. Japan, however, may experience an adverse effect, at least in the short run, because the elimination of some barriers to imports that have long protected such Japanese industries as steel, agricultural, processed food, and dairy products will open these markets to outside competition. Some U.S. industries are also dissatisfied with the Uruguay Round because they face continued barriers. The motion picture industry, for example, had hoped to gain greater access to European markets, and pharmaceutical companies are concerned about the additional ten years during which developing countries can pirate drugs without penalty. Moreover, GATT will initially cost revenue to participating countries from the loss of tariffs. Economists estimate that $12–13 billion will be lost over the next five years, but as exports grow under an expanded GATT, higher corporate profits will eventually cause tax revenues to rise.[35]

Each of the previous GATT rounds has reduced trade barriers and has introduced a period of strong economic growth. By the year 2002, falling trade barriers are expected to add $250 billion to the value of goods and services worldwide, which translates into an 8 percent boost in the global domestic product.[36] It is hoped that by reducing trade barriers, nations will develop closer relationships, and as this happens, global markets should become not only more profitable but also more efficient.

Developing Organizational Structures for International Marketing

*T*he level of commitment to international marketing is a major variable in deciding what kind of involvement is appropriate. A firm's options range from occasional exporting to expanding overall operations (production and marketing) into other countries. In this section we examine exporting, licensing, joint ventures, trading companies, direct ownership, and other approaches to international involvement.

■ Exporting

Exporting is the lowest level of commitment to international marketing and the most flexible approach. A firm may find an exporting intermediary to take over most marketing functions associated with selling to other countries. This approach entails minimum effort and cost. Modifications in packaging, labeling, style, or color may be the major expenses in adapting a product. However, there is limited risk in using export agents and merchants because no direct investment in the foreign country is required.

Export agents bring together buyers and sellers from different countries; they collect a commission for arranging sales. Export houses and export merchants purchase products from different companies and then sell them to foreign countries. They are specialists at understanding foreign customers' needs.

Foreign buyers from companies and governments provide a direct method of exporting and eliminate the need for an intermediary. They encourage international exchange by contacting domestic firms about their needs and the opportunities available in exporting. A study of minority firms' participation in international marketing indicated that only

10 percent reported previous exporting experience, but 70 percent expressed an interest in exporting. These firms identify limited experience and lack of knowledge as the major barriers to getting involved in exporting.[37] Domestic firms that want to export with a minimum of effort and investment should seek out foreign importers and buyers.

■ *Trading Companies*

Trading company A company that links buyers and sellers in different countries

Marketers sometimes employ a **trading company,** which links buyers and sellers in different countries but is not involved in manufacturing or owning assets related to manufacturing. Trading companies buy goods in one country at the lowest price consistent with quality and sell them to buyers in another country. An important function of trading companies is taking title to products and performing all the activities necessary to move the products from the domestic country to a foreign country. For example, large grain-trading companies operating out of home offices in both the United States and overseas control a major portion of the world's trade in basic food commodities. These trading companies sell agricultural commodities that are homogeneous and can be stored and moved rapidly in response to market conditions.

Trading companies reduce risk for firms interested in getting involved in international marketing. A trading company will assist producers with information about products that meet quality and price expectations in domestic or international markets. Additional services a trading company may provide include consulting, marketing research, advertising, insurance, product research and design, legal assistance, warehousing, and foreign exchange.

In 1982, the Export Trading Company Act was passed to facilitate the efficient operation of trading companies in the United States. Besides allowing banks to invest in trading companies, the act created a new certification procedure that enables companies to apply for limited protection from antitrust laws when conducting export operations. The program has been less successful than the government had hoped. The best-known U.S. trading company is Sears World Trade, which specializes in consumer goods, light industrial items, and processed foods. A trading company acts like a wholesaler, taking on much of the responsibility of finding markets while facilitating all marketing aspects of a transaction.

■ *Licensing*

Licensing An alternative to direct investment requiring a licensee to pay commissions or royalties on sales or supplies used in manufacturing

When potential markets are found across national boundaries—and when production, technical assistance, or marketing know-how is required—**licensing** is an alternative to direct investment. The licensee (the owner of the foreign operation) pays commissions or royalties on sales or supplies used in manufacturing. An initial down payment or fee may be charged when the licensing agreement is signed. Exchanges of management techniques or technical assistance are primary reasons for licensing agreements. Yoplait yogurt is a French yogurt that is licensed for production in the United States; the Yoplait brand tries to maintain a French image.

Licensing is an attractive alternative to direct investment when the political stability of a foreign country is in doubt or when resources are unavailable for direct investment. Licensing is especially advantageous for small manufacturers wanting to launch a well-known brand internationally. For example, all Spalding sporting products are licensed worldwide; the Questor Corporation owns the Spalding name but produces not a single golf club or tennis ball itself. Lowenbrau has used licensing agreements, including one with Miller in the United States, to increase sales worldwide without committing capital to building breweries.

■ *Joint Ventures*

Joint venture Partnership between a domestic firm and a foreign firm

In international marketing, a **joint venture** is a partnership between a domestic firm and a foreign firm or government. Joint ventures are especially popular in industries that call for large investments, such as natural resources extraction or automobile manufacturing. Control of the joint venture can be split equally, or one party may control decision making. Joint ventures are often a political necessity because of nationalism and governmental restrictions on foreign ownership. They also provide legitimacy in the eyes of the host country's citizens. Local partners have firsthand knowledge of the economic and sociopolitical environment, access to distribution networks, or privileged access to local resources (raw material, labor management, contacts, and so on). Moreover, entrepreneurs in many less-developed countries actively seek associations with a foreign partner as a ready means of implementing their own corporate strategy.[38]

Joint ventures are assuming greater global importance because of cost advantages and the number of inexperienced firms entering foreign markets. They may be the result of a tradeoff between a firm's desire for completely unambiguous control of an enterprise and its quest for additional resources. They may occur when internal development or acquisition is not feasible or is unavailable or when the risks and constraints leave no other alternative. As project sizes increase in the face of global competition and firms attempt to spread the huge costs of technological innovation, there is a stronger impetus to form joint ventures.[39]

Strategic alliances
Partnerships formed to create competitive advantage on a worldwide basis

Increasingly, once a joint venture succeeds, nationalism spurs a trend toward expropriating or purchasing foreign shares of the enterprise. On the other hand, a joint venture may be the only available means for entering a foreign market. For example, American construction firms bidding for business in Saudi Arabia have found that joint ventures with Arab construction companies gain local support among the handful of people who make the contracting decisions.

Strategic alliances, the newest form of international business structure, are partnerships formed to create competitive advantage on a worldwide basis. They are very similar to joint ventures. The number of strategic alliances is growing at an estimated rate of about 20 percent per year.[40] In fact, in some industries, such as automobiles and computers, strategic alliances are becoming the predominant means of competing. International competition is so fierce and the costs of competing on a global basis so high that few firms have the individual resources to do it alone. Thus individual firms that lack all the internal resources essential for international success may seek to collaborate with other companies.[41] In Figure 4.7, Delta announces its strategic alliance with Virgin Atlantic to provide its domestic customers service to London. Through its Worldwide Partners program, Delta has formed many strategic alliances, allowing it to provide more nonstops to more European cities than any other domestic airline.

The partners forming international strategic alliances often retain their distinct identities, and each brings a distinctive competence to the union. However, the firms share common long-term goals. As might be imagined, this "marriage" of two firms from different cultures is not without problems. Interestingly, research has shown that the firm experiencing the highest levels of conflict and lowest levels of satisfaction is often the company from the host country.[42] What distinguishes international strategic alliances from other business structures is that member firms in the alliance may have been traditional rivals competing for market share in the same product class.[43] An example of such an alliance is the New United Motor Manufacturing, Inc. (NUMMI), formed by Toyota and General Motors to make Chevrolet Novas and Toyota Tercels. This alliance united the quality engineering of Japanese cars with the marketing expertise and market access of General Motors.

Figure 4.7
A Strategic Alliance
Delta announces its partnership with Virgin Atlantic to provide its U.S. customers service to London.

■ *Direct Ownership*

Direct ownership A situation in which a company owns subsidiaries or other facilities overseas

Once a company makes a long-term commitment to marketing in a foreign nation that has a promising political and economic environment, **direct ownership** of a foreign subsidiary or division is a possibility. For example, FedEx has made a strong commitment to the global marketplace through direct investment overseas (see Figure 4.8). Most discussions of foreign investment concern only manufacturing equipment or personnel because the expenses of developing a separate foreign distribution system can be tremendous. The opening of retail stores in Europe, Canada, or Mexico can require a staggering financial investment in facilities, research, and management.

Multinational enterprise A company with operations or subsidiaries in many countries

The term **multinational enterprise** refers to firms that have operations or subsidiaries located in many countries. Often the parent company is based in one country and carries on production, management, and marketing activities in other countries. The firm's subsidiaries may be quite autonomous to be able to respond to the needs of individual international markets. Firms such as General Motors, Citicorp, ITT, and Ford are multinational companies with worldwide operations.

A wholly owned foreign subsidiary may be allowed to operate independently of the parent company so that its management can have more freedom to adjust to the local environment. Cooperative arrangements are developed to assist in marketing efforts, production, and management. A wholly owned foreign subsidiary may export products to the home country. Some American automobile manufacturers, for example, import cars built by their foreign subsidiaries. A foreign subsidiary offers important tax, tariff, and other operating advantages. One of the greatest advantages is the cross-cultural approach. A subsidiary usually operates under foreign management, so that it can develop a local identity. The greatest danger in such an arrangement comes from political uncertainty: a firm may lose its foreign investment.

Figure 4.8
Direct Ownership
FedEx operates a worldwide delivery service through direct ownership and global service participants.

SUMMARY

Marketing activities performed across national boundaries are usually significantly different from domestic marketing activities. International marketers must have a profound awareness of the foreign environment. The marketing strategy ordinarily is adjusted to meet the needs and desires of foreign markets.

The level of involvement in international marketing can range from casual exporting to globalization of markets. Although most firms adjust their marketing mixes for differences in target markets, some firms standardize their marketing efforts worldwide. Traditional full-scale international marketing involvement is based on products customized according to cultural, regional, and national differences. Globalization, however, involves developing marketing strategies as if the entire world (or regions of it) were a single entity; a globalized firm markets standardized products in the same way everywhere.

A detailed analysis of the environment is essential before a company enters a foreign market. Environmental aspects of special importance include cultural, social, economic, political, legal, and technological forces. Cultural aspects of the environment that are most important to international marketers include customs, concepts, values, attitudes, morals, and knowledge. Marketing activities are primarily social in purpose; therefore they are influenced by the institutions of family, religion, education, health, and recreation. The most prominent economic forces that affect international marketing are those that can be measured by income and resources. Credit, buying power, and income distribution are aggregate measures of market potential. Political and legal forces include the political system, national laws, regulatory bodies, special interest groups, and courts. Foreign policies of all nations that are involved in trade determine how marketing can be conducted. The level of technology helps define economic development within a nation and indicates the existence of methods to facilitate marketing.

Although the world is beginning to be viewed as one huge marketplace, various regional trade alliances and specific markets create both difficulties and opportunities for companies engaging in international marketing. These alliances and markets include the North American Free Trade Agreement (NAFTA) between the United States, Canada, and Mexico; the European Union; the Pacific Rim nations; changing conditions in Eastern Europe and the former Soviet Republics; and the General Agreement on Tariffs and Trade (GATT).

There are several ways of getting involved in international marketing. Exporting is the easiest and most flexible method. Trading companies are experts at buying products in the domestic market and selling to foreign markets, thereby assuming most of the risk in international involvement. Licensing is an alternative to direct investment; it may be necessitated by political and economic conditions. Joint ventures and strategic alliances are often appropriate when outside resources are needed, when governmental restrictions hinder foreign ownership, or when changes in global markets encourage competitive consolidation. Direct ownership of foreign divisions or subsidiaries is the strongest commitment to international marketing and involves the greatest risk. When a company has operations or subsidiaries located in many countries, it is termed a multinational enterprise.

IMPORTANT TERMS

International marketing	NAFTA	Trading company	Strategic alliances
Globalization	GATT	Licensing	Direct ownership
Gross domestic product (GDP)	Dumping	Joint venture	Multinational enterprise

DISCUSSION AND REVIEW QUESTIONS

1. How does international marketing differ from domestic marketing?
2. What factors must marketers consider as they decide whether to become involved in international marketing?
3. Why are the largest industrial corporations in the United States so committed to international marketing?
4. Why was so much of this chapter devoted to an analysis of the international marketing environment?
5. A manufacturer recently exported peanut butter with a green label to a nation in the Far East. The product failed because it was associated with jungle sickness. How could this mistake have been avoided?
6. How do religious systems influence marketing activities in foreign countries?
7. If you were asked to provide a small tip (or bribe) to have a document approved in a foreign nation where this practice was customary, what would you do?
8. In marketing dog food to Latin America, what aspects of the marketing mix would a U.S. firm need to alter?
9. What should marketers consider as they decide whether to license or to enter into a joint venture in a foreign nation?
10. Discuss the impact of strategic alliances on marketing strategies.

96

APPLICATION QUESTIONS

1. Procter & Gamble has made a substantial commitment to foreign markets and especially to Latin America. Its actions may be described as a "globalization of marketing." Describe how a firm such as a shoe manufacturer would go from domestic marketing, to limited exporting, to international marketing, and finally to a globalization of marketing. Give examples of some of the activities that might be involved in this process.

2. Understanding the complexities of the marketing environment is necessary if a marketer is to successfully implement marketing strategies in the international marketplace. Which environmental forces (cultural/social, economic, political/legal, and technological) might a marketer need to consider when marketing the following products in the international marketplace and why?

   a. Barbie doll
   b. beer
   c. financial services
   d. television sets

3. Many firms, like Procter & Gamble, FedEx, and Occidental Petroleum, wish to do business in Eastern Europe and the countries formerly part of the Soviet Union. What events could occur which would make marketing in these countries more difficult? easier?

4. Various organizational approaches to international marketing are discussed in the chapter. Which would be the best arrangements for international marketing of the following products and why?

   a. construction equipment manufacturing
   b. cosmetics
   c. automobiles

Case 4.1 20 Years of Innovation: There Is No Finish Line for Nike

Named for the Greek goddess of victory invoked by the legendary runner from Marathon, Nike has an atmosphere of electricity that has been embedded in its corporate culture by Chairman and CEO Phil Knight. Along with Bill Bowerman, Knight's track coach at the University of Oregon, Knight founded Nike in 1968, driven by a desire to help athletes perform at their highest potential. Knight's passion and drive for excellence has been passed on to Nike's employees; the company dominates the global athletic footwear market with a 30 percent share.

The winning climate at Nike is exemplified by the athletes it sponsors, such as John McEnroe and Michael Jordan. Employees are encouraged to compete, but in a way that promotes the spirit of corporate family. As one employee says, "It's an atmosphere that allows you to dream, and come up with some good ideas and possibly some bad ideas; no idea is a stupid idea here at Nike." Employees whose product ideas are accepted have the opportunity to become a project manager for their brainchild. Development staff, designers, and marketers work closely as a team to form the nucleus of smaller business units. This culture has provided Nike with many product market leaders like the basketball shoe "Air Jordan," named after the basketball star, and the "Cross Trainer."

Nike faces tremendous challenges in its global marketing efforts, particularly in China, where it began selling shoes and clothing in 1984. Although China's more than 1.2 billion consumers represent a promising market, U.S. marketers must brave a poor transportation infrastructure, burglars, pirates, and a casual—if not contemptuous—attitude toward contracts by both the government and business partners. Other problems include uncooperative customs agents and trade officials who, for example, forced one company to revise an advertising campaign because the map of China on its posters did not include Hong Kong and Taiwan. Such problems make China an unpredictable and often humbling place for a company that pioneers a new product. After assessing the market, Nike concluded that only 15 percent of the consumers could afford Nike footwear. These people live mainly in cities and could be reached through advertising, especially sponsorship of athletic teams.

The Chinese sportswear market is fragmented with no dominant sales leader. Today, Chinese companies and joint ventures sell products at significantly lower prices than Nike. Western athletic shoes such as Nike and Reebok may sell for as much as 1,000 yuan (about $120) a pair, whereas names like Torch, a Chinese company marketing Shanghai-made trainers, cost from 120 to 200 yuan a pair. One of the most popular brands is Geant, a mid-price shoe produced by a Chinese–Hong Kong joint venture.

China's hottest American import is professional basketball, and the Chicago Bulls are current favorites. Jackets with the Bulls logo have become fashionable, and counterfeiters are churning out imitations. Sporting goods stores display posters of NBA stars like

Shaquille O'Neal and Michael Jordan rather than China's few basketball stars. The sudden popularity of basketball in China has been a boon to Nike, which manufactures tens of millions of shoes in China for world export. In fact, China accounts for about 30 percent of all Nike manufacturing worldwide—1 million pairs of athletic shoes a month at its Fujian province factories alone.

The competition between Nike and Reebok to attract China's sports fans and running shoe buyers is escalating. Nike is providing running shoes for 1996 Chinese Olympic athletes. However, it lost its sponsorship agreement with the Chinese track and field team to a rival after a major marketing push gained Reebok the right to be the exclusive supplier of shoes and clothing to the 600 track and field athletes, coaches, and officials. Nike still sponsors China's national basketball and tennis teams and various professional and semi-professional soccer teams.

Both Nike and Reebok believe that China's vast 1.2 billion person shoe market is worth a considerable investment. A pair of running shoes for many Chinese can currently cost several months' salaries, but as the economy improves, more people will be able to afford the product, and will be buying. Given Nike's manufacturing presence, international celebrity connections, and aggressive athletic sponsorships, the company is well positioned to be the premier global marketer of athletic shoes.[44]

Questions for Discussion

1. Why are athletic shoes ideal for global marketing?
2. What advantages does Nike have in its competition with Reebok to obtain leadership in the Chinese athletic shoe market?
3. What risks does Nike face in investing its resources in manufacturing and marketing athletic shoes in China?

Case 4.2   KLM Flies High with Global Alliances

Koninklijke Luchtvaart Maatschappij (KLM Royal Dutch Airlines), the world's oldest international airline, serves 150 cities on six continents, with 1994 revenues of $4.6 billion. It is number one in offering service between the Netherlands and the United States. The Dutch government owns 38.2 percent of the Amsterdam-based airline but stays out of management decisions.

KLM was founded in 1919 in The Hague by flight lieutenant Albert Plesman. The title of Koninklijke, or "royal," was bestowed on the fledgling firm by Queen Wilhelmina. With regal blessing and Plesman at the helm, KLM quickly established service between Amsterdam and London (1920), then Copenhagen (1920), Brussels (1922), Paris (1923), Zurich (1928), Rome (1931), Prague (1935), Vienna (1936), and Oslo (1939). In 1927, it inaugurated the longest air route in the world—8,700 miles—from Amsterdam to Indonesia. However, Hitler's occupation of Holland during World War II terminated KLM's European operations in 1940, and Plesman himself was imprisoned by the Germans from 1940 to 1942. Service resumed quickly after the war, and by the mid-1950s, KLM had expanded to Africa and North and South America. KLM was also one of the first European airlines to offer service to Taiwan, starting in 1983.

Because air traffic into Amsterdam is relatively light compared to other world capitals, KLM has been forced to think globally and to diversify creatively. Today, it has interests in businesses such as computer

reservation systems, helicopter ferrying, regional airlines, forwarding, and trucking. In 1954, the company formed a separate subsidiary for aerial photography and surveying, KLM Aerocarto. KLM Helicopters was established in 1965 to serve offshore drilling platforms in the North Sea. KLM Dutch Airlines (later renamed NLM CityHopper) was launched in 1966 to provide commuter services within the Netherlands. KLM's aggressive cargo-carrying strategy has made it the fifth-largest cargo carrier in the world, even against stiff competition from UPS and FedEx. In fact, 16 percent of KLM revenues derive from carrying mail and cargo.

To become more competitive and gain more passengers in key markets, KLM started looking for partners in the late 1980s. For example, it bought 10 percent of Covia Partnership, which owns and operates United Airlines' Apollo computer reservation system, in 1988. KLM also owns a majority stake in Transavia, a Dutch charter airline, and equity interests in Air Littoral, a French regional airline, and ALM Antillean Airlines. Deregulation of the European airline industry further spurred airline industry efforts to develop strategic alliances—partnerships formed to create competitive advantage on a global scale. KLM has established alliances with several firms, including Singapore Airlines and Japan Airlines, and has interests in several U.K., Dutch, and Caribbean airlines.

KLM's most significant strategic alliance to date, and the one most closely watched by the airline industry, is its partnership with U.S.-based Northwest

Airlines, in which it holds a 25 percent equity stake. The alliance allows the two carriers to share some operations and pool resources. They can set prices together and conduct joint marketing campaigns. For example, in the spring of 1994, they started a common business class, with identical seats, food, and service on international flights. They also have plans to introduce a common international economy class with video screens on the back of every seat to give passengers a choice of movies and games. The partners may eventually adopt a single name. They are able to do all this partly because they won exemption from U.S. antitrust laws and partly because a Dutch–American "open skies" treaty permits airlines of both countries to fly unrestricted into each other's markets.

The KLM–Northwest alliance has not been trouble-free. KLM, hurt by Northwest's huge losses in 1992, had to write off its initial investment of $400 million in Northwest (Northwest has since returned to profitability). In the fall of 1995, KLM filed a lawsuit against Northwest over the terms of their partnership. KLM wanted to prevent Northwest from curtailing its previously agreed-upon voting rights and to fight a "poison pill" takeover defense. Moreover, the two firms have vastly different cultures. Northwest, for example, hands out rock-and-roll CDs to business-class passengers, whereas KLM offers tiny china houses filled with Dutch gin. A KLM executive accustomed to formal Dutch cabin attendants labels Northwest's too "enthusiastic" for European tastes. KLM's chairman, Pieter Bouw, hopes to train crews together to meld a happy medium.

He also hopes to standardize more elements of the services offered by the two airlines.

Bickering aside, the alliance has helped both firms prosper. For example, trade barriers prevented Northwest from flying into Rome, but KLM, with its European Union advantages, serves Rome on Northwest's behalf, much to the dismay of Italy's government. KLM, in turn, has gained greater access via Northwest to the North American market. Northwest has a strong presence in North Asia, while KLM has a solid system in Southeast Asia; both hope to build sales on the other's foundation. KLM's well-established flights to the Middle East, Africa, and Southeast Asia are helping Northwest sell more tickets to faraway destinations. Capitalizing on each other's strengths has helped KLM and Northwest together become the world's third-largest carrier in revenues, after American and United. Grouses an executive of American Airlines, "They're taking revenues from us." As such, the strategic alliance between KLM and Northwest stands as a successful model that other airlines would like to emulate in the highly competitive global airline industry.[45]

Questions for Discussion

1. How is KLM using strategic alliances to expand internationally?
2. What environmental forces have affected KLM's ability to expand and its partnership with Northwest?
3. What strategy does KLM seem to be using in world markets?

Kentucky Fried Chicken Expands Globally

During the 1960s and 1970s, Kentucky Fried Chicken Corporation (KFC) pursued an aggressive strategy of restaurant expansion, quickly establishing itself as one of the largest fast-food chains in the United States. KFC was also one of the first U.S. fast-food chains to expand overseas. By 1990, restaurants located outside the United States were generating over 50 percent of KFC's total profits. By 1995, KFC was operating in 68 foreign countries and was one of the three largest fast-food chains operating outside the United States.

Japan, Australia, and the United Kingdom accounted for the greatest share of KFC's international expansion during the 1970s and 1980s. During the 1990s, other markets became attractive. China, with a population of over 1 billion, as well as Europe and Latin America, offered expansion opportunities. By 1996, KFC had established 158 company-owned restaurants and franchises in Mexico. In addition to Mexico, KFC was operating 220 restaurants in the Caribbean, and Central and South America.

Company History

Fast-food franchising was still in its infancy in 1954 when Harland Sanders began his cross-country travels to market "Colonel Sanders' Recipe Kentucky Fried Chicken." By 1963, the number of KFC franchises numbered over 300. Tiring of running the daily operations of his business, Colonel Sanders sold his company in 1964 at the age of 74 to two Louisville businessmen—Jack Massey and John Young Brown, Jr.—for $2 million. Brown, who later became governor of Kentucky, was named president, and Massey was named chairman; "the Colonel" stayed on in a public relations capacity.

In 1966, Massey and Brown took KFC public, and the company was listed on the New York Stock Exchange. During the late 1960s, Massey and Brown turned their attention to international markets and signed a joint venture with Mitsuoishi Shoji Kaisha Ltd. in Japan. Subsidiaries were also established in Great Britain, Hong Kong, South Africa, Australia, New Zealand, and Mexico. In the late 1970s, Brown's desire to seek a political career led him to seek a buyer for KFC. Soon after, KFC merged with Heublein, Inc., a producer of alcoholic beverages with little restaurant experience. Conflicts quickly arose between Heublein management and Colonel Sanders, who was concerned about quality control issues and restaurant cleanliness. In 1977, Heublein sent in a new management team to redirect KFC's strategy. New unit construction was discontinued until existing restaurants could be upgraded and operating problems eliminated. The overhaul emphasized cleanliness, service, profitability, and product consistency. By 1982, KFC was once again aggressively building new restaurant units.

In October 1986, Kentucky Fried Chicken was sold to PepsiCo. First incorporated in Delaware in 1919, Pepsi-Cola Co. acquired Frito-Lay in 1965, creating one of the largest consumer companies in the United States. PepsiCo first entered the restaurant business in 1977 when it acquired Pizza Hut's 3,200 units. In 1978, Taco Bell was added. Marketing fast food complemented PepsiCo's consumer product orientation and followed much the same pattern as marketing soft drinks and snack foods. Pepsi soft drinks and fast-food products could be marketed together in the same restaurants and through coordinated national advertising, providing higher returns for each advertising dollar.

The Kentucky Fried Chicken acquisition gave PepsiCo the leading market share in three of the four largest and fastest-growing segments in the U.S. quick-service industry. By the end of 1995, Pizza Hut held a 28 percent share of the $18.5 billion U.S. pizza segment, Taco Bell held 75 percent of the $5.7 billion Mexican food segment, and KFC held 49 percent of the $7.7 billion U.S. chicken fast-food segment.

The Fast-Food Industry

Six major business segments make up the fast-food market of the food service industry. Sandwich chains comprise the largest segment. Many have recently expanded menu offerings to include fried chicken (Hardee's and McDonald's), fried clams and shrimp (Burger King), and chicken teriyaki (Jack in the Box). In an effort to broaden its customer base, McDonald's has installed 400 restaurants in Wal-Mart stores across the country. Co-branding is also a potential source of expansion for many food chains. PepsiCo plans to add Taco Bell signs and menus to approximately 800 existing KFC restaurants over the next few years, increasing Taco Bell's 4,500 unit system by almost 18 percent.

The second largest fast-food segment is pizza, long dominated by Pizza Hut, whose sales were $5.4 billion in 1995. Little Caesar's and Domino's are the other primary players in this market. The success of home delivery has driven competitors to look for new methods of increasing their customer base by, for example, diversifying into nonpizza items, nontraditional units (airport kiosks and university campus stores), and special promotions.

The highest growth segment is the chicken segment, where sales were expected to increase by 14.3 percent in 1995. KFC continues to dominate here, with sales in 1995 of $3.7 billion. KFC's closest competitors are

Boston Market and Popeye's Famous Fried Chicken. Despite KFC's long supremacy in the chicken segment, it has lost market share over the last two years to new restaurant chains that emphasize roasted chicken over traditional fried chicken. In order to expand distribution to new customers, many chains have begun to offer home delivery and home-replacement take-out meals (KFC's $14.99 megameal, for example).

Intense marketing by the leading chain will no doubt continue to stimulate demand for fast food. However, a number of demographic and societal changes are likely to affect the future demand for fast food in different directions. On the one hand, demand should be stimulated by the rise in number of dual-income families and by increased disposable income given the increase in single-person households (approximately 25 percent of U.S. households). Americans are expected to spend 55 percent of their food dollars at restaurants, up from 34 percent in 1970. On the other hand, the proliferation of microwaves into approximately 70 percent of all U.S. homes has resulted in a shift in the types of products sold for home preparation and consumption. In addition, the aging American population may increase the frequency with which people patronize more upscale restaurants.

Although the number of fast-food outlets is near saturation in the United States, fast-food chains are relatively scarce internationally. The United States represents the largest consumer market in the world, accounting for over one-fifth of the world's gross domestic product. Many other cultures have strong culinary traditions that have not been easy to penetrate. KFC previously failed in the German market because Germans were not accustomed to take-out food or to ordering food over a counter. KFC has been more successful in the Asian markets, where chicken is a staple dish. Aside from cultural factors, international business carries risks not present in the U.S. market. Long distances between headquarters and foreign franchises often make it difficult to control the quality of individual franchises. Long distances also cause transportation, servicing, and support problems.

Marketing Strategy

As KFC entered 1996, it grappled with a number of important issues. During the 1980s, consumers began to demand healthier foods, and KFC's limited menu consisting mainly of fried foods was a distinct liability. In order to soften its fried chicken chain image, the company changed its name and logo from Kentucky Fried Chicken to KFC in 1991. In addition, it responded to consumer demands for greater variety by introducing several new products. Consumers have also become more mobile, demanding fast food in a variety of nontraditional locations such as grocery stores, restaurants, airports, and outdoor events. This has

forced fast-food restaurant chains in general to investigate nontraditional distribution channels and restaurant designs. Additionally, families continue to seek greater value in the food they buy, further increasing the pressure on fast-food chains to reduce operating costs and prices.

Many of KFC's problems during the late 1980s surrounded its limited menu and its inability to bring new products to market quickly. The popularity of its Original Recipe fried chicken allowed KFC to expand through the 1980s without significant competition from other chicken competitors. As a result, new-product introductions were never an important part of KFC's overall strategy. However, the introduction of chicken sandwiches and fried chicken by hamburger chains has changed the make-up of KFC's competitors. Most important, McDonald's introduced its McChicken sandwich to the U.S. market in 1989, while KFC was still testing its version. By beating KFC to the counter, McDonald's was able to develop a strong consumer awareness for its sandwich. This setback significantly complicated KFC's task of developing consumer awareness for its chicken sandwich, which was introduced several months later.

The growing popularity of healthier foods and consumers' increasing demand for greater variety have led to a number of changes in KFC's menu offerings. In 1992, KFC introduced Oriental Wings, Popcorn Chicken, and Honey BBQ Chicken as alternatives to its Original Recipe fried chicken. It also introduced a dessert menu that included a variety of pies and cookies. In 1993, KFC rolled out its Rotisserie Chicken and began to promote its lunch and dinner buffet. The buffet, which includes thirty items, had been introduced into almost 1,600 KFC restaurants in twenty-seven states by the end of 1993.

One aggressive strategy employed by KFC was its "Neighborhood Program." By mid-1993, almost 500 company-owned restaurants in New York, Chicago, Philadelphia, Washington, D.C., St. Louis, Los Angeles, Houston, and Dallas had been outfitted with special menu offerings to appeal to the African-American community. Menus were beefed up with side dishes such as greens, macaroni and cheese, sweet-potato pie, and red beans and rice. In addition, restaurant employees have been outfitted with African-inspired uniforms. The introduction of the Neighborhood Program has increased sales by 5–30 percent in restaurants catering directly to the African-American community. KFC is currently testing Hispanic-oriented restaurants in the Miami area, which offer such side dishes as fried plantains, flan, and très leches.

As the growth in sales of traditional, freestanding fast-food restaurants has slowed during the last decade, consumers have demanded quick meals in more and more nontraditional locations. As a result, distribution has taken on increasing importance. KFC is relying on nontraditional units to spur much of its future growth. The chicken giant is currently testing such unusual distribution channels as mall stores, cafeteria snack shops, kiosks in airports, amusement parks, supermarkets, and office buildings; and mobile units that can be transported to outdoor concerts and fairs. Moreover, Taco Bell and KFC plan to add the Taco Bell menu to existing KFC restaurants in 1996 and 1997. This "dual branding" strategy would help PepsiCo improve economies of scale within its restaurant operations and enable KFC to strengthen its customer base by widening its menu offerings.

Although marketing and operating strategies can improve sales and profitability in existing outlets, an important part of success in the quick-service industry is investment growth. KFC is now the third-largest quick-service, and largest chicken, restaurant system in the world. In the future, KFC's international operations will be called on to provide an increasing percentage of KFC's overall sales and profit growth as the U.S. market continues to mature.

Mexico and Latin America

KFC was operating 205 company-owned restaurants and 173 franchises in Mexico, the Caribbean, and Latin America at the end of 1995. Through 1990, KFC has concentrated its company operations in Mexico and Puerto Rico, and its franchisee operations in the Caribbean and Central America. By 1994, KFC had altered its Latin American strategy to begin franchising in Mexico, expand its company-owned restaurants in the Caribbean, and reestablish a subsidiary in Venezuela.

Franchising, though popular in the United States, was virtually unknown in Mexico until 1990, when a new law governing franchising resulted in an explosion of fast-food restaurants, services, hotels, and retail outlets. Mexico is a potentially profitable location for U.S. direct investment and trade. With a population of over 91 million, Mexico is approximately one-third the size of the United States. Its geographical proximity makes transportation costs minimal, increasing the competitiveness of U.S. goods over those from Asia or Europe. The United States is Mexico's largest trading partner, accounting for over 65 percent of its imports. Mexico in turn, exports about 69 percent of its goods to the United States. Despite the importance of the U.S. market to Mexico, it still represents a small percentage of overall U.S. trade and investment, largely because of Mexico's history of restrictions on trade and foreign direct investment. In 1988, the government of Carlos Salenas embarked on an ambitious restructuring of the Mexican economy. Foreign firms are now allowed to buy up to 100 percent of the equity in many Mexican firms, tax rates were reduced, and restrictions on foreign investment were relaxed.

Prior to 1989, Mexico levied high tariffs on most imported goods, and many others were subjected to quotas, licensing requirements, and other nontariff trade barriers. The 1994 North American Free Trade Agreement (NAFTA) created a trading block with a larger population and gross domestic product than the European Union. Mexico should benefit from the lower cost of imported goods and increased employment from higher investment from Canada and the United States. Canada and the United States should benefit from lower labor and transportation costs related to investments in Mexico.

In 1994, Ernesto Zedillo was elected as Mexico's new president. Zedillo's objective was to maintain stability in prices, wages, and exchange rates. However, Salinas had achieved stability largely on the basis of price, wage, and foreign exchange controls. Giving the appearance of stability, an overvalued peso continued to encourage imports, which exacerbated Mexico's balance of trade deficit. Anticipating a devaluation of the peso, investors began to move capital into U.S. dollar investments at the end of 1994. The continued devaluation of the peso in early 1995 resulted in higher import prices, runaway inflation, destabilization of the stock market, and exorbitant interest rates. The peso crisis led to a recession in Mexico and left KFC managers uncertain about Mexico's economic and political future.

KFC's approach to investment in Mexico was to remain conservative, at least until greater economic and political stability was achieved. Although resources could be redirected toward other investment areas with less risk, such as Japan, Australia, China, and Europe, KFC still views Mexico as its most important foreign growth market. Significant opportunities also exist for KFC to expand its franchise base throughout the Caribbean and South America. PepsiCo's commitments to these markets are unlikely to be affected by its investment decisions in Mexico. The danger in taking a conservative approach in Mexico is the potential loss of market share in a country where KFC enjoys enormous popularity.

QUESTIONS FOR DISCUSSION

1. What are KFC's greatest marketing challenges in the domestic fast-food market?
2. What is the role of globalization of marketing in KFC's plans to expand sales? Can KFC use the same marketing strategies worldwide?
3. Why are environmental forces so important to KFC's sales success in Latin America and Mexico?

SOURCE: This case was prepared by Jeffrey Krug, The University of Memphis. Research assistance was provided by Phylis Mansfield, The University of Memphis. All rights reserved by Jeffrey Krug.

Part 2

Buyer Behavior and Target Market Selection

*P*art 2 focuses on the buyer. The development of a marketing strategy begins with the buyer. Chapter 5 provides a foundation for analyzing buyers through a discussion of marketing information systems and the basic steps in the marketing research process. Understanding elements that affect buying decisions enables marketers to better analyze customers' needs and evaluate how specific marketing strategies can satisfy those needs. In Chapter 6 we examine consumer buying decision processes and factors that influence buying decisions. Then, in Chapter 7, we stress organizational markets, organizational buyers, the buying center, and the organizational buying decision process. Chapter 8 focuses on one of the major steps in the development of a marketing strategy: selecting and analyzing target markets.

Chapter 5

Information Systems and Marketing Research

OBJECTIVES

- To be able to describe the nature and importance of information systems in marketing decision making

- To explore how tools such as databases, electronic bulletin boards, online information services, and the Internet facilitate marketing research

- To learn the five basic steps for conducting a marketing research project

- To become familiar with the fundamental methods of gathering data for marketing research

- To understand the importance of ethics in marketing research

Consumers crave low-fat potato chips.

*B*etcha can't eat just one. At least that's what Frito-Lay hopes is true of its new Baked Lay's Potato Crisps. The new chips have 1.5 grams of fat per serving, compared with 10 grams for a serving of the firm's all-American favorite Lay's Potato Chips. In 1994, 1,439 low-fat products hit the marketplace, up from 626 in 1989, and there are certainly plenty of low-fat corn chips, pretzels, and other snacks on the market, but until January 1996, there was no low-fat potato chip.

In the early 1990s, marketing researchers at Frito-Lay found that most consumers disliked low-fat chips because, frankly, they tasted like cardboard. Karen Snepp, Frito-Lay's vice president of customer and consumer insights says, "Yet even as our focus groups told us they hated low-fat chips, they also kept saying that they would do anything for a low-fat potato chip with a decent taste."

Thus was born Project Liberty, a play on Frito's goal of liberating potato chips from the deep-fat fryer. After three years of extensive research into different types of potatoes, oils, slicing and baking methods, and taste tests, a potato chip worthy of the name Lay's emerged from test ovens. But the research wasn't over. The new Baked Lay's Potato Crisps next went to test marketing in Midland, Texas, and Cedar Rapids, Iowa, because the incomes, ethnic mix, and average number of kids per family in those communities represent what Frito-Lay considers mainstream America. When executives saw sales in the two cities jump by 15 to 20 percent, they knew they had a hit.

Frito-Lay projected national sales of Baked Lay's to reach $200 million by the end of 1996, which would set a record for a first-year product in the snack-food business. The company is also researching other low-fat temptations, including low-fat granola bars, and it has already introduced a Ruffles Reduced Fat Chip. In fact, expecting that low-fat snacks will comprise a third of its business by 1998 (up from 10 to 15 percent today), Frito-Lay is investing $225 million to build factories and add fifteen manufacturing lines to existing plants to handle the new products. Their optimism is reflected in the new dare: "Betcha can't eat just one . . . bag."[1]

The marketing research conducted by Frito-Lay demonstrates that in order to implement the marketing concept, marketers require information about the characteristics, needs, and wants of their target markets. Such information, well used, fosters relationship marketing by helping marketers fashion their efforts toward meeting and even anticipating the needs of their customers. In fact, "Know thy customer" may well be "the first commandment of successful marketing in the 1990s."[2] Marketing research and information systems that can provide practical and objective information to help firms develop and implement marketing strategies are therefore essential to effective marketing.

In this chapter, we focus on how marketers gather information needed to make marketing decisions. We first define marketing research and marketing information systems and distinguish between them. Next we look at how technology, particularly the evolution of the Internet, is facilitating marketing research and marketing information systems. Then we examine the individual steps of the marketing research process, including various methods of collecting data. Finally, we consider the importance of ethics in marketing research.

Marketing Research and Marketing Information Systems

Marketing research The systematic design, collection, interpretation, and reporting of marketing information

Marketing research is the systematic design, collection, interpretation, and reporting of information to help marketers solve specific marketing problems or take advantage of marketing opportunities. As the word *research* implies, it is a process for gathering information not currently available to decision makers. Marketing research is conducted on a special-project basis, with the research methods adapted to the problems being studied and to changes in the environment. The American Marketing Association defines marketing research as follows:

> Marketing research is the function which links the consumer, customer, and public to the marketer through information—information used to identify and define marketing opportunities and problems; generate, refine, and evaluate marketing actions; monitor marketing performance; and improve understanding of marketing as a process. Marketing research specifies the information required to address these issues; designs the method for collecting information; manages and implements the data collection process; analyzes the results; and communicates the findings and their implications.[3]

Marketing information system (MIS) A framework for the management and structuring of information gathered regularly from sources inside and outside an organization

A **marketing information system (MIS)** is a framework for the day-to-day management and structuring of information gathered regularly from sources both inside and outside an organization. As such, an MIS provides a continuous flow of information about prices, advertising expenditures, sales, competition, and distribution expenses. Kraft General Foods, Inc., for example, operates one of the largest marketing information systems in the food industry, maintaining, using, and sharing information with others in ways that increase the value of what the company offers consumers. Kraft seeks to develop a dialogue with consumers by providing toll-free numbers. It receives about half a million calls a year from consumers who ask questions and express concerns about products.[4]

The main focus of the marketing information system is on data storage and retrieval, as well as on computer capabilities and management's information requirements. Regular reports of sales by product or market categories, data on inventory levels, and records of salespersons' activities are all examples of information that is useful in making decisions. In the MIS, the means of *gathering* data receive less attention than do the procedures for expediting the *flow* of information.

An effective marketing information system starts by determining the objective of the information—that is, by identifying decision needs that require certain information. Then the firm can specify an information system for continuous monitoring to provide regular, pertinent information on both the external and internal environment. FedEx, for example, has developed interactive marketing systems to provide instantaneous communication between the company and its customers. Through the telephone and computer information services, customers can track their packages and receive immediate feedback concerning delivery. Online services provide information to FedEx about customer usage,

Figure 5.1
Marketing Information
Maritz and LEXIS-
NEXIS are two
companies that provide
market research and
marketing information
systems.

and FedEx can find out directly what consumers think about company services. The evolving development of telecommunications and computer technology is allowing marketing information systems to cultivate one-to-one relationships with customers.

The main difference between marketing research and marketing information systems is that marketing research is an information-gathering process for specific situations, whereas an MIS is a system that provides continuous data input for an organization. Nonrecurring decisions that deal with the dynamics of the marketing environment often call for a data search structured according to a specific problem and decision. Marketing research is usually characterized by in-depth analyses of a major problem or issue. Often the information needed is available only from sources outside an organization's formal channels of information. For instance, an organization may want to know something about its competitors or may need to gain an unbiased understanding of its own customers. Such information objectives may require an independent investigation by a marketing research firm.

The real value of marketing research and marketing information systems is measured by improvements in a marketer's ability to make decisions. Marketers should treat information in the same manner as other resources utilized by the firm, and they must weigh the costs of obtaining information against the benefits derived. Information is judged worthwhile if it results in marketing activities that better satisfy the needs of the firm's target markets, that lead to increased sales and profits, or that help the firm achieve some other goal. In Figure 5.1, creative advertisements from Maritz and LEXIS-NEXIS reinforce the importance of marketing research information.

Capitalizing on New Technologies for Marketing Research

*T*echnology is making information for marketing decisions ever more accessible. The ability of firms to track customer buying behavior and better discern what customers want is changing the nature of marketing. For example, the airlines have discovered that many of their most desirable customers have computers and can communicate with the carriers online. Frequent flyers—people who fly ten or more times a year—account for just 8 percent of all airline customers but book 44 percent of all trips. With interactive communication through devices such as fax, telephone, and computer online access, Northwest Airlines invited customers to take part in survey research. From this research, Northwest learned that its affluent frequent flyers travel at Christmas, like beach vacations, and most important, want flights to be on time.[5]

The integration of various types of telecommunications and computing technologies is allowing marketers to access a growing array of valuable information sources related to industry forecasts, business trends, and customer buying behavior. Electronic communication tools can be effectively utilized to gain accurate information with minimal customer interaction. Most marketing researchers have E-mail, voice mail, teleconferencing, video conferences, and faxes at their disposal.[6] Because some of these communications tools—particularly databases, electronic bulletin boards, online services, and the Internet—are radically changing the way marketers conduct research, we'll take a closer look at them now.

■ *Databases*

Database A collection of information arranged for easy access and retrieval

A **database** is a collection of information arranged for easy access and retrieval. Databases allow marketers to tap into an abundance of information useful in making marketing decisions: internal sales reports, newspaper articles, company news releases, government economic reports, bibliographies, and more, often accessed through a computer system.

Many marketing researchers use commercial databases developed by information research firms to obtain useful information for marketing decisions. Some of the databases supplied by CompuServe, DIALOG, NEXIS, and Dow Jones News Retrieval are outlined in Table 5.1. These commercial online databases are accessible via a telephone hookup for a fee. They can also be obtained in printed form or on computer compact discs (CD-ROMs). In most commercial databases, the user typically does a computer search on a key word, topic, or company, and the database service generates abstracts, articles, or reports that can then be printed out. Accessing multiple reports or a complete article may cost extra.

CompuServe, for example, has a special neighborhood report option that provides summaries of demographics for any ZIP code in the United States. In addition, a menu allows the researcher to select demographic, sales potential, or neighborhood reports, but these carry a surcharge. For example, two sales potential reports for the automotive parts market cost approximately $100. Medical/health insurance data for a ZIP code in Ohio costs $25. CENDATA, another database available through CompuServe, allows marketers to access 1990 U.S. Census Bureau data in both tabular and report form. It also lists names, addresses, and phone numbers for local, regional, and national census offices. CENDATA supplies statewide population and housing characteristics for variables such as income, education, and language spoken, as well as others.[7]

Single-source data Information provided by a single marketing research firm

Information provided by a single firm on household demographics, purchases, television viewing behavior, and responses to promotions such as coupons and free samples is called **single-source data**.[8] For example, Behavior Scan, offered by Information Resources, Inc., screens about 60,000 households in twenty-six U.S. markets. This single-source information service monitors consumer household televisions and records the programs and commercials watched. When consumers from these households shop in stores equipped with scanning registers, they present Hotline cards (similar to credit cards) to cashiers. This enables each customer's identification to be electronically coded so that the firm can track each product they purchase.

Many marketers also develop their own databases. An example is NSS, a firm that markets software to banks. Facing a challenge of qualifying thousands of new sales leads, NSS developed a database program to track customers and prospects according to specified criteria. NSS's database provides detailed data that ranks prospects in terms of those who can make a buying decision within a year and those who can make one within two years or more. Such information gives NSS greater control in managing its sales force.[9]

Finally, firms can also sell their databases to other firms. *Reader's Digest,* for example, markets a database that includes 100 million households. One of the best databases available to assess potential markets for consumer products, it lets *Reader's Digest* management know the likes and dislikes of many of its readers. It also permits a linkup to test

Table 5.1 Databases for Marketing Information

CompuServe

Business Demographics: "Business to Business Report" details number of employees and states percentages for all SIC codes."Advertisers Service Reports" provides employee counts and number of establishments by employee size for retail trade businesses. Both are available for various geographic units.

IQuest: A gateway to more than 850 databases, including magazines, newspapers, indexes, conference proceedings, newsletters, government documents, and patent records.

Magazine Database Plus: Full-text magazine articles from more than 90 magazines.

Marketing/Management Research Center: Indexes and full text of major business magazines, indices to market and industry research reports, and company news releases.

Neighborhood Report: Summaries of the demographics of any zip code in the U.S. Information provided includes population, race, age, occupation, and housing patterns.

DIALOG

ABI/INFORM®: Information on business management and administration from approximately 800 publications.

ARTHUR D. LITTLE/ONLINE: Industry forecasts, technology assessments, product and market overviews, and public opinion surveys.

BUSINESS SOFTWARE DATABASE™: Information on computer software for micro-, mini-, and mainframe computers. Each record contains a description of the software, the producer's name/address/telephone number, price, number of installations, and hardware requirements.

D&B-DONNELLY DEMOGRAPHICS: Demographic data from the 1980 Census and selected portions of the 1990 Census, as well as proprietary estimates and projections.

D&B-DUN'S ELECTRONIC BUSINESS DIRECTORY: Information for over 8.7 million businesses and professionals in the U.S. Includes address, telephone number, SIC code and description, and number of employees.

EMPLOYEE BENEFITS INFOSOURCE™: Comprehensive information on all aspects of employee benefit plans.

INVESTEXT®: More than 320,000 full-text reports written by analysts at investment banks and research firms worldwide.

MOODY'S® CORPORATE FILES: Descriptive and financial information on all companies traded on the New York and American Stock Exchanges, as well as 1,300 other companies traded over the counter.

PTS NEWSLETTER DATABASE™: Full text from over 500 business and trade newsletters covering 50 industries.

PUBLIC OPINION ONLINE (POLL): Full-text collection of public opinion surveys conducted in the U.S.

NEXIS

Analyst Research: Brokerage house reports on companies and industries, structured by data type or category.

Computers and Communications: Over 40 full-text sources for information on computers and communications.

Company: Over 170 files of business and financial information, including thousands of in-depth company and industry research reports from worldwide investment banks, research firms, SEC filings, Standard & Poor's, and more.

Consumer Goods: Information from over 40 trade publications and brokers' reports on the cosmetics, drugs, electronics, food, beverages, retail, and apparel industries.

LEXPAT®: Full text of U.S. patents issued since 1975 by the U.S. Patent and Trademark Office.

Marketing: Information from trade publications and other sources on advertising, marketing, market research, public relations, sales and selling, promotions, consumer attitudes and behavior, demographics, product announcements, and reviews.

PROMT/PLUS: Overview of markets and technology. Tracks competitors, identifies and monitors trends, analyzes specific companies and industries, and assesses various advertising and promotion techniques.

Dow Jones News Retrieval

Comprehensive Company Reports: Detailed financial and business information on public companies.

Dow Jones Business Newswires: Continuously updated news from seven different news wires.

Dow Jones Text Library: Full-text articles from nearly 500 local, regional, and national publications and over 600 newsletters and two news wires.

Dun & Bradstreet Financial Profiles & Company Reports: In-depth financial, historical, and operational reports for public and private companies.

Japanese Business News: Same-day coverage of major Japanese business, financial, and political news.

Statistical Comparisons of Companies & Industries: Comparative stock price, volume, and fundamental data on companies and industries.

Standard & Poor's Profiles and Earnings Estimates: Company reports with descriptive and statistical data.

Top Business, Financial & Economic News: Summaries of the day's business and financial stories.

Source: Reprinted from *Sales and Marketing Management* (Jan. 1993), p. 40. Copyright © 1993 Sales and Marketing Management. Used with permission.

products, assess retailers, examine media alternatives, and evaluate the effectiveness of promotions. In fact, the *Reader's Digest* database is possibly as valuable to the company as the magazine itself.[10]

■ *Electronic Bulletin Boards*

Computer networks (systems that link multiple computers through phone lines or satellite) allow marketers to interface with data sources and customers with almost instantaneous information about products and sales performance. Through such networks, firms can exchange electronic mail (E-mail) internally, among their employees, and externally, with suppliers and customers. *Electronic bulletin boards (BBSs)* are another method of communicating through computers. BBSs enable users to post a message for any participant to read and discuss, just as if they had tacked a handwritten notice to an actual bulletin board in an office hallway for all to see. Many business computer networks include a BBS for employees to pose questions, discuss work (and sometimes nonwork) issues, and air grievances. For example, Texas Instruments Incorporated maintains a bulletin board on which employees can anonymously express concerns and complaints. Their messages can be routed to executives who coordinate and integrate the firm's efforts to develop positive customer relations. One frequent reader of the Texas Instruments bulletin board is Jerry Junkins, the company's chief executive.[11]

More firms are also installing BBSs that can be accessed by customers to develop information for the marketing information system, which assists in developing marketing strategies. Some companies even use bulletin boards to answer customer questions. Pharmaceutical companies have long relied on them to monitor patients' reactions to new drugs. Most large computer software and hardware companies operate bulletin boards to help their customers solve problems. Compaq Computer Corporation's bulletin board receives about 500 messages a week, which Compaq then compiles and evaluates as a way to monitor product quality, company productivity, and service needs.[12] Currently, 13.5 million people use electronic bulletin boards, and the number rises 70 percent a year.[13] Some firms' bulletin boards allow customers to exchange ideas for creative problem solving related to products. Customers learn from one another, and the firm gains new insights into the marketing of its products.

■ *Online Information Services*

A technological step above electronic bulletin boards are online information services, such as CompuServe, Delphi, Prodigy, GEIS, DIALOG, and NEXIS. These services typically offer their subscribers access to E-mail, discussion groups (depending on the service, these may be called bulletin boards, forums, or newsgroups), files for downloading, chat rooms (where users can converse with each other in "real time" like a telephone call, except the conversation is typed instead of spoken), news, databases and related research materials, and other services, such as airline reservations. Accessing online services is as simple as calling in, hitting the return key, and typing in a password (once the user has arranged payment). Marketers can subscribe to "mailing lists" that periodically deliver electronic newsletters to their computer screens, and they can participate in on-screen discussions with thousands of network users. This enhanced communication with a firm's customers, suppliers, and employees provides a high-speed link that boosts the capabilities of a firm's marketing information system.

■ *The Internet*

Previously, we defined the Internet as a network of business, university, government, and other networks. In essence, the Internet is a collection of computers hooked together with telephone lines that enables users to communicate and share information around the globe. Whereas the online information services (such as CompuServe and America Online) limit their services to subscribers, the Internet permits the exchange of E-mail, global discussion through public forums called newsgroups on everything ranging from *Star Trek* (the original cybertopic) to presidential elections and just about everything in

Figure 5.2
The Internet
The Internet provides today's businesses with unlimited opportunities for market research.

between with participants around the world, as well as files for downloading, chat rooms, and more.

Although the Internet has been in existence for several decades, it was not until 1992, with the development of the World Wide Web (WWW, or "the Web"), that the Internet became significant as a medium for obtaining marketing information (see Figure 5.2). The WWW organizes much of the vast array of information available on the Internet into a series of interconnected "pages" that may include text, graphics, sound, and video. The introduction in 1994 of Mosaic, a popular software program for navigating the Web, has turned WWW into a true multimedia communication tool. Today, some 37 million North Americans have access to the Internet, and that number will have grown considerably by the time you read this.[14] Experts believe there will be more than 100 million users around the world on the Internet by the year 2000. Table 5.2 is an overview of who has access to the Internet and how they are using it. Based on the developments of the last few years, the pace of Internet growth will only accelerate.

The Internet has evolved as the most powerful communication medium, linking customers and companies around the world via computer networks. An entire industry is emerging to make marketing information easily accessible to both marketing firms and customers.[15] Nordstrom's, a large department store, has set up an interactive shopping effort through E-mail that links frequent customers with a personal shopper. Nordstrom's keeps personal information such as shirt and shoe size on file for easy reordering. In addition, Nordstrom's marketing information system tracks the changing desires and buying habits of its most valued customers.[16]

While most WWW home pages are open to anyone with Internet access, big companies like U.S. West are creating internal Web pages, called "intranets," that allow employees to access internal data such as customer profiles and product inventory—information once hidden in databases only technicians could unlock. Such sensitive corporate information can be protected from outside users of the World Wide Web by special security software called "firewalls." Turner Broadcasting System uses intranets to test products during the development phase. Marketing department employees can view animated clips and listen to sound bites from popular cartoon talk shows. Employees can then express their opinions by E-mailing the animators directly. The animators use this feedback to revise the cartoon before moving onto the firm's public cartoon site on America Online. Most marketers who get in the habit of accessing their companies' internal Web pages often move on to seek information externally via the rest of the WWW as well.[17]

Perhaps the ultimate in relationship marketing is giving customers access to nonproprietary internal information. FedEx, for example, allows customers to track their packages by logging onto FedEx's Web home page, which is linked to the company's internal database. Netscape, which markets a World Wide Web navigator, or browser, offers

Table 5.2 Internet Use in North America	
People 16 and older with access to the Internet	37 million
Number who have used the World Wide Web in the past three months	18 million
Average time a user spends on the Internet per week	5.5 hours
Female Internet users	35 percent
Users who have purchased goods or services through the World Wide Web	14 percent

Source: Commercenet Consortium/Nielsen Media Research, in "Who's on the Web?" *Newsweek*, Nov. 13, 1995, p. 14. Copyright © 1995, Newsweek, Inc. All rights reserved. Reprinted by permission.

Table 5.3   World Wide Web Page Addresses Useful for Marketing Research

To view these pages, you'll need access to a computer with a modem and software for browsing the Web.

http://www.yahoo.com/	A huge index of WWW pages
http://www.webcrawler.com/	A "search engine" to find useful WWW pages; allows you to search for Web pages on topics you specify
http://lycos.cs.cmu.edu	Another Web searching tool
http://www.whitehouse.gov	Links to electronic government information
gopher://gopher.cenus.gov/	Employment statistics in the U.S. Census Bureau's main database
http://www.ama.org/	American Marketing Association's home page
http://www.adage.com/	*Advertising Age*'s home page
http://nsns.com/MouseTracks/	Marketing conferences
http://www.nielsen.com/	Nielsen marketing research
http://www.hoovers.com	Company and industry profiles

rewards as incentives for users of its software to report product deficiencies.[18] Table 5.3 lists the "addresses" of some marketing-research-related World Wide Web pages.

The U.S. Census Bureau also employs WWW pages to disseminate information that may be useful to marketing researchers. Data can be accessed by Data Map and 1990 Census Lookup. Data Map enables users to view profiles of states and counties in both tabular and graphic form. Researchers can select which state to display simply by clicking on a map. The Census Lookup option allows marketing researchers to create their own customized information. With this online tool, researchers can select tables by clicking boxes to select the state and then within the state, the county, place, and urbanized area or metropolitan statistical area to be examined.

The Marketing Research Process

arketing research, as described earlier, is the systematic design, collection, interpretation, and reporting of information to help marketers solve specific marketing problems or take advantage of marketing opportunities. The difference between good and bad research is the quality of the input, which includes effective control over the entire marketing research process. To maintain the control needed for obtaining accurate information, marketers approach marketing research in logical steps. Figure 5.3 presents the five steps of the marketing research process: (1) defining and locating problems, (2) designing the research project, (3) collecting data, (4) interpreting research findings, and (5) reporting research findings. These five steps should be viewed as an overall approach to conducting research rather than as a rigid set of rules to be followed in each project. In planning research projects, marketers must consider each of the steps carefully and determine how they can best be adjusted to resolve the particular problems at hand.

Figure 5.3
The Five Steps of the Marketing Research Process

| 1 Defining and locating problems | 2 Designing the research project | 3 Collecting data | 4 Interpreting research findings | 5 Reporting research findings |

Defining and Locating Problems

Problem definition First step in finding a solution or launching a research study; focuses on uncovering the nature and boundaries of a negative, or positive, situation or question

Problem definition, the first step toward finding a solution or launching a research study, focuses on uncovering the nature and boundaries of a negative, or positive, situation or question. The first sign of a problem is usually a departure from some normal function, such as conflicts between or failures in attaining objectives. If a corporation's objective is a 12 percent sales increase and the result is 6 percent, this discrepancy should be analyzed. It is a symptom that something inside or outside the organization has blocked the attainment of the desired goal or that the goal is unrealistic. Declining sales, increasing expenses, or decreasing profits also signal problems. Conversely, when an organization experiences a dramatic rise in sales, or some other positive event, it may conduct marketing research to discover the reasons and maximize the opportunities stemming from them.

To pin down the specific causes of the problem through research, marketers must define the problem and its scope in a way that requires probing beneath the superficial symptoms. The interaction between the marketing manager and the marketing researcher should yield a clear definition of the problem. Researchers and decision makers should remain in the problem definition stage until they have determined precisely what they want from the research and how they will use it.

The research objective specifies what information is needed to solve the problem. Deciding how to refine a broad, indefinite problem into a precise, researchable statement is a prerequisite for the next step in planning the research: designing the research project.

Designing the Research Project

Reliability A condition existing when use of a research technique produces almost identical results in successive repeated trials

Validity A condition existing when a research method measures what it is supposed to measure, not something else

Hypothesis An informed guess or assumption about a certain problem or set of circumstances

Once the problem has been defined, an overall plan for obtaining the information needed to address it must be formulated. In designing research, marketing researchers must ensure that research techniques are both reliable and valid. A research technique has **reliability** if it produces almost identical results in successive repeated trials. But a reliable technique is not necessarily valid. To have **validity,** the method must measure what it is supposed to measure, not something else. A study to measure the effectiveness of advertising would be valid if advertising could be isolated from other factors or variables that affect sales. It would be reliable if the study or experiment on the effectiveness of advertising could be repeated in successive trials.

The objective statement of a marketing research project should include hypotheses drawn from both previous research and expected research findings. A **hypothesis** is an informed guess or assumption about a certain problem or set of circumstances. It is based on all the insight and knowledge available about the problem or circumstances from previous research studies and other sources. As information is gathered, a researcher can test the hypothesis. For example, a consumer food products manufacturer such as H. J. Heinz might propose the hypothesis that children today have more influence on their families' buying decisions for ketchup and other grocery products. A marketing researcher would then gather data, perhaps through surveys of children and their parents, and draw conclusions as to whether the hypothesis is correct. Sometimes several hypotheses are developed during the actual study; the hypotheses that are accepted or rejected become the study's chief conclusions.

Exploratory studies
Research conducted when more information is needed about a problem and the tentative hypothesis needs to be made more specific

Descriptive studies
Research undertaken when marketers need to understand the characteristics of certain phenomena to solve a particular problem; may require statistical analysis and predictive tools

The kind of hypothesis being tested determines which approach will be used for gathering general data: exploratory, descriptive, or causal. When marketers need more information about a problem or want to make a tentative hypothesis more specific, they may conduct **exploratory studies.** For instance, they may review the information in the firm's database or examine publicly available data. Questioning knowledgeable people inside and outside the organization may also yield new insights into the problem. An advantage of the exploratory approach is that it permits marketers to conduct ministudies with a very restricted database.

If marketers need to understand the characteristics of certain phenomena to solve a particular problem, **descriptive studies** can aid them. Such studies may range from general surveys of consumers' education, occupation, or age to specifics on how many consumers purchased Ford Explorers last month or how many adults between the ages of 18 and 30 eat a microwaved meal at least three times a week. Some descriptive studies require statistical analysis and predictive tools. For example, a researcher trying to find out how many people will vote for a certain political candidate may have to survey registered voters to predict the results. Descriptive studies generally demand much prior knowledge and assume that the problem is clearly defined. The marketers' major task is to choose adequate methods for collecting and measuring data.

Causal studies Studies in which it is assumed that a particular variable *X* causes a variable *Y*

Hypotheses about causal relationships call for a more complex approach than a descriptive study. In **causal studies,** it is assumed that a particular variable *X* causes a variable *Y*. Marketers must plan the research so that the data collected prove or disprove that *X* causes *Y*. To do so, marketers must try to hold constant all variables except *X* and *Y*. For example, to find out whether new carpeting, miniblinds, and ceiling fans increase the number of rentals in an apartment complex, marketers need to keep all variables constant except the new furnishings.

Collecting Data

Primary data Data observed and recorded or collected directly from respondents

Secondary data Data compiled inside or outside the organization for some purpose other than the current investigation

*M*arketing researchers have two types of data at their disposal. **Primary data** are observed and recorded or collected directly from respondents. This type of data must be gathered by observing phenomena or surveying respondents. **Secondary data** are compiled inside or outside the organization for some purpose other than the current investigation. Secondary data include general reports supplied to an enterprise by various data services and internal and online databases. Such reports might concern market share, retail inventory levels, and consumers' buying behavior. Commonly, secondary data are already available in private or public reports or have been collected and stored by the organization itself. In the next section we discuss the methods of gathering both secondary and primary data. In the early 1990s, about 70 percent of marketing information was based on primary research. By the year 2000, however, it is estimated that the scales will be reversed: 60 percent or more of all marketing research data is expected to come from secondary sources.[19]

■ *Secondary Data Collection*

Marketers often begin the marketing research process by gathering secondary data. They may use available reports and other information from both internal and external sources to study a marketing problem.

Internal sources of secondary data can contribute tremendously to research. An organization's marketing database may contain information about past marketing activities, such as sales records and research reports, which can be used to test hypotheses and pinpoint problems. Accounting records are also an excellent source of data but, strangely enough, are often overlooked. The large volume of data an accounting department collects does not automatically flow to the marketing area. As a result, detailed information about costs, sales, customer accounts, or profits by product category may not be part of the MIS. This condition develops particularly in organizations that do not store marketing information on a systematic basis.

Secondary data can also be gleaned from periodicals, government publications, unpublished sources, and online databases. Periodicals such as *Business Week, The Wall Street Journal, Sales & Marketing Management, American Demographics, Marketing Research,* and *Industrial Marketing* print general information that helps in defining problems and developing hypotheses. *Survey of Buying Power,* an annual supplement to *Sales & Marketing Management,* contains sales data for major industries on a county-by-county basis. Many marketers consult federal government publications such as the *Statistical Abstract of the United States,* the *Census of Business,* the *Census of Agriculture,* and the *Census of Population,* available from the Superintendent of Documents in Washington,

Table 5.4 Guide to External Sources of Secondary Data	
Databases	Many databases are a collection of information arranged for easy access and retrieval through online information services or the Internet. Users select key words (such as the name of a subject) to search a database and generate references.
Government	The federal government, through its various departments and agencies, collects, analyzes, and publishes statistics on practically everything. Many government agencies have data available online.
Periodical Indexes	The library's reference section contains indexes on virtually every discipline. *The Business Periodicals Index,* for example, indexes each article in all major business publications.
Trade Journals	Virtually every industry or type of business is covered by a trade journal. These journals give a feel for the industry—its size, degree of competition, range of companies involved, and problems. To find trade journals in the field of interest, check *Ulrich's,* a reference book that lists U.S. and foreign periodicals by subject.
Trade Associations	Almost every industry, product category, and profession has organized its own association. These often conduct research, publish journals, provide training sessions, and hold conventions. To find out which associations serve which industries, check the *Encyclopedia of Associations.*
WWW pages	Many companies have established "home pages" on the Internet's World Wide Web for disseminating information on their products and activities.

D.C.; some of these government resources are available through online information services or the Internet World Wide Web. Table 5.4 summarizes the major external sources of secondary data, excluding syndicated services.

■ *Primary Data Collection*

The collection of primary data is a more lengthy and complex process than the collection of secondary data. The acquisition of primary data utilizes survey methods, sampling procedures, and observation methods.

Survey methods
Data-gathering methods that include interviews by mail, telephone, E-mail, and personal interviews

Survey Methods **Survey methods** include interviews by mail, telephone, E-mail, and personal interviews. Survey results are used to describe and analyze consumer behavior. Selection of a survey method depends on the nature of the problem, the data needed to test the hypothesis, and the resources, such as funding and personnel, available to the researcher. Table 5.5 summarizes and compares the advantages of the various survey methods.

Gathering information through surveys is becoming more difficult because response rates are declining. Many researchers believe that nonresponse is the single biggest problem facing the research industry.[20] Some causes of nonresponse are fear of invasion of privacy, overly long questionnaires, dull topics, time pressures, and general skepticism regarding the personal benefits of participating in a research study.[21] Moreover, fear of crime makes respondents unwilling to trust personal interviewers. The use of sales techniques disguised as market surveys has also contributed to decreased respondent cooperation.

In *mail surveys,* questionnaires are sent to respondents, who are encouraged to complete and return them. Mail surveys are used most often when the individuals chosen for questioning are spread over a wide area and funds for the survey are limited. A mail survey is the least expensive survey method as long as the response rate is high enough to produce reliable results. The main disadvantages of this method are the possibility of a low response rate or of misleading results if respondents are significantly different from the population being sampled.

Premiums or incentives encouraging respondents to return questionnaires have been effective in developing panels of respondents who are regularly interviewed by mail.

Table 5.5 Comparison of the Three Basic Survey Methods

	Mail and E-Mail Surveys	Telephone Surveys	Personal Interview Surveys
Economy	Potentially the lowest cost per interview if there is an adequate return rate.	Avoids interviewers' travel expenses; less expensive than in-home interviews.	In-home interviewing is the most expensive interviewing method; shopping mall, focus-group interviewing lower costs.
Flexibility	Inflexible; questionnaire must be short, easy for respondents to complete.	Flexible because interviewers can ask probing questions, but observations are impossible.	Most flexible method; respondents can react to visual materials, demographic data are more accurate; in-depth probes are possible.
Interviewer Bias	Interviewer bias eliminated; questionnaires can be returned anonymously.	Some anonymity; may be hard to develop trust in respondents.	Refusals may be decreased by interviewers' rapport-building efforts.
Sampling and Respondents' Cooperation	Obtaining a complete mailing list is difficult; nonresponse is a major disadvantage; E-mail surveys require computer and online access.	Sample must be limited to respondents with telephones; telephone answering machines used to screen calls, busy signals, and refusals are problems.	Not-at-homes are more difficult to deal with; focus-group, shopping mall interviewing may overcome these problems.

Mail panels, which are selected to represent a market or market segment, are especially useful for evaluating new products, providing general information about consumers, and providing records of consumers' purchases. Consumer mail panels and consumer purchase diaries are much more widely used than custom mail surveys, but both have shortcomings. Research indicates that the people who take the time to fill out a consumer diary have higher income and are more educated than the general population. If researchers include less educated consumers in the panel, they must risk poorer response rates.[22]

In *telephone surveys,* respondents' answers to a questionnaire are recorded by interviewers on the phone. A telephone survey has some advantages over a mail survey. The rate of response is higher because it takes less effort to answer the telephone and talk than to fill out a questionnaire and return it. If there are enough interviewers, telephone surveys can be conducted very quickly. Thus they can be used by political candidates or organizations seeking an immediate reaction to an event. In addition, this survey technique permits interviewers to gain rapport with respondents and ask probing questions. According to a survey by the Council of American Survey Research Organizations (CASRO), telephone interviewing is the preferred survey method in more than 40 percent of the projects conducted by commercial survey research firms.[23]

However, as Figure 5.4 indicates, only a small proportion of the population likes to participate in telephone surveys. By contrast, over three-fourths of us feel indifferent toward telephone surveys or don't like them at all.[24] This poor image can significantly limit participation and distort representation in a telephone survey. Moreover, telephone surveys are limited to oral communication; visual aids or observation cannot be included. Interpreters of results must make adjustments for subjects who are not at home or who do not have telephones. Many households are excluded from telephone directories by choice (unlisted numbers) or because the residents moved after the directory was published. Telephone answering machines are often used to screen calls and prevent access to potential respondents.

These findings have serious implications for the use of telephone samples in conducting surveys. Some adjustment must be made for groups of respondents that may be undersampled because of a smaller-than-average incidence of telephone listings. Nondirectory telephone samples can overcome such bias. Various methods are available, including random-digit dialing (adding random numbers to the telephone prefix) and

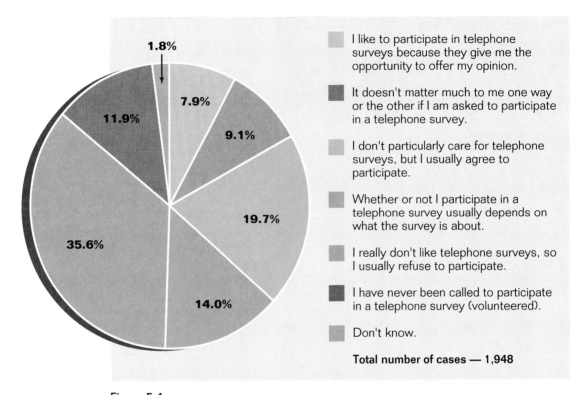

1.8%

7.9%

11.9%

9.1%

35.6%

19.7%

14.0%

I like to participate in telephone surveys because they give me the opportunity to offer my opinion.

It doesn't matter much to me one way or the other if I am asked to participate in a telephone survey.

I don't particularly care for telephone surveys, but I usually agree to participate.

Whether or not I participate in a telephone survey usually depends on what the survey is about.

I really don't like telephone surveys, so I usually refuse to participate.

I have never been called to participate in a telephone survey (volunteered).

Don't know.

Total number of cases — 1,948

Figure 5.4
Attitudes Toward Telephone Survey Participation
Source: Peter S. Tuckel and Harry W. O'Neill, "Call Waiting," *Marketing Research*, Spring 1995, p. 8.
Used by permission of American Marketing Association.

plus-one telephone sampling (adding one to the last digit of a number in the directory). These methods make it feasible to dial any working number, whether or not it is listed in a directory.

Voice mail has much potential for asking simple questions and obtaining quick responses. Questions can be communicated by voice mail, and voice mail messages may be saved, passed along, or returned. Voice mail thus permits efficient survey participation without wasting respondents' time.[25]

Telephone surveys, like mail and personal interview surveys, are sometimes used to develop panels of respondents who can be interviewed repeatedly to measure changes in attitudes or behavior. Reliance on such panels is increasing.

E-mail surveys are evolving as an alternative to telephone surveys. Questionnaires can be transmitted to respondents who have provided their E-mail addresses and agree to be contacted individually. Moreover, because E-mail is semi-interactive, recipients can ask for clarification of specific questions or pose questions of their own.[26] The potential advantages of E-mail interviewing are quick response and lower cost than traditional mail and telephone surveys, but these advantages have not yet been realized because of limited access to respondents and unreliable response rates.[27]

Given the growing number of households owning PCs and connected to online information services or the Internet, marketing research is likely to rely heavily on E-mail surveys in the future. And, as negative attitudes toward telephone surveys render that technique less representative and more expensive, the integration of E-mail, fax, and voice mail functions into one PC-based system provides a promising opportunity for survey research. E-mail surveys have especially strong potential within organizations whose employees are networked and for associations that publish members' E-mail addresses. However, there are some ethical issues to consider when using E-mail for marketing research, as discussed in Ethical Challenges on the following page.

Marketing researchers have traditionally favored the *personal interview survey*, chiefly because of its flexibility. Various audiovisual aids—pictures, products, diagrams, or prerecorded advertising copy—can be incorporated into a personal interview. Rapport

ETHICAL CHALLENGES

Marketing Research Ethics and E-Mail

Although the Internet seems like a fantastic "place" both to sell products to specific target markets and to learn about the needs and wants of those markets, marketers must take care to observe traditional practices and "netiquette" when using the Net. E-mail, for example, is a popular means of communicating among coworkers, friends, family, and even customers. However, marketers must consider ethical issues associated with conducting marketing research via E-mail.

Many Internet users pay for their Internet access and E-mail privileges, usually by the hour, and they may also pay to store data (including E-mail) on their access provider's host computer. Consequently, users may be annoyed by unsolicited E-mail from marketers, whether it be advertisements or survey questionnaires. In fact, some long-time Net users regard unsolicited E-mail, particularly that of a commercial nature, as theft—of their time and of the money it costs them to read and store messages they didn't initiate and don't appreciate.

There are also privacy issues associated with E-mail. Some people view marketing-related E-mail much as they do junk mail in their "snail-mail" boxes or telephone sales calls that intrude on the dinner hour; they simply don't want to be bothered.

The Internet *is* a powerful medium that is rapidly changing the way people get information. However, if abused, the use of E-mail for marketing research and promotion could be curtailed by legislation. Many companies have discovered that the World Wide Web is a promising venue for exposing their products and messages. With the Web, consumers can seek out information that interests them and ignore whatever doesn't. Thus, companies doing marketing research can post surveys on their Web pages, and consumers can decide whether or not to take part. Until the ethical issues of using the Net for marketing research are resolved, marketers should proceed cautiously, learning what practices are acceptable and which are not, before they dive in.

Source: Contributed by Gwyneth M. Vaughn, freelance editor/writer.

---

gained through direct interaction usually permits more in-depth interviewing, including probes, follow-up questions, or psychological tests. In addition, because personal interviews can be longer, they can yield more information. Finally, respondents can be selected more carefully, and reasons for nonresponse can be explored. In one study, it was found that respondents questioned by personal contact methods had the most favorable attitudes toward survey research in general. The respondent liked seeing the person who was asking the questions and having the personal contact that is part of the interview.[28]

One such research technique is the *in-home (door-to-door) interview*. The in-home interview offers a clear advantage when thoroughness of self-disclosure and the elimination of group influence are important. In an in-depth interview of forty-five to ninety minutes, respondents can be probed to reveal their real motivations, feelings, behaviors, and aspirations.

The object of a *focus-group interview* is to observe group interaction when members are exposed to an idea or concept. Often these interviews are conducted informally, without a structured questionnaire. Consumer attitudes, behavior, lifestyles, needs, and desires can be explored in a flexible and creative manner through focus-group interviews. Questions are open-ended and stimulate consumers to answer in their own words. Researchers can ask probing questions to clarify something they do not fully understand or something unexpected and interesting that may help explain consumer behavior. Cadillac used information obtained from focus groups to change its advertising to emphasize the luxury car's safety features. The new advertisements increased Cadillac sales by 36 percent in test markets.[29] JRP Marketing Services, Inc. and QCS (Quality Controlled Services) are two marketing research firms that arrange for and conduct focus-group interviews (see Figure 5.5). Inside Marketing (on page 120) describes current trends in focus-group research.

The nature of personal interviews has changed. In the past, most personal interviews, which were based on random sampling or prearranged appointments, were conducted in

Figure 5.5
Focus Groups
These two advertisements acknowledge the importance of focus groups for providing in-depth data collection.

the respondent's home. Today most personal interviews are conducted in shopping malls. *Shopping mall intercept interviews* involve interviewing a percentage of persons passing by certain "intercept" points in a mall. Although there are many variations of this technique, the reaction toward mall intercept research is mixed, nearly equally split among positive, negative, and neutral. Almost half of major consumer goods and services companies use this technique and report shopping mall intercept interviewing as their major expenditure on survey research.[30]

Like any face-to-face interviewing method, mall intercept interviewing has many advantages. The interviewer is in a position to recognize and react to respondents' nonverbal indications of confusion. Respondents can be shown product prototypes, videotapes of commercials, and the like, and reactions can be sought. The mall environment lets the researcher deal with complex situations. For example, in taste tests, researchers know that all the respondents are reacting to the same product, which can be prepared and monitored from the mall test kitchen or some other facility. In addition, lower cost, greater control, and the ability to conduct tests requiring bulky equipment make shopping mall intercept interviews popular.

On-site computer interviewing, a variation of the mall intercept interview, consists of respondents completing a self-administered questionnaire displayed on a computer monitor. A computer software package can be used to conduct such interviews in shopping malls. After a brief lesson on how to operate the software, respondents can proceed through the survey at their own pace. Adaptive design questionnaires may be developed so that the respondent sees only those questionnaire items (usually a subset of an entire scale) that provide useful information about the respondent's attitude.[31]

Questionnaire Construction   A carefully constructed questionnaire is essential to the success of any survey. Questions must be designed to elicit information that meets the study's data requirements. These questions must be clear, easy to understand, and directed toward a specific objective. Researchers need to define the objective before trying to develop a questionnaire because the objective determines the substance of the questions and the amount of detail. A common mistake in constructing questionnaires is to ask questions that interest the researchers but do not yield information useful in deciding whether to accept or reject a hypothesis. Finally, the most important rule in composing questions is to maintain impartiality.

The questions are usually of three kinds: open-ended, dichotomous, and multiple-choice.

INSIDE MARKETING

Trends in Focus Groups

Because focus groups help marketing researchers gain information about consumers' attitudes and motivations, they are one of the most frequently used marketing research tool. Researchers are therefore constantly looking for ways to make focus groups even more effective.

One significant trend is the use of smaller focus groups of six to eight participants instead of the traditional ten to twelve. Minigroups of two to five are also becoming more common, as are one-on-one interviews. Researchers are finding that participants in smaller groups respond more thoughtfully and substantively, whereas respondents in larger groups are more prone to give one-word answers, and more reserved people may not get a word in at all. Minigroups may be even more cost-effective than larger focus groups when greater depth is needed. Smaller groups are also easier for researchers to recruit, host, and moderate, and may be more comfortable for participants.

Another trend is the increasing use of videoconferencing. For example, FocusVision Network, a Stamford, Connecticut, research firm, can hold a focus group in one facility while, through videoconferencing, clients and others can observe the session from their own company offices. Observers can even feed follow-up questions to the moderator.

Videoconferencing can be cost-effective because observers don't have to fly to each focus group site to view the sessions. FocusVision sessions cost about $1,000 more than traditional focus groups, but the company claims it can save a company that sponsors sixty focus groups a year $79,000 in travel expenses and 120 staff days.

Another trend in focus groups is literally going on the road to interview consumers. Marketing researcher Liz DiPilli criss-crosses the country talking to Generation Xers (21- to 29-year-olds) about their lifestyles and attitudes for clients such as Comedy Central, Ralph Lauren, and Evian. On her latest trip, DiPilli interviewed sixty people and conducted twelve focus groups in Atlanta, Portland (Oregon), Kansas City (Missouri), San Francisco, and New York. The focus groups were conducted in trendy hotel suites; the interviews, at parks, college campuses, pizzerias, clubs, rollerblade rental stands, volleyball games, and malls. "It's more casual, but it's more informative," she says.

Sources: Don L. Boroughs, "A High-Technology Meeting of Minds," *U.S. News & World Report,* June 5, 1995, pp. 46–48; Leslie M. Harris, "Technology, Techniques Drive Focus Group Trends," *Marketing News,* February 27, 1995, p. 8; Cyndee Miller, "Researcher Reaches Xers with Her Focus Groups on the Road," *Marketing News,* January 2, 1995, p. 10; and Carol Z. Shea, "Thinking About Focus Groups? Think Small for Big Results," *Marketing News,* August 28, 1995, p. 19.

OPEN-ENDED QUESTION
What is your general opinion of the American Express Optima Card?

_____
_____
_____

DICHOTOMOUS QUESTION
Do you presently have an American Express Optima Card?

Yes_____   No_____

MULTIPLE-CHOICE QUESTION
What age group are you in?

Under 20 _____   40–49   _____
20–29   _____   50–59   _____
30–39   _____   60 and over _____

Researchers must be very careful about questions that a respondent might consider too personal or that might require him or her to admit activities that other people are likely to condemn. Questions of this type should be worded in such a way as to make them less offensive.

Population All the elements, units, or individuals of interest to researchers for a specific study

Sampling Because the time and the resources available for research are limited, it is almost impossible to investigate all the members of a population. A **population,** or "universe," includes all the elements, units, or individuals that are of interest to researchers for

Sample A limited number of units that represents the characteristics of a total population

Sampling The selection of representative units from a total population

Random sampling A type of sampling in which all the units in a population have an equal chance of appearing in the sample

Stratified sampling A type of sampling in which the population of interest is divided into groups according to a common characteristic or attribute and then a probability sample is conducted within each group

Area sampling A variation of stratified sampling, with geographic areas serving as the segments, or primary units, used in sampling

Quota sampling Nonprobability sampling in which the final choice of respondents is left to the interviewers

Observation methods Research methods in which researchers record respondents' overt behavior, taking note of physical conditions and events

a specific study. For example, for a Gallup poll designed to predict the results of a presidential election, all registered voters in the United States would comprise the population. By systematically choosing a limited number of units—a **sample**—to represent the characteristics of a total population, marketers can project the reactions of a total market or market segment. In the case of the Gallup presidential poll, for example, a representative national sample of several thousand registered voters would be selected and surveyed to project the probable voting outcome. (Of course, the projection would be based on the assumption that no major political events would occur between survey time and the election.) The objective of **sampling** in marketing research, therefore, is to select representative units from a total population. Sampling procedures are used in studying the likelihood of events based on assumptions about the future. Sampling techniques allow marketers to predict buying behavior fairly accurately on the basis of the responses from a representative portion of the population of interest.

When marketers employ **random sampling,** all the units in a population have an equal chance of appearing in the sample. Random sampling is basic probability sampling. The various events that can occur have an equal or known chance of taking place. For example, a specific card in a regulation deck should have a 1/52 probability of being drawn at any one time. Similarly, if each student at a university or college has a unique identification number and these numbers are mixed up in a large basket, each student's number would have a known probability of being selected. Sample units are ordinarily chosen by selecting from a table of random numbers statistically generated so that each digit, zero through nine, will have an equal probability of occurring in each position in the sequence. The sequentially numbered elements of a population are sampled randomly by selecting the units whose numbers appear in the table of random numbers.

In **stratified sampling,** the population of interest is divided into groups according to a common characteristic or attribute, and then a probability sample is conducted within each group. The stratified sample may reduce some of the error that could occur in a simple random sample. By ensuring that each major group or segment of the population receives its proportionate share of sample units, investigators avoid including too many or too few sample units from each group. Usually, samples are stratified when researchers believe that there may be variations among different types of respondents. For example, many political opinion surveys are stratified by sex, race, and age.

Area sampling involves two stages: (1) selecting a probability sample of geographic areas, such as blocks, census tracts, or census enumeration districts, and (2) selecting units or individuals within the selected geographic areas for the sample. This approach is a variation of stratified sampling, with the geographic areas serving as the segments, or primary units, used in sampling. To select the units of individuals within the geographic areas, researchers may choose every *n*th house or unit, or random selection procedures may be used to pick out a given number of units or individuals from a total listing within the selected geographic areas. Area sampling may be used when a complete list of the population is not available.

Quota sampling differs from other forms of sampling in that it is judgmental—that is, the final choice of respondents is left to the interviewers. A study of consumers who wear eyeglasses, for example, may be conducted by interviewing any person who wears eyeglasses. In quota sampling, there are some controls—usually limited to two or three variables, such as age, sex, and education—over the selection of respondents. The controls attempt to ensure that representative categories of respondents are interviewed.

Quota samples are unique because they are not probability samples; not everyone has an equal chance of being selected. Therefore, sampling error cannot be measured statistically. Quota samples are used most often in exploratory studies, when hypotheses are being developed. Often a small quota sample will not be projected to the total population, although the findings may provide valuable insights into a problem. Quota samples are useful when people with some common characteristic are found and questioned about the topic of interest. A probability sample used to study people allergic to cats would be highly inefficient.

Observation Methods In using **observation methods,** researchers record respondents' overt behavior, taking note of physical conditions and events. Direct contact with respondents is avoided; instead, their actions are examined and noted systematically. For example, researchers might use observation methods to answer the question "How long does the average McDonald's restaurant customer have to wait in line before being served?"

Observation may also be combined with interviews. For example, during personal interviews, the condition of a respondent's home or other possessions may be observed and recorded, and demographic information such as race, approximate age, and sex can be confirmed by direct observation.

Data gathered through observation can sometimes be biased if the respondent is aware of the observation process. An observer can be placed in a natural market environment, such as a grocery store, without biasing or influencing shoppers' actions. However, if the presence of a human observer is likely to bias the outcome or if human sensory abilities are inadequate, mechanical means may be used to record behavior. Mechanical observation devices include cameras, recorders, counting machines, and equipment to record physiological changes in individuals. For instance, a special camera can be used to record eye movements of respondents looking at an advertisement; the sequence of reading and the parts of the advertisement that receive greatest attention can be detected. Electronic scanners in supermarkets are mechanical observation devices that offer an exciting opportunity for marketing research. Scanner technology can provide accurate data on sales and consumers' purchase patterns, and marketing researchers may buy such data from the supermarket.

Observation is straightforward and avoids a central problem of survey methods: motivating respondents to state their true feelings or opinions. However, observation tends to be descriptive. When it is the only method of data collection, it may not provide insights into causal relationships. Another drawback is that analyses based on observation are subject to the biases of the observer or the limitations of the mechanical device.

Interpreting Research Findings

Statistical interpretation
An interpretation that focuses on what is typical or what deviates from the average and so indicates how widely responses vary and how they are distributed in relation to the variable being measured

*A*fter collecting data to test their hypotheses, marketers interpret the research findings. Interpretation of the data is easier if marketers carefully plan their data analysis methods early in the research process. They should also allow for continual evaluation of the data during the entire collection period. They can then gain valuable insight into areas that ought to be probed during the formal interpretation. In Figure 5.6, Red Brick Systems promotes its leadership in providing software that allows companies to better interpret their data.

The first step in drawing conclusions from most research is displaying the data in table format. If marketers intend to apply the results to individual categories of the things or people being studied, cross tabulation may be quite useful, especially in tabulating joint occurrences. For example, using the two variables, gender and purchase rates of automobile tires, a cross tabulation could show how men and women differ in purchasing automobile tires.

After the data are tabulated, they must be analyzed. **Statistical interpretation** focuses on what is typical or what deviates from the average. It indicates how widely responses vary and how they are distributed in relation to the variable being measured. Moreover, when they interpret statistics, marketers must take into account estimates of expected error or deviation from the true values of the population. The

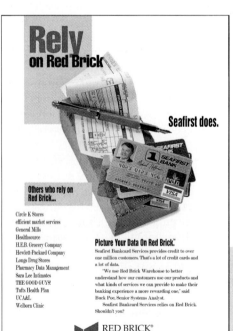

Circle K Stores
efficient market services
General Mills
Healthsource
H.E.B. Grocery Company
Hewlett-Packard Company
Longs Drug Stores
Pharmacy Data Management
Sara Lee Intimates
THE GOOD GUYS!
Tufts Health Plan
UCA&L
Welborn Clinic

Figure 5.6
Interpreting Data   Red Brick Systems provides a relational database management system specialized for data warehousing, which allows users to ask complex business questions.

Figure 5.7
Data Interpretation   SPSS assists in analyzing and interpreting marketing research findings.

analysis of data may lead researchers to accept or reject the hypothesis being studied.

Data require careful interpretation by the marketer. If the results of a study are valid, the decision maker should take action; however, if it is discovered that a question has been incorrectly worded, the results should be ignored. For example, if a study by an electric utility company reveals that 50 percent of its customers believe that meter readers are "friendly," is that finding good, bad, or indifferent? Two important benchmarks help interpret the result: how the 50 percent figure compares with that for competitors and how it compares with a previous time period. Managers must understand the research results and relate the results to a context that permits effective decision making.[32] Statistical interpretation is facilitated by data analysis packages such as SPSS (see Figure 5.7).

Reporting Research Findings

*T*he final step in the marketing research process is reporting the research findings. Before preparing the report, the marketer must take a clear, objective look at the findings to see how well the gathered facts answer the research question or support or negate the hypotheses posed in the beginning. In most cases it is extremely doubtful that the study can provide everything needed to answer the research question. Thus, the researcher must point out the deficiencies, and the reasons for them, in the report.

The report presenting the results is usually a formal, written document. Researchers must allow time for the writing task when they plan and schedule the project. Because the report is a means of communicating with the decision makers who will use the research findings, researchers need to determine beforehand how much detail and supporting data to include. They should keep in mind that corporate executives prefer reports that are short, clear, and simply expressed. Often researchers will give their summary and recommendations first, especially if decision makers do not have time to study how the results were obtained. A technical report allows its users to analyze data and interpret recommendations because it describes the research methods and procedures and the most important data gathered. Thus researchers must recognize the needs and expectations of the report user and adapt to them.

When marketing decision makers have a firm grasp of research methods and procedures, they are better able to integrate reported findings and personal experience. If marketers can spot limitations in research from reading the report, then personal experience assumes additional importance in the decision-making process. For example, it is important for marketing decision makers who are studying potential markets in Russia to know that marketing research in Russia is made extremely difficult by the magnitude of product shortages. In Russia the last brand purchased is more of an indication of availability than of brand preference. In fact, brand names have little meaning to the average Russian consumer, although country of origin does have significance.[33]

A major problem comes from bias and distortion because the researcher wants to obtain favorable results. Consider the following examples: (1) Levi Strauss purportedly asked students which clothes would be most popular this year. Ninety percent said Levis 501 jeans. However, Levi's were apparently the only jeans on the list for students to select. (2) A Gallup poll sponsored by the disposable diaper industry asked: "It is estimated that disposable diapers account for less than 2 percent of the trash in today's landfills. In contrast, beverage containers, third-class mail, and yard waste are estimated to account for about 21 percent of the trash in landfills. Given this, in your opinion, would it be fair to ban disposable diapers?" Eighty-four percent of those interviewed said no.[34] These findings of both surveys would be positive, but of what value?

These examples illustrate research conducted for public consumption and to further the interests of the parties conducting the research. Most research for internal decision making is conducted objectively. Marketing researchers want to know about behavior and opinions, and they want accurate data to help in making decisions. Careful wording of questions is very important because a biased or emotional word can change the results tremendously. Marketing research and marketing information systems provide the organization with accurate and reliable customer feedback, without which a marketer cannot understand the dynamics of the marketplace. As managers recognize its benefits, they assign marketing research a much larger role in decision making.

Marketers who cannot understand basic statistical assumptions and data gathering procedures may misuse research findings. Consequently, report writers should be aware of the backgrounds and research abilities of those who will rely on the report in making decisions. Clear explanations presented in plain language make it easier for decision makers to apply the findings and diminish the chances of a report being misused or ignored. Talking with potential research users before writing a report can help researchers supply information that will indeed improve decision making.

The Importance of Ethical Marketing Research

*M**arketing* research and systematic information gathering make successful marketing more likely. In fact, many companies, and even entire industries, have failed because of a lack of marketing research. Marketing managers and other professionals are relying more and more on marketing research to make better decisions. Clearly, marketing research and information systems are vital to marketing decision making. It is therefore essential that professional standards be established by which such research may be judged reliable.

Professional standards are necessary in marketing research because of the ethical and legal issues that develop in gathering data. In addition, the relationships between research suppliers, such as marketing research agencies, and the marketing managers who make strategy decisions require ethical behavior. Organizations like the Marketing Research Association have developed guidelines and practices to promote ethical marketing research. For codes of conduct to be effective, they must instruct those who participate in marketing research activities how to avoid misconduct. Table 5.6, for example, recommends the explicit steps an interviewer should follow when introducing a questionnaire.

The ethical and legal considerations of telephone and Internet privacy are taking shape slowly. The use of current technology such as E-mail surveys may create privacy issues that both professional marketing research associations and marketing research companies will have to address in the future.

Because so many parties are involved in the marketing research process, developing shared ethical concern is difficult. The relationships among respondents who cooperate and share information, interviewing companies, marketing research agencies that manage projects, and organizations that use the data are interdependent and complex. Trust and the perceived quality of interaction between information users and information providers have been found to contribute significantly to research utilization.[35] Ethical conflict typically occurs because the parties involved in the marketing research process often have different objectives. For example, the organization that uses data tends to be result-oriented, and success is often based on performance rather than a set of standards. On the other hand, a data-gathering subcontractor is evaluated based on the ability to follow a specific set of standards or rules. The relationships among all participants in marketing research must be understood so that decision making becomes ethical. Without clear understanding and agreement, including mutual adoption of standards, ethical conflict will lead to mistrust and questionable research results.[36]

Table 5.6   Guidelines for Questionnaire Introduction by Interviewer
Questionnaire introduction should: • Allow for the interviewer to introduce him/herself by name.   • State the name of the research company.   • Indicate this is a marketing research project.   • Explain there will be no sales involved.   • Note the general topic of discussion (if this is a problem in a "blind" study, a statement such as "consumer opinion" is acceptable).   • State the likely duration of the interview.   • Assure the anonymity of the respondent and confidentiality of all answers.   • State the honorarium if applicable (for many business-to-business and medical studies this is done up front for both qualitative and quantitative studies).   • Reassure the respondent with a statement such as, "There are no right or wrong answers, so please give thoughtful and honest answers to each question" (recommended by many clients).   Source: Reprinted with permission of Marketing Research Association, P.O. Box 230, Rocky Hill, CT 06067-0230, (860)257-4008.

Summary

When implementing the marketing concept, marketers need information about the characteristics, needs, and wants of their target markets. Marketing research and information systems that furnish practical, unbiased information help firms avoid the assumptions and misunderstandings that could lead to poor marketing performance. Indeed, information is often the key to a successful marketing strategy.

Marketing research is the systematic design, collection, interpretation, and reporting of information to help marketers solve specific marketing problems or take advantage of marketing opportunities. It is a process for gathering information that decision makers do not have. A marketing information system (MIS) is the framework for gathering and managing information from sources both inside and outside an organization. An MIS provides a continuous flow of information about prices, advertising expenditures, sales, competition, consumer behavior, and distribution expenses. The main difference between marketing research and marketing information systems is that marketing research is an information gathering process for specific situations, whereas an MIS provides continuous data input. The real value of marketing research information is measured by improvements in a marketer's ability to make decisions. Marketers treat information like other resources utilized by the firm and weigh the costs of obtaining information against the benefits derived.

Technology and databases allow marketers to retrieve a variety of information that is useful in making marketing decisions. Databases may include newspaper articles, company news releases, government reports, economic data, or bibliographies and are typically accessed electronically, through computer systems. Many firms install electronic bulletin boards to communicate

with employees and customers and to develop information for the marketing information system. Online information services and the Internet also enable marketers to communicate with customers and obtain information.

The five steps of the marketing research process are (1) defining and locating problems, (2) designing the research project, (3) collecting data, (4) interpreting research findings, and (5) reporting the findings.

Defining and locating the problem, the first step toward finding a solution or launching a research study, focuses on uncovering the nature and boundaries of a negative, or positive, situation or question. After defining the problem, marketing researchers must formulate an overall plan for obtaining needed information—that is, design the project. They must also ensure that the research techniques are both reliable and valid. A technique is reliable if it produces almost identical results in successive repeated trials; it is valid if it measures what it is supposed to measure and not something else. The objective statement of a marketing project should include hypotheses. A hypothesis is an informed guess or assumption about a problem or set of circumstances. It is based on insight and knowledge gleaned from earlier research studies and other sources. The type of hypothesis being tested dictates which of three approaches will be used for gathering general data: exploratory, descriptive, or causal studies.

For the third step, collecting data, two types of data are available: primary and secondary. Primary data are observed and recorded or collected directly from respondents. Secondary data may be collected from an organization's database and other internal sources; from periodicals, government publications, and unpublished sources. Methods for collecting primary data include surveys, sampling, and observation. Survey methods range from mail surveys, telephone surveys, E-mail surveys, personal interview surveys, and shopping mall intercept interviews to on-site computer interviews, focus-group interviews, and in-home interviews. Questionnaires are instruments used to obtain information that meets the study's data requirements. A carefully constructed questionnaire is essential to the success of any survey. Sampling involves selecting representative units from a total population. Four sampling techniques are random sampling, stratified sampling, area sampling, and quota sampling. In using observation methods, researchers record respondents' overt behavior and take note of physical conditions and events but avoid direct contact with respondents. They may use mechanical observation devices, such as cameras, recorders, and other equipment.

To apply research data to decision making, marketers must interpret and report their findings properly—the final two steps in the research process. The first step in drawing conclusions is displaying the data in table format. After tabulation, data must be analyzed. Statistical interpretation focuses on what is typical or what deviates from the average. After interpreting the research findings, the researchers must prepare a report on the findings that the decision makers can understand and use. Researchers must also take care to avoid bias and distortion.

Marketing research and systematic information gathering increase the probability of successful marketing. Indeed, marketing research is essential for planning and developing marketing strategies. Consequently, eliminating unethical marketing research practices and establishing generally acceptable procedures for conducting research are important goals. Because so many parties are involved in the marketing research process, developing shared ethical concern is difficult. It is thus crucial that the relationships among all participants in marketing research, as well as their different objectives, be clearly understood. Mutual trust and quality of interaction between users and providers of information help considerably in the undertaking and utilizing of research.

IMPORTANT TERMS

Marketing research	Reliability	Primary data	Random sampling
Marketing information system (MIS)	Validity	Secondary data	Stratified sampling
	Hypothesis	Survey methods	Area sampling
Database	Exploratory studies	Population	Quota sampling
Single-source data	Descriptive studies	Sample	Observation methods
Problem definition	Causal studies	Sampling	Statistical interpretation

DISCUSSION AND REVIEW QUESTIONS

1. What is a marketing information system and what should it provide? How is the value of a marketing information system measured?
2. Where are data for a marketing information system obtained? Give examples of internal and external data.
3. Define database. What is its purpose and what does it include?
4. How can marketers use online services and the Internet to obtain information for decision making?
5. Name the five steps in the marketing research process.
6. What is the difference between defining a research problem and developing a hypothesis?
7. Describe the different types of studies in marketing research and indicate when they should be used.
8. What are the major limitations of using secondary data to solve marketing problems?
9. In what situation would it be best to use random sampling? quota sampling? stratified or area sampling?
10. Make some suggestions for ways to encourage respondents to cooperate in mail surveys.
11. If a survey of all homes with listed telephone numbers is conducted, what sampling design should be used?
12. Describe some marketing problems that could be solved through information gained from observation.

APPLICATION QUESTIONS

1. After observing traffic patterns, Bashas' Markets repositioned the greeting card section in its stores, and card sales increased substantially. When considering marketing research, what information from consumers might be useful in increasing sales for the following types of companies?

   a. furniture stores
   b. gasoline outlets/service stations
   c. investment companies
   d. medical clinics

2. When a company wants to conduct research, a problem or potential problem must be recognized or

possible opportunities must exist to market its goods or services. Choose a company in your city that you think might benefit from a research project. Develop a research question and outline a method to approach this inquiry. Explain why you think the research question is relevant to the organization and why the particular methodology is suited to the question and the company.

3. Input for marketing information systems can come from internal or external sources. Nielsen Marketing Research is the largest provider of single-source marketing research in the world. Indicate two firms or companies in your city that might utilize internal sources and two that would benefit from external sources and explain why they would benefit. Suggest the type of information each should gather.

4. Texas Instruments utilizes an internal computer network bulletin board on which employees can make suggestions or air complaints. Choose a company with which you are familiar and write a memo to the president that would persuade him or her to install a similar system in that company.

5. Suppose that you were opening a health insurance brokerage firm and wanted it to market your services to small businesses with under fifty employees. Determine which database for marketing information you would use in your marketing efforts and tell why you would use it.

Case 5.1 Marketing Research for V-8 Vegetable Juice, Maidenform, and AT&T 800 Service Advertising

Marketing research is the systematic design, collection, interpretation, and reporting of information to help marketers solve specific problems or take advantage of market opportunities. The development of an advertising campaign involves a series of steps starting with the identification of the right target market. Advertisers research and analyze various audiences or markets to determine factors such as buying behavior, geographic distribution of the target group, demographic factors such as age, income, sex, and education, and consumer attitudes regarding purchase and use of both the advertiser's products and competing products. The exact kinds of information an organization finds useful depend on the type of product being advertised, the characteristics of the target market, and the type and amount of competition. Generally, the more an advertiser knows about the target market, the more likely the firm is to develop an effective advertising campaign. When the advertising target is not precisely identified and properly analyzed, the campaign may not succeed. The following case examples show how marketing research improved advertising for three products.

Case One: Campbell's V-8 Vegetable Juice

Marketing research was undertaken to develop a new advertising campaign to reverse the trend of decreasing sales. Research indicated that consumers needed to be reminded to purchase V-8 because of competition and the many choices available to beverage purchasers. In-depth consumer interviews probed consumers' childhood memories to try to understand their thinking about V-8. Consumers were asked to express their thoughts and feelings about the V-8 brand. The technique was to ask the same question over and over again: "What do you really want in a V-8?" Four factors came out of the research: the overall healthiness of V-8;

V-8 is healthy relative to other types of foods; V-8 contains beta carotene (disease preventive); and the vegetable goodness of V-8. A test TV commercial was produced using the research results.

Marketing research on test TV commercials indicated that the four-factor strategy in an actual advertising situation was confusing to consumers. Therefore, a new creative concept was developed. Additional research recast the message. Advertising needed to focus on the product as healthy, while conveying a simpler, clearer message about V-8. When the message was simplified to stress taste and health benefits, the advertising campaign resulted in double-digit increases in sales as long as it ran. The key to success in this case was marketing research to help refine a message so that it was simple, easy to understand, and had a call for action to purchase the product.

Case Two: Maidenform

Historically, Maidenform felt certain that it stood for women's self-esteem. Nevertheless, the company needed to know more about the Maidenform consumer and her purchasing habits. Maidenform wanted to do a broad-based check on who buys lingerie and why. The company began with mall intercepts. Interviewers went into shopping malls and spoke to over 3,000 women between 18 and 65 years of age who had purchased two or more bras recently. Each interview lasted 45 minutes, long enough for a thorough discussion of lingerie purchasing behavior.

The results were surprising. There turned out to be far more lapsed purchasers of Maidenform than current purchasers. Many women had heard of Maidenform but had never bought a Maidenform bra and had little perception of the product. This finding amazed Maidenform product managers. Startling numbers of women were not aware of Maidenform at all or associated the name more with their mothers than with contemporary lifestyles. The company wrongly assumed that Maidenform was a highly regarded brand name with fabulous, obvious attributes. Maidenform was so overwhelmed by the findings that the researchers conducted a second study to clarify the results.

After analyzing the second confirming study, the company decided on a new creative strategy to promote its products. Generating trial of the product was determined to be the most important objective based on the research. Confidence and self-esteem were considered the best positioning message for advertising.

Case Three: AT&T 800 Numbers

Prior to 1993, 800 numbers were assigned by long-distance carrier, but since then, 800 numbers have been portable; that is, users can take their number and change carriers. The 800 number business is worth several billion dollars to AT&T, Sprint, and MCI. Therefore, a market share loss of even a few percentage points could mean millions of dollars of loss to AT&T. Following the change in regulations, AT&T decided to do research to determine which hot buttons might cause its customers to either change companies or stay with AT&T. If they could anticipate what their competitors might do, then they could better defend and protect their market share. Marketing research was needed to identify a pool of messages that could work to retain customers.

A strategic understanding of the 800 number concept was developed from personal interviews with business customers using 800 service. The design was to gain insights into how AT&T should respond to the competition's expected tactics. The research firm went

to Boston, where large, medium, and small companies could be interviewed. Business executives were surveyed to get a sense of what AT&T's strongest and most effective message could be to keep its 800 customers. Without an effective marketing research effort to determine how to preempt competitors' moves, AT&T could not hope to develop a strong advertising campaign.

The research found that reliability was very important; therefore, promotional messages were developed to show what AT&T does to maintain reliability and depict the cost to a company of a breakdown in reliability. AT&T produced twenty-two TV commercials, which were tested along with their competitors' ads among 800 service customers. By doing in-depth interviews with executives and showing them potential commercial messages, they were able to confirm that reliability was the key factor triggering business use of AT&T's 800 service. Acting on this research, AT&T achieved a major victory. They retained most of their 800 users and made millions of dollars. The whole mindset of the study was an attempt to hold on to existing customers, but the research actually helped AT&T gain new customers.[37]

Questions for Discussion

1. How did marketing research help increase the sales of V-8?
2. What surprising discovery did research reveal to Maidenform? Why had this information been overlooked by managers?
3. Of what value were the personal interviews conducted with business executives in formulating the AT&T advertising message?

Case 5.2 Chrysler Reinvents Itself Through Primary Research

Chrysler Corporation manufactures cars, trucks, and minivans under the Chrysler, Dodge, Plymouth, Jeep, and Eagle insignias. In the last few years, the firm has been responsible for such acclaimed vehicles as the Dodge Intrepid, Chrysler Concorde, Eagle Vision, Jeep Grand Cherokee, and Viper sports car. These, along with the company's best-selling minivans, propelled the firm to profits of $3.7 billion on sales of $52.2 billion in 1994, an increase of 54 percent and 20 percent, respectively, from the previous year. Although Chrysler continues to lag behind General Motors and Ford in terms of sales, it has come a long way since it nearly failed and had to be bailed out by the federal government in the 1970s. After extremely difficult times in the 1970s and 1980s, Chrysler set out to reinvent itself for

the 1990s by restructuring to become more efficient and shifting its focus to the needs of its consumers.

One key to the turnaround at Chrysler was its restructuring into "platform teams"—empowered teams of workers from all levels of the organization focused on producing a certain type of vehicle. The four platform teams created—one each for large cars, small cars, minivans, and Jeeps/trucks—were not arranged along departmental or functional lines, as they might have been in the past. Instead, they were formed in accordance with the input of actual customers who told Chrysler what they wanted in a new vehicle.

To shift toward a customer orientation, Chrysler implemented a highly integrated marketing research effort, employing multiple forms of primary data collection aimed at putting the customer first. For example, it now routinely brings together groups of potential customers in focus groups and shows them small-scale models and drawings of future vehicles in order to gauge reactions to product ideas at the earliest possible stages of development. When introduced, this practice marked a radical change; previously, vehicles were designed and then shown to the customer for evaluation in near-final form. Research was geared primarily toward creating advertising and other promotional appeals to market the product. The new focus on gathering primary data from customers at the earliest possible time enables Chrysler to avoid costly product modifications. Even more important, the automaker isn't trying to sell customers something they do not want.

Chrysler also seeks to collect consumer input in the early stages of product development in other ways. For example, during industry trade shows, the company solicits comments from prospective customers about the potential models on display. Customer letters to the company are taken seriously, as are various focus-group sessions, which are taped and later reviewed by a wide range of Chrysler employees. One series of focus-group interviews dealing with customer complaints about auto dealerships led Chrysler to implement an incentive program for dealers. The manufacturer now rewards dealers not on the basis of sales volume, but rather on their ability to satisfy customers based on levels of CSI— customer satisfaction index— scores.

Collecting primary marketing research information does not stop at the product design stage. The company also contacts buyers of its vehicles thirty days and again one year after the sale to ensure that the vehicle is receiving proper service. Through such inquiry, Chrysler can also uncover any common problems that certain vehicles may be experiencing. For example, after owners of Chrysler minivans complained about awkward-to-use power-window switches and easy-to-bump power-door locks, the company spent $300,000 to move the window switches and safeguard the locks on its minivans—even though a full model redesign was just a year away. Poor rankings of several Chrysler vehicles by J. D. Power & Associates and *Consumer Reports* also spurred Chrysler to spend millions to boost product quality and design higher levels of quality into vehicles in development. These efforts show that marketing research activities at the new Chrysler are directed not just to make a sale. Rather, they are designed to garner useful information that helps build long-term relationships with customers.

As Chrysler was reinventing itself, it cast its information net beyond consumers. To gain competitive information, it bought products of other automakers, disassembled them, and carefully analyzed how they were built. For example, Chrysler engineers dissected the popular Toyota Camry to learn how one of the top-selling models in the class in which its New Yorker and LHS models would be competing was constructed. Their work with the Camry taught Chrysler not only what to do, but also what *not* to do. They concluded, for instance, that injecting foam into door moldings to deaden road noise was a useless and potentially costly activity.

Gathering primary data from parts and equipment suppliers is another vital aspect of the new Chrysler. Whereas in the past Chrysler often told its suppliers what to make and how to make it, it now welcomes suppliers' input as to what might work best in certain situations. Its relationships with suppliers such as Johnson Controls (seats) and the Prince Corporation (headliners) were once on an "us" versus "them" basis. Now they have established long-term interactive partnerships to facilitate the timely and efficient production of vehicles according to the needs of Chrysler's customers.

Chrysler's new structure and customer focus are having a definite impact on its bottom line. For example, the Dodge Intrepid, Chrysler Concorde, and Eagle Vision took just forty months to go from conception to showroom floor, a full year faster than previous models. Chrysler's hot new Plymouth Prowler, a retro-style, two-seat roadster, went through development in record time and at a relatively low cost of $75 million. Moreover, the Prowler—expected to sell for $35,000 when it goes on sale in 1997—is the product of unprecedented cooperation between the company and its suppliers. Chrysler executives hope the sleek roadster will inject new life and excitement into the Plymouth brand, which research indicates has little identity among the first-time car buyers that Chrysler desires. Additionally, Chrysler's restructuring efforts have shaved some $3 billion from its operating costs, boosting profits.

Chrysler's new customer orientation, based on the continual gathering of timely primary data, has altered marketing at the company. It is no longer primarily a post-production, and thus highly sales-oriented, undertaking. Instead, marketing has vital input into final product decisions. Through marketing research efforts, marketing has become the driving force behind Chrysler's phenomenal resurgence. Its success stems from allowing the voice of the customer to be heard throughout the product design, sales, and service cycle.[38]

Questions for Discussion

1. What methods of primary research collection does Chrysler use to design and market its new automobiles?
2. What survey methods are employed by Chrysler? Evaluate their success.
3. Discuss how the use of primary research has been integrated into the new corporate atmosphere at Chrysler.

Chapter 6

Consumer Buying Behavior

OBJECTIVES

- To understand what consumer markets and consumer buying behavior are

- To learn about the types of consumer problem-solving processes

- To recognize the stages of the consumer buying decision process

- To explore how personal factors may affect the consumer buying decision process

- To learn about the psychological factors that may affect the consumer buying decision process

- To examine the social factors that influence the consumer buying decision process

For busy families, Boston Market means home cooking away from home.

*T*he last thing Mom and Dad want to do after working all day is race around the kitchen cooking dinner, so they decide to pick up the kids and go out to eat. Dad wants chicken, but the kids don't; and Mom wants everyone to have a healthy meal. They decide to eat at Boston Market®. The National Restaurant Association recently reported that Americans eat about four meals a week away from home, but like this family, a growing number of them want to combine the convenience of fast food with the variety of sit-down restaurants. Observing these changing consumer desires, the 900-restaurant chain Boston Chicken® changed its name to Boston Market and expanded its menu so that Mom, Dad, and the kids could all get what they want at one restaurant.

When Boston Chicken asked its customers, "If you hadn't come here, where would you have gone?" more than half replied, "Home to cook." The company's executives are determined to give these hungry customers what they want. To promote its new broader menu, the chain scratched the word *chicken* from its name and *rotisserie* from its sign, replacing them with *market* and *home style meals*. To live up to its new slogan, Boston Market began offering more than rotisserie chicken, serving double-glazed smoked ham, boneless roasted turkey, even meatloaf. Instead of the ho-hum side dishes such as French fries offered by competitors, they added zucchini marinara and pasta salad. Recently, Boston Market expanded to hand-carved meats and deli-type sandwiches. Some outlets even sold whole and half hams at Easter, tempting many customers to zip in and pick up no-fuss holiday dinners. Declared one Boston Market executive, "We have the food for people who want to make believe they are having a home-cooked meal."

The success of home-style, quick-service restaurants like the Boston Market is influencing the entire food industry. There is hardly a supermarket that doesn't offer some variety of cooked food, from sweet-and-sour meatballs to barbecued ribs. Even traditional fast-food franchises are experimenting with family meals. KFC, for example, added reduced-fat rotisserie chicken and healthier side dishes such as squash. Because of the growing number of two-career families and the increasingly hurried lifestyles of many Americans, the battle for the largest share of the $80-billion dollar meal-replacement segment will continue heating up. Its knack for providing convenience and tasty food is likely to make Boston Market one of the winners.[1]

132

Marketers at successful companies like Boston Market make a considerable effort to determine their customers' needs and gain a better grasp of their customers' buying behavior. Marketers attempt to understand consumer buying behavior for several reasons. First, consumers' reactions to an organization's marketing efforts have great impact on its success. Second, understanding how consumers make purchasing decisions helps marketers to create marketing mixes that satisfy customers. Third, by understanding the factors that influence consumers, marketers are in a better position to predict how consumers will respond to marketing strategies.

In this chapter we begin by defining consumer markets and consumer buying behavior. We examine how the customer's level of involvement affects the type of problem solving employed and then discuss the types of consumer problem-solving processes. We then analyze the major stages of the consumer buying decision process, beginning with problem recognition, information search, and evaluation of alternatives and proceeding through purchase and postpurchase evaluation. Next, we examine personal factors—demographic, lifestyle, and situational—that influence purchasing decisions. We go on to consider psychological factors influencing purchasing decisions: perception, motives, learning, attitudes, and personality and self-concept. We conclude with a discussion of social factors that influence buying behavior. These include roles and family influences, reference groups and opinion leaders, social classes, and culture and subcultures.

Consumer Markets and Consumer Buying Behavior

Market An aggregate of individuals and/or organizations that have needs for products in a product class and have the ability, willingness, and authority to purchase such products

Consumer market
Purchasers and household members who intend to consume or benefit from the purchased products and who do not buy products for the main purpose of making profits

A **market** is an aggregate of individuals and/or organizations that have needs for products in a product class and have the ability, willingness, and authority to purchase these products. Markets can be divided into two categories: consumer markets and organizational, or industrial, markets. (Organizational markets are discussed in Chapter 7.) This division is based on the characteristics of the individuals and groups that make up specific markets and the purposes for which they buy products. A **consumer market** consists of purchasers and household members who intend to consume or benefit from the purchased products and who do not buy products for the main purpose of making profits. Thus we belong to numerous consumer markets for products such as housing, food, clothing, vehicles, personal services, appliances, furniture, and recreational equipment. **Consumer buying behavior** is the decision processes and acts of ultimate consumers involved in buying and using products.[2]

Types of Consumer Problem-Solving Processes

Consumer buying behavior
The decision processes and acts of ultimate consumers involved in buying and using products

Level of involvement
An individual's intensity of interest in a product and the importance of the product for that person

A consumer generally tries to acquire and maintain an assortment of products that satisfy his or her current and future needs. To do so, a consumer engages in problem solving. For example, to solve problems, people purchase products such as food, clothing, shelter, medical care, education, recreation, or transportation. When making these purchases, they engage in different types of problem-solving processes. The amount of effort, both mental and physical, that buyers expend in solving problems varies considerably. A major determinant of the type of problem-solving process employed depends on the customer's **level of involvement**—the individual's degree of interest in a product and the importance he or she places on this product. High-involvement products tend to be those that are visible to others (such as clothing, furniture, or automobiles) and products that are expensive. Expensive bicycles, for example, are usually high-involvement products. Low-involvement products tend to be those that are less expensive and have less social risk associated with them (such as many grocery items). When a person's interest in a product category is ongoing and long-term, it is referred to as *enduring involvement*. In contrast, *situational involvement* is temporary and dynamic and results from a particular set of circumstances. Involvement level, as well as other factors, affects a consumer's selection of one of three types of consumer problem solving: routinized response behavior, limited problem solving, or extended problem solving.

Figure 6.1
Routinized Response Behavior
Most buyers employ routinized response behavior when purchasing cereal.

A consumer uses **routinized response behavior** when buying frequently purchased, low-cost items needing very little search-and-decision effort. When buying such items, a consumer may prefer a particular brand but is familiar with several brands in the product class and views more than one as being acceptable. Typically, low-involvement products are bought through routinized response behavior almost automatically. Most buyers, for example, do not spend much time or effort selecting a soft drink or a brand of cereal (see Figure 6.1). If the nearest soft drink machine does not offer Sprite, they will likely choose 7Up instead.

Buyers engage in **limited problem solving** when buying products occasionally and when they need to obtain information about an unfamiliar brand in a familiar product category. This type of problem solving requires a moderate amount of time for information gathering and deliberation. For example, if Procter & Gamble introduces an improved Tide laundry detergent, buyers will seek additional information about the new product, perhaps by asking a friend who has used the product or watching a commercial, before making a trial purchase.

The most complex type of problem solving, **extended problem solving,** occurs when unfamiliar, expensive, or infrequently bought products are purchased—for instance, cars, homes, or a college education. The buyer uses many criteria to evaluate alternative brands or choices and spends much time seeking information and deciding on the purchase. Extended problem solving is frequently used for purchasing high-involvement products.

Purchase of a particular product does not always elicit the same type of problem-solving process. In some instances we engage in extended problem solving the first time we buy a certain product but find that limited problem solving suffices when we buy it again. If a routinely purchased, formerly satisfying brand no longer pleases us, we may use limited or extended problem solving to switch to a new brand. Thus, if we notice that the gasoline brand we normally buy is making our automobile's engine knock, we may seek out a higher-octane brand through limited problem solving. Most consumers occasionally make purchases solely on impulse, and not on the basis of any of these three problem-solving processes. **Impulse buying** involves no conscious planning but rather results from a powerful urge to buy something immediately.

Extended problem solving, as already indicated, requires a great deal of conscious effort. We now examine the specific steps by which a consumer makes purchase decisions when engaged in extended problem solving.

Routinized response behavior A type of consumer problem-solving process used when buying frequently purchased, low-cost items that require very little search-and-decision effort

Limited problem solving A type of consumer problem-solving process that buyers engage in when they purchase products occasionally and need to obtain information about an unfamiliar brand in a familiar product category

Extended problem solving A type of consumer problem-solving process employed when unfamiliar, expensive, or infrequently bought products are purchased

Impulse buying An unplanned buying behavior involving a powerful urge to buy something immediately

Consumer Buying Decision Process

Consumer buying decision process A five-stage purchase decision process that includes problem recognition, information search, evaluation of alternatives, purchase, and postpurchase evaluation

The **consumer buying decision process,** shown in Figure 6.2, includes five stages: (1) problem recognition, (2) information search, (3) evaluation of alternatives, (4) purchase, and (5) postpurchase evaluation. Before we examine each stage, consider these important points. First, the actual act of purchasing is only one stage in a process, and usually not the first stage. Second, even though we indicate that a purchase occurs, not all decision processes lead to a purchase; individuals may end the process at

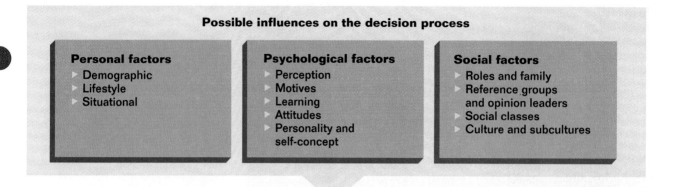

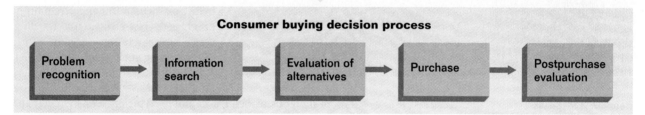

Figure 6.2
Consumer Buying Decision Process and Possible Influences on the Process

any stage. Finally, all consumer decisions do not always include all five stages. Persons engaged in extended problem solving usually go through all stages of this decision process, whereas those engaged in limited problem solving and routinized response behavior may omit some stages.

■ *Problem Recognition*

Problem recognition occurs when a buyer becomes aware of a difference between a desired state and an actual condition. For example, consider a marketing student who wants a reliable advanced calculator for use in a finance course. When her old calculator breaks down, she recognizes that a difference exists between the desired state—a reliable calculator—and the actual condition—a nonworking calculator. She therefore decides to buy a new calculator.

The speed of consumer problem recognition can be quite rapid or rather slow. Sometimes a person has a problem or need but is unaware of it. Marketers use sales personnel, advertising, and packaging to help trigger recognition of such needs or problems. For example, a university bookstore may advertise business and scientific calculators in the university newspaper at the beginning of the term. Students who see the advertisement may recognize that they need calculators for their course work. As shown in Figure 6.3, the Austin Gym helps individuals to recognize that they may have weight and fitness problems and suggests the use of its facilities as a solution to these problems.

■ *Information Search*

After recognizing the problem or need, buyers (if continuing the decision process) search for product information that helps resolve the problem or satisfy the need. For example, the above-mentioned student, after recognizing the need for a calculator, may search for information about different types and brands of calculators. She acquires information over time from her surroundings. However, the information's impact depends on how the consumer interprets it.

There are two aspects to an information search. In the **internal search,** buyers search their memories for information about products that might solve the problem. If they cannot retrieve enough information from their memory for a decision, they seek additional information in an **external search.** The external search may focus on communication

Internal search An information search in which buyers search their memories for information about products that might solve their problem

External search An information search in which buyers seek information from outside sources

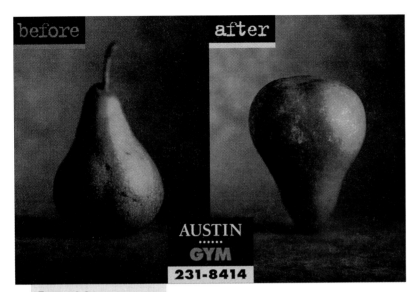

Figure 6.3
Recognizing a Problem
Through this advertisement, the Austin Gym is attempting to help individuals recognize weight and fitness problems.

with friends or relatives, comparison of available brands and prices, marketer-dominated sources, and/or public sources. An individual's personal contacts—friends, relatives, associates—often are credible sources of information because the consumer trusts and respects them. A consumer study has shown that word-of-mouth communication has a stronger impact on consumer judgments about products than printed communication, unless the buyer has a well-defined prior impression of a product or unless printed information about a product is extremely negative.[3] Utilizing marketer-dominated sources of information—such as salespersons, advertising, package labeling, and in-store demonstrations and displays—typically does not require much effort on the consumer's part. Buyers also obtain information from public sources—for instance, government reports, news presentations, publications such as *Consumer Reports,* and reports from product-testing organizations. Consumers frequently view information from public sources as highly credible because of its factual and unbiased nature.

Repetition, a technique well known to advertisers, increases consumer learning of information. When seeing or hearing an advertising message for the first time, recipients may not grasp all its important details but learn more details as the message is repeated. Nevertheless, even when commercials are initially effective, repetition eventually may cause wearout, meaning that consumers pay less attention to the commercial and respond to it less favorably than they did at first.

The format in which information is transmitted to the buyer may also determine its use. Information can be presented verbally, numerically, or visually. For a wide variety of consumer tasks, pictures are remembered better than words, and the combination of pictures and words further enhances learning.[4] Consequently, marketers pay great attention to creation of the visual components of their advertising materials.

A successful information search yields a group of brands that a buyer views as possible alternatives. This group of products is sometimes called the buyer's *evoked set.* For example, an evoked set of calculators might include those made by Texas Instruments, Hewlett-Packard, Sharp, and Casio.

■ *Evaluation of Alternatives*

Evaluative criteria Objective and subjective characteristics that are important to a buyer

To assess the products in his or her evoked set, the buyer uses **evaluative criteria,** which are objective (such as an EPA mileage rating) and subjective (such as style) characteristics that are important to a buyer. For example, one calculator buyer may want a solar-powered unit with a large display and large buttons, whereas another may have no size preferences but happens to dislike solar-powered calculators. The buyer also assigns a certain level of importance to each criterion; some features and characteristics carry more weight than others. Using the criteria, a buyer rates and eventually ranks brands in the evoked set. The evaluation stage may yield no brand the buyer is willing to purchase; in that case, a further information search may be necessary.

Marketers influence consumers' evaluation by *framing* the alternatives—that is, by the manner in which the marketer describes the alternative and its attributes. Framing can make a characteristic seem more important to a consumer and facilitate its recall from memory. For example, by stressing a car's superior safety features over those of a competitor's, a car maker can direct consumers' attention toward this point of superiority. Framing probably influences the decision processes of inexperienced buyers more than those of experienced ones. If the evaluation of alternatives yields one or more brands that the consumer is willing to buy, the consumer is ready to move on to the next stage of the decision process—the purchase.

■ *Purchase*

In the purchase stage, the consumer chooses the product or brand to be bought. Selection is based on the outcome of the previous evaluation stage and on other dimensions. Product availability may influence which brand is purchased. For example, if the brand ranked highest in evaluation is unavailable, the buyer may purchase the brand ranked second. If a consumer wants a black pair of Nikes and cannot find them in her size, she might buy a black pair of Reeboks.

During this stage, the buyer also picks the seller from whom he or she will buy the product. The choice of seller may affect final product selection—and so may the terms of sale, which, if negotiable, are determined during the purchase decision stage. Other issues such as price, delivery, warranties, maintenance agreements, installation, and credit arrangements are settled. Finally, the actual purchase takes place during this stage, unless the consumer terminates the buying decision process before reaching that point.

■ *Postpurchase Evaluation*

After the purchase, buyers begin evaluating the product to ascertain if its actual performance meets expected levels. Many criteria used in evaluating alternatives are applied again during postpurchase evaluation. The outcome of this stage is either satisfaction or dissatisfaction, which influences whether consumers complain, communicate with other possible buyers, and repurchase the brand or product.

Cognitive dissonance
A buyer's doubts shortly after a purchase about whether it was the right decision

Shortly after purchase of an expensive product, postpurchase evaluation may result in **cognitive dissonance**—doubts in the buyer's mind about whether the right decision was made in purchasing the product. For example, after buying a pair of $169 in-line skates, a person may feel guilty about the purchase or wonder whether she purchased the right brand and quality. Cognitive dissonance is most likely to arise when a person has recently bought an expensive, high-involvement product that does not have some of the desirable features of the unpurchased competing brands. A buyer experiencing cognitive dissonance may attempt to return the product or seek positive information about it to justify that choice. Marketers sometimes attempt to reduce cognitive dissonance by having salespeople telephone recent purchasers to make sure that they are satisfied with their new purchases. At times, recent buyers are sent results of studies showing that consumers are very satisfied with the brand.

As shown in Figure 6.2, three major categories of influences are believed to affect the consumer buying decision process: personal, psychological, and social factors. The remainder of this chapter focuses on these factors. Although we discuss each major factor separately, their effects on the consumer decision process are interrelated.

Personal Factors Influencing the Buying Decision Process

Personal factors
Factors that are unique to a particular individual

*P*ersonal factors are those unique to a particular person. Numerous personal factors influence purchasing decisions. In this section we consider three types of them: demographic, lifestyle, and situational.

■ *Demographic Factors*

Demographic factors
Individual characteristics such as age, sex, race, ethnicity, income, family life cycle, and occupation

Demographic factors are individual characteristics, such as age, sex, race, ethnicity, income, family life cycle, and occupation. (These and other characteristics are discussed in Chapter 8 as possible variables for market segmentation purposes.) Demographic factors have a bearing on who is involved in family decision making. For example, children are assuming more responsibility and taking part in more purchase decisions, from groceries to clothes and even family vacations.[5] Teenagers have considerable financial resources, as well as strong feelings about exercising brand choices. When redecorating a home, husbands are much more likely to be concerned about the decor of the den, whereas women show the greatest concern about the appearance of the living room.[6] Demographic factors may also affect behavior during a specific stage of the decision process. During the information stage, for example, a person's age and income may affect the number and types of information sources used and the amount of time devoted to seeking information.

Demographic factors also affect the extent to which a person uses products in a specific product category. Consumers aged 15 to 24 purchase more fast-food products than elderly consumers. Older consumers are more concerned with the levels of fat, cholesterol, and sodium in their diets.[7] Brand preferences, store choice, timing of purchases, and inclination to shop at all are other areas on which demographic factors have impact.

Occupation clearly affects consumer buying behavior. Consider, for example, how differences in occupation result in variations in product needs. A financial analyst may earn the same amount as a plumber. Yet the financial analyst and the plumber spend their incomes differently because product needs arising from these two occupations vary. Although both occupations require purchase of work clothes, the financial analyst purchases suits, and the plumber buys overalls and work shirts. The types of vehicles they drive also vary to some extent. The plumber is more likely to drive a truck or van, whereas the financial analyst is more likely to drive a car. Finally, the tools they purchase and use in their work are not the same.

◼ *Lifestyles*

Lifestyle An individual's pattern of living expressed through activities, interests, and opinions

A **lifestyle** is an individual's pattern of living expressed through activities, interests, and opinions. Lifestyle patterns include the ways people spend time, the extent of their interaction with others, and their general outlook on life and living. People partially determine their own lifestyles, but the pattern is also affected by personality, as well as by demographic factors such as age, education, income, and social class. Lifestyles are measured through lengthy series of questions.

Lifestyles have a strong impact on many aspects of the consumer buying decision process—from problem recognition to postpurchase evaluation. Lifestyles influence consumers' product needs, (see Technology in Marketing on the next page) brand preferences, types of media used, and how and where they shop. In Chapter 8 we discuss lifestyles in more detail as they relate to market analysis.

◼ *Situational Factors*

Situational factors Influences resulting from circumstances, time, and location that affect the consumer buying decision process

Situational factors are influences resulting from circumstances, time, and location that affect the consumer buying decision process. For example, buying an automobile tire after noticing while washing your car that the tire was badly worn is a different experience than buying a tire right after a blowout on the highway derails your vacation. Situational factors can influence the buyer during any stage of the consumer buying decision process and may cause the individual to shorten, lengthen, or terminate the process. As shown in Figure 6.4, pet ownership at times leads to troubling situations. The Washington Emergency Clinic for Animals suggests the use of its veterinary services for these pet emergencies.

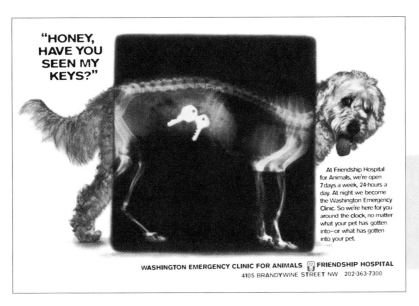

"HONEY, HAVE YOU SEEN MY KEYS?"

At Friendship Hospital for Animals, we're open 7 days a week, 24-hours a day. At night we become the Washington Emergency Clinic. So we're here for you around the clock, no matter what your pet has gotten into–or what has gotten into your pet.

WASHINGTON EMERGENCY CLINIC FOR ANIMALS ⬛ FRIENDSHIP HOSPITAL
4105 BRANDYWINE STREET NW   202-363-7300

Figure 6.4
Situational Factors Affecting the Consumer Buying Decision Process
The Washington Emergency Clinic for Animals suggests the use of its services for resolving troublesome situations associated with pets.

■ TECHNOLOGY IN MARKETING ■

High-Tech Helps to Satisfy Entertainment Needs

A college student hears a great CD and decides she must have it. She turns on her computer, slides in a blank disk, keys in commands, and in a few minutes has her own copy. After dinner, a couple settles in to watch an old movie, but instead of Clark Gable and Claudette Colbert, they want to see Brad Pitt and Winona Ryder in the leading roles. By pushing a few buttons on their "Plototronic," a device that lets viewers change a movie's plot, characters, or actors, the couple enjoys an old romance starring hot new actors. Although these technological advances in entertainment are still in the development stage, multidisc compact disc players, interactive TV, CD-ROM multimedia computers, online services, pay-per-view movies at home, and a host of other high-tech forms of entertainment are already part of mainstream American life.

Americans spend about one-third of their time being entertained. While some consumer purchases, such as food, clothing, and shelter, fulfill basic human needs, entertainment helps fulfill desires. More and more, consumers are finding that entertainment and technology go hand in hand. From the printing press to motion pictures, from home movies to home theaters, technology has changed the way people spend their free time.

Entertainment technology marketers have long recognized, however, that Americans don't buy the latest entertainment innovation simply because it exists. It took eighteen years before 40 percent of American households owned color television sets and ten years for CD players to reach that same level. However, when consumers believe that a new technological product can entertain them in novel and interesting ways, they go for it. When satellite television systems first became available, for example, skeptics warned that consumers would never spend $700 to $900 for an 18-inch dish plus $50 every month to receive programs. Today, these prolific dishes are popular enough to challenge cable television.

Consumers already have a difficult time deciding which gadgets to buy, and considering the technological innovations on the horizon, their choices are only going to get harder. If these new technologies successfully fulfill consumers' desires, they might develop into entertainment must-haves like televisions, CD players, and videogames.

Sources: Thomas R. King, "What's Entertainment?" *Wall Street Journal*, Sept. 15, 1995, pp. R1, R6; Robert J. Toth, "From Caves to Computers," *Wall Street Journal*, Sept. 15, 1995, p. R4; David Blum, "Stardate 2005," *Wall Street Journal*, Sept. 15, 1995, p. R12; Jeffrey A. Trachtenberg, "Homeward Bound," *Wall Street Journal*, Sept. 15, 1995, p. R15; and Anne Gregor, "Decisions, Decisions," *Wall Street Journal*, Sept. 15, 1995, p. R21.

Situational factors can be classified into five categories: physical surroundings, social surroundings, time perspective, task definition, and antecedent states.[8] Physical surroundings refer to location, store atmosphere, aromas, sounds, lighting, weather, and other factors in the physical environment in which the decision process occurs. Marketers at some restaurants, banks, department stores, and specialty stores go to considerable trouble and expense to create physical settings conducive to making purchase decisions. Clearly, in an outdoor setting there are several dimensions, such as weather, traffic sounds, and odors, that marketers cannot control; instead they must try to make customers more comfortable.

Social surroundings include characteristics and interactions of other consumers who are present when a purchase decision is being made—friends, relatives, salespeople, and other customers. The buyer may feel pressured to behave in a certain way because of the composition of the people who are in the location where the decision is being made such as in a restaurant, store, or sports arena. Thoughts about who will be around when the product is used or consumed is also a dimension of the social setting.

The time dimension, too, influences the buying decision process in several ways, such as the amount of time required to become knowledgeable about a product, to search for it, and to buy it. Time plays a major role in that the buyer considers the possible frequency of product use, the length of time required for the product to be used, and the length of the overall life of the product. Other time dimensions can include time of day, day of the week or month, seasons, or holidays.

Task definition raises the question of what exactly the product purchase should accomplish. Generally, consumers make a purchase for their own use, for someone in the household, or for someone not in the household. The item may be bought for specific household use, for individual use, or perhaps for a gift.

The buyer's antecedent state also has a bearing on the buying decision process. Antecedent states are momentary moods (such as anger, anxiety, contentment) or momentary conditions (fatigue, illness, being flush with cash). These moods or conditions immediately precede the current situation and are not chronic. Any of these moods or conditions can affect a person's ability and desire to seek information, receive information, or look for and evaluate alternatives. They can also significantly influence a consumer's postpurchase evaluation.

Psychological Factors Influencing the Buying Decision Process

Psychological factors
Factors that operate within individuals and in part determine their general behavior, thus influencing their behavior as consumers

Perception   The process of selecting, organizing, and interpreting information inputs to produce meaning

Information inputs
Sensations received through the sense organs

Selective exposure   The process of selecting some inputs to be exposed to our awareness while ignoring others

Selective distortion
An individual's changing or twisting of received information when it is inconsistent with personal feelings or beliefs

Psychological factors operating within individuals partly determine people's general behavior and thus influence their behavior as consumers. Primary psychological influences on consumer behavior are (1) perception, (2) motives, (3) learning, (4) attitudes, and (5) personality and self-concept. Even though these psychological factors operate internally, they are also very much affected by social forces outside the individual.

■ *Perception*

Are the horsemen in Figure 6.5 riding to the left or the right? It could be either way depending on how you perceive the riders. Different people perceive the same thing at the same time in different ways. Similarly, the same individual at different times may perceive the same item in a number of ways. **Perception** is the process of selecting, organizing, and interpreting information inputs to produce meaning. **Information inputs** are sensations received through sight, taste, hearing, smell, and touch. When we hear an advertisement, see a friend, smell polluted air or water, or touch a product, we receive information inputs.

As the definition indicates, perception is a three-step process. Although we receive numerous pieces of information at once, only a few reach awareness. We select some inputs and ignore others because we do not have the ability to be conscious of all inputs at one time. This phenomenon is sometimes called **selective exposure** because we select inputs that are to be exposed to our awareness. If you are concentrating on this paragraph, you probably are not aware that cars are outside making noise, that the light is on, or that you are touching this page. Even though you receive these inputs, they do not reach your awareness until they are mentioned.

Besides selective exposure, the selective nature of perception may also result in two other conditions: selective distortion and selective retention. **Selective distortion** is changing or twisting currently received information; it occurs when a person receives information that is inconsistent with personal feelings or beliefs. For example, on seeing an advertisement promoting a disliked brand, a viewer may distort the information to make it more consistent with prior views. This distortion substantially lessens the effect of the advertisement on the

Figure 6.5
Are the Horsemen Riding to the Left or to the Right?

Selective retention
Remembering information inputs
that support personal feelings
and beliefs and forgetting inputs
that do not

individual. In the case of **selective retention,** a person remembers information inputs that support personal feelings and beliefs and forgets inputs that do not. After hearing a sales presentation and leaving a store, a customer may forget many selling points if they contradict already held beliefs.

Information inputs that do reach awareness are not received in an organized form. To produce meaning, an individual must take the second step of the perceptual process—organize and integrate new information with what is already stored in memory. Ordinarily, organizing is done rapidly.

Interpretation—the third step in the perceptual process—is the assignment of meaning to what has been organized. A person bases interpretation on what he or she expects or what is familiar. For this reason, a manufacturer that changes a package design faces a major problem. Since people look for the product in the old, familiar package, they might not recognize it in the new one. For instance, when Smucker's recently redesigned its packaging, marketers told designers that although they wanted a more contemporary package design, they also wanted a classic look so that consumers would perceive their products to be the familiar ones that they have been buying for years.[9] Unless a package change is accompanied by a promotional program that makes people aware of the change, a firm may lose sales.

Although marketers cannot control people's perceptions, they often try to influence them. Several problems may arise from such attempts, however. First, a consumer's perceptual process may operate so that a seller's information never reaches that person. For example, a buyer may block out a store clerk's sales presentation. Second, a buyer may receive a seller's information but perceive it differently than was intended. For example, when a toothpaste producer advertises that "35 percent of the people who use this toothpaste have fewer cavities," a customer could infer that 65 percent of those using the product have more cavities. Third, a buyer who perceives information inputs inconsistent with prior beliefs is likely to forget the information quickly. Thus if a salesperson tells a prospective car buyer that a particular model is highly reliable and requires few repairs, but the customer does not believe it, the customer probably will not retain the information very long.

■ *Motives*

Motive   An internal energizing
force that directs a person's
behavior toward satisfying needs
or achieving goals

A **motive** is an internal energizing force that orients a person's activities toward satisfying needs or achieving goals. Buyers' actions are affected by a set of motives rather than by just one motive. At a single point in time, some of a person's motives are stronger than others. For example, a person's motives for having a cup of coffee are much stronger right after waking up than just before going to bed. Motives also affect the direction and intensity of behavior. Some motives may help an individual achieve his or her goals whereas others create barriers to goal achievement.

Patronage motives   Motives
that influence where a person
purchases products on a regular
basis

Motives that influence where a person purchases products on a regular basis are called **patronage motives.** A buyer may shop at a specific store because of such patronage motives as price, service, location, product variety, or friendliness of salespeople. Because buyer enthusiasm for Afrocentric products is booming, several major retailers are attempting to cater to African-Americans. JC Penney opened African boutiques in more than three hundred stores. The boutiques feature items that are or resemble authentic African clothes and accessories.[10] To capitalize on patronage motives, marketers try to determine why regular customers patronize a store and to emphasize these characteristics in the store's marketing mix.

Depth interviews   Lengthy
personal interviews used to study
motives in which the interviewer
poses nondirected questions and
then probes the responses

Marketers conduct motivation research to analyze major motives influencing consumers to buy or not buy their products. Motives that operate at a subconscious level are difficult to measure. People often do not even know what motivates them, so marketers cannot simply ask them about their motives. Most motivation research relies on interviews or projective techniques.

Group interviews   Interviews
used to uncover people's motives
in which an interviewer generates
discussion on one or more topics
among the six to twelve people
in the group

When researchers study motives through interviews, they may use depth interviews, group interviews, or a combination. In **depth interviews,** researchers try to get subjects to talk freely about anything to create an informal atmosphere. The researcher may ask general, nondirected questions and then probe the subject's answers by asking for clarification. A depth interview may last several hours. In **group interviews,** interviewers— through somewhat unstructured leadership—generate discussion about one or several topics among a group of six to twelve people. From what is said in the discussion, the interviewer attempts to discover people's motives relating to some issue, such as use of a product. Researchers usually cannot probe as far in a group interview as in a depth interview.

Projective techniques are tests in which subjects are asked to perform specific tasks for particular purposes while in fact they are evaluated for other purposes. Such tests are based on the assumption that subjects unconsciously "project" their motives as they perform required tasks. Researchers trained in projective techniques analyze the materials a subject produces and make inferences about the person's subconscious motives. Some common types of projective techniques are word-association tests and sentence-completion tests. Marketers attempt to use projective techniques to make advertising more effective.[11]

Motivation research techniques, though reasonably effective, are far from perfect. Marketers hoping to research people's motives should obtain the services of psychologists skilled in motivation research methods.

■ *Learning*

Learning refers to changes in a person's behavior caused by information and experience. Consequences of behavior strongly influence the learning process. Behaviors that result in satisfying consequences tend to be repeated. For example, a consumer who buys a Snickers candy bar and enjoys the taste is more likely to buy a Snickers again. In fact, the individual will probably continue to purchase that brand until it no longer provides satisfaction. But when effects of the behavior are no longer satisfying, the person may switch brands or stop eating candy bars altogether.

When making purchasing decisions, buyers must process information. Individuals have differing abilities in this regard. Inexperienced buyers may use different types of information than experienced shoppers familiar with the product and purchase situation. Inexperienced buyers use price as an indicator of quality more frequently than buyers with some knowledge of a particular product category.[12] Thus two potential purchasers of an antique desk may use different types of information in making their purchase decisions. The inexperienced buyer is likely to judge the desk's value by price, whereas the more experienced buyer may seek information about the manufacturer, period, and place of origin to judge the desk's quality and value. Consumers lacking experience may seek advice of others when making a purchase or take along a "purchase pal." More experienced buyers have greater self-confidence and more knowledge about the product or service, recognizing which product features are reliable cues to product quality.

Marketers also help customers learn about their products by letting them gain experience with them. Free samples successfully encourage trial and reduce purchase risk. Because some consumers are wary of exotic foods, restaurants have begun offering free samples. For example, at Solera, a Spanish restaurant in New York City, eggplant spread on bread is offered to potential customers.[13] In-store demonstrations foster knowledge of product uses. Paul Mace Software uses point-of-sale product demonstrations to introduce a multimedia animation product.[14] Test drives give new car purchasers some experience with an automobile's features. Recognizing that a spin around the block is an insufficient product trial, Chrysler is now offering two-day test drives.[15]

Consumers also learn by experiencing products indirectly, through information from salespersons, advertisements, friends, and relatives. Through sales personnel and advertisements, marketers offer information before (and sometimes after) purchases to influence what consumers learn and create a more favorable attitude toward the products. Yet their efforts are seldom fully successful. Marketers encounter problems in attracting and holding consumers' attention, providing consumers with important information for making purchase decisions, and convincing them to try the product.

■ *Attitudes*

An **attitude** is an individual's enduring evaluation, feelings, and behavioral tendencies toward an object or idea. The objects toward which we have attitudes may be tangible or intangible, living or nonliving. For example, we have attitudes toward sex, religion, politics, and music, just as we do toward cars, football, and what we eat for breakfast. Over the

Projective techniques Tests in which subjects are asked to perform specific tasks for particular purposes while in fact they are evaluated for other purposes, the assumption being that subjects unconsciously project their motives

Learning Changes in an individual's behavior caused by information and experience

Attitude An individual's enduring evaluation, feelings, and behavioral tendencies toward an object or idea

last twenty-five years, Americans have increased their per capita consumption of corn cereals by 97 percent and oat cereals by 93 percent, and cut their per capita consumption of milk by 18 percent, coffee by 22 percent, and eggs by 24 percent.[16] Although attitudes do change, an individual's attitudes remain generally stable and do not vary from moment to moment. However, a person's attitudes do not all have equal impact at any one time; some are stronger than others. Individuals acquire attitudes through experience and interaction with other people.

An attitude consists of three major components: cognitive, affective, and behavioral. The cognitive component is a person's knowledge and information about the object or idea, whereas the affective component comprises feelings and emotions toward the object or idea. The behavioral component is composed of the action tendencies one exhibits toward this object or idea. Changes in one of these components may or may not alter the other components. Thus consumers may become more knowledgeable about a specific brand without changing the affective or behavioral components of their attitude toward that brand.

Consumer attitudes toward a company and its products greatly influence success or failure of the firm's marketing strategy. When consumers have strong negative attitudes toward one or more aspects of a firm's marketing practices, they may not only stop using its product, but also urge relatives and friends to do likewise.

Because attitudes play such an important part in determining consumer behavior, marketers should measure consumer attitudes toward prices, package designs, brand names, advertisements, salespeople, repair services, store locations, features of existing or proposed products, and social responsibility efforts. Several methods help marketers gauge these attitudes. One of the simplest ways is to question people directly. An attitude researcher for Keytronics, a computer keyboard manufacturer, for example, might ask respondents what they think about the style and design of Keytronics' newest keyboard. Projective techniques used in motivation research can also measure attitudes.

Attitude scale Means of measuring consumer attitudes by gauging the intensity of individuals' reactions to adjectives, phrases, or sentences about an object

Marketers also evaluate attitudes through attitude scales. An **attitude scale** usually consists of a series of adjectives, phrases, or sentences about an object. Respondents indicate the intensity of their feelings toward the object by reacting to the adjectives, phrases, or sentences in a certain way. For example, a marketer measuring people's attitudes toward shopping might ask respondents to indicate the degree to which they agree or disagree with a number of statements, such as "Shopping is more fun than watching television." By using an attitude scale, the consulting firm of Management Horizons was able to classify six major shopper types of clothing purchasers. The scale was based on attributes found to be predictive of shopping behavior, as profiled by demographics, media use, and purchase behavior.[17]

When marketers determine that a significant number of consumers have negative attitudes toward an aspect of a marketing mix, they may try to change those attitudes to make them more favorable. This task is generally long, expensive, and difficult and may require extensive promotional efforts. For example, the California Prune Growers, an organization of prune producers, has tried to use advertising to change consumers' attitudes toward prunes by presenting them as a nutritious snack.[18] To alter consumers' responses so that more of them buy a given brand, a firm might launch an information-focused campaign if it wants to change the cognitive component of a consumer's attitude, or a persuasive (emotional) campaign if it wants to influence the affective component. Distributing free samples might help change the behavioral component. Both business and nonbusiness organizations try to change people's attitudes about many things, from health and safety to prices and product features.

■ *Personality and Self-Concept*

Personality A set of internal traits and distinct behavioral tendencies that result in consistent patterns of behavior

Personality is a set of internal traits and distinct behavioral tendencies that result in consistent patterns of behavior in certain situations. An individual's personality arises from hereditary characteristics and personal experiences that make the individual unique. Personalities typically are described as having one or more characteristics such as compulsiveness, ambition, gregariousness, dogmatism, authoritarianism, introversion, extroversion, and competitiveness. Marketing researchers look for relationships among such characteristics and buying behavior. Even though a few links among several personality

Figure 6.6
Expression of Personality and Self-Concept
Wanting to own, ride, and work on a Harley is partially affected by one's personality and is also an expression of one's self-concept.

"FINE, WE'LL JUST EAT WITHOUT YOU THEN!"

traits and buyer behavior have been determined, results of many studies have been inconclusive. The weak measured association between personality and buying behavior may be the result of unreliable measures, and not a lack of a relationship. A number of marketers are convinced that consumers' personalities do influence types and brands of products purchased. For example, the type of clothing, jewelry, or automobile a person buys may reflect one or more personality characteristics.

At times, marketers aim advertising at certain types of personalities. For example, certain cigarette brand ads are directed toward specific types of personalities. Marketers focus on positively valued personality characteristics, such as security consciousness, gregariousness, independence, or competitiveness, not negatively valued ones like insensitivity or timidity.

Self-concept One's own perception or view of oneself

A person's self-concept is closely linked to personality. **Self-concept** (sometimes called self-image) is a person's view or perception of himself or herself. Individuals develop and alter their self-concept based on an interaction of psychological and social dimensions. Research shows that a buyer purchases products that reflect and enhance the self-concept and that purchase decisions are important to the development and maintenance of a stable self-concept. Consumers' self-concept may influence whether they buy a product in a specific product category and may have an impact on brand selection as well. As alluded to in the advertisement in Figure 6.6, one's willingness to spend a great deal of time with a Harley Davidson motorcycle is, to some degree, determined by one's personality and self-concept.

Social Factors Influencing the Buying Decision Process

Social factors The forces that other people exert on one's buying behavior

*F*orces that other people exert on buying behavior are called **social factors.** As shown in Figure 6.2, they are grouped into four major areas: (1) roles and family influences, (2) reference groups and opinion leaders, (3) social classes, and (4) culture and subcultures.

■ Roles and Family Influences

Role Actions and activities that a person in a particular position is supposed to perform, based on expectations of the individual and surrounding persons

All of us occupy positions within groups, organizations, and institutions. Associated with each position is a **role**—a set of actions and activities a person in a particular position is supposed to perform, based on expectations of both the individual and surrounding persons. Because people occupy numerous positions, they have many roles. For example, a

Figure 6.7
Role and Family
Influences At an early
age children influence
the selection of the
types and brands of
clothing purchased for
their use.

Consumer socialization
The process through which a
person acquires the knowledge
and skills to function as a
consumer

Reference group Any group
that positively or negatively
affects a person's values,
attitudes, or behavior

man may perform the roles of son, husband, father, employee or employer, church member, civic organization member, and student in an evening college class. Thus there are multiple sets of expectations placed on each person's behavior.

An individual's roles influence both general behavior and buying behavior. The demands of a person's many roles may be inconsistent and confusing. To illustrate, assume that the man mentioned above is thinking about buying a boat. While he wants a boat for fishing, his children want one suitable for water skiing. His wife wants him to delay the boat purchase until next year. A coworker insists that he should buy a particular high-performance brand. Thus input and opinions of family and friends have a bearing on an individual's buying behavior.

Family influences have a very direct impact on the consumer buying decision process. Parents teach children how to cope with a variety of problems, including those dealing with purchase decisions. **Consumer socialization** is the process through which a person acquires the knowledge and skills to function as a consumer. Often children gain this knowledge and set of skills by observing parents and older siblings in purchase situations and through their own purchase experiences. Children observe brand preferences and family buying practices in their primary families and, as adults, use some of these brand preferences and buying practices as they establish and raise their own families. Buying decisions made by a family are a combination of group decision making and individual decision making.

Although female roles continue to change, women still make buying decisions related to many household items, including health care products, laundry supplies, paper products, and foods. Spouses participate jointly in the purchase of a variety of products, especially durable goods. Children make many purchase decisions and influence numerous household purchase decisions. At an early age children often influence the selection of their own clothing, as indicated in the Healthtex advertisement in Figure 6.7.

The extent to which either one or both of the two adult family members take part in family decision making varies among families and product categories. Traditionally, family decision-making processes have been grouped into four categories: autonomic, husband-dominant, wife-dominant, and syncratic. Autonomic decision making means that an equal number of decisions are made by each adult household member. In husband-dominant or wife-dominant decision making, the husband or the wife makes most of the family decisions. Syncratic decision making means that most decisions concerning purchases are made jointly by both partners. The type of family decision making employed depends on the values and attitudes of family members.

When two or more family members participate in a purchase, their roles may dictate that each is responsible for performing certain purchase-related tasks such as initiating the idea, gathering information, determining if the product is affordable, deciding whether to buy the product, or selecting the specific brand. The specific purchase tasks performed depend on the types of products being considered, the kind of family purchase decision process typically employed, and the amount of influence that children have in the decision process. Thus different family members may play different roles in the family buying process. To develop a marketing mix that precisely meets the needs of target market members, marketers must know not only who does the actual buying, but also which other family members perform purchase-related tasks.

■ *Reference Groups and Opinion Leaders*

A **reference group** is any group that positively or negatively affects a person's values, attitudes, or behavior. Reference groups can be large or small. Most people have several reference groups, such as families, work-related groups, fraternities, sororities, civic clubs, professional organizations, or church-related groups.

In general, there are three major types of reference groups: membership, aspirational, and disassociative. A membership reference group is one to which an individual actually belongs; the individual identifies with group members strongly enough to take on the values, attitudes, and behaviors of people in that group. An aspirational reference group is a group to which one aspires to belong; one desires to be like those group members. A group that a person does not wish to be associated with is a disassociative reference group; the individual does not want to take on the values, attitudes, and behavior of group members.

A reference group may serve as an individual's point of comparison and source of information. A customer's behavior may change to be more in line with actions and beliefs of group members. For example, a person might stop buying one brand of shirts and switch to another based on reference-group members' advice. An individual may also seek information from the reference group about other factors regarding a prospective purchase, such as where to buy a certain product.

The extent to which a reference group affects a purchase decision depends on the product's conspicuousness and on an individual's susceptibility to reference group influence. Generally, the more conspicuous a product, the more likely that the purchase decision will be influenced by reference groups. The degree of a product's conspicuousness is determined by whether it can be seen by others and whether it can attract attention. Reference groups can affect whether you do or do not buy a product at all, buy a type of product within a product category, or buy a specific brand.

A marketer sometimes tries to use reference-group influence in advertisements by suggesting that people in a specific group buy a product and are highly satisfied with it. In this type of appeal, the advertiser hopes that many will accept the suggested group as a reference group and buy (or react more favorably to) the product. Whether this kind of advertising succeeds depends on three factors: how effectively the advertisement communicates the message, the type of product, and the individual's susceptibility to reference-group influence.

In most reference groups, one or more members stand out as opinion leaders. An **opinion leader** provides information about a specific sphere that interests reference-group participants who seek information. Opinion leaders are viewed by other group members as being well informed about a particular area and easily accessible. An opinion leader is not the foremost authority on all issues. However, because such individuals know that they are opinion leaders, they feel a responsibility to remain informed about their sphere of interest and thus seek out advertisements, manufacturers' brochures, salespeople, and other sources of information.

> **Opinion leader** The reference group member who provides information about a specific sphere that interests reference group participants

An opinion leader is likely to be most influential when consumers have high product involvement but low product knowledge, when they share the opinion leader's values and attitudes, and when the product details are numerous or complicated.

■ *Social Classes*

In all societies, people rank others into higher or lower positions of respect. This ranking results in social classes. A **social class** is an open group of individuals with similar social rank. A class is referred to as "open" because people can move into and out of it. Criteria for grouping people into classes vary from one society to another. In the United States, we take into account many factors, including occupation, education, income, wealth, race, ethnic group, and possessions. A person who is ranking someone does not necessarily apply all of a society's criteria. Sometimes, too, the role of income in social class determination tends to be overemphasized. Although income does help determine social class, the other factors mentioned also figure in social class assessment. Within social classes, both incomes and spending habits differ significantly among members.

> **Social class** An open group of individuals with similar social rank

Analyses of social class commonly divide people in the United States into three to seven categories. Social scientist Richard P. Coleman suggests that for purposes of consumer analysis the population be divided into the four major status groups shown in Table 6.1, but he cautions marketers that considerable diversity exists in people's life situations within each status group.

To some degree, persons within social classes develop and assume common behavioral patterns. They may have similar attitudes, values, language patterns, and possessions. Social class influences many aspects of our lives. For example, it affects our chances of having children and their chances of surviving infancy. It influences our childhood training, choice of religion, selection of occupation, and leisure time activities. Because social class has a bearing on so many aspects of a person's life, it also affects buying decisions.

Class (% of Population)	Behavioral Traits	Buying Characteristics
Upper (14%); includes upper-upper, lower-upper, upper-middle	Income varies among the groups, but goals are the same Various lifestyles: preppy, conventional, intellectual, etc. Neighborhood and prestigious schooling important	Prize quality merchandise Favor prestigious brands Products purchased must reflect good taste Invest in art Spend money on travel, theater, books, and tennis, golf, and swimming clubs
Middle (32%)	Often in management Considered white collar Prize good schools Desire an attractive home in a nice, well-maintained neighborhood Often emulate the upper class Enjoy travel and physical activity Often very involved in children's school and sports activities	Like fashionable items Consult experts via books, articles, etc, before purchasing Will spend for experiences they consider worthwhile for their children (e.g., ski trips, college education) Tour packages; weekend trips Attractive home furnishings
Working (38%)	Emphasis on family, especially for economic and emotional supports (e.g., job opportunity tips, help in times of trouble) Blue collar Earn good incomes Enjoy mechanical items and recreational activities Enjoy leisure time after working hard	Buy vehicles and equipment related to recreation, camping, and selected sports Strong sense of value Shop for best bargains at off-price and discount stores Purchase automotive equipment for making repairs Enjoy local travel; recreational parks
Lower (16%)	Often down and out through no fault of their own (e.g., layoffs, company takeovers) Can include individuals on welfare; the homeless Often have strong religious beliefs May be forced to live in less desirable neighborhoods In spite of their problems, often good-hearted toward others Enjoyment of everyday activities when possible	Most products purchased are for survival Ability to convert good discards into usable items

Source: Adapted with permission from Richard P. Coleman, "The Continuing Significance of Social Class to Marketing," *Journal of Consumer Research*, pp. 265–280, 1983, 10 (December), with data from J. Paul Peter and Jerry C. Olson, *Consumer Behavior: Marketing Strategy Perspective* (Homewood, Ill.: Irwin, 1987), p. 433.

Social class influences people's spending, saving, and credit practices. It determines to some extent the type, quality, and quantity of products that a person buys and uses. For example, it affects our purchases of clothing, foods, financial and health care services, travel, recreation, entertainment, and home furnishings. Social class also affects an individual's shopping patterns and types of stores patronized. In some instances marketers attempt to focus on certain social classes through store location and interior design, product design and features, pricing strategies, advertising, and personal sales efforts.

■ Culture and Subcultures

Culture The values, knowledge, beliefs, customs, objects, and concepts of a society

Culture is the accumulation of values, knowledge, beliefs, customs, objects, and concepts that a society uses to cope with its environment and passes on to future generations. Examples of the objects are foods, furniture, buildings, clothing, and tools. Concepts include education, welfare, and laws. Culture also includes core values and the degree of acceptability of a wide range of behaviors in a specific society. For example, in our culture not only are businesspeople expected to behave ethically, but customers are expected to meet ethical standards as well.

GLOBAL PERSPECTIVE

What's for Dinner? Different Cultures Have Different Answers

In Bucharest, Romania, a young couple settles in for a quiet evening at home. They prepare a traditional homemade Romanian dinner of stuffed cabbage and sit down to watch not-so-traditional MTV and *Beverly Hills 90210*. Even though American cuisine is not as popular overseas as American television, this couple could soon be substituting frozen pizza or microwaveable burritos for cabbage.

To succeed in global food marketing takes more than knowing a little of the local language. Companies need to be aware of the tastes typical to each of their markets. The Foreign Agricultural Services agency recommends that food producers conduct marketing research in those countries in which they are involved. Almost every country has its own special tastes. In the Netherlands, spicy Tex-Mex foods are big sellers, and in Denmark, demand is increasing for low-fat foods like turkey and chicken. In Singapore, consumers are hungry for bite-size snack foods like chips, candy, popcorn, and crackers.

CPC International, Inc., maker of Knorr soups, Hellmann's mayonnaise, and Skippy peanut butter, has been extremely successful in marketing foods all over the world, primarily because the company pays close attention to national taste differences. For example, in Brazil, Hellmann's mayonnaise is more lemony, in Britain, more vinegary. Thai consumers prefer Knorr soup's "tom yam" bouillon cubes to the more familiar chicken flavor. Rich Products Corporation, maker of nondairy whipped topping, does 10 percent of its business in fifty foreign countries, striving to adapt its product to the unique flavor and visual preferences of its global customers. Mexicans like their whipped cream white and sweet, for example; New Zealanders, accustomed to dairy products colored by the high levels of carotene in their cattle food, prefer yellow cream. To sell ice cream in Tokyo, Dreyer's modifies its formula to suit Japanese consumers, who prefer their frozen desserts less sweet.

International markets for food are opening fast. Only those companies that tailor their products to specific cultural tastes can hope to win the hearts and satisfy the appetites of hungry global consumers.

Sources: "Singapore: Bite-Size Market Shows a Taste for Snacks," *AgReporter,* Oct. 1994, pp. 4–7; "Marketing Tips for Consumer-Oriented Product Exporters," *AgReporter,* Oct. 1994, pp. 8–9; Richard Gibson, "Gerber Missed the Boat in Quest to Go Global," *Wall Street Journal,* May 24, 1994, pp. A1, A8; Peter Hollingsworth, "Global Opportunities," *Food Technology,* Mar. 1994, pp. 65–68; Amy Feldman, "Have Distribution, Will Travel," *Forbes,* June 20, 1994, pp. 44–45; Cyndee Miller, "Going Overseas Requires More Than a New Language," *Marketing News,* Mar. 28, 1994, pp. 8, 13; Clifford Carlsen, "Asia Adds International Flavor to Dreyer's Sales," *San Francisco Business Times,* Aug. 12, 1994, p. 5; Richard Schroeder, "*Rich Products in Its 50th Year,*" *Buffalo News,* Mar. 26, 1995, p. B13; and Susanna Person, "Success Is Saucy for Aggie Entrepreneur," *Austin Business Journal,* Apr. 28, 1995, p. 10.

Culture influences buying behavior because it permeates our daily lives. Our culture determines what we wear and eat, where we reside and travel. Society's interest in the healthfulness of food affects companies' approaches to developing and promoting their products. It also influences how we buy and use products and our satisfaction from them.

Because culture to some degree determines product purchases and uses, cultural changes affect product development, promotion, distribution, and pricing. Food marketers, for example, have made a multitude of changes in their marketing efforts. Thirty years ago, most families in our culture ate at least two meals a day together, and the mother spent four to six hours a day preparing those meals. Now more than 75 percent of women between the ages of 25 and 54 work outside the home, and average family incomes have risen considerably. These shifts, along with the problem of time scarcity, have resulted in dramatic changes in the national per capita consumption of certain foods: take-out foods, frozen dinners, and shelf-stable foods.

When U.S. marketers sell products in other countries, they realize the tremendous impact that culture has on product purchases and use. Global marketers find that people in other regions of the world have different attitudes, values, and needs, which call for different methods of doing business, as well as different types of marketing mixes. (See Global Perspective for a discussion of the challenges faced by global food marketers.)

Some international marketers fail because they do not or cannot adjust to cultural differences. The effect of culture on international marketing programs is discussed in greater detail in Chapter 4.

A culture consists of various subcultures. **Subcultures** are groups of individuals who have similar values and behavior patterns and differ from people in other groups of the same culture. Subcultural boundaries are usually based on geographic designations and demographic characteristics such as age, religion, race, and ethnicity. Our culture is marked by a number of different subcultures, among them, West Coast, teenage, Asian-American, and college students. Within subcultures, greater similarities exist in people's attitudes, values, and actions than within the broader culture. Relative to other subcultures, individuals in one subculture may have stronger preferences for specific types of clothing, furniture, or foods. For example, a significant proportion of college students (about one-half of the women and one-third of the men) support the concept of vegetarianism although their diets are not strictly meatless. However, among similar-aged persons not attending college, the percentage of people eating primarily vegetarian diets is considerably less.[19]

Marketers recognize that the growth in the number of U.S. subcultures has resulted in considerable variation in what products people buy, as well as differences in how and when people make purchases. To deal effectively with these differences, marketers may have to alter products, promotion, distribution systems, or price to satisfy members of particular subcultures.[20] AT&T, for example, has developed "Klub Filipino" aimed at Filipino Americans because they often maintain very strong emotional ties to their homeland. Club members receive a magazine about Filipino personalities, history, and culture and chances to win free trips to the Philippines.[21]

Subcultures Groups of individuals who have similar values and behavior patterns within the group but differ from people in other groups of the same culture

SUMMARY

A consumer market consists of purchasers and household members who intend to consume or benefit from the purchased products and who do not buy products for the main purpose of making profits. Consumer buying behavior is the decision processes and acts of people involved in buying and using products and refers to the buying behavior of ultimate consumers.

An individual's level of involvement—the importance and intensity of interest in a product in a particular situation—affects the type of problem-solving process used. Enduring involvement is an ongoing interest in a product class because of personal relevance, whereas situational involvement is a temporary interest stemming from the particular circumstance or environment in which buyers find themselves. There are three kinds of consumer problem solving: routinized response behavior, limited problem solving, and extended problem solving. Consumers rely on routinized response behavior when buying frequently purchased, low-cost items requiring little search-and-decision effort. Limited problem solving is used for products purchased occasionally and when buyers need to acquire information about an unfamiliar brand in a familiar product category. Consumers engage in extended problem solving when purchasing an unfamiliar, expensive, or infrequently bought product. Purchase of a certain product does not always elicit the same type of decision making. Impulse

buying is not a consciously planned buying behavior but involves a powerful urge to buy something immediately.

The consumer buying decision process includes five stages: problem recognition, information search, evaluation of alternatives, purchase, and postpurchase evaluation. Not all decision processes culminate in a purchase, nor do all consumer decisions always include all five stages. Problem recognition occurs when buyers become aware of a difference between a desired state and an actual condition. After recognizing the problem or need, buyers search for information about products to help resolve the problem or satisfy the need. In the internal search, buyers search their memories for information about products that might solve the problem. If they cannot retrieve from memory enough information for a decision, they seek additional information through an external search. A successful search yields a group of brands, called an evoked set, that a buyer views as possible alternatives. To evaluate the products in the evoked set, a buyer establishes certain criteria by which to compare, rate, and rank different products. Marketers can influence consumers' evaluation by framing alternatives.

In the purchase stage, consumers select products or brands on the basis of results from the evaluation stage and on other dimensions. Buyers also choose the seller from whom they will buy the product. After the purchase, buyers evaluate the product to determine if its actual performance meets expected levels. Shortly after the purchase of an expensive product, for example, the postpurchase evaluation may result in cognitive dissonance, which is dissatisfaction brought on by the consumer's doubts as to whether he or she should have bought the product in the first place or would have been better off buying another desirable brand.

Three major categories of influences affect the consumer buying decision process: personal, psychological, and social factors. A personal factor is unique to a particular person. Personal factors include demographic, lifestyle, and situational factors. Demographic factors are individual characteristics such as age, gender, race, ethnicity, income, family life cycle, and occupation. Lifestyle is an individual's pattern of living expressed through activities, interests, and opinions. Lifestyle factors affect consumers' needs, brand preferences, and how and where they shop. Situational factors are external circumstances or conditions, such as time and location, existing when a consumer makes a purchase decision. Situational factors can be classified into five categories including physical surroundings, social surroundings, time perspective, task definition, and antecedent state.

Psychological factors operating within individuals partly determine people's general behavior, thus influencing their behavior as consumers. The primary psychological influences on consumer behavior are perception, motives, learning, attitudes, and personality and self-concept. Perception is the process of selecting, organizing, and interpreting information inputs (sensations received through sight, taste, hearing, smell, and touch) to produce meaning. The three steps in the perceptual process are exposure, organization and integration, and interpretation. Individuals have numerous perceptions of packages, products, brands, and organizations, which affect their buying decision processes. A motive is an internal energizing force that orients a person's activities toward satisfying needs or achieving goals. Learning refers to changes in a person's behavior caused by information and experience. Marketers try to influence what consumers learn in order to influence what they buy. An attitude is an individual's enduring evaluation, feelings, and behavioral tendencies toward an object or idea. An attitude refers to positive or negative feelings about an object or activity and consists of three major components: cognitive, affective, and behavioral. Personality is all the traits and behaviors that make a person unique. A person's self-concept is closely linked to his or her personality. Self-concept is a person's view or perception of himself or herself. Research indicates that buyers purchase products that reflect and enhance their self-concept.

Forces that other people exert on buying behavior are called social factors. Social factors include the influence of roles and families, reference groups and opinion leaders, social class, and culture and subcultures. Everyone occupies positions within groups, organizations, and institutions, and each position has a role—a set of actions and activities that a person in a particular position is supposed to perform, based on expectations of both the individual and surrounding persons. A reference group is any group that positively or negatively affects a person's values, attitudes, or behavior. The three major types of reference groups are membership, aspirational, and disassociative. In most reference groups, one or more members stand out as opinion leaders, or those who furnish requested information to reference group participants. A social class is an open group of individuals with similar social rank. Social class influences people's spending, saving, and credit practices. Culture is the accumulation of values, knowledge, beliefs, customs, objects, and concepts that a society uses to cope with its environment and passes on to future generations. A culture is made up of subcultures. A subculture is a group of individuals who have similar values and behavior patterns within the group and differ from people in other groups of the culture.

IMPORTANT TERMS

Market	Internal search	Selective distortion	Social factors
Consumer market	External search	Selective retention	Role
Consumer buying behavior	Evaluative criteria	Motive	Consumer socialization
	Cognitive dissonance	Patronage motives	Reference group
Level of involvement	Personal factors	Depth interviews	Opinion leader
Routinized response behavior	Demographic factors	Group interviews	Social class
	Lifestyle	Projective techniques	Culture
Limited problem solving	Situational factors	Learning	Subcultures
Extended problem solving	Psychological factors	Attitude	
Impulse buying	Perception	Attitude scale	
Consumer buying decision process	Information inputs	Personality	
	Selective exposure	Self-concept	

DISCUSSION AND REVIEW QUESTIONS

1. How does a consumer's level of involvement affect his or her choice of a problem-solving process?
2. Name the types of consumer problem-solving processes. List some products that you have bought using each type. Have you ever bought a product on impulse? Describe the circumstances.
3. What are the major stages in the consumer buying decision process? Are all these stages used in all consumer purchase decisions? Why or why not?
4. What personal factors affect the consumer buying decision process? How do they affect the process?
5. What are the five categories of situational factors that influence consumer buying behavior? Explain how each of these factors influences buyers' decisions.
6. What is selective exposure? Why do people engage in it?
7. How do marketers attempt to shape consumers' learning?
8. Why are marketers concerned about consumer attitudes?
9. How do roles and family influences affect a person's buying behavior?
10. Describe reference groups. How do they influence buying behavior? Name some of your own reference groups.
11. How does an opinion leader influence the buying decision process of reference group members?
12. In what ways does social class affect a person's purchase decisions?
13. What is culture? How does it affect a person's buying behavior?
14. Describe the subcultures to which you belong. Identify buying behavior that is unique to one of your subcultures.

APPLICATION QUESTIONS

1. Consumers use one of three problem-solving processes when purchasing goods or services: (1) routinized response behavior, (2) limited problem solving, or (3) extended problem solving. Describe three buying experiences you have had (one for each type of problem solving) and identify which problem-solving type you used. Discuss why that particular process was appropriate.
2. The consumer buying process consists of five stages: (1) problem recognition, (2) information search, (3) evaluation of alternatives, (4) purchase, and (5) post-purchase evaluation. Not every consumer goes through all five stages, and the process does not necessarily conclude in a purchase. Interview a fellow student about the last purchase he or she made. Report the stages used and skipped.
3. Attitudes toward products or companies often affect consumer behavior. The three components of an attitude are cognitive, affective, and behavioral. Briefly describe how a beer company might alter the cognitive and affective components of consumer attitudes toward beer products and the company.
4. An individual's roles influence that person's buying behavior. Identify two of your roles and give an example of how they have influenced your buying decisions.
5. The ethical behavior of consumers increasingly has become a concern of marketers and society. Locate an article in a newspaper or magazine that relates to ethical or unethical behavior of consumers. Describe the behavior the article discusses and explain how it is ethical or unethical.

Case 6.1   In Japan, an End to All Work and No Play

Every year about 100 million Japanese spend about $75 dollars to see Mickey Mouse and wait two hours in line to rocket through Space Mountain at Tokyo Disneyland. They flock to hear Aron Narikiyo, "Elvis-san," a wildly popular Elvis impersonator. They ski, attend cultural events, go bowling, take juggling lessons, and play pachinko, a vertical version of pinball. What they also do in great numbers is shop. One hundred and twenty million Japanese consumers with rising disposable incomes translates into lots of buying power. Long considered a society of all work and no play, Japan finds both its culture and its consumers changing.

In the conventional picture of modern Japan, men work most of the time, and women are relegated to background positions of stay-at-home wives and mothers. Indeed, many older Japanese accept without complaint endless, unquestioned hard work. But the old ways are changing. Japanese men are discovering that fun is sometimes more important than earnest dedication to the workplace. And Japanese women are assuming professional roles outside the home. Declaring that its citizens should start enjoying life, the government officially shortened the workweek from forty-eight hours to forty and funded the Leisure

Research and Development Center to teach its citizens the value of leisure time. With more money to spend and more time in which to spend it, the Japanese are becoming active and experienced consumers, dedicated to making their country a *seikatsu taikoku*—a "lifestyle superpower."

Two of the most powerful groups of Japanese consumers are the more than 8 million *Dankai Juniors,* children of Japan's postwar baby boom, and women, whose status and affluence continue to grow. Raised during a prosperous time in an affluent society, young Japanese spend a lot of money on sports, audiovisual equipment, entertainment, and fashion. Although looking for value more than they did in the 1980s, these young consumers still splurge on new products that improve the quality of their leisure time. One of their favorite places to go for fun is Namco's Wonder Eggs, an arcade specializing in virtual reality games. As for tastes in fashion, this group prefers American and European styles and colors. To attract these trendy customers, some small shops in areas frequented by young people carry only imported clothing.

In today's Japan, women comprise about 40 percent of the country's 64.5-million-person work force, and more than 50 percent of mothers work outside the home. Following the Equal Employment Law of 1986, women began to pursue more education, entered a variety of professions, began earning their own salaries, and became champion consumers. Besides attending concerts and plays, traveling, engaging in sports, and frequenting "relaxation parlors," where the sounds of birds singing or waves crashing on the shore relieve stress, Japanese women shop. Choosy about labels, many Japanese women favor distinctive brands, such as Armani suits, Yves St. Laurent towels, and $1,600 Gucci handbags.

Benefiting from Japan's growing appetite for consumption, retailing—both upscale and value-oriented—is booming. To attract customers by providing more spacious and attractive surroundings, venerable department stores such as Mitsukoshi and Takashima are remodeling and modernizing their interiors. New specialty shops are springing up, as are large shopping centers with avenues of stores and abundant parking space. Although many Japanese equate a good product with a high price tag, many others are becoming increasingly value-conscious, looking for high quality at low prices. Retailers are responding by opening giant discount stores. One of them, I World, is recording annual sales of over $180 million on discounted top-of-the-line brands such as Nordica and Sony. What the Japanese call "roadside chains," freestanding retail buildings, are springing up in the suburbs. Two such competing chains, Aoyama and Aoki, sell name brand men's clothing at lower-than-department-store prices.

When Japanese leaders commanded the country to relax, the leisure industry rushed to provide places to do it. Just as retailing is profiting from larger numbers of Japanese shoppers, the leisure industry is profiting from the greater amount of time that Japanese are spending on recreation. In one year alone, two hundred companies applied for permits to develop new theme parks. To enable ski enthusiasts to make one-day trips from Tokyo, a bullet train station opened at a popular ski resort, Gala Yuzawa. For those who prefer to schuss in climate-controlled comfort, indoor ski slopes are available within city limits. Built on top of one of Tokyo's numerous skyscrapers, the International Aquarium gives city dwellers a chance to escape temporarily to an undersea world. Having discovered the pleasures of camping, Japanese are pursuing this pastime in record numbers. American commercial campground developer KOA recently opened its first Japanese campground in Okayama. Vacationers can swim, play tennis, visit the mini zoo, or join in recreational group singing at the Karoake Kabin.

With all these choices and more, people don't have trouble deciding how to have fun on a day off or a week-long break, but the Japanese are still novices at "hanging out." A Leisure Development Center survey revealed that 40 percent of respondents wouldn't know what to do with a month off. To help them, the National Recreation Association offers a one-year course on how to enjoy life. Many Japanese, however, are convinced that the art of having fun is "Made in the U.S.A."[22]

Questions for Discussion

1. In what ways have the changing roles of Japanese women influenced their buying behavior?
2. To increase leisure facilities in Japan, which buyer behavior variables should be of greatest concern to marketers? Discuss.
3. Are high-involvement and low-involvement products approximately the same for both U.S. and Japanese consumers? Explain.

Case 6.2 Watercress and Duck Gizzard Soup: Mmm, Mmm, Good

152

Over 120 years ago, Campbell Soup Company introduced canned condensed soup and gave the world its first convenience food. Those well-known red and white labels and the words, "Mmmm, mmmm, good" joined baseball and apple pie as symbols of American culture. However, today's increasingly health-conscious consumers often spurn canned soup in favor of those made with fresh ingredients, and Americans also have a growing appetite for spicier seasoned and ethnic soups. Faced with declining domestic sales, the $7 billion New Jersey–based company is shaking up what many consider a food industry icon. It has added color photos to can labels, changed its slogan from "M-m! M-m! Good" to "Never underestimate the power of Campbell's," and added several new spicier ethnic-based selections. Campbell's is also turning to global markets for growth. Company executives hope that by the year 2000, more than half of the firm's profits will come from sales outside the United States.

Experts caution that strong cultural and regional tastes and preferences make food more difficult to translate to foreign markets than soft drinks or laundry detergent. Just because Americans love to ladle out chicken noodle and tomato soup by the bowlful doesn't mean those same flavors appeal to customers around the world. Marketers at Campbell recognize that demographics, lifestyle, and geography influence customer choices. To avoid potential pitfalls that differences often create, Campbell conducts extensive research in its specific consumer segments before generating and marketing brands.

All over the globe, Campbell's research and taste-tests are resulting in new, locally pleasing recipes. In Argentina, consumers shun the perennial American favorite, chicken noodle, but they do like split pea with ham. Emphasizing "Sopa de Campbell's" fresh ingredients, regional ads proclaim it "the real soup." Polish soup-lovers, who eat an average of five bowls of soup each week, can choose from eight varieties of Campbell's *zupa*, including *flaki*, tripe soup spiced with lots of pepper. To please Mexican palates, Campbell came up with its hot and spicy Cream of Chile Poblano.

In its Hong Kong test kitchen, the company cooked up some recipes it hoped would appeal to about 2 billion Asian consumers. What did the Campbell chefs come up with? Successes include watercress and duck gizzard soup, radish-carrot soup, fig soup, and date soup, varieties that Americans will probably not look for or find on neighborhood grocery shelves. Although willing to experiment even with snake, Campbell balked when it came to using ingredients from endangered species, such as shark's fin. What the company discovered is that Chinese consumers are willing to buy soup in a can if the right soup is inside.

Encouraged by its Hong Kong success, Campbell launched seventeen varieties of soup in the Chinese province of Guandong. Product sampling suggested that mainland Chinese would buy the same brands already popular in Hong Kong. Campbell's toughest competitor is homemade soup, as much a staple in China as rice. Company executives hope that as more Chinese adopt a faster-paced, more Westernized lifestyle, they will come to accept convenience foods in the form of canned soup. Backed by a $465,000 ad campaign, Campbell plans to make its product available in about 570 retail food outlets in Guandong.

Since joining the company, Campbell's CEO has aggressively pushed his global strategy, most recently acquiring Australia's 127-year-old cookie and cracker company, Arnotts Ltd., for $200 million. Campbell has no intention of foisting American tastes on Australians and will continue offering Arnotts' well-loved Milk Arrowroot cookies and Sao Water Crackers. In its drive to become a major player in the global soup market, however, Campbell's faces stiff competition. British consumers have known and preferred Heinz canned soups for many years, and CPC International already markets its popular Knorr dried soup mixes in every foreign country Campbell is targeting. In Argentina, for example, CPC controls 80 percent of the market. Soup rival Grand Metropolitan PLC is intensifying the global marketing of Progresso Soups, which it recently acquired by purchasing Pet, Inc.

Is the world ready for Campbell's soup? The company's CEO believes the answer is yes. His considerable global experience—as a former marketing executive with Colgate-Palmolive in South Africa and with Parke-Davis in Hong Kong—tells him that being responsive to consumer preferences leads to increased sales.[23]

Questions for Discussion

1. What fundamental behavioral issue is of greatest importance to marketers at Campbell Soup in introducing canned soup to mainland Chinese?
2. Which buying behavior variables are most likely to influence preferences for soup flavors?
3. Does the type of consumer problem-solving process vary from one culture to another when it comes to buying soup? Discuss.

Chapter 7

Organizational Markets and Buying Behavior

OBJECTIVES

- To become familiar with the various types of organizational markets

- To be able to identify the major characteristics of organizational buyers and transactions

- To understand several attributes of organizational demand

- To become familiar with the major components of a buying center

- To understand the stages of the organizational buying decision process and the factors that affect this process

- To become aware of the Standard Industrial Classification (SIC) system and explain how it can be used to identify and analyze organizational markets

Planning and customer service power up Emerson Electric.

*E*merson Electric Company, manufacturer of a broad range of electrical and electronic equipment such as appliance motors, process controls, thermostats, and ultrasonic welders, does what every company would like to do—it keeps getting more successful. In fiscal year 1995, Emerson recorded thirty-eight uninterrupted years of increased earnings. Eighty-seven percent of its products (3000 of them) rank first or second in U.S. markets. In 1970, Emerson ranked third in the appliance motor market. Twenty-five years later, competing with industry giants such as Hitachi, Mitsubishi, and General Electric, Emerson has become the number one motor manufacturer. Remarked one industry analyst of the company, "They find a way to make money no matter what is going on in the economy."

St. Louis-based Emerson Electric was founded in 1890 by two inventors developing applications for electric motors. The electric fan they introduced in 1892 was their best-known product, but the pair also put motors in hair dryers, sewing machines, water pumps, and player pianos. During World War II, the company adapted electric motors for the military effort, powering gun turrets for the B-24 bomber,

among other uses. In 1954, a new company president and a series of acquisitions turned Emerson into a major manufacturer of electrical products. The company's annual sales in fiscal 1995 reached $10 billion, with over half of its profits generated from sales of process-control products and systems, large industrial motors, and other electrical equipment in its commercial and industrial segment.

Industry experts attribute Emerson's stellar performance to the company's painstaking planning efforts with respect to long-term and daily operations, its ability to make every procedure cost effective, and its commitment to customer satisfaction. By facilitating communication between Emerson's engineers, marketers, and salespeople and their industrial customers, the company solves problems and responds to customers quickly. And at Emerson, communication means more than a phone call. Many of its suppliers have offices in Emerson's facilities, and Emerson in turn has offices in many of its chief customers' buildings. Electronic data transfer enhances rapid communication and timely product delivery. Customers are often on hand at the factory to watch prototypes being created, and they receive immediate feedback to their questions and suggestions.

In recent years, Emerson has intensified its global presence, especially in Asia, opening offices and factories throughout the region. Forty-four percent of the company's sales in fiscal 1995 were from foreign markets.[1]

An understanding of organizational markets and the buying decision process is required to effectively serve those markets. Emerson Electric Company marketers' understanding of their organizational buyers allows them to more effectively market their products to several different types of organizational markets. Like consumer marketers, organizational marketers are concerned about satisfying their customers.

In this chapter we look at organizational markets and organizational buying decision processes. We first discuss various kinds of organizational markets and types of buyers making up these markets. Next, we explore several dimensions of organizational buying, such as characteristics of transactions, attributes and concerns of buyers, methods of buying, and distinctive features of demand for products sold to organizational purchasers. Then we examine how organizational buying decisions are made and who makes the purchases. Finally, we consider how organizational markets are analyzed.

Organizational Markets

Organizational, or industrial, markets
Individuals or groups that purchase a specific kind of product for resale, direct use in producing other products, or use in general daily operations

*A*n **organizational,** or **industrial, market** consists of individuals or groups that purchase a specific kind of product for one of three purposes: resale, direct use in producing other products, or use in general daily operations. The four categories of organizational, or industrial, markets are producer, reseller, government, and institutional. In the remainder of this section, we discuss each of these types of organizational markets.

■ Producer Markets

Producer markets
Individuals and business organizations that purchase products to make profits by using them to produce other products or by using them in their operations

Individuals and business organizations that purchase products for the purpose of making a profit by using them to produce other products or by using them in their operations are classified as **producer markets.** Producer markets include buyers of raw materials, as well as purchasers of semifinished and finished items used to produce other products. For example, manufacturers buy raw materials and component parts for direct use in product production. Grocery stores and supermarkets are part of producer markets for numerous support products, such as paper and plastic bags, counters, and scanners. Farmers are part of producer markets for farm machinery, fertilizer, seed, and livestock. A broad array of industries make up producer markets; these industries range from agriculture, forestry, fisheries, and mining to construction, transportation, communications, and utilities. As Table 7.1 indicates, the number of business units in national producer markets is enormous.

Manufacturers are geographically concentrated. More than half are located in only seven states: New York, California, Pennsylvania, Illinois, Ohio, New Jersey, and Michigan. This concentration sometimes enables industrial marketers to serve customers more efficiently. Within certain states, production in just a few industries may account for a sizable proportion of total industrial output. As discussed in Inside Marketing (on the next page), automakers who buy air bags from Breed Technologies comprise a producer market.

Table 7.1 Number of Establishments in Industry Groups	
Industry	**Number of Establishments**
Agriculture, forestry, fishing	91,000
Mining	30,000
Construction	578,000
Manufacturing	374,000
Transportation, public utilities	245,000
Finance, insurance, real estate	577,000
Services	2,142,000

Source: *Statistical Abstract of the United States,* 1994, p. 546.

INSIDE MARKETING

Breed Technologies Succeeds by Breaking the Rules

In automobile collisions, air bags save lives. Within 25 milliseconds of impact, they pop out from steering wheels and dashboards and inflate to cushion drivers' and passengers' heads. To make their products safer, you might think that car manufacturers would have been eager to install air bags as soon as the technology became available. They were not. For ten years, Allen Breed, founder and president of Breed Technologies, tried to interest automakers in his company's sensing device for inflating air bags, but they wanted nothing to do with sensors or air bags. Snazzy hubcaps or state-of-the-art stereo systems attracted customers, not safety, they argued. For ten years, Breed heard all the objections: "They won't work," "It costs too much," and "No one wants a balloon exploding out of the steering wheel." Although many of his competitors gave up on the idea, Breed never did. By holding on to the product instead of selling the technology to another manufacturer, Breed was way ahead of potential competitors when the federal government mandated air bags for all cars made or sold in the United States.

Industry experts agree that one of Breed Technologies' strengths is its manufacturing strategy. To respond more readily both to individual customer needs and to new product development, Breed practices what it calls "intelligent automation," automating only to the degree that equipment can be easily modified. To keep costs manageable, Breed makes many of its own product components, including filters, propellants, and small metal sensor parts. So while competitors were paying suppliers $2 each for sensor tubes, Breed was turning them out for about 45 cents.

Today, Breed Technologies offers a complete range of air bag products, from electronic and electromechanical sensors that "tell" bags when to inflate to complete front and side impact systems. Breed operates facilities in the United States, Mexico, Great Britain, Finland, France, Germany, and Italy. The company's most impressive statistic? Twenty-one of the world's car manufacturers are Breed customers.

Sources: Anne Murphy, "Entrepreneur of the Year," *Inc*, Dec. 1995, pp. 38–40, 43–44, 46–48, 50; Breed Technologies, Inc., *1995 Annual Report;* Breed Technologies, Inc., "Advanced Technology for Occupant Safety Systems," company brochure; Junius Ellis, "As Air-bag Makers Head for a Pileup, Consider Selling TRW, Morton, and Hi-Shear," *Money*, Sept. 1995, pp. 31–32.

■ *Reseller Markets*

Reseller markets
Intermediaries that buy finished goods and resell them to make profits

Reseller markets consist of intermediaries, such as wholesalers and retailers, who buy finished goods and resell them for profit. (Wholesalers and retailers are discussed in Chapters 14 and 15.) Aside from making minor alterations, resellers do not change physical characteristics of products they handle. Except for items that producers sell directly to consumers, all products sold to consumer markets are first sold to reseller markets.

Wholesalers purchase products for resale to retailers, to other wholesalers, and to producers, governments, and institutions. Of the 492,000 wholesalers in the United States, a large percentage are located in New York, California, Illinois, Texas, Ohio, Pennsylvania, and New Jersey.[2] Although some technical products are sold directly to end users, many products are sold through wholesalers who, in turn, sell products to other firms in the distribution system. Thus wholesalers are very important in helping get a producer's product to customers. Professional buyers and buying committees make wholesalers' initial purchase decisions. Reordering is often automated.

Retailers purchase products and resell them to final customers. There are approximately 1.6 million retailers in the United States employing almost 20 million people and generating over $2.2 trillion in annual sales.[3] Some retailers carry a large number of items. Drugstores may stock up to 12,000 items, and some supermarkets handle as many as 20,000 different products. In small, individually owned retail stores, owners frequently make purchasing decisions. In chain stores, a central office buyer or buying committee frequently decides whether a product will be made available for selection by store managers. For most products, however, local store management makes the actual buying decisions for a particular store.

Table 7.2   Annual Expenditures by Government Units for Selected Years (in billions of dollars)

Year	Total Government Expenditures	Federal Government Expenditures	State and Local Expenditures
1970	$ 333	$ 185	$ 148
1975	560	292	268
1980	959	526	432
1985	1,581	1,032	658
1990	2,047	1,155	1,032
1992	2,488	1,527	1,355

Source: *Statistical Abstract of the United States*, 1994, p. 297.

When making purchase decisions, resellers consider several factors. They evaluate the level of demand for a product to determine in what quantity and at what prices the product can be resold. Wal-Mart recently stopped carrying some of Rubbermaid's products because the vendor's prices were too high. Rubbermaid marketers were quite concerned about Wal-Mart's response to price increases because Wal-Mart is Rubbermaid's biggest customer.[4] Retailers assess the amount of space required to handle a product relative to its potential profit. In fact, they sometimes evaluate products on the basis of sales per square foot of selling area. Because customers often depend on resellers to have products when needed, resellers typically appraise a supplier's ability to provide adequate quantities when and where wanted. Resellers also take into account the ease of placing orders and the availability of technical assistance and training programs from the producer. When resellers consider buying a product not previously carried, they try to determine whether the product competes with or complements products the firm currently handles. These types of concerns distinguish reseller markets from other markets.

■ *Government Markets*

Government markets
Federal, state, county, and local governments that buy goods and services to support their internal operations and to provide products to their constituencies

Federal, state, county, and local governments make up **government markets.** They spend billions of dollars annually for a variety of goods and services to support internal operations and provide citizens with such products as highways, education, water, energy, and national defense. For example, the U.S. federal government spends about $325 billion annually on defense.[5] Government expenditures annually account for about 20 percent of the U.S. gross national product.

Besides the federal government, there are 50 state governments, 3,043 county governments, and 83,649 other local governments.[6] The amount spent by federal, state, and local units during the last thirty years has increased rapidly because the total number of government units and the services they provide have both increased. Costs of providing these services have also increased. As noted in Table 7.2, the federal government spends over half of the total amount spent by all governments. As shown in Figure 7.1, FedEx provides a package of special services specifically for government units.

Figure 7.1
Targeting Government Markets
FedEx provides a specific package of services for government units.

158

The types and quantities of products bought by government markets reflect societal demands on various government agencies. As citizens' needs for government services change, so does demand for products by government markets. Not all government expenditures are for big-ticket, high-tech products. Recently, Maple Donuts, Inc., one of the largest donut producers in Pennsylvania, was awarded a contract to supply fortified donuts to all schools in the Chicago school system for one-half cent per donut.[7]

Because government agencies spend public funds to buy the products needed to provide services, they are accountable to the public. This accountability explains their relatively complex set of buying procedures. Some firms do not even try to sell to government buyers because they want to avoid the tangle of red tape. However, many marketers have learned to deal efficiently with government procedures and do not find them a stumbling block. Recently, for instance, Canada Inc. Apple, the Canadian division of Apple Computer, has decided to pursue government markets more aggressively. For certain products, such as defense-related items, the government may be the only customer. The U.S. Government Printing Office publishes and distributes several documents explaining buying procedures and describing types of products various federal agencies purchase.

The government makes purchases through bids or negotiated contracts. Although companies may be reluctant to approach government markets because of the complicated bidding process, once the rules of this process are understood, it can become routine for some firms to penetrate government markets.[8] To make a sale under the bid system, firms must apply for and be approved to be placed on a list of qualified bidders. When a government unit wants to buy, it sends out a detailed description of the products to qualified bidders. Businesses wishing to sell such products submit bids. The government unit is usually required to accept the lowest bid.

When buying nonstandard or highly complex products, a government unit often uses a negotiated contract. Under this procedure, the government unit selects only a few firms and then negotiates specifications and terms; it eventually awards the contract to one of the negotiating firms. Most large defense-related contracts once held by such companies as McDonnell Douglas, General Dynamics, and Northrop were negotiated in this fashion. However, as the number and size of government contracts has declined, these companies have had to strengthen their marketing efforts and look to other markets.[9] Although government markets can impose intimidating requirements, they can also be very lucrative.

**Figure 7.2
Institutional Customer**
Smith College is an institutional customer that has purchased Pella windows for Seelye Hall.

■ *Institutional Markets*

Organizations with charitable, educational, community, or other nonbusiness goals constitute **institutional markets.** Members of institutional markets include churches, some hospitals, fraternities and sororities, charitable organizations, and private colleges (see Figure 7.2). Institutions purchase millions of dollars' worth of products annually to provide goods, services, and ideas to congregations, students, patients, and others. Because institutions

Institutional markets
Organizations with charitable, educational, community, or nonbusiness goals

often have different goals and fewer resources than other types of organizations, marketers may use special marketing efforts to serve this segment. Sam's Club, a division of Wal-Mart Stores, Inc., targets institutional markets and other organizational markets. Giant warehouse outlets permit institutional as well as other qualified members to purchase supplies on a self-service cash basis at prices lower than those charged by high-service wholesalers.

Dimensions of Organizational Buying

*H*aving considered different types of organizational customers, we turn to the dimensions of organizational buying. We examine several characteristics of organizational transactions and then discuss attributes of organizational buyers, as well as some of their primary concerns when making purchase decisions. Next we consider organizational buying methods and major types of purchases. We conclude this section with a discussion of the characteristics of demand for industrial products.

■ *Characteristics of Organizational Transactions*

Organizational transactions differ from consumer sales in several ways. Orders by organizational buyers tend to be much larger than individual consumer sales. Suppliers often must sell products in large quantities to make profits; consequently, they prefer not to sell to customers who place small orders. For example, Airborne competes successfully against FedEx, UPS, and DHL by providing overnight delivery services primarily to businesses that buy such services in high volume for low prices.[10]

Some organizational purchases involve expensive items, such as computers. IBM Direct, for instance, sells mainframe computers in the $85,000 to $100,000 range (over the phone).[11] Other products, such as raw materials and component items, are used continuously in production and the supply may need frequent replacing. However, the contract regarding terms of sale of these items is likely to be a long-term agreement.

Discussions and negotiations associated with organizational purchases can require considerable marketing time and selling efforts. Purchasing decisions are often made by committee; orders are frequently large and expensive; and products may be custom-built. Several people or departments in the purchasing organization will probably be involved. One department might express a need for a product; a second department might develop the specifications; a third might stipulate maximum expenditures; and a fourth might place the order.

Reciprocity An arrangement unique to organizational marketing in which two organizations agree to buy from each other

One practice unique to organizational markets is **reciprocity,** an arrangement in which two organizations agree to buy from each other. Although such cooperation brings risks, companies that develop long-term relationships based on reciprocity and trust find cooperation to be an effective competitive tool.[12] Reciprocal agreements that threaten competition are illegal. The Federal Trade Commission and the Justice Department take action to stop anticompetitive reciprocal practices. Nonetheless, a certain amount of reciprocal activity occurs among small businesses and, to a lesser extent, among larger companies. Because reciprocity influences purchasing agents to deal only with certain suppliers, it can lower morale among agents and lead to less-than-optimal purchases.

■ *Attributes of Organizational Buyers*

Organizational buyers differ from consumer buyers in their purchasing behavior because they are better informed about the products they purchase. They demand detailed information about products' functional features and technical specifications to ensure that they meet the organization's needs. Personal goals, however, may also influence organizational buyers' behavior. Most organizational purchasing agents seek psychological satisfaction that comes with organizational advancement and financial rewards. Agents who consistently exhibit rational organizational buying behavior are likely to attain these personal goals because they help their firms achieve organizational objectives. Suppose, though, that an organizational buyer develops a close friendship with a certain supplier. If the buyer values friendship more than organizational promotion or financial rewards, he or she may behave irrationally from the firm's point of view.

■ *Primary Concerns of Organizational Buyers*

Today organizational buying behavior is influenced more by longer-term strategic considerations than by short-term operational concerns. This is because companies purchase more of the products they use and sell, and rapidly changing technology and global competition put more pressure on decision makers.[13] When making purchasing decisions, organizational customers take into account a variety of factors. Among their chief considerations are price, product quality, and service.

Price matters greatly to organizational customers because it influences operating costs and costs of goods sold, and these costs affect a customer's selling price, profit margin, and ultimately, ability to compete. When purchasing major equipment, an industrial buyer views price as the amount of investment necessary to obtain a certain level of return or savings. An organizational purchaser is likely to compare the price of the equipment with the value of the benefits that the equipment will yield.

Most organizational customers try to achieve and maintain a specific level of quality in the products they offer. To achieve this goal, most firms establish standards (usually stated as a percentage of defects allowed) for these products, buying them on the basis of a set of expressed characteristics, commonly called *specifications*. An organizational buyer evaluates the quality of the products being considered to determine whether they meet specifications. If a product fails to meet specifications and malfunctions for the ultimate consumer, the organizational customer may drop that product's supplier and switch to a different one. On the other hand, organizational customers are ordinarily cautious about buying products that exceed specifications because such products often cost more, thus increasing an organization's overall costs. As customer wants are evaluated, specifications that do not contribute to meeting these wants are considered wasteful.

Organizational buyers value service. Services offered by suppliers influence directly and indirectly organizational customers' costs, sales, and profits. In some instances, the mix of customer services is the major way marketers gain a competitive advantage. The organizational marketers shown in Figure 7.3 have created a specific mix of services to meet their specific customers' needs. Services are only as good as customers' evaluations say they are.

Typical services desired by customers are market information, inventory maintenance, on-time delivery, and repair services. Organizational buyers are likely to need technical product information, data regarding demand, information about general economic conditions, or supply and delivery information. Maintaining adequate inventory is critical because it helps make products accessible when an organizational buyer needs them

Figure 7.3
Customer Services
Providing the appropriate mix of customer services is important to organizational customers.

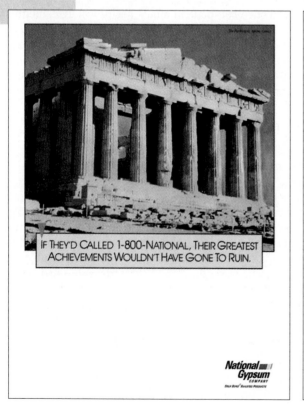

and reduces the buyer's inventory requirements and costs. Since organizational buyers are usually responsible for ensuring that products are on hand and ready for use when needed, on-time delivery is crucial. Furthermore, reliable, on-time delivery saves organizational customers money because it enables them to carry less inventory. Purchasers of machinery are especially concerned about obtaining repair services and replacement parts quickly because inoperable equipment is costly. Caterpillar Inc., manufacturer of earth-moving, construction, and materials-handling machinery, has built an international reputation, as well as a competitive advantage, by providing prompt service and replacement parts for its products around the world.

Service quality has become a critical issue because customer expectations about service have broadened. Approaching service quality based on traditional manufacturing and accounting systems is not enough. Communication channels that allow customers to ask questions, complain, submit orders, and trace shipments are indispensable components of service. Consider how Telogy has improved service quality by means of a data-synchronization system, described in Technology in Marketing. Marketers should strive for uniformity of service, simplicity, truthfulness, and accuracy. They should also develop

TECHNOLOGY IN MARKETING

Technology Enhances Customer Service at Telogy

When companies such as Boeing, Honeywell, IBM, McDonnell Douglas, and Westinghouse need amplifiers, calibrators, dataloggers, oscilloscopes, thermal array recorders, signal generators, attenuators, spectrum analyzers, or one of fifteen varieties of thermometers, they call Telogy. Since 1984, California-based Telogy has purchased, refurbished, sold, leased, and managed electronic testing equipment for businesses large and small all over the world. Keeping its 15,000 customers informed about the description, function, price, and availability of over 3,000 testing and measurement products makes marketing complicated at Telogy. Thanks to the company's data synchronization system, however, salespeople have more control over their jobs, and customers receive better, faster service.

Before 1993, none of Telogy's databases were integrated, making it impossible for departments to share information electronically. Pricing information, for example, was in one database, and customer information in another. When a person called telemarketing, the sales representative had no way of knowing whether the caller was a current customer or a prospective one. If callers were known customers, the salesperson couldn't easily access the types of products they had previously leased or problems they had experienced.

To improve its customer service, Telogy invested $500,000 in "database synchronization," a global link of all its computer information systems. Using a centralized database of worldwide inventory, manufacturing, and pricing information, sales staff can handle every step of the sales process from identifying customers to quoting prices. Field sales people, known at Telogy as equipment management consultants, carry HP OmniBooks with built-in modems, word processing softwear, Excell spreadsheets, and E-mail, all of which expedite communication with the home office.

Now, if a customer calls one department to report an equipment problem and decides to place an order at the same time, the customer service representative can alert both the repair technician and the sales rep. When making a sale, an outside salesperson can instantly transfer comprehensive customer information to inside support staff back in California. When the service department gets a call, a technician can immediately get online technical information for every piece of equipment Telogy sells or leases, facilitating quick, efficient repairs.

Since the new system's implementation, Telogy's salespeople spend more time selling and talking to customers and less time logging paperwork. The company processes orders in record time, and sales have increased by 15 percent.

Sources: "Telogy: Unique Test Equipment Solutions to Suit the Changing Needs of Today's Business Environment," company brochure; Melissa Campanelli, "On the Right Track," *Sales & Marketing Management*, Aug. 1995, pp. 47–48, 50–51; Kevin Strehlo, "Round the Clock Offsourcing," *Datamation*, Dec. 1, 1994, 44; and Telogy product catalog, 1995.

customer service objectives and monitor customer service programs. Firms can monitor service by formally surveying customers or informally calling on customers and asking questions about the service they receive. Taking the time and making the effort to ensure that customers are happy can greatly benefit marketers by increasing customer retention. One study found that boosting customer retention 2 percent can have the same effect as cutting costs by 10 percent.[14] Proper complaint handling helps to retain a customer and significantly reduces the likelihood that he or she will tell eleven or twelve other customers about a negative experience (which *does* occur when a customer is very dissatisfied).[15]

To ensure that their concerns are met, a number of organizational customers are indicating their expectations or requirements to their potential suppliers; that is, they are engaging in reverse marketing. **Reverse marketing** is a process through which an organizational buyer develops a relationship with a supplier that shapes the products, services, operations, and capabilities of the supplier to better satisfy the buyer's requirements.[16] For example, the customer may require, and even train, suppliers to provide just-in-time delivery, higher-quality products, and lower-cost products that are no less profitable for the supplier. Reverse marketing efforts are frequently a part of long-term partnership programs involving organizational buyers and sellers.

Reverse marketing
A process through which an organizational buyer develops a relationship with a supplier that shapes the products, services, operations, and capabilities of the supplier to better satisfy the buyer's needs

■ *Methods of Organizational Buying*

Although no two organizational buyers do their jobs the same way, most use one or more of the following purchase methods: *description, inspection, sampling,* and *negotiation.* When products being purchased are commonly standardized according to certain characteristics (such as size, shape, weight, and color) and are normally graded using such standards, an organizational buyer may be able to purchase simply by describing or specifying quantity, grade, and other attributes. Agricultural products often fall into this category. Sometimes buyers specify a particular brand or its equivalent when describing the desired product. Purchases on the basis of description are especially common between a buyer and seller with an ongoing relationship built on trust.

Certain products, such as industrial equipment, used vehicles, and buildings, have unique characteristics and may vary regarding their condition. For example, a particular used truck might have a bad transmission. Consequently, organizational buyers of such products must base purchase decisions on inspection.

In buying based on sampling, a sample of the product is taken from the lot and evaluated on the assumption that its characteristics represent the entire lot. This method is appropriate when the product is homogeneous—for instance, grain—and examining the entire lot is not physically or economically feasible.

Some industrial purchasing is based on negotiated contracts. In certain instances, organizational buyers describe exactly what is needed and then ask sellers to submit bids. Buyers may take the most attractive bids and negotiate with those suppliers. In other cases, the buyer may not be able to identify specifically what is to be purchased but can provide only a general description—as might be the case for a special piece of custom-made equipment. A buyer and seller might negotiate a contract that specifies a base price and provides for the payment of additional costs and fees. These contracts are most commonly used for one-time projects, such as buildings, capital equipment, and special projects. For example, the prices that Orbital Sciences Corporation charges its customers for launching and placing satellites in orbit are established through negotiated contracts.

■ *Types of Organizational Purchases*

Most organizational purchases are one of three types: new-task purchase, modified rebuy purchase, or straight rebuy purchase. In a **new-task purchase,** an organization makes an initial purchase of an item to be used to perform a new job or solve a new problem. A new-task purchase may require development of product specifications, vendor specifications, and procedures for future purchases of that product. To make the initial purchase, the organizational buyer usually needs much information. New-task purchases are important to suppliers, for if organizational buyers are satisfied with the products, suppliers may be able to sell buyers large quantities of them for many years.

New-task purchase
An initial purchase by an organization of an item to be used to perform a new job or solve a new problem

Modified rebuy purchase
A new-task purchase that is changed on subsequent orders or when the requirements of a straight rebuy purchase are modified

Straight rebuy purchase
A routine purchase of the same products by an organizational buyer

In a **modified rebuy purchase,** a new-task purchase is changed the second or third time it is ordered or requirements associated with a straight rebuy purchase are modified. An organizational buyer might seek faster delivery, lower prices, or a different quality level of product specifications. A modified rebuy situation may cause regular suppliers to become more competitive to keep the account. Competing suppliers may have the opportunity to obtain the business.

A **straight rebuy purchase** occurs when buyers purchase the same products routinely under approximately the same terms of sale. Buyers require little information for these routine purchase decisions and tend to use familiar suppliers that have provided satisfactory service and products in the past. These suppliers try to set up automatic reordering systems to make reordering easy and convenient for organizational buyers. A supplier may even monitor the organizational buyer's inventories and indicate to the buyer what should be ordered and when.

■ *Demand for Industrial Products*

Products sold to organizational customers are called industrial products; consequently, demand for these products is called industrial demand. Unlike consumer demand, industrial demand is (1) derived, (2) inelastic, (3) joint, and (4) fluctuating.

Derived demand   Demand for industrial products that stems from demand for consumer products

Inelastic demand   Demand that is not significantly altered by a price increase or decrease

Derived Demand   Because organizational customers, especially producers, buy products for direct or indirect use in the production of goods and services to satisfy consumers' needs, the demand for industrial products derives from the demand for consumer products; therefore it is called **derived demand.** In the long run, no industrial demand is totally unrelated to the demand for consumer goods. The derived nature of industrial demand is usually multilevel. Industrial sellers at different levels are affected by a change in consumer demand for a particular product. For instance, consumers today are more concerned with health and good nutrition than ever before, and as a result are purchasing more products with less fat, cholesterol, and salt. When consumers reduced their purchases of high-fat foods, the demand then changed for products marketed by food processors, equipment manufacturers, suppliers of raw materials, and even fast-food restaurants. When consumer demand for a product changes, a wave is set in motion that affects demand for all firms involved in the production of that consumer product. For example, Malden Mills, the maker of Polartec Climate Control Fabrics, promotes consumer products made of Polartec fabric, as shown in Figure 7.4. Assuming that such promotion generates demand for consumer products made of Polartec, it indirectly generates derived demand for Polartec Climate Control Fabrics in general.

Inelastic Demand   **Inelastic demand** for many industrial products means that a price increase or decrease will not significantly alter demand for the item. (The concept of price elasticity of demand is discussed further in

What I throw on when I feel like bike-riding 277 days to see hippos, water buffaloes and the entire African continent.
—Dan Buettner

STAYING COMFORTABLE IN THE SADDLE ON A 12,107-MILE CYCLING TRIP FROM THE SAHARA TO SOUTH AFRICA IS NO MEAN FEAT. BUT DAN BUETTNER ACHIEVED IT WITH SHIRTS MADE OF POLARTEC XT™ FABRIC AND JACKETS OF POLARTEC SERIES 200 FABRIC, THE VIBRANT COLORS DELIGHTED EVEN THE HIPPOS.

POLARTEC
Climate Control Fabrics
MAKE SURE YOUR OUTDOOR GARMENT HAS THIS LABEL.

Figure 7.4
Derived Demand   Malden Mills®, the maker of Polartec® Climate Control Fabrics①, promotes its products at the consumer level to generate consumer demand, which will in turn create derived demand for Polartec fabrics.
(Malden Mills is a registered trademark. Polartec is a registered trademark for fabrics available only from Malden Mill Industries, Inc).

Chapter 21.) Because many industrial products contain a number of parts, price increases affecting only one or two parts of the product may yield only a slightly higher per-unit production cost. When a sizable price increase for a component represents a large proportion of the product's cost, then demand may become more elastic because the price increase in the component causes the price at the consumer level to rise sharply. For example, if aircraft engine manufacturers substantially increase the price of engines, forcing Boeing to raise the prices of the aircraft it manufactures, the demand for airliners may become more elastic as airlines reconsider whether they can afford to buy new aircraft. An increase in the price of windshields, however, is unlikely to greatly affect the price of airliners or the demand for them.

Inelasticity applies only to industry demand for industrial products, not to the demand curve faced by an individual firm. Suppose that a spark plug producer increases the price of spark plugs sold to manufacturers of small engines, but its competitors continue to maintain lower prices. The spark plug company would probably experience reduced unit sales because most small-engine producers would switch to lower-priced brands. A specific firm is vulnerable to elastic demand, even though industry demand for a particular product is inelastic.

Joint demand Demand involving the use of two or more items in combination to produce a product

Joint Demand   Demand for certain industrial products, especially raw materials and components, is subject to joint demand. **Joint demand** occurs when two or more items are used in combination to produce a product. For example, a firm that manufactures axes needs the same number of ax handles as it does ax blades; these two products are demanded jointly. If a shortage of ax handles exists, then the producer buys fewer ax blades. Understanding the effects of joint demand is particularly important for a marketer selling multiple jointly demanded items. Such a marketer realizes that when a customer begins purchasing one of the jointly demanded items, a good opportunity exists for selling related products.

Demand Fluctuation   As already mentioned, the demand for industrial products may fluctuate enormously because it is derived from consumer demand. In general, when particular consumer products are in high demand, their producers buy large quantities of raw materials and components to ensure meeting long-run production requirements. In addition, these producers may expand production capacity, which entails acquiring new equipment and machinery, more workers, and more raw materials and component parts. Conversely, a decline in demand for certain consumer goods significantly reduces demand for industrial products used to produce those goods.

Marketers of industrial products may notice changes in demand when customers change inventory policies, perhaps because of expectations about future demand. For example, if several dishwasher manufacturers who buy timers from one producer increase their inventory of timers from a two-week to a one-month supply, the timer producer will have a significant immediate increase in demand.

Sometimes price changes lead to surprising temporary changes in demand. A price increase for an industrial item may initially cause organizational customers to buy more of the item because they expect the price to rise further. Similarly, demand for an industrial product may be significantly lower following a price cut because buyers are waiting for further price reductions. Fluctuations in demand can be significant in industries in which prices change frequently.

Organizational Buying Decisions

Organizational buying behavior The purchase behavior of producers, government units, institutions, and resellers

*O*rganizational buying behavior refers to the purchase behavior of producers, resellers, government units, and institutions. Although several of the factors affecting consumer buying behavior (discussed in Chapter 6) also influence organizational buying behavior, a number of factors are unique to the latter. We first analyze the buying center to learn who participates in organizational purchase decisions. Then we focus on the stages of the buying decision process and the factors affecting it.

■ *The Buying Center*

Buying center The group of people within an organization, including users, influencers, buyers, deciders, and gate-keepers, who are involved in making organizational purchase decisions

Relatively few organizational purchase decisions are made by just one person; mostly, they are made through a buying center. The **buying center** is the group of people within an organization who make organizational purchase decisions. They include users, influencers, buyers, deciders, and gatekeepers.[17] One person may perform several roles. These participants share some goals and risks associated with their decisions.

Users are the organization members who actually use the product being acquired. They frequently initiate the purchase process and/or generate purchase specifications. After the purchase, they evaluate product performance relative to the specifications. Influencers are often technical personnel, such as engineers, who help develop the specifications and evaluate alternative products. Technical personnel are especially important influencers when products being considered involve new, advanced technology.

Buyers select suppliers and negotiate terms of purchase. They may also become involved in developing specifications. Buyers are sometimes called purchasing agents or purchasing managers. Their choices of vendors and products, especially for new-task purchases, are heavily influenced by persons occupying other roles in the buying center. For straight rebuy purchases, the buyer plays a major role in vendor selection and negotiations. Deciders actually choose the products. Although buyers may be deciders, it is not unusual for different people to occupy these roles. For routinely purchased items, buyers are commonly deciders. However, a buyer may not be authorized to make purchases exceeding a certain dollar limit, in which case higher-level management personnel are deciders. Gatekeepers, such as secretaries and technical personnel, control the flow of information to and among persons who occupy other roles in the buying center. Buyers who deal directly with vendors also may be gatekeepers because they can control information flows. The flow of information from supplier sales representatives to users and influencers is often controlled by personnel in the purchasing department.

The number and structure of an organization's buying centers are affected by the organization's size and market position, the volume and types of products being purchased, and the firm's overall managerial philosophy regarding exactly who should be involved in purchase decisions. The size of a buying center is influenced by the stage of the buying decision process and the type of purchase (new-task, straight rebuy, or modified rebuy).[18] Varying goals among members of a buying center can have both positive and negative effects on the purchasing process.

A marketer attempting to sell to an organizational customer should determine who is in the buying center, the types of decisions each individual makes, and which individuals are most influential in the decision process. Because in some instances many people make up the buying center, marketers cannot contact all participants; instead, they must be certain to contact a few of the most influential.

■ *Stages of the Organizational Buying Decision Process*

Like consumers, organizations follow a buying decision process, summarized in the lower portion of Figure 7.5. In the first stage, one or more individuals recognize that a problem or need exists. Problem recognition may arise under a variety of circumstances—for instance, when machines malfunction or a firm modifies an existing product or introduces a new one. Individuals in the buying center—such as users, influencers, or buyers—may be involved in problem recognition, but it may be stimulated by external sources, such as sales representatives.

The second stage of the process, development of product specifications, requires that organizational participants assess the problem or need and determine what is necessary to resolve or satisfy it. During this stage, users and influencers, such as technical personnel and engineers, often provide information and advice for developing product specifications. By assessing and describing needs, the organization should be able to establish product specifications.

Searching for possible products to solve problems and locating suppliers is the third stage in the decision process. Search activities may involve looking in company files and trade directories, contacting suppliers for information, soliciting proposals from known

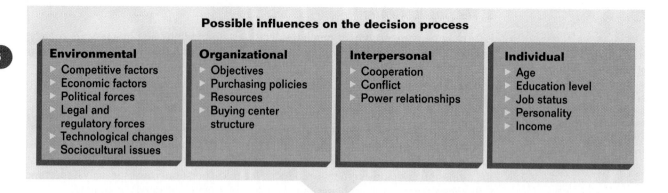

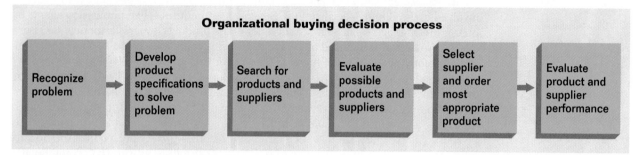

Figure 7.5
Organizational Buying Decision Process and Factors That May Influence It
Source: Frederick E. Webster, Jr., and Yoram Wind, *Organizational Buying Behavior*, © 1972, pp. 33–37. Adapted by permission of Prentice Hall, Upper Saddle River, New Jersey.

Value analysis An evaluation of each component of a potential purchase

vendors, and examining catalogs and trade publications. Figure 7.6 is an example of information available in trade publications. During this stage some organizations engage in **value analysis,** an evaluation of each component of a potential purchase. Value analysis examines quality, designs, materials, and possibly item reduction or deletion in order to acquire the product in the most cost-effective way. Some vendors may not be deemed acceptable because they are not large enough to supply needed quantities; others may be excluded because of poor delivery and service records. Sometimes the product is not available from any existing vendor and the buyer must find an innovative company, like 3M, to design and make the product. Some organizations, such as IBM, actually advertise their intention to build partnerships with certain types of vendors (see Figure 7.7).

If all goes well, the search stage results in a list of several alternative products and suppliers. The fourth stage is evaluating products on the list to determine which ones (if any) meet product specifications developed in the second stage. At this point, various suppliers are judged according to multiple criteria. A number of firms employ **vendor analysis.**

Vendor analysis A formal, systematic evaluation of current and potential vendors

Vendor analysis is a formal, systematic evaluation of current and potential vendors, focusing on a variety of characteristics including price, product quality, delivery service, product availability, and overall reliability.

Multiple sourcing
An organization's decision to use several suppliers

Sole sourcing
An organization's decision to use only one supplier

Results of deliberations and assessments in the fourth stage are used during the fifth stage to select the product to be purchased and the supplier from which to buy it. In some cases the buyer selects and uses several suppliers, which is known as **multiple sourcing.** In others only one supplier is selected—a situation known as **sole sourcing.** Sole sourcing has traditionally been discouraged except when a product is available from only one company. Firms with federal government contracts are required to have several sources for an item. Sole sourcing is considerably more common today, partly because such an arrangement means better communications between buyer and supplier, stability and higher profits for suppliers, and often lower prices for buyers. However, many organizations still prefer multiple sourcing because this approach lessens the possibility of disruption caused by strikes, shortages, or bankruptcies. The actual product is ordered in this

Figure 7.6
Trade Publication Information 3M uses an advertisement in a trade publication to promote packaging made with Scotchban Protector, which resists ruin from leaking bags or boxes. When searching for products to solve problems, organizational customers often consult trade publications.

Figure 7.7
Vendor Search
IBM promotes its willingness to establish partnerships with vendors that are small or minority-owned businesses.

fifth stage, and specific details regarding terms, credit arrangements, delivery dates and methods, and technical assistance are finalized.

During the sixth stage, the product's performance is evaluated by comparing it with specifications. Sometimes, even though the product meets the specifications, its performance does not adequately solve the problem or satisfy the need recognized in the first stage. In that case product specifications must be adjusted. The supplier's performance is also evaluated during this stage. If supplier performance is inadequate, the organizational purchaser seeks corrective action from the supplier or searches for a new one. Results of the evaluation become feedback for the other stages and influence future organizational purchase decisions.

This organizational buying decision process is used in its entirety primarily for new-task purchases. Several stages, but not necessarily all, are used for modified rebuy and straight rebuy situations.

■ *Influences on Organizational Buying*

Figure 7.5 also lists four major categories of factors that influence organizational buying decisions: environmental, organizational, interpersonal, and individual.

Environmental factors are forces such as competitive and economic factors, political forces, legal and regulatory forces, technological changes, and sociocultural issues. These forces generate considerable amounts of uncertainty for an organization, and uncertainty can make individuals in the buying center apprehensive about certain types of purchases. Changes in one or more environmental forces can create new purchasing opportunities and threats. For example, changes in competition and technology can make buying decisions difficult in the case of products like computers, a field in which competition is increasingly affected by new cooperative strategies between companies. Compaq Computer, for instance, grew into a billion-dollar company by competing primarily against IBM and developing cooperative relationships with several other potential competitors.[19]

Organizational factors influencing the organizational buying decision process include the buyer's objectives, purchasing policies, and resources, as well as the size and composition of its buying center. An organization may have certain buying policies to which buying center participants must conform. For instance, a firm's policies may mandate long-term contracts, perhaps longer than most sellers desire. An organization's financial resources may require special credit arrangements. Any of these conditions could affect purchase decisions.

Interpersonal factors are the relationships among people in the buying center. Use of power and level of conflict among buying center participants influence organizational buying decisions. Certain persons in the buying center may be better communicators than others and may be more persuasive. Often these interpersonal dynamics are hidden, making them difficult for marketers to assess.

Individual factors are personal characteristics of individuals in the buying center, such as age, education, personality, income, and position in the organization. For example, a fifty-five-year-old manager who has been in the organization for twenty-five years may affect decisions made by the buying center differently than a thirty-year-old person employed only two years. How influential these factors are depends on the buying situation, the type of product being purchased, and whether the purchase is new-task, modified rebuy, or straight rebuy. Negotiating styles of people vary within an organization and from one organization to another. To be effective, marketers must know customers well enough to be aware of these individual factors and the effects they may have on purchase decisions.

Using Standard Industrial Classification (SIC) Codes

*M*arketers have easy access to a considerable amount of information about potential organizational customers, for much of this information appears in government and industry publications. Marketers use this information to (1) identify potential organizational customers and (2) estimate their purchase potential.

■ Identifying Potential Organizational Customers

Standard Industrial Classification (SIC) system
The federal government system for classifying selected economic characteristics of industrial, commercial, financial, and service organizations

Much information about organizational customers is based on the **Standard Industrial Classification (SIC) system,** which the federal government developed to classify selected economic characteristics of industrial, commercial, financial, and service organizations. Table 7.3 shows how the SIC system can be used to categorize products. Various types of business activities are separated into lettered divisions, and each division is divided into numbered two-digit major groups. For example, major group 22 includes all firms that manufacture textile mill products. Each major group is divided into three-digit-coded subgroups, and each subgroup is separated into detailed industry categories coded with four-digit numbers. The most recent *SIC Manual* lists 83 major groups, 596 subgroups, and 1005 detailed industry categories.[20] To categorize manufacturers in more detail, the *Census of Manufacturers* further subdivides manufacturers (Division D) into five- and seven-digit-coded groups. The fifth digit denotes the product category, and the sixth and seventh digits designate specific products.

The SIC system is a ready-made tool allowing marketers to divide organizations into groups based mainly on the types of products manufactured or handled. Although the SIC

Table 7.3   Example of Product Classification in the Standard Industrial Classification System

Level	SIC Code	Description
Division	D	Manufacturing
Major group	22	Textile mill products
Industry subgroup	225	Knitting mills
Detailed industry	2251	Women's full-length and knee-length hosiery
Product category	22513	Women's finished seamless hosiery
Product item	2251311	Misses' finished knee-length socks

Sources: *1987 Standard Industrial Classification Manual*, U.S. Office of Management and Budget; and *Census of Manufacturers 1987*, U.S. Bureau of the Census.

system is a vehicle for segmentation, it is most appropriately used in conjunction with other types of data to enable a specific marketer to determine exactly how many and which customers it can reach.

Input-output analysis works well in conjunction with the SIC system. This type of analysis is based on the assumption that the output or sales of one industry are the input or purchases of other industries. **Input-output data** tell what types of industries purchase products of a particular industry. A major source of national input-output data is the *Survey of Current Business*, published by the Office of Business Economics, U.S. Department of Commerce. After learning which industries purchase the major portion of an industry's output, the next step is finding the SIC numbers for those industries. Because firms are grouped differently in input-output tables and the SIC system, ascertaining SIC numbers can be difficult. However, the Office of Business Economics provides some limited conversion tables with input-output data. These tables can help marketers assign SIC numbers to industry categories used in input-output analysis. For example, the motor vehicle and equipment industry, an industry that buys significant quantities of paint and related products, can be converted into SIC categories 3711 and 3715.

Having determined the SIC codes of industries that buy the firm's output, a marketer is in a position to ascertain the number of organizations that are potential buyers nationally, by state, and by county. Government publications such as the *Census of Business,* the *Census of Manufacturers,* and *County Business Patterns* report the number of establishments, the value of industry shipments, the number of employees, percentage of imports and exports, and industry growth rates within SIC classifications. Commercial directories and other trade publications also contain information about organizations classified by SIC codes.

A marketer can take several approaches to determine the identities and locations of organizations in specific SIC groups. One approach is to use state directories or commercial industrial directories such as *Standard & Poor's Register* and Dun & Bradstreet's *Million Dollar Directory.* These sources contain such information about a firm as its name, SIC number, address, phone number, and annual sales. By referring to one or more of these sources, marketers isolate organizational customers that have SIC numbers, determine their locations, and develop lists of potential customers by city, county, and state. A more expedient, although more expensive, approach is to use a commercial data service. Dun & Bradstreet, for example, can provide a list of organizations that fall into a particular four-digit SIC group. For each company on the list, Dun & Bradstreet gives the name, location, sales volume, number of employees, type of products handled, names of chief executives, and other pertinent information. Either method can effectively identify and locate a group of potential customers. However, a marketer probably cannot pursue all organizations on the list. Because some companies have greater purchase potential than others, marketers must determine which customer or customer group to pursue.

Input-output data
Information that tells what types of industries purchase the products of a particular industry

■ *Estimating Purchase Potential*

To estimate the purchase potential of organizational customers or groups of customers, a marketer must find a relationship between the size of potential customers' purchases and a variable available in SIC data, such as the number of employees. For example, a paint manufacturer might attempt to determine the average number of gallons purchased by a specific type of potential customer relative to the number of persons employed. A marketer with no previous experience in this market segment will probably have to survey a random sample of potential customers to establish a relationship between purchase sizes and numbers of persons employed. Once this relationship is established, it can be applied to potential customer groups to estimate their purchases. After deriving these estimates, a marketer is in a position to select the customer groups with the most sales and profit potential.

Despite their usefulness, SIC data pose several problems. First, a few industries do not have specific SIC designations. Second, because a transfer of products from one establishment to another is counted as a part of total shipments, double counting may occur when products are shipped between two establishments within the same firm. Third, because the Census Bureau is prohibited from publishing data that identifies specific business organizations, some data—such as value of total shipments—may be understated. Finally, because government agencies provide SIC figures, a significant lag usually exists between data collection time and publication time.

SUMMARY

Organizational markets consist of individuals and groups that purchase a specific kind of product for resale, direct use in producing other products, or use in day-to-day operations. Producer markets include those individuals and business organizations purchasing products for the purpose of making a profit by using them to produce other products or by using them in their operations. Intermediaries that buy finished products and resell them to make a profit are classified as reseller markets. Government markets consist of federal, state, and local governments, which spend billions of dollars annually for goods and services to support internal operations and provide citizens with needed services. Organizations that seek to achieve charity, education, community, or other not-for-profit goals constitute institutional markets.

Organizational transactions differ from consumer transactions in several ways. Organizational transactions tend to be larger, and negotiations occur less frequently, though they are often lengthy. Organizational transactions sometimes involve more than one person or department in the purchasing organization. They may also involve reciprocity, an arrangement in which two organizations agree to buy from each other. Organizational customers are usually better informed than ultimate consumers and more likely to seek information about a product's features and technical specifications.

When purchasing products, organizational customers are particularly concerned about quality, service, and price. Quality is important because it directly affects the quality of products the buyer's firm produces. To achieve an exact level of quality, organizations often buy products on the basis of a set of expressed characteristics, called specifications. Because services have such a direct influence on a firm's costs, sales, and profits, such matters as market information, on-time delivery, and availability of parts are crucial to an organizational buyer. Although organizations' customers do not depend solely on price to decide which products to buy, price is of prime concern because it directly influences profitability.

Organizational buyers use several purchasing methods, including description, inspection, sampling, and negotiation. Most organizational purchases are new-task, modified rebuy, or straight rebuy. In new-task purchases, organizations make an initial purchase of items to be used to perform new jobs or solve problems. In a modified rebuy purchase, a new-task purchase is changed the second or third time it is ordered or requirements associated with a straight rebuy purchase are modified. A straight rebuy purchase occurs when buyers purchase the same products routinely under approximately the same terms of sale.

Industrial demand differs from consumer demand along several dimensions. Industrial demand derives from demand for consumer products. At the industry level, industrial demand is inelastic. If an industrial item's price changes, product demand will not change as much proportionally. Some industrial products are subject to joint demand, which occurs when two or more items are used in combination to make a product. Finally, because organizational demand derives from consumer demand, the demand for organizational products can fluctuate widely.

Organizational buying behavior refers to purchase behavior of producers, resellers, government units, and institutions. Organizational purchase decisions are made through a buying center—the group of people involved in making organizational purchase decisions. Users are those in the organization who actually use the product. Influencers help develop specifications and evaluate alternative products for possible use. Buyers select suppliers and negotiate purchase terms. Deciders choose the products. Gatekeepers control flow of information to and among persons occupying other roles in the buying center.

The stages of the organizational buying decision process are problem recognition, development of product specifications to solve problems, search for products and suppliers, evaluation of products relative to specifications, selection and ordering of the most appropriate product, and evaluation of the product's and supplier's performance.

Four categories of factors influence organizational buying decisions: environmental, organizational, interpersonal, and individual. Environmental factors include politics, laws and regulations, sociocultural factors, eco-nomic conditions, competitive forces, and technological changes. Organizational factors influencing the organizational buying decision process include the buyer's objectives, purchasing policies, and resources, as well as size and composition of its buying center. Interpersonal factors are the relationships among people in the buying center. Individual factors are personal characteristics of individuals in the buying center, such as age, education, personality, position in the organization, and income.

Organizational marketers have a considerable amount of information available for use in planning marketing strategies. Much of this information is based on the Standard Industrial Classification (SIC) system, which categorizes businesses into major industry groups, industry subgroups, and detailed industry categories. The SIC system provides marketers with information needed to identify organizational customer groups. It can best be used for this purpose in conjunction with other information, such as input-output data. After identifying target industries, a marketer can obtain the names and locations of potential customers by using state or commercial industrial directories or through a commercial data service. Marketers then must estimate potential purchases of organizational customers by finding a relationship between a potential customer's purchases and a variable available in published sources.

IMPORTANT TERMS

Organizational, or industrial, market	Reverse marketing	Organizational buying behavior	Standard Industrial Classification (SIC) system
Producer markets	New-task purchase	Buying center	Input-output data
Reseller markets	Modified rebuy purchase	Value analysis	
Government markets	Straight rebuy purchase	Vendor analysis	
Institutional markets	Derived demand	Multiple sourcing	
Reciprocity	Inelastic demand	Sole sourcing	
	Joint demand		

DISCUSSION AND REVIEW QUESTIONS

1. Identify, describe, and give examples of the four major types of organizational markets.
2. Regarding purchasing behavior, why are organizational buyers generally considered more rational than ultimate consumers?
3. What are the primary concerns of organizational buyers?
4. List several characteristics that differentiate organizational transactions from consumer ones.
5. What are the commonly used methods of organizational buying?
6. Why do buyers involved in a straight rebuy purchase require less information than those making a new-task purchase?
7. How does industrial demand differ from consumer demand?

8. What are the major components of an organization's buying center?
9. Identify the stages of the organizational buying decision process. How is this decision process used when making straight rebuys?
10. How do environmental, organizational, interpersonal, and individual factors affect organizational purchases?
11. What function does the SIC system help marketers perform?
12. List some sources that an organizational marketer can use to determine the names and addresses of potential organizational customers.

APPLICATION QUESTIONS

1. Identify organizations in your area that fit each organizational market category (producer, reseller, government, institutional). Explain your classifications.

2. Indicate the most likely method of buying (description, inspection, sampling, negotiation) an organization might use when purchasing each of the following items. Defend your selection.
   a. a building for the home office of a light bulb manufacturer
   b. wool for a clothing manufacturer
   c. an Alaskan cruise for a company retreat, assuming that a regular travel agency is used
   d. one-inch nails for a building contractor

3. Purchases by organizations may be described as new-task, modified rebuy, or straight rebuy. Categorize the following purchase decisions and explain your choice.
   a. Bob has purchased toothpicks from Smith Restaurant Supply for twenty-five years and recently placed an order for yellow toothpicks rather than the usual white ones.

   b. Jill's investment company has been purchasing envelopes from AAA Office Supply for a year and now needs to purchase boxes to mail year-end portfolio summaries to clients. Jill calls AAA to purchase these boxes.
   c. Reliance Insurance has been supplying its salespeople with a small personal computer to assist in their sales efforts. The company recently agreed to begin supplying them with faster, more sophisticated computers with color monitors rather than black and white ones.

4. Identifying qualified customers is important to the survival of any organization. The Standard Industrial Classification (SIC) system provides helpful information about many different organizations. Find the SIC manual at the library and identify the SIC code for the product item, category, detailed industry, major group, and division for the following items.
   a. chocolate candy bars
   b. automobile tires
   c. men's athletic running shoes

Case 7.1   Intel Builds Brand Awareness from the Inside Out

In 1986, thirty years after leaving his native Hungary, Andy Grove founded Intel Corp., pioneer of the microprocessing chips that provide the brainpower for most personal computers. The company's 8086 and 8088 chips powered early IBM personal computers, and today, its 486 and Pentium microprocessors dominate the market. Every year some 40 million personal computers are sold, and inside almost every one, including such well-known brands as IBM and NextStep, is at least one Intel chip. Revenues of almost $5 billion, earnings that grew more than 30 percent in one year, and innovative new products have earned Intel its place near the top of "The Business Marketing 100" list.

When personal computing was in its infancy, companies designed, built, and sold completely integrated systems, including chips, software, and disk drives. Buyers had to choose a whole package or nothing. Because today's most successful products are all compatible, original equipment manufacturers can assemble computers with parts from various firms. A new computer might well be a hybrid of Intel processor, Sharp display, Toshiba memory, U.S. Robotics modem, and Microsoft operating system. Although Intel continues to maintain its near monopoly of the microprocessor market, competition from firms such as Digital Equipment and Advanced Micro Devices is now making it necessary to differentiate Intel chips from clones.

Recognizing that most PC users never check their computers to see which microprocessors constitute the brains, Intel decided to make sure users think twice about whose silicon chips are in there. To boost brand awareness and preference for its products, Intel launched its $250 million global "Intel Inside" campaign. First, Intel created a logo, the words *Intel Inside* surrounded by an oval that doesn't quite close. In partnership with original equipment manufacturers (OEMs), the company is working to make that logo a symbol of quality and proven performance. Every time a participating manufacturer's advertisement for 486sx or Pentium products incorporates the "Intel Inside" logo, Intel reimburses that manufacturer for up to 50 percent of its media placement costs. About a hundred OEMs, including industry frontrunners IBM, Zenith Data Systems, NCR, and Dell Computer, feature Intel's logo in their advertisements, and another two hundred firms have signed up for the program. IBM's first "Intel Inside" ad, launched in computer and business magazines, bore the caption "How to spot the very best PCs."

Intel provides detailed and uncompromising guidelines for using the logo, including reproduction, placement, and even color. It does not reimburse OEMs for ads containing competing products. OEMs must always identify the Intel logo as a registered trademark of the Intel Corp. Official logo colors are blue, red, and green only. Using supplied logo sheets, advertisers may not add graphics to the logo, place it on a patterned background, reduce its size, connect it to any other logo or type, or otherwise alter it. If firms put removable logo stickers on their products, they must place them on the top right- or left-hand corner, but not on the monitor, keyboard, or other peripheral components.

Besides trade advertising, the logo can strengthen other marketing efforts, such as brochures and trade show displays and consumer advertising. At COMDEX, the computer industry's largest trade show, billboards (and a huge banner hung outside the entrance) amplified Intel's presence by displaying the increasingly well-known symbol. High-tech television commercials carrying the logo and animated by George Lucas's Industrial Light and Magic illustrate how Intel chips streamline computers. Print versions appear in intensely circulated publications such as *The Wall Street Journal, Business Week, Fortune,* and *PC World.*

By developing close partnerships with OEMs and directing them in effective logo use, Intel has heightened brand awareness and increased its customers' preference for Intel components. When they spot the "Intel Inside" logo, says the firm's marketing director, customers instantly recognize the quality product with an Intel chip inside. Although participating computer firms claim that the logo has boosted their advertising effectiveness, industry skeptics predict that the campaign will not establish long-term brand loyalty. Recently, Compaq Computer began using Pentium-class microprocessors from NexGen, the first major endorsement of a Pentium rival. Smart customers, experts insist, will realize that there are no important

differences between Intel and NexGen brands and will choose whichever is more economical.

Intel may have recently regretted its brand's high profile. When Intel's Pentium chip made some errors in math-intensive calculations, consumers identified the processor's brand and company from the "Intel Inside" campaign. Some industry analysts even contend that the Pentium controversy neutralizes the company's investment in the "Intel Inside" program, because with trust in the Intel brand tarnished, customers have no reason to choose an Intel product over any other.

These days, Intel is too busy staying ahead of the market to pay much attention to these dire predictions. The company recently announced another record quarter with sales of its Pentium chip topping those of the older 486 for the first time. Intel's president asserts that two essential steps will help the company maintain its preeminent status: continuing to pioneer better microprocessing technology and making sure that customers know Intel products are better. Intel believes that its marketing investment in the "Intel Inside" campaign will help it achieve the second goal.[21]

Questions for Discussion

1. What types of organizational markets does Intel serve?
2. What are the characteristics of the demand for Intel computer chips?
3. To what extent is it possible for Intel to create customer loyalty toward its computer chips?
4. Identify and evaluate other producers' attempts to stimulate customer preference for components of finished goods.

Case 7.2   WMX Technologies, Inc.: Turning Trash into Cash

Getting rid of garbage isn't as simple as it used to be. Recycling is virtually mandated, environmental protection regulations are extremely rigorous, landfills are overburdened, and waste disposal incinerators are as welcome in many communities as nuclear power plants. For years, WMX Technologies grew and profited by acquiring and operating landfills all over the United States. With the greening of America, however, company executives recognized the need to change and expand their services. Providing solid and hazardous waste management programs and environmental technologies has helped propel WMX from a $180-million-a-year garbage hauler to a $10-billion-a-year environmental services company. WMX collects recyclables from about 11 million residential and 1 million commercial and industrial customers in the United States,

Canada, Europe, South America, the Pacific Rim, and the Middle East.

By the year 2000, about forty U.S. states will have enacted laws requiring that 10 to 50 percent of all trash be diverted from traditional methods of waste disposal. For WMX, these impending requirements mean strategic changes. Many waste-generating companies will be forced to find new ways to deal with the byproducts of their operations. WMX has responded by moving aggressively into recycling, forming joint ventures to supply paper, can, and plastics manufacturers with recyclable materials collected from firms that generate them. By managing all in-house waste disposal, WMX believes it can solve its customers' problems while saving them money. Alcoa, Boeing, Du Pont, General Electric, General Motors, and other

Fortune 500 companies have contracted with WMX to oversee hazardous waste disposal, water and air treatment, and recycling. At GM's Saturn plant, for example, WMX sells metal to a local recycler, trucks wooden shipping pallets to a distillery for use as boiler fuel, and ships foundry sand to a concrete block company.

Although WMX can point to several successful operations, the company is faced with problems that are squeezing its profits. Industry experts insist that although recycling is environmentally responsible, it is not necessarily economically viable. Company executives report that they must spend $175 to collect and sort 1 ton of recyclable material, but can sell it for only about $40. Still, WMX must continue providing a potentially unprofitable service because the public approves of recycling, and in many cities garbage collection and recycling are part of the same system.

Environmental problems have tarnished the company's reputation and pose an even more immediate threat to its success than do financial woes. WMX ran a hazardous waste disposal facility in Chicago that was once the nation's largest. It was also a model of safe hazardous waste disposal, boasting state-of-the-art technology. But after a 1991 incinerator explosion released toxic fumes and brought a barrage of allegations of environmental and worker safety violations, the organization suspended operations pending a full investigation. In addition, WMX's San Diego unit came under government scrutiny for similar allegations.

Meanwhile, WMX must also cope with intense industry competition, especially from its chief rival, Browning-Ferris Industries. BFI operates in 545 locations in North America, Australia, Europe, the Middle East, and South America. To keep its operations as simple as possible, and to avoid the environmental entanglements that are choking WMX, Browning-Ferris got out of the hazardous waste business altogether. The company's manager of marketing and operations for recycling systems recently announced the opening of a $10 million recycling facility in Silicon Valley, California. Built primarily to handle commercial waste, the BFI superplant already lists Sun Microsystems, Del-Monte, and Toyota among its accounts. State-of-the-art

sorters reclaim recyclables from about 96 tons of commercial waste a day. In addition, the company has residential contracts with cities, including San Jose, to collect curbside glass, tin and aluminum cans, plastic, and newspaper.

To remain competitive, WMX has slashed spending, consolidated its complex corporate structure, and enlarged its operations. A major new recycling program in Fort Worth is Texas's largest. In a move designed to capture a share of the $1 billion New York City trash-hauling business, WMX recently purchased a 14-acre trash-handling plant in the Bronx. The organization's global ventures include a waste sorting plant in Nice, France, a $150-million plant in Hong Kong, and one of the world's largest recycling facilities in the world in the Netherlands.

In all of its expansion efforts, WMX must be able to assure potential customers that it can and will comply with environmental laws. Any doubts on the customer's part could delay or even doom a project. Stringent landfill and incinerator regulations, which have closed down about 14,000 small municipal dumps, have hurt WMX, too. For example, state officials in Indiana decided to re-review WMX's application to expand an existing waste disposal facility until they could be certain that the plans met all applicable regulations.

For several years, losses painted a cloudy picture for WMX's future. However, the company's recent fourth-quarter revenues rose 11 percent. Analysts attribute this positive sign to two trends: (1) a more favorable economy and increased markets for recycled materials in general, and (2) WMX's revamped internal programs for becoming more competitive.[22]

Questions for Discussion

1. Identify the types of organizational markets served by WMX.

2. What types of issues or concerns are of greatest importance to WMX's customers?

3. What are your recommendations for solving some of WMX's problems?

Chapter 8

Target Markets: Segmentation and Evaluation

OBJECTIVES

- To learn what a market is

- To understand the differences among general targeting strategies

- To be familiar with the major segmentation variables

- To know what segment profiles are and how they are used

- To understand how to evaluate market segments

- To be aware of the factors that influence the selection of specific market segments for use as target markets

- To become familiar with sales forecasting methods

What's on TV?
Something for everyone.

*T*here was a time when American television viewers had three networks to choose from: NBC, CBS, and ABC. Then came cable television. Today, two-thirds of American homes with televisions subscribe to cable services, plugging into dozens of channels, such as CNN, ESPN, USA, TBS, TNT, MTV, Discovery, The Weather Channel, CSpan, and the Nashville Network. By segmenting the mass television market into specific audiences and offering programming geared to their interests, cable TV is luring more and more consumers away from the Big Three.

The cable industry is replete with examples of cable networks, both famous and obscure, that target specific market segments. The Cartoon Network and spectacularly successful Nickelodeon target children. Lifetime proclaims itself the "network for women." The growing Hispanic market has spawned Spanish-language channels such as MTV Latino, HBO's Olé, and Telecompras Shopping Network. One relative newcomer, CNBC, has carved out a niche serving upscale viewers eager for financial and business information.

Experts agree that knowing its audience is the key to cable television's ability to build viewer loyalty. After researching the general television public, cable networks divide viewers into smaller groups with identifiable demographic or psychological characteristics and then formulate a program line-up that appeals to viewers in that population. Surveys of cable subscribers often facilitate this segmentation. For example, one recent poll divides adult viewers into "Broadcast TV Fans," "All-Around Viewers," "Moderate Viewers," "Basic Cable Fans," and "Premium Cable Fans." Another study by Discovery Communications segments cable audiences based on interests in specific kinds of information programming. "Entertain-Mes" hold traditional values and watch TV for entertainment. "Boy Toys," affluent, young, white-collar men, like programs about airplanes, military technology, and space. Ethnically diverse "Here and Nows" prefer realistic topics dealing with lifestyles and current events.

With the arrival of direct broadcast satellite (DBS) and other emerging technologies, 500-channel television will soon be a reality. Although cable networks are adept at catering to many precisely defined markets, industry analysts question whether there are enough unique audiences to go around.[1]

To compete effectively, ESPN, CNN, USA, and TBS single out groups of customers for their specific types of programming and direct their marketing activities at those groups. Any organization that wants to succeed must do the same. These organizations attempt to develop and maintain marketing mixes that satisfy the needs of their customer groups.

In this chapter we explore markets and market segmentation. Initially, we define the term *market* and discuss the major requirements of a market. Then we examine the steps in the target market selection process, including identifying the appropriate targeting strategy; determining which variables to use for segmenting consumer and organizational markets; developing market segment profiles; evaluating relevant market segments; and selecting target markets. Finally, we discuss various methods for developing sales forecasts.

What Are Markets?

*T*he word *market* has a number of meanings. People sometimes use it to refer to a specific location where products are bought and sold—for example, a flea market. A large geographic area may also be called a market. Sometimes the word refers to the relationship between supply and demand of a specific product, as in the question "How is the market for disposable cameras?" *Market* may also be used as a verb, meaning to sell something.

Market An aggregate of people who have needs for products in a product class and who have the ability, willingness, and authority to purchase such products

We define a **market** as an aggregate of people who, as individuals or as organizations, have needs for products in a product class and have the ability, willingness, and authority to purchase such products. In general use, the term *market* sometimes refers to the total population—or mass market—that buys products. However, our definition is more specific; it refers to persons seeking products in a specific product category. For example, students are part of the market for textbooks, as well as the markets for software, pens, paper, food, music, and other products. Obviously, there are many different markets in our complex economy.

For a group of people to be a market, they must meet the following four requirements. First, the people must have needs for a specific product in a product category. If they do not, then that group is not a market. Second, the people in the group must have the ability to purchase the product. Ability to purchase is a function of their buying power, which consists of resources, such as money, goods, and services, that can be traded in an exchange situation. Third, the people in the group must be willing to use their buying power. Finally, they must have the authority to buy the specific products. For, example, high school students may have the desire, money, and willingness to buy alcoholic beverages, but liquor producers do not consider them a market because, until students are 21 years old, they are prohibited by law from buying alcoholic beverages. An aggregate of people lacking any one of the four requirements does not constitute a market.

Target Market Selection Process

*I*n Chapter 1 we indicate that the first of two major components for developing a marketing strategy is to select a target market. Although marketers may employ several methods for target market selection, generally they use a five-step process. This process is shown in Figure 8.1, and we discuss it in the rest of this section.

Figure 8.1
Target Market Selection Process

| 1 Identify the appropriate targeting strategy | 2 Determine which segmentation variables to use | 3 Develop market segment profiles | 4 Evaluate relevant market segments | 5 Select specific target market(s) |

Step 1: Identify the Appropriate Targeting Strategy

*A*s you may recall from Chapter 1, a target market is a group of persons or organizations for which a business creates and maintains a marketing mix that is specifically designed to satisfy the needs of group members. The strategy used to select a target market is affected by target market characteristics, product attributes, and the organization's objectives and resources. Figure 8.2 illustrates the three basic targeting strategies: undifferentiated, concentrated, and differentiated.

■ *Undifferentiated Strategy*

Undifferentiated targeting strategy   A strategy in which an organization defines an entire market for a particular product as its target market, designs a single marketing mix, and directs it at that market

An organization sometimes defines an entire market for a particular product as its target market. When a company designs a single marketing mix and directs it at the entire market for a particular product, it is using an **undifferentiated targeting strategy.** As Figure 8.2 shows, the strategy assumes that all customers in the target market for a specific kind of product have similar needs, and so the organization can satisfy most customers with a single marketing mix. This mix consists of one type of product with little or no variation, one price, one promotional program aimed at everybody, and one distribution system to reach most customers in the total market. Products marketed successfully through the undifferentiated strategy include staple food items, such as sugar and salt, and certain kinds of farm produce.

Homogeneous market
A market in which a large proportion of customers have similar needs for a product

The undifferentiated targeting strategy is effective under two conditions. First, a large proportion of customers in a total market must have similar needs for the product—a situation termed a **homogeneous market.** A marketer using a single marketing mix for a total market of customers with a variety of needs would find that the marketing mix satisfies very few people. A "universal car" meant to satisfy everyone would satisfy very few customers' needs for cars because it would not provide the specific attributes that a specific person wants. Second, the organization must be able to develop and maintain a single marketing mix that satisfies customers' needs. The company must be able to identify a set of needs common to most customers in a total market and have the resources and managerial skills to reach a sizable portion of that market.

Although customers may have similar needs for a few products, for most products their needs decidedly differ. In such instances a company should use a differentiated or a concentrated strategy.

■ *Concentrated Strategy Through Market Segmentation*

Heterogeneous markets
Markets made up of individuals or organizations with diverse product needs for products in a specific product class

Markets made up of individuals or organizations with diverse product needs are called **heterogeneous markets.** Not everyone wants the same type of car, furniture, or clothes. For example, some individuals want an economical car, others desire a status symbol, and still others seek a roomy and comfortable automobile. The automobile market, then, is heterogeneous.

Market segmentation
The process of dividing a total market into groups with relatively similar product needs in order to design a marketing mix that matches those needs

Market segment   Individuals, groups, or organizations with one or more similar characteristics that make them have similar product needs

For such heterogeneous markets, market segmentation is appropriate. **Market segmentation** is the process of dividing a total market into market groups consisting of people or organizations with relatively similar product needs. The purpose is to enable a marketer to design a marketing mix that more precisely matches the needs of consumers in a selected market segment. A **market segment** consists of individuals, groups, or organizations with one or more similar characteristics that cause them to have relatively similar product needs. For instance, the cola market could be divided into segments consisting of diet cola drinkers and regular cola drinkers. The main rationale for segmenting heterogeneous markets is that a company is better able to develop a satisfactory marketing mix for a relatively small portion of a total market than to develop a mix meeting the needs of all people. Market segmentation is widely used. Fast-food chains, soft drink companies, magazine publishers, hospitals, and banks are just a few types of organizations that employ market segmentation.

For market segmentation to succeed, five conditions must exist. First, consumers' needs for the product must be heterogeneous; otherwise there is little reason to segment the market. Second, segments must be identifiable and divisible. The company must find

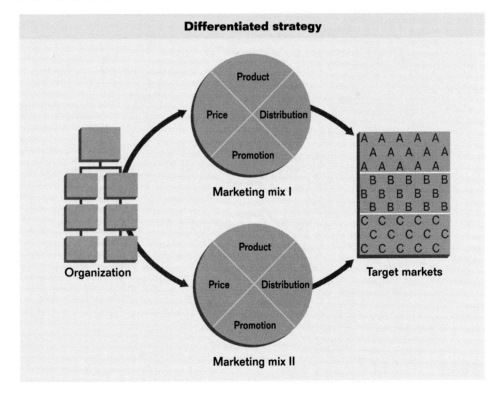

Figure 8.2
Targeting Strategies
The letters in each target market represent potential customers. Customers that have the same letters have similar characteristics and similar product needs.

a characteristic or variable for effectively separating individuals in a total market into groups containing people with relatively uniform needs for the product. Third, the total market should be divided so that segments can be compared with respect to estimated sales potential, costs, and profits. Fourth, at least one segment must have enough profit potential to justify developing and maintaining a special marketing mix. Finally, the company must be able to reach the chosen segment with a particular marketing mix. Some

There's a point when your boss will be happy with it, your partner will be happy with it, and your client will be happy with it. That was two hours ago.

INTRODUCING METROPOLIS*
by Cross

For those of you in the business of thinking, Cross presents Metropolis. A new line of writing instruments with an unquestioned, lifetime mechanical guarantee. From $30 to $60, manufacturer's suggested retail price.

CROSS
METROPOLIS

There's work to be done.

market segments may be difficult or impossible to reach because of legal, social, or distribution constraints. For instance, marketers of Cuban rum and cigars cannot sell to U.S. consumers because of political and trade restrictions.

When an organization directs its marketing efforts toward a single market segment using one marketing mix, it is employing a **concentrated targeting strategy.** Porsche focuses on the luxury sports car segment and directs all its marketing efforts toward high-income individuals who want to own high-performance sports cars. Pen manufacturer A.T. Cross aims its products at the upscale gift segment of the pen market and does not compete with Bic or Papermate, which focus on less expensive pen segments (see Figure 8.3). Notice in Figure 8.2 that the organization using the concentrated strategy is aiming its marketing mix only at "B" customers. The chief advantage of the concentrated strategy is that it allows a firm to specialize. The firm analyzes characteristics and needs of a distinct customer group and then focuses all its energies on satisfying that group's needs. A firm can generate a large sales volume by reaching a single segment. In addition, concentrating on a single segment permits a firm with limited resources to compete with much larger organizations, which may have overlooked some smaller segments.

Specialization, however, means that a company puts all its eggs in one basket, which can be hazardous. If a company's sales depend on a single segment and the segment's demand for the product declines, the company's financial strength also declines. Moreover, when a firm penetrates one segment and becomes well entrenched, its popularity may keep it from moving into other segments. For example, in the automobile market, Subaru, known for its small, low-price four-wheel-drive vehicles, may have trouble moving into the more affluent car segment, whereas Ferrari would find it difficult to enter the utilitarian, inexpensive automobile segment.

Concentrated targeting strategy A strategy in which an organization targets a single market segment using one marketing mix

■ *Differentiated Strategy Through Market Segmentation*

Differentiated targeting strategy A strategy in which an organization targets two or more segments by developing a marketing mix for each segment

With a **differentiated targeting strategy** (see Figure 8.2), an organization directs its marketing efforts at two or more segments by developing a marketing mix for each. After a firm uses a concentrated strategy successfully in one market segment, it sometimes expands its efforts to additional segments. For example, Fruit of the Loom underwear has traditionally been aimed at one segment: men. However, the company now markets underwear for women and children as well. Marketing mixes for a differentiated strategy may vary as to product features, distribution methods, promotion methods, and prices. A comparison of the two advertisements in Figure 8.4 illustrates that Wrangler aims multiple marketing mixes at multiple target markets, thus employing a differentiated targeting strategy.

A firm may increase sales in the aggregate market through a differentiated strategy because its marketing mixes are aimed at more people. For example, The Gap, which established its retail clothes reputation by targeting people under 25, now targets several segments that include infants to people over 60. A company with excess production capacity may find a differentiated strategy advantageous because the sale of products to additional segments may absorb excess capacity. On the other hand, a differentiated strategy often demands more production processes, materials, and people; thus production and costs may be higher than with a concentrated strategy.

Have We Made
Our Relaxed Fit Jeans
Too Comfortable?

Our classic 22MWZ jeans have extra room in the seat and thigh. Perfect for sitting around on leather covered rocking chairs.

Wrangler
The Western Original

Button fly jeans for women. Coming soon.

Wrangler
The Western Original

Figure 8.4
Differentiated Targeting Strategy
Using multiple marketing mixes aimed at multiple target markets. Wrangler employs a differentiated targeting strategy based on variation in product features, promotional methods, and prices.

Step 2: Determine Which Segmentation Variables to Use

Segmentation variables
Characteristics of individuals, groups, or organizations used to divide a market into segments

Segmentation variables are the characteristics of individuals, groups, or organizations used for dividing a market into segments. For example, location, age, gender, or rate of product usage can all be a means of segmenting.

To select a segmentation variable, several factors are considered. The segmentation variable should relate to customers' needs for, uses of, or behavior toward the product. Stereo marketers might segment the stereo market based on income and age—but not on religion, because people's stereo needs do not differ due to religion. Furthermore, if individuals or organizations in a total market are to be classified accurately, the segmentation variable must be measurable. Age, location, and gender are measurable because such information can be obtained through observation or questioning. But segmenting a market on the basis of intelligence is extremely difficult because this attribute is harder to measure accurately.

A company's resources and capabilities affect the number and size of segment variables used. The type of product and degree of variation in consumers' needs also dictate the number and size of segments a particular firm targets. In short, there is no best way to segment markets.

Choosing a segmentation variable or variables is a critical step in targeting a market. Selecting an inappropriate variable limits the chances of developing a successful marketing strategy. To help you better understand possible segmentation variables, we examine the major types of variables used to segment consumer markets and the types used to segment organizational markets.

■ Variables for Segmenting Consumer Markets

A marketer using segmentation to reach a consumer market can choose one or several variables from an assortment of possibilities. As shown in Figure 8.5, segmentation variables can be grouped into four categories: (1) demographic, (2) geographic, (3) psychographic, and (4) behavioristic.

Demographic Variables   Demographers study aggregate population characteristics, such as the distribution of age and gender, fertility rates, migration patterns, and mortality rates. Demographic characteristics that marketers commonly use in segmenting

182

Demographic variables
- Age
- Gender
- Race
- Ethnicity
- Income
- Education
- Occupation
- Family size
- Family life cycle
- Religion
- Social class

Geographic variables
- Region
- Urban, suburban, rural
- City size
- County size
- State size
- Market density
- Climate
- Terrain

Psychographic variables
- Personality attributes
- Motives
- Lifestyles

Behavioristic variables
- Volume usage
- End use
- Benefit expectations
- Brand loyalty
- Price sensitivity

Figure 8.5
Segmentation Variables
for Consumer Markets

markets include age, gender, race, ethnicity, income, education, occupation, family size, family life cycle, religion, and social class. Marketers rely on these demographic characteristics because they are often closely linked to customers' needs and purchasing behavior and can be readily measured. Like demographers, a few marketers even use mortality rates. Service Corporation International (SCI), the largest U.S. funeral services company, attempts to locate its facilities in higher income suburban areas with high mortality rates. SCI operates 771 funeral homes, 204 cemeteries, and 68 crematoriums.[2]

Because age is a commonly used variable for segmentation purposes, marketers need to be aware of age distribution and how that distribution is changing. All age groups (except the 5 to 13 group) that include persons now 34 years old or younger are expected to decrease, and all other age categories are expected to increase by the year 2000. In 1970, the average age of a U.S. citizen was 27.9; currently, it is about 32. According to projections, the average age in the year 2000 will be 35.5. In an attempt to reach the growing elderly market, Wal-Mart is using a number of marketing efforts to attract retirees to its stores.[3] Figure 8.6 visually illustrates age-based segmentation: Oshkosh clothing is promoted for young children, whereas the advertisement for Cigna is aimed at senior citizens. Playskool

Figure 8.6
Age-Based Segmentation
Oshkosh and Cigna are
two companies that use
age-based segmentation
to define their markets.

aims its Tinkertoy products at children ages 3 and older. As discussed in Inside Marketing, Playtex targets the Wonderbra at women in the 35–49 age group.

Marketers are recognizing the purchase influence of children and targeting more marketing efforts at them. Teenagers spend $33.5 billion on family grocery shopping. In households with only one parent or where both parents work, children take on additional responsibilities such as cooking, cleaning, and grocery shopping. Moreover, the 44 million children under age 12 have about $17.1 billion to spend on their own. Children are believed to influence household purchases in excess of $167 billion annually.[4]

Gender is another demographic variable commonly used to segment markets, including clothes, soft drinks, nonprescription medications, toiletries, magazines, and even cigarettes. The U.S. Census Bureau reports that girls and women account for 51.2 percent and boys and men for 48.8 percent of the total U.S. population.[5] Some deodorant marketers utilize gender segmentation—Secret deodorant is marketed specifically to women, whereas Old Spice deodorant is directed toward men.

Marketers also choose race and ethnicity as means of segmenting markets for goods such as food, music, clothing, and cosmetics and for services such as banking and insurance. The U.S. Hispanic population illustrates the importance of ethnicity as a segmentation variable. Made up of people of Mexican, Cuban, Puerto Rican, and Central and South

183

INSIDE MARKETING

Lo and Behold, It's the Wonderbra!

With all the hoopla of a Hollywood premiere, Playtex, a division of Sara Lee Corp., introduced the Wonderbra. While Wonderbra's marketing manager celebrated its virtues on *Donahue,* armored vehicles delivered the first shipment to three swank New York department stores. Macy's sold one Wonderbra every fifteen seconds, and many stores had to limit sales to one per customer. What is this underwear item that made the list of top ten new products in *Fortune, USA Today, U.S. News & World Report, Time, Newsweek,* and *Advertising Age*? Likened to a suspension bridge with padding, the Wonderbra is a high-tech bra with forty-six wire, lace, and fabric components that simultaneously push in and push up.

What is making so many women eager to wear a bra that lifts, separates, and creates drop-dead cleavage? Some women concede that they are eager to buy a product that can give them fuller-looking breasts without the potential dangers of silicon implants. Fashion consultants suggest that the Wonderbra has emerged at a turning point in the fashion world when women are rejecting the waif look and opting for more curves. The market that many experts credit with fueling the Wonderbra's popularity, however, is baby boomers in the 35 to 49 age group. By taking advantage of baby boomers' search for youthfulness, Playtex has been able to boost U.S. bra sales, which have been flat for years.

To promote the Wonderbra, Playtex launched a multimillion dollar print and billboard campaign. Double-page ads in *Vanity Fair, Mademoiselle, Cosmopolitan, Vogue,* and *Glamour* feature the Wonderbra model and ask "Who Cares If It's A Bad Hair Day?" Traffic-stopping billboards in Los Angeles, San Francisco, Miami, Houston, and six other major U.S. cities bear the model and the motto, "Hello Boys."

Playtex's all-out advertising efforts are part of Wonderbra's frontal assault in what has become the battle of the bras. Wonderbra's major competitor is the British Super-Uplift bra, whose campaign slogan is "Say goodbye to your feet." Victoria's Secret offers women the Miracle Bra, which promises women that they will appear one full size larger. Other contenders in the "clash of the cleavagemakers" include Loveable's IncrediBra, Vanity Fair's It Must Be Magic, Lily's La Lift, and Maidenform's Really Works.

Sources: Joshua Levine, "Bra Wars," *Forbes,* Apr. 25, 1994, p. 120; Elaine Underwood, "Victoria Pits Miracle vs. Sara," *Brandweek,* Sept. 19, 1994, p. 16; Judith Schoolman, "Cleavage Makes a Comeback as Underwear Takes Center Stage," *Reuter Business Report,* May 9, 1994; Lisa Anderson, "U.S. Next Beachhead in 'Bra Wars,'" *Chicago Tribune,* May 1, 1994; Lisa Pollak, "Pair Pressure," *The News and Observer,* Apr. 25, 1994; Jonathan Shalit, "Wonderbra," *Marketing,* Jan. 19, 1995, p. 9; Christina Duff, "Women's Lingerie Is All the Fashion," *Wall Street Journal,* Mar. 29, 1994, p. B7; and Jennifer DeCoursey, "Maidenform Fashions Wonderbra Challenger," *Advertising Age,* Feb. 20, 1995, p. 24.

184

Figure 8.7
Family Life
Cycle Segmentation
Oscar Mayer uses
family life cycle
segmentation and aims
Lunchables at families
with school-age
children.

American heritage, this ethnic group is growing five times faster than the general population. Consequently, Campbell Soup, Procter & Gamble, and other companies target Hispanic consumers, viewing this segment as attractive because of its size and growth potential. However, targeting Hispanic customers is not an easy task. For example, although marketers have long believed that Hispanic consumers are exceptionally brand loyal and prefer Spanish-language broadcast media, recent research does not support these assumptions. Not only do advertisers disagree about the merits of Spanish-language media, they also realize that they cannot effectively advertise to Mexicans, Puerto Ricans, and Cubans using a common Spanish language.[6]

Because it strongly influences people's product needs, income often provides a way of dividing markets. It affects ability to buy (discussed in Chapter 2) and aspirations to certain lifestyles. Product markets segmented by income include sporting goods, housing, furniture, cosmetics, clothing, food, home appliances, automobiles, and jewelry.

Among the factors influencing household income and product needs are marital status and the presence and age of children. These characteristics, often combined and called the *family life cycle,* affect needs for housing, appliances, food, automobiles, recreational equipment, and many other products. As shown in Figure 8.7, Oscar Mayer employs family life cycle segmentation for its Lunchable products, which are aimed at families with school-age children.

Family life cycle can be broken down in various ways. Figure 8.8 shows a breakdown into nine categories. As the figure shows, the composition of the American household in relation to family life cycle is changing. The "typical" American family of a single-earner married couple with children dropped from 21 percent of all households in 1970 to just 8 percent in 1990, and the number of households in which one person lives alone or with unrelated people increased from 23 percent to 35 percent. Unmarried adults under age 45 headed just 3 percent of the households in 1970, but their share increased to 9 percent by 1990.[7] Persons in a particular life cycle stage may have very specific needs that can be satisfied by precisely designed marketing mixes.

Marketers also apply many other demographic variables. For instance, encyclopedia and dictionary and computer companies segment markets by education level. Time Insurance Company segments its market using occupation, targeting health insurance products at college students and at younger workers whose employers are small and do not provide health coverage.[8]

Marketers must recognize that some of the demographic groups they target may be rather vulnerable. In such instances, marketers should exercise a degree of caution. This issue is discussed further in Ethical Challenges on the next page.

Geographic Variables   Geographic variables—climate, terrain, natural resources, population density, and subcultural values—also influence consumer product needs. Markets may be divided into regions because one or more geographic variables cause customers to differ from one region to another. A company selling products to a national market might divide the United States into the following regions: Pacific, Southwest, Central, Midwest, Southeast, Middle Atlantic, and New England. A firm operating in one of several states might regionalize its market by counties, cities, zip code areas, or other units.

Marketers sometimes segment on the basis of state populations, using population figures to estimate demand. Between 1980 and 1990, the U.S. population grew by 10 percent, but the population in all regions did not grow proportionally. While the South and West registered significant increases, the Midwest and East experienced only minor gains. To analyze and segment the market accurately, marketers must be aware of both current population patterns and projected changes in these patterns.

City size can be an important segmentation variable. Some marketers focus efforts on cities of a certain size. For example, one franchised restaurant organization will not locate in cities of less than 200,000 people. It concluded that a smaller population base would not result in adequate profits. Other firms, however, seek opportunities in smaller towns. A classic example is Wal-Mart, which initially located only in smaller towns.

Because cities often cut across political boundaries, the U.S. Census Bureau developed a system to classify metropolitan areas (any area with a city or urbanized area of at least 50,000 population and a total metropolitan population of at least 100,000). Metropolitan areas are categorized as one of the following: a metropolitan statistical area (MSA), a primary metropolitan statistical area (PMSA), or a consolidated metropolitan statistical area (CSMA). An MSA is an urbanized area encircled by nonmetropolitan counties and is neither socially nor economically dependent on any other metropolitan area. A metropolitan area within a complex of at least 1 million inhabitants can elect to be named a PMSA. A CMSA is a metropolitan area of at least 1 million consisting of two or more PMSAs. Of the twenty CMSAs, the five largest—New York, Los Angeles, Chicago, San Francisco, and Philadelphia—account for 20 percent of the U.S. population. The federal

Figure 8.8
The Nine Family Life Cycle Stages as a Percentage of All Households for 1970 and 1990
Source: Bureau of the Census, Current Population Survey, 1970 and 1990.

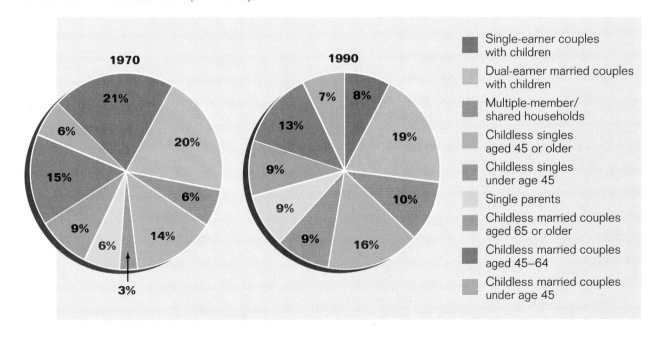

Targeting Vulnerable Groups: Is It Ethical?

Using the sophisticated tools at their disposal, marketers are very successfully identifying, understanding, and reaching narrow groups of potential consumers. Targeting precise markets with certain product ads and promotions is not intrinsically improper or unethical. However, what if relatively uneducated poor consumers are the target market for the state lottery, or children the target of cigarette advertising? When marketers target vulnerable groups, such as the elderly, disabled, racial and ethnic minorities, or young children, the ethics of their practices can become questionable.

Industry experts define as *vulnerable* any group that can too easily be taken advantage of because its members have little chance of making informed choices. A new study of tobacco trade publications and other recently disclosed documents reveals that from 1920 to the present, the cigarette industry has persistently and purposefully targeted youth. The National Food Alliance's "Project on Food Marketing and Advertising to Children" recently pointed out the proliferation of ads for fatty, sugary foods directed at children.

Because of their relative lack of experience and insight, children and young people obviously fit into the vulnerable category. Industry analysts insist, however, that there are also vulnerable adult markets. For example, many state lotteries heavily target people in poor neighborhoods with the message

that buying a lottery ticket will free them from their financial burdens. Is it ethical to persuade people to gamble their grocery money on a lottery ticket? Liquor manufacturers intensely promote malt liquor, a beverage with a much higher alcohol content than regular beer, to African-Americans.

To defend segmented promotion of their products, business organizations have posed a question of their own. Is it ethical to label certain groups incompetent to make rational decisions in the marketplace? Other defenses of their practices include their constitutional guarantee of free speech; the assertion that if selling a product is legal, promoting that product is also legal; and their insistence that people don't have to buy anything they don't want to. Critics of the practice of targeting vulnerable groups counter with the argument that legal is not synonymous with ethical. Because various types of promotional efforts associated with targeting certain groups can shape beliefs, they maintain, industries should refrain from irresponsible actions that have the potential to do harm.

Sources: Geoffrey Cannon, "Food Advertisers Resort to Tricks of Tobacco Trade," *Marketing,* May 4, 1995, p. 14; Richard W. Pollay, "Targeting Tactics in Selling Smoke," *Journal of Marketing Theory & Practice,* Winter 1995, pp. 1–22; Kirk Davidson, "Targeting Is Innocent Until It Exploits the Vulnerable," *Marketing News,* Sept. 11, 1995, pp. 4, 10; James M. Stearns, and Shaheen Borna, "The Ethics of Lottery Advertising: Issues and Evidence," *Journal of Business Ethics,* Jan. 1995, pp. 43–51; and Rance Crain, "Not All Emotional Appeals Are Equal," *Advertising Age's Business Marketing,* Apr. 1995, p. 9.

---

government provides a considerable amount of socioeconomic information about MSAs, PMSAs, and CMSAs that can aid market analysis and segmentation.

Market density The number of potential customers within a unit of land area

Market density refers to the number of potential customers within a unit of land area, such as a square mile. Although market density relates generally to population density, the correlation is not exact. For example, in two different geographic markets of approximately equal size and population, market density for office supplies might by much higher in one area than in another if one area contains a much greater proportion of business customers. Market density may be a useful segmentation variable because low-density markets often require different sales, advertising, and distribution activities than do high-density markets.

Geodemographic segmentation Marketing segmentation that divides people into ZIP code areas and smaller neighborhoods based on lifestyle and demographic information

Over the last few years a number of marketers have begun using what is called geodemographic segmentation. **Geodemographic segmentation** clusters people in ZIP code areas and even smaller neighborhood units based on lifestyle information and especially demographic data such as income, education, occupation, type of housing, ethnicity, family life cycle, and level of urbanization. These small, precisely described population clusters help marketers isolate demographic units as small as neighborhoods where the demand for specific products is strongest. Information companies such as Donnelley Marketing Information Services, Claritas, and C.A.C.I., Incorporated, provide geodemographic data services called ClusterPlus, PRIZM, and Acorn, respectively. PRIZM is based on a classification of the over 500,000 U.S. neighborhoods into one of forty cluster types such as "shotguns and pickups," "money and brains," and "gray power."

Micromarketing An approach to market segmentation in which organizations focus precise marketing efforts on very small geographic markets

Geodemographic segmentation allows marketers to engage in micromarketing. **Micromarketing** is the focusing of precise marketing efforts on very small geographic markets, such as local and even neighborhood markets. Providers of financial and health care services, retailers, and consumer products companies use micromarketing. Special advertising campaigns, promotions, retail site location analyses, special pricing, and unique retail product offerings are a few examples of micromarketing facilitated through geodemographic segmentation. Target Stores Inc. relies heavily on micromarketing, especially for determining the specific mix of products for each store. The products sold at the Scottsdale store are different from those offered in the Phoenix east-side store, which is only fifteen minutes away. For example, the Scottsdale store carries stocks of in-line skates for its affluent shoppers whereas the Phoenix store stocks only a few pair. The Phoenix store's customers have an average household income 42 percent below that of the Scottsdale store customers. The Phoenix store stocks a large inventory of religious candles to serve its many Hispanic Catholic customers. Only a few religious candles are carried at the Scottsdale store.[9]

Climate is commonly used as a geographic segmentation variable because of its broad impact on people's behavior and product needs. Product markets affected by climate include air-conditioning and heating equipment, clothing, gardening equipment, recreational products, and building materials.

Psychographic Variables Marketers sometimes use psychographic variables, such as personality characteristics, motives, and lifestyles, to segment markets. A psychographic dimension can be used by itself to segment a market or combined with other types of segmentation variables.

Personality characteristics can be useful for segmentation when a product resembles many competing products and consumers' needs are not greatly affected by other segmentation variables. However, segmenting a market according to personality traits can be risky. Although marketing practitioners have long believed that consumer choice and product use vary with personality, until recently marketing research had indicated only weak relationships. It is hard to measure personality traits accurately—especially since most personality tests were developed for clinical use, not for segmentation purposes. New, more reliable measurements devised for personality characteristics indicate a stronger association between personality and consumer behavior.[10]

When appealing to a personality characteristic, marketers almost always select one that many people view positively. Individuals with this characteristic, as well as those who would like to have it, may be influenced to buy that marketer's brand. Marketers taking this approach do not worry about measuring how many people have the positively valued characteristic; they assume that a sizable proportion of people in the target market either have or want to have it.

Motives are another means of segmenting markets. A market is divided according to consumers' needs associated with making a purchase. Personal appearance, affiliation, safety, or status are examples of motives affecting the types of products purchased and the choice of stores in which they are bought. For example, two possible motives for purchasing dieting-related products are appearance and health.

Lifestyle segmentation groups individuals according to how they spend their time, importance of things in their surroundings (homes or jobs, for example), beliefs about themselves and broad issues, and some demographic characteristics, such as income and education.[11] For example, because some adults are content to spend time at home, toy companies like Mattel and Nintendo are trying such segmentation to reach homebody adults.[12] As Figure 8.9 indicates, Chrysler uses lifestyle segmentation for the Jeep Cherokee. Lifestyle analysis

Figure 8.9
Lifestyle Segmentation
The Jeep Cherokee is aimed at a lifestyle segment that favors an outdoor, adventuresome, fun-seeking style of life.

Table 8.1 Lifestyle Dimensions

Activities	Interests	Opinions
Work	Family	Themselves
Hobbies	Home	Social issues
Social events	Job	Politics
Vacation	Community	Business
Entertainment	Recreation	Economics
Club membership	Fashion	Education
Community	Food	Products
Shopping	Media	Future
Sports	Achievements	Culture

Source: Reprinted, adapted, from Joseph Plummer, "The Concept and Application of Life Style Segmentation," *Journal of Marketing*, (Jan. 1974): 34, published by the American Marketing Association. Used by permission.

provides a broad view of buyers because it encompasses numerous characteristics related to people's activities, interests, and opinions. Table 8.1 charts the factors that make up the major dimensions of lifestyle.

One of the more popular studies of lifestyle is conducted by the Stanford Research Institute's Value and Lifestyle Program (VALS). This program surveys American consumers to select groups with identifiable values and lifestyles. It has identified three broad consumer groups: Outer-Directed, Inner-Directed, and Need-Driven consumers. A VALS 2 classification categorizes consumers into five basic lifestyle groups: Strugglers, Action-Oriented, Status-Oriented, Principle-Oriented, and Actualizers. The VALS studies have been used to create products as well as to segment markets. While VALS studies are widely used for segmenting consumers by lifestyle, many other lifestyle classification systems exist.

Even though psychographic variables can effectively divide a market, they are less often used than some of the other variables. They are harder to measure accurately, their links to consumers' needs are sometimes obscure and unproven, and segments based on these variables may not be reachable. Thus a marketer may determine that highly compulsive individuals want a certain type of clothing, but no specific stores or specific media—such as television or radio programs, newspapers, or magazines—appeal precisely to this group and this group alone.

Behavioristic Variables   Firms can divide a market according to some feature of consumer behavior toward a product, commonly involving some aspect of product use. For example, a total market may be separated into users, classified as heavy, moderate, or light, and nonusers. To satisfy a specific group, such as heavy users, marketers may create a distinctive product, set special prices, or initiate special promotion and distribution activities. Per capita consumption data help to identify different levels of usage. For example, economic census data show that per capita spending on building supplies at building material stores varies widely across the United States, ranging from $537 per resident in New Hampshire to $29 per resident in Wyoming. This information helps companies like Home Depot plan expansion and resource allocation.

How customers use or apply products may also determine segmentation. To satisfy customers who use a product in a certain way, some feature—say, packaging, size, texture, or color—may be designed precisely to make the product easier to use, safer, or more convenient. For instance, Crest, Colgate, and other brands of toothpaste are now packaged in stand-up dispensers because consumers wanted easier-to-use containers. In addition, special distribution, promotion, or pricing activities may have to be created.

Benefit segmentation is the division of a market according to benefits that consumers want from the product. Although most types of market segmentation assume a

Benefit segmentation
The division of a market according to the various benefits that customers want from the product

relationship between the variable and customers' needs, benefit segmentation is different in that the benefits customers seek *are* their product needs. Thus individuals are segmented directly according to their needs. By determining the desired benefits, marketers may be able to divide people into groups seeking certain sets of benefits. The effectiveness of such segmentation depends on three conditions: the benefits sought must be identifiable; using these benefits, marketers must be able to divide people into recognizable segments; and one or more of the resulting segments must be accessible to the firm's marketing efforts. Both Timberland and Avia, for example, segment the foot apparel market based on benefits sought.

As this discussion shows, consumer markets can be divided according to numerous characteristics. Some of these variables, however, are not particularly helpful for segmenting organizational markets.

■ *Variables for Segmenting Organizational Markets*

Like consumer markets, organizational markets are frequently segmented. Marketers segment organizational markets according to geographic location, type of organization, customer size, and product use.

Geographic Location   We noted that the demand for some consumer products can vary considerably among geographic areas because of differences in climate, terrain, customer preferences, or similar factors. Demand for organizational products also varies according to geographic location. For example, producers of certain types of lumber divide their markets geographically because their customers' needs vary from region to region. Geographic segmentation may be especially appropriate for reaching industries concentrated in certain locations. Furniture and textile producers, for example, are concentrated in the Southeast.

Type of Organization   A company sometimes segments a market by types of organizations within that market. Different types of organizations often require different product features, distribution systems, price structures, and selling strategies. Given these variations, a firm may either concentrate on a single segment with one marketing mix (concentration strategy) or focus on several groups with multiple mixes (multisegment strategy). A carpet producer could segment potential customers into several groups, such as automobile makers, commercial carpet contractors (firms that carpet large commercial buildings), apartment complex developers, carpet wholesalers, and large retail carpet outlets.

Customer Size   An organization's size may affect its purchasing procedures and the types and quantities of products it wants. Size can thus be an effective variable for segmenting an organizational market. To reach a segment of a particular size, marketers may have to adjust one or more marketing mix components. For example, customers who buy in extremely large quantities are sometimes offered discounts. In addition, marketers must often expand personal selling efforts to serve larger organizational buyers properly. Because the needs of larger and smaller buyers tend to be quite distinct, marketers frequently use different marketing practices to reach various customer groups.

Product Use   Certain products, especially basic raw materials such as steel, petroleum, plastics, and lumber, are used in numerous ways. How a company uses products affects the types and amounts of products purchased, as well as the purchasing method. For example, computers are used for engineering purposes, basic scientific research, and business operations, such as word processing, bookkeeping, and telephone service. A computer producer may segment the computer market by types of use because organizations' needs for computer hardware and software depend on the purpose for which products are purchased.

190

Table 8.2   Market Segment Profiles of Golfers

Golfer Segment	% of Golfers	Gender	Average Age	Average Household Income	Golf Spending per Year	Rounds per Year
Swinging Seniors (57% of rounds on private course, almost 50% belong to private clubs)	6.1%	Female	56.8	$31,144	$1,625	42.3
Country Club Traditionals (86% of their rounds on private courses)	9.2%	Male	52.6	$77,323	$4,413	68.9
Public Pundits (zealous golfers, 88% of rounds on public courses)	13.1%	Male	44.5	$50,629	$1,999	44.5
Junior Leaguers (less enthusiastic than income would allow)	13.2%	Female	42.6	$57,832	$1,604	42.6
Pull-Carts (60% retired or unemployed)	15.3%	Male	51.7	$32,212	$1,367	51.7
Tank Tops 'n' Tennis Shoes (very casual golfers, most golfing while on vacation)	16.6%	Male	34.8	$36,716	$565	12.9
Dilettante Duffers (weekend-athlete approach to golf, only 8% belong to a golf club, spend larger than average portion of annual vacation golfing)	26.5%	Male	40.6	$64,180	$1,149	15.6

Sources: Deborah Bosanko, "Seven Ways to Swing a Club," *American Demographics* (July 1995) 16–18; and Don Jozwiak, "All About Golf: Who Are Your Customers?" *PGA Magazine*, Special Report (Nov. 1994).

Step 3: Develop Market Segment Profiles

A market segment profile describes the similarities among potential customers within a segment and explains the differences among people and organizations in different segments. A profile may cover such aspects as demographic characteristics, geographic factors, product benefits sought, lifestyles, brand preferences, and usage rates. Individuals and organizations within segments should be quite similar with respect to several characteristics and product needs and differ considerably from individuals or organizations within other market segments. Table 8.2 illustrates market segment profiles resulting from a Professional Golfers' Association study of golfers' lifestyles. Marketers use market segment profiles to assess the degree to which the organization's possible products can match or fit potential customers' product needs. Market segment profiles provide marketers with an understanding of how an organization can use its capabilities to serve potential customer groups.

Step 4: Evaluate Relevant Market Segments

*A*fter analyzing the market segment profiles, a marketer is likely to identify several relevant market segments for which further analysis is required and to eliminate certain segments from consideration. To further assess relevant market segments, several important factors, including sales estimates, competition, and estimated costs associated with each segment should be determined and analyzed.

■ Sales Estimates

Potential sales for a segment can be measured along several dimensions, including product level, geographic area, time, and level of competition.[13] With respect to product level, potential sales can be estimated for a specific product item (for example, Diet Coke) or an entire product line (for example, Coca-Cola Classic, Caffeine-Free Coke, Diet Coke, Caffeine-Free Diet Coke, Cherry Coca-Cola, and Diet Cherry Coca-Cola comprise one product line). A manager must also determine the geographic area to be included in the estimate. In relation to time, sales estimates can be short-range (one year or less), medium-range (one to five years), or long-range (longer than five years). The competitive level specifies whether sales are being estimated for a single firm or for an entire industry.

Market potential The total amount of a product that customers will purchase within a specified period at a specific level of industrywide marketing activity

Market potential is the total amount of a product, for all firms in an industry, that customers will purchase within a specified period at a specific level of industrywide marketing activity. Market potential can be stated in terms of dollars or units. A segment's market potential is affected by economic, sociocultural, and other marketing environment forces. Marketers must assume a certain general level of marketing effort in the industry when they estimate market potential. The specific level of marketing effort varies from one firm to another, but the sum of all firms' marketing activities equals industry marketing efforts. A marketing manager must also consider whether and to what extent industry marketing efforts will change.

Company sales potential The maximum percentage of market potential that an individual firm can expect to obtain for a specific product

Company sales potential is the maximum percentage of market potential that an individual firm within an industry can expect to obtain for a specific product. Several factors influence company sales potential for a market segment. First, the market potential places absolute limits on the size of the company's sales potential. Second, the magnitude of industrywide marketing activities has an indirect but definite impact on the company's sales potential. Those activities have a direct bearing on the size of the market potential. When Domino's Pizza advertises home-delivered pizza, for example, it indirectly promotes pizza in general; its commercials may even help sell Pizza Hut's and other competitors' home-delivered pizza. Third, the intensity and effectiveness of a company's marketing activities relative to those of its competitors affect the size of the company's sales potential. If a company spends twice as much as any of its competitors on marketing efforts and if each dollar spent is more effective in generating sales, the firm's sales potential will be quite high compared with that of its competitors.

Breakdown approach Measuring company sales potential based on a general economic forecast for a specific time period and the market potential derived from it

There are two general approaches to measuring company sales potential: breakdown and buildup. In the **breakdown approach,** the marketing manager first develops a general economic forecast for a specific time period. Next, market potential is estimated on the basis of this economic forecast. The company's sales potential is then derived from the general economic forecast and estimate of market potential. In the **buildup approach,** an analyst begins by estimating how much of a product a potential buyer in a specific geographic area, such as a sales territory, will purchase in a given period. Then the analyst multiplies that amount by the total number of potential buyers in that area. The analyst performs the same calculation for each geographic area in which the firm sells products and then adds the totals for each area to calculate market potential. To determine company sales potential, the analyst must estimate, based on planned levels of company marketing activities, the proportion of the total market potential the company can obtain.

Buildup approach Measuring company sales potential by estimating how much of a product a potential buyer in a specific geographic area will purchase in a given time period, multiplying the estimate by the number of potential buyers, and adding the totals of all the geographic areas considered

■ Competitive Assessment

Besides obtaining sales estimates, it is crucial to assess competitors already operating in the segments being considered. Unless they are tempered with competitive information, sales estimates may be misleading. A market segment that seems attractive based on sales estimates may prove to be much less so when a competitive assessment is made. In such an assessment, several questions must be asked about competitors: How many of them are there? What are their strengths and weaknesses? Do several competitors have major market shares and together dominate the segment? Can our company create a marketing mix to compete effectively against competitors' marketing mixes? Is it likely that new competitors will enter this segment? If so, how will they affect our firm's ability to compete successfully? Answers to such questions are important for proper assessment of the competition in relevant market segments.

The actions of a national company that considered entering the dog food market illustrate the importance of competitive assessment. Through a segmentation study, the food processor determined that dog owners can be divided into three segments according to how they viewed their dogs and dog foods. One group saw their dogs as performing a definite utilitarian function, such as protecting family members, playing with children, guarding the property, or herding farm animals. These people wanted a low-priced, nutritional dog food and were not interested in a wide variety of flavors. The second segment of dog owners treated their dogs as companions and family members. These individuals were willing to pay relatively high prices for dog foods and wanted a variety of types and flavors so that their dogs would not get bored. Dog owners in the third segment had negative feelings and, in fact, were found to hate their dogs. These people wanted the cheapest dog food they could buy and were not concerned with nutrition, flavor, or variety. The food company examined the extent to which competitive brands were serving all these dog owners. It found that in each segment there were at least three well-entrenched competing brands, which together dominated the segment. The food company's management decided not to enter the dog food market because of the strength of the competing brands.

■ *Cost Estimates*

To fulfill the needs of a target segment, an organization must develop and maintain a marketing mix that precisely meets the wants and needs of individuals and organizations in that segment. Developing and maintaining such a mix can be expensive. Distinctive product features, attractive package design, generous product warranties, extensive advertising, attractive promotional offers, competitive prices, and high-quality personal service consume considerable organizational resources. Indeed, to reach certain segments, the costs may be so high that a marketer may see the segment as inaccessible. Another cost consideration is whether an organization can effectively reach a segment at costs equal to or below competitors' costs. If the firm's cost are likely to be higher, it will not be able to compete in that segment in the long run.

Step 5: Select Specific Target Markets

*A*n important initial issue to consider in this step is whether there are enough differences in customers' needs to warrant the use of market segmentation. If segmentation analysis shows customer needs to be fairly homogeneous, a firm's management may decide to use the undifferentiated approach, discussed earlier. However, if customer needs are heterogeneous, which is much more likely, then one or more target markets must be selected. On the other hand, marketers may decide not to enter and compete in any of the segments.

Assuming that one or more of the segments offer significant opportunities for the organization to achieve its objectives, marketers must decide which segments to participate in. Ordinarily, information gathered in the previous step—about sales estimates, competitors, and cost estimates—requires critical consideration in this final step to determine long-term profit opportunities. Also, the firm's management must investigate whether the organization has financial resources, managerial skills, labor expertise, and facilities allowing entry and effective competition in selected segments. Furthermore, the requirements of some market segments might be at odds with the firm's overall objectives, and the possibility of legal problems, conflicts with interest groups, and technological

Coffee, Tea or Duvet.

Announcing British Airways First Class Sleeper Service.™ It puts you in total control of your flight. Choose all your in-flight options before you board, slip into one of our special sleeper suits and relax. You see, we've finally put to bed the notion that airline seats can't be slept in. *It's the way we make you feel* that makes us the world's favourite airline.

BRITISH AIRWAYS
The world's favourite airline™

Figure 8.10
Selecting Specific Target Markets   British Airways designed its First Class Sleeper Service for travelers who desire all the comforts of home as they travel overseas by night.

advancements could make certain segments unattractive. In addition, when prospects for long-term growth are taken into account, some segments might appear very attractive and others less desirable.

Selecting appropriate target markets is important to an organization's adoption and use of the marketing concept philosophy. For example, British Airways carefully selected the target market for its First Class Sleeper Service (see Figure 8.10). Identifying the right target market is the key to implementing a successful marketing strategy, whereas failure to do so can lead to low sales, high costs, and severe financial losses. A careful target market analysis places an organization in a better position both to serve customers' needs and to achieve its objectives.

Developing Sales Forecasts

Sales forecast The amount of a product a company expects to sell during a specific period at a specified level of marketing activities

A **sales forecast** is the amount of a product the company actually expects to sell during a specific period at a specified level of marketing activities. The sales forecast differs from the company sales potential. It concentrates on what the actual sales will be at a certain level of company marketing effort, whereas the company sales potential assesses what sales are possible at various levels of marketing activities, assuming that certain environmental conditions will exist. Businesses use the sales forecast for planning, organizing, implementing, and controlling their activities. The success of numerous activities depends on this forecast's accuracy. Common problems in companies that fail are improper planning and lack of realistic sales forecasts. Overly ambitious sales forecasts lead to overbuying, overinvestment, and higher costs.

To forecast sales, a marketer can choose from a number of forecasting methods, some arbitrary, and others more scientific, complex, and time-consuming. A firm's choice of method or methods depends on the costs involved, type of product, market characteristics, time span of the forecast, purposes of the forecast, stability of the historical sales data, availability of required information, and forecasters' expertise and experience.[14]

Common forecasting techniques fall into five categories: executive judgment, surveys, time series analysis, regression analysis, and market tests.

■ *Executive Judgment*

Executive judgment Sales forecasting based on the intuition of one or more executives

At times, a company forecasts sales chiefly on the basis of **executive judgment,** the intuition of one or more executives. This approach is highly unscientific but expedient and inexpensive. Executive judgment may work reasonably well when product demand is relatively stable and the forecaster has years of market-related experience. However, because intuition is swayed most heavily by recent experience, the forecast may be overly optimistic or overly pessimistic. Another drawback to intuition is that the forecaster has only past experience as a guide for deciding where to go in the future.

■ *Surveys*

Another way to forecast sales is to question customers, sales personnel, or experts regarding their expectations about future purchases.

Customer forecasting survey A survey of customers regarding the quantities of products they intend to buy during a specific period

In a **customer forecasting survey,** marketers ask customers what types and quantities of products they intend to buy during a specific period. This approach may be useful to a business with relatively few customers. For example, a manufacturer such as Intel that is marketing to a limited number of companies (primarily computer manufacturers) could conduct customer forecasting surveys. PepsiCo, though, has millions of customers and cannot feasibly use a customer survey to forecast future sales.

Customer surveys have several drawbacks. Customers must be able and willing to make accurate estimates of future product requirements. Although industrial buyers can sometimes estimate their anticipated purchases accurately from historical buying data and their own sales forecasts, many cannot make such estimates. In addition, customers may not want to take part in a survey. Occasionally, a few respondents give answers they know are incorrect, making survey results inaccurate. Moreover, customer surveys reflect buying intentions, not actual purchases. Customers' intentions may not be well formulated, and even when potential purchasers have definite buying intentions, they do not necessarily follow through on them. Finally, customer surveys consume much time and money.

Sales-force forecasting survey Estimates by members of a firm's sales force of the anticipated sales in their territories for a specified period

In a **sales-force forecasting survey,** members of the firm's sales force estimate anticipated sales in their territories for a specified period of time. The forecaster combines these territorial estimates to arrive at a tentative forecast.

A marketer may survey the sales staff for several reasons. The most important is that the sales staff is closer to customers on a daily basis than other company personnel; therefore, it should know more about customers' future product needs. Moreover, when sales representatives assist in developing the forecast, they are more likely to work toward its achievement. Another advantage of this method is that forecasts can be prepared for single territories, divisions consisting of several territories, regions made up of multiple divisions, and the total geographic market. Thus the method provides sales forecasts from the smallest geographic sales unit to the largest.

Despite these benefits, a sales-force survey has certain limitations. Salespeople can be too optimistic or pessimistic because of recent experiences. In addition, salespeople tend to underestimate sales potential in their territories when they believe that their sales goals will be determined by their forecasts. They also dislike paperwork because it takes up the time that could be spent selling. If preparation of a territorial sales forecast is time-consuming, the sales staff may not do the job adequately.

Nonetheless, sales-force surveys can be effective under certain conditions. First of all, the salespeople as a group must be accurate—or at least consistent—estimators. If the aggregate forecast is consistently over or under actual sales, then the marketer who develops the final forecast can make the necessary adjustments. Assuming that the survey is well administered, the sales force can have the satisfaction of helping to establish reasonable sales goals and the assurance that its forecasts are not being used to set sales quotas.

Expert forecasting survey Sales forecasts prepared by experts such as economists, management consultants, advertising executives, college professors, or other persons outside the firm

When a company wants an **expert forecasting survey,** it hires professionals to help prepare the sales forecast. These experts are usually economists, management consultants, advertising executives, college professors, or other persons outside the firm with solid experience in a specific market. Drawing on this experience and their analyses of available information about the company and the market, experts prepare and present forecasts or answer questions regarding a forecast. Using experts is expedient and relatively inexpensive. However, because they work outside the firm, these forecasters may not be as motivated as company personnel to do an effective job.

Delphi technique A procedure in which experts create initial forecasts, submit them to the company for averaging, and then refine the forecasts

A more complex form of the expert forecasting survey is to incorporate the Delphi technique. The **Delphi technique** is a procedure in which experts create initial forecasts, submit them to the company for averaging, and have the results returned to them so that they can make individual refined forecasts. The premise is that the experts will use the averaged results when making refined forecasts and that these forecasts will be in a narrower range. The procedure may be repeated several times until the experts—each working separately—reach a consensus on the forecasts. The ultimate goal in using the Delphi technique is to develop a highly accurate sales forecast.

Time Series Analysis

Time series analysis A forecasting method that uses historical sales data to discover patterns in the firm's sales over time and generally involves trend, cycle, seasonal, and random factor analyses

Trend analysis An analysis that focuses on aggregate sales data over a period of many years to determine general trends in annual sales

Cycle analysis An analysis of sales figures for a period of three to five years to ascertain whether sales fluctuate in a consistent, periodic manner

Seasonal analysis An analysis of daily, weekly, or monthly sales figures to evaluate the degree to which seasonal factors influence sales

Random factor analysis An analysis attempting to attribute erratic sales variation to random, nonrecurrent events

With **time series analysis,** the forecaster uses the firm's historical sales data to discover a pattern or patterns in the firm's sales over time. If a pattern is found, it can be used to forecast sales. This forecasting method assumes that past sales patterns will continue in the future. The accuracy, and thus usefulness, of time series analysis hinges on the validity of this assumption.

In a time series analysis, a forecaster usually performs four types of analyses: trend, cycle, seasonal, and random factor. **Trend analysis** focuses on aggregate sales data, such as a company's annual sales figures, from a period of many years to determine whether annual sales are generally rising, falling, or staying about the same. Through **cycle analysis,** a forecaster analyzes sales figures (often monthly sales data) from a period of three to five years to ascertain whether sales fluctuate in a consistent, periodic manner. When performing **seasonal analysis,** the analyst studies daily, weekly, or monthly sales figures to evaluate the degree to which seasonal factors, such as climate and holiday activities, influence sales. **Random factor analysis** is an attempt to attribute erratic sales variations to random, nonrecurrent events, such as a regional power failure, a natural disaster, or political unrest in a foreign market. After performing each of these analyses, the forecaster combines the results to develop the sales forecast. Time series analysis is an effective forecasting method for products with reasonably stable demand but not for products with highly erratic demand.

Regression Analysis

Regression analysis A method of predicting sales based on finding a relationship between past sales and one or more variables, such as population or income

Like time series analysis, regression analysis requires the use of historical sales data. In **regression analysis,** the forecaster seeks to find a relationship between past sales (the dependent variable) and one or more independent variables, such as population, per capita income, or gross national product. Simple regression analysis uses one independent variable while multiple regression analysis includes two or more independent variables. The objective of regression analysis is to develop a mathematical formula that accurately describes a relationship between the firm's sales and one or more variables; however, the formula indicates only an association, not a causal relationship. Once an accurate formula is established, the analyst plugs the necessary information into the formula to derive the sales forecast.

Regression analysis is useful when a precise association can be established. However, a forecaster seldom finds a perfect one. Furthermore, this method can be used only when available historical sales data are extensive. Thus regression analysis is futile for forecasting new-product sales.

Market Tests

Market test Making a product available to buyers in one or more test areas and measuring purchases and consumer responses

Conducting a **market test** involves making a product available to buyers in one or more test areas and measuring purchases and consumer responses to distribution, promotion, and price. Test areas are often cities with populations of 200,000 to 500,000, but can be larger metropolitan areas or towns with populations of 50,000 to 200,000. A market test provides information about consumers' actual, rather than intended, purchases. In addition, purchase volume can be evaluated in relation to the intensity of other marketing activities—advertising, in-store promotions, pricing, packaging, distribution, and the like. Forecasters base their estimate of product sales for larger geographic units on customer response in test areas.

Because it does not require historical sales data, a market test is effective for forecasting sales of new products or sales of existing products in new geographic areas. A market test also gives a marketer an opportunity to test various elements of the marketing mix. But these tests are often time-consuming and expensive. In addition, a marketer cannot be certain that consumer response during a market test represents the total market response or that such a response will continue in the future.

■ *Using Multiple Forecasting Methods*

Although some businesses depend on a single sales forecasting method, most firms use several techniques. A company is sometimes forced to use several methods when marketing diverse product lines, but even for a single product line several forecasts may be needed, especially when the product is sold to different market segments. Thus a producer of automobile tires may rely on one technique to forecast tire sales for new cars and on another to forecast sales of replacement tires. Variation in the length of needed forecasts may call for several forecasting methods. A firm that employs one method for a short-range forecast may find it inappropriate for long-range forecasting. Sometimes a marketer verifies results of one method by using one or several other methods and comparing outcomes.

SUMMARY

A market is an aggregate of people who, as individuals or as organizations, have needs for products in a product class and who have the ability, willingness, and authority to purchase such products.

In general, marketers employ a five-step process when selecting a target market. Step 1 is to identify the appropriate targeting strategy. When a company designs a single marketing mix and directs it at the entire market for a particular product, it is using an undifferentiated targeting strategy. The undifferentiated strategy is effective in a homogeneous market, whereas a heterogeneous market needs to be segmented through a concentrated targeting strategy or a differentiated targeting strategy. Both these strategies divide markets into segments consisting of individuals, groups, or organizations that have one or more similar characteristics and so can be linked to similar product needs. When using a concentrated strategy, an organization directs marketing efforts toward a single market segment through one marketing mix. With a differentiated targeting strategy, an organization directs customized marketing efforts at two or more segments.

Certain conditions must exist for effective market segmentation. First, customers' needs for the product should be heterogeneous. Second, the segments of the market should be identifiable and divisible. Third, the total market should be divided so that segments can be compared with respect to estimated sales, costs, and profits. Fourth, at least one segment must have enough profit potential to justify developing and maintaining a special marketing mix for that segment. Fifth, the firm must be able to reach the chosen segment with a particular marketing mix.

Step 2 is determining which segmentation variables to use. Segmentation variables are the characteristics of individuals, groups, or organizations used to divide a total market into segments. The segmentation variable should be related to customers' needs for, uses of, or behavior toward the product. Segmentation variables for consumer markets can be grouped into four categories: demographic (age, gender, income, ethnicity, family life cycle), geographic (population, market density, climate), psychographic (personality traits, motives, lifestyle), and behavioristic (volume usage, end use, expected benefits, brand loyalty, price sensitivity). Variables for segmenting organizational markets include geographic location, type of organization, customer size, and product use.

Step 3 in the target market selection process is to develop market segment profiles. Profiles describe the similarities among potential customers within a segment and explain the differences among people and organizations in different market segments. Step 4 is evaluating relevant market segments, which requires that several important factors—including sales estimates, competition, and estimated costs associated with each segment—be determined and analyzed. Step 5 involves the final selection of specific target markets. In this final step, companies consider whether enough differences in customers' needs exist to warrant segmentation and which segments to focus on.

A sales forecast is the amount of a product the company actually expects to sell during a specific period at a specified level of marketing activities. To forecast sales, marketers can choose from a number of methods depending on costs involved, type of product, market characteristics, and time span and purposes of the forecast. There are five categories of forecasting techniques: executive judgment, surveys, time series analysis, regression analysis, and market tests. Executive judgment is based on the intuition of one or more executives. Surveys include customer forecasting surveys and sales-force forecasting surveys. Time series analysis uses the firm's historical sales data to discover any patterns in the firm's sales over time and comprises four major types of analyses: trend, cycle, seasonal, and random factor. With regression analysis, forecasters attempt to find a relationship between past sales and one or more independent variables. Market testing involves making a product available to buyers in one or more test areas and measuring purchases, as well as consumer responses to distribution, promotion, and price. Many companies employ multiple forecasting methods by combining one or more of the above types.

IMPORTANT TERMS

Market	Differentiated targeting strategy	Company sales potential	Expert forecasting survey
Undifferentiated targeting strategy	Segmentation variables	Breakdown approach	Delphi technique
Homogeneous market	Market density	Buildup approach	Time series analysis
Heterogeneous market	Geodemographic segmentation	Sales forecast	Trend analysis
Market segmentation	Micromarketing	Executive judgment	Cycle analysis
Market segment	Benefit segmentation	Customer forecasting survey	Seasonal analysis
Concentrated targeting strategy	Market potential	Sales-force forecasting survey	Random factor analysis
			Regression analysis
			Market test

DISCUSSION AND REVIEW QUESTIONS

1. What is a market? What are the requirements for a market?
2. In your local area, can you identify a group of people with unsatisfied product needs who represent a market? Could this market be reached by a business organization? Why or why not?
3. Outline the five major steps in the target market selection process.
4. What is an undifferentiated strategy? Under what conditions is it most useful? Describe a present market situation in which a company is using an undifferentiated strategy. Is the business successful? Why or why not?
5. What is market segmentation? Describe the basic conditions required for effective segmentation. Identify several firms that use market segmentation.
6. List the differences between concentrated and differentiated strategies, and describe the advantages and disadvantages of each.
7. Identify and describe four major categories of variables that can be used to segment consumer markets. Give examples of product markets that are segmented by variables in each category.
8. What dimensions are used to segment organizational markets?

9. Define geodemographic segmentation. Name several types of firms that might employ this type of market segmentation, and explain why.
10. What is a market segment profile? Why is it an important step in the target market selection process?
11. Describe the important factors that marketers should analyze in order to evaluate market segments.
12. Why is a marketer concerned about sales potential when trying to find a target market?
13. Why is selecting appropriate target markets important to an organization that wants to adopt the marketing concept philosophy?
14. What is a sales forecast? Why is it important?
15. What are the two primary types of surveys a company might use to forecast sales? Why would a company use an outside expert forecasting survey?
16. Under what conditions are market tests useful for sales forecasting? Discuss the advantages and disadvantages of market tests.
17. Discuss the benefits of using multiple forecasting methods.

APPLICATION QUESTIONS

1. MTV Latino targets the growing Hispanic market in the United States. Identify another product marketed to a distinct target market. Identify the target market, and describe how the marketing mix appeals specifically to that group.

2. Generally, marketers use one of three basic targeting strategies to focus on a target market: (1) undifferentiated, (2) concentrated, or (3) differentiated. Locate an article that describes the targeting strategy of a particular company or organization. Describe the target market, and explain the strategy being used to reach that market.

3. The stereo market may be segmented according to income and age. Name two ways the market for each of the following products might be segmented.
   a. candy bars
   b. travel agency services
   c. bicycles
   d. hair spray

4. If you were using a time series analysis to forecast sales for your company for the next year, how would you use the following sets of sales figures?

   a.

1987	$145,000	1992	$149,000
1988	$144,000	1993	$148,000
1989	$147,000	1994	$180,000
1990	$145,000	1995	$191,000
1991	$148,000	1996	$227,000

   b.

	1994	*1995*	*1996*
Jan.	$12,000	$14,000	$16,000
Feb.	$13,000	$14,000	$15,500
Mar.	$12,000	$14,000	$17,000
Apr.	$13,000	$15,000	$17,000
May	$15,000	$17,000	$20,000
June	$18,000	$18,000	$21,000
July	$18,500	$18,000	$21,500
Aug.	$18,500	$19,000	$22,000
Sep.	$17,000	$18,000	$21,000
Oct.	$16,000	$15,000	$19,000
Nov.	$13,000	$14,000	$19,000
Dec.	$14,000	$15,000	$18,000

   c. 1994 sales increased 21.2% (opened additional store in 1994)

   1996 sales increased 18.8% (opened another store in 1996)

Case 8.1   Ryka Athletic Shoes: By Women, For Women, Helping Women

Sheri Poe is the founder and CEO of Ryka, Inc., manufacturer of women's shoes for aerobics, step aerobics, walking, running, hiking, and cross-training. Knowing it wouldn't be easy for an upstart like Ryka to compete with giants like Reebok and Nike for a share in the $11 billion athletic footwear industry, Poe from the start resorted to some unusual marketing strategies. For example, she had her British distributor deliver several pairs of Rykas with a personal note to fitness enthusiast Princess Diana. The royal trainer told Ryka that the princess not only liked the fit, but was also moved by the company's donation of part of its profits toward stopping violence against women. Ryka is Poe's way of fulfilling her dream—running a business and also helping women who are victims of rape, assault, and abuse.

The Ryka phenomenon began when Poe and several of her aerobics classmates realized that they were experiencing back pain because their shoes didn't fit right. Poe surveyed department stores and athletic footwear shops, asking customers and salespeople what kinds of shoes they wanted. She discovered that no one was paying attention to the women's market. The majority of women's shoes were designed simply as scaled-down versions of men's shoes. To get a proper and painless fit, women needed athletic shoes with higher arches and thinner heels, but couldn't find them. Poe decided that there was a future for a company that made athletic shoes just for women.

Rather than cater to the whims of fashion, Ryka concentrates on manufacturing only high-performance athletic shoes that fit a woman's foot. Rykas are anatomically correct for women's feet, and the company's patented Nitrogen E/S system provides cushioning and shock absorption for the heel and ball of the foot. Ryka Ultra-Lite aerobics shoes weigh only 7.7 ounces, about one-third that of regular aerobic shoes. Ryka was the first athletic shoe producer to develop and market lightweight shoes specifically designed for the ups and downs of step aerobics.

What sets Ryka apart from other athletic shoe companies, though, is not only its unique product line. The real soul of Ryka is its commitment to being a socially responsible company. When Sheri Poe was a young college student, she was assaulted and raped. In launching Ryka, Poe was determined that her company find ways to help women who, like her, had been victims of violent crimes. Seven percent of Ryka Shoes' pretax profits goes to the ROSE Fund, *rose* standing for "restoring one's self-esteem." When women buy a pair of Rykas, they know that some of their money provides educational material and supports battered women's shelters, violence-prevention programs, and nonprofit treatment centers. A card attached to shoelaces outlines physical safety tips for women. Ryka reminds retailers that carry its shoes, "You and your customers can make a difference."

From the beginning, Ryka battled for every small success. Until it found a quality manufacturer in Korea, Ryka shoes often either didn't fit or fell apart. Until Poe hired a vice president of marketing and sales who shifted the company's marketing emphasis from its

cause to its shoes, many retailers wouldn't carry Ryka because it wasn't a nationally recognized brand. Despite Sheri Poe's remarkable energy and devotion to her company and her cause, Ryka has continued to struggle for survival. In 1995, a planned merger with L.A. Gear fell through. But such hurdles don't cause Poe to lose stride; her dream is still alive. As long as women buy Ryka brands, part of the profits will support the ROSE Fund.[15]

Questions for Discussion

1. What type of general targeting strategy is Ryka using? Explain

2. Which segmentation variables is Ryka using?

3. Evaluate the sales and marketing vice president's decision to shift the company's marketing focus from its cause (preventing violence against women) to its shoes.

Case 8.2   Sports Illustrated Scores Through Segmentation

Sports fans come in all shapes and sizes. Aware that they also come in all ages and live in all regions, *Sports Illustrated* offers an assortment of publications created to attract diverse groups of sports enthusiasts. From the middle-aged Monday-morning quarterback to the 8-year-old future quarterback, Time Warner's *Sports Illustrated* segments its market to offer something for everyone.

Although the main body of the magazine remains the same in issues sold throughout the United States, each *Sports Illustrated* allots some space for regional advertising and often includes one or two articles of special interest to specific regions. The publication's managing editor can also elect to develop issues that focus entirely on one region. The number of regional issues varies from year to year; selected areas are usually associated with a major sports event, such as the city that won the Superbowl or the university whose team captured the national college basketball title. For example, when the University of Nebraska earned the title of America's number one college football team, *Sports Illustrated* produced a regional edition devoted exclusively to that state. Such specials sell heavily in the highlighted market.

Besides the more than 3 million Americans who subscribe to *Sports Illustrated*, fans all over the world enjoy the magazine. In Canada alone there are almost 150,000 subscribers. To appeal more directly to its

North American neighbors, *Sports Illustrated* introduced a separate Canadian edition that is printed in Canada, has its own distinct cover, and includes special articles aimed at the Canadian audience. The premier issue was a spring baseball preview featuring expanded coverage of the Montreal Expos and the Toronto Blue Jays.

Operating with the strategy that today's little sports enthusiasts are tomorrow's adult sports enthusiasts and hoping to establish brand loyalty at an early age, Time Warner launched *Sports Illustrated for Kids* in 1989. The publishers strive to get their magazine to youngsters, whether by traditional methods or by offering free subscriptions on the back of Wheaties cereal boxes or by distributing 250,000 free copies nationwide to low-income school districts. Although many industry experts were skeptical in the beginning, circulation has reached over 1 million. Recognizing how effectively the magazine reaches the powerful children's market, advertisers increased the number of print ads appearing in *Sports Illustrated for Kids* by 55.7 percent in one year.

When conducting early focus groups for its children's spinoff, *Sports Illustrated* learned that research into its potential audience is essential because children's tastes, habits, and opinions change often and quickly. From both an editorial and a marketing standpoint, assert the publishers, they can never know too much about kids. To learn about its readers, *Sports Illustrated for Kids* employs subscriber studies, personal interviews, focus groups, and other research methods. Sending questionnaires to subscribers and their parents on a regular basis, the magazine gathers information on household demographics and buying habits. The publishers also established what they call "lab schools"—learning centers where magazine staff observe and visit with children as they read the magazine.

Encouraged by the success of *Sports Illustrated for Kids*, *Sports Illustrated* decided to target the opposite end of the market's spectrum, older adults. *Sports Illustrated Classic* is a rendition of the standard magazine filled with nostalgic articles about games and players familiar to older audiences. To attract the growing number of technophiles, *Sports Illustrated* recently came out with a CD-ROM version, offering individual issues as well as the popular *Year in Review* and *Media Gallery*, a collection of over 600 of the magazine's award-winning photographs.

Recently, *Advertising Age* presented *Sports Illustrated* with its "Magazine of the Year" award. It honored *SI*'s ability to keep a mature magazine thriving by creating spinoff titles and custom publishing products that successfully attract new audiences.[16]

Questions for Discussion

1. What type of targeting strategy is *Sports Illustrated* using?
2. Which kinds of segmentation variables are being employed by *Sports Illustrated?*
3. What other types of segmentation might *Sports Illustrated* marketers consider?

STRATEGIC CASE 2

Black & Decker Goes after Serious Do-It-Yourselfers

Between the professional contractor and the entry-level putterer is a growing home improvement market, the "serious do-it-yourselfer." A person in this market segment may have rewired a light switch successfully and feels confident enough to tackle the installation of a garage door opener. Known in the industry as SDIYers, this consumer group has advanced beyond the starter tool kit and the $25 electric screwdriver but isn't ready to pay $300 for a professional-quality saw. The Black & Decker Corporation, the world's largest manufacturer and marketer of power tools and electric lawn and garden products, responded to the 22 million customers in the segment. After conducting extensive consumer research, Black & Decker created Quantum, a line of power tools priced from $60 to $100.

Background

After World War II, the United States entered the power tool era, in which machines simultaneously enhanced worker skills and conserved energy. By that time, Black & Decker had already produced tools that defined the industry. Started in 1910 by S. Duncan Black and Alonzo G. Decker, the company produced the first portable electric drill in 1916. With a pistol grip and trigger switch, it offered a level of safety and ease of use never before available to nonprofessionals. Black & Decker continued to market standard-setting tools, including the first portable electric screwdriver, the first electric hammer, finishing sanders, jigsaws, and the nearly indispensable Dustbuster. Today, Black & Decker Corporation is a global company with widely recognized brand names, worldwide distribution, 8 number one selling products, and annual sales of almost $5 billion.

Consumer Input Shapes the Quantum Line

Despite its successes, Black & Decker remained number three behind Japan's Makita and Sears' Craftsman. Industry research suggested that many nonprofessional consumers were dissatisfied with available economy-priced tools but unwilling to pay top dollar for top-of-the-line items. Quantum was Black & Decker's way of meeting the needs of those SDIYers while also luring market share from its competitors.

Before creating Quantum, Black & Decker hired an independent research firm to assemble a "living laboratory" composed of fifty male homeowners, aged 25 to 54, who owned more than six power tools. Over a three-month period, researchers questioned them about their tools and the particular brands they chose. Questions such as "What was your first project?" and "How did you feel about doing it?" were designed to elicit candid discussion. Black & Decker's own market-

ing executives also visited members of the group at their homes and workshops to watch them use their tools, find out how comfortably they handled their tools, and observe how they cleaned their work spaces. Black & Decker marketers even went along on shopping trips to monitor what the do-it-yourselfers bought and how much they spent.

Black & Decker's research revealed that SDIYers wanted a cordless drill with enough power to finish a job without requiring a recharge; a safety feature that stops a saw blade as soon as it's switched off rather than letting it spin dangerously for more than ten seconds; and something to help clean up sawdust. Armed with the research results, Black & Decker was ready to start developing.

Building What Customers Want

Instead of following Black & Decker's customary slow procedure for bringing new products to the market, the company's CEO put product development on the fast track. He created the "Fusion Team," made up of eighty-five engineers, designers, finance people, and marketers from around the world and charged them with getting the Quantum line to customers as soon as possible. The team came up with a powerful drill with a detachable battery pack that recharges completely in one hour rather than overnight; an automatic braking system that stops saw blades in two seconds; and a sander and circular saw equipped with a mini-vacuum bag to suck up sawdust. To ensure that Quantum buyers get quality service as well as quality tools, Black & Decker introduced "PowerSource," a free maintenance check for Quantum tool owners. A toll-free hotline providing answers to home-repair questions helps customers use Quantum tools effectively.

To iron out the final details of the Quantum line, Black & Decker again turned to its potential customers. The Fusion Team chose deep green for the Quantum line because consumers associate the color with quality and reliability. Although some members suggested "Excell" and "Excalibur" as code names, the team kept Quantum because customer research found it was the most popular. The Black & Decker trademark appeared on the packaging and products because a customer survey revealed that do-it-yourselfers respect the name.

Introducing the Quantum Line

Quantum's public debut was made at a New York City "build-a-thon" to benefit a municipal homeless shelter. Movie stars and famous athletes used Quantum saws and drills to build enough furniture, such as closets, tables, and benches, to fill six 40-foot trucks. At the three-day National Hardware Show, about 3,000 hardware manufacturers and retailers chose Quantum for the Retailer's Choice award. A $10 million advertising campaign promoted Quantum on television and in print with the slogan "Serious Tools for Serious Projects."

Targeting Other Market Segments

Black & Decker is increasing its emphasis on market segmentation. To attract midrange professionals, who had shunned the company's products, Black & Decker launched the DeWalt line of professional power tools. Upscale, precision-engineered, rugged, DeWalt tools cost over $100 each. By pricing these products higher, changing their color from black (the color of Black & Decker's regular line) to yellow, and displaying the DeWalt name prominently, the company made the superior line easily distinguishable from the SDIYers line. In addition, Black & Decker more effectively reached its target market by offering DeWalt tools at outlets such as The Home Depot and not at mass merchandisers such as Wal-Mart.

To market irons, Black & Decker targets customers according to demographics. For younger customers it offers the Wild 'N Steamy iron in teal, fuchsia, and "hot blue." For nostalgic baby boomers, there is the Classic, weighing a hefty three-and-a half pounds. For those who prefer the top of the line, Black & Decker offers the SurgeXpress, a lightweight iron designed to emit more steam than any other it manufactures. Television ads for this model parallel those for high-performance automobiles.

Power tools account for $1.364 billion of Black & Decker's revenues, but Black & Decker also sells millions of dollars worth of household appliances, security hardware, outdoor products, plumbing accessories, fastening systems, information services and systems, and more. By dividing each market into segments, Black & Decker successfully satisfies the needs of more people and therefore sells more products.

Questions for Discussion

1. What approach has Black & Decker management taken in selecting and analyzing the target market for Quantum tools?
2. What information did Black & Decker acquire through marketing research, and how was that information used?
3. What specific customer needs did Black & Decker attempt to satisfy
4. Which factors are most likely to influence the consumer buying decision process for Black & Decker Quantum tools?

Sources: Susan Caminiti, "A Star Is Born," *Fortune*, Autumn/Winter 1993, pp. 44–47; Jessica Hall, "Black & Decker's New Line Hits Stores Next Month," *Baltimore Business Journal*, Aug. 13, 1993; Kim Clark, "B & D to Introduce Midpriced Power Tools," *Baltimore Sun*, Apr. 28, 1993; Terry Lefton, "B & D Retools with Quantum," *Brandweek*, July 5, 1993, p. 1; Gary Hoover, Alta Campbell, and Patrick J. Spain, eds., *Hoover's Handbook of American Business 1995* (Austin, Texas: Reference Press, 1995), pp. 284–285; Lisa Kempger, "Ironing Out Design Analysis," *Computer-Aided Engineering*, July 1995, p. 10; Norton Pale, "Back From the Dead," *Sales & Marketing Management*, July 1995, pp. 30–31; and Joseph Weber, "A Better Grip on Hawking Tools," *Business Week*, June 5, 1995, p. 99.

Part 3

Product Decisions

*W*e are now prepared to analyze the decisions and activities associated with developing and maintaining effective marketing mixes. In Parts 3 through 6 we focus on the major components of the marketing mix: product, distribution, promotion, and price. Specifically, in Part 3 we explore the product ingredient of the marketing mix. Chapter 9 introduces basic concepts and relationships that must be understood if one is to make effective product decisions. In Chapter 10 we analyze a variety of dimensions regarding product management, including product modification, new product development, and product elimination. Branding, packaging, and labeling are discussed in Chapter 11. The nature, importance, and classification of services are explored in Chapter 12.

Chapter 9

Product Concepts

OBJECTIVES

- To understand the concept of a product

- To understand how to classify products

- To become familiar with the concepts of product item, product line, and product mix and understand how they are connected

- To understand the concept of product life cycle

- To become familiar with the concepts of product differentiation, product quality, product design, and product support services

- To become aware of how products are positioned and repositioned

- To gain insight into the types of organizational structures used for managing products

Customers trail SnackWell's delivery trucks to the supermarket.

*I*n our never-ending quest to be thin, Americans don't count calories as much as we used to—we count fat grams instead. In response, the food industry has inundated grocery stores with products promising to reduce the fat in our diets. Most celebrated and successful among these is RJR Nabisco's SnackWell's line of cookies, crackers, and more. In its first two years on the market, SnackWell's grew from new product, to hot brand, to line extensions, to a $400-million megabrand phenomenon. Recently, SnackWell's topped venerable Oreos and Ritz to become America's number one brand of cookies and crackers.

First, Nabisco introduced SnackWell's Devil's Food Cookie Cakes. These no-fat, no-cholesterol treats quickly became so popular that the cookie maker couldn't keep up with demand. Diet-conscious consumers resorted to following SnackWell's delivery trucks to supermarkets, not just in the amusing "cookie-man" commercials, but in real life. To satisfy demand for the cocoa-and-marshmallow-covered chocolate cookie, Nabisco increased production capacity to nine times the original, but it still wasn't enough. Nabisco product developers were convinced; consumers clearly craved more SnackWell's. Next came wheat crackers, oatmeal raisin cookies, chocolate chip cookies, and low-fat chocolate and vanilla sandwich cookies. All were successful. It was time to grow beyond the cookie aisle.

Nabisco's director for wellness brands asserts that the company is looking for more markets where SnackWell's can meet consumer desire for low-fat healthy snacks. SnackWell's nonfat apple, strawberry, and blueberry cereal bars and fat-free toaster pastries satisfy the need for a healthy breakfast alternative. In its first foray into the dairy case, SnackWell's introduced six flavors of no-fat chocolate yogurt. Number three novelty marketer Eskimo Pie Corp. recently signed a licensing agreement with SnackWell's to develop several low-fat ice cream and frozen yogurt desserts containing SnackWell's cookie bits. Nabisco is also rolling out SnackWell's 50 percent reduced-fat pies in stores and bakeries. Snack-Well's also offers nonfat granola bars and has plans for cheesecake, pie shells, and cookie mixes.

SnackWell's spectacular success has sounded a wake-up call for its competitors. Number two Keebler now serves a plateful of fat-free and low-fat products such as Delights Fruitastic fruit bars and fat-free devil's food cookies. Frito-Lay expects that its new low-fat pretzels, chips, and similar snacks will soon account for almost one-third of its sales. Wal-Mart stores is introducing an exclusive line of low-fat/no-fat fruit bars, devil's food cookies, popcorn, pretzels, and other snacks. As the industry plays catch-up with SnackWell's, the smorgasbord becomes more laden with consumer-pleasing choices.[1]

The product is an important variable in the marketing mix. Products such as SnackWell's can be a firm's most important asset and visible contact with buyers. If a company's products do not meet its customers' desires and needs, the company will fail unless it makes adjustments. Developing successful products, as Nabisco does, requires knowledge of fundamental marketing and product concepts.

In this chapter we first introduce and define what a product is and how buyers view products. Next we examine the concepts of product line and product mix to help us understand product planning. We then explore the stages of the product life cycle. Each life cycle stage generally requires a specific marketing strategy, operates within a certain competitive environment, and has its own sales and profit pattern. Next, we examine product differentiation, looking closely at product quality, product design, and product features. We then discuss product positioning and repositioning and conclude the chapter with a look at several organizational approaches used to manage products.

What Is a Product?

Product Anything, tangible or intangible, received in an exchange

Good A tangible physical entity

Service An intangible result of the application of human and mechanical efforts to people or objects

Ideas Concepts, philosophies, images, or issues

A **product** is anything you receive in an exchange. This can be either tangible or intangible and includes functional, social, and psychological utilities or benefits. A product can be an idea, a service, a good, or any combination of these three. This definition also covers supporting services that go with goods, such as installation, guarantees, product information, and promises of repair or maintenance. A **good** is a tangible physical entity, such as a Black & Decker drill or a Big Mac. A **service,** by contrast, is intangible; it is the result of the application of human and mechanical efforts to people or objects. Examples of services include a game at Madison Square Garden between the New York Knicks and the Boston Celtics, medical examinations, child day care and real estate services (see Figure 9.1). (Chapter 12 provides a detailed discussion of services.) **Ideas** are concepts, philosophies, images, or issues. They provide the psychological stimulation that aids in solving problems or adjusting to the environment. For example, MADD (Mothers Against Drunk Driving) promotes safe consumption of alcohol and stricter enforcement of laws against drunk driving (see Figure 9.1).

**Figure 9.1
Examples of a Services Marketer and a Marketer of Ideas**
REMAX is a marketer of real estate services and MADD is primarily a marketer of ideas.

When buyers purchase a product, they are really buying the benefits and satisfaction they think the product will provide. A Rolex watch, for example, is purchased to make a statement of success, not just for telling time. Services, in particular, are purchased on the basis of promises of satisfaction. Promises, suggested by images and symbols, help consumers make judgments about tangible and intangible products.[2] Often, symbols and cues are used to make intangible products more tangible or real to the consumer. Allstate Insurance Co., for example, uses giant hands to symbolize security, strength, and friendliness.

Classifying Products

Consumer Products
Products purchased to satisfy personal and family needs

Organizational products
Products bought to use in a firm's operations, to resell, or to make other products

*P*roducts fall into one of two general categories. Products purchased to satisfy personal and family needs are **consumer products.** Those bought to use in a firm's operations, to resell, or to make other products are **organizational products.** Consumers buy products to satisfy their personal wants, whereas business buyers seek to satisfy the goals of their organizations.

The same item can be both a consumer product and an organizational product. For example, when consumers buy a computer disk for their home computer, it is classified as a consumer product. However, when a large corporation purchases computer disks for office use, they are considered organizational products because they are used in the daily operations of the firm. Thus the buyer's intent—or the ultimate use of the product—determines whether an item is classified as a consumer or an organizational product.

Why do we need to know about product classifications? The main reason is that classes of products are aimed at particular target markets, and this affects distribution, promotion, and pricing decisions. Furthermore, the types of marketing efforts needed differ among the classes of consumer or organizational products. In short, the entire marketing mix can be affected by how a product is classified. In the next section we examine the characteristics of consumer and organizational products and explore the marketing activities associated with some of them.

■ Consumer Products

The most widely accepted approach to classifying consumer products is based on characteristics of consumer purchasing behavior. It divides products into four categories: convenience, shopping, specialty, and unsought products. However, not all buyers behave in the same way when purchasing a specific type of product. Thus a single product can fit into several categories. To minimize this problem, marketers think in terms of how buyers *generally* behave when purchasing a specific item. In addition, they recognize that the "correct" classification can be determined only by considering a particular firm's intended target market. With these thoughts in mind, let us examine the four traditional categories of consumer products.

Convenience products
Relatively inexpensive, frequently purchased items for which buyers exert minimal purchasing effort

Convenience Products Convenience products are relatively inexpensive, frequently purchased items for which buyers exert only minimal purchasing effort. They range from bread, soft drinks, and chewing gum to gasoline and newspapers. The buyer spends little time planning the purchase or comparing available brands or sellers. Even a buyer who prefers a specific brand will readily choose a substitute if the preferred brand is not conveniently available.

Classifying a product as a convenience product has several implications for a firm's marketing strategy. A convenience product is normally marketed through many retail outlets. Because sellers experience high inventory turnover, per-unit gross margins can be relatively low. Producers of convenience products, such as Wrigley's chewing gum and Mennen's Speed Stick antiperspirant expect little promotional effort at the retail level and thus must provide it themselves with advertising and sales promotion. Packaging is also an important element of the marketing mix for convenience products. The package may have to sell the product because many convenience items are available only on a self-service basis at the retail level.

Shopping products Items for which buyers are willing to expend considerable effort in planning and making the purchase

Shopping Products

Shopping products are items for which buyers are willing to expend considerable effort in planning and making the purchase. Buyers allocate much time for comparing stores and brands with respect to prices, product features, qualities, services, and perhaps warranties. Appliances, furniture, stereos, cameras, and bicycles exemplify shopping products. These products are expected to last a fairly long time and thus are purchased less frequently than convenience items. Even though shopping products are more expensive than convenience products, few buyers of shopping products are particularly brand loyal. If they were, they would be unwilling to shop and compare among brands.

To market a shopping product effectively, a marketer considers several key issues. Shopping products require fewer retail outlets than convenience products. Because shopping products are purchased less frequently, inventory turnover is lower, and middlemen expect to receive higher gross margins. Although large sums of money may be required to advertise shopping products, an even larger percentage of resources is likely to be used for personal selling. Usually, the producer and the middlemen expect some cooperation from one another with respect to providing parts and repair services and performing promotional activities.

Specialty products Items that have unique characteristics and that buyers are willing to expend considerable effort to obtain

Specialty Products

Specialty products possess one or more unique characteristics, and a significant group of buyers is willing to expend considerable effort to obtain them. Buyers actually plan the purchase of a specialty product; they know exactly what they want and will not accept a substitute. Examples of specialty products include a Mont Blanc pen or a one-of-a-kind piece of baseball memorabilia, such as a ball signed by Babe Ruth. When searching for specialty products, buyers do not compare alternatives; they are concerned primarily with finding an outlet that has a preselected product available.

The fact that an item is a specialty product can affect a firm's marketing efforts in several ways. Specialty products are often distributed through a limited number of retail outlets. Like shopping products, they are purchased infrequently, causing lower inventory turnover and thus requiring relatively high gross margins.

Unsought products Products purchased to solve a sudden problem, products of which customers are unaware, and products that people do not necessarily think about buying

Unsought Products

Unsought products are products purchased when a sudden problem must be solved, products of which customers are unaware, and products that people do not necessarily think of purchasing. Emergency automobile repairs and some types of auto accessories, such as snow chains, are examples of products needed quickly to solve a problem. Life insurance is a product that individuals may not necessarily think about buying.

■ *Organizational Products*

Organizational, or industrial, products are usually purchased on the basis of an organization's goals and objectives. Generally, the functional aspects of the product are more important than the psychological rewards sometimes associated with consumer products. Organizational products can be classified into seven categories according to their characteristics and intended uses: raw materials, major equipment, accessory equipment, component parts, process materials, consumable supplies, and organizational services.[3]

Raw materials Basic natural materials that become part of a physical product

Raw Materials

Raw materials are the basic natural materials that actually become part of a physical product. They include minerals, chemicals, agricultural products, and materials from forests and oceans. They are usually bought and sold according to grades and specifications, and in relatively large quantities.

Major equipment Large tools and machines used for production purposes

Major Equipment

Major equipment includes large tools and machines used for production purposes, such as cranes and stamping machines. Normally, major equipment is expensive and intended to be used in a production process for a considerable length of time. Some major equipment is custom-made to perform specific functions for a particular organization, but other items are standardized and perform similar tasks for many types of firms. Because major equipment is so expensive and normally a long-term investment of capital, purchase decisions are often made by high-level management. Marketers of major equipment frequently must provide a variety of services, including installation, training, repair and maintenance assistance, and even aid in financing the purchase.

Accessory equipment
Equipment used in production or office activities

Accessory Equipment   **Accessory equipment** does not become a part of the final physical product but is used in production or office activities. Examples include file cabinets, fractional-horsepower motors, calculators, and tools. Compared with major equipment, accessory items are usually much cheaper; purchased routinely, with less negotiation; and treated as expense items rather than capital items because they are not expected to last as long. Accessory products are standardized items that can be used in several aspects of a firm's operations. More outlets are required for distributing accessory equipment than for major equipment, but sellers do not have to provide the multitude of services expected of major equipment marketers.

Component parts   Items that become part of the physical product and are either finished items ready for assembly or ones that need little processing before assembly

Component Parts   **Component parts** become a part of the physical product and are either finished items ready for assembly or products that need little processing before assembly. Although they become part of a larger product, component parts can often be easily identified and distinguished. Spark plugs, tires, clocks, and switches are all component parts of the automobile. Buyers purchase such items according to their own specifications or industry standards. They expect the parts to be of specified quality and delivered on time so that production is not slowed or stopped. Producers that are primarily assemblers, such as most lawn mower or computer manufacturers, depend heavily on the suppliers of component parts.

Process materials   Materials used directly in the production of other products

Process Materials   **Process materials** are used directly in the production of other products. Unlike component parts, however, process materials are not readily identifiable. For example, Reichhold Chemicals, Inc., markets a treated fiber product— a phenolic-resin sheet-molding compound—that is used in the production of aircraft flight deck instrument panels and cabin interiors. Although the material is not identifiable in the finished aircraft, it retards burning, smoke, and formation of toxic gas if molded components are subjected to fire or high temperatures. As with component parts, process materials are purchased according to industry standards or the purchaser's specifications.

Consumable supplies
Items that facilitate production and operations but do not become part of the finished product

Consumable Supplies   **Consumable supplies** facilitate production and operations but do not become part of the finished product. Paper, pencils, oils, cleaning agents, and paints are in this category. The Hammermill paper advertised in Figure 9.2 is a consumable supply. Because such supplies are standardized items used in a variety of situations, they are purchased by many different types of organizations. Consumable supplies are commonly sold through numerous outlets and are purchased routinely. To ensure that supplies are available when needed, buyers often deal with more than one seller. Because these supplies can be divided into three subcategories—maintenance, repair, and operating (or overhaul) supplies—they are sometimes called **MRO items.**

MRO items   Maintenance, repair, and operating (or overhaul) supplies

Organizational services
The intangible products, or industrial services, that many organizations use in their operations

Organizational Services   Organizational services (also called industrial services) are the intangible products that many organizations use in their operations. They include financial, legal, and marketing research, computer programming and operation, and janitorial services. Firms must decide whether to provide their own services internally or obtain them outside the organization. This decision depends on the costs associated with each alternative and how frequently the services are needed.

Figure 9.2
Consumable Supply
Hammermill paper is a consumable supply.

Product Line and Product Mix

Product item   A specific version of a product

Product line   A group of closely related product items viewed as a unit because of marketing, technical, or end-use considerations

*M*arketers must understand the relationships among all the products of their organization if they are to coordinate the marketing of the total group of products. The following concepts help describe the relationships among an organization's products. A **product item** is a specific version of a product that can be designated as a distinct offering among an organization's products. An L.L. Bean chamois cloth shirt represents a product item. A **product line** includes a group of closely related product items that are considered to be a unit because of marketing, technical, or end-use considerations. For example, L.L. Bean has launched a product line of children's clothing. The clothes are designed for 6- to 12-year-olds and represent a product line different from the firm's traditional outdoor outfitters' clothing for adults.[4] The exact boundaries of a product line (although sometimes confusing) are usually indicated by using descriptive terms such as "frozen dessert" product line or "shampoo" product line. To come up with the optimum product line, marketers must understand buyers' goals. Specific product items in a product line usually reflect the desires of different target markets or the different needs of consumers. By developing a number of products, a company can appeal to consumers operating on perceived price-quality relationships. In fact, consumers often rely on the brand name of a product rather than price as an indicator of quality.[5]

Product mix   The total group of products that an organization makes available to customers

Depth of product mix
The number of different products offered in each product line

Width of product mix
The number of product lines a company offers

A **product mix** is the composite, or total, group of products that an organization makes available to customers. For example, all the health care, beauty care, laundry and cleaning, food and beverage, paper, cosmetic, and fragrance products that Procter & Gamble manufactures constitute its product mix. A representative sample of Classico's product mix is shown in Figure 9.3. The **depth of product mix** is measured by the number of different products offered in each product line. The **width of product mix** is measured by the number of product lines a company offers. Figure 9.4 illustrates these concepts by showing the width of the product mix and the depth of each product line for selected Procter & Gamble products. Procter & Gamble is known for using distinctive branding, packaging, and consumer advertising to promote individual items in its detergent product line. Tide, Bold, Gain, Dash, Cheer, and Era—all Procter & Gamble detergents—share the same distribution channels and similar manufacturing facilities. Yet each is promoted as distinctive, and this claimed uniqueness adds depth to the product line. Procter & Gamble has introduced product items in cosmetic areas such as lipstick to meet the needs of minority women, particularly African-American, Asian-American, and Hispanic. The products' formulations, and the marketing of the products, are adapted to appeal to a diverse group of customers with varying complexions and hair colors.[6]

Figure 9.3
Product Mix   A representation of Classico's product mix of Italian sauces.

Laundry detergents	Toothpastes	Bar soaps	Deodorants	Shampoos	Tissue/Towel
Oxydol 1914	Gleem 1952	Ivory 1879	Old Spice 1948	Prell 1946	Charmin 1928
Ivory Snow 1930	Crest 1955	Camay 1926	Secret 1956	Pantene 1947	Puffs 1960
Dreft 1933		Zest 1952	Sure 1972	Head & Shoulders 1961	Bounty 1965
Tide 1946		Safeguard 1963		Vidal Sassoon 1974	Summit 1100's 1992
Cheer 1950		Coast 1974		Pert Plus 1979	
Dash 1954		Oil of Olay 1993		Ivory 1983	
Bold 1965					
Gain 1966					
Era 1972					

Product line depth (vertical axis) — *Product mix width* (horizontal axis)

Figure 9.4
The Concepts of Product Mix Width and Depth Applied to Selected Procter & Gamble Products
Source: From "Facts About Procter & Gamble," March 1996. Used by permission of Procter & Gamble.

Product Life Cycles

Product life cycle
The progression of a product through four stages: introduction, growth, maturity, and decline

*J*ust as biological cycles progress through growth and decline, so do product life cycles. As Figure 9.5 shows, a **product life cycle** has four major stages: (1) introduction, (2) growth, (3) maturity, and (4) decline. As a product moves through its cycle, the strategies relating to competition, promotion, distribution, pricing, and market information must be periodically evaluated and possibly changed. Astute marketing managers use the life cycle concept to make sure that the introduction, alteration, and termination of a product are timed and executed properly. By understanding the typical life cycle pattern, marketers are better able to maintain profitable products and drop unprofitable ones. (Marketing strategies for different life cycle stages are discussed in Chapter 10.)

■ *Introduction*

Introduction stage
The initial stage of a product's life cycle—its first appearance in the marketplace—when sales are zero and profits are negative

The **introduction stage** of the life cycle begins at a product's first appearance in the marketplace, when sales are zero and profits are negative. Profits are below zero because initial revenues are low while the company generally must cover large expenses for

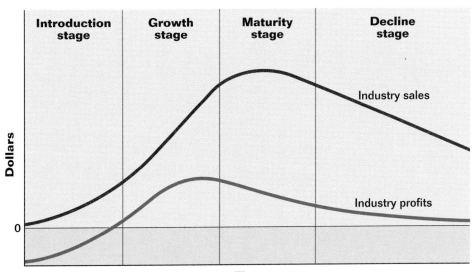

Figure 9.5
The Four Stages of the Product Life Cycle

Figure 9.6
Product Introduction
Seiko promotes its new kinetic watch, which is the first quartz watch to generate and store electrical energy through human motion.

Growth stage The stage of a product's life cycle when sales rise rapidly and profits reach a peak and then start to decline

Maturity stage The stage of a product's life cycle when the sales curve peaks and starts to decline as profits continue to decline

promotion and distribution. Notice in Figure 9.5 how sales should move upward from zero, and profits should also move upward from a position in which profits are negative because of high expenses.

Developing and introducing a new product can mean an outlay of $20 million or more. The risk of new product failure is quite high, depending on the industry and how product failure is defined. Because of high risks and costs, few product introductions represent revolutionary inventions. More typically, product introductions involve a new packaged convenience food, a new year model of automobile, or a new fashion in clothing rather than a major product innovation. For example, Figure 9.6 shows a product that has been introduced as "new," although what is new is not the concept of the watch but the way the watch works.

Potential buyers must be made aware of the new product's features, uses, and advantages. Two difficulties may arise at this point. First, only a few sellers may have the resources, technological knowledge, and marketing know-how to launch the product successfully. And second, the initial product price may have to be high to recoup expensive marketing research or development costs. Given these difficulties, it is not surprising that many products never get beyond the introduction stage.

■ *Growth*

During the **growth stage,** sales rise rapidly and profits reach a peak and then start to decline (see Figure 9.5). The growth stage is critical to a product's survival because competitive reactions to the product's success during this period will affect the product's life expectancy. For example, the maker of Tabasco successfully marketed the first hot pepper sauce but today competes against numerous other brands. Profits begin to decline late in the growth stage as more competitors enter the market, driving prices down and creating the need for heavy promotional expenses. At this point a typical marketing strategy encourages strong brand loyalty and competes with aggressive emulators of the product. During the growth stage, an organization tries to strengthen its market share and develop a competitive niche by emphasizing the product's benefits. Aggressive pricing, including price cuts, is also typical during this stage. For example, the multifunctional office machine (it phones, faxes, scans, copies, and prints) is in its growth stage. Hewlett-Packard has gained a strong market position for its OfficeJet by providing a quality product at a competitive price.[7]

■ *Maturity*

During the **maturity stage,** the sales curve peaks and starts to decline and profits continue to decline (see Figure 9.5). This stage is characterized by intense competition, as many brands are in the market. Competitors emphasize improvements and differences in their versions of the product. As a result, during the maturity stage weaker competitors are squeezed out or lose interest in the product. For example, some brands of VCRs will perish as the VCR moves through the maturity stage.

During the maturity phase, the producers who remain in the market must make fresh promotional and distribution efforts. Advertising and dealer-oriented promotions are typical during this stage of the product life cycle. Marketers must also take into account that, as the product reaches maturity, buyers' knowledge of it attains a high level. Consumers of the product are no longer inexperienced generalists but instead experienced specialists. Marketers of mature products sometimes expand distribution into global markets. Often, the products have to be adapted to more precisely fit differing needs of global customers as discussed in Global Perspective.

GLOBAL PERSPECTIVE

Frito-Lay Targets Snackers Worldwide

Six months after PepsiCo Food International (PFI), Frito-Lay's overseas snack division, introduced Chee-tos in China, the brand was so popular that the company could barely keep up with demand. How did PFI convince so many Chinese—who eat almost no snack foods—to indulge in the crunchy, salty morsels? Before marketing its product, PFI conducted extensive research and development, testing 100 brand names and 600 flavors. In China, as in all of its global markets, Frito-Lay's key to success is understanding each market and adapting products to local tastes. This strategy has made the company the world's largest snack food enterprise outside of the United States, owning 35 percent of the global snack market, and offering products in thirty-four countries from the Netherlands to Korea to Brazil.

The strategy has been shaped by bitter experience. When the company introduced Chee-tos to Great Britain without doing consumer research, the product failed. In Spain, adults loved PFI's "Matutano" snacks, which they bought in grocery stores and restaurants. Children, however, couldn't get Matutanos in the outdoor kiosks where they typically buy snacks and couldn't afford to buy them elsewhere. To increase acceptance among children, the company packaged the chips in single-serving bags, expanded distribution to smaller outlets, and increased outdoor advertising. These mistakes taught Frito-Lay's marketers to become experts in distinctive local tastes and behaviors. Today, the company makes essential changes in seasonings, textures, product positioning, and promotion based on brand managers' information about markets and consumer snacking habits.

Frito-Lay now knows that British snackers favor salted potato chips, Germans prefer paprika flavoring, and Koreans like cuttlefish peanut snacks. The company gave Britons a thinner, lighter-textured Dorito, more like the potato chips they love. A $9 million ad campaign and sampling that reached 7 million consumers boosted British sales of Doritos to over $100 million in the first year. In China, the company took the cheese out of Chee-tos because dairy products are not a staple in Chinese diets. Instead, Chinese snackers can munch on popcorn flavored Savory American Creams or teriyaki tasting Zesty Japanese Steak. The company supported the product launch with an aggressive marketing campaign comprised of television ads, massive product sampling, and consumer promotions featuring spokescartoon Chester Cheetah, or Qi Duo Bao as he is known in China. Six months after Chinese Chee-tos rolled onto the market, stores were selling out.

Building on global successes like these, the snack food giant plans to introduce Chee-tos, Doritos, and other snacks in Eastern Europe, India, and the Middle East.

Sources: Karen Benezra, "Fritos 'Round the World," *Brandweek,* Mar. 27, 1995, pp. 32, 35; Lara Mills, "Hostess Reformulates With Famous Faces," *Marketing Magazine,* Mar. 6, 1995, p. 4; and Anita Sharp, "Pepsico's Net Jumped 16% in 4th Quarter," *Wall Street Journal,* Feb. 8, 1995, p. A4.

■ *Decline*

Decline stage   The stage of a product's life cycle when sales fall rapidly

During the **decline stage,** sales fall rapidly (see Figure 9.5). New technology or a new social trend may cause product sales to take a sharp turn downward. When this happens, the marketer considers pruning items from the product line to eliminate those not earning a profit. At this time, too, the marketer may cut promotion efforts, eliminate marginal distributors, and, finally, plan to phase out the product.

Because most businesses have a product mix consisting of multiple products, a firm's destiny is rarely tied to one product. A composite of life cycle patterns is formed when various products in the mix are at different cycle stages. As one product is declining, other products are in the introduction, growth, or maturity stage. Marketers must deal with the dual problem of prolonging the life of existing products and introducing new products to meet organizational sales goals. In Chapter 10 the management of products in various life cycle stages is discussed.

Product Differentiation

Product differentiation
The process of creating and designing products so that consumers perceive them as different from competing products

*S*ome of the most important characteristics of products are the elements that distinguish them from one another. **Product differentiation** is the process of creating and designing products so that customers perceive them as different from competing products. The idea of consumer perception is critically important in differentiating products because the differences between products can be either real or perceived. Real differences might include quality, features, styling, or price. Differences created by perceptions (subjective or imaginary) are typically based on a product's image. Whether the differences between products are real or only the customer's perceptions, all marketers take steps to ensure that these differences do exist. A crucial element that differentiates one product from another is the brand. Although branding is very important, the brand itself is not a part of the physical creation and design of a product. We discuss branding in Chapter 11.

In this section we examine three physical aspects of product differentiation that companies must consider when creating and offering products for sale: product quality, product design and features, and product support services. These aspects involve the company's attempt to create real differences between products. Later in this chapter, we discuss how companies position their products in the marketplace based on these three aspects.

■ *Product Quality*

Quality   The overall characteristics of a product that allow it to perform as expected in satisfying customer needs

Quality refers to the overall characteristics of a product that allow it to perform as expected in satisfying customer needs. The words *as expected* are very important to this definition because quality usually means different things to different customers. For some, durability signifies quality. Among the most durable products on the market today is the Craftsman line of tools at Sears. Indeed, Sears provides a lifetime guarantee on the durability of these tools. For other consumers, a product's ease of use may indicate quality. Apple's Macintosh line of personal computers, for example, is widely known as the easiest computer to set up, learn to use, and use.

The concept of quality also varies between consumer and organizational markets. According to one study, American consumers consider high-quality products to have these characteristics (in order): reliability, durability, ease of maintenance, ease of use, a known and trusted brand name, and reasonable price.[8] For organizational markets, product characteristics such as technical suitability, ease of repair, and company reputation are important. Unlike consumers, most organizations place far less emphasis on price than on product quality.

Level of quality   The amount of quality possessed by a product

Two important dimensions of quality are level and consistency. The **level of quality** is the amount of quality a product possesses. The concept is a relative one. That is, the quality level of one product is difficult to describe unless it is compared with that of other products. For example, most consumers would consider the quality level of Timex watches to be good, but when they compare Timex to Rolex, most consumers would say that a Rolex's level of quality is higher. **Consistency of quality** refers to the degree to which a product is the same level of quality over time. Consistency means giving consumers the quality they expect every time they purchase the product. Like the level of quality, consistency is a relative concept; however, it implies a quality comparison within the same brand over time. The quality level of McDonald's French fries is generally consistent from one location to another. If FedEx delivers more than 99 percent of overnight packages on time, then its service has consistent quality.

Consistency of quality
The degree to which a product is the same over time

The consistency of product quality can also be compared across competing products. It is at this stage that consistency becomes critically important for a company's success. Companies that can provide quality on a consistent basis have a major competitive advantage over their rivals. FedEx is viewed as more consistent in delivery schedules than the U.S. Postal Service. In simple terms, no company has ever succeeded by creating and marketing low-quality products. (As discussed in Ethical Challenges, some companies have experienced major legal problems when the quality or design of their products was questioned.) Many companies have taken major steps, such as implementing total quality management (TQM), to improve the quality of their products. (TQM is discussed further in Chapter 23.) However, 71 percent of Americans believe that the quality of American-made products continues to erode.[9]

By and large, higher product quality (real or perceived) means that marketers will charge a higher price for the product. This fact forces marketers to consider quality carefully in their product-planning efforts. Not all customers want or can afford the highest-quality products available. Thus many companies offer products in a wide range of quality.

■ ETHICAL CHALLENGES ■

Product Liability: Ethical Choices for Businesses and Customers

Americans initiate more product liability lawsuits than do customers in any other country in the world. Since 1974, the number of product liability cases heard in U.S. federal courts has increased by an incredible 983 percent. Reports of multimillion dollar awards to customers are daily fare in the press and on television. Alarmed lawmakers are working to reign in what seems to be a runaway number of frivolous product liability lawsuits. Ultimately, though, the ethical issues surrounding product liability cannot be legislated. Questions of responsibility and fairness are in the hands of businesses and customers.

Studies show that most product-related injuries result from inadequate guarding, design defects, and inadequate or nonexistent warnings. Businesses are responsible for minimizing the occurrence of such problems by improving the safety of existing products and considering customer safety when developing new products. Manufacturers should also provide clear and adequate safety instructions and hazard warnings, and must avoid false or misleading advertising claims.

Most Americans agree that companies should be held responsible for injuries caused by their products. Is it ethical, however, for a restaurant customer to sue the restaurant if she burns herself by spilling hot coffee in her lap? Is it ethical for my neighbor to sue a lawn mower manufacturer if he severely injures his hands while using the lawn mower to trim the hedge instead of mow the lawn? Is it ethical for

a smoker who develops lung cancer to sue the cigarette manufacturer when the dangers of smoking are widely recognized and packages and advertisements carry unmistakable warnings? Americans demand—and fight for—the rights to be informed, warned, protected, and adequately compensated when harmed. But don't they also have ethical responsibilities to use products as intended, pay attention to instructions and warnings, and refrain from initiating unfair or unwarranted lawsuits if injuries occur?

Although there are a small number of unethical organizations that knowingly market defective products, cover up problems, and deny responsibility, the vast majority of American companies manufacture or sell safe products and inform customers about any potential dangers involved with their use. And despite the uproar in Congress and the media hype over high-profile cases, product liability lawsuits are the exception rather than the rule. According to a recent survey, most Americans with product-related injuries do not file lawsuits or make any type of compensation claim, and most injured people blame themselves or bad luck rather than the manufacturer.

Sources: Randall Goodden, "Be Informed About Product Liability," *Quality*, Mar. 1995, p. 88; Paula Mergenbagen, "Product Liability: Who Sues?" *American Demographics*, June 1995, pp. 48–54; Robert Klitzman, "Contract on the Consumer," *New York Times*, Mar. 4, 1995, p. 19; Daniel Gross, "Deflating Product Liability," *CFO*, Apr. 1995, pp. 70–72, 75; and Kenneth Ross, "Warnings Are a Must," *Appliance Manufacturer*, Apr. 1995, p. 6.

■ *Product Design and Features*

Product design   How a
product is conceived, planned,
and produced

Product design refers to how a product is conceived, planned, and produced. Design is a very complex topic because it involves the total sum of all the product's physical characteristics. Many companies are known for the outstanding designs of their products: Sony for personal electronics, Hewlett-Packard for laser printers, Levi Strauss for clothing, and JanSport for backpacks. Good design is one of the best competitive advantages any brand can possess.

Styling   The physical
appearance of a product

One component of design is **styling,** or the physical appearance of the product. The style of a product is one design feature than can cause certain products to sell very rapidly. Good design, however, means more than just appearance; it also involves functionality and usefulness. For example, a pair of jeans may look great, but if it falls apart after three washes, clearly its design was poor. Most consumers seek out products with good looks and functionality.

Product features   Specific
design characteristics that allow
a product to perform certain
tasks

Product features are specific design characteristics allowing a product to perform certain tasks. By adding or subtracting features, a company can differentiate its products from those of the competition. Chrysler Corp. promotes its line of minivans as having more features related to passenger safety—dual air bags, steel-reinforced doors, and integrated child safety seats—than any other company. As shown in Figure 9.7, both Mita and Dremel employ multiple product features to differentiate their products from competitors. Product features can also be used to differentiate products within the same company. For example, Nike offers both a walking shoe and a run-walk shoe for specific consumer needs. In these cases, the company's products are sold with a wide range of features, from low-priced "base" or "stripped-down" versions to high-priced and prestigious "feature-packed" ones. The automotive industry regularly sells products with a wide range of features. In general, the more features a product has, the higher its price and often the higher the perceived quality.

For a brand to have sustainable competitive advantage, marketers must determine the product designs and features that customers desire. Information from marketing research efforts and from databases can be used in helping to assess customers' product

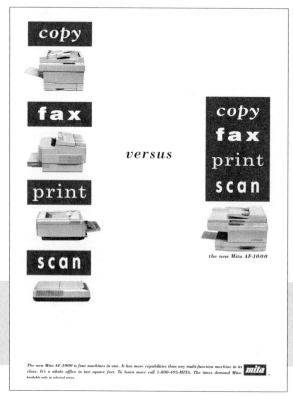

Figure 9.7
Product Differentiation
Both Mita and Dremel
use multiple features to
differentiate their products.

design and feature preferences. Samsonite Corporation, the Denver-based luggage manufacturer, uses three databases to determine what customers do and don't like about their own brands and competing brands. Samsonite shares this information with its dealers so that they can better serve customers.[10] Being able to meet customers' desires for product design and features at prices that they can afford is crucial to a product's long-term success.

■ *Product Support Services*

Customer services Human or mechnical efforts or activities that add value to the product

Many companies differentiate their product offerings by providing support services. These services are usually referred to as **customer services** and include any human or mechanical efforts or activities a company provides that add value to that product.[11] Examples of customer services include delivery and installation, financing arrangements, customer training, warranties and guarantees, repair, lay-a-way plans, convenient hours of operation, adequate parking, and information through toll-free numbers. For example, Nike's 800 number provides callers with product information and pre-recorded messages from Nike athletes. Nike plans to expand this option to twelve other countries and uses this support service to build customer databases.[12]

Whether as a major or a minor part of the total product offering, all marketers of goods sell customer services. In some cases, providing good customer service may be the only way a company can differentiate its products when all products in a market have essentially the same quality, design, and features. This is especially true in the computer industry. When consumers buy a personal computer, they shop more for fast delivery, technical support, warranties, and price than for product quality and design. Through research, a company can discover the types of services that customers want and need. For example, some customers are more interested in financing, whereas others may be more concerned with installation and training. When Black & Decker introduced its DeWalt line of premium-priced professional power tools to compete with Makita, the market leader at the time, it did customer research to determine which support services were needed. The set of support services that Black & Decker provides includes quick response order processing, efficient inquiry/complaint handling, protected distribution for resellers, and job site product demonstrations. Today, Black & Decker's DeWalt line is the market leader.[13] Companies like Black & Decker must design their customer support services with as much care as they design their products.

Product Positioning and Repositioning

Product positioning The decisions and activities that create and maintain a certain concept of the firm's product in customers' minds

*P*roduct **positioning** refers to the decisions and activities intended to create and maintain a certain concept of the firm's product (relative to competitive brands) in customers' minds. When marketers introduce a product, they try to position it so that it seems to possess the characteristics the target market most desires. This projected image is crucial. Crest is positioned as a fluoride toothpaste that fights cavities, and Close-Up is positioned as a whitening toothpaste that enhances the user's sex appeal. Based on FDA approval, Tagament HB is positioned as a heartburn medication to be taken prior to eating, whereas both Tagament and Maalox are positioned as medications that provide heartburn relief (see Figure 9.8).

Product position is customers' perceptions of a product's attributes relative to those of competitive brands. Buyers make a large number of purchase decisions on a regular basis. To avoid a continuous reevaluation of numerous products, buyers tend to group, or "position," products in their minds to simplify buying decisions. Rather than allowing customers to position products independently, marketers often try to influence and shape consumers' concepts or perceptions of products through advertising. Marketers sometimes analyze product positions by developing perceptual maps, as shown in Figure 9.9. Perceptual maps are created by questioning a sample of consumers regarding their perceptions of products, brands, and organizations with respect to two or more dimensions. To develop a perceptual map like the one in Figure 9.9, respondents would be asked how

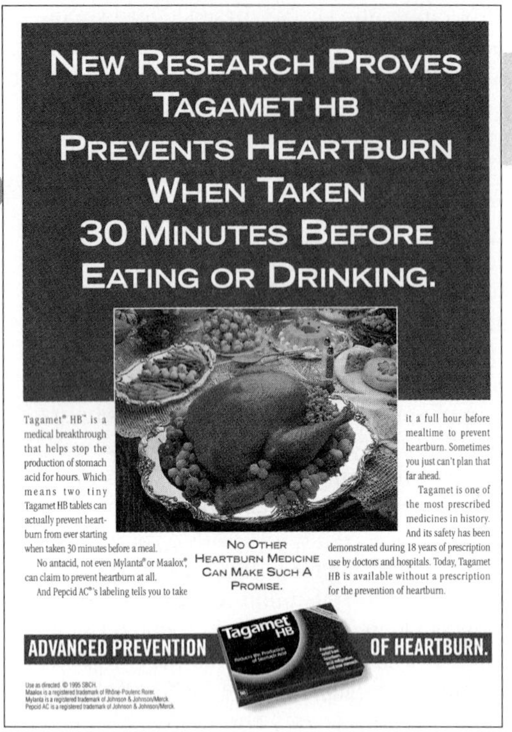
NEW RESEARCH PROVES TAGAMET HB PREVENTS HEARTBURN WHEN TAKEN 30 MINUTES BEFORE EATING OR DRINKING.
Tagamet® HB™ is a medical breakthrough that helps stop the production of stomach acid for hours. Which means two tiny Tagamet HB tablets can actually prevent heartburn from ever starting when taken 30 minutes before a meal.
No antacid, not even Mylanta® or Maalox®, can claim to prevent heartburn at all.
And Pepcid AC®'s labeling tells you to take it a full hour before mealtime to prevent heartburn. Sometimes you just can't plan that far ahead.
Tagamet is one of the most prescribed medicines in history. And its safety has been demonstrated during 18 years of prescription use by doctors and hospitals. Today, Tagamet HB is available without a prescription for the prevention of heartburn.
NO OTHER HEARTBURN MEDICINE CAN MAKE SUCH A PROMISE.
ADVANCED PREVENTION
Tagamet HB
OF HEARTBURN.
Use as directed. © 1995 SBCH.
Maalox is a registered trademark of Rhône-Poulenc Rorer.
Mylanta is a registered trademark of Johnson & Johnson/Merck.
Pepcid AC is a registered trademark of Johnson & Johnson/Merck.

Figure 9.8
Product Positioning Tagamet HB is positioned as a medication that prevents heartburn as well as providing heartburn relief.

they perceive selected pain relievers in regard to price and type of pain for which they are used. Also, respondents would be asked about their preferences for product features to establish "ideal points" or "ideal clusters," which represent a consensus view of what a specific group of customers desire in terms of product features. Then, a marketer can compare how his or her brand is perceived compared to the ideal points.

Product positioning is a part of a natural progression when market segmentation is used. Segmentation lets the firm aim a given brand at a portion of the total market. Effective product positioning helps serve a specific market segment by creating an appropriate concept in the minds of customers in that market segment. A firm can position a product to compete head-on with another brand, as PepsiCo has done against Coca-Cola, or to avoid competition, as 7Up has done relative to other soft drink producers. Head-to-head competition may be a marketer's positioning objective if the product's performance characteristics are at least equal to competitive brands and if the product is priced lower. Head-to-head positioning may be appropriate even when the price is higher if the product's performance characteristics are superior. Conversely, positioning to avoid competition may be best when the product's performance characteristics do not differ significantly from competing brands. Moreover, positioning a brand to avoid competition may be appropriate when that brand has unique characteristics that are important to some buyers. Volvo, for example, has for years positioned itself away from competitors by focusing on the safety characteristics of its cars. Competitors sometimes mention safety issues in their advertisements but are more likely to focus on style, fuel efficiency, or performance.

Avoiding competition is critical when a firm introduces a brand into a market in which it already has one or more brands. Marketers usually want to avoid cannibalizing

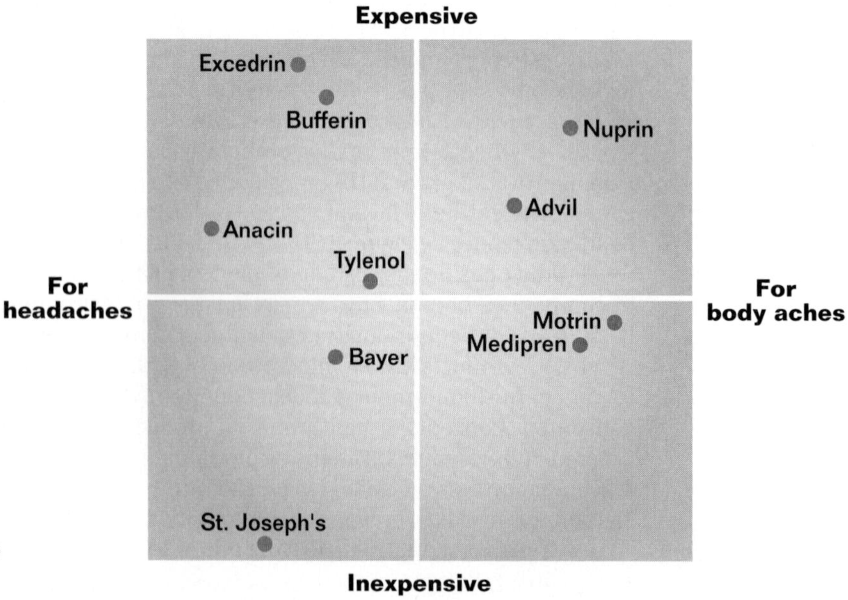
Expensive
Excedrin
Bufferin
Nuprin
Advil
Anacin
Tylenol
For headaches
For body aches
Motrin
Medipren
Bayer
St. Joseph's
Inexpensive

Figure 9.9
Hypothetical Perceptual Map for Pain Relievers

sales of their existing brands, unless the new brand generates substantially larger profits. Sometimes attempts to avoid cannibalization can be troublesome. Tylenol was a brand leader in the analgesic market for many years until ibuprofen products, like Advil, were introduced. To remain competitive, Johnson & Johnson (the maker of Tylenol) introduced Medipren, an ibuprofen brand. Since Tylenol was positioned as a headache remedy, Johnson & Johnson positioned Medipren for body aches and pains to avoid cannibalization. Even with a $40 million advertising campaign for Medipren's introductory year, consumers were confused about its uses. Many consumers believed the Medipren was for menstrual pain. Thus Advil took considerable share from Tylenol. Johnson & Johnson should have positioned Medipren for headache pain. Even though this positioning would have cannibalized some Tylenol sales, Johnson & Johnson would have kept a larger share of the total analgesic market.[14]

If a product has been planned properly, its features and brand image will give it the distinct appeal needed. Style, shape, construction, quality of work, and color help create the image and the appeal. If the benefits can be easily identified, then of course buyers are more likely to purchase the product. When the new product does not offer certain preferred attributes, there is room for another new product.

Positioning decisions are not just for new products. Evaluating the positions of existing products is important because a brand's market share and profitability may be strengthened by product repositioning. For example, several years ago Kraft was on the verge of discontinuing Cheez Whiz because its sales had declined considerably. Kraft marketers repositioned Cheez Whiz as a fast, convenient microwavable cheese sauce, causing its sales to rebound to new heights. When introducing a new product into a product line, one or more existing brands may have to be repositioned to minimize cannibalization of established brands and to assure a favorable position for the new brand.

Repositioning can be accomplished by physically changing the product, its price, or its distribution. Rather than making any of these changes, marketers sometimes reposition a product by changing its image through promotional efforts directed at customers (which was the case with Cheez Whiz). Of course, products can be repositioned through both physical and image changes.

Organizing to Manage Products

*A*fter reviewing the concepts of product line and mix, life cycles, positioning, and repositioning, it should be obvious that managing products is a complex task. Often the traditional functional form of organization—in which managers specialize in business functions such as advertising, sales, and distribution—does not fit a company's needs. Consequently, management must find an organizational approach that accomplishes the tasks necessary to develop and manage products. Alternatives to functional organization include the product manager approach, the market manager approach, and the venture team approach.

Product manager
The person within an organization responsible for a product, a product line, or several distinct products that make up a group

Brand manager   The person responsible for a single brand

A **product manager** is responsible for a product, a product line, or several distinct products that make up an interrelated group within a multiproduct organization. A **brand manager,** on the other hand, is responsible for a single brand. General Foods, for example, has one brand manager for Maxim coffee and one for Maxwell House coffee. A product or brand manager operates cross-functionally to coordinate the activities, information, and strategies involved in marketing an assigned product. Product managers and brand managers plan marketing activities to achieve objectives by coordinating a mix of distribution, promotion (especially sales promotion and advertising), and price. They must consider packaging and branding decisions and work closely with personnel in research and development, engineering, and production. Marketing research helps product managers to understand consumers and find target markets. The product or brand manager approach to organization is used by many large, multiple-product companies in the consumer packaged goods business.

Market manager   The person responsible for managing the marketing activities that serve a particular group of customers

A **market manager** is responsible for managing the marketing activities that serve a particular group or class of customers. This organizational approach is particularly effective when a firm engages in different types of marketing activities to provide products to diverse customer groups. A company might have one market manager for industrial markets and another for consumer markets. These broad market categories might be broken down into more limited market responsibilities.

Venture team   A cross-functional group that creates entirely new products that may be aimed at new markets

A **venture team**'s purpose is to create entirely new products that may be aimed at new markets. Some firms have set goals for divisions that require a certain percentage of annual revenue to be generated by new products introduced within specific time periods. For example, 3M Company now requires 30 percent of annual revenue to be accounted for by new products introduced within the last four years. The goal may be impossible to reach without unique organizational structures focused on developing new products. A venture team is such a structure.[15]

Unlike a product or market manager, a venture team is responsible for all aspects of a product's development: research and development, production and engineering, finance and accounting, and marketing. Venture teams work outside established divisions to create inventive approaches to new products and markets. As a result of this flexibility, new products can be developed to take advantage of opportunities in highly segmented markets.

The members of a venture team come from different functional areas of an organization. When the commercial potential of a new product has been demonstrated, the members may return to their functional areas, or they may join a new or existing division to manage the product. The new product may be turned over to an existing division, market manager, or a product manager. Venture teams can be especially useful for well-established firms operating primarily in mature markets. These companies must take a dual approach to marketing organization. They must accommodate the management of mature products and also encourage the development of new ones.

SUMMARY

A product is anything you receive in an exchange. This can be either tangible or intangible and includes functional, social, and psychological utilities or benefits. A product can be an idea, a service, a good, or any combination of these three. When consumers purchase a product, they are buying the benefits and satisfaction that they think the product will provide.

Products can be classified on the basis of the buyer's intentions. Thus consumer products are those purchased to satisfy personal and family needs. Organizational products, on the other hand, are purchased for use in a firm's operations, to resell, or to make other products. Consumer products can be subdivided into convenience, shopping, specialty, and unsought products. Organizational products can be divided into raw materials, major equipment, accessory equipment, component parts, process materials, consumable supplies, and organizational services.

A product item is a specific version of a product that can be designated as a distinct offering among an organization's products. A product line is a group of closely related product items that are considered a unit because of marketing, technical, or end-use considerations. The composite, or total, group of products that an organization makes available to customers is called the product mix. The depth of a product line is measured by the number of different products offered in each product line. The width of the product mix is measured by the number of product lines a company offers.

The product life cycle describes how product items in an industry move through (1) introduction, (2) growth, (3) maturity, and (4) decline. The life cycle concept is used to make sure that the introduction, alteration, and termination of a product are timed and executed properly. The sales curve is at zero at introduction, rises at an increasing rate during growth, peaks at maturity, and then declines. Profits peak toward the end of the growth stage of the product life cycle. The life expectancy of a product is based on buyers' wants, the availability of competing products, and other environmental conditions. Most businesses have a composite of life cycle patterns for various products. It is important to manage existing products and develop new ones to keep the overall sales performance at a desired level.

Product differentiation focuses on the elements of a product that make it different from competing products. Products can be differentiated through physical aspects, such as a product's quality, its specific design and features, and product support services. Product quality can have various meanings, especially when comparing consumer and organizational markets. In the consumer market, quality generally connotes reliability, durability, ease of use and maintenance, a trusted brand name, and low price. In organizational markets, quality usually refers to technical suitability, ease of repair, and company reputation. Product quality can be described in terms of level, or amount of quality, and in terms of consistency, or the ability of the product to provide the same level of quality over time. In general, higher quality (real or perceived) yields higher prices in consumer markets and repeat purchases by organizational markets. Product differentiation through design can refer to the overall style and appearance of a product. Specific product features allow a product to perform certain functions that may not be available on competing products. Another way of differentiating a product is by the support, or customer services, offered. These services range from delivery and installation, customer training, and financing arrangements to warranties, repairs, and convenient hours of operation.

Product positioning refers to the decisions and activities intended to create and maintain a certain concept of the firm's product (relative to competitive brands) in customers' minds. Product positioning is part of a natural progression when market segmentation is used. A firm can position a product to compete head-on with another brand or to avoid competition. Existing products are sometimes repositioned to make them more competitive.

Developing and managing products is critical to an organization's survival and growth. The various approaches available for organizing product management share common activities, functions, and decisions necessary to guide a product through its life cycle. A product manager is responsible for a product, a product line, or several distinct products that make up an interrelated group within a multiproduct organization. A brand manager is a product manager who is responsible for a single brand. Market managers are responsible for managing the marketing activities that serve a particular group or class of customers. A venture team is sometimes used to create entirely new products that may be aimed at new markets.

IMPORTANT TERMS

Product	Major equipment	Width of product mix	Styling
Good	Accessory equipment	Product life cycle	Product features
Service	Component parts	Introduction stage	Customer services
Ideas	Process materials	Growth stage	Product positioning
Consumer products	Consumable supplies	Maturity stage	Product manager
Organizational products	MRO items	Decline stage	Brand manager
Convenience products	Organizational services	Product differentiation	Market manager
Shopping products	Product item	Quality	Venture team
Specialty products	Product line	Level of quality	
Unsought products	Product mix	Consistency of quality	
Raw materials	Depth of product mix	Product design	

DISCUSSION AND REVIEW QUESTIONS

1. List the tangible and intangible attributes of a pair of Nike athletic shoes. Compare the benefits of the Nike shoes with those of an intangible product, such as a hairstyling in a salon.
2. A product has been referred to as a "psychological bundle of satisfaction." Is this a good definition of a product? Why or why not?
3. Is a personal computer sold at a retail store a consumer product or an organizational product? Defend your answer.
4. How do convenience products and shopping products differ? What are the distinguishing characteristics of each type of product?
5. In the category of organizational products, how do component parts differ from process materials?
6. How does an organization's product mix relate to its development of a product line? When should an enterprise add depth to its product lines rather than width to its product mix?

7. How do industry profits change as a product moves through the four stages of its life cycle?
8. What is the relationship between the concepts of product mix and product life cycle?
9. What type of organization might use a venture team to develop new products? What are the advantages and disadvantages of such a team?
10. Describe the various ways in which a camcorder can be differentiated from its competitors. Are these characteristics real or perceived?
11. Explain how the term *quality* has been used to differentiate products in the automobile industry in recent years. What are some of the makes and models of automobiles that come to mind when you hear the terms *high quality* and *poor quality*?

APPLICATION QUESTIONS

1. Name a product that could be described as both a consumer and an organizational product and discuss why. Describe its uses and product perceptions by customers in both markets.

2. Choose a familiar clothing store. Describe its product mix, including its depth and width. Evaluate the mix and make suggestions to the owner.

3. Tabasco is a product that has entered the maturity stage of the product life cycle. Name products that would fit into each of the four stages (introduction, growth, maturity, and decline). Describe them and explain why they fit in that stage.

4. Product positioning aims to create a certain concept of a product in the mind of the consumer relative to its competition. Pepsi positions itself in direct competition with Coca-Cola, whereas Volvo has traditionally positioned itself away from its competitors by emphasizing its safety features. Below are several distinct positions in which an organization may place its product. Identify a product that would fit into each of them.
   a. high-price/high-quality
   b. low-price
   c. convenient
   d. unique

5. Select an organization that you think should reposition itself in the eye of the consumer. Identify where it is currently positioned, and make recommendations for repositioning. Explain and defend your suggestions.

Case 9.1   Positioning the New American Heritage Dictionary

What are the exact meanings of *cyberpunk, liposuction, arbitrage, triathlete, sound bite,* or *hip-hop*? To find the definitions of these and almost 16,000 other brand-new words, just look them up in the latest edition of *The American Heritage Dictionary*. Curious readers can also learn about words that have meanings unique to specific U.S. geographical regions, like *bodacious, gum band,* and *hoagie*. Other improvements over previous editions of the dictionary include more than 400 new word histories, better and more complete appendixes, and higher-quality illustrations. People responded so positively to these changes that the new *American Heritage Dictionary* spent sixteen weeks on *The New York Times* bestseller list. The 250,000 copies sold in its debut year put the dictionary among the ranks of must-read adventure stories, romance novels, and scandal-filled biographies. Industry experts attribute the dictionary's phenomenal success to a creative and effective marketing strategy and unique product positioning.

After 175 specialists worked for four years to put it together, Houghton Mifflin Company launched the third edition of *The American Heritage Dictionary,* tackling *Merriam-Webster's Collegiate Dictionary,* the industry leader, head on. Long dominating the U.S. dictionary market, *Webster* has become almost synonymous with *dictionary*. Houghton Mifflin, however, was convinced that its dictionary's unique positioning would enable it to win the war of the words. Before the arrival of the latest AHD, dictionary-buyers had basically two choices. On the one hand were highly detailed, unabridged dictionaries about 4,000 pages long and priced at about $90; at the other extreme, smaller condensed versions containing from 700 to 800 pages sold for around $20. *The American Heritage Dictionary,* Third Edition, however, is positioned in between. It has just under 1,000 pages and sells for about $45. To emphasize its difference from all the others, Houghton chose a black book jacket instead of the red one sported by virtually every other dictionary on the market.

Supporting the positioning strategy was a creative $1.5 million advertising and promotion program designed to deliver the message that *The American Heritage Dictionary* is not just another boring reference book. In fact, television and radio ads for the book carried the tag line, "There Is a Difference." Print ads in *Vanity Fair, New Age Journal, People,* and many other mass publications, carried the same slogan. Bookstores and other retail outlets displayed *The American Heritage Dictionary* on free-standing kiosks instead of crowded, cluttered bookshelves.

The list of creative promotions is long. The company set up a toll-free phone line—1-800-NEW-WORD—to answer consumer questions about new entries. Houghton Mifflin's marketers composed a rap song rhyming dozens of the new words in the dictionary. Understanding lyrics such as "Prequels, sequels, liposuction, pixels, O-rings, quasars, quark," requires looking them up in the new *American Heritage Dictionary*. The publisher established connections with popular television game shows. On *Jeopardy,* the dictionary was identified on air as the source for verifying certain answers, and *Wheel of Fortune* not only advertised the dictionary but gave it away as a gift to contestants. The executive editor of the new *American Heritage*

Dictionary praised its features on ABC's *Good Morning, America* and *Larry King Live.* Arsenio Hall brought it onto his show to look up *nerd.* In the movie *Wolf,* Jack Nicholson kept the dictionary on his desk just in case he needed to check out the word *lycanthropy.* By sending a newsletter entitled "World of Words" to radio stations throughout the country, Houghton Mifflin's publicity department generates interviews with the dictionary's chief lexicographer, who discusses recently added words such as *criminalist, latte,* and *domestic partner.*

The new *American Heritage*'s early and enormous success has spawned a line of related products. *The American Heritage College Dictionary* came out about a year after the original, and other Houghton Mifflin lexicon products have followed the leader, including dictionaries for high school students and children. In addition, the publisher came out with a full-featured electronic version of the dictionary. Available on computer disk and as part of software packages such as Word for Windows, the paperless high-tech AHD

became a top seller in the retail computer software market. Was all the effort Houghton Mifflin put into its new product worthwhile? After all, it's just a dictionary. Given that dictionaries can generate sales for ten years or more, the publisher answers with a resounding yes.[16]

Questions for Discussion

1. Did Houghton Mifflin position its third edition of *The American Heritage Dictionary* to avoid or to facilitate direct competition with other dictionaries in the marketplace? What rationale would justify this positioning strategy?
2. On what product characteristics was the new *American Heritage Dictionary* differentiated from the competition? Discuss briefly how marketers achieved this differentiation.
3. What type of consumer product is *The American Heritage Dictionary*?

Case 9.2 Schwinn: Reviving a Classic American Brand

For decades, American children yearned for Schwinn bicycles. Kids who rode Schwinn Excelsiors, Phantoms, and Sting-Rays were the envy of their neighborhood. In the United States, *Schwinn* meant *bicycle.* Today, however, if you ask people under 30 to name a popular brand of bicycle, they would probably come up with Trek or Cannondale, but not Schwinn. When consumer tastes changed from sturdy low-cost bikes to trendy high-priced bikes, the company's sales plummeted. Unwilling to let Schwinns disappear with Smith-Corona typewriters and Zenith televisions, the venerable bicycle maker has launched an all-out effort to bring back the best-known brand name on two wheels.

Over one hundred years ago, Iganz Schwinn founded his bicycle company and built it into the most prestigious in the industry. For years, Schwinn ruled as the number one U.S. bicycle brand. In the late 1970s and early 1980s, however, cyclists got serious. To pedal off sidewalks and roads and into the mountains and woods, they wanted upright handlebars, fat tires, and additional climbing gears. They also wanted the state-of-the-art technology provided by Cannondale, Giant, Waterloo, and market-leading Trek. Through most of the 1980s, however, Schwinn wasn't paying attention. But by 1993, two-thirds of bikes sold were mountain bikes, and the once-mighty Schwinn filed for bankruptcy. Believing in Schwinn's name and reputation,

Sam Zell bought the company, moved its headquarters to Boulder, Colorado, and formulated a strategy for driving Schwinn to the top of a crowded bicycle market.

Zell's goal is to get the Schwinn name on everything from $100 children's bicycles to $2,500 mountain bikes. The first step toward that goal was to upgrade the entire product line. To make its bicycles stronger and lighter, for example, Schwinn turned to EMF Industries, a company whose new electromagnetic process for forming aluminum makes bicycle frames much stronger. Adding vibrant colors and eye-catching graphics, Schwinn also restyled all forty-eight of its models to make them attractive to today's customers.

One of Schwinn's hottest new products is its Cruiser, a retro-style one-speed model with a wide seat and balloon tires, which sells for about $200. Unless Schwinn moves upscale, however, and persuades cyclists to spend more for its high-end, higher-priced mountain bikes, it cannot compete successfully. The company's previous management didn't believe that anyone would buy a Schwinn-brand $1,500 mountain bike, but today's management hopes its new Homegrown line of racing and all-terrain bikes, handmade in the U.S., will put the company back in high gear.

It won't be easy for Schwinn to transform its image from stodgy to stylish. Toward that end, the company launched a $10 million advertising campaign and several creative promotional efforts. Print ads feature enthusiasts mountain biking and racing on Schwinn bicycles, and Schwinn's professional mountain bike team races every weekend between April and September. To generate positive word of mouth about its products, Schwinn developed "Project Underground." Through this program, the company sells its elite models at lower-than-cost prices to Schwinn dealer employees before their general release. When a customer comes into shop looking for a new bicycle, those employees can rave about Schwinn bikes based on personal experience.

Although industry experts agree that market segmentation is the best strategy for most bicycle manufacturers, not everyone agrees that Schwinn should target upscale consumers. Skeptics argue that, even in their glory days, Schwinn bikes were never on the cutting edge. The company's CEO remains optimistic. He believes that because of its status as an American icon, even its competitors are rooting for Schwinn.[17]

Questions for Discussion

1. How would Schwinn mountain bicycles be classified?
2. In what stage of the product life cycle is the bicycle industry? Explain.
3. Evaluate Schwinn management's decision to launch the Cruiser.

Chapter 10

Developing and Managing Products

OBJECTIVES

- To become aware of how companies manage existing products through line extensions and product modifications

- To understand the importance and role of product development in the marketing mix

- To gain insight into how businesses develop a product idea into a commercial product

- To acquire knowledge about the management of products during various life cycle stages

- To learn how product elimination can be used to improve product mixes

Hummer drivers take their fun seriously.

226

A garden variety, four-wheel-drive sport utility vehicle—nonchalant toward gravel, slush, and puddles—is suddenly confronted with a massive mud slide, or a knee-high brick wall, or a dirt road that dissolves into a rocky stream bed. Time to turn around. However, if that vehicle is a 3-ton, 7-foot-wide Hummer with 16-inch ground clearance, the driver can just step on the gas and drive over everything in the way. Manufactured by Indiana-based AM General, the Hummer was originally designed explicitly to take soldiers across almost any kind of terrain. Since 1992, however, AM General has sold about 1,000 Hummers a year to military wannabees, outdoor enthusiasts, and rugged celebrities, including Indianapolis 500 champion Al Unser and superstar Arnold Schwarzenegger, who owns five.

Since production began in 1983, AM General has sold 110,000 Hummers to the military. Known as a Humvee, a military acronym for "high-mobility, multipurpose wheeled vehicle," more than 20,000 Humvees served as everything from ambulances to missile launchers in the Gulf War. The Gulf War ended, however, and so did the Cold War, resulting in drastic cutbacks in military spending. Seeking new markets for the Hummer, AM General faced the challenge of transforming a military product into a commercial and recreational one.

When designing a vehicle for the military, the company cared little about size and appearance. The Hummer is huge—over 15 feet long and over 6 feet wide—and covered inside and out with hundreds of rivets. To appeal to the civilian population, AM General invested a considerable amount in design changes, adding a roof, upgrading the paint, and softening seats and interior trim. Today, the public can choose from six Hummer styles, some of them containing CD players, carpeting, and lighted vanity mirrors. Unique features include shuttered headlights and a dashboard switch that automatically deflates the tires for increased traction and a smoother ride on poor surfaces and pumps air back into them again, all without even a tap on the brakes.

Although industries requiring sturdy vehicles, such as mining, logging, and utilities, are purchasing Hummers for commercial use, they are becoming popular with individuals. Of course, with a price tag ranging from $39,000 for a two-door pickup to $75,000 for a loaded four-door model, not everyone can afford to park a Hummer in the garage, even if it would fit. Typical Hummer owners earn about $300,000 a year and have two or three other cars. Attracting more of these upscale buyers is the goal of Hummer's first consumer advertising campaign message: Hummers are serious trucks—and fun playthings.[1]

To compete effectively and achieve their goals, organizations such as AM General, the maker of Hummer, must be able to adjust their product mixes in response to changes in customers and customers' needs. A firm often has to introduce new products, modify existing products, or eliminate products that were successful perhaps only a few years ago. To provide products that satisfy target markets and achieve the organization's objectives, a marketer must develop, alter, and maintain an effective product mix. An organization's product mix may need several types of adjustments. Because customers' attitudes and product preferences change over time, their desire for certain products may wane.

In some cases a company needs to alter its product mix for competitive reasons. A marketer may have to delete a product from the mix because a competitor dominates the market for that product. Similarly, a firm may have to introduce a new product or modify an existing one, as AM General has done with the Hummer, to compete more effectively. A marketer may expand a firm's product mix to take advantage of excess marketing and production capacity.

Regardless of the reasons for altering a product mix, the product mix must be managed. In strategic market planning, many marketers rely on the portfolio approach for managing the product mix. The product portfolio approach tries to create specific marketing strategies to achieve a balanced mix of products that will bring maximum profits in the long run. (We examine product portfolio models in Chapter 22 in the discussion of strategic market planning.) This chapter examines several ways to improve an organization's product mix, including managing existing products, developing new products from idea generation to commercialization, and eliminating weak products from the product mix. We also consider issues and decisions associated with managing products during life cycle stages.

Managing Existing Products

*A*n organization can benefit by capitalizing on its existing products. By assessing the composition of the current product mix, a marketer can identify weaknesses and gaps. This analysis can then lead to improvement of a product mix through line extension and through product modification.

■ Line Extensions

Line extension A product that is closely related to existing products in the line, but meets different customer needs

A **line extension** is the development of a product that is closely related to one or more products in the existing product line but is designed specifically to meet somewhat different needs of customers. For example, the maker of Comet cleanser has extended this line to include Liquid Comet and Comet Gel. Many of the so-called new products introduced each year by organizations are in fact line extensions. Line extensions are more common than new products because they are a less expensive, lower risk alternative for increasing sales. A line extension may focus on a different market segment or may be an attempt to increase sales within the same market segment by more precisely satisfying the needs of people in that segment. For example, the Coca-Cola company extended its Fruitopia beverage line to include four ready-to-drink fruit teas including Born Raspberry, Peaceable Peach, Lemon Berry Intuition, and Curious Mango.[2]

■ Product Modifications

Product modification Changing one or more characteristics of a product

Product modification means changing one or more characteristics of a firm's product. A product modification differs from a line extension in that the original product that is modified does not remain in the line. For example, U.S. automakers use product modifications annually when they create new models of the same brand. Once the new models are introduced, the manufacturers stop producing last year's model. Like line extensions, however, product modifications entail less risk than developing new products.

Product modification can indeed improve a firm's product mix, but only under the following conditions. First, the product must be modifiable. Second, customers must be able to perceive that a modification has been made. Third, the modification should make

228

Figure 10.1
Product Modifications
Mapleleaf is engaging in product modification to be more competitive.

the product more consistent with customers' desires so that it provides greater satisfaction. The product in Figure 10.1 is the result of product modification. There are three major ways to modify products: quality modifications, functional modifications, and aesthetic modifications.

Quality modifications
Changes relating to a product's dependability and durability

Quality Modifications   **Quality modifications** are changes that relate to a product's dependability and durability. Usually the changes are executed by altering the materials or the production process.

Reducing a product's quality may allow an organization to lower its price and direct the item at a different target market. In contrast, increasing the quality of a product may give a firm an advantage over competing brands. In fact, over the last twenty years, increased global competition, rapid technological changes, and more demanding customers have forced marketers to improve product integrity to remain competitive.[3] Higher quality may enable a company to charge a higher price by creating customer loyalty and by lowering customer sensitivity to price. However, higher quality may require the use of more expensive components and processes, thus forcing the organization to cut costs in other areas. Some firms, such as Caterpillar, are finding ways to both increase quality and reduce costs.

Functional modifications
Changes affecting a product's versatility, effectiveness, convenience, or safety

Functional Modifications   Changes that affect a product's versatility, effectiveness, convenience, or safety are called **functional modifications;** they usually require that the product be redesigned. Typical product categories that have undergone considerable functional modifications include office and farm equipment, appliances, and cleaning products. Procter & Gamble, for example, modified Tide by adding bleach, which improved the detergent's effectiveness. Panasonic modified one of its camcorders by adding a stabilization feature. Functional modifications can make a product useful to more people and thus enlarge its market. This type of change can place a product in a favorable competitive position by providing benefits that competing brands do not offer. Functional modifications can also help an organization achieve and maintain a progressive image. Sometimes functional modifications are made to reduce the possibility of product liability lawsuits.

Aesthetic modifications
Changes to the sensory appeal of a product

Aesthetic Modifications   **Aesthetic modifications** change the sensory appeal of a product by altering its taste, texture, sound, smell, or appearance. A buyer making a purchase decision is swayed by how a product looks, smells, tastes, feels, or sounds. Thus an aesthetic modification may strongly affect purchases. For years automobile makers have relied on aesthetic modifications.

Through aesthetic modifications, a firm can differentiate its product from competing brands and thus gain a sizable market share. The major drawback in using aesthetic modifications is that their value is determined subjectively. Although a firm may strive to improve the product's sensory appeal, customers may actually find the modified product to be less attractive.

Developing New Products

A firm develops new products as a means of enhancing its product mix and/or adding depth to a product line. Developing and introducing new products is frequently expensive and risky. Thousands of new products are introduced annually, and many of them fail. In fact, of the approximately 22,000 products introduced in 1994, 90 percent failed, at a cost to U.S. companies of about $30 billion.[4] Table 10.1 shows examples of recent product failures and product successes. Lack of research is a leading cause of new-product failure. Other often-cited causes are technical problems in design or production and errors in timing the product's introduction. Although new-product development is risky, so is failure to introduce new products. For example, the makers of Timex watches gained a large share of the U.S. watch market through effective marketing strategies during the 1960s and early 1970s. By 1983, Timex's market share had slipped considerably, in part because Timex had failed to introduce new products. In recent times, however, Timex has introduced a number of new products and regained market share.

The term *new product* can have more than one meaning. A genuinely new product—such as the car navigation system shown in Figure 10.2—offers innovative benefits. But products that are different and distinctly better are often viewed as new. The following items (listed in no particular order) are product innovations of the last thirty years: Post-it note pads, fax machines, birth-control pills, personal computers, felt-tip pens, disposable razors, quartz watches, and camcorders. Thus a new product can be an innovative product that has never been sold by any organization, such as Polaroid's Captiva camera, which holds the developed photos inside the camera. It can also be a product that a given firm has not marketed previously, although similar products may have been available from other companies (see the Wenger watch example in Figure 10.2). Eddie Bauer, best known for its rugged outdoor wear, extended this image with the introduction of a new line of men's cologne. This introduction is considered a new product because Eddie Bauer

Table 10.1 Product Successes and Failures

Product Successes	Product Failures
Mars Milky Way Lite reduced fat candy bar	Mars Milky Way II reduced fat candy bar
International's Hellmann's One-Step Dressings	Gerber Singles jarred food for adults
3M Active Strips flexible bandages	Saratoga Sweets Chocolate Salsa
Dexus Laboratories Pantyhose Savers portable run-stopper	Wisconsin Pharmacal's Reality Female Condom
Prepaid calling cards	Cosmo Cosmetics Scent Coatier perfumed nail polish
AriZona Iced Tea	Varaflame adjustable flame butane candles
Nabisco Reduced Fat Oreos	Nestlé Tea-Whiz
Nestlé Butterfinger BBs	R.J. Reynolds Premier smokeless cigarettes
Baby Think It Over virtual reality parenting programmed doll	Reddi-Whip Reddi-Bacon

Sources: Pam Weisz, "1994's New Products Winners and Sinners, a la Consumer Panels," *Brandweek,* Dec. 12, 1994, pp. 22–24; Neil Steinberg, "Famous Flops," *Reader's Digest,* pp. 29–32; "Edison Best New Products," *Marketing News,* May 8, 1995, pp. E4–E8; "The Best of 1994: Managers/New Products/Entrepreneurs," *Business Week,* Jan. 9, 1995, pp. 101–119; and Wilton Woods, "1994 Products of the Year," *Fortune,* Dec. 12, 1994, pp. 198–208.

Figure 10.2

Types of New Products   The Delco Telepath 100 Navigation System is a new innovative type of product. The Wenger Watch can also be viewed as a new product because the watch is a new product for the Wenger organization, which has traditionally been known as the maker of the genuine Swiss Army knife.

has not previously marketed cologne or cosmetics.[5] Finally, a product can be viewed as new when it is brought to one or more markets from another. For example, making the Dodge minivan available in Japan is viewed as a new-product introduction in Japan.

New-product development process   A seven-phase process for introducing products

Before a product is introduced, it goes through the seven phases of the **new-product development process** shown in Figure 10.3: (1) idea generation, (2) screening, (3) concept testing, (4) business analysis, (5) product development, (6) test marketing, and (7) commercialization. A product may be dropped, and many are, at any stage of development. In this section, we look at the process through which products are developed, from idea inception to fully commercialized product.

■ *Idea Generation*

Idea generation   Seeking product ideas to achieve objectives

Businesses and other organizations seek product ideas that will help them achieve their objectives. This activity is **idea generation.** The fact that only a few ideas are good enough to be commercially successful underscores the difficulty of the task. Although some organizations get their ideas almost by chance, firms that are trying to manage their product mixes effectively usually develop systematic approaches for generating new product ideas. At the heart of innovation is a purposeful, focused effort to identify new ways to serve a market. Unexpected occurrences, incongruities, new needs, industry and market changes, and demographic changes all may indicate new opportunities.[6]

New product ideas can come from several sources. They may come from internal sources—marketing managers, researchers, sales personnel, engineers, or other organizational personnel. Brainstorming and incentives or rewards for good ideas are typical intrafirm devices for stimulating the development of ideas. For example, the idea for 3M Post-it adhesive-backed notes came from an employee. As a church choir member, he used slips of paper for marking songs in his hymnal. Because the pieces of paper fell out, he suggested developing an adhesive-backed note. New product ideas may also arise from sources outside the firm—customers, competitors, advertising agencies, management

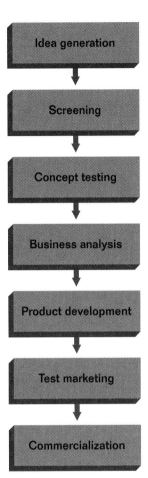

Figure 10.3
Phases of New-Product Development

Screening Choosing the most promising ideas for further review

Concept testing Seeking potential buyers' responses to a product idea

Business analysis Assessing the potential of a product idea in regard to the firm's sales, costs, and profits

consultants, and private research organizations. In a single year, organizations have provided marketing research firms with more than $3.5 billion to gain greater insights into what customers want.[7] Asking customers what they want from products and organizations has helped many firms to become successful and to remain competitive.

■ *Screening*

In the process of **screening,** the ideas with the greatest potential are selected for further review. During screening, product ideas are analyzed to determine whether they match the organization's objectives and resources. If a product idea results in a product that is similar to the firm's existing products, marketers must assess the degree to which the new product could cannibalize the sales of current products. The company's overall abilities to produce and market the product are also analyzed. Other aspects of an idea that should be weighed are the nature and wants of buyers and possible environmental changes. At times a checklist of new-product requirements is used when making screening decisions. It encourages evaluators to be systematic and so reduces the chances of their overlooking some pertinent fact. Compared with other phases, the largest number of new-product ideas are rejected during the screening phase.

■ *Concept Testing*

To evaluate ideas properly, it may be necessary to test product concepts. **Concept testing** is a phase in which a small sample of potential buyers is presented with a product idea through a written or oral description (and perhaps a few drawings) to determine their attitudes and initial buying intentions regarding the product. For a single product idea, an organization can test one or several concepts of the same product. Concept testing is a low-cost procedure that lets an organization determine customers' initial reactions to a product idea before it invests considerable resources in research and development. The results of concept testing can be used by product development personnel to better understand which product attributes and benefits are most important to potential customers.

Figure 10.4 shows a concept test for a proposed tick and flea control product. Notice that the concept is briefly described; then a series of questions is presented. The questions asked vary considerably depending on the type of product being tested. The typical questions are these: In general, do you find this proposed product attractive? Which benefits are especially attractive to you? Which features are of little or no interest to you? Do you feel that this proposed product would work better for you than the product that you currently use? Compared with your current product, what are the primary advantages of the proposed product? If this product were available at an appropriate price, would you buy it? How often would you buy this product? How could this proposed product be improved?

■ *Business Analysis*

During the **business analysis** stage, the product idea is evaluated to determine its potential contribution to the firm's sales, costs, and profits. In the course of a business analysis, evaluators ask a variety of questions: Does the product fit in with the organization's existing product mix? Is demand strong enough to justify entering the market and will the demand endure? What types of environmental and competitive changes can be expected, and how will these changes affect the product's future sales, costs, and profits? Are the organization's research, development, engineering, and production capabilities adequate? If new facilities must be constructed, how quickly can they be built and how much will they cost? Is the necessary financing for development and commercialization on hand or obtainable at terms consistent with a favorable return on investment?

In the business analysis stage, firms seek market information. The results of consumer polls, along with secondary data, supply the specifics needed for estimating potential sales, costs, and profits.

For many products in this stage (when they are still just product ideas), forecasting sales accurately is difficult. This is especially true for innovative and new-to-the-world products. Marketers sometimes employ break-even analysis (discussed in Chapter 21) to

Product description

An insecticide company is considering the development and introduction of a new tick and flea control product for pets. This product would consist of insecticide and a liquid dispensing brush for applying the insecticide to dogs and cats. The insecticide is in a cartridge that is installed in the handle of the brush. The insecticide is dispensed through the tips of the bristles when they touch the pet's skin (which is where most ticks and fleas are found). The actual dispensing works very much like a felt-tip pen. Only a small amount of insecticide actually is dispensed on the pet because of this unique dispensing feature. Thus the amount of insecticide that is placed on your pet is minimal compared to conventional methods of applying a tick and flea control product. One application of insecticide will keep your pet free from ticks and fleas for fourteen days.

Please answer the following questions:

1. In general, how do you feel about using this type of product on your pet?

2. What are the major advantages of this product compared with the existing product that you are currently using to control ticks and fleas on your pet?

3. What characteristics of this product do you especially like?

4. What suggestions do you have for improving this product?

5. If it is available at an appropriate price, how likely are you to buy this product?

          Very likely   Semi-likely   Not likely

6. Assuming that a single purchase would provide 30 applications for an average-size dog or 48 applications for an average-size cat, approximately how much would you pay for this product?

Figure 10.4
Concept Test for a Tick and Flea Control Product

determine how many units would have to be sold in order for the organization to begin to make a profit. At times, an organization also uses payback analysis, in which marketers compute the time period required to recover the funds that would be invested in developing the new product. Because break-even and payback analyses are based on estimates, they are usually viewed as useful but not particularly precise during this stage.

■ *Product Development*

Product development
The phase in which the firm finds out if producing a product is feasible and cost-effective

Product development is the phase in which the organization finds out if it is technically feasible to produce the product and if it can be produced at costs low enough to make the final price reasonable. To test its acceptability, the idea or concept is converted into a prototype, or working model. The prototype should reveal tangible and intangible attributes associated with the product in consumers' minds. The product's design, mechanical features, and intangible aspects must be linked to wants in the marketplace. Through marketing research and concept testing, product attributes that are important to buyers are identified. These characteristics must be communicated to customers through the design of the product.

After a company has developed a prototype, its functionality must be tested. This means that its performance, safety, convenience, and other functional qualities are tested in a laboratory as well as in the field. Functional testing should be rigorous and long enough to test the product thoroughly. For example, in Figure 10.5, the makers of Breathe *Right* tested this product's functionality.

A crucial question that arises during product development is how much quality to build into the product. For example, a major dimension of quality is durability. Keds, well

It's almost elegant in its simplicity. If you have a hard time breathing, especially at night, Breathe Right strips hold your nasal passages open so you breathe easier. And for lots of people, that's something to smile about. Breathe Right strips. In cough and cold sections everywhere.

Breathe Right

Don't Laugh. It Works.

Figure 10.5
Product Development The maker of Breath *Right®* tested the functionality of its product, a key element in product development.

known for its tennis shoes, decided to enhance product durability by developing a highly durable, washable leather. Higher quality often calls for better materials and more expensive processing, which increase production costs and, ultimately, the product's price. In determining the specific level of quality, a marketer must ascertain approximately what price the target market views as acceptable. In addition, a marketer usually tries to set a quality level for a specific product that is consistent with the firm's other products that carry a similar brand. Obviously, the quality of competing brands is also a consideration.

The development phase of a new product is frequently lengthy and expensive; thus a relatively small number of product ideas are put into development. If the product appears sufficiently successful during this stage to merit test marketing, then during the latter part of the development stage marketers begin to make decisions regarding branding, packaging, labeling, pricing, and promotion for use in the test marketing stage.

■ *Test Marketing*

Test marketing Limited introduction of a product to gauge the extent to which potential customers will actually buy the product

A limited introduction of a product in geographic areas chosen to represent the intended market is called **test marketing.** Its aim is to determine the extent to which potential customers will buy the product. For example, Coca-Cola test marketed PowerAde, a sports drink created to compete with Gatorade for the $750 million market. PowerAde was originally available only through restaurants but, after successful tests, is now marketed with other soft drinks throughout the country.[8] Test marketing is not an extension of the development stage; it is a sample launching of the entire marketing mix. Test marketing should be conducted only after the product has gone through development and after initial plans regarding the other marketing mix variables have been made. Numerous pizza and breakfast food companies have test marketed breakfast varieties of pizza with limited success.

Companies of all sizes use test marketing to lessen the risk of product failure. The dangers of introducing an untested product include undercutting already profitable products and, should the new product fail, loss of credibility with distributors and customers. R.J. Reynolds Premier cigarettes never made it out of the test market and now have a spot in the New Products Showcase and Learning Center in Ithaca, New York, where product successes and failures are displayed. Premier was a smokeless cigarette that appealed only to nonsmokers—hardly the target market for the product.[9]

Test marketing provides several benefits. It lets marketers expose a product in a natural marketing environment to gauge its sales performance. While the product is being marketed in a limited area, the company can strive to identify weaknesses in the product or in other parts of the marketing mix. Frito-Lay, Inc., and Taco Bell Corp., subsidiaries of PepsiCo, Inc., joined to produce Mexican-style products to sell in supermarkets. Initially, eighteen different items under the Taco Bell name were tested in one thousand stores in Georgia and Ohio. After the initial testing, the product line was reduced to reflect the test results. The successful Taco Bell products are distributed to grocers' warehouses by Frito-Lay.[10] A product weakness discovered after a nationwide introduction can be expensive to correct. Moreover, if consumers' early reactions are negative, marketers may not be able to convince consumers to try the product again. Thus making adjustments after test marketing can be crucial to the success of a new product. On the other hand, testing may be successful enough to cause a company to accelerate the introduction of a new product. Test marketing also allows marketers to experiment with variations in advertising, pricing, and packaging in different test areas and to measure the extent of brand awareness, brand switching, and repeat purchases that result from alterations in the marketing mix.

The accuracy of test marketing results often hinges on where the tests are conducted. Selection of appropriate test areas is very important. The validity of test market results depends heavily on selecting test sites that provide accurate representation of the intended target market. Table 10.2 lists some of the most popular test market cities. The criteria used for choosing test cities depend on the product's characteristics, the target market's characteristics, and the firm's objectives and resources.

Test marketing is not without risks, however. Not only is it expensive, but a firm's competitors may try to interfere. A competitor may attempt to "jam" the test program by increasing advertising or promotions, lowering prices, and offering special incentives—all to combat the recognition and purchase of a new brand. Any such tactics can invalidate test results. Sometimes, too, competitors copy the product in the testing stage and rush to introduce a similar product. It is therefore desirable to move quickly and commercialize as soon as possible after successful testing. Clorox spent over four years and several million dollars test marketing a detergent with bleach. During this period Procter & Gamble launched and went national with Tide with Bleach. Several other brands were also introduced during this period, and Clorox withdrew from the detergent market.[11]

Because of these risks, many companies are using alternative methods to measure customer preferences. One such method is simulated test marketing. Typically, consumers at shopping centers are asked to view an advertisement for a new product and are given a free sample to take home. These consumers are subsequently interviewed over the phone and asked to rate the product. The major advantages of simulated test marketing are quicker speed, lower costs, and tighter security, which reduces the flow of information to competitors and reduces jamming. For example, Gillette's Personal Care Division spends less than $200,000 for a simulated test that takes three to five months. A live test market costs Gillette $2 million, counting promotion and distribution, and takes one to two years to complete.[12] Several marketing research firms, such as A. C. Nielsen Company, offer test marketing services to help provide independent assessment of proposed products.

■ *Commercialization*

Commercialization The phase of deciding on full-scale manufacturing and marketing plans and preparing budgets

During the **commercialization** phase, plans for full-scale manufacturing and marketing must be refined and settled, and budgets for the project must be prepared. Early in the commercialization phase, marketing management analyzes the results of test marketing to find out what changes in the marketing mix are needed before the product is introduced. For example, the results of test marketing may tell the marketers to change one or more of the product's physical attributes, modify the distribution plans to include more retail outlets, alter promotional efforts, or change the product's price. However, as more

Table 10.2 Popular Test Markets in the United States			
Tulsa, OK	Wichita, KS	Longview, TX	Pittsfield, MA
Charleston, WV	Bloomington, IL	Lafayette, LA	Jacksonville, FL
Midland, TX	Oklahoma City, OK	Omaha, NE	Edmond, OK
Springfield, IL	Indianapolis, IN	Phoenix, AZ	Hight Point, NC
Lexington-Fayette, KY	Rockford, IL	Gastonia, NC	Salt Lake City, UT
Eau Claire, WI	Grand Junction, CO	Rome, GA	Marion, IN
Cedar Rapids, IA	Visalia, CA		

Source: Strategic Mapping, Inc., Santa Clara, Calif., and Betsy Spethmann, "Test Market USA," *Brandweek*, May 8, 1995, p. 42.

and more changes are made based on test marketing findings, the test marketing projections may become less valid.

During the early part of this stage, marketers must not only gear up for larger-scale production, but also make decisions about warranties, repairs, and replacement parts. The type of warranty a firm provides can be a critical issue for buyers, especially when expensive, technically complex goods such as appliances are involved. Maytag, for example, provides a money-back guarantee on its refrigerators, and Land's End and L. L. Bean offer a no-questions, full-refund guarantee on their products. Establishing an effective system for providing repair services and replacement parts is necessary to maintain favorable customer relationships. Although the producer may furnish these services directly to buyers, it is more common for the producer to provide such services through regional service centers. Regardless of how services are provided, it is important to customers that they be performed quickly and correctly.

The product enters the market during the commercialization phase. One study suggests that only 8 percent of new-product projects initiated by major companies actually reach this stage.[13] When introducing a product, a firm spends enormous sums of money for advertising, personal selling, and other types of promotion. These expenses, together with capital outlays for plant and equipment, can make commercialization costly; such expenditures may not be recovered for several years. Smaller organizations may find the commercializing of a product especially difficult. Consider the challenge of commercializing Prison Blues as discussed in Inside Marketing on the next page.

Products are not usually launched nationwide overnight but are introduced through a process called a *roll-out*. Through a roll-out, a product is introduced in stages, starting in a set of geographic areas and gradually expanding into adjacent areas. It may take several years to market the product nationally. Sometimes the test cities are used as initial marketing areas, and the introduction becomes a natural extension of test marketing. A product test-marketed in Sacramento, Fort Collins, Dallas, St. Louis, and Jacksonville, as the map in Figure 10.6 shows, could be introduced first in those cities. After the stage 1 introduction is complete, stage 2 could include market coverage of the states in which the test cities are located. In stage 3, marketing efforts could be extended into adjacent states.

Figure 10.6
Stages of Expansion into a National Market During Commercialization

Source: Adapted from Herbert G. Hicks, William M. Pride, and James D. Powell, *Business: An Involvement Approach*. Copyright © 1975. Reproduced with permission of The McGraw-Hill Companies.

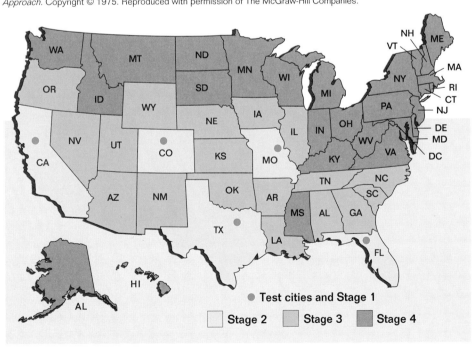

Always Look for the Prison Label

All 7,000 inmates at the Eastern Oregon Correctional Institute wear blue jeans and white T-shirts as uniforms. Although Lee, Wrangler, or Levi's used to be the label of choice, everyone now wears the Prison Blues brand. They don't just wear them, however. They also make them. Inmates at this medium-security prison produce Prison Blues, a line of jeans, denim jackets and shirts, caps, and T-shirts bearing slogans like "Made on the Inside to Be Worn on the Outside" and "Sentenced to Life on the Planet Earth."

Federal law prohibits sale of federal prison products to the private sector, but states can get permission to sell state prison products to private businesses. Unigroup, Oregon's governmental division overseeing prison work programs, secured approval to produce and market clothing directly to retailers and consumers. In 1990 the Oregon State Department of Corrections built a 47,000-square-foot factory at the prison. Inmates who work in the factory cutting, sewing, and inspecting the clothing earn up to $6.50 an hour, a large portion of which goes toward room and board, taxes, and victims' compensation.

The factory's original sewing team of ten inmates has now grown to sixty-seven. Annual sales have climbed to over $1 million. Priced between $11 and $50, Prison Blues apparel is sold in over 500 specialty clothing stores in the United States, Japan, Italy, Germany, and Switzerland. Prison Blues has

been the focus of television programs such as *Entertainment Tonight* and *Donahue* and of a segment on the *CBS Evening News*. *People* magazine and *The New York Times* have also carried feature stories about the operation.

Media attention and international distribution have not translated into profits, however. Convinced that inadequate marketing has been the stumbling block for Prison Blues, Unigroup recently asked a Portland advertising agency to intensify promotional activities and to function as the group's sales representatives. The agency already designs point-of-purchase materials, direct mail ads, and trade show booths for the line. Now they have created a special division, "The Big House," to market Prison Blues to retailers nationwide using telephone and direct mail. In addition, the new Prison Blues mail order catalog allows customers anywhere to buy its products.

If major department stores begin carrying the label and catalog sales take off, Prison Blues is ready to add a hundred more inmate workers and a second shift. But with powerhouse brands such as Levis, Bugle Boy, and Guess already entrenched in the $7-billion U.S. jeans industry, it won't be easy for Prison Blues to compete.

Sources: Katie Hanigan, "Dalbey & Dalbey Division Sings Prison Blues Refrain," *Business Journal—Portland*, Feb. 10, 1995, p. 6; Susan G. Hauser, "Leisure & Arts: Look for the Prison Label," *Wall Street Journal*, Apr. 21, 1995, p. 8; and Michelle Trappen, "Buying at the Big House," *Oregonian*, Feb. 16, 1995.

All remaining states would then be covered in stage 4. Gradual product introductions do not always occur state by state, however; other geographic combinations are used as well, such as groups of counties that overlap across state borders.

Gradual product introduction is desirable for several reasons. It reduces the risks of introducing a new product. If the product fails, the firm will experience smaller losses if the item has been introduced in only a few geographic areas than if it has been marketed nationally. Furthermore, a company cannot introduce a product nationwide overnight because the system of wholesalers and retailers, necessary to distribute a product, cannot be established that quickly. The development of a distribution network may take considerable time. Keep in mind also that the number of units needed to satisfy the national demand for a successful product can be enormous, and a firm usually cannot produce the required quantities in a short time.

Despite the good reasons for introducing a product gradually, marketers realize that this approach creates some competitive problems. A gradual introduction allows competitors to observe what a firm is doing and to monitor results, just as the firm's own marketers are doing. If competitors see that the newly introduced product is successful, they may enter the same target market quickly with similar products. In addition, as a product is introduced region by region, competitors may expand their marketing efforts to offset promotion of the new product.

Product Adoption Process

Product adoption process
The stages buyers go through in accepting a product.

*T*he acceptance of new products—especially new-to-the-world products—usually doesn't happen overnight, and it can take a very long time. People are sometimes cautious or even skeptical about adopting new products, as indicated by some of the remarks quoted in Table 10.3. Customers who eventually accept a new product do so through an adoption process. The following stages of the **product adoption process** are generally recognized as those that buyers go through in accepting a product:

1. *Awareness.* The buyer becomes aware of the product.
2. *Interest.* The buyer seeks information and is receptive to learning about the product.
3. *Evaluation.* The buyer considers the product's benefits and determines whether to try it.
4. *Trial.* The buyer examines, tests, or tries the product to determine its usefulness relative to his or her needs.
5. *Adoption.* The buyer purchases the product and can be expected to use it when the need for this general type of product arises again.[14]

In the first stage, when individuals become aware that the product exists, they have little information about it and are not concerned about obtaining more. For example, one might be aware that Polaroid offers a talking camera that has built-in recorded comic messages to evoke smiles, but have no plans to gather more information about it. Consumers enter the interest stage when they are motivated to get information about the product's features, uses, advantages, disadvantages, price, or location. During the evaluation stage, individuals consider whether the product will satisfy certain criteria that are crucial for meeting their specific needs. In the trial stage, they use or experience the product for the first time, possibly by purchasing a small quantity, by taking advantage of a free sample or demonstration, or by borrowing the product from someone. Supermarkets, for instance, frequently offer special promotions to encourage consumers to taste products. During this stage, potential adopters determine the usefulness of the product under the specific

---

Table 10.3   Most New Ideas Have Their Skeptics

"I think there is a world market for maybe five computers."
—Thomas Watson, Chairman of IBM, 1943

"This 'telephone' has too many shortcomings to be seriously considered as a means of communication. The device is inherently of no value to us."
—Western Union internal memo, 1876

"The wireless music box has no imaginable commercial value. Who would pay for a message sent to nobody in particular?"
—David Sarnoff's associates in response to his urgings for investment in the radio in the 1920s

"The concept is interesting and well-formed, but in order to earn better than a 'C,' the idea must be feasible."
—A Yale University management professor in response to Fred Smith's paper proposing reliable overnight delivery service (Smith went on to found Federal Express Corp.)

"Who the hell wants to hear actors talk?"
—H. M. Warner, Warner Brothers, 1927

"A cookie store is a bad idea. Besides, the market research reports say America likes crispy cookies, not soft and chewy cookies like you make."
—Banker's response to Debbie Fields's idea of starting Mrs. Fields' Cookies

"We don't like their sound, and guitar music is on the way out."
—Decca Recording Co. rejecting the Beatles, 1962

Figure 10.7
Encouraging Product Trial   The maker of Silken Mist is attempting to encourage trial by a $1.00 mail order offer.

conditions for which they need it. The company in Figure 10.7 is encouraging product trial by providing a special promotional offer.

Individuals move into the adoption stage by choosing the specific product when they need a product of that general type. However, because a person enters the adoption process does not mean that she or he will eventually adopt the new product. Rejection may occur at any stage, including adoption. Both product adoption and product rejection can be temporary or permanent.

This adoption model has several implications for the commercialization phase. First, the company must promote the product to create widespread awareness of its existence and its benefits. Samples or simulated trials should be arranged to help buyers make initial purchase decisions. At the same time, marketers should emphasize quality control and provide solid guarantees to reinforce buyer opinion during the evaluation stage. Finally, production and physical distribution must be linked to patterns of adoption and repeat purchases.

When an organization introduces a new product, people do not all begin the adoption process at the same time, nor do they move through the process at the same speed. Of those who eventually adopt the product, some enter the adoption process rather quickly, whereas others start considerably later. For most products, too, there is a group of nonadopters who never begin the process.

Depending on the length of time it takes them to adopt a new product, people can be divided into five major adopter categories: innovators, early adopters, early majority, late majority, and laggards.[15] Figure 10.8 illustrates each adopter category and the percentage of total adopters that it typically represents. **Innovators** are the first to adopt a new product; they enjoy trying new products and tend to be venturesome. **Early adopters** choose new products carefully and are viewed as "the people to check with" by persons in the remaining adopter categories. Persons in the **early majority** adopt just prior to the average person; they are deliberate and cautious in trying new products. **Late majority**

Innovators   First adopters of new products

Early adopters   Careful choosers of new products

Early majority   Those adopting new products just before the average person

Late majority   Skeptics who adopt new products when they feel it is necessary

Figure 10.8
Distribution of Product Adopter Categories
Source: Reprinted with permission of The Free Press, a division of Simon & Schuster, from *Diffusion of Innovations*, Fourth Edition by Everett M. Rogers. Copyright © 1995 by Everett M. Rogers. Copyright © 1962, 1971, 1983 by The Free Press.

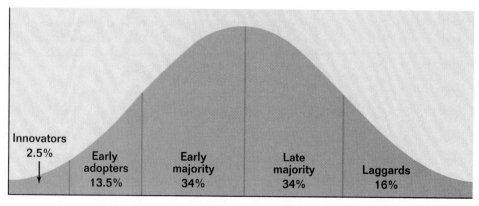

Innovators
2.5%

Early adopters
13.5%

Early majority
34%

Late majority
34%

Laggards
16%

Laggards The last adopters, who distrust new products

people, who are quite skeptical of new products, eventually adopt new products because of economic necessity or social pressure. **Laggards,** the last to adopt a new product, are oriented toward the past. They are suspicious of new products, and when they finally adopt the innovation, it may already have been replaced by a new product.

Product Life Cycle Management

*M*ost new products start off slowly and seldom generate enough sales to bring immediate profits. As buyers learn about the new product, marketers should be alert for product weaknesses and make corrections quickly to prevent its early demise. Marketing strategy should be designed to attract the segment that is most interested and has the fewest objections. If any of these marketing factors need adjustment, this action, too, must be taken quickly to sustain demand. As the sales curve moves upward and the break-even point is reached, the growth stage begins.

■ Marketing Strategy in the Growth Stage

As sales increase, management must support the momentum by adjusting the marketing strategy. The goal is to establish the product's position and to fortify it by encouraging brand loyalty. As profits increase, the organization must brace itself for the entrance of aggressive competitors, who may make specialized appeals to selected market segments.

During the growth stage, product offerings may have to be expanded. To achieve greater penetration of an overall market, segmentation may have to be used more intensely. That would require developing product variations to satisfy the needs of people in several different market segments. Marketers should also analyze the competing brands' product position relative to their own brands and take corrective actions.

Gaps in the marketing channels should be filled during the growth period. Once a product has won acceptance, new distribution outlets may be easier to obtain. Sometimes marketers tend to move from an exclusive or selective exposure to a more intensive network of dealers to achieve greater market penetration. Marketers must also make sure that the physical distribution system is running efficiently and delivering supplies to distributors before their inventories are exhausted. Because competition increases during the growth period, service adjustments and prompt credit for defective products are important marketing tools.

Advertising expenditures may be lowered slightly from the high level of the introductory stage but are still quite substantial. As sales increase, promotion costs should drop as a percentage of total sales. A falling ratio between promotion expenditures and sales should contribute significantly to increased profits. The advertising messages should stress brand benefits. Coupons and samples may be used to increase market share.

After recovering development costs, a business may be able to lower prices. As sales volume increases, efficiencies in production can result in lower costs. These savings may be passed on to buyers. If demand remains strong and there are few competitive threats, prices tend to remain stable. If price cuts are feasible, they can improve price competition and discourage new competitors from entering the market.

■ Marketing Strategy for Mature Products

Because many products are in the maturity stage of their life cycle, marketers must know how to deal with these products and be prepared to adjust their marketing strategies. Characteristics of the maturity stage include slower market growth, increased competitive actions with some competitors being forced out, and a greater emphasis on changing a product's price, promotion, and distribution. There are many approaches to altering marketing strategies during the maturity stage. Some of these are shown in Table 10.4.

One way to increase sales of mature products is to suggest new uses of the products. Arm & Hammer has boosted demand for its baking soda by this method. Kraft General Foods continues to stimulate sales of Jell-O by promoting new uses. It has been suggested that as a product matures, its customers become more experienced and specialized

240

Table 10.4   Selected Approaches for Managing Products in the Maturity Stage

Approaches	Examples
Develop new product uses	Use Knox gelatin as a plant food. Market Arm & Hammer baking soda as a refrigerator deodorant. Promote Cheez Whiz as a microwavable cheese sauce.
Increase product usage among current users	Use multiple packaging for products in which a larger supply at the point of consumption actually increases consumption (such as for soft drinks or beer).
Increase the number of users	Pursue global markets or small niches in domestic markets.
Add product features	CD-ROM built into computers. Dual airbags for automobiles.
Change package sizes	Single-serving sizes. Travel-size packages of personal care products.
Increase product quality	Increased life of light bulbs. Increased reliability and durability of U.S.-made automobiles.
Change nonproduct marketing mix variables—promotion, price, distribution	Dr Pepper shifts the focus of its advertisements from teenagers to people 18–54 years of age. Offer a package of dishwasher detergent containing one-third more product for the same price. Market computer hardware through mail order outlets.

(particularly for industrial products). As these customers gain knowledge, the benefits they seek may change as well, necessitating product modifications. For example, consumers who have long enjoyed Kraft or Campbell products may now prefer lower fat versions of these products (see Figure 10.9).

Finding new product uses and users can play a major role in remaining competitive in the maturity stage. As discussed in Global Perspective, Gillette is a strong competitor in some mature markets because of its global vision.

During the maturity stage of the life cycle, marketers actively encourage dealers to support the product. Dealers may be offered promotional assistance in lowering their inventory costs. In general, marketers go to great lengths to serve dealers and provide incentives for selling the manufacturer's brand.

Figure 10.9
Effective Management of a Mature Product
One way to stimulate sales of mature food products is to offer low-fat versions of these products.

GLOBAL PERSPECTIVE

Gillette's Products: A Global Success Story

Gillette markets an extraordinary array of products in over 200 countries. Although in some parts of the world the name *Gillette* has become synonymous with the words *razor blades,* this organization markets much more than sharpened steel. In addition to razors and blades, Gillette's product offerings include Parker and Paper Mate pens, Liquid Paper, Oral-B toothbrushes, Braun small appliances, and toiletries such as Right Guard deodorant and Foamy shaving cream. Although it does sell razors in Russia and blades in Bulgaria, the company also sells toothbrushes in Turkey and pens in Panama. In each of its divisions and in all of its international markets, Gillette's strategy is the same—aggressively roll out new products.

For over a hundred years, ever since King C. Gillette came up with the idea for disposable razor blades in 1895, the Gillette Company has been a world-class product innovator. While other organizations die out, asserts Gillette's president, his company thrives by continuously rejuvenating and reinventing its products. In its personal care products division, Gillette originated clear gel deodorant and strengthened its brand image among women by introducing women's shave gel. In its shaving division, Gillette won't launch a product unless there is another new one already under development.

In addition to new-product introductions, expansion into international markets is fueling Gillette's phenomenal growth in sales and profits. Today, almost 70 percent of the company's sales come from outside the United States. Gillette's strategy for global expansion is to enter into joint ventures with local organizations. Penetrating the Russian and Eastern European markets, however, was not easy. Politics and currencies were unstable, borders were still evolving, and communication systems were unreliable at best. Gillette forged ahead, however, recognizing that if it waited for stability, its competitors would have a head start.

In a joint venture with a Russian government group, Gillette invested about $60 million to construct a factory that produces blades and razors. Responding to modest Russian incomes, Gillette altered its product mix to feature lower-end razors and more affordable packages containing fewer blades. To reach Russian shoppers, Gillette sells its brands in free-standing marketplace kiosks. By acquiring 80 percent of a Polish razor-blade company, Gillette was recently able to expand its operations to Poland. Several new joint ventures are on the drawing boards, and experts agree, Gillette's brand name recognition and distribution expertise virtually guarantee success in other foreign markets, as long as it keeps the new products coming.

Based on information from Clive Chajet, "Breaking Down Image Barriers," *Executive Speeches,* Feb./Mar. 1995, pp. 32–35; Pam Weisz, "The Razor's Edge," *Brandweek,* Apr. 24, 1995, pp. 26–28, 30, 32; Gary Hoover, Alta Campbell, and Patrick J. Spain, *Hoover's Handbook of American Business 1995* (Austin, Texas: Reference Press, Inc., 1995), pp. 560–561; "The Process View: How Marketing Needs To Change," *Planning Review,* Mar./Apr. 1995, p. 11; John Wyatt, "Biggest U.S. Companies Promise You a Profitable Year," *Fortune,* May 15, 1995, pp. 65–66; Avraham Shama, "Entry Strategies of U.S. Firms to the Newly Independent States, Baltic States, and Eastern European Countries," *California Management Review,* Spring 1995, pp. 90–109; Alex Pham, "Seventh Annual Globe 100," *Boston Globe,* May 23, 1995, p. 36; and Tom Nutile, "Gillette's Product Development a Key," *Boston Herald,* Mar. 13, 1995, p. 23.

To maintain market share during the maturity stage requires moderate and sometimes large advertising expenditures. Advertising messages focus on differentiating a brand from the field of competitors, and sales promotion efforts are aimed at both consumers and resellers.

A greater mixture of pricing strategies is used during the maturity stage. Strong price competition is likely and may ignite price wars. Firms also compete in other ways than price, such as through product quality or service. For example, during the 1980s Cameron Balloons, a hot-air balloon producer located in Ann Arbor, Michigan, successfully competed against nine other balloon manufacturers by providing customers with high quality inflatables. During the early 1990s the balloon market matured and adverse economic conditions led to a decline in sales. Rather than reducing quality to be able to lower its prices to a more competitive level, Cameron cut its work force size and kept its focus on providing top-quality balloons. The emphasis on quality worked. Cameron has survived a market shake-out and now has only four competitors.[16]

Marketers develop price flexibility to differentiate offerings in product lines. Mark downs and price incentives are more common. Procter & Gamble lowered prices on Pampers (5 percent) and Luvs (16 percent) to reduce the widening gap between its diapers and the generic brands. Prices may rise, however, if distribution and production costs increase.

■ *Marketing Strategy for Declining Products*

As a product's sales curve turns downward, industry profits continue to fall. A business can justify maintaining a product as long as it contributes to profits or enhances the over-all effectiveness of a product mix. In this stage, marketers must determine whether to eliminate the product or seek to reposition it to extend its life. Usually, a declining product has lost its distinctiveness because similar competing products have been introduced. Competition engenders increased substitution and brand switching as buyers become insensitive to minor product differences. For these reasons, marketers do little to change a product's style, design, or other attributes during its decline. New technology, product substitutes, or environmental considerations may also indicate that the time has come to delete a product.

During a product's decline, outlets with strong sales volumes are maintained, and unprofitable outlets are weeded out. An entire marketing channel may be eliminated if it does not contribute adequately to profits. Sometimes a new marketing channel, such as a factory outlet, will be used to liquidate remaining inventory of an obsolete product. As sales decline, the product becomes more obscure, but loyal buyers seek out dealers who carry it.

Advertising expenditures are at a minimum. Advertising of special offers may slow the rate of decline. Sales promotions, such as coupons and premiums, may temporarily regain buyers' attention. As the product continues to decline, the sales staff shifts its emphasis to more profitable products.

To have a product return a profit may be more important to a firm than to maintain a certain market share through repricing. To squeeze out all possible remaining profits, marketers may maintain the price despite declining sales and competitive pressures. Prices may even be increased as costs rise if a loyal core market still wants the product. In other situations, the price may be cut to reduce existing inventory so that the product can be deleted. Severe price reductions may be required if a new product is making an existing product obsolete.

Product Elimination

Product elimination
Deleting a declining product from the product mix

*G*enerally, a product cannot satisfy target market customers and contribute to the achievement of an organization's overall goals indefinitely. **Product elimination** is the process of deleting a product from the product mix when it no longer satisfies a sufficient number of customers. A declining product reduces an organization's profitability and drains resources that could be used instead to modify other products or develop new ones. A marginal product may require shorter production runs, which can increase per-unit production costs. Finally, when a dying product completely loses favor with customers, the negative feelings may transfer to some of the company's other products.

Most organizations find it difficult to eliminate a product. A decision to drop a product may be opposed by management and other employees who feel the product is necessary in the product mix. Salespeople who still have some loyal customers are especially upset when a product is dropped. Considerable resources and effort are sometimes spent trying to change a slipping product's marketing mix to improve its sales and thus avoid having to eliminate it.

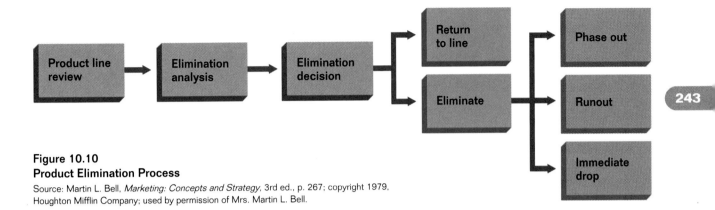

Figure 10.10
Product Elimination Process

Source: Martin L. Bell, *Marketing: Concepts and Strategy*, 3rd ed., p. 267; copyright 1979, Houghton Mifflin Company; used by permission of Mrs. Martin L. Bell.

243

Some organizations delete products only after they have become heavy financial burdens. A better approach is some form of systematic review in which each product is evaluated periodically to determine its impact on the overall effectiveness of the firm's product mix. Such a review should analyze a product's contribution to the firm's sales for a given period and include estimates of future sales, costs, and profits associated with the product. It should also gauge the value of making changes in the marketing strategy to improve the product's performance. A systematic review allows an organization to improve product performance and to ascertain when to eliminate products. Although many companies do systematically review their product mixes, relatively few have formal, written policies on the process of deleting products.

Basically, there are three ways to eliminate a product: phase it out, run it out, or drop it immediately (see Figure 10.10). A *phase out* approach allows the product to decline without a change in the marketing strategy. No attempt is made to give the product new life. A *runout* policy exploits any strengths left in the product. Intensifying marketing efforts in core markets or eliminating some marketing expenditures, such as advertising, may cause a sudden jump in profits. This approach is commonly taken for technologically obsolete products, such as older models of computers and calculators. Often the price is reduced to get a sales spurt. The third alternative, *dropping* an unprofitable product immediately, is the best strategy when losses are too great to prolong the product's life.

SUMMARY

Organizations must be able to adjust their product mixes to compete effectively and achieve their goals. A product mix can be improved through line extension and through product modification. A line extension is the development of a product that is closely related to one or more products in the existing line, but is designed specifically to meet different customer needs.

Product modification is the changing of one or more characteristics of a firm's product. This approach to altering a product mix can be effective when the product is modifiable, when customers can perceive the change, and when customers want the modification. Quality modifications are changes that relate to a product's dependability and durability. Changes that affect a products' versatility, effectiveness, convenience, or safety are called functional modifications. Aesthetic modifications change the sensory appeal of a product.

Developing new products is a way of enhancing a firm's product mix and/or adding depth to the product line. A new product may be an innovation that has never been sold by any organization; a product that a given firm has not marketed previously, although similar products may have been available from other organizations; or a product brought from one market to a new market.

Before a product is introduced, it goes through the seven phases of the new-product development process. In the idea generation phase, new-product ideas may come from internal or external sources. In the process of screening, ideas with the greatest potential are selected for further review. There are several key questions a company should ask when reviewing an idea for a new product. What will the concept of the product be in the mind of the consumer? What sales and promotional methods will be appropriate and how profitable will the product be? Does the product fit within the company's current mission, purpose, and product portfolio? Who is the target market for the product and how long is the demand expected to continue? Who are the current and possible future competitors? And what is the overall probability of its success? Concept testing, the third phase, involves having a small sample of potential customers review a brief description of the product idea to determine their initial perceptions of the proposed product and their early buying intentions. During the business analysis stage, the product idea is evaluated to determine its potential contribution to the firm's sales, costs, and profits. Product development is the stage in which the organization finds out if it is technically feasible to produce the product and if it can be produced at a cost low enough to make the final price reasonable. Test marketing is a limited introduction of a product in areas chosen to represent the intended market. The decision to enter the commercialization phase means that full-scale production of the product begins and a complete marketing strategy is developed.

The process that buyers go through in accepting a product includes awareness, interest, evaluation, trial, and adoption. Adopters fall into five main categories: innovators, the first to adopt a new product; early adopters, who

select new products carefully; early majority, which adopts just before the average person; late majority, the skeptics who adopt new products because of economic necessity or social pressure; and laggards, who adopt last.

As a product moves through its life cycle, marketing strategies may require continual adaptation. In the growth stage, it is important to develop brand loyalty and a market position. In the maturity stage, a product may be modified, or new market segments may be developed to rejuvenate its sales. A product that is declining may be maintained as long as it makes a contribution to profits or enhances the product mix. Marketers must determine whether to eliminate the declining product or try to modify and reposition it to extend its life.

Product elimination is the process of deleting a product that no longer satisfies a sufficient number of customers. Although a firm's personnel may oppose product elimination, weak products are unprofitable, consume too much time and effort, may require shorter production runs, and can create an unfavorable impression of the firm's other products. A product mix should be systematically reviewed to determine when to delete products. Products to be eliminated can be phased out, run out, or dropped immediately.

IMPORTANT TERMS

Line extension	Idea generation	Commercialization	Laggards
Product modification	Screening	Product adoption process	Product elimination
Quality modifications	Concept testing	Innovators	
Functional modifications	Business analysis	Early adopters	
Aesthetic modifications	Product development	Early majority	
New-product development process	Test marketing	Late majority	

DISCUSSION AND REVIEW QUESTIONS

1. Compare and contrast the three major ways of modifying a product.
2. Identify and briefly explain the seven major phases of the new-product development process.
3. Do small companies that manufacture one or two products need to be concerned about developing and managing products? Why or why not?
4. Why is product development a cross-functional activity within an organization? That is, why must finance, engineering, manufacturing, and other functional areas be involved?
5. What is the major purpose of concept testing, and how is it accomplished?
6. What are the benefits and disadvantages of test marketing?
7. Why does the process of commercialization sometimes take a considerable amount of time?

8. What are some of the ways in which a company can improve new-product implementation success?
9. What are the stages in the product adoption process, and how do they affect the commercialization phase?
10. What are the five major adopter categories that describe the length of time required for a consumer to adopt a new product, and what are the characteristics of each?
11. In what ways does the marketing strategy for a mature product differ from the marketing strategy for a growth product?
12. What types of problems are caused by a weak product in a product mix?
13. Describe the most effective approach for eliminating weak products from a product mix.

APPLICATION QUESTIONS

1. When developing a new product, a company often test markets the proposed product in a specific area or location. Coca-Cola did this with its sports drink, PowerAde. Suppose you wish to test-market your new revolutionary SuperWax car wax, which requires only one application for a lifetime finish. Where and how would you test market your new product?

2. Generally, buyers go through a product adoption process before becoming a loyal consumer. Describe your experience adopting a product you now use consistently. Did you go through all the stages?

3. Identify and describe a friend or family member who fits into each of the following adopter categories for purchasing clothes. How would you use this information if you were product manager for a fashion-oriented, medium-priced retailer such as J. Crew or JC Penney?
   a. innovator
   b. early adopter
   c. early majority
   d. late majority
   e. laggard

4. A product manager may make quality, functional, or aesthetic modifications when modifying a product. Identify a familiar product that recently has been modified, categorize the modification (quality, functional, or aesthetic), and describe how you would have modified it differently.

5. Phasing out a product from the product mix often is difficult for an organization. Sears's elimination of its "Big Book" catalogs is a good example. Visit a restaurant and a retail store in your area. Ask the manager of each what products he/she has had to discontinue in the recent past. Find out what determined the elimination and who was involved in the decision. Ask the manager to identify any products that should be but have not been eliminated, and try to ascertain the reason.

Case 10.1 Product Management at Outboard Marine Corporation

In the fiercely competitive, $11 billion U.S. boating industry, Outboard Marine Corporation (OMC) and Brunswick Corporation dominate the market. Even these two powerhouses, however, are susceptible to ups and downs in the economy. When the economy falters, boat and motor sales tumble. In fact, according to industry experts, the marine industry almost more than any other is inextricably linked to consumer confidence. When pleasure powerboat sales plunged 47 percent between 1988 and 1992, Outboard Marine struggled. Although sales of engines and powerboats are now on the rise again, Outboard Marine is looking for ways to protect itself from unpredictable economic turns. According to company executives, skilled and creative product management is one way of keeping Outboard Marine afloat during both prosperous and adverse economic conditions.

In 1936, Outboard Marine and Manufacturing Company was born. A few years after acquiring Evinrude Motors, the company joined with Johnson Motor Company and in 1956 adopted its present name. The company manufactures and markets marine engines, boats, and boat accessories for recreational use. From headquarters located in Waukegan, Illinois, Outboard Marine operates plants all over the world, including Canada, Mexico, Brazil, France, Sweden, Australia, and China. Although the company is the number two pleasure boat maker behind giant Brunswick Corporation,

it is number one in sales of marine engines, controlling over 40 percent of the market. Despite its prominent market position and $1 billion in annual sales, Outboard Marine's recent difficulties persuaded company executives to adopt an aggressive strategy for managing its products.

According to company marketers, bass fisherman, who constitute the great majority of OMC's customers, had become disenchanted with the company's 150-horsepower marine engine. This engine had outlived its ability to generate excitement in the marketplace. Instead of following the traditional method of boosting sales of a product in this stage, which might have included modifying the engine or repositioning it for a new market, OMC adopted what it call a "leapfrog strategy." The company introduced its 175-horsepower engine, a new product it believes is the biggest advance in recreational boating since the invention of the outboard engine in 1909.

One of Outboard Marine's greatest strengths is its superior technology, and the company used that technology to create its new engine. As a result, its two-stroke model has a smoother idle, is quieter, increases fuel efficiency by about 30 percent, and is much cleaner, spewing 70 to 80 percent fewer hydrocarbons into the atmosphere than previous models. With the Environmental Protection Agency mandating lower marine engine emissions, OMC believes that its low-emission, high-performance engine gives the company a huge competitive advantage.

During the introduction of its new engine, the company launched an aggressive advertising campaign and sponsored fishermen in bass tournaments around the United States to demonstrate the engine's superiority. When boaters and fishermen shop for new engines, OMC offers two choices—the old model at lower-than-competitors' prices, or the lighter, quicker, better looking, fuel efficient, environmentally responsible upgraded model for a little more. In this way, the company can market both the familiar, lower-priced models and the technologically advanced higher-priced models.

Company executives are also examining other ways to increase sales and improve customer service. Toward that end, OMC recently initiated a study of its strengths and weaknesses. One deficiency they discovered was a lack of feedback from retailers or customers before going ahead with new-product development. For example, one of OMC 's biggest Chris-Craft boat dealers

recently complained about being presented with the new product line without ever having given any input to OMC regarding his customers' likes and dislikes. To facilitate communication, the company invested $1 million in additional toll-free lines for customers and dealers. In addition to opening communication, Outboard Marine is striving to achieve better coordination of boat and engine products to intensify strategic planning efforts.[17]

Questions for Discussion

1. Is OMC's new 175-horsepower engine a modified product, a line extension, or a new product? Explain.
2. What are the strengths and weaknesses of the process that OMC used to develop the new 175-horsepower engine?
3. Evaluate OMC's approach of selling its older models at competitive prices while making the newer engine available at a higher price.

Case 10.2   Pepsi-Cola Struggles with Product Introductions

Pepsi-Cola markets Diet Pepsi, Crystal Pepsi, Lipton Teas, Ocean Spray juices, Mountain Dew, Mug root beer, All Sport, Pepsi Max, Slice, and of course, its original brand, Pepsi. Calling itself a total beverage company, Pepsi's strategy is to expand with new products in fast-growing categories. Regardless of how many products it introduces, however, Pepsi-Cola has spent its life playing second fiddle to number one soft drink marketer, Coca-Cola. Domestic sales of Pepsi have declined for five straight years, and in international markets, Coke outsells Pepsi three to one. In its never-ending battle to quench its rival, Pepsi is willing to be innovative and take risks, primarily because it has so much to gain. After all, the soft drink market is a $48-billion industry.

Pepsi repeatedly gambles on new-product introductions to reach the elusive top spot. But the gamble doesn't pay off when the product fizzles. In 1977, Pepsi tried to tempt cola fans to reduce their sugar and calorie intake by drinking Pepsi Light, a low-sugar, but not a no-sugar, cola. According to industry experts, Pepsi Light failed because the weight-conscious wanted a no-calorie drink, and everyone else wanted the original calorie-laden version. Another of Pepsi's unmemorable cola offerings, Jake's, never made it past the test marketing stage.

When increasing numbers of thirsty Americans began drinking sparkling juices and bottled spring water instead of colas, Pepsi saw an opportunity to try another new product. What the company came up with was a clear, caffeine-free, preservative-free, 130-calorie cola. During test marketing, Crystal Pepsi performed beyond expectations, and three months after its national roll-out, it had captured over 2 percent of national supermarket soft drink sales. Pepsi believed it had a winner at last. However, initial excitement about the product waned, and although the company hasn't stopped producing Crystal Pepsi, the clear cola is hardly an overwhelming success. Some industry analysts insist that if Crystal Pepsi's packaging and advertising had told consumers more about the product, cola drinkers would not have been disappointed that Crystal Pepsi didn't taste like Pepsi, and the product might have been a hit.

This string of product failures did not persuade Pepsi's executives to quit gambling on new products, concentrate on its tried-and-true offerings, and remain content with its number two position. Hoping to reinvigorate cola sales, the company spent $1.5 million to develop Pepsi XL, a half-sugar, half-artificial-sweetener cola with half the calories of regular Pepsi. Some people don't like the taste of artificial sweeteners; some won't drink anything labeled diet. Pepsi marketers believe that Pepsi XL meets the needs of these finicky cola drinkers perfectly. What about the dismal performance of Pepsi Light? What about warnings that sales of Pepsi

XL will cannibalize sales of Pepsi and Diet Pepsi? With no diet leader of its own, Pepsi is willing to take a risk on adding a second low-calorie drink to its product line. As one Pepsi executive said, "It's worth a shot."

In keeping with its strategy, Pepsi is adding several new non-cola beverages to its already impressive list of drink categories. It is test marketing a new fruit drink made from the guarana, an exotic red berry from the Brazilian rain forest. Hoping to capture a significant share of the $1.8 billion ready-to-drink tea market, Pepsi joined with Lipton to market Lipton Original in bottles. Pepsi also introduced Aquafina, its own brand of bottled water. Single-serving Aquafinas will cost substantially less than upscale name-brand competitors. The soft drink marketer believes that offering bottled water gives the company another chance to recapture customers who have cut their cola consumption in recent years. If Aquafina flops, joke some industry analysts, Pepsi can always concentrate on milk. And in fact PepsiCo's beverage unit recently announced test mar-keting of Smooth Moos Smoothies, low-fat milk shakes in chocolate, vanilla, and strawberry flavors. Pepsi is heading for the dairy case hoping to build brand identity in what the company's vice president of marketing calls "the last underdeveloped beverage frontier."

No matter what new beverage frontier is discovered, Pepsi-Cola is sure to blaze a trail. The company believes that only by innovation and new-product introduction can it eventually become the number one soft drink marketer in the world, a position it has sought for almost 100 years.[18]

Questions for Discussion

1. Cola-flavored soft drinks are in which stage of the product life cycle?
2. From the perspective of Pepsi employees, was Crystal Pepsi a new product or a modified product? Discuss.
3. Evaluate Pepsi's use of new-product development as a means of competing with Coca-Cola.

Chapter 11

Branding and Packaging

O B J E C T I V E S

- To recognize the types of brands and their benefits

- To gain an understanding of brand loyalty

- To analyze the major components of brand equity

- To understand how to select, protect, and license brands

- To become aware of the major packaging functions and design considerations and how packaging is used in marketing strategies

- To examine the functions of labeling and the legal issues associated with labeling

Doritos sports new package, new shape, same old position: number one with snackers.

*I*n the snack food market, Frito-Lay's Doritos Tortilla Chips is a superstar brand with annual sales of $1.3 billion. What in the world would prompt makers of Doritos to change the chips and redesign the logo and package? According to Frito-Lay, sometimes revolutionary changes are required. With competition from private-label and trendy new brands intensifying, the snack food giant hopes that the changes will make Doritos more exciting and accelerate sales growth beyond the current annual rate of about 3 percent.

For two years, Frito-Lay conducted focus groups, asking about 5,000 participants to describe the perfect snack chip. The result was new Doritos—rounder, larger, thinner, and coated with more seasonings. To make consumers aware that something new was inside the bag, Frito-Lay changed the outside of the bag, the fourth design change since Doritos chips were introduced in 1967. The company conducted two years of research to ensure that the new packaging enhanced the associations consumers had with the decades-old brand. Gone are the orange and brown tiles behind the brand name; added is the newly created "signature chip," a hand-drawn, graffiti-like red, orange, and yellow triangle. Company officials believe that the redesigned logo not only matches the product's shape, it reinforces the "high-energy irreverent personality" of the Doritos brand, something the older designs ignored.

To announce the arrival of the reborn Doritos, Frito-Lay launched a $50-million marketing campaign, the largest in company history. Seven thousand Frito-Lay delivery trucks sport the new Dorito look on bright side panels. Eight thousand retail outlets across the U.S. display snack aisle signs bearing the new package. In the first new TV spot, recently ousted governors Mario Cuomo and Ann Richards look for a change . . . and find it—in new Doritos.

Frito-Lay executives are pleased with a recent survey indicating that consumers like new Doritos and the new logo. They hope that the changes will make it even harder for other snack-food marketers to compete. Competing with Doritos was already a difficult assignment. Even with pointy corners and a ho-hum package, Doritos was the best-selling snack in the U.S.[1]

Brands and packages (such as the new Doritos bag) are part of a product's tangible features, the verbal and physical cues that help customers identify the products they want and influence their choices when they are unsure. As such, branding and packaging play an important role in marketing strategy. A good brand is distinct and memorable; without one, firms could not differentiate their products, and shoppers' choices would essentially be arbitrary. A good package design is cost-effective, safe, environmentally responsible, and is valuable as a promotional tool, as the new Doritos package is proving to be.

In this chapter we discuss branding, including its value to customers and marketers, brand loyalty, and brand equity. Next we examine the various types of brands. We then consider how companies choose and protect brands, the various branding policies employed, and brand licensing. We look at packaging's critical role as part of the product and how it is marketed. The functions of packaging, issues to consider in packaging design, how the package can be a major element in marketing strategy, and packaging criticisms are also explored. We conclude with a discussion of labeling and other product-related features, including the product's physical characteristics and supportive product-related services.

Branding

Brand   An identifying name, term, design, or symbol

Brand name   The part of a brand that can be spoken

Brand mark   The part of a brand not made up of words

Trademark   A legal designation of exclusive use of a brand

*M*arketers must make many decisions about products, including branding choices such as brands, brand names, brand marks, trademarks, and trade names. A **brand** is a name, term, design, symbol, or any other feature that identifies one seller's good or service as distinct from those of other sellers. A brand may identify one item, a family of items, or all items of that seller.[2] A **brand name** is that part of a brand that can be spoken—including letters, words, and numbers—such as 7Up. A brand name is often a product's only distinguishing characteristic. Without the brand name, a firm could not identify its products. To consumers, brand names are as fundamental as the product itself. Indeed, many brand names have become synonymous with the product itself, such as Scotch tape and Xerox copiers. Through promotional activities, these companies try to protect their brand names from being generic names for tape and photocopiers. Table 11.1 lists the top ten brand names in terms of perceived brand quality.

The element of a brand that is not made up of words, but is often a symbol or design, is called a **brand mark.** One example is the Golden Arches, which identify McDonald's restaurants and can be seen on patches worn by athletic teams—from the U.S. Olympic teams to little league softball teams—sponsored by McDonald's. In Figure 11.1, Citgo's pyramid and eagle are brand marks, and the Maxwell House's tipped-over coffee cup and drop is also a brand mark. A **trademark** is a legal designation indicating that the owner has

Table 11.1 Top Ten Names in Brand Quality*	
Brand Name	**Product**
Kodak	Film
Disney World	Theme park
Mercedes-Benz	Luxury automobile
Disneyland	Theme park
Hallmark	Greeting cards
Fisher-Price	Toys
Levi's	Jeans
UPS	Delivery service
Arm & Hammer	Baking soda
Reynolds Wrap	Aluminum foil

*Based on a survey of 2,000 respondents.
Source: T. L. Stanley, "How They Rate," *Brandweek*, Apr. 3, 1995, pp. 45–48.

Figure 11.1
Brandmarks
Citgo employs a three-sided pyramid and an eagle as brand marks, and Maxwell House uses a tipped coffee cup and drop as a brand mark.

Trade name Full legal name of an organization

exclusive use of a brand or a part of a brand and that others are prohibited by law from using it. To protect a brand name or brand mark in the United States, an organization must register it as a trademark with the U.S. Patent and Trademark Office. As of 1994, the Patent and Trademark Office had 928,613 trademark registrations.[3] Finally, a **trade name** is the full and legal name of an organization, such as Ford Motor Company, rather than the name of a specific product.

■ *Value of Branding*

Both buyers and sellers benefit from branding. Brands help buyers identify specific products that they do and do not like, which in turn facilitates the purchase of items that satisfy their needs and reduces the time required to purchase the product. Without brands, product selection would be quite random because buyers could have no assurance that they were purchasing what they preferred. The purchase of certain brands can be a form of self-expression. Table 11.2 indicates that clothing brand names are important to teenagers (especially boys). Names such as Tommy Hilfiger, Polo, Champion, Guess, and Nike give manufacturers an advantage in the marketplace. A brand also helps buyers evaluate the quality of products, especially when they are unable to judge a product's characteristics. That is, a brand may symbolize a certain quality level to a customer, and in turn

Table 11.2 Importance of Brand Name Clothing to Teenagers		
How important to you is the brand name on clothes you buy?		
	Boys	**Girls**
Very important	21%	13%
Somewhat important	40%	31%
Only a little important	23%	28%
Not at all important	16%	28%
Source: USA Today/CNN/Gallup poll of 803 teenagers, aged 13–17, conducted Aug. 1993.		

252

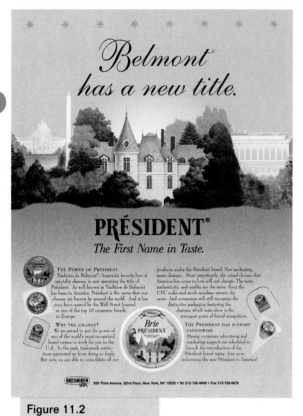

Figure 11.2
Changing Brand Names
Changing a brand name can be a difficult decision because the value in the old brand must be sacrificed for the opportunity to build greater value in the new brand.

the person lets that perception of quality represent the quality of the item. A brand helps to reduce a buyer's perceived risk of purchase. In addition, a psychological reward may come from owning a brand that symbolizes status. The Mercedes-Benz brand is an example.

Sellers benefit from branding because each company's brands identify its products, which makes repeat purchasing easier for customers. Branding helps a firm introduce a new product that carries the name of one or more of its existing products because buyers are already familiar with the firm's existing brands. Branding also facilitates promotional efforts because the promotion of each branded product indirectly promotes all other products that are similarly branded. Coca-Cola's brand extensions—additional products marketed under the Coca-Cola brand—improved its market share from 36 percent in the early 1980s to 42 percent in the 1990s. Branding also helps sellers by fostering brand loyalty. To the extent that buyers become loyal to a specific brand, the company's market share for that product achieves a certain level of stability, allowing the firm to use its resources more efficiently. Once a firm develops some degree of customer loyalty for a brand, it can maintain a fairly consistent price rather than continually cutting the price to attract customers. A brand is valuable to an organization. It is just as much of an asset as the company's building or machinery. When marketers at a company build a brand, thus increasing the brand's value, they also are raising the total asset value of the organization. (We discuss brand value in more detail later in this chapter.) At times marketers must decide whether or not to change a brand name. This is a difficult decision because the value in the existing brand name must be given up in order to gain the potential for building a higher value in a new brand name. As shown in Figure 11.2, the producer of Tradition de Belmont Brie cheese decided to change its U.S. brand name to Président because Président is the name used on its cheeses around the world. The Président brand name is one of the top consumer brands in Europe. Marketers of this product decided that they wanted to put the power of one of the world's most recognized names to work in the United States.

■ *Brand Loyalty*

Brand loyalty   A customer's favorable attitude toward a specific brand

As mentioned earlier, creating and maintaining customer loyalty toward a brand is a major benefit of branding. **Brand loyalty** is a customer's favorable attitude toward a specific brand and, depending on loyalty strength, some likelihood of consistent purchase of this brand when needs for a product in this product category arise. Although brand loyalty may not result in a customer purchasing a specific brand every time a need for that product category occurs, the brand is at least considered as a potentially viable brand in the set of brands being considered for purchase. Development of brand loyalty by a customer reduces his or her risks and shortens the time spent buying the product. As the data in Figure 11.3 indicate, the degree of brand loyalty for products varies. Thus the extent to which an organization can develop brand loyalty differs from one product category to another. Levels of brand loyalty also vary by country. Customers in France, Germany, and the United Kingdom tend to be less brand loyal than U.S. customers.

There are three degrees of brand loyalty: recognition, preference, and insistence.

Brand recognition
A customer's awareness that a brand exists and is an alternative to purchase

Brand recognition exists when a customer is aware that the brand exists and views it as an alternative to purchase if the preferred brand is unavailable or if the other available brands are unfamiliar to the customer. This is the mildest form of brand loyalty. The term *loyalty* clearly is being used very loosely here. One of the initial objectives of a marketer introducing a new brand is to create widespread awareness of the brand in order to generate brand recognition.

Brand preference
The degree of brand loyalty in which a customer prefers one brand over competitive offerings

Brand preference is a stronger degree of brand loyalty in which a customer definitely prefers one brand over competitive offerings and will purchase this brand if available.

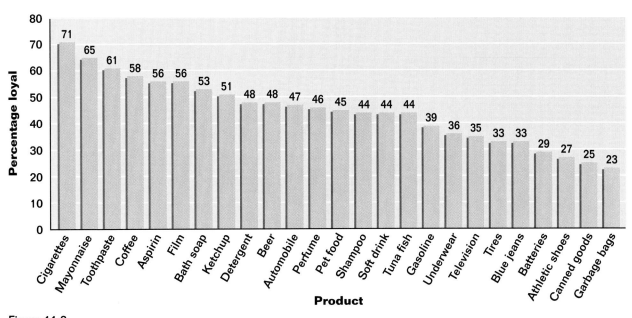

Figure 11.3
Percentage of Users of Selected Products Who Are Loyal to One Brand
Source: Reprinted by permission of *Wall Street Journal,* © 1989 Dow Jones & Company, Inc. All rights reserved worldwide.

Brand insistence
The degree of brand loyalty in which a customer strongly prefers a specific brand and will accept no substitute

However, if the brand is not available, the customer will accept a substitute brand rather than expend additional effort finding and purchasing the preferred brand. A marketer is likely to be able to compete effectively in a market when a number of customers have developed brand preference for its specific brand.

Brand insistence is the degree of brand loyalty in which a customer strongly prefers a specific brand, will accept no substitute, and is willing to spend a great deal of time and effort to acquire that brand. If a brand-insistent customer goes to a store and finds the brand unavailable, rather than purchasing a substitute brand the customer will seek the brand elsewhere. Brand insistence is the strongest degree of brand loyalty. It is a brander's dream. However, it is the least common type of brand loyalty. Customers vary considerably regarding the product categories for which they may be brand insistent. Can you think of products for which you are brand insistent? Perhaps a deodorant or soft drink brand? As indicated in Figure 11.4, pets have preferences for certain brands of cat food; thus their owners may exhibit brand preference or even brand insistence for cat food brands.

Brand loyalty, in general, seems to be declining, partly because of marketers' increased reliance on sales, coupons, and other short-term promotions, and partly because of the sometimes overwhelming array of similar new products from which customers can choose. A *Wall Street Journal* survey found that 12 percent of consumers are not loyal to any

For them, there is Fancy Feast. The gourmet cat food. Exceptionally moist. Uniquely delicious. And only Fancy Feast offers so many extraordinary varieties to satisfy even the most discriminating connoisseurs. Fancy Feast gourmet cat food.

Good taste is easy to recognize.

There are those among us with very simple tastes.

They only want the best.

Figure 11.4
Brand Loyalty Some cat owners will exhibit brand preference or even brand insistence for a particular cat food brand such as Fancy Feast, because their cats have strong taste preferences.

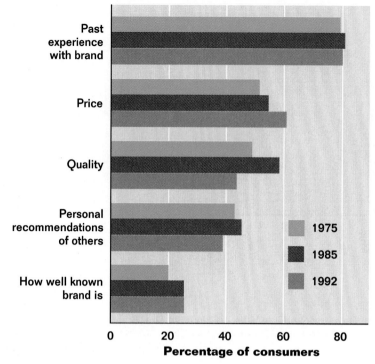

Figure 11.5
Changes in the Importance of Factors Affecting Brand Choice
Source: *Brandweek*, June 7, 1993. Copyright © 1993 by Roper Starch Worldwide. Used
with permission.

brand, whereas 17 percent are brand loyal for one to five product types. Only 2 percent of
the respondents were brand loyal for more than sixteen product types (see Figure 11.3).
The Roper Organization asked consumers which of a dozen factors are most important in
their decisions to buy a particular brand; respondents rated past experience with the
brand (cited by 80 percent) as more important than other factors, such as price, quality,
recommendations of others, and brand awareness.[4] Figure 11.5 provides the results of this
Roper poll, indicating changes in brand choice criteria.

Building brand loyalty is a major challenge for many marketers. However, it is an
extremely important issue. The creation of brand loyalty significantly contributes to an
organization's ability to achieve a sustainable competitive advantage.

■ *Brand Equity*

Brand equity The marketing
and financial value associated
with a brand's strength in a
market

A well-managed brand is an asset to an organization. The value of this asset is often
referred to as brand equity. **Brand equity** is the marketing and financial value associated
with a brand's strength in a market. Besides the actual proprietary brand assets, such as
patents and trademarks, four major elements underlie brand equity. These components
are brand name awareness, brand loyalty, perceived brand quality, and brand associations, as shown in Figure 11.6.[5]

Being aware of a brand leads to brand familiarity, which in turn results in a level of
comfort with the brand. A familiar brand is more likely to be selected than an unfamiliar
brand because the familiar brand often is viewed as reliable and of acceptable quality
compared to the unknown brand. The familiar brand is likely to be in a customer's evoked
set whereas the unfamiliar brand is not.

Brand loyalty is a valued component of brand equity because it reduces a brand's vulnerability to competitors' actions. Brand loyalty allows an organization to keep its existing
customers and not have to spend enormous amounts of resources gaining new customers. Loyal customers provide brand visibility and reassurance to potential new customers. And because customers expect their brand to be available when and where they
shop, retailers strive to carry the brands known for their strong customer following.

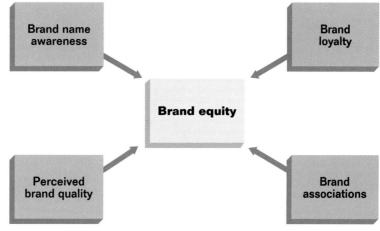

**Figure 11.6
Major Elements of Brand Equity**

Source: Adapted with the permission of The Free Press, a division of Simon & Schuster, from *Managing Brand Equity: Capitalizing on the Value of a Brand Name* by David A. Aaker. Copyright © 1991 by David A. Aaker.

Customers associate a certain level of perceived overall quality with a brand. A brand name itself actually stands for a certain level of quality in a customer's mind and is used as a substitute for actual judgment of quality. In many cases customers can't actually judge the quality of the product for themselves and instead must rely on the brand as a quality indicator. Perceived high brand quality helps to support a premium price, allowing a marketer to avoid severe price competition. Also, favorable perceived brand quality can ease the introduction of brand extensions, as the high regard for the brand will likely translate into high regard for the related products.

The set of associations linked to a brand is another key component of brand equity. At times a marketer works to connect a lifestyle, or in some instances a certain personality type, with a particular brand. For example, customers associate Michelin tires with protecting family members, a De Beers diamond with a loving, long-lasting relationship (a diamond is forever), and Dr Pepper with a unique taste. These types of brand associations contribute significantly to the brand's equity.

Although difficult to measure, brand equity represents the value of a brand to an organization. An organization may buy a brand from another company at a premium price because outright brand purchase may be less expensive and less risky than creating and developing a brand from scratch. Brand equity helps to give a brand the power to capture and maintain a consistent market share, which provides stability to an organization's sales volume. The top ten brands with the highest economic value are shown in Table 11.3. The values in Table 11.3 were determined by multiplying a brand's net profits by the brand's strength index.[6] Any company that owns a brand listed in Table 11.3 would agree that the economic value of that brand is likely to be the greatest single asset in the organi-

Table 11.3 The World's Most Valuable Brands	
Brand	**Brand Value (in millions)**
Marlboro	$44,614
Coca-Cola	43,427
McDonald's	18,920
IBM	18,491
Disney	15,358
Kodak	13,267
Kellogg's	11,409
Budweiser	11,026
Nescafé	10,527
Intel	10,499

Source: Kurt Bradenhausen, "Blind Faith," *Financial World*, Jul. 8, 1996, p. 53.

zation's possession. A brand's overall economic value rises and falls with the brand's profitability, brand awareness, brand loyalty, perceived brand quality, and the strength of positive brand associations.

■ *Types of Brands*

Manufacturer brands
Brands initiated by producers

There are three categories of brands: manufacturer brands, private distributor brands, and generic brands. **Manufacturer brands** are initiated by producers and ensure that producers are identified with their products at the point of purchase—for example, Green Giant, Apple Computer, and Levi's jeans. A manufacturer brand usually requires a producer to become involved in distribution, promotion, and, to some extent, pricing decisions. Brand loyalty is encouraged by promotion, quality control, and guarantees; it is a valuable asset to a manufacturer. The producer tries to stimulate demand for the product, which tends to encourage sellers and resellers to make the product available.

Private distributor brands
Brands initiated and owned by resellers

Private distributor brands (also called **private brands, store brands,** or **dealer brands**) are initiated and owned by resellers—wholesalers or retailers. The major characteristic of private brands is that the manufacturers are not identified on the products. Retailers and wholesalers use private distributor brands to develop more efficient promotion, to generate higher gross margins, and to improve store image. Private distributor brands give retailers or wholesalers freedom to purchase products of a specified quality at the lowest cost without disclosing the identity of the manufacturer. Wholesaler brands include IGA (Independent Grocers' Alliance) and Topmost (General Grocer). Familiar retailer brand names include Sears' Kenmore and J. C. Penney's Arizona. Many successful private brands are distributed nationally. Kenmore washers are as well known as most manufacturer brands. Sometimes retailers with successful distributor brands start manufacturing their own products to gain more control over product costs, quality, and design with the hope of increasing profits. Although one might think that store brands have their strongest appeal among lower-income shoppers, studies indicate that private brand buyers have characteristics that match those of the overall population.[7]

Generic brands Brands indicating only the product category

Some marketers of products that have traditionally been branded have embarked on a policy of not branding, often called generic branding. **Generic brands** indicate only the product category (such as aluminum foil) and do not include the company name or other identifying terms. Usually generic brands are sold at lower prices than comparable branded items. Although at one time generic brands may have represented as much as 10 percent of all retail grocery sales, today they account for considerably less. Private brands account for roughly 15 percent of all grocery sales.[8] Supermarket private brands are even more popular globally. In the United Kingdom, private brand products generate over 30 percent of supermarket revenue and in other countries as follows: France, 25 percent; Belgium and Germany, over 22 percent; Holland, 18 percent; Spain, 10 percent; and Italy, 8 percent.[9]

Competition between manufacturer brands and private distributor brands (sometimes called "the battle of the brands") is intensifying in several major product categories. Figure 11.7 shows the percentage of private brand expenditures for top ten packaged goods items by heavy, occasional, and infrequent private brand buyers. Note that milk and bread products are the most heavily purchased private-branded products. For manufacturers, developing multiple manufacturer brands and distribution systems has been an effective means of combating the increased competition from private brands. By developing a new brand name, a producer can adjust various elements of a marketing mix to appeal to a different target market. The growth of private brands has been steady, but the rate of growth is slowing because some manufacturer brand makers have stopped price increases or even cut their prices, which has narrowed the price gap, the major advantage of buying a private brand. Private brands traditionally cost 25–30 percent less than manufacturer brands. Today, the difference is about 10 percent.[10]

Manufacturers find it hard to ignore the marketing opportunities that come from producing private distributor brands for resellers. If a manufacturer refuses to produce a private brand for a reseller, a competing manufacturer will. Moreover, the production of private distributor brands allows the manufacturer to use excess capacity during periods when its own brands are at nonpeak production. The ultimate decision whether to produce a private or a manufacturer brand depends on a company's resources, production capabilities, and goals.

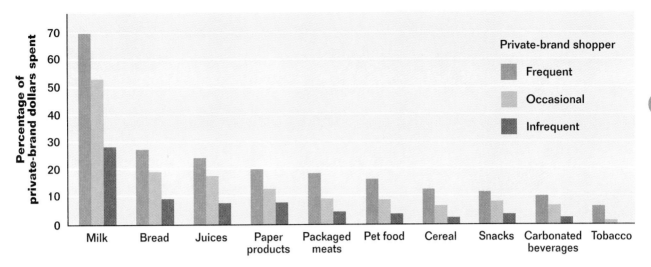

Figure 11.7

Top Ten Private-Branded Product Groups Percentage of private-label dollars spent for top-ten packaged-goods items, by heavy, occasional, and infrequent private-label shoppers.

Source: A. C. Neilson, Neilson Consumer Information Services, reported in Marcia Mogelonsky, "When Stores Become Brands," *American Demographics*, Feb. 1995, p. 34. Reprinted with permission.

◼ *Selecting a Brand Name*

Marketers consider a number of factors in selecting a brand name. The name should be easy for customers (including foreign buyers, if the firm intends to market its products in other countries) to say, spell, and recall. Short, one-syllable names such as Cheer often satisfy this requirement. The brand name should indicate the product's major benefits and, if possible, should suggest in a positive way the product's uses and special characteristics; negative or offensive references should be avoided. For example, household cleaning products have brand names that show strength and effectiveness, such as Ajax dishwashing liquid, Vanish toilet bowl cleaner, Formula 409 multipurpose cleaner, Cascade dishwasher detergent, and Wisk laundry detergent. The brand in Figure 11.8 relates directly to the product's benefits and special characteristics. The brand should be distinctive, to set it apart from competing brands. If a marketer intends to use a brand for a product line, it must be compatible with all products in the line. Finally, a brand should be designed so that it can be used and recognized in all the various types of media. Finding the right brand name has become a challenging task because many obvious product names have already been used. In 1994, the U.S. Patent and Trademark Office issued 59,797 new trademarks.[11]

How are brand names derived? Brand names can be created from single or multiple words—for example, Bic or Dodge Grand Caravan. Initials,

Find the Fountain of Youth for newer no-wax floors.

Mr. Clean it to the ultra Shine.

Figure 11.8

Brand Name That Highlights Product Features

Mr. Clean for Newer Floors relates its brand name to its product's benefits and special features.

258

numbers, or sometimes combinations are used to create brands such as IBM PC or PS 2. At times, words, numbers, and initials are combined to yield brand names such as Mazda RX7 or Mitsubishi 3000GT. To avoid terms that have negative connotations, marketers sometimes use fabricated words that have absolutely no meaning at the point when they are created—for example, Kodak and Exxon. Occasionally, a brand is simply brought out of storage and used as is or modified. Firms often maintain banks of registered brands, some of which may have been used in the past. Cadillac, for example, has a bank of approximately 360 registered trademarks. The LaSalle brand, used in the 1920s and 1930s, could be called up for a new Cadillac model in the future. Possible brand names sometimes are tested in focus groups or in other settings to assess customers' reactions.

Who actually creates brand names? Brand names can be created internally by the organization. Sometimes a name is suggested by individuals who are close to the development of the product. Some organizations have committees that participate in brand name creation and approval. Large companies that introduce numerous new products annually are likely to have a department that develops brand names. At times, outside consultants are used in the process of developing brand names. An organization may also hire a company (see Figure 11.9) that specializes in brand name development. When General

Figure 11.9
Brand Name Specialist
Organizations such as Manhattan-based Wallace and Church Associates specialize in developing brand imagery, package design, and brand naming. Firms like this become strategic marketing partners with major brand manufacturers.

Motors was trying to find a name for its new subcompact product line, it looked for a single word that would say "world" or "Asian" to attract consumers resistant to domestic automobiles. It wanted a name that reflected its emphasis on designs with a more international look. The Name Lab, a research firm that creates brand names for products, chose the word *Geo* because it is a word component that means "world" in many different languages.[12]

Even though most of the important branding considerations apply to both goods and services, services branding has some additional dimensions. The brand of the service is usually the same as the company name. Financial companies such as Fidelity Investments and Charles Schwab Discount Brokerage have established strong brand recognition. These companies have used their names to create an image of value and customer service through friendly, timely, responsible, accurate, and knowledgeable assistance. Service providers (such as United Air Lines) are perceived by customers as having one brand name, even though they offer multiple products (first class, business class, and coach). Because the service brand name and company name are so closely interrelated, a service brand name must be flexible enough to encompass a variety of current services, as well as new ones that the company might offer in the future. Geographical references like "western" and descriptive terms like "trucking" limit the scope of associations that can be made with the brand name. Because Southwest Airlines now flies to many parts of the country, its name has become too limited in its scope of associations. But "Humana," with its connotations of kindness and compassion, is flexible enough to encompass all services that the company offers—hospitals, insurance plans, and health care memberships.[13] Frequently, a service marketer will employ a symbol along with its brand name to make the brand distinctive and to communicate a certain image. For example, the Wausau Insurance Company's constant advertising of its distinctive name and brand logo (a train station) has increased its response rates to direct mail and increased general consumer acceptance of the company.[14]

■ *Protecting a Brand*

A marketer should also design a brand that can be protected easily through registration. A series of court decisions has created a broad hierarchy of protection based on brand type. From most protectable to least protectable, these brand types are fanciful (Exxon), arbitrary (Dr Pepper), suggestive (Spray 'n Wash), descriptive (Minute Rice), and generic (aluminum foil). Generic words are not protectable. Surnames and descriptive geographic or functional names are difficult to protect.[15] Because of their designs, some brands can be legally infringed upon more easily than others. Although registration protects trademarks domestically for ten years and can be renewed indefinitely, a firm should develop a system for ensuring that its trademarks will be renewed as needed.

To protect its exclusive rights to a brand, the company must make certain that the selected brand is not likely to be considered an infringement on any existing brand already registered with the U.S. Patent and Trademark Office. This task may be complex because infringement is determined by the courts, which base their decisions on whether a brand causes consumers to be confused, mistaken, or deceived about the source of the product. McDonald's is one company that aggressively protects its trademarks against infringement; it has brought charges against a number of companies with "Mc" names because it fears that the use of the prefix will give consumers the impression that these companies are associated with or owned by McDonald's. In 1982, Auto Shack changed its name to AutoZone when faced with legal action from the Tandy Corp., owners of Radio Shack. Tandy maintained that they owned the name "Shack." After research showed that virtually every auto supply store in the country used "auto" in its name, "zone" was deemed the best word to pair with *auto*. A brand name research firm found that *zone* suggests technology and energy. Also, the name is associated with auto parts and can be easily remembered by potential customers.[16]

If possible, a marketer must guard against allowing a brand name to become a generic term used to refer to a general product category. Generic terms cannot be protected as exclusive brand names. For example, names such as aspirin, escalator, and shredded wheat—all brand names at one time—eventually were declared generic terms that refer to product classes; thus they no longer could be protected. To keep a brand name from becoming a generic term, the firm should spell the name with a capital letter and use it as an adjective to modify the name of the general product class, as in Kool-Aid Brand Soft Drink Mix.[17] Including the word *brand* just after the brand name is also helpful. An organization can deal with this problem directly by advertising that its brand is a trademark and should not be used generically. The firm can also indicate that the brand is a registered trademark by using the symbol ®.

In the interest of strengthening trademark protection, Congress enacted the 1988 Trademark Law Revision Act, which is the only major federal trademark legislation since the Lanham Act passed in 1946. The purpose of this recent legislation is to increase the value of the federal registration system for U.S. firms relative to foreign competitors and to better protect the public from counterfeiting, confusion, and deception.[18]

A U.S. firm that tries to protect a brand in a foreign country frequently encounters problems. In many countries, brand registration is not possible; the first firm to use a brand in such a country has the rights to it. In some instances, a U.S. company actually had to buy its own brand rights from a firm in a foreign country because the foreign firm was the first user in that country.

Marketers trying to protect their brands must also contend with brand counterfeiting. In the United States, for instance, one can purchase counterfeit General Motors parts, Cartier watches, Jordache jeans, Louis Vuitton handbags, Walt Disney character dolls, Warner Brothers clothing, Mont Blanc pens, and a host of other products illegally marketed by manufacturers that do not own the brands. Many counterfeit products are manufactured overseas—in South Korea, Italy, or Taiwan, for example—but some are counterfeited in the United States. Counterfeit branded products are often lookalikes hard to distinguish from the real products. Microsoft, maker of MS-DOS, Windows, and other software, estimates that its revenues would double if counterfeiting of its brand name products was eliminated. Some $40 billion a year is lost in the computer software business because of counterfeit and pirated products. Annual losses caused by counterfeit products in other product categories likely exceed $75 billion.

260

■ *Branding Policies*

Before establishing branding policies, a firm must first decide whether to brand its products at all. If a company's product is homogeneous and similar to competitors' products, it may be difficult to brand. Raw materials—such as coal, sand, and farm produce—are hard to brand because of the homogeneity of such products and their physical characteristics.

Individual branding
A policy of naming each product differently

If a firm chooses to brand its products, it may opt for one or more of the following branding policies: individual, family, and brand-extension branding. **Individual branding** is a policy of naming each product differently. Lever Bros. Co. relies on an individual branding policy for its line of detergents, which includes Wisk, Surf, and All. A major advantage of individual branding is that if an organization introduces a poor product, the negative images associated with it do not contaminate the company's other products. An individual branding policy may also facilitate market segmentation when a firm wishes to enter many segments of the same market. Separate, unrelated names can be used, and each brand can be aimed at a specific segment. Sara Lee utilizes individual branding among its many divisions. Sara Lee markets Coach luggage, Hanes underwear, L'eggs pantyhose, Champion sportswear, and other vastly different brands. Connecting these products' names with the Sara Lee brand name, which is associated with desserts, would not make sense to consumers.[19]

Family branding   Branding all of a firm's products with the same name

In **family branding,** all of a firm's products are branded with the same name or at least part of the name, such as Kellogg's Frosted Flakes, Kellogg's Rice Krispies, and Kellogg's Corn Flakes. In some cases, a company's name is combined with other words to brand items. Arm & Hammer uses its name on all its products, along with a generic description of the item, such as Arm & Hammer Heavy Duty Detergent, Arm & Hammer Pure Baking Soda, and Arm & Hammer Carpet Deodorizer. Unlike individual branding, family branding means that the promotion of one item with the family brand promotes the firm's other products. Family branding has been practiced by major companies such as Mitsubishi, Kodak, and Fisher-Price. These firms have a basic philosophy that—in terms of marketing—the brand is more important than the product.[20]

Brand-extension branding
Using an existing brand name for an improved or new product

Brand-extension branding occurs when a firm uses one of its existing brand names as part of a brand for an improved or new product that is usually in the same product category as the existing brand. McNeil Consumer Products, the makers of Tylenol and Extra Strength Tylenol, also introduced Extra Strength Tylenol P.M., extending the Tylenol brand product line.

An organization is not limited to a single branding policy. A company that primarily uses individual branding for many of its products may also use brand extensions. Branding policy is influenced by the number of products and product lines the company produces, the characteristics of its target markets, the number and types of competing products available, and the size of its resources.

■ *Brand Licensing*

A recent trend in branding strategies involves the licensing of trademarks. By means of a licensing agreement, a company may permit approved manufacturers to use its trademark on other products for a licensing fee. Royalties may be as low as 2 percent of wholesale revenues or higher than 10 percent. The licensee is responsible for all manufacturing, selling, and advertising functions and bears the costs if the licensed product fails. Not long ago, only a few firms licensed their corporate trademarks, but today licensing is a multi-billion dollar business. The retail value of licensed products was over $70 billion in 1994.[21] Several companies have become very effective in licensing their brands. For example, in 1994 Marvel Entertainment, the world's largest comic book publisher, generated over $20 million in revenues from licensing.[22] As indicated in Inside Marketing, Nickelodeon licenses approximately 450 products that are distributed in forty-five countries.

The advantages of licensing range from extra revenues and low cost to free publicity, new images, and trademark protection. For example, Coca-Cola has licensed its trademark for use on glassware, radios, trucks, and clothing in the hope of protecting its trademark. However, brand licensing is not without drawbacks. The major disadvantages are a lack of manufacturing control, which could hurt the company's name, and bombarding

Nick's Knack for Licensing Its Brand

Founded in 1979, the Nickelodeon cable television channel reaches 60 million American homes with programming that includes game, news, and variety shows, original series and classic reruns, and a line-up of original animated series called "Nicktoons." But "Nick," as it is affectionately known, is more than a television channel. Through a growing number of licensing agreements, Nickelodeon is putting its splashy orange signature on a huge assortment of products. Licensing experts agree that the organization's remarkable talent for transferring its offbeat personality to licensed goods is building Nickelodeon into a blockbuster brand.

Nick's Consumer Products Division has licensing agreements with over one hundred manufacturers who distribute more than 450 Nick brand products in forty-five countries worldwide. Leading licensees include well-known companies such as Sony, Hasbro's Playskool, Viacom, Sega, Dakin, Marvel, Simon and Schuster, and Mattel. From these manufacturers come Nickelodeon sports and activity toys, stuffed animals, CD-ROMs and video games, home videos and audio tapes, gift items, books, and apparel. Toys 'R' Us recently held a ten-week promotion showcasing over 150 Nick products at its in-store "Nickelodeon Toy Factory," and fun emporium FAO Schwarz is carving out departments devoted exclusively to Nickelodeon-branded products. Right next door to the Barbie boutique will be stuffed versions of Nick's crazed chihuahua Ren and his side-kick Stimpy from the cult cartoon hit *Ren and Stimpy,* action tykes based on characters from *Rug Rats,* and a rainbow selection of GAK.

One of Nick's most successful licensing arrangements is with megatoymaker Mattel, which has licensed the rights, not only to specific characters, but to the Nickelodeon brand. Some of Mattel's most popular licensed products from Nickelodeon include GAK, a squishy, stretchy compound; Floam, a molding substance studded with tiny styrofoam balls that make it bounce; and Zog Logs, potato-based construction toys that stick together when moistened. Because of Nickelodeon's popularity with 7–9-year-olds, Mattel's executives believe Nick and Mattel make a perfect match. That Nick products accounted for $100 million in Mattel sales in one year confirms the conviction.

Although Nickelodeon faces stiff competition from such other licensing phenomena as Disney and Warner Brothers, industry experts agree that no other company has taken its brand name into the marketplace like Nickelodeon. However, despite innumerable offers from companies that want to use its name, McDonald's and Kellogg's among them, Nick has no intention of saturating the market with its licensed products. Asserted the company's licensing vice president, "Our brand is sacred."

Sources: Laura Liebeck, "Theatrical Displays Enliven Merchandising," *Discount Store News,* Aug. 7, 1995, p. 45; Jim Eskridge, "Licensing '95: Mattel," *Brandweek,* June 19, 1995, pp. 28–29; Karen Benezra and Elaine Underwood, "Nick Takes Kid Franchise Into Apparel," *Brandweek,* May 8, 1995, p. 6; "Marketing and Media: Viacom's Nickelodeon Sets Venture to Make Children's Products," *Wall Street Journal,* May 11, 1995, p. B2; Karen Benezra, "Toys 'R' Us Gets Nick Knack," *Brandweek,* July 31, 1995, pp. 1, 6; and Karen Benezra, "Brand Nick Is a Program of Its Own," *Brandweek,* June 19, 1995, p. 34.

consumers with too many unrelated products bearing the same name. Licensing arrangements can also fail because of poor timing, inappropriate distribution channels, or mismatching of product and name.

Packaging

Packaging involves the development of a container and a graphic design for a product. A package can be a vital part of a product, making it more versatile, safer, or easier to use. Like a brand name, a package can influence customers' attitudes toward a product and so affect their purchase decisions. For example, several producers of jellies, sauces, and ketchups have packaged their products in squeezable containers to make use and storage more convenient. Package characteristics help shape buyers' impressions of a product at the time of purchase or during use. In this section we examine the main functions of packaging and consider several major packaging decisions. We also analyze the role of the package in a marketing strategy.

Packaging Functions

Effective packaging means more than simply putting products in containers and covering them with wrappers. First of all, packaging materials serve the basic purpose of protecting the product and maintaining its functional form. Fluids such as milk, orange juice, and hair spray need packages that preserve and protect them; the packaging should prevent damage that could affect the product's usefulness and thus lead to higher costs. Since product tampering has become a problem for marketers of many types of goods, several packaging techniques have been developed to counter this danger. Some packages are also designed to deter shoplifting.

Another function of packaging is to offer convenience for consumers. For example, small aseptic packages—individual-sized boxes or plastic bags that contain liquids and do not require refrigeration—strongly appeal to children and young adults with active lifestyles. Action Snacks is testing a freeze-dried cheese pizza with a shelf life of seven years. The special product packaging permits the pizza to require no refrigeration.[23] The size or shape of a package may relate to the product's storage, convenience of use, or replacement rate. Small, single-serving cans of vegetables, for instance, may prevent waste and make storage easier. A third function of packaging is to promote a product by communicating its features, uses, benefits, and image. At times, a reusable package is developed to make the product more desirable. For example, the Cool Whip package doubles as a food-storage container. A recent phenomenon in the music industry is the packaging of classic music into compact disc compilation packages. Though the 1971 Led Zeppelin album, *Stairway to Heaven,* was a big hit, in recent years the rock group had sold relatively few recordings. To boost sales, the group's works were recompiled and packaged in a $70 boxed set of compact discs. The set went platinum, selling over a million copies. Other artists with renewed sales as a function of boxed set packaging include The Police, Elvis Presley, Elton John, Pink Floyd, and The Beatles.[24]

Major Packaging Considerations

As they develop packages, marketers must take many factors into account. Obviously, one major consideration is cost. Although a variety of packaging materials, processes, and designs are available, costs vary greatly. In recent years, buyers have shown a willingness to pay more for improved packaging, but there are limits. Marketers should try to determine, through research, just how much customers are willing to pay for effective and efficient package designs.

As already mentioned, developing tamper-resistant packaging is very important for certain products. Although no package is tamper-proof, marketers can develop packages that are difficult to tamper with. At a minimum, all packaging must comply with the Food and Drug Administration's packaging regulations. However, packaging should also make any product tampering evident to resellers and consumers. An example of a tamper evident package is shown in Figure 11.10. Although effective tamper-resistant packaging may be expensive to develop, when balanced against the costs of lost sales, loss of consumer confidence and company reputation, and potentially expensive product liability lawsuits, the costs of ensuring consumer safety are minimal.

Figure 11.10
Tamper Evident Packaging   Many tamper-proof packages are protected with a plastic tamper evident seal that must be removed in order to open the package.

Marketers should consider how much consistency is desirable among an organization's package designs. No consistency may be the best policy, especially if a firm's products are unrelated or aimed at vastly different target markets. To promote an overall company image, a firm may decide that all packages are to be similar or include one major element of the design. This approach is called **family packaging.** Sometimes it is used only for lines of products, as with Campbell's soups, Weight Watcher's foods, and Planter's nuts.

Family packaging
Making an organization's packages similar or at least containing a common element

A package's promotional role is an important consideration. Through verbal and non-verbal symbols, the package can inform potential buyers about the product's content, features, uses, advantages, and hazards. A firm can create desirable images and associations by its choice of color, design, shape, and texture. Many cosmetics manufacturers, for example, design their packages to create impressions of richness, luxury, and exclusiveness. A package performs a promotional function when it is designed to be safer or more convenient to use, if such characteristics help stimulate demand.

To develop a package that has a definite promotional value, a designer must consider size, shape, texture, color, and graphics. Beyond the obvious limitation that the package must be large enough to hold the product, a package can be designed to appear taller or shorter. Lighter-colored packaging may be used to make a package appear larger, and darker colors minimize the perceived size.

Colors on packages are often chosen to attract attention. People associate specific colors with certain feelings and experiences. Red, for example, is linked with fire, blood, danger, and anger; yellow suggests sunlight, caution, warmth, and vitality; blue can imply coldness, sky, water, and sadness.[25] A trend toward colorless packages stems from the New Age mentality. The clear products and packaging give consumers the impression of a pure, natural product. Procter & Gamble decided to change the milky-white formula that has marked its Ivory Liquid dishwashing detergent since 1957 to a clear product and packaging. A company spokesperson says that the clear product and packaging are designed to emphasize Ivory's improved grease-cutting ability.[26] When opting for color on packaging, marketers must judge whether a particular color will evoke positive or negative feelings when it is linked to a specific product. Rarely, for example, do processors package meat or bread in green materials because customers may associate green with mold. Marketers must also determine whether a specific target market will respond favorably or unfavorably to a particular color. Cosmetics for women are more likely to be sold in pastel packaging than are personal-care products for men. Packages designed to appeal to children often use primary colors and bold designs.

Packaging must also meet the needs of resellers. Wholesalers and retailers consider whether a package facilitates transportation, storage, and handling. Resellers may refuse to carry certain products if their packages are cumbersome. Concentrated versions of laundry detergents and fabric softeners aid retailers in offering more product diversity within the existing shelf space.

A final consideration is whether to develop packages that are environmentally responsible. Nearly one-half of all garbage consists of discarded plastic packaging, such as polystyrene containers, plastic soft drink bottles, carryout bags, and other packaging. Plastic packaging material does not biodegrade, and paper requires the destruction of valuable forests. Consequently, a number of companies have changed to environmentally sensitive packaging; they are also recycling more materials. Procter & Gamble markets several cleaning products in a concentrated form, which requires less packaging than the ready-to-use version; H. J. Heinz is looking for alternatives to its plastic ketchup squeeze bottles. Other companies are searching for alternatives to environmentally harmful packaging. In some instances, customers have objected to such switches because the new environmentally responsible packaging may be less effective or more inconvenient. Thus marketers must carefully balance society's desires to preserve the environment against customers' desires for convenience.

■ *Packaging and Marketing Strategy*

Packaging can be a major component of a marketing strategy. A new cap or closure, a better box or wrapper, or a more convenient container may give a product a competitive advantage. The right type of package for a new product can help it gain market recognition very quickly. In the case of existing brands, marketers should reevaluate packages periodically. Especially for consumer convenience products, marketers should view

Table 11.4 Companies That Spend The Most on Packaging		
Rank	**Company**	**Expenditures ($ millions)**
1	Coca-Cola	856.25
2	PepsiCo	754.25
3	Procter & Gamble	682.72
4	Anheuser-Busch	484.25
5	Kraft USA	412.50
6	Campbell Soup	400.31
7	Coca-Cola Foods	358.00
8	Kraft General Foods	331.50
9	General Mills	312.26
10	Miller Brewing	282.50

Source: *Packaging Magazine*, Jan. 1994.

packaging as a major strategic tool. For example, in the consumer food industry, jumbo and larger package sizes have been very successful with products such as hot dogs, pizzas, English muffins, frozen dinners, and biscuits. When considering the strategic uses of packaging, marketers must also analyze the cost of packaging and package changes. The biggest packaging spenders are listed in Table 11.4. In this section we examine several ways in which packaging can be used strategically.

Altering the Package   At times, a marketer changes a package because the existing design is no longer in style, especially when compared with competitive products. Arm & Hammer now markets a refillable plastic shaker for its baking soda. Quaker Oats hired a package design company to redesign its Rice-A-Roni package to give the product the appearance of having evolved with the times but still retaining its traditional taste appeal. Rice-A-Roni had been experiencing a lag in sales because of increased competition. An overhaul of the product packaging to a refreshing and more up-to-date look was credited with a 20 percent increase in sales compared with the previous year. Similarly, Del-Monte introduced a contemporary look for its tomato products and experienced a double-digit gain in the first year. Survey results show that 75 percent of consumers make their product purchase decisions in the supermarket while looking at the packaging, not as a response to advertising. A package may also be redesigned because new product features need to be highlighted or because new packaging materials have become available. An organization may decide to change a product's packaging to make the product more convenient or safer to use or to reposition the product.

Secondary-Use Packaging   A secondary-use package is one that can be reused for purposes other than its initial function. For example, a margarine container can be reused to store leftovers, and a jelly container can be used as a drinking glass. Secondary-use packages can be viewed by customers as adding value to products. If customers value this type of packaging, then its use should stimulate unit sales.

Category-Consistent Packaging   Category-consistent packaging means that the product is packaged in line with the packaging practices associated with a particular product category. Some product categories—for example, mayonnaise, mustard, ketchup, and peanut butter—have traditional package shapes. Other product categories are characterized by recognizable color combinations—red and white for soup; red, white, and blue for Ritz-like crackers. When an organization introduces a brand in one of these product categories, marketers will often use traditional package shapes and color combinations to ensure that customers will recognize the new product as being in that specific product category.

Figure 11.11
Innovative Packages
Unique packaging makes these products
distinctive and easier to use.

Innovative Packaging   Sometimes, a marketer will employ a unique cap, design, applicator, or other feature to make the product competitively distinctive. Using such packaging can be effective when the innovation makes the product safer or easier to use or when the unique package provides better protection for the product. For example, the packages in Figure 11.11 make the products distinctive and easier to use. In some instances, marketers use innovative or unique packages that are inconsistent with traditional packaging practices to make the brand stand out relative to its competitors. To distinguish their products, marketers in the beverage industry have used innovative shapes and packaging materials. The packaging for K-Cider glows in the dark.[27] Unusual packaging generally requires a considerable amount of resources, not only in package design, but also in making customers aware of the unique package and its benefit.

Multiple Packaging   Rather than packaging a single unit of the product, marketers sometimes use twin packs, tri-packs, six-packs, or other forms of multiple packaging. For certain types of products, multiple packaging is used to increase demand because it increases the amount of the product available at the point of consumption (in one's house, for example). However, multiple packaging does not work for all types of products. One would not use additional table salt simply because an extra box is in the pantry. Multiple packaging can make products easier to handle and store, as in the case of six-packs for soft drinks; it can also facilitate special price offers, such as two-for-one sales. In addition, multiple packaging may increase consumer acceptance of the product by encouraging the buyer to try the product several times.

Handling-Improved Packaging   Packaging of a product may be changed to make it easier to handle in the distribution channel—for example, changing the outer carton, special bundling, shrink-wrapping, or palletizing. In some cases the shape of the package may need to be changed. An ice-cream producer, for instance, may change from a cylindrical package to a rectangular one to facilitate handling. In addition, at the retail level, the ice-cream producer may be able to get more shelf-facings with a rectangular package as opposed to a round one. Outer containers for products are sometimes changed so that they will proceed more easily through automated warehousing systems.

As package designs improve, it becomes harder for any one product to dominate because of packaging. However, marketers still try to gain a competitive edge through packaging. Skilled artists and package designers who have experience in marketing research test packaging to see what sells well, not just what is eye-catching or aesthetically appealing. Since the typical large store stocks fifteen thousand items or more, products that stand out are more likely to be bought.

■ Criticisms of Packaging

The last several decades have brought a number of improvements in packaging. However, some packaging problems still need to be resolved.

Some packages suffer from functional problems in that they simply do not work well. The packaging for flour and sugar is, at best, poor. Both grocers and consumers are very much aware that these packages leak and are easily torn. Can anyone open and close a bag of flour without spilling at least a little bit? Certain packages such as refrigerated biscuit cans, milk cartons with foldout spouts, and potato chip bags are frequently difficult to open. The traditional shapes of packages for products such as ketchup and salad dressing make the product inconvenient to use. Have you ever wondered when tapping on a ketchup bottle why the producer didn't put ketchup in a mayonnaise jar?

Although many steps have been taken to make packaging safer, critics still focus on the safety issues. Containers with sharp edges and easily broken glass bottles are sometimes viewed as a threat to safety. Certain types of plastic packaging and aerosol containers represent possible health hazards.

At times, packaging is viewed as being deceptive. Package shape, graphic design, and certain colors may be used to make a product appear larger than it actually is. The inconsistent use of certain size designations—such as giant, economy, family, king, and super—can certainly lead to customer confusion. Although customers in this country traditionally have liked attractive, effective, convenient packaging, the cost of such packaging is high.

Labeling

Labeling   Providing identifying, promotional, or other information on package labels

Labeling is very closely interrelated with packaging and can be used in a variety of promotional, informational, and legal ways. The label can be used to facilitate the identification of a product by presenting the brand and a unique graphic design. For example, Heinz ketchup is easy to identify on a supermarket shelf because the brand name is easy to read and is coupled with a distinctive crown-like graphic design. Labels have a descriptive function. For certain types of products—especially canned fruit—the label indicates the grade of the product. Labels can describe the source of the product, its contents and major features, how to use the product, how to care for it, nutritional information, type and style of the product, and size and number of servings. The label can play a promotional function through the use of graphics that attract attention.

Several federal laws deal directly or indirectly with packaging and labeling. For instance, federal laws require disclosure of such information as textile identification, potential hazards, and nutritional information. Although consumers have responded favorably to this type of information on labels, evidence as to whether they actually use it has been mixed. Several studies indicate that consumers do not use nutritional information, whereas other studies indicate that they do. In 1966, Congress passed the Fair Packaging and Labeling Act, one of the most comprehensive pieces of labeling and packaging legislation. This law focuses on mandatory labeling requirements, voluntary adoption of packaging standards by firms within industries, and the provision of power to the Federal Trade Commission and the Food and Drug Administration to establish and enforce packaging regulations. The Nutrition Labeling and Education Act of 1990 required the FDA to review current food labeling and packaging focusing on nutrition content, label format, ingredient labeling, food descriptions, and health messages. Based on this legislation, the Food and Drug Administration has established labeling guidelines that require food processors to indicate the number of calories and the amount of protein, fat, carbohydrates, and vitamins contained in a product. Ethical Challenges discusses questionable labeling practices that still persist.

▪ ЕТHICAL CHALLENGES ▪

What You See Is Not Necessarily What You Get

U.S. lawbooks are loaded with regulations pertaining to the information shown on product labels. These laws mandate the inclusion of certain information, such as health hazards or nutritional values, and forbid other items, such as false claims. However, between what is strictly legal and what is clearly illegal, is a gray area. For example, when the label on a breakfast cereal sports a "Low in sugar" banner, can a diabetic safely start the day with a bowlful?

The problems associated with nutrition and other health-related claims made on food labels did not end when Congress passed the Nutrition Labeling and Education Act, which regulates much, but not all, of this information. The Center for Science in the Public Interest recently asked the Food and Drug Administration to ban from food labels misleading claims and illustrations about fruit, vegetables, whole wheat, and other ingredients not covered under the 1990 act. The center questions the ethics of naming a product "Strawberry Frozen Yogurt Bars" when it contains strawberry flavoring but no strawberries, or of calling a breakfast cereal "lightly sweetened" when sugar makes up 22 percent of its ingredients. In addition, a growing number of consumers trying to reduce their intake of fat are being misled by labels claiming "low fat" and "reduced fat." The meaning of these terms is vague, and the amount of fat actually depends on the so-called serving size, which is usually smaller than what most people eat.

A second area in which labels often misinform customers is that of environmental responsibility. The U.S. Public Interest Research Group accuses manufacturers of "greenwashing" consumers, playing on their concern for the environment to sell products, even if the claimed benefits are bogus. First on the group's "Don't Be Fooled" list is S.C. Johnson and Sons Windex cleaner. Although containers carry the recycling symbol (three arrows chasing each other in a circle), Windex containers are made of polyvinyl chloride plastic, which cannot be recycled in the vast majority of American communities. Putting the recycling symbol on containers is not a lie, but it certainly misleads consumers about the ease with which they can recycle the package.

Consumers who are committed to making socially responsible purchasing decisions are also often fooled by labels. For five years, the label on Ben & Jerry's Rainforest Crunch ice cream claimed that "money from these nuts will help Brazilian forest people start a nut shelling cooperative." Ice cream lovers who wanted to support Amazon tribes felt good about buying Rainforest Crunch. However, Ben & Jerry's actually purchased 95 percent of its nuts from huge Brazilian agribusinesses and only 5 percent from the Xapuri natives. Granted, the ice cream manufacturer didn't lie to consumers (*some* money *did* go to the forest people), but it certainly gave an inaccurate impression.

Although marketers acknowledge the importance of many labeling laws, they question how far they have to go to protect customers. Is it unethical for New Balance athletic shoes to say "Made in the U.S.A." if the rubber soles on some of its shoes come from China? Is it misleading if the manufacturer of a Batman costume fails to attach a label warning, "Caution—For Play Only: Cape does not enable wearer to fly"? Where do marketers' responsibilities end and customers' responsibilities begin?

Sources: Jacqueline Gaulin, "U.S. Manufacturers Protest as FTC Tightens 'Made in the USA' label law," *Washington Times,* Feb. 9, 1995, p. B7; "FDA Asked to Tighten Labeling Rules," *Supermarket Business,* Sept. 1995, p. 9; Kit Smith, "Group Lists Firms That Play 'Dirty': Environmental Claims Misleading," *Honolulu Advertiser,* Apr. 1, 1995, p. C1; R. L. King, "More Consumers Crave Low-Fat Snacks," *Detroit News,* Mar. 31, 1995, p. E1; Stephen Advokat, "Kids, Don't Try This At Home," *Reader's Digest,* June 6, 1995, pp. 133–134; and Jeff Glasser, "Not Exactly a Shell Game: Ben & Jerry's Shelves Inaccurate Rainforest Pitch," *Boston Globe,* July 27, 1995, p. 35.

Universal product code (UPC) A series of lines identifying a product and containing inventory and pricing information

The label for many products includes a **universal product code (UPC),** which is a series of thick and thin lines that identifies the product and provides inventory and pricing information that is read by an electronic scanner. The UPC is electronically read at the retail checkout counter. This information is used by retailers and producers for price and inventory control purposes.

SUMMARY

A brand is a name, term, design, symbol, or any other feature that identifies one seller's good or service and distinguishes it from those of other sellers. A brand name is that part of a brand that can be spoken; the element that cannot be spoken is called a brand mark. A trademark is a legal designation indicating that the owner has exclusive use of a brand or part of a brand and that others are prohibited by law from using it. A trade name is the legal name of an organization. Branding helps buyers identify and evaluate products, helps sellers facilitate repeat purchasing and product introduction, and fosters brand loyalty.

Brand loyalty is a customer's favorable attitude toward a specific brand. Depending on loyalty strength, there is some likelihood that a customer will purchase this brand consistently when needs for a product in this product category arise. The three degrees of brand loyalty are recognition, preference, and insistence. Brand recognition exists when a customer is aware that the brand exists and views it as an alternative to purchase if the preferred brand is unavailable. Brand preference is the degree of brand loyalty in which a customer prefers one brand over competing brands and will purchase it if available. Brand insistence is the degree of brand loyalty in which a customer will accept no substitute.

Brand equity is the marketing and financial value associated with a brand's strength. It represents the value of a brand to an organization. The four major elements underlying brand equity include brand name awareness, brand loyalty, perceived brand quality, and brand associations.

A manufacturer brand, initiated by the producer, makes it possible to associate the firm more easily with its products at the point of purchase. A private distributor brand is initiated and owned by a reseller, sometimes taking on the name of the store or distributor. A generic brand indicates only the product category and does not include the company name or other identifying terms. Manufacturers combat the growing competition from distributor brands by developing multiple brands.

When selecting a brand name, a marketer should choose one that is easy to say, spell, and recall and that alludes to the product's uses, benefits, or special characteristics. Additional considerations are required if the brand is to be sold outside the country of origin. Brand names are created inside an organization by individuals, committees, or branding departments, or by outside consultants. Brand names can be devised from words, initials, numbers, nonsense words, or a combination of these. Services as well as products are branded, often with the company name and an accompanying symbol that makes the brand distinctive or conveys a desired image.

Producers protect ownership of their brands through registration with the U.S. Patent and Trademark Office.

Marketers at a company must make certain that their selected brand name does not infringe on an already registered brand by confusing or deceiving consumers about the source of the product. In most foreign countries, brand registration is on a first-come, first-served basis, making protection more difficult. Brand counterfeiting, increasingly common, can undermine consumers' confidence in a brand and diminish their loyalty to it. Companies brand their products in several ways. Individual branding designates a unique name for each of a company's products; family branding identifies all of a firm's products with the single name; and brand-extension branding applies an existing name to a new or improved product. Trademark licensing enables producers to earn extra revenue, receive low-cost or free publicity, and protect their trademarks. Through a licensing agreement, and for a licensing fee, a firm may permit approved manufacturers to use its trademark on other unrelated products.

Packaging involves development of a container and a graphic design for a product. Effective packaging offers protection, economy, safety, and convenience. It can influence a customer's purchase decision by promoting features, uses, benefits, and image. When developing a package, marketers must consider the value to the customer of efficient and effective packaging, offset by the cost that the customer is willing to pay. Other considerations include how to make the package tamper-resistant, whether to use multiple packaging and family packaging, how to design the package as an effective promotional tool, how best to accommodate resellers, and whether to develop environmentally responsible packaging. Packaging can be an important part of an overall marketing strategy and can be used as a way to target certain market segments, such as singles, children, or senior citizens. Modifications in packaging can revive a mature product and extend its product life cycle. Firms choose particular colors, designs, shapes, and textures to create desirable images and associations. Producers alter packages to convey new features or to make them safer or more convenient. If a package has a secondary use, the product's value to the consumer may be increased. Category-consistent packaging makes products more easily recognized by consumers, and innovative packaging enhances a product's distinctiveness. Consumers may criticize packaging that does not work well, poses health or safety problems, is deceptive in some way, or is not biodegradable or recyclable.

Labeling is an important aspect of packaging for promotional, informational, and legal reasons. Various regulatory agencies can require that products be labeled or marked with warnings, instructions, certifications, nutritional information, and manufacturer's identification.

IMPORTANT TERMS

Brand
Brand name
Brand mark
Trademark
Trade name

Brand loyalty
Brand recognition
Brand preference
Brand insistence
Brand equity

Manufacturer brands
Private distributor brands
Generic brands
Individual branding
Family branding

Brand-extension branding
Family packaging
Labeling
Universal product code
  (UPC)

DISCUSSION AND REVIEW QUESTIONS

1. What is the difference between a brand and a brand name? Compare and contrast the terms "brand mark" and "trademark."
2. How does branding benefit consumers? marketers?
3. What are the three major degrees or levels of brand loyalty?
4. What is brand equity? Identify and explain the major elements that underlie brand equity.
5. Compare and contrast manufacturer brands, private distributor brands, and generic brands.
6. Identify the factors that a marketer should consider in selecting a brand name.
7. The brand name Xerox is sometimes used generically to refer to photocopying and Kleenex is used to refer to tissues. How can these corporations protect their brand names, and why should they want to?
8. What are the major advantages and disadvantages of licensing?
9. Describe the functions that a package can perform. Which function is most important? Why?
10. When developing a package, what are the main factors that a marketer should consider?
11. In what ways can packaging be used as a strategic tool?
12. What are the major criticisms of packaging?
13. What are the major functions of labeling?
14. In what ways can labeling requirements impact an industry?

APPLICATION QUESTIONS

1. Brand names help consumers identify products they like, reducing time spent on the decision process. Identify two products you purchase without a search. Why do you no longer use other brands? Why did you begin using your brand?
2. General Motors introduced the subcompact Geo with a name that appeals to a world market. Invent a brand name for a line of luxury sports cars that also would appeal to an international market. Suggest a name that implies quality, luxury, and value.
3. When a firm decides to brand its products, it may choose one of several different strategies. Name one company that utilizes each of the following strategies. How does each strategy help the company?
   a. individual branding
   b. family branding
   c. brand-extension branding
4. Packaging provides product protection, customer convenience, and promotion of image, key features, and benefits. Identify a product that utilizes packaging in each of these ways and evaluate the effectiveness of the package.
5. McDonald's has replaced Styrofoam packaging with environmentally friendly paper. How does this benefit McDonald's? Name another company that has shown similar social responsibility, and describe its actions.

Case 11.1   Labeling Requirements in the Red Meat Industry

The 1980s witnessed a drastic decline in red meat consumption in the United States. This downward trend was due largely to the fact that consumers had become more health-conscious and began to perceive red meat as an "unhealthy" food, high in fat and cholesterol. Despite the efforts of the beef and pork producers to improve the quality of their product, as well as promote its nutritional value, the negative perceptions of red meat have persisted well into the 1990s.

The meat industry has traditionally been characterized by a somewhat confusing federal regulatory environment. For example, the Food and Drug Administration is in charge of regulating the quality of all food items sold in supermarkets except fresh meat, which is the responsibility of the Department of Agriculture. But the Agriculture Department also promotes the fresh meat industry; hence conflicts of interest can arise within the agency. One deleterious result, as far as consumers and consumer advocacy groups are concerned, was labeling information that consumers could misconstrue. In the past, marketers expressed fat content as a percentage of total product weight, but consumers often took this measure to be the same as another, more meaningful, one: fat as a percentage of total calorie content. Although expressing the fat content as a percentage of total weight was not illegal on the part of meat marketers, critics saw it as highly misleading and therefore harmful to consumers.

In 1990, Congress, pressured by a coalition of twenty-five consumer and medical organizations, established guidelines for meat labeling under the Nutrition Labeling and Education Act. These guidelines were to eliminate confusion by mandating a universal set of standards for providing consumers with nutritional information regarding fresh meat products. Many retailers and red meat industry leaders voiced their disapproval of the proposed labeling requirements on the grounds that they would greatly increase costs.

However, others in the red meat industry viewed the new labeling regulations as an opportunity to regain some of the sales lost in the past decade and improve the image of red meat in the eyes of the consuming public. Better breeding and feeding techniques had greatly improved the nutritional quality of red meat. For example, Department of Agriculture representatives reported that certain cuts of beef were surrounded by 27 percent less fat than they had been in the 1970s; during the same period, many cuts of pork had decreased in fat content by more than 30 percent.

At the forefront of the effort to revitalize the red meat industry was the National Live Stock and Meat Board (NLSMB), a coalition of fresh meat producers and marketers. Regarding the potential high cost of the new labeling regulations, the NLSMB suggested that failing to provide such information as proposed might cost more in the end. According to the NLSMB, research had consistently shown that consumers want complete point-of-purchase nutritional information. By supplying such information, meat retailers and producers would be reminding consumers that meat is a vital part of a healthy diet.

One major challenge anticipated by the NLSMB was the difficulty of communicating information successfully to the diverse range of customers buying meat in supermarkets and other retail outlets. Labeling would have to transmit nutritional information about the product to customers of many different cultural backgrounds speaking nearly as many different languages.

The fresh meat industry thus had to deal with an intriguing dilemma. On the one hand, a seemingly golden opportunity had arisen for the industry to inform consumers about the relative merits of its products. On the other hand, in seizing the opportunity, red meat producers, marketers, and retailers would have to cope with the difficulties of presenting the required information, physically altering the packaging and labeling used in the industry, and effectively serving diverse consumer segments.

As the meat industry waited to see if the regulations proposed as part of the Nutrition Labeling and Education Act would indeed become law, it was struck another blow. In late 1993, Agriculture Secretary Mike Espy announced an additional labeling requirement: within just sixty days, all fresh meat products would have to carry labeling warning consumers that the meat may contain harmful bacteria if it had been improperly handled. The labels were also to advise consumers to (1) keep raw meat refrigerated or frozen, (2) thaw it in a refrigerator or microwave, and (3) keep meat separate from other food products. This announcement was one of several responses by the Agriculture Department to outbreaks of food poisoning traced to a particularly infectious strain of *E. coli* bacteria in undercooked meat. Warning labels for meat had been considered for years. The decision to require them was part of what Secretary Espy referred to as an effort to reinvent and rethink every aspect of meat inspection.[28]

Questions for Discussion

1. How do the functional and promotional aspects of packaging and labeling interact in this case?
2. How might the benefits of the labeling regulations proposed in the Nutrition Labeling and Education Act outweigh their initial costs to both fresh meat retailers and producers? Should meat marketers wait for these labeling regulations to be passed into law before taking action?
3. Discuss how retailers and producers of red meat might use the proposed labeling requirements to help them compete against other protein products, such as chicken, turkey, or fish, perceived by the public as being healthier.

Case 11.2   Evian's New Bottle Promises Marketing and Environmental Benefits

In the 1970s, millions of Americans quenched their thirst with soft drinks. In the 1980s, they switched in large numbers to diet soft drinks. But the 1990s is the decade of bottled water. According to the International Bottled Water Association, Americans drink about 2.5 billion gallons of bottled water a year. People seeking healthy beverages that are free from everything—calories, caffeine, and artificial sweeteners, flavors, and colors—can find an ever-growing number of brands of bottled water from which to choose. As competition intensifies in the $3-billion-a-year bottled water business, companies struggle to distinguish their products from those of competitors. Marketers at Evian Natural Spring Water believe they have found a way. They are convinced that their unique new bottle will make Evian stand out on increasingly crowded grocery shelves.

Discovered in 1789 in the mountains overlooking the French city of Evian, the spring water was sold as "Source Cachat Water" in Paris and Geneva by the early 1800s. It wasn't until 1978, however, that Evian spring water flowed to the United States. Imported by Great Brands of Europe, Evian was initially available solely in one-liter glass bottles in upscale Miami Beach restaurants. Despite skeptics who argued that Americans would never pay for water, Evian was a regional hit. To expand distribution into grocery and specialty food stores all over the country, the company wanted a lighter container. In 1980 Evian introduced its first packaging innovation to the American beverage industry, the PET (polyethylene terephthalate) container. Today, the 1.5-liter PET bottle is the industry standard, and about 700 brands across the United States are packaged in bottles similar to Evian's.

With so many look-alike bottled water brands, Evian needed to distinguish itself. Spending several years and $40 million to develop its patented design, Evian created a collapsible bottle that incorporates an impression of the French Alps carved in plastic. Sculpted swirls represent the mountain aquifer from which the water comes, and the label, which is placed lower on the bottle like the label on premium wines, depicts those same mountains. The swirls are more than artistic, though—they contribute to the ease with which the bottle compacts. Called by designers "the spiral of weakness," the shape allows Evian bottles to collapse from the top down like an accordion, without sacrificing strength.

Evian's new package design unifies image and function. Its graphic mountain scene clearly conveys the water's source and heritage and reinforces its upscale positioning, which attracts the sophisticated and educated consumers who comprise the majority of Evian purchasers. The bottle's collapsibility makes it easier to recycle, and the new design uses 14 percent less plastic than the old one. These features make Evian packaging more environmentally friendly, which attracts customers who view themselves as environmentally concerned.

Evian marketers believe that the bottle plays a key promotional role in making the brand visible. Even if consumers miss a commercial or flip past a magazine advertisement, they can see the bottle every time they shop for food. Was a bottle design worth such a fortune? A study conducted by Evian's marketers revealed that changing from the old bottle to the new one raised purchasing intent by 20 percent. Among loyal Evian drinkers, a positive attitude about the bottle increased by 40 percent. Of those who do not currently purchase Evian, half said that, based on the new bottle, they'd be likely to consider doing so.

Positioned as a superpremium product, Evian costs significantly more than store-brand bottled waters. But even at as much as $1.89 a liter, Americans buy enough Evian to make it the third-largest selling bottled water in the United States.[29]

Questions for Discussion

1. Compared to the old Evian package, what major packing functions does the new Evian package perform especially well?
2. Which packaging strategies discussed in this chapter are most consistent with what Evian hopes to achieve with its new package?
3. In what ways is Evian's new package environmentally sensitive? Evaluate Evian marketers' view that bottled water drinkers are likely to be concerned about environmental issues and thus may be influenced to buy Evian because of its package.

Chapter 12

Services

OBJECTIVES

- To understand the nature and importance of services

- To become familiar with the characteristics of services that differentiate them from goods

- To examine how services are classified

- To become aware of the importance of service quality and be able to explain how to deliver exceptional service quality

- To explore the nature of nonprofit marketing

Online services beckon customers into cyberspace.

Although occasional skirmishes still flare in the Coke and Pepsi duel and the fast-food fray, the fiercest contest of the 1990s is shaping up to be the online service wars. Prodigy, America Online, Compu-Serve, Delphi, GEnie, AT&T Interchange, and Microsoft Network have all mustered for combat. While these services were formulating battle plans to defeat their commercial rivals, however, the Internet outmaneuvered them all to become the "in" place to be in cyberspace.

In the 1960s, the Defense Department created the Internet to link government labs, contractors, and military installations. Today, computer users all over the world use it to link files, get information, and relay messages. The World Wide Web, an information space on the Internet, opens the information highway to any-one wanting to publish information or promote products. Long considered forbiddingly techni-cal, the Web makes the Internet very appealing to customers and marketers, forcing online services to scramble for ways to provide subscribers Internet access and give them a reason to choose one service over another.

A recent survey reveals that 40 percent of per-sonal computer owners cannot name a single online service. Experts predict, however, that when the smoke of battle clears, only three or four online services will remain standing. Thus it is a matter of survival for these services to distin-guish themselves in the minds of customers. In addition, they must provide access to the Internet while making their own services seem more user-friendly and customer-oriented than those of competitors.

To link subscribers owning IBM compatible computers to the Net, Prodigy offers add-on Web-browser software. The company launched an advertising campaign with the slogan, "InterNET . . . Prodigy—InterNOT . . . America Online, CompuServe, Microsoft." Contrary to Prodigy's ad, though, America Online, Microsoft, and CompuServe, America's oldest commercial online service, all *do* provide Internet access. America Online's new Internet-only service is called Global Network Navigator; Microsoft Network limits subscribers to keep customer service quality high; and CompuServe sells sim-plicity by promising the "Internet Made Easy."

Is the Internet worth all the effort? Micro-soft's online services general manager responds by saying, "Unless we get the content of the Internet on our services, we'll be hosed."[1]

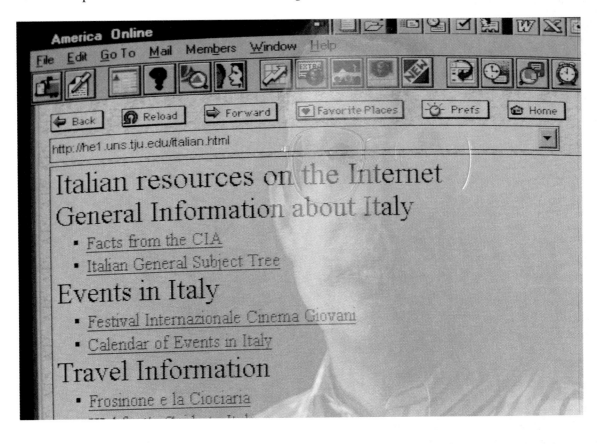

The products offered by online companies such as Prodigy, America Online, and CompuServe are primarily services, not tangible goods. This chapter presents concepts that apply specifically to products that are services. Service products involve marketing in for-profit areas such as financial, personal, and professional services, as well as in not-for-profit organizations, such as educational institutions, churches, charities, and governments.

The first section focuses on the growing importance of service industries in our economy. It addresses the unique characteristics of services and the problems these characteristics present to marketers. Next the chapter outlines various classification schemes that can help service marketers develop marketing strategies. We then consider how customers judge service quality and discuss the importance of delivering high-quality services. Finally, we define nonprofit marketing and examine the development of nonprofit marketing strategies.

The Nature and Importance of Services

Service An intangible product involving a deed, performance, or effort that cannot be physically possessed

*A*s noted in Chapter 9, all products—goods, services, or ideas—are to some extent intangible. A **service** is an intangible product involving a deed, a performance, or an effort that cannot be physically possessed.[2] Services are usually provided through the application of human and/or mechanical efforts directed at people or objects. For example, a service like education involves the efforts of service providers (teachers) directed at customers (students). In janitorial and interior decorating services, the efforts of service providers are directed at objects. Services can also involve the use of mechanical efforts directed at people (air transportation) or at objects (freight transportation). A wide variety of services, such as health care or landscaping, involve both human and mechanical efforts. Thus many services are provided through the use of tangible components like tools and machinery. However, the primary difference between a good and a service is that a service is dominated by the intangible portion of the total product.

Services as products should not be confused with the related topic of customer services. As discussed in Chapter 9, customer service involves any human or mechanical activity that adds value to the product.[3] Although customer service is typically associated with the marketing of goods, service marketers also provide customer services. For example, many service companies offer guarantees to their customers in an effort to increase value. Hampton Inns, a national chain of mid-price hotels, gives its guests a free night if they are not 100 percent satisfied with their stay.[4] In some cases, the 100 percent satisfaction guarantee or a similar service commitment may motivate employees to provide high-quality service, not because failure to do so leads to personal penalities but because they are proud to be part of an organization that provides such a strong service promise.

The increasing importance of services in the U.S. economy has led many people to call the United States the world's first service economy. Service industries account for 74 percent of the country's gross domestic product (GDP) and 76 percent of its nonfarm jobs.[5] Between 1990 and 1995, service industry employment grew by an average of 8 percent,[6] and service employment is expected to continue to grow.[7] These industries have absorbed much of the influx of women and minorities into the work force.

One major catalyst of the growth in consumer services has been long-term economic growth in the United States, which has led to increased interest in financial services, travel, entertainment, and personal care. Lifestyle changes have similarly encouraged expansion of the service sector. In the past forty years, the number of women in the work force has more than doubled. With approximately 70 percent of the women between the ages of 18 and 34 now working, the need for child care, domestic services, and other time-saving services has increased. Consumers want to avoid such tasks as meal preparation, house cleaning, home maintenance, and tax preparation; consequently, franchise operations, such as Subway, Merry Maids, Chemlawn, and H&R Block, have experienced rapid growth. Furthermore, Americans have become more fitness- and recreation-oriented, and so the demand for fitness and recreational facilities has escalated. In terms of demographics, the U.S. population is growing older, and this change has promoted tremendous expansion of health care services. Finally, the increasing number and complexity of high-tech goods have spurred demand for repair services.

Not only have consumer services grown in our economy; business services have prospered as well. Business or industrial services include repairs and maintenance, consulting, installation, equipment leasing, marketing research, advertising, temporary office personnel, and janitorial services. Expenditures for business and industrial services have risen even faster than expenditures for consumer services. For example, the recent trend in downsizing among many U.S. companies has dramatically raised the demand for temporary office personnel. This growth in business services has been attributed to the increasingly complex, specialized, and competitive business environment.

Characteristics of Services

*T*he issues associated with marketing service products are not exactly the same as those associated with marketing goods. To understand these differences, it is first necessary to understand the distinguishing characteristics of services. Services have six basic characteristics: (1) intangibility, (2) inseparability of production and consumption, (3) perishability, (4) heterogeneity, (5) client-based relationships, and (6) customer contact.[8] Table 12.1 summarizes these characteristics and the marketing problems they entail.

Table 12.1   Service Characteristics and Marketing Problems

Unique Service Characteristics	Resulting Marketing Problems
Intangibility	Difficult for consumer to evaluate Marketer is forced to sell a promise Difficult to advertise and display Prices are difficult to set and justify
Inseparability of production and consumption	Service providers are critical to delivery Consumer must participate in production Other consumers affect service outcomes Consumer does not take physical possession Services are difficult to distribute
Perishability	Services cannot be inventoried Very difficult to balance supply and demand Unused capacity is lost forever Demand is very time-sensitive
Heterogeneity	Service quality is difficult to control Difficult to standardize service delivery
Client-based relationships	Success depends on satisfying and keeping customers in the long term Generating repeat business is challenging Relationship marketing becomes critical
Customer contact	Service providers are critical to delivery High levels of service employee training and motivation are required Changing a high-contact service into a low-contact service to achieve lower costs without reducing customer satisfaction

Sources: Adapted from J. Paul Peter and James H. Donnelly, Jr., *A Preface to Marketing Management*, 5th ed. (Homewood, Ill.: Irwin, 1991), pp. 200–218; Valarie A. Zeithaml, A. Parasuraman, and Leonard L. Berry, *Delivering Quality Service: Balancing Customer Perceptions and Expectations* (New York: Free Press, 1990); Leonard L. Berry and A. Parasuraman, *Marketing Services: Competing Through Quality* (New York: Free Press, 1991), p. 5; and A. Parasuraman, Leonard L. Berry, and Valarie A. Zeithaml, "An Empirical Examination of Relationships in an Extended Service Quality Model," *Marketing Science Institute Working Paper Series*, Report no. 90–122 (Cambridge, Mass.: Marketing Science Institute, 1990), p. 29.

■ *Intangibility*

Intangibility Being
unperceivable by the senses

As already noted, the major characteristic that distinguishes a service from a good is intangibility. **Intangibility** means that a service cannot be seen, touched, tasted, or smelled. For example, it is impossible to see, touch, taste, or smell the education that students derive from attending classes. In addition, services cannot be physically possessed by consumers in the way that a good can be possessed. Thus students cannot possess an education like they can possess a stereo or a car.

Intangibility creates many problems for service marketers. Since a service cannot be examined by customers' senses, the service becomes very difficult for customers to evaluate before they actually purchase it. When a person evaluates a pair of jeans, she can try them on before buying. But how does a person evaluate the haircut he will get before actually having the service performed? This problem forces service marketers such as hairstylists to actually sell promises to customers. The customer is also forced to place some degree of trust in the service provider to perform the service correctly. This problem for both marketers and customers would not exist if services were not intangible.

Another major problem posed by intangibility is how to advertise a service effectively. Because a service cannot be pictured in an advertisement or displayed in a store, the marketer faces the difficult task of explaining the service to customers. Consequently, advertising of services typically includes tangible cues that symbolize the service. For example, Transamerica uses its "pyramid" shaped building to symbolize strength, security, and reliability, which are important features associated with insurance and other financial services (see Figure 12.1). Likewise, Allstate shows the "good hands" to symbolize personalized service and trustworthy, caring representatives. While these symbols have nothing to do with the actual service, they make it much easier for consumers to understand the intangible features associated with insurance.

Intangibility can result in services pricing problems. Marketers often base the price of a physical good on its costs of production (materials and labor). However, determining the costs of producing and delivering a service is very difficult. Service marketers also have a hard time justifying their prices to customers since the service cannot be evaluated before actual consumption. Consumers of legal or medical services, for instance, often do not know the prices of these services in advance of delivery.

Figure 12.1
Tangibilizing a Service
Transamerica uses its "Pyramid" to tangibilize its financial services by symbolizing this service provider's strength, security, and reliability.

■ *Inseparability of Production and Consumption*

Inseparability Being produced and consumed at the same time

Another important characteristic of services, **inseparability,** refers to the fact that the production of a service cannot be separated from its consumption by customers. In other words, services are produced and consumed simultaneously. In goods marketing, customers can purchase the good from a store, take it home with them, and store it until such time that the good is consumed. This cannot take place in services marketing. This inseparable, or indivisible, nature of services causes problems for marketers.

One of the crucial problems caused by inseparability is the increased importance of the service provider in the delivery process. For such services as hairstyling, education, and health care, the service provider *is* the service in the eyes of the consumer.[9] This forces the service marketer to pay careful attention to the training of service personnel.[10] Inseparability also means that the customer must participate in the production of a service. For example, a doctor cannot conduct an adequate medical examination without the participation of the patient. The outcome of the service also depends on the participation of the customer.

The fact that customers take part in the production of a service means that other customers can affect the outcome of a service. For instance, if a nonsmoker dines in a restaurant without a no-smoking section, then the overall quality of service experienced by the nonsmoking customer declines. This is the reason why many restaurants have no-smoking sections or have prohibited smoking in their establishments. Service marketers can reduce these problems by encouraging customers to cooperate in sharing the responsibility of maintaining an environment that allows all participants to receive the intended benefits of the service.

■ *Perishability*

Perishability
The impossibility of storing unused service capacity for future use

Because their production and consumption are simultaneous, services are also characterized by **perishability**: that is, the unused service capacity of one time period cannot be stored for use in future time periods. For this reason, service marketers face several hurdles in trying to balance supply and demand. Goods marketers handle the supply-demand problem through production scheduling and inventory techniques. Service marketers, however, do not have the same advantage.

Consider the supply-demand problems faced by the airlines. Each carrier maintains a sophisticated reservation system to juggle ticket prices in an effort to fill every seat on every flight. On a single day, each airline makes thousands of fare changes to maximize the use of its seating capacity and thus maximize its revenues. This practice usually leads to overbooking, or selling more tickets than the number of seats available in order to compensate for customers who fail to show up for a particular flight. Other service marketers face similar difficulties. Movie theaters are often empty during matinees but sold out at night, whereas evening sections of college courses often have seats available, while the daytime sections are full.

Peak demand The point in time when consumers want to use a service

Service marketers pay careful attention to the supply-demand problem for one simple reason: any unused capacity cannot be stored and is therefore lost forever. Every empty seat on an airline flight or in a movie theater represents lost revenue. This example illustrates another problem caused by perishability—namely, that service demand is very time-sensitive. Service activities are typically performed when consumers want to use them. This point in time is called **peak demand**. For an airline, peak demand times are usually early and late in the day. For cruise lines, peak demand occurs in the winter for Caribbean cruises and in the summer for Alaskan cruises. The prices for services during peak demand are typically higher than at other times. As a result, a service company brings in most of its revenues during peak demand times. The problem, however, is how to eliminate unused capacity during **off-peak demand**, or when customers do not want to use the service. Many service marketers offer lower prices during times of off-peak demand to encourage more consumers to use the service. This is why the price of a matinee movie is often half the price of the same movie shown at night. Service marketers can also attempt to control these fluctuations in demand by substituting machine labor for human labor. Many banks have installed automated teller machines (ATMs) to more efficiently serve customers during peak demand times and to lower their labor costs during off-peak times.

Off-peak demand The time when consumers do not want to use the service

277

■ *Heterogeneity*

Heterogeneity Variation in quality

Services that are people-based are susceptible to **heterogeneity**, or variation in quality. Because of the nature of human behavior, it is very difficult for service providers to always deliver a service consistently. This variation in quality can occur in at least four different ways: (1) from one organization to another, (2) from one service to another within the same organization, (3) from one outlet to another within the same organization, or (4) the service that a single employee provides can vary from customer to customer, day to day, or even hour to hour. As a result, standardization and service quality are very difficult to control.

Denny's, a family restaurant chain, provides an example of the difficulties involved in the control of heterogeneity. Recently, Denny's introduced a new menu that offers more than 150 choices for breakfast, lunch, dinner, and late-night dining. With most outlets open twenty-four hours a day, Denny's usually serves thousands of customers daily. In performance of their numerous duties, Denny's 47,000 employees can deliver quality service to restaurant customers, or can fail to do so. With so many menu items, operating hours, and employees, the possibility of service mistakes is high. To cope with uncontrolled service heterogeneity, Denny's instituted changes throughout its 1,500 U.S. outlets. Denny's restructured restaurant management so that regional managers are accountable for the service in all restaurants, whether franchised or company owned. Now both individual restaurant managers and field managers earn bonuses for quality service. The restaurant manager training course has been lengthened from seven to thirteen weeks. To free restaurant managers from excessive administrative functions, automated systems order inventory and schedule labor. To improve service speed and meal consistency, Denny's is testing new kitchen technology including cooking by computer.[11]

Heterogeneity actually provides one advantage to service marketers. Because services are very difficult to standardize, they can be customized to match the specific needs of any customer. Health care is an example of an extremely customized service, with the activities of the service provider totally different from one patient to another. However, customized services are very expensive for both the provider and the customer. Thus many service marketers face a dilemma: how to provide efficient, standardized service at an acceptable level of quality while simultaneously treating every customer as unique. This is precisely the type of debate going on in the health care industry today.

■ *Client-Based Relationships*

Client-based relationships Interactions that result in satisfied customers who repeatedly use a service over time

The success of many services depends on creating and maintaining **client-based relationships,** or interaction with customers that results in satisfied customers who repeatedly use a service over time.[12] In fact, service providers such as lawyers, accountants, and financial advisers actually call their customers clients. Service providers like these are successful only to the degree that they can maintain a group of clients who use their services on an ongoing basis. For example, a doctor may serve a family in his or her area for decades. If the family likes the quality of the services delivered by the doctor, they are likely to recommend him or her to other families. Once this positive word of mouth is repeated for several different families, it does not take long for the doctor to acquire a long list of satisfied clients.

This process is the very essence of creating and maintaining client-based relationships. However, the service provider must take steps to ensure that the process actually occurs. The process of creating and maintaining client-based relationships is called relationship marketing. The goal of relationship marketing is to satisfy customers so well that they become very loyal to the provider and unlikely to switch to a competitor. For example, the United Services Automobile Association (USAA), one of the largest U.S. insurance companies, has built a very loyal following of customers by focusing its efforts on customer service. USAA targets its financial services to military families by customizing services to match the specific needs of these customers. This concentrated effort to provide quality customer service to a specific target market makes USAA customers very loyal. Inside Marketing demonstrates how USAA maintains strong customer loyalty through superior customer service.

INSIDE MARKETING

USAA: Dedicated to Customer Service

USAA is the fourth-largest homeowner's insurer and fifth-largest automobile insurer in the United States, serving over 2.8 million people, most of them present or former military personnel and their dependents. In addition to insurance, USAA's divisions include USAA Life Insurance, USAA Investment Management, USAA Federal Savings Bank, USAA, Buying Services Group, and USAA Real Estate.

Analysts agree that USAA's dedication to providing quality customer service has propelled it to the forefront of the insurance and financial services industry. To provide what has become the industry's standard of excellent service, USAA learns as much as it can about its customers. From sales and marketing offices in Texas, California, Colorado, Florida, Virginia, London, and Frankfurt, 6,000 customer service representatives talk on the phone with members every day. The question they ask their customers most often is, "What do you need?"

Every year, the company conducts about one hundred phone and mail surveys and focus groups asking thousands of customers to judge new services and to suggest others they'd like to see offered. For example, when its customers complained about confusing long-distance telephone rates, USAA conducted a customer needs survey and then established a special arrangement with Sprint. Within a few years, 600,000 members enrolled.

Among its many customer-friendly services, USAA Federal Savings and Loan provides free checking with no minimum balance, five free monthly withdrawals from any ATM, convenient banking by computer, and low-interest loans. By making one phone call to USAA's centralized service center, customers can get policy changes made immediately; agents don't need to call other branches or ship files around the country.

Despite the ongoing military cuts that have been steadily shrinking its customer base, USAA membership continues to grow by about 100,000 members a year. USAA's superior service has earned it unwavering customer loyalty and numerous industry awards. USAA boasts a 95 percent customer retention rate, and a recent customer satisfaction survey indicates that almost 98 percent of those surveyed are satisfied or highly satisfied. *CIO* magazine listed USAA among America's top customer-service companies, and *Money* magazine named USAA the "Best Bank in America" based on criteria such as generous savings rates, unparalleled convenience, and excellent service.

Sources: USAA Fact Sheet, Oct. 16, 1995; Carol Hildebrand, "CIO 100—Best Practices: Satisfaction Guaranteed," *CIO*, Aug. 1995, pp. 98–100; Vanessa O'Connell, "The Best Bank in America," *Money*, June 1995, pp. 126–133; David Gertz, "Beating the Odds," *Journal of Business Strategy*, July/Aug. 1995, pp. 20–24; and Shep Montgomery, "Merchants & Farmers Bank Named Mississippi's Best Bank," *Mississippi Business Journal*, June 19, 1995, p. 9.

■ *Customer Contact*

Customer contact
Interaction between provider and customer needed to deliver the service

Not all services require a high degree of customer contact, but many do. **Customer contact** refers to the necessary interaction between service provider and customer in order for the service to be delivered. For this reason, service employees become a very important ingredient in creating satisfied customers. One of the main principles of customer contact is that satisfied employees lead to satisfied customers, and vice versa. In fact, recent research indicates that employee satisfaction is the single most important factor in providing high service quality.[13] Thus, to minimize the problems created by customer contact, service organizations must take steps to understand and meet the needs of employees by training them, giving them more freedom to make decisions, and rewarding them for customer-oriented behaviors.[14] The importance of employees also creates a second problem related to customer contact: high-contact services are very expensive to deliver because they are labor-intensive.

Service companies can minimize many of the problems caused by customer contact by changing high-contact services into low-contact services.[15] The banking industry has undergone major changes to decrease customer contact. By installing ATMs, many banks eliminated the need for employees to interact with customers in order to deliver service.

Likewise, many banking services are now available by phone. Each of these innovations helped to standardize banking services and lower costs by eliminating the need for human tellers. However, changing a high-contact service into a low-contact service can actually create another problem: the service becomes less personalized. Therefore, when designing methods for service delivery, service marketers must pay attention to the degree of personalization desired by customers.

Classification of Service Products

*S*ervices are a very diverse group of products, and an organization may provide more than one kind. Examples of services include car rentals, repairs, health care, barber shops, health spas, tanning salons, amusement parks, day care, domestic services, legal counsel, banking, insurance, air travel, education, business consulting, dry cleaning, and accounting. Nevertheless, services can be meaningfully analyzed in two ways: (1) as a continuum of pure goods to pure services and (2) by service categories.

■ The Service Continuum

Figure 12.2 depicts the continuum of pure goods (tangible) to pure services (intangible). Pure goods typically do not exist in today's business environment since practically all goods marketers provide customer services. For example, a tangible, good-dominant product like sugar must still be delivered to the store, priced, and placed on the shelf before a customer can purchase it. Thus practically all makers of goods are also providers of services.

Intangible, service-dominant products like education or health care are clearly service products. But what about the products near the center of the service continuum? Is a restaurant like Red Lobster a goods marketer or a service marketer? Knowing where the product lies on the service continuum is an important step in creating marketing strategies for service-dominant products. The further a product is on the intangible side of the continuum, the more an organization must understand the important characteristics of services discussed previously in the chapter.

Figure 12.2
The Service Continuum

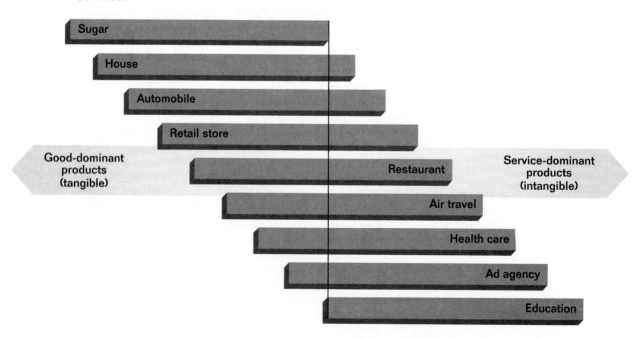

Table 12.2   Categories of Services

Category	Examples
Type of Market	
Consumer	Repairs, child care, lawn care
Business	Consulting, janitorial services, temporary workers
Degree of Labor-Intensiveness	
People-based	Repairs, education, haircuts
Equipment-based	Telecommunications, health spas, public transportation
Degree of Customer Contact	
High contact	Health care, hotels, real estate
Low contact	Tax preparation, dry cleaning, postal service
Skill of the Service Provider	
Professional	Legal counsel, health care, accounting services
Nonprofessional	Domestic services, dry cleaning, public transportation
Goal of the Service Provider	
Profit	Financial services, insurance, health care
Nonprofit	Health care, education, government

■ *Categories of Services*

Services can also be classified according to different categories. Table 12.2 describes this classification scheme.

Services can be viewed in terms of the market or type of customer they serve—consumer or business. The implications of this distinction are very similar to those for all products and therefore are not discussed here.

A second way to classify services is by degree of labor-intensiveness. Many services, such as repairs, education, and hair care, rely heavily on human labor. Other services, such as telecommunications, health clubs, and public transportation, are more equipment-intensive. People-based services are often prone to fluctuations in quality from one time period to the next. For example, the fact that a customer receives a good haircut today does not guarantee a haircut of equal quality at a later date. This happens because the performance of the same hairstylist can change. Equipment-based services do not suffer from this problem to the same degree as people-based services.

The third way services can be classified is by customer contact. High-contact services include health care (see Figure 12.3), real estate agencies, and hair care. An example of a high-contact service is the one provided by Cleo Hodde of Kelso, Washington. She

Figure 12.3 High Contact Service Provider   Health care organizations are providers of high-contact services.

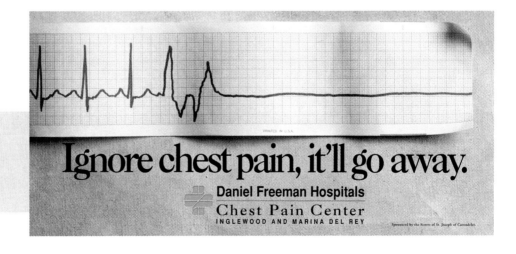

Ignore chest pain, it'll go away.

Daniel Freeman Hospitals
Chest Pain Center
INGLEWOOD AND MARINA DEL REY

282

operates a one-woman traveling massage business, scheduling up to twenty-five appointments a day, primarily in area businesses. Most of her customers are women.[16] Low contact services include tax preparation, movie theaters, dry cleaning, and spectator sports. Note that high-contact services generally involve actions directed toward individuals. Because these services are directed at people, the customer must be present during production. Although it is sometimes possible for the service provider to go to the customer, high-contact services typically require that the customer go to the production facility. Thus the physical appearance of the facility may be a major component of the customer's overall evaluation of the service. Because the customer must be present during production of a high-contact service, the process of production may be just as important as its final outcome. Low-contact services, in contrast, usually do not require the physical presence of the customer during delivery. The customer, however, may need to be present in order to initiate and/or terminate the service.

Skill of the service provider is a fourth way to classify services. Professional services tend to be more complex and more highly regulated than nonprofessional services. In the case of legal counsel, for example, consumers often do not know what the actual service will involve or how much it will cost until the service is completed because the final product is very situation-specific. Additionally, attorneys are regulated both by law and by professional associations. Health care is another service that requires a high degree of skill and is highly regulated. As you can see in Technology in Marketing, eye surgery is an example of a high-skill health service.

Finally, services can be classified according to the goal of the service provider—profit or nonprofit. The Big Brother and Big Sister organizations are nonprofit service providers (see Figure 12.4). Later in this chapter we examine nonprofit marketing. Many nonprofit organizations provide services.

Figure 12.4
Nonprofit Service Providers   The Big Brother and Big Sister organizations are nonprofit service providers.

TECHNOLOGY IN MARKETING

Marketing High-Tech Surgery for Nearsightedness

In 1978, nearsighted Americans were introduced to radial keratotomy (RK), a procedure in which an ophthalmologist uses a scalpel to make spoke-like incisions into the cornea to flatten it. A more recent surgery, photorefractive keratotomy (PRK), employs a laser to remove tissue from the central cornea. Unlike glasses and contact lenses, which are products to correct nearsightedness, RK and PRK are techniques that cure it. Despite a potentially huge market (about 60 million people), nearsighted Americans must be persuaded to spend between $2,600 and $4,000 for elective surgery that is not covered by most health insurance programs.

Ophthalmologists and eye centers are using various marketing efforts to sell their high-tech surgery. Thanks in large part to aggressive newspaper and radio advertising, public awareness of the procedure has convinced over 450,000 Americans to have radial keratotomies performed. PRK doctors and clinics, hoping to top those numbers, are aggressively promoting their ability to free patients more quickly and painlessly from the hassle of glasses or contact lenses. They believe that, from the customer's standpoint, the newer laser technology has more appeal—because it involves less risk—than a procedure that slices 80 percent of the cornea.

One of the most aggressive marketing campaigns for PRK has been generated by Summit Technologies, which not only invented the technique but operates surgery centers around the country. Summit promotions are designed to stimulate demand for the surgery at the consumer level. People will be informed about the procedure and told to see an eye care specialist for more information. Summit's promotion is accomplished primarily through public relations efforts targeting forty major U.S. cities. The company sends local newspapers prepared press packs with information about the technique. Company representatives appear on network talk television to discuss the procedure. Interested consumers can call toll-free to order a PRK educational resource guide. In 1996, the company launched its first paid television ads.

Some industry experts are concerned that as high-tech surgery becomes more popular, unscrupulous providers will inappropriately advertise the benefits by omitting facts or making false claims. In addition, many analysts doubt that marketing efforts alone will ever attract many customers. They contend that people are too wary of anyone touching their eyes to be swayed solely by a television advertisement.

Sources: Press pack, Summit Technology, Inc., Nov. 1995; Adam Goodman, "Entrepreneur Has an Eye on Laser Surgery Center," *St. Louis Post-Dispatch,* June 5, 1995, p. B3; Kevlin C. Haire, "Surgery Chain Eyed for Region," *Baltimore Business Journal,* Oct. 28, 1994, p. 3; Seth Shulman, "High-tech Help for the Nearsighted," *Technology Review,* Apr. 1995, pp. 18–19; Susan Caminiti, "Focusing on Laser Surgery," *Fortune,* Feb. 20, 1995, p. 31; Art Chamberlain, "Seeing a Way to Profit: Laser Surgery to Correct Near-sightedness Is One of the Fastest Growing Medical Areas," *Toronto Star,* Jan. 23, 1995, p. E1; "Eye-Surgery Marketing Is Scrutinized," *Wall Street Journal,* Mar. 2, 1995, p. B1; and phone interview with Mike Barra, Summit Technologies, Inc., Marketing Department, Nov. 7, 1995.

Service Quality

Service quality Customers' perception of how well a service meets or exceeds their expectations

The delivery of high-quality services is one of the most important and most difficult tasks that any service organization faces. Because of their unique characteristics, services are very difficult to evaluate. Hence customers must look closely at service quality when comparing services. **Service quality** is defined as customers' perception of how well a service meets or exceeds their expectations.[17] Note that service quality is judged by customers, not the organization. This distinction is critical because it forces service marketers to examine their quality from the customer's viewpoint. For example, a bank may view service quality as having friendly and knowledgeable employees. However, the customers of this bank may be more concerned with waiting time, ATM access, and security, as well as statement accuracy. Thus it is important for service organizations to determine what customers expect and then develop service products that meet or exceed those expectations.

■ *Customer Evaluation of Service Quality*

Search qualities
Tangible attributes that can be judged before the purchase of a product

Experience qualities
Attributes gaugeable only during purchase and consumption of a service

Credence qualities
Attributes that customers may be unable to evaluate even after purchasing and consuming a service

The biggest obstacle for customers in evaluating service quality is the intangible nature of the service. How can customers evaluate something that they cannot see, feel, taste, or hear? The evaluation of a good is much easier because all goods possess **search qualities,** or tangible attributes such as color, style, size, feel, or fit, which can be evaluated prior to the purchase of a product. Trying on a new coat or taking a car for a test drive are examples of how customers evaluate search qualities. Services, on the other hand, have very few search qualities; instead, they abound in experience and credence qualities. **Experience qualities**, such as taste, satisfaction, or pleasure, are attributes that can be assessed only during the purchase and consumption of a service.[18] Restaurants and vacations are examples of services that are high in experience qualities. **Credence qualities** are attributes that customers may be unable to evaluate even after the purchase and consumption of the service. Examples of services high in credence qualities are surgical operations, automobile repairs, consulting, and legal representation. Most consumers lack the knowledge or the skills to evaluate the quality of these types of services. Consequently, they must place a great deal of faith in the integrity and competence of the service provider.

Despite the difficulties in evaluating quality, service quality may be the only way customers can choose one service over another. For this reason, service marketers live or die by understanding how consumers judge service quality. Table 12.3 defines five dimensions that consumers use when evaluating service quality: tangibles, reliability, responsiveness, assurance, and empathy. Note that all of them have links to employee performance. Of the five, reliability is the most important in determining customer evaluations of service quality.[19]

Table 12.3   Dimensions of Service Quality

Dimension	Evaluation Criteria	Examples
Tangibles: Physical evidence of the service	Appearance of physical facilities Appearance of service personnel Tools or equipment used to provide the service	A clean and professional-looking doctor's office A clean and well-dressed college professor The quality of food in a restaurant The equipment used in a medical exam
Reliability: Consistency and dependability in performing the service	Accuracy of billing or record keeping Performing services when promised	An accurate bank statement A confirmed hotel reservation An airline flight departing and arriving on time
Responsiveness: Willingness or readiness of employees to provide the service	Returning customer phone calls Providing prompt service Handling urgent requests	A waiter refilling a customer's glass of tea without being asked An ambulance arriving within 3 minutes
Assurance: Knowledge/competence of employees and ability to convey trust and confidence	Knowledge and skills of employees Company name and reputation Personal characteristics of employees	A highly trained financial adviser A known and respected service provider A doctor's bedside manner
Empathy: Caring and individual attention provided by employees	Listening to customer needs Caring about the customer's interests Providing personalized attention	A store employee listening to and trying to understand a customer's complaint A nurse counseling a heart patient

Sources: Adapted from Leonard L. Berry and A. Parasuraman, *Marketing Services: Competing Through Quality* (New York: Free Press, 1991); Valarie A. Zeithaml, A. Parasuraman, and Leonard L. Berry, *Delivering Quality Service: Balancing Customer Perceptions and Expectations* (New York: Free Press, 1990); and A. Parasuraman, Leonard L. Berry, and Valarie A. Zeithaml, "An Empirical Examination of Relationships in an Extended Service Quality Model," *Marketing Science Institute Working Paper Series*, Report no. 90-122 (Cambridge, Mass.: Marketing Science Institute, 1990), p. 29.

Service marketers pay a great deal of attention to the tangibles dimension of service quality. Tangible elements, such as the appearance of facilities and employees, are often the only aspects of a service that can be viewed before purchase and consumption. Therefore, service marketers must ensure that these tangible elements are consistent with the overall image of the service product. For example, Direct Tire Sales, an independent tire and automotive service center in Watertown, Massachusetts, understands the importance of appearances. The customer lounge is kept spotless and stocked with fresh coffee, real cream, and fresh croissants on a daily basis. The lounge also has an aquarium. Sales employees are required to wear a tie as part of their uniform. Just providing the coffee and croissants costs the company $3,800 a year. However, these tangible elements are also backed by exceptional service. Direct Tire Sales guarantees many of its services for the life of the car.[20]

Except for the tangibles dimension, the criteria that customers use to judge service quality are intangible. For instance, how does a customer judge reliability? Since dimensions such as reliability cannot be examined with the senses, consumers must rely on other ways of judging service criteria. One of the most important factors in customer judgments of service quality is service expectations. Service expectations are influenced by past experiences with the service, word-of-mouth communication from other customers, and the service company's own advertising. For example, customers are usually eager to try a new restaurant, especially when friends recommend it. These same customers may have also seen advertisements placed by the restaurant. As a result, these customers have an idea of what to expect when they visit the restaurant for the first time. When they finally dine at the restaurant, the quality they experience will change the expectations they have for their next visit. That is why providing consistently high service quality is important. If the quality of a restaurant, or any service marketer, begins to deteriorate, customers will alter their own expectations and word-of-mouth communication to others accordingly.

■ Delivering Exceptional Service Quality

Providing high-quality service on a consistent basis is very difficult. All consumers have experienced examples of poor service: long checkout lines in a store, late airline departures and arrivals, inattentive waiters in a restaurant, and rude bank employees. Obviously, it is impossible for a service organization to ensure exceptional service quality 100 percent of the time. However, there are many steps that an organization can take to increase the likelihood of providing high-quality service. First, though, the service company must understand the four factors that affect service quality. As shown in Figure 12.5 they are (1) understanding customer expectations, (2) service quality specifications, (3) employee performance, and (4) managing service expectations.[21]

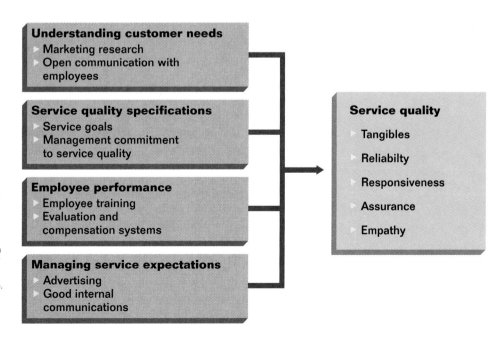

Figure 12.5
Service Quality Model

Understanding Customer Expectations   As mentioned earlier, providers need to understand customer expectations when designing a service to meet or exceed those expectations. Only then can they deliver good service. Customers usually have two levels of expectations—desired and acceptable. The desired level of expectations is what the customer really wants. If this level of expectations is provided, the customer would be very satisfied. The acceptable level is viewed as a reasonable level of performance that the customer views as being adequate. The difference between these two levels of expectations is called the customer's zone of tolerance.[22]

Service companies sometimes use marketing research, such as surveys and focus groups, as a means of discovering customer needs and expectations. Other service marketers, especially restaurants, use comment cards, on which customers can complain or provide suggestions. Still another approach is to ask employees. Because customer-contact employees interact daily with customers, they are in a good position to know what customers want from the company. Service managers should regularly interact with their employees by asking their opinions on how to best serve customers.

Service Quality Specifications   Once an organization understands its customers' needs, it must establish goals to help ensure good service delivery. These goals, or service specifications, are typically set in terms of employee or machine performance. For example, a bank may require its employees to conform to a dress code. Likewise, the bank may require that all incoming phone calls be answered by the third ring. Specifications like these can be very important in providing quality service as long as they are tied to the needs expressed by customers.

Perhaps the most critical aspect of service quality specifications is managers' commitment to service quality. Service managers who are committed to quality become role models for all employees in the organization.[23] Such commitment motivates contact employees to comply with service specifications. It is also crucial that all managers within the organization embrace this commitment—especially front-line managers, who are much closer to customers than higher-level managers.

Employee Performance   Once an organization sets service quality standards and managers are committed to them, the organization must find ways to ensure that customer-contact employees perform their jobs well. Contact employees in most service industries—bank tellers, flight attendants, waiters, sales clerks—are often the least-trained and lowest-paid members of the organization. What service organizations must realize is that contact employees are the most important link to the customer, and thus their performance is critical to customer perceptions of service quality.[24] The means to ensure that employees perform well is to train them well so that they understand how to do their jobs. Providing information about customers, service specifications, and the organization itself during the training promotes this understanding.[25]

The evaluation and compensation system used by the organization also plays a part in employee performance. Many service employees are evaluated and rewarded on the basis of output measures such as sales volume (automobile salespeople) or the lack of errors during work (bank tellers). But systems using output measures overlook other major aspects of job performance: friendliness, teamwork, effort, and customer satisfaction. Thus customer-oriented measures of performance may be a better basis of evaluation and reward. For example, Dun and Bradstreet has tied employee commissions to customer satisfaction surveys rather than sales volume.[26] This type of system stimulates employees to take care of customer needs rather than focus solely on sales or profits.

Managing Service Expectations   Because expectations are so significant in customer evaluations of service quality, service companies recognize that they must set realistic expectations about the service they can provide. They can set these expectations through advertising and good internal communication. In their advertisements, service companies make promises about the kind of service they will deliver (see Figure 12.6). In fact, a service company is forced to make promises since the intangibility of services prevents it from showing them in the advertisement. However, the advertiser should not promise more than it can deliver; doing otherwise may mean disappointed customers.

To the frequent flyers who voted us number one in *Inside Flyer* magazine, thanks. We're tickled pink. And rest assured, it's just the start of what employee-ownership is going to mean for you. Come fly our friendly skies.

✈ **UNITED AIRLINES**

MILEAGE PLUS®
Program of the Year
Best Customer Service
Best Elite Program

Stop, you're making us blush.

Figure 12.6
Establishing Realistic Service Expectations
Service providers often use advertisements to establish expectations about the quality of services they intend to deliver.

To deliver on promises made, a company needs to have good internal communication among its departments—especially management, advertising, and store operations. Assume, for example, that a restaurant's radio advertisements guaranteed service within five minutes or the meal would be free. If top management or the advertising department failed to inform store operations about the five-minute guarantee, the restaurant very likely would not meet its customers' service expectations. Even though customers might appreciate a free meal, the restaurant would lose some credibility.

As mentioned earlier, word-of-mouth communication from other customers also shapes customer expectations. However, service companies cannot manage this "advertising" directly. The best way to ensure positive word-of-mouth communication is to provide exceptional service quality. It has been estimated that customers tell four times as many people about bad service as they do about good service. Consequently, service marketers must provide four good service experiences for every bad experience just to break even.

Nonprofit Marketing of Services

*E*arlier in the text, we broadly defined marketing as the process of creating, distributing, promoting, and pricing goods, services, and ideas to facilitate satisfying exchange relationships in a dynamic environment. Most of the previously discussed concepts and approaches to service products also apply to nonprofit organizations. Indeed, many nonprofit organizations provide mainly service products.

Nonprofit marketing includes marketing activities conducted by individuals and organizations to achieve some goal other than ordinary business goals of profit, market share, or return on investment. Nonprofit marketing can be divided into two categories: nonprofit-organization marketing and social marketing. Nonprofit-organization marketing is the use of marketing concepts and techniques by organizations whose goals do not include making profits. Social marketing is attempting to influence the acceptability of social ideas, such as contributing to a foundation for AIDS research or getting people to engage in recycling.

In this section we examine the concept of nonprofit marketing to determine how it differs from marketing activities in for-profit business organizations. Next we explore the overall objectives of nonprofit organizations, their marketing objectives, and the development of their product strategies.

Nonprofit marketing
Marketing conducted to achieve some goal other than ordinary business goals of profit, market share, or return on investment

■ Why Is Nonprofit Marketing Different?

Many nonprofit organizations strive for effective marketing activities. Charitable organizations and supporters of social causes are major nonprofit marketers in this country. Political parties, unions, religious sects, and fraternal organizations also perform marketing activities, yet they are not considered businesses. Whereas the chief beneficiary of a

Seven Continents on Central Park West *For 125 years, we've traveled to the farthest corners of the earth to bring you the world.*

American Museum of Natural History

Central Park West at 79th Street, New York City - For information, call 212-769-5100

Figure 12.7
Nonprofit Service
The American Museum of Natural History is a nonprofit cultural and educational institution and a major center for scientific research.

business enterprise is whoever owns or holds stock in it, in theory the only beneficiaries of a nonprofit organization are its clients, its members, or the public at large. The American Museum of Natural History is a nonprofit service organization (see Figure 12.7).

Nonprofit organizations have a greater opportunity for creativity than most for-profit business organizations, but trustees or board members of nonprofit organizations are likely to have trouble judging performance when services can be provided only by trained professionals. It is harder for administrators to evaluate the performance of professors or social workers than it is for sales managers to evaluate the performance of salespersons in a for-profit organization.

Another way in which nonprofit marketing differs from for-profit marketing is that nonprofit marketing is sometimes quite controversial. Nonprofit organizations such as Greenpeace, the National Rifle Association, and the National Organization for Women spend lavishly on lobbying efforts to persuade Congress, the White House, and even the courts to support their interests, in part because acceptance of their aims by all of society is not always guaranteed. However, marketing as a field of study does not attempt to state what an organization's goals should be or to debate the issue of nonprofit versus for-profit business goals. Marketing tries only to provide a body of knowledge and concepts to help further an organization's goals. Individuals must decide whether they approve or disapprove of a particular organization's goal orientation. Most marketers would agree that profit and consumer satisfaction are appropriate goals for business enterprises, but there would probably be considerable disagreement about the goals of a controversial nonprofit organization.

■ *Nonprofit Marketing Objectives*

The basic aim of nonprofit organizations is to obtain a desired response from a target market. The response could be a change in values, a financial contribution, the donation of services, or some other type of exchange. Nonprofit marketing objectives are shaped by the nature of the exchange and the goals of the organization. Nonprofit marketing objectives should state the rationale for an organization's existence. An organization that defines its marketing objective as providing a product can be left without a purpose if the product becomes obsolete. However, servicing and adapting to the perceived needs and wants of a target public, or market, enhances an organization's chance to survive and achieve its goals.

■ *Developing Nonprofit Marketing Strategies*

Nonprofit organizations must also develop marketing strategies by defining and analyzing a target market and creating and considering the total marketing mix that appeals to that market.

Target public People interested in or concerned about an organization, product, or social cause

Target Markets   We must revise the concept of target markets slightly to apply it to nonprofit organizations. Whereas a business is supposed to have target groups that are potential purchasers of its product, a nonprofit organization may attempt to serve many diverse groups. For our purposes, a **target public** is broadly defined as a collective of individuals who have an interest in or concern about an organization, a product, or a social cause. The terms *target market* and *target public* are difficult to distinguish for many nonprofit organizations. The target public of the Partnership for a Drug Free America is parents, adults, and concerned teenagers. However, the target market for the organization's advertisements is potential and current drug users. When an organization is concerned about changing values or obtaining a response from the public, it views the public as a market.[27]

Client publics Direct consumers of a product

General publics Indirect consumers of a product

In nonprofit organizations, direct consumers of the product are called **client publics** and indirect consumers are called **general publics.**[28] For example, the client public for a university is its student body, and its general public includes parents, alumni, and trustees. The client public usually receives most of the attention when an organization develops a marketing strategy. The techniques and approaches to segmenting and defining target markets discussed in Chapter 8 apply also to nonprofit target markets.

Developing a Marketing Mix A marketing mix strategy limits alternatives and directs marketing activities toward achieving organizational goals. The strategy should outline or develop a blueprint for making decisions about product, distribution, promotion, and price. These decision variables should be blended to serve the target market.

In developing the product, nonprofit organizations usually deal with ideas and services. Problems may evolve when an organization fails to define what is being provided. What product does the Peace Corps provide? Its services include vocational training, health services, nutritional assistance, and community development. It also markets the ideas of international cooperation and the implementation of U.S. foreign policy. The Peace Corps' product is more difficult to define than the average business product. As indicated in the first part of this chapter, services are intangible and therefore need special marketing efforts. The marketing of ideas and concepts is likewise more abstract than the marketing of tangibles, and it requires much effort to present benefits.

**Figure 12.8
Nonprofit Marketers of Ideas** Some nonprofit marketers promote ideas to combat social ills.

Perfume won't hide it.

SMOKELINE 0800 84 84 84 ⊛ HEALTH EDUCATION BOARD FOR SCOTLAND

Because most nonprofit products are ideas and services, distribution decisions relate to how these ideas and services will be made available to clients. If the product is an idea, selecting the right media to communicate the idea will facilitate distribution. In Figure 12.8, for example, the anti-smoking poster by the Health Education Board of Scotland targets preteen and teenage girls. The availability of services is closely related to product decisions. By nature, services consist of assistance, convenience, and availability. Availability is part of the total service. For example, making a product such as health services available calls for knowledge of such retailing concepts as site location analysis.

Developing a channel of distribution to coordinate and facilitate the flow of nonprofit products to clients is a necessary task, but in a nonprofit setting the traditional concept of the marketing channel may need to be revised. The independent wholesalers available to a business enterprise do not exist in most nonprofit situations. Instead, a very short channel—nonprofit organization to client—is prevalent because production and consumption of ideas and services are often simultaneous.

Making promotional decisions may be the first sign that nonprofit organizations are performing marketing activities. Nonprofit organizations use advertising and publicity to communicate with clients and the public. Direct mail remains the primary means of fundraising for social services such as those provided by the Red Cross and Special Olympics. Personal selling is also used by many nonprofit organizations, although it may be called something else. Churches and charities rely on personal selling when they send volunteers to recruit new members or request donations. The U.S. Army uses personal selling when its recruiting officers attempt to convince men and women to enlist. Special events to obtain funds, communicate ideas, or provide services are also effective promotion activities. Amnesty International, for example, has held worldwide concert tours, featuring well-known musical artists to raise funds and increase public awareness of political prisoners around the world.

Although product and promotion techniques might require only slight modification when applied to nonprofit organizations, pricing is generally quite different and the decision making more complex. The different pricing concepts that the nonprofit organization faces include pricing in user and donor markets. There are two types of monetary pricing: *fixed* and *variable.* There may be a fixed fee for users, or the price may vary depending on the user's ability to pay. When a donation-seeking organization will accept any size contribution, variable pricing is being used.

The broadest definition of price (valuation) must be used to develop nonprofit marketing strategies. Financial price, an exact dollar value, may or may not be charged for a nonprofit product. Economists recognize the giving up of alternatives as a cost. **Opportunity cost** is the value of the benefit that is given up by selecting one alternative rather than another. This traditional economic view of price means that if a nonprofit organization can convince someone to donate time to a cause or to change his or her behavior, then the alternatives given up are a cost to (or a price paid by) the individual. Volunteers who answer phones for a university counseling service or suicide hotline, for example, give up the time they could have spent studying or doing other things and the income they might have earned from working at a for-profit business organization.

For other nonprofit organizations, financial price is an important part of the marketing mix. Nonprofit organizations today are raising money by increasing the prices of their services or starting to charge for services if they have not done so before. They are using marketing research to determine what kinds of products people will pay for. Pricing strategies of nonprofit organizations often stress public and client welfare over equalization of costs and revenues. If additional funds are needed to cover costs, then donations, contributions, or grants may be solicited.

Opportunity cost Value of the benefit given up by choosing one alternative over another

Summary

Services are intangible products involving deeds, performances, or efforts that cannot be physically possessed. They are the result of applying human or mechanical efforts to people or objects. Services are a growing part of the U.S. economy. Services have six fundamental characteristics: intangibility, inseparability of production and consumption, perishability, heterogeneity, client-based relationships, and customer contact. Intangibility means that a service cannot be seen, touched, tasted, or smelled. Inseparability refers to the fact that the production of a service cannot be separated from its consumption by customers. Perishability means that unused service capacity of one time period cannot be stored for use in future time periods. Heterogeneity is variation in service quality. Client-based relationships are interactions with customers that lead to the repeated use of a service over time. Customer contact is the interaction between providers and customers needed to deliver a service.

Services are a very diverse group of products and can be classified along several dimensions. They can be viewed in terms of the market or type of customer they serve, degree of labor-intensiveness, degree of customer contact, skill of the service provider, or goal of the service

provider. Type of market can be either consumer or business. Degree of labor-intensiveness refers to people-based labor or equipment-based labor. Customer contact can be either high or low. Service providers can be either professionals or nonprofessionals. The service provider can have profit-related goals or nonprofit goals.

Service quality is the perception of how well a service meets or exceeds customer expectations. Service quality, although one of the most important aspects of services marketing, is very difficult for customers to evaluate. The reason for this difficulty is that services render benefits impossible to assess prior to the actual purchase and consumption—these include experience qualities, such as taste, satisfaction, or pleasure, and credence qualities, which customers may not be able to evaluate even after consumption. When competing services are very similar, service quality may be the only way for customers to distinguish between them. Service marketers can increase the quality of their services by following the four-step process of understanding customer needs, setting service specifications, ensuring good employee performance, and managing customers' service expectations.

Nonprofit marketing is marketing aimed at nonbusiness goals such as social causes. Nonprofit marketing uses most of the same concepts and approaches that apply to business situations. The chief beneficiary of a business enterprise is whoever owns or holds stock in the business, but the beneficiary of a nonprofit enterprise should be its clients, its members, or its public at large. The goals of a nonprofit organization reflect its unique philosophy or mission. Some nonprofit organizations have very controversial goals, but many organizations exist to further generally accepted social causes.

The marketing objective of nonprofit organizations is to obtain a desired response from a target market. Developing a nonprofit marketing strategy consists of defining and analyzing a target market and creating and maintaining a marketing mix. In nonprofit marketing, the product is usually an idea or a service. Distribution is not involved as much with movement of goods as with communication of ideas and the delivery of services. The result is a very short marketing channel. Promotion is very important to nonprofit marketing. Nonprofit organizations use advertising, publicity, and personal selling to communicate with clients and the public. Direct mail remains the primary means of fundraising for social services. Price is more difficult to define in nonprofit marketing because of opportunity costs and the difficulty of quantifying the values exchanged.

IMPORTANT TERMS

Service	Off-peak demand	Search qualities	Client publics
Intangibility	Heterogeneity	Experience qualities	General publics
Inseparability	Client-based relationships	Credence qualities	Opportunity cost
Perishability	Customer contact	Nonprofit marketing	
Peak demand	Service quality	Target public	

DISCUSSION AND REVIEW QUESTIONS

1. Identify the major unique service characteristics, and discuss the marketing problems that derive from these unique characteristics.
2. Choose a service product, then explain how the major unique characteristics of services in general relate to this particular service.
3. Discuss the major ways by which service products can be classified.
4. Analyze a cleaning service in terms of the five classification schemes and discuss the implications for marketing mix development.
5. What is service quality?
6. Why do customers experience difficulty in judging service quality?
7. Identify and discuss the five components of service quality. How do customers evaluate these components?
8. What is the significance of tangibles in service marketing?
9. How do search, experience, and credence qualities affect the way customers view and evaluate services?
10. What steps should a service company take to provide exceptional service quality?
11. How does nonprofit marketing differ from marketing in for-profit organizations?
12. What are the differences among clients, publics, and customers? What is the difference between a target public and a target market?
13. Discuss the development of a marketing strategy for a university. What marketing decisions must be made as the strategy is developed?

APPLICATION QUESTIONS

1. You are the owner of a new service business. What is your service? Be creative. What are some of the most important considerations in developing the service, training salespeople, and communicating to potential customers about your service?
2. Service products may be categorized by market, degree of labor intensiveness, intensity of customer contact, provider skill level, and goal of provider. Identify a service product in each category and indicate why it would be classified in that category.
3. In advertising intangible services, a company often must use symbols to represent the offered product. Identify three service product organizations you see in outdoor advertising. What symbols are used to represent their services? What message do the symbols convey to potential customers?
4. Delivering consistently high-quality service is difficult for service marketers. Describe an instance when you received high-quality service and an instance when you experienced low-quality service. What contributed to your perception of high quality? of low quality?

Case 12.1 Fireworks by Grucci Entertains America

Accompanied by the sounds of Jerry Lee Lewis's "Great Balls of Fire," showers of red, blue, green, and white fill the night sky. Golden comets criss-cross the dark to Bruce Springsteen's "Born in the U.S.A." Startled crowds gasp in admiration as Fireworks by Grucci does business as usual. For almost 150 years, the Grucci family has been in the business of entertaining audiences with fireworks displays. At the Olympics, three U.S. presidential inaugurations, the Columbus Voyage Quincentennial, even at an Yves Saint Laurent champagne gala, Fireworks by Grucci was there.

In 1900, the family-owned, family-run firm moved to New York from Bari, Italy, where Angelo Lanzetta had established it in 1850. In 1929, Lanzetta's nephew, Felix Grucci, took over the organization, renaming it the New York Pyrotechnic Company. Over the next two decades, Grucci gained a reputation as a master of his art, inventing the stringless shell, which made fireworks less dangerous by eliminating burning fallout, and creating inventive and unique displays. Although many fireworks producers disappeared during the 1960s, when demand for fireworks displays waned, Fireworks by Grucci, as the company was by then called, survived.

In the 1970s, two events transformed Grucci from a moderately successful mom-and-pop operation into a world-class, world-renowned firm. In 1976, cities across America booked Grucci for U.S. Bicentennial celebrations. In 1979, the company became the first American entry to win the Gold Medal at the Monte Carlo International Fireworks Championship, defeating competitors from Denmark, France, Italy, and Spain. Winning this competition earned Grucci the title "First Family of Fireworks." Although the Grucci family was struck by tragedy when two family members died in an explosion that destroyed the Grucci factory, the company was able to recover from its losses. Today, Fireworks by Grucci employs 30 full-time and 400 part-time workers and stages about 300 shows a year.

Grucci's clients have come to expect dazzling pyrotechnics, stunning choreography, and precise synchronization between music and visual displays. To meet these expectations, Grucci custom designs every production. Each firework is hand built, and music is recorded and edited at a professional sound studio. Grucci specialties include split comets, ring shells, butterflies with crosses, swaying leaves and meteors, splendid white flowers, serpents, and happy gates (boxes that fire a hundred shells of various colors simultaneously). To set up a major fireworks production involving such unique creations, Grucci's trained pyrotechnicians require about 7 miles of cable, 25 tons of sand, enough lumber to build a small home, as many as 6,000 launching tubes, and about 200 hours of labor.

Although productions start at about $4,000, city- and state-class events cost about $800 a minute. For a twenty-minute fireworks display, this rate adds up to nearly $16,000. To stage world-class productions, such as a presidential inauguration, the Grucci meter ticks away at $2,000 per minute. Along with stunning and memorable spectacles, part of Grucci's service to its clients is to provide them with fireworks display liability insurance, along with advice on publicizing their events.

To promote the company's products, the Gruccis rely primarily on word-of-mouth communication and on brand awareness established by media coverage of their premier shows. They do not advertise. When the vice president for marketing meets with potential clients, whether they be communities or businesses, he uses a videotape of previous productions to help him explain the firm's services. This low-key approach has persuaded customers like Lever Brothers, PepsiCo, and Maxwell House Coffee to pay $20,000 to $50,000 for shows at sales meetings and other corporate events.

In the $75-million-a-year fireworks market, the Gruccis compete with the Souza family's Pyro-Spectaculars, and the Zambelli's International Fireworks. When economic conditions worsen, the competition stiffens. Many communities can no longer afford to pay for the kind of extravaganza these companies produce. Nevertheless, Grucci's vice president declares that his family members are entertainers whose shows will go on in rain, snow, sleet, wind, and cold—everything except fog. States Felix Grucci, Jr., "It is gratifying when you can deliver smiles on faces."[29]

Questions for Discussion

1. Discuss the six characteristics of services shown in Table 12.1 as they relate to the services provided by Fireworks by Grucci.
2. In what ways do customers evaluate the quality of Grucci's service?
3. Evaluate the methods that Fireworks by Grucci uses to promote its services.

Case 12.2   **Harrah's Casinos Gambles on Its Strategy**

Americans who love to gamble have many legal ways to indulge. They can buy a lottery ticket at the local supermarket, cruise for an evening on a gambling riverboat, or fly to Las Vegas for three days of casino games. In fact, to find a casino, bettors don't even have to go to Las Vegas or Atlantic City anymore. Twenty-six states permit casino gambling in some form, and more Americans go to gambling casinos each year than attend major league baseball games or applaud Broadway shows. Eighty-two percent of those responding to a recent study agreed that going to a casino would be "a fun night out." Harrah's Entertainment Company, America's largest casino enterprise, welcomes the growing appeal of casino gaming. The company's goal is to establish itself as a nationally recognized brand name casino operation in a highly-competitive market by delivering quality entertainment and superior customer service.

Gambling has been part of life in the United States since the country began. The funds to launch the *Mayflower*, raise the colonial army, and found Harvard, Yale, and Dartmouth came from lotteries. Until the early twentieth century, legal gaming flourished all over the United States. However, when Americans began associating gaming with corruption and violence, the law stepped in. In 1931, Nevada legalized casino gambling and maintained a monopoly on betting until 1976, when New Jersey became the second state to make the activity legal. Between 1982 and 1994, U.S. casino revenues rose from $1.5 billion to $16.5 billion a year. Because of the growing number of gambling alternatives and intense industry competition, assert many experts, the days are over when companies could simply open a casino and be certain people would come.

In operation since 1937, Harrah's today competes with gaming giants such as Circus Circus, Caesar's World, Mirage Resorts, Bally's, Hilton, and many others, including a growing number of Native American–run casinos. To make their hotels or resorts appeal to the largest audience, many casino companies are marketing themselves as family vacation destinations complete with theme parks and children's activities. What these organizations are quickly discovering is that families come, but after a day of entertaining kids, parents are too worn out to try their luck in the casino at night.

Harrah's is convinced that people don't go to casinos to zip down waterslides or play virtual reality video games; they go to interact with adults and enjoy themselves gambling. Harrah's executive vice president of marketing reports that his company doesn't urge Mom and Dad to bring the kids. Instead, the company focuses on making gaming inside the casino an exciting entertainment experience for adults. Harrah's executives believe that gambling is not about getting rich—it is about having fun. At the front entrance to Harrah's Las Vegas casino, dealers "capture" passersby, encouraging them to come in. Inside, dealers in the Fun Pit joke with customers, ring bells, whack players on the head with rubber hammers, and joust with collapsible swords. "Celebration stations" serve drinks and cake, and the "win committee" sprinkle's "lucky dust" on winners and awards medals reading, "I won at Harrah's." When someone hits the jackpot at the slot machines, Harrah's employees bring over a cellular phone, and the winner can call anyone, anywhere.

To set themselves apart from an ever-increasing crowd of rivals, Caesar's World is putting a Planet Hollywood restaurant in each of its casinos, Hilton and Viacom's Paramount Parks are teaming up to create a Star Trek Virtual Reality attraction in Las Vegas, and Harrah's is concentrating on providing the highest standard of customer service. It maintains a guest satisfaction rating that tracks customer opinions and is the first casino to extend to its customers an "unconditional guarantee of service excellence." During one recent six-month period, the company surveyed 13,000 patrons concerning their Harrah's experience. Seventy-eight percent of those who visited land-based casinos and 74 percent of those who played on the company's riverboats reported that their overall experience had been one of the best or better than at Harrah's competitors.

Not every Harrah's effort is quite as satisfying. For example, attendance at Harrah's New Orleans casino during its first four months of operation fell far below expectations. The casino's executives blame flooding, the slow summer season, and insufficient marketing for grand opening difficulties. Although they plan to step up marketing efforts, they don't plan to change the company's strategy.[30]

Questions for Discussion

1. Using the categories in Table 12.2, classify the gaming services provided by Harrah's.
2. Describe Harrah's attitude toward the service quality issue.
3. What strategy is Harrah's using to differentiate its product mix from those of its competitors? Evaluate this strategy.

STRATEGIC CASE 3

Mattel Toys Sings, "Oh, You Beautiful Doll!"

Teenage Mutant Ninja Turtles are on their way out. Mighty Morphin Power Rangers are fading fast. Toys are a notoriously fickle business, and trying to predict which toy is going to be popular is more an art than a science. Last year's hit can turn into this year's loser. Mattel's Barbie doll, however, goes on and on. When Mattel introduced Barbie, toy buyers dismissed her as a passing fad. More than thirty-seven years have passed since then, and enough Barbies have been sold to circle the earth more than three and a half times if laid head to pointed toe. What makes Barbie the most successful brand name toy ever sold? By continually reinventing Barbie and by introducing imaginative brand extensions, Mattel keeps Barbie forever young.

Barbie Is Born

Mattel, Inc. started in 1945 as a small California toy manufacturer operating out of a converted garage. The company's first product was toy furniture. By 1952, Mattel was recording annual sales of more than $5 million and had expanded its line to include burp guns and musical toys. In 1959, Mattel changed forever the way little girls played with dolls by introducing the golden-haired Barbie doll, named after the owner's daughter. Along with her extensive and fashionable wardrobe and countless accessories, Barbie was an instant hit. Soon afterward, she acquired boyfriend Ken, named for the owner's son. Although her outfits have changed over the years, Barbie is still at the top of her form. Best friend to millions of girls around the world, the foot-high doll with the improbable figure generates annual sales of $1.4 billion worldwide. Thanks primarily to Barbie, Mattel has become the toy industry's market leader.

A Barbie for Everyone

Although the best-selling Barbie in history is Totally Hair Barbie, a doll with floor-length hair that turns pink when sprayed, there are more than ninety versions of the doll, priced anywhere from $8 to $250. Barbie comes as an astronaut, a doctor, a horsewoman, a presidential candidate, an air force lieutenant colonel, an Egyptian queen, or even an Olympic gymnast. Super Barbie comes complete with a pink holographic cape. Wearing a purser's outfit, Carnival Barbie carries a tote bag that prominently displays the Carnival Cruise Line logo. Mattel recently introduced Baywatch Barbie, based on the popular syndicated television show. Portrayed as an animal lover and ecocrusader, Baywatch Barbie takes her role as a beach beauty seriously.

When Barbie turned 35, Mattel introduced a reproduction of the original model complete with pony tail and black and white striped bathing suit. A talking teacher Barbie says "Great answer!" or "Try again" when a child pushes her hidden button. There is a soft-body version called Bedtime Barbie and a child-size Barbie in a wearable wedding dress. Barbie's outfits (some of which are created by fashion designers like Christian Dior, Yves St. Laurent, and Donna Karan) all have catchy names such as "Easter Parade," and "Roman Holiday."

To keep Barbie company, Mattel added not only Ken, but also an ever-expanding and diverse group of friends and relatives. There are also Barbie dollhouses, Barbie sports cars, Barbie grocery stores and fast-food restaurants, and even Barbie motor homes that come with camping equipment and glow-in-the-dark stick-on stars. In the works is a piece of Barbie computer software called Barbie Fashion Designer. Girls will be able to print out fashions on fabric, cut them out, and dress their dolls.

With so many dolls and accessories available, toy store giant F.A.O. Schwarz recently designated an entire section of its New York store as the Barbie Boutique. The boutique carries products designed for the traditional little girl market as well as a section of products targeting older girls. In addition to the designated Barbie areas in Toys "R" Us outlets, Mattel plans to launch Barbie shops in 500 U.S. department stores.

Barbie's Plans for the Future

After conquering the hearts of preteen girls in the United States and Western Europe, Barbie went to Asia. When Mattel first brought her to Japan in 1979, the toy manufacturer had to make some changes in the all-American doll. Her face was too sophisticated and her makeup too heavy for Japanese tastes, so Barbie acquired a more wide-eyed, innocent look that appealed to Japanese consumers. Encouraged by Barbie's global successes, Mattel launched Barbie in Argentina, Venezuela, Portugal, and thirty-one other countries, including China, where she has been manufactured for years but never sold.

The fastest-growing segment of the Barbie empire is the collector market. For example, when Bloomingdale's offered limited-edition Donna Karan designer Barbies, stores sold 30,000 in three weeks. Although fans have sought vintage Barbies and accessories for years through collector's networks, until recently Mattel hasn't zealously targeted adults.

Increasingly aware of Barbie's appeal to grown-ups, however, Mattel launched its first-ever advertising campaign targeting nostalgic collectors who once played with the original. Print ads in *People* and women's magazines bear the tag line "You're never too old for Barbie," and a sweepstakes supports the campaign. Infomercials are proving to be a successful format for marketing collectible Barbie products, and Mattel hopes Barbie's new web site will succeed as well. Counting on the enthusiasm of the 53 million women outside the United States who enjoyed Barbies when they were younger, Mattel is also going after the international collectors market.

Barbie is aging well. The most successful brand-name toy ever sold, her appeal spans generations. Over 1.5 million Barbie dolls are sold every week, and the average three-to-ten-year-old American girl acquires two to three new Barbies a year. A recent study reveals that 98 percent of American households recognize the Barbie name. A doting 200,000 collectors hold conventions, join clubs, publish Barbie magazines, and advertise on the Internet. In an era of computer games and other battery-powered high-tech toys, a doll from the 1950s still accounts for over 37 percent of Mattel's sales.

Questions for Discussion

1. What actions have Mattel marketers taken to extend the life of Barbie and to maintain this product's success?
2. Describe the product positioning of Barbie.
3. Evaluate the brand equity of the Barbie brand.

295

Sources: Larry Carlat, "Queen of the Aisles," *Brandweek*, Feb. 12, 1996, pp. 20–22, 24, 26; Gary Hoover, Alta Campbell, and Patrick J. Spains, eds., *Hoover's Handbook of American Business* (Austin, Texas: Reference Press, 1995), pp. 732–734; Karen Benezra, "Toymakers & Animated Friends Take Heroic Steps Toward Girls," *Brandweek*, Feb. 20, 1995, p. 9; Elizabeth Stephenson, "Mattel Dolls Up Barbie for Adult Collectors," *Advertising Age*, Oct. 9, 1995, p. 44; James Bernstein, "Barbie's Still Queen in Retail Toyland," *Newsday*, Nov. 23, 1995, p. 57; Karen Benezra, "No Stopping the Rangers," *Adweek*, Superbrands Supplement, 1995, pp. 135–137; Elaine Underwood, "Carnival as Scent and as Barbie," *Brandweek*, Sept. 18, 1995, p. 4; Barbara Lippert, "Barb-Watch," *Adweek*, July 17, 1995, p. 54; "Toy Fair Attracts 120,000 Products and 22,000 Buyers," *Drug Topics*, Mar. 21, 1994, pp. 65–66; Eric Schine, "Mattel's Wild Race to Market," *Business Week*, Feb. 21, 1994, pp. 62–63; Judy Feldman, "The Top 10 Boomer Toys," *Money*, May 1994, p. 159; Cyndee Miller, "Finding Next Big Toy Is Not Child's Play," *Advertising Age*, May 23, 1994, p. 2; and Ann Marie Angebrandt, "An Old Friend Makes Good," *Asian Business*, Feb. 1994, p. 46.

Part 4

Distribution Decisions

Developing products that satisfy customers is important but not enough to guarantee successful marketing strategies. These products must also be available in adequate quantities in accessible locations at the times when customers desire them. The chapters in Part 4 deal with the distribution of products and the marketing channels and institutions that provide the structure for making products available. In Chapter 13 we discuss the structure and functions of marketing channels and present an overview of institutions that make up these channels. In Chapter 14 we analyze the types of wholesalers and their functions. In Chapter 15 we focus on retailing and retailers. Specifically, we examine the types of retailers, nonstore retailing, and strategic retailing issues. Finally, in Chapter 16 we analyze the decisions and activities associated with the physical distribution of products, such as order processing, materials handling, warehousing, inventory management, and transportation.

Chapter 13

Marketing Channels

O B J E C T I V E S

- To describe the nature and functions of marketing channels

- To identify the types of marketing channels

- To examine the major levels of marketing coverage

- To explain how supply chain management can facilitate distribution for the benefit of all channel members, especially customers

- To specify how channel integration can improve channel efficiency

- To explore the concepts of cooperation, conflict, and leadership in channel relationships

- To examine the legal issues affecting channel management

Electronics Boutique delivers the goods—wherever and whenever consumers desire.

*E*lectronics Boutique, based in West Chester, Pennsylvania, is a specialty retailer of video games, computer software and hardware, and accessories. Its 527 stores in the United States, Puerto Rico, United Kingdom, and Canada stock up to 2,500 different products from 250 suppliers. Getting the right product from the right supplier to the right store at the right time is crucial. Sales of video games, in particular, peak within the first week or two after release. When customers learn of the latest video game, they want it *now,* and if they don't find it at an Electronics Boutique outlet, they'll go to Software Etc., Babbage's, Toys "R" Us, or some other competitor. Distribution is therefore a critical element of Electronics Boutique's strategy for success. To ensure that the latest products are available in its stores, Electronics Boutique restocks each store daily and tries to get the hottest new releases into stores overnight.

One key to the chain's outstanding distribution strategy is the teamwork among its buyers and distribution staff. The relationship among these departments at other retailers is often adversarial, but at Electronics Boutique, they meet together daily to examine the previous day's sales records for each store, review new releases, map out a strategy for the day, and plan for next week and next month. The company refills part of its stock from a 120,000-square-foot distribution center in West Chester, which runs on a computerized order management program. The system also helps guide regional allocation, getting, for example, hockey-based games to New England and baseball games to Puerto Rico. However, new releases of video games are often shipped directly from the supplier to individual stores through a third-party shipping company, and even overnight through Airborne Express, to ensure the products are on the shelf.

Electronics Boutique's strategy has pushed its revenues sky high while helping hold its distribution costs to 2.8 percent of sales. Because of its leadership in fast cycle times, rapid restocking, and thorough customer service, Electronics Boutique was chosen as one of only three retailers to get advance releases of Sega's latest game, Saturn.[1]

Distribution The activities that make products available to customers when and where they want to purchase them

The rapid growth of Electronics Boutique is partially due to wise distribution decisions that led to changes in the company's marketing channels. The **distribution** component of the marketing mix focuses on the decisions and actions involved in making products available to consumers when and where they want to purchase them. Choosing which channels of distribution to use is a major decision in the development of marketing strategies.

This chapter describes and analyzes marketing channels. After discussing the nature of marketing channels and the need for intermediaries, we analyze the primary functions they perform. Next, we outline the types of marketing channels and explore how marketers determine the appropriate intensity of market coverage for a product. We also consider supply chain management and several forms of channel integration. Finally, after examining behavioral patterns within marketing channels, we look at several legal issues affecting channel management.

The Nature of Marketing Channels

Marketing channel A group of individuals and organizations directing products from producers to customers

A marketing channel (also called a channel of distribution or distribution channel) is a group of individuals and organizations that directs the flow of products from producers to customers. The major role of marketing channels is to make products available at the right time at the right place in the right quantities. Providing customer satisfaction should be the driving force behind marketing channel decisions. Buyers' needs and behavior are therefore important concerns of channel members.

Marketing intermediary A middleman linking producers to other middlemen or ultimate consumers through contractual arrangements or through the purchase and resale of products

Some marketing channels are direct—from producer straight to customer—but most channels of distribution have marketing intermediaries. A **marketing intermediary** (middleman) links producers to other middlemen or to ultimate consumers through contractual arrangements or through the purchase and reselling of products. Marketing intermediaries perform the activities described in Table 13.1. Wholesalers and retailers are examples of intermediaries. Wholesalers buy and resell products to other wholesalers, to retailers, and to industrial customers. Retailers purchase products and resell them to ultimate consumers. Chapters 14 and 15 discuss in greater detail the functions of wholesalers and retailers in marketing channels.

Marketing intermediaries, or channel members, share certain significant characteristics. Each member has different responsibilities within the overall structure of the channel. Mutual profit and success for channel members can be attained most readily when channel members cooperate to deliver satisfying products to customers.

Table 13.1 Marketing Channel Activities Performed by Intermediaries

Category of Marketing Activities	Possible Activities Required
Marketing information	Analyze information such as sales data in databases and information systems Perform or commission marketing research
Marketing management	Establish strategic plans for developing customer relationships and organizational productivity
Facilitating exchanges	Choose product assortments that match the needs of customers Cooperate with channel members to develop partnerships
Promotion	Set promotional objectives Coordinate advertising, personal selling, sales promotion, publicity, and packaging
Price	Establish pricing policies and terms of sales
Physical distribution	Manage transportation, warehousing, materials handling, inventory control, and communication

Although distribution decisions need not precede other marketing decisions, they are a powerful influence on the rest of the marketing mix. Channel decisions are critical because they determine a product's market presence and buyers' accessibility to the product. One reason that Nintendo of America has been more successful than its rival Sega is that Nintendo has a distribution advantage. Twenty-five percent of Nintendo's volume is sold at retailers where Sega is not on the shelves.[2] The strategic significance of channel decisions is further heightened because they entail long-term commitments. For example, it is usually easier to change prices or promotion than to change marketing channels.

Marketing channels serve many functions. Although some of these functions may be performed by a single channel member, most functions are accomplished through both independent and joint efforts of channel members. These functions include creating utility and facilitating exchange efficiencies.

■ *Marketing Channels Create Utility*

Marketing channels create three types of utility: time, place, and possession. Time utility is having products available when the customer wants them. Place utility is created by making products available in locations where customers wish to purchase them. Possession utility is created by the customer having access to the product to use or to store for future use. Possession utility can occur through ownership or through arrangements such as lease or rental agreements that give the customer the right to use the product. Channel members sometimes create form utility by assembling, preparing, or otherwise refining the product to suit individual customer needs.

■ *Marketing Channels Facilitate Exchange Efficiencies*

Marketing intermediaries can reduce the costs of exchanges by efficiently performing certain services or functions. Even if producers and buyers are located in the same city, there are costs associated with exchanges. As Figure 13.1 shows, when four buyers seek products from four producers, sixteen transactions are possible. If one intermediary serves

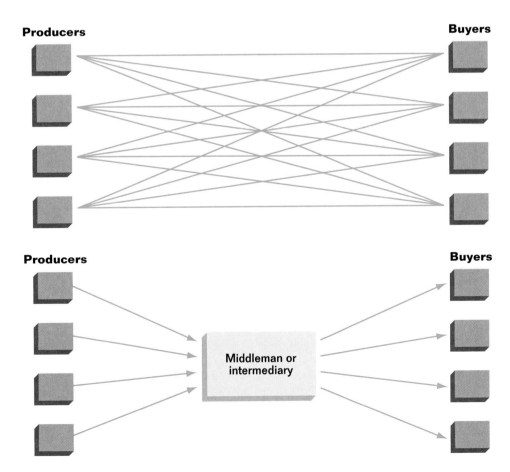

Figure 13.1
Efficiency in Exchanges Provided by an Intermediary

302

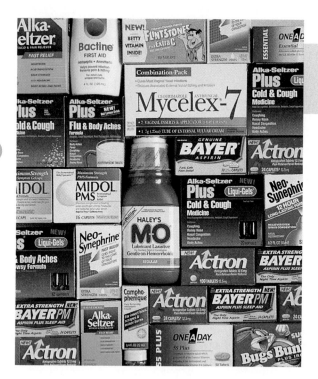

Figure 13.2
Wholesalers Provide Efficient Distribution
Bayer provides diverse consumer care products and promotes its line to wholesalers.

both producers and buyers, the number of transactions can be reduced to eight. Intermediaries are specialists in facilitating exchanges. They provide valuable assistance because of their access to, and control over, important resources used in the proper functioning of marketing channels. Bayer Corporation is able to provide a diverse line of consumer care products because of the efficient distribution of these products by wholesalers (see Figure 13.2).

Nevertheless, the press, consumers, public officials, and other marketers freely criticize intermediaries, especially wholesalers. Critics accuse wholesalers of being inefficient and parasitic. Consumers often wish to make the distribution channel as short as possible, assuming that the fewer the intermediaries, the lower the price. Because suggestions to eliminate wholesalers come from both ends of the marketing channel, they must be careful to perform only those marketing activities that are truly desired. To survive, they must be more efficient and more customer-focused than alternative marketing institutions.

Critics who suggest that eliminating wholesalers would lower consumer prices do not recognize that this would not eliminate the need for services that wholesalers provide. Although wholesalers can be eliminated, the functions they perform cannot. Other channel members would have to perform those functions, and customers would still have to fund them. In addition, all producers would have to deal directly with retailers or consumers, meaning that every producer would have to keep voluminous records and hire enough personnel to deal with a multitude of customers. Customers might end up paying a great deal more for products because prices would reflect the costs of less efficient channel members.

To illustrate wholesalers' efficient services, assume that all wholesalers have been eliminated. Because there are more than 1.5 million retail stores, a widely purchased consumer product—say, candy—would require an extraordinary number of sales contacts, possibly more than a million, to maintain the current level of product exposure. For example, Mars, Incorporated, would have to deliver candy, purchase and service thousands of vending machines, establish warehouses all over the country, and maintain fleets of trucks. Selling and distribution costs for candy would skyrocket. Instead of a few contacts with food brokers, large retail organizations, and merchant wholesalers, candy manufacturers would face thousands of expensive contacts with and shipments to smaller retailers. Such an operation would be highly inefficient, and costs would be passed on to consumers. Candy bars would cost more and be harder to find. Wholesalers are often more efficient and less expensive.

Types of Marketing Channels

*B*ecause marketing channels appropriate for one product may be less suitable for others, many different distribution paths have been developed. The various marketing channels can be classified generally as channels for consumer products or channels for industrial products.

■ *Channels for Consumer Products*

Figure 13.3 illustrates several channels used in the distribution of consumer products. Channel A describes the direct movement of goods from producer to consumers. Producers that sell goods directly from their factories to end users and ultimate customers are using direct-marketing channels. Although these channels are the simplest, they are not necessarily the most effective distribution method. Faced with the strategic choice of going directly to the customer or using intermediaries, a firm must evaluate the benefits to consumers from going direct to the market versus the transaction costs involved in using intermediaries.[3]

Channel B, which moves goods from the producer to a retailer and then to consumers, is a frequent choice of large retailers, for they can buy in quantity from manufacturers. Retailers such as Kmart and Sears sell clothing, stereos, and many other items purchased directly from producers. New automobiles and new college-level textbooks are also sold through this type of marketing channel. Primarily nonstore retailers such as L.L. Bean (see Inside Marketing on the next page) and J. Crew also use this type of channel.

A long-standing distribution channel, especially for consumer products, Channel C takes goods from the producer to a wholesaler, then to a retailer, and finally to consumers. It is a practical option for producers that sell to hundreds of thousands of consumers through thousands of retailers. A single producer finds it hard to do business directly with thousands of retailers. For example, consider the number of retailers marketing Wrigley's chewing gum. It would be extremely difficult, if not impossible, for Wrigley's to deal directly with each retailer that sells its brand of gum. Manufacturers of tobacco products, some home appliances, hardware, and many convenience goods sell their products to wholesalers, who then sell to retailers, who in turn do business with individual consumers.

Channel D—through which goods pass from producer to agents to wholesalers to retailers and then to consumers—is frequently used for products intended for mass distribution, such as processed foods. For example, to place its cracker line in specific retail outlets, a food processor may hire an agent (or a food broker) to sell the crackers to wholesalers. Wholesalers then sell the crackers to supermarkets, vending machine operators, and other retail outlets.

Contrary to popular opinion, then, a long channel may be the most efficient distribution channel for some consumer goods. When several channel intermediaries perform specialized functions, costs may be lower than when one channel member tries to perform them all.

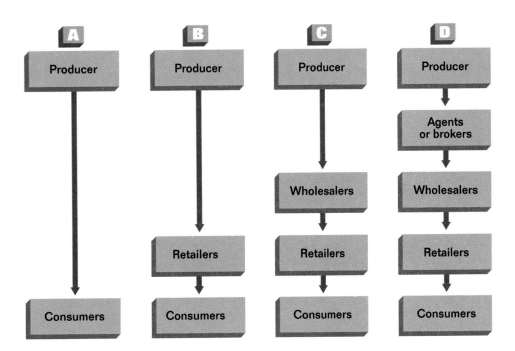

Figure 13.3
Typical Marketing Channels for Consumer Products

303

304

INSIDE MARKETING

At L.L. Bean, Quality and Service Never Go Out of Style

For more than eighty years, L.L. Bean's customers have eagerly pored over its catalogs, selecting from such outdoor items as the original Maine hunting shoe, the chamois cloth shirt, dog beds, and hand-painted cork decoys. Confident of receiving ordered items promptly, they know that if they are dissatisfied with a purchase for any reason, they can return it with no questions asked. What Leon Leonwood Bean knew when he started his company in 1912 has today become a watchword of American business—success depends on providing quality products and excellent customer service.

After suffering through too many hunting trips with wet feet, L.L. Bean created the waterproof, brown and blue Maine hunting shoe. He went on to develop and market other outdoor gear, for years testing each product himself before selling it. Today L.L. Bean offers 5,000 different products in twenty-three different catalogs, distributing about 100 million catalogs and filling more than 10 million orders a year. Yet experts and employees (even the president) continue to field-test every item L.L. Bean offers, and the firm maintains its 100 percent satisfaction guarantee.

Open for business 24 hours a day, 365 days a year, L.L. Bean's customer service department takes orders, handles returns, and provides order status information. It consistently ranks among the best companies providing telephone customer service. To minimize turnaround time between receiving orders and shipping them, L.L. Bean's central distribution center maintains a bar-coded inventory of all company products, processes all incoming and outgoing packages, and houses facilities for all monogramming and other customized finishing work.

L.L. Bean's slogan, "Get It Right the First Time," reflects its commitment to delivering orders both promptly and accurately. Even during a recent Christmas season when it was shipping some 134,000 packages a day, L.L. Bean maintained a 99 percent accuracy rate. Though faced with increasing competition and stagnant sales, L.L. Bean remains focused on quality merchandise, reasonable prices, and superior customer service.

Sources: Phyllis Berman and Amy Feldman, "Trouble in Bean Land," *Forbes,* July 6, 1992, pp. 42–43; Susan Chandler, "Strategies for the New Mail Order," *Business Week,* Dec. 19, 1994, p. 82; "L.L. Bean," *Direct Marketing,* Feb. 1992, pp. 16–17; L.L. Bean, press kit, 1993; Otis Port and Geoffrey Smith, "Quality: Small and Midsize Companies Seize the Challenge—Not a Moment Too Soon," *Business Week,* Nov. 30, 1992, pp. 66–72, 74–75; and "To Scream, Press '0'," *Business Week,* May 29, 1995, p. 4.

■ *Channels for Industrial Products*

Figure 13.4 shows four of the most common channels for industrial products. As with consumer products, manufacturers of industrial products sometimes work with more than one level of wholesalers.

Channel E illustrates the direct channel for industrial products. In contrast to consumer goods, more than half of all industrial products—especially expensive equipment (see Figure 13.5)—are sold through direct channels. Industrial buyers like to communicate directly with producers, especially when expensive or technically complex products are involved. For this reason, business buyers prefer to purchase expensive and highly complex mainframe computers directly from IBM, Cray, and other mainframe producers. Intel Corp. is establishing direct-marketing channels for selling its microprocessor chips to computer manufacturers.[4] In these circumstances, a customer wants the technical assistance and personal assurances that only a producer can provide.

The second industrial distribution channel (Channel F) involves an industrial distributor to facilitate exchanges between the producer and customer. An **industrial distributor** is an independent business organization that takes title to products and carries inventories. Industrial distributors usually sell standardized items, such as maintenance supplies, production tools, and small operating equipment. Some industrial distributors carry a wide variety of product lines; others specialize in one or a small number of lines. Industrial distributors can be most effectively used when a product has broad

Industrial distributor
An independent business organization that takes title to industrial products and carries inventories

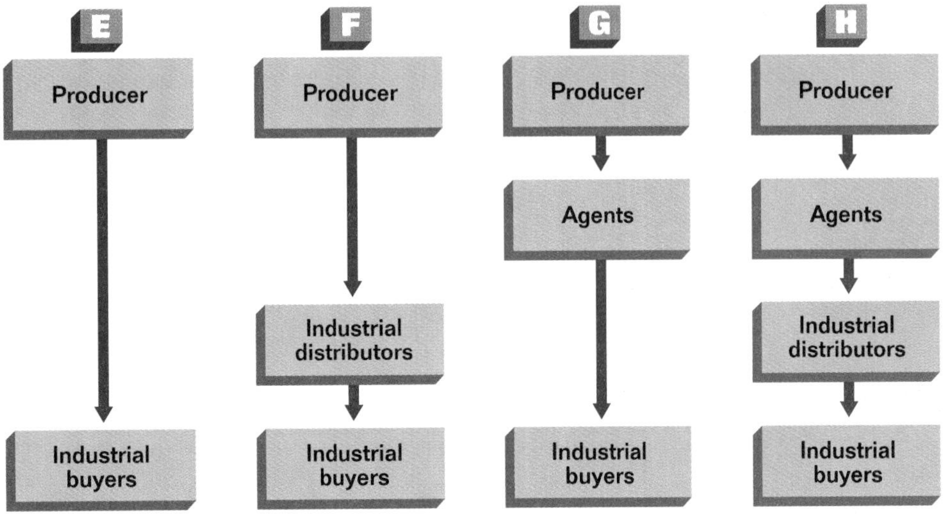

E F G H

Producer	Producer	Producer	Producer
		Agents	Agents
	Industrial distributors		Industrial distributors
Industrial buyers	Industrial buyers	Industrial buyers	Industrial buyers

Figure 13.4
Typical Marketing Channels for Industrial Products

market appeal, is easily stocked and serviced, is sold in small quantities, and is needed on demand to avoid high losses (as is a part for an assembly line machine).[5]

Industrial distributors offer sellers several advantages. They can perform the needed selling activities in local markets at relatively low cost to a manufacturer and reduce a producer's financial burden by providing customers with credit services. And because industrial distributors usually maintain close relationships with their customers, they are aware of local needs and can pass on market information to producers. By holding adequate inventories in their local markets, industrial distributors reduce the producers' capital requirements.

Using industrial distributors has several disadvantages, however. Industrial distributors may be difficult to control since they are independent firms. Because they often stock competing brands, an industrial producer cannot depend on them to sell a specific brand aggressively. Furthermore, industrial distributors maintain inventories, for which they incur numerous expenses; consequently, they are less likely to handle bulky items or

Figure 13.5
Direct Industrial Channel
Ford markets heavy duty cargo trucks directly to businesses for industrial uses.

306

items that are slow sellers relative to profit margin, need specialized facilities, or require extraordinary selling efforts. In some cases, industrial distributors lack the technical knowledge necessary to sell and service certain products.

The third industrial channel (Channel G) employs a manufacturers' agent or representative, an independent businessperson who sells complementary products of several producers in assigned territories and is compensated through commissions. Unlike an industrial distributor, a manufacturers' agent does not acquire title to the products and usually does not take possession. Acting as a salesperson on behalf of the producers, a manufacturers' agent has little or no latitude in negotiating prices or sales terms.

Using manufacturers' agents can benefit an industrial marketer. These agents usually possess considerable technical and market information and have an established set of customers. For an industrial seller with highly seasonal demand, a manufacturers' agent can be an asset because the seller does not have to support a year-round sales force. That manufacturers' agents are paid on a commission basis may also be an economical alternative for a firm that has highly limited resources and cannot afford a full-time sales force.

Certainly, the use of manufacturers' agents is not problem-free. Even though straight commissions may be cheaper, the seller may have little control over manufacturers' agents. Because of the compensation method, manufacturers' agents generally want to concentrate on their larger accounts. They are often reluctant to spend adequate time following up sales, to put forth special selling efforts, or to provide sellers with market information when such activities reduce the amount of productive selling time. Because they rarely maintain inventories, manufacturers' agents have a limited ability to provide customers with parts or repair services quickly.

Finally, Channel H includes both a manufacturers' agent and an industrial distributor between the producer and the industrial customer. This channel may be appropriate when the industrial marketer wishes to cover a large geographic area but maintains no sales force because of highly seasonal demand or because the firm cannot afford a sales force. This type of channel can also be useful for an industrial marketer that wants to enter a new geographic market without expanding the firm's existing sales force.

■ *Multiple Marketing Channels and Channel Alliances*

To reach diverse target markets, manufacturers may use several marketing channels simultaneously, each channel involving a different group of intermediaries. For example, a manufacturer uses multiple channels when the same product is directed to both consumers and industrial customers. When Del-Monte markets ketchup for household use, it is sold to supermarkets through grocery wholesalers or, in some cases, directly to retailers, whereas ketchup going to restaurants or institutions follows a different distribution channel. In some instances, a producer may prefer **dual distribution**: the use of two or more marketing channels for distributing the same products to the same target market. An example of dual distribution is a retailer that operates specialty stores and sends sale catalogs to customers according to their purchase habits. Catalogs that target mail-order customers may also influence store traffic. Through dual distribution, the firm can maximize market exposure.[6] Kellogg sells its cereals directly to large retail grocery chains and to food wholesalers that, in turn, sell them to retailers. Dual distribution can cause dissatisfaction among wholesalers and smaller retailers when they must compete with large retail grocery chains that make direct purchases from manufacturers like Kellogg. The practice of dual distribution recently has drawn considerable scrutiny from those who consider it anticompetitive.[7] The legal dimensions of dual distribution are discussed later in this chapter.

A **strategic channel alliance** exists when the products of one organization are distributed through the marketing channels of another organization. The products are often similar with respect to target markets or product uses, but they are not direct competitors. For example, a brand of bottled water might be distributed through a marketing channel for soft drinks, or a domestic cereal producer might form a strategic channel alliance with a European food processor. Alliances can provide benefits for both the organization that owns the marketing channel and the company whose brand is being distributed through the channel.

Dual distribution
The use of two or more channels to distribute the same product to the same target market

Strategic channel alliance
Distributing the products of one organization through the marketing channels of another

Intensity of Market Coverage

*I*n addition to deciding which marketing channels to use to distribute a product, marketers must determine the intensity of coverage a product should get—that is, the number and kinds of outlets in which it will be sold. This decision depends on the characteristics of the product and the target market. To achieve the desired intensity of market coverage, distribution must correspond to behavior patterns of buyers. Chapter 9 divided consumer products into three categories—convenience products, shopping products, and specialty products—according to how consumers make purchases. In considering products for purchase, consumers take into account replacement rate, product adjustment (services), duration of consumption, time required to find the product, and similar factors.[8] These variables directly affect the intensity of market coverage. Three major levels of market coverage are intensive, selective, and exclusive distribution.

■ *Intensive Distribution*

Intensive distribution
Using all available outlets to distribute a product

In **intensive distribution,** all available outlets are used for distributing a product. Intensive distribution is appropriate for convenience products such as bread, chewing gum, beer, and newspapers. Convenience products have a high replacement rate and require almost no service. To meet these demands, intensive distribution is necessary, and multiple channels may be used to sell through all possible outlets. To consumers, availability means a store located nearby and minimum time necessary to search for the product at the store. Sales may have a direct relationship to availability. Successful sale of products such as bread and milk at service stations or of gasoline at convenience grocery stores illustrates that availability of these products is more important than the nature of the outlet. Producers of consumer packaged items such as Procter & Gamble rely on intensive distribution for many of their products (for example, soaps, detergents, food and juice products, and personal care products) because consumers want availability provided quickly.

■ *Selective Distribution*

Selective distribution
Using only some available outlets to distribute a product

In **selective distribution,** only some available outlets in an area are chosen to distribute a product. Selective distribution is appropriate for shopping products. Durable goods such as television sets and stereos usually fall into this category. These products are more expensive than convenience goods, and consumers are willing to spend more time visiting several retail outlets to compare prices, designs, styles, and other features.

Selective distribution is desirable when a special effort—such as customer service from a channel member—is important. Shopping products require differentiation at the point of purchase. To motivate retailers to provide adequate presale service, selective distribution and company-owned stores are often used. Many industrial products are sold on a selective basis to maintain some control over the distribution process. For example, agricultural herbicides are distributed on a selective basis because dealers must offer services to buyers, such as instructions about how to apply herbicides safely or the option of having the dealer apply the herbicide. Evinrude outboard motors are sold by dealers on a selective basis.

■ *Exclusive Distribution*

Exclusive distribution
Using a single outlet in a fairly large geographic area to distribute a product

In **exclusive distribution,** only one outlet is used in a relatively large geographic area. Exclusive distribution is suitable for products purchased rather infrequently, consumed over a long period of time, or requiring service or information to fit them to buyers' needs. It is also used for expensive, high-quality products such as Porsche automobiles (see Figure 13.6). It is not appropriate for convenience products and many shopping products.

Exclusive distribution is often used as an incentive to sellers when only a limited market is available for products. For example, automobiles such as the Bentley, made by Rolls-Royce, are sold on an exclusive basis. Exclusive distribution affords a company tighter

Figure 13.6
Exclusive Distribution
Porsche utilizes
exclusive distribution
for its luxury cars.

**Like peanut butter
to the roof of your mouth.**

image control because the types of distributors and retailers that distribute the product are closely monitored.[9] A producer using exclusive distribution generally expects dealers to carry a complete inventory, send personnel for sales and service training, participate in promotional programs, and provide excellent customer service. Some products are appropriate for exclusive distribution when first introduced, but as competitors enter the market and the product moves through its life cycle, other types of market coverage and distribution channels often become necessary. A problem that can arise with exclusive distribution (and also selective distribution) is that unauthorized resellers acquire and sell products, violating the agreement between a manufacturer and its exclusive authorized dealers.

Supply Chain Management

Supply chain management
Long-term partnerships among
marketing channel members to
reduce inefficiencies, costs, and
redundancies in order to satisfy
customers

*A*n important function of the marketing channel is the joint effort of all channel members to create a supply chain, a total distribution system that serves customers and creates a competitive advantage. **Supply chain management** refers to long-term partnerships among channel members working together to reduce inefficiencies, costs, and redundancies in the entire marketing channel in order to satisfy customers.[10]

Supply chain management involves manufacturing, research, sales, advertising, shipping, and most of all, cooperation and understanding of tradeoffs throughout the whole channel to achieve the optimal level of efficiency and service.[11] Traditional marketing channels tend to focus on producers, wholesalers, retailers, and customers, whereas the supply chain is a broader concept that also includes facilitating agencies such as component parts suppliers, shipping companies, communication companies, and other organizations that take part in marketing exchanges. Thus, the supply chain includes all entities that facilitate product distribution and benefit from cooperative efforts.

Traditionally, buyers and sellers have taken an adversarial approach to negotiating purchases, with the seller striving to minimize costs and maximize revenue from the sale, and the buyer trying to minimize both.[12] Supply chain management, however, is helping more firms realize that optimizing the supply chain costs through partnerships will improve all members' profits. All parties should focus on cooperating to reduce the costs of all affected channel members. When the buyer, the seller, marketing intermediaries, and facilitating agencies work together, the cooperative relationship results in compromise and adjustments that meet customers' needs regarding delivery, scheduling, packaging, or other requirements.

Supply chains start with the customer and require the cooperation of channel members to satisfy customer requirements. For example, Home Depot, North America's largest home-improvement retailer, is re-engineering itself to become more efficient in inventory control, security, and information systems. The company's goal is to help its suppliers improve their productivity and thereby supply Home Depot with better quality products at less cost for the benefit of its customers. In an effort that includes about twenty competitors, including Wal-Mart, Handy Andy, and other home centers, the company has suggested a cooperative partnership so that regional trucking companies making deliveries can provide better service, faster delivery, and greater efficiency in their operations. Home Depot also made suggestions for standardizing packaging and delivery that saved its suppliers millions of dollars.[13]

Most companies do not set out to develop a supply chain, but like Home Depot they see a need to rework the way they serve their customers. Often, there is a need to increase the quality of a good or service, which results in improvement goals such as reducing the time from production to customer purchase, reducing transportation costs, or reducing information management or administrative costs. Achieving these goals for a more competitive position often requires that channel members cooperate and share information, as well as accommodate one another's needs.

Technology has dramatically improved the capability for supply chain management on a global basis. The information technology revolution, in particular, has created a virtually seamless distribution process for matching inventory needs to customers' requirements.[14] With integrated information sharing among channel members, costs can be reduced, service can be improved, and value provided to the customer can be enhanced (see Figure 13.7). Through supply chain management, Wal-Mart has all but eliminated the statement, "Sorry, this item is not in stock." The key to Wal-Mart's success is the use of bar-code and electronic data interchange (EDI) technology, extending from the firm's suppliers to the warehouse to the customer at the store checkout. Tools such as electronic billing, purchase order verification, bar-code technology, and image processing integrate needed data into the supply chain and improve overall performance.[15]

Supply chain management should not be considered just a new buzzword. Reducing inventory and transportation costs, speeding order cycle times, cutting administrative and handling costs, and improving customer service—these improvements provide rewards for *all* channel members.[16] The rewards will come as companies determine their position in the supply chain, identify their partners and their roles, and establish partnerships that focus on customer relationships.

Figure 13.7
Integrated Information
Sharing Computer Associates has developed an inventory management software allowing SEGA of America, Inc. to fill its orders to retailers faster and more accurately.

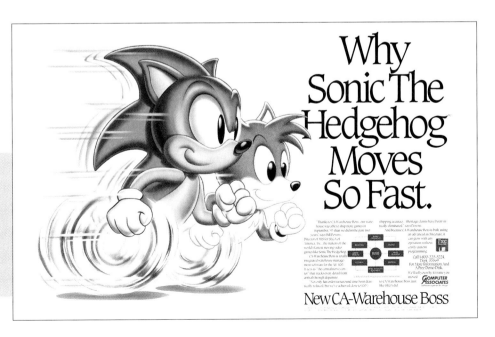

To fulfill the potential of effective supply chain management may require consolidation of channels (through channel integration) as well as channel cooperation, management of channel conflict, and channel leadership.

■ *Channel Integration*

Channel functions may be transferred between intermediaries and to producers and even customers. Channel members can either combine and control most activities or pass them on to another channel member. However, the channel member cannot eliminate functions; unless buyers themselves perform the functions, they must pay for the labor and resources needed for the functions to be performed.

Many marketing channels are determined by consensus. Producers and intermediaries coordinate efforts for mutual benefit. Some marketing channels, however, are organized and controlled by a single leader, which can be a producer, a wholesaler, or a retailer. Channel leaders may establish channel policies and coordinate development of the marketing mix. Wal-Mart, for example, is a channel leader for many of its Sam's brand private label products. But Wal-Mart has more of a partnership relationship with Procter & Gamble for P&G's consumer products.

Various channel links or stages may be combined under the management of a channel leader either horizontally or vertically. Integration may stabilize supply, reduce costs, and increase coordination of channel members.

Vertical Channel Integration   **Vertical channel integration** combines two or more stages of the channel under one management. This may occur when one member of a marketing channel purchases the operations of another member or simply performs the functions of another member, eliminating the need for that intermediary as a separate entity. For example, Warner Bros., the television and movie production unit of Time Warner, Inc., sells items such as cookie jars, puzzles, photo albums, and stuffed animals featuring its popular Animaniacs cartoon characters directly through its own retail outlets. Warner has also created distribution systems to get its cartoon characters, such as Pinky and the Brain and Sylvester and Tweety, directly to the public. Previously broadcasting many of its children's cartoon programs over the Fox network, Warner now runs these shows on its own recently launched WB network.[17]

Whereas members of conventional channel systems work independently, participants in vertical channel integration coordinate efforts to reach a desired target market. In this more progressive approach to distribution, channel members regard other members as extensions of their own operations. Vertically integrated channels are often more effective against competition because of increased bargaining power, the ability to inhibit competitors, and the sharing of information and responsibilities.[18] At one end of an integrated channel, a manufacturer might provide advertising and training assistance, and the retailer at the other end would buy the manufacturer's products in large quantities and actively promote them.

In the past, integration has been successfully institutionalized in marketing channels called **vertical marketing systems (VMS),** in which a single channel member coordinates or manages channel activities to achieve efficient, low-cost distribution aimed at satisfying target market customers. Vertical integration brings most or all stages of the marketing channel under common ownership or control. The Limited, a retail clothing chain, uses a wholly owned subsidiary, Mast Industries, as its primary supply source. Such marketing channel partnerships strive for some of the same efficiencies of a vertically integrated marketing system but without common ownership.[19] Radio Shack operates as a vertical marketing system, encompassing both wholesale and retail functions. Because efforts of individual channel members are combined in a VMS, marketing activities can be coordinated for maximum effectiveness and economy, without duplication of services. Vertical marketing systems are also competitive, accounting for a growing share of retail sales in consumer goods.

Most vertical marketing systems take one of three forms: corporate, administered, or contractual. The *corporate VMS* combines all stages of the marketing channel, from producers to consumers, under a single owner. For example, The Limited established a corporate VMS operating corporate-owned production facilities and retail stores.

Vertical channel integration Combining two or more stages of the marketing channel under one management

Vertical marketing systems (VMS) Marketing channels managed by a single channel member

Supermarket chains that own food-processing plants, as well as large retailers that purchase wholesaling and production facilities, are other examples of corporate VMSs.

In an *administered VMS*, channel members are independent, but a high level of interorganizational management is achieved by informal coordination. Members of an administered VMS may, for example, adopt uniform accounting and ordering procedures and cooperate in promotional activities for the benefit of all partners. Although individual channel members maintain autonomy, as in conventional marketing channels, one channel member (such as a producer or large retailer) dominates the administered VMS, so that distribution decisions take into account the whole system. Because of its size and power, Intel exercises a strong influence over distributors and manufacturers in its marketing channels, as do Kellogg (cereal) and Magnavox (television and other electronic products).

Under a *contractual VMS*, the most popular type of vertical marketing system, channel members are linked by legal agreements spelling out each member's rights and obligations. Franchise organizations, such as McDonald's and KFC, are contractual VMSs. Other contractual VMSs include wholesaler-sponsored groups, such as IGA (Independent Grocers' Alliance) stores, in which independent retailers band together under the contractual leadership of a wholesaler. Retailer-sponsored cooperatives, which own and operate their own wholesalers, are a third type of contractual VMS.

Horizontal channel integration Combining institutions at the same level of operation under one management

Horizontal Channel Integration   Combining institutions at the same level of operation under one management constitutes **horizontal channel integration.** An organization may integrate horizontally by merging with other organizations at the same level in a marketing channel. The owner of a dry cleaning firm might buy and combine several other existing dry cleaning establishments. Horizontal integration may enable a firm to generate sufficient sales revenue to integrate vertically as well.

Although horizontal integration permits efficiencies and economies of scale in purchasing, marketing research, advertising, and specialized personnel, it is not always the most effective method of improving distribution. Problems of size often follow, resulting in decreased flexibility, difficulties in coordination, and the need for additional marketing research and large-scale planning. Unless distribution functions for the various units can be performed more efficiently under unified management than under the previously separate managements, horizontal integration will neither reduce costs nor improve the competitive position of the integrating firm.

■ *Channel Cooperation, Conflict, and Leadership*

Each channel member performs a different role in the system and agrees (implicitly or explicitly) to accept certain rights, responsibilities, rewards, and sanctions for nonconformity. Moreover, each channel member holds certain expectations of other channel members. Retailers, for instance, expect wholesalers to maintain adequate inventories and deliver goods on time. Wholesalers expect retailers to honor payment agreements and keep them informed of inventory needs.

Channel partnerships facilitate effective supply chain management, with each partner agreeing on objectives, policies, and procedures for ordering and physical distribution of the supplier's products.[20] A primary goal of channel partnerships is to re-engineer processes to decrease the overall costs of the distribution system, shorten the time required to replenish inventories, and reduce the amount of inventory carried in the marketing channel.[21] Such partnerships eliminate redundancies and reassign tasks for maximum systemwide efficiency. One of the best-known partnerships is the relationship between Wal-Mart and Procter & Gamble. P&G locates some of its staff near Wal-Mart's purchasing department in Bentonville, Arkansas, to establish and maintain the supply chain. P&G has also assigned a separate sales team to Kmart. At this point, most suppliers have not been willing or able to make this level of commitment. In this section we discuss channel member behavior, including cooperation, conflict, and leadership, which marketers must understand in order to make effective channel decisions.

Channel Cooperation   Channel cooperation is vital if each member is to gain something from other members.[22] By cooperating, retailers, wholesalers, and suppliers can speed up inventory replenishment, improve customer service, and cut the costs of bringing products to the consumer.[23] Without cooperation, neither overall channel goals nor member goals can be realized. All channel members must recognize and understand that the success of one firm in the channel depends, in part, on other firms in the channel. Thus marketing channel members should take actions that provide a coordinated effort to satisfy market requirements. Channel cooperation leads to greater trust among channel members and improves the overall functioning of the channel.[24] Increased cooperation also leads to more satisfying relationships among channel members.[25]

There are several ways to improve channel cooperation. If a marketing channel is viewed as a unified supply chain, competing with other systems, then individual members will be less likely to take actions that create disadvantages for other members. Similarly, channel members should agree to direct efforts toward common objectives so that channel roles can be structured for maximum marketing effectiveness, which in turn can help members achieve individual objectives. This cooperative spirit has led VF Corporation, Levi Strauss, and other leading manufacturers to form "quick response partnerships" with both discounters and department stores to replenish inventory and develop joint promotion with advertisements in trade publications.[26] It is crucial to define each channel member's tasks precisely. This provides a basis for reviewing the intermediaries' performance and helps reduce conflicts because each channel member knows exactly what is expected of it.

**Figure 13.8
Avoiding Channel
Conflict** Meyer
Tomatoes offers a
direct sales program
and specialized con-
sumer packaging,
bypassing wholesalers.

Channel Conflict   Although all channel members work toward the same general goal—distributing products profitably and efficiently—members may sometimes disagree about the best methods for attaining this goal. However, if self-interest creates misunderstanding about role expectations, the end result is frustration and conflict for the whole channel. Inside Marketing describes a channel conflict between Rubbermaid and Wal-Mart. For individual organizations to function together, each channel member must clearly communicate and understand role expectations. Communication difficulties are a potential form of channel conflict because ineffective communication leads to frustration, misunderstandings, and ill-coordinated strategies.[27]

Channel conflicts also arise when dealers overemphasize competing products or diversify into product lines traditionally handled by other, more specialized, intermediaries. Sometimes conflict develops because producers strive to increase efficiency by circumventing intermediaries, as is happening in marketing channels for microcomputer software. Many software-only stores are establishing direct relationships with software producers, bypassing wholesale distributors altogether. Some dishonest retailers are also pirating software or making unauthorized copies, thus cheating other channel members out of their due compensation. Produce companies sometimes promote directly to retailers, also bypassing wholesalers (see Figure 13.8).

When a producer that traditionally used franchised dealers broadens its retailer base to include other types of retailer outlets, considerable conflict can arise. Goodyear intensified its market coverage by allowing Sears and Discount Tire to market Goodyear tires. While this action significantly increased the company's sales revenues, it also greatly angered 2,500 independent Goodyear dealers.[28]

Although there is no single method for resolving conflict, partnerships can be reestablished if two conditions are met. First, the role of each channel member must be specified. To minimize misunderstanding, all members must be able to expect unambiguous, agreed-on performance levels

**YOU'VE BEEN BUYING
MEYER TOMATOES
FOR MORE THAN
40 YEARS**

As one of the largest grower/shippers of tomatoes in the West, it's likely that if you sell tomatoes, you've bought some of ours. Now, our direct sales program makes that easier to do.

We grow and ship the high quality, long-shelf-life tomato varieties you're accustomed to handling –

mature greens, vine-ripes, cherry tomatoes and romas – and we can supply them in a variety of packages convenient to the way you do business.

For quality supply year round, call the people who know tomatoes. Meyer. For more than forty years, the leader in quality produce.

MEYER

For information on our Consumer Packaging
Call Dave Golla, Director of Sales at 800-835-3231

Meyer Tomatoes · King City, CA 93930 · Tel. 408-385-4047 · Fax 408-385-3883

INSIDE MARKETING

Can Rubbermaid Bounce Back?

Rubbermaid produces 5,000 products, from household goods such as ice cube trays and wastebaskets to specialty products like equipment carts for janitors and bathtub seats for the elderly. These products are sold through 100,000 Wal-Mart, Kmart, and other retail stores. Wal-Mart, in fact, accounts for 15 percent of Rubbermaid's sales through its 2,180 U.S. stores and is Rubbermaid's biggest customer. Although Rubbermaid generates sales of $2.2 billion, it must meet a demanding goal—to grow by 15 percent annually, or to double in size every five years. That goal has recently brought the firm into conflict with some of its retailer customers.

Most of Rubbermaid's products are made from pellets of petroleum-based resins, which it buys by the railcar load—100 railcars a week. However, in 1994, increasing global demand for resins drove up their price to the point where it almost doubled in eighteen months. With resins comprising about a third of the cost of making a typical Rubbermaid product, Rubbermaid couldn't meet its goals without both cutting costs *and* raising prices.

Wal-Mart and other retailers were unwilling to pass on Rubbermaid's higher prices to their own customers, particularly when competitors' products were improving in quality but not increasing in price as quickly as Rubbermaid's. So they declined to restock Rubbermaid products and turned to competing products from Sterilite and Tucker. Wal-Mart even omitted Rubbermaid from promotional materials it hands out to customers, touting Sterilite's houseware line instead.

To resolve the situation, Rubbermaid CEO Wolfgang Schmitt fired the head of the Home Products division and took over that job as well as his own. While waiting for resin prices to stabilize, Rubbermaid is also relying on its research and development staff to come up with exciting new products not offered by competitors, such as a cooler with wheels that can be rolled along on picnics and a plastic toolshed. Whether these efforts will appease Wal-Mart and other retailers remains to be seen. As one industry analyst says, "Wal-Mart can live without Rubbermaid, but the opposite is not necessarily true."

Sources: "The Customer with Clout," *Fortune*, October 2, 1995, p. 100; and Lee Smith, "Rubbermaid Goes Thump," *Fortune*, October 2, 1995, pp. 90–104.

from each other. Second, channel members must institute certain measures of channel coordination, which requires leadership and benevolent exercise of control.[29] To prevent channel conflict, producers, or other channel members, may provide competing resellers with different brands, allocate markets among resellers, define direct-sales policies to clarify potential conflict over large accounts, negotiate territorial issues between regional distributors, and provide recognition to certain resellers for their importance in distributing to others. Hallmark, for example, distributes its Ambassador greeting-card line in discount stores and its name brand Hallmark line in upscale department stores and Hallmark stores, thus limiting the amount of competition between retailers carrying its products.[30]

Channel power The ability of one channel member to influence another channel member's goal achievement

Channel Leadership   Marketing channel effectiveness hinges on channel leadership, even in partnerships. Producers, retailers, or wholesalers may assume this leadership. To become a leader, a channel member must want to influence overall channel performance. To attain desired objectives, the leader must possess **channel power,** which is the ability to influence another channel member's goal achievement. The member who becomes the channel leader will accept the responsibilities and exercise the power associated with this role.[31] To strive for higher-quality products, for example, GM has announced that it will select only suppliers that can provide the highest-quality parts at the lowest cost, including parts made by GM.[32]

A manufacturer—whose large-scale production efficiency demands increasing sales volume—may exercise power by giving channel members financing, business advice, ordering assistance, advertising, and support materials. After Rubbermaid increased product distribution from 60,000 to 100,000 outlets, it improved cooperative advertising plans and increased channel members' margins, both to motivate new channel members and to appease older channel members which now had to compete with more outlets carrying Rubbermaid products.[33] Coercion causes dealer dissatisfaction that is stronger than any impact from rewards, so use of coercion can be a major cause of channel conflict.[34] The use of noncoercive strategies, less frequent use of coercive strategies, lower conflict, and more favorable evaluation of marketing channel partner performance are associated with mutual dependence and a strong relationship that provides greater rewards for channel members.[35]

Retailers can also function as channel leaders and, with the rise of national chain stores and private brand merchandise, are increasingly doing so. Small retailers, too, may share in leadership roles when they gain strong customer loyalty in local or regional markets. These retailers control many brands and sometimes replace uncooperative producers. Increasingly, leading retailers are concentrating their buying power with fewer suppliers and, in the process, improving their market effectiveness and efficiency. Single-source supply relationships are often successful, whereas multiple-source supply relationships based on price competition are decreasing. Long-term commitments enable retailers to place smaller and more frequent orders as needed rather than waiting for large volume discounts or placing huge orders early in the season and assuming the risks associated with carrying an unsold inventory.[36]

Wholesalers assume channel leadership roles as well, although they were more powerful decades ago, when most manufacturers and retailers were small, underfinanced, and widely scattered. Today wholesaler leaders may form voluntary chains with several retailers, which they supply with bulk buying or management services; these chains may also market their own brands. In return, retailers shift most of their purchasing to the wholesaler leader. The Independent Grocers' Alliance (IGA) is one of the best-known wholesaler leaders in the United States. IGA's power is based on the expert advertising, pricing, and purchasing knowledge it makes available to independent business owners. Other wholesaler leaders might also help retailers with store layouts, accounting, and inventory control.

Legal Issues in Channel Management

*T*he multitude of federal, state, and local laws governing channel management are based on the general principle that the public is best served by protecting competition and free trade. Under the authority of such federal legislation as the Sherman Antitrust Act and the Federal Trade Commission Act, courts and regulatory agencies determine under what circumstances channel management practices violate this underlying principle and must be restricted. Although channel managers are not expected to be legal experts, they should be aware that attempts to control distribution functions may have legal repercussions. The following practices are among those frequently subject to legal restraint.

■ *Dual Distribution*

A producer that distributes the same product through two or more different channel structures or sells the same or similar products through different channels under different brand names is engaging in dual distribution.[37] Louis Vuitton, for example, makes its products available through both department stores and its own retail outlets (see Figure 13.9). Courts do not consider this practice illegal when it promotes competition. For example, a manufacturer can legally open its own retail outlets where no other retailers are available to carry its products. But the courts view as a threat to competition a manufacturer who uses company-owned outlets to dominate or drive out of business independent retailers or distributors who handle its products. In such cases, dual distribution violates the law. To avoid this interpretation, producers should use outlet prices that do not severely undercut independent retailers' prices.

Profoundly masculine. Taïga by Louis Vuitton.

Available exclusively in Louis Vuitton shops and select department stores.
For more information or the store nearest you, please call: 1-800-409-9456.

Louis Vuitton
The spirit of travel

Figure 13.9
Dual Distribution
Louis Vuitton offers dual distribution for its products—select department stores and Louis Vuitton boutiques.

■ *Restricted Sales Territories*

To tighten control over distribution of its products, a manufacturer may try to prohibit intermediaries from selling its products outside designated sales territories. Intermediaries themselves often favor this practice because it gives them exclusive territories, letting them avoid competition for the producer's brands within these territories. In recent years, the courts have adopted conflicting positions in regard to restricted sales territories. Although the courts have deemed restricted sales territories a restraint of trade among intermediaries handling the same brands (except for small or newly established companies), they have also held that exclusive territories can actually promote competition between dealers handling different brands. At present, the producer's intent in establishing restricted territories and the overall effect of doing so on the market must be evaluated for each case individually.

■ *Tying Agreements*

Tying agreement Requiring a channel member to buy other products from a supplier besides the one it wants

When a supplier (usually a manufacturer or franchiser) furnishes a product to a channel member stipulating that the channel member must purchase other products as well, a **tying agreement** exists.[38] Suppliers, for instance, may institute tying arrangements to move weaker products along with more popular items, or a franchiser may tie purchase of equipment and supplies to the sale of franchises, justifying the policy as necessary for quality control and protection of the franchiser's reputation.

A related practice is *full-line forcing,* in which a supplier requires that channel members purchase the supplier's entire line to obtain any of the supplier's products. Manufacturers sometimes use full-line forcing to ensure that intermediaries accept new products and that a suitable range of products is available to customers.

The courts accept tying agreements when the supplier alone can provide products of a certain quality, when the intermediary is free to carry competing products as well, and when a company has just entered the market. Most other tying agreements are considered illegal.

■ *Exclusive Dealing*

Exclusive dealing Forbidding an intermediary to carry products of a competing manufacturer

When a manufacturer forbids an intermediary to carry products of competing manufacturers, the arrangement is called **exclusive dealing.** Manufacturers receive considerable market protection in an exclusive dealing arrangement and may cut off shipments to intermediaries who violate the agreement.

The legality of an exclusive dealing contract is generally determined by applying three tests. If the exclusive dealing blocks competitors from as much as 10 percent of the market, if the sales revenue involved is sizable, and if the manufacturer is much larger (and thus more intimidating) than the dealer, the arrangement is considered anticompetitive.[39] If dealers and customers in a given market have access to similar products or if the exclusive dealing contract strengthens an otherwise weak competitor, the arrangement is allowed.

■ *Refusal to Deal*

For over seventy years, courts have held that producers have the right to choose channel members with which they will do business (and the right to reject others). Within existing distribution channels, however, suppliers may not refuse to deal with wholesalers or dealers just because these wholesalers or dealers resist policies that are anticompetitive or in restraint of trade. Suppliers are further prohibited from organizing some channel members in refusal-to-deal actions against other members that choose not to comply with illegal policies.[40]

SUMMARY

A marketing channel, or channel of distribution, is a group of individuals and organizations that directs the flow of products from producers to customers. The major role of marketing channels is to make products available at the right time at the right place in the right amounts. In most channels of distribution, producers and consumers are linked by marketing intermediaries, or middlemen. Of the two major types of intermediaries, retailers purchase products and resell them to ultimate consumers, and wholesalers buy and resell products to other wholesalers, retailers, and industrial customers.

Marketing channels serve many functions. They create time, place, and possession utility by making products available when and where customers want them and providing customers with access to product use through sale or rental. Marketing intermediaries facilitate exchange efficiencies, often reducing the costs of exchanges by performing certain services and functions. Although critics suggest eliminating wholesalers, their functions must be performed by someone in the marketing channel. Because intermediaries serve both producers and buyers, they reduce the total number of transactions that would otherwise be needed to move products from producer to ultimate users.

Channels of distribution are broadly classified as channels for consumer products or channels for industrial products. Within these two broad categories, different marketing channels are used for different products. Although consumer goods can move directly from producer to consumers, consumer product channels including wholesalers and retailers are usually more economical and efficient. Distribution of industrial products differs from that of consumer products in the types of channels used; the kinds of intermediaries available; and transportation, storage, and inventory policies. A direct distribution channel is common in industrial marketing. Also used are channels containing manufacturers' agents, industrial distributors, or both agents and distributors. Most producers have dual or multiple channels so that the distribution system can be adjusted for various target markets.

A marketing channel is managed so that products receive appropriate market coverage. In choosing intensive distribution, producers strive to make a product available to all possible dealers. In selective distribution, only some outlets in an area are chosen to distribute a product. Exclusive distribution usually gives one dealer exclusive rights to sell a product in a large geographic area.

Supply chain management refers to long-term partnerships among channel members working together to reduce inefficiencies, costs, and redundancies in the entire marketing channel in order to satisfy customers. The supply chain includes all entities—shippers and other firms that facilitate distribution as well as producers, wholesalers, and retailers—that distribute products and benefit from cooperative efforts. Supply chains start with the customer and require the cooperation of channel members to satisfy customer requirements.

Integration of marketing channels brings various activities under one channel member's management. Vertical integration combines two or more stages of the channel under one management. The vertical marketing system (VMS) is managed centrally for the mutual benefit of all channel members. Vertical marketing systems may be corporate, administered, or contractual. Horizontal integration combines institutions at the same level of channel operation under a single management.

Channels function most efficiently when members cooperate, but when they deviate from their roles, channel conflict can arise. Effective marketing channels are usually a result of channel leadership. Producers are in an excellent position to structure channel policy and use technical expertise and consumer acceptance to influence other channel members. Retailers gain channel control through consumer confidence, wide product mixes, and intimate knowledge of consumers. Wholesalers become channel leaders when they have expertise that other channel members value and when they can coordinate functions to match supply with demand.

Federal, state, and local laws regulate channel management to protect competition and free trade. Courts may prohibit or permit a given practice depending on whether it violates this underlying principle. Various procompetitive legislation applies to distribution prac-

tices. Channel management practices frequently subject to legal restraint include dual distribution, restricted sales territories, tying agreements, exclusive dealing, and refusal to deal. When these practices strengthen weak competitors or increase competition among dealers, they may be permitted; in most other cases, when competition may be weakened considerably, they are deemed illegal.

IMPORTANT TERMS

Distribution
Marketing channel
Marketing intermediary
(middleman)
Industrial distributor

Dual distribution
Strategic channel alliance
Intensive distribution
Selective distribution
Exclusive distribution

Supply chain management
Vertical channel
integration
Vertical marketing systems
(VMS)

Horizontal channel
integration
Channel power
Tying agreement
Exclusive dealing

DISCUSSION AND REVIEW QUESTIONS

1. Describe the major functions of marketing channels. Why are these functions better accomplished through combined efforts of channel members?
2. Can one channel member perform all channel functions?
3. "Shorter channels are usually a more direct means of distribution and therefore are more efficient." Comment on this statement.
4. Why do consumers often blame intermediaries for distribution inefficiencies? List several of the reasons.
5. Compare and contrast the four major types of marketing channels for consumer products. Through which type of channel is each of the following products most likely to be distributed?
   a. new automobiles
   b. saltine crackers
   c. cut-your-own Christmas trees
   d. new textbooks
   e. sofas
   f. soft drinks
6. Outline the four most common channels for industrial products. Describe the products and/or

situations that lead marketers to choose each channel.
7. Describe an industrial distributor. What types of products are marketed through an industrial distributor?
8. Under what conditions is a producer most likely to use more than one marketing channel?
9. Explain the differences between intensive, selective, and exclusive methods of distribution.
10. Name and describe firms that use (a) vertical integration and (b) horizontal integration in their marketing channels.
11. Explain the major characteristics of each of the three types of vertical marketing systems (VMSs)— corporate, administered, and contractual.
12. "Channel cooperation requires that members support the overall channel goals to achieve individual goals." Comment on this statement.
13. Under what conditions are tying agreements, exclusive dealing, and dual distribution judged illegal?

APPLICATION QUESTIONS

1. Supply chain management refers to long-term partnerships among channel members working together to reduce inefficiencies, costs, and redundancies in the entire marketing channel. Select one of the following companies and explain how supply chain management could increase marketing productivity.
   a. Dell Computer
   b. Federal Express
   c. Nike
   d. Taco Bell
2. Wholesalers and intermediaries facilitate the exchange process by creating efficiencies and lowering costs. Of the examples below, which organization

would benefit most from using intermediaries and why?
   a. passenger aircraft manufacturer
   b. soft drink producer
   c. insurance company
3. Organizations often form strategic channel alliances when they find it more profitable or convenient to distribute their products through the marketing channel of another organization. Find an article in the newspaper or library that describes such a strategic channel alliance. Briefly summarize the article and indicate the benefits each organization expects to gain.

4. There are three major levels of market coverage from which to select when determining the number and kinds of outlets in which a product will be sold: (1) intensive, (2) selective, and (3) exclusive. Characteristics of the product and its target market determine the intensity of coverage a product should receive. Indicate the intensity level best suited for the following products and tell why it is appropriate.
   a. personal computer
   b. deodorant

c. collector baseball autographed by Babe Ruth
d. Windows 95 computer software

5. Describe the decision process that you might go through if you were attempting to determine the most appropriate distribution channel for one of the following:
   a. shotguns for hunters
   b. women's lingerie
   c. telephone systems for small businesses
   d. toy trucks for 2-year-olds

Case 13.1   CUTCO Cutlery: Differentiation via Direct Sales

The fastest growing segment of the $240 million cutlery industry is in high-quality, relatively high-priced knives and accessories used primarily in cooking/kitchen applications. Typically, high-quality knives from manufacturers such as Henckels, Wusthof, Sabatier/Cuisine de France, and Chicago Cutlery can be purchased in fine department stores or in cutlery shops specializing in such goods. CUTCO Cutlery has used a different marketing channel to develop a successful marketing strategy. The Alcas Corporation, manufacturer of CUTCO knives, has succeeded in differentiating its products from others in the upscale end of the cutlery industry by employing a unique method of sales and distribution—direct selling—used most notably by encyclopedia marketers, vacuum cleaner manufacturers, and cosmetic firms such as Avon and Mary Kay, as well as by Amway, a marketer of household products.

The Alcas Corporation has manufactured and marketed CUTCO Cutlery since 1949. As a result of several corporate restructurings, Alcas now exists essentially as a holding company composed of two wholly owned operating subsidiaries: (1) the CUTCO Cutlery Corporation, manufacturer of CUTCO Cutlery, and (2) the Vector Marketing Corporation, a direct and exclusive sales agent for CUTCO products in North America. Alcas has experienced consistent growth over the last ten years, with annual sales expanding by an average of 22 percent since 1985. Sales in 1995 were projected to top the $80 million mark.

The CUTCO product line consists of a wide variety of kitchen (food preparation and table) cutlery, hunting, fishing, and utility pocket knives, as well as related accessories like wood chopping blocks. The CUTCO product line comprises over fifty individual items, most ranging in price from $30 to $80, which are often sold in sets and gift packs priced from $160 to $680. Pricing is consistent with that of other high-quality cutlery products such as those made by Henckels and Wusthof. CUTCO Cutlery products are promoted as "CUTCO—

The World's Finest Cutlery" and are sold on the basis of quality and performance tests against competitive products and a lifetime guarantee.

Unlike its competitors, who sell and distribute their cutlery through fine department stores and specialty shops, CUTCO, via its Vector Marketing sales subsidiary, engages in direct selling through one-to-one in-home demonstrations. The CUTCO sales force is made up primarily of college students recruited during summer vacation months. In 1995, Vector Marketing recruited more than 35,000 salespeople, between 85 and 90 percent of them college students. The recruiting, training, and ongoing counseling of salespeople, all of whom work as independent contractors, is done in decentralized fashion, utilizing approximately 165 district sales and distribution managers located strategically in communities across the United States and Canada. During its peak summer months, Vector also opens up an additional 200 temporary "branch offices" staffed by college students with prior selling and management experience.

One reason for the effectiveness of CUTCO's direct sales and distribution approach is that the high price of its products necessitates that potential buyers see them in use before committing to purchase. CUTCO's competitors usually address this issue by using in-store sales specialists or interactive video demonstrations.

One-to-one in-home or workplace selling is the most popular form of direct selling. Between 1987 and 1992, the number of persons involved in direct selling increased from 3.6 million to 5 million, with the total volume of sales made rising from $8.8 million to over $14 million. However, some experts have criticized direct sales and distribution as being limited in today's increasingly competitive and high-tech business environment. Specifically, they suggest that direct sellers expand the number of channels through which their products are offered. As evidence, they cite the problems faced by the Encyclopedia Britannica

Corporation. The 225-year-old company, analysts contend, lost market share and profits to competitors not only because it failed to offer its encyclopedias in a much less costly CD-ROM format, but also because it continued to market its products exclusively through its direct sales network. These analysts suggested that Encyclopedia Britannica would have been well advised to diversify its sales and distribution approach, as had competitors, by marketing its products through retail outlets, direct mail, telemarketing, and online computer marketing.

In the face of stagnant growth in the early 1990s CUTCO did indeed experience problems trying to expand its operations exclusively through direct selling. In 1993, Vector Marketing was cited by the Wisconsin State Department of Agriculture, Trade, and Consumer Protection for overly aggressive salesperson recruitment. As a result, Vector was ordered to disclose in more exacting detail to its young recruits the nature of positions offered. The dispute centered around three issues: (1) some recruits were led to believe that they would be working for Vector when in fact they were to work as independent sales contractors, (2) the company failed to tell potential recruits that they "would be strongly urged" to purchase a $200 sales kit, and (3) Vector did not inform recruits that they would not be paid until a minimum number of sales demonstrations had been made.

As a result of these problems, Vector might consider exploring other means of product sales and distribution to supplement its current direct approach. One promising alternative is marketing its products directly to potential buyers online. Not only would such an approach allow the all-important demonstration of CUTCO products, but it would also facilitate customer convenience (as opposed to the sometimes intrusive in-home sales call), instant order transmission, and greater marketer efficiency (by reducing sales and commissions costs).

In 1990, Alcas established Vector Canada as a distinct international marketing entity utilizing the direct sales and distribution approach used in its domestic operations. Vector Canada has been a highly successful venture. Vector Korea was set up in similar fashion in 1992. The decision to enter Korea was made partly on the basis of the availability of U.S.–trained, Korean-born managers. Alcas's direct sales and distribution approach proved not to be as effective in Korea as it was in Canada, with the company experiencing losses in 1992, 1993, 1994, and 1995 totaling $2.5 million. As a result, in February 1995, Vector Korea supplemented direct selling by hiring Korean housewives as the recruiting base for a "party plan" approach most notably used by marketers of Tupperware home products. This tactic has proven very successful; the party plan approach accounted for 65 percent of Korean sales in 1995. Vector Korea plans to move exclusively to the party plan sales and distribution approach in 1996.[41]

Questions for Discussion

1. Discuss the strengths and weaknesses associated with Alcas's direct selling approach to the sales and distribution of CUTCO Cutlery.
2. Is the marketing channel traditionally employed for CUTCO products vertically or horizontally integrated?
3. Discuss the level and nature of channel power now held by Alcas. What would be the impact on the firm's power of diversifying to include online marketing?

Case 13.2 New Distribution Channels for Automobiles

If the idea of buying a used car brings to your mind overbearing salespeople pitching dishonest praise about rundown jalopies, you are certainly not alone. One major auto industry executive agrees: "If you look into all of the buying processes in this country, the used car buying process image ranks close to the bottom." However, sticker shock over new car prices is driving more and more consumers to used car lots. According to the National Automobile Dealers Association, the average price of a new vehicle in 1995 was $20,270, compared to $10,980 for a used vehicle sold by a franchised dealer. Moreover, thanks to the popularity of short-term leases, there are more two- and three-year-old, low-mileage cars and trucks than ever on the market. As a result, Americans are buying about 35 million used cars and trucks each year, compared to about 14.8 million new light vehicles. Customer dissatisfaction over used car sales tactics, and over new car prices, has created a market opportunity for savvy firms to develop new channels for marketing used cars.

For example, Circuit City Stores, Inc., which operates consumer electronics superstores throughout the nation, is applying its expertise in customer service, logistics, sales of high-dollar merchandise, and financing to develop a chain of CarMax Auto Superstores. It has already opened four—one in Richmond, Virginia, two in Atlanta, and one in Raleigh, North Carolina—with a fifth slated for Charlotte, North Carolina, in 1996. At these superstores, customers can browse an electronic car lot of hundreds of used cars and trucks by using touch-screen computer terminals. Circuit City senior vice president W. Austin Ligon says, "Our focus is on cars one to five years old with less than 70,000 miles. . . . We try to have almost everything you'd want to choose from in one location." CarMax reconditions each vehicle and offers a five-day money-back guarantee as well as a thirty-day warranty. Longer warranties are available at extra cost. CarMax tries to ease the stressful car-buying experience in several ways. Vehicle prices are fixed, so negotiating is eliminated. Salespeople earn salaries instead of commissions, so they provide assistance and advice rather than high-pressure sales tactics. Customer-friendly amenities such as nanny-supervised child-care areas and coffee bars also help alleviate shoppers' anxiety.

Circuit City's ideas for selling used cars seem to be working well. CarMax sold an estimated $288 million worth of vehicles at its four stores in 1995. And, more important from the customer's point of view, it did so with a 98 percent customer satisfaction rating; traditional dealerships satisfy only 65 to 85 percent of their used car customers.

Thus far, Circuit City views CarMax as an experiment, but potential competitors are taking notice. H. Wayne Huizenga, the entrepreneur who built Blockbuster Entertainment, has assembled a group of investors to open twenty-five Auto Nation used car superstores in twenty-five cities. Several large U.S. franchise car dealers have also joined forces to build 100 Driver's Mart used car superstores across the nation over the next five years. Another firm has opened two CarChoice superstores in Michigan and Texas.

Auto industry executives are also paying close attention to the CarMax experiment. GM, for example, plans to offer more extensive used car warranty programs to compete with the new retailers. Richard E. Colliver, senior vice president of American Honda Motor Co., believes CarMax and its competitors will persuade traditional car dealers to focus more on serving used car customers. Chrysler Corp. is so intrigued that it has given CarMax a new car franchise in Northcross, Georgia, where it will sell new Chryslers, Jeeps, and Eagles. Chrysler sales vice president E. Thomas Pappert says, "It is our plan to observe the CarMax process to determine what application, if any, these policies might have in the new car sales process."

Although CarMax and its competitors have thus far limited their operations to used vehicles, their success and the interest of automobile manufacturers' in their techniques have many new car dealers worried, perhaps with good reason. In fact, J.D. Power, who ranks annual car buyer satisfaction, predicts that within ten years, auto manufacturers may begin to bypass the tra-

ditional franchise dealer system and open factory sales outlets and other channels of distribution through national retailers such as Sears or Wal-Mart. Other industry observers foresee automotive supermarkets where consumers will be able to comparison shop through aisles of new Ford Escorts, Toyota Corollas, and GMC trucks, much as they do televisions or stereos at Circuit City. Already, United Auto, a franchise chain, permits consumers to shop for twenty-two brands of new cars from 8:00 A.M. to midnight and offers full-service cafeterias, playgrounds, and plush waiting rooms to satisfy customers.

Other new marketing channels are also opening up. Consumers can already shop for vehicles via the Internet, through brokers such as AutoByTel, which helped customers negotiate more than 25,000 car purchases in 1995. AutoByTel runs a free referral service with a network of 1,400 dealers through the World Wide Web. Auto-buying clubs, which help consumers negotiate new car purchases, are also increasing. One such venture, Consumers Car Club, negotiated $250 million worth of car sales in 1995 and plans to go online through the Internet in 1996.

The success of these new channels of distribution carries one message to new car dealers: change or die. Many, pushed by auto manufacturers, are experimenting with new car-selling approaches such as computerizing displays, no-haggle pricing, greater selection, and customer-friendly amenities. Several dealers have established an individual presence on the Internet's World Wide Web. Some have even joined forces as DealerNet, a "virtual showroom," that allows World Wide Web browsers to click on words, pictures, sounds, and video in interactive displays that link buyers to dozens of dealerships. DealerNet eventually hopes to become a computerized locator service for new and used cars and parts, through which consumers can not only find the car they want, but also negotiate features, prices, and warranties, and possibly even shop for financing as well. Whether or not these experiments succeed, customers will be the big winners with more choices in shopping for both new and used vehicles.[42]

Questions for Discussion

1. Why is CarMax using a "new" marketing channel for automobiles?
2. How does a new-car franchise dealer's marketing channel differ from the "new" marketing channels?
3. What would happen if auto manufacturers bypassed their traditional dealer system and used multiple channels (i.e., Sears, Wal-Mart, etc.) to distribute cars?

Chapter 14

Wholesaling

OBJECTIVES

- To understand the nature of wholesaling in the marketing channel

- To learn about wholesalers' functions

- To understand how wholesalers are classified

- To examine organizations that are facilitating agencies

- To explore changing patterns in wholesaling

Frieda's fresh ideas are as appealing as her fresh produce.

321

*T*hanks in large part to Frieda's Finest, trendsetting wholesaler of exotic fruits and vegetables, shoppers throughout the United States and Canada can find taro root, passion fruit, habanero chilies, coquito nuts, enoki mushrooms, purple potatoes, and burpless cucumbers, to name a few, in the produce sections of their supermarkets. Bringing new ideas to fruit and vegetable wholesaling, company founder Frieda Caplan built Frieda's Finest by offering the kinds of produce that its mainstream competitors such as Dole and Chiquita decline to stock.

In the 1960s, the only mushrooms available to most grocery shoppers were found in cans. By launching a wholesale produce business specializing in fresh mushrooms, Frieda Caplan helped transform an unusual vegetable into a well-accepted regular on American tables. She did the same for alfalfa sprouts and a variety of squash. When a buyer from a large national supermarket chain asked Frieda if she could supply Chinese gooseberries, she had never heard of them. Soon afterward, however, some New Zealand fruit growers offered her 2,400 pounds of the fuzzy, brown-skinned fruit with the strawberry-banana-melon-pineapple flavor. Frieda took the fruit, renamed it "kiwi" after the national bird of New Zealand, sold it to chains all over the United States, and again changed the look of America's supermarket produce sections. Says company president Karen Caplan (daughter of founder Frieda), "We take every customer request seriously. By using these tools of communication, we have established ourselves as experts in exotic fruits and vegetables."

What is the key to the company's wholesaling success? Many buyers report that although they could often purchase exotic fruits and vegetables at lower prices from other wholesalers, they buy from Frieda's because of excellent service. In addition to maintaining consistent quality standards that produce buyers have come to rely on, the company offers strong retail support. It conducts seminars for produce buyers and managers and provides merchandising bulletins, displays, and promotion packages. Frieda's weekly newsletter and fact sheets keep produce retailers informed about what is selling, what is available, and what consumers say in the hundreds of letters Frieda's receives every week.

Frieda Caplan acknowledges that once a specialty becomes a staple, her company can no longer compete with wholesaling giants. Frieda's Finest kiwis and common mushrooms no longer dominate the market. By turning instead to unique fruits like the prickly pear cactus and the kiwano, Frieda's records annual sales of over $23 million and continues "changing the way America eats."[1]

Frieda's Finest has succeeded as a wholesaler because of its ability to compete and to satisfy its customers through effective marketing strategies. It is maintaining a strong position as a wholesaler, which is not the case for wholesalers in general. Currently, a number of wholesalers are changing their way of doing business in order to survive and adjust to restructuring of marketing channels.

This chapter focuses on wholesaling activities within a marketing channel. We view wholesaling as all exchanges among organizations and individuals in marketing channels except transactions with ultimate consumers. We examine the importance of wholesalers and their functions, noting the services they render to producers and retailers. We then classify various types of wholesalers and facilitating organizations. Finally, we explore changing patterns in wholesaling.

The Nature and Importance of Wholesaling

Wholesaling All transactions in which products are bought for resale, for making other products, or for general business operations

Wholesaler An individual or organization that facilitates and expedites wholesale transactions

Wholesaling refers to all transactions in which products are bought for resale, for making other products, or for general business operations. It does not include exchanges with ultimate consumers. A **wholesaler** is an individual or organization that facilitates and expedites exchanges that are primarily wholesale transactions. In other words, wholesalers buy products and sell them directly to reseller, government, and institutional users. For example, SYSCO, the nation's number one food-service distributor, supplies everything from frozen and fresh food and paper products to medical and cleaning supplies to restaurants, hotels, schools, industrial caterers, and hospitals. It supplies goods (many of them well-known name brands) and services to 245,000 dining sites outside the home, or about 10 percent of the market.[2] Rarely does a wholesaler engage in retail transactions to ultimate consumers. There are approximately 492,000 wholesaling establishments in the United States,[3] and approximately 60 percent of all products sold in the United States pass through these firms.[4] The effective functioning of wholesalers as a part of the marketing channel, especially in developing countries, contributes directly to a country's economic potential and growth by providing links to an expanded market base.[5]

Distribution of all goods requires wholesaling activities, whether or not a wholesaling firm is involved. Wholesaling activities are not limited to goods; service companies, such as financial institutions, also use active wholesale networks. For example, some banks buy loans in bulk from other financial institutions rather than originate loans from their own retail customers.

Table 14.1 lists major activities wholesalers perform, but individual wholesalers may perform more or fewer functions than the table shows. Wholesalers perform functions or services to organizations above and below them in the marketing channel. They bear the primary responsibility for physical movement of goods from manufacturers to retailers. In addition, they may establish decision support systems that satisfy manufacturers' and retailers' warehouse expectations, including a set of delivery requirements in terms of time and frequency of deliveries.[6] Wholesalers provide essential services for both producers/manufacturers and retailers.

■ *Services for Producers*

Wholesalers provide many services to producers. By selling diverse products to retailers and by initiating sales contacts with the manufacturer, wholesalers serve as an extension of the producer's sales force. Wholesalers also provide financial assistance: (1) they often pay for transporting goods; (2) they reduce a producer's warehousing expenses and inventory investment by holding goods in inventory; (3) they extend credit and assume losses from buyers who turn out to be poor credit risks; and (4) when they buy a producer's entire output and pay promptly or in cash, they are a source of working capital. Wholesalers also serve as conduits for information within the marketing channel, keeping producers up-to-date on market developments and passing along the manufacturers' promotional plans to other intermediaries. Using wholesalers therefore gives producers a distinct advantage because the specialized services performed by wholesalers allow producers to

Table 14.1   Major Wholesaling Functions

Supply Chain Management	Creating long-term partnerships among channel members
Promotion	Providing a sales force, advertising, sales promotion, and publicity
Warehousing, Shipping, and Product Handling	Receiving, storing, and stockkeeping Packaging Shipping outgoing orders Materials handling Arranging and making local and long-distance shipments
Inventory Control and Data Processing	Processing orders Controlling physical inventory Recording transactions Tracking sales data for financial analysis
Taking Risks	Assuming responsibility for theft, product obsolescence, and excess inventories
Financing and Budgeting	Extending credit Borrowing Making capital investments Forecasting cash flow
Marketing Research and Information Systems	Providing information about markets Conducting research studies Managing computer networks to facilitate exchanges and relationships

concentrate on developing and manufacturing products that match consumers' needs and wants.

Many producers would prefer more direct interaction with retailers. Wholesalers, however, are more likely to have closer contact with retailers because of their strategic position in the marketing channel. Although a producer's own sales force is probably more effective at selling, the costs of maintaining a sales force and performing functions normally done by wholesalers are sometimes higher than the benefits received from an independent sales staff. Wholesalers can spread sales costs over many more products than most producers, resulting in lower costs per product unit. For these reasons, many producers shift market information, transportation, warehousing, and financing tasks to wholesalers. Thus the wholesaler often becomes a major partner in supply chain management.

■ *Services for Retailers*

Through partnerships, wholesalers and retailers can establish successful relationships for the benefit of consumers. A wholesaler supports retailers by assisting with marketing strategy, especially the marketing channel component. Wholesalers also help retailers select inventory. Wholesalers are often specialists in understanding market conditions and experts at negotiating final purchases. In industries in which obtaining supplies is important, skilled buying is indispensable. For example, Atlanta-based Genuine Parts Co. (GPC), the nation's top automotive parts wholesaler, has more than sixty-five years experience in the auto parts business; this experience helps it serve its customers effectively. GPC obtains more than 150,000 replacement parts from 150 different suppliers and resells them to retail stores and job shops (which in turn resell to garages) in the United States, Canada, and Mexico.[7] Effective wholesalers make an effort to understand the businesses of their customers. A retailer's buyer can thus avoid the responsibility of looking for and coordinating supply sources. If the wholesaler purchases for several different buyers, expenses can be shared by all customers. Another advantage is that a manufacturer's salesperson offers retailers only a few products at a time, but independent wholesalers always have a wide range of products available.

Figure 14.1
Services for Retailers
Fleming, a grocery wholesaler, offers ordering and inventory management services to retailers to control costs.

By buying in large quantities and delivering to customers in smaller lots, wholesalers perform physical distribution activities—such as transportation, materials handling, inventory planning, communication, and warehousing (covered in Chapter 16)—more efficiently. They furnish more service than might be feasible for a producer's or retailer's own physical distribution system. Furthermore, wholesalers offer quick and frequent delivery even when demand fluctuates. They can provide fast delivery at low cost, which lets the producer and the wholesalers' customers avoid risks associated with holding large inventories (see Figure 14.1).

Because they carry products for many customers, certain types of wholesalers maintain broad product lines at relatively low costs. Tempe, Arizona-based MicroAge, for example, concentrates on reselling high-tech products manufactured by Apple, Compaq, Hewlett-Packard, Packard Bell, and IBM through its own network of franchised stores (MicroAge Network), as well as to other resellers. It also provides services such as systems integration, technical support, and its own ZDATA electronic ordering and product information system for customers.[8] Often wholesalers can perform storage and warehousing activities more efficiently, permitting retailers to concentrate on other marketing activities. When wholesalers provide storage and warehousing, they generally take on ownership as well, an arrangement freeing retailers' and producers' capital for other purposes. Through computer networks, wholesalers are also helping their supply chain partners to better satisfy their own customers. Cardinal Health, Inc., for example, provides purchasing and information systems to 3,300 hospitals, doctors' offices, and pharmacies, and, in some cases, handles the telemarketing operations of manufacturers.[9]

Classifying Wholesalers

*T*here are many types of wholesalers to meet the varying needs of producers and retailers. In addition, new institutions and establishments develop in response to producers and retail organizations wanting to take over wholesaling functions. Wholesalers adjust their functions as the contours of the marketing environment change.

Wholesalers are classified along several dimensions. Whether a producer owns the wholesaler influences how it is classified. Wholesalers are also grouped as to whether they take title to (actually own) the products they handle. The range of services provided is another criterion used for classification. Finally, wholesalers are classified according to the breadth and depth of their product lines. Using these dimensions, we discuss three general types of wholesaling establishments: (1) merchant wholesalers, (2) agents and brokers, and (3) manufacturers' sales branches and offices.

■ *Merchant Wholesalers*

Merchant wholesalers
Independently owned businesses that take title to goods, assume ownership risks, and buy and resell products to industrial or retail customers

Merchant wholesalers are independently owned businesses that take title to goods and assume risks associated with ownership and generally buy and resell products to industrial or retail customers. A producer is likely to rely on merchant wholesalers when selling directly to customers would be economically unfeasible. Merchant wholesalers are also valuable for providing market coverage, making sales contacts, storing inventory, handling orders, collecting market information, and furnishing customer support.[10] Some merchant wholesalers are even involved in packaging and developing private brands to help retailer customers be competitive. Merchant wholesalers go by various names, including wholesaler, jobber, distributor, assembler, exporter, and importer. They fall into one of two broad categories: full-service and limited-service (Figure 14.2).

Full-service wholesalers
Marketing intermediaries providing the widest range of wholesaling functions

Full-Service Merchant Wholesalers **Full-service wholesalers** are intermediaries offering the widest possible range of wholesaling functions. Customers rely on them for product availability, suitable assortments, bulk breaking (breaking large quantities into smaller ones), financial assistance, and technical advice and service.[11] Universal Corporation, for example, is the world's largest buyer and processor of leaf tobacco. The Richmond, Virginia-based firm buys, ships, packs, processes, and resells tobacco, and provides financing for its customers, which include cigarette manufacturers such as Philip Morris (which accounts for 41 percent of Universal's sales). Universal is also involved in sales of lumber, rubber, tea, nuts, dried fruit, and other products and has operations in thirty-three countries.[12] Full-service wholesalers provide numerous marketing services to interested customers. Many large grocery wholesalers help retailers with store design, site selection, personnel training, financing, merchandising, advertising, coupon redemption, and scanning. Although full-service wholesalers often earn higher gross margins than other wholesalers, their operating expenses are also higher because they perform a wider range of functions. Full-service merchant wholesalers (categorized as general-merchandise, limited-line, or specialty-line wholesalers) handle either consumer or industrial products.

General-merchandise wholesalers Full-service wholesalers with a wide product mix but limited depth within product lines

General-merchandise wholesalers carry a wide product mix but offer limited depth within product lines. They deal in such products as drugs, nonperishable foods, cosmetics, detergents, and tobacco. General-merchandise wholesalers develop strong, mutually beneficial relationships with their typical customers—neighborhood grocery stores,

Figure 14.2
Types of Merchant Wholesalers

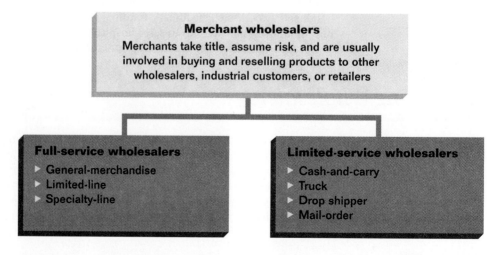

Merchant wholesalers
Merchants take title, assume risk, and are usually involved in buying and reselling products to other wholesalers, industrial customers, or retailers

Full-service wholesalers
▸ General-merchandise
▸ Limited-line
▸ Specialty-line

Limited-service wholesalers
▸ Cash-and-carry
▸ Truck
▸ Drop shipper
▸ Mail-order

326

Figure 14.3
Limited-Line Wholesaler
Super Valu is a large
limited-line food wholesaler.

hardware and appliance shops, and local department stores. Small retailers often obtain everything they need from these wholesalers. General-merchandise wholesalers for industrial customers provide supplies and accessories and are sometimes called *industrial distributors* or *mill supply houses.*

Limited-line wholesalers
Full-service wholesalers that carry only a few product lines, but offer an extensive assortment of products within those lines

Limited-line wholesalers carry only a few product lines—such as groceries, lighting fixtures, or oil-well drilling equipment—but offer an extensive assortment of products within those lines. They provide a range of services similar to those of general wholesalers. Super Valu, for example, is a large limited-line food wholesaler (see Figure 14.3). Limited-line wholesalers for industrial goods serve relatively large geographic areas and provide technical expertise; for consumer goods, they supply single- or limited-line retailers. Bergen Brunswig Corporation, for example, is a limited-line wholesaler of pharmaceuticals and health and beauty aids. Inside Marketing (on the next page) discusses Bergen Brunswig's continuous quality improvement program.

Specialty-line wholesalers
Full-service wholesalers that carry only a single product line or a few items within a product line

Of all wholesalers, **specialty-line wholesalers** offer the narrowest range of products, usually a single product line or a few items within a product line. Wholesalers that specialize in shellfish, fruit, or other food delicacies are specialty-line wholesalers. Specialty-line wholesalers understand particular requirements of ultimate buyers and offer customers detailed product knowledge and depth of choice. To provide sales assistance to retailers, specialty wholesalers may set up displays and arrange merchandise. In industrial markets, specialty wholesalers often are better able than manufacturers to give customers technical advice and service.

Rack jobbers   Full-service specialty-line wholesalers that own and maintain display racks in stores

Rack jobbers are full-service specialty-line wholesalers that own and maintain display racks in supermarkets and discount, drug, and variety stores. They specialize in high-profit-margin, nonfood items, such as health and beauty aids, books, magazines, hardware, and housewares. Rack jobbers set up displays, mark merchandise, stock shelves, and keep billing and inventory records; retailers need only furnish space. Most rack jobbers operate on consignment and take back unsold products.

Limited-service wholesalers
Intermediaries providing some services and specializing in a few functions

Limited-Service Merchant Wholesalers   **Limited-service wholesalers** provide some marketing services and specialize in a few functions. Producers perform the remaining functions or pass them on to customers or to other middlemen. Limited-service wholesalers take title to merchandise but often do not deliver merchandise, grant credit, provide marketing information, store inventory, or plan ahead for customers' future needs. Because they offer only restricted services, limited-service wholesalers are compensated with lower rates and earn smaller profit margins than full-service wholesalers.

Bergen Brunswig Corporation's Prescriptions for Quality

Pharmaceutical wholesaler Bergen Brunswig Corporation purchases prescription anti-ulcer medication, antidepressants, and antibiotics from giant drug manufacturers such as Merck, Lilly, Pfizer, and Roche, as well as over-the-counter health and beauty aids, and distributes them to over eleven thousand hospitals and pharmacies throughout the United States. Guided by the company's stated principles of acting ethically, respecting individuals, and satisfying customers, Bergen continually strives to provide quality that surpasses customer expectations.

At Bergen, continuous quality improvement (CQI) is more than lip service to a business trend. It is the firm's systematic and ongoing program that encourages employees to make changes improving product and service quality. Chief among the program's methods are the use of customer satisfaction surveys and its team-based, four-phase problem-solving process. Each company division develops specific targeted customer satisfaction performance levels. Using what it calls a satisfaction index, Bergen measures customer satisfaction four times a year to assess its success in meeting those standards. When the surveys indicate problems, the continuous quality improvement teams get to work solving them.

More than a hundred teams, composed of associates from several departments and sometimes including suppliers and customers, work through Bergen's four-phase problem-solving process. Their goal is to identify and set in motion ways to improve quality and efficiency. The first step is defining the problem and identifying its causes. In the next stage, team members develop actions and calculate the costs of implementing them. After the new procedures are in place, the team tracks their success, measuring performance against predetermined quality goals. Finally, the team is empowered to standardize the new procedures and encouraged to share the lessons they have learned with other teams.

CQI projects have improved order-filling accuracy, speeded up the delivery process, cut down the time it takes to process customer credit, and reduced waste disposal through conservation and recycling. Bergen's Pine Brook division reduced stock-outs by 68 percent. In Tulsa, the organization reduced order-filling errors by 73 percent. The Dallas branch reduced ordering errors for narcotics by 91 percent. Its Valencia division improved the cycle time on customer credits by 66 percent. Overall, Bergen Brunswig's CQI has meant better quality, lower costs, more satisfied customers, and $7.6 billion in annual sales.

Sources: Bergen Brunswig Corporation, *1992 Annual Report;* Bergen Brunswig Corporation, "Quality Process Brochure," 1993; Rob Perez, "Bergen, French Firm Join in Bid for Distributor OCP," *Journal of Commerce,* Apr. 29, 1993, p. 7A; and "The Business Week 1000," *Business Week,* Mar. 27, 1995, p. 138.

Although certain types of limited-service wholesalers are few in number (and not even categorized separately by the Census Bureau), they are important in the distribution of such products as specialty foods, perishable items, construction materials, and coal. In this section we discuss specific functions of four typical limited-service wholesalers: cash-and-carry wholesalers, truck wholesalers, drop shippers, and mail-order wholesalers. (Table 14.2 summarizes services these wholesalers provide.)

Cash-and-carry wholesalers are intermediaries whose customers—usually small retailers and small industrial firms—pay cash and furnish transportation. Cash-and-carry wholesaling developed after 1920, when independent retailers began experiencing competitive pressure from large chain stores. Today, cash-and-carry wholesaling offers advantages because these wholesalers have no expenditures for outside salespersons, marketing research, promotion, credit, or delivery. Customers benefit from lower prices and immediate access to products. Cash-and-carry wholesalers usually handle a limited line of products with a high turnover rate—for instance, groceries, building materials, electrical supplies, or office supplies. Many small retailers whose accounts are refused by other wholesalers survive because of cash-and-carry wholesalers.

Truck wholesalers, sometimes called truck jobbers or wagon jobbers, transport a limited line of products directly to customers for on-the-spot inspection and selection.

Cash-and-carry wholesalers
Limited-service wholesalers whose customers pay cash and furnish transportation

Truck wholesalers
Limited-service wholesalers that transport products directly to customers for inspection and selection

328

Table 14.2 Various Services That Limited-Service Merchant Wholesalers Provide

	Cash-and Carry	Truck	Drop Shipper	Mail-Order
Physical possession of merchandise	Yes	Yes	No	Yes
Personal sales calls on customers	No	Yes	No	No
Information about market conditions	No	Some	Yes	Yes
Advice to customers	No	Some	Yes	No
Stocking and maintenance of merchandise in customers' stores	No	No	No	No
Credit to customers	No	Some	Yes	Some
Delivery of merchandise to customers	No	Yes	No	No

They are often small operators who own and drive their own trucks. They usually have regular routes, calling on retailers and other institutions to determine their needs. Truck wholesalers play an important part in supplying small grocery stores with perishables, such as fruits and vegetables, which other wholesalers often do not carry. They may also sell meat, service station supplies, and tobacco products. Although truck wholesalers sell, promote, and transport goods, they are generally classified as limited-service wholesalers because they do not extend credit. Their low-volume sales and wide range of customer services result in high operating costs.

Drop shippers

Limited-service wholesalers that take title to products and negotiate sales but never take actual possession of products

Drop shippers, also known as desk jobbers, take title to goods and negotiate sales but never take actual possession of products. They forward orders from retailers, industrial buyers, or other wholesalers to manufacturers and arrange for carload shipments of items to be delivered directly from producers to these customers. They assume responsibility for products during the entire transaction, including the costs of any unsold goods. Drop shippers are most commonly used in large-volume purchases of bulky goods, such as coal, oil, chemicals, lumber, and building materials, which are expensive to handle and ship relative to their unit value. Drop shippers incur no inventory costs and provide only minimal promotional assistance. They have low operating costs and pass along some of the savings to customers. Some drop shippers offer planning services, credit, and personal selling.

Mail-order wholesalers

Limited-service wholesalers that sell products through catalogs

Mail-order wholesalers use catalogs instead of sales forces to sell products to retail, industrial, and institutional buyers (see Figure 14.4). Wholesale mail-order houses generally feature cosmetics, specialty foods, sporting goods, office supplies, and automotive

**Figure 14.4
Mail-Order Wholesaler**
Grainger provides maintenance, repair, and operations products through its mail-order catalog.

Part 4 Distribution Decisions

parts. They usually require payment in cash or by credit card, and may discount large orders. Mail-order wholesalers hold goods in inventory and offer some planning services but seldom provide assistance with promotional efforts. Mail-order wholesaling enables buyers to choose and order particular catalog items for delivery through United Parcel Service, the U.S. Postal Service, or other carriers. This is a convenient and effective method of selling small items to customers in remote areas that other wholesalers might find unprofitable to serve.

■ *Agents and Brokers*

Functional middlemen
Intermediaries that negotiate purchases and expedite sales for a fee but do not take title to products

Agents Functional middlemen representing buyers or sellers on a permanent basis

Brokers Functional middlemen that bring buyers and sellers together temporarily and help negotiate exchanges

Agents and brokers (see Figure 14.5) negotiate purchases and expedite sales but do not take title to products. They are **functional middlemen,** intermediaries that perform a limited number of services in exchange for a commission, which is generally based on the product's selling price. **Agents** are middlemen representing buyers or sellers on a permanent basis. **Brokers** are usually middlemen that either buyers or sellers employ temporarily.

Although agents and brokers perform even fewer functions than limited-service wholesalers, they are usually specialists in particular products or types of customers and can provide valuable sales expertise. They know their markets well and often form long-lasting associations with customers. Agents and brokers enable manufacturers to expand sales when resources are limited, to benefit from the services of a trained sales force, and to hold down personal selling costs. However, despite the advantages they offer, agents and brokers face increased competition from merchant wholesalers, manufacturers' sales branches and offices, and direct-sales efforts.

We look here at three types of agents: manufacturers' agents, selling agents, and commission merchants. We also examine the brokers' role in bringing about exchanges between buyers and sellers. Table 14.3 summarizes these services.

Manufacturers' agents
Independent middlemen representing more than one seller and offering complete product lines

Manufacturers' Agents **Manufacturers' agents**—accounting for over half of all agent wholesalers—are independent middlemen that represent two or more sellers and usually offer customers complete product lines. They sell and take orders year-round, much like a manufacturer's sales force. Restricted to a particular territory, a manufacturers' agent handles noncompeting and complementary products. The relationship between the agent and each manufacturer is governed by written agreements explicitly outlining territories, selling price, order handling, and terms of sale relating to delivery, service, and warranties. Manufacturers' agents have little or no control over producers' pricing and marketing policies. They do not extend credit and may not be able to provide

Figure 14.5
Types of Agents and Brokers

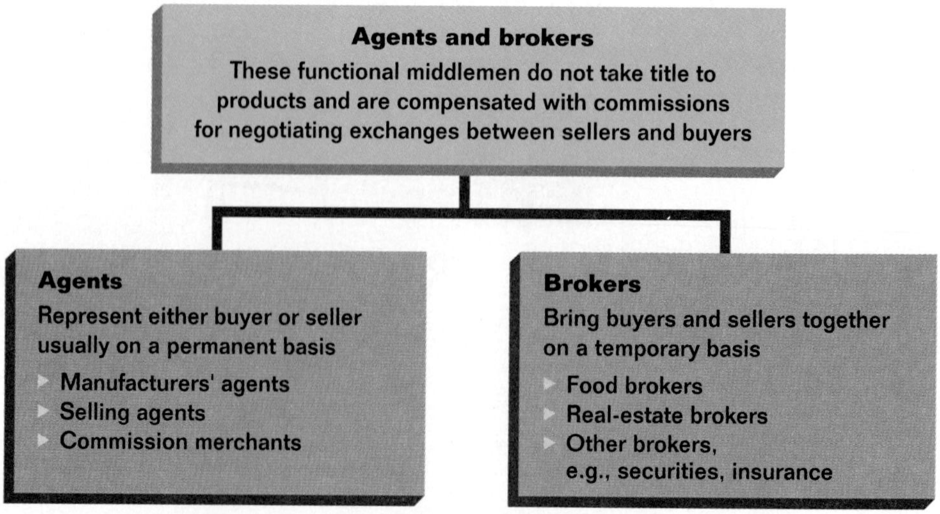

Agents and brokers
These functional middlemen do not take title to products and are compensated with commissions for negotiating exchanges between sellers and buyers

Agents
Represent either buyer or seller usually on a permanent basis
▷ Manufacturers' agents
▷ Selling agents
▷ Commission merchants

Brokers
Bring buyers and sellers together on a temporary basis
▷ Food brokers
▷ Real-estate brokers
▷ Other brokers, e.g., securities, insurance

Table 14.3   Various Services Agents and Brokers Provide

	Manufacturers' Agents	Selling Agents	Commission Merchants	Brokers
Physical possession of merchandise	Some	No	Yes	No
Long-term relationship with buyers or sellers	Yes	Yes	Yes	No
Representation of competing product lines	No	No	Yes	Yes
Limited geographic territory	Yes	No	No	No
Credit to customers	No	Yes	Some	No
Delivery of merchandise to customers	Some	Yes	Yes	No

technical advice. They do occasionally store and transport products, assist with planning, and provide promotional support. Some agents help retailers advertise and maintain a service organization. The more services offered, the higher is the agent's commission. Manufacturers' agents are commonly used in sales of apparel, machinery and equipment, steel, furniture, automotive products, electrical goods, and certain food items.

Agents' major advantages are their wide range of contacts and strong customer relationships. These intermediaries help large producers minimize the costs of developing new sales territories and adjust sales strategies for different products in different locations. Agents are also useful to small producers that cannot afford outside sales forces of their own because the producers incur no costs until the agents have sold something. Agents also spread operating expenses among noncompeting products, thus offering each manufacturer lower prices for services rendered.

The chief disadvantage of using agents is the higher commission rate (usually 10 to 15 percent) for new-product sales. When sales of a new product begin building, total selling costs go up, and producers sometimes transfer the selling function to in-house sales representatives. For this reason, agents avoid depending on a single product line; most work for more than one manufacturer.

Selling agents Middlemen marketing a whole product line or a manufacturer's entire output

Selling Agents   **Selling agents** market either all of a specified product line or a manufacturer's entire output. They perform every wholesaling activity except taking title to products. Selling agents usually assume the sales function for several producers at a time and are often used in place of marketing departments. In contrast to other agent wholesalers, selling agents generally have no territorial limits and have complete authority over prices, promotion, and distribution. They play a key role in advertising, marketing research, and credit policies of the sellers they represent, at times even advising on product development and packaging.

Selling agents are used most often by small producers or by manufacturers that have difficulty maintaining a marketing department because of seasonal production or other factors. Producers having financial problems may also engage selling agents. By so doing, producers relinquish some control of the business but may gain working capital by avoiding immediate marketing costs.

To avoid conflicts of interest, selling agents represent noncompeting product lines. Agents play an important part in distribution of coal and textiles, and also sometimes handle canned foods, household furnishings, clothing, lumber, and metal products. In these businesses, competitive pressures increase the importance of marketing relative to production, and selling agents are sources of essential marketing and financial expertise.

Commission merchants Agents that receive goods on consignment and negotiate sales in large markets

Commission Merchants   **Commission merchants** receive goods on consignment from local sellers and negotiate sales in large central markets. Most often found in agricultural marketing, commission merchants take possession of truckload quantities of commodities, arrange for necessary grading or storage, and transport the commodities to auction or markets where they are sold. When sales are completed, the agents deduct commission, plus the expense of making the sale, and then turn over profits to the producer.

Sometimes called factor merchants, these agents may have broad powers regarding prices and terms of sale. They specialize in obtaining the best price possible under market conditions. Commission merchants offer planning assistance and sometimes extend credit but usually do not provide promotional support. Because commission merchants deal in large volumes, their per-unit costs are generally low. Their services are most useful to small producers that must get products to buyers but do not field a sales force or accompany goods to market. In addition to farm products, commission merchants may handle textiles, art, furniture, or seafood products.

Businesses—including farms—that use commission merchants have little control over pricing, although the seller can specify a minimum price. Generally, the seller can supervise the agent's actions by checking commodity prices published regularly in newspapers. Large producers, however, maintain closer contact with the market and therefore have limited need for commission merchants.

Brokers Brokers seek buyers or sellers and help negotiate exchanges. A broker's primary purpose is to bring buyers and sellers together. Thus brokers perform fewer functions than other intermediaries. They are not involved in financing or physical possession, have no authority to set prices, and assume almost no risks. Instead, they offer customers specialized knowledge of a particular commodity and a network of established contacts.

Brokers are especially useful to sellers of certain types of products, such as supermarket products and real estate. They must assess and understand the needs and objectives of manufacturers and retailers. Brokers often provide consumer profiles and purchase patterns to identify target markets for specific products of their customers. For example, a Dallas broker identified the target market for Combat bug aerosol and helped the manufacturer increase sales by 25 percent.[13] The party engaging the broker's services—usually the seller—pays the broker's commission when the transaction is completed.

Food brokers sell food and general merchandise items to retailer-owned and merchant wholesalers, grocery chains, industrial buyers, and food processors. In fact, brokers handle 55 percent of all products sold in supermarkets. Food brokers enable buyers and sellers to adjust to fluctuating market conditions, provide assistance in grading, negotiating, and inspecting foods, and sometimes store and deliver products. Because of the seasonal nature of food production, the association between food broker and producer is temporary. Many mutually beneficial broker-producer relationships, however, are resumed year after year. Because food brokers provide a range of services on a somewhat permanent basis and operate in specific geographic territories, they are more accurately described as manufacturers' agents.

Food brokers Intermediaries selling food and general merchandise to merchant wholesalers, grocery chains, industrial buyers, and food processors

■ *Manufacturers' Sales Branches and Offices*

Sometimes called manufacturers' wholesalers, manufacturers' sales branches and offices resemble merchant wholesalers' operations.

Sales branches are manufacturer-owned middlemen selling products and providing support services to the manufacturer's sales force, especially in locations where large customers are concentrated and demand is high. They offer credit, deliver goods, give promotional assistance, and furnish other services. In many cases, they carry inventory (although this practice often duplicates functions of other channel members and is now declining). Customers include retailers, industrial buyers, and other wholesalers. Branch operations are common in the electrical supplies (Westinghouse Electric Corp.), plumbing (Crane Co. and American Standard Inc.), lumber, and automotive parts industries.

Sales branches Manufacturer-owned middlemen selling products and providing support services to the manufacturer's sales force

Sales offices are manufacturer-owned operations that provide services normally associated with agents. Like sales branches, they are located away from manufacturing plants, but unlike branches, they carry no inventory. A manufacturer's sales office or branch may sell products that enhance the manufacturer's own product line. Companies such as Campbell Soup Company provide diverse services to their wholesale and retail customers (see Figure 14.6). Hiram Walker, a liquor producer, imports wine from Spain to increase the number of products its sales offices can offer wholesalers.

Sales offices Manufacturer-owned operations providing services normally associated with agents

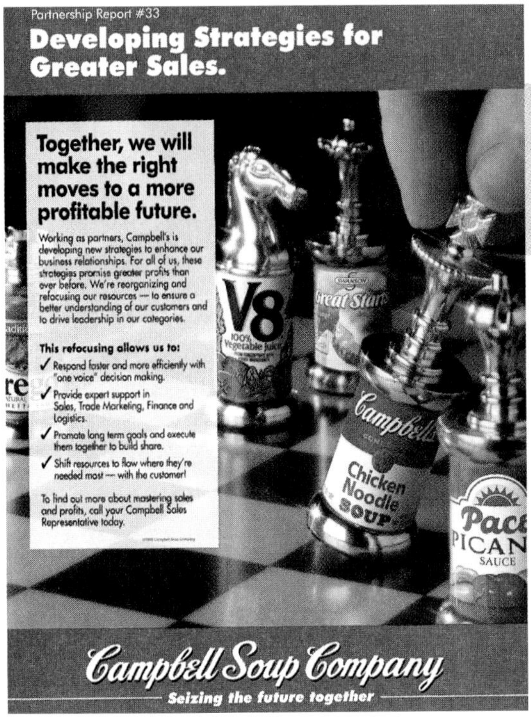
Partnership Report #33
Developing Strategies for Greater Sales.
Together, we will make the right moves to a more profitable future.
Working as partners, Campbell's is developing new strategies to enhance our business relationships. For all of us, these strategies promise greater profits than ever before. We're reorganizing and refocusing our resources — to ensure a better understanding of our customers and to drive leadership in our categories.
This refocusing allows us to:
✓ Respond faster and more efficiently with "one voice" decision making.
✓ Provide expert support in Sales, Trade Marketing, Finance and Logistics.
✓ Promote long term goals and execute them together to build share.
✓ Shift resources to flow where they're needed most — with the customer!
To find out more about mastering sales and profits, call your Campbell Sales Representative today.
V8
100% Vegetable
Campbell's
Chicken Noodle Soup
Pace
Picante Sauce
Campbell Soup Company
Seizing the future together

Figure 14.6
Manufacturers' Sales Office Services
Campbell Soup Company provides retail and wholesale businesses with many support services.

Manufacturers may set up sales branches or sales offices in order to reach their customers more effectively by performing wholesaling functions themselves. A manufacturer may also set up these branches or offices when specialized wholesaling services are not available through existing middlemen. In some situations, a manufacturer may bypass its wholesaling organization entirely—for example, if the producer decides to serve large retailer customers directly. One major distiller bottles private brand bourbon for California supermarkets and separates this operation completely from its sales office, which serves other retailers.

Facilitating Agencies

Facilitating agencies
Organizations engaging in activities that support channel functions

The supply chain is more than a marketing channel linking producer, intermediary, and buyer. **Facilitating agencies**—transportation companies, insurance companies, advertising agencies, marketing research agencies, and financial institutions—engage in activities that support channel functions (see Figure 14.7). Any of the functions these facilitating agencies perform, however, may be assumed by regular marketing intermediaries in the marketing channel.

The basic difference between channel members and facilitating agencies is that channel members perform negotiating functions (buying, selling, and transferring title), whereas facilitating agencies do not.[14] Facilitating agencies assist in channel operations but do not sell products. Channel managers may view facilitating agencies as subcontractors to which various distribution tasks can be farmed out according to the principle of specialization and division of labor.[15] Channel members (producers, wholesalers, or retailers) may rely on facilitating agencies because they believe that these independent businesses perform various activities more efficiently and effectively than they themselves could. Facilitating agencies are functional specialists performing special tasks for channel members without directing or controlling channel decisions. The following sections describe ways in which facilitating agencies expedite the flow of products through marketing channels.

Public Warehouses

Public warehouses are storage facilities available for a fee. Producers, wholesalers, and retailers rent space in warehouses instead of constructing their own facilities or using a merchant wholesaler's storage services. Many warehouses also process orders, deliver, collect accounts, and maintain display rooms where potential buyers inspect products.

When goods are used as collateral for a loan, channel members may place them in a bonded warehouse. If it is too impractical or expensive to transfer goods physically, channel members may arrange for a public warehouse to verify that goods are in the member's own facilities and then issue receipts for lenders.[16] Under this arrangement, the channel member retains possession of the products, but the warehouser has control. Many public warehousers know where clients can borrow working capital and are sometimes able to arrange low-cost loans.

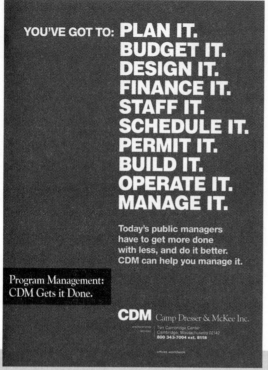

Figure 14.7
Facilitating Agencies   Facilitating agencies, such as CDM (Camp Dresser & McKee Inc.) and GE Information Services, provide support to marketing channel members.

■ *Finance Companies*

Wholesalers and retailers may also obtain financing by transferring product ownership to sales finance companies, banks, or savings and loan associations, while retaining physical possession of the goods. Often called "floor planning," this form of financing enables wholesalers and retailers—especially automobile and appliance dealers—to offer a greater selection of products and thus increase sales. When a product is sold, the dealer may have to pay off the loan immediately. Products financed through floor plans are usually well known, sell relatively easily, and present little risk.

Other financing functions are performed by factors—organizations providing clients with working capital by buying their accounts receivable or by loaning money, using the accounts receivable as collateral. Most factors minimize their risks by specializing in particular industries, making it easier to evaluate more accurately individual channel members within those industries. They may help clients improve their credit and collection policies and provide management expertise.

■ *Transportation Companies*

Rail, truck, air, and other carriers are facilitating organizations that help manufacturers and retailers transport products. Each form of transportation has advantages, which we will consider in Chapter 16. Transportation companies sometimes take over the functions of other middlemen. Because of the ease and speed of using air transportation for certain types of products, air freight companies can eliminate the need for maintaining large inventories and branch warehouses. In other cases, freight forwarders combine less-than-full shipments into full loads and pass on the savings to customers—perhaps charging a carload rate rather than a less-than-carload rate.

■ *Trade Shows and Trade Marts*

Trade shows   Industry exhibitions offering both selling and nonselling benefits

Trade shows and trade marts enable manufacturers or wholesalers to exhibit products to potential buyers and thus help selling and buying functions. **Trade shows** are industry exhibitions offering both selling and nonselling benefits.[17] Trade shows allow exhibitors to identify prospects; gain access to key decision makers; disseminate facts about their products, services, and personnel; and actually sell products and service current accounts through contacts at the show.[18] Nonselling benefits include opportunities to maintain the company image with competitors, customers, and the industry; gather information about competitors' products and prices; and identify potential channel partners.[19] Excluding the sales force, trade shows represent the second-largest promotional expenditure in a manufacturer's budget, second only to advertising in business publications.[20]

Trade show attendees come to find solutions to problems, evaluate potential suppliers, meet experts in specialized areas, and check out new developments in their industry.[21] According to a survey conducted by Simmons Market Research Bureau, 91 percent of respondents said they find trade shows to be "extremely useful" sources of purchasing information and that trade shows are the best way to view products and evaluate competitors.[22]

Trade shows permit direct buyer-seller interaction and may eliminate the need for agents. Companies exhibit at trade shows because of the high concentration of prospective buyers for their products. Studies show that it takes, on average, 5.1 sales calls to close an industrial sale but less than 1 sales call (0.8) to close a trade show lead, largely because more than half of the customers who purchase a product based on information gained at a trade show do so by mail or by phone after the show. When customers use these more impersonal information-gathering methods, the need for multiple sales calls to provide such information is eliminated.

International trade shows are important in developing global marketing opportunities. Exhibiting in an overseas trade show can be the most cost-effective way for a business to either initiate or extend its export activities in a business-to-business market.[23]

Trade marts Facilities that firms rent to exhibit products year-round

Trade marts are relatively permanent facilities that firms rent to exhibit products year round. At these marts, such products as furniture, home decorating supplies, toys, clothing, and gift items are sold to wholesalers and retailers. In the United States, trade marts are located in several major cities, including New York, Chicago, Dallas, High Point (North Carolina), Atlanta, and Los Angeles. The Dallas Market Center—which includes the Dallas Trade Mart, the Home-Furnishing Mart, the World Trade Center, the Decorative Center, Market Hall, InfoMart, and the Apparel Mart—is housed in six buildings designed specifically for the convenience of professional buyers.

Changing Patterns in Wholesaling

Wholesaling has become extremely competitive in the 1990s. The distinction between wholesaling services performed by many businesses and those provided by traditional wholesalers is blurring. Changes in the competitive nature of business, especially the growth of strong retailers such as Wal-Mart, Home Depot, Best Buy, and Circuit City, are changing supply chain relationships. In many product categories, such as electronics, furniture, and even food products, retailers have discovered that they may be able to deal directly with producers, performing the wholesaler's job themselves at a lower cost. For instance, retailers are increasingly relying on computer technology to expedite ordering, delivery, and handling of goods. Technology is thus allowing retailers to take over many wholesaling functions. Three noteworthy trends in wholesaling today are (1) consolidation of the wholesaling industry, (2) development of improved quality and productivity, and (3) globalization of wholesale markets.

■ *Wholesaler Consolidation*

Like most major industries, the wholesale industry is experiencing many buyouts and mergers. As examples, Super Valu, the nation's second-largest food wholesaler, acquired Wetterau, Inc., a rival; and Union Pacific Corp., a rail transport company, plans to merge with Southern Pacific Rail Corp.[24] (Inside Marketing on the next page profiles Super Valu.) Particularly in the health care industry, producers are acquiring wholesalers to control market share for their products and otherwise improve their operations. In two such cases, pharmaceuticals manufacturer Merck acquired Medco Containment Services, a

INSIDE MARKETING

Super Valu Excels at Supply Chain Management

Super Valu's revenues of $16.5 billion make it the second-largest food wholesaler in the United States. Super Valu provides wholesale services for 4,600 independent grocers, ranging in size from corner convenience stores to giant supermarkets. It supplies these retailer customers not only with thousands of grocery and nongrocery items—produce, meat, dairy products, paper goods, household items—but also with buying clout to compete against larger chain grocers. Super Valu distributes national brands, as well as its own private brand products, at prices comparable to those at larger stores. Furthermore, retailing experience gained in operating more than 300 grocery stores of its own means that Super Valu truly understands its customers.

Supply chain management involves the distribution of products and/or information that assists the manufacturer, wholesaler, and retailer, and provides value and service for the consumer. Super Valu is a specialist at integrating activities and developing partnerships across firms in the supply chain and eliminating services and activities that do not add value. It works closely with its retail partners to eliminate inefficiencies, costs, and redundancies in the marketing channel. Such coordination of activities and management of relationships in the supply chain can be a significant source of competitive advantage and can bring additional value to the customer. Cooperative relationships exist from linkages with suppliers to the development of financing, staff training, and store design for retail customers. Super Valu keeps its focus on supplying independent grocery retailers, helping them to compete by driving down costs, and offering value-added services such as electronic ordering.

Wholesalers are seeing a blurring between their traditional functions and the functions of their retailer customers, and Super Valu is caught between the profit margins of manufacturers and retailers facing a highly competitive market. To remain competitive, the company is continuing to add services such as a payroll system and insurance to keep retailers satisfied. At Super Valu, supply chain management is not just today's buzz word; it is a way of doing business that cuts across organizational and company boundaries to create a total system that serves customers and builds competitive advantage.

Sources: "The Business Week 1000," *Business Week,* Mar. 25, 1996, p. 126; Lisa Harrington, "How to Join the Supply Chain Revolution," *Inbound Logistics,* Nov. 1995, pp. 20–21; Jennifer Patterson, "Adding Value by Managing Supply Chain Activities," *Marketing News,* July 17, 1995, p. 6; Super Valu, *1995 Annual Report;* Harlan S. Byrne, "Super Valu Stores: Food Wholesaler Gives Thanks for Its Retail Operations," *Barron's,* Nov. 19, 1990, pp. 51–52; *Hoover's Company Profile* database (Austin, Texas: Reference Press, Inc., 1995), via America Online.

drug-benefits manager and mail-order distributor, and Eli Lilly, another pharmaceutical firm, bought PCS Health Systems, a managed-care firm.[25] Wholesalers that grow through geographic expansion, merger or acquisition, or improved productivity will control most of the wholesale business by the year 2000.[26] Wholesaling firms acquire or merge with other firms primarily to achieve more efficiency in the face of declining profit margins. Consolidation also gives larger wholesalers more pricing power over producers. Some analysts express concern that wholesalers' increased clout will increase the number of single-source supply deals.

On the other hand, wholesalers' larger customers, such as John Deere and Maytag, are demanding consolidation. These firms want to deal with a few suppliers that provide quality services at low prices.[27] As partnerships are developed through supply chain management, some companies want to purchase from just one supplier.

The wave of consolidation in the wholesale industry has caused more wholesalers to specialize. For example, McKesson Corp. once distributed chemicals, wines, and spirits but now focuses only on drugs. New larger wholesalers can also afford to purchase and use advanced technology to physically manage inventories, provide computerized ordering services, and help manage retail customers' operations.

■ *Productivity and Quality*

A major trend influencing business today is improving quality and productivity, or making the most efficient use of available resources to lower costs and increase value to customers. Companies are streamlining the way products move through the marketing channel to reduce costs, increase service, and improve profits to gain a competitive advantage. Thus, efforts to improve quality and productivity are likely to be a key trend in wholesaling in the immediate future. Efficient supply chain management will become a necessity to remain competitive.

To improve productivity and increase customer service, wholesalers are forging new relationships with both manufacturers and retailers. Wholesalers, in order to survive, must consistently, reliably, and profitably provide value to their customers. The use of new technology, especially in the area of information technology, has enormous potential to improve the outlook for wholesalers. Wholesalers are benefiting from computer networks that allow various organizations in the supply chain to share information and coordinate distribution based on long-term partnerships. Many wholesalers are using online services and/or the Internet to allow their employees, customers, and suppliers to share information between intermediaries and facilitating agencies. For example, FedEx, which serves as a facilitating agency in providing overnight or even same-day delivery of packages, provides online tracking of packages for the benefit of its customers. Other firms are making their databases and marketing information systems available to their supply chain partners to facilitate order processing, shipping, and product development, and to share information about changing market conditions and consumer desires.

■ *Global Expansion*

Wholesalers are very important as a means of reaching global markets. Approximately 85 percent of all prescription drugs sold in Europe go through wholesalers that are within national borders of the country in which the products are sold.[28] Encouraged by developments such as the North American Free Trade Agreement (NAFTA), increasing numbers of U.S. wholesalers are seeking opportunities in other countries. For example, Genuine Parts Co. (GPC) now owns a 49 percent interest in Canadian distributor UAP/NAPA and is a joint venture partner with Auto Todo, which operates six distribution centers in Mexico.[29] To facilitate their foreign operations, wholesalers seek help from local residents. Drug wholesaler McKesson Corp., for example, relies almost entirely on Canadians to manage its operations in Canada.[30] In the future, more wholesalers will probably penetrate global markets by operating without considering national borders. Some analysts predict that wholesalers who avoid foreign markets may find growth difficult.[31]

SUMMARY

Wholesaling includes all transactions in which the purchaser intends to use the product for resale, for making other products, or for general business operations. It does *not* include exchanges with ultimate consumers. Wholesalers are individuals or organizations that facilitate and expedite primarily wholesale transactions.

More than half of all goods are exchanged through wholesalers, although distribution of any product requires some wholesaling functions, whether or not a wholesaling institution is involved. For producers, wholesalers perform specialized accumulation and allocation functions for a number of products, letting the producers concentrate on manufacturing products. For retailers, wholesalers provide buying expertise, wide product lines, efficient distribution, and warehousing and storage.

Various types of wholesalers serve different market segments. How a wholesaler is classified depends on whether the wholesaler is owned by a producer, whether it takes title to products, what range of services it provides, and how broad and deep are its product lines. The three general categories of wholesalers are merchant wholesalers, agents and brokers, and manufacturers' sales branches and offices.

Merchant wholesalers are independently owned businesses that take title to goods and assume risk. They are either full-service wholesalers, offering the widest possible range of wholesaling functions, or limited-service wholesalers, providing only some marketing services and specializing in a few functions. Full-service merchant wholesalers include general-merchandise wholesalers offering a wide but relatively shallow product mix, limited-line wholesalers offering extensive assortments in a few product lines, and specialty-line wholesalers offering depth in a single product line or in a few items within a line. Rack jobbers are specialty-line wholesalers that own and service display racks in supermarkets and drugstores. There are four types of limited-service merchant wholesalers. Cash-and-carry wholesalers sell to small businesses, require payment in cash, and do not deliver. Truck wholesalers sell a limited line of products from their own trucks directly to customers. Drop shippers own goods and negotiate sales but never take possession of products. Mail-order wholesalers sell to retail, industrial, and institutional buyers through direct-mail catalogs.

Agents and brokers, sometimes called functional middlemen, negotiate purchases and expedite sales but do not take title to products. They are usually specialists, providing valuable sales expertise. Agents represent buyers or sellers on a permanent basis. Manufacturers' agents offer customers the complete product lines of two or more sellers; selling agents market a complete product line or a producer's entire output and perform every wholesaling function except taking title to products;

commission merchants receive goods on consignment from local sellers and negotiate sales in large central markets. Brokers negotiate exchanges between buyers and sellers on a temporary basis.

Manufacturers' sales branches and offices are vertically integrated units owned by manufacturers. Branches sell products and provide support services for the manufacturer's sales force in a given location. Sales offices carry no inventory and function much as agents do.

Facilitating agents do not buy, sell, or take title but perform certain wholesaling functions. They include public warehouses, finance companies, transportation companies, and trade shows and trade marts. These organizations sometimes eliminate the need for a wholesaling establishment.

The wholesaling industry is changing in response to changes in the marketing environment. The main changes are greater consolidation of the wholesaling industry; an increasing focus on improving quality and productivity, especially through information technology; and the growing importance of wholesalers as a means of reaching global markets.

IMPORTANT TERMS

Wholesaling	Specialty-line wholesalers	Drop shippers	Commission merchants
Wholesaler	Rack jobbers	Mail-order wholesalers	Food brokers
Merchant wholesalers	Limited-service wholesalers	Functional middlemen	Sales branches
Full-service wholesalers		Agents	Sales offices
General-merchandise wholesalers	Cash-and-carry wholesalers	Brokers	Facilitating agencies
Limited-line wholesalers	Truck wholesalers	Manufacturers' agents	Trade shows
		Selling agents	Trade marts

DISCUSSION AND REVIEW QUESTIONS

1. Is there a distinction between wholesalers and wholesaling? If so, what is it?
2. Would it be appropriate for a wholesaler to stock both interior wall paint and office supplies? Under what circumstances would this product mix be logical?
3. What services do wholesalers provide to producers and retailers?
4. Drop shippers take title to products but do not accept physical possession, and commission merchants take physical possession of products but do not accept title. Defend the logic of classifying drop shippers as wholesale merchants and commission merchants as agents.
5. What are the advantages of using agents to replace merchant wholesalers? What are the disadvantages?
6. What, if any, are the differences in the marketing functions that manufacturers' agents and selling agents perform?

7. Why are manufacturers' sales offices and branches classified as wholesalers? Which independent wholesalers are replaced by manufacturers' sales branches? Which independent wholesalers are replaced by manufacturers' sales offices?
8. "Public warehouses are really wholesale establishments." Comment on this statement.
9. Explain the role of facilitating organizations. Identify three facilitating organizations, and explain how each type performs this role.
10. Discuss the major trends in wholesaling today. How do these changes provide opportunities for growth of wholesaling?

APPLICATION QUESTIONS

1. Contact a local retailer with which you do business, and ask the manager to describe the relationship the store has with one of its wholesalers. Using Table 14.1 as a guide, identify the activities performed by the wholesaler. Are any of the functions shared by both the retailer and the wholesaler?

2. Review the section in the text entitled Classifying Wholesalers. Identify which type of wholesaling establishment is described below and explain your answer.

   Martin's Produce purchases fresh vegetables and fruit from the farmers' market and ships the goods to grocery stores, school cafeterias, and restaurants. Martin's also warehouses some of the produce at a central location for retailers who need to make emergency purchases, which they may do by picking up the merchandise themselves and paying for it with cash.

3. For each of the following, identify a specific facilitating agency: public warehouse, finance company, transportation company, trade show, and trade mart. Contact these organizations and ask the managers what services they provide for their customers. Summarize your findings.

4. Recent international developments such as NAFTA have provided global opportunities for many wholesalers. Find an article in the library that describes the efforts of a wholesaler in the international marketplace. How is the organization attempting to establish itself internationally?

Case 14.1 Fleming: Success Through Service

In one out of ten supermarkets in the United States, shoppers select food, household items, and health and beauty products supplied by wholesale food distributor Fleming Companies, Inc. Retailers count on Fleming to provide national and private brands, fresh meat, produce, dairy products, and frozen foods, as well as a huge assortment of nonfood items, from vitamins to videos. Of 240 U.S. wholesalers, Oklahoma-based Fleming is the largest, employing about 23,000 people and serving more than 4,800 retail outlets in thirty-six states. What gives Fleming an edge over competitors such as Super Valu is the exceptional service it provides retailers.

When O. A. Fleming, Gene Wilson, and Sam Lux incorporated Lux Mercantile in Topeka, Kansas, in 1915, they probably couldn't predict that by the 1990s the company would be recording annual sales of almost $16 billion. Facing powerful competition from chain stores, Fleming's founders created a partnership with other independent wholesale grocers to offer retailers help with mass merchandising, advertising, and efficient store operations. Renamed Fleming Companies, Inc., in 1941, the organization continues to grow by acquiring supermarkets, as well as other wholesale food distributors. With its purchase of Malone & Hyde, America's sixth-largest food distributor, Fleming became the largest wholesale food distributor in the United States, a title it has never relinquished.

In addition to being the biggest, Fleming strives to be the best. Its computerized, fuel-efficient fleet of nineteen hundred vehicles keeps costs low, a saving that Fleming passes on to its customers. Employing state-of-the-art technology helps the company dispense fast, efficient service at manageable prices. Computerized ordering systems and inventory control, such as Efficient Consumer Response, mechanized order selection and loading, and laser scanning expedite delivery from Fleming's warehouse and distribution centers, which are strategically located around the country. After placing an order, supermarkets can count on delivery in under twenty hours and often in as few as twelve.

Reasonable prices and prompt delivery are only part of the service picture at Fleming. Over the years, the wholesaler has discovered that its customers benefit from and welcome an array of support services. As one of Fleming's executive vice presidents noted, the more a wholesaler can do for retailers, the more time retailers have to concentrate on selling. To give its customers a competitive edge, Fleming offers them numerous private brand product lines. By spending less for these high-quality products, retailers can realize higher profits. Through retail counseling, the firm provides customers with its merchandising, management, and operations know-how. Fleming furnishes retailers with electronic services, including order entry and scanning equipment and computer software to manage shelves and regulate store operations. The company also offers employee training programs. Fleming helps retailers grow by providing them with location studies, aiding them in selecting sites for optimum new-store placement, and assisting them in designing individual stores. Fleming also provides financial services, including loans for equipment and inventory, store leasing, and fiscal counseling.

Even in a time of economic slowdown and corporate downsizing, Fleming is proceeding full steam ahead with growth and acquisition. In one recent year, the company added 136 stores. It also bought the largest supermarket chain in Puerto Rico, with operations in Florida and the U.S. Virgin Islands. To reduce expenses,

Fleming closed its southern California warehouse. To keep its customers supplied, Fleming still has to purchase some 600 million pounds of meat, 60 million cases of produce, and 450 million cases of grocery, frozen food, and dairy items a year.[32]

Questions for Discussion

1. How would you classify Fleming as to type of wholesaler?
2. In what ways is Fleming trying to gain an edge over its competitors?
3. What services is Fleming providing to its customers?

Case 14.2   McKesson Drug Company Prepares for the Twenty-First Century

Although McKesson Corporation owns Armor All automotive appearance products and McKesson Water Products bottled water, 97 percent of the company's $13 billion in annual revenues comes from its McKesson Drug Company. In the United States, pharmaceutical and health and beauty care wholesaling is a $35-billion-a-year industry, and McKesson Drug leads it. Every day McKesson serves two thousand pharmacies and sixteen thousand chain and independent drugstores from its thirty-nine nationwide distribution centers. As the United States enters a new generation of health care, McKesson is prepared to provide high-quality, low-cost products and services.

America's health care system is already changing, and more dramatic reforms are on the horizon. The market for pharmaceuticals will continue to expand. The U.S. population is aging, researchers are developing new, higher-priced drugs, and more employers are offering prescription benefits as part of their managed care programs. If the federal government includes pharmaceuticals in its health care reforms, about 72 million more Americans will be covered for prescription drugs. At the same time, costs of providing health care are skyrocketing and pressure to come up with cost-effective programs and products is intensifying. To face the changes ahead, McKesson Drug is enhancing its customer support, increasing its operating efficiency, restructuring its organizations, and strengthening its management.

McKesson is directing substantial energy and resources toward helping all its customers succeed. Econolink, McKesson's computer-based system of order entry and inventory control for institutional customers, helps pharmacists at hospitals, oncology clin-

ics, and nursing homes keep costs and inventory low while remaining responsive to their customers' needs. With the system in place, pharmacists can immediately locate and reserve inventory from the nearest McKesson distribution center, confirm orders, and schedule delivery for the next day. Largely as a result of Econolink, McKesson's institutional sales doubled in five years, reaching $1.5 billion. In addition, a newly organized fifty-five-person sales force works solely with McKesson's institutional customers to help them meet their changing needs.

Whatever its retail chain pharmacies need in terms of technology, programs, and services, McKesson tries to provide. When it doesn't offer a needed service, the company tries to implement it. For example, McKesson helped its customer, Med-X, a Tulsa, Oklahoma, chain of twenty drugstores, design in-house point-of-sale scanning and pharmacy computer systems. To help its retail chain pharmacies contain costs, reduce inventory, and retrieve information, McKesson established a retail version of Econolink.

The advent of managed health care, such as health maintenance organizations (HMOs) and other preferred provider plans, has made independent drugstores especially vulnerable. Under managed care, retail pharmacies will almost certainly have to align themselves in networks that can keep performance standards high while controlling costs. McKesson is aiding them in this effort. To help independent pharmacies, its largest customer group, remain competitive, McKesson created a new unit which offers innovative marketing programs and business counseling services. It also revitalized its line of generic drugs, whose lower prices meet the demands of managed care. In addition,

McKesson sponsors Valu-Rite, the largest voluntary association of independent drugstores in the United States.

To increase its own operating efficiency, McKesson consolidated its distribution centers, improved its inventory management, and streamlined its organizational structure. These changes have led to a shorter order-delivery cycle, expanded reach of service, lower transportation and handling costs, and increased order-filling accuracy.

In the opinion of McKesson Drug's executives, using technology effectively is the key to increasing operating efficiency. Almost 65 percent of McKesson's orders are filled by computer-controlled machinery. Computers communicate with one another using McKesson's warehouse management system. After bar codes are read with scanners, boxes are loaded onto conveyers, taken to automatic pickup machines, and put on storage shelves. At a distribution center in Spokane, Washington, McKesson's data management system and hands-free portable bar code scanner, called Acumax, have worked together to reduce mispicks by 72 percent. Because each avoided mispick saves McKesson about $80 in correction procedures, the company saves $9,000 in one month.

McKesson Drug's road into the twenty-first century is not totally smooth. In 1994, McKesson sold its PCS Health Care Systems division, a drug management program for health care systems, to Eli Lilly to avoid conflicts with McKesson Drug. McKesson is doing well among retail giants such as Wal-Mart, where it records annual sales of $1 billion; but as discounters swallow smaller independents, relying on a few huge customers will be risky. What happens if McKesson loses its Wal-Mart contract or Wal-Mart enters the pharmaceutical business itself? Perhaps the biggest threat to the organization is the growing mail-order drug business. One such firm, MedCo Containment, has grown almost 40 percent in the last five years.

Whatever the challenges, McKesson Drug continues pursuing growth through new contracts and acquisitions. In a single year, the U.S. government awarded McKesson six contracts with the Department of Defense, the Bureau of Prisons, and the Bureau of Veterans Affairs. In 1995, McKesson signed a $1 billion contract to supply Albertson's grocery stores with pharmaceuticals and other products. To become international leaders in pharmaceutical wholesaling, the organization acquired 23 percent of Nadro S.A. de C.V., Mexico's leading pharmaceutical distributor, and Medis Health, Canada's foremost pharmaceutical distributor. With most of the Western Hemisphere as its marketplace, McKesson Drug may realize its vision of becoming a "world-class provider of health care products and services for the emerging era of managed care."[33]

Questions for Discussion

1. What type of wholesaler is McKesson Drug Company?
2. What services does McKesson provide to producers and to retailers?
3. Why is McKesson so focused on helping drug retailers, such as Med-X, remain successful?

Chapter 15

Retailing

O B J E C T I V E S

- To understand the purpose and function of retailers in the marketing channel

- To be able to identify the major types of retailers

- To recognize the various forms of nonstore retailing

- To examine the types of franchising and its benefits and weaknesses

- To explore strategic issues in retailing

When Talbots steps out, consumers know what to expect.

*T*albots sells classic women's and children's apparel through 431 retail outlets in the United States, Canada, and the United Kingdom, as well as through private-label catalogs. It currently operates 308 Talbots Misses stores, 64 Talbots Petites stores, and four Talbots Intimates stores for women, in addition to 45 Talbots Kids stores and 10 Talbots Surplus stores. The retailer has succeeded by concentrating on classic sportswear designs, racking up $879 million in sales in 1994, up 19 percent from the previous year, compared to a 6.2 percent gain among other women's apparel retailers. The firm has decided to capitalize on the strength of its name by expanding into two new types of stores—boutiques for accessories and shoes, to be called Talbots Accessories and Shoes, and a Talbots Babies collection of infant clothing.

In leveraging its name in new areas, Talbots is following the lead of several other chains, including Ann Taylor, The Gap, and The Limited. Those three chains have started bath-and-body-care lines, and The Gap has also expanded into children's clothing, shoes, accessories, and active wear. Talbots already has some experience spinning off its name: in 1992, it launched a fragrance, and in 1994, it opened the first of its Talbots Kids stores with a line of apparel for older children. The firm is also looking into opening separate outlets for menswear and home furnishings, which competitors Calvin Klein and Liz Claiborne have already pioneered. Clark Hinkley, Talbots' COO says, "We think Talbots is a brand that could be transportable to almost anything connoting classic quality merchandise."

To test new product categories, Talbots first introduces them in its catalogs. For example, based on more than a year of catalog tests, which revealed sales increases that were exceeding the 9.5 percent comparable store sales gained at retail, the company decided to proceed with the launch of Talbots Accessories and Shoes. Only time and consumers' tastes will determine whether Talbots' plans for the future are on the right track. However, as Wendy Liebmann, a retail marketing consultant says, "Talbots is classic apparel for people who like a classic life. The opportunity to leverage it into a lifestyle is logical."[1]

Retailers such as Talbots are the most visible and accessible channel members to consumers. They are an important link in the marketing channel because they are both marketers for and customers of producers and wholesalers. They perform many marketing functions, such as buying, selling, grading, risk taking, and developing and maintaining information databases about customers. Retailers are in a strategic position to develop relationships with consumers and develop strategic partnerships with producers and intermediaries in the marketing channel.

In this chapter we examine the nature of retailing and its importance in supplying consumers with goods and services. We discuss the major types of retail stores and describe several forms of nonstore retailing. We also look at franchising, a retailing form that continues to grow in popularity. Finally, we present several strategic issues in retailing: location, retail positioning, store image, scrambled merchandising, and the wheel of retailing.

The Nature of Retailing

Retailing Transactions in which ultimate consumers are the buyers

Retailer An organization that purchases products for the purpose of reselling them to ultimate consumers

Retailing includes all transactions in which the buyer intends to consume the product through personal, family, or household use. Buyers in retail transactions are therefore the ultimate consumers. A **retailer** is an organization that purchases products for the purpose of reselling them to ultimate consumers. Although most retailers' sales are directly to the consumer, nonretail transactions occasionally occur when retailers sell products to other businesses. Retailing often takes place in stores or service establishments, but it also occurs through direct selling, direct marketing, and vending machines outside stores.

Retailing is important to the national economy. There are approximately 1.55 million retailers operating in the United States.[2] This number has remained relatively constant for the past twenty years, but sales volume has increased more than fourfold. Most personal income is spent in retail stores, and nearly one of every seven persons employed in the United States works in a retail store.

Retailers add value, provide services, and assist in making product selections. Retailer image can enhance the value of the product through the shopping experience, availability, or convenience, such as home shopping. Through its location, a retailer can facilitate comparison shopping. For example, it is not unusual for car dealerships to cluster in the same general vicinity. Product value is also enhanced as retailers offer services, such as technical advice, delivery, credit, and repair services. Finally, retail sales personnel can demonstrate to customers how a product can help address their needs or solve a problem.

The value added by retailers is significant for both producers and ultimate consumers. Retailers are the critical link between producers and ultimate consumers because they provide the environment in which exchanges with ultimate consumers occur. Ultimate consumers benefit through retailers' performance of marketing functions that result in the availability of broader arrays of products. As discussed in Chapter 13, retailers play a major role in creating time, place, and possession utility and, in some cases, form utility.

Leading retailers such as Wal-Mart, The Home Depot, Macy's, and Toys "R" Us offer consumers a place to browse and compare merchandise to find just what they need. However, such traditional retailing is being challenged by direct marketing channels that provide home shopping through catalogs, television, and even the Internet. Traditional retailers are responding to this change in the retail environment in various ways. Wal-Mart, for example, has joined forces with fast-food giants like McDonald's and PepsiCo to attract consumers and offer them the added convenience of eating where they shop.[3] Nordstrom's has developed around-the-clock access to apparel, shoes, and accessories through an electronic online mail system over the Internet.[4]

New store formats and advances in information technology are making the retail environment highly dynamic and competitive. The key to success in retailing is first to have a strong customer focus with a retail strategy that provides the appropriate level of service, product quality, and innovativeness that consumers desire. Partnerships among noncompeting retailers and other marketing channel members are providing new opportunities for retailers. For example, airports are leasing space to retailers such as The Sharper Image, McDonald's, Burger King, The Body Shop, and others.[5] The Kroger Co. and Nordstrom's have developed joint cobranded credit cards that provide rebates to customers at participating stores. The Kroger Mastercard provides a 1 percent rebate toward future Kroger grocery purchases.[6]

Retailers are also finding global opportunities. For example, Toys "R" Us is now opening more international units than domestic stores, a trend that is likely to continue for the foreseeable future.[7] Wal-Mart and Home Depot are rapidly opening stores in Canada and Mexico. McDonald's is growing faster outside the United States and even has stores in Russia and China.

Major Types of Retail Stores

Independent store
A single retail outlet owned by an individual, partnership, or corporation

Chain store   A retail outlet that is part of a multiple-outlet organization

Portfolio retailing
A situation in which one company owns multiple chains of stores

Franchise store   A store owned by a franchisee who has contracted with the parent company to market specific products under conditions specified by the franchiser

General merchandise retailer   A retail establishment that offers a variety of product lines, which are stocked in depth

Department stores
Large retail organizations characterized by wide product mixes and organized into separate departments to facilitate marketing efforts and internal management

There are many different types of retail stores. One way to classify them is by form of ownership. An **independent store** is a single retail outlet owned by an individual, partnership, or corporation. Most independent retailers tend to be small stores owned by individuals, such as a local hardware store, bakery, dry cleaning establishment, or bookstore. A **chain store** is a retail outlet that is part of a multiple-outlet organization, often owned by a corporation. The Gap, Radio Shack, and JC Penney are examples of chain stores. A company can also own multiple chains, which is referred to as **portfolio retailing.** For example, Dayton Hudson Corporation owns many chains, including Target, Mervyn's, Marshall Field's, Dayton's, and Hudson's. A **franchise store** is owned by a franchisee who has contracted with the parent company (called a franchiser) to market specific products under conditions specified by the franchiser. The parent company may also own similar stores. Franchising is discussed in more detail later in this chapter.

Retailers are also categorized based on the breadth of products offered. Two general categories include general merchandise retailers and specialty retailers.

◼ General Merchandise Retailers

A retail establishment that offers a variety of product lines, stocked in considerable depth, is referred to as a **general merchandise retailer.** The types of product offerings, the mixes of customer services and the operating styles of retailers in this category vary considerably. The primary types of general merchandise retailers are department stores, discount stores, supermarkets, superstores, hypermarkets, warehouse clubs, and warehouse and catalog showrooms (Table 15.1).

Department Stores   **Department stores** are large retail organizations employing at least 25 people and characterized by wide product mixes. To facilitate marketing efforts and internal management in these stores, related product lines are organized into separate departments such as cosmetics, housewares, apparel, home furnishings, and appliances. Often each department functions as a self-contained business, and buyers for individual departments are fairly autonomous.

Department stores are distinctly service-oriented. Their total product includes credit, delivery, personal assistance, merchandise returns, and a pleasant atmosphere. Although some so-called department stores are actually large, departmentalized specialty stores, most department stores are shopping stores. Consumers can compare price, quality, and service at one store with those at competing stores. Along with large discount stores, department stores are often considered retailing leaders in a community and are found in most communities with populations of more than fifty thousand.

Typical department stores—Macy's, Sears, Marshall Field's, Dillard's and Neiman Marcus—obtain a large proportion of sales from apparel, accessories, and cosmetics. Figure 15.1 shows an advertisement for Nordstrom's department stores. Other products these stores carry include gift items, luggage, electronics, home accessories, and sports equipment. Some department stores offer services such as automotive insurance, hair

Table 15.1 General Merchandise Retailers

Type of Retailer	Description	Examples
Department store	Large organization offering wide product mix and organized into separate departments	Macy's, JC Penney, Sears
Discount store	Self-service, general merchandise store offering brand name and private name products at low prices	Wal-Mart, Target, Kmart
Supermarket	Self-service store offering complete line of food products and some nonfood products	Kroger, Albertson's, Winn-Dixie
Superstore	Giant outlet offering all food and nonfood products found in supermarkets, as well as most routinely purchased products	Meijer-Thrifty Acres
Hypermarket	Combination supermarket and discount shopping, larger than a superstore	Carrefours
Warehouse club	Large-scale, members-only establishments combining cash-and-carry wholesaling with discount retailing	Sam's Club, Price-Costco
Warehouse showroom	Facility in a large, low-cost building with large on-premises inventories and minimum service	Levitz Furniture
Catalog showroom	Type of warehouse showroom where consumers shop from a catalog and products are stored out of buyers' reach and provided in manufacturer's carton	Service Merchandise

care, and travel, optical, and income tax preparation services. In some cases, space for these specialized services is leased out, with proprietors managing their own operations and paying rent to department stores.

Department stores have encountered problems in recent years. Overhead and operating expenses (about 35 percent of sales) are higher than those of most other retailers, partly because of the variety of services offered. Some have been forced into bankruptcy or near bankruptcy and have streamlined their product offerings, modified their appeal, or undergone major remodeling to sustain and generate profitability. Some are expanding budget-priced lines to ease competitive pressure from discount and specialty stores. Population growth is now centered in the suburbs; to stay close to their customers, many department stores have opened stores in outlying shopping centers and malls. In recent years, department stores have lost customers to specialty retailers, discounters, and direct marketers.[8]

Figure 15.1
Department Stores A department store, such as Nordstrom's, provides broad product mixes.

Discount stores
Self-service, general-merchandise stores offering brand name and private brand products at low prices

Discount Stores   Discount stores are self-service, general-merchandise outlets regularly offering brand name and private brand products at low prices. Discounters accept lower margins than conventional retailers in exchange for high sales volume. To keep turnover high, they carry a wide but carefully selected assortment of products, from appliances to housewares and clothing. Major discount establishments also offer foods, toys, automotive services, garden supplies, and sports equipment. Wal-Mart, Target, and Kmart are the three largest discount stores. Many discounters are regional organizations such as Venture, Bradlees, and Meuer. Most operate in large (50,000 to 80,000 square feet) no-frills facilities. Discount stores usually offer everyday low prices rather than relying on sales events.

347

Discount retailing developed on a large scale in the early 1950s, when postwar production began catching up with consumer demand for appliances, home furnishings, and other hard goods. Discount stores were often cash-only operations in warehouse districts, offering goods at savings of 20 to 30 percent over conventional retailers. Facing increased competition from department stores and other discount stores, some discounters have improved store services, atmosphere, and location, raising prices and sometimes blurring the distinction between discount stores and department stores. Other discounters continue to focus on price alone.

Supermarkets   Large, self-service stores that carry a complete line of food products, along with some nonfood products

Supermarkets   Supermarkets are large, self-service stores that carry a complete line of food products, as well as some nonfood products, such as cosmetics and nonprescription drugs. Supermarkets are arranged in departments for maximum efficiency in stocking and handling products but have central checkout facilities. They offer lower prices than smaller neighborhood grocery stores, usually provide free parking, and may also cash checks. Supermarkets may be independently owned but are often part of a chain operation. Top U.S. supermarket chains include Kroger (see Figure 15.2), Safeway, and A & P.

Today consumers make more than three-quarters of all grocery purchases in supermarkets. Even so, supermarkets' total share of the food market is declining because consumers now have widely varying food preferences and buying habits, and in most communities shoppers can choose from a number of convenience stores, discount stores, and specialty food stores, as well as a wide variety of restaurants.

Figure 15.2
Supermarket   Kroger provides diverse services, such as catering.

To remain competitive, some supermarkets are cutting back services, emphasizing low prices, and using promotion methods such as games or coupons. Other supermarkets have converted to discount or warehouse retailing. Still others have taken the opposite approach, dramatically expanding both services and product mixes. For example, at Gromer's Super Market in Elgin, Illinois, customers can use the post office, pay utility bills, buy lottery tickets, get documents notarized or photocopied, have film processed, pick up license plates and transfer auto titles, cash checks, use an automatic teller machine, rent rug-cleaning machines, and even get fingerprinted. However, a survey by the Food Marketing Institute found that few shoppers take advantage of some of these extras. For example, only 11 percent of supermarket shoppers say they buy videos there, usually because of limited selection. Other less-than-popular frills include supermarket floral and catering services. One convenience that consumers *do* like is ATM machines located in supermarkets. Supermarket ATMs are used almost as much as machines located adjacent to banks.[9]

Supermarkets also try to increase efficiency and competitiveness through technological changes. Most supermarkets use electronic scanners, which identify and record purchases via bar codes on products. Such detailed sales data allow management to maintain inventories, track unit sales and consumer preferences, and improve store and shelf layouts. Regardless of the technology used, supermarkets must operate efficiently because net profits after taxes are usually less than 1 percent of sales.

Superstores Giant retail outlets that carry food and nonfood products found in supermarkets, as well as most routinely purchased consumer products

Superstores Superstores—which originated in Europe—are giant retail outlets that carry not only food and nonfood products ordinarily found in supermarkets, but also many routinely purchased consumer products. Besides a complete food line, superstores sell housewares, hardware, small appliances, clothing, personal-care products, garden products, and tires—about four times as many items as supermarkets. Services available at superstores include dry cleaning, automotive repair, check cashing, bill paying, and snack bars.

Superstores combine features of discount stores and supermarkets. Examples include Meijer-Thrifty Acres in Michigan, some Kroger stores, and Super Kmart Centers. To cut handling and inventory costs, they use sophisticated operating techniques and often tall shelving that displays entire assortments of products. Superstores can have an area of as much as 100,000 square feet (compared with 20,000 square feet in supermarkets). Sales volume is two to three times that of supermarkets, partly because locations near good transportation networks help generate in-store traffic needed for profitability.

Consumers are attracted to superstores by lower prices and one-stop shopping. Consequently, other food retailers have started handling general merchandise because gross margin and net profit are higher on those items than on food. Several supermarket chains, including Vons, have added supersized units. Its Expo stores combine warehouse pricing and value-packs with standard grocery items.[10] But superstores require large investments, stringent cost controls, appropriate facilities, and managers who can coordinate broad product assortments. Conventional supermarkets, hampered by economic uncertainty and lack of space for physical expansion, find it difficult to compete effectively with superstores.

Hypermarkets Stores that combine supermarket and discount shopping in one location

Hypermarkets Hypermarkets combine supermarket and discount store shopping in one location. Larger than superstores, they range from 225,000 to 325,000 square feet and offer 45,000 to 60,000 different types of low-priced products. They commonly allocate 40 to 50 percent of their space to grocery products and the remainder to general merchandise, including athletic shoes, designer jeans, and other apparel; refrigerators, televisions, and other appliances; housewares; cameras; toys; jewelry; hardware; and automotive supplies. Many lease space to noncompeting businesses, such as banks, optical shops, and fast-food restaurants. All hypermarkets focus on low prices and vast selection. Although Kmart, Wal-Mart, and Carrefours (a French retailer) have operated hypermarkets in the United States, most of these stores have been unsuccessful and have closed. Such stores are too big for time-constrained U.S. shoppers. However, hypermarkets are quite successful in Europe and South America.[11]

Warehouse clubs Large-scale, members-only establishments that combine features of cash-and-carry wholesaling with discount retailing

Warehouse Clubs Warehouse clubs, a rapidly growing form of mass merchandising, are large-scale, members-only selling operations combining cash-and-carry wholesaling with discount retailing. For a nominal annual fee (usually about $25), small retailers purchase products at wholesale prices for business use or for resale. Warehouse clubs also sell to ultimate consumers affiliated with government agencies, credit unions, schools, hospitals, and banks, but instead of paying a membership fee, individual consumers pay about 5 percent more on each item than do business customers.

Sometimes called buying clubs, warehouse clubs offer the same types of products as discount stores but in a limited range of sizes and styles. Whereas most discount stores carry 40,000 items, a warehouse club handles only 3,500 to 5,000 different products, usually acknowledged brand leaders.[12] Warehouse clubs offer a broad product mix, including nonperishable foods, beverages, books, appliances, housewares, automotive parts, hardware, and furniture. In the United States, more than 21 million people belong to warehouse clubs. These clubs generate over $34 billion a year in sales.[13] Warehouse clubs appeal to many price-conscious consumers and small retailers unable to obtain wholesaling services from larger distributors. The average warehouse club shopper has more education, higher income, and a larger household than the average supermarket shopper.[14]

To keep prices 25 to 30 percent lower than those of supermarkets and discount stores, warehouse clubs provide few services.[15] They generally do not advertise, except through direct mail. Their facilities, often located in industrial areas, have concrete floors and aisles wide enough for forklifts. Merchandise is stacked on pallets or displayed on pipe racks. All payments must be in cash, and customers must transport purchases themselves.

The warehouse club concept, which has spread widely in the last few years, was pioneered by Price Co. After a fiercely tough competitive war among twenty firms, there are two remaining major competitors: Wal-Mart's Sam's Club and Price-Costco.[16]

Warehouse and Catalog Showrooms   **Warehouse showrooms** are retail facilities with five basic characteristics: (1) large, low-cost buildings, (2) warehouse materials-handling technology, (3) vertical merchandise displays, (4) large on-premises inventories, and (5) minimum services.

Warehouse showrooms Retail facilities in large, low-cost buildings with large on-premise inventories and minimum services

Although some superstores, hypermarkets, and discount supermarkets have used warehouse retailing, most of the best-known showrooms are operated by large furniture retailers. Wickes Furniture and Levitz Furniture Corporation brought sophisticated mass merchandising to the highly fragmented furniture industry. These high-volume, low-overhead operations stress fewer personnel and services. Lower costs are possible because some marketing functions have been shifted to consumers, who must transport, finance, and perhaps store merchandise. Most consumers carry away purchases in the manufacturer's carton, although stores will deliver for a fee.

Catalog showrooms A form of warehouse showroom, where consumers shop from a catalog and where products are stored out of buyers' reach

In **catalog showrooms,** one item of each product is displayed, often in a locked case, with remaining inventory stored out of the buyer's reach. Using catalogs that have been mailed to their homes or are on store counters, customers order products by phone or in person. Clerks fill orders from the warehouse area, and products are presented in the manufacturer's carton. In contrast to traditional catalog retailers, which offer no discounts and require that customers wait for delivery, catalog showrooms regularly sell below list price and often provide goods immediately.

Catalog showrooms usually sell jewelry, luggage, photographic equipment, toys, small appliances and housewares, sporting goods, and power tools. They advertise extensively and carry established brands and models that are not likely to be discontinued. Because catalog showrooms have higher product turnover, fewer losses through shoplifting, and lower labor costs than department stores, they are able to feature lower prices. They offer minimal services, however. Customers may have to stand in line to examine items or place orders. Pressure is being applied to catalog showrooms by rapid growth of discounters and warehouse clubs. Service Merchandise (the market leader), Best Products, and Consumer Distributing are examples of catalog showroom retailers.

■ *Specialty Retailers*

In contrast to general merchandise retailers with their broad product mixes, specialty retailers emphasize narrow and deep ones. Despite their name, specialty retailers do not sell specialty items (except when specialty goods complement the overall product mix). Instead, they offer substantial assortments in a few product lines. We examine three types of specialty retailers: traditional specialty retailers, off-price retailers, and category killers.

Traditional specialty retailers Stores that carry a narrow product mix with deep product lines

Traditional Specialty Retailers   **Traditional specialty retailers** are stores carrying a narrow product mix with deep product lines. Sometimes called *limited-line retailers,* they may be referred to as *single-line retailers* if they carry unusual depth in one main product category. Specialty retailers commonly sell shopping goods such as apparel, jewelry, sporting goods, fabrics, computers, and pet supplies. The Limited, Radio Shack, Hickory Farms, The Gap, and The Disney Store are examples of retailers offering limited product lines but great depth within those lines (see Figure 15.3).

Although the number of chain specialty stores is increasing, most specialty stores are independently owned. They occupy about two-thirds of the space in most shopping centers and malls, accounting for 40 to 50 percent of all general merchandise sales.[17] Florists, bakery shops, and bookstores are among the small independent specialty retailers that appeal to local target markets, although these stores can be owned and managed by large corporations. Even if this kind of retailer adds a few supporting product lines, the store may still be classified as a specialty store.

Figure 15.3
Specialty Retailers
Specialty retailers like The Disney Store offer limited product lines with greater product depth.

Because they are usually small, specialty stores may have high costs in proportion to sales, and satisfying customers may require carrying some products with low turnover rates. However, these stores sometimes obtain lower prices from suppliers by purchasing limited lines of merchandise in large quantities. Successful specialty stores understand their customer types and know what products to carry, thus reducing the risk of unsold merchandise. Specialty stores usually offer better selections and more sales expertise than department stores, their main competitors. By capitalizing on fashion, service, personnel, atmosphere, and location, specialty retailers position themselves strategically to attract customers in specific market segments. They may even become exclusive dealers in their markets for certain products. Through specialty stores, small-business owners provide unique services to match consumers' varied desires. For consumers dissatisfied with the impersonal nature of large retailers, the close, personal contact offered by a small specialty store can be a welcome change. For example, Run-Tex, an independent specialty store in Austin, Texas, focuses solely on shoeing runners, joggers, and walkers. Owners Sheila and Paul Carrozza, runners themselves, provide their customers with the widest selection of shoes and related running apparel available, as well as expert advice. Run-Tex also sponsors clinics and marathons and donates used shoes to the poor and homeless of their community (customers who trade in an old pair of shoes for donation receive $10 off each pair they buy). The store's selection, expertise, races, and charitable activities have brought it recognition from well beyond Austin; *Runner's World* magazine named Run-Tex "the country's best running store."[18]

Off-price retailers
Stores that buy manufacturers' seconds, overruns, returns, and off-season merchandise for resale to consumers at deep discounts

Off-Price Retailers   **Off-price retailers** are stores that buy manufacturers' seconds, overruns, returns, and off-season production runs at below-wholesale prices for resale to consumers at deep discounts. Unlike true discount stores, which pay regular wholesale prices for goods and usually carry second-line brand names, off-price retailers offer limited lines of national-brand and designer merchandise, usually clothing, shoes, or housewares. The number of off-price retailers has grown since the mid-1980s and now includes such major chains as T. J. Maxx, Stein Mart, Burlington Coat Factory, and Marshalls.

Off-price stores charge 20 to 50 percent less than do department stores for comparable merchandise but offer few customer services. They often feature community dressing rooms, central checkout counters, and no credit, returns, or exchanges. Off-price stores may or may not sell goods with original labels intact (Filene's Basement Stores do, Loehmann's outlets do not). They turn over their inventory nine to twelve times a year, three times as often as traditional specialty stores. They compete with department stores for the same customers: price-conscious members of suburban households who are knowledgeable about brand names. Another form of off-price retailer is the manufacturer's outlet mall, which makes available manufacturer overstocks and unsold merchandise from other retail outlets. Prices are low, and diverse manufacturers are represented in

Best Buy Co.: Using Technology to Sell Technology

Best Buy Company, Inc., based in Eden Prairie, Minnesota, is one of the leading U.S. consumer electronics retailers with 1995 sales of $5 billion and profits of nearly $58 million. By strategically locating its more than 250 superstores and offering strong customer service with home delivery, car stereo installation, technical repair, and a private label credit card, Best Buy has achieved remarkable success as a "category killer."

Best Buy was founded in 1966 in Minnesota by Richard Schulze (now CEO) as the Sound of Music, a home- and car-stereo store. From the beginning, Schulze emulated Wal-Mart, concentrating on keeping prices low by working faithfully to improve efficiency. When Schulze realized that his target customer population, 15-to-18-year-old males, was shrinking, he began targeting older, more affluent customers by broadening the product line to include appliances and VCRs. The name was changed to Best Buy in 1983. To further differentiate Best Buy from stiff competition such as Circuit City, Schulze developed a new store concept. At Best Buy's first Concept II store in Minneapolis–St. Paul, customers could buy products in just one step, taking the goods from the aisle to the cash register. Believing customers didn't need or want a lot of high-pressure sales help, Schulze took his sales staff off commission and reduced the number of employees per store.

Schulze did not rest with the success of the Concept II stores. He began to develop an even more consumer-driven concept patterned after such winning models as Toys 'R' Us and The Home Depot. At these Concept III stores, interactive Answer Center kiosks allow customers to access information about product functions, features, and prices. The new stores also provide demonstration areas for surround sound, simulated, life-size car displays to demonstrate car stereo speakers, fun and games areas, 100 CD listening posts, 65,000 music titles, 12,000 video titles, and 2,000 computer software titles.

Best Buy has also introduced computers to its product line and is now the nation's top retailer of personal computers to the home user market. Best Buy has been so successful at selling PCs that, in 1994, Intel named Best Buy "the Number One Pentium Processor Retailer in the World."

Source: Best Buy 1995 Annual Report; Hoover's Handbook database (Austin, TX: The Reference Press, 1995), via America Online.

these malls. Sales at factory outlet malls have more than doubled in the last five years to $13 billion.[19]

To ensure a regular flow of merchandise into their stores, off-price retailers establish long-term relationships with suppliers that can provide large quantities of goods at reduced prices. Manufacturers may approach retailers with samples, discontinued products, or items that have not sold well; or retailers may seek out producers, offering to pay cash for goods produced during the manufacturers' off season. Although manufacturers benefit from such arrangements, they also risk alienating their specialty and department store customers. Department stores tolerate off-price stores as long as they do not advertise brand names, limit merchandise to lower-quality items, and are located away from the department stores. When off-price retailers obtain large stocks of in-season, top-quality merchandise, tension builds between department stores and manufacturers.

Category killer A very large specialty store concentrating on a single product line and competing on the basis of low prices and product availability

Category Killers   Over the last decade, a new breed of specialty retailer, the category killer, has evolved. A **category killer** is a very large specialty store that concentrates on a single product line and competes on the basis of low prices and enormous product availability. These stores are referred to as category killers because they expand rapidly and gain sizable market shares, taking business away from smaller, high-cost retail outlets. Examples of category killers include The Home Depot (building materials), Office Depot (office supplies and equipment), Toys "R" Us (toys), and Sports Authority (sports equipment). Sports equipment superstores are expected to triple their current 5 percent share of the $31 billion sports retail market in the next five years, perhaps at the expense of smaller sports-equipment outlets. Sports Authority, with 120 stores and plans to open about 50 more by the end of 1996, has the highest inventory turnover and sales per store of all the superstore chains.[20] Technology in Marketing profiles Best Buy Co.

Nonstore Retailing

Nonstore retailing
The selling of products outside the confines of a retail facility

Nonstore retailing is the selling of products outside the confines of a retail facility. This form of retailing accounts for an increasing percentage of total sales. Three factors are spurring its growth. Consumers—especially women, because of their increased participation in the work force—have less time for shopping in retail stores. Some retail store salespeople are poorly informed and therefore less able to assist shoppers. Finally, the number of older consumers is rising, and they are less prone to shop in stores. Approximately 15 percent of all consumer purchases are made through nonstore retailing. The three major types of nonstore retailing are direct selling, direct marketing, and automatic vending.

■ *Direct Selling*

Direct selling
The marketing of products to ultimate consumers through face-to-face sales presentations at home or in the workplace

Direct selling is the marketing of products to ultimate consumers through face-to-face sales presentations at home or in the workplace. Traditionally called door-to-door selling, direct selling began in our country with the peddler over a century ago and has grown into a sizable industry of several hundred firms. Although direct selling retailers historically used a cold canvass door-to-door approach for finding prospects, many companies today, such as World Book, Kirby, Mary Kay, Amway, and Avon, use other approaches. They initially identify customers through mail, telephone, and shopping mall intercepts and set appointments. Probably less than 1 percent of total direct selling purchases result from sales efforts without prearranged appointments.

The party plan is sometimes used in direct selling and can occur in homes or in the workplace. When a party plan is used, a consumer acts as a host and invites a number of friends and associates to view merchandise in a group setting, where a salesperson is available to demonstrate products. The congenial party atmosphere overcomes customers' suspicions and encourages them to buy. Direct selling through the party plan requires effective salespersons, who can identify hosts and provide encouragement and incentives for them to organize a gathering of friends and associates. Companies that commonly use the party plan include Tupperware, Stanley Home Products, and Sarah Coventry.

Direct selling has both benefits and limitations. It provides the marketer with an opportunity to demonstrate the product in an environment—customers' homes—where it would most likely be used. The door-to-door seller can give the customer personal attention, and the product can be presented to the customer at a convenient time and location. Personal attention to the customer is the foundation on which some direct sellers, such as Mary Kay, have built their businesses. Because salesperson commissions are so high, ranging from 30 to 50 percent of the sales price, and great effort is required to isolate promising prospects, overall costs of direct selling make it the most expensive form of retailing. Furthermore, some customers view direct selling negatively, owing to unscrupulous and fraudulent practices used by direct sellers in the past. Some communities even have local ordinances that control or, in some cases, prohibit direct selling.

■ *Direct Marketing*

Direct marketing   The use of the telephone and nonpersonal media to introduce products to consumers, who then can purchase them by mail or telephone

Direct marketing is the use of the telephone and nonpersonal media to communicate product and organizational information to customers, who then can purchase products by mail, E-mail, or telephone. Direct marketing can occur through catalog marketing, direct-response marketing, telemarketing, home shopping, and online marketing.

Catalog marketing   A type of marketing where an organization provides a catalog from which customers make selections and place orders by mail or telephone

Catalog Marketing   In **catalog marketing** an organization provides a catalog from which customers make selections and place orders by mail or telephone. Catalog marketing began in 1872, when Montgomery Ward issued its first catalog to rural families. Today there are over 7,000 catalog marketing companies in the United States, as well as a number of retailers, such as JC Penney, that engage in catalog marketing. Some organizations, such as Spiegel (see Figure 15.4) and JC Penney offer a broad array of products spread over multiple product lines. Catalog companies such as L.L. Bean, The Pottery Barn (see Figure 15.4), and J. Crew offer considerable depth in one major line of products. Still other catalog companies specialize in only a few products within a single line.

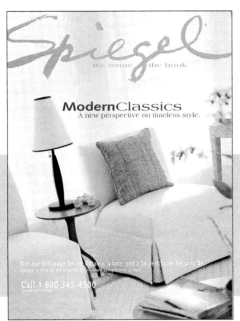 

Figure 15.4
Catalog Retailers
Spiegel offers a broad product mix, comprising many product lines. The Pottery Barn's product mix consists of a few product lines and a great deal of depth.

The advantages of catalog retailing include efficiency and convenience for customers. The retailer can benefit by locating in remote, low-cost areas, saving on expensive store fixtures, and reducing personal selling expenses, as well as store operating expenses. On the other hand, catalog retailing is inflexible, provides limited service, and is most effective for a selected set of products. Some catalog retailers—for instance, Crate and Barrel and The Sharper Image—have opened stores in major metropolitan areas.

Consumer mail-order catalog sales are about $130 billion each year, the equivalent of every American spending about $500 annually on catalog purchases.[21] Even though the cost of mailing catalogs continues to rise, catalog sales are growing at double the rate of over-the-counter retailing in the U.S.[22] Williams-Sonoma sells kitchenware and home and garden products through five catalogs including Pottery Barn, Gardeners' Eden, and Williams-Sonoma. Sales have been increasing due to the convenience of catalog shopping. Product quality is often high, and because consumers can call toll-free 24 hours a day, charge the purchase to a credit card, and have the merchandise delivered to their door in one to two days, such shopping is much easier than going to a store.[23]

Direct-response marketing
A type of marketing that occurs when a retailer advertises a product and makes it available through mail or telephone orders

Direct-Response Marketing   **Direct-response marketing** occurs when a retailer advertises a product and makes it available through mail or telephone orders. Generally, a purchaser may use a credit card, but other forms of payment are acceptable. Examples of direct-response marketing include a television commercial offering a recording artist's musical collection available through a toll-free number, a newspaper or magazine advertisement for a series of children's books available by filling out the form in the ad or calling a toll-free number, and even a billboard promoting floral services by calling 1-800-FLOWERS. Direct-response marketing can also be achieved by sending letters, samples, brochures, or booklets to prospects on a mailing list and asking that they order the advertised products by mail or telephone. In general, products must be priced above $20 to justify the advertising and distribution costs associated with direct-response marketing.

Telemarketing
The performance of marketing-related activities by telephone

Telemarketing   A number of organizations, including Merrill Lynch, Allstate, Avis, Ford, Time, and American Express, use the telephone to strengthen the effectiveness of traditional marketing methods. **Telemarketing** is the performance of marketing-related activities by telephone. Some organizations use a prescreened list of prospective clients, whereas others rely primarily on a cold canvass approach using telephone directories. Telemarketing can also help generate sales leads, improve customer service, speed up payment on past-due accounts, raise funds for nonprofit organizations, and gather marketing data. It is often combined with other marketing efforts, and both nonstore retailers and retailers with establishments use it.

354

Television home shopping
A form of selling in which products are presented to television viewers, who buy them by calling a toll-free number and paying with credit cards

Television Home Shopping   **Television home shopping** presents products to television viewers, urging buyers to order through toll-free numbers and use credit cards. Home Shopping Network in Florida originated and popularized this format. Today there are numerous home shopping cable channels, several of them specializing in certain product categories. The most popular products sold through television home shopping are jewelry (40 percent of total sales), clothing, housewares, and electronics.

Home shopping channels have grown so rapidly in recent years that more than 60 percent of all U.S. households have access to home shopping programs. Home Shopping Network and QVC are two of the largest home shopping networks. Approximately 60 percent of home shopping sales revenues come from repeat purchasers. When asked why they purchase through television home shopping, shoppers indicate that they perceive the prices to be lower, the service more prompt, and the sales personnel friendlier and better informed about the products.[24]

The television home shopping format offers several benefits. Products can be easily demonstrated, and an adequate amount of time can be spent showing the product so that viewers are well informed. The length of time that a product is shown depends not only on the time required for doing demonstrations, but also on whether the product is selling. Once the calls peak and begin to decline, then a new product is shown. Another benefit is that customers can shop at their convenience from the comfort of their own homes.

Online retailing   Makes products available between buyers and sellers through computer connections

Online Retailing   **Online retailing** makes products available between buyers and sellers through computer connections. The phenomenal growth of online information services (CompuServe, America Online) and the Internet has created new retailing opportunities. In addition, banks and brokerage firms have established direct connections for transactions. Many retailers are setting up "home pages" on the Internet's World Wide Web to disseminate information about their companies and products. Although most companies are currently using the Web just to promote products, some companies, including Borders bookstores and OfficeMax, actually sell merchandise online.[25] Land's End, for example, has an electronic catalog on the Internet featuring eighty-three of the mail-order retailer's best-selling products. Land's End also sells merchandise through CompuServe and Prodigy.[26] Table 15.2 provides "addresses" of the home pages of a sampling of retailers with an online presence.

Although online retailing represents a major new retailing venue, security remains a significant barrier to selling online. Many customers choose to order by telephone because of the potential for credit card security problems. However, many organizations are working to find ways to secure online transactions, and once the issue of credit card security is resolved, direct marketing online is expected to grow rapidly.

Table 15.2   World Wide Web Pages for Major Retailers

Borders	http://www.borders.com/
Dillards	http://www.azstarnet.com/dillards/holidays.html
Egghead	http://www.egghead.com/
The Home Depot	http://www.HomeDepot.com/
Imaginarium	http://oldwww.tig.com/Imaginarium/
JC Penney	http://www.jcpenney.com/
J. Sainsbury's	http://www.j-sainsbury.co.uk/
Kmart	http://www.kmart.com/
Land's End	http://www.landsend.com/
L.L. Bean	http://www.llbean.com/
OfficeMax	http://www2.pcy.mci.net/marketplace/ofcmax/
Pier 1 Imports	http://www.pier1.com/
Service Merchandise	http://www.svcmerch.com/service/svcmerch.html
The Sharper Image	http://www.sharperimage.com/tsi/
Target Stores	http://www.targetstores.com/
Wal-Mart	http://www.wal-mart.com/

■ *Automatic Vending*

Automatic vending is the use of machines to dispense products selected by customers when money is inserted. It accounts for less than 2 percent of all retail sales. Video game machines provide an entertainment service, and many banks now offer automatic teller machines (ATMs), which dispense cash or offer other services.

Automatic vending is one of the most impersonal forms of retailing. Small, standardized, routinely purchased products (chewing gum, candy, newspapers, cigarettes, soft drinks, coffee) can be sold in machines because consumers usually buy them at the nearest available location. Machines in areas of heavy traffic provide efficient and continuous services to consumers. Such high-volume areas may have more diverse product availability—for example, hot and cold sandwiches, as well as soups. Since vending machines need only a small amount of space and no sales personnel, this retailing method has some advantages over stores. The advantages are partly offset, however, by the high costs of equipment and frequent servicing and repairs.

355

Franchising

Franchising is an arrangement whereby a supplier, or franchiser, grants a dealer, or franchisee, the right to sell products in exchange for some type of consideration. The franchiser may receive some percentage of total sales in exchange for furnishing equipment, buildings, management know-how, and marketing assistance to the franchisee. The franchisee supplies labor and capital, operates the franchised business, and agrees to abide by the provisions of the franchise agreement. With changes in the international marketplace, shifting employment options in the United States, the expanding U.S. service economy, and corporate interest in more joint venture activity, franchising is rapidly increasing. A new franchise opens somewhere in the United States every 6½ minutes, every business day.[27] Franchising accounts for $900 billion annually, or 40 percent of all U.S. retail sales, and revenues are expected to reach $1 trillion by the year 2000.[28] In this section we look at major types of retail franchises and the advantages and disadvantages of franchising.

■ *Major Types of Retail Franchises*

Retail franchise arrangements fall into three general categories. In one type of arrangement, a manufacturer authorizes a number of retail stores to sell a certain brand name item. This franchise arrangement, one of the oldest, is common in the sales of cars and trucks, farm equipment, shoes, paint, earth-moving equipment, and petroleum. About 90 percent of all gasoline is sold through franchised independent retail service stations, and franchised dealers handle virtually all sales of new cars and trucks. A second type of retail franchise involves a producer licensing distributors to sell a given product to retailers. This arrangement is common in the soft drink industry. Most national manufacturers of soft drink syrups—Coca-Cola, Dr Pepper, Pepsi-Cola—franchise independent bottlers, which then serve retailers. In the third type of retail franchise, a franchiser supplies brand names, techniques, or other services, instead of complete products. The franchiser may provide certain production and distribution services, but its primary role in the arrangement is careful development and control of marketing strategies. This approach to franchising, most typical today, is used by many organizations, including Holiday Inn, AAMCO, McDonald's, Dairy Queen, KFC, and H&R Block.

■ *Advantages and Disadvantages of Franchising*

Franchising offers several advantages to both the franchisee and the franchiser. It enables a franchisee to start a business with limited capital and use the business experience of others. Moreover, nationally advertised retailers, such as ServiceMaster and Burger King, are often assured of customers as soon as they open. If business problems arise, the franchisee can obtain guidance and advice from the franchiser at little or no cost. Franchised outlets are generally more successful than independently owned businesses. Less than 10 percent of franchised retail businesses fail during the first two years of operation, whereas approximately half of independent retail businesses fail during that period. The franchisee also receives materials to use in local advertising and can take part in national promotional campaigns sponsored by the franchiser.

The franchiser gains fast and selective product distribution through franchise arrangements without incurring the high cost of constructing and operating its own outlets. The franchiser therefore has more capital for expanding production and advertising. It can also ensure, through the franchise agreement, that outlets are maintained and operated by its own standards. The franchiser benefits from the fact that the franchisee, being a sole proprietor in most cases, is likely to be very highly motivated to succeed. Success of the franchise means more sales, which translate into higher royalties for the franchiser.

Despite numerous advantages, franchise arrangements have several drawbacks. The franchiser can dictate many aspects of the business: decor, design of employees' uniforms, types of signs, and numerous details of business operations. In addition, franchisees must pay to use the franchiser's name, products, and assistance. Usually, there is a one-time franchise fee and continuing royalty and advertising fees, often collected as a percentage of sales. For example, Subway requires franchisees to come up with $40,000 to $80,000 in startup costs. Franchisees often must work very hard, putting in ten- to twelve-hour days, six days a week. In some cases, franchise agreements are not uniform; one franchisee may pay more than another for the same services. The franchiser also gives up a certain amount of control when entering into a franchise agreement. Consequently, individual establishments may not be operated exactly the way that the franchiser would like.

Strategic Issues in Retailing

Consumers often have vague reasons for making retail purchases. Whereas most industrial purchases are based on economic planning and necessity, consumer purchases may result from social influences and psychological factors. Because consumers shop for a variety of reasons—to search for specific items, escape boredom, or learn about something new—retailers must do more than simply fill space with merchandise. They must make desired products available, create stimulating shopping environments, and develop marketing strategies that increase store patronage. Inside Marketing describes how some government agencies are doing just that. In this section we discuss how store location, retail positioning, store image, scrambled merchandising, and the wheel of retailing affect retailing objectives.

■ *Location*

Location, the least flexible of the strategic retailing issues, is one of the most important because location dictates the limited geographic trading area from which a store draws its customers. Retailers consider a variety of factors when evaluating potential locations, including location of the firm's target market within the trading area, kinds of products being sold, availability of public transportation, customer characteristics, and competitors' locations.

In choosing a location, retailers evaluate the relative ease of movement to and from the site, including pedestrian and vehicular traffic, parking, and transportation. Most retailers prefer sites with high pedestrian traffic. Preliminary site investigations often include a pedestrian count to determine how many passersby are truly prospective customers. The nature of the area's vehicular traffic is analyzed. Certain retailers, such as service stations and convenience stores, depend on large numbers of driving customers but try to avoid overly congested locations. Parking space must be adequate for projected demand, and transportation networks (major thoroughfares and public transit) must accommodate customers and delivery vehicles.

Retailers also evaluate the characteristics of the site itself: types of stores in the area; size, shape, and visibility of the lot or building under consideration; and rental, leasing, or ownership terms. Retailers also look for compatibility with nearby retailers because stores

INSIDE MARKETING

Government Agencies Master the Lessons of Marketing

Although you may not think of them as retailers, your state's department of motor vehicles and the U.S. Postal Service distribute products (driver's licenses and mail service) through retail outlets. Both agencies probably bring to mind grim images: inconvenient hours and lousy locations, long lines, surly employees, and that photo of a stranger on your driver's license. But confronted with ever-tightening budgets, angry taxpayers who want more for less money, and, in the case of the Postal Service, stiff competition from private carriers and fax machines, these organizations are taking a few lessons from marketers to make life easier for their "customers."

To remain competitive, the U.S. Postal Service is opening up new outlets in unusual places, such as Furr's supermarkets and Kmart stores, sprucing up old offices, and improving customer services. For example, 200 of the nation's 40,000 local post offices have already been remodeled with better lighting and are training sales clerks to be friendlier and more helpful. The new "stores" have seen sales rise 20 percent over the offices they replaced. Customers can also purchase stamps through ATMs, by phone, and with credit cards. Some post offices are extending their hours, especially during busy holiday seasons. Says Postmaster General Marvin T. Runyon, "We just can't sit here and say to people, 'Here are our hours and, if you feel like it, bring your mail to us.' We need to get [market share] back."

Connecticut's Department of Motor Vehicles has also turned to nontraditional quarters, opening license-renewal branches in several shopping malls. For a fee, large firms like General Electric and Aetna Life & Casualty can arrange for DMV clerks to make regular "house calls" to their offices for their employees' convenience. Virginia, Washington, and California are developing ATM-like systems where drivers can transact DMV business. Florida is working with Time Warner Inc. to develop an interactive cable channel to provide information and enable drivers to take written driving tests and to call up records, outstanding tickets, and renewal dates. Such strategies not only improve service to DMV "customers," but also save money in an era of increasing fiscal constraint.

Sources: Pam Black, "Finally, Human Rights for Motorists," *Business Week*, May 1, 1995, 45; and Mark Lewyn, "Repackaging the Post Office," *Business Week*, Jan. 8, 1996, p. 39.

---

that complement each other draw more customers for everyone. When making site location decisions, retailers select from among several general types of locations: freestanding structures, traditional business districts, neighborhood shopping centers, community shopping centers, regional shopping centers, or nontraditional shopping centers.

Free-Standing Structures   Free-standing structures are buildings unconnected to other buildings. Organizations may build structures or lease or buy them. A retailer, for example, may find that it is most successful when stores are in free-standing structures close to a shopping mall but not in the mall. Use of free-standing structures allows retailers to physically position themselves away from or close to competitors. It is not unusual for quick-service oil change dealers and fast-food restaurants to use free-standing structures and locate close to each other.

Traditional Business Districts   Traditional business districts consist of structures usually attached to one another and located in a central part of a town or city. Often these structures are older. In some cities traditional business districts are decaying and are not seen as viable locations for retailers. However, a number of towns and cities are preserving or revitalizing traditional business districts, thus making them attractive locations for certain types of retailers. Some cities have enclosed walkways, shut off streets from traffic, and provided free parking and trolley systems to help traditional business districts compete with shopping malls more effectively.

Neighborhood shopping centers Shopping centers usually consisting of several small convenience and specialty stores and serving consumers within ten minutes' driving time from the center

Community shopping centers Shopping centers with one or two department stores, some specialty stores, and convenience stores, which serve several neighborhoods and draw consumers who are not able to find desired products in neighborhood shopping centers

Regional shopping centers A type of shopping center with the largest department stores, the widest product mix, and the deepest product lines of all shopping centers

Figure 15.5 Regional Shopping Centers Regional shopping centers, such as Copley Place in Boston's Back Bay, provide many and varied product lines.

I will go to symphony.
I will attend the ballet.
I will pursue my cultural side.
I will do it all.

After I go shopping at Copley Place.

C O P L E Y P L A C E
IN BOSTON'S BACK BAY
Neiman Marcus • Tiffany & Co. • 100 shops, restaurants and theatres

Neighborhood Shopping Centers **Neighborhood shopping centers** usually consist of several small convenience and specialty stores, such as small grocery stores, gas stations, and fast-food restaurants. They serve consumers living within ten minutes' driving time from the center. Many of these retailers consider their target markets to be consumers who live within a two- to three-mile radius of their stores. Because most purchases are based on convenience or personal contact, there is usually little coordination of selling efforts within a neighborhood shopping center. Generally, product mixes consist of essential products, and depth of the product lines is limited. Convenience stores are most successful when they are closer to consumers than, for example, supermarkets. A good strategy for neighborhood centers is to locate near hotels, or interstate highways, or on the route to regional shopping centers.

Community Shopping Centers **Community shopping centers** include one or two department stores and some specialty stores, as well as convenience stores. They serve a larger geographic area and draw consumers looking for shopping and specialty products not available in neighborhood shopping centers. Consumers drive longer distances to community shopping centers than to neighborhood shopping centers. Community shopping centers are planned and coordinated to attract shoppers. Special events, such as art exhibits, automobile shows, and sidewalk sales, stimulate traffic. Overall management of a community shopping center looks for tenants that complement the center's total assortment of products. Such centers have wide product mixes and deep product lines.

Regional Shopping Centers **Regional shopping centers** usually have the largest department stores, the widest product mixes, and the deepest product lines of all shopping centers (see Figure 15.5). Many shopping malls are regional shopping centers, although some are community shopping centers. Regional shopping centers carry most products found in a downtown shopping district. With 150,000 or more consumers in their target market, regional shopping centers must have well-coordinated management and marketing activities. Target markets may include consumers traveling from a distance to find products and prices not available in their hometowns.

Because of the expense of leasing space in regional shopping centers, tenants are more likely to be national chains than small independent stores. Large centers usually advertise, have special events, furnish transportation to some consumer groups, maintain their own security forces, and carefully select the mix of stores. Mall of America, near Minneapolis, is one of the largest shopping malls in the world. It contains eight hundred stores, including Nordstrom's and Bloomingdale's, and one hundred restaurants and nightclubs. The shopping center features Camp Snoopy, a theme park based on Charlie Brown's famous dog, as well as hotels, miniature golf courses, and water slides.[29]

Nontraditional Shopping Centers Three new types of discount malls or shopping centers are emerging that differ significantly from traditional shopping centers. Factory outlet malls feature discount and factory outlet stores carrying traditional manufacturer brands, such as Van Heusen, Levi Strauss, HealthTex, and Wrangler. Manufacturers own these stores and make a special effort to avoid conflict with traditional retailers of their products. Manufacturers claim that their stores are in noncompetitive locations, and indeed most factory outlet malls are located outside metropolitan areas. Not all factory outlets stock closeouts and irregulars, but most avoid comparison with discount houses. Factory outlet malls attract customers because of lower prices for quality and major brand names. They operate in much the same way as regional shopping centers but probably draw traffic from a larger shopping radius. Promotional activity is at the heart of these shopping centers. Craft and antique shows, contests, and special events attract a great deal of traffic.

Another nontraditional shopping center is the miniwarehouse mall. These loosely planned centers sell space to retailers, who operate what are essentially retail stores out of warehouse bays. Developers of the

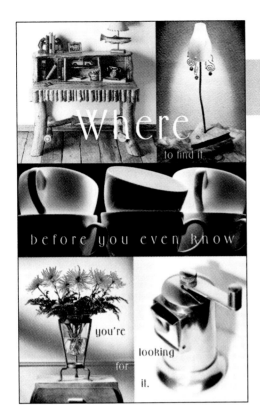

Figure 15.6
Nontraditional Shopping Centers   The Galleria is an upscale specialty center with approximately 75 stores.

miniwarehouse mall may also sell space to wholesalers or to light manufacturers that maintain a retail facility in their warehouse bay. Some of these miniwarehouses are located in high-traffic areas and provide ample customer parking, as well as display windows that can be seen from the street. Home improvement materials, specialty foods, pet supplies, and garden and yard supplies are often sold in these malls. Unlike traditional shopping centers, miniwarehouse malls usually do not have coordinated promotional programs and store mixes. These nontraditional shopping centers come closest to neighborhood or community shopping centers.

A third type of emerging shopping center is one that does not include a traditional anchor department store (see Figure 15.6). Most malls have one to three main anchor department stores to ensure a continuous stream of mall traffic. With traditional mall sales declining, this new type of shopping mall may be anchored by a store like The Gap. One such mall in Wheaton, Illinois, has a 17,000-square-foot Gap and is surrounded by other specialty stores, such as Banana Republic and GapKids. Other likely stores for the new malls include Toys "R" Us, Circuit City, and The Home Depot.

Shopping center developers are combining off-price stores with category killers in "power center" formats. Off-price centers are expanding rapidly, resulting in a variety of formats vying for the same retail dollar. To compete regional malls will have to adapt by changing their store mix.[30]

◼ *Retail Positioning*

Retail positioning
Identifying an unserved or underserved market niche, or segment, and serving it through a strategy that distinguishes the retailer from others in the minds of persons in that segment

Emergence of new types of stores (warehouse clubs, combination stores, and category killers) and expansion of product offerings by traditional stores have intensified retailing competition. Management, therefore, must consider the retail organization's market positioning. **Retail positioning** involves identifying an unserved or underserved market niche, or segment, and serving the segment through a strategy that distinguishes the retailer from others in the minds of persons in that segment (see Figure 15.7).[31] In international marketing, understanding the target market is critical. Several Canadian firms have found marketing their products in the United States quite difficult. In Canada, competition is more limited, and prices are higher than in the United States. To succeed in exporting their products to the United States, Canadian retailers must position themselves differently than at home.[32]

The ways in which retailers position themselves vary. A retailer may position itself as a seller of high-quality, premium-priced products and provide many services. Neiman Marcus, specializing in expensive high-fashion clothing and jewelry, sophisticated electronics, and exclusive home furnishings, might be expected to provide wrapping and delivery, valet parking, and personal shopping consultants. Von Maur, a high-quality midwestern department store, emphasizes topnotch service. It

Figure 15.7
Retail Positioning   CENTURY 21 positions its home selling service as large, responsive, and number one in the nation.

wraps and mails packages at no charge all over the country during the holidays and even hires pianists to play in the main lobbies of its stores. Another type of retail organization may be positioned as a marketer of reasonable-quality products at everyday low prices.

■ *Store Image*

To attract customers, a retail store must project an image—a functional and psychological picture in the consumer's mind—that is acceptable to its target market. Store environment, merchandise quality, and service quality are key determinants of store image.[33]

Atmospherics, the physical elements in a store's design that appeal to consumers' emotions and encourage buying, helps to create an image and position a retailer. Exterior atmospheric elements include the appearance of the storefront, display windows, store entrances, and degree of traffic congestion. Exterior atmospherics are particularly important to new customers, who tend to judge an unfamiliar store by its outside appearance and may not enter if they feel intimidated by the building or inconvenienced by the parking lot. Interior atmospheric elements include aesthetic considerations, such as lighting, wall and floor coverings, dressing facilities, and store fixtures. Interior sensory elements also contribute significantly to atmosphere. Color, for example, can attract shoppers to a retail display. Many fast-food restaurants use bright colors, such as red and yellow, because these have been shown to make customers feel hungrier and eat faster, which increases turnover. Sound is another important sensory component of atmosphere and may consist of silence, soft music, or even noise. A store's layout—arrangement of departments, width of aisles, grouping of products, and location of checkout areas—is another determinant of atmosphere. Department stores, restaurants, hotels, service stations, and shops combine these elements in different ways to create specific atmospheres that may be perceived as warm, fresh, functional, or exciting.

Retailers must assess the atmosphere the target market seeks and then adjust atmospheric variables to encourage desired consumer awareness and action. High-fashion boutiques generally strive for an atmosphere of luxury and novelty. Ralph Lauren's Polo Shops offer limited merchandise in large open areas, with props such as saddles or leather chairs adding to the exclusive look and image. On the other hand, discount department stores must *not* seem too exclusive and expensive. To appeal to multiple market segments, a retailer may create different atmospheres for different operations within the store; for example, the discount basement, the sports department, the housewares department, and the women's shoe department may each have a unique atmosphere.

Although heavily dependent on atmospherics, a store's image is also shaped by its reputation for integrity, number of services offered, location, merchandise assortments, pricing policies, promotional activities, and community involvement. Characteristics of the target market—social class, lifestyle, income level, and past buying behavior—help form store image as well. How consumers perceive the store can be a major determinant of store patronage. Consumers from lower socioeconomic groups tend to patronize small, high-margin, high-service food stores and prefer small, friendly loan companies over large, impersonal banks, even though these companies charge high interest. Affluent consumers look for exclusive establishments offering high-quality products and prestigious labels. Retailers should be aware of the multiple factors contributing to store image and recognize that perceptions of image vary.

■ *Scrambled Merchandising*

When retailers add unrelated products and product lines—particularly fast-moving items that can be sold in volume—to an existing product mix, they are practicing **scrambled merchandising.** For example, a convenience store might start selling lawn fertilizer. Retailers adopting this strategy hope to accomplish one or more of the following: (1) convert stores into one-stop shopping centers, (2) generate more traffic, (3) realize higher profit margins, and (4) increase impulse purchases. In scrambling merchandising, retailers must deal with diverse marketing channels. The practice can also blur a store's image in consumers' minds, making it more difficult for a retailer to succeed in today's highly competitive, saturated markets. Finally, scrambled merchandising intensifies competition among traditionally distinct types of stores and forces suppliers to adjust distribution systems to accommodate new channel members.

Atmospherics The physical elements in a store's design that appeal to consumers' emotions and encourage buying

Scrambled merchandising The addition of unrelated products and product lines to an existing product mix, particularly fast-moving items that can be sold in volume

■ *The Wheel of Retailing*

As new types of retail businesses come into being, they strive to fill niches in a dynamic retailing environment. One hypothesis regarding the evolution and development of new types of retail stores is the **wheel of retailing.** According to this theory, new retailers often enter the marketplace with low prices, margins, and status. New competitors' low prices are usually the result of innovative cost-cutting procedures and soon attract imitators. Gradually, as these businesses attempt to broaden their customer base and increase sales, their operations and facilities become more elaborate and more expensive. They may move to more desirable locations, begin to carry higher-quality merchandise, or add services. Eventually, they emerge at the high end of the price/cost/service scales, competing with newer discount retailers following the same evolutionary process.[34]

For example, supermarkets have undergone many changes since their introduction in 1921. Initially, they provided limited services in exchange for lower food prices. However, over time they developed a variety of new services, including free coffee, gourmet food sections, and children's play areas. Now supermarkets are challenged by superstores and combination stores, which offer more product choices than the original supermarkets and have undercut supermarket prices.

Figure 15.8 illustrates the wheel of retailing for department stores and discount houses. Department stores such as Sears started out as high-volume, low-cost merchants competing with general stores and other small retailers; discount stores developed later, in response to rising expenses of services in department stores. Many discount outlets now appear to be following the wheel of retailing by offering more services, better locations, quality inventories, and therefore higher prices. Some discount stores are almost indistinguishable from department stores.

The wheel of retailing, along with other changes in the marketing environment and buying behavior itself, requires that retailers adjust in order to survive and compete.

Figure 15.8

The Wheel of Retailing, Which Explains the Origin and Evolution of New Types of Retail Stores   If the "wheel" is considered to be turning slowly in the direction of the arrows, then the department stores around 1900 and the discounters later can be viewed as coming on the scene at the low end of the wheel. As it turns slowly, they move with it, becoming higher-price operations, and at the same time leaving room for lower-price firms to gain entry at the low end of the wheel.

Source: Adapted from Robert F. Hartley, *Retailing: Challenge and Opportunity*, 3rd ed., p. 42. Copyright © 1984 by Houghton Mifflin Company. Used by permission.

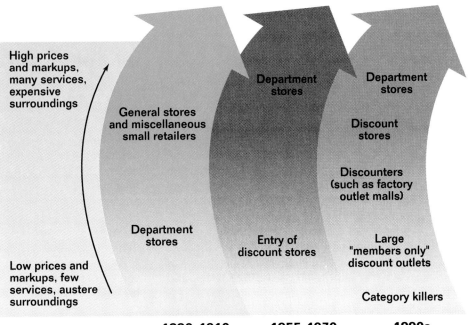

Consumers have less time than ever to shop and seem less interested in the shopping experience. Shopping today centers on "needs fulfillment" and thus is more utilitarian and work-oriented, a fact that many major retailing executives have noticed. About 95 percent of all products sold in 1995 did not require the services of a sales associate. As one retail consultant says, "People don't want to be sold anything. All they want is help buying the products they already know they need."[35] Consequently, consumers desire less personal service and more "assisted self-service." These changes in retailing and buying behavior mean retailers must change as well.[36] As consumers have less time to shop, more direct routes to manufacturers, and greater access to more sophisticated technology, retailing venues such as catalog retailing, television home shopping, and the Internet's World Wide Web will take on greater importance. New retailers will evolve to capitalize on these opportunities and respond to these challenges, while those retailers that cannot adapt will not survive.

SUMMARY

Retailing includes all transactions in which buyers intend to consume products through personal, family, or household use. Retailers—organizations that sell products primarily to ultimate consumers—are important links in the marketing channel because they are both marketers for and customers of wholesalers and producers. Although retailing often takes place inside stores or service establishments, it also occurs through direct selling, direct marketing, and vending machines. Retail institutions provide place, time, and possession utilities and, in some cases, form utility.

Retail stores can be classified by form of ownership. The three major forms are independent, chain, and franchise stores.

Retail stores can also be classified according to the breadth of products offered. Two general categories include general merchandise retailers and specialty retailers. The primary types of general merchandise retailers include department stores, discount stores, supermarkets, superstores, hypermarkets, warehouse clubs, and warehouse and catalog showrooms. Department stores are large retail organizations employing at least twenty-five people and characterized by wide product mixes in considerable depth for most product lines. Their products are organized into separate departments, which function like self-contained businesses. Discount stores are self-service, low-price, general merchandise outlets. Supermarkets are large, self-service food stores that also carry some nonfood products. Superstores are giant retail outlets carrying all the products found in supermarkets and many consumer products purchased on a routine basis. Hypermarkets offer supermarket and discount store shopping at one location. Warehouse clubs are large-scale, members-only discount operations, and warehouse and catalog showrooms are low-cost operations characterized by warehouse methods of materials handling and display, large inventories, and minimum services.

Specialty retailers offer substantial assortments in a few product lines. They include traditional specialty retailers, which carry narrow product mixes with deep product lines; off-price retailers, which sell brand name manufacturers' seconds and production overruns at deep discounts; and category killers—large specialty stores that concentrate on a single product line and compete on the basis of low prices and enormous product availability.

Nonstore retailing is selling goods or services outside the confines of a retail facility. The three major types of nonstore retailing include direct selling, direct marketing, and automatic vending. Direct selling is the marketing of products to ultimate consumers through face-to-face sales presentations at home or in the workplace. Direct marketing is the use of telephone and nonpersonal media to communicate product and organizational information to consumers who then can purchase products by mail or telephone. Forms of direct marketing include catalog marketing, direct-response marketing, telemarketing, television home shopping, and on-line retailing. Automatic vending is the use of machines to dispense products selected by customers when money is inserted.

Franchising is an arrangement whereby a supplier grants a dealer the right to sell products in exchange for some type of consideration. Retail franchises are of three general types: a manufacturer may authorize a number of retail stores to sell a certain brand name item; a producer may license distributors to sell a given product to retailers; or a franchiser may supply brand names, techniques, or other services instead of a complete product. Franchise arrangements have a number of advantages and disadvantages over traditional business forms, and their use is increasing.

To increase sales and store patronage, retailers must consider strategic issues. Location determines the trading area from which a store draws its customers and should be evaluated carefully. When evaluating potential sites, retailers take into account a variety of factors, including the location of the firm's target market within the trading area, the kinds of products being sold, the availability of public transportation, customer characteristics, and competitors' locations. Retailers can choose among several types of locations: free-standing structures, traditional business districts, neighborhood shopping centers, community shopping centers, regional shopping centers, or nontraditional shopping centers.

Retail positioning involves identifying an unserved or underserved market niche, or segment, and serving the segment through a strategy that distinguishes the retailer from others in people's minds. Store image, which various consumers perceive differently, derives not only from atmosphere, but also from location, products offered, customer services, prices, promotion, and the store's overall reputation. Atmospherics comprises the physical elements of a store's design that can be adjusted to appeal to consumers' emotions and thus induce consumers to buy. Scrambled merchandising adds unrelated product lines to an existing product mix and is being used by a growing number of stores to generate sales.

The wheel-of-retailing hypothesis holds that new retail institutions start as low-status, low-margin, and low-price operations. As they develop, they increase service and prices and eventually become vulnerable to newer institutions, which enter the market and repeat the cycle.

IMPORTANT TERMS

Retailing	Supermarkets	Nonstore retailing	Neighborhood shopping
Retailer	Superstores	Direct selling	centers
Independent store	Hypermarkets	Direct marketing	Community shopping
Chain store	Warehouse clubs	Catalog marketing	centers
Portfolio retailing	Warehouse showrooms	Direct-response marketing	Regional shopping centers
Franchise store	Catalog showrooms	Telemarketing	Retail positioning
General merchandise	Traditional specialty	Television home shopping	Atmospherics
retailer	retailers	Online retailing	Scrambled merchandising
Department stores	Off-price retailers	Automatic vending	Wheel of retailing
Discount stores	Category killer	Franchising	

DISCUSSION AND REVIEW QUESTIONS

1. What value is added to the product by retailers? What value is added by retailers for producers and for ultimate consumers?
2. Differentiate between the two general categories of retail stores based on breadth of product offering.
3. What are the major differences between discount stores and department stores?
4. How does a superstore differ from a supermarket?
5. How can department stores continue to compete effectively against discount stores, superstores, and warehouse clubs?
6. In what ways are traditional specialty stores and off-price retailers similar? How do they differ?
7. Describe the three major types of nonstore retailing. List some products you have purchased through nonstore retailing in the last six months. Why did you choose this method for making your purchases instead of going to a retail outlet?
8. Why is door-to-door selling a form of retailing? Some consumers feel that direct-response orders skip the retailer. Is this true?
9. Evaluate the following statement: Telemarketing, television home shopping, and online retailing will eventually eliminate the need for traditional forms of retailing.
10. If you were to open a retail business, would you prefer to open an independent store or to own a store under a franchise arrangement? Explain your preference.
11. What major issues should be considered when determining a retail site location?
12. Describe the three major types of shopping centers. Give an example of each type in your area.
13. Discuss the major factors that help determine a retail store's image.
14. How does atmosphere add value to products sold in a store? How important is atmospherics for convenience stores?
15. Is it possible for a single retail store to have an overall image that appeals to sophisticated shoppers, extravagant buyers, and bargain hunters? Why or why not?
16. In what ways does the use of scrambled merchandising affect a store's image?

APPLICATION QUESTIONS

1. Juanita wants to open a small retail store that specializes in high-quality, high-priced children's clothing. What concerns should Juanita have in the competitive retail environment? Specifically, with what competitors or types of competitors should she be concerned? Why?

2. Location of retail outlets is an issue in strategic planning. What initial steps would you recommend to Juanita (in question 1) when she considers a location for her store?

3. Godiva Chocolate stores offer a very narrow assortment of products but provide great depth. Different types of stores offer various breadth and depth of assortments. Visit a discount store, a specialty store, or a department store. Report the number of different product lines offered and the depth within each line. Identify the name and type of store you visited.

4. Atmospherics is an important tool used by retailers in their efforts to position stores. Visit a retail store you shop in regularly or one in which you would like to shop. Identify the store and describe the atmospherics. Be specific about both exterior and interior elements and indicate how the store is being positioned through its use of atmospherics.

Case 15.1   The Container Store: The Definitive Place to Get Organized

To put some order into their lives, many people head for The Container Store, where they can find over 10,000 products to put things in, including trash containers and recycling bins, desktop and closet organizers, boxes and wrapping paper, 35 types of shoe racks, 100 varieties of coat hangers, 261 different jars and bottles, 500 kinds of pantry organizers, and more. Customers can spend as little as $2 for a pocket change organizer or as much as several hundred dollars for a system to organize an entire wardrobe closet. Designating itself the "ultimate organization store," the $60-million-a-year retail chain offers its customers storage and organization products in an attractive atmosphere and is staffed by knowledgeable salespeople. In a poll of industry experts, The Container Store was unanimously acclaimed as "the most innovative storage merchandiser in the nation."

When The Container Store's founders, Garrett Boone and Kip Tindell, opened their first outlet in 1978, they had two employees, an innovative idea, and no retail experience. At the time, durable, well-designed, reasonably priced storage and organization merchandise was available only in commercial markets serving offices, factories, and hospitals. Boone and Tindell wanted to provide those same products for home use. Proposing their pioneering concept for a retail container store to investors earned them responses such as "You're going to open a store that sells empty boxes?" Despite the skeptics, the two persisted and opened their first store in Dallas, Texas. Six months later sales hit $200,000.

In the early days, Boone and Tindell worried that because their operation was very specialized, as soon as people bought what they needed the market would be saturated. Not so. New stores continue to attract new customers, and seasoned customers come back for new products or new ways to use old ones. In fact, every day about a thousand customers, some of them driving for over an hour, flock to Container Stores to satisfy their organizational and storage needs. Experiencing annual growth of some 30 percent, three times the industry average, Container Stores now open their doors to shoppers in Texas, Georgia, and Virginia. Florida, Southern California, and Illinois are next in line.

Container Stores are usually distinct free-standing buildings in shopping centers with other high-quality affordably priced outlets. Opening only one or two stores a year, management is very particular when it comes to finding the right location. In Texas, company executives waited nine years for one site they wanted, which was across the street from an upscale Houston mall.

To the company's owners, mass merchandising does not mean dreary surroundings. The Container Store customers are treated to blue ceilings and pale gray carpet and surrounded by natural light from skylights and floor-to-ceiling windows. Shoppers seeking general purpose items, such as tubs, baskets, and bins, can easily locate them in the center of the store. To find specialized items, they just look for the big bold banners that identify sections such as "Kitchen," "Closet," "Packaging," "Leisure," or "Bath." Although store size is growing along with the number of products offered, the basic design and arrangement remain the same.

What distinguishes The Container Store among retailers is the versatility of the products it sells. Because there were few storage products manufactured specifically for home use when Boone and Tindell first started out, they often bought commercial products that could double as consumer products. A mason's tool bag was a fine overnight bag and an egg basket worked well as a carryall. The company's owners recognized the sales potential of offering multipurpose products. Today a laundry hamper can easily function as a recycling bin, and a cosmetics organizer works as a tackle box. To encourage creative product use, The Container Store merchandisers display many items in seven or eight sections throughout the store. In the closet storage section, customers can design their own unique storage system with the store's best-selling line, Elfa wire drawers and shelves. They can even use a drill and a piece of dry wall to practice installing their new wares.

From the sales floor to the warehouse, The Container Store reflects its owners' conviction that quality customer service translates into business success. Boone and Tindell like to say that regardless of the job description every Container Store employee works in customer service. Computerized inventory control and excellent delivery mean that outlets replenish their shelves every two days with the exact items sold over that two-day period. Customers are never disappointed by out-of-stock conditions. With the help of

ongoing training and new-product fact sheets, salespeople acquire the skills and knowledge to help their customers make smart buying choices without feeling pushed into a sale.

Attracted by the chain's extraordinary success, several major corporations have approached Boone and Tindell, hoping to buy the company. They have refused. They want to continue doing business their way: flexible, friendly, and customer-oriented.[37]

Questions for Discussion

1. What type of retail store is The Container Store?
2. Using each retailing strategic issue discussed in this chapter, describe The Container Store's strategy.
3. So far Boone and Tindell have not tried franchising. Would you advise them to start using franchising for developing new stores rather than relying strictly on expansion through company stores? Why, or why not?

Case 15.2   Walt Disney Co.

If it seems as if everyone is going to Disneyland, perhaps it is because Disney has such a global presence these days. The Walt Disney Company entertains millions of guests each year at 350 retail stores, 16 resort hotels, and several theme parks located around the world, such as EuroDisney in Paris, Magic Kingdom, EPCOT Center, and Disney-MGM Studios Theme Park. Disney also plans to open a water-oriented theme park at the turn of the century in Tokyo, tentatively called Tokyo DisneySea. Disney also owns movie production companies, the ABC television network, cable channels (ESPN, Lifetime, A&E, and Disney), television and radio stations, newspapers in thirteen states, publishing companies, and real estate (such as the New Amsterdam Theater in New York). These far-flung entertainment businesses generated revenues of $19.3 billion for the Walt Disney Co. in 1994.

Guests at Disney's theme parks, resorts, and other outlets often comment on three aspects of Disney's service: cleanliness, quality, and friendliness. Disney recognizes that it has an energetic, loyal audience with high expectations. Meeting these expectations requires more than just adherence to a policy manual. Disney executives realize they can't possibly supervise all their employees all the time, so quality must be ingrained in the organization's culture. Quality service becomes a way of life in the company; employees follow the guidelines implicit in the culture. For example, Disney University in Orlando puts new theme park employees

through an intensive three-day training program to familiarize them with Disney practices, the company's history, its mission and objectives, and its emphasis on quality service. Disney theme park employees routinely converse using the Disney language of "guests," "cast members," "on stage" (working), and "off stage" (not working).

The emphasis of Disney's approach is simple: Make people happy. But beyond that simplicity is a strategy based on hard work, attention to detail, and exceeding customer expectations. Disney's approach to entertaining guests can be summarized in four principles taught at Disney University.

1. *Know your customers.* Disney maintains guest information in areas such as demographics, evaluation of current marketing strategies, attraction evaluations, payment preferences, price sensitivities, and the economy. It receives more than 600,000 letters each year, which are summarized for top management, who then take corrective action to resolve any problems. Disney also hires professionals to attend and evaluate the theme parks.

2. *Empower your employees and treat them with care.* Disney provides a positive work environment to make employees happy; happy employees enjoy providing quality service.

3. *Build delivery systems to ensure quality service.* Frontline employees at Disney's theme parks have the authority to resolve customer problems; customers can

ask questions by using telephones placed throughout the park that are connected to a centralized question-and-answer line.

4. *Create a simple service theme that can be understood by everyone.* Disney's theme: "We create happiness by providing the finest in family entertainment."

Disney is applying its expertise in creating positive entertainment atmospherics to resorts and real estate development as well. For example, Disney's new Vero Beach, Florida, resort is patterned after the glamorous elegance of an old southern inn. A nine-hole miniature golf course, playground, pool, and "wet deck" with a shipwreck and water cannons delight children, all within view of a parent's poolside lounge chair. Themed restaurants and snack bars also please both parents and children. And if that's not enough, guests can visit the beach, play basketball or tennis, ride bikes, or spend the day at one of Disney's nearby theme parks.

One of Disney's most ambitious projects is Celebration, Florida, a residential community fifteen minutes from Orlando. The 4,900-acre development is the vision of Walt Disney himself, though it has taken years of planning to reach fruition. Celebration is a master-planned community modeled after World War II southeastern towns, featuring specific architectural styles and integrating residential, retail, and recreation areas. Disney has employed some of the best-known architects and planners in the country to design Celebration's homes, offices, and recreation. Celebration is not the first "neotraditional" development, but it is the largest contemplated thus far.

Whereas most master-planned communities zone businesses and residences into separate locations, Celebration mingles inexpensive townhouses, apartments, and upscale homes into the same neighborhoods. The townhouses start at $127,000, while "cottage homes" run from $150,000 to $600,000. The houses, of varying architectural styles, will all have wide front porches and garages in the rear. In fact, builders must adhere to "pattern books" that specify everything from ceiling height to facade detailing. Disney eventually plans 8,000 residential units for Celebration, with the first opening in 1996.

Plans for Celebration also include a "town center," with shops, a bank, health center, and cinema, all within walking distance of most homes. The health center, Celebration Health, will focus on wellness programs. Residents can patronize their own golf course, hike and bike trails, parks, and public school. The school will include adult-education programs, as well as Celebration Teaching Academy, where teachers can learn innovative teaching methods. Everything in Celebration will be linked with fiber-optic cables.

Some critics wonder if an entertainment company can handle the myriad details of managing a huge residential community, but many people familiar with Disney's products want to give it a try. Even before Celebration's preview center opened, it received more than 2,000 inquiries; 4,000 visitors turned up its first weekend in operation.

Celebration is just one example of Disney's wide, and growing, reach. In 1995, Disney acquired Capital Cities/ABC, itself owner of the ABC television network, for $19 billion, to create one of the largest media empires to date at a time when entertainment is one of the fastest-growing segments of global business. The acquisition not only gives Disney ownership of a thriving network, but also distribution experience and more outlets for airing its movies and television programs.

The Walt Disney Company plans to continue its aggressive growth strategy based on quality service in all its businesses throughout its domestic and international markets. Chief executive Michael Eisner wants to enhance the Disney name in foreign markets so that he can export even more theme parks. Says Eisner, "... I'm thinking about the millennium change. I've got to protect the Disney brand well into the future."[38]

Questions for Discussion

1. How is Disney positioning itself?
2. Describe how Disney uses atmospherics to create a positive entertainment experience for its guests.
3. How does Disney's culture contribute to its success?

Chapter 16

Physical Distribution

OBJECTIVES

- To be able to recognize how physical distribution activities are integrated into marketing channels and overall marketing strategies

- To examine three important physical distribution components: customer service, total distribution costs, and cycle time

- To understand how efficient order processing expedites product flow

- To understand inventory management decisions about when and how much to order to maintain adequate product assortments that meet or exceed customer service standards

- To learn about the role of materials handling in physical distribution activities

- To explore how warehousing facilitates the storage and movement functions in physical distribution

- To be able to summarize the primary strengths and weaknesses of major transportation modes and examine the basic criteria that marketers use to select them

Distribution experts help Weight Watchers shed inefficiency.

*P*rior to 1990, Weight Watchers International, a division of H. J. Heinz Company, was a weight-loss service firm. However, competition from Nutri/Systems and Jenny Craig, as well as over-the-counter liquid weight-loss products, prompted Weight Watchers to launch Personal Cuisine, its own line of healthy weight-loss food products. Literally overnight, the firm had to build a supply chain and a logistics organization from scratch.

Michael Beall, marketing manager, says, "The challenge for our organization—with no [distribution] structure—was to find a way to get 69 products from 17 points of manufacture to 30 points of sale to test the concept and see if it would work." The company manufactured products all over the country and then shipped them to various small local wholesalers. On the East Coast, for example, the company moved products through a handful of local ice-cream wholesalers. However, this "bubble gum and baling wire" distribution system failed to provide an adequate level of service, much less optimal cost, largely because there were no links between production planning, inventory deployment, and product demand.

Weight Watchers then turned to a consulting company to help it design an effective physical distribution system. After assessing the situation, the consultant made several suggestions for short-term adjustments, including using the information collected from point-of-sale systems in each store to determine volume and forecast demand, and then to guide Weight Watchers' restocking strategies. For the long run, the consultant advised Weight Watchers to find a logistics firm to manage the movement of food from the last level of distribution network to the stores, and a food wholesaler to be its sole supplier of the Personal Cuisine line. Weight Watchers implemented these suggestions, retaining Christian Salveson to handle logistics services and The Food Company, a wholesaler, as its sole supplier for foods and other retail products.

Weight Watchers now benefits from an integrated physical distribution system that it built from the ground up. This effective system helped Weight Watchers cook up sales of $1.6 billion from class fees and food sales, while helping its customers achieve their own goal of losing weight.[1]

Without an effective system to move and handle physical distribution, organizations such as Weight Watchers will not be able to provide a level of service that satisfies customers. Even though physical distribution is costly, it creates time and place utility, which maximizes the value of products by delivering them when and where they are wanted.

This chapter describes how marketing decisions are related to physical distribution. After considering basic physical distribution concepts, we outline the major objectives of physical distribution and examine each major distribution function: order processing, inventory management, materials handling, warehousing, and transportation. We end with a discussion of marketing strategy considerations in physical distribution. Throughout, we stress the importance of customer service to physical distribution and supply chain management.

The Importance of Physical Distribution

Physical distribution
Activities used to move products from producers to consumers and other end users

Physical distribution refers to the activities—order processing, inventory management, materials handling, warehousing, and transportation—used to move products from producers to consumers and other end users. Planning an efficient physical distribution system is crucial to developing an effective marketing strategy. Companies that have the right goods in the right place, at the right time, in the right quantity, and with the right support services are able to sell more than competitors that do not. Physical distribution is an important element in a marketing strategy because it can decrease costs and increase customer satisfaction. Speed of delivery, service, and dependability are often as important to customers as costs.

Physical distribution deals with physical movement and inventory holding (storing and tracking inventory until it is needed) both within and among marketing channel members. Often, one channel member manages physical distribution for all channel members involved in exchanges. In fact, there is a trend toward centralizing, with one marketing channel member of the supply chain assuming the responsibility and authority for physical distribution for the entire chain.[2]

Physical distribution systems must meet the needs of the supply chain as well as customers. A construction equipment dealer with a low inventory of replacement parts requires fast, dependable service from component suppliers when it needs parts not in stock. Even when the demand for products is unpredictable, suppliers must be able to respond quickly to inventory needs.[3] In such cases, the distribution costs may be a minor consideration when compared with service, dependability, and timeliness.

For most companies, the main objectives of physical distribution are decreasing costs and transit time while increasing customer service (see Figure 16.1). However, few

**Figure 16.1
Meeting Customer Service Standards**
Motor Freight offers strong customer service through logistics management and customized problem solving.

distribution systems achieve these goals in equal measure. The large inventories and rapid transportation necessary for good customer service drive up costs. Physical distribution managers therefore strive for a reasonable balance among service, costs, and resources. They determine what level of customer service is acceptable and realistic, then develop a "system" outlook to minimize total distribution costs and cycle time. In this section, we examine these three performance objectives.

■ Meeting Customer Service Standards

All organizations strive to satisfy customer needs and wants through a set of activities known collectively as customer service. The level and quality of service that a firm's management aims to provide for its customers comprise the organization's customer service standards. Many companies claim that customer service is their top priority, and clearly, without customers there would be no sales or profits. Service may therefore be as important in attracting customers and building sales as are the cost and quality of the organization's products.

Customers require a variety of services. At the most basic level, they need fair prices, acceptable product quality, and dependable deliveries. In the physical distribution area, availability, timeliness, and quality are important dimensions of customer service and frequently determine whether customers are satisfied with a supplier.[4] To keep the nation's farmers, lawn-care firms, and other agricultural and industrial firms at work, John Deere sets rigorous distribution objectives. Deere expects its dealers to be able to fulfill 80 to 85 percent of orders from their own stock, 85 percent of orders from one of Deere's eleven regional depots in the U.S. and Canada, and 95 percent from its parts distribution center located in Milan, Illinois. Although Deere could reduce its distribution costs significantly by cutting these inventories, it would not then be able to meet its strict customer service standards. When a part is not in a dealer's stock, Deere is committed to shipping the part from one of its distribution centers the same day it is ordered. As a result, Deere ships more than 99 percent of orders the same day, and most orders are received within one day.[5]

Customers seeking a higher level of customer service may also want sizable inventories, efficient order processing, availability of emergency shipments, progress reports, postsale services, prompt replacement of defective items, and warranties. Customers' inventory requirements influence the expected level of physical distribution service. For example, customers seeking to minimize inventory storage and shipping costs may want suppliers to take responsibility for maintaining inventory in the marketing channel or to assume the cost of premium transportation.[6] Because service needs vary from customer to customer, companies must analyze—and adapt to—customer preferences. Attention to customer needs and preferences is crucial to increasing sales and obtaining repeat orders. A company's failure to provide the desired level of service may mean loss of customers.

Companies must also examine the service levels competitors offer and match or exceed those standards when the costs of providing the services can be justified by the sales generated. Many companies guarantee service performance to win customers. Services are provided most effectively when service standards are developed and stated in measurable terms—for example, "98 percent of all orders filled within 48 hours." Standards should be communicated clearly to both customers and employees and diligently enforced. Many service standards also outline delivery times and specify provisions for backordering, returning goods, and obtaining emergency shipments.

■ Reducing Total Distribution Costs

Although physical distribution managers try to minimize the costs associated with order processing, inventory management, materials handling, warehousing, and transportation, decreasing costs in one area often raises them in another. (Figure 16.2 shows the percentage of total costs that each physical distribution function represents.) By using a total cost approach to physical distribution, managers view physical distribution as a system rather than a collection of unrelated activities. This shifts the emphasis from lowering the separate costs of individual activities to minimizing overall distribution costs.

The total cost approach involves analyzing the costs of all distribution alternatives, even those considered too impractical or expensive. Total cost analyses weigh inventory levels against warehousing expenses, materials costs against various modes of trans-

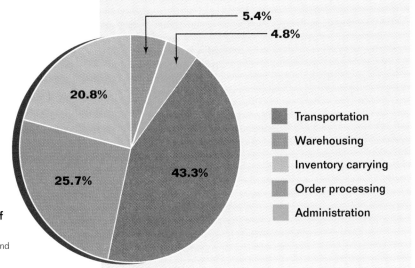

Figure 16.2
Proportional Cost of Each Physical Distribution Function as a Percentage of Total Distribution Costs
Source: Data from 1995 Physical Distribution Cost and Service Memorandum 4–63, Herbert W. Davis and Company, Mar. 19, 1996, p. 2.

portation, and all distribution costs against customer service standards. Costs of potential sales losses from lower performance levels must also be considered. In many cases, accounting procedures and statistical methods are used to figure total costs. Where hundreds of combinations of distribution variables are possible, computer simulations are helpful. A distribution system's lowest total cost is never the result of using a combination of the cheapest functions; instead, it is the lowest overall cost compatible with the company's stated service objectives.

Distribution managers must be sensitive to the issue of cost tradeoffs. Higher costs in one function area of a distribution system may be necessary to achieve lower costs in another. Tradeoffs are strategic decisions to combine (and recombine) resources for greatest cost-effectiveness. When distribution managers regard the system as a network of integrated functions, tradeoffs become useful tools in implementing a unified, cost-effective distribution strategy.

Cycle time
The time it takes to complete a process

■ Reducing Cycle Time

Another important goal of physical distribution involves reducing **cycle time,** the time it takes to complete a process, so as to reduce costs and/or increase customer service.[7] Many companies, particularly overnight delivery firms, major news media, and publishers of hot-topic books, are using cycle-time reduction to gain a competitive advantage. FedEx believes so strongly in this concept that it conducts research on reducing cycle time and identifying new management techniques and procedures to help it be the fastest overnight delivery service provider. The package-tracking software it offers to customers was one result of these streamlining efforts. In 1995, FedEx and rival United Parcel Service began to offer same-day delivery service, for those times when speed, not cost, counts most to customers.[8] Figure 16.3 shows how Ryder Systems, a transportation firm, is trying to help its partners in the supply chain reduce cycle times and costs.

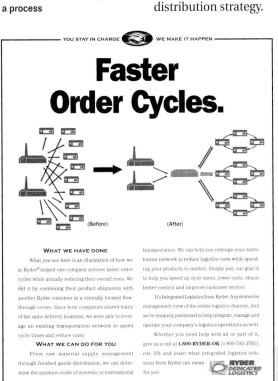

Figure 16.3
Reducing Cycle Time   Ryder assists customers in reducing their cycle time.

Order Processing

Order processing
The receipt and transmission of sales order information in the physical distribution process

*O*rder processing, an important physical distribution function, is the receipt and transmission of sales order information. Although management sometimes overlooks the importance of these activities, efficient order processing facilitates product flow. Computerized order processing provides a database for all supply chain members to increase their productivity. When carried out quickly and accurately, order processing contributes to customer satisfaction, decreased costs and cycle time, and increased profits.

There are three main tasks in order processing: order entry, order handling, and order delivery. Order entry begins when customers or salespersons place purchase orders by mail, telephone, or computer. Graybar, for example, provides electronic ordering systems for its customers (see Figure 16.4). This shifts the emphasis from time-consuming paper-based purchase ordering systems to electronic ordering, which reduces procurement costs. In some companies, sales representatives receive and enter orders personally, also handling complaints, preparing progress reports, and forwarding sales order information.

Order handling involves several tasks. Once an order is entered, it is transmitted to the warehouse, where product availability is verified, and to the credit department, where prices, terms, and the customer's credit rating are checked. If the credit department approves the purchase, warehouse personnel (sometimes assisted by automated equipment) pick and assemble the order. If the requested product is not in stock, a production order is sent to the factory or the customer is offered a substitute.

Electronic data interchange (EDI) A means of integrating order processing with production, inventory, accounting, and transportation

When the order has been assembled and packed for shipment, the warehouse schedules delivery with an appropriate carrier. If the customer pays for rush service, priority transportation is used. The customer is sent an invoice, inventory records are adjusted, and the order is delivered.

Order processing can be manual or electronic, depending on which method provides the greatest speed and accuracy within cost limits. Manual processing suffices for small-volume orders and is more flexible in special situations. **Electronic data interchange (EDI)** integrates order processing with production, inventory, accounting, and transportation. EDI is an information system for the supply chain that links marketing channel members and facilitating agencies together. It allows members of the supply chain to reduce paperwork and share information on invoices, orders, payments, inquiries, and scheduling among all channel members.

Many companies are pushing their suppliers toward EDI to reduce distribution costs and cycle times. At FedEx, for example, more than 70 percent of the company's major business customers carry out transactions via EDI. AutoZone and Dobbs International have all their merchandising vendors on EDI systems and request that other vendors be EDI-capable. The U.S. government has set 1997 for EDI requirements for procurement transactions with all federal government departments and agencies. The U.S. Air Force expects to save $135 million annually by reducing technical documentation as a result of using EDI to exchange product data with defense contractors.[9] For smaller companies, it generally takes about $5,000 to set up an EDI on a PC-based system. Setting up supply chain partners on software and computers as well as training employees to manage and monitor the EDI may initially increase costs, but may save money in the long run.[10]

The Internet represents another opportunity for EDI systems. The Internet is expected to lower costs and make it easier for all supply chain members to be online. Although electronic commerce poses some security problems, the opportunity to develop Internet links for EDI whenever customers want access will certainly enhance productivity in physical distribution. Channel members and facilitating agencies will be able to assess information and supply feedback

Figure 16.4
Order Processing
Graybar's online order entry system for Windows® helps customers lower their costs.

directly. For example, a database of information for trucking may provide online service that will allow carriers to schedule their travel times through high-traffic or limited-capacity zones in cities or industrial areas.[11]

Inventory Management

Stockouts Shortages of a product resulting from carrying too few products in inventory

Reorder point The inventory level that signals the need to place a new order

Order lead time The average time lapse between placing the order and receiving it

Usage rate The rate at which a product's inventory is used or sold per time period

Safety stock The amount of extra inventory a firm keeps to guard against stockouts

Fixed order-interval system Ordering products at predetermined intervals

*I*nventory management involves developing and maintaining adequate product assortments that meet customers' needs. Because a firm's investment in inventory usually represents a significant portion of its total assets, inventory decisions have a major impact on physical distribution costs and the level of customer service provided. When too few products are carried in inventory, the result is **stockouts,** or shortages of products, causing brand switching, lower sales, and loss of customers. When too many products (or too many slow-moving products) are carried, costs increase, as do risks of product obsolescence, pilferage, and damage. The objective of inventory management is to minimize inventory costs while maintaining an adequate supply of goods. To achieve this objective, marketers focus on two major issues: when to order and how much to order.

To determine when to order, a marketer calculates the reorder point. The **reorder point** is an inventory level that signals the need to place a new order. To calculate the reorder point, the marketer must know the order lead time, the usage rate, and the amount of safety stock required. The **order lead time** is the average time lapse between placing the order and receiving it. The **usage rate** is the rate at which a product's inventory is used or sold during a specific time period. **Safety stock** is the amount of extra inventory that a firm keeps to guard against stockouts resulting from above-average usage rates and/or longer than expected lead times. The reorder point can be calculated using the following formula:

$$\text{Reorder Point} = (\text{Order Lead Time} \times \text{Usage Rate}) + \text{Safety Stock}$$

Thus, if order lead time is 10 days, usage rate is 3 units per day, and safety stock is 20 units, then the reorder point is 50 units.

In some instances marketers employ the fixed order-interval system instead of the reorder point approach. The **fixed order-interval system** is an approach in which products are ordered at predetermined intervals, such as every two days, twice a week, or once a month. This approach works well when usage rate is relatively constant and the unit cost of the item is quite small.

To decide how much to order, two sets of costs must be analyzed: inventory-carrying costs and order-processing costs (see Figure 16.5). Inventory-carrying costs include warehousing and interest costs, insurance expenses, and the cost of obsolescence, product

Figure 16.5
Economic Order Quantity (EOQ) Model

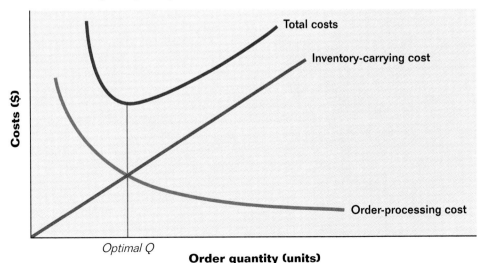

GLOBAL PERSPECTIVE

Transporting Perishable Products

With consumers becoming ever more concerned about health and nutrition, the volume of perishable commodities being transported around the globe has accelerated in recent years. However, if fruits, vegetables, seafood, meat, or flowers are left too long in the sun or not properly handled, packaged, or stored during shipment, product quality suffers and consumers will refuse to buy the goods. Shippers are therefore developing new technologies and services to move perishables quickly and safely.

For example, Maersk Line, a Danish ocean shipper, transports perishables such as meat and fruit from the United States to Europe. To ensure freshness, Maersk uses refrigerated containers called reefers that maintain constant temperature and humidity. When shipping pulp cargo, Maersk inserts probes, which are connected to a data logger, a computer that monitors and records the air circulating inside the container, as well as readings from the probes, during every hour of the voyage at sea and on shore. If necessary, Maersk can take immediate corrective action.

SAS Cargo Systems, an air freight firm, moves seafood, fruits, and vegetables from the United States to Scandinavia. It stores most perishables on wooden pallets that hold as much as 4,000 kilograms and loads them into the cargo hold of its planes. SAS relies on "Cool Guard," a foil-backed insulation material that maintains ideal temperatures as the cargo comes in to be assembled in lower-deck containers.

For Lep Profit International, a distributor of seafood to Europe and Asia, time is critical. To ship fresh monkfish, which is popular in Korea, Lep packs shipments with ice and frozen gel packs and transports them in wax styrofoam boxes that prevent leakage. These are put into reefers, trucked to New York, and then flown to Seoul, arriving 24 hours later. Temperatures must be monitored constantly to ensure the fish remains fresh, but not frozen. Freight tracing is also vital. If bad weather or cancelled flights cause any delays, Lep quickly makes alternative arrangements—or risks losing the whole cargo.

Source: Patricia B. Demetrio, "A Race Against Time," *Inbound Logistics*, June 1994, pp. 40–48.

---

deterioration, and pilferage. This set of costs encourages marketers to maintain a relatively low inventory by placing small orders quite frequently. On the other hand, order-processing costs include counting inventory to determine how much is needed, filling out purchase orders, and computer and communication expenses. This set of costs would encourage a marketer to place larger orders because the cost per unit ordered goes down as the order size increases. When both sets of costs are considered, the lowest-cost order size is the minimum point on the total cost curve shown in Figure 16.5. This point is also referred to as the economic order quantity. The **economic order quantity (EOQ)** is the order size that has the lowest total of both order-processing costs and inventory-carrying costs.[12] Fundamental relationships underlying the widely accepted EOQ model are the basis of many inventory control systems. However, the objective of minimizing total inventory costs must be balanced against meeting or exceeding a prescribed customer service standard. To meet or exceed a certain customer service standard, a marketer may have to place larger orders than those specified by the EOQ model, which may raise the overall costs associated with inventory management.

Some organizations have abandoned the use of EOQ and are using a just-in-time approach instead. The **just-in-time (JIT)** approach means that products arrive just as they are needed for use in production or for resale. When using the JIT approach, companies maintain low inventory levels and purchase products and materials in small quantities whenever they are needed. Usually, there is no safety stock. Suppliers are expected to provide consistent, high-quality products. When Chrysler implemented a JIT system in a Jeep plant, efficiency improved immediately. About 87 percent of the valve parts that go into a Grand Cherokee arrive at the plant less than six hours before they are needed.[13] Just-in-time inventory management depends on a high level of coordination between producers and suppliers, but this approach eliminates waste and reduces inventory costs

Economic order quantity (EOQ) The order size minimizing the total cost of ordering and carrying inventory

Just-in-time (JIT) Making products and materials available just when needed for production or resale

significantly. With just-in-time inventory, supply chain network relationships often result in suppliers moving close to their customers. For example, Japanese auto parts suppliers often send engineers to work at their customers' sites or locate plants near their customers' facilities. This results in low transportation and inventory costs and improved product development coordination.[14]

Materials Handling

Materials handling
Physical handling of products

Unit loading   Grouping one or more boxes on a pallet or skid

Containerization   The practice of consolidating many items into one container, which is sealed at the point of origin and opened at the destination

Materials handling, or physical handling of products, is important for efficient warehouse operations, as well as in transportation from points of production to points of consumption. Product characteristics often determine handling. For example, bulk liquids and gases have unique characteristics that determine how they can be moved and stored. Global Perspective describes how several shipping firms are meeting the challenge of hauling perishable goods.

Materials handling procedures and techniques should increase the usable warehouse capacity, reduce the number of times a good is handled, improve customer service, and increase customer satisfaction. Packaging, loading, movement, and labeling systems must be coordinated to maximize cost reduction and customer satisfaction.

Internal packaging is also an important consideration in materials handling. Goods must be packaged correctly to prevent damage or breakage during handling and transportation. Most companies employ packaging consultants to help them decide which packaging materials and methods would result in the most efficient physical handling.

Materials handling equipment is used in designing handling systems. **Unit loading** is grouping one or more boxes on a pallet or skid, permitting movement of efficient loads by mechanical means, such as forklifts, trucks, or conveyer systems. **Containerization** is the consolidating of many items into a single large container, which is sealed at its point of origin and opened at its destination. Containers are usually eight feet wide, eight feet high, and ten, twenty, twenty-five, or forty feet long. They can be conveniently stacked and shipped via rail or waterway. Once containers reach their destinations, wheel assemblies can be added to make them suitable for ground transportation. Because individual items are not handled in transit, containerization greatly increases efficiency and security in shipping (see Figure 16.6).

Figure 16.6
Containerization Steamship services and containerization provide cost-effective access to many international markets.

Warehousing

Warehousing Designing and operating facilities for storing and moving goods

Warehousing, the design and operation of facilities for storing and moving goods, is an important physical distribution function. Warehousing provides time utility by enabling firms to compensate for dissimilar production and consumption rates. When mass production creates a greater stock of goods than can be sold immediately, companies may warehouse the surplus until customers are ready to buy. Warehousing also helps stabilize prices and availability of seasonal items. In this section we describe the basic functions of warehouses and the different types of warehouses available. We also examine the distribution center concept, a special warehouse operation designed to move goods rapidly.

■ *Warehousing Functions*

Warehousing is not simply the storage of products. When warehouses receive goods by carloads or truckloads, they break down the shipments into smaller quantities (the operation is sometimes called breaking bulk) for individual customers; when goods arrive in small lots, warehouses sometimes consolidate them into bulk loads that can be shipped more economically (see Figure 16.7).[15] Warehouses perform the following basic distribution functions:

1. *Receiving goods.* Products are accepted, and the warehouse assumes responsibility for them.
2. *Identifying goods.* Appropriate stockkeeping units are recorded, along with the quantity of each item received. Items may be marked with physical codes, tags, or other labels or may be identified by item codes (codes on carriers or containers) or by physical properties.
3. *Sorting goods.* Products are sorted for storage in appropriate areas.
4. *Dispatching goods to storage.* Products are put away for later retrieval when necessary.
5. *Holding goods.* Products are kept in storage and properly protected until needed.
6. *Recalling and picking goods.* Items customers have ordered are efficiently retrieved from storage and readied for the next step.
7. *Collecting the shipment.* Items making up a single shipment are brought together and checked for completeness or explainable omissions. Order records are prepared or modified as necessary.
8. *Dispatching the shipment.* The consolidated order is packaged suitably and directed to the right transport vehicle. Necessary shipping and accounting documents are prepared.[16]

■ *Types of Warehouses*

Choice of warehouse facilities is an important strategic consideration. By using the right warehouse, a company may reduce transportation and inventory costs or improve service to customers; the wrong warehouse may drain company resources. Besides deciding how many facilities to operate and where to locate them, a company must determine which type of warehouse is most appropriate. Warehouses fall into two general categories, private and public. In many cases, a combination of private and public facilities provides the most flexible warehousing approach.

Figure 16.7 Warehousing Functions Warehousing services can greatly reduce inventory costs for customers. Millbrook Distribution Services is one company that provides these services for its customers.

Private warehouses
Facilities operated by organizations for distributing their own products

Private Warehouses   **Private warehouses** are operated by companies for shipping and storing their own products. Private warehouses are usually leased or purchased when a firm's warehouse needs in given geographic markets are substantial and stable enough to make a long-term commitment to fixed facilities. They are also appropriate for firms requiring special handling and storage features and wanting to control warehouse design and operation.

Some of the largest users of private warehouses are retail chain stores. Retailers such as Sears, Radio Shack, and Kmart find it economical to integrate warehousing with purchasing for and distribution to retail outlets. When sales volumes are fairly stable, ownership and control of a private warehouse may provide benefits, such as property appreciation. Private warehouses, however, face fixed costs, such as insurance, taxes, maintenance, and debt expense. They also allow little flexibility when firms wish to move inventories to more strategic locations. Before tying up capital in a private warehouse or entering into a long-term lease, a company considers its resources, level of expertise in warehouse management, and the role of the warehouse in overall marketing strategy. Many private warehouses are being eliminated by direct linkages and reduced cycle time between production and purchase. In an effort to reduce inventory costs, businesses are trying to move products as quickly and directly as possible from the manufacturer to customers.[17]

Public warehouses
Organizations that rent storage and related physical distribution facilities

Public Warehouses   **Public warehouses** rent storage space and related physical distribution facilities to other companies, sometimes providing distribution services, such as receiving and unloading products, inspecting, reshipping, filling orders, financing, displaying products, and coordinating shipments. They are especially useful to firms with seasonal production or low-volume storage needs, companies with inventories that must be maintained in many locations, firms that are testing or entering new markets, and business operations that own private warehouses but occasionally require additional storage space. Public warehouses also serve as collection points during product-recall programs. Whereas private warehouses have fixed costs, public warehouses have variable (and often lower) costs because users rent space and purchase warehousing services only as needed. Because public warehouses generally offer greater flexibility and more value-added services, more companies are shifting their warehouse usage from private to public warehouses.[18]

Field public warehouses
Warehouses established by a public warehouse at the owner's inventory location

Bonded storage   A storage service whereby goods are not released until their owners pay U.S. customs duties, taxes, or other fees

Many public warehouses furnish security for products being used as collateral for loans, a service provided at either the warehouse or the site of the owner's inventory. **Field public warehouses** are warehouses established by public warehouses at the owner's inventory location. The warehouser becomes custodian of the products and issues a receipt that can be used as collateral for a loan. Public warehouses also provide **bonded storage,** a warehousing arrangement under which imported or taxable products are not released until the owners of the products pay U.S. customs duties, taxes, or other fees. Bonded warehouses enable firms to defer tax payments on such items until they are delivered to customers.

Distribution centers   Large, centralized warehouses that concentrate on moving rather than storing goods

Distribution Centers   **Distribution centers** are large, centralized warehouses that receive goods from factories and suppliers, regroup them into orders, and ship them to customers quickly, the focus being on movement of goods rather than storage.[19] Distribution centers are specially designed for rapid flow of products. They are usually one-story buildings (to eliminate elevators) with access to transportation networks, such as major highways or railway lines. Many distribution centers are highly automated, with computer-directed robots, forklifts, and hoists collecting and moving products to loading docks. Although some public warehouses offer such specialized services, most distribution centers are privately owned. They serve customers in regional markets and in some cases function as consolidation points for a company's branch warehouses.

Distribution centers offer several benefits, the foremost being improved customer service. Distribution centers ensure product availability by maintaining full product lines. The speed of operations cuts delivery time to a minimum. Distribution centers also reduce costs. Instead of making many smaller shipments to scattered warehouses and customers, factories ship large quantities of goods directly to distribution centers at bulk-load rates, lowering transportation costs; furthermore, rapid inventory turnover lessens

■ **TECHNOLOGY IN MARKETING** ■

The Future of Warehousing

Technological advances and faster, more reliable transportation that make it possible for companies to operate with much smaller inventories are transforming the nature of warehousing. To survive in today's competitive marketplace, traditional inventory storehouses are making radical changes to become effective supply chain partners.

For example, one significant trend is the increased use of cross-docking, an approach whereby products received at a warehouse are immediately shipped out without ever being put into storage. With computerized information systems, warehouses can pre-assign a shipping door for each inbound carton. When the shipment arrives, a receiving dock employee can quickly apply a bar-coded shipping label that includes destination data, and place the carton directly on an outbound vehicle. Cross-docking greatly reduces labor and time associated with handling materials. Cross-docking is even changing the configuration of the warehouse. Although traditional warehouses are square, with truck doors on one side and rail doors on the other, combination storage/cross-dock warehouses look more like a modified *U* with storage at either end and cross-docking areas in the center. Goods

are received through the cross-dock area and moved directly to shipping doors or, if necessary, to short-term storage, which minimizes the distance goods have to travel within the warehouse.

Warehouses are also providing more value-added services such as packaging, assembly, consolidation, end-aisle display creation, labeling, bar coding, and automatic shipment notifications. Warehouses can often provide these services to manufacturers at a lower cost than the manufacturers could manage themselves. For many public warehouses, these services comprise as much as 50 percent of their activities.

With more and more companies eliminating inventory, warehouses are performing fewer storage functions. Instead, they are growing adept at keeping products moving quickly and accurately. This requires sophisticated computer information systems (and computer-literate warehouse employees) to minimize storage costs and time while maximizing quality service to warehouse customers. The best warehouses are therefore reinventing their role as supply chain partners by becoming expertly managed "flow-through" centers.

Source: Lisa H. Harrington, "Taking Stock of Warehousing," *Inbound Logistics*, July 1995, pp. 24–28.

the need for warehouses and cuts storage costs. Philips Lighting Co., a subsidiary of Dutch-based Philips Electronics N.V., has twenty-one factories in the United States manufacturing lighting and electrical products. To improve service to its customers, Philips recently established a national distribution center in Memphis, Tennessee, to concentrate on handling the distribution of "slow movers" (products at the bottom of Philips's sales line), while five satellite distribution centers handle "fast movers" (products in at least 20 percent of the sales lines). By separating the slow movers from the fast movers, Philips can more efficiently match shipments to orders for the benefit of customers and its own bottom line.[20] Technology in Marketing describes other changes in warehousing. Some distribution centers also facilitate production by receiving and consolidating raw materials and providing final assembly for some products. The development of distribution centers in Germany by Coca-Cola's German subsidiary has helped the company reach a previously untapped market.

Transportation

Transportation Moving a product from where it is made to where it is purchased and used

Transportation adds time and place utility to a product by moving it from where it is made to where it is purchased and used.[21] Transportation is the most expensive physical distribution function. Because product availability and timely deliveries are dependent on transportation functions, choice of transportation directly affects customer service. A firm may even build its distribution and marketing strategy around a

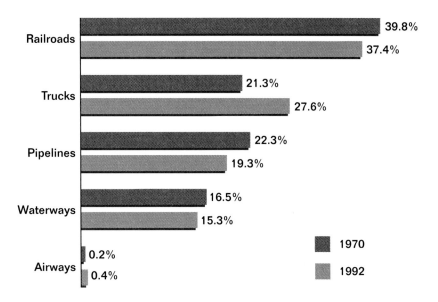

Figure 16.8
Proportion of Intercity Freight Carried by Various Transportation Modes, 1970 and 1992
Source: *Statistical Abstract of the United States, 1994*, 114th ed., p. 622.

unique transportation system if on-time deliveries, which that system ensures, give the firm a competitive edge. In this section we consider the principal modes of transportation, the criteria companies use to select one transportation mode over another, and several methods of coordinating transportation services.

■ *Transportation Modes*

Transportation modes
The means of moving goods from one location to another

There are five major **transportation modes,** or means of moving goods: railroads, trucks, waterways, airways, and pipelines. Each mode offers distinct advantages. Many companies adopt physical handling procedures that facilitate the use of two or more modes in combination. Figure 16.8 indicates the percentage of intercity freight carried by each transportation mode for 1970 and 1992. Table 16.1 illustrates typical transportation modes for various products.

Railroads   Railroads carry heavy, bulky freight that must be shipped long distances overland (see Figure 16.9). Railroads commonly haul minerals, sand, lumber, chemicals, and farm products, as well as low-value manufactured goods and an increasing number of automobiles. They are especially efficient for transporting full carloads, which can be shipped at lower rates than smaller quantities because they require less handling. Many companies locate factories or warehouses near major rail lines or on spur lines for convenient loading and unloading.

Table 16.1 Typical Transportation Modes for Various Products				
Railroads	**Trucks**	**Waterways**	**Airways**	**Pipelines**
Coal	Clothing	Petroleum	Flowers	Oil
Grain	Paper goods	Chemicals	Perishable food	Processed coal
Chemicals	Computers	Iron ore	Instruments	Natural gas
Lumber	Books	Bauxite	Emergency parts	Water
Automobiles	Livestock	Grain	Overnight mail	Chemicals
Steel				

380

**Figure 16.9
Railroads**
Norfolk Southern offers
rail service to its
customers.

Although railroads haul more intercity freight than other modes of transportation, accounting for more than one-third of all cargo ton-miles carried, their share of the transportation market declined from a high of 75 percent in the 1920s to 35 percent in the 1990s.[22] High fixed costs, shortages of rail cars during peak periods, poor maintenance of tracks and equipment, and increased competition from other carriers, mainly trucks, have plagued railroad companies and diminished profits.

Trucks   Trucks provide the most flexible schedules and routes of all major transportation modes because they can go almost anywhere. Trucks usually haul small shipments of high-value goods over short distances. Because trucks have a unique ability to move goods directly from factory or warehouse to customer, they are often used in conjunction with other forms of transport that cannot provide door-to-door deliveries.

The Interstate Commerce Commission (ICC) classifies trucks as common, contract, private, or exempt carriers. Common carriers are legally obligated to serve all customers requesting services, assuming that carriers have the necessary equipment. For example, CF MotorFreight is a common carrier. Contract carriers function similarly to private transportation systems, only hauling freight for customers with written agreements. Private carriers are company-owned transport systems; although they are not economically regulated by the ICC, they are subject to safety regulations and prohibited from carrying other companies' products. Exempt carriers are freight haulers that carry products exempted from regulation, such as unprocessed agricultural goods. Brokers bring together those wanting transport services and those providing them.

Although trucks usually travel much faster than trains, they are more expensive and somewhat more vulnerable to bad weather. Trucks are also subject to size and weight restrictions of products they carry. Trucks, especially common carriers, are sometimes criticized for high levels of loss and damage to freight and for delays from rehandling small shipments. In response, the trucking industry is turning to computerized tracking of shipments and developing new equipment to speed up loading and unloading.

Waterways   Water transportation is the cheapest method of shipping heavy, low-value, nonperishable goods, such as ore, coal, grain, and petroleum products. Water carriers offer considerable capacity. Powered by tugboats and towboats, barges that travel along intercoastal canals, inland rivers, and navigation systems can haul at least ten times the weight of one rail car, and ocean-going vessels can haul thousands of containers.

Many markets are inaccessible by water transportation unless it is supplemented by rail or truck. Furthermore, water transport is extremely slow and sometimes comes to a standstill during freezing weather. Companies depending on water may ship their entire inventory during the summer and then store it for winter use. Droughts and floods also create difficulties for users of inland waterway transportation. Nevertheless, because water transportation is extremely fuel-efficient, its use will increase in the future.

Airways   Air transportation is the fastest and most expensive form of shipping. It is used most often for perishable goods; for high-value, low-bulk items; and for products requiring quick delivery over long distances, such as emergency shipments. The success of many businesses is now based on the availability of overnight delivery that air transportation can offer. Air transport capacity is limited only by the capacity of individual aircraft. Medium-range jets can haul about 60,000 pounds of freight, and some new jet cargo planes equipped to carry containers accommodate more than 220,000 pounds.[23] Some air carriers transport combinations of passengers, freight, and mail.

Although air transport accounts for only 2 percent of total ton-miles carried, its importance as a mode of transportation is growing. Despite its expense, air transit can reduce warehousing and packaging costs and losses from theft and damage, thus helping lower total costs (but truck transportation needed for pickup and final delivery adds to cost and transit time). Examples of air transportation organizations include Airborne, FedEx, DHL, UPS, RPS Air, and the U.S. Postal Service.

Pipelines   Pipelines, the most automated transportation mode, usually belong to the shipper and carry the shipper's products. Most pipelines carry petroleum products or chemicals. The Trans-Alaska Pipeline, owned and operated by a consortium of oil companies including Exxon, Mobil, and British Petroleum, transports crude oil from remote oil-drilling sites in central Alaska to shipping terminals on the coast. Slurry pipelines carry pulverized coal, grain, or wood chips suspended in water. There are over 440,000 miles of intercity pipelines in the United States. Even though pipelines have limited accessibility because of their fixed routes, pipeline use accounts for about 22 percent of all intercity ton-miles.[24]

Pipelines move products slowly but continuously and at relatively low cost. They are dependable and ensure low product damage and theft. However, contents are subject to as much as 1 percent shrinkage, usually from evaporation. Pipelines have also been a concern to environmentalists, who fear that installation and leaks could harm plants and animals.

■ Criteria for Selecting Transportation Modes

Marketers select a transportation mode based on cost, speed, dependability, load flexibility, accessibility, and frequency.[25] Table 16.2 shows relative ratings of each transportation mode by selection criteria.

Cost   Marketers compare alternative transportation modes to determine whether benefits from a more expensive mode are worth higher costs. Air freight carriers—for instance, United Parcel Service—promise many benefits, such as speed, availability, and dependability, but at higher costs relative to other transportation modes. When speed is less important, marketers prefer lower costs. Bicycles are often shipped by rail because an unassembled bicycle can be shipped more than a thousand miles on a train for as little as

381

Table 16.2   Relative Ratings of Transportation Modes by Selection Criteria

Mode	Cost	Speed	Dependability	Load Flexibility	Accessibility	Frequency
Railroads	Moderate	Average	Average	High	High	Low
Trucks	High	Fast	High	Average	Very high	High
Waterways	Very low	Very slow	Average	Very high	Limited	Very low
Airways	Very high	Very fast	High	Low	Average	Average
Pipelines	Low	Slow	High	Very low	Very limited	Very high

$3.60. Bicycle wholesalers plan purchases far enough in advance to capitalize on this cost advantage.

Marketers have cut expenses and increased efficiency since transportation was deregulated in the late 1970s and early 1980s. Railroads, airlines, trucks, barges, and pipeline companies are all more competitive and more responsive to customers' needs. For some products, deregulation cut transportation costs as much as 50 percent.

Speed   Speed is measured by the total time a carrier has possession of goods, including the time required for pickup and delivery, handling, and movement between points of origin and destination. Speed obviously affects a marketer's ability to provide service, but there are some less obvious implications as well. Shippers take advantage of transit time to process orders for goods en route, a capability especially important to agricultural and raw materials shippers. Some railroads also let carloads in transit be redirected for maximum flexibility in selecting markets. A carload of peaches may be shipped to a closer destination if the fruit is in danger of ripening too quickly.

Dependability   Dependability of a transportation mode is determined by the consistency of service provided (see Figure 16.10). Marketers must be able to count on carriers to deliver goods on time and in an acceptable condition. Along with speed, dependability affects a marketer's inventory costs, including sales lost when merchandise is not available. Undependable transportation necessitates higher inventory levels so that stockouts are avoided, whereas reliable delivery service enables customers to carry smaller inventories at lower cost. To maintain desired inventory levels, Wal-Mart ships more than 75 percent of its stock through its own distribution network, including twenty-two distribution centers and a private fleet of trucks.[26]

Security problems vary considerably among transportation modes and are a major consideration in carrier selection. A firm does not incur costs directly when goods are lost or damaged because the common carrier is usually held liable. Nevertheless, poor service and lack of security indirectly lead to increased costs and lower profits because damaged or lost goods are not available for immediate sale or use.

Figure 16.10
Dependability
The U.S. Postal Service promotes the reliability of its Parcel Post service.

Harry and David. Parcel Post reliability is at the core of their success.

Over 40 years ago, Harry and David® turned to the United States Postal Service to help grow their business. It was a smart solution. And they're still depending on the mail — both to generate orders and deliver the goods.

This year, Parcel Post will deliver over 4 million packages of Royal Riviera® pears and other perishable Harry and David gifts. On time, in shape — and for about $1 less per parcel than other carriers would charge.

Get a free Parcel Services Business Kit that shows ways we'll deliver for you — reliably and economically. Mail the reply card or call **1 800 THE USPS, Ext. 1184.**

PARCEL POST
UNITED STATES POSTAL SERVICE™

Load Flexibility   Load flexibility is the degree to which a transportation mode can provide appropriate equipment and conditions for moving specific kinds of goods and can be adapted for moving other products. Many products must be shipped under controlled temperature and humidity. Other products, such as liquids or gases, require special equipment or facilities for shipment. In the railroad industry, a shipper with unusual transport needs can consult the *Official Railway Equipment Register,* which lists various types of cars and equipment each railroad owns. Generally, motor vehicle and railroads have greater load flexibility than pipelines.

Accessibility   A carrier's ability to move goods over a specific route or network (rail lines, waterways, or truck routes) is its accessibility. For example, marketers evaluating transportation modes for reaching Great Falls, Montana, consider rail lines, truck routes, and scheduled airline service but would eliminate water-borne carriers because Great Falls is inaccessible by water.

Some carriers differentiate themselves by serving areas competitors do not. After deregulation many large railroad companies sold off or abandoned unprofitable routes, making rail service inaccessible to shippers located on spur lines. Some shippers were forced to buy their own truck fleets to get their products to market. In recent years, small, short-line railroad companies have started buying up track and creating networks of low-cost feeder lines to reach underserved markets.

Frequency   Frequency is how often a company can send shipments by a specific transportation mode. When using pipelines, shipments can be continuous. A shipper using railroads or water must cope with limited schedules of possible shipping times between two cities.

■ *Coordinating Transportation Services*

To take advantage of the benefits various types of carriers offer and to compensate for deficiencies, marketers often combine and coordinate two or more transportation modes. In recent years, **intermodal transportation,** as this integrated approach is sometimes called, has become easier because of new developments within the transportation industry.

Intermodal transportation
Two or more transportation modes used in combination

Several kinds of intermodal shipping are available, all combining the flexibility of trucking with the low cost or speed of other forms of transport. Containerization facilitates intermodal transportation by consolidating shipments into sealed containers for transport by piggyback (shipping that combines truck trailers and railway flatcars), fishyback (truck trailers and water carriers), and birdyback (truck trailers and air carriers). As transportation costs increase, intermodal services gain popularity. Intermodal services are estimated to cost 25 to 40 percent less than all-highway transport and account for about 12 to 16 percent of total freight transportation business.[27]

Freight forwarders
Businesses that consolidate shipments from several firms into efficient lot sizes

Specialized agencies, **freight forwarders,** provide other forms of transport coordination. These firms combine shipments from several organizations into efficient lot sizes. Small loads (less than five hundred pounds) are much more expensive to ship than full carloads or truckloads, frequently requiring consolidation. Freight forwarders take small loads from various shippers, buy transport space from carriers, and arrange for goods to be delivered to respective buyers. Freight forwarders' profits come from the margin between higher, less-than-carload rates charged to each shipper and lower carload rates the agency pays. Because large shipments require less handling, use of freight forwarders can speed delivery. Freight forwarders can also determine the most efficient carriers and routes and are useful for shipping goods to foreign markets. Some shippers prefer to use freight forwarders because they provide door-to-door service.

Megacarriers   Freight transportation firms that provide several methods of shipment

One other transportation innovation is the development of **megacarriers,** freight transportation companies providing several shipment methods such as rail, truck, and air service. CSX, for example, has trains, barges, container ships, trucks, and pipelines, thus offering a multitude of transportation services. Air carriers have increased their ground transportation services. As they expand the range of transportation alternatives, carriers also put greater stress on customer service.

Strategic Issues in Physical Distribution

*P*hysical distribution functions discussed in this chapter—order processing, inventory management, materials handling, warehousing, and transportation—account for about half of all marketing costs. Moreover, these functions have a significant impact on customer service and satisfaction, which are of prime importance to marketers.

The strategic importance of physical distribution is evident in all elements of the marketing mix. Product design and packaging must allow for efficient stacking, storage, and transport. Differentiating products by size, color, and style must take into account additional demands placed on warehousing and shipping facilities. Competitive pricing may depend on a firm's ability to provide reliable delivery or emergency shipments of replacement parts; firms trying to lower inventory costs may offer quantity discounts to encourage large purchases. Promotional campaigns must be coordinated with distribution functions so that advertised products are available to buyers. Order-processing departments must handle additional sales order information efficiently. Supply chain members must consider warehousing and transportation costs, which may influence a firm's policy on stockouts or its choice to centralize (or decentralize) inventory.

Improving physical distribution starts by closing the gap with customers. The entire supply chain must understand and meet customers' requirements. Another major opportunity for improving physical distribution is integrating processes across the boundaries of all members of the supply chain. The full scope of the physical distribution process includes suppliers, manufacturers, transportation firms, and warehouses. To work well, it requires a formal, integrated plan to balance supply and demand within a defined time period. Physical distribution can also be improved by developing cooperative relationships with suppliers of component parts and services that emphasize joint improvement rather than just transferring costs and inefficiencies from one party to another.[28]

No single distribution system is ideal for all situations, and any system must be evaluated continually and adapted as necessary. Pressures to adjust service levels or reduce costs may lead to totally restructuring supply chain relationships; changes in transportation, warehousing, materials handling, and inventory may affect speed of delivery, reliability, and economy of service. Marketing strategists consider customers' changing needs and preferences, recognizing that changes in any major distribution function may affect all other functions. Customer-oriented marketers analyze the characteristics of their target markets and plan distribution systems to provide products in the right place, at the right time, and at acceptable cost.

Summary

Physical distribution is a set of activities that moves products from producers to consumers, or end users. These activities include order processing, inventory management, materials handling, warehousing, and transportation. An effective physical distribution system can be an important component of an overall marketing strategy because it can decrease costs and increase customer satisfaction. Physical distribution activities should be integrated with marketing channel decisions and adjusted to meet unique needs of a channel member.

The main objective of physical distribution is to decrease costs and time while increasing customer service. Physical distribution managers strive to balance service, distribution costs, and resources. Companies must adapt to customers' needs and preferences, offer service comparable to or better than their competitors, and develop and communicate desirable customer service policies. Costs of providing service are minimized most effectively through the total-cost approach, which evaluates costs of the system as a whole rather than as a collection of separate activities. Reducing cycle time, the time it takes to complete a process, is also important.

Order processing, the first stage in a physical distribution system, is the receipt and transmission of sales order information. Order processing consists of three main tasks. Order entry is placing purchase orders from customers or salespersons by mail, telephone, or computer. Order handling involves checking customer credit, verifying product availability, and preparing products for shipping. Order delivery is provided by the carrier most suitable for a desired level of customer service. Order processing may be done manually or electronically through an EDI network, depending on which

method gives greatest speed and accuracy within cost limits.

The objective of inventory management is to minimize inventory costs while maintaining a supply of goods adequate for customers' needs. All inventory costs—carrying and order-processing costs—must be controlled for profit goals to be met. To avoid stockouts without tying up too much capital in inventory, firms must have systematic methods for determining a reorder point, the inventory level at which more inventory is ordered. To calculate the reorder point, marketers must know the order lead time, the usage rate, and the amount of safety stock required. The order lead time is the average amount of time between placing the order and receiving it. The usage rate is the rate at which a product's inventory is used or sold during a specific time period. Safety stock is the amount of extra inventory that a firm keeps to guard against stockouts. Some marketers use the fixed order-interval system instead of the reorder-point approach. The fixed order-interval system is an approach in which products are ordered based on a predetermined interval. Two sets of costs must be analyzed when deciding how much to order: inventory-carrying costs and order-processing costs. The order size that has the lowest total of both order-processing costs and inventory costs is called the economic order quantity (EOQ). Some organizations have abandoned EOQ and use the just-in-time (JIT) approach instead. The just-in-time approach means that products arrive just as they are needed for use in production or resale.

Materials handling, or physical handling of products, is an important element of physical distribution. Packaging, loading, and movement systems must be coordinated to take into account both cost reduction and customer requirements. Basic handling systems include unit loading on pallets or skids, movement by mechanical devices, and containerization.

Warehousing involves the design and operation of facilities for storing and moving goods. Private warehouses are owned and operated by a company for the purpose of distributing its own products. Public warehouses are business organizations renting storage space and related physical distribution facilities to other firms. Public warehouses may furnish security for products that are being used as collateral for loans by establishing field warehouses. They may also provide bonded storage for companies wishing to defer tax payments on imported or taxable products. Distribution centers are large, centralized warehouses, specially designed for rapid movement of goods to customers. In many cases, a combination of private and public facilities is the most flexible warehousing approach.

Transportation adds time and place utility to a product by moving it from where it is made to where it is purchased and used. The five major modes of transporting goods in the United States are railroads, trucks, water-

ways, airways, and pipelines. Marketers evaluate transportation modes with respect to costs, speed, dependability, load flexibility, accessibility, and frequency. Final selection of a transportation mode involves many tradeoffs. Intermodal transportation allows marketers to combine advantages of two or more modes of transport; it is facilitated by containerization; freight forwarders, which coordinate transport by combining small shipments from several organizations into efficient lot sizes; and megacarriers, freight transportation companies that offer several shipment methods.

Physical distribution affects every element of the marketing mix: product, price, promotion, and distribution. To give customers products at acceptable prices, marketers consider consumers' changing needs and shifts within major distribution functions. Then they adapt existing physical distribution systems for greater effectiveness. Physical distribution functions account for about half of all marketing costs and have significant impact on customer satisfaction. Therefore, effective marketers are actively involved in design and control of physical distribution systems.

IMPORTANT TERMS

Physical distribution	Usage rate	Materials handling	Bonded storage
Cycle time	Safety stock	Unit loading	Distribution centers
Order processing	Fixed order-interval	Containerization	Transportation
Electronic data	system	Warehousing	Transportation modes
interchange (EDI)	Economic order quantity	Private warehouses	Intermodal transportation
Stockouts	(EOQ)	Public warehouses	Freight forwarders
Reorder point	Just-in-time (JIT)	Field public warehouses	Megacarriers
Order lead time			

DISCUSSION AND REVIEW QUESTIONS

1. Discuss the cost and service tradeoffs in developing a physical distribution system.
2. What factors must physical distribution managers consider when developing a customer service mix?
3. Why should physical distribution managers develop customer service standards?
4. What is the advantage of using a total distribution cost approach?
5. What are the main tasks involved in order processing?
6. Discuss the advantages of using an electronic order-processing system. Which types of organizations are most likely to utilize electronic order processing?
7. Describe the costs associated with inventory management.
8. Explain the tradeoffs inventory managers face when reordering products or supplies. How is the reorder point computed?
9. How can managers improve inventory control? Give specific examples of techniques.

10. How does a product's package affect materials handling procedures and techniques?
11. What is containerization? Discuss its major benefits.
12. Explain the major differences between private and public warehouses. What is a field public warehouse?
13. Under what circumstances should a firm use a private warehouse instead of a public one?
14. The focus of distribution centers is on active movement of goods. Discuss how distribution centers are designed for the rapid flow of products.
15. Compare the five major transportation modes as to costs, speed, dependability, load flexibility, accessibility, and frequency.
16. Discuss the ways marketers can combine or coordinate two or more modes of transportation. What is the advantage of doing so?
17. Identify the types of containerized shipping available to physical distribution managers.

385

APPLICATION QUESTIONS

1. Assume you are responsible for the distribution of computers at a mail-order company. What would you do to ensure the availability, timeliness, and quality of the product for your customers?

2. Wal-Mart's use of EDI has lowered its costs and increased efficiencies in its distribution systems. What should be an organization's major consideration when attempting to follow Wal-Mart's example? Why?

3. The type of warehouse facilities chosen has important strategic implications for a firm. What type of warehouse would be most appropriate for the following situations and why?

   a. A propane gas company recently entered the market in the state of Washington. The company's customers need varied quantities of propane on a timely basis and, at times, on short notice.

   b. A suntan lotion manufacturer has little expertise in managing warehouses and needs storage space in several locations in the Southeast.

   c. A shampoo manufacturer must have short cycle time to its customers and needs to send its products to many different retailers.

4. Determine the reorder point for a jeans retailer's inventory given the following information. The retail outlet wants to have forty pairs of jeans on hand at all times and sells an average of five pairs per day. An order takes seven days to be received from the day it is ordered.

5. Modes of transportation are shown in Table 16.2. Marketers select the transportation mode based on cost, speed, dependability, load flexibility, accessibility, and frequency. Identify a product and then select a mode of transportation based on the criteria above. Explain your choice.

Case 16.1   **Airborne's Competitive Dogfight**

By spending the last ten years grabbing corporate business from rivals Federal Express and United Parcel Service, Airborne Express has transformed itself from a virtual unknown into a formidable competitor in the express delivery industry with sales of $2 billion. Attributing this achievement to its focus on one goal, delivering packages where they should be, on time, all of the time, Airborne takes pride in providing superior service at low prices in over 200 countries around the world.

Founded in 1946 as a freight forwarder, the Seattle-based company entered the express delivery business in 1980. From the beginning, Airborne established a reputation for reliable on-time delivery and customer satisfaction. By handling only small packages, Airborne avoided the expense of installing cargo doors on its planes. By targeting business shippers exclusively, the firm didn't require as extensive and costly a delivery system as Federal Express and UPS. Savings for the company meant savings for customers, making Airborne an attractive alternative for corporations doing business with its rivals. It was exactly these corporations Airborne went after, winning contracts with some of Federal Express's biggest customers, such as IBM. By 1990, Airborne had secured contracts with *Fortune* 500 companies, such as Merrill Lynch, McDonald's, and Xerox, and operated 8,000 trucks and vans and ninety-seven aircraft.

Every day Airborne handles over 500,000 packages. To facilitate speed and dependability, the firm relies on state-of-the-art technology. Bar code scanning permits almost instantaneous package tracking, and electronic data entry eliminates hours of paperwork. Airborne's innovative Libre computer-based shipment processing system allows customers to weigh, route, label, invoice, and track packages from their own locations, and its Linkage System connects Airborne's computers with those of its customers.

What company executives insist sets Airborne apart from the competition even more than cutting-edge technology and more than speed and efficiency is its emphasis on personal service. When customers have questions, they speak with representatives at their local customer service centers who know how local traffic and weather conditions will affect delivery. When customers call as late as 2 A.M. with urgent requests to have parts delivered the next day, Airborne accommodates them.

For years, Airborne was the fastest-growing company in the industry. Since 1984, the organization has not lost one day of service. Its private airport, centralized warehouse and distribution center, and highly trained technicians who maintain and repair company aircraft all contributed to this "zero down time" record. Despite excellent and uninterrupted service, however, Airborne is now struggling to maintain its 16 percent market share. To save money, many shippers are switching to less expensive two- or three-day delivery services. UPS and the U.S. Postal Service are encroaching on Airborne's territory by aggressively pursuing corporate accounts. Federal Express, which used to charge up to 50 percent more than Airborne, recently lowered prices for large-volume customers. Underbidding Airborne by $31.3 million earned Federal Express a five-year contract with the federal government, and its new lower prices also lured Apple Computer and General Electric away from Airborne. Losing General Electric alone could cost the company about $7 million a year.

To fight back, Airborne is expanding services, targeting new customers, and cutting expenses. For cost-conscious customers, Airborne now offers lower-priced next-afternoon service. Its "flight-ready express packs," available in many retail outlets, afford small businesses the convenience of using prepaid shipping envelopes they themselves can prepare for overnight delivery. Airborne's sales force is making more than a thousand calls a day to small and midsize companies, many of them Federal Express customers. The company is also offering discounts through trade organizations, such as state bar associations.

Industry analysts assert that despite its current challenges Airborne remains a serious contender in the air express business. One edge Airborne maintains is its small but profitable international operation. Although UPS has a powerful global presence, Federal Express is dramatically reducing its overseas service. Airborne is positioned to step in and grow.[29]

Questions for Discussion

1. On which transportation selection criteria would Airborne be rated high? On which would it be rated low?
2. In what ways has Airborne managed to keep its costs low? What benefits has that brought?
3. Can the use of overnight express services result in suboptimization? Explain.

Case 16.2   The Home Depot Initiates New Cooperation in Supply Chain Management

Atlanta-based Home Depot is the leading chain of home-improvement stores in the United States with sales of $15.4 billion and profits of $731.5 million. With more than 350 stores in the United States and Canada, The Home Depot ranks among the twenty largest U.S. retailers. It plans to double its number of stores by 1998, including new locations in Mexico and overseas. *Fortune* magazine named Home Depot "America's most admired retailer" in both 1994 and 1995, and it consistently makes *Fortune*'s list of "America's most admired corporations."

Home Depot was founded in 1978 by Bernard Marcus, Arthur Blank, and Ronald Brill, all former Handy Dan Home Improvement Centers executives. Their first three stores opened in the Atlanta area in 1979, and they added a fourth in 1980. Over the years, the firm has acquired Bowater Home Centers (with stores in Texas, Louisiana, and Alabama), Modell's Shoppers World stores (Long Island), and Aikenhead, a Canadian home-improvement retailer. In 1987, the chain initiated its policy of "low day-in day-out pricing."

The typical Home Depot store stocks more than 40,000 to 50,000 home improvement materials, building supplies, and lawn and garden items in more than 100,000 square feet. To cater to both do-it-yourselfers and professional contractors, the stores follow a strategy of providing superior customer service, low prices, and a broad product assortment. They also offer product installation services, free professional consultation on home improvement projects, and how-to seminars on a variety of do-it-yourself projects.

Several new Home Depot outlets opened in the 1990s with Expo Design Centers, which offer upscale interior design products and services. The company has also developed a new concept store for rural areas, called CrossRoads, which will offer farming and ranching supplies as well as building and home improvement products. The first CrossRoads opened in 1995 in Quincy, Illinois. Also in 1995, the firm launched Right at Home, a line of coordinated home furnishings, including textiles, wall coverings, floor tiles, and lighting fixtures.

As a leader in both its supply chain and its industry, Home Depot is using re-engineering to become more efficient in physical distribution—particularly logistics, inventory control, security, and electronic data interchange systems—in order to help manufacturers improve their productivity and thereby supply Home Depot with better quality products at less cost. After recognizing that it needed to implement a core carrier program (with 89 percent of its deliveries going direct from vendor to store, store receiving docks were often overwhelmed with incoming trucks from multiple carriers), Home Depot required its suppliers to switch to designated regional and national carriers. This stipulation was met with substantial resistance for several years until Home Depot began listening to vendors' concerns and implementing some of their suggestions. Home Depot now offers two choices of carriers in each region.

Its success has led Home Depot to form the Inbound Logistics Consortium, a cooperative partnership of retailers such as Wal-Mart, Handy Andy, Caldor, Rickels, Target, Venture, Lowes, HomeQuarters, and others, in which regional trucking companies making deliveries can provide better service, faster delivery, and greater efficiency in their operations. "We think Wal-Mart and The Home Depot can help each other," insists Rebecca Nash, director of traffic. Home Depot has also made suggestions for standardizing packaging and delivery that saves its suppliers millions of dollars.

Another radical change was Home Depot's insistence that its 5,000 vendors switch from shipping products on wooden pallets to plastic slipsheets. Slipsheets cost about one-sixth as much as wooden pallets and, because they are thin, take up less room in storage and on trucks, allowing more goods to be transported at one time. According to Pete Cleaveland, Home Depot's vice president for traffic and distribution, "The slipsheeting program will result in significant cost and manpower savings for our industry." If it had not switched to slipsheeting, in 1994 alone Home Depot would have paid carriers more than $700,000 to haul away pallets. To motivate suppliers to switch to slipsheets, Home Depot distributed a humorous promotional video to vendors and conducted seminars stressing the advantages of slipsheeting. The company also has a toll-free answer line for vendors converting to slipsheeting and is working with its core carriers to help vendors convert to the new system. It has also founded a Slipsheet Retailer Coalition to share the benefits and expand the uses of slipsheeting throughout the retail industry. Says Nash, "We want to share our experience with other retailers. We went to the vendor community and said, 'We want to sell your stocks and reduce your lead time.'"

Home Depot is also making greater use of Electronic Data Interchange (EDI), a paperless system that electronically processes orders from stores to manufacturers, alerts stores when merchandise is scheduled to arrive, and transmits invoice data. The system helps Home Depot avoid stockouts and allows it to track shipments almost instantly, resulting in better customer service.

Home Depot is also trying to persuade the retail industry to standardize other elements, such as UPC (bar code) symbols and security devices. Such standardization and re-engineering will enable Home Depot to become even more efficient in its role as supply chain leader while providing better value and service to its customers.[30]

Questions for Discussion

1. Explain why physical distribution is so important in Home Depot's marketing strategy.
2. How has Home Depot positioned itself as a leader of supply chain management in the home improvement industry?
3. Why do you think Home Depot has formed a cooperative partnership with Wal-Mart and other competitors?

STRATEGIC CASE 4

Goodyear Breaks with Tradition

To replace Goodyear tires, customers no longer have to find a Goodyear tire outlet. They can go to Sears, Kmart, or Wal-Mart instead. In a break with its almost century-long practice of marketing tires exclusively through its dealer network, Goodyear Tire and Rubber Company also is selling through tire franchises and multibrand discount stores. Convinced that Goodyear needed wider distribution than its independent dealers could provide, CEO Stanley Gault made the dramatic change in 1991. Although many industry experts believed that opening new distribution channels would boost the company's market share, others warned that Goodyear would risk alienating once-loyal dealers. Gault's successor, Samir Gibara, sought a compromise in 1996, announcing that certain new tire models would be available only at Goodyear dealers.

Goodyear Gets Rolling

Founded in 1898, Goodyear got its start manufacturing tires for bicycles and carriages. Soon afterward, the organization turned its attention to the expanding American automobile industry. With its 1903 introduction of the Quick Detachable Tire and the Universal Rim, Goodyear was catapulted into the position of the world's largest tire manufacturer. Goodyear continued to lead the industry, introducing pneumatic truck tires, establishing its own rubber plantations, and in 1930, inaugurating what became its global symbol, the Goodyear Blimp. As a testament to the dependability of Goodyear tires, the *Apollo XIV* Lunar Landing Module rolled over the moon's surface on them.

While Goodyear was enjoying its number one status, rival Michelin changed the tire industry by introducing radial tires in 1966. Ten years after their introduction, radials accounted for about 45 percent of all American tire sales. Scrambling to catch up, Goodyear introduced a variety of new tires, including its all-weather Tiempo and other brands such as Eagle, Arriva, and Wrangler. The company temporarily regained its market-leading position, but by 1990 had fallen to number three behind France's Michelin and Japan's Bridgestone. By the time Stanley Gault took over as CEO, the company was struggling.

Distribution Changes

Stanley Gault believed the key to Goodyear's long-term profitability was in its ability to change. The most significant change he instituted was to increase the availability of Goodyear tires. To do this, the company focused on the $13 billion replacement market instead of the original equipment market and made Goodyear tires available in more outlets. Instead of concentrating on selling tires to automobile manufacturers who put them on new cars, the tire producer was trying to make sure that owners in need of new tires would choose Goodyear. To attract potential customers, Goodyear introduced a stream of new products, including the simultaneous launch of four new tires in 1991–1992—three times the industry average.

One of these tires, the innovative Aquatred, is designed to channel water away from the tread. With its better-than-average traction on wet surfaces, Aquatred is particularly attractive to safety-conscious consumers. Company executives are convinced that Aquatred is a popular brand despite its $95-per-tire price tag because it was designed with customer expectations in mind.

Goodyear also is taking consumer preferences into account by widening distribution. According to *Modern Tire Dealer* magazine, the number of consumers buying tires at chain stores and warehouse clubs has grown 30 percent. At the same time, the number buying at tire dealerships has decreased 4 percent. In addition, 51 percent of new tire purchases occur within two days of a decision that they are needed. These impulse buyers are unlikely to seek out specialty tire dealers, going instead to the nearest, and usually cheapest, available outlet. To better meet the changing needs of consumers, Gault was determined to make Goodyear tires available in more places.

The organization initiated its strategy by selling seven Goodyear brands through 875 Sears outlets. Depending on the size of the store, Sears kept an inventory of 300 to 500 Goodyear tires, including Arriva, Corsa CT, two types of Wrangler, and three styles of Eagle. They did not, however, carry a complete range of sizes for any of these lines—a policy that remains intact. Encouraged by sales at Sears, Goodyear widened distribution to include Wal-Mart, Kmart, Discount Tire, and other outlets. To serve the Goodyear franchises, which continue to sell almost 50 percent of the company's replacement tires, Goodyear began supplying them with competitive low-end Goodyear tires.

Response to the Changes

At the time of the announced change in distribution strategy, one industry expert believed that Goodyear's arrangement with Sears could result in significant benefits. Sears then controlled about 10 percent of the replacement market. If it were to capture 20 percent, Goodyear's sales would increase by 3 million tires a

390

year. Others, however, were not as optimistic. The director of Fundamental Research in Cleveland, Ohio, predicted that loss of business from Goodyear's dealers would cancel at least one-third of any gains from other outlets. He suggested that Sears might lure customers with the respected Goodyear name and sell its own Roadhandler brand instead, and that alienated dealers would begin offering rival brands or higher profit margin private-label brands.

Reported dealer responses such as "I feel like they stabbed me in the back" and "We went with them through thick and thin, and now they're going to drown us," served as a warning flag to Goodyear. One dealer in Flagstaff, Arizona, said he was shocked and angered by a Discount Tire newspaper advertisement featuring Goodyear Wrangler tires priced $17 less than he paid Goodyear for the same tires. Disgruntled dealers also are complaining because Goodyear is allowing Sears to sell the popular Aquatred, a line they hoped to sell exclusively.

CEO Gault stated that he wanted to support Goodyear dealers, not take business away from them. According to distributors and analysts, however, a growing number of Goodyear's once-loyal dealers were selling other brands. One large Goodyear dealer in Melbourne, Florida, markets a line of private-brand tires. The owner says that although he sells 20 percent fewer Goodyear tires, his profits are up. A Detroit-based distributor and retailer of Michelin, Uniroyal, and Firestone tires claims that about half of the Goodyear dealers in the region have approached his company about becoming dealers for one or more of these brands.

Goodyear's response to this criticism and dealer activity was to give their dealers exclusive sales rights to newly introduced tire models. New CEO Gibara, for example, announced in early 1996 that the company's latest release, the lifetime-warrantied Infinitred tire, would be sold exclusively through the company's 5,000 dealers and company-owned stores. To further support the launch of the Infinitred, Goodyear announced a generous package of cooperative promotional incentives available to dealers.

Whatever the final outcome of Goodyear's new distribution strategy, the company's executives believe they have no choice. Depending solely on Goodyear dealerships for market share is no longer viable. For now, the company characterized by its former CEO as "the last bastion of the American-owned tire industry" is holding its own. It operates 32 plants in the United States and 42 more in 29 countries around the world, its annual sales exceed $12 billion, and its blimps sport new colors and a bolder logo to remind the world that Goodyear is still flying high.

Questions for Discussion

1. Identify the major sources of channel conflict between Goodyear and its franchised dealers.
2. What steps did Goodyear take to reduce the conflict with its Goodyear franchised dealers?
3. What are the major benefits to Goodyear of maketing its tires through retailers such as Sears, Wal-Mart, Discount Tire, and Kmart?
4. Which organization(s) is the channel leader and what are its sources of power? Is the channel leader likely to change? Explain.

Sources: *Hoover's Company Profile* database (Austin, Texas: Reference Press, 1996), via America Online; Jeff Higley, "Warranty Key to Firm's Latest Marketing Blitz," *Rubber and Plastics*, Feb. 19, 1996, p. 4; Dave Zielasko, "Infinitred Launch to Top Aquatred's," *Tire Business*, Feb. 19, 1996, p. 22; Fara Warner, "Straight Talk from Stan Gault," *Brandweek*, Nov. 23, 1992, pp. 16–18; Zachary Schiller, "Goodyear Is Gunning Its Marketing Engine," *Business Week*, Mar. 16, 1992, p. 42; Dana Milbank, "Independent Tire Dealers Rebelling Against Goodyear," *Wall Street Journal*, July 7, 1992, p. B4; Peter Nulty, "The Bounce Is Back at Goodyear," *Fortune*, Sept. 7, 1992, pp. 70–72; and Seth Lubove, "The Last Bastion," *Forbes*, Feb. 14, 1994, pp. 56, 58.

Part 5

Promotion Decisions

*P*art 5 focuses on communication with target market members. A specific marketing mix cannot satisfy people in a particular target market unless they are aware of the product and where to find it. Some promotion decisions relate to a specific marketing mix, whereas others, broader in scope, are geared to promoting the whole organization. Chapter 17 presents an overview of promotion. We describe the communication process and the major promotion methods that can be included in promotion mixes. In Chapter 18, we analyze the major steps required to develop an advertising campaign, and we explain what public relations is and how it can be used. Chapter 19 deals with the management of personal selling and the role it can play in a firm's promotion mix. This chapter also explores the general characteristics of sales promotion and sales promotion techniques.

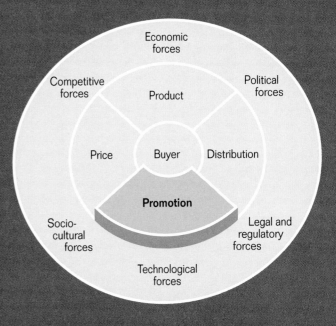

Chapter 17

Promotion:
An Overview

O B J E C T I V E S

- To understand the role of promotion in the marketing mix

- To examine the process of communication

- To understand the objectives of promotion

- To explore the elements of the promotion mix

- To acquire an overview of the major methods of promotion

- To explore factors that affect the choice of promotional methods

- To examine criticisms and defenses of promotion

Columbia Sportswear's secret weapon, Mother Boyle, captures consumers' affection.

*T*o outdoor enthusiasts, dressed for success is likely to mean dressed in Columbia Sportswear. Maker of hunting jackets, skiwear, snowboarder clothing, rainwear, footgear, and casual sports attire, Columbia Sportswear is the world's largest outerwear manufacturer. Among its most famous customers are former presidents and avid fly fishermen Jimmy Carter and George Bush, both loyal fans of Columbia's multipocketed fishing vest. Established in 1938 as a family hat manufacturing business, today the company has over 900 employees and sells its rugged fashions in the United States, Canada, Europe, Asia, South America, Australia, New Zealand, and China. Its Bugaboo parka is the best-selling ski parka in apparel history. Thanks in large part to its unconventional boss and its extensive promotional program, Columbia boasts annual sales of $316 million, far ahead of its closest competitor, Patagonia.

Gert Boyle is known from New York to New Zealand as Columbia's tough CEO with the "born to nag" tattoo on her arm. Her slogan—"Early to bed, early to rise, work like hell, and advertise"—is borne out in the company's multimillion dollar advertising campaign. Columbia consistently reaches millions of consumers with ads appearing in international print and broadcast media including *GQ, Rolling Stone,* and *Ski* magazines, during *The Late Show with David Letterman,* and on cable networks ESPN and MTV. One ad features Mother Boyle subjecting her son to inhumane weather conditions that demonstrate the durability of Columbia garb. Another is a photo of Gert facing off with a huge bonefish; the caption reads, "What's tough, silver, and always looking for a fight?"

Public relations, sales promotion, and aggressive personal selling efforts also build Columbia's brand awareness and drive sales. Chatting on television talk shows one day and mingling with bikers at motorcycle rallies the next, Gert comfortably navigates the globe to foster favorable public relations. High-profile sponsorships, such as being the official outerwear supplier to CBS Sports for the 1994 Winter Olympics and outfitting the first all-female America's Cup sailboat racing team, also create positive publicity. In the United States, Europe, Asia, Latin America, Australia, and New Zealand, Columbia works with sixteen independent sales agencies to bring its products to retail outlets. In the Netherlands, Austria, and France, the company maintains its own sales offices. Sales personnel strive to make sure that products look good in stores, providing retailers with Columbia's "Merchandising Manual," visual merchandising accessories, and in-store signage bearing Gert Boyle's imposing—but apparently irresistible—face.[1]

Mother Gert Boyle, Chairman, Columbia Sportswear

"MOTHER ALWAYS HAS A HAND IN DESIGN."

–Tim Boyle, President, Columbia Sportswear

My mother may not be a goddess, but it appears that she has eight arms. Otherwise, how do you explain the fact that while creating this Hoodoo Parka™ she sealed seams, finessed the pull-out hood and checked the Radial Sleeves™ Simultaneously. And she still managed to add a draw-cord waist with an internal powder skirt. In fact, Mother always tackles the task of building the world's most technical parkas head-on. Her search for maximum waterproof/breathability led to the Mini-Oxford Omni-Tech™ outershell in this Hoodoo Parka. So why should you care that Mother is a hands-on person? The answer will become obvious the next time you're out in a storm.

Hoodoo Parka," with mesh fleece-lined, zip-out HydroPlus" liner.

Columbia Sportswear Company

6600 N. Baltimore, Portland, Oregon 97203. For the dealer nearest you in the U.S. and Canada, call 1-800-MA BOYLE.

Organizations such as Columbia Sportswear employ a variety of promotional methods to communicate with their target markets. Providing information to customers is vital to maintaining strong customer relationships.

This chapter looks at the general dimensions of promotion. First we define and examine the role of promotion. Next, to understand how promotion works, we analyze the meaning and process of communication, as well as the objectives of promotion. Then we consider the major types of promotional methods and the factors that influence marketers' decisions to use particular methods. Finally, the criticisms and defenses of promotion are explored.

The Role of Promotion

Promotion Communication that facilitates exchanges by influencing the audience to accept a product

Promotion means communicating with individuals, groups, or organizations to directly or indirectly facilitate exchanges by informing and persuading one or more audiences to accept an organization's products. A variety of organizations spend considerable resources on promotion. Marketers indirectly facilitate exchanges by focusing information about company activities and products on interest groups (such as environmental and consumer groups), current and potential investors, regulatory agencies, and society in general. Some marketers use *cause-related marketing,* which links purchase of their products to philanthropic efforts for a particular cause favored by their target market. Cause-related marketing often helps marketers boost sales and generate goodwill through contributions to causes that members of its target markets support.[2] Marketers also sponsor special events, often leading to news coverage and positive promotion of an organization and its brands.

From this wider perspective, promotion plays a comprehensive communication role. Some promotional activities help a company justify its existence and maintain positive, healthy relationships between itself and various groups. For example, Coors Brewing Company is sponsoring a five-year, $40 million program aimed at teaching half a million American adults to read. Allstate Insurance Company encourages people to make sure that the batteries in their smoke detectors are working. Searle Canada, a pharmaceutical company, has designed for physicians' offices a poster that encourages abused women to seek help (see Figure 17.1).

Although companies can direct a single type of communication—such as an advertisement—toward numerous audiences, marketers often design a communication precisely for a specific target market. A firm frequently communicates several different messages concurrently, each to a different group. McDonald's may direct one communication toward its Big Mac customers, a second toward investors about the firm's stable growth, and a third toward society in general regarding the company's social awareness in supporting Ronald McDonald Houses, which aid families of children suffering from cancer.

Sometimes love hits like a ton of bricks.

It doesn't hurt to talk to your doctor.

Figure 17.1
Promoting Socially Responsible Causes   Searle Canada sponsors a poster for physicians' offices, which is designed to encourage women abused by their spouses to seek help.

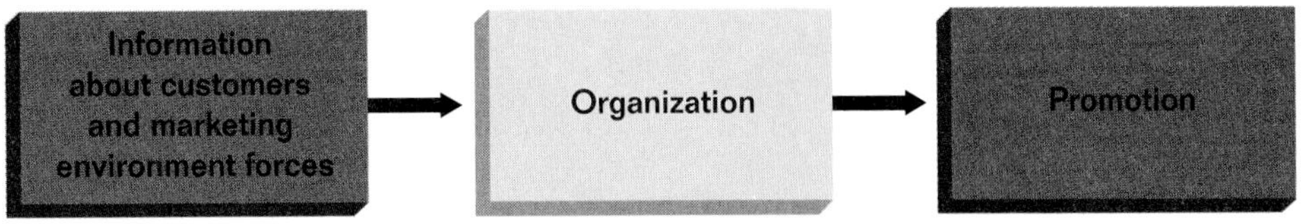

Figure 17.2
Information Flows Into and Out of an Organization

For maximum benefit from promotional efforts, marketers strive to properly plan, implement, coordinate, and control communications. Effective promotional activities are based on information about customers and the marketing environment, often obtained from an organization's marketing information system (see Figure 17.2). How successfully marketers use promotion to maintain positive relationships depends largely on the quantity and quality of information an organization receives. Because promotion's basic role is communication, we should analyze what communication is and how the communication process works.

Promotion and the Communication Process

*C*ommunication can be viewed as the transmission of information. For communication to take place, both the sender and receiver of information must share some common ground. They must share a common understanding of the symbols, words, and pictures used to transmit information. An individual transmitting the following message may believe he or she is communicating with you:

在工廠吾人製造化粧品,在商店吾人銷售希望。

However, communication has not taken place because few of you understand the intended message.[3] Thus we define **communication** as a sharing of meaning.[4] Implicit in this definition is the notion of transmission of information because sharing necessitates transmission.

As Figure 17.3 shows, communication begins with a source. A **source** is a person, group, or organization with a meaning it intends and attempts to share with an audience. A source could be a salesperson wishing to communicate a sales message or an organization wanting to send a message to thousands of customers through an advertisement. A **receiver** is the individual, group, or organization that decodes a coded message, and an audience is two or more receivers. The intended receivers or audience of an advertisement for Motorola cellular telephones, for example, might be businesspersons who frequently travel by car.

Communication
A sharing of meaning

Source A person, group, or organization with a meaning it wants and tries to share with an audience

Receiver The individual, group, or organization that decodes a coded message

Figure 17.3
The Communication Process

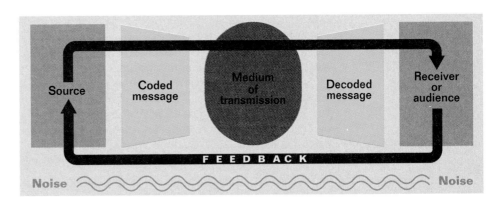

396

Coding process Converting meaning into a series of signs

To transmit meaning, a source must convert the meaning into a series of signs representing ideas or concepts. This is called the **coding process,** or *encoding*. When coding meaning into a message, a source must consider certain characteristics of the receiver or audience. To share meaning, the source should use signs that are familiar to the receiver or audience. Marketers who understand this realize how important it is to know their target market and to make sure that an advertisement, for example, uses a language that the target market understands. Thus, when DuPont advertises its Stainmaster carpeting, it does not mention the chemical used to make the carpet resistant to spotting because it would have little meaning to consumers. There have been some notable problems in translating English advertisements into other languages to communicate with customers in global markets. For example, Budweiser has been advertised in Spain as the "Queen of Beers," and the Chinese have been encouraged to "eat their fingers off" when receiving KFC's slogan "Finger-Lickin' Good."[5] Clearly, it is important that people understand the language used in promotion.

When coding a meaning, a source needs to use signs that the receiver or audience uses for referring to the concepts the source intends to convey. Marketers try to avoid signs that may have several meanings for an audience. For example, *soda* as a general term for soft drinks might not work well in national advertisements. Although in some parts of the United States the word means "soft drink," in other regions it may connote bicarbonate of soda, an ice cream drink, or something one mixes with Scotch whisky.

Medium of transmission The means of carrying the coded message from the source to the receiver

To share a coded meaning with the receiver or audience, a source selects and uses a medium of transmission. A **medium of transmission** carries the coded message from the source to the receiver or audience. Transmission media include ink on paper, air wave vibrations produced by vocal cords, chalk marks on a chalkboard, and electronically produced vibrations of air waves—in radio and television signals, for example.

When a source chooses an inappropriate medium of transmission, several problems may arise. A coded message may reach some receivers, but not the right ones. Suppose a community theater spends most of its advertising dollars on radio advertisements. If theatergoers depend mainly on newspapers for information about local drama, then the theater will not reach its intended target audience. Coded messages may also reach intended receivers in incomplete form because the intensity of the transmission is weak. For example, radio signals are received effectively only over a limited range, which varies depending on climatic conditions. Members of the target audience living on the fringe of the broadcast area may receive a weak signal; others well within the broadcast area may also receive an incomplete message if they listen to radios while busy driving or studying.

Decoding process Converting signs into concepts and ideas

Noise Whatever reduces a communication's clarity and accuracy

In the **decoding process,** signs are converted into concepts and ideas. Seldom does a receiver decode exactly the same meaning that a source coded. When the result of decoding is different from what was coded, noise exists. **Noise** is anything that reduces the clarity and accuracy of the communication; it has many sources and may affect any or all parts of the communication process. Noise sometimes arises within the medium of transmission itself. Radio static, faulty printing processes, and laryngitis are sources of noise. Noise also occurs when a source uses signs that are unfamiliar to the receiver or that have a different meaning from the one intended. Noise also may originate in the receiver. A receiver may be unaware of a coded message when perceptual processes block it out.

Feedback The receiver's response to a message

The receiver's response to a message is **feedback** to the source. The source usually expects and normally receives feedback, although perhaps not immediately. During feedback, the receiver or audience is the source of a message directed toward the original source, which then becomes a receiver. Feedback is coded, sent through a medium of transmission, and decoded by the receiver, the source of the original communication. Thus communication is a circular process.

During face-to-face communication, such as a personal selling situation or product sampling, verbal and nonverbal feedback can be immediate. Instant feedback lets communicators adjust messages quickly to improve the effectiveness of their communication. For example, when a salesperson realizes through feedback that a customer does not understand a sales presentation, the salesperson adapts the presentation to make it more meaningful to the customer. In interpersonal communication, feedback occurs through talking, touching, smiling, nodding, eye movements, and other body movements and postures.

When mass communication such as advertising is used, feedback is often slow and difficult to recognize. If Disney World increased advertising to attract more visitors, it might be six to eighteen months before the firm could notice the effects of expanded advertising. Although it is harder to discern, feedback does exist for mass communication. Advertisers obtain feedback in the form of changes in sales volume or in consumers' attitudes and awareness levels.

Channel capacity The limit on the volume of information a communication channel can handle effectively

Each communication channel has a limit on the volume of information it can handle effectively. This limit, called **channel capacity,** is determined by the least efficient component of the communication process. Consider communications that depend on vocal speech. An individual source can talk only so fast, and there is a limit to how much an individual receiver can take in aurally. Beyond that point, additional messages cannot be decoded; thus meaning cannot be shared. Although a radio announcer can read several hundred words a minute, a one-minute advertising message should not exceed 150 words because most announcers cannot articulate words into understandable messages at a rate beyond 150 words per minute. Marketers should keep this limit in mind when developing radio commercials. At times, a firm creates a television advertisement containing several types of visual materials and several forms of audio messages, all transmitted to viewers at the same time. Such communication may not be totally effective because receivers cannot decode all messages simultaneously.

Objectives of Promotion

*P*romotional objectives differ considerably from one organization to another and within organizations over time. Large organizations with multiple promotional programs operating simultaneously may have quite varied promotional objectives. For the purpose of analysis we focus on the eight promotional objectives shown in Table 17.1. Although the list is not exhaustive, one or more of these objectives underlie many promotional programs.

■ *Create Awareness*

A considerable amount of promotion is directed at creating awareness. For an organization introducing a new product, new brand, or brand extension, making customers aware is crucial to initiating the product adoption process. A marketer that has invested heavily in product development strives to create product awareness quickly in order to generate revenues to offset the high costs of product development and introduction. As discussed in Inside Marketing (on the following page), companies sometimes use movie tie-ins, gearing products to capitalize on the pre-existing awareness of a movie.

Creating awareness is important for existing products, too. Promotional efforts may be aimed at increasing brand awareness, product feature awareness, awareness of image-related issues (such as organizational size or socially responsive behavior), or awareness of operational characteristics (such as store hours, locations, and credit availability). Some organizations are unsuccessful because marketers fail to generate awareness of critical issues among a significant portion of target market members.

Table 17.1 Possible Objectives of Promotion

- Create awareness
- Stimulate demand
- Encourage product trial
- Identify prospects
- Retain loyal customers
- Facilitate reseller support
- Combat competitive promotional efforts
- Reduce sales fluctuations

397

Movie Tie-Ins: Taking Hollywood Home

Although every toy manufacturer dreams of creating the next Frisbee, Etch-A-Sketch, or Barbie doll, the reality is that about 90 percent of new non-Hollywood–related products fail. Having learned it is less risky to ride the cape-tails of Batman, the Power Rangers, and Walt Disney, toy makers are becoming increasingly dependent on Hollywood for ideas and sales. With annual sales of licensed merchandise in the U.S. and Canada topping $17 billion, movie tie-ins are serious business.

Movie marketing boosts toys sales. In one summer alone, toy companies recorded sales of $300 million tied to the *Mighty Morphin Power Rangers,* $130 million tied to *Batman Forever,* and $100 million from Disney's *Pocahontas,* who appeared with her friends as 50 million kid's meal trinkets at Burger King, on a new line of Payless footwear, and on countless licensed toys from Mattel. Because toy sales also generate excitement about movies, movie makers benefit as well, paving the way for toy manufacturers to exert increasing influence over what viewers ultimately see on the screen. When Warner Brothers planned the look of the new Batmobile, it first checked the design with Hasbro, the toy company licensed to manufacture and sell Batman gadgetry. In addition to suggesting a longer hood for the car, Hasbro asked the film maker to put the Riddler in tights, because his traditional baggy pants just don't suit toy action figures. There are reports that to facilitate sales of its "Braided Beauty" Pocahontas doll, Mattel asked Disney to add a scene in which Pocahontas briefly wears her hair in a braid.

Encouraged by the enormous success of marketing tie-ins with children's movies, adult-oriented movie makers are getting into the act, too. Yves St. Laurent introduced a bright red lipstick called "007" tied to the James Bond movie *GoldenEye,* and Omega features scenes from *Apollo 13* in its ads for the Omega Speedmaster Chronograph, the first watch on the moon. Many experts agree that grown-up tie-ins are a good idea. If parents buy movie tie-in action figures, lunch boxes, and sleeping bags for their children, why not drinking glasses, night shirts, or perfume tied to their own favorite films for themselves?

Because product sales are usually linked to a movie's success, depending on tie-ins can be risky business. If a movie bombs, the manufacturer can lose millions of dollars spent on design, production, distribution, and advertising. One industry expert asserted that dust moved more quickly than products tied to box office failures such as *Pagemaster, The Jetsons,* and *Congo.* Given the potential success of movie tie-ins, however, film fans are sure to be able to take home lunch boxes, key rings, beach towels, stuffed animals, and action figures based on heroes and villains of the next Disney movie.

Sources: Fara Warner, "Move Tie-Ins Now Aimed at Adults as Well as Kids," *Wall Street Journal,* June 23, 1995, pp. B1, B9; T. L. Stanley, "Rangers Flick Hits $200M—in Promo$," *Brandweek,* May 29, 1995, pp. 1, 6; Joseph Pereira and Lisa Bannon, "Goodbye Dolly? Toy Makers' Addition to Hollywood Figures Reshapes Kids' Play," *Wall Street Journal,* July 13, 1995, pp. A1, A6; Kevin Goldman, "Like the Film? You Will Love the Lunch Box," *Wall Street Journal,* June 20, 1995, pp. B1, B12; and T. L. Stanley, "Disney Resets Tie-In Bar with $125M Consortium," *Brandweek,* Mar. 13, 1995, pp. 1, 6.

■ *Stimulate Demand*

Primary demand
Demand for a product category rather than for a specific brand

Pioneer promotion
Promotion that informs consumers about a new product

When an organization is the first to introduce an innovative product, it tries to stimulate **primary demand**—demand for a product category rather than for a specific brand of product—through pioneer promotion. **Pioneer promotion** informs potential customers about the product: what it is, what it does, how it can be used, and where it can be purchased. Because pioneer promotion is used in the introductory stage of the product life cycle, which means that there are no competing brands, it neither emphasizes brand names nor compares brands. The first company to introduce the compact disc player, for instance, initially attempted to stimulate primary demand by emphasizing the benefits of compact disc players in general rather than the benefit of its specific brand.

Primary demand stimulation is not just for new products. At times an industry trade association, rather than a single firm, uses promotional efforts to stimulate primary demand. For example, to stimulate primary demand for flowers, the American Floral Marketing Council sponsors advertisements promoting flowers as gifts. As shown in Figure 17.4, the California Fluid Milk Advisory Board is attempting to stimulate primary demand for milk through its "Got Milk?" campaign.

**Figure 17.4
Stimulating Demand**
The California Fluid Milk
Processors Advisory
Board attempts to stim-
ulate primary demand for
milk with its "Got Milk?"
campaign.

Selective demand
Demand for a specific brand

To build **selective demand,** which is demand for a specific brand, a marketer employs promotional efforts based on the strengths and benefits of a specific brand. Building selective demand requires promotional efforts that single out attributes important to potential buyers and the specific attributes of the brand. Promotional techniques are sometimes used to stimulate selective demand by differentiating the product from competing brands in the minds of potential buyers. Stimulating selective demand by increasing the number of product uses is sometimes accomplished through advertising campaigns, as well as through free samples, coupons, and consumer contests and sweepstakes. Promotions for large package sizes or multiple-product packages are directed at increasing consumption, which in turn can stimulate demand.

■ *Encourage Product Trial*

When attempting to move customers through the product adoption process, a marketer may be successful at creating awareness and interest, but then a significant proportion of customers stall during the evaluation stage. Thus certain types of promotion, such as free samples, coupons, test drive or limited free-use offers, contests, and games, are employed to encourage product trial. A magazine publisher, for example, might offer several free issues to entice potential readers to become new subscribers. Regardless of whether a marketer's product is the first of a new product category or a new brand in an existing category (in which case customers are familiar with competing brands), trial-inducing promotional efforts aim at making product trial convenient and low risk for potential customers.

■ *Identify Prospects*

Certain types of promotional efforts are directed at identifying customers who are interested in the firm's product and are most likely to buy. A marketer may utilize a magazine advertisement with a direct response information form, requesting the reader to complete and mail the form to receive additional information. In some cases advertisements have toll-free numbers to facilitate direct customer response. Customers who fill out information blanks or call the organization usually have higher interest in the product, which makes them possible sales prospects. The organization can respond with phone calls, follow-up letters, and in some instances, personal contact by salespeople.

■ *Retain Loyal Customers*

Clearly, maintaining long-term customer relationships is a major goal of most marketers, because such relationships are quite valuable. Recently, a major pizza chain, for example, determined that the lifetime receipts from one loyal pizza customer amount to $8,000.[6] Promotional efforts directed at customer retention can help an organization control its costs because the costs of retaining customers are usually considerably lower than those of acquiring new ones. Frequent user programs, such as those relied on by airlines, car rental agencies, and hotels, aim at rewarding loyal customers and encouraging them to remain loyal. Some organizations employ special offers that can only be used by their existing customers. To retain loyal customers, marketers not only advertise loyalty programs but also use reinforcement advertising, which assures current users that they have made the right brand choice and tells them how to get the most satisfaction from the product.

■ *Facilitate Reseller Support*

Reseller support is a two-way street. Producers generally want to provide support to resellers to maintain sound working relationships, and producers, in turn, expect to get support for their products from resellers. When a manufacturer advertises a product to consumers, this promotion should be viewed by resellers as being strong manufacturer support. In some instances, a producer agrees to pay a certain proportion of retailers' advertising expenses for promoting the producer's products. When a manufacturer is introducing a new consumer brand in a highly competitive product category, one difficulty is convincing supermarket managers to carry this brand. If the manufacturer promotes the new brand with free sample and coupon distribution in the retailer's area, a supermarket manager views these actions as strong support and is much more likely to handle the product. To encourage wholesalers and retailers to increase their inventories, the manufacturer may provide special offers and buying allowances to resellers. In certain industries a producer's salesperson may provide support to a wholesaler by working with the wholesaler's customers (retailers) in the presentation and promotion of the products. Strong relationships with resellers are important to a firm's capability to maintain a sustainable competitive advantage. The use of various promotional methods can help an organization achieve this goal.

■ *Combat Competitive Promotional Efforts*

At times a marketer's objective in using promotion is to offset or lessen the effect of a competitor's promotional program. This type of promotional activity does not necessarily increase the organization's sales or market share, but it may prevent a sales or market share loss. A combative promotional objective is used most often by firms in extremely competitive consumer products markets, such as the fast-food industry, or in local competitive markets. For example, a local supermarket may mail out store coupons to residents living within a two-mile radius of the store. Coupons might be redeemable only Tuesdays and Wednesdays for the purchase of common items such as milk, bread, or eggs at very low prices. To offset the effects of these coupons, a competing store could advertise in the newspaper that it will accept any store's coupons on any day of the week.

■ *Reduce Sales Fluctuations*

Demand for many products varies from one month to another because of factors such as climate, holidays, and seasons. A business, however, cannot operate at peak efficiency when sales fluctuate rapidly. Changes in sales volume translate into changes in production, inventory levels, personnel needs, and financial resources required. To the extent that marketers can generate sales during slow periods, they can reduce the fluctuations. When promotional techniques reduce fluctuations, a manager can use the firm's resources more efficiently.

Promotional techniques are often designed to stimulate sales during sales slumps. For example, advertisements promoting price reduction of lawn care equipment can increase sales during fall and winter months. On occasion, an organization advertises that customers can be better served by coming in on certain days rather than other days. During peak season periods, a marketer may refrain from advertising to prevent overstimulating sales to the point that the firm cannot handle all the demand. A pizza outlet might distribute coupons that are valid only Monday through Thursday because Friday through Sunday the restaurant is extremely busy.

To achieve the major objectives of promotion discussed here, companies must develop appropriate promotional programs. In the next section we consider the basic components of such programs: the promotion mix elements.

The Promotion Mix

Promotion mix A combination of promotional methods used to promote a specific product

*S*everal promotional methods can be used to communicate with individuals, groups, and organizations. When an organization combines specific elements to promote a particular product, that combination constitutes the promotion mix for that product. The four possible elements of a **promotion mix** are advertising, personal selling, public relations, and sales promotion (see Figure 17.5). For some products, firms use all four ingredients; for others, only two or three.

■ *Advertising*

Advertising is a paid nonpersonal communication about an organization and its products that is transmitted to a target audience through a mass medium such as television, radio, newspapers, magazines, direct mail, mass transit vehicles, or outdoor displays. Individuals and organizations use advertising to promote goods, services, ideas, issues, and people. Being highly flexible, advertising can reach an extremely large target audience or focus on a small, precisely defined segment. For instance, Burger King's advertising focuses on a large audience of potential fast-food customers, ranging from children to adults, whereas advertising for corporate jets focuses on a much smaller and more specialized target market.

Advertising offers several benefits. It can be extremely cost-efficient because it can reach a vast number of people at a low cost per person. For example, the cost of a four-color, one-page advertisement in *Time* magazine is $150,000. Because the magazine reaches 4 million subscribers, the cost of reaching a thousand subscribers is only $37.50. Advertising also lets the user repeat the message several times. Levi Strauss, for example, advertises on television, in magazines, and through outdoor advertising. Furthermore, advertising a product a certain way can add to its value. The visibility that an organization gains from advertising can enhance its image. At times, a firm tries to enhance the company's or product's image by including celebrity endorsers in its advertisements (see Global Perspective on the next page).

Advertising has disadvantages as well. Even though the cost per person reached may be low, the absolute dollar outlay can be extremely high, especially for commercials during popular television shows. High costs can limit, and sometimes prevent, use of advertising in a promotion mix. Moreover, advertising rarely provides rapid feedback. Measuring its effect on sales is difficult, and it is ordinarily less persuasive than personal selling. In many instances the time available to communicate a message to customers is limited to seconds since people look at a print advertisement for only a few seconds and most broadcast commercials are thirty seconds or less. Of course, the use of infomercials can increase advertisement exposure time for viewers.

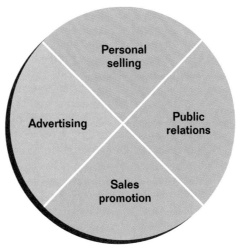

Figure 17.5
The Four Possible Elements of a Promotion Mix

Celebrity Endorsers: Does Star Power Translate Around the World?

Every year, companies pay actors, singers, athletes, and other celebrities millions of dollars to endorse their products. Supermodel Cindy Crawford campaigns for Revlon cosmetics. Candice Bergen pushes Sprint, Jerry Seinfeld is the American Express ambassador, and Michael Jordan has endorsed more than a dozen companies' products from Wheaties and Gatorade, to Hanes underwear and Rayovac batteries. Many studies have shown that celebrity endorsements make advertisements more believable, enhance message recall, aid in brand name recognition, and create positive attitudes toward brands. What companies want to know is how well star power pays off in the global marketplace.

In England, several NBA stars endorse Converse athletic shoes, and tennis star Andre Agassi praises Pepsi Max internationally. Nike's European advertising campaign, appearing on MTV Europe and Eurosport Cable, features Nike endorsers playing tragic figures in operettas performed in native languages with subtitles. In one Italian spot featuring Charles Barkley, the basketball star must give up his Nikes as punishment for killing the referee. Of all celebrities endorsing products globally today, the best known is Michael Jordan. His return to basketball excited fans the world over, including China, where Qiao Dan, as he is known, has enough notoriety to successfully recommend American products in the gradually opening Chinese market.

Because people around the world are more familiar with American trends and celebrities than Americans are with headliners of other countries, celebrity product endorsements don't usually travel well into the United States. For example, in Europe, where Formula I racing is enormously popular, race car drivers like Michael Schumacher and Gerhard Berger are in demand as endorsers. Few Americans, however, have heard of these figures, rendering their product endorsements in the United States far less effective.

Satellite and cable television networks such as Cable News Network International and MTV have spawned a generation of global consumers who listen to the same music, cheer the same sporting events, and buy the same products. The director of MTV Europe asserts that "18-year-olds in Paris have more in common with 18-year-olds in New York than with their own parents." With the media becoming increasingly international and tastes becoming increasingly homogenized, it seems likely that the same sports figure who endorses a brand of soft drink in the United States could successfully do so from Alberta to Zaire, and everywhere in between.

Sources: Jagdish Agrawal and Wagner A. Kamakura, "The Economic Worth of Celebrity Endorsers: An Event Study Analysis," *Journal of Marketing*, July 1995, pp. 56–62; Jeff Jensen, "MJ Draws All Levels of Fans to His Net," *Advertising Age*, Mar. 27, 1995, pp. 3, 6; "Converse Debuts U.K. Shop-In-Store," *Footwear News*, May 8, 1995, p. 4; Randall Lane, "Mr. Overexposure?" *Forbes*, Dec. 18, 1995, p. 14; and "Pepsi, Agassi Sign Two-Year Endorsement," *Nation's Restaurant News*, Sept. 25, 1995, p. 100.

■ *Personal Selling*

Personal selling is a paid personal communication that seeks to inform customers and persuade them to purchase products in an exchange situation. The phrase *purchase products* is interpreted broadly to encompass acceptance of ideas and issues. Telemarketing, described in Chapter 15 as direct selling over the telephone, relies heavily on personal selling.

Personal selling has both advantages and limitations when compared with advertising. Advertising is general communication aimed at a relatively large target audience, whereas personal selling involves more specific communication aimed at one or several persons. Reaching one person through personal selling costs considerably more than through advertising, but personal selling efforts often have greater impact on customers. Personal selling also provides immediate feedback, allowing marketers to adjust their messages to improve communication. It helps them determine and respond to customers' information needs.

When a salesperson and customer meet face to face, they use several types of interpersonal communication. The predominant communication form is language—both speech and writing. A salesperson and customer frequently use **kinesic communication,** which is communication through the movement of head, eyes, arms, hands, legs, or torso.

Kinesic communication
Communication through the movement of head, eyes, arms, hands, legs, or torso

Winking, head nodding, hand gestures, and arm motions are forms of kinesic communication. A good salesperson can often evaluate a prospect's interest in a product or presentation by noting eye contact and head nodding. **Proxemic communication,** a less obvious form of communication used in personal selling situations, occurs when either person varies the physical distance separating them. When a customer backs away from a salesperson, for example, that individual may be displaying a lack of interest in the product or expressing dislike for the salesperson. Touching, or **tactile communication,** is also a form of communication, although less popular in the United States than in many other countries. Handshaking is a common form of tactile communication both in the United States and elsewhere.

Proxemic communication
Varying the physical distance in face-to-face interactions

Tactile communication
Communication through touching

403

■ *Public Relations*

While many promotional activities are focused on a firm's customers, clearly other groups or publics are important to an organization as well. These include suppliers, employees, stockholders, the media, educators, potential investors, government officials, and society in general. To communicate with customers as well as one or more of these publics, a company employs public relations. Public relations is a broad set of communication efforts used to create and maintain favorable relationships between an organization and its publics. Maintaining a positive relationship with one or more publics can affect a firm's current sales and profits, as well as its long-term survival.

Public relations can be achieved through the use of a variety of tools including annual reports, brochures, event sponsorship, and sponsorship of socially responsible programs aimed at protecting the environment or helping disadvantaged individuals. Other tools arise from the use of publicity, which is a part of public relations. Publicity is nonpersonal communication in news story form about an organization, its products, or both that is transmitted through a mass medium at no charge. A few examples of publicity-based public relations tools would be news releases, press conferences, and feature articles. Ordinarily, public relations efforts are planned and implemented to be consistent with and support other elements of the promotion mix. Public relations efforts may be the responsibility of an individual or a department within an organization, or an organization may hire an independent public relations agency. Unpleasant situations and negative events such as a product tampering may provoke unfavorable public relations for an organization. To minimize the damaging effects of unfavorable coverage, effective marketers have policies and procedures in place to help manage any public relations problems.

Public relations should not be viewed as a set of tools to be used only during crises. To get the most from the use of public relations, an organization should have someone responsible for public relations either internally or externally and should have an ongoing public relations program.

■ *Sales Promotion*

Sales promotion is an activity or material that acts as a direct inducement, offering added value, or incentive for the product, to resellers, salespersons, or consumers.[7] Examples include free samples, rebates, sweepstakes, contests, premiums, and coupons (see Figure 17.6). *Sales promotion* should not be confused with *promotion;* sales

Figure 17.6
Sales Promotion Coupon The publishers of *Animals* magazine promote their publication by offering a coupon for a free trial issue.

promotion is a part of the more comprehensive area of promotion. Currently, marketers spend about $3 on sales promotion for every $1 spent on advertising. Sales promotion appears to be growing in use more than advertising.

Generally, when companies employ advertising or personal selling, they either depend on them continuously or cyclically. However, a marketer's use of sales promotion tends to be irregular. Many products are seasonal. A company such as Toro may offer more sales promotions in July and August than in the peak selling season of April or May, when more people buy tractors, lawn mowers, and other gardening equipment. Marketers frequently rely on sales promotion to improve the effectiveness of other promotion mix ingredients, especially advertising and personal selling.

An effective promotion mix requires the right combination of components. To see how such a mix is created, we examine the factors and conditions affecting the selection of promotional methods that an organization uses for a particular product.

Selecting Promotion Mix Elements

*M*arketers vary the composition of promotion mixes for many reasons. Although all four elements can be included in a promotion mix, frequently a marketer selects fewer than four. Many firms that market multiple product lines use several promotion mixes simultaneously.

When making decisions about the composition of promotion mixes, marketers must recognize that commercial messages, whether from advertising, personal selling, sales promotion, or public relations, are limited in the extent to which they can inform and persuade customers and move them closer to making purchases. Depending on the type of customers and the products involved, buyers to some extent rely on word-of-mouth communication from personal sources such as family members and friends. Over 40 percent of Americans seek information from friends and family members when buying medical, legal, and auto repair services. Word-of-mouth communication is also very important when people are selecting restaurants, entertainment, banking, and personal services such as hair care. Effective marketers who understand the importance of word-of-mouth communication attempt to isolate advice-givers and encourage them to talk about their products. For example, Chrysler did this when it introduced the Dodge Intrepid, Chrysler Concorde, and Eagle Vision. Chrysler dealers in a multistate region offered these models for a weekend to over 6,000 opinion leaders (advice-givers), resulting in over 32,000 exposures of these new models.[8] Marketers must not underestimate the importance of both word-of-mouth communication and personal influence, nor should they have unrealistic expectations about the performance of commercial messages.

When selecting promotion methods to include in promotion mixes, it is important to strive for **integrated marketing communication,** which is the coordination of promotional elements and other marketing efforts that communicate with customers to maximize total informational and promotional impact on customers. Integrated marketing communication requires a marketer to look at the broad perspective when planning marketing and promotional programs and coordinating the total set of communication functions.[9]

Integrated marketing communication Coordination of promotional elements and other marketing efforts to maximize total informational and promotional impact

■ *Promotional Resources, Objectives, and Policies*

The quality of an organization's promotional resources affects the number and relative intensity of promotional methods included in a promotion mix. If a company's promotional budget is extremely limited, the firm is likely to rely on personal selling because it is easier to measure a salesperson's contribution to sales than to measure the effect of advertising. Businesses must have sizable promotional budgets to use regional or national advertising. Organizations with extensive promotional resources generally include more elements in their promotion mixes, but having more promotional dollars to spend does not necessarily mean using more promotional methods.

An organization's promotional objectives and policies also influence the types of promotion selected. If a company's objective is to create mass awareness of a new convenience good, such as a breakfast cereal, its promotion mix probably leans heavily toward advertising, sales promotion, and possibly public relations. If a company hopes to educate consumers about the features of a durable good, such as a home appliance, its promotion mix may combine a moderate amount of advertising, possibly some sales promotion efforts designed to attract customers to retail stores, and a great deal of personal selling because this method is an excellent way to inform customers about these types of products. If a firm's objective is to produce immediate sales of consumer nondurables, the promotion mix will probably stress advertising and sales promotion.

■ *Characteristics of the Target Market*

Size, geographic distribution, and demographic characteristics of an organization's target market also help dictate the methods to be included in a product's promotion mix. To some degree, market size determines composition of the mix. If the size is quite limited, the promotion mix will probably emphasize personal selling, which can be quite effective for reaching small numbers of people. Organizations selling to industrial markets and firms marketing products through only a few wholesalers frequently make personal selling the major component of their promotion mixes. When a product's market consists of millions of customers, organizations rely on advertising and sales promotion because these methods reach masses of people at a low cost per person.

Geographic distribution of a firm's customers affects the combination of promotional methods used. Personal selling is more feasible if a company's customers are concentrated in a small area than if they are dispersed across a vast region. When the company's customers are numerous and dispersed, advertising may be more practical.

Distribution of a target market's demographic characteristics, such as age, income, or education, may affect the types of promotional techniques a marketer selects. For example, personal selling may be more successful than print advertisements for communicating with less-educated people.

■ *Characteristics of the Product*

Generally, promotion mixes for industrial products concentrate on personal selling. However, advertising plays a major role in promoting consumer goods. This generalization should be treated cautiously, though. Industrial marketers use some advertising to promote products. Advertisements for computers, road-building equipment, and aircraft are not uncommon, and some sales promotion is used occasionally to promote industrial products. Personal selling is used extensively for consumer durables, such as home appliances, automobiles, and houses, and consumer convenience items are promoted mainly through advertising and sales promotion. Public relations appears in promotion mixes for both industrial and consumer products.

Marketers of highly seasonal products often emphasize advertising, and possibly sales promotion, because off-season sales generally will not support an extensive year-round sales force. Although toy producers by and large have sales forces to sell to resellers, many of these companies depend chiefly on advertising to promote their products.

A product's price also influences the composition of the promotion mix. High-priced products call for personal selling because consumers associate greater risk with the purchase of such products and usually want advice from a salesperson. Few of us, for example, are willing to purchase a refrigerator from a self-service establishment. For low-priced convenience items, marketers use advertising rather than personal selling at the retail level.

A further consideration in creating an effective promotion mix is the stage of the product life cycle. During the introduction stage, much advertising may be necessary for both industrial and consumer products to make potential users aware of them. For many products, personal selling and sales promotion are helpful as well in this stage. In the case of consumer nondurables, the growth and maturity stages require heavy emphasis on advertising. Industrial products often require a concentration of personal selling and some sales promotion efforts during these stages. In the decline stage, marketers usually decrease promotional activities, especially advertising. Promotional efforts in the decline stage often center on personal selling and sales promotion.

Intensity of market coverage is another factor affecting composition of the promotion mix. When products are marketed through intensive distribution, firms depend strongly on advertising and sales promotion. Many convenience products, such as lotions, cereals, and coffee, are promoted through samples, coupons, and money refunds. When marketers choose selective distribution, marketing mixes vary considerably as to type and amount of promotional methods. Items handled through exclusive distribution frequently demand more personal selling and less advertising. Expensive watches, furs, and high-quality furniture are typical products promoted heavily through personal selling.

A product's use also affects the combination of promotional methods. Manufacturers of highly personal products, such as laxatives, nonprescription contraceptives, feminine hygiene products, and hemorrhoid medications, depend on advertising for promotion because many customers do not want to talk with salespersons about these products (see Figure 17.7).

■ Costs and Availability of Promotional Methods

Costs of promotional methods are major factors to analyze when developing a promotion mix. National advertising and sales promotion efforts require large expenditures. However, if these efforts are effective in reaching extremely large audiences, the cost per individual reached may be quite small, possibly a few pennies per person. Not all forms of advertising are expensive. Many small, local businesses advertise products through local newspapers, magazines, radio and television stations, and outdoor and transit signs.

Another consideration that marketers explore when formulating a promotion mix is availability of promotional techniques. Despite the tremendous number of media vehicles in the United States, a firm may find that no available advertising medium effectively reaches a certain market. Some companies promote media availability as well as media capabilities for reaching specific markets, as shown in Figure 17.8. The problem of media

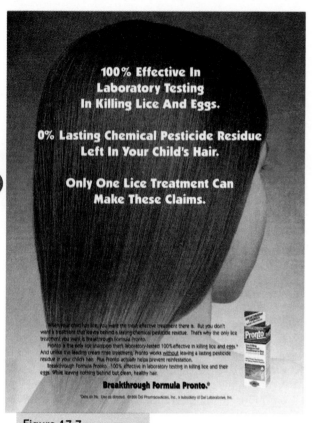

Figure 17.7
Promoting Personal Products
Manufacturers rely heavily on advertising to promote highly personal products.

406

Figure 17.8
Media Availability
Turner Broadcasting is promoting the availability of specific media.

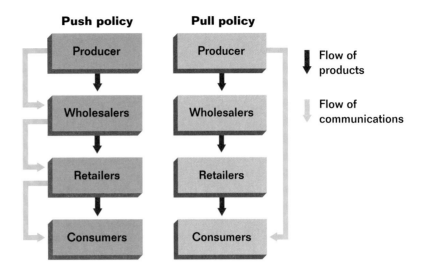

Figure 17.9
Comparison of Push and Pull Promotional Strategies

availability becomes more pronounced when marketers advertise in foreign countries. Some media, such as television, simply may not be available. Available media may not be open to certain types of advertisements. In Germany, advertisers are forbidden to make brand comparisons on television. Other promotional methods also have limitations. A firm may wish to increase its sales force but be unable to find qualified personnel.

■ *Push and Pull Channel Policies*

Push policy Promoting a product only to the next institution down the marketing channel

Pull policy Promoting a product directly to consumers to develop strong consumer demand that pulls products through the marketing channel

Another element marketers consider when planning a promotion mix is whether to use a push policy or a pull policy. With a **push policy,** the producer promotes the product only to the next institution down the marketing channel. In a marketing channel with wholesalers and retailers, the producer promotes to the wholesaler because in this case the wholesaler is the channel member just below the producer (see Figure 17.9). Each channel member in turn promotes to the next channel member. A push policy normally stresses personal selling. Sometimes sales promotion and advertising are used in conjunction with personal selling to push the products down through the channel.

As Figure 17.9 shows, a firm using a **pull policy** promotes directly to consumers to develop a strong consumer demand for the products. It does so primarily through advertising and sales promotion. Because consumers are persuaded to seek the products in retail stores, retailers in turn go to wholesalers or the producer to buy the products. This policy is intended to pull the goods down through the channel by creating demand at the consumer level. For example, if marketers at Post Cereals were launching a new cereal such as Frosted Grape-Nuts, they would likely use a pull policy, aiming a large amount of advertising toward consumers and encouraging them to look for Frosted Grape-Nuts at their favorite stores. Consumers are told that if the stores don't have it, ask them to get it. Stimulating demand at the consumer level for Frosted Grape-Nuts causes the product to be pulled through the channel. Push and pull policies are not mutually exclusive. At times an organization uses both simultaneously.

Criticisms and Defenses of Promotion

*E*ven though promotional activities can help consumers make informed purchasing decisions, social scientists, consumer groups, government agencies, and members of society in general have long criticized promotion. There are two main reasons for such criticism: promotion does have flaws, and it is a highly visible business activity that pervades our daily lives. Although people almost universally complain that there is simply too much promotional activity, a number of more specific criticisms have been lodged. In this section we discuss some of the criticisms and defenses of promotion.

■ *Is Promotion Deceptive?*

One common criticism is that promotion is deceptive or unethical. During the nineteenth and early twentieth centuries, much promotion was blatantly deceptive. Although no longer widespread today, some deceptive promotional activities continue to occur. Critics of some state lottery advertisements claim the ads are deceptive because they overemphasize the lottery as the solution to financial problems and downplay the odds against winning.[10] Metropolitan Life and other insurers have employed questionable selling techniques to disguise whole-life insurance policies.[11] American Family Publishers has been accused of using deceit and trickery to sell magazines through its $10 million sweepstakes.[12] Questionable weight loss claims are made about various exercise devices and diet programs. Some promotions are unintentionally deceiving. For instance, when advertising to children, it is easy to mislead them because they are more naive and less able to separate fantasy from reality. A promotion may also mislead some receivers because words can have diverse meanings for different people. All promotion, however, should not be condemned because some is flawed. The increased number of laws, the efforts of government regulatory agencies, and self-regulation have caused a decrease in deceptive promotion.

■ *Does Promotion Increase Prices?*

Promotion is also castigated for raising prices. The ultimate purpose of promotion is to stimulate demand. If it does, then a business should be able to produce and market products in larger quantities and thus reduce per-unit production and marketing costs, which can result in lower prices. For example, as demand and competition have increased for personal computers and compact disc players, their prices have dropped. When promotion fails to stimulate demand, then the price of the promoted product increases because promotion costs must be added to other costs. Promotion also helps keep prices lower by facilitating price competition (see Figure 17.10). When firms advertise prices, their prices tend to remain lower than when prices are not promoted. Gasoline pricing illustrates how promotion fosters price competition. Service stations with the highest prices seldom have highly visible price signs.

Figure 17.10
Promoting Price Competition
Promotion of prices stimulates price competition and helps to keep prices lower.

■ *Does Promotion Create Needs?*

Critics claim that promotion manipulates consumers by persuading them to buy products they do not need, hence creating need. In his theory of motivation, A. H. Maslow indicates that an individual tries to satisfy five levels of needs: (1) physiological needs such as hunger, thirst, and sex; (2) safety needs; (3) needs for love and affection; (4) needs for self-esteem and respect from others; and (5) self-actualization needs (that is, the need to realize one's potential).[13] When needs are viewed in this context, it is difficult to demonstrate that promotion creates them. If there were no promotional activities, people still would have needs for food, water, sex, safety, love, affection, self-esteem, respect from others, and self-actualization.

Even though promotion does not create needs, it does capitalize on them (which may be why some critics feel promotion creates needs). Many marketers base their appeals on these needs. For example, several mouthwash, toothpaste, and perfume advertisements associate these products with needs for love, affection, and respect. These advertisers rely on human needs in their messages, but they do not create the needs.

■ *Does Promotion Encourage Materialism?*

Another frequent criticism of promotion is that it leads to materialism. The purpose of promoting goods is to persuade people to buy them, and so if promotion works, consumers will want to buy more and more things. Marketers assert that values are instilled in the home and that promotion does not change people into materialistic consumers. However, the behavior of today's children and teenagers contradicts this view; they insist on high-priced, name-brand apparel, such as Girbeaud, Nike, and Guess?.

■ *Does Promotion Help Consumers Without Costing Too Much?*

Every year firms spend billions of dollars for promotion. The question is whether promotion helps consumers enough to be worth the cost. Consumers do benefit, for promotion informs them about products' uses, features, advantages, prices, and locations. Consumers thus gain more knowledge about available products and can describe more precisely the ones they seek. Promotion also informs consumers about services—for instance, health care, educational programs, and day care—as well as about important social and political issues.

■ *Should Potentially Harmful Products Be Promoted?*

Finally, some critics of promotion, including consumer groups and government officials, suggest that certain products should not be promoted at all. Primary targets are products associated with violence, sex, and unhealthy activities—products such as handguns, alcohol, tobacco, and gambling. Cigarette advertisements, for example, promote smoking, a behavior proven harmful, even deadly. In a recent study released by the Robert Wood Johnson Foundation, a philanthropic organization that studies health-related issues, 88 percent of those interviewed want to eliminate the sampling of cigarettes, 70 percent want to prohibit mail-order premiums that display tobacco company logos, and 55 percent would prohibit tobacco company sponsorship advertising at sports and entertainment events.[14] Tobacco industry executives have countered criticism of their promotions by pointing out that promoters of butter and red meat are not censured despite the fact that their cholesterol-filled products might cause heart disease. Recently, a few publishers of selected newspapers and magazines have adopted guidelines stating that they will not publish tobacco-related advertisements with cartoonlike characters (such as Joe Camel) if they could be interpreted to be targeted at children or teenagers.[15] Those who defend such promotion assert that as long as it is legal to sell a product, promoting that product should be allowed.

SUMMARY

Promotion is communicating with individuals, groups, or organizations in the environment to directly or indirectly facilitate exchanges.

Communication is a sharing of meaning. The communication process involves several steps. First the source translates meaning into code, a process known as coding or encoding. The source should employ signs familiar to the receiver or audience. The coded message is sent through a medium of transmission to the receiver or audience. The receiver or audience then decodes the message and usually supplies feedback to the source. When the decoded message differs from the encoded one, a condition called noise exists.

Although promotional objectives vary from one organization to another and within organizations over time, there are eight primary objectives that underlie many promotional programs. Promotion aims to create awareness of a new product, new brand, or existing product; stimulate primary and secondary demand; encourage product trial through the use of free samples, coupons, limited free use offers, contests, and games; identify prospects; retain loyal customers; facilitate reseller support; combat competitive promotional efforts; and reduce sales fluctuations.

The promotion mix for a product may include four major promotional methods: advertising, personal selling, public relations, and sales promotion. Advertising is a paid form of nonpersonal communication about an organization and its products transmitted to a target audience through a mass medium. Personal selling is personal, paid communication that attempts to inform customers and persuade them to purchase products in an exchange situation. Publicity is nonpersonal communication in news story form, regarding an organization, its products, or both, transmitted through a mass medium at no charge. Sales promotion is an activity or material that acts as a direct inducement and offers added value or incentive for the product, to resellers, salespersons, or consumers.

There are several major determinants of what promotional methods to include in a product's promotion mix: the organization's promotional resources, objectives, and policies; the characteristics of the target market; characteristics of the product; and cost and availability of promotional methods. Marketers also consider whether to use a push policy or a pull policy. With a push policy, the producer promotes the product only to the next institution down the marketing channel. Normally, a push policy stresses personal selling. Firms that use a pull policy promote directly to consumers, with the intention of developing strong consumer demand for the products. Once consumers are persuaded to seek products in retail stores, retailers go to wholesalers or the producer to buy the products.

Promotional activities can help consumers make informed purchasing decisions, but they have also evoked many criticisms. Promotion has been accused of deception. Although some deceiving or misleading promotions do exist, government and local regulatory agencies, as well as industry self-regulation, minimize deceptive promotion. Promotion has been blamed for increasing prices, but it usually tends to lower them. When demand is high, production and marketing costs decrease, which can result in lower prices. Moreover, promotion helps keep prices lower by facilitating price competition. Other criticisms of promotional activity are that it manipulates consumers into buying products they do not need; that it leads to a more materialistic society; and that consumers do not benefit sufficiently from promotional activity to justify its high cost. Finally, some critics of promotion suggest that potentially harmful products, especially those associated with violence, sex, and unhealthy activities, should not be promoted at all.

IMPORTANT TERMS

Promotion	Decoding process	Selective demand	Integrated marketing
Communication	Noise	Promotion mix	communication
Source	Feedback	Kinesic communication	Push policy
Receiver	Channel capacity	Proxemic communication	Pull policy
Coding process	Primary demand	Tactile communication	
Medium of transmission	Pioneer promotion		

DISCUSSION AND REVIEW QUESTIONS

1. What is the major task of promotion? Do firms ever use promotion to accomplish this task and fail? If so, give several examples.
2. What is communication? Describe the communication process. Is it possible to communicate without using all the elements in the communication process? If so, which ones can be omitted?
3. Identify several causes of noise. How can a source reduce noise?
4. Describe the possible objectives of promotion and discuss the circumstances under which each of these objectives might be used.
5. Identify and briefly describe the four major promotional methods in an organization's promotion mix.

6. What forms of interpersonal communication besides language can be used in personal selling?

7. How do market characteristics determine which promotional methods to include in a promotion mix? Assume that a company is planning to promote a cereal to both adults and children. Along what major dimensions would these two promotional efforts have to be different?

8. How can a product's characteristics affect the composition of its promotion mix?

9. Evaluate the following statement: "Appropriate advertising media are always available if a company can afford them."

10. Explain the difference between a pull policy and a push policy. Under what conditions should each policy be used?

11. Which criticisms of promotion do you believe to be the most valid? Why?

12. Should organizations be allowed to promote offensive, violent, sexual, or unhealthy products and services that can be legally sold and purchased? Support your answer.

411

APPLICATION QUESTIONS

1. One of the objectives of promotion is to stimulate demand for a product. Through television advertising, the American Dairy Association promotes the benefits of drinking milk, which is aimed at stimulating primary demand. Advertisements for a specific brand of milk are aimed at stimulating selective demand. Identify two television commercials, one aimed at stimulating primary demand and one aimed at stimulating selective demand. Describe each and discuss how they attempt to achieve these objectives.

2. Developing a promotion mix is contingent upon many factors. The type of product and the attributes of that product influence the mix. Which of the promotional methods (advertising, personal selling, public relations, or sales promotion) would you emphasize if you were developing the promotion mix for the products listed below? Explain your answer.

   a. washing machine
   b. cereal
   c. Halloween candy
   d. compact disc

3. Marketers at Falcon International Corporation have come to you for recommendations on how they should promote their products. They are interested in developing a comprehensive promotional campaign and have a generous budget with which to implement their plans. What questions would you ask them, and what would you suggest they consider before developing a promotional program?

4. Marketers must consider whether to use a push or a pull policy when deciding on a promotion mix (see Figure 17.4). Identify a product for which marketers should use each of these and a third product that might best be promoted using a mix of the two policies. Explain your answers.

Case 17.1   National Pork Producers Promote "The Other White Meat"

A television commercial portrays patrons at an upscale restaurant asking a waiter to substitute pork for chicken in the dishes they order; they want "pork tetrazzini," "pork cacciatore," "pork divan," and "pork kiev." Since 1987, consumer demand for pork has steadily risen, and Americans today are each eating about fifty pounds of it a year. Many now view pork, like chicken, as nutritional white meat. What is convincing so many people to discard pork's long-standing image as an unhealthy, fat-laden and cholesterol-filled, disease-bearing food? Through an intense campaign of advertising and retail and food service promotions, the National Pork Producers Council (NPPC) is successfully repositioning pork in consumers' minds.

During the 1980s, increasingly health-conscious Americans began eating less high-fat and high-cholesterol food, including red meat. From 1981 through 1986, national pork consumption decreased about 3.5 percent a year. The National Pork Producers Council fought back aggressively. Recognizing that white meat had a more positive image than red, and armed with the United States Department of Agriculture's assessment that today's pork is 50 percent leaner than twenty years ago, the NPPC began promoting pork as "The Other White Meat." Launched in 1987, the $15-million-a-year advertising campaign includes network and cable television, radio, magazine, newspaper, and outdoor ads.

The television commercials provide consumers with information about calories and nutrition. One spot identifies eight cuts of pork below 180 calories a serving. Ads also present pork being grilled, sautéed, braised, stir-fried, ground for sausage and meat loaf, and roasted whole, often substituting for chicken but never as plain boring chops. Print ads in national magazines such as *Family Circle, Better Homes and Gardens, Bon Appetit,* and *Southern Living* give recipes for pork that range from down-home ethnic to elegant gourmet. When the Pork Council introduced pork as "The Other White Meat" in 1987, the response from the beef industry, also suffering from reduced consumption, was "Who do they think they're kidding?" No one is skeptical now. During the campaign's first two years, pork sales rose more than $1 billion. When the campaign began, about 10 percent of Americans considered pork a white meat; now, about 75 percent do.

To enhance consumer recognition of new, healthier cuts of pork, the NPPC introduced trademark cuts. More than 50,000 supermarkets across the nation now regularly use the trademark names America's Cut and Chef's Prime on pork in their meat cases. One meat director recently reported that in one year alone, sales of Chef's Prime rose 500 percent. When pork producers expressed concern that pork might lose its reputation as a hearty and satisfying main course for a meal, a new commercial, showing a ravenous cowboy devouring a hunk of pork, touted America's Cut as "a new kind of steak."

To increase retail pork sales, the NPPC operates an aggressive sales promotion program, working in close partnership with supermarkets. The council encourages meat managers to enlarge their pork departments and take part in promotional programs. In turn, retailers let the NPPC know which promotions are most useful, and the Pork Council makes them available. "Take-One" illustrated recipe cards and other point-of-sale advertising are particularly successful in attracting customers and strengthening stores' marketing efforts. Samples, coupon, and tie-ins with products such as Bull's-Eye Barbecue Sauce, Weber grills, and Shake-and-Bake are also very popular.

"Shopping by Shape" is a sales promotion designed to give customers new ideas about cooking pork. At the meat case, grocers display pictures of the six basic shapes of pork—roasts, ribs, cutlets, chops, strips, and cubes—as well as supply recipes and serving suggestions.

Working to get pork on more restaurant menus, the Pork Council generates advertising, promotions, and public relations programs specifically for the food service segment. To show restaurant owners that pork dishes can satisfy their calorie- and health-conscious customers, the NPPC distributes recipes and places inserts in food service publications. Promotions such as the "Pork Recipe" and "Restaurant of the Year" contests highlight restaurants offering innovative and creative pork dishes. Some of the recent winning recipes include Spicy Adobo Grilled Pork with green chile tamale and anchovy-mushroom sauce and Black Pepper Brioche-wrapped Roast Pork Loin. According to a recent National Restaurant Association Menu Analysis, 42 percent of menus surveyed include pork.

Since "The Other White Meat" ads and the NPPC's intense promotion efforts debuted more Americans are choosing more pork from meat counters and menus. Other food industry groups have been paying attention. When the National Turkey Foundation (NTF) held its annual meeting recently, it invited the NPPC's chief consumer promotion specialist to talk about "The Other White Meat" campaign. One NTF source asserted that if turkey boasted an equally strong slogan, its sales, like those of pork, would mount. Perhaps television voice-overs and supermarket banners will soon ask consumers to buy "Turkey: The Real White Meat."[16]

Questions for Discussion

1. What promotional objectives is the National Pork Producers Council pursuing?
2. Which promotion mix elements does the NPPC include in its promotion mix?
3. What recommendations would you make to the NPPC regarding its promotional programs?

Case 17.2 Anheuser-Busch Tackles America's Alcohol-Related Problems

According to a recent Harvard School of Public Health study, 44 percent of college students consume more than five alcoholic drinks in a row in any given two-week period. The National Institute of Alcohol Abuse and Alcoholism estimates that alcohol disorder rates are highest among 18-to-29-year-olds. These statistics reveal that, although educational efforts by alcoholic beverage companies have helped reduce drunk driving in the United States, there is much more work to be done. Today, these companies are addressing not only the problem of drunk driving, but also the issues of alcohol abuse and underage drinking, and other alcohol-related concerns.

As early as the turn of the century, Anheuser-Busch, the world's largest brewer, advocated moderation in drinking. Its 1982 launch of the "Know When To Say When" advertising campaign was an industry first. Using educational videos, community outreach programs, television advertising, and public service announcements, the brewer now leads the industry in promoting alcohol awareness and education. In the last seven years, Anheuser-Busch has invested over $140 million in preventing misuse of its products.

To deliver its message about personal responsibility at home, at school, and where alcohol is served, Anheuser-Busch administers and supports more than a dozen community-based alcohol awareness and education programs. "Family Talk About Drinking" provides free guidebooks and video materials to help parents talk with their children about family rules, respect for the law, and dealing with peer pressure. To educate high school and college students about the consequences of underage drinking and drunk driving, the company produced the video "Make the Right Call." Anheuser-Busch is a major supporter of alcohol education on American college campuses, creating programs such as "BACCHUS," a peer network designed to boost awareness of alcohol's effect on health, and sponsoring National Collegiate Alcohol Awareness Week.

Since 1989, "Alert Cab" has taxied over 140,000 people home safely. Alert Cab brings together alcohol retailers and cab companies to provide free rides home to bar and restaurant patrons. Anheuser-Busch also works with tens of thousands of wholesalers to promote use of designated drivers through its "I'm Driving" program. At bars and restaurants, those who volunteer to be designated drivers and not drink alcohol receive free O'Doul's, Anheuser-Busch's nonalcoholic beer, and coupons for free food. Its "ServSafe" program has trained over 115,000 bartenders and store clerks to serve and sell alcohol safely, avoid abuse situations, prevent drunk driving, and spot fake IDs.

To amplify these and other programs, as well as get their messages across to millions of Americans, Anheuser-Busch advertises using print, billboards, and national television and radio. Television commercials feature celebrities and run during some of America's most-watched programs. Through advertising, the company has brought its message about the potential dangers of alcohol abuse to 75 percent of America's beer drinkers.

Anheuser-Busch isn't alone among alcoholic beverage companies in its efforts. *Beer Marketer's Insights,* an industry trade publication, reports that brewers' promotional activities have changed. Most brewers no longer hire student representatives to promote beer brands on campuses, a common practice until recently. In addition, alcohol marketers are increasingly aiming ads that say "we don't want your business" at underage consumers. The Century Council, an industry supported group, engages in community-oriented alcohol awareness projects such as the "Sober Graduation and Prom" program, which reaches about 8,000 U.S. high schools. The Distilled Spirits Council has revised its code of good marketing and advertising practices to discourage alcohol ads in college newspapers and bar contests that invite drinking.

Anheuser-Busch believes that its work, along with that of other companies and organizations, has led to some encouraging changes. The U.S. Department of Transportation recently reported that in one decade, drunk driving deaths fell 32 percent, and studies at the University of Michigan indicate that the level of drinking by high school seniors is at its lowest in twenty years.[17]

Questions for Discussion

1. Why is Anheuser-Busch engaging in promotional efforts to reduce underage drinking and alcohol abuse?
2. What are the major components of the promotion mix being used by Anheuser-Busch in its campaign to reduce alcohol abuse?
3. Evaluate the effectiveness of Anheuser-Busch and other organizations in tackling alcohol-related issues.

Chapter 18

Advertising and Public Relations

OBJECTIVES

- To explore the nature and types of advertising

- To become aware of the major steps involved in developing an advertising campaign

- To find out who is responsible for developing advertising campaigns

- To gain an understanding of public relations

- To analyze how public relations is used and evaluated

Perfect publicity pushes posh Pink Palace: pampered patrons praise premiere.

*I*n 1912, it cost $500,000 to build the Beverly Hills Hotel. For $18, celebrities could spend a night at what became the most famous landmark on Sunset Boulevard. For over eighty-five years, the "Pink Palace" survived major earthquakes, the Great Depression, and a string of owners from a Hollywood film producer to an infamous Wall Street securities trader to a Middle East sultan. After closing its doors in 1992 for multimillion dollar renovations that included 1,600 gallons of pink paint and a new gold-leaf Steinway piano, the Beverly Hills Hotel recently reopened. To herald the event, California-based public relations firm The Blaze Company created and administered a ten-month, multifaceted promotional campaign culminating in an extravagant grand opening party.

In crafting the promotional program, The Blaze Company positioned the Beverly Hills Hotel as a "living legend." Press releases, advertisements, and television features all assured people that, although the refurbished hotel is more modern and efficiently run, the elements loved by generations remain the same. Company representatives arranged coverage of the hotel's opening with editors of magazines such as *The New Yorker, Forbes, Vanity Fair,* and *People.* The Blaze Company compiled a comprehensive press kit full of historical information and hotel trivia. Press releases included items such as the head chef's biography, renovation highlights, and "Legends of the Beverly Hills Hotel." For six months prior to the reopening, press releases tantalized the public by announcing tidbits one at a time—opening date, new room rates, date of the opening party, and a list of expected celebrities. Television coverage of the renovations and reopening included segments on *Good Morning America, CBS Evening News, Entertainment Tonight,* and many others, both in the United States and in Great Britain, Germany, France, and Spain.

The CEO of the Beverly Hills Hotel got what he told Blaze he wanted—an utterly unforgettable party. In attendance at the gala were Hollywood stars, such as Denzel Washington, Steve Martin, Marisa Tomei, and Jay Leno, and 1,500 other local, national, and international guests and media representatives. In addition to cocktails and hors d'oeuvres, musical entertainment, and an official ribbon cutting, guests feasted on a $1,000-a-plate dinner to benefit the Academy of Motion Picture Arts and Sciences.

What are the results of The Blaze Company's efforts? The firm estimates that pre-event coverage reached millions. Major feature stories about the Beverly Hills Hotel opening appeared in 174 newspapers, including nineteen stories in the *Los Angeles Times* and nine in *USA Today.* More tangible results include record-level occupancy and packed hotel restaurants and bars.[1]

Organizations like the Beverly Hills Hotel sometimes use public relations, along with other promotional efforts such as advertising, to change the corporate image, launch new products (such as Microsoft's Windows 95), or promote current brands. This chapter explores many dimensions of advertising and public relations. Initially, we focus on the nature and types of advertising. Next, we examine the major steps in developing an advertising campaign and describe who is responsible for developing such campaigns. We then discuss the nature of public relations and how public relations is used. We examine various public relations tools and ways to evaluate the effectiveness of public relations. Finally, we focus on how companies deal with unfavorable public relations.

The Nature and Types of Advertising

*A*dvertising permeates our daily lives. At times we may view it positively; at other times we tune it out or avoid it by taping television programs and then zipping over commercials with the VCR fast-forward button. Some advertising informs, persuades, or entertains us; some bores and even offends us.

As mentioned in Chapter 17, **advertising** is a paid form of nonpersonal communication that is transmitted through mass media such as television, radio, newspapers, magazines, direct mail, mass transit vehicles, and outdoor displays. Organizations use advertising to reach a variety of audiences, ranging from small, specific groups, such as stamp collectors in Idaho, to extremely large groups, such as all athletic shoe purchasers in the United States.

When people are asked to name major advertisers, most immediately mention business organizations. However, many types of organizations—including governments, churches, universities, and charitable organizations—take advantage of advertising. In 1994, the U.S. government was the fortieth-largest advertiser in the country, spending $343 million on advertising.[2] Even though we analyze advertising in the context of business organizations here, much of what we say applies to all types of organizations.

Advertising is used to promote goods, services, ideas, images, issues, people, and anything that advertisers want to publicize or foster. Depending on what is being promoted, advertising can be classified as institutional or product advertising. **Institutional advertising** promotes organizational images, ideas, or political issues. Institutional advertising can be used to create or maintain an organizational or family brand image. Such advertisements might deal with broad image issues such as organizational strength, family brand quality and durability, or the friendliness of employees. Institutional advertisements could be aimed at making noncustomer groups such as shareholders, consumer advocacy group members, potential stockholders, or the general public view the organization more favorably. When a company promotes its position on a public issue—for instance, a tax increase, abortion, welfare, or international trade coalitions—this type of institutional advertising is referred to as **advocacy advertising.** Institutional advertising may also be used to promote socially approved behavior like recycling and moderation in consuming alcoholic beverages. This type of advertising not only has societal benefits but also helps build an organization's image.

Product advertising promotes the uses, features, and benefits of products (see Figure 18.1). There are two types of product advertising: pioneer and competitive. **Pioneer advertising** focuses on stimulating demand for a product category (rather than a specific brand) by informing potential customers about the product's features, uses, and benefits. This type of advertising is employed when the product is in the introductory stage of the product life cycle.

The second type of product advertising, **competitive advertising,** attempts to stimulate demand for a specific brand by indicating a brand's features, uses, and advantages sometimes through indirect or direct comparisons with competing brands. To make direct product comparisons, marketers use a form of competitive advertising called **comparative advertising,** in which two or more specified brands are compared on the basis of one or more product characteristics. Often, the brands promoted through comparative advertisements are the ones with lower market shares and are being compared with competitors that have the highest market shares in a product category. The Healthy Choice

Advertising
Paid nonpersonal communication about an organization transmitted to a target audience through mass media

Institutional advertising
Promotes organizational images, ideas, and political issues

Advocacy advertising
Promotes a company's position on a public issue

Product advertising
Promotes products' uses, features, and benefits

Pioneer advertising
Tries to spark demand for a product category rather than a specific brand by informing potential buyers about the product

Competitive advertising
Points out a brand's special features and advantages relative to competing brands

Comparative advertising
Compares product characteristics of two or more specific brands on the basis of one or more product characteristics

Figure 18.1
Product Advertising
This Timberland advertisement promotes the appearance and overall image of ruggedness of this Timberland shoe.

Reminder advertising
Reminds consumers about an established brand's uses, characteristics, and benefits

Reinforcement advertising
Assures users that they chose the right brand and tells them how to get the most satisfaction from it

advertisement in Figure 18.2 is a comparative advertisement. Competitive industries in which comparative advertising is common include soft drinks, toothpaste, pain relievers, tires, automobiles, and detergents. Under the provisions of the 1988 Trademark Law Revision Act, marketers using comparative advertisements must not misrepresent the qualities or characteristics of competing products. Other forms of competitive advertising include reminder and reinforcement advertising. **Reminder advertising** tells customers that an established brand is still around and that it has certain characteristics, uses, and advantages. **Reinforcement advertising** assures current users that they have made the right brand choice and tells them how to get the most satisfaction from that brand.

Figure 18.2
Comparative Advertisement
This Healthy Choice comparative advertisement challenges its competitor Lean Cuisine on the issue of the number of fat grams per serving.

Developing an Advertising Campaign

Advertising campaign
The creation and execution of a series of advertisements to communicate with a particular target audience

*A*n **advertising campaign** involves designing a series of advertisements and placing them in various advertising media to reach a particular target market. As Figure 18.3 indicates, the major steps in creating an advertising campaign are (1) identifying and analyzing the target audience, (2) defining the advertising objectives, (3) creating the advertising platform, (4) determining the advertising appropriation, (5) developing the media plan, (6) creating the advertising message, (7) executing the campaign, and (8) evaluating advertising effectiveness. The number of steps and the exact order in which they are carried out may vary according to an organization's resources, the nature of its product, and the types of target markets or audiences to be reached. These general guidelines for developing an advertising campaign are appropriate for all types of organizations.

■ *Identifying and Analyzing the Target Audience*

Target audience
The group of people at which advertisements are aimed

The **target audience** is the group of people at which advertisements are aimed. Advertisements for Barbie cereal are targeted toward young girls who play with Barbie dolls, whereas those for Special K cereal are directed at health-conscious adults. Identifying and analyzing the target audience are critical processes; the information yielded helps determine other steps in developing the campaign. The target audience often includes everyone in a firm's target market. Marketers may, however, direct a campaign at only a portion of the target market.

Advertisers research and analyze advertising targets to establish an information base for a campaign. Information commonly needed includes location and geographic distribution of the target group; the distribution of demographic factors such as age, income, race, sex, and education; and consumer attitudes regarding purchase and use of both the advertiser's products and competing products. The exact kinds of information an organization finds useful depend on the type of product being advertised, the characteristics of the target audience, and the type and amount of competition. Generally, the more an advertiser knows about the target audience, the more likely the firm is to develop an effective advertising campaign. When the advertising target is not precisely identified and properly analyzed, the campaign may not succeed.

1. Identify and analyze target audience
2. Define advertising objectives
3. Create advertising platform
4. Determine advertising appropriation
5. Develop media plan
6. Create advertising message
7. Execute campaign
8. Evaluate advertising effectiveness

Figure 18.3
General Steps for Developing and Implementing an Advertising Campaign

■ *Defining the Advertising Objectives*

The advertiser's next step is determining what the firm hopes to accomplish with the campaign. Because advertising objectives guide campaign development, advertisers should define objectives carefully. Advertising objectives should be stated clearly, precisely, and in measurable terms. Precision and measurability allow advertisers to evaluate advertising success at the end of the campaign, assessing whether or not objectives have been met. To provide precision and measurability, advertising objectives should contain benchmarks and indicate how far the advertiser wishes to move from these benchmarks. The advertiser should state the current sales level (the benchmark) and the amount of sales increase that is sought through advertising. An advertising objective should also specify a time frame, so that advertisers know exactly how long they have to accomplish the objective. An advertiser with average monthly sales of $450,000 (the benchmark) might set the following objective: "Our primary advertising objective is to increase average monthly sales from $450,000 to $540,000 within twelve months."

If an advertiser defines objectives on the basis of sales, the objectives focus on raising absolute dollar sales, increasing sales by a certain percentage, or increasing the firm's market share. Even though an advertiser's long-run goal is to increase sales, not all campaigns are designed to produce immediate sales. Some campaigns are designed to increase product or brand awareness, make consumers' attitudes more favorable, or increase consumers' knowledge of product features. The

Coming June 2

American Muse of Natural Histc

Central Park West at 79th Street, New York City For information, call 212-769-5100

Figure 18.4
Advertisement Based on a Communications
Objective   The objective of this advertisement was to increase awareness of the American Museum of Natural History's new dinosaur halls.

advertisement in Figure 18.4 attempts to achieve an objective of increasing product awareness. These objectives are stated in terms of communication. A specific communication objective might be to increase product feature awareness from 0 to 40 percent in the target audience by the end of six months.

■ *Creating the Advertising Platform*

Before launching a political campaign, party leaders develop a political platform, stating major issues that are the basis of the campaign. Like a political platform, an **advertising platform** consists of the basic issues or selling points that an advertiser wishes to include in the advertising campaign. A single advertisement in an advertising campaign may contain one or several issues from the platform. Although the platform sets forth the basic issues, it does not indicate how to present them.

Advertising platform
Basic issues or selling points to be included in the advertising campaign

A marketer's advertising platform should consist of issues that are important to consumers. One of the best ways to determine those issues is to survey consumers about what they consider most important in the selection and use of the product involved. Selling features must not only be important to customers; if possible, they should also be features that competitive products lack.

Although research is the most effective method for determining what issues to include in an advertising platform, it is expensive. Therefore, an advertising platform is most commonly based on opinions of personnel within the firm and of individuals in the advertising agency, if an agency is used. This trial-and-error approach generally leads to some successes and some failures.

Because the advertising platform is a base on which to build the message, marketers should analyze this stage carefully. A campaign can be perfect as to the selection and analysis of its target audience, statement of its objectives, its media strategy, and the form of its message. But the campaign will still fail if the advertisements communicate information that consumers do not deem important when selecting and using the product.

■ *Determining the Advertising Appropriation*

Advertising appropriation
Advertising budget for a specified period of time

The **advertising appropriation** is the total amount of money a marketer allocates for advertising for a specific time period. It is hard to decide how much to spend on advertising for a specific period of time because the potential effects of advertising are so difficult to measure precisely.

Many factors affect a firm's decision about how much to appropriate for advertising. Geographic size of the market and the distribution of buyers within the market have a great bearing on this decision. As Table 18.1 shows, both the type of product advertised and a firm's sales volume relative to competitors' sales volumes also play a part in determining what proportion of a firm's revenue is spent on advertising. Advertising appropriations for industrial products are usually quite small relative to product sales, whereas consumer convenience items, such as soft drinks, soaps, and cosmetics, generally have large appropriations.

Table 18.1 Twenty Leading National Advertisers

		Advertising Expenditures ($ millions)	Sales ($ millions)	Advertising Expenditures as Percentage of Sales
1	Procter & Gamble	$2,689.8	$ 16,213.0	16.5%
2	Philip Morris Companies	2,418.8	40,878.0	5.9
3	General Motors	1,929.4	122,387.2	1.5
4	Ford Motor	1,186.0	90,364.0	1.3
5	Sears, Roebuck	1,134.1	54,559.0	2.0
6	AT&T	1,102.7	6,776.9	16.2
7	PepsiCo	1,097.8	20,246.4	5.4
8	Chrysler	971.6	45,855.0	2.1
9	Walt Disney	934.8	7,697.6	12.1
10	Johnson & Johnson	933.7	7,812.0	11.9
11	Nestlé SA	894.2	9,185.0	9.7
12	Time Warner	860.0	11,711	7.3
13	Warner-Lambert Co.	831.2	2,954.0	28.1
14	Toyota Motor	766.1	54,747.6*	1.4*
15	Grand Metropolitan	764.3	7,045.8	10.8
16	McDonald's	763.7	4,155.5	18.3
17	Kellogg	732.9	3,840.8	19
18	Unilever NV	654.7	8,976.0	7.2
19	JC Penney	621.7	21,082.0	2.9
20	Federated Stores	614.0	7,080.0	8.6

Source: Reprinted with permission from the Sept. 27, 1995 issue of *Advertising Age*. Copyright, Crain Communications, Inc. 1995.

*Estimates

Objective-and-task approach Budgeting for an advertising campaign by first determining its objectives and then the cost of all the tasks needed to attain them

Percent-of-sales approach Budgeting for an advertising campaign by multiplying the firm's past and expected sales by a standard percentage

Competition-matching approach Determining an advertising budget by trying to match competitors' ad outlays

Of the many techniques used to determine the advertising appropriation, one of the most logical is the **objective-and-task approach.** Using this approach, marketers determine the objectives that a campaign is to achieve and then attempt to list the tasks required to accomplish them. The costs of the tasks are then calculated and added to arrive at the total appropriation. This approach has one main problem; marketers sometimes have trouble accurately estimating the level of effort needed to attain certain objectives. A coffee marketer, for example, might find it extremely difficult to determine how much to increase national television advertising to raise a brand's market share from 8 to 10 percent.

In the more widely used **percent-of-sales approach,** marketers simply multiply a firm's past sales, plus a factor for planned sales growth or decline, by a standard percentage based on both what the firm traditionally spends on advertising and the industry average. This approach, too, has a major flaw: it is based on the incorrect assumption that sales create advertising rather than the reverse. A marketer using this approach during declining sales will reduce the amount spent on advertising, but such a reduction may further diminish sales. Though illogical, this technique has been favored because it is easy to use.

Another way to determine advertising appropriation is the **competition-matching approach.** Marketers following this approach try to match their major competitors' appropriations in absolute dollars or to allocate the same percentage of sales for advertising as their competitors do. Although a wise marketer should be aware of what competitors spend on advertising, this technique should not be used alone because a firm's competitors probably have different advertising objectives and different resources available for advertising. Many companies and advertising agencies engage in quarterly competitive spending reviews, comparing competitors' dollar expenditures in print, radio, and television with their own spending levels. Competitive tracking of this nature occurs at both the national and regional levels.

At times, marketers use the **arbitrary approach,** which usually means that a high-level executive in the firm states how much to spend on advertising for a certain time period. The arbitrary approach often leads to underspending or overspending. Although hardly a scientific budgeting technique, it is expedient.

Arbitrary approach
A high-level executive in the firm states how much to spend on advertising for a certain time period

Deciding how large the advertising appropriation should be is critical. If the appropriation is set too low, the campaign cannot achieve its full potential. When too much money is appropriated, overspending results and financial resources are wasted.

■ *Developing the Media Plan*

As Table 18.2 shows, advertisers spend tremendous amounts of money on advertising media. These amounts have grown rapidly during the past two decades. To derive maximum results from media expenditures, marketers must develop effective media plans. A **media plan** sets forth the exact media vehicles to be used (specific magazines, television stations, newspapers, and so forth) and the dates and times that the advertisements will appear. The plan's effectiveness determines how many people in the target audience will be exposed to the message. It also determines, to some degree, the effects of the message on those individuals. Media planning is a complex task requiring thorough analysis of the target audience. Sophisticated computer models have been developed in an attempt to maximize the effectiveness of an organization's media plan.[3]

Media plan   Specifies media vehicles and schedule for running the advertisements

To formulate a media plan, the planners select the media for a campaign and prepare a time schedule for each medium. The media planner's primary goal is to reach the largest number of persons in the advertising target per dollar spent on media. A secondary goal is to achieve the appropriate message reach and frequency for the target audience while staying within budget. *Reach* refers to the percentage of consumers in the target audience actually exposed to a particular advertisement in a stated time period. *Frequency* is the number of times these targeted consumers are exposed to the advertisement.

Media planners begin with broad decisions but eventually make very specific choices. Planners first decide which kinds of media to use: radio, television, newspapers, magazines, direct mail, outdoor displays, transit vehicles, and the Internet. As discussed in Technology in Marketing (on the following page), a growing number of organizations are advertising on the Internet. They are assessing different formats and approaches to determine which are the most effective. Some media plans are quite focused and use just one medium. For example, the Burlington, Vermont–based rock-and-roll band Phish communicates with about 100,000 fans through direct mail.[4] The media plans of consumer packaged goods companies can be quite complex and dynamic. Currently, some of these companies, like Kraft and Procter & Gamble, are changing their media plans to include considerably larger expenditures on direct mail.[5]

Table 18.2   Total Advertising Expenditures (in millions of dollars)

	1975	1980	1985	1990	1995
Newspapers	$ 8,234	$14,794	$25,170	$ 32,281	$ 36,317
Magazines	1,539	3,279	5,341	6,803	8,580
Television	5,263	11,366	20,738	28,405	36,246
Radio	1,980	3,777	6,490	8,726	11,338
Outdoor	335	600	945	1,084	1,263
Direct mail	4,124	7,596	15,500	23,370	32,866
Business press	919	1,674	2,375	2,875	3,559
Miscellaneous	5,558	10,767	18,159	25,096	20,232
Total	$27,952	$53,853	$94,718	$128,640	$160,920

Source: DDB Needham, *Worldwide Media Trends*, 1987 Edition; Robert J. Coen, "Coen: Little Ad Growth," *Advertising Age*, May 6, 1991, pp. 1, 16; and Robert J. Coen, "96 Expected to Deliver Energetic Ad Growth," *Advertising Age*, May 20, 1996, p. 22.

TECHNOLOGY IN MARKETING

Advertising Online: New Frontiers for Advertisers and Customers

While flipping through a magazine in a doctor's waiting room, a patient might run across an advertisement for Club Med. At home, a television viewer might see Club Med's 30-second commercial. But computer users with access to the information highway have another alternative for checking out the vacation packages. They can type http://www.hotwired.com/Coin/Spnsers/Clubmed and get information on eighteen Club Med resorts plus a map to locate destinations. It's not only high-tech marketers such as IBM and Microsoft that promote products on commercial online services. It's also Embassy Suites, Volvo, JC Penney, Reebok, and many others.

When marketers decide to launch into cyberspace, they can choose from a variety of online services. The World Wide Web, a portion of the Internet, is an information space where marketers can place advertising "home pages." America Online (AOL), currently the fastest-growing commercial online service, offers the Marketplace where advertisers can set up bulletin boards, run promotions, distribute brochures, and poll users. Major cybercompetitors, including Prodigy and CompuServe, and smaller players such as General Electric's GEnie have similar offerings.

How do marketers advertise in cyberspace? Some experts insist that providing useful information about the company and its products works better than an obvious advertisement. Others insist that straight product information is out; entertainment, service, and free samples are in. On the World Wide Web, Ragu spaghetti sauces offers downloadable coupons and recipes, holds a sweepstakes, and even gives Italian lessons. Norwegian Cruise Lines displays pictures of its ships and cabins, lists departure dates and times, and gives rate information. Saturn Corporation's "electronic showroom" advertises its newest line of automobiles. American Express allows computer users to communicate with the company, apply for a credit card, and participate in special promotions.

Some marketers aren't convinced that online advertising—with its high costs and small target audiences—yields results. Skeptics point out, for example, that while 34 million people watch *Seinfeld* each week, only about 2 million cruise the Internet. Proponents of the high-tech medium acknowledge the criticism, but they are quick to respond that for about $150,000 marketers can set up an advertising site on the Web at which visitors can linger five minutes or longer and to which they can return over and over. Compare that to a single 30-second spot on *Seinfeld,* which costs $500,000 and which viewers will miss if they're in the kitchen getting a snack.

Sources: Mary Kuntz, "Burma Shave Signs On the I-Way," *Business Week,* Apr. 17, 1995, pp. 102, 104; Scott Donaton, "Commercial Services or the Web?" *Advertising Age,* Feb. 20, 1995, p. 18; Andy Cohen, "Attitudes Vary On Internet Ads," *Sales & Marketing Management,* Mar. 1995, p. 12; "Making Moves on the Internet," *Advertising Age,* Jan. 9, 1995, p. 22; "Who's On the 'Net: A Graphic Guide," *Advertising Age,* Jan. 9, 1995, pp. 22, 24; Scott Donaton, "AOL Seeks Big Bucks for Ads," *Advertising Age,* Jan. 23, 1995, p. 15; Scott Donaton, "Mucking Up Marketing on the 'Net," *Advertising Age,* Jan. 23, 1995, p. 18; and "Ad Age Names Awards and Finalists," *Advertising Age,* Feb. 27, 1995, pp. 12–14.

Media planners take many factors into account when devising a media plan. They analyze location and demographic characteristics of people in the target audience because the various media appeal to particular demographic groups in particular locations. There are radio stations especially for teenagers, magazines for men aged 18 to 34, and television programs aimed at adults of both sexes. Media planners also consider the sizes and types of audiences that specific media reach. Several data services collect and periodically provide information about circulations and audiences of various media.

The content of the message sometimes affects media choice. Print media can be used more effectively than broadcast media to present many issues or numerous details in single advertisements. If an advertiser wants to promote beautiful colors, patterns, or textures, media offering high-quality color reproduction—magazines or television—

Figure 18.5
Black and White Versus Color Advertisements
This example highlights the importance of using color in advertisements for certain types of products such as foods.

should be used instead of newspapers. For example, food can be effectively promoted in full-color magazine advertisements, but would be far less effective in black and white. Compare the black-and-white and color versions of the same advertisement in Figure 18.5.

The cost of media is an important but troublesome consideration. Planners try to obtain the best coverage possible for each dollar spent. Yet there is no accurate way of comparing the cost and impact of a television commercial with the cost and impact of a newspaper advertisement. A **cost comparison indicator** lets an advertiser compare the costs of several vehicles within a specific medium (such as two magazines) in relation to the number of persons reached by each vehicle. The "cost per thousand" (CPM) is the cost comparison indicator for magazines; it shows the cost of exposing a thousand persons to a one-page advertisement.

Table 18.2 shows that the extent to which each medium is used varies quite a bit and that the pattern of use has changed over the years. For example, the proportion of total media dollars spent on television since 1975 has risen to equal that spent on newspapers. The proportion of total advertising dollars spent on direct mail has risen considerably since 1985. Media are selected by weighing various characteristics, advantages, and disadvantages of each (see Table 18.3).

Cost comparison indicator Lets an advertiser compare the cost of vehicles in a specific medium in relation to the number of people reached

■ *Creating the Advertising Message*

The basic content and form of an advertising message are a function of several factors. Products' features, uses, and benefits affect the content of the message. Characteristics of the people in the target audience—their gender, age, education, race, income, occupation, and other attributes—influence both content and form. When Procter & Gamble promotes its Crest toothpaste to children, the company emphasizes daily brushing and cavity control. When Crest is marketed to adults, tartar and plaque are discussed. To communicate effectively, advertisers use words, symbols, and illustrations that are meaningful, familiar, and attractive to people in the target audience.

An advertising campaign's objectives and platform also affect the content and form of its messages. If a firm's advertising objectives involve large sales increases, the message demands hard-hitting, high-impact language and symbols. When campaign objectives aim at increasing brand awareness, the message may use much repetition of the brand name and words and illustrations associated with it. Thus the advertising platform is the foundation on which campaign messages are built.

Table 18.3   Characteristics, Advantages, and Disadvantages of Major Advertising Media

Medium	Types	Unit of Sale	Factors Affecting Rates
Newspaper	Morning Evening Sunday Sunday supplement Weekly Special	Agate lines Column inches Counted words Printed lines	Volume and frequency discounts Number of colors Position charges for preferred and guaranteed positions Circulation level
Magazine	Consumer Farm Business	Pages Partial pages Column inches	Circulation level Cost of publishing Type of audience Volume discounts Frequency discounts Size of advertisement Position of advertisement (covers) Number of colors Regional issues
Direct mail	Letters Catalogs Price lists Calendars Brochures Coupons Circulars Newsletters Postcards Booklets Broadsides Samplers	Not applicable	Cost of mailing lists Postage Production costs
Radio	AM FM	Programs: sole sponsor, cosponsor, participative sponsor Spots: 5, 10, 20, 30, 60 seconds	Time of day Audience size Length of spot or program Volume and frequency discounts
Television	Network Local CATV	Programs: sole sponsor, cosponsor, participative sponsor Spots: 5, 10, 15, 30, 60 seconds	Time of day Length of program Length of spot Volume and frequency discounts Audience size
Inside transit	Buses Subways	Full, half, and quarter showings are sold on a monthly basis	Number of riders Multiple-month discounts Production costs Position
Outside transit	Buses Taxicabs	Full, half, and quarter showings; space also rented on per-unit basis	Number of advertisements Position Size
Outdoor	Papered posters Painted displays Spectaculars	Papered posters; sold on monthly basis in multiples called "showings" Painted displays and spectaculars: sold on per-unit basis	Length of time purchased Land rental Cost of production Intensity of traffic Frequency and continuity discounts Location

Cost Comparison Indicator	Advantages	Disadvantages
Milline rate = cost per agate line × 1,000,000 divided by circulation	Reaches large audience; purchased to be read; national geographic flexibility; short lead time; frequent publication; favorable for cooperative advertising; merchandising services	Not selective for socioeconomic groups; short life; limited reproduction capabilities; large advertising volume limits exposure to any one advertisement
Cost per thousand (CPM) = cost per page × 1,000 divided by circulation	Demographic selectivity; good reproduction; long life; prestige; geographic selectivity when regional issues are available; read in leisurely manner	High absolute dollar cost; long lead time
Cost per contact	Little wasted circulation; highly selective; circulation controlled by advertiser; few distractions; personal; stimulates actions; use of novelty; relatively easy to measure performance; hidden from competitors	Expensive; no editorial matter to attract readers; considered junk mail by many; criticized as invasion of privacy
Cost per thousand (CPM) = cost per minute × 1,000 divided by audience size	Highly mobile; low-cost broadcast medium; message can be quickly changed; reaches large audience; geographic selectivity; demographic selectivity	Provides only audio message; has lost prestige; short life of message; listeners' attention limited because of other activities while listening
Cost per thousand (CPM) = cost per minute × 1,000 divided by audience size	Reaches large audience; low cost per exposure; uses audio and video; highly visible; high prestige; geographic and demographic selectivity	High dollar costs; highly perishable message; size of audience not guaranteed; amount of prime time limited
Cost per thousand riders	Low cost; "captive" audience; geographic selectivity	Does not reach many professional persons; does not secure quick results
Cost per thousand exposures	Low cost; geographic selectivity; reaches broad, diverse audience	Lacks demographic selectivity; does not have high impact on readers
No standard indicator	Allows for repetition; low cost; message can be placed close to point of sale; geographic selectivity; operable 24 hours a day	Message must be short and simple; no demographic selectivity; seldom attracts readers' full attention; criticized as traffic hazard and blight on countryside

Sources: Information from Dean M. Krugman, Leonard N. Reid, S. Watson Dunn, and Arnold M. Barban, *Advertising: Its Role in Modern Marketing*, 8th ed. (Forth Worth, Tex.: Dryden Press, 1993); and Anthony F. McGann and J. Thomas Russell, *Advertising Media* (Homewood, Ill.: Irwin, 1981).

425

Choice of media obviously influences the content and form of the message. Effective outdoor displays and short broadcast spot announcements require concise, simple messages. Magazine and newspaper advertisements can include considerable detail and long explanations. Because several different kinds of media offer geographic selectivity, a precise message can be tailored to a particular geographic section of the target audience. Some magazine publishers produce **regional issues,** in which advertisements and editorial content of copies appearing in one geographic area differ from those appearing in other areas. As Figure 18.6 shows, *Sports Illustrated* publishes five regional issues. A clothing manufacturer advertising in *Sports Illustrated* might decide to use one message in the western region and another in the rest of the nation. A company may also choose to advertise in only one region. Such geographic selectivity lets a firm use the same message in different regions at different times.

Regional issues   Versions of a magazine that differ across geographic regions

The basic components of a print advertising message are shown in Figure 18.7. Messages for most advertisements depend on the use of copy and artwork. Let us examine these two elements in more detail.

Copy   Copy is the verbal portion of an advertisement including headlines, subheadlines, body copy, and the signature (see Figure 18.7). When preparing advertising copy, marketers attempt to move readers through a persuasive sequence called AIDA: attention, interest, desire, and action. Not all copy need be this extensive. Marketers should give readers or listeners something that will appeal to them. Important points should be clear and understandable.[6]

Copy   The verbal portion of advertisements

The headline is critical because often it is the only part of the copy that people read. It should attract readers' attention and create enough interest to make them want to read the body copy. The subheadline, if there is one, links the headline to the body copy and sometimes is used to explain the headline.

Body copy for most advertisements consists of an introductory statement or paragraph, several explanatory paragraphs, and a closing paragraph. Some copywriters have adopted guidelines for developing body copy systematically: (1) identify a specific desire or problem, (2) recommend the product as the best way to satisfy that desire or solve that problem, (3) state product advantages and benefits and indicate why the product is best

Figure 18.6
Geographic Divisions for *Sports Illustrated* Regional Issues
Source: *Sports Illustrated.*

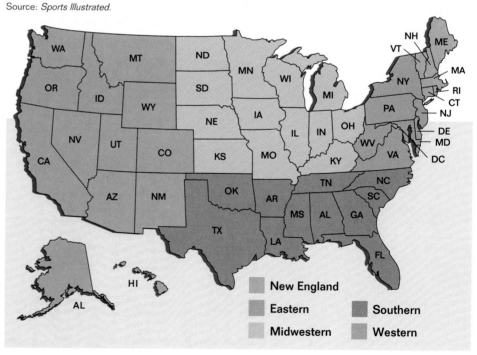

Figure 18.7
Components of a Print Advertisement This advertisement includes all the major components of a print advertisement.

for the buyer's particular situation, (4) substantiate advertising claims, and (5) ask the buyer for action. When substantiating claims, it is important to present the substantiation in a credible manner. The proof of claims should strengthen product and company integrity.

The signature identifies the advertisement's sponsor. It may contain several elements, including the firm's trademark, logo, name, and address. The signature should be attractive, legible, distinctive, and easy to identify in a variety of sizes.

Because radio listeners often are not fully "tuned in" mentally, radio copy should be informal and conversational to attract listeners' attention, resulting in greater impact. Radio messages are highly perishable and should consist of short, familiar terms. The length should not require a rate of speech exceeding approximately two and one-half words per second.

In television copy, the audio material must not overpower the visual material and vice versa. However, a television message should make optimal use of its visual portion, which can be very effective for product demonstrations. Television commercials with product demonstrations are significantly more persuasive than those without demonstrations.[7] As Figure 18.8 illustrates, copy for a television commercial is initially written in parallel script form. Video is described in the left column and audio in the right. When the parallel script is approved, the copywriter and artist combine copy with visual material by using a **storyboard** (see Figure 18.9), which depicts a series of miniature television screens showing the sequence of major scenes in the commercial. Beneath each screen is a description of the audio portion to be used with the video message shown. Technical personnel use the storyboard as a blueprint when producing the commercial.

Storyboard A mockup combining copy and visual material to show the sequence of major scenes in the commercial

Little Caesars Pizza

Title: "Cheeser-Cheeser The Stretch" :30 seconds

Visual	Audio
Kid reaching for pizza in kitchen	SFX: Children are heard playing in other room; cat meows
Kid picks up slice of pizza	
Kid walks away with pizza stretching	SFX: Stretchy sound is heard as boy stretches pizza
Children continue to play	Continued SFX as boy walks down hall
Boy hands little girl in high chair pizza	
Little girl is pulled by "Rubber Band" cheese	SFX: Ricochet sound as little girl is pulled by "Rubber Band" cheese
Little girl being pulled down the hall	SFX: Sonic swish as she is pulled down hall: she giggles hysterically
Little boy watches as she circles over and over	
She flies out the door	
He picks her up out of high chair	MAN: Well look who's here! SFX: High chair shoots back into house and breaks window
Close-up of pizza pie	MALE ANNCR: Little Caesars Cheeser-Cheeser. Not one but two pizzas with extra cheese, up to four toppings, and free Crazy Bread for $8.98.
Little Caesars cartoon with words "2 Pizzas, Extra Cheese, up to 4 Toppings and <u>Free</u> Crazy Bread for $8.98."	LITTLE CAESARS: Cheeser-Cheeser!

Figure 18.8

Example of a Parallel Script   In a parallel script, the audio and video components of a television commercial are presented.

Used by permission of Little Caesar Enterprises, Inc. © 1991, Little Caesar Enterprises, Inc.

Artwork
An ad's illustration and layout

Illustrations
Photos, drawings, graphs, charts, and tables used to spark audience interest

Artwork   **Artwork** consists of the advertisement's illustration and layout (see Figure 18.7). Although **illustrations** are often photographs, they can also be drawings, graphs, charts, and tables. Illustrations are used to attract attention, encourage audiences to read or listen to the copy, communicate an idea quickly, or communicate ideas that are difficult to put into words.[8] They are especially important because consumers tend to recall the visual portion of advertisements better than verbal portions. Advertisers use a variety of illustration techniques, including showing the product alone, in a setting, or being used, or showing the results of its use. Illustrations can also be in the form of comparisons, contrasts, diagrams, and testimonials.

Layout
The physical arrangement of an ad including the illustration, headline, subheadline, body copy, and signature

The **layout** of an advertisement is the physical arrangement of the illustration, headline, subheadline, body copy, and signature. Arrangement of these parts in Figure 18.7 is only one possible layout. These same elements could be arranged in many ways. The final layout is the result of several stages of layout preparation. As it moves through these stages, the layout helps people developing the advertising campaign to exchange ideas and provides instructions for production personnel.

■ *Executing the Campaign*

Execution of an advertising campaign requires extensive planning and coordination because many tasks must be completed on time and many people and firms are involved in a campaign's execution. Production companies, research organizations, media firms,

Figure 18.9
Storyboard
This is a storyboard for a Little Caesar Enterprises advertisement.

printers, photoengravers, and commercial artists are just a few of the people and firms contributing to a campaign.

Implementation requires detailed schedules to ensure that various phases of the work are done on time. Advertising management personnel must evaluate the quality of the work and take corrective action when necessary. In some instances, changes are made during the campaign so that it meets objectives more effectively. Sometimes one firm develops a campaign, but another executes it. McCann-Erickson and Creative Artists Agency collaborated recently for Coca-Cola. Creative Artists Agency developed Coca-Cola's worldwide strategy, and McCann-Erickson executed it.[9]

■ *Evaluating Advertising Effectiveness*

There are a variety of ways to test the effectiveness of advertising. They include measuring achievement of advertising objectives; assessing effectiveness of copy, illustrations, or layouts; and evaluating certain media.

Advertising can be evaluated before, during, and after the campaign. Evaluations performed before the campaign begins are **pretests** and usually attempt to evaluate the effectiveness of one or more elements of the message. To pretest advertisements, marketers sometimes use a **consumer jury,** a number of actual or potential buyers of the advertised product. Jurors judge one or several dimensions of two or more advertisements. Such tests are based on the belief that consumers are more likely than advertising experts to know what influences them.

To measure advertising effectiveness during a campaign, marketers usually take advantage of "inquiries." In a campaign's initial stages, an advertiser may use several

Pretest   Evaluation of ads performed before a campaign begins

Consumer jury   A panel of a product's actual or potential buyers used to pretest ads

advertisements simultaneously, each containing a coupon or a form requesting information. The advertiser records the number of coupons returned from each type of advertisement. If an advertiser receives 78,528 coupons from advertisement A, 37,072 coupons from advertisement B, and 47,932 coupons from advertisement C, advertisement A is judged superior to advertisements B and C.

Posttest Evaluation of advertising effectiveness after the campaign

Evaluation of advertising effectiveness after the campaign is called a **posttest.** Advertising objectives often indicate what kind of posttest is appropriate. If the objectives are in terms of communication—product awareness, brand awareness, or attitude change—then the posttest should measure changes in these dimensions. Advertisers sometimes use consumer surveys or experiments to evaluate a campaign based on communication objectives. These methods are costly, however.

For campaign objectives stated in terms of sales, advertisers should determine the change in sales or market share attributable to the campaign. However, changes in sales or market share brought about by advertising cannot be measured precisely; many factors independent of advertisements affect a firm's sales and market share. Competitive actions, government actions, and changes in economic conditions, consumer preferences, and weather are only a few factors that might enhance or diminish a company's sales or market share. By using data about past and current sales and advertising expenditures, advertisers can make gross estimates of the effects of a campaign on sales or market share.

Recognition test A posttest in which individuals are shown the actual ad and asked whether they recognize it

Because consumer surveys and experiments are expensive and because it is difficult to determine the direct effects of advertising on sales, many advertisers evaluate print advertisements according to how well consumers can remember them. Posttest methods based on memory include recognition and recall tests. Such tests are usually performed by research organizations through consumer surveys. If a **recognition test** is used, respondents are shown the actual advertisement and asked whether they recognize it. If they do, the interviewer asks additional questions to determine how much of the advertisement each respondent read. When recall is evaluated, the respondents are not shown the actual advertisement but instead are asked about what they have seen or heard recently.

Unaided recall test
A posttest that asks subjects to identify recently seen ads but does not provide any clues

Aided recall test
A posttest that asks subjects to identify recently seen ads and provides clues to jog memory

Recall can be measured through either unaided or aided recall methods. In an **unaided recall test,** subjects identify advertisements that they have seen recently but are not shown any clues to help them remember. A similar procedure is used with an **aided recall test,** but subjects are shown a list of products, brands, company names, or trademarks to jog their memories. Several research organizations, including Daniel Starch and Gallup & Robinson, provide research services that test recognition and recall of advertisements.

The major justification for using recognition and recall methods is that people are more likely to buy a product if they can remember an advertisement about it than if they cannot. However, recalling an advertisement does not necessarily lead to buying the product or brand advertised. Researchers also use a sophisticated technique called single-source data to help evaluate advertisements. With this technique, individuals' behaviors are tracked from television sets to checkout counters. Monitors are placed in preselected homes, and microcomputers record when the television set is on and which station is being viewed. At the supermarket checkout, the individual in the sample household presents an identification card. Checkers then record the purchases by scanner, and data are sent to the research facility. This technique is now bringing more insight into people's buying patterns than ever before.

Who Develops the Advertising Campaign?

*A*n advertising campaign may be handled by an individual or a few persons within the firm, an advertising department within the organization, or an advertising agency.

In very small firms, one or two individuals are responsible for advertising (and many other activities as well). Usually these individuals depend heavily on personnel at local newspapers and broadcast stations for copywriting, artwork, and advice about scheduling media.

In certain large businesses—especially the larger retail organizations—advertising departments create and implement advertising campaigns. Depending on the size of the advertising program, an advertising department may consist of a few multiskilled persons or a sizable number of specialists, such as copywriters, artists, media buyers, and technical production coordinators. Advertising departments sometimes obtain the services of independent research organizations and hire freelance specialists when a particular project requires it.

When an organization uses an advertising agency, the firm and the agency usually develop the advertising campaign jointly. How much each participates in the campaign's total development depends on the working relationship between the firm and the agency. Ordinarily, a firm relies on the agency for copywriting, artwork, technical production, and formulation of the media plan. Consumer products companies rely the most on advertising agencies for the development and implementation of advertising campaigns, whereas wholesalers, in particular, but also industrial products organizations rely on them less.[10]

Advertising agencies assist businesses in several ways. An agency, especially a larger one, supplies the firm with services of highly skilled specialists—not only copywriters, artists, and production coordinators, but also media experts, researchers, and legal advisers. Agency personnel often have broad advertising experience and are usually more objective than a firm's employees about the organization's products.

Because an agency traditionally receives most of its compensation from a 15 percent media commission on media purchases, firms can obtain some agency services at low or moderate cost. If an agency contracts for $400,000 of television time for a firm, it receives a commission of $60,000 from the television station. Although the traditional compensation method for agencies is changing and now includes other factors, media commissions still offset some costs of using an agency.

Like advertising, public relations can be a vital element in a promotion mix. We turn to it next.

Public Relations

Public relations
Communications activities used to create and maintain favorable relations between an organization and its publics

Public relations is a broad set of communication efforts used to create and maintain favorable relationships between an organization and its publics. An organization communicates with various publics, both internal and external. Public relations efforts can be directed toward any and all of these. A firm's publics can include customers, suppliers, employees, stockholders, the media, educators, potential investors, government officials, and society in general.

Public relations efforts can be used to promote people, places, ideas, activities, and even countries. Public relations focuses on enhancing the image of the total organization. Assessing public attitudes and creating a favorable image are no less important than direct promotion of an organization's products. Because the public's attitudes toward a firm are likely to affect the sales of its products, it is very important for firms to maintain positive public perceptions. In addition, employee morale is strengthened if the firm is perceived positively by the public.[11] Although public relations can make people aware of a company's products, brands, or activities, it can also create specific company images, such as innovativeness or dependability. Ben and Jerry's ice cream has a reputation for being socially responsible not only because this organization engages in socially responsive behavior, but because this behavior is reported through news stories and other public relations efforts. By getting the media to report on a firm's accomplishments, public relations also helps a company maintain positive public visibility. Some firms use public relations for a single purpose and others for several purposes.

■ *Public Relations Tools*

Companies use a variety of public relations tools to convey messages and to create images. Public relations professionals prepare written materials, such as brochures, newsletters, company magazines, news releases, and annual reports, that reach and influence their

**Figure 18.10
Annual Report Used as
a Communications Tool**
In its annual report (front
and back cover shown
here), Marvel Entertainment
Group Inc. explains results
in a comic book form to
demonstrate the enter-
tainment value of Marvel
characters. The report also
contains standard financial
information.

various publics. As shown in Figure 18.10, Marvel Entertainment Group Inc. conveys the company's creative image to its stockholders by producing a unique annual report that is written like a comic book complete with super heros who convey financial information in word balloons. Public relations personnel also create corporate identity materials, such as logos, business cards, stationery, and signs, that make firms immediately recognizable. Speeches are another public relations tool. Because what a company executive says publicly at meetings or to the media can affect the organization's image, his or her speech must convey the desired message clearly.

Event sponsorship, in which a company pays for part or all of a special event, such as a benefit concert or a tennis tournament, is another public relations tool. Examples are Eastman Kodak's sponsorship of the Olympic games and Evian bottled water's sponsorship of the *Food and Wine* magazine classic, a convention for gourmet food lovers and chefs. Sponsoring special events is an effective means of increasing brand recognition with relatively minimal investment. Except for the initial underwriting cost, event sponsorship can provide companies with considerable amounts of free media coverage. Organizations try to make sure that their product and the sponsored event target a consistent audience. Associating a 10-kilometer race with a sports drink such as Gatorade is more consistent than associating it with a brand of baby food. Public relations personnel can also organize unique events to "create news" about the company. These can include grand openings with celebrities, prizes, hot-air balloon rides, and other attractions that appeal to their publics. Sega earned *Advertising Age*'s Promotional Marketer of the Year award for its long list of specials, including a nationwide videogame tournament to launch its new "Sonics and Knuckles" game. The contest involved hundreds of thousands of videogame players with the finalists facing off in a showdown held on Alcatraz Island and televised live on MTV.[12]

Certain public relations tools have traditionally been associated specifically with publicity, which is a part of public relations. **Publicity** is communication in news story form, about an organization, its products, or both, that is transmitted through a mass medium at no charge. Although public relations has a larger, more comprehensive communication function than publicity, publicity is a very important aspect of public relations. Publicity can be used to provide information about goods or services, to announce expansions, acquisitions, research, or new-product launches, or to enhance a company's image. When Microsoft introduced Windows 95, the company received a tremendous amount of international publicity by lighting up the side of a New York skyscraper with the Windows 95 logo and sailing a huge facsimile of the Windows 95 box into Tokyo Harbor.

Publicity A news story type of communication transmitted through a mass medium at no charge

News release
A short piece of copy publicizing an event or a product

The most common publicity-based public relations tool is the **news release,** sometimes called a press release, which is usually a single page of typewritten copy containing fewer than 300 words. A news release also gives the firm's or agency's name, address, phone number, and contact person, as shown in Figure 18.11. Automakers, as well as other manufacturers, sometimes use news releases when introducing new products. When Wal-Mart made a special effort to carry environmentally safe products and packaging, its public relations department sent out news releases to various newspapers, magazines, television contacts, and suppliers, resulting in public relations in the form of magazine articles, newspaper acknowledgements, and television coverage. As Table 18.4 shows, news releases tackle a multitude of specific issues. A **feature article** is a longer manuscript (up to 3,000 words) prepared for a specific publication. A **captioned photograph** is a photograph with a brief description explaining the picture's content. Captioned photographs are effective for illustrating new or improved products with highly visible features.

Feature article A longer manuscript prepared for a specific publication

Captioned photograph
A photo with a brief description of its contents

Press conference
A meeting used to announce major news events

There are several other kinds of publicity-based public relations tools. A **press conference** is a meeting called to announce major news events. Media personnel are invited to a press conference and are usually supplied with written materials and photographs. Letters to the editor and editorials are sometimes prepared and sent to newspapers and magazines. Video- and audiotapes may be distributed to broadcast stations in the hope that they will be aired.

The use of publicity-based public relations tools has several advantages including credibility, news value, significant word-of-mouth communications, and a perception of being endorsed by the media. The public may consider the news more truthful and credible than an advertisement because the media is not paid to provide the information. In addition, stories regarding a new-product introduction or a new environmentally responsible company policy, for example, are handled as news items and are likely to receive notice. Finally, the cost of publicity is low compared to the cost of advertising.[13]

Publicity-based public relations tools do have some limitations. Media personnel must judge company messages to be newsworthy if they are to be published or broadcast at all. Consequently, messages must be timely, interesting, accurate, and in the public interest. Many communications do not qualify. It may take a great deal of time and effort to convince media personnel of the news value of publicity releases. Although public relations personnel usually encourage the media to air publicity releases at certain times, they control neither the content nor the timing of the communications. Media personnel alter length and content of publicity releases to fit publishers' or broadcasters' requirements and may even delete parts of messages that company personnel view as most important. Furthermore, media personnel use publicity releases in time slots or positions most convenient for them. Thus messages sometimes appear in locations or at times that may not reach the firm's target audiences. Although these limitations can be frustrating, properly managed publicity-based public relations tools offer an organization substantial benefits.

News Release

Unisys Corporation
PO Box 500
Blue Bell PA 19424 0001

UNISYS

Contact: Pete Cavanaugh, 215-986-7884
Internet : cavanaug@po7.bb.unisys.com

U.K.'S MIDLAND BANK OUTSOURCES DATA CENTER MAINTENANCE TO UNISYS IN $15 MILLION AWARD

Unisys to manage support of IBM and Amdahl mainframe computers in broad single-source, multivendor services contract.

BLUE BELL, PA, SEPTEMBER 12, 1995 -- Midland Bank, one of the largest retail banks in the United Kingdom, has awarded Unisys Corporation a three-year, $15 million contract to maintain and support the bank's data centers. Midland is the first major retail bank in the U.K. to outsource its data center maintenance and support requirements.

Midland selected Unisys for its service management expertise and proven ability to deliver quality multivendor support solutions. Under the agreement, Unisys will ensure high availability of business-critical systems running on Amdahl and IBM mainframes, Unisys enterprise servers, and equipment from Digital, Memorex and StorageTek.

Unisys is a leading provider of innovative support solutions for multivendor computing environments. The company provides single-source support solutions to a range of organizations worldwide, including Abbey National, Aetna Life and Casualty, Bass Taverns, Chemical Bank, Pitney Bowes, TSB Bank and many others.

Unisys -- The information management company
As an information management company, Unisys acts as a solutions and systems integrator for business and government, complementing those integration skills with a full range of consulting and implementation services, information technology and vertical industry expertise. The company's perspective extends beyond supplying technology to delivering comprehensive information management solutions. Access the Unisys home page on the World Wide Web -- http://www.unisys.com -- for further information.

###
RELEASE NO.: 0995/5881

Unisys is a registered trademark of Unisys Corporation. All other brands and products reference herein are acknowledged to be trademarks or registered trademarks of their respective holders.

Figure 18.11
Example of a News Release   Unisys issued this information release to publicize its new online banking facilities to credit union members.
Reprinted with permission of Unisys Corporation.

433

Table 18.4   Possible Issues for Publicity Releases

Changes in marketing personnel	New products
Support of a social cause	Creation of a new slogan
Improved warranties	Research developments
Reports on industry conditions	Company's history and development
New uses for established products	Employment, production, and sales records
Product endorsements	Award of contracts
Winning of quality awards	Opening of new markets
Company name changes	Improvements in financial position
Interviews with company officials	Opening of an exhibit
Improved distribution policies	History of a brand
International business efforts	Winners of company contests
Athletic event sponsorship	Logo changes
Visits by celebrities	Speeches of top management
Reports on new discoveries	Merit awards to the organization
Innovative marketing activities	Anniversary of inventions
Economic forecasts	
Packaging changes	

■ Evaluating Public Relations Effectiveness

Because of the potential benefits of good public relations, it is essential that organizations evaluate the effectiveness of their public relations campaigns. Research can be conducted to determine how well a firm is communicating its messages or image to its publics. Environmental monitoring identifies changes in public opinion affecting an organization. A public relations audit is used to assess an organization's image among its publics or to evaluate the effect of a specific public relations program. A communications audit can include a content analysis of messages, a readability study, or a readership survey. If an organization wants to measure the extent to which publics view it as being socially responsible, it can conduct a social audit.

One approach to measuring the effectiveness of publicity-based public relations is to count the number of exposures in the media. To monitor print media and determine which releases are published and how often, an organization can hire a clipping service, a firm that clips and sends news releases to client companies. To measure the effectiveness of television coverage, a firm can enclose a card with its publicity releases, requesting that the station record its name and the dates when the news item is broadcast, although station personnel do not always comply. Though some television and radio tracking services exist, they are extremely costly.

Counting the number of media exposures does not reveal how many people actually read or heard a company's message, or what they thought about the message afterward. However, measuring changes in product awareness, knowledge, and attitudes resulting from the publicity campaign does. To assess these changes, companies must measure these levels before and after public relations campaigns. Although precise measures are difficult to obtain, a firm's marketers should attempt to assess the impact of its public relations efforts on the organization's sales.

■ Dealing with Unfavorable Public Relations

Until now we have discussed public relations as a planned promotion mix element. However, companies may have to deal with unfavorable public relations regarding an unsafe product, an accident, controversial actions of employees, or some other negative event or situation. For example, an airline that experiences a plane crash is faced with a very tragic, and distressing, situation. Reports of Chrysler minivan rear doors flying open on impact raised public concern and generated unfavorable public relations for Chrysler Corporation. The public's image of The Body Shop as a socially responsible company

GLOBAL PERSPECTIVE

Greenpeace Versus Royal Dutch/Shell: A Public Relations Lesson

For weeks, Greenpeace, one of the world's best-known environmental groups, had been protesting Royal Dutch/Shell's plan to dispose of the Brent Spar oil rig by sinking it deep into the Atlantic. Greenpeace warned that the rig's toxic and radioactive sludge would wreak havoc on the ocean's environment. Then, television viewers around the world saw a band of Greenpeace activists trying to land on the rig in the North Sea. To fend off this small band of ecowarriors, mighty Shell Oil blasted them with high-powered water cannons. These pictures left viewers with the negative image of a huge multinational oil company bullying a squad of brave environmentalists. Losing what became a public opinion battle, Shell was forced to halt its dumping plans. Greenpeace's victory over Shell illustrates the power of effective public relations, and Greenpeace's ability to use it well.

Prior to the Brent Spar events, Shell had scuttled many rigs, usually with environmentalists' approval because the rigs create artificial reefs. When the oil giant initiated plans to sink the Brent Spar, the announcement stirred very little news coverage. Although Greenpeace believed that the Brent Spar's 100 tons of oil, arsenic, cadmium, PCBs, lead, and

radioactive waste potentially made it more harmful than other scuttled rigs, the group knew that only strong public sentiment could stop Shell. To get it, Greenpeace decided not only to board the rig, but to acquire satellite communications and video equipment so the entire world could see them do it. It was this footage of soaked Greenpeace activists on the six o'clock news that sparked a public uproar. In addition to its highly visible live-action storming of the rig, Greenpeace kept its story on the front page of newspapers by issuing over thirty follow-up news releases. These included photos of Shell employees harassing Greenpeace activists and reports of Shell's attempts to get courts to stop the press from covering the story. Using emotionally charged language such as "Shell is so ashamed of what they are doing," and "Shell is cashing in at the expense of the North Sea environment," Greenpeace was able to increase international pressure on the oil company. After repeatedly refusing to explain its decision or to budge, Shell gave in to Greenpeace demands and agreed to dispose of the Brent Spar on land.

Sources: Bhushau Bahree, Kyle Pope, and Allanna Sullivan, "How Greenpeace Sank Shell's Plan to Dump Big Oil Rig in Atlantic," *Wall Street Journal*, July 7, 1995, pp. A1, A3; "Greenpeace Brent Spar Protest in the North Sea," World Wide Web, http://www.greenpeace.org/comms/brent/brent.html., Oct. 10, 1995; and Anastasia Toufexis, "It's Not Easy Being Greenpeace," *Time*, Oct. 16, 1995, p. 86.

diminished considerably when it was reported that the company's actions were not as socially responsible as its promotion promised. Unfavorable coverage can have quick and dramatic effects. Consider the magnitude of the effects of negative coverage on Royal Dutch/Shell as discussed in Global Perspective. A single negative event that produces unfavorable public relations can wipe out a company's favorable image and destroy positive customer attitudes that took years to build through expensive advertising campaigns and other types of promotional efforts. Moreover, today's mass media, including online services and the Internet, disseminate information faster than ever before. Bad news generally receives considerable media attention.

To protect an organization's image, it is important to avoid unfavorable public relations or at least to lessen its effects. First and foremost, organizations can directly reduce negative incidents and events through safety programs, inspections, and effective quality control procedures. Secondly, because negative events can happen to even the most cautious of firms, organizations should have predetermined plans in place to handle them when they occur. Firms need to establish policies and procedures for news coverage of a crisis or controversy. These policies should aim at reducing the adverse impact. In most cases, organizations should expedite news coverage of negative events rather than trying to discourage or block them. If news coverage is squelched, rumors and misinformation may replace facts and be passed along anyway. An unfavorable event can easily balloon into ugly problems or public issues and become quite damaging. By being forthright with the press and public and taking prompt action, firms may be able to convince the public of their honest attempts to deal with the situation, and news personnel might be more willing to help explain complex issues to the public. Dealing effectively with a negative event allows an organization to lessen, if not eliminate, the impact on the organization's image.

SUMMARY

Advertising is a paid form of nonpersonal communication transmitted to consumers through mass media, such as television, radio, newspapers, magazines, direct mail, mass transit vehicles, outdoor displays, and the Internet. Both nonbusiness and business organizations use advertising. Institutional advertising promotes organizational images, ideas, or political issues. When a company promotes its position on a public issue such as taxation, institutional advertising is referred to as advocacy advertising. Product advertising promotes uses, features, and benefits of products. The two types of product advertising are pioneer advertising, which focuses on stimulating demand for a product category rather than a specific brand, and competitive advertising, which attempts to stimulate demand for a specific brand by indicating a brand's features, uses, and advantages. To make direct product comparisons, marketers use comparative advertising, in which two or more brands are compared. Two other forms of competitive advertising are reminder advertising, which tells customers that an established brand is still around, and reinforcement advertising, which assures current users that they have made the right brand choice.

Although marketers may vary in how they develop advertising campaigns, they should follow a general pattern. First, they must identify and analyze the target audience—the group of people at which advertisements are aimed. Second, they should establish what they want the campaign to accomplish by defining advertising objectives. Objectives should be clear, precise, and presented in terms that can be measured. The third step is creating the advertising platform, which contains basic issues to be presented in the campaign. Advertising platforms should consist of issues that are important to consumers. Fourth, advertisers must decide how much money to spend on the campaign; they arrive at this decision through the objective-and-task approach, percent-of-sales approach, competition-matching approach, or arbitrary approach.

Then advertisers must develop a media plan by selecting and scheduling media to use in the campaign. Some of the factors affecting the media plan are location and demographic characteristics of people in the target audience, content of the message, and cost of the various media. Advertisers use copy and artwork to create the message. Basic content and form of the message are affected by product features, uses, and benefits; characteristics of the people in the target audience; the campaign's objectives and platform; and the choice of media. The execution of an advertising campaign requires extensive planning and coordination. Finally, advertisers must devise one or more methods for evaluating advertisement effectiveness. Evaluations performed before the campaign begins are called pretests; those after the campaign are called posttests. Two types of posttests are a recognition test, in which respondents are shown the actual advertisement and asked whether they recognize it, and recall tests. In aided recall tests, subjects are shown a list of products, brands, company names, or trademarks to jog their memories. In unaided tests, no clues are given.

Advertising campaigns can be developed by personnel within the firm or in conjunction with advertising agencies. When a campaign is created by the firm's personnel, it may be developed by only a few people, or it may be the product of an advertising department within the firm. Use of an advertising agency may be advantageous to a firm because an agency provides highly skilled, objective specialists with broad experience in advertising at low to moderate costs to the firm.

Public relations is a broad set of communication efforts used to create and maintain favorable relationships between an organization and its publics. Public relations can be used to promote people, places, ideas, activities, and countries and can also be used to create and maintain a positive image. Some firms use public relations for a single purpose and others for several purposes. Public relations tools include written materials such as brochures, newsletters, and annual reports; corporate identity materials such as business cards and signs; speeches; event sponsorships; and special events. Some public relations tools are associated with publicity. Publicity is communication in news story form, about an organization, its products, or both, that is transmitted through a mass medium at no charge. Publicity-based public relations tools include news releases, feature articles, captioned photographs, and press conferences. Problems that organizations confront in using publicity-based public relations include reluctance of media personnel to print or air releases and lack of control over timing and content of messages.

To evaluate the effectiveness of their public relations programs, companies conduct research to determine how well their messages are reaching their publics. Environmental monitoring, public relations audits, counting the number of media exposures, and monitoring print media are all means of evaluating public relations effectiveness. Organizations should avoid negative public relations by minimizing the number of negative events resulting in unfavorable publicity. To diminish the impact of unfavorable public relations, organizations should institute policies and procedures for dealing with news personnel and the public when negative events occur.

IMPORTANT TERMS

Advertising	Target audience	Cost comparison indicator	Recognition test
Institutional advertising	Advertising platform	Regional issues	Unaided recall test
Advocacy advertising	Advertising appropriation	Copy	Aided recall test
Product advertising	Objective-and-task	Storyboard	Public relations
Pioneer advertising	approach	Artwork	Publicity
Competitive advertising	Percent-of-sales approach	Illustrations	News release
Comparative advertising	Competition-matching	Layout	Feature article
Reminder advertising	approach	Pretest	Captioned photograph
Reinforcement advertising	Arbritrary approach	Consumer jury	Press conference
Advertising campaign	Media plan	Posttest	

DISCUSSION AND REVIEW QUESTIONS

1. What is the difference between institutional and product advertising?
2. When should advertising be used to stimulate primary demand? When should advertising be used to stimulate selective demand?
3. What are the major steps in creating an advertising campaign?
4. What is a target audience? How does a marketer analyze the target audience after it has been identified?
5. Why is it necessary to define advertising objectives?
6. What is an advertising platform, and how is it used?
7. What factors affect the size of an advertising budget? What techniques are used to determine an advertising budget?
8. Describe the steps required in developing a media plan.
9. What is the function of copy in an advertising message?
10. What role does an advertising agency play in developing an advertising campaign?
11. Discuss several ways to posttest the effectiveness of advertising.
12. What is public relations? Whom can an organization reach through public relations?
13. How do organizations use public relations tools? Give several examples that you have observed recently.
14. Explain the problems and limitations associated with publicity-based public relations.
15. In what ways is the effectiveness of public relations evaluated?
16. What are some of the sources of negative public relations? How should an organization deal with negative public relations?

APPLICATION QUESTIONS

1. An organization must define its objectives carefully when developing an advertising campaign. Listed below are several advertising objectives developed by a firm for the coming year. Which will be most useful for the company and why?
   a. The organization will spend $1 million in order to move from second in market share to market leader.
   b. The organization wants to increase sales from $1.2 million to $1.5 million this year, which will give them the lead in market share.
   c. The advertising objective is to gain as much market share as possible within the next twelve months.
   d. The advertising objective is to increase sales by 15 percent.
2. Copy is the verbal portion of print advertising and is used to move readers through a persuasive sequence called AIDA: attention, interest, desire, and action. To achieve this, some copywriters have adopted guidelines for developing the copy in an advertise-

ment. Select a print ad and identify the copy that does the following: (1) identifies a specific problem, (2) recommends the product as the best solution to the problem, (3) states the product's advantages and benefits, (4) substantiates the ad's claims, and (5) asks the reader to take action.
3. Advertisers use several types of publicity mechanisms. Look through several recent newspapers and magazines, and identify a news release, a feature article, and a captioned photograph used as publicity mechanisms for a particular product. Describe the type of product or service.
4. Negative public relations, if not dealt with properly, can be harmful to an organization's marketing efforts. Identify a company that recently has been the target of negative public relations. Describe the situation and discuss the company's response. What did marketers at this company do well? What would you recommend that they change about their response?

Case 18.1   The Advertising Council: Advertising for Good, Not for Gain

Advertising, we say, is sexist or racist; ads make people want what they don't need and can't afford; commercials are provocative, explicit, intrusive, irritating, or just plain lies. Americans have long criticized the advertising industry for promoting greed and consumption. What many don't realize is that advertising can sell cars, but it can also sell responsible driving. Ads can sell cigarettes, but they can also sell the dangers of smoking. From preventive health treatments such as vaccinations and prenatal care to complex and controversial issues such as racial intolerance, mental illness, and AIDS, the Advertising Council develops campaigns that confront some of America's vital concerns. For over half a century, this nonprofit organization has demonstrated that advertising can inform, educate, and unite people, change attitudes, and combat social problems.

In 1942, after the attack on Pearl Harbor plunged the United States into World War II, the government established the War Advertising Council. Inaugurating public service advertising, the council had as its purpose encouraging Americans to help the war effort by buying war bonds, planting "victory gardens," saving metals and rubber, and conserving fuel. How effective was the campaign? By the end of the war, advertisers and the media had donated about $1 billion worth of time and space for war-related messages, and Americans had purchased $35 billion worth of war bonds, planted 50 million victory gardens, and salvaged millions of pounds of rubber, tin, and steel. Convinced by these results that advertising could be a powerful tool for public good, the War Advertising Council became the Advertising Council in 1945 and prepared to take on America's postwar problems.

Planning, creating, and implementing advertising nationally, the Advertising Council selects issues that the federal government or nonprofit social agencies suggest. To maintain autonomy, the council raises all funds from private sources and allows no public officials on its board of directors. Over 400 prominent national manufacturers and marketers such as Johnson & Johnson, RJR Nabisco, Procter & Gamble, Coca-Cola, and Time Warner sponsor council projects. Advertising agencies create campaigns, with national advertisers directing the process and providing financial support. The media provides about 30,000 print, broadcast, outdoor, and transit outlets with an average of $25 million dollars donated per campaign. In one year alone, donations totaled over $600,000 million in media space and time and thousands of hours of advertising agency services.

To help select noncommercial, nonpolitical, nondenominational problems to tackle, the Advertising Council's board of directors gets help from its Advisory Committee on Public Issues and from yearly briefings with staff, directors, business leaders, and government officials. Campaigns must address problems faced by all areas of the United States, be conducive to effective advertising, and suggest specific actions individuals can take to change the status quo. However, a campaign must not promote an organization itself. For example, the Ad Council would not promote the American Heart Association but might create an ad that stresses healthy eating as a way to avoid heart attacks.

In its fifty years, the Advertising Council has created award-winning campaigns on numerous issues. The council's early crusades dealt with uncomplicated issues. Smokey the Bear cautioned, "Only You Can Prevent Forest Fires," and children sang "Please, please, don't be a litterbug" to Keep America Beautiful. Advertisements also reminded people to give money for foreign hunger relief, to get regular chest x-rays and vaccinations, and to buckle their seat belts. In the late 1960s, however, America's concerns changed, and with them the Ad Council's focus. Social ills and controversial issues took center stage, issues such as drinking and driving, alcoholism, drugs, child abuse, rape, cancer, AIDS, and mental illness.

Recently, the Advertising Council announced "Commitment 2000: Raising a Better Tomorrow." This new set of Ad Council guidelines states that all campaigns will focus on benefiting the health and well-being of America's youth age 0 to 21. To clarify this initiative, the council's chairman issued a Statement of Commitment, which reads, "The Ad Council is committed to making a longer-lasting impact on society by helping all of our children have a better chance to achieve their full potential." New campaigns will address social issues from health care and education to family and community concerns, providing Americans with specific steps and preventive actions to improve the lives of children and youth living in the United States. The campaign agenda for Commitment 2000 includes improving math and science education, preventing child abuse, and eliminating hunger.

For those skeptics who doubt that advertising is powerful enough to inspire people to act against inhumanity, discrimination, and spread of disease, statistics are convincing. Since the Advertising Council began its "A Mind Is a Terrible Thing to Waste" ads in 1971, the United Negro College Fund has seen an 800 percent increase in donations. In one year, a million children called the Runaway Teen Hotline after seeing the council's posters and billboards. An Ad Council research study on the effects of its campaign to prevent colon cancer reveals that awareness of the disease rose 30 percent in one year.

The Advertising Council's president recently acknowledged that, because of the types of foes her organization plans to tackle, unequivocal victories will be rare. However, that will not stop the council from taking on tough-to-solve problems and exploring new ways to publicize them. The council is using nontraditional methods including sports arena signage and advertising in high school and college newspapers, in movie theaters, and on MTV. To supplement conventional 30-second spots and print ads, the council plans to employ media talk shows, infomercials, and interactive computer information services. The council's president promises that the Advertising Council will continue doing what it has accomplished so successfully for fifty years—turning social causes into major national issues by using the power of advertising.[14]

Questions for Discussion

1. In what ways might the process for developing Ad Council campaigns differ from the process discussed in this chapter?
2. Who selects the topics for the Ad Council campaigns and who creates the campaigns?
3. Does publicity play a role in the Ad Council campaigns? Explain.
4. How is the advertising effectiveness of the Ad Council campaigns measured?

439

Case 18.2   Marvel Entertainment's Public Relations Efforts Keep Its Heroes Flying High

During the dark days of Nazi conquest and looming world war, Martin Goodman founded Marvel Comics and introduced Captain America, a hero who symbolized America's strength and honor. Years later, Marvel pitted Spider Man, an anxiety-ridden character always threatening to quit the superhero business, against DC Comics' invulnerable Superman. Although the Man of Steel might win a contest of strength, when it comes to profits and market share, Marvel Entertainment Group is on top. In a $700-million-a-year industry, Marvel owns 32 percent. Calling itself a "youth entertainment company," Marvel's product mix includes television programs and movies, trading cards, toys, T-shirts, video game software, and, of course, comic books, of which they sell about 15 million a month.

Why have Marvel's revenues skyrocketed and earnings recently doubled? Acquiring Fleer Corporation, marketer of sports trading cards and bubble gum, and owning tremendously popular comic books such as the *X-Men*, which outsells *Superman* by 5 to 1, certainly help. Licensing and merchandising its 3,500 characters put a Marvel action hero on stickers, POGs, cereal boxes, candy wrappers, fast-food containers, and even telephone cards. In addition, savvy public relations efforts keeps 6- to 18-year-olds demanding, "Make Mine Marvel."

Although Marvel employs an outside agency to administer some of its public relations activities, its in-house public relations department handles the bulk of its efforts. Doing no consumer advertising, Marvel is able to keep its cast of characters in the public eye by issuing press releases on a wide range of Marvel-related activities. When Marvel introduced CD-ROM interactive comics, when it debuted the Marvel Interactive Battle Pack that allows comic fans to interact with superheroes over the phone, when it acquired Malibu Comics, when it opened the Marvel Boutique at New York's F.A.O. Schwarz, and when it hired Aerosmith guitarist Joe Perry to write the theme song for the Spider Man cartoon series, the company issued press releases to let the world know.

Press releases announced that two artists who left Marvel in 1992 are returning. Their mission is to update classic characters such as Captain America, The Avengers, and Iron Man so that they are fully prepared to fight twenty-first-century evil. Recently, Planet Hollywood teamed up with Marvel to launch "Marvel Mania," a restaurant with a Marvel Comics character theme. Press releases let people know that at Marvel Mania restaurants in London, New York, or Las Vegas, they can dine among animated Marvel characters displayed on video screens, eat from creative menu offerings such as dessert fajitas with fruit-flavored tortillas, and purchase Marvel merchandise on the way out.

Publicity is another of Marvel's vital public relations tools. Marvel characters often appear at store and restaurant openings and at charity events, creating positive publicity for the company. One of Marvel's best publicity generators is its comic book–style annual report. Containing the same detailed full-color art as comic books, the first part of the report features a host of Marvel's famous characters dispensing financial information in comic book story and format. Amid descriptions of expansion plans and market share, heroes such as Thor, Wolverine, and the Scarlet Witch do battle with archvillains such as Hypnotia, The Grey Gargoyle, and Venom. Even charts and graphs employ comic book lettering and drawings. Newspapers like

440

USA Today and *The Wall Street Journal* and cable news networks have featured stories on Marvel's unique annual report, which stockholders eagerly await and for which collectors pay as much as $80.

Hoping to generate the kind of publicity received by DC Comics over the death of Superman, Marvel recently introduced a plot twist in the story line of its long-running Spider Man. His creators revealed that Peter Parker, the person we all knew for over thirty years as Spider Man's secret identity, was not a human at all, but a test-tube created clone. Although the story line generated a great deal of publicity, unfortunately for Marvel, most of it wasn't good. Outraged fans formed protest groups and cancelled subscriptions, causing sales of Spider Man comics to plummet. In response, Marvel has already changed the story line to cast doubt on the so-called tests that proved Parker's laboratory origins.

Although Marvel currently dominates the market, hungry competitors aren't settling for the status quo. Relative newcomer Image Comics recently topped DC to become the number two comic book publisher, claiming eight of the ten best-selling titles. In addition, Viz Comics and Dark Horse Comics are grabbing increasing market share. One of the ways Marvel hopes to hold on to its number one spot is by keeping its characters visible through sustained public relations efforts. Can Marvel, like its superheroes, remain invincible? To be continued.[15]

Questions for Discussion

1. What are the major public relations tools being used by Marvel Entertainment?
2. Describe and evaluate Marvel Entertainment's use of its annual report as a public relations tool.
3. Marvel Entertainment's revelation that Peter Parker was a test-tube created clone, rather than a human, resulted in negative public relations for the company. What actions could Marvel take to turn this set of circumstances into a positive situation with the potential for favorable public relations?

Chapter 19

Personal Selling and Sales Promotion

O B J E C T I V E S

- To understand the major purposes of personal selling

- To learn the basic steps in the personal selling process

- To be able to identify the types of sales force personnel

- To gain insight into sales management decisions and activities

- To become aware of what sales promotion activities are and how they can be used

- To become familiar with specific consumer and trade sales promotion methods

IBM's sales force under-stands its products . . . and its customers.

442

*S*ince its launch in 1914, International Business Machines (IBM) has transformed the public's perception of "salesman" from shady character to knowledgeable professional. IBM sales personnel understood their customers' needs and worked with them to show how computers could solve their business problems. On the strength of its technology and its sales force, IBM became an international computer powerhouse. During the 1980s, however, IBM began selling hardware rather than solutions, and its prominence began to fade. When GTE, one of IBM's top customers, wanted to switch from a mainframe system to a less expensive network of personal computers, IBM representatives tried to dissuade the company from changing. GTE switched not only systems but suppliers, opting for Hewlett-Packard. After suffering a number of such staggering losses, IBM re-engineered its 35,000-person sales force to better meet its customers' needs.

What IBM recognized is that having talented and hardworking salespeople isn't enough to maintain a competitive advantage. To help its sales staff win and keep customers, the company reorganized its field force by industry instead of by geography. In what industry experts call IBM's biggest restructuring in decades, the company established fourteen industry areas—banking, retail, travel, insurance, and others. Instead of selling a huge and confusing array of IBM products to all customers within a geographical area, salespeople specialize in specific industries, developing expertise in the businesses they serve. They know their customers better and are more familiar with the specific products that satisfy their needs. According to the company's CEO, re-engineering has transformed IBM sales personnel from order takers into business advisers.

It appears that the changes are beginning to pay off. IBM's workstation sales grew by 47 percent in one year, taking business away from market leader Sun Microsystems, Inc. Kansas City Southern Railway Co. recently reported that the IBM people calling on them are more attuned to what the railroad does and what it needs. Stated the company's president, "We don't have to explain to them what's going on."[1]

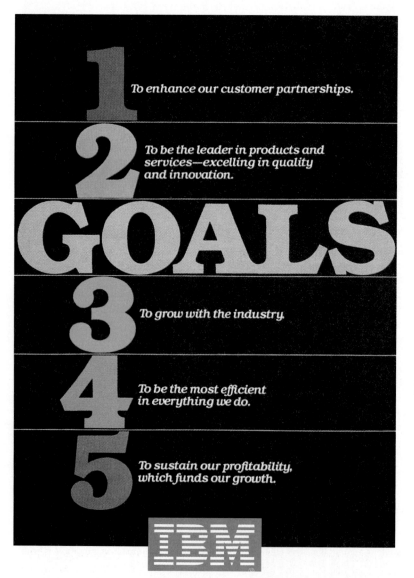

1 To enhance our customer partnerships.

2 To be the leader in products and services—excelling in quality and innovation.

GOALS

3 To grow with the industry.

4 To be the most efficient in everything we do.

5 To sustain our profitability, which funds our growth.

IBM

IBM's re-engineered, industry-focused sales force plays a major role in maintaining long-term satisfying customer relationships, which, in turn, contributes to the company's success. As indicated in Chapter 17, personal selling and sales promotion are two possible elements in a promotion mix. Sometimes personal selling is a company's sole promotional tool, although it is generally used in conjunction with other promotion mix elements. Personal selling is becoming more professional and sophisticated, with sales personnel acting more as consultants and advisers. Sales promotion, too, plays an increasingly important role in marketing strategies.

This chapter focuses on personal selling and sales promotion. We consider the purposes of personal selling, its basic steps, the types of salespersons, and how they are selected. We also discuss major sales force management decisions, including setting objectives for the sales force and determining its size; recruiting, selecting, training, compensating, and motivating salespeople; managing sales territories; and controlling and evaluating sales personnel. We then examine several characteristics of sales promotion, reasons for using sales promotion, and sales promotion methods available for use in a promotion mix.

The Nature of Personal Selling

Personal selling Personal, paid communication that informs customers and persuades them to buy products

Personal selling is personal, paid communication that attempts to inform customers and persuade them to purchase products in an exchange situation. A salesperson describing the benefits of a Kenmore dryer to a customer in a Sears store engages in personal selling. Personal selling gives marketers the greatest freedom to adjust a message to satisfy customers' information needs. Compared with other promotion methods, personal selling is the most precise, enabling marketers to focus on the most promising sales prospects. Other promotion mix elements are aimed at groups of people, some of whom may not be prospective customers. However, a major disadvantage of personal selling is cost. Generally, it is the most expensive element in the promotion mix.

Millions of people, including increasing numbers of women, earn their living through personal selling. Mary Kay Cosmetics, for example, has a sales force of several hundred thousand individuals, most of whom are women. Sales careers can offer high income, a great deal of freedom, a high level of training, and a high level of job satisfaction. Although personal selling is sometimes viewed negatively, major corporations, professional sales associations, and academic institutions are trying to change negative stereotypes of salespeople.

Personal selling goals vary from one firm to another. However, they usually involve finding prospects, convincing prospects to buy, and keeping customers satisfied. Identifying potential buyers interested in an organization's products is critical. Because most potential buyers seek information before making purchases, salespersons can ascertain prospects' informational needs and then provide relevant information. To do so, sales personnel must be well trained regarding both their products and the selling process in general.

Salespeople must be aware of their competitors. They must monitor new products being developed and know about competitors' sales efforts in their sales territories— salespeople should know how often and when the competition calls on their accounts and what the competition is saying about their product in relation to its own.[2] Salespeople must emphasize the benefits their products provide, especially when competitors' products do not offer those specific benefits.

Few businesses survive solely on profits from one-sale customers. For long-run survival, most marketers depend on repeat sales and thus need to keep their customers satisfied. Besides, satisfied customers provide favorable word-of-mouth communications, attracting new customers. Even though the whole organization is responsible for providing customer satisfaction, much of the burden falls on salespeople since they are almost always closer to customers than anyone else in the company and often provide buyers with information and service after the sale. Such contact gives salespeople an opportunity to generate additional sales and offers them a good vantage point for evaluating the

■ TECHNOLOGY IN MARKETING ■

Using Technology to Improve Customer Service

Someday, salespeople using technology may talk to their computers and their computers will talk back. Acting like digital mentors, the machines will suggest ideas and strategies. Computers will function as electronic receptionists, taking calls, prioritizing appointments, and reminding sales reps of staff meetings. When reps are ready to make a sales call, their computers will even provide automated driving directions. While many sales forces already use computers in some capacity, Microsoft, AT&T, and many other companies are working on advanced technology that will help salespeople further increase productivity and better serve their customers.

The potential of sales force automation is enormous. Tapping into the company's network, salespeople provide customers with up-to-the-minute inventory, shipping, and pricing figures. Through their databases, sales personnel have information about sales and special promotions at their fingertips. Because information is so readily accessible, salespeople no longer need to postpone deals because of slow credit checks, lose dissatisfied customers to competitors when service problems aren't resolved promptly, or spend endless hours doing paperwork instead of helping customers.

From global giants to small local operations, companies are improving customer service by automating their sales forces. Gillette, top marketer of razors and other health and beauty aids, reports that its sales reps equipped with pen-based computers called "GriD PAD Hds" spend more time in the field satisfying customers. An architectural firm offers clients more input into the design process by using software to show designs in progress, which both parties view simultaneously on their own computer screens. To save customers time, salespersons at Tops Appliance City communicate sales orders directly to warehouse staff using hand-held computers. By the time customers have paid at the counter, items are ready to pick up.

A vast array of sales-enhancing hardware and software is available today. Experts suggest one major guideline for companies leaning toward automation. Keep the customer in mind—the chosen technology should improve customer service.

Sources: "Improving Customer Service for the Crucial Few," *Inc.* 17, no. 9, 1995, p. 38; Mindy Blodgett, "Guide Ranks Sales Software," *Computerworld,* June 19, 1995, p. 53; "Tops Looks to Informix System To Enhance Customer Service," *Chain Store Age,* Sept. 1995, pp. 8B–9B; John J. Xenakis, "First Steps," *CFO,* Sept. 1995, pp. 75–82; Tony Seideman, "Reps' Needs Drive Gillette's System," *Sales & Marketing Management,* June 1994, p. 22; and Tony Seideman, "On the Cutting Age," *Sales & Marketing Management,* June 1994, pp. 18–23.

strengths and weaknesses of the company's products and other marketing mix components. Their observations help develop and maintain a marketing mix that better satisfies both customers and the firm. As discussed in Technology in Marketing, salespeople in some organizations are assisted by technologically advanced hardware and software.

Elements of the Personal Selling Process

*T*he specific activities involved in the selling process vary among salespersons and selling situations. No two salespersons use exactly the same selling methods. Nonetheless, many salespersons move through a general selling process as they sell products. This process consists of seven elements, or steps, outlined in Figure 19.1: prospecting, preapproach, approach, making the presentation, overcoming objections, closing the sale, and following up.

■ Prospecting

Prospecting Developing a list of potential customers

Developing a list of potential customers is called **prospecting.** Salespeople seek names of prospects from company sales records, referrals, trade shows, commercial databases

1 Prospecting

2 Preapproach

3 Approach

4 Making the presentation

5 Overcoming objections

6 Closing the sale

7 Following up

Figure 19.1
General Steps in the Personal Selling Process

(see Figure 19.2), newspaper announcements (of marriages, births, deaths, and so on), public records, telephone directories, trade association directories, and many other sources. Sales personnel also use responses to advertisements that encourage interested persons to send in information request forms (see Figure 19.2). Seminars and meetings targeted at particular types of clients, such as attorneys or accountants, may also produce leads.

Some organizations use their databases to identify prospects. John Deere used its database of 750,000 farm equipment owners to find prospects for its retail dealers' parts and service businesses. By researching owners of older equipment, John Deere isolated prospects and, through special offers, enticed them to go to John Deere dealers for parts and service.[3]

Consistent activity is critical to successful prospecting. Salespersons must actively prospect the customer base for qualified prospects that fit the target market profile. After developing the prospect list, a salesperson evaluates whether each prospect is able, willing, and authorized to buy the product. Based on this evaluation, prospects are ranked according to desirability or potential.

■ *Preapproach*

Before contacting acceptable prospects, a salesperson finds and analyzes information about each prospect's specific product needs, current use of brands, feelings about available brands, and personal characteristics. The most successful salespeople are thorough in their preapproach, which involves identifying key decision makers, reviewing account histories and problems, contacting other clients for information, assessing credit histories and problems, preparing sales presentations, identifying product needs, and obtaining relevant literature. A salesperson with a lot of information about a prospect is better equipped to develop a presentation that precisely communicates with the prospect.

445

Figure 19.2
Sources of Prospects   Marketers employ commercial databases as well as advertising to identify prospects.

■ *Approach*

The **approach**—the manner in which a salesperson contacts a potential customer—is a critical step in the sales process. In more than 80 percent of initial sales calls, the purpose is to gather information about the buyer's needs and objectives. Creating a favorable impression and building rapport with prospective clients are also important tasks in the approach because the prospect's first impressions of the salesperson are usually lasting ones. During the initial visit, the salesperson strives to develop a relationship rather than just push a product. The salesperson may have to call on a prospect several times before the product is considered. The approach must be designed to deliver value to targeted customers. If the sales approach is inappropriate, the salesperson's efforts are likely to result in a mediocre performance.

One type of approach is based on referrals. The salesperson approaches the prospect and explains that an acquaintance, associate, or relative suggested the call. The salesperson who uses the cold canvass method calls on potential customers without prior consent. Repeat contact is another common approach; when making the contact, the salesperson mentions a prior meeting. The exact type of approach depends on the salesperson's preferences, the product being sold, the firm's resources, and the prospect's characteristics.

■ *Making the Presentation*

During the sales presentation, the salesperson must attract and hold the prospect's attention, stimulating interest and sparking a desire for the product. The salesperson should have the prospect touch, hold, or use the product. If possible, the salesperson should demonstrate the product. Audiovisual equipment and software may also enhance the presentation (as shown in Figure 19.3).

During the presentation, the salesperson must not only talk but also listen. The sales presentation gives the salesperson the greatest opportunity to determine the prospect's specific needs by listening to questions and comments and observing responses. Even though the salesperson plans the presentation in advance, she or he must be able to adjust the message to meet the prospect's information needs.

■ *Overcoming Objections*

An effective salesperson usually seeks out a prospect's objections in order to address them. If they are not apparent, the salesperson cannot deal with them, and the prospect may not buy. One of the best ways to overcome objections is to anticipate and counter them before the prospect raises them. However, this approach can be risky because the salesperson may mention objections that the prospect would not have raised. If possible, the salesperson should handle objections when they arise. They also can be addressed at the end of the presentation.

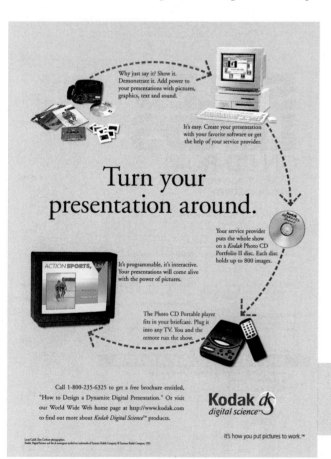

Figure 19.3
Enhancing Sales Presentations Audiovisual equipment and software assist salespeople in sales presentations.

■ *Closing the Sale*

Closing   The stage in the selling process when the salesperson asks the prospect to buy the product

Closing is the part of the selling process when the salesperson asks the prospect to buy the product. During the presentation, the salesperson may use a "trial close" by asking questions that assume the prospect will buy the product. The salesperson might ask the potential customer about financial terms, desired colors or sizes, or delivery arrangements. Reactions to such questions usually indicate how close the prospect is to buying. Properly asked, questions may allow prospects to uncover their own problems and identify solutions themselves. One questioning approach uses broad questions (what, how, why) to probe or gather information and focused questions (who, when, where) to clarify and close the sale.[4] A trial close allows prospects to indicate indirectly that they will buy the product without having to say those sometimes difficult words, "I'll take it."

A salesperson should try to close at several points during the presentation because the prospect may be ready to buy. One closing strategy involves asking the potential customer to place a low-risk tryout order. An attempt to close the sale may result in objections. Thus closing can uncover hidden objections, which can then be addressed.

■ *Following Up*

After a successful closing, the salesperson must follow up the sale. In the follow-up stage, the salesperson determines whether the order was delivered on time and installed properly, if installation was required. He or she should contact the customer to learn what problems or questions have arisen regarding the product. The follow-up stage is also used to determine customers' future product needs.

Types of Salespersons

*T*o develop a sales force, a marketing manager decides what kind of salesperson will sell the firm's products most effectively. Most business organizations use several different kinds of sales personnel. Based on the functions performed, salespersons can be classified into three groups: order getters, order takers, and support personnel. One salesperson can, and often does, perform all three functions.

■ *Order Getters*

Order getter   The salesperson who sells to new customers and increases sales to current ones

To obtain orders, a salesperson informs prospects and persuades them to buy the product. The **order getter**'s job is to increase sales by selling to new customers and by increasing sales to present customers. This task sometimes is called creative selling. It requires that salespeople recognize potential buyers' needs and give them necessary information. Order getting is sometimes divided into two categories: current-customer sales and new-business sales.

Current-Customer Sales   Sales personnel who concentrate on current customers call on people and organizations that have purchased products from the firm before. These salespeople seek more sales from existing customers by following up previous sales. Current customers can also be sources of leads for new prospects.

New-Business Sales   Business organizations depend to some degree on sales to new customers. New-business sales personnel locate prospects and convert them into buyers. Salespersons in many industries help generate new business, but industries depending in large part on new-customer sales are real estate, insurance, appliances, heavy industrial machinery, and automobiles.

■ *Order Takers*

Order taker   The salesperson who primarily seeks repeat sales

Taking orders is a repetitive task salespersons perform to perpetuate long-lasting, satisfying customer relationships. **Order takers** seek repeat sales. One major objective is to be

447

certain that customers have sufficient product quantities where and when needed. Most order takers handle orders for standardized products purchased routinely and not requiring extensive sales efforts. The role of order takers is changing, however. Now and in the future they will probably serve as identifiers and problem solvers to better meet the needs of their customers.[5] There are two groups of order takers: inside order takers and field order takers.

Inside Order Takers   In many businesses, inside order takers, who work in sales offices, receive orders by mail and telephone. Certain producers, wholesalers, and even retailers have sales personnel who sell from within the firm rather than in the field. That does not mean that inside order takers never communicate with customers face to face. For example, retail salespersons are classified as inside order takers.

Field Order Takers   Salespersons who travel to customers are outside, or field, order takers. Often customers and field order takers develop interdependent relationships. The buyer relies on the salesperson to take orders periodically (and sometimes to deliver them), and the salesperson counts on the buyer to purchase a certain quantity of products periodically. Use of small computers has improved the field order taker's inventory and order tracking capabilities.

Field and inside order takers are not passive functionaries who simply record orders in a machinelike manner. Order takers generate the bulk of many organizations' total sales.

■ Support Personnel

Support personnel Sales staff members who facilitate the selling function but usually are not involved solely with making sales

Support personnel facilitate selling but usually are not involved solely with making sales. They are engaged primarily in marketing industrial products, locating prospects, educating customers, building goodwill, and providing service after the sale. Although there are many kinds of sales support personnel, the three most common are missionary, trade, and technical.

Missionary salespersons Support salespeople who assist the producer's customers in selling to their own customers

Missionary Salespersons   Missionary salespersons, usually employed by manufacturers, assist the producer's customers in selling to their own customers. Missionary salespersons may call on retailers to inform and persuade them to buy the manufacturer's products. When they succeed, retailers purchase products from wholesalers, who are the producer's customers. Manufacturers of medical supplies and pharmaceuticals often use missionary salespersons, called detail reps, to promote their products to physicians, hospitals, and retail druggists.

Trade salespersons Salespeople mainly involved in helping a producer's customers promote a product

Trade Salespersons   Trade salespersons are not strictly support personnel because they usually take orders as well. However, they direct much effort toward helping customers, especially retail stores, promote the product. They are likely to restock shelves, obtain more shelf space, set up displays, provide in-store demonstrations, and distribute samples to store customers. Food producers and processors commonly employ trade salespersons.

Technical salespersons Support salespeople who give technical assistance to a firm's current customers

Technical Salespersons   Technical salespersons give technical assistance to the organization's current customers, advising them on product characteristics and applications, system designs, and installation procedures. Because this job is often highly technical, the salesperson usually has formal training in one of the physical sciences or in engineering. Technical sales personnel often sell technical industrial products, such as computers, heavy equipment, and steel.

When hiring sales personnel, marketers seldom restrict themselves to a single category because most firms require different types. Several factors dictate how many of each type of salesperson a particular company should have. Product use, characteristics, complexity, and price influence the kind of sales personnel used, as do the number of customers and their characteristics. The types of marketing channels and the intensity and type of advertising also affect the composition of a sales force.

Management of the Sales Force

*T*he sales force is directly responsible for generating one of an organization's primary inputs: sales revenue. Without adequate sales revenue, businesses cannot survive. In addition, a firm's reputation is often determined by the ethical conduct of the sales force. The morale, and ultimately success, of a firm's sales force depend in large part on adequate compensation, room for advancement, adequate training, and management support—all key areas of sales management. When these elements do not satisfy salespeople, they may leave. It is important to evaluate the input of salespeople because effective sales force management has a strong bearing on a firm's success.

We explore eight general areas of sales management: (1) establishing sales force objectives, (2) determining sales force size, (3) recruiting and selecting salespeople, (4) training sales personnel, (5) compensating salespeople, (6) motivating salespeople, (7) managing sales territories, and (8) controlling and evaluating sales force performance.

■ *Establishing Sales Force Objectives*

To manage a sales force effectively, sales managers must develop sales objectives. Sales objectives tell salespersons what they are expected to accomplish during a specified time period. They give the sales force direction and purpose and serve as performance standards for evaluating and controlling sales personnel. Sales objectives should be stated in precise, measurable terms and should specify the time period and geographic areas involved.

Sales objectives are usually developed for both the total sales force and each salesperson. Objectives for the entire force are normally stated in terms of sales volume, market share, or profit. Volume objectives refer to dollar or unit sales. For example, the objective for an electric drill producer's sales force might be to sell $10 million worth of drills or 600,000 drills annually. When sales goals are stated in terms of market share, they usually call for an increase in the proportion of the firm's sales relative to the total number of products sold by all businesses in that industry. When sales objectives are based on profit, they are generally stated in terms of dollar amounts or return on investment.

Sales objectives, or quotas, for individual salespersons are commonly stated in terms of dollar or unit sales volume. Other bases used for individual sales objectives include average order size, average number of calls per time period, and ratio of orders to calls.

■ *Determining Sales Force Size*

Deciding how many salespersons to use is important because it influences the company's ability to generate sales and profits. Moreover, size of the sales force affects the compensation methods used, salespersons' morale, and overall sales force management. Sales force size must be adjusted periodically because a firm's marketing plans change, as do markets and forces in the marketing environment. One danger is to cut back the size of the sales force to increase profits. The sales organization could lose strength and resiliency, preventing it from rebounding when growth occurs or better market conditions prevail.

There are several analytical methods for determining optimal sales force size. One method involves determining how many sales calls per year are necessary for an organization to serve customers effectively and then dividing this total by the average number of sales calls that a salesperson makes annually. A second method is based on marginal analysis, whereby additional salespeople are added to the sales force until the costs of an additional salesperson equals the additional sales generated by that person. Although marketing managers may use one or several analytical methods, they normally temper decisions with subjective judgment.

■ *Recruiting and Selecting Salespeople*

Recruiting Developing a list of qualified applicants for sales positions

To create and maintain an effective sales force, sales managers must recruit the right type of salespeople. **Recruiting** is a process by which the sales manager develops a list of

450

applicants for sales positions. Costs of hiring and training a salesperson are soaring—they are reaching over $60,000 in some industries. Thus recruiting errors are expensive.

To ensure that the recruiting process results in a pool of qualified salespersons from which to hire, a sales manager establishes a set of qualifications before beginning to recruit. Although for years marketers have tried to identify a set of traits characterizing effective salespeople, there is still no set of generally accepted characteristics. A sales manager must determine what set of traits best fits the sales tasks in a particular company. Two activities help establish this set of required attributes. The sales manager should prepare a job description listing specific tasks salespersons are to perform. The manager also should analyze characteristics of the firm's successful salespersons, as well as those of ineffective sales personnel. From the job description and analysis of traits, the sales manager should be able to develop a set of specific requirements and be aware of potential weaknesses that could lead to failure.

A sales manager generally recruits applicants from several sources: departments within the firm, other firms, employment agencies, educational institutions, respondents to advertisements, and individuals recommended by current employees. The specific sources depend on the type of salesperson required and the manager's experiences with particular sources.

The process of recruiting and selecting salespersons varies considerably from one company to another. Companies intent on reducing sales force turnover are likely to have strict recruiting and selection procedures. State Farm Life Insurance Co., for example, strives to retain customers by having low sales force turnover. Applicants for the job of State Farm Insurance agents must endure a yearlong series of interviews, tests, and visits with agents before finding out if they have been hired. In the near future anyone who wants to become a State Farm agent will need to work three years in claims, underwriting, or another department at the national State Farm headquarters. This stringent procedure for recruiting and selection of agents is highly effective in reducing turnover. At State Farm, 80 percent of new agents are still employed four years after being hired. The industry average is only 30 percent retention after four years.[6]

Sales management should design a selection procedure that satisfies the company's specific needs. The process should include steps that yield the information required for making accurate selection decisions. However, because each step incurs a certain amount of expense, there should be no more steps than necessary. Stages of the selection process should be sequenced so that the more expensive steps, such as a physical examination, are near the end. Fewer people will then move through higher-cost stages.

Recruitment should not be sporadic; it should be a continuous activity aimed at reaching the best applicants. The selection process should systematically and effectively match applicants' characteristics and needs with the requirements of specific selling tasks. Finally, the selection process should ensure that new sales personnel are available where and when needed.

■ *Training Sales Personnel*

Many organizations have formal training programs; others depend on informal on-the-job training. Some systematic training programs are quite extensive, whereas others are rather short and rudimentary. Whether the training program is complex or simple, developers must consider what to teach, whom to train, and how to train them.

A sales training program can concentrate on the company, products, or selling methods. Training programs often cover all three. Training for experienced company salespersons usually emphasizes product information, although salespeople must also be informed about new selling techniques and changes in company plans, policies, and procedures. Training programs can be aimed at newly hired salespeople, experienced salespersons, or both. Ordinarily, new sales personnel require comprehensive training, whereas experienced personnel need both refresher courses about established products and training regarding new-product information. Training programs can be directed at the entire sales force or at a segment of it.

Sales training may be done in the field, at educational institutions, in company facilities, or in several of these locations. Some firms train new employees before assign-

The all-new *Professional Selling Skills* (PSS) system—training to build successful business relationships with today's tough customers.

His name is Allan.
He's the prospect of the '90s.

He doesn't play golf
with vendors.
He plays hardball.

He was brought in to get
results. He expects the same
from you.

Do your salespeople know
how to sell to him?

The old approaches to selling don't cut it anymore. Customers today are more knowledgeable, more sophisticated, more demanding. To be effective, your salespeople must become trusted business consultants and advisors, and at the same time, make their numbers.

The *Professional Selling Skills* system helps your salespeople build mutually beneficial business relationships — relationships that produce results for you and your customers.

The all-new system enables your salespeople to identify and understand customer needs — and the business objectives behind them. It teaches them how to offer relevant solutions that position your capabilities in distinctive and compelling ways. And it shows them how to respond to customer indifference and concerns that can stall or block a sale.

Comprised of integrated components for salespeople, sales managers, and trainers, the PSS system ensures that concepts and skills are transferred to the job — and continuously refined.

Built on the skills and strategies that have benefited more than two million sales professionals worldwide, this is the training you need to turn tough prospects like Allan into loyal customers.

For a free brochure that describes the *Professional Selling Skills* system and how it can benefit you and your customers, call or write:

Learning International
225 High Ridge Road
Stamford, CT 06905
1-800-456-9390
extension 56

**Figure 19.4
Provider of Sales
Training Programs**
A number of organizations specialize in providing sales training programs for different types of companies.

**Straight salary
compensation plan**
Paying salespeople a specific amount per time period

**Straight commission
compensation plan**
Paying salespeople according to the amount of their sales in a given time period

**Combination compensation
plan** Paying salespeople a fixed salary plus a commission based on sales volume

ing them to a specific sales position. Others, however, put them into the field immediately, providing formal training only after new salespersons gain a little experience. Training programs for new personnel can be as short as several days or as long as three years; some are even longer. Sales training for experienced personnel is often scheduled when sales activities are not too demanding. Because training of experienced salespeople usually recurs, a firm's sales management must determine the frequency, sequencing, and duration of these efforts.

Sales managers, as well as other salespeople, often engage in sales training—whether daily on the job or periodically during sales meetings. Salespeople sometimes receive training from technical specialists within their own organizations. In addition, a number of outside companies specialize in providing sales training programs (see Figure 19.4). Appropriate materials for sales training programs range from films, texts, manuals, and cases to programmed learning devices and audio- and videocassettes. Lectures, demonstrations, simulation exercises, and on-the-job training can all be effective teaching methods. Choice of methods and materials for a particular sales training program depends on type and number of trainees, program content and complexity, length and location, size of the training budget, number of teachers, and teacher preferences.

■ *Compensating Salespeople*

To develop and maintain a highly productive sales force, a business must formulate and administer a compensation plan that attracts, motivates, and retains the most effective individuals. The plan should give sales management the desired level of control and provide sales personnel with acceptable levels of freedom, income, and incentive. It should be flexible, equitable, easy to administer, and easy to understand. Good compensation programs facilitate and encourage proper treatment of customers. Obviously, it is quite difficult to incorporate all of these requirements into a simple program.

Developers of compensation programs must determine the general level of compensation required and the most desirable method of calculating it. In analyzing the required compensation level, sales management must ascertain a salesperson's value to the company on the basis of the tasks and responsibilities associated with the sales position. Sales managers may consider a number of factors, including salaries of other types of personnel in the firm, competitors' compensation plans, costs of sales force turnover, and nonsalary selling expenses.

Sales compensation programs usually reimburse salespersons for selling expenses, provide some fringe benefits, and deliver the required compensation level. To do that, a firm may use one or more of three basic compensation methods: straight salary, straight commission, or a combination of salary and commission. In a **straight salary compensation plan,** salespeople are paid a specified amount per time period. This sum remains the same until they receive a pay increase or decrease. In a **straight commission compensation plan,** salespeople's compensation is determined solely by sales for a given time period. A commission may be based on a single percentage of sales or on a sliding scale involving several sales levels and percentage rates. In a **combination compensation plan,** salespeople receive a fixed salary plus a commission based on sales volume. Some combination programs require that a salesperson exceed a certain sales level before earning a commission; others offer commissions for any level of sales. Table 19.1 lists major characteristics of each sales force compensation method. Notice that the combination method

451

Table 19.1   Characteristics of Sales Force Compensation Methods

Compensation Method	Frequency of Use (%)*	When Especially Useful	Advantages	Disadvantages
Straight salary	14.6	Compensating new salespersons; firm moves into new sales territories that require developmental work; sales requiring lengthy presale and postsale services	Gives salesperson security; gives sales manager control over salespersons; easy to administer; yields more predictable selling expenses	Provides no incentive; necessitates closer supervision of salespersons; during sales declines, selling expenses remain constant
Straight commission	19.7	Highly aggressive selling is required; nonselling tasks are minimized; company uses contractors and part-timers	Provides maximum amount of incentive; by increasing commission rate, sales managers can encourage salespersons to sell certain items; selling expenses relate directly to sales resources	Salespersons have little financial security; sales manager has minimum control over sales force; may cause salespeople to give inadequate service to smaller accounts; selling costs less predictable
Combination	65.7	Sales territories have relatively similar sales potentials; firm wishes to provide incentive but still control sales force activities	Provides certain level of financial security; provides some incentive; can move sales force efforts in profitable direction	Selling expenses less predictable; may be difficult to administer

*The figures are computed from *Dartnell's 28th Sales Force Compensation Survey,* Dartnell Corporation, Chicago, 1994.

Source: Charles Futrell, *Sales Management* (New York: Dryden Press, 1994), pp. 475–487.

is most popular. When selecting a compensation method, sales management weighs advantages and disadvantages shown in Table 19.1.

■ *Motivating Salespeople*

A sales manager should develop a systematic approach for motivating salespersons to be productive. Motivating should not be reserved for periods of sales decline. Effective sales force motivation is achieved through an organized set of activities performed continuously by the company's sales management. An example of a company engaged in effective sales force motivation is discussed in Inside Marketing (on page 454).

Although financial compensation is important, motivational programs must also satisfy nonfinancial needs. Sales personnel, like other people, join organizations to satisfy personal needs and achieve personal goals. Sales managers must recognize their personnel's motives and goals and attempt to create an organizational climate that lets salespeople satisfy personal needs. Recognition of individual goals is becoming more challenging as cultural diversity increases.

A sales manager can use a variety of positive motivational incentives other than financial compensation. Enjoyable working conditions, power and authority, job security, and opportunity to excel are effective motivators. Salespeople can be motivated by company efforts to make their jobs more productive and efficient.

Sales contests and other incentive programs can also be effective motivators. Sales contests can motivate salespersons to focus on increasing sales or adding new accounts, promote special items, achieve greater volume per sales call, cover territories better, and increase activity in new geographic areas.[7] Some companies find such incentive programs to be powerful motivating tools that marketing managers can use to achieve corporate goals. The advertisements in Figure 19.5 show examples of two incentive programs.

Figure 19.5
Incentive Programs
Companies have access to a variety of incentive programs aimed at motivating salespeople.

Properly designed, incentive programs pay for themselves many times over. In fact, sales managers are relying on incentives more than ever. Recognition programs that acknowledge outstanding performance with symbolic awards, such as plaques or rings, can also be effective. Although some experts believe that the best recognition programs reward less than 30 percent of the sales force at one time, some research efforts indicate that the most successful recognition programs reward 30 to 50 percent.[8] Some organizations use negative motivational measures: financial penalties, demotions, even terminations.

■ Managing Sales Territories

Effectiveness of a sales force that must travel to customers is somewhat influenced by management's decisions regarding sales territories. Sales managers deciding on territories must consider size, shape, routing, and scheduling.

Creating Sales Territories   Several factors enter into designing sales territory size and shape. First, sales managers must construct territories so that sales potentials can be measured. Sales territories often consist of several geographic units for which market data are obtainable, such as census tracts, cities, counties, or states. Sales managers usually try to create territories with similar sales potentials or requiring about the same amount of work. If territories have equal sales potentials, they will almost always be unequal in geographic size. Salespersons with larger territories have to work longer and harder to generate a certain sales volume. Conversely, if sales territories requiring equal amounts of work are created, sales potentials for those territories will often vary. If sales personnel are partially or fully compensated through commissions, they will have unequal income potentials. Many sales managers try to balance territorial workloads and earning potentials by using differential commission rates. Although a sales manager seeks equity when developing and maintaining sales territories, some inequities always prevail.

A territory's size and shape should also help the sales force provide the best possible customer coverage and minimize selling costs. Territory size and shape should take into account customer density and distribution.

Routing and Scheduling Salespeople   Geographic size and shape of a sales territory are the most important factors affecting routing and scheduling sales calls. Next are number and distribution of customers within the territory, followed by sales call frequency and duration. Those in charge of routing and scheduling must consider the sequence in which customers are called on, specific roads or transportation schedules to be used, number of calls to be made in a given period, and time of day calls will occur. In

INSIDE MARKETING

Invacare's Sales Force Never Rests

People with disabilities are leading more active lives, from working outside the home to playing basketball and tennis. What this adds up to is a flourishing U.S. market for wheelchairs, walkers, and other home care and medical equipment. In this intensely competitive field, Invacare Corporation is the world leader, offering over 300 products such as standard, power, superlight, and sports wheelchairs, crutches, canes, walkers, home care beds, and respiratory aids. When Mal Mixon bought Invacare from Johnson & Johnson in 1979, the company was a David dominated by Sunrise Medical, a Goliath six times its size. Its products were limited to standard wheelchairs and a small line of patient aids. Mal Mixon made lowering costs, developing new products, and forming an aggressive sales force his priorities, and at the end of his first year of management, sales had reached $25 million. Since 1979, Invacare has experienced an average 23 percent annual sales growth.

Mixon readily acknowledges that he likes to win, and he conveys that message clearly to his sales force. The company's vice president of sales summarizes Mixon's philosophy as "Sell faster. Sell more. Don't slow down until the customer is happy . . . and the competition is conquered." Invacare believes that its sales force is the best in the industry, characterizing it as a group of resourceful, aggressive, confident "millionaire wannabees." The average annual sales quota is $3.5 million per salesperson, and compensation is based on a 50-50 combination of salary and bonus.

In addition, each Invacare representative is responsible for selling *all* of the more than 300 products that the company manufactures. Invacare's competitors, as well as some industry experts, question whether the company's sales force can maintain expertise in so many product areas. They also question whether sales people can continually thrive under such high pressure to perform. Indeed, Invacare has a reputation for high turnover. Ask those who remain, however, and they report satisfaction with the pace, the compensation, and the unfailing support they get from management.

Sources: Charles Butler, "Mal Bonding," *Sales & Marketing Management*, July 1995, pp. 66–72; Invacare Corporation, press kit; Invacare Corporation, *1994 Annual Report*; and Felicia Paik, "Medical Device Suppliers Show Recovery Signs," *Wall Street Journal*, Jan. 9, 1995, p. B7E.

some firms, salespeople plan their own routes and schedules with little or no assistance from the sales manager; in other organizations, the sales manager draws up the routes and schedules. No matter who plans the routing and scheduling, the major goals should be minimizing salespersons' nonselling time (time spent traveling and waiting) and maximizing selling time. Planners should try to achieve these goals so that a salesperson's travel and lodging costs are held to a minimum.

■ Controlling and Evaluating Sales Force Performance

To control and evaluate sales force activities properly, sales management needs information. A sales manager cannot observe the field sales force daily and so relies on call reports, customer feedback, and invoices. Call reports identify customers called on and present detailed information about interaction with those clients. Traveling sales personnel often must file work schedules indicating where they plan to be during specific time periods.

Dimensions used to measure a salesperson's performance are determined largely by sales objectives, normally set by the sales manager. If an individual's sales objective is stated in terms of sales volume, then that person should be evaluated on the basis of sales volume generated. Even though a salesperson may be assigned a major objective, he or she is ordinarily expected to achieve several related objectives as well. Thus salespeople are often judged along several dimensions. Sales managers evaluate many performance indicators, including average number of calls per day, average sales per customer, actual sales relative to sales potential, number of new-customer orders, average cost per call, and average gross profit per customer.

To evaluate a salesperson, a sales manager may compare one or more of these dimensions with predetermined performance standards. However, sales management commonly compares one salesperson's performance with the performance of other employees operating under similar selling conditions or compares current performance with past performance. Sometimes management judges factors with less direct bearing on sales performance, such as personal appearance, product knowledge, and competitors.

After evaluating salespeople, sales managers take any needed corrective action to improve sales force performance. They may adjust performance standards, provide additional training, or try other motivational methods. Corrective action may demand comprehensive changes in the sales force.

The Nature of Sales Promotion

Sales promotion An activity and/or material meant to induce resellers or salespersons to sell a product or consumers to buy it

As defined in Chapter 17, **sales promotion** is an activity or material (or both) that acts as a direct inducement, offering added value or incentive for the product, to resellers, salespersons, or consumers. It encompasses all promotional activities and materials other than personal selling, advertising, and publicity. In competitive markets, where products are very similar, sales promotion provides additional inducements that encourage product trial and purchase. For example, while keeping its advertising budget about the same, Estée Lauder has increased expenditures on direct-mail sampling and on off-site sampling, such as in health clubs, to generate more product trial.[9]

The use of sales promotion has risen dramatically over the last fifteen years, primarily at the expense of advertising. Figure 19.6 shows the proportion of total promotional dollars spent on sales promotion and advertising. Notice that the proportion spent on sales promotion generally has increased whereas the percentage spent on advertising has declined. This shift in how promotional dollars are used has occurred for several reasons. Heightened concerns about value have made consumers more responsive to promotional offers, especially price promotions, coupons, and point-of-purchase displays. Because of their sheer size and access to scanner data, retailers have become much more powerful relative to manufacturers and are placing greater demands on manufacturers for trade sales promotion efforts that generate retailer profits. Declines in brand loyalty have produced an environment in which sales promotions aimed at convincing customers to

Figure 19.6

Proportion of Promotional Expenditures Allocated to Advertising, Consumer Sales Promotion, and Trade Sales Promotion

Source: From the *"18th Annual Survey of Promotional Practices"* by Carol Wright Promotions, Inc., 1996. Used by permission of Carol Wright Promotions, Inc.

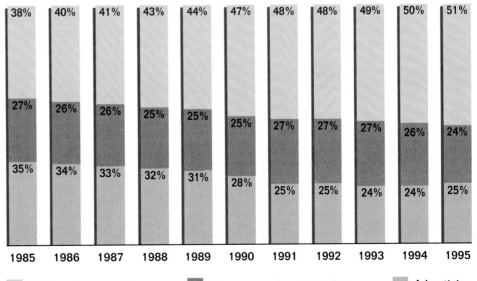

switch brands are more effective. Finally, the stronger emphasis placed on improving short-term performance results calls for greater use of sales promotion methods that yield quick (although perhaps short-lived) sales increases.[10]

An organization often uses sales promotion together with other promotional efforts to facilitate personal selling, advertising, or both. Companies sometimes use advertising and personal selling to support sales promotion activities. For example, marketers frequently use advertising to promote contests, free samples, and premiums. The most effective sales promotion efforts are highly interrelated with other promotional activities. Decisions regarding sales promotion often affect advertising and personal selling decisions, and vice versa.

Sales Promotion Opportunities and Limitations

*S*ales promotion can increase sales by providing extra purchasing incentives. There are many opportunities to motivate consumers, resellers, and salespeople to take desired actions. Some kinds of sales promotion are designed specifically to stimulate resellers' demand and effectiveness; some are directed at increasing consumer demand; and others focus on both resellers and consumers. Regardless of the purpose, marketers must ensure that sales promotion objectives are consistent with the organization's overall objectives, as well as its marketing and promotion objectives.

Although sales promotion can support brand image, excessive price-reduction sales promotion efforts, such as coupons, can negatively affect brand image. Indeed, in the future brand advertising may become more important than sales promotion. Some firms that shifted from brand advertising to sales promotion have lost market share. For example, Minute Maid orange juice (owned by Coca-Cola Foods) experienced its most dramatic sales declines after shifting the majority of advertising spending to sales promotion while one of its major competitors, Tropicana, continued to focus on brand advertising. Tradeoffs exist between these two forms of promotion, and marketing managers must determine the right balance to achieve maximum promotional effectiveness.

Sales Promotion Methods

Consumer sales promotion methods Ways of encouraging consumers to patronize specific stores or to try and/or buy particular products

Trade sales promotion methods Ways of persuading wholesalers and retailers to carry a producer's products and market them aggressively

*M*ost sales promotion methods can be grouped into consumer sales promotion and trade sales promotion. **Consumer sales promotion methods** encourage or stimulate consumers to patronize specific retail stores or try particular products. **Trade sales promotion methods** stimulate wholesalers and retailers to carry a producer's products and to market these products more aggressively.

In deciding which sales promotion methods to use, marketers must take several factors into account. They must consider both product characteristics (size, weight, costs, durability, uses, features, and hazards) and target market characteristics (age, sex, income, location, density, usage rate, and shopping patterns). How products are distributed and the number and types of resellers may determine the type of method used. The competitive and legal environment may also influence the choice.

We examine several consumer and trade sales promotion methods to learn what they entail and what goals they can help marketers achieve.

■ Consumer Sales Promotion Methods

Consumer sales promotion methods used by retailers are often aimed at attracting customers to specific locations, whereas those used by manufacturers are generally directed at introducing new products or promoting established brands. In this section we discuss coupons, demonstrations, frequent-user incentives, point-of-purchase displays, free samples, money refunds, premiums, cents-off offers, and consumer contests and sweepstakes.

Coupons A written price reduction used to encourage consumers to buy a specific product

Coupons Coupons reduce a product's price and are used to prompt customers to try new or established products, to increase sales volume quickly, to attract repeat purchasers, or to introduce new package sizes or features. Savings may be deducted from the purchase price or offered as cash. For best results, the coupons should be easy to recognize and state the offer clearly. The nature of the product (seasonality, maturity, frequency of purchase) is the prime consideration in setting up a coupon promotion.

Coupons are the most widely used consumer sales promotion technique. In 1994, manufacturers distributed over 327 billion coupons. About 88 percent of all consumers use them, and their 1992 savings from coupons amounted to $4.2 billion. When selecting a grocery item brand, 39 percent of survey respondents said that a coupon is very important and 46 percent agreed it is somewhat important.[11]

Coupons are distributed on and in packages, through free-standing inserts (FSIs), print advertising, direct mail, and in stores through shelf dispensers (see Figure 19.7), electronic dispensers, and at check-out counters. According to a recent survey, consumers' preferred methods of receiving coupons are through color leaflets in Sunday newspapers (67 percent) and by mail (59 percent).[12]

When deciding on the proper vehicle for coupons, marketers should consider strategies and objectives, redemption rates, availability, circulation, and exclusivity. The coupon distribution and redemption arena has become very competitive. To draw customers to their stores, grocers double and sometimes even triple the value of customers' coupons.

There are several advantages to using coupons. Print advertisements with coupons are often more effective than nonpromotional advertising for generating brand awareness. Generally, the larger the coupon's cash offer, the better the recognition generated. Another advantage is that coupons reward present product users, win back former users, and encourage purchases in larger quantities. Because they are returned, coupons also let a manufacturer determine whether it reached the intended target market.

Drawbacks of coupon use include fraud and misredemption, which can be expensive for manufacturers. The approximate redemption rate is 2.3 percent, with 25 percent of coupons accepted being misredemptions.[13] Another disadvantage, according to some experts, is that coupons are losing their value: because so many manufacturers offer them, consumers have learned not to buy without some incentive, whether it be a coupon, rebate, or refund. Furthermore, brand loyalty among heavy coupon users has diminished, and many consumers only redeem coupons for products they normally buy. It is believed

**Figure 19.7
Shelf Dispenser for Coupons**
Shelf dispensers of coupons are available in a number of stores.

that about three-fourths of coupons are redeemed by people already using the brand on the coupon. Thus coupons have questionable success as an incentive for consumers to try a new brand or product and then continue using it. An additional problem with coupons is that stores often do not have enough of the coupon item in stock. This situation generates ill will toward both the store and the product.

Demonstrations A sales promotion method manufacturers use temporarily to encourage trial use and purchase of the product or to show how the product works.

Demonstrations   Demonstrations are excellent attention getters. Manufacturers offer them temporarily to encourage trial use and purchase of the product or to show how the product works. Because labor costs can be extremely high, demonstrations are not used widely. They can be highly effective for promoting certain types of products, such as appliances, cosmetics, and cleaning supplies. Cosmetics marketers such as Clinique (owned by Estée Lauder), for example, sometimes offer potential customers "makeovers" to demonstrate product benefits and proper application.

Frequent-User Incentives   Many firms develop incentive programs to reward customers who engage in repeat (frequent) purchases. For example, most major airlines offer frequent-flyer programs through which customers who have flown a specified number of miles are rewarded with free tickets for additional travel. It is estimated that travelers have stockpiled as many as 1.2 trillion miles since the programs began in the early 1980s.[14] Frequent-user incentives foster customer loyalty to a specific company or group of cooperating companies that provide extra incentives for patronage. They are favored by service businesses, such as auto rental agencies, hotels, and credit card companies as well as by consumer goods marketers. An example of a successful frequent-user program is Subway's Sub Club cards; customers earn card stamps with each purchase and redeem completed cards for free sandwiches.

Point-of-purchase (P-O-P) materials Signs, window displays, display racks, and similar means used to attract customers

Point-of-Purchase Displays   Point-of-purchase (P-O-P) materials include outside signs, window displays, counter pieces, display racks, and self-service cartons. Innovations in P-O-P displays include sniff-teasers, which give off a product's aroma in the store as consumers walk within a radius of four feet, and computerized interactive displays. These items, often supplied by producers, attract attention, inform customers, and encourage retailers to carry particular products. A retailer is likely to use point-of-purchase materials if they are attractive, informative, well-constructed, and in harmony with the store. Marketers spend over $16 billion annually on point-of-purchase materials.[15]

Free samples Samples of product given out to encourage trial and purchase

Free Samples   Marketers use **free samples** for several reasons: to stimulate trial of a product, to increase sales volume in the early stages of a product's life cycle, or to obtain desirable distribution. L'Oréal, in launching a line of new foam leave-in conditioners, relied heavily on free samples to increase product awareness.[16] Sampling is the most expensive of all sales promotion methods because production and distribution—at local events, by mail or door-to-door delivery, in stores, and on packages—entail very high costs. In-store sampling is the most frequently used distribution method, although most consumers prefer to get their samples by mail.[17] In designing a free sample, marketers should consider certain factors, such as seasonality of the product, market characteristics, and prior advertising. Free samples usually are not appropriate for slow-turnover products. Despite high costs, use of and expenditures on sampling are increasing. In a given year, it is not unusual for three-fourths of all consumer product companies to use sampling.

Money refunds A sales promotion technique offering consumers some money when they mail in a proof of purchase usually for multiple product purchases

Rebates A customer is sent a specific amount of money for purchasing a single product

Money Refunds and Rebates   With **money refunds,** consumers submit proof of purchase and are mailed a specific amount of money. Usually, manufacturers demand multiple product purchases before consumers qualify for refunds. With **rebates,** the customer is sent a specified amount of money for making a single purchase. These methods, used primarily to promote trial use of a product, are relatively low in cost. Nevertheless, because money refunds sometimes generate a low response rate, they have limited impact on sales.

One of the problems with money refunds and rebates is that many people perceive the redemption process as too complicated. Consumers also have negative perceptions of manufacturers' reasons for offering rebates. They may believe that these are new, untested products or products that haven't sold well. If these perceptions are not changed, rebate offers may degrade the image and desirability of the products being promoted.

Premiums   Items offered free or at a minimum cost as a bonus for purchasing a product

Premiums   **Premiums** are items offered free or at minimum cost as a bonus for purchasing a product. They are used to attract competitors' customers, introduce different sizes of established products, add variety to other promotional efforts, and stimulate consumer loyalty. Inventiveness is necessary, however; if an offer is to stand out and achieve a significant number of redemptions, the premium must match both the target audience and the brand's image. To be effective, premiums must be easily recognizable and desirable. Premiums are placed on or in packages and can also be distributed by retailers or through the mail. Examples include a service station giving free glasses with a fill-up, a free toothbrush available with a tube of toothpaste, or a free plastic storage box given with the purchase of Kraft Cheese Singles.

Cents-off offers   Letting buyers pay less than the regular price to encourage purchase

Cents-Off Offers   When a **cents-off offer** is used, buyers pay a certain amount less than the regular price shown on the label or package. Similar to coupons, this method can be a strong incentive for trying products; it can stimulate product sales, yield short-lived sales increases, and promote products in off-seasons. It is an easy method to control and is often used for specific purposes. However, if used on an ongoing basis, cents-off offers reduce the price for customers who would buy at the regular price and may also cheapen a product's image. In addition, the method often requires special handling by retailers.

Consumer contests   Competitions for prizes intended to generate retail traffic

Consumer Contests and Sweepstakes   In **consumer contests,** individuals compete for prizes based on analytical or creative skills. This method generates retail traffic. Marketers should exercise care in setting up a contest. Problems or errors may anger consumers or result in lawsuits. Contestants are usually more involved in consumer contests than in sweepstakes, even though total participation may be lower. Contests may be used in conjunction with other sales promotion methods, such as coupons.

Consumer sweepstakes   A sales promotion in which entrants submit their names for inclusion in a drawing for prizes

Entrants in **consumer sweepstakes** submit their names for inclusion in a drawing for prizes (see Figure 19.8). Sweepstakes are used to stimulate sales and, as with contests, are sometimes teamed with other sales promotion methods. Sweepstakes are used more often than consumer contests and tend to attract a greater number of participants. Sweepstakes cost considerably less than contests. Successful sweepstakes can generate widespread interest and short-term increases in sales or market share. However, some states prohibit sweepstakes.

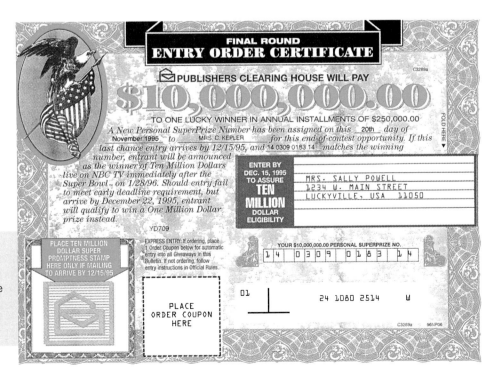

Figure 19.8
Consumer Sweepstakes
Consumer sweepstakes are employed to stimulate sales and are sometimes linked to other promotion methods.

459

■ *Trade Sales Promotion Methods*

To encourage resellers, especially retailers, to carry their products and promote them effectively, producers use sales promotion methods. These include buy-back allowances, buying allowances, scan-back allowances, count and recount, free merchandise, merchandise allowances, cooperative advertising, dealer listings, premium or push money, sales contests, and dealer loaders.

Buy-back allowance Money given to a reseller for each unit bought after an initial deal is over

Buy-Back Allowances A **buy-back allowance** is a sum of money given to a reseller for each unit bought after an initial deal is over. This method is a secondary incentive in which the total amount of money that resellers receive is proportional to their purchases during an initial trade deal, such as a coupon offer. Buy-back allowances foster cooperation during an initial sales promotion effort and stimulate repurchase afterward. The main drawback of this method is expense.

Buying allowance A temporary price reduction to resellers for purchasing specified quantities of a product

Buying Allowances A **buying allowance** is a temporary price reduction to resellers for purchasing specified quantities of a product. A soap producer, for example, might give retailers $1 for each case of soap purchased. Such offers may be an incentive to handle new products, achieve temporary price reductions, or stimulate purchase of items in larger than normal quantities. The buying allowance, which takes the form of money, yields profits to resellers and is simple and straightforward. There are no restrictions on how resellers use the money, which increases the method's effectiveness. One hazard of buying allowances is that customers will buy forward, meaning that they buy large amounts that keep them supplied for many months. Another problem is that competition can match (or beat) the reduced price, which can lower profits for all sellers.[18]

Scan-back allowance A reward given by manufacturers to retailers based on the number of pieces scanned

Scan-Back Allowances A **scan-back allowance** is a manufacturer's reward to retailers based on the number of pieces moved through their scanners during a specific time period. To participate in scan-back programs, retailers usually are expected to pass along savings to consumers through special pricing. Scan-backs are becoming widely used by manufacturers because they directly link trade spending to product movement at the retail level.

Count and recount Payment of a specific amount of money for each product unit moved from a reseller's warehouse in a given period of time

Count and Recount The **count-and-recount** promotion method is based on payment of a specific amount of money for each product unit moved from a reseller's warehouse in a given time period. Units of a product are counted at the start of the promotion and again at the end to determine how many units have moved through the warehouse. This method can reduce retail stockouts by moving inventory out of warehouses and can also clear distribution channels of obsolete products or packages and reduce warehouse inventories. The count-and-recount method might benefit a producer by decreasing resellers' inventories, making resellers more likely to place new orders. However, this method is often difficult to administer and may not appeal to resellers with small warehouses.

Free merchandise A reward given to resellers for purchasing a stated quantity of products

Free Merchandise Free merchandise is sometimes offered to resellers who purchase stated quantities of the same or different products. Occasionally, free merchandise is used as payment for allowances provided through other sales promotion methods. To avoid handling and bookkeeping problems, the giving of free merchandise is usually accomplished by reducing the invoice.

Merchandise allowance A manufacturer's agreement to help resellers pay for special promotional efforts

Merchandise Allowances A **merchandise allowance** is a manufacturer's agreement to pay resellers certain amounts of money for providing promotional efforts, such as advertising or displays. This method is best suited to high-volume, high-profit, easily handled products. Its major drawback is that some retailers perform activities at a minimally acceptable level simply to obtain allowances. Before paying retailers, manufacturers usually verify their performance. Manufacturers hope that retailers' additional promotional efforts will yield substantial sales increases.

Cooperative advertising Sharing of media costs by manufacturer and retailer for advertising the manufacturer's products

Cooperative Advertising Cooperative advertising is an arrangement whereby a manufacturer agrees to pay a certain amount of a retailer's media costs for advertising the manufacturer's products. The amount allowed is usually based on the quantities purchased. Before payment is made, a retailer must show proof that advertisements did appear. These payments give retailers additional funds for advertising. Some retailers exploit cooperative advertising programs by crowding too many products into one advertisement. Surprisingly, not all available cooperative advertising dollars are used. Some retailers cannot afford to advertise; others can afford it but do not want to advertise. A large proportion of all cooperative advertising dollars are spent on newspaper advertisements.

Dealer listings
Ads promoting a product and identifying retailers that sell it

Dealer Listings **Dealer listings** are advertisements promoting a product and identifying participating retailers that sell the product. Dealer listings can influence retailers to carry the product, build traffic at the retail level, and encourage consumers to buy the product at participating dealers.

Premium, or push, money
Extra compensation to sales people for pushing a line of goods

Premium, or Push, Money **Premium,** or **push, money** is additional compensation provided to salespeople by the manufacturer in order to push a line of goods. This promotion method is appropriate when personal selling is an important part of the marketing effort; it is not effective for promoting products sold through self-service. The method often helps manufacturers obtain commitment from the sales force, but it can be very expensive.

Sales contest A means of motivating distributors, retailers, and salespeople by recognizing outstanding achievements

Sales Contests A **sales contest** is designed to motivate distributors, retailers, and sales personnel by recognizing outstanding achievements. To be effective, this method must be equitable for all salespersons involved. One advantage of the method is that it can achieve participation at all distribution levels. However, positive effects may be temporary, and prizes are usually expensive.

Dealer loader
A gift, often part of a display, offered to a retailer who purchases a specified quantity of merchandise

Dealer Loaders A **dealer loader** is a gift to a retailer who purchases a specified quantity of merchandise. Often dealer loaders are used to obtain special display efforts from retailers by offering essential display parts as premiums. For example, a manufacturer might design a display that includes a sterling silver tray as a major component and give the tray to the retailer. Marketers use dealer loaders to obtain new distributors and push larger quantities of goods.

SUMMARY

Personal selling is the process of informing customers and persuading them to purchase products through personal communication in an exchange situation. The three general purposes of personal selling are finding prospects, convincing them to buy, and keeping customers satisfied.

Many salespersons—either consciously or unconsciously—move through a general selling process as they sell products. In prospecting, the salesperson develops a list of potential customers. Before contacting prospects, the salesperson conducts a preapproach that involves finding and analyzing information about prospects and their needs. Approach is the way in which a salesperson contacts potential customers. During the sales presentation, the salesperson must attract and hold the prospect's attention to stimulate interest and desire for the product. If possible, the salesperson should handle objections when they arise. Closing is the stage in the selling process when the salesperson asks the prospect to buy the product or products. After a successful closing, the salesperson must follow up the sale.

In developing a sales force, marketing managers must consider which types of salespersons will sell the firm's products most effectively. The three classifications of salespersons are order getters, order takers, and support personnel. Order getters inform both current customers and new prospects and persuade them to buy. Order takers seek repeat sales and fall into two categories: inside order takers and field order takers. Sales support personnel facilitate selling, but their duties usually extend beyond making sales. The three types of support personnel are missionary, trade, and technical salespersons.

Effectiveness of sales force management is an important determinant of a firm's success because the sales force is directly responsible for generating an organization's sales revenue. Major decision areas and activities on which sales managers must focus are establishing sales force objectives, determining sales force size, recruiting, selecting, training, compensating, and motivating salespeople, managing sales territories, and controlling and evaluating the sales force.

Sales objectives should be stated in precise, measurable terms and specify the time period and geographic areas involved. The size of the sales force must be adjusted occasionally because a firm's marketing plans change, as do markets and forces in the marketing environment.

Recruiting and selecting salespeople involves attracting and choosing the right type of salesperson to maintain an effective sales force. When developing a training program, managers must consider a variety of dimensions, such as who should be trained, what should be taught, and how training should occur. Compensation of salespeople involves formulating and administrating a compensation plan that attracts, motivates, and holds the right types of salespeople for the firm. Motivation of salespeople should allow the firm to attain high productivity. Managing sales territories, another aspect of sales force management, focuses on such factors as size, shape, routing, and scheduling. To control and evaluate sales force performance, sales managers must use information obtained through salespersons' call reports, customer feedback, and invoices.

Sales promotion is an activity or material (or both) that acts as a direct inducement, offering added value or incentive for the product, to resellers, salespersons, or consumers. Marketers use sales promotion to identify and attract new customers, introduce new products, and increase reseller inventories. Sales promotion techniques fall into two general categories: consumer and trade. Consumer sales promotion methods encourage consumers to trade at specific stores or try a specific product. These methods include coupons, demonstrations, frequent-user incentives, free samples, money refunds, premiums, cents-off offers, and consumer sweepstakes and contests. Trade sales promotion techniques stimulate resellers to handle a manufacturer's products and market those products aggressively. These techniques include buy-back allowances, buying allowances, scan-back allowances, count and recount, free merchandise, merchandise allowances, cooperative advertising, dealer listings, premium, or push, money, sales contests, and dealer loaders.

IMPORTANT TERMS

Personal selling
Prospecting
Approach
Closing
Order getter
Order taker
Support personnel
Missionary salespersons
Trade salespersons
Technical salespersons
Recruiting

Straight salary
    compensation plan
Straight commission
    compensation plan
Combination
    compensation plan
Sales promotion
Consumer sales
    promotion methods
Trade sales promotion
    methods

Coupons
Demonstrations
Point-of-purchase (P-O-P)
    materials
Free samples
Money refunds
Rebates
Premiums
Cents-off offers
Consumer contests
Consumer sweepstakes

Buy-back allowance
Buying allowance
Scan-back allowance
Count and recount
Free merchandise
Merchandise allowance
Cooperative advertising
Dealer listings
Premium, or push, money
Sales contest
Dealer loader

DISCUSSION AND REVIEW QUESTIONS

1. What is personal selling? How does personal selling differ from other types of promotional activities?
2. What are the primary purposes of personal selling?
3. Identify the elements of the personal selling process. Must a salesperson include all these elements when selling a product to a customer? Why or why not?
4. How does a salesperson find and evaluate prospects? Do you consider any of these methods questionable ethically? Explain.
5. Are order getters more aggressive or creative than order takers? Why or why not?
6. Identify several characteristics of effective sales objectives.
7. How should a sales manager establish criteria for selecting sales personnel? What do you think are the general characteristics of a good salesperson?
8. What major issues or questions should management consider when developing a training program for the sales force?

9. Explain the major advantages and disadvantages of the three basic methods of compensating salespersons. In general, which method would you prefer? Why?
10. What major factors should be taken into account when designing the size and shape of a sales territory?
11. How does a sales manager—who cannot be with each salesperson in the field on a daily basis—control the performance of sales personnel?
12. What is sales promotion? Why is it used?
13. For each of the following, identify and describe three techniques and give several examples: (a) consumer sales promotion methods and (b) trade sales promotion methods.
14. What types of sales promotion methods have you observed recently? Comment on their effectiveness.

APPLICATION QUESTIONS

1. Briefly describe an experience you have had with a salesperson at a clothing store or when buying an automobile. Identify the steps used by the salesperson and describe them. Did the salesperson skip any steps? What did the salesperson do well? not so well?

2. Refer to your answer to question 1. Would you describe the salesperson as an order getter, an order taker, or a support salesperson? Why? Did the salesperson perform more than one of these functions?

3. Leap Athletic Shoe, Inc., a newly formed company, is in the process of developing a sales strategy. Market research indicates sales management should segment the market into five regional territories. The sales potential for the North region is $1.2 million, $1 million for the West region, $1.3 million for the Central region, $1.1 million for the South Central region, and $1 million for the Southeast region. The firm wishes to maintain some control over the training and sales processes because of the unique features of its new product line, but Leap marketers realize that the salespeople need to be fairly aggressive in their efforts to break into these markets. They would like to provide the incentive needed for the extra selling effort that will be required. What type of sales force compensation method would you recommend to Leap? Why?

4. Consumer sales promotions are aimed at increasing the sales of a particular retail store or product. Identify a familiar type of retail store or product. Recommend at least three sales promotion methods that should be used to promote the store or product. Explain why you would use these methods.

5. Trade sales promotions are used by producers to encourage resellers to promote their products more effectively. Identify which method or methods of sales promotion a producer might use in the following situations, and explain why the method would be appropriate.
   a. a golf ball manufacturer wants to encourage retailers to add a new type of golf ball to current product offerings
   b. a life insurance company wants to increase sales of its universal life products, which have been lagging in sales recently (the company has little control over sales activities)
   c. a light bulb manufacturer with an overproduction of 100-watt bulbs wants to encourage its grocery store chain resellers to increase their bulb inventories

Case 19.1 Chili's Restaurants Take Training Seriously

At Chili's* restaurants, waiters don't usually ask customers, "Have you decided yet?" They are more likely to say something like "How about some spicy chicken wings and cheese fries while you're deciding?" Called "suggestive selling," this technique is one of many that Chili's restaurants train their employees to use. Chili's restaurants are convinced that their well-trained, competent, and friendly staff provide customers with the best service in the restaurant industry, and, at Chili's restaurants, excellent service leads to success. With ten years of consecutive sales increases and average annual sales of over $2 million per restaurant, Chili's restaurants are to casual dining what McDonald's is to fast-food—the one competitors imitate.

For over thirty years, the founder of Chili's restaurants, Norman Brinker, has been shaping the restaurant industry. Convinced that people who eat out want something more upscale than fast-food but more affordable than fine cuisine, Brinker opened Brink's Coffee Shop, offering quality at moderate prices. In the 1970s, he turned a midmarket steakhouse into a nationally successful chain with the creation of Steak & Ale,† and in the 1980s, he bought a Dallas-based gourmet burger chain called Chili's Restaurant. Today,

casual dining is the fastest growing restaurant market in the United States, and Chili's is the market leader. To maintain its number one spot, Chili's continually strives for improvement, whether by adding menu items, increasing portions, or enhancing service through employee training.

To help its staff improve customer service as well as increase sales, Chili's developed a suggestive selling program. Suggestive selling is a set of techniques for recommending menu items without being pushy. Techniques include upgrading, being specific, assuming guests want to buy, describing food, and using props. Upgrading involves encouraging customers to add something to their orders. For example, a server might ask, "Would you like soup with that," or "Be sure to leave room for one of our delicious desserts." By suggesting specific menu items and by learning to describe menu items in creative ways, servers become skilled at whetting customers' appetites.

Chili's employees learn suggestive selling from coworkers, through management supervision, and through training that includes a company-produced video dramatizing the techniques. Training goals include helping employees develop a "selling attitude," building self-confidence, improving appearance, and conveying the meaning of good customer service. To assist managers, Chili's has created a suggestive selling guide that outlines a step-by-step training agenda. During training, managers define suggestive selling, show the videotape, discuss the five suggestive selling techniques, and administer a series of exercises. Managers are sure to highlight the "don'ts" of suggestive selling: don't be pushy; don't stop giving good service if the customer says no; and don't worry if the customer doesn't like a suggestion.

Always looking for ways to enhance its customers' satisfaction, Chili's has created "Sizzle Service," a habit of approaching service that lets customers know that restaurant staff is there to help in any way they can. As part of their Sizzle Service training servers are taught to acknowledge customers quickly, try to take their orders on their first visit to the table, turn in orders before serving appetizers, and return change or charge slips quickly. Training even includes hints for serving specific groups, such as families with children or groups of teenagers. Employees proficient in the steps of Sizzle Service handle their stations more smoothly, help guests choose the best items from the menu, and in general provide customers with an enjoyable dining experience.

Believing that managers are an essential link in creating the Sizzle experience, Chili's provides them with written Sizzle Service guidelines and holds manager-training workshops. Guidelines contain Chili's objec-

tives, an explanation of why managers' attitudes are critical, employee rating forms, sample applicant interviews, and interviewing pointers. At workshops, managers role-play interviews, get tips for judging the friendliness of their staff, and learn how to run training sessions.

Food service workers have one big advantage over other sales personnel. People who walk into a restaurant have already made a decision to buy something. At Chili's restaurants, however, the intent is to do more than sell food. Chili's wants to provide customers with the kind of service that will make them return again and again and bring their friends. The company's extensive training at all levels of employment has been the key to accomplishing this goal.[19]

Questions for Discussion

1. Are the Chili's Restaurant servers order getters, order takers, or support personnel?
2. How do Chili's restaurants motivate their server sales force?
3. What is the role of training efforts at Chili's restaurants, and how important is training to the success of Chili's restaurants?

*Chili's is a registered trademark of Brinker Restaurant Corporation.

†Steak & Ale is a registered trademark of S&A Restaurant Corp.

Case 19.2 Nintendo Competes Through Sales Promotion Efforts

When Hiroshi Yamauchi was 21 years old, he inherited his grandfather's playing card company, Nintendo, Inc., and built it into a videogame empire. By the beginning of the 1990s, Nintendo owned 90 percent of the videogame business and recorded annual sales of $4.7 billion. Among American children, Nintendo's Super Mario character had become more popular than Mickey Mouse. Then, videogame company Sega Systems stormed into the United States with products and promotions that challenged rival Nintendo head on. In just a few years, Nintendo lost half of its European and American market shares to Sega. The once-dominant videogame marketer also found itself scrapping with Sony, PC software developers, and the Internet for a piece of the $15 billion electronic fun industry. To reverse its downward trend, Nintendo turned to numerous sales promotions designed to increase sales and retail visibility and to attract new customers through hands-on play.

Billed as the "largest videogame competition in history," Nintendo's Powerfest was the company's most lavish sales promotion event ever. The videogame tour, which included thirty-eight free-play sampling stations where participants could try new Nintendo games and in-store attractions with premium give-aways and sweepstakes, included cities all over the United States and culminated in a world championship tournament.

From time to time, Nintendo does stage grand-scale promotions such as Powerfest, but its fundamental strategy is to link specific sales promotions to specific products. For example, when the company introduced its Ken Griffey Jr. Major League Baseball videogame, it packed a Griffey baseball card inside the first 500,000 games shipped. To interest kids in the new brightly colored edition of its hand-held video system, the "Play it Loud" Game Boy, Nintendo held a national promotion called "Made in the Shade." At company-sponsored body painting contests using the game's red, yellow, green, and black signature colors, participants sampled the Game Boy system. Those who purchased a Play it Loud Game Boy during the promotion received free Terminator-style sunglasses and an opportunity to buy logo-bearing tank tops, caps, and beach towels at reduced prices.

To launch its Donkey Kong Country II videogame, Nintendo joined Kellogg to create a $15 million promotion that included sweepstakes and premiums. Packages of Apple Jacks, Corn Pops, Frosted Mini-Wheats, and Frosted Flakes contained entries for the Donkey Kong Sweepstakes offering 10,000 prizes including Nintendo systems and games. Cereal buyers could also find free premiums inside boxes of Corn Flakes, Raisin Bran, and four other Kellogg cereals. To maintain interest in the game after its introduction, Nintendo unveiled "Banana Bucks," a sales promotion offering a variety of premiums such as Donkey Kong figurines, apparel, and CDs in exchange for points earned when buying Donkey Kong Country. Many retailers offered special Donkey Kong Land phone cards good for ten minutes of free calls to Nintendo's game tips hotline.

Nintendo of Canada teamed up with General Mills and Smiles 'N Chuckles candy to promote the game in that country. Specially marked packages of several varieties of General Mills cereals contained "Diddy Koins" that customers could redeem for Donkey Kong merchandise. For example, nine coins earned a set of Donkey Kong collectible cards, and thirty-five coins a subscription to the company's monthly magazine, *Nintendo Power*. In addition, everyone mailing in a Diddy Koin merchandise order automatically entered a sweepstakes. Collecting and mailing in points found on Smiles 'N Chuckles candy wrappers earned customers a $10 rebate on the purchase price of a Donkey Kong Country game pack.

Although Nintendo strongly believes in sales promotions that feature premiums and sweepstakes, company executives are convinced that a videogame's most powerful sales promotion tool is sampling. A teenager who plays a game at a mall display is much more likely to want to own it than a teenager who sees a picture of the game in a magazine ad or on a TV commercial. In the case of Virtual Boy, Nintendo's new portable three-dimensional game system, hands-on sampling is essential. Print ads can't display the technology, and even television can't adequately convey the 3-D experience. To give videogame lovers experience with Virtual Boy, Nintendo teamed up with Blockbuster Entertainment for a $5 million sales promotion. At 3,000 Blockbuster stores, customers can rent a Virtual Boy system and two games for two days for $9.99. Renters also get a coupon for $10 off the Virtual Boy $179.95 purchase price.

Recent studies indicate that Americans' interest in videogames is still high, but with so many competitors battling for market share, experts predict that some companies will not survive. To remain a contender in the industry it almost single-handedly created, Nintendo continues to count on successful sales promotion efforts.[20]

Questions for Discussion

1. What types of sales promotion methods has Nintendo employed?
2. In what ways do Nintendo's specific sales promotion efforts provide benefits to the company?
3. Evaluate Nintendo's practice of using product-specific sales promotion efforts rather than linking a sales promotion effort to a broader product line or its total product mix.

STRATEGIC CASE 5

The American Dairy Industry: Got Promotion?

A television commercial begins by panning a room full of papers and artifacts relating to the notorious duel between Aaron Burr and Alexander Hamilton. At a table sits a man spreading peanut butter on a slice of bread. As he takes a big bite, the radio announces the day's random telephone trivia question worth $10,000 to the person answering correctly. The question is, "Who shot Alexander Hamilton in that famous duel?" The phone rings and, of course, the man knows the answer. However, thanks to his mouthful of peanut butter, the words come out sounding like "Awuh Bwuh." Frantically, he tries to pour a glass of milk to wash down his sticky sandwich, but the carton is empty. The radio announcer hangs up. As a dial tone sounds and the scene fades, on the screen appears this phrase: "Got Milk?" In magazine advertisements and on billboards from New York to Hollywood, celebrities like Kate Moss and Pete Sampras proudly wear something mothers have been wiping off children's faces for centuries—milk mustaches. These examples of creative advertising for milk illustrate only a small portion of the American dairy industry's aggressive promotional program designed to increase milk consumption.

Dairy Promoters Struggle to Make Milk Popular

For generations, milk was synonymous with health and nutrition in the minds of Americans. What conveyed the all-American image more than the milkman delivering bottles of fresh milk at dawn or Mom pouring tall, cold glasses of milk to go with her children's after-school snack? Although this image might endure, U.S. milk consumption has been in a steady decline since the 1960s, largely the result of increasing concerns for more healthy eating and the perception that milk contains large amounts of fat.

During the 1980s, national milk promoters tried to counter those perceptions with advertising that touted milk's healthy attributes. Fresh faces and wholesome beauties drank frothy glasses of milk and assured consumers, "Milk. It Does a Body Good." Research revealed that the ads successfully heightened awareness of milk's healthy qualities and convinced many Americans that they should be drinking milk. Despite the dairy industry's investment of millions of dollars to promote its product, however, milk consumption continued to decline. Americans agreed milk did a body good, but each of them continued to drink about sixteen fewer gallons of it every year. Concerned about the failure of past efforts, various organizations within the dairy industry—including the National Dairy Board,

the American Dairy Association, the National Dairy Promotion and Research Board, the United Dairy Industry Association, the Fluid Milk Processor's Association, and various state and local organizations—have banded together in an all-out effort to promote milk as the perfect drink for people of all ages.

Advertising Efforts

Because milk is not a cool or trendy drink, competing with soft drinks is bound to be a losing battle. Therefore, advertising agencies for the dairy industry decided to position milk as an accompaniment to foods that just aren't the same without it. The Got Milk? campaign was born because milk, not Diet Coke or Snapple, is the drink people want with brownies or breakfast cereal. A number of television spots kicked off the $72 million campaign, each one depicting the predicaments of people who need milk but don't have it. A man with a mouthful of chocolate cake pounds on a vending machine that won't release a container of milk. A man who believes he has gone to heaven realizes that he has really gone the other direction when he discovers that all the milk cartons in a giant refrigerator are empty. Although the campaign relies predominantly on television, there are also billboards showing brownies, cookies, and peanut butter sandwiches missing big bites, and the simple tag line, "Got Milk?" Television spots and billboards never mention calcium, strong bones, or healthy skin.

The Got Milk? campaign has won many awards, including an Obie for excellence in outdoor advertising. Follow-up studies show that three months after the premiere of the Got Milk? campaign consumption of milk in one twenty-four-hour period rose 2 percent. Now planning tie-in spots with Nestlé, General Mills, Nabisco, and Kraft, new ads will center around foods people wouldn't think of eating without milk. For example, the long-suffering Trix Rabbit, who has tried all his animated life to steal Trix cereal, finally succeeds. The victory is hollow, however, because when he gets home, he finds he is out of milk.

Unlike the Got Milk? campaign, the dairy industry's $52 million milk mustache advertising campaign *does* focus on the health advantages of drinking skim and low-fat milk. Ads that run in major monthly magazines feature sports figures, musicians, movie stars, and television personalities wearing very noticeable milk mustaches. In slightly humorous ways, each ad highlights a particular health feature that milk provides and includes the tag line, "Milk. What a surprise!" Ice skater Kristi Yamaguchi advocates milk for its potassium and vitamin content. Billy Ray Cyrus promotes milk as a way to reduce dietary fat. Vanna White credits milk's calcium with giving her the perfect white teeth in her famous smile. Model Christie Brinkley reminds pregnant women and nursing mothers that they need extra calcium, and milk is the best way to get it.

Follow-up research reveals that the milk mustache campaign is having an impact on how people perceive milk. In an independent nationwide survey, *USA Today* discovered that of the 523 women polled, 60 percent had seen the ads and 69 percent considered them effective. In addition, the number of respondents who believe milk is good after exercising rose 22 percent, and the number who believe milk is an adult drink rose 22 percent. Encouraged by the campaign's success, the dairy industry plans to expand the program's target audience to include teenage girls and younger women and men. Ads in teen and men's magazines will focus on getting people to substitute milk for water in preparing foods like soups and hot chocolate. Mustaches in those ads will be colored instead of white—red for tomato soup or brown for chocolate milk, for example. Although the campaign will be primarily print-based, marketers plan to increase the number of billboards and bus-stop signage.

Sales Promotion Efforts

To stimulate milk sales and reinforce its advertising message, the dairy industry developed several sales promotions, including contests, sweepstakes, premiums, and rebates. The Milk Mustache Contest asked people to submit photos of themselves wearing milk mustaches. Prizes included cameras and film, with the winner's picture appearing in *Life* magazine. By sending in their answers to three "Test Your Milk Mustache IQ" questions, consumers entered a sweepstakes for a $500 health club membership. Chocolate milk drinkers could receive a premium of fifteen free removable tattoos by sending in proofs of purchase from two gallons of chocolate milk, or a self-liquidating premium of a cow puppet with proofs of purchase and $4.50. To receive a $13 rebate off the price of Reebok sports and fitness videos, milk drinkers could submit proof-of-purchase seals from milk cartons.

Public Relations Efforts

In addition to the extremely visible advertising campaigns and very successful sales promotions, the dairy industry conducts lower-profile but equally important public relations efforts. These keep milk in the spotlight and make it easier for people to learn about milk's positive health attributes. The milk mustache campaign generated a great deal of publicity, showing up on David Letterman's Top 10 List, as an answer on *Jeopardy,* in Jay Leno's *Tonight Show* monologue, and as

a story on the *Saturday Night Live* "Weekend Update." When one of the characters in an episode of Fox Broadcasting's popular family program *Party of Five* looked in the refrigerator and asked, "Got milk?" the resulting publicity augmented the national launch of the Got Milk? print and television campaign.

The dairy industry's public relations efforts also include organized events to generate news about milk and an extensive public education program. National Milk Mustache Week, officially proclaimed in major U.S. cities including New York, Chicago, San Francisco, St. Louis, and Seattle, is a week-long celebration of milk's contribution to women's health. About eighty media markets cover events like the Milk Mustache March in New York City. The industry's toll-free hotline, 1-800-WHY-MILK, provides information about milk ranging from nutritional data to recipes. Consumers who call in can listen to recorded messages on milk-related topics, get answers to specific questions from registered dieticians and nurses, and order free informative brochures such as "Trim with Skim," "Milk. What a Surprise," and "Milk Matters to Mothers-To-Be." In its first year of operation, the toll-free milk line received 72,000 calls, and to date, over 7 million brochures have been distributed.

For years, Americans harbored a number of negative attitudes toward milk: milk is fatty; milk is a kid's drink; milk doesn't taste good; milk causes heart disease. Thanks to the American dairy industry's promotional efforts, these misperceptions are finally fading. For example, more young women believe milk is good for their health, and more people identify milk as a thirst-quenching drink after a workout. Whether positive attitudes toward milk will translate into long-term increased milk consumption is not yet clear.

Questions for Discussion

1. What types of promotional objectives is the American dairy industry attempting to achieve?
2. Assess the dairy industry's approach of advertising milk as an indispensable accompaniment to foods that traditionally go with a glassful, such as brownies and cereal.
3. Why have the milk mustache and Got Milk? campaigns generated significant publicity?
4. Do you believe that the American dairy industry's current promotional efforts will increase long-term milk consumption? Explain your answer.

Sources: National Fluid Milk Processor Promotion Board, press kit, 1995; Wisconsin Milk Marketing Board, press kit; Anthony Vagnoni, "The 1995 Obie Awards," *Advertising Age,* May 8, 1995, p. 66; International Dairy Foods Association, press kit, 1996; National Fluid Milk Processor Promotion Board, *Dairy Foods,* Feb. 1996, pp. 1–7; Ann Hennessey, "Truck Ads Put Milk on the Moove," *Press Enterprise* (Riverside, California), Sept. 29, 1995, p. E1; Betsy Spethmann, "'Got' Goes National," *Brandweek,* Oct. 2, 1995, pp. 20, 24; and T. L. Stanley, "Fox, Dairies Plot Moo Juice Party," *Brandweek,* Oct. 30, 1995, p. 34.

467

Part 6

Pricing Decisions

*I*f an organization is to provide a satisfying marketing mix, the price must be acceptable to target market members. Pricing decisions can have numerous effects on other parts of the marketing mix. For example, a product's price can influence how customers perceive it, what types of marketing institutions are used in distributing the product, and how the product is promoted. In Chapter 20, we discuss the importance of price and look at some of the characteristics of price and nonprice competition. We then examine the major factors that affect marketers' pricing decisions. Eight major stages in the process used by marketers to establish prices are discussed in Chapter 21.

Chapter 20

Pricing Concepts

O B J E C T I V E S

- To understand the nature and importance of price

- To become aware of the characteristics of price and nonprice competition

- To become familiar with various pricing objectives

- To explore key factors that may influence marketers' pricing decisions

- To consider issues affecting the pricing of products for organizational markets

Consumers fill their cereal bowls without emptying their wallets.

*T*o save money, cereal lovers can buy Tootie Fruities instead of Froot Loops, Coco Roos instead of Cocoa Puffs, and Toasty O's instead of Cheerios. They won't find free prizes inside the box as they often do in well-known cereals from Kellogg or General Mills. In fact, these low-cost clones don't even come in boxes, but in clear plastic bags. What they *will* get is a high-quality product for about $1 less a package than they would have paid for their more expensive counterparts. With the price of name brand cereals as high as $5 for a 20-ounce box, increasing numbers of consumers are choosing value-priced, ready-to-eat cereals like those in bags produced by Malt-O-Meal.*

Malt-O-Meal, which has marketed hot cereal since 1919, ventured into the ready-to-eat market in 1975 when it began producing Toasty O's and store brands for Kroger, Safeway, and SuperValu. According to the company's marketing manager, Malt-O-Meal's mission has always been to deliver high quality at low prices. "We sold value," he says, "before value was trendy." Unable to compete with cereal giants like Kellogg, General Mills, and Post when it comes to ad budgets, promotional efforts, and name recognition, Malt-O-Meal competes through price. Company executives are convinced that low prices tempt shoppers to try a bagged cereal, and high quality transforms them into loyal customers. With sales increasing 34.2 percent in one year, Malt-O-Meal's strategy is working.

One of Malt-O-Meal's competitors, Quaker Oats, agrees. To vie for economy-minded shoppers, the number four cereal maker recently began marketing six value-priced cereals packaged in polyurethane bags bearing its smiling logo. Quaker marketers are counting on the Quaker name to attract shoppers and are confident that potential gains will offset the risk of eroding sales of its name brand boxed cereals.

Although Kellogg and Post have recently lowered prices on their cereals, many industry experts—and consumers—believe that these companies are still charging too much. Since 1983, the price of breakfast cereal has risen 90 percent, twice the rate of food overall. Remarked one analyst, "Why should a box of cereal, made of cardboard and containing nothing more than flakes, cost an arm and a leg?" Malt-O-Meal responds that it shouldn't, and prices its cereals accordingly.[1]

*Tootie Fruities, Coco Roos, Toasty O's, and Malt-O-Meal are registered trademarks of the Malt-O-Meal Company.

Malt-O-Meal is using pricing as a tool to compete effectively against the cereal giants. This approach to pricing is successful because the large cereal producers have raised their prices by 90 percent since 1983, and today's value-conscious customers want an affordable selection. In this chapter we focus first on the nature of price and its importance to marketers. We then consider some characteristics of price and nonprice competition. Next we explore the various types of pricing objectives that marketers may establish, and we examine in some detail the numerous factors that can influence pricing decisions. Finally, we discuss selected issues related to the pricing of products for organizational markets.

The Nature of Price

Price Value exchanged for products in a marketing exchange

*T*he purpose of marketing is to facilitate satisfying exchange relationships between buyer and seller. **Price** is the value that is exchanged for products in a marketing transaction. In most marketing situations, the price is very evident, and buyers and sellers are aware of the amount of value that each must give up in order to complete the exchange.[2] However, it is a mistake to believe that price is always money paid. In fact, trading of products—**barter**—is the oldest form of exchange. Money may or may not be involved.

Barter The trading of products

Buyers' interest in price stems from their expectations about the usefulness of a product or the satisfaction they may derive from it. Because buyers have limited resources, they must allocate these resources so that they can obtain the most desired products. Buyers must decide whether the utility gained in an exchange is worth the buying power sacrificed. Almost anything of value—ideas, services, rights, and goods—can be assessed by a price because in our society the financial price is the measurement of value commonly used in exchanges. Consider the value that consumers around the world place on breakfast, as discussed in Global Perspective.

■ Terms Used to Describe Price

Value can be expressed in different terms for different marketing situations. For instance, students pay *tuition* for a college education. Automobile insurance companies charge a *premium* for protection from the cost of injuries or repairs stemming from an automobile accident. An officer who stops you for speeding writes a ticket that requires you to pay a *fine*. If a lawyer defends you, a *fee* is charged, and if you use a railway or taxi, a *fare* is charged. A *toll* is charged for the use of bridges or turnpikes. *Rent* is paid for the use of equipment or an apartment. A *commission* is remitted to a broker for the sale of real estate. *Dues* are paid for membership in a club or group. A *deposit* is made to hold or lay away merchandise. A *tip* helps pay waitresses or waiters for their services. *Interest* is charged for a loan, and *taxes* are paid for government services. Although price may be expressed in a variety of ways, it is important to remember that the purpose of this concept is to quantify and express the value of the items in a market exchange.

■ The Importance of Price to Marketers

As pointed out in Chapter 10, developing a product may be a lengthy process. It takes time to plan promotion and to communicate benefits. Distribution usually requires a long-term commitment to dealers that will handle the product. Often price is the only thing a marketer can change quickly to respond to changes in demand or to the actions of competitors. Under certain circumstances, however, the price variable may be relatively inflexible.

Price is also a key element in the marketing mix because it relates directly to the generation of total revenue. The following equation is an important one for the entire organization:

$$\text{Profits} = \text{Total Revenues} - \text{Total Costs}$$

or

$$\text{Profits} = (\text{Prices} \times \text{Quantities Sold}) - \text{Total Costs}$$

The Price of Breakfast Around the World

At the Third Empire hotel in France, the cheapest room costs $330 a night, and dinner for two with wine can run as high as $500. The next morning, boiled and scrambled eggs with chives, marinated raw salmon, smoked ham, salami, a platter of cheeses, fresh and preserved fruits, and bread costs $36 a person. On the other hand, at a little diner in Montreal a breakfast platter of two eggs, bacon, toast, hash brown potatoes, and juice costs under $2. From country to country and city to city around the world, the price of breakfast varies dramatically, even for the same food.

A recent study compared the price of a breakfast consisting of toast, cereal, eggs, and milk in the United States and ten other countries. To get each item separately at the lowest price would require traveling around the world. Bread is least expensive in London, eggs in Bangkok, and milk in Mexico. To buy all of the ingredients for this breakfast in the United States, grocery shoppers pay about $9.79. Breakfast in Rome or Tokyo costs more. For the same items in Rome, the cash register receipt totals $11.60, and in Tokyo a very expensive $23.12. Shoppers in Mexico City and London, however, get breakfast for the bargain price of under $7.

To make breakfast more interesting, several U.S. cereal makers are using ingredients such as pecans, almonds, dried blueberries, cherries, and exotic grains. Packaged elegantly with gold foil in boxes adorned with watercolor art, some upscale varieties cost breakfast eaters about $5 for a 12-to-16-ounce package. Although this price seems high to Americans, Tokyo residents have to pay almost $8 for a 16-ounce box of plain old corn flakes or boring bran. In Manila and Singapore as well, shoppers pay premium prices for ordinary cereals. Paying only $1.85 for a 16-ounce box, Londoners get the best cereal deal of all the cities surveyed.

Why does the price of a simple meal range from affordable to outrageous depending on where you eat it? Several factors affect the price of an American-style breakfast in foreign countries. First, the exchange rate for U.S. dollars affects prices. For example, when the dollar's value fell in Europe, the price of breakfast in Brussels rose about $3. Second, a locale's cost of living in general influences the cost of specifics such as breakfast food. Finally, breakfast costs are determined by supply and demand. In Japan, for example, because milk and cereal are not popular foods, supplies of these American breakfast staples are limited and prices high.

Sources: Jennifer Fulkerson, "The Continental Breakfast," *American Demographics,* July 1995, pp. 18–20; Jonathan Dahl, " Travel: Shop Around to Avoid Europe's High Prices," *Wall Street Journal,* Apr. 14, 1995, p. B9; Betsy Spethmann, "Cereal Chic," *Brandweek,* Aug. 7, 1995, pp. 26–28; Anthony Marshall, "It Doesn't Take a Fool to Spy Erratic Pricing," *Hotel & Motel Management,* Apr. 24, 1995, p. 13; Jacqueline Simmons, "Travel: Canada, A Welcome Break for Americans," *Wall Street Journal,* June 23, 1995, p. B11; and Paul Levy, "The Mobile Guide: Three Stars, Three Figures," *Wall Street Journal,* May 17, 1995, p. A18.

Prices affect an organization's profits in several ways since price is a major component of the profit equation and can be a major determinant of the quantities sold. Furthermore, total costs are influenced by quantities sold.

Because price has a psychological impact on customers, marketers can use it symbolically. By pricing high, they can emphasize the quality of a product and try to increase the prestige associated with its ownership. By lowering a price, marketers can emphasize a bargain and attract customers who go out of their way to save a small amount of money. Thus, as this chapter details, price can have a strong effect on a firm's sales and profitability.

Price and Nonprice Competition

*T*he competitive environment strongly influences the marketing mix decisions associated with a product. Pricing decisions are often made according to the price or nonprice competitive situation in a particular market. Price competition exists when consumers have difficulty distinguishing competitive offerings and marketers emphasize low prices. Nonprice competition involves a focus on marketing mix elements other than price.

THE SUGGESTED RETAIL PRICE OF THIS SHIRT IS $125. WE HAVE A SUGGESTION FOR WHOEVER SUGGESTED IT.

Designer clothes 40-75% off, every day. New York City, Manhasset, L.I. & New Jersey.

DAFFY'S

CLOTHES THAT WILL MAKE YOU, NOT BREAK YOU.

Figure 20.1
Price Competition
Daffy's, an off-price specialty store, engages in price competition.

474

■ *Price Competition*

Price competition
Emphasizing price and matching or beating competitors' prices

When engaging in **price competition,** a marketer emphasizes price as an issue and matches or beats the prices of competitors (see Figure 20.1). To compete effectively on a price basis, a firm should be the low-cost seller of the product. If all firms producing goods in an industry charge the same price, the firm with the lowest costs is the most profitable. Firms that stress low price as a key element in the marketing mix tend to market standardized products. A seller competing on price may change prices frequently or at least must be willing and able to do so. Whenever competitors change their prices, the seller usually responds quickly and aggressively.

Price competition gives a marketer flexibility. Prices can be altered to account for changes in the firm's costs or in demand for the product. If competitors try to gain market share by cutting prices, an organization competing on a price basis can react quickly to such efforts. However, a major drawback of price competition is that competitors, too, have the flexibility to adjust their prices. Thus they can quickly match or beat a company's price cuts and a price war may ensue. Chronic price wars, such as those in the airline industry, can substantially weaken organizations.

■ *Nonprice Competition*

Nonprice competition
Emphasizing factors other than price in relation to competitors' products

Nonprice competition occurs when a seller decides not to focus on price and instead emphasizes distinctive product features, service, product quality, promotion, packaging, or other factors to distinguish its product from competing brands. Thus nonprice competition allows a company to increase its brand's unit sales through means other than changing the brand's price. A major advantage of nonprice competition is that a firm can build customer loyalty toward its brand. If customers prefer a brand because of nonprice factors, they may not be easily lured away by competing firms and brands. But when price is the primary reason that customers buy a particular brand, a competitor is able to attract such customers through price cuts.

Nonprice competition is workable under the right conditions. A company must be able to distinguish its brand through unique product features, higher product quality, promotion, packaging, or excellent customer service. For example, through research that included a survey of 2,000 motorists, Mobil determined that only about 20 percent of gasoline purchasers are highly price-sensitive. Based on this research, Mobil introduced its "friendly serve" concept, which includes free full service, immaculate restrooms, occasional free coffee or newspapers, and calling regular customers by name.[3] Buyers not only must be able to perceive these distinguishing characteristics but must also view them as important. The distinguishing features that set a particular brand apart from its competitors should be difficult, if not impossible, for competitors to imitate. Finally, the organization must extensively promote the distinguishing characteristics of the brand to establish its superiority and to set it apart from competitors in the minds of buyers.

Still, a marketer trying to compete on a nonprice basis cannot simply ignore competitors' prices. It must be aware of them and will probably price its brand near or slightly above competing brands. Therefore, price remains a crucial marketing mix component even in environments that call for nonprice competition.

Pricing Objectives

Pricing objectives
Overall goals that describe what a firm wants to achieve through pricing efforts

Pricing objectives are overall goals that describe what the firm wants to achieve through its pricing efforts. Because pricing objectives influence decisions in many functional areas, including finance, accounting, and production, the objectives must be consistent with the organization's overall mission and goals. Besides short- and long-term pricing objectives, a marketer may also use multiple pricing objectives. For instance, a firm may wish to increase market share by 18 percent over the next three years, achieve a 15 percent return on investment, and promote an image of quality in the marketplace. In this section, we examine a few of the pricing objectives that companies might set for themselves. The major pricing objectives and typical actions associated with them are shown in Table 20.1.

■ *Survival*

A fundamental pricing objective is survival. Most organizations will tolerate difficulties, such as short-run losses and internal upheaval, if they are necessary for survival. Because price is a flexible variable, it is sometimes used to increase sales volume to levels that match the organization's expenses.

■ *Profit*

Although businesses may claim that their objective is to maximize profits for their owners, the objective of profit maximization is rarely operational because its achievement is difficult to measure. Because of this difficulty, profit objectives tend to be set at levels that the owners and top-level decision makers view as satisfactory. Specific profit objectives may be stated in terms of actual dollar amounts or in terms of percentage change relative to profits of a previous period.

Table 20.1   Pricing Objectives and Typical Actions Taken to Achieve Them

Objective	Possible Action
Survival	Adjust price levels so that firm can increase sales volume to match organizational expenses
Profit	Identify price and cost levels that allow firm to maximize profit
Return on investment	Identify price levels that enable firm to yield targeted ROI
Market share	Adjust price levels so that firm can maintain or increase sales relative to competitors' sales
Cash flow	Set price levels to encourage rapid sales
Status quo	Identify price levels that help stabilize demand and sales
Product quality	Set prices to recover research and development expenditures and establish high-quality image

■ *Return on Investment*

Pricing to attain a specified rate of return on the company's investment is a profit-related pricing objective. Most pricing objectives based on return on investment (ROI) are achieved by trial and error because not all cost and revenue data needed to project the return on investment are available when prices are set. General Motors uses ROI pricing objectives.

■ *Market Share*

Market share, which is a product's sales in relation to total industry sales, can be an appropriate pricing objective. Many firms establish pricing objectives to maintain or increase market share. For years both Coca-Cola and PepsiCo have set pricing objectives aimed at gaining market share. Many firms recognize that high relative market shares often translate into higher profits. The Profit Impact of Market Strategies (PIMS) study conducted over the last twenty-five years has shown that both market share and product quality heavily influence profitability.[4] Thus marketers often use increasing market share as a primary pricing objective.

Maintaining or increasing market share need not depend on growth in industry sales. Remember that an organization can increase its market share even though sales for the total industry are decreasing. On the other hand, an organization's sales volume may increase while its market share within the industry decreases if the overall market is growing.

■ *Cash Flow*

Some organizations set prices to recover cash as fast as possible. Financial managers are understandably interested in quickly recovering capital spent to develop products. This objective may have the support of the marketing manager who anticipates a short product life cycle.

Although it may be acceptable in some situations, the use of cash flow and recovery as an objective oversimplifies the value of price in contributing to profits. A disadvantage of this pricing objective could be high prices, which might allow competitors with lower prices to gain a large share of the market.

■ *Status Quo*

In some cases, an organization may be in a favorable position and, desiring nothing more, may set an objective of status quo. Status quo objectives can focus on several dimensions—maintaining a certain market share, meeting (but not beating) competitors' prices, achieving price stability, or maintaining a favorable public image. A status quo pricing objective can reduce a firm's risks by helping stabilize demand for its products. The use of status quo pricing objectives sometimes minimizes pricing as a competitive tool, leading to a climate of nonprice competition in an industry.

■ *Product Quality*

A company might have the objective of product quality leadership in the industry. This goal normally dictates a high price to cover the high product quality and, in some instances, the high cost of research and development. Crayola Tempera and Canon products are priced to reflect and emphasize high product quality (see Figure 20.2). As previously mentioned, the PIMS study has shown that both product quality and market share are good indicators of profitability. The products and brands that customers perceive to be of high quality are more likely to survive in a competitive marketplace. High quality usually enables a marketer to charge higher prices for the product. For example, Bill McAlpin, owner of a 1,000-acre coffee plantation in Costa Rica, developed a higher-quality coffee bean, which allowed him to charge coffee roasters $3.50 per pound of beans instead of the $1 market price.[5] However, marketers cannot continue to raise prices unless they simultaneously improve their relative quality.[6]

476

Figure 20.2
Product Quality
Pricing Objectives
Pricing of these products is based on product quality pricing objectives.

Factors Affecting Pricing Decisions

*P*ricing decisions can be complex because of the number of factors that must be considered. Frequently, there is considerable uncertainty about the reactions to price on the part of buyers, channel members, competitors, and others. Price is also an important consideration in marketing planning, market analysis, and sales forecasting. It is a major issue when assessing a brand's position relative to competing brands. Most factors that affect pricing decisions can be grouped into one of the eight categories shown in Figure 20.3. In this section we explore how each of these eight groups of factors enters into price decision making.

Figure 20.3
Factors That Affect Pricing Decisions

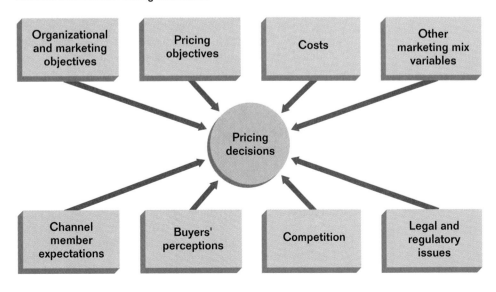

■ *Organizational and Marketing Objectives*

Marketers should set prices that are consistent with the organization's goals and mission. For example, a retailer trying to position itself as value-oriented may wish to set prices that are quite reasonable relative to product quality. In this case, a marketer would not want to set premium prices on products but would strive to price products in line with this overall organizational goal.

The firm's marketing objectives must also be considered. Decision makers should make pricing decisions that are compatible with the organization's marketing objectives. Say, for instance, that one of a producer's marketing objectives is a 12 percent increase in unit sales by the end of the next year. Assuming that buyers are price-sensitive, increasing the price or setting a price above the average market price would not be in line with the firm's sales objective.

■ *Types of Pricing Objectives*

The type of pricing objectives a marketer uses obviously has considerable bearing on the determination of prices. An objective of a certain target return on investment requires that prices be set at a level that will generate a sales volume high enough to yield the specified target. A market share pricing objective usually causes a firm to price a product below competing brands of similar quality to attract competitors' customers to the company's brand. A marketer sometimes uses temporary price reductions in the hope of gaining market share. A cash flow pricing objective may cause an organization to set a relatively high price, which can place the product at a competitive disadvantage. However, this type of objective is more likely to be addressed by using temporary price reductions, such as sales, rebates, and special discounts.

■ *Costs*

Clearly, costs must be an issue when establishing price. A firm may temporarily sell products below cost to match competition, to generate cash flow, or even to increase market share, but in the long run it cannot survive by selling its products below cost. Even when a firm has a high-volume business, it cannot survive if each item is sold slightly below what it costs. A marketer should be careful to analyze all costs so that they can be included in the total cost associated with a product.

To maintain market share and revenue in an increasingly price-sensitive market, many marketers have concentrated on reducing costs. Labor-saving technologies, a focus on quality, and efficient manufacturing processes have brought productivity gains that translate into reduced costs and lower prices for customers. In an industry ravaged by labor concerns and monetary losses, Southwest Airlines has managed to stay one step ahead of its larger rivals. Southwest is the low-fare leader on more of the top one hundred routes in the United States than the three largest airlines, American, Delta, and United. One reason for the Texas-based airline's success is its ability to control costs. It costs Southwest 7 cents to fly one seat one mile versus 8.5 cents for American and 9 cents for United and Delta. Southwest's cost savings are then passed on to the air traveler.[7]

Besides considering the costs associated with a particular product, marketers must also take into account the costs that the product shares with others in the product line. Products often share some costs, particularly the costs of research and development, production, and distribution. Most marketers view a product's cost as a minimum, or floor, below which the product cannot be priced. We discuss cost analysis in more detail in Chapter 21.

■ *Other Marketing Mix Variables*

All marketing mix variables are highly interrelated. Pricing decisions can influence decisions and activities associated with product, distribution, and promotion variables. A product's price frequently affects the demand for the item. A high price, for instance, may result in low unit sales, which in turn may lead to higher production costs per unit.

Conversely, lower per-unit production costs may result from a low price. For many products, buyers associate better product quality with a high price and poorer product quality with a low price. This perceived price/quality relationship influences customers' overall image of products or brands. Sony, for example, prices its television sets higher than average to help communicate that Sony television sets are high-quality electronic products. Consumers recognize the Sony brand name, its reputation for quality, and the prestige associated with buying the product. Individuals who associate quality with a high price are likely to purchase products with well-established and recognizable brand names.[8]

The price of a product is linked to several dimensions of its distribution. Premium-priced products are often marketed through selective or exclusive distribution; lower-priced products in the same product category may be sold through intensive distribution. For example, Cross pens are distributed through selective distribution, and Bic pens through intensive distribution. When setting a price, the profit margins of marketing channel members, such as wholesalers and retailers, must be considered. Channel members must be adequately compensated for the functions they perform.

Price may determine how a product is promoted. Bargain prices are often included in advertisements, whereas premium prices are less likely to appear in advertising messages. Premium price is sometimes included in advertisements for upscale items, such as luxury cars or fine jewelry. Higher-priced products are more likely to require personal selling efforts than lower-priced ones. Furthermore, the price structure can affect a salesperson's relationship with customers. A complex pricing structure takes longer to explain to customers, is more likely to confuse the buyer, and may cause misunderstandings that result in long-term customer dissatisfaction. For example, the pricing structures of many airlines are complex and frequently confuse ticket sales agents and travelers alike.

■ *Channel Member Expectations*

When making price decisions, a producer must consider what distribution channel members expect. A channel member certainly expects to receive a profit for the functions it performs. The amount of profit expected depends on what the intermediary could make if it were handling a competing product instead. Also, the amount of time and the resources required to carry the product influence intermediaries' expectations.

Channel members often expect producers to give discounts for large orders and prompt payment. At times, resellers expect producers to provide several support activities, such as sales training, service training, repair advisory service, cooperative advertising, sales promotions, and perhaps a program for returning unsold merchandise to the producer. These support activities clearly have costs associated with them, and a producer must consider these costs when determining prices.

■ *Buyers' Perceptions*

When making price decisions, marketers should pose this vital question: How important is the price to people in the target market? The importance of price can vary from market segment to market segment and from person to person. It can also vary across different product categories, and buyers may have a range of acceptable prices for different product categories. Furthermore, consumers' perceptions of price may be influenced by all the products in a firm's product line. The perception of price depends on a product's actual price and consumers' expectations regarding price. For example, customers expect that most new cars are priced too high and that car dealers will sell their cars for lower negotiated prices. As discussed in Inside Marketing (on the following page), car buyers can use car-buying services on the Internet, such as AutoAdvantage or AutoMall and get no-haggle prices, thus avoiding price negotiations.

Buyers' perceptions of a product relative to competing products may allow a firm to set a price that differs significantly from the prices of competing products. If the product is deemed superior to most of the competition, a premium price may be feasible. However, even products with superior quality can be overpriced. Columbia Sportswear had to discontinue its upscale youth sportswear line because it was priced too high.[9] Strong brand loyalty sometimes provides the opportunity to charge a premium price. On

479

INSIDE MARKETING

Buying a Car on the Internet: No Pressure, No Haggling

According to a recent survey, Americans find purchasing an automobile "the most anxiety-provoking and least satisfying of any retail experience." They dislike tenacious salespeople wielding high-pressure tactics; they quake at haggling over what seem to be arbitrary prices; and in the end, they know they'll drive off wondering, "Did I pay too much?" What many prospective car buyers are discovering, however, is that there is a less traumatic way to shop. They can go instead to the Internet to purchase a new car from a vast selection at no-haggle prices. On the cutting edge of this new kind of auto retailing are Auto-By-Tel, AutoAdvantage, and AutoMall.

Shopping for new cars over the Internet allows some consumers to save as much as $1,500 off the lowest price they could get by going to a regular auto dealer. Many consumers make poor decisions on auto price negotiations because they lack adequate information. Over one-third of all new car purchases are made by consumers without any negotiating for a lower price. Compared with the dreaded ordeal of negotiating with every auto dealer in town, the Internet is providing a powerful and persuasive tool for getting the best price. An Internet search engine, All Things Automotive Directory, provides addresses and "hot links" to connect the consumer with most automobile addresses on the Internet. The All Things Automotive Directory's Internet address is xwww.webcom.com/autodir.

Objective online information is available about prices and options, including four-color photos of models. AutoAdvantage and AutoMall, two of the better-known buying services, promise to get buyers the best price on new cars and light trucks. These services may charge a fee or require the consumer to join a club. Auto-By-Tel, which helps customers negotiate a final price, earns its fee from dealers who have signed on with the firm. The customer picks up the car at the designated local dealer. Auto-By-Tel promises to deliver the lowest price with the least amount of stress that a consumer can have in purchasing an automobile. Consumers can key in exactly what they are looking for—model, year, options, even color—and within forty-eight hours, they get a call-back with a no-haggle price. Even for consumers who opt for the traditional purchase through a dealership, the online services provide valuable information for securing the lowest price.

Sources: Keith Naughton, Kathleen Kerwin, Bill Vlasic, Lori Bongiorno, and David Leonhardt, "Revolution in the Showroom," *Business Week,* Feb. 19, 1996, pp. 70–76; Jesse Birnbaum, "No Need to Kick the Tires," *Time,* Feb. 19, 1996, p. 50; and Paul A. Eisenstein, "Car Shopping on the Internet," *World Traveler,* Apr. 1996, pp. 10, 12, 77.

---

the other hand, if buyers view the product unfavorably (assuming that they are not extremely negative), a lower price may be required to generate sales. There is a considerable body of research on the relationship between price and consumers' perceptions of quality. Consumers use price as an indicator of quality when brands are unfamiliar and the perceived risk of making unsatisfactory choices is high. They also rely on price if there is little information available and a product's attributes are difficult to judge.[10]

Buyers can be characterized according to their degree of value consciousness, price consciousness, and prestige sensitivity. Marketers who understand these characteristics are better able to set pricing objectives and policies. **Value-conscious** consumers are concerned about both price and quality aspects of a product. On the other hand, **price-conscious** individuals strive to pay low prices. Individuals who are **prestige-sensitive** focus on purchasing products that signify prominence and status.[11]

■ *Competition*

A marketer needs to know competitors' prices so that the firm can adjust its own prices accordingly. This does not mean that a company will necessarily match competitors' prices; it may set its price above or below theirs. However, for some organizations (such as airlines), matching competitors' prices is an important strategy for survival.

Value-conscious
Concerned about price and quality aspects of a product

Price-conscious
Striving to pay low prices

Prestige-sensitive
Drawn to products that signify prominence and status

When adjusting prices, a marketer must assess how competitors will respond. Will competitors change their prices and, if so, will they raise or lower them? In Chapter 2 we describe several types of competitive market structures. The structure that characterizes the industry to which a firm belongs affects the flexibility of price setting. For example, due to reduced pricing regulation, firms in the telecommunications industry have moved from a monopolistic market structure to an oligopolistic market structure, which has resulted in significant price flexibility and price competition (see Figure 20.4).

When an organization operates as a monopoly and is unregulated, it can set whatever prices the market will bear. However, the company may avoid pricing the product at the highest possible level for fear of inviting government regulation or in order to penetrate a market by using a lower price. If the monopoly is regulated, it normally has less pricing flexibility; the regulatory body lets it set prices that generate a reasonable, but not excessive, return. A government-owned monopoly may price products below cost to make them accessible to people who otherwise could not afford them. Transit systems, for example, are sometimes operated this way. However, government-owned monopolies sometimes charge higher prices to control demand. In states with state-owned liquor stores, the price of liquor tends to be higher than in states where liquor stores are not owned by a government body.

In an oligopoly, there are only a few sellers and the barriers to competitive entry are high. The automotive, mainframe-computer, and steel industries exemplify oligopolies. A company in such industries can raise its price, hoping that its competitors will do the same. When an organization cuts its price to gain a competitive edge, other companies are likely to follow suit. Thus very little advantage is gained through price cuts in an oligopolistic market structure.

481

Figure 20.4

Changes in Competitive Market Structure Leads to Greater Price Flexibility   Changes in the competitive market structure of the telecommunications industry over the last 15 years have led to greater price flexibility and competition.

A market structure characterized by monopolistic competition means numerous sellers with differentiated product offerings. The products are differentiated by physical characteristics, features, quality, and brand images. The distinguishing characteristics of its product may allow a company to set a different price than its competitors. However, firms in a monopolistic competitive market structure are likely to practice nonprice competition, discussed earlier in this chapter.

Under conditions of perfect competition, there are many sellers. Buyers view all sellers' products as the same. All firms sell their products at the going market price, and buyers will not pay more than that. This type of market structure, then, gives a marketer no flexibility in setting prices.

■ Legal and Regulatory Issues

As discussed in Chapter 2, legal and regulatory issues can influence pricing decisions. To curb inflation, the federal government may invoke price controls, freeze prices at certain levels, or determine the rates at which prices can be increased. In some states, regulatory agencies set prices on such products as insurance, dairy goods, and electricity.

Many regulations and laws affect pricing decisions and activities. The Sherman Antitrust Act prohibits conspiracies to control prices, and in interpreting the act, courts have ruled that price fixing among firms in an industry is illegal. Marketers must refrain from fixing prices by developing independent pricing policies and setting prices in ways that do not even suggest collusion. Both the Federal Trade Commission Act and the Wheeler-Lea Act prohibit deceptive pricing. In establishing prices, marketers must guard against deceiving customers.

The Robinson-Patman Act has had a strong impact on pricing decisions. For various reasons, marketers may wish to sell the same type of product at different prices. Provisions in the Robinson-Patman Act, as well as those in the Clayton Act, limit the use of such price differentials. The practice of providing price differentials that tend to injure competition by giving one or more buyers a competitive advantage relative to other buyers is called **price discrimination**; it is prohibited by law. However, not all price differentials are discriminatory. Marketers can use them if the price differentials do not hinder competition, if the price differentials result from differences in the costs of selling or transportation to various customers, or if the price differentials arise because the firm has had to cut its price to a particular buyer to meet competitors' prices.

Price discrimination
Practice of providing price differentials that injure competition by giving one or more buyers a competitive advantage

Pricing for Organizational Markets

*O*rganizational markets consist of individuals and organizations that purchase products for resale, for use in their own operations, or for producing other products. Establishing prices for this category of buyers is sometimes different from setting prices for consumers. Organizational markets have experienced much change because of economic uncertainty, sporadic supply shortages, and an increasing interest in service. Differences in the size of purchases, geographic factors, and transportation considerations require sellers to adjust prices. In this section, we discuss several issues unique to the pricing of organizational products, including discounts, geographic pricing, and transfer pricing.

■ Price Discounting

Producers commonly provide intermediaries with discounts or reductions from list prices. Although there are many types of discounts, they usually fall into one of five categories: trade, quantity, cash, seasonal, and allowances.

Trade, or functional, discount A reduction off the list price given by a producer to an intermediary for performing certain functions

Trade Discounts   A reduction off the list price given by a producer to an intermediary for performing certain functions is called a **trade, or functional, discount.** A trade discount is usually stated in terms of a percentage or series of percentages off the list price. Intermediaries are given trade discounts as compensation for performing various functions, such as selling, transporting, storing, final processing, and perhaps providing credit services. Although certain trade discounts are often a standard practice within an industry, discounts do vary considerably among industries. It is important that a manufacturer provide a trade discount large enough to offset the intermediary's costs, plus a reasonable profit, to entice the reseller to carry the product. For example, QMS, Inc., a producer of high-quality, moderately priced laser-jet printers, offered retailers a trade discount that was too low to cover retailers' costs of ordering, displaying, and selling QMS printers. Thus retailers simply did not order the printer, leaving $71 million in printers in QMS warehouses. QMS had to borrow money to help cover the carrying costs of this excess inventory.[12]

Quantity discounts
Deductions from list price for purchasing large quantities

Cumulative discounts
Quantity discounts aggregated over a stated period of time

Noncumulative discounts
One-time reductions in price based on specific factors

Cash discount
A price reduction given to buyers for prompt payment or cash payment

Seasonal discount
A price reduction given to buyers for purchasing goods or services out of season

Allowance A concession in price to achieve a desired goal

Quantity Discounts   Deductions from list price that reflect the economies of purchasing in large quantities are called **quantity discounts.** Price quantity discounts are used to pass to the buyer cost savings gained through economies of scale.

Quantity discounts can be either cumulative or noncumulative. **Cumulative discounts** are quantity discounts aggregated over a stated period of time. Purchases of $10,000 in a three-month period, for example, might entitle the buyer to a 5 percent, or $500, rebate. Such discounts are supposed to reflect economies in selling and encourage the buyer to purchase from one seller. **Noncumulative discounts** are one-time reductions in prices based on the number of units purchased, the dollar value of the order, or the product mix purchased. Like cumulative discounts, these discounts should reflect some economies in selling or trade functions.

Cash Discounts   A **cash discount,** or price reduction, is given to a buyer for prompt payment or cash payment. Accounts receivable are an expense and a collection problem for many organizations. A policy to encourage prompt payment is a popular practice and sometimes a major concern in setting prices.

Discounts are based on cash payments or cash paid within a stated time. For example, "2/10 net 30" means that a 2 percent discount will be allowed if the account is paid within ten days. However, if the buyer does not make payment within the ten-day period, the entire balance is due within thirty days without a discount. If the account is not paid within thirty days, interest may be charged.

Seasonal Discounts   A price reduction to buyers who purchase goods or services out of season is a **seasonal discount.** As shown in Figure 20.5, for example, the Chase Development Center offers a lower price during July and August due to reduced demand for its facilities during this time. These discounts let the seller maintain steadier production during the year. For example, automobile rental agencies offer seasonal discounts in winter and early spring to encourage firms to use automobiles during the slow months of the automobile rental business.

Allowances   Another type of reduction from the list price is an **allowance,** or concession in price to achieve a desired goal. Trade-in allowances, for example, are price reductions granted for turning in a used item when purchasing a new one. Allowances help give the buyer the ability to make the new purchase. This type of discount is popular in the aircraft industry. Another example is promotional allowances, which are price reductions granted to dealers for participating in advertising and sales support programs intended to increase sales of a particular item.

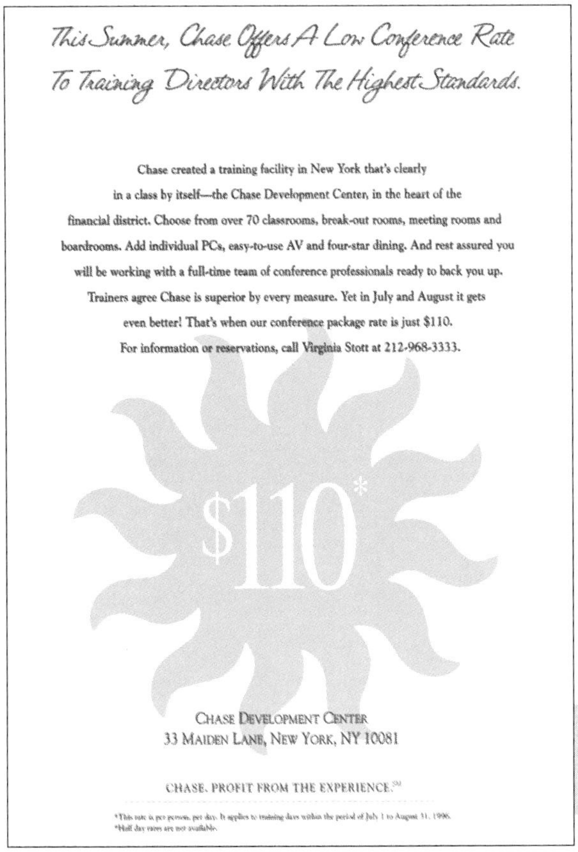

Figure 20.5
Seasonal Discounts   The Chase Development center offers a price reduction during July and August.

■ *Geographic Pricing*

Geographic pricing
Reductions for transportation and other costs due to the physical distance between buyer and seller

Geographic pricing involves reductions for transportation costs or other costs associated with the physical distance between the buyer and the seller. Prices may be quoted as being F.O.B. (free-on-board) factory or destination. An **F.O.B. factory** price indicates the price of the merchandise at the factory, before it is loaded onto the carrier vehicle, and thus excludes transportation costs. The buyer must pay for shipping. An **F.O.B. destination** price means that the producer absorbs the costs of shipping the merchandise to the customer. This policy may be used to attract distant customers. Although F.O.B. pricing is an easy way to price products, it is sometimes difficult for marketers to administer, especially when a firm has a wide product mix or when customers are dispersed widely. Because customers will want to know about the most economical method of shipping, the seller must keep abreast of shipping rates.

F.O.B. factory The price of the merchandise at the factory, before shipment

F.O.B. destination A price indicating that the producer is absorbing shipping costs

Uniform geographic pricing
Charging all customers the same price, regardless of geographic location

To avoid the problems involved in charging different prices to each customer, **uniform geographic pricing,** sometimes called postage-stamp pricing, may be used. The same price is charged to all customers regardless of geographic location, and the price is based on average shipping costs for all customers. Gasoline, paper products, and office equipment are often priced on a uniform basis.

Zone pricing Adjusting regional prices for major geographic zones as the transportation costs increase

In **zone pricing,** regional prices take advantage of a uniform pricing system; prices are adjusted for major geographic zones as the transportation costs increase. For example, a Florida manufacturer's prices may be higher for buyers on the Pacific Coast and in Canada than for buyers in Georgia.

Base-point pricing
Geographic pricing combining factory price and freight charges from the base point nearest the buyer

Base-point pricing is a geographic pricing policy that includes the price at the factory, plus freight charges from the base point nearest the buyer. This approach to pricing has virtually been abandoned because its legal status has been questioned. The policy resulted in all buyers paying freight charges from one location, such as Detroit or Pittsburgh, regardless of where the product was manufactured.

Freight absorption pricing
Absorption of all or part of the actual freight costs by the seller

When the seller absorbs all or part of the actual freight costs, **freight absorption pricing** is being used. The seller might choose this method because it wishes to do business with a particular customer or to get more business; more business will cause the average cost to fall and counterbalance the extra freight cost. This strategy is used to improve market penetration and to retain a hold in an increasingly competitive market.

■ *Transfer Pricing*

Transfer pricing
Prices charged in sales between an organization's units

When one unit in an organization sells a product to another unit, **transfer pricing** occurs. The price is determined by one of the following methods:

Actual full cost: calculated by dividing all fixed and variable expenses for a period into the number of units produced

Standard full cost: calculated on what it would cost to produce the goods at full plant capacity

Cost plus investment: calculated as full cost, plus the cost of a portion of the selling unit's assets used for internal needs

Market-based cost: calculated at the market price less a small discount to reflect the lack of sales effort and other expenses

The choice of a method of transfer pricing depends on the company's management strategy and the nature of the units' interaction. An organization must also ensure that transfer pricing is fair to all units involved in the purchases.

Summary

Price is the "value" that is exchanged for products in marketing transactions. Price is not always money paid; barter, the trading of products, is the oldest form of exchange. Price is a key element in the marketing mix because it relates directly to the generation of total revenue. The profit factor can be determined mathematically by multiplying price by quantity sold to get total revenues, and then subtracting total costs. Price is the only variable in the marketing mix that can be adjusted quickly and easily to respond to changes in the external environment.

A product offering can compete on either a price or a nonprice basis. Price competition emphasizes price as the product differential. Prices fluctuate frequently, and price competition among sellers is aggressive. Nonprice competition emphasizes product differentiation through distinctive features, services, product quality, or other factors. Establishing brand loyalty by using nonprice competition works best when the product can be physically differentiated and the customer can recognize these differences.

Pricing objectives are overall goals that describe the role of price in a firm's long-range plans. The most fundamental pricing objective is the organization's survival. Price can be easily adjusted to increase sales volume or to combat competition so that the organization can stay alive. Profit objectives, which are usually stated in terms of sales dollar volume or percentage change, are normally set at a satisfactory level rather than at a level designed for profit maximization. A sales growth objective focuses on increasing the profit base by increasing sales volume. Pricing for return on investment (ROI) has a specified profit as its objective. A pricing objective to maintain or increase market share implies that market position is linked to success. Other types of pricing objectives include cash flow and recovery, status quo, and product quality.

Eight factors enter into price decision making: organizational and marketing objectives, pricing objectives, costs, other marketing mix variables, channel member expectations, buyers' perceptions, competition, and legal and regulatory issues. When setting prices, marketers should make decisions consistent with the organization's goals and mission. Pricing objectives heavily influence price-setting decisions. Most marketers view a product's cost as the floor below which a product cannot be priced. Because of the interrelation of the marketing mix variables, price can affect product, promotion, and distribution decisions. The revenue that channel members expect for their functions must also be considered when making price decisions.

Buyers' perceptions of price vary. Some consumer segments are sensitive to price, but others may not be; thus before determining price, a marketer needs to be aware of its importance to the target market. Knowledge of the prices charged for competing brands is essential for the firm so that it can adjust its prices relative to those of competitors. Government regulations and legislation influence pricing decisions. Congress has enacted several laws to enhance competition in the marketplace by outlawing price fixing and deceptive pricing. Legislation also restricts price differentials that injure competition and sometimes result in price discrimination. Moreover, the government can invoke price controls to curb inflation.

Unlike consumers, organizational buyers purchase products to use them in their own operations or for producing other products. When adjusting prices, organizational sellers take into consideration the size of the purchase, geographic factors, and transportation requirements. Producers commonly provide discounts off list prices to intermediaries. The categories of discounts include trade, quantity, cash, seasonal, and allowances. A trade discount is a price reduction for performing such functions as storing, transporting, final processing, or providing credit services. If an intermediary purchases in large enough quantities, the producer gives a quantity discount, which can be either cumulative or noncumulative. A cash discount is a price reduction for prompt payment or payment in cash. Buyers who purchase goods or services out of season may be granted a seasonal discount. A final type of reduction from the list price is an allowance, such as a trade-in allowance.

Geographic pricing involves reductions for transportation costs or other costs associated with the physical distance between the buyer and the seller. A price quoted as F.O.B. factory means that the buyer pays for shipping from the factory. An F.O.B. destination price means that the producer pays for shipping; this is the easiest way to price products, but it is difficult for marketers to administer. When the seller charges a fixed average cost for transportation, the practice is known as uniform geographic pricing. Zone prices take advantage of a uniform pricing system adjusted for major geographic zones as the transportation costs increase. Base-point pricing resembles zone pricing; prices are adjusted for shipping expenses incurred by the seller from the base point nearest the buyer. A seller who absorbs all or part of the freight costs is using freight absorption pricing.

IMPORTANT TERMS

Price	Prestige-sensitive	Cash discount	Uniform geographic
Barter	Price discrimination	Seasonal discount	pricing
Price competition	Trade, or functional,	Allowance	Zone pricing
Nonprice competition	discount	Geographic pricing	Base-point pricing
Pricing objectives	Quantity discounts	F.O.B. factory	Freight absorption pricing
Value-conscious	Cumulative discounts	F.O.B. destination	Transfer pricing
Price-conscious	Noncumulative discounts		

DISCUSSION AND REVIEW QUESTIONS

1. Why are pricing decisions so important to an organization?
2. Compare and contrast price and nonprice competition. Describe the conditions under which each form works best.
3. How does a pricing objective of sales growth and expansion differ from an objective to increase market share?
4. Why must marketing objectives and pricing objectives be considered when making pricing decisions?
5. In what ways do other marketing mix variables affect pricing decisions?
6. What types of expectations may channel members have about producers' prices, and how do these expectations affect pricing decisions?
7. How do legal and regulatory forces influence pricing decisions?
8. Compare and contrast a trade discount and a quantity discount.
9. What is the reason for using the term F.O.B.?
10. What are the major methods used for transfer pricing?

APPLICATION QUESTIONS

1. Price competition is evident in industries such as fast-food, air travel, and personal computers. Discuss a recent situation in which companies had to meet or beat a competitor's price in a price competitive industry. Did you benefit from this situation? Did it change your perception of the companies and/or their products?
2. Buyers' perceptions of a product and its price are an important influence on marketers' pricing decisions. Value consciousness, price consciousness, and prestige sensitivity are three ways of describing these perceptions. Discuss how these three characteristics influence the buying decision process for the following products:

   a. a new house
   b. weekly groceries for a family of five
   c. an airline ticket
   d. a soft drink from a vending machine

3. Organizations often use multiple pricing objectives. Locate an organization that uses several pricing objectives, and discuss how this approach influences marketing mix decisions. Are some objectives oriented toward the short term and others toward the long term? How does the marketing environment influence these objectives?

Case 20.1   Low Prices and Fun: The Winning Combination at Southwest Airlines

The 1980s and early 1990s were tough times for the U.S. airline industry. Fierce price competition—"price wars"—in which one company would announce drastic price cuts only to have them matched by already troubled rivals, was commonly cited as leading to the downfall of many industry members. Between 1990 and 1992 alone, companies representing roughly 40 percent of the total capacity of the airline industry either ceased operations or began operating under Chapter 11 bankruptcy protection. Most of the companies that somehow did manage to survive this brutally competitive period lost enormous sums of money. However, one industry competitor, Southwest Airlines, seemed consistently to fly high above the rest of the struggling field, showing a profit for twenty-one consecutive years.

In 1967, Texas businessman Rollin King and lawyer Herb Kelleher established Air Southwest Company. Originally, King and Kelleher planned to fly only within Texas, linking Dallas, San Antonio, and Houston with low-priced, frequent flights. Almost immediately, airline companies then serving the Texas market filed suit against the upstart competitor, claiming that the market was already sufficiently served. However, after several years of legal maneuvering, the Texas Supreme Court ruled in favor of the newly renamed Southwest Airlines, and the company made its initial flight between Dallas and San Antonio. At that time, the fledgling carrier had just three Boeing 737s in its fleet.

Playing on the name of its home airport—Dallas's Love Field—Southwest initially featured "love" as the theme of ad campaigns, while flight attendants clad in hot pants served "love potions" (drinks) and "love bites" (peanuts) on early company flights. Such unconventional practices established Southwest as a maverick in the airline industry. Much to both the surprise and the disappointment of its competitors, the tiny airline not only survived the early years, but proceeded to cultivate a loyal following in its home state as an underdog up against "the big airlines." Today, Southwest owns more than 140 Boeing 737s, employs more than 13,000 people, flies to over forty U.S. cities coast to coast, and serves its passengers almost 50 million bags of peanuts a year.

In 1978, the company's present CEO, Herb Kelleher, took over the company and quickly gained the spotlight as what some might call a master of the bizarre. One Southwest advertisement featured Kelleher—dressed as Elvis, with sideburns and white jumpsuit—dancing about an airport. Unlike most airlines, whose ticket agents and flight attendants must dress in businesslike uniforms, Southwest allows personnel to wear casual clothing like polo shirts, shorts, and sneakers. Southwest may be the only U.S. company that requires its employees to laugh. Two interview questions asked of potential employees are (1) Tell me how you recently used your sense of humor in a work environment, and (2) Tell me how you have used humor to defuse a difficult situation. When the company became the official airline of San Antonio–based Sea World (Texas) in 1986, it painted a 737 to resemble Shamu, the park's famous killer whale. That same year, the company introduced its highly successful Fun Fares program featuring bargain basement prices—some fares as low as $19—to encourage customers to fly "just for the fun of it."

Industry experts acknowledge that Southwest Airlines has permanently changed air travel in the United States. Value-conscious consumers now drive the market, and Southwest gives them plenty of bargains from which to choose. Without advance purchase, they can fly one-way from Cleveland to Baltimore for $19, or from Chicago to Baltimore for $29. From Los Angeles, commuters can get a one-way ticket to San Jose for $29. The airline also has twenty-one-day, advance-purchase fares that are half the price of its regular fares. Asked if such pricing practices are meant to harm competitors and if Southwest could make money with such a low pricing structure, Kelleher explained that the company can indeed turn a profit—it had done so before when

charging even lower prices. In a nationally run advertisement, Kelleher vows to "nuke" the competition in any and all fare wars.

Southwest's phenomenal success, however, has spawned several imitators, intensifying competition and threatening its profitability and position as America's top airline. USAir, Continental, United, and Delta are all trying Southwest's formula for success: low fares, on-time flights, and no-frills service. In addition, three airline reservation systems partially owned by Southwest's rivals ousted the airline from their computer systems, making it difficult for travel agents to make reservations or write tickets for Southwest. In 1994, the company's fourth-quarter earnings fell 47 percent below those for the same period the previous year. As a result, Southwest raised its fares $3 to $7 on some routes in some markets. Fares on its 465 daily flights in the highly competitive California market, however, did not go up. In addition, Southwest made all advance-purchase tickets nonrefundable.

While an uncertain future looms for both the airline industry and many of the individual companies in it, Southwest stands out as an exception. Its emphasis on giving customers what they want and no more—low prices and basic but personal service—keeps it the industry's benchmark for thrifty operating costs and enviable profitability. According to the 1994 Airlines Quality Rating, Southwest is the nation's number one major airline based on fares, on-time performance, customer satisfaction, number of accidents, financial viability, baggage complaints, and age of the fleet.[13]

Questions for Discussion

1. Price competition within the industry has driven many airlines out of business or into bankruptcy protection. Why has Southwest Airlines been so successful in competing on the basis of price?
2. What are Southwest's primary pricing objectives?
3. Discuss any possible negative aspects of the low market-entry pricing strategy employed by Southwest.

Case 20.2   Denny's Competes Through Value Pricing

In recent years, customers have been deserting moderately priced family restaurants for one of two types of establishments. Those who want a quick meal at low prices go to fast-food giants like McDonald's, Taco Bell, and Burger King. Those who want atmosphere and don't mind paying higher prices go to casual dining chains such as Applebee's and Chili's. To fight back, many family restaurants are doing one of two things. Some are

going after upscale diners by improving service and atmosphere. Others, such as Denny's, leader of the mid-range family restaurant segment, are taking on the fast-food business primarily by competing through price.

Serving more than 1 million customers a day, Denny's is the largest full-service family restaurant chain in the United States. Since its introduction of the Grand Slam Breakfast in the late 1970s, Denny's has been whetting appetites for lower-priced meals. Its offer of two eggs, two pancakes, and two pieces of bacon or sausage for $1.99 set the industry standard for the value-meal concept. In the early 1990s, Denny's rolled back the price of the Grand Slam Breakfast to its original price and, more recently, introduced five additional breakfast entrees under $1.99 and fourteen other breakfast value meals. Available from 5:00 A.M. until 10:00 P.M., these "Breakaway Value Meals" include choices such as the $2.99 Super Slam, like the original but with three of everything; a three-egg omelet stuffed with cheddar cheese, hash browns, and homestyle buttermilk biscuits for $2.99; the French Slam featuring French toast; and such other "slams" as the Southern, Harvest, and Grand Slam Slugger. To promote its new breakfast menu, Denny's launched a new advertising campaign featuring television and radio spots as well as print ads. Gone is the old slogan, "$1.99—are you out of your mind?" Underscoring the greater variety of penny-pinching breakfast combinations is the new slogan, "Have You Ever Had to Make Up Your Mind?"

Recently, Denny's has expanded its breakfast value strategy to include lunch and dinner. Lunch Basket Specials include a choice of three entrees—hamburger, popcorn shrimp, or a chicken pita sandwich—each for $2.99. For $2.99, $3.99, or $4.99, lunchtime customers can also choose from ten different Breakaway Lunch Values, such as a basket of chicken strips or a freshly made deli salad. At dinner, Denny's has even introduced prime rib for $5.99.

Although few family restaurants are going head-to-head with Denny's Grand Slam prices, many are countering with similar value-oriented promotions. International House of Pancakes features its "Rooty Tooty Fresh 'N Fruity" breakfast for $2.99, and Houston-based Kettle restaurants lowered prices on four breakfast combinations to $1.99 to match Denny's price. In addition, Kettle introduced $2.99 lunch specials and $3.99 dinner specials.

With competition intensifying, Denny's realizes that to maintain its leadership position, price is not enough. In response to a customer survey revealing that people perceive Denny's restaurants as old and tired looking, the company is updating the decor in all of its 1,500 restaurants in 49 states. Trendy new colors, brighter lighting, and a new logo are all part of the makeover.

Industry analysts applaud improvements in Denny's ambiance, but at the same time they recognize that Denny's most effective means of competing is its value-pricing strategy, and the chain's management agrees. According to a Denny's spokesperson, reviving the Grand Slam Breakfast helped increase Denny's traffic 8.6 percent in one year. By reinforcing its commitment to serving quality food at low prices, Denny's has solidified its reputation as the segment's low-price leader.[14]

Questions for Discussion

1. What are the major benefits of value pricing? the major drawbacks?
2. In what ways are Denny's marketers assessing the chain's target market's evaluation of price?
3. What type of pricing method does Denny's primarily use?

Chapter 21

Setting Prices

OBJECTIVES

- To understand eight major stages of the process used to establish prices

- To explore issues connected with developing pricing objectives

- To grasp the importance of identifying the target market's evaluation of price

- To gain insight into demand curves and the price elasticity of demand

- To examine the relationships among demand, costs, and profits

- To learn about analyzing competitive prices

- To understand the different types of pricing policies

- To become familiar with the major kinds of pricing methods

For thrifty consumers, Lamborghini's new economy model is a bargain at $85,000.

*T*he same person who thinks nothing of spending $3,200 for an Armani suit would probably have no trouble writing a $245,000 check for a Lamborghini Diablo SE. After all, what is "too much" to pay for an automobile that has been described as "kinetic sculpture," "a car and an amusement park ride wrapped into one," and "ranking up there with a room full of Van Gogh originals"? Anyone who has to ask the price of a Lamborghini sports car probably cannot afford one.

Ferruccio Lamborghini, an Italian tractor manufacturer, introduced Lamborghini sports cars in 1963. Until 1987, the company never had an organized sales and marketing program in North America. The sports cars sold themselves, with distributors and individual dealers importing cars for specific customers. These buyers were paying for vertical hydraulic doors, glove-like leather seats, and breath-taking performance—the car reaches 110 mph without shifting into fifth gear. On today's vehicles, for $5,000 more they could add a rear wing, and for $900 a CD player, raising the total price to about a quarter of a million dollars.

In the value-sensitive 1990s, Lamborghini has had a difficult time maintaining sales for models that can cost as much $320,000. To counter consumer concerns about affordability, the company has taken several steps. For instance, Lamborghini plans to introduce two new, lower-priced models: one of its sports cars will sell for around $110,000, and a sport utility vehicle will be priced close to $85,000, which is slightly higher than its nearest competitor. Those who cannot afford to buy a Lamborghini Diablo VT can lease one for a $52,000 down payment and $2,999 a month.

Intensifying its marketing efforts, Lamborghini advertises in elite business and travel publications such as *Departures,* a magazine for American Express Platinum Card members. A direct mail campaign targets 50,000 households with incomes of at least $1.5 million. Sales promotions include offering reporters Diablo VT test drives and teaming up with Circuit City to display the sports car in its stores.

Lamborghini sells about 300 Diablo cars worldwide each year, about 120 of them to American customers. By 2000, the company hopes to have established thirty American dealerships and to have sold 1,500 cars in the United States. With a minimum sticker price of almost $100,000, accomplishing that goal certainly presents a challenge for Lamborghini.[1]

1 **Development of pricing objectives**

2 **Assessment of target market's evaluation of price**

3 **Determination of demand**

4 **Analysis of demand, cost, and profit relationships**

5 **Evaluation of competitors' prices**

6 **Selection of a pricing policy**

7 **Selection of a pricing method**

8 **Determination of a specific price**

Figure 21.1
Stages for Establishing Prices

The price of a Lamborghini is clearly a distinguishing component of this product's marketing mix. The car's price alone sets it apart from every other auto on the market, giving it an ultra-exclusive image. Setting prices of products requires careful analysis of numerous issues. In this chapter we examine eight stages of a process that marketers can use when setting prices. Figure 21.1 illustrates these eight stages. Stage 1 is the development of a pricing objective that is congruent with the organization's overall objectives and its marketing objectives. In stage 2, the target market's evaluation of price must be assessed. Then, in stage 3, marketers should examine the nature and price elasticity of demand. Stage 4, which consists of analyzing demand, cost, and profit relationships, is necessary for estimating the economic feasibility of alternative prices. Evaluation of competitors' prices, which constitutes stage 5, helps determine the role of price in the marketing strategy. Stage 6 is the selection of a pricing policy, or the guidelines for using price in the marketing mix. Stage 7 involves choosing a method for calculating the price charged to customers. Stage 8, determining the final price, depends on environmental forces and marketers' understanding and use of a systematic approach to establishing prices. These stages are not rigid steps that all marketers must follow but rather guidelines that provide a logical sequence for establishing prices.

Development of Pricing Objectives

*I*n Chapter 20 we discussed the various types of pricing objectives. Developing pricing objectives is an important task because pricing objectives form the basis for decisions about other stages of pricing. Thus pricing objectives must be stated explicitly, and the statement should include the time frame for accomplishing them.

Marketers must make sure that the pricing objectives they set fit in with the organization's overall objectives and marketing objectives. Inconsistent objectives cause internal conflicts and confusion and can prevent the organization from achieving its overall goals. Normally, organizations have multiple pricing objectives, some short-term and others long-term. In response to changing market conditions, a marketer typically alters pricing objectives over time.

Figure 21.2
Target Market's Evaluation of Price Customers may expect prices of products to be lower for children and seniors than for adults who are not senior citizens.

ADULTS $8. CHILDREN $5.
SENIOR CITIZENS $5. SALMON FREE.

Grizzly Bears. Now At The NC Zoo, Asheboro.

Assessment of the Target Market's Evaluation of Price

Despite the general assumption that price is a major issue for buyers, the importance of price depends on the type of product, the type of target market, and the purchase situation. For example, buyers are probably more sensitive to gasoline prices than to luggage prices. With respect to the type of target market, non-senior adults may have to pay more than seniors or children for the same products (see Figure 21.2). The purchase situation also affects the buyer's view of price. Most moviegoers would never pay in other situations the prices charged for soft drinks, popcorn, and candy at movie concession stands. By assessing the target market's evaluation of price, a marketer is in a better position to know how much emphasis to put on price. Information about the target market's price evaluation may also help a marketer determine how far above the competition a firm can set its prices.

The 1990s has become the "born-to-bargain-hunt" decade, as customers demand lower prices, shop warehouse clubs, and patronize supermarkets offering double coupons. Because consumers are making do with less expensive products and shopping more selectively, manufacturers and retailers are focusing on the value of their products. Value combines a product's price and quality attributes, which are used by consumers to differentiate competing brands. Consumers are looking for a good deal on a product that provides a better value for their money.[2] As discussed in Global Perspective, Japanese consumers are attracted to larger-size General Electric refrigerators sold at lower prices because of the value associated with these appliances. Understanding the importance of a product to customers, as well as their expectations of quality, helps marketers correctly assess the target market's evaluation of price.

Determination of Demand

Determining the demand for a product is the responsibility of marketing managers, who are aided in this task by marketing researchers and forecasters. Marketing research and forecasting techniques yield estimates of sales potential, or the quantity of a product that could be sold during a specific period. These estimates are helpful in establishing the relationship between a product's price and the quantity demanded.

GE and Kojima: Big Size Plus Low Price Equals Great Value

It is generally assumed that Japanese consumers prefer small refrigerators manufactured by Japanese appliance companies such as Hitachi, Matsushita, Sharp, or Toshiba. Conventional wisdom dictates that in Japan, bulky American refrigerators will not sell at any price. Experts were surprised, therefore, when Kojima, Japan's second-largest appliance retailer, made a deal to sell General Electric refrigerators in its 159-store chain throughout Japan.

Because of space constraints in their homes and their habit of shopping daily, most Japanese have traditionally purchased smaller refrigerators than Americans do, and they pay high prices to get them. For a small apartment-size model, Japanese shoppers spend about $1,300. Japan, however, is changing. A slowing economy is creating demand for cheaper products, and an increasing number of working women means fewer are buying groceries every day. Big, inexpensive refrigerators make sense, but Japanese manufacturers don't make them. Enter Kojima Corporation.

When Kojima approached GE, the American company already had an arrangement with Toshiba to guide its appliances through Japan's complicated distribution system. Toshiba's strategy, however, was to market refrigerators as luxury items at about $2,400 each. Persuading General Electric to sell 100,000 refrigerators directly to the retailer, Kojima devised a distribution system that facilitates quick shipment in large quantities at relatively low cost. The first GE refrigerators introduced were two side-by-side models priced at $800 each, about one-fourth the price of a similar Japanese version manufactured by Matsushita. In four months, Japanese consumers bought 53,000 of them. Remarked one buyer, "At this price, who could pass it up?"

Today, Kojima sells ten different GE refrigerator models and three GE freezer models. Although GE was the first American manufacturer to market appliances in Japan through a direct arrangement with a major retailer, it is no longer the only one. Encouraged by GE's success through price competitiveness, Whirlpool Corporation has inked a similar deal with Kojima to sell washers and dryers.

Sources: Ric Manning, "GE Has Deal for Selling Appliances in Japan," *Courier Journal*, June 2, 1995, p. C1; "Endaka and Refrigerators," *Tokyo Business Today*, Sept. 1995, p. 19; Norihiko Shirouzu, "Flouting 'Rules' Sells GE Fridges in Japan," *Wall Street Journal*, Oct. 31, 1995, p. B1; and Richard J. Babyak, "Strategic Imperative," *Appliance Manufacturer*, Feb. 1995, pp. W19–W24.

493

■ *The Demand Curve*

For most products, the quantity demanded goes up as the price goes down, and as the price goes up, the quantity demanded goes down. Thus there is an inverse relationship between price and quantity demanded. As long as the marketing environment and buyers' needs, ability (purchasing power), willingness, and authority to buy remain stable, this fundamental inverse relationship will continue.

Figure 21.3 illustrates the effect of one variable—price—on the quantity demanded. The classic **demand curve** (D_1) is a graph of the quantity of products expected to be sold

Demand curve A graph of the quantity of products expected to be sold at various prices, if other factors remain constant

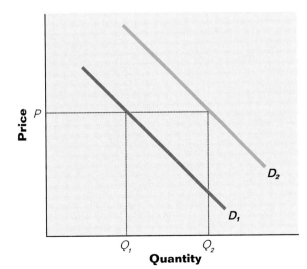

**Figure 21.3
Demand Curve Illustrating the Price/Quantity Relationship and Increase in Demand**

494

Figure 21.4
Prestige Products
Expensive plumbing
fixtures and jewelry are
examples of prestige
products.

at various prices, if other factors remain constant.[3] It illustrates that as price falls, the quantity demanded usually rises. Demand depends on other factors in the marketing mix, including product quality, promotion, and distribution. An improvement in any of these factors may cause a shift to, say, demand curve D_2. In such a case, an increased quantity (Q_2) will be sold at the same price (P).

There are many types of demand and not all conform to the classic demand curve shown in Figure 21.3. Prestige products, such as selected perfumes and jewelry, seem to sell better at high prices than at low ones. These products are desirable partly because their expense makes buyers feel elite. For example, in Figure 21.4, the Kohler plumbing fixtures and the Harry Winston watches are examples of prestige products. If the price fell drastically and many people owned these products, they would lose some of their appeal.

The demand curve in Figure 21.5 shows the relationship between price and quantity demanded for prestige products. Quantity demand is greater, not less, at higher prices. For a certain price range—from P_1 to P_2—the quantity demanded (Q_1) goes up to Q_2. After a certain point, however, raising the price backfires. If the price of a product goes too high, the quantity demanded goes down. The figure shows that if the price is raised from P_2 to P_3, the quantity demanded goes back down from Q_2 to Q_1.

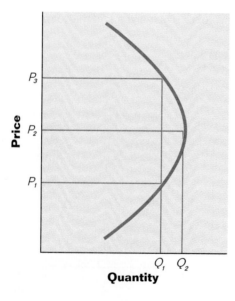

Figure 21.5
Demand Curve Illustrating the
Relationship Between Price and
Quantity for Prestige Products

■ *Demand Fluctuations*

Changes in buyers' needs, variations in the effectiveness of other marketing mix variables, the presence of substitutes, and dynamic environmental factors can influence demand. Restaurants and utility companies experience large fluctuations in demand daily. Toy manufacturers, fireworks suppliers, and air-conditioning and heating contractors also face demand fluctuations because of the seasonal nature of their products. The demand for fax machines, single-serving low-calorie meals, and fur coats has changed significantly over the last few years. In some cases, demand fluctuations are predictable. It is no surprise to restaurants and utility company managers that demand fluctuates. However, changes in demand for other products may be less predictable, and this leads to problems for some companies. Other organizations anticipate demand fluctuations and develop new products and prices to meet consumers' needs. For instance, instead of pizza, pasta, tablecloths, and dim lights, McDonald's discovered that cheaper food was what boosted evening business. The fast-food restaurateur marketed extra-value meals at discount prices, $1.99 Happy Meals for kids, and larger versions of traditional Big Macs for the dinnertime crowd.[4]

■ *Gauging Price Elasticity of Demand*

Price elasticity of demand
A measure of the sensitivity of demand to changes in price

Up to this point, we have been discussing how marketers identify the target market's evaluation of price and its ability to purchase and how they examine demand to learn whether price is related inversely or directly to quantity. The next step is to gauge price elasticity of demand. **Price elasticity of demand** provides a measure of the sensitivity of demand to changes in price. It is formally defined as the percentage change in quantity demanded relative to a given percentage change in price (see Figure 21.6).[5] The percentage change in quantity demanded caused by a percentage change in price is much greater for elastic demand than for inelastic demand. For a product such as electricity, demand is relatively inelastic. When its price is increased, say, from P_1, to P_2, quantity demanded goes down only a little, from Q_1 to Q_2. For products such as recreational vehicles, demand is relatively elastic. When price rises sharply, from P_1 to P_2, quantity demanded goes down a great deal, from Q_1 to Q_2.

If marketers can determine the price elasticity of demand, then setting a price is much easier. By analyzing total revenues as prices change, marketers can determine whether a product is price-elastic. Total revenue is price times quantity; thus 10,000 rolls of wallpaper sold in one year at a price of $10 per roll equals $100,000 of total revenue. If demand is *elastic,* a change in price causes an opposite change in total revenue: an increase in price will decrease total revenue, and a decrease in price will increase total revenue. *Inelastic* demand results in a change in the same direction in total revenue: an

Figure 21.6
Elasticity of Demand

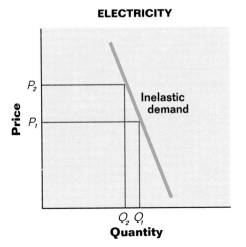

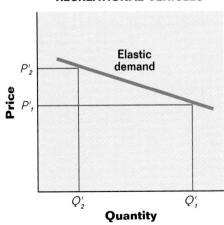

increase in price will increase total revenue, and a decrease in price will decrease total revenue. The following formula determines the price elasticity of demand:

$$\text{Price Elasticity of Demand} = \frac{\text{\% Change in Quantity Demanded}}{\text{\% Change in Price}}$$

For example, if demand falls by 8 percent when a seller raises the price by 2 percent, the price elasticity of demand is -4 (the negative sign indicating the inverse relationship between price and demand). If demand falls by 2 percent when price is increased by 4 percent, then elasticity is $-\frac{1}{2}$. The less elastic the demand, the more beneficial it is for the seller to raise the price. Products without readily available substitutes and for which consumers have strong needs (for example, electricity or appendectomies) usually have inelastic demand.

Marketers cannot base prices solely on elasticity considerations. They must also examine the costs associated with different volumes and see what happens to profits.

Analysis of Demand, Cost, and Profit Relationships

*T*he analysis of demand, cost, and profit is important because customers are becoming less tolerant of price increases and thus forcing manufacturers to find new ways to cut costs. In the past, many customers desired premium brands and were willing to pay extra for these products. Today customers pass up certain brand names if they can pay less without sacrificing quality. The proliferation of private brands in most consumer goods categories has narrowed the quality gap between these moderately priced goods and premium brands.[6] To stay in business, a company has to set prices that not only cover its costs, but also meet customers' expectations. This section explores two approaches to understanding demand, cost, and profit relationships: marginal analysis and breakeven analysis.

■ Marginal Analysis

Marginal analysis is the examination of what happens to a firm's costs and revenues when production (or sales volume) is changed by one unit. Both production costs and revenues must be evaluated. To determine the costs of production, it is necessary to distinguish among several types of costs. **Fixed costs** do not vary with changes in the number of units produced or sold. The cost of renting a factory does not change because production increases from one shift to two shifts a day or because twice as much wallpaper is sold. Rent may go up, but not because the factory has doubled production or revenue. **Average fixed cost** is the fixed cost per unit produced and is calculated by dividing fixed costs by the number of units produced.

Variable costs vary directly with changes in the number of units produced or sold. The wages for a second shift and the cost of twice as much paper are extra costs that occur when production is doubled. Variable costs are usually constant per unit; that is, twice as many workers and twice as much material produces twice as many rolls of wallpaper. **Average variable cost,** the variable cost per unit produced, is calculated by dividing the variable costs by the number of units produced.

Total cost is the sum of average fixed costs and average variable costs times the quantity produced. The **average total cost** is the sum of the average fixed cost and the average variable cost. **Marginal cost (MC)** is the extra cost a firm incurs when it produces one more unit of a product. Table 21.1 illustrates various costs and their relationships. Notice that the average fixed cost declines as the output increases. The average variable cost follows a U shape, as does the average total cost. Because the average total cost continues to fall after the average variable cost begins to rise, its lowest point is at a higher level of output than that of the average variable cost. The average total cost is lowest at 5 units at a cost of $22.00, whereas the average variable cost is lowest at 3 units at a cost of $11.67. As shown in Figure 21.7, marginal cost equals average total cost at the latter's lowest level. In Table 21.1 this occurs between 5 and 6 units of production. Average total cost decreases as

Fixed costs   Costs that do not vary with changes in the number of units produced or sold

Average fixed cost   The fixed cost per unit produced

Variable costs   Costs that vary directly with changes in the number of units produced or sold

Average variable cost   The variable cost per unit produced

Total cost   The sum of average fixed and average variable costs times the quantity produced

Average total cost   The sum of the average fixed cost and the average variable cost

Marginal cost (MC)   The extra cost a firm incurs by producing one more unit of a product

Table 21.1   Costs and Their Relationships

1	2	3	4	5	6	7
Quantity	Fixed Cost	Average Fixed Cost (2) ÷ (1)	Average Variable Cost	Average Total Cost (3) + (4)	Total Cost (5) × (1)	Marginal Cost
1	$40	$40.00	$20.00	$60.00	$60	
						$10
2	40	20.00	15.00	35.00	70	
						5
3	40	13.33	11.67	25.00	75	
						15
4	40	10.00	12.50	22.50	90	
						20
5	40	8.00	14.00	22.00	110	
						30
6	40	6.67	16.67	23.33	140	
						40
7	40	5.71	20.00	25.71	180	

long as the marginal cost is less than the average total cost, and it increases when marginal cost rises above average total cost.

Marginal revenue (MR) is the change in total revenue that occurs when a firm sells an additional unit of a product. Figure 21.8 depicts marginal revenue and a demand curve. Most firms in the United States face downward-sloping demand curves for their products. In other words, they must lower their prices to sell additional units. This situation means that each additional product sold provides the firm with less revenue than the previous unit sold. MR then becomes less than average revenue, as Figure 21.8 shows. Eventually, MR reaches zero, and the sale of additional units actually hurts the firm.

However, before the firm can determine whether a unit makes a profit, it must know its cost, as well as its revenue, because profit equals revenue minus cost. If MR is a unit's addition to revenue and MC is a unit's addition to cost, then MR minus MC tells us whether the unit is profitable or not. Table 21.2 illustrates the relationships among price, quantity sold, total revenue, marginal revenue, marginal cost, and total cost. It indicates where maximum profits are possible at various combinations of price and cost.

Profit is maximized where MC = MR (see Table 21.2). In this table MC = MR at four units. The best price is $33.75 and the profit is $45.00. Up to this point, the additional

Marginal revenue (MR)
The change in total revenue made by the sale of an additional unit of a product

Figure 21.7
Typical Marginal Cost and Average Total Cost Relationship

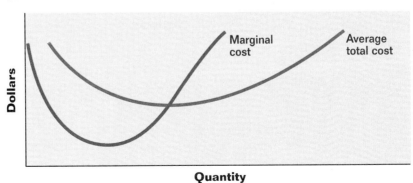

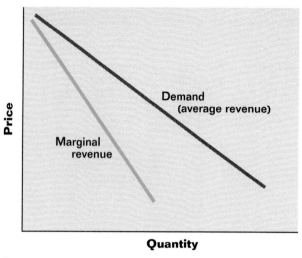

Figure 21.8
Typical Marginal Revenue and Average Revenue Relationship

revenue generated from an extra unit sold exceeds the additional total cost. Beyond this point, the additional cost of another unit sold exceeds the additional revenue generated, and profits decrease. If the price was based on minimum average total cost—$22.00 (Table 21.1)—it would result in less profit: only $40.00 (Table 21.2) for five units at a price of $30.00 versus $45.00 for four units at a price of $33.75.

Graphically combining Figures 21.7 and 21.8 into Figure 21.9 shows that any unit for which MR exceeds MC adds to a firm's profits, and any unit for which MC exceeds MR subtracts from a firm's profits. The firm should produce at the point where MR equals MC because this is the most profitable level of production.

This discussion of marginal analysis may give the false impression that pricing can be highly precise. If revenue (demand) and cost (supply) remained constant, then prices could be set for maximum profits. In practice, however, cost and revenue change frequently. The competitive tactics of other firms or government action can quickly undermine a company's expectations of revenue. Thus marginal analysis is only a model from which to work. It offers little help in pricing new products before costs and revenues are established. On the other hand, in setting prices of existing products, especially in competitive situations, most marketers can benefit by understanding the relationship between marginal cost and marginal revenue.

Table 21.2 Marginal Analysis: Method of Obtaining Maximum Profit-Producing Price

1	2	3	4	5	6	7
Price	Quantity Sold	Total Revenue (1) × (2)	Marginal Revenue	Marginal Cost	Total Cost	Profit (3) − (6)
$57.00	1	$ 57	$57	$ —	$ 60	−$ 3
55.00	2	110	53	10	70	40
40.00	3	120	10	5	75	45
33.75*	**4**	**135**	**15**	**15**	**90**	**45**
30.00	5	150	15	20	110	40
27.00	6	162	12	30	140	22
25.00	7	175	13	40	180	−5

*Boldface indicates best price-profit combination.

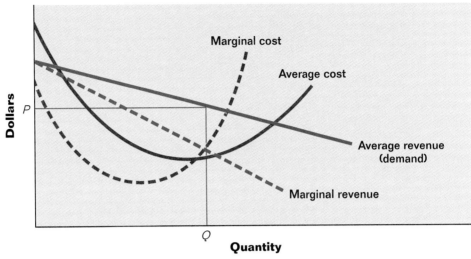

Figure 21.9
Combining the Marginal Cost and Marginal Revenue Concepts for Optimal Profit

■ *Breakeven Analysis*

The point at which the costs of producing a product equal the revenue made from selling the product is the **breakeven point.** If a wallpaper manufacturer has total annual costs of $100,000 and the same year it sells $100,000 worth of wallpaper, then the company has broken even.

Figure 21.10 illustrates the relationships of costs, revenue, profits, and losses involved in determining the breakeven point. Knowing the number of units necessary to break even is important in setting the price. If a product priced at $100 per unit has an average variable cost of $60 per unit, then the contribution to fixed costs is $40. If total fixed costs are $120,000, here is the way to determine the breakeven point in units:

$$\text{Breakeven Point} = \frac{\text{Fixed Costs}}{\text{Per Unit Contribution to Fixed Costs}}$$

$$= \frac{\text{Fixed Costs}}{\text{Price} - \text{Variable Costs}}$$

$$= \frac{\$120,000}{\$40}$$

$$= 3,000 \text{ Units}$$

Figure 21.10
Determining the Breakeven Point

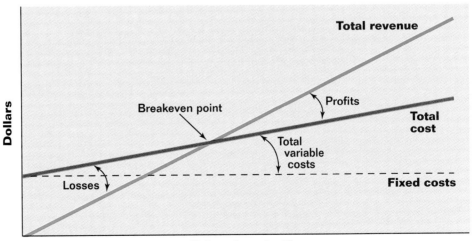

To calculate the breakeven point in terms of dollar sales volume, multiply the breakeven point in units by the price per unit. In the preceding example, the breakeven point in terms of dollar sales volume is 3,000 (units) times $100, or $300,000.

To use breakeven analysis effectively, a marketer should determine the breakeven point for each of several alternative prices. This determination allows the marketer to compare the effects on total revenue, total costs, and the breakeven point for each price under consideration. Although this comparative analysis may not tell the marketer exactly what price to charge, it will identify highly undesirable price alternatives that should definitely be avoided.

Breakeven analysis is simple and straightforward. It does assume, however, that the quantity demanded is basically fixed (inelastic) and that the major task in setting prices is to recover costs. It focuses more on how to break even than on how to achieve a pricing objective, such as percentage of market share or return on investment. Nonetheless, marketing managers can use this concept to determine whether a product will achieve at least a breakeven volume.

Evaluation of Competitors' Prices

*I*n most cases, marketers are in a better position to establish prices when they know the prices charged for competing brands. Learning competitors' prices may be a regular function of marketing research. Some grocery and department stores, for example, have full-time comparative shoppers who systematically collect data on prices. Companies may also purchase price lists, sometimes weekly, from syndicated marketing research services.

Finding out what prices competitors are charging is not always easy, especially in producer and reseller markets. Competitors' price lists are often closely guarded. Even if a marketer has access to competitors' price lists, these lists may not reflect the actual prices at which competitive products are sold because those prices may be established through negotiation.

Knowing the prices of competing brands can be very important for a marketer. Competitors' prices and the marketing mix variables that they emphasize partly determine how important price will be to customers. Marketers in an industry in which nonprice competition prevails need competitive price information to ensure that their organization's prices are the same as its competitors' prices.

In some instances, an organization's prices are designed to be slightly above competitors' prices to give its products an exclusive image. Alternately, another company may use price as a competitive tool and price its products below those of competitors. Category killers like Toys 'R' Us and The Home Depot rely heavily on the strategy of everyday low prices and have acquired large market shares through highly competitive pricing. Currently, several category killers such as The Home Depot, Wal-Mart, The Sports Authority, and Party City are expanding into Canada because they believe that certain Canadian markets are less price competitive.[7]

Selection of a Pricing Policy

Pricing policy A guiding philosophy or course of action designed to influence and determine pricing decisions

A **pricing policy** is a guiding philosophy or course of action designed to influence and determine pricing decisions. Pricing policies set guidelines for achieving pricing objectives. They are an important component of an overall marketing strategy. Generally, pricing policies should answer this recurring question: How will price be used as a variable in the marketing mix? This question may relate to (1) introduction of new products, (2) competitive situations, (3) government pricing regulations, (4) economic conditions, or (5) implementation of pricing objectives. Pricing policies help marketers solve the practical problems of establishing prices. Table 21.3 lists the five most common pricing policies, and we discuss them in the rest of this section.

Table 21.3 Common Pricing Policies	
Pioneer Pricing	**Professional Pricing**
Price Skimming	**Promotional Pricing**
Penetration Pricing	Price Leaders
Psychological Pricing	Special-Event Pricing
Odd-Even Pricing	Superficial Discounting
Customary Pricing	**Experience Curve Pricing**
Prestige Pricing	
Price Lining	

■ *Pioneer Pricing Policies*

Pioneer pricing—setting the base price for a new product—is a necessary part of formulating a marketing strategy. The base price is easily adjusted (in the absence of government price controls), and its establishment is one of the most fundamental decisions in the marketing mix. The base price can be set high to recover development costs quickly or to provide a reference point for developing discount prices to different market segments.

When marketers set base prices, they also consider how quickly competitors will enter the market, whether they will mount a strong campaign on entry, and what effect their entry will have on the development of primary demand. If competitors will enter quickly, with considerable marketing force, and with limited effect on the primary demand, then a firm may adopt a penetration pricing policy by setting a base price that will discourage their entry.[8]

Price skimming Charging the highest possible price that buyers who most desire the product will pay

Price Skimming **Price skimming** is charging the highest possible price that buyers who most desire the product will pay. This pioneer approach provides the most flexible introductory base price. Demand tends to be inelastic in the introductory stage of the product life cycle.

Price skimming can provide several benefits, especially when a product is in the introductory stage of its life cycle. A skimming policy can generate much-needed initial cash flows to help offset sizable developmental costs. When introducing a new model of camera, Polaroid initially uses a skimming price to defray large research and development costs. Price skimming protects the marketer from problems that arise when the price is set too low to cover costs. When a firm introduces a product, its production capacity may be limited. A skimming price can help keep demand consistent with a firm's production capabilities. The use of a skimming price may attract competition into an industry because the high price makes that type of business appear to be quite lucrative.

Penetration pricing Pricing below the prices of competing brands; designed to penetrate a market and produce a larger unit sales volume

Penetration Pricing **Penetration pricing** is pricing below the prices of competing brands and is designed to penetrate a market and produce a larger unit sales volume. When introducing a product, a marketer sometimes uses penetration pricing to gain a large market share quickly. This approach is less flexible for a marketer than is price skimming because it is more difficult to raise a penetration price than to lower or discount a skimming price. It is not unusual for a firm to use a penetration price after having skimmed the market with a higher price.

Penetration pricing can be especially beneficial when marketers suspect that competitors could enter the market easily. First, if penetration pricing lets one marketer gain a large market share quickly, competitors might be discouraged from entering the market. Second, entering the market may be less attractive to competitors when penetration pricing is used because the lower per-unit price results in lower per-unit profit; this may cause competitors to view the market as not being especially lucrative. Some credit unions, for example, use penetration pricing to establish a foothold in the financial services marketplace. They underprice competitors on loan and fee services and overprice them on deposit rates to penetrate their market and provide value to customers.[9]

■ *Psychological Pricing*

Psychological pricing encourages purchases based on emotional rather than rational responses. It is used most often at the retail level. Psychological pricing has limited use for organizational (industrial) products.

Psychological pricing
Encourages purchases based on emotional rather than rational responses

Odd-Even Pricing   Through **odd-even pricing**—ending the price with certain numbers—marketers try to influence buyers' perceptions of the price or the product.[10] Odd pricing assumes that more of a product will be sold at $99.95 than at $100. Supposedly, customers will think, or at least tell friends, that the product is a bargain—not $100, but $99 and change. Also, customers are supposed to think that the store could have charged $100 but instead cut the price to the last cent, to $99.95. Some claim, too, that certain types of customers are more attracted by odd prices than by even ones. However, there are no substantial research findings that support the notion that odd prices produce greater sales. Nonetheless, even prices are far less common today than odd prices.

Odd-even pricing   Influencing the buyers' perceptions of the price or the product by ending the price with certain numbers

Even prices are often used to give a product an exclusive or upscale image. An even price supposedly will influence a customer to view the product as being a high-quality, premium brand. A shirt maker, for example, may print on a premium shirt package a suggested retail price of $32.00 instead of $31.95; the even price of the shirt is used to enhance its upscale image.

Customary Pricing   In **customary pricing,** certain goods are priced primarily on the basis of tradition. Recent economic uncertainties have made most prices fluctuate fairly widely, but the classic example of the customary, or traditional, price is the candy bar. For years, the price of a candy bar was 5 cents. A new candy bar would have had to be something very special to sell for more than a nickel. This price was so sacred that rather than change it, manufacturers increased or decreased the size of the candy bar itself as chocolate prices fluctuated. Now, of course, the nickel candy bar has disappeared, probably forever. Yet most candy bars still sell at a consistent but obviously higher price. Thus customary pricing remains the standard for this market.

Customary pricing
Pricing on the basis of tradition

Prestige Pricing   In **prestige pricing,** prices are set at an artificially high level to provide prestige or a quality image. Prestige pricing is used especially when buyers associate a higher price with higher quality.[11] Pharmacists report that some consumers complain when a prescription does not cost enough. Apparently, some consumers associate a drug's price with its potency. Typical product categories in which selected products are prestige-priced include perfumes, automobiles, liquor, and jewelry. If producers that use prestige pricing lowered their prices dramatically, it would be inconsistent with the perceived high-quality images of such products.

Prestige pricing   Prices set at an artificially high level to provide prestige or a quality image

Price Lining   When an organization sets a limited number of prices for selected groups or lines of merchandise, it is using **price lining.** A retailer may have various styles and brands of similar quality men's shirts that sell for $15. Another line of higher-quality shirts may sell for $22. Price lining simplifies customers' decision making by holding constant one key variable in the final selection of style and brand within a line.

Price lining   Setting a limited number of prices for selected groups or lines of merchandise

The basic assumption in price lining is that the demand is inelastic for various groups or sets of products. If the prices are attractive, customers will concentrate their purchases without responding to slight changes in price. Thus a women's dress shop that carries dresses priced at $85, $55, and $35 might not attract many more sales with a drop to, say, $83, $53, and $33. The "space" between the price of $65 and $45, however, can stir changes in consumer response. With price lining, the demand curve looks like a series of steps, as shown in Figure 21.11.

■ *Professional Pricing*

Professional pricing is used by persons who have great skill or experience in a particular field or activity. Some professionals who provide such products as medical services feel that their fees (prices) should not relate directly to the time and involvement in specific cases; rather, a standard fee is charged regardless of the problems involved in performing the job. Some doctors' and lawyers' fees are prime examples: $55 for a checkup, $500 for an appendectomy, and $399 for a divorce. Other professionals set prices in other ways.

Professional pricing
Fees set by persons with great skill or experience in a particular field or activity

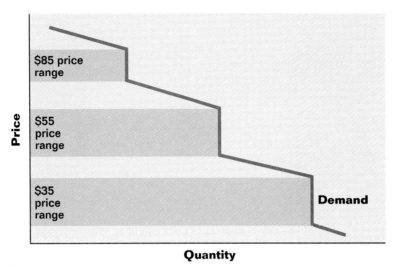

Figure 21.11
Price Lining

The concept of professional pricing carries with it the idea that professionals have an ethical responsibility not to overcharge unknowing customers. In some situations, a seller can charge customers a high price and continue to sell many units of the product. Medicine offers several examples. If a diabetic requires one insulin treatment per day to survive, the individual will buy that treatment whether its price is $1 or $10. In fact, the patient surely would purchase the treatment even if the price went higher. In these situations sellers could charge exorbitant fees. Drug companies claim that despite their positions of strength in this regard, they charge ethical prices rather than what the market will bear. The discussion in Ethical Challenges (on the following page) raises questions over the professional pricing of contact lenses by Bausch & Lomb.

■ Promotional Pricing

Price, as an ingredient in the marketing mix, is often coordinated with promotion. The two variables sometimes are so interrelated that the pricing policy is promotion-oriented. Some examples of promotional pricing include price leaders, special-event pricing, and superficial discounting.

Price leaders Products priced below the usual markup, near cost, or below cost

Price Leaders Sometimes a firm prices a few products below the usual markup, near cost, or below cost, which results in prices known as **price leaders.** This type of pricing is used most often in supermarkets and restaurants to attract customers by giving them especially low prices on a few items (see Figure 21.12). Management hopes that sales of regularly priced products will more than offset the reduced revenues from the price leaders.

Figure 21.12
Promotional Pricing
Denny's uses pricing to stimulate demand and to encourage customers to choose its restaurants.

ETHICAL CHALLENGES

A Closer Look at Bausch & Lomb Prices

During World War I, Bausch & Lomb supplied the U.S. military with lenses for binoculars and telescopes. In the 1950s, Bausch & Lomb won an Oscar for developing the Cinemascope lens. In the 1960s, the company contributed innovative technology to U.S. satellite and missile systems. However, recent allegations about the ethics of the company's pricing practices are threatening to tarnish its admirable image.

For years, Bausch & Lomb had a monopoly on soft contact lenses, sales of which propelled the company into the *Fortune* 500. Bausch & Lomb markets a variety of lenses, priced differently, apparently according to type of use. Conventional daily-wear lenses cost about $250 a year including cleaners; frequent-replacement lenses run about $350 a year; and disposable lenses, between $400 and $500 a year. However, a recent *Business Week* investigation contends that Bausch & Lomb sells identical lenses for far-from-identical prices; the only real difference among them is packaging. For example, customers pay $40 a lens for the company's Optima FW, $9 a lens for its Medalist, and $4 a lens for its See-Quence 2, but all three lenses are exactly the same product.

Largely as a result of this revelation, a group of Bausch & Lomb customers initiated a lawsuit against the company alleging that Bausch & Lomb has committed fraud by misrepresenting its lenses. Recently, a federal judge issued notification of the suit to buyers who purchased Medalist and Optima FW contact lenses. Bausch & Lomb concedes that the lenses are the same, but insists that the suit is without merit. Eye care professionals, the company asserts, are the ones who direct patients to wear lenses for varying lengths of time and who set the final price.

Several ethical questions remain. Is it ethical for the company to assign different names—and different prices—to one product? Are customers deceived when a different name—and a different price—does *not* signify a different product? The courts may force Bausch & Lomb to address these questions. The potential costs to Bausch & Lomb are not only monetary, but also a diminished reputation and loss of customer trust.

Sources: Gary Hoover, Alta Campbell, and Patrick J. Spain, *Hoover's Handbook of American Business 1995* (Austin, Texas: Reference Press, 1995), pp. 260–261; Kenneth N. Gilpin, "Suit Against Bausch & Lomb Is Judged a Class Action," *New York Times,* Nov. 3, 1994, p. D5; Mark Maremont, "Eyeway Robbery?" *Business Week,* Feb. 27, 1995, p. 48; "Health Brief—Bausch & Lomb Inc.: Judge Clarifies Categories of Lens Buyers Tied to Suit," *Wall Street Journal,* Apr. 3, 1995; and Lesley Alderman, "How to Save Dollars and Make Sense When You Buy Contact Lenses," *Money,* May 1994, pp. 156–157.

Special-event pricing
Advertised sales or price cutting linked to a holiday, season, or event

Special-Event Pricing   To increase sales volume, many organizations coordinate price with advertising or sales promotions for seasonal or special situations. **Special-event pricing** involves advertised sales or price cutting linked to a holiday, season, or event. If the pricing objective is survival, then special sales events may be designed to generate the necessary operating capital. Special-event pricing also entails coordination of production, scheduling, storage, and physical distribution. Whenever there is a sales lag, special-event pricing is an alternative that marketers should consider.

Superficial discounting
Fictitious comparative pricing

Superficial Discounting   **Superficial discounting,** sometimes called "was-is pricing," is fictitious comparative pricing—for example, "Was $259, Is $199." The Federal Trade Commission and the Better Business Bureau discourage these deceptive markdowns. Legitimate discounts are not questioned, but when a pricing policy gives only the illusion of a discount, it is unethical and in some states illegal.

As an example of superficial discounting, consider one retailer that sells 93 percent of its power tools on sale, with discounts ranging from 10 to 40 percent. The retailer's frequent special events or sales mean that the tools are sold at sale prices most of the year. To combat such superficial discounting, Canada requires retailers to post a base price for at least six months before discounting a product.

■ *Experience Curve Pricing*

In **experience curve pricing,** a company fixes a low price that high-cost competitors cannot match and thus expands its market share. This practice is possible when a firm gains cumulative production experience and is able to reduce its manufacturing costs at a predictable rate through improved methods, materials, skills, and machinery. Texas Instruments used this strategy in marketing its calculators. The experience curve depicts the inverse relationship between production costs per unit and cumulative production quantity. To take advantage of the experience curve, a company must gain a dominant market share early in a product's life cycle. An early market share lead, with the greater cumulative production experience that it implies, will place a company further down the experience curve than its competitors. To avoid antitrust problems, companies must objectively examine the competitive structure of the market before and after implementing the experience curve strategy. The strategy should not be anticompetitive, and the company must have specific and accurate data that will be unshakable in a court of law.

505

Development of a Pricing Method

After selecting a pricing policy, a marketer must choose a **pricing method,** a mechanical procedure for setting prices on a regular basis. The pricing method structures the calculation of the actual price. The nature of a product, its sales volume, or the amount of product the organization carries will determine how prices are calculated. For example, a procedure for pricing the thousands of products in a supermarket must be simpler and more direct than that for calculating the price of a new earthmoving machine manufactured by Caterpillar. In this section we examine three types of market-oriented pricing methods: cost-oriented, demand-oriented, and competition-oriented pricing.

■ *Cost-Oriented Pricing*

In **cost-oriented pricing,** a dollar amount or percentage is added to the cost of a product. The method thus involves calculations of desired margins or profit margins. Cost-oriented pricing methods do not necessarily take into account the economic aspects of supply and demand, nor do they necessarily relate to a specific pricing policy or ensure the attainment of pricing objectives. They are, however, simple and easy to implement. Two common cost-oriented pricing methods are cost-plus and markup pricing.

Cost-Plus Pricing   In **cost-plus pricing,** the seller's costs are determined (usually during a project or after a project is completed), and then a specified dollar amount or percentage of the cost is added to the seller's cost to set the price. When production costs are difficult to predict, cost-plus pricing is appropriate. Custom-made equipment and commercial construction projects are often priced by this method. The government frequently uses such cost-oriented pricing in granting defense contracts. One pitfall for the buyer is that the seller may increase costs to establish a larger profit base. Furthermore, some costs, such as overhead, may be difficult to determine. In periods of rapid inflation, cost-plus pricing is popular, especially when the producer must use raw materials that are fluctuating in price. For industries in which cost-plus pricing is common and sellers have similar costs, price competition may not be especially intense.

Markup Pricing   A common pricing method among retailers is **markup pricing.** In markup pricing, a product's price is derived by adding a predetermined percentage of the cost, called *markup,* to the cost of the product. Although the percentage markup in a retail store varies from one category of goods to another (35 percent of cost for hardware items and 100 percent of cost for greeting cards, for example), the same percentage often is used to determine the price on items within a single product category, and the same or similar percentage markup may be standardized across an industry at the retail level. Using a rigid percentage markup for a specific product category reduces pricing to a routine task that can be performed quickly.

Markup can be stated as a percentage of the cost or as a percentage of the selling price. The following example illustrates how percentage markups are determined and points out the differences in the two methods. Assume that a retailer purchases a can of tuna at 45 cents, adds 15 cents to the cost, and then prices the tuna at 60 cents. Here are the figures:

$$\text{Markup as a Percentage of Cost} = \frac{\text{Markup}}{\text{Cost}}$$

$$= \frac{15}{45}$$

$$= 33.3\%$$

$$\text{Markup as a Percentage of Selling Price} = \frac{\text{Markup}}{\text{Selling Price}}$$

$$= \frac{15}{60}$$

$$= 25.0\%$$

Obviously, when discussing a percentage markup, it is important to know whether the markup is based on cost or selling price.

Markups normally reflect expectations about operating costs, risks, and stock turnovers. Wholesalers and manufacturers often suggest standard retail markups that are considered profitable. An average percentage markup on cost may be as high as 100 percent or more for jewelry or as low as 20 percent for the textbook you are reading. To the extent that retailers use similar markups for the same product category, price competition is reduced. In addition, using rigid markups is convenient and is the major reason that retailers, who face numerous pricing decisions, favor this method.

■ *Demand-Oriented Pricing*

Demand-Oriented pricing
A pricing method based on the level of demand for the product

Rather than basing the price of a product on its cost, marketers sometimes use a pricing method based on the level of demand for the product: **demand-oriented pricing.** This method results in a high price when demand for the product is strong and a low price when demand is weak. For example, many metropolitan hotels, which attract numerous business travelers during the week, use special rates to stimulate demand on the weekends (see Figure 21.13). Most long-distance telephone companies, such as MCI, Sprint, and AT&T, use demand-oriented pricing. MCI tries to influence demand for its 1-800-COLLECT service by promoting its low cost. To use this method, a marketer must be able to estimate the amounts of a product that consumers will demand at different

Figure 21.13
Demand-Oriented Pricing
The Marriott, which caters to many business travelers during the week, offers special rates to encourage nonbusiness customers to visit the city and stay at its hotels during the weekends.

506

prices. The marketer then chooses the price that generates the highest total revenue. Obviously, the effectiveness of this method depends on the marketer's ability to estimate demand accurately.

A marketer may favor a demand-oriented pricing method called **price differentiation** when the firm wants to use more than one price in the marketing of a specific product. Price differentiation can be based on such considerations as type of customer, type of distribution channel used, or the time of the purchase. For example, a 12-ounce canned soft drink costs less from a supermarket than from a vending machine. Florida hotel accommodations are more expensive in the winter than in the summer. A home owner pays more for air-conditioner filters than does an apartment complex owner, who purchases the same-size filters in greater quantity. Christmas tree ornaments are usually cheaper on December 26 than on December 16.

For price differentiation to work properly, the marketer must be able to segment a market on the basis of different strengths of demand, then keep the segments separate enough so that segment members who buy at lower prices cannot then sell to buyers in segments that are charged a higher price. This isolation could be accomplished, for example, by selling to geographically separated segments. Price differentiation can also be based on employment in a public service position. For example, most airlines permit 50 percent off each regular one-way or roundtrip fare for all U.S. military personnel on active duty, leave, furlough, or a pass.

Compared with cost-oriented pricing, demand-oriented pricing places a firm in a better position to reach higher profit levels, assuming that buyers value the product at levels sufficiently above the product's cost. To use demand-oriented pricing, however, a marketer must be able to estimate demand at different price levels, which is often difficult to do accurately.

■ *Competition-Oriented Pricing*

In using **competition-oriented pricing,** an organization considers costs and revenue as secondary to competitors' prices. The importance of this method increases if competing products are almost homogeneous and the organization is serving markets in which price is the key variable of the marketing strategy. A firm that uses competition-oriented pricing may choose to price below competitors' prices, above competitors' prices, or at the same level. In Figure 21.14, both GM Goodwrench and USAir are promoting and emphasizing their prices in these advertisements, indicating that they are competing (obviously not with each other) through competition-oriented pricing. The airlines also use competition-oriented pricing and often charge identical fares on the same routes.

Although not all introductory marketing texts have exactly the same price, they do have similar prices. The price that the bookstore paid to the publishing company for this textbook was determined using competition-oriented pricing. Competition-oriented pricing should help a firm achieve the pricing objective of increasing sales or market share. Competition-oriented pricing may necessitate frequent price adjustments but can also lead to price stability. For example, for some routes, air fares are adjusted often, whereas for other routes, the fares remain the same for long periods.[12] Competition-oriented pricing methods may be combined with cost approaches to arrive at price levels necessary for a profit.

Determination of a Specific Price

A pricing method (or combination of them) will yield a certain price. However, this price is likely to need refinement. The price may need alteration to make it consistent with pricing practices in a particular market or industry. For example, a manager may set the final retail price of a handblown glass vase at $180.00 if the pricing method resulted in an initial price of $177.61.

Pricing policies and methods should help in setting a final price. If they are to do so, it is important for marketers to establish pricing objectives, to know something about the

508

Figure 21.14
Competition-Oriented
Pricing Both GM
Goodwrench and
USAir use competition-
oriented pricing.

target market, and to determine demand, price elasticity, costs, and competitive factors. Also, the way that pricing is used in the marketing mix will affect the final price.

Although we suggest a systematic approach to pricing, in practice prices often are finalized after only limited planning, or they may be set without planning, just by trial and error. Then marketers determine whether revenue, minus costs, yields a satisfactory profit. This approach to pricing is not recommended because it makes it difficult to discover pricing errors.

In the absence of government price control, pricing remains a flexible and convenient way to adjust the marketing mix. In most situations, prices can be adjusted quickly—in a matter of minutes or over a few days. This flexibility and freedom do not characterize the other components of the marketing mix.

SUMMARY

The eight stages in the process of establishing prices are (1) selecting pricing objectives; (2) assessing the target market's evaluation of price; (3) determining demand; (4) analyzing demand, cost, and profit relationships; (5) evaluating competitors' prices; (6) selecting a pricing policy; (7) choosing a pricing method; and (8) determining a specific price.

The first stage, setting pricing objectives, is critical because pricing objectives form a foundation on which the decisions of subsequent stages are based. Organizations may use numerous pricing objectives: short-term and long-term ones, and different ones for different products and market segments.

The second stage in establishing prices is an assessment of the target market's evaluation of price. This stage

tells a marketer how much emphasis to place on price and may help the marketer determine how far above the competition the firm can set its prices. Understanding how important a product is to the customers in comparison with other products as well as customers' expectations of quality helps marketers correctly assess the target market's evaluation of price.

In the third stage, the organization must determine the demand for its product. The classic demand curve is a graph of the quantity of products expected to be sold at various prices, if other factors hold constant. It illustrates that, as price falls, the quantity demanded usually increases. However, for prestige products, there is a direct positive relationship between price and quantity demanded: demand increases as price increases. Next, price elasticity of demand—the percentage change in quantity demanded relative to a given percentage change in price—must be determined. If demand is elastic, a change in price causes an opposite change in total revenue. Inelastic demand results in parallel change in total revenue when a product's price is changed.

Analysis of demand, cost, and profit relationships—the fourth stage of the process—can be accomplished through marginal analysis or breakeven analysis. Marginal analysis is the examination of what happens to a firm's costs and revenues when production (or sales volume) is changed by one unit. Marginal analysis combines the demand curve with a firm's costs to develop an optimum price for maximum profit. Fixed costs do not vary with changes in the number of units produced or sold; average fixed cost is the fixed cost per unit produced. Variable costs vary directly with changes in the number of units produced or sold. Average variable cost is the variable cost per unit produced. Average total cost is the sum of average fixed cost and average variable cost times the quantity produced. The optimum price is the point at which marginal cost (the cost associated with producing one more unit of the product) equals marginal revenue (the change in total revenue that occurs when one additional unit of the product is sold). Marginal analysis is only a model; it offers little help in pricing new products before costs and revenues are established.

Breakeven analysis (determining the number of units necessary to break even) is important in setting the price. The point at which the costs of production equal the revenue from selling the product is the breakeven point. To use breakeven analysis effectively, a marketer should determine the breakeven point for each of several alternative prices. This determination makes it possible to compare the effects on total revenue, total costs, and the breakeven point for each price under consideration. However, this approach assumes that the quantity demanded is basically fixed and that the major task is to set prices to recover costs.

A marketer needs to be aware of the prices charged for competing brands. This allows a firm to keep its prices the same as competitor's prices when nonprice competition is used. If a company uses price as a competitive tool, it can price its brand below competing brands.

A pricing policy is a guiding philosophy or course of action designed to influence and determine pricing decisions. Pricing policies help marketers solve the practical problems of establishing prices. Two types of pioneer pricing policies are price skimming and penetration pricing. With price skimming, an organization charges the highest price that buyers who most desire the product will pay. A penetration price is a lower price designed to penetrate the market and produce a larger unit sales volume. Psychological pricing, another pricing policy, encourages purchases that are based on emotional rather than rational responses. It includes odd-even pricing, customary pricing, prestige pricing, and price lining. A third pricing policy, professional pricing, is used by people who have great skill or experience in a particular field. Promotional pricing, in which price is coordinated with promotion, is another type of pricing policy. Price leaders, special-event pricing, and superficial discounting are examples of promotional pricing. Experience curve pricing fixes a low price that high-cost competitors cannot match. Experience curve pricing is possible when experience reduces manufacturing costs at a predictable rate.

A pricing method is a mechanical procedure for assigning prices to specific products on a regular basis. Three types of pricing methods are cost-oriented, demand-oriented, and competition-oriented pricing. In using cost-oriented pricing, a firm determines price by adding a dollar amount or percentage to the cost of the product. Two common cost-oriented pricing methods are cost-plus and markup pricing. Demand-oriented pricing is based on the level of demand for the product. To use this method, a marketer must be able to estimate the amounts of a product that buyers will demand at different prices. Demand-oriented pricing results in a high price when demand for a product is strong and a low price when demand is weak. In the case of competition-oriented pricing, costs and revenues are secondary to competitors' prices. Competition-oriented pricing and cost approaches may be combined to arrive at price levels necessary for a profit.

Once a price is determined by using one or more pricing methods, it will need to be refined to a final price consistent with the pricing practices in a particular market or industry.

IMPORTANT TERMS

Demand curve	Marginal revenue (MR)	Price lining	Markup pricing
Price elasticity of demand	Breakeven point	Professional pricing	Demand-oriented pricing
Fixed costs	Pricing policy	Price leaders	Price differentiation
Average fixed cost	Price skimming	Special-event pricing	Competition-oriented
Variable costs	Penetration pricing	Superficial discounting	pricing
Average variable cost	Psychological pricing	Experience curve pricing	
Total cost	Odd-even pricing	Pricing method	
Average total cost	Customary pricing	Cost-oriented pricing	
Marginal cost (MC)	Prestige pricing	Cost-plus pricing	

DISCUSSION AND REVIEW QUESTIONS

1. Identify the eight stages that make up the process of establishing prices.
2. Why do most demand curves demonstrate an inverse relationship between price and quantity?
3. List the characteristics of products that have inelastic demand. Give several examples of such products.
4. Explain why optimum profits should occur when marginal cost equals marginal revenue.
5. The Chambers Company has just gathered estimates for doing a breakeven analysis for a new product. Variable costs are $7 a unit. The additional plant will cost $48,000. The new product will be charged $18,000 a year for its share of general overhead. Advertising expenditures will be $80,000, and $55,000 will be spent on distribution. If the product sells for $12, what is the breakeven point in units? What is the breakeven point in dollar sales volume?
6. Why should a marketer be aware of competitors' prices?
7. For what type of products would a pioneer price-skimming policy be most appropriate? For what type of products would penetration pricing be more effective?
8. Why do customers associate price with quality? When should prestige pricing be used?
9. Are price leaders a realistic approach to pricing?
10. What are the benefits of cost-oriented pricing?
11. Under what conditions is cost-plus pricing most appropriate?
12. A retailer purchases a can of soup for 24 cents and sells it for 36 cents. Calculate the markup as percentage of cost and as percentage of selling price.

APPLICATION QUESTIONS

1. Price skimming and penetration pricing are two policies commonly used when setting the base price of a new product. Which policy would be most appropriate for the following products? Explain your answer.
   a. short flights between cities in Florida offered by an airline
   b. a laser disc player
   c. a backpack or book bag with a lifetime warranty
   d. season tickets for a newly franchised NBA basketball team
2. Price lining is used to set a limited number of price for selected lines of merchandise. Visit local retail stores to find instances of price lining policies. For what types of products and stores is this most common? For what products and stores is price lining not typical or usable?
3. Professional pricing is used by persons who have great skill in a particular field, such as doctors, lawyers, and business consultants. Find examples (advertisements, personal contacts) that reflect a professional pricing policy. How is the price established? Are there any restrictions on the services performed at that price?

Case 21.1 Steinway: Price Supported by over 140 Years of Quality

Heinrich Englehard Steinweg came to the United States from Germany in the early 1850s and began to redesign and improve the piano, an instrument that Beethoven and Chopin had complained sounded "tinny" and "thin." Shortly after his arrival, he changed his family name to Steinway, the name that has become synonymous with quality in the piano industry. Some thirty years and a hundred patents later, the modern piano was born from Steinway's efforts. Like no pianos of their time, the handcrafted instruments of Heinrich Steinway and his sons were true works of art. They could fill concert halls with powerful sound, yet were sensitive enough to handle the most delicate and intricate of musical inflections.

The company's success peaked in the early 1900s, a success symbolized by construction of the elegant Steinway Hall on New York's West 57th Street in 1925. Like many companies of the time, Steinway and Sons struggled through the Great Depression. (Between 1927 and 1931, the company's rate of production plummeted.) During this difficult period, however, the company held firm to its rich legacy. When approached by a home appliance maker and offered $500,000—a monumental sum of money at the time—for use of the Steinway and Sons name to help sell refrigerators and stoves, Theodore E. Steinway refused. "We are makers of pianos," he stated, "and the Steinway name will never grace anything but the finest pianos."

Determined to maintain its traditional method of constructing pianos instead of mass producing them to meet a lower price, the standard of excellence and product quality in piano design and workmanship that

Steinway established remains the industry benchmark. This quality is reflected in the prices charged for Steinway pianos—typically among the highest in the industry. The company's top-of-the-line, 9-foot-long, 45,000-pound concert grand, for instance, carries a price tag of approximately $70,000. Other models in the Steinway grand piano line sell for between $25,000 and $53,000. More affordable are the company's upright pianos, which are priced between $11,000 and $17,000. Overall, the base price of Steinway pianos averages about $25,000. At additional cost, the company offers special finishes on its pianos, ranging in price from a $900 satin lustre finish on its two lowest-priced upright models, to a $9,600 high-polish finish on the concert grand.

Most of Steinway and Sons' competitors employ much more competitive pricing methods. For example, in the 1980s and 1990s, the world market saw a great influx of Asian piano makers offering high-quality, yet relatively low-priced instruments. In fact, new market entrants such as Japan's Yamaha and Kawai and Korea's Young Chang have come to dominate the mid-price piano market, typically selling grands and uprights for about $9,600 and $4,000 respectively. To the untrained ear, these less expensive instruments offer a clean and generally acceptable sound. However, many accomplished pianists claim that these mostly machine-made pianos sound shallow compared to hand-assembled Steinways.

Each year New York–based Steinway and Sons handcrafts and sells roughly 2,500 pianos, a relatively low number in this age of mass production and mass marketing. Yamaha, for example, produces well over 200,000 pianos a year. To put this difference in perspective, consider that it took Steinway and Sons 135 years to produce its 500,000th piano—approximately the two-year output of one of its leading Asian competitors.

The painstaking attention to detail that goes into each Steinway piano reflects its strategy: build to a standard, not to a price. Each Steinway takes nearly two full years to prepare and make. Seasoning the wood alone takes up to twelve months. The crafting of a Steinway involves 120 separate steps in which some 12,000 parts are carefully assembled according to guidelines established by Heinrich Steinway himself almost 150 years ago.

Steinway and Sons spares no expense in gathering together the materials that go into the making of its esteemed instruments. For example, the wood, which constitutes 85 percent of each Steinway, is selected from only the highest-grade poplar, rock maple, and spruce. The outer rim of a Steinway grand piano consists of eighteen layers of hard rock maple that are bent as a unit and then clamped onto presses over 100 years old. The rigid arch thus formed can bear more than 45,000 pounds of tension when strung—strength

unparalleled in the piano industry. To ensure optimal transmission of vibrations to the soundboard, as many as 243 pure Swedish steel strings are custom-fitted across a bell-quality, cast-iron frame to bear down on the bridge of the piano with up to 1,200 pounds of pressure.

From a more aesthetic perspective, each Steinway is built to exceed the requirements of even the most demanding concert pianist. Steinway and Sons' patented keyboard technology, for instance, ensures that each key returns as rapidly as possible to the playing position after being struck. Also, the unique touch of the Steinway keyboard is impervious to changes in temperature or humidity, thanks to the company's patented tubular metallic action frame. As a result of this obsession with product quality, 93 percent of all piano soloists performing with major symphony orchestras choose to play exclusively on Steinway pianos. The director of London's Sotheby's asserts that Steinway is the most sought-after name by those attending the organization's prestigious auctions. To the buyer of a Steinway, the price paid represents not a cost, but an investment in what is for most a family heirloom, a standard of excellence and good taste.

Independent research supports this perception. *Forbes* magazine, for example, found that a Steinway concert grand increases in retail value nearly 200 percent after ten years of ownership. Steinway concert grands sell for an average of 430 percent of their original retail price, and uprights for 220 percent over their original cost. *Business Week* reported that a medium grand purchased in 1975 for $5,920 would sell for about $12,000 today.

To complement the company's pricing methods and policies, other marketing activities engaged in by Steinway and Sons are generally discrete and aimed at individuals who can afford the relatively high initial product cost. For example, prospective buyers are targeted through use of a "catalog offer" advertisement in upscale magazines such as the *New Yorker, Architectural Digest,* and *Town and Country.*

Despite its reputation as the maker of the finest pianos in the world, the company faces critical challenges. In some ways, Steinway is its own biggest competitor. Because they are constructed so well, Steinways built as far back as the 1800s are still in use today and do not need replacing. Technology and lower-priced competitors also make times difficult for Steinway. For example, in 1991, Yamaha introduced its revolutionary Disklavier. For about $9,000, this computer-age instrument plays like a regular piano, connects to a synthesizer, records what is played, and plays it back.

To keep the company successful in the face of these challenges, Steinway strengthened its marketing program. While several piano manufacturers have been forced into bankruptcy, Steinway has been achieving record-breaking sales. From 1986 through 1991, the company sold more grand pianos in North America than it had in the past fifty years. Today, revenues have reached $125 million, giving the company its most profitable year in its 143-year history. Although Steinway's owner recently agreed to merge with Selmer Company, maker of band and orchestral instruments, the company's president insists that the two firms will continue operating as individual entities so that the venerable piano maker can maintain the quality, workmanship, and prized reputation it has earned.[13]

Questions for Discussion

1. Are the assumptions of the classic demand curve likely to hold true for the products of Steinway and Sons? If not, what would the demand curve for these products look like? Explain in terms of elasticity of demand.
2. Why doesn't Steinway and Sons lower its prices to be more competitive with other piano makers? What factors, if any, serve to justify the high relative prices of Steinway pianos?
3. In terms of both pricing policy and method, how should Steinway and Sons respond to low-priced, high-tech competition such as Yamaha's Disklavier?

512

Case 21.2   Back Yard Burgers: Fresh Gourmet Food at a Competitive Price

Since its first outlet opened in 1987 in Cleveland, Mississippi, Back Yard Burgers has grown into a significant competitor in the fast-food service industry in the southern United States. The company moved its headquarters to Memphis in 1990 and went public in 1993. Early investors were so optimistic about the company's chances for long-term success that shares of its stock sold for nearly twice their initial price in the first day of over-the-counter trading. By the end of 1994, there were over sixty-five Back Yard Burgers locations and plans for even more rapid expansion in coming years. The company's success has come in part from its ability to maintain competitive prices while offering a nonstandard, premium product in a very price-sensitive industry.

In the late 1980s and early 1990s, the fast-food business became intensely price-competitive, with what was termed "value pricing" characterizing the industry. Value pricing entails delivering high-quality, low-price products on a regular basis, not just during sales or as specials. Fast-food operators marketing all types of foods joined the value-pricing battle. In Mexican-style food, Taco Bell succeeded by grouping most of its menu items into three categories, all priced under $1. Its three-tier, price-based groupings—59, 79, and 99 cents—established Taco Bell's "value menu" as the leader in value pricing. Other food categories followed suit. McDonald's, Burger King, and Wendy's all introduced burger choices selling for under $1 or repriced popular items under this figure.

Back Yard Burgers' founder, Lattimore Michael, created the company to introduce upscale products—gourmet hamburgers and chicken filet sandwiches—into an industry characterized by standard fare. Moreover, the company brought these nonstandard products into what was then the fastest growing segment in the fast-food industry—double-drive-through restaurants. Back Yard Burgers specializes in healthier, leaner offerings. Everything but the French fries is cooked on a slanted grill so the fat runs off. Menu items include grilled-to-order 1/3-pound and 2/3-pound hamburgers, seven types of 1/3-pound Gourmet

Burgers, five kinds of charbroiled chicken filet sandwiches, and Gardenburgers, meatless and soyless vegetarian patties, all priced to compete with top-of-the-line offerings of fast-food rivals. One-third- and two-third-pound Back Yard Burgers are priced at $1.89 and $2.99, and all seven Gourmet Burgers sell for $2.49. Customers can also order a wide variety of side-order items like cole slaw, fries, and salads.

Because of the highly price-competitive nature of the fast-food industry, Back Yard Burgers also offers several value-priced items. The Back Yard Dog—grilled, all-beef hotdogs—sells for 98 cents. Other value-priced products are chili dogs, chili-cheese fries, and all-beef chili. Additionally, the company often runs specials on these items, offering them in combination or in larger quantity at low prices.

With its diverse range of nonstandard gourmet products, faster-than-average service, and competitive pricing, Back Yard Burgers competes with the four largest U.S. hamburger chains—McDonald's, Burger King, Wendy's, and Hardees. The big four, much larger than their upstart competitor, are capable of accessing far greater financial resources. However, with its 1994 net income 31 times greater than the previous year, Back Yard Burgers continues to grow. Undaunted by the fast-food dynasties, Back Yard Burgers targets those customers who want something a notch above typical fast food and a good value at the same time.[14]

Questions for Discussion

1. What type of psychological pricing is most evident in the fast-service food industry? How might this present problems for Back Yard Burgers, given the company's pricing objectives?
2. Discuss the effects of both fixed and variable costs on Back Yard Burgers' ability to compete successfully on price with other fast-food establishments.
3. How might demand factors figure into the prices set at Back Yard Burgers? Are the resulting individual demand curves for the various products offered by the company likely to differ? Explain.

STRATEGIC CASE 6

United States Postal Service Competes Through Pricing

As far back as 2000 B.C., historians can find references to mail delivery through a structured postal system. Although Ancient Egypt and China both operated rudimentary forms of such systems, the modern concept of mail delivery wasn't born until the late 1600s. By 1753, the American colonies boasted a fairly extensive, frequent, and speedy mail service, and by 1775, the new nation had not only its independence, but its first postmaster general, Benjamin Franklin. Mail reforms during the late 1800s brought mail within reach of masses of people by establishing cheap and uniform rates, and the range of services available has been growing steadily since. The Postal Reorganization Act of 1970 transformed the U.S. Post Office into a government-owned corporation called the United States Postal Service (U.S.P.S.). Although Congress no longer sets postal rates, it does retain the power to approve or veto them.

Product Mix and Prices

When the U.S.P.S. was created, its directive was to provide universal service for every class of mail and to price letter mail uniformly. The growing number and types of mail service, however, have led to an assortment of pricing programs. In addition to first-, second-, third-, and fourth-class mail, which are priced according to content, there are also Priority and Express Mail services, which are priced according to timing. Express Mail service guarantees overnight delivery of domestic letters and packages, even on Saturdays, Sundays, and holidays. Priority Mail, expedited delivery of first-class mail, promises delivery in two days. Costing $3 for mail weighing up to 2 pounds and $6 for packages up to 5 pounds Priority Mail is significantly less expensive than are competing overnight services. Today, Priority Mail is one of the Postal Service's most popular and fastest growing products, producing almost three times the annual revenue raised by the more expensive Express Mail.

The "What's Your Priority?" Promotional Campaign

During the 1980s, Federal Express, the Postal Service's fiercest competitor, capitalized on the free-spending mood of that decade to become the world leader in overnight mail delivery. Businesses, for example, were willing to spend more money if it meant closing a deal quickly and successfully. With the slower economy of the more value-conscious 1990s, Americans are becoming increasingly attracted to the lower-priced choice offered them by the U.S.P.S.'s Priority Mail. In response, the U.S.P.S. has created a multimedia promo-

tional campaign designed to increase its current 50 percent share of the two-day market.

Positioning Priority Mail as the low-priced alternative to premium second-day services, ads focus on the Postal Service's competitive advantages, including price, Saturday delivery, and—with the largest number of facilities, trucks, and airplanes—convenience. The campaign, which includes cable, spot, and national television, print, direct mail, radio, and outdoor ads, emphasizes price and uses it as the one easy-to-remember thematic link. Although each of six television commercials highlights a different, little-recognized fact about Priority Mail, they all focus on price by including the same $12-$6-$3 comparison among Federal Express, United Parcel Service, and the Postal Service. Postal Service marketers believe that once potential customers know the facts, the decision to use Priority Mail is a "no-brainer."

Print ads with the same $12-$6-$3 theme appear in major newspapers such as *The Wall Street Journal* and *The New York Times*, in business publications such as *Business Week*, and in other magazines, like *Inc.*, that target small businesses. Seven 60-second radio spots, termed "factoid commercials" by creators, also remind listeners that they can choose to pay one of three prices, $12, $6, or $3. In the campaign's first direct mail effort, launched during tax season, the $12-$6-$3 theme was intensified by including the message, "Don't give away more than you already have to." In none of these advertising media does the Postal Service even hint at its comparative disadvantages, which include no tracking or tracing and no on-time guarantee.

Although many customers believe that Priority Mail's price is right, they are sometimes dissatisfied when the Postal Service does not fulfill its promise of two-day delivery. To overcome this problem, the Postal Service recently announced that it will test a new method for handling Priority Mail. Even though regular post offices will continue accepting Priority Mail Letters and packages, they will be dispatched to separate processing centers handling solely this class of mail. If the year-long test of ten sites meets its 98-percent-in-two-days delivery goal, the Postal Service will add fifty sites all over the United States.

Changing Services and Changing Prices

For some time, the Postal Service has wanted to restructure the way in which it prices all classes of mail, moving away from prices based on mail content and toward a system based on delivery time. In this way, insist U.S.P.S. officials, its prices, like those of competitors Federal Express and United Parcel Service, will be more market-based. One such proposal includes consolidating all mail into four classes: Expedited Mail (combining Express and Priority Mail services); First Class; Second Class (including all periodicals); and Standard (combining third and fourth class). Not only will this simplified system be more in line with the market, asserts the Postal Service, it will increase customer satisfaction.

At the opposite end of the spectrum from this uncomplicated approach is a vast and dizzying array of other Postal Service plans. Hoping to increase customer service, the U.S.P.S. is testing "Pack & Send" centers at some post office locations. With prices based on three elements—packaging, postage, and labor—customers will be able to have their packages boxed and shipped in one stop. Two business-oriented, service-enhancing proposals are "Fastnet" and "Neighborhood Mail." With Fastnet, businesses would be able to contract with the post office for next-day product shipments but pay regular parcel post prices. Neighborhood Mail would allow businesses to send advertising pieces for as little as eleven cents each. In addition, the Postal Service has proposed the Worldpost Priority Letter, offering four-day delivery service at an economical flat rate, launched a multimillion dollar research project aimed at establishing the Postal Service as a major player in the E-mail business, and explored the possibility of selling long-distance phone cards in a partnership with American Express. Quipped one industry analyst, "We're told that the Postal Service plans to continue selling stamps and delivering letters."

The Challenge of Pricing Decisions

Federal Express recently added $159 same-day delivery. United Parcel Service meanwhile increased its shipping rates, basing them on distance as well as weight. The Postal Service, however, must wait up to a year for approval of a one-cent hike in the price of sending a postcard. When the Postal Service's competitors want to add products or change prices, their executives decide and proceed. Because of its unique relationship with the United States government, the Postal Service is unable to take such quick and decisive action. To increase its flexibility in changing prices and introducing new products and services, the postmaster general is seeking legislation that will grant the agency greater freedom. With domestic and foreign postal competitors and electronic communication vying for market share, the Postal Service wants to convince Congress that giving it more freedom translates into giving it a chance to succeed.

Questions for Discussion

1. How might buyers' perceptions affect the pricing of Priority Mail service?
2. Do U.S.P.S. and Federal Express have similar pricing objectives when pricing their similar services? Explain.
3. Which pricing method is U.S.P.S. using?
4. What types of issues will U.S.P.S. officials have to cope with when making future pricing decisions?

Sources: Bill McAllister, "Postal Service to Make 2-Day Parcels a Priority," *Washington Post*, Jan. 22, 1996, p. A17; Ho Rodney, "UPS Raising Rates, But Customer Impact Varies," *Atlanta Constitution*, Jan. 4, 1996, p. F1; Mario C. Aguilera, "Post Office Tries New Services to Get an Edge," *San Diego Daily Transcript*, Oct. 18, 1995, p. A1; Dorothy Gjiobbe, "Postal Service Plans Unaddressed Saturation Program," *Editor & Publisher*, Sept. 9, 1996, p. 24; Jim McTeague, "D.C. Current: Runyonesque Approach Would Let the Post Office Borrow in the Credit Markets, Expand into Other Services," *Barron's*, Nov. 27. 1996, p. 35; Bill McAllister, "Postal Service Projects Surplus of $1.8 Billion," *Washington Post*, Sept. 13, 1995, p. A17; Bill McAllister, "Postal Service Seeks to Cut Rates for Biggest Customers," *Washington Post*, March 14, 1995, pp. D1, D7; Asra Q. Nomani, "Postal Service Proposes Increase in Postcard Rates," *Wall Street Journal*, Mar. 14, 1995, p. B2; Robert Frank, "Federal Express, Battling Against UPS, Will Offer Same-Day Delivery Service," *Wall Street Journal*, Apr. 12, 1995, p. A2; United States Postal Service, *Consumer's Guide to Postal Rates and Fees*, July 1995; United States Postal Service, *Classification Reform Overview*, June 1995; and phone interview with David Shinnenbarger, Expedited and Package Services Marketing Manager, April 11, 1996.

Marketing
Management

*W*e have divided marketing into several sets of variables and have discussed the decisions and activities associated with each variable. By now, you should understand (1) how to analyze marketing opportunities and (2) the components of the marketing mix. It is time to put all these components together in a discussion of marketing management issues. In Chapter 22 we discuss strategic market planning; the role of the mission statement; how organizational opportunities affect the planning process; corporate, business-unit, and marketing strategies; and creating the marketing plan. Chapter 23 deals with other marketing management issues, including implementation and control. It explores approaches

to organizing a marketing unit, issues regarding strategy implementation, and techniques for controlling marketing strategies.

Chapter 22

Strategic Market Planning

OBJECTIVES

- To be able to describe the strategic market planning process

- To understand the role of the mission statement in strategic market planning

- To be able to explain how organizational opportunities and resources affect the planning process

- To examine corporate, business-unit, and marketing strategy

- To learn about the process of creating the marketing plan

King Ranch diversifies from cattle roundups to corporate spinoffs.

*T*he King Ranch was founded in 1853 by steamboat captain Richard King, on the advice of his friend Robert E. Lee. Today, 60,000 "Running W"–branded cattle roam the King Ranch's 825,000 acres—roughly the size of Rhode Island—within 2,000 miles of fencing. The King Ranch has developed many elements of modern cattle ranching while contending, over the years, with Union and Mexican soldiers, overseas expansion and retrenchment, drought, diminishing revenues from its oil and gas leases, declining beef consumption, and family members who sought to break up and sell the historic ranch. It has been especially vulnerable to the volatile cycles of the cattle and energy industries, as well as the whims of the arid South Texas weather. To mini-mize the effects of these cycles and to position itself for the next century, King Ranch, Inc., is capitalizing on the strength of its size and resources by developing new market opportunities and diversifying.

The King Ranch Saddle Shop, which once produced tack solely for ranch hands, now sells upscale clothing and luggage to the public through two stores in Texas as well as direct mail and telemarketing. The ranch also offers eco-tours where the public can observe the ranch's unique variety of birds and wildlife, as well as traditional ranching activities. Hunters in pursuit of white-tail deer, javelina, wild turkeys, and doves bring in $3 million a year from leases on 435,000 acres of ranch land. Favorable market conditions, particularly rising cotton prices, have led ranch managers to engage in land management by planting approximately 63,000 acres in cotton and milo. And although oil revenues have long been important, the company is now employing advanced technology to find new sources of oil and gas in Texas, Oklahoma, and under the Gulf of Mexico.

In addition, the ranch continues to experiment with new types of grasses, genetic research, and creative ways to market beef. Although the King Ranch will always be best known for cattle ranching, the company's spinoff businesses now comprise about 60 percent of its revenues. Stephen J. "Tio" Kleberg, the ranch's vice president in charge of agribusiness, and the great-great-grandson of Captain King, says, "We no longer see ourselves in the cattle business, as such. We are in the resource-management business."[1]

517

The continuing success of the King Ranch will depend on its ability to determine and implement comprehensive and well-designed strategic market plans. With competition increasing, many companies are spending more time and resources on strategic market planning, that is, determining how to use their resources and abilities to reach a specific target market. To understand the tools for strategic market planning, it is important to recognize that strategic market planning takes into account all aspects of a firm's strategy in the marketplace. Most of this book deals with marketing decisions and strategies. This chapter focuses on the recognition that all functional activities—including marketing, research and development, production, finance, and human resources—must be coordinated to reach organizational goals.

We begin this chapter with an overview of the strategic market planning process, including the development of a mission statement and organizational goals. We also examine the role of organizational opportunities and resources in strategic market planning. After discussing the development of both corporate and business-unit strategy, we explore the nature of marketing strategy and the creation of the marketing plan. The implementation, evaluation, and control of marketing strategies are covered in Chapter 23.

518

Defining Strategic Market Planning

Strategic market plan
An outline of the methods and resources needed to achieve a firm's goals in a specific target market

Strategic business unit (SBU)   A division, product line, or other profit center within the parent company

Strategic market planning
A process yielding a marketing strategy that is the framework for a marketing plan

Marketing program
Marketing strategies to be implemented and used at the same time

A **strategic market plan** is an outline of the methods and resources required to achieve an organization's goals within a specific target market. It takes into account not only marketing, but also all functional aspects of a business unit that must be coordinated. These functional aspects include production, finance, and human resources management. Environmental issues are also an important consideration.

The concept of the strategic business unit is used to define areas for consideration in a specific strategic market plan. Each **strategic business unit (SBU)** is a division, product line, or other profit center within the parent company. Borden's strategic business units, for example, consist of dairy products, snacks, pasta, niche grocery products such as ReaLemon juice and Cremora coffee creamer, and other units such as glue and paints. Each sells a distinct set of products to an identifiable group of customers, and each competes with a well-defined set of competitors. Each SBU's revenues, costs, investment, and strategic plans can be separated from those of the parent company and evaluated. SBUs operate in a variety of markets, which have differing growth rates, opportunities, degrees of competition, and profit-making potential. Strategic planners therefore must recognize the different performance capabilities of each SBU and carefully allocate scarce resources among these divisions.

The process of **strategic market planning** yields a marketing strategy that is the framework for a marketing plan, which was defined in Chapter 1 as a written document that specifies the activities to be performed to implement and control an organization's marketing activities. Thus a strategic market plan is *not* the same as a marketing plan; it is a plan of *all* aspects of an organization's strategy in the marketplace. A marketing plan, in contrast, deals primarily with implementing the market strategy as it relates to target markets and the marketing mix.[2]

Figure 22.1 shows the components of strategic market planning. The process is based on the establishment of an organization's overall goals, and it must stay within the bounds of the organization's opportunities and resources. When the firm has determined its overall goals and identified its resources, it can then assess its opportunities and develop an overall corporate strategy. Marketing objectives must be designed so that their achievement will contribute to the corporate strategy and so that they can be accomplished through efficient use of the firm's resources.

To achieve its marketing objectives, an organization must develop a marketing strategy, or a set of marketing strategies, as shown in Figure 22.1. The set of marketing strategies that are implemented and used at the same time is referred to as the organization's **marketing program.** As we have mentioned before, to formulate a marketing strategy, the marketer identifies and analyzes the target market and develops a marketing mix to satisfy individuals in that market. Marketing strategy is best formulated when it reflects the

Figure 22.1
Components of Strategic Market Planning

overall direction of the organization and is coordinated with all the firm's functional areas. Through the process of strategic market planning, an organization can develop marketing strategies that, when properly implemented and controlled, will contribute to the achievement of its marketing objectives and its overall goals.

As indicated in Figure 22.1, the strategic market planning process is based on an analysis of the environment, by which it is very much affected. Environmental forces can constrain an organization and possibly influence its overall goals; they also affect the amount and type of resources that a firm can acquire. However, these forces can create favorable opportunities as well—opportunities that can be translated into overall organizational goals and marketing objectives. Inside Marketing (on the next page) describes how MCI plans to take advantage of such a favorable opportunity.

Marketers differ in their viewpoints concerning the effect of environmental variables on marketing planning and strategy. Some take a deterministic perspective, believing that firms must react to external conditions and tailor their strategies and organizational structures to deal with these conditions. According to others, however, companies can influence their environments by choosing what markets to compete in. Furthermore, they can change the structures of their industries, engaging in activities such as mergers and acquisitions, demand creation, or technological innovation.[3]

Regardless of which viewpoint is adopted, environmental variables play a part in the creation of a marketing strategy. When environmental variables affect an organization's overall goals, resources, opportunities, or marketing objectives, they also affect its marketing strategies, which are based on these factors. Environmental forces more directly influence the development of a marketing strategy through their impact on consumers' needs and desires. In addition, these forces have a bearing on marketing mix decisions. For instance, competition strongly influences marketing mix decisions. The organization must diagnose the marketing mix activities it performs, taking into account competitors' marketing mix decisions, and develop some competitive advantage to support a strategy. Thus as Nissan and Toyota entered the luxury automobile market with the Infiniti and Lexus models, European car makers BMW, Mercedes-Benz, and Jaguar had to change their marketing strategies to maintain their market shares. First, they lowered prices to compete with the new Japanese models. Mercedes also developed the new Mercedes E class and Mercedes sport utility vehicle models to maintain a competitive advantage.

MCI Rolls Up Its Sleeves

MCI handles 20 percent of all long-distance telephone calls in the United States, ringing up 1995 revenues of $15.3 billion and profits of $1.07 billion. In fact, the "Big Three"—MCI together with AT&T and Sprint—command 90 percent of the $75 billion long-distance market. That domination may soon be diluted, however, by 1996 legislation that deregulated the telecommunications industry, allowing long-distance firms, local phone companies, and cable-TV providers to enter one another's markets for the first time. Deregulation will forever change the way telecommunications firms do business. To survive, MCI is developing new plans and strategies.

MCI intends to focus on selling as many communications-related services as possible, including Internet connections, satellite TV, and local, long-distance, and international phone calls. It wants to provide one-stop shopping for long-distance and local phone calls, and video, data, and wireless services. Already, its MCI Metro subsidiary is building a fiber-optic network in major cities that will connect businesses directly to its long-distance network. MCI has also acquired Nationwide Cellular to gain quick entry into the cellular resale business, and its purchase of SHL Systemhouse gives it an opportunity to handle corporate telecom networks. According to MCI chairman/CEO Bert C. Roberts Jr., "We want to get as many hooks into each of our customers as possible." However, AT&T, Sprint, cable-TV providers, and other firms are thinking along the same lines. Moreover, many new companies will soon be entering the long-distance market, driving down prices and forcing up marketing costs.

To compete in the new deregulated marketplace, MCI is looking for partners to spread out its risks. It has already completed deals for a Microsoft Corp. online partnership, a direct broadcast satellite (DBS) venture with News Corp., and another with British Telecom to offer global networking services to major corporations. It has also held preliminary talks with AT&T about forming an alliance to build local calling networks. MCI executives believe these moves and savvy marketing will give the firm a sharp edge in the cutthroat telecommunications industry.

Sources: Catherine Arnst, "MCI Is Swarming Over the Horizon," *Business Week,* Feb. 19, 1996, pp. 68–69; and Catherine Arnst, "Operator, Please Connect Me," *Business Week,* Feb. 26, 1996, p. 33.

In the next sections we discuss the major components of the strategic market planning process: organizational mission and goals, organizational opportunities and resources, and corporate and business-unit strategy, as well as some of the tools used in strategic market planning. Later, we examine marketing strategy and the role of the marketing plan.

Establishing an Organizational Mission and Goals

Mission statement
A long-term view of what the organization wants to become

*T*he goals of any organization should be derived from its mission. Most successful organizations put their missions in writing in the form of a **mission statement,** which is a long-term view, or vision, of what the organization wants to become. Defense contractor Lockheed Martin, for example, defines its mission as forging strong partnerships with government and commercial customers throughout the world, with technology that ranges from aeronautics and electronics to information services and space communication (see Figure 22.2).

When an organization decides on its mission, it really answers two questions: What is our business? and What should our business be?[4] Although these questions seem very simple, they are in fact two of the hardest yet most important questions that any business can answer. Creating or revising a mission statement is very difficult because of the many complex variables that must be examined. However, having a mission statement can greatly benefit the organization in at least five ways.[5]

520

Our mission is to forge strong partnerships with governments and companies throughout the world. With technology ranging from aeronautics and electronics to information services and space communications. Our customers count on us to meet their needs for affordable solutions that get results. Working together with our customers, we turn opportunity into reality.

LOCKHEED MARTIN
Mission Success

Figure 22.2
Mission Statement
Lockheed Martin, a large defense contractor, promotes its aeronautics and electronics capabilities to solve government and commercial customers' needs.

- A mission statement gives the organization a clear purpose and direction. Thus it keeps the organization on track, preventing it from drifting.
- It describes the unique focus of the organization that helps to differentiate it from similar competing organizations.
- It keeps the organization focused on customer needs rather than its own abilities. This ensures that the organization remains externally rather than internally focused.
- It provides specific direction and guidelines to top managers for selecting from among alternative courses of action. Thus it helps them decide which business opportunities to pursue, as well as which opportunities not to pursue.
- It provides guidance to all employees and managers of an organization, even if they work in different parts of the world. As a result, the mission statement acts like glue to hold the organization together.

The wording of Federal Express's mission statement (Figure 22.3) is directly related to the five benefits mentioned above. For example, the mission statement directly explains what business Federal Express competes in. It also focuses on customer needs and the

Figure 22.3
Federal Express Corporate Mission Statement

Source: *Federal Express Information Book*, Copyright © 1993. Reprinted courtesy of Federal Express Corporation.

Mission Statement

Federal Express is committed to our People-Service-Profit philosophy. We will produce outstanding financial returns by providing totally reliable, competitively superior global air-ground transportation of high priority goods and documents that require rapid, time-certain delivery. Equally important, positive control of each package will be maintained, utilizing real time electronic tracking and tracing systems. A complete record of each shipment and delivery will be presented with our request for payment. We will be helpful, courteous and professional to each other and the public. We will strive to have a satisfied customer at the end of each transaction.

Distinctive competency
Something that a firm does extremely well, which may give it a competitive advantage

company's distinctive competencies. A **distinctive competency** is something that an organization does extremely well—sometimes so well that it gives the company an advantage over its competition.[6] An organization's goal can be focused on a distinctive competency to meet a market need. For example, Martha and Ralph Stewart market designer paints at $110 per gallon to people who want the highest-quality paint and unique colors. The Stewarts developed their colors—such as Crested Butte, Porch Awning, Dressage Red, and Spinnaker Blue—from the blue-, green-, and brown-hued eggshells produced by Martha's Araucana and Ameraucana chickens at her Westport, Connecticut, home. They believe the high prices are justified because their paints last longer and cover more. When 85 percent of the cost of painting is labor, why not use the very best paint possible?[7] The FedEx mission statement mentions two distinctive competencies: electronic tracking systems and employee relations. These advantages make FedEx one of the top companies in the business of document and package delivery. The mission statements of most successful companies are built around one or more distinctive competencies.

An organization's goals, which are derived from its mission, guide the remainder of its planning efforts. Goals focus on the end results sought by the organization. Examples of organizational goals include profit, return on investment, or an increase in market share. The Federal Express mission statement incorporates the company's goal of striving for customer satisfaction.

Organizations can have short-term and long-term goals. Companies experiencing financial difficulty may be forced to focus solely on the short-term results necessary to stay in business, such as increasing cash flow by lowering prices or selling off parts of the business. Other organizations may have more optimistic, long-term goals. In many cases, companies that pursue long-term goals have to sacrifice short-term results to achieve them. For example, General Motors created the Saturn division in the late 1980s with the long-term goal of having Saturn become the number one automobile in the small-car market. However, the short-term results of the Saturn Corp. have been reduced profits and large investments to maintain quality.[8]

Making the Most of Organizational Opportunities and Resources

*O*nce an organization has established its mission and goals, it must then take stock of its opportunities, as well as the resources it has available to take advantage of those opportunities. There are three major considerations in assessing opportunities and resources: environmental scanning, evaluating market opportunities, and understanding the firm's capabilities and resources.

■ *Environmental Scanning*

In Chapter 2 we defined environmental scanning as the process of collecting information about forces in the marketing environment because such knowledge helps marketers identify opportunities and assists in planning. Some companies have derived substantial benefits from establishing an "environmental scanning (or monitoring) unit" within the strategic planning group or including line management in teams of committees to conduct environmental analysis. Results of forecasting research show that even simple quantitative forecasting techniques outperform the unstructured intuitive assessments of experts.[9]

Environmental scanning to detect changes in the environment is extremely important if a firm is to avoid crisis management. An environmental change can suddenly alter a firm's opportunities or resources. Reformulated, more effective strategies may then be needed to guide marketing efforts. For example, California passed legislation that requires all automakers to convert 2 percent of their yearly sales to zero-emission vehicles by 1998 and 10 percent by 2003. Eleven other states are considering similar legislation.[10] Because automobile manufacturers had been scanning their environment for the possibility of this type of legislation, they had already begun developing plans for emission-free vehicles.

The Big Three U.S. automakers are cooperating on the production of a battery-powered car. However, since consumers have yet to fully accept the idea of electric vehicles, the jury is still out on the ultimate success of such a venture.[11]

■ *Market Opportunities*

Chapter 1 defined a market opportunity as the right combination of circumstances and timing that permit an organization to take action toward reaching a target market. An opportunity provides a favorable chance or opening for the firm to generate sales from identifiable markets. Being the very first to take advantage of a new market opportunity is expensive and risky but can be very rewarding. The lead time that a trailblazer company has over later entrants can create an advantage in terms of obtaining supplies, reducing costs, improving quality, and gaining commitment from supply chain partners. For example, Xerox gained long-term strategic advantage by being first in the photocopier market. On the other hand, later entrants to a market may be able to leap-frog over the errors of pioneers with better technology and better consumer understanding to produce a more successful product.[12] Many marketers are poised to take advantage of the growth of the Internet's World Wide Web. The Yahoo guide, an index to many WWW sites, currently lists nearly 25,000 companies. CDNow, for example, markets more than 165,000 CDs and other products on its Web site, which is visited by more than 10,000 Internet users a day. Sun Microsystems' Web page permits customers to obtain product information, documentation, and software updates; it saves the company nearly $1 million a year in toll-free calls. With more than 18 million people in the United States and Canada accessing the World Wide Web, and more coming online every day, the Web represents a huge opportunity for marketers to reach current and potential customers.[13] Opportunities like these are often called **strategic windows,** or temporary periods of optimum fit between the key requirements of a market and the particular capabilities of a firm competing in that market.[14] Taking advantage of strategic windows is easier for a company already established in a particular market. When Duncan Hines launched Angel Cups, a fat-free, one-minute cupcake mix, the product was an instant success. It appealed to customers' desires to eliminate fat and preparation time from tasty desserts, and shoppers trusted the Duncan Hines label on a new product more than they might have a no-name cake mix company.[15]

Strategic windows
Temporary periods of optimum fit between the requirements of a market and the capabilities of a firm

The attractiveness of market opportunities is determined by market factors, such as size and growth rate, as well as competitive, economic, political, legal and regulatory, technological, and sociocultural forces. Because each industry and product are somewhat different, the factors that determine attractiveness tend to vary.

Market requirements
Relate to customers' needs or desired benefits

Market requirements relate to customers' needs or desired benefits. Market requirements are satisfied by components of the marketing mix that provide buyers with these benefits. Of course, buyers' perceptions of what requirements fulfill their needs and provide the desired benefits determine the success of any marketing effort. Marketers must devise strategies to outperform competitors by finding out what product attributes buyers use to select products. An attribute must be important and differentiating if it is to be useful in strategy development. When marketers fail to understand buyers' perceptions and market requirements, the result may be failure.

■ *Capabilities and Resources*

A firm's capabilities relate to distinctive competencies that it has developed to do something well and efficiently. Some firms use their competencies to create a competitive advantage over their rivals. A **competitive advantage** is created when a company matches its distinctive competency to the opportunities it has discovered in the market.[16] Ford Motor Company, for example, invests in racing design and development, which results in a competitive advantage in auto and truck performance (see Figure 22.4). In some cases, a company may possess manufacturing, technical, or marketing skills that can be matched to market opportunities in order to create a competitive advantage. Microsoft, for example, used its marketing and technical skills to create Windows to make computers easier to use. Although Windows is now pre-installed on most personal computers, Microsoft continues to work to maintain its competitive advantage by improving Windows and introducing Windows-compatible software.

Competitive advantage
Matching a distinctive competency to the opportunities in the market

Figure 22.4
Competitive Advantage
By investing in racing car technology, new-product developments are transferred back to consumer cars and trucks, giving Ford a competitive advantage.

Significant competitive advantages are associated with positive brand equity. Once a brand is established as providing unique benefits, it can resist or blunt competitive threats such as price wars or new-product introductions. In extreme situations, strong brand equity helps a brand survive a crisis that would destroy a weaker competitor.[17] For example, Tylenol faced a severe threat when it had to recall all of its capsule products because of tampering. A weaker brand probably would have been destroyed by such a calamity; Tylenol not only survived, but thrived.

Developing Corporate and Business-Unit Strategies

*I*n any organization, there are essentially three levels of strategic market planning: corporate strategy, business-unit strategy, and marketing strategy. The outcomes of each planning stage must be consistent with the stage that precedes it. That is, marketing strategy must be consistent with the business-unit and corporate strategies, and business-unit strategy must be consistent with the corporate strategy. Although corporate strategy is the broadest stage in strategic market planning, it must be developed with the organization's overall mission in mind. The relationships between these planning levels are shown in Figure 22.5. Before we examine marketing strategy, we must first discuss the broader topics of corporate and business-unit strategy.

■ *Corporate Strategy*

Corporate strategy
Determines the means for utilizing resources in various functional areas to reach the firm's goals

Corporate strategy determines the means for utilizing resources in the areas of production, finance, research and development, human resources, and marketing to reach the organization's goals. A corporate strategy determines not only the scope of the business but also its resource deployment, competitive advantages, and overall coordination of production, finance, marketing, and other functional areas. As such, the corporate strategy more specifically addresses the two questions that we first answered in the organization's mission statement: What is our business? and What should our business be?[18] The term *corporate* in this context does not apply only to corporations; corporate strategy is used by all organizations, from the smallest sole proprietorship to the largest multinational corporation.

Corporate strategy planners are concerned with issues such as diversification, competition, differentiation, interrelationships between business units, and environmental issues. They attempt to match the resources of the organization with the opportunities and risks in the environment. Corporate strategy planners are also concerned with defining the scope and role of the strategic business units of the firm so that they are coordinated to reach the ends desired.

A number of tools have been proposed to aid corporate managers in their planning efforts. Based on ideas used in the management of financial portfolios, several models that classify an organization's product portfolio have been proposed. Just as financial

Figure 22.5
Levels of Strategic Market Planning

investors have different investments with varying risks and rates of return, firms have a portfolio of products characterized by different market growth rates and relative market shares. These models allow strategic business units or products to be classified and visually displayed according to the attractiveness of various markets and the business's relative market share within those markets. One of the most helpful of these is **product-portfolio analysis,** the Boston Consulting Group (BCG) approach, which is based on the philosophy that a product's market growth rate and its relative market share are important considerations in determining its marketing strategy. All the firm's products should be integrated into a single, overall matrix and evaluated to determine appropriate strategies for individual SBUs and the overall portfolio strategies. Managers can use these models to determine and classify each product's expected future cash contributions and future cash requirements. Generally, managers who use a portfolio model must examine the competitive position of a product (or product line) and the opportunities for improving that product's contribution to profitability and cash flow.[19] The BCG analytical approach is more of a diagnostic tool than a guide for making strategy prescriptions.

Figure 22.6, which is based on work by the BCG, enables the marketing manager to classify a firm's products into four basic types: stars, cash cows, dogs, and problem children.[20] Stars are products with a dominant share of the market and good prospects for growth. However, they use more cash than they generate to finance growth, add capacity,

Product-portfolio analysis
A strategic planning approach based on the philosophy that a product's market growth rate and its relative market share are important in its marketing strategy

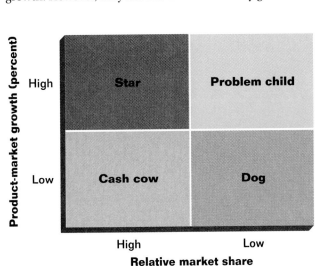

Figure 22.6
Illustrative Growth-Share Matrix Developed by the Boston Consulting Group

Source: *Perspectives,* No. 66, "The Product Portfolio." Reprinted by permission from The Boston Consulting Group, Inc., Boston, MA. © Copyright 1970.

and increase market share. Cash cows have a dominant share of the market but low prospects for growth; typically, they generate more cash than is required to maintain market share. Dogs have a subordinate share of the market and low prospects for growth; these products are often found in mature markets. Problem children, sometimes called "question marks," have a small share of a growing market and generally require a large amount of cash to build share. Figure 22.7 suggests marketing strategies appropriate for cash cows, stars, dogs, and problem children.

The long-term health of an organization depends on having some products that generate cash (and provide acceptable profits) and others that use cash to support growth. Among the indicators of overall health are the size and vulnerability of the cash cows, the

Figure 22.7
Characteristics and Strategies for the Four Basic Product Types in the Growth-Share Matrix
Source: Adapted from George S. Day, "Diagnosing the Product Portfolio," *Journal of Marketing,* Apr. 1977, pp. 30–31.

Product-market growth

High

Stars

Characteristics
▷ Market leaders
▷ Fast growing
▷ Substantial profits
▷ Require large investment to finance growth

Strategies
▷ Protect existing share
▷ Reinvest earnings in the form of price reductions, product improvements, providing better market coverage, production efficiency, etc.
▷ Obtain a large share of the new users

Example
▷ GM's Saturn Division

Problem children

Characteristics
▷ Rapid growth
▷ Poor profit margins
▷ Enormous demand for cash

Strategies
▷ Invest heavily to get a disproportionate share of new sales
▷ Buy existing market shares by acquiring competitors
▷ Divestment (see Dogs)
▷ Harvesting (see Dogs)
▷ Abandonment (see Dogs)
▷ Focus on a definable niche where dominance can be achieved

Example
▷ Electric cars

Cash cows

Characteristics
▷ Profitable products
▷ Generate more cash than needed to maintain market share

Strategies
▷ Maintain market dominance
▷ Invest in process improvements and technological leadership
▷ Maintain price leadership
▷ Use excess cash to support research and growth elsewhere in the company

Example
▷ Chrysler's Minivan Division

Low

Dogs

Characteristics
▷ Greatest number of products fall in this category
▷ Operate at a cost disadvantage
▷ Few opportunities for growth at a reasonable cost
▷ Markets are not growing; therefore, little new business

Strategies
▷ Focus on a specialized segment of the market that can be dominated and protected from competitive inroads
▷ Harvesting—cut back all support costs to a minimum level; supports cash flow over the product's remaining life
▷ Divestment—sale of a growing concern
▷ Abandonment—elimination from the product line

Example
▷ Typewriters

High   **Low**

Relative market share

prospects for the stars, if any, and the number of problem children and dogs. Particular attention must be paid to those products with large cash appetites. Unless the company has an abundant cash flow, it cannot afford to sponsor many such products at one time. If resources, including debt capacity, are spread too thin, the company will end up with too many marginal products and will be unable to finance promising new product entries or acquisitions in the future.

■ *Business-Unit Strategy*

After analyzing corporate operations and performance, the next step in strategic market planning is to determine future business directions and develop business-unit strategies. From a corporate strategy perspective, strategic business units need to be developed according to how well the company's skills and expertise fit with the strategic business unit's needs and success. Is the strategic business unit enhanced because the corporate strategy can contribute to the critical success factors of that unit?[21] A business may choose one or more competitive strategies, including intensive growth or diversified growth. Figure 22.8 shows these competitive strategies on a product-market matrix. This matrix can help in determining growth that can be implemented through marketing strategies.

Intensive growth Growth occurring when current products and markets have potential for increasing sales

Intensive Growth   **Intensive growth** can take place when current products and current markets have the potential for increasing sales. There are three main strategies for intensive growth: market penetration, market development, and product development.

Market penetration is a strategy of increasing sales in current markets with current products. For example, Philip Morris cut prices on its Marlboro cigarette brands to enlarge its market share in the increasingly competitive tobacco industry.

Market development is a strategy of increasing sales of current products in new markets. Arm & Hammer baking soda, for instance, successfully introduced its basic product into several new markets, such as toothpaste, laundry detergent, carpet deodorizer, and cat litter. Likewise, whenever a company introduces its products into international markets for the first time, it is engaging in market development.

Product development is a strategy of increasing sales by improving present products or developing new products for current markets. Oral-B, known for its toothbrushes, is developing markets for its new oral hygiene products, such as toothpaste and antiplaque rinses. In Figure 22.9, Kodak offers a new, smaller disposable camera that provides more ease of use and a new digital camera that provides exceptional digitized pictures. Perhaps the most common example of product development occurs in the automobile industry, in which car manufacturers regularly introduce redesigned or completely new models to their current markets.

Diversified growth Growth occurring when new products are developed to be sold in new markets

Diversified Growth   **Diversified growth** occurs when new products are developed to be sold in new markets. Firms have become increasingly diversified since the 1960s. Diversification offers some advantages over single-business firms because it allows firms to spread their risk across a number of markets. More importantly, it allows firms to make

Figure 22.8
Intensive Growth Strategies
Source: H. I. Ansoff, *New Corporate Strategy* (New York: Wiley, 1988), p. 109.

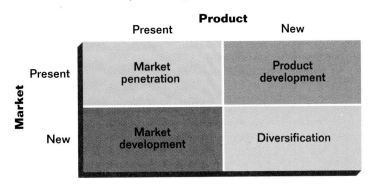

527

Figure 22.9
Product Development
Kodak introduces a smaller disposable camera, which increases its convenience, as well as a new type of digital camera that provides superior images that can easily be transferred to a personal computer.

better and wider use of their management, technical, and financial resources. For example, marketing expertise can be used across businesses, and they may also share advertising themes, distribution channels, warehouse facilities, or even sales forces.[22] Technology in Marketing describes Packard Bell's effort to diversify to gain new products and markets. The four forms of diversification are horizontal, concentric, conglomerate, and integrated. Figure 22.10 shows these diversification strategies in a product-market matrix similar to the previous matrix.

Horizontal diversification results when new products that are not technologically related to current products are introduced into current markets. When Sony Corp. purchased Columbia Pictures, it gained access to a library of almost three thousand movies and tens of thousands of television episodes. While these products are not technologically related to Sony's electronic products, the acquisition allowed Sony to diversify into other areas that could help the sales of its current products.

In *concentric diversification*, the marketing and technology of new products are related to current products, but the new ones are introduced into new markets. For example, Kmart Corp. is most widely known for its chain of Kmart discount stores. However, the retailer is highly diversified into other retail markets. Kmart also owns Waldenbooks, OfficeMax (office supplies), Sports Authority (sporting goods), Builders Square (home improvement centers), and PayLess Drug. It is no surprise that Kmart is regarded as the most diversified retailer in the industry.[23]

Figure 22.10
Diversified Growth Strategies

		Markets	
		Current	New
New products	Unrelated to current products	Horizontal diversification	Conglomerate diversification
	Related to current products	Integrated diversification	Concentric diversification

Packard Bell Makes a Smart Purchase

With half of all personal computers sold in chain stores carrying a Packard Bell label, Packard Bell has become the country's leading manufacturer of PCs. Founded in 1986 (the name—a well-known TV brand in the 1950s—was acquired from Teledyne, Inc.), the company grew to sales of $4.5 billion in 1995. Part of its success stems from quickly integrating the latest technology into its products, especially Intel's Pentium chip. To ensure its continued success in the face of intense competition, Packard Bell acquired Zenith Data Systems, a unit of France's Groupe Bull, in 1996.

The Zenith merger represents a good match for Packard Bell in many ways. Until recently, Packard Bell has focused on home PC users, whereas Zenith sells almost exclusively to companies and government agencies. Zenith makes notebook computers and network servers, higher-margin products that Packard Bell lacks. Packard Bell has been wanting to expand internationally—less than 10 percent of its sales are overseas—and Zenith did more than half of its $1.3 billion in sales outside the United States in 1995.

Even before acquiring Zenith, Packard Bell was planning international expansion. It opened a factory in France in 1994, started building computers in Brazil in 1995, and set up a Singapore-based Asian division in 1995. The company has also been working on expanding to include business accounts, even forming a technical support group dedicated to corporate buyers. CEO Beny Alagem says, "We have always sold PCs to small and medium-sized corporations through our retailers. But as we go forward, we will put more emphasis on our relationship with corporate resellers."

In the business market, Packard Bell can expect fierce competition from IBM, Compaq, and Dell, who are likely to match any price cuts Packard Bell offers. However, by giving it new products and markets, the acquisition of Zenith helps put Packard Bell in a better position in an industry that may be slowing down. Promises Alagem, "What you're seeing is the beginning of the second phase of Packard Bell's growth."

Sources: Larry Armstrong, "More Red Meat, Please," *Business Week*, May 22, 1995, pp. 132, 134; and Larry Armstrong, with Peter Elstrom, "Packard Bell and Zenith Data: The Tortoise and the Tortoise?" *Business Week*, Feb. 19, 1996, p. 30.

529

Conglomerate diversification occurs when new products are unrelated to current technology, products, or markets and are introduced into markets new to the firm. For example, Seagram Co., which markets alcoholic beverages, acquired MCA, which produces movies and television shows, and owns publishing houses, theme parks, and movie theaters.

Integrated diversification typically occurs within the same industry or product market when one company buys or merges with another. This integration can be forward, backward, or horizontal. A company growing through forward integration takes ownership or increased control of its distribution system. For example, a shoe manufacturer might start selling its products through wholly owned retail outlets. In backward integration, a firm takes ownership or increased control of its supply systems. A newspaper company that buys a paper mill is integrating backward. Horizontal integration occurs when a firm takes ownership or control of one of its competitors.

Developing a Marketing Strategy

*T*he next phase in strategic market planning is the development of a sound marketing strategy. A marketing strategy is typically designed around two components: (1) the selection of a target market and (2) the creation of a marketing mix that will satisfy the needs of the chosen target market. A marketing strategy is also a detailed explanation of how an organization will achieve its marketing objectives. Once properly implemented, a good marketing strategy enables a company to achieve its business-unit and corporate objectives. While corporate, business-unit, and marketing strategies all overlap to some extent, the marketing strategy is the most detailed and specific of the three.

All good marketing strategies begin with an understanding of consumers and their needs. When a company truly understands the needs of its target market or markets, it can use its own strengths or distinctive competencies to fill those needs better than any other company. Meeting consumer needs better than competitors is another way of creating a competitive advantage. In addition, a superior marketing strategy that differentiates a firm's product can generate higher margins via premium pricing, which depends on loyal customers whose brand preferences make them relatively price insensitive. An effective marketing strategy opens doors so that a firm can get a boost from an enthusiastic sales force and from retailers who provide space for the established product.[24]

■ *Target Market Selection*

Selecting an appropriate target market may be the most important decision a company has to make in the planning process. This is so because the target market has to be chosen before the organization can adapt its marketing mix to meet this market's needs and preferences. Defining the target market and developing the appropriate marketing mix are the keys to strategic success. Alamo Rent-A-Car, Inc., grew from a very small regional company to the nation's fourth-largest daily car rental company by defining its market as leisure travelers while its major competitors focused on business travelers. Alamo introduced such concepts as unlimited mileage and developed strong ties to travel agents and tour operators to dominate the leisure traveler market.[25] Should the company select the wrong target market, all other marketing decisions will be a waste of time. An organization must also examine whether it possesses the necessary resources and skills to create a marketing mix that will satisfy the needs of its target market. Organizations that do not possess the resources or skills to meet the needs of a particular target market are usually better off finding a different market to serve.

Organizations must also choose their target markets carefully because of the drastic changes taking place in the U.S. population. For example, because many adults are becoming more concerned about their diet, Planters introduced lower-fat content peanuts, whereas 3 Musketeers reminded consumers that its candy bars, which now come in a new miniature size, have always had less fat than competitive chocolate bars (see Figure 22.11). Organizations that have served the needs of baby boomers find that their market is aging. As they age, baby boomers tend to buy fewer products like homes or home furnishings and more products like financial services (for retirement) and health-related products. The population group behind the baby boomers—usually referred to as Generation X, or those between the ages of 18 and 29—also creates many problems and

**Figure 22.11
Anticipating Target
Market Needs**
Planters and 3 Musketeers promote products that appeal to health-conscious adults.

opportunities for marketers. This market of over 47 million consumers is more ethnically diverse than any previous generation.[26] MCI has taken that into account in promoting its 1-800-COLLECT service, which is targeted directly at the Generation X market, for MCI's research has shown that 72 percent of all collect calls are made by people under the age of 34. In its ads, MCI shows a diverse group of young people, along with the 1-800-COLLECT logo on everything from blimps to graffiti on an inner-city wall. This type of advertising is necessary because of the ethnic diversity of this target market.[27]

■ *Creating the Marketing Mix*

The selection of a target market serves as the basis for the creation of the marketing mix to satisfy the needs of that market. The elements of the marketing mix—product, distribution, promotion, and price—are sometimes referred to as marketing mix variables because each can be varied or changed to accommodate the needs of the target market. The term *mix* aptly describes the decisions that must be made because each element of the marketing mix must be precisely matched not only with each other, but also with the needs of the target market as perceived by the organization.

The decisions made in creating a marketing mix are only as good as the organization's understanding of the target market. This understanding typically comes from careful and in-depth research into the characteristics of the target market. Thus, while demographic information is important, the organization must also analyze consumer needs, preferences, and wants with respect to product design, pricing, distribution, and promotion.

Marketing mix decisions must also have two other characteristics: consistency and flexibility. All marketing mix decisions must be consistent with the marketing, business-unit, and corporate strategies. This consistency allows the organization to achieve its objectives on all three levels of planning. Flexibility, on the other hand, lets the organization alter the marketing mix to match changes in market conditions, competition, and consumer needs.

Table 22.1 provides some examples of how the marketing mix can be altered to match certain business-unit and marketing strategies. In market penetration, the goal of all

531

Table 22.1   Matching the Marketing Mix to Intensive Growth Strategies

Business-Unit Strategy	Marketing Strategy	Marketing Mix			
		Product	**Pricing**	**Distribution**	**Promotion**
Market Penetration	Increase sales of brand X	Increase quality	Lower prices	Make available at more outlets	Offer coupons; advertise new prices
	Increase sales in the 18–24 age group	Add features desired by this segment	Lower prices	Make available in outlets visited by this segment	Target advertising to this group via media selection
Market Development	Find new uses for the product; seek out new markets; move into global markets	Conduct research to discover new uses; add features desired by new markets	Changes will depend on new uses and new markets	Seek distribution outlets in new markets; find global distribution partners	Educate consumers on new uses via advertising; create new advertising appeals for new markets
Product Development	Improve existing products or develop new products	Invest in consumer research and product development	Increase prices on improved products	New products will require shelf space; gain the cooperation of retailers	Educate consumers on improvements; use advertising and sales promotion to introduce new products

marketing efforts is to increase sales of a particular brand or to increase sales within a specific target market segment. Some of the most common marketing mix decisions aimed at increasing sales volume include making the product more desirable, lowering prices, expanding the product's distribution, and engaging in sales promotion activities. For example, General Mills added X's to Cheerios, its O-shaped cereal, for a short period of time to help increase sales of the brand. The company also placed a detachable game board at the back of the cereal box so that consumers could use the X and O shapes to play games. This change in product design was the first for Cheerios since it was introduced in 1941.[28]

Different elements of the marketing mix can be changed to accommodate different marketing strategies. The strategy of market development, for example, often involves moving into global markets in an effort to expand market share. One of the most important marketing decisions in global markets is the choice of distribution channels. In some cases, U.S. companies create partnerships with foreign companies in order to gain access to distribution networks. This is precisely what Anheuser-Busch did when it formed a joint venture with the Kirin Brewery, Japan's number one beer maker, which has an extensive distribution network already in place. By forging an alliance with Kirin, Anheuser-Busch can move into foreign distribution more quickly and efficiently. Anheuser-Busch has plans to become the first foreign brewer to establish its own distribution network in Japan.[29]

Organizations must always strive to create a very strong marketing mix. The success of the marketing mix depends on the combination of all four elements. Each of the marketing mix elements must work together with the others. For example, to work effectively, pricing efforts must complement an overall marketing strategy by sending a message that reinforces the company's desired product image. A company needs to assess its customers to discover how the product is valued in order to make beneficial pricing, promotion, and distribution decisions.[30] If one marketing mix element is improperly matched to the others or to the target market, the product is likely to fail.

Creating the Marketing Plan

Marketing planning
Process of assessing opportunities and resources, setting objectives, defining strategies, and establishing guidelines for the marketing program

The final stage of the strategic market planning process is **marketing planning,** or the systematic process of assessing market opportunities and resources, determining marketing objectives, defining marketing strategies, and establishing guidelines for implementation and control of the marketing program. The outcome of marketing planning is the development of a marketing plan. As already noted, the marketing plan is a formal, written document that outlines and explains all the activities necessary to implement marketing strategies.

Figure 22.12 illustrates the **marketing planning cycle,** which is a circular process. As the feedback lines in the figure indicate, planning is not unidirectional. Feedback is used to coordinate and synchronize all stages of the planning cycle.

Marketing planning cycle
A circular process using feedback to coordinate and synchronize all stages

Short-range plans
Plans covering one year or less

Medium-range plans
Plans covering two to five years

Long-range plans
Plans extending beyond five years

The duration of marketing plans varies. Plans that cover a period of one year or less are called **short-range plans. Medium-range plans** usually encompass two to five years. Marketing plans that extend beyond five years are generally viewed as **long-range plans.** These plans can sometimes cover a period as long as twenty years. Marketing managers may have short-, medium-, and long-range plans all at the same time. Long-range plans are relatively rare. However, as the marketing environment continues to change and business decisions become more complex, profitability and survival will depend more and more on the development of long-range plans.[31]

The extent to which marketing managers develop and use plans also varies. A firm should have a plan for each marketing strategy it develops. Because such plans must be changed as forces in the firm and in the environment change, marketing planning is a continuous process.

Although planning provides numerous benefits, some managers do not use formal marketing plans because they spend almost all their time dealing with daily problems, many of which would be eliminated by adequate planning. However, planning is becoming more important to marketing managers, who realize that planning is necessary to develop, coordinate, and control marketing activities effectively and efficiently. When formulating a marketing plan, a new enterprise or a firm with a new product does not have

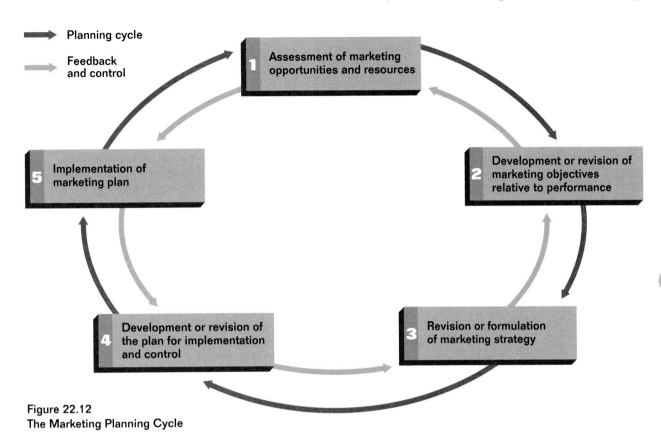

Planning cycle

Feedback and control

Figure 22.12
The Marketing Planning Cycle

current performance to evaluate or an existing plan to revise. Therefore, its marketing planning centers on analyzing available resources and options to assess opportunities. Managers can then develop marketing objectives and a strategy. In addition, many firms recognize the need to include information systems in their plans so that they can have continuous feedback and keep their marketing activities oriented toward objectives. (Information systems were discussed in Chapter 5.)

■ Components of the Marketing Plan

Organizations use many different formats when devising marketing plans. Plans may be written for strategic business units, product lines, individual products or brands, or specific markets. Most plans share some common ground, however, by including many of the same components (see Table 22.2). In the following sections we consider the major parts of a typical marketing plan, as well as the purpose that each part serves.

Table 22.2 Components of the Marketing Plan	
I. Executive Summary	VII. Marketing Implementation
II. Environmental Analysis	A. Marketing organization
A. The marketing environment	B. Activities and responsibilities
B. Target market(s)	C. Implementation timetable
C. Current marketing objectives and performance	VIII. Evaluation and Control
III. Strengths and Weaknesses	A. Performance standards
IV. Opportunities and Threats	B. Financial controls
V. Marketing Objectives	C. Monitoring procedures (audits)
VI. Marketing Strategies	
A. Target market	
B. Marketing mix	

533

Executive Summary   The executive summary is a synopsis (often only one or two pages long) of the entire report. It includes an introduction, an explanation of the major aspects of the marketing plan, and a statement about the costs of implementing the plan. The executive summary should not provide detailed information but rather should give an overview of the plan so that its readers can identify key issues pertaining to their roles in the planning and implementation process.[32]

The executive summary is one of the most important parts of the marketing plan because it is often furnished to people outside the organization. For example, the executive summary may be useful to the organization's financial institution when it becomes involved in the financial aspects of the marketing plan. In other instances, suppliers or investors may be given access to the executive summary if they play a pivotal role in implementing the plan.

Environmental Analysis   The environmental analysis provides information about the company's current situation with respect to the marketing environment, the target market, and the firm's current objectives and performance. The information needed for environmental analysis is obtained from both the internal and external environments, usually through the firm's marketing information system. However, if the required information is not available, it may have to be collected through marketing research. The environmental analysis phase is one of the most difficult parts of the marketing plan and often illustrates the need for an ongoing effort at collecting and organizing environmental data. Having this sort of information readily available also makes the other parts of the marketing plan easier to develop.

The first issue in environmental analysis is an assessment of the marketing environment. In this section, the organization must look at all of the external factors—competitive, economic, political, legal and regulatory, technological, and sociocultural—that can affect marketing activities. As we discussed in Chapter 2, these factors can exert considerable direct and indirect pressures on marketing activities. In addition, the firm must also assess its internal marketing environment to collect information about such matters as the firm's current political environment, the availability and deployment of human resources, the age and capacity of equipment or technology, and the availability of financial resources.

In the second part of environmental analysis, the organization must examine the current situation with respect to its target markets. This section explains the current needs of each target market, anticipated changes in these needs, and how well the organization's products are meeting these needs. In assessing its target markets, the firm must try to understand all relevant consumer behavior variables and product usage statistics. Organizations that successfully practice the marketing concept should know their consumers well enough to have access to this type of information. Organizations that do not have this information may have to conduct marketing research to fully understand the current situation of its target markets.

The final aspect of environmental analysis is a critical evaluation of the firm's current marketing objectives and performance. All organizations should periodically examine their marketing objectives to ensure these objectives remain consistent with the changing marketing environment. This analysis yields important input for later stages of the marketing plan. The organization should also evaluate its current performance with respect to changes in the environment and the target markets. Poor or declining performance may be caused by holding on to marketing objectives that do not consider the current realities of the marketing environment.

Strengths and Weaknesses   This section of the marketing plan marks the first part of the SWOT analysis. SWOT stands for strengths, weaknesses, opportunities, and threats. The analysis of strengths and weaknesses focuses on internal factors that give the organization certain advantages and disadvantages in meeting the needs of its target markets. These factors are derived from the environmental analysis in the preceding portion of the marketing plan. Strengths and weaknesses should also be analyzed relative to market needs and competition. This allows the organization to determine what it does well and what it needs to improve.[33]

534

1-800-645-3142

Figure 22.13
Competitive Strength   Nike's strength is its strong name recognition and consumer acceptance of its many products.

535

Strengths refer to competitive advantages or distinctive competencies that give the firm an advantage in meeting the needs of its target markets. As shown in Figure 22.13, Nike has strong name recognition and customer demand for its athletic shoes and clothing. Any analysis of company strengths must be customer-focused because strengths are only meaningful when they assist the firm in meeting customer needs. For example, a firm may possess a highly trained and capable sales force, which would be considered a major strength in many industries. However, if customers are more interested in product quality or price, then a good sales force may do little to help satisfy customer needs. Strengths that are more related to quality and price might include production efficiency or low-cost distribution.

Weaknesses refer to any limitations that a company might face in marketing strategy development or implementation. Weaknesses should also be examined from a customer perspective because customers often perceive weaknesses that the company cannot see. For example, recent research suggests that the logos used by many organizations actually downgrade the image of the company's brands. Based on in-depth consumer research, the two poorest-performing logos were those of British Airways and American Express. The three highest-performing logos were those of Borden, IBM, and Mercedes-Benz.[34]

Taking a customer-oriented approach toward the examination of strengths and weaknesses does not mean that strengths and weaknesses that are not customer-oriented should be forgotten. Rather, it suggests that all firms should tie their strengths and weaknesses to customer requirements. Only those strengths that relate to satisfying customers should be considered true competitive advantages. Likewise, weaknesses that directly affect customer satisfaction should be considered competitive disadvantages.

Opportunities and Threats   The second section of the SWOT analysis examines the opportunities and threats that exist in the environment. It focuses on factors that are external to the organization. Both opportunities and threats exist independently of the firm; however, they can greatly affect its operations. The way to differentiate a strength or weakness from an opportunity or threat is to ask the question, Would this issue exist if the company did not exist? If the answer is yes, then the issue should be considered external to the firm.[35] Because opportunities and threats are external to the firm, they represent issues to be considered by all organizations, even those that do not compete with the firm. These issues are also derived from the environmental analysis in the preceding portion of the marketing plan. Like strengths and weaknesses, opportunities and threats should be analyzed relative to market needs and the capabilities of competitors.

Opportunities refer to favorable conditions in the environment that could produce rewards for the organization if acted upon properly. That is, opportunities are situations that exist but must be acted upon in order to benefit the firm. **Threats,** on the other hand, refer to conditions or barriers that may prevent the firm from reaching its objectives. Like opportunities, threats must be acted upon to prevent them from limiting the capabilities of the organization.

Strengths   Competitive advantages or distinctive competencies giving the firm an advantage in its target markets

Weaknesses   Any limitations a firm might face in marketing strategy development or implementation

Opportunities   Favorable environmental conditions that could bring the firm rewards if acted upon properly

Threats   Conditions or barriers that may prevent the firm from reaching its objectives

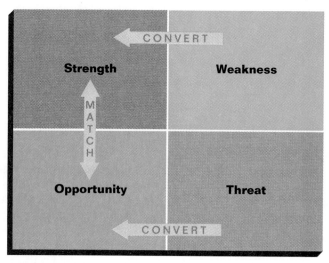

Figure 22.14
The Four-Cell SWOT Matrix
Source: Adapted from Nigel F. Piercy, *Market-Led Strategic Change*, copyright © 1992 Butterworth-Heinemann Ltd., p. 371. Used with permission.

Opportunities and threats can stem from many sources within the environment. When a company is threatened by a competitor's new-product introduction, a defensive strategy may be required. In some cases, such a threat can be transformed into an opportunity if the firm can develop and launch a new product that meets or exceeds the competition's offering.[36] Because of competition from low-cost carriers such as Southwest Airlines, Delta Airlines has dramatically cut costs and is even launching a no-frills service to compete directly with its discounting competitors. In fact, discount airlines are advancing steadily in 60 percent of Delta's market. Although some Delta customers complain that service and on-time performance are declining, the competitive threat of discounters requires that Delta move quickly to maintain its markets.[37]

Figure 22.14 depicts a four-cell SWOT matrix that can help managers in the planning process. As indicated in the figure, when internal strengths are matched to external opportunities, the organization creates capabilities that can be used to create competitive advantages in meeting the needs of customers. In addition, actions should be taken to convert internal weaknesses into strengths and external threats into opportunities. Toyota and Nissan converted the threats posed by luxury automobiles into opportunities when they introduced the Lexus and Infiniti, respectively. A firm that lacks adequate marketing skills can hire outside consultants to help convert a weakness into a strength.

The SWOT analysis framework has gained widespread acceptance because it is both a simple and a powerful tool for marketing strategy development. However, like any planning tool, SWOT is only as good as the information contained within it. Thorough marketing research and accurate information systems are essential if the SWOT analysis is to identify key issues in the environment.

Marketing objective
States what is to be accomplished through marketing activities

Marketing Objectives   This section of the marketing plan describes the marketing objectives that underlie the plan. A **marketing objective** states what is to be accomplished through marketing activities. This statement should be based on a careful study of the SWOT analysis and should contain objectives related to matching strengths to opportunities and/or the conversion of weaknesses or threats. Marketing objectives can be stated in terms of product introduction, product improvement or innovation, sales volume, profitability, market share, pricing, distribution, advertising, or employee training activities.

Marketing objectives should possess certain characteristics. First, a marketing objective should be expressed in clear, simple terms so that all marketing personnel understand exactly what they are trying to achieve. Second, an objective should be written so that it can be measured accurately. This allows the organization to determine if and when the objective has been achieved. For example, if a firm has an objective of increasing market share by 10 percent, the firm should be able to measure market share changes accurately. Third, a marketing objective should specify a time frame for its accomplishment. For example, a firm that sets an objective of introducing a new product should state the time period in which this is to be done. Finally, a marketing objective should be consistent with both business-unit and corporate strategy. This ensures that the firm's mission is carried out at all levels of the organization.

Marketing Strategies   This section of the marketing plan outlines ways of achieving the marketing objectives. As already noted, marketing strategy consists of two components: target market selection and the development of a marketing mix. In a broader sense, however, marketing strategy refers to how the firm will manage its relationships with customers so that it gains an advantage over the competition. Target market selection is the first stage of this process. Target markets must be clearly defined in terms of the segmentation variables discussed earlier—demographics, geography, psychographics, product usage, and so on. This step is extremely important because a marketer must understand the needs of its customers before it can develop a marketing mix to satisfy those needs. In developing a marketing mix, the firm must determine how the elements of the mix—product, distribution, promotion, and price—will work together to satisfy the needs of the target market.

It is at the marketing mix level that the firm will detail how it will achieve a competitive advantage. To gain an advantage, the firm must do something better than the competition. In other words, its products must be of higher quality, its prices must be consistent with the level of quality (value), its distribution methods must be efficient and cost as little as possible, and its promotion must be more effective. AT&T, for example, has expanded its marketing mix to better satisfy the needs of international callers (see Figure 22.15). It is also important that the firm attempt to make these advantages sustainable. A **sustainable competitive advantage** is one that cannot be copied by the competition. For example, Wal-Mart maintains a sustainable advantage over Kmart because of its very efficient and low-cost distribution system. This advantage allows Wal-Mart to offer lower prices. However, Kmart has a sustainable advantage over Wal-Mart in terms of store locations. Since Kmart stores were in most urban areas before Wal-Mart began moving from rural areas, Kmart stores are typically in better and more convenient locations. In fact, location is often referred to as the most sustainable competitive advantage because it is almost impossible for competitors to change or copy it.[38]

Sustainable competitive advantage   One that cannot be copied by the competition

**Figure 22.15
Marketing Strategies**
AT&T's Language Line provides translations of international phone calls for customers' convenience, thereby satisfying the needs of the international caller target market.

Marketing implementation
Putting marketing strategies into action

Marketing Implementation   This section outlines how the marketing strategies will be implemented. **Marketing implementation** is the process of putting marketing strategies into action. This section of the marketing plan answers many of the questions about the marketing activities outlined in the preceding section. What specific actions will be taken? How will these activities be performed? When will these activities be performed? Who is responsible for the completion of these activities? And how much will these activities cost? Without a workable plan for implementation, the success of the marketing strategy is in jeopardy. For this reason, the implementation phase of the marketing plan is just as important as the planning phase.

Because implementation is so important, we devote all of Chapter 23 to a discussion of issues in marketing implementation. In that discussion, we examine how the organization of the marketing function affects the implementation of marketing strategy. We also consider the importance of employees to marketing implementation. When discussing implementation, it is important to remember this fact: organizations do not implement strategies; people do. Thus Chapter 23 addresses employee motivation, communication, and training as key factors in the implementation of marketing strategy.

Evaluation and Control   This final section of the marketing plan details how the results of the plan will be measured and evaluated. The control phase of this section includes the actions that can be taken to reduce the differences between planned and actual performance. First, standards for assessing the actual performance need to be established. These standards can be based on sales volume increases, profitability, or market share increases; they can even be advertising standards, such as brand name recognition or recall. The second part of the control process deals with the financial data that can be used to evaluate whether the marketing plan is working. Finally, if the marketing plan is not living up to expectations, the firm can use a number of monitoring procedures to pinpoint potential causes for the discrepancies. One such procedure is the marketing audit, which can help isolate weaknesses in the marketing plan and recommend actions to help improve performance. Because evaluation and control procedures are directly related to marketing implementation, they are discussed in detail in Chapter 23.

■ *Using the Marketing Plan*

The creation and implementation of a complete marketing plan will allow the organization not only to achieve its marketing objectives, but its business-unit and corporate objectives as well. However, it is important to understand that the marketing plan is only as good as the information it contains and the effort and creativity that went into its development. As a result, the importance of having a good marketing information system cannot be overstated. Equally important is the role of managerial judgment throughout the strategic market planning process. Managers must always weigh any information against its accuracy and their own intuition when making marketing decisions.

We should also note that the marketing plan outline in Table 22.2 should serve as a structure for the written document rather than as a series of sequential planning steps. In actual practice, many of the elements in the outline are decided on simultaneously. For example, the actual development of marketing strategies must take into account how those strategies will be implemented. This is one of the realities of marketing planning discussed in Chapter 23. It is also important to realize that most organizations have their own unique format and terminology to describe the marketing plan. For that reason, the outline in Table 22.2 should not be regarded as the only correct format for the creation of a marketing plan. Every marketing plan is and should be unique to the organization for which it was created.

While the creation of a marketing plan is an important milestone in strategic market planning, it is by no means the final step. Some of the information used to create the plan may turn out to be inaccurate. Many of the managerial assumptions or projections used in the analysis often turn out differently when the plan is put into practice. These realities underscore the need to make the marketing plan flexible enough so that it can be adjusted on a daily basis. This adjusting process is a vital element of marketing implementation and control, to which we turn our attention in the next chapter.

SUMMARY

A strategic market plan is an outline of the methods and resources required to achieve the organization's goals within a specific target market; it takes into account all functional areas of a business unit that must be coordinated. A strategic business unit (SBU) is a division, product line, or other profit center within the parent company and is used to define areas for consideration in a specific strategic market plan. The process of strategic market planning yields a marketing strategy that is the framework for a marketing plan. A marketing plan includes the framework and entire set of activities to be performed; it is the written document or blueprint for implementing and controlling an organization's marketing activities.

Through the process of strategic market planning, an organization can develop marketing strategies that, when properly implemented and controlled, will contribute to achieving the organization's overall goals. The set of marketing strategies that are implemented and used at the same time is referred to as the organization's marketing program. Environmental forces are important in the strategic market planning process and very much affect it. These forces imply opportunities and threats that influence an organization's overall goals.

A firm's organizational goals should be derived from its mission, the broad long-term view of what the organization wants to become. The mission statement answers two questions: What is our business? and What should our business be? A mission statement that is well thought-out and well formulated has a number of benefits for an organization, including the identification of its distinctive competencies, which enable the organization to achieve a competitive advantage.

There are three major considerations in assessing opportunities and resources: monitoring of environmental forces, evaluation of market opportunities, and understanding the firm's capabilities and resources. Environmental scanning is a search for information about events and relationships in a company's outside environment; such information aids marketers in planning. A market opportunity, or strategic window, opens when the right combination of circumstances occurs at the right time, and an organization can take action toward a target market. An opportunity offers a favorable chance for the company to generate sales from markets. Market requirements relate to the customers' needs or desired benefits. The market requirements are satisfied by components of the marketing mix that provide buyers with these benefits. A firm's capabilities relate to distinctive competencies that it has developed to do something well and efficiently. A company will be likely to enjoy a differential advantage in an area where its competencies outmatch those of its potential competition.

Corporate strategy determines the means for utilizing resources in the areas of production, finance, research and development, human resources, and marketing to reach the organization's goals. A number of tools have been developed to aid corporate managers in their planning efforts, including the Boston Consulting Group (BCG) product-portfolio analysis. The BCG approach is based on the philosophy that a product's market growth rate and its market share are key factors influencing marketing strategy. All the firm's products are integrated into a single, overall matrix and evaluated to determine appropriate strategies for individual SBUs and the overall portfolio strategies.

After corporate strategy, organizations can pursue a number of business-unit strategies to aid in the marketing of each SBU's products within its target markets. Intensive growth strategies include market penetration, market development, and product development. Strategic business units can also pursue a number of diversified growth strategies, including horizontal, concentric, conglomerate, or integrated diversification.

After business-unit strategies, all organizations must develop a sound marketing strategy. Marketing strategy is composed of two elements: the selection of a target market and the creation of a marketing mix that will satisfy the needs of the chosen target market. If implemented properly, a good marketing strategy helps a company achieve its business-unit and corporate objectives. While corporate, business-unit, and marketing strategies all overlap to some extent, the marketing strategy is the most detailed and specific of the three.

One of the final stages in strategic market planning is marketing planning, or the systematic process of assessing market opportunities and resources, determining marketing objectives, defining marketing strategies, and establishing guidelines for implementation and control of the marketing program. Short-range marketing plans cover one year or less; medium-range plans, two to five years; and long-range plans, more than five years.

A marketing plan is the written document, or blueprint, for implementing and controlling an organization's marketing activities. A well-written plan clearly specifies when, how, and who is to perform marketing activities. Typical marketing plans include an executive summary, environmental analysis, SWOT analysis, marketing objectives, marketing strategies, and statements of marketing implementation, as well as evaluation and control procedures. Any marketing plan is only as good as the information it contains and the effort and creativity that was put into its development. Therefore, marketing information systems and managerial judgment are also important in creating a complete and workable marketing plan. The marketing plan must be flexible enough to be adjusted on a daily basis. It is important that every marketing plan be unique to the organization for which it is created.

539

IMPORTANT TERMS

Strategic market plan
Strategic business unit
  (SBU)
Strategic market planning
Marketing program
Mission statement
Distinctive competency

Strategic windows
Market requirements
Competitive advantage
Corporate strategy
Product-portfolio analysis
Intensive growth
Diversified growth

Marketing planning
Marketing planning cycle
Short-range plans
Medium-range plans
Long-range plans
Strengths
Weaknesses

Opportunities
Threats
Marketing objective
Sustainable competitive
  advantage
Marketing
  implementation

DISCUSSION AND REVIEW QUESTIONS

1. Identify the major components of strategic market planning, and explain how they are interrelated.
2. Describe the characteristics of a good mission statement. What role does the mission statement play in strategic market planning?
3. What are some of the issues that must be considered in analyzing a firm's opportunities and resources? How do these issues affect marketing objectives and market strategy?
4. Why is market opportunity analysis necessary? What are the determinants of market opportunity?
5. In relation to resource constraints, how can environmental scanning affect a firm's long-term strategic market planning?
6. Explain how an organization can create a competitive advantage at the corporate, business-unit, and marketing strategy levels.
7. Give examples of intensive and diversified growth strategies that are being used by today's firms. Which strategy appears to be the most effective in today's environment? Why?

8. Describe the role of the marketing plan in developing marketing strategy. How important is the SWOT analysis to the marketing planning process?
9. How should an organization establish marketing objectives?
10. Refer to question 6. How can an organization make its competitive advantages sustainable over time? How difficult is it to create sustainable competitive advantages?
11. What benefits do marketing managers gain from planning? Is planning necessary for long-run survival? Why or why not?

APPLICATION QUESTIONS

1. Organizational goals are necessary for a firm to achieve success in a dynamic marketing environment. Contact three companies or organizations that appear to be successful. Talk with one of the managers or executives in the company, and ask if he or she would share with you the company's mission statement or organizational goals. Obtain as much information as possible about the statement and the organizational goals. Discuss how the statement matches the criteria outlined in the text.
2. Short-term goals help a firm reach its long-term goals. Assume that you own a new family-style restaurant that will open for business in the next year. Formulate a long-term goal for the company, and then develop short-term goals that will assist you in achieving the long-term goal.
3. The QVC home shopping network identified an opportunity to capitalize on a desire of many consumers to shop at home. This strategic window

gave the network a very competitive position in a new market. Consider the opportunities that may be present in your city, region, or the United States as a whole. Identify a strategic window, and discuss how a company could take advantage of this opportunity. What kind of distinctive competencies are necessary?
4. The selection of a target market may be one of the most important decisions a marketer makes. McDonald's has been very successful in identifying and satisfying the needs of its target market. Identify the target market of the companies below.
   a. American Express
   b. Nike
   c. Walt Disney
   d. CompuServe

Case 22.1   PETsMART: Looking to Be Man's Second-Best Friend

More than 50 percent of U.S. households have at least one pet, and more than twice as many households have a pet as those that have a child under the age of 18. The growth of pet ownership is being stoked by aging baby boomers and the rising proportion of the elderly. According to the Pet Industry Joint Advisory Council, pet owners spent about $17 billion on their furry friends in 1994, with an additional $10 billion going toward pet health care. These trends in pet ownership have caught the attention of several retailers and fed the growth of a new form of retail category killer—the pet-supply superstore.

During the early 1980s, most pet owners shopped for pet food and other supplies at the supermarket, which accordingly held 95 percent of the share of the pet food market. Although many pet owners still go to the supermarket to buy pet food, that number is ebbing. When Fluffy, Fido, or Tweety run low on chow, pet owners today are likely to head to the nearest pet-supply superstore where they can shop 25,000-square-foot, warehouse-like facilities for a huge variety of pet food, as well as over 10,000 different pet toys and non-food items, and onsite services such as grooming, obedience classes, and even good-health clinics, discounted versions of the annual checkups provided by veterinarians. In the six years since the superstores first began to appear, ten major retailers have opened close to 600 such megamarts across the United States, and another 500 will be open by 1997. These superstores have taken a bite out of supermarket pet food sales, reducing their share to less than two-thirds of total pet food sales. One pet superstore estimates that nearly half its food sales are for items not available in supermarkets or other mass merchandise outlets. The superstores also stock a variety of nonfood supplies, such as leashes, shampoos, carriers, toys, and the like, which have not traditionally been stocked by grocery stores.

Phoenix-based PETsMART, Inc., one of the leaders of this retailing revolution, wants to be for pet lovers what The Home Depot is to homeowners. PETsMART superstores offer more than 12,000 different products and pet foods, including a line of pet colognes, shampoos, conditioners, and health-maintenance items such as eardrops and eyedrops. Like many of its competitors, PETsMART stores invite their human customers to bring their furred, feathered, and scaled companions to browse the aisles together. With 180 superstores throughout the West, Midwest, and South, PETsMART dominates the pet superstore industry, with sales climbing from $29.3 million in 1990 to over $1 billion in 1995. Its closest competitor, Petco, projected sales of $188 million at 219 stores during 1995. PETsMART executives estimate the chain had leashed nearly 5 per-

cent of the total pet industry market by 1995, second only to Wal-Mart/Sam's Clubs.

PETsMART was founded by Jim and Janice Dougherty as The Pet Food Warehouse in 1987, with two stores in Arizona. However, after growing to seven stores in just two years, the firm began to lose money. Controlling investors ousted the Doughertys and brought in Sam Parker, a former executive of the Jewel supermarket chain, as chairman in 1990. Under Parker's guidance, the chain spruced up its stores, widening the aisles, brightening the lighting, and adding more product variety. By the end of 1993, when the company went public, the chain had 106 stores. In 1994, PETsMART acquired the Petzazz superstore chain, the nation's third largest, adding an additional thirty stores throughout the Midwest, and in Kentucky and Pennsylvania. The purchase also gave PETsMART instant access into Chicago, where it previously lacked a presence.

To achieve its corporate objective of being the dominant retailer of pet foods and supplies in the United States, PETsMART has adopted a step-by-step approach. During its first year of operation, its strategy was simply to introduce itself and create an awareness of PETsMART in consumers' minds. Advertising focused on PETsMART's wide selection of products and low prices, hoping to encourage consumers to check out the store. The chain also capitalized on the strong emotional bond that exists between people and their pets with commercials featuring owner testimonials and comments such as, "I'd do anything to keep her happy, anything." Advertising slogans like "More than low prices, a whole lot more" and "PETsMART has thousands of things to keep your pet happy—for less" reinforced the emotional link.

In its second year of operation, PETsMART began to implement a branding strategy by focusing on identification of its trademark, recall of its commercials, and encouraging repeat customer visits. Research found PETsMART commercials in the top 5 percent of all filmed advertisements tested. It also indicated that 27 percent of occasional shoppers could be motivated to increase their number of visits. PETsMART continued to focus on the bond between owners and their pets with such advertising taglines as "When is a pet more than a pet? When it's a friend" and "PETsMART—where pets are family."

Reinforcing the emotional ties between owners and their pets, while appealing to the social responsibility some animal lovers feel, PETsMART has a policy of not selling puppies or kittens, citing the overpopulation of these animals in the United States. Instead, it has instituted an Adopt-a-Pet program, in which it features several dogs and cats from local animal shelters weekly in its stores, in hopes of attracting adoptive families. Television commercials touting the program tell viewers, "We don't sell pets, but we help save thousands of them each year."

The estimated 50 million companion pets in this country have been associated with increased health and well-being of their owners, especially by helping to lower blood pressure and relieve stress. This has prompted PETsMART to target a very special segment of the market, senior citizens, with commercials featuring older pet owners. Advertising slogans strengthen this tie with the tagline, "There's no greater gift than love that's shared."

PETsMART has stated that its number one goal is to be the best in its class—the industry leader. To achieve this goal, the company offers a wider variety of products at lower prices than do grocery stores. But to ensure that it satisfies its customers, it further differentiates itself from other pet stores and mass merchandisers by focusing on emotional, nonprice issues as well.[39]

Questions for Discussion

1. Describe PETsMART's target market and marketing mix.
2. What general type of strategy did PETsMART use during its first year of operation? its second year? What strategy might it employ next?
3. Does PETsMART's advertising seem to be consistent with its overall strategies and objectives? Explain.

Case 22.2   Anheuser-Busch Returns to Its Roots

The "King of Beers," St. Louis-based Anheuser-Busch Cos., is the largest brewer in the United States, with 44 percent of the domestic market. The company also is the world's second-largest theme park operator, owning Busch Gardens, Adventure Island, Cypress Gardens, Sea World, and others. In recent years, Anheuser-Busch, like many companies, has diversified as a growth strategy. However, cold facts have forced the company to shelve that strategy and return to its roots: brewing beer and entertaining people.

Anheuser-Busch started out as the Bavarian Brewery, founded by George Schneider in St. Louis in 1852. Aberhard Anheuser acquired the brewery in 1860 and was joined five years later by his son-in-law Adolphus Busch. Busch helped restaurateur Carl Conrad develop a new light beer like those brewed in the Bohemian town of Budweis, from which the new brew took its name. The little brewery grew rapidly on the strength of Budweiser's popularity. After Busch died in 1913, his son August took over the company, which became Anheuser-Busch Inc., in 1919. When the brewery couldn't sell beer during Prohibition (1920–1933), August Busch kept the company afloat by selling yeast, refrigeration units, truck bodies, syrup, and soft drinks. He quickly resumed beer making after Prohibition was repealed, even delivering a case of Budweiser to President Franklin Roosevelt in a wagon drawn by Clydesdale horses, which became Anheuser-Busch's symbol.

In the years since, Anheuser-Busch has grown to more than $10 billion in sales through new products and diversification. It became the number one U.S. brewer in 1957, overtaking Schlitz. The firm acquired the St. Louis Cardinals major league baseball team in 1953 and established its Busch Entertainment theme park division in 1959. Miller Brewing Co., owned by tobacco giant Philip Morris, has been nipping at Anheuser's market share since the 1970s, but Anheuser-Busch was the first brewer to sell 40 million barrels. The firm diversified further with the creation of its Eagle snack foods unit in 1979 and the purchase of Campbell Taggart, a bakery, in 1982.

At the time, August Busch believed getting into bread and snacks to be a smart strategy. As a brewer, Anheuser-Busch knew a great deal about yeast, a key ingredient in bread, and he figured beer distributors could deliver Eagle snacks on their regular routes to bars, clubs, and supermarkets. However, the synergies Busch hoped for never developed. Distribution turned out to be complicated, partly because the three products—beer, snacks, and bread—go into different areas of grocery stores and convenience stores and are ordered by different buyers. The result was a costly patchwork distribution system, with some Eagle snack distributors also carrying beer, some also carrying Campbell Taggart bread, some independent.

During the same period, Frito-Lay, PepsiCo's snack division, zoomed into marketing overdrive. launching many successful new snack products (including its new low-fat baked chips), while upgrading its distribution and cutting costs. As a more cost-efficient marketer, Frito was able to cut prices, escalating its share of the snack market to around 50 percent; Eagle's never passed 6 percent. Against the onslaught of Frito-Lay and various regional competitors, the less efficient Eagle was never able to make a profit. In 1995, Eagle lost $25 million on sales of just $400 million. Eagle's problems may also have distracted executives from their other products. Anheuser's profits from beer sales of $7.8 billion fell 5 percent to $1.6 billion in 1995, while market share declined by 0.3 percent in the face of deflating consumer demand for beer and fierce competition from Miller and regional brewers.

In 1995, CEO August A. Busch III, the fourth-generation Busch to head the company, decided to refocus Anheuser-Busch and get back to beer and entertainment. The company sold the Cardinals to an investor group for $150 million and spun off the marginally profitable Campbell Taggart baking division to shareholders. Eagle Snacks Inc., hemorrhaging red ink from the beginning, was not so easy to dispatch, however. Anheuser put Eagle up for sale in 1995. Although several firms, including Nabisco, took a look, no serious offers were made. In February 1996, Busch announced that Anheuser was getting out of the snack food business and closing down Eagle. Although the sale of four Eagle plants to Frito-Lay for $135 million took some of the sting out of the painful decision, the firm was still forced to take a $206 million write-off.

Now, the company is focusing its efforts on staying on top of the competitive brewing industry, a challenge in itself as domestic beer sales have been flat for years. More than half of Anheuser-Busch's sales come from its flagship Budweiser brand. The company has launched several new products, including Bud Ice, Red Wolf, and Crossroads, a wheat-based beer, to boost domestic sales. To compete with popular regional brews, Anheuser-Busch has started to develop regional brands of its own, such as ZiegenBoch, a dark beer that will go head-to-head in Texas against that state's hot-selling Shiner Boch. It has also acquired a 25 percent stake in Seattle's Redhook Ale microbrewery and the rights to distribute Redhook products, including its Elk Mountain brew. Anheuser plans to spend heavily to promote its brands at home, especially Budweiser and Bud Light—more than $70 million, for example, to be associated with the 1996 Olympics in Atlanta.

Anheuser-Busch is also looking across the sea for growth. Although the company sells beer in more than seventy countries, it holds just 9 percent of the international market. It is widening its reach through acquisitions and alliances. For example, in 1993, the brewer bought 18 percent of Mexico's Grupo Modelo, which markets Corona, Mexico's best-selling beer. It has formed partnerships with Brazil's Companhia Antarctica Paulista, and with China's Tsingtao and Zhongde breweries. It has established distribution partnerships with local firms, such as Kirin in Japan, Peroni in Italy, Kronenbourg in France, and Shaw Wallace in India. In 1995, Anheuser-Busch formed a joint venture with UK-based Courage Ltd. to operate London's Stag Brewery. Never ignoring its flagship brand, Anheuser-Busch has pumped up its marketing muscle to propel Budweiser to become Western Europe's fastest-growing brand and Japan's top-selling import. Overseas sales have been climbing at a rate of about 20 percent a year and now contribute about $80 million, or 5 percent, to Anheuser's operating profits.

Although Anheuser-Busch's foray into snacks, bread, and baseball seemed to make sense in an era in which diversification was a common strategy, the brewer never developed successful marketing mixes to achieve the synergy necessary in a conglomerate multinational enterprise. By returning to focus on the products it knows best and applying its marketing expertise to satisfy customers in the markets it knows best, Anheuser-Busch is once again enjoying the heady taste of success in the competitive beer wars.[40]

Questions for Discussion

1. Why did Anheuser-Busch abandon its diversification strategy?
2. Describe Anheuser-Busch's corporate strategy for growth.
3. Discuss the current marketing strategy for developing various brands to compete with popular regional brews.

Chapter 23

Marketing Implementation and Control

OBJECTIVES

- To be able to describe the marketing implementation process, as well as the major approaches to marketing implementation

- To understand the components of the marketing process

- To learn about the role of the marketing unit in a firm's organizational structure

- To be able to identify the alternatives for organizing a marketing unit

- To understand the control processes used in managing marketing strategies

- To learn how cost and sales analyses can be used to evaluate the performance of marketing strategies

- To become aware of the major components of a marketing audit

Neiman Marcus nurtures customer relationships by offering nothing but the best.

*N*eiman Marcus is a clear leader in upscale retailing to affluent customers. To maintain its position, the Neiman Marcus plan is to develop the most attractive stores of any national retailer, and to support them by a highly efficient retail infrastructure and strong relationships with the world's leading designers of fine merchandise.

To carry out this plan, Neiman Marcus is not resting on its elite reputation. In the last eight years, the company has remodeled or built new one-half of its total store square footage. The remodeling and expansion program has created the most modern and attractive national store network in the industry and has enabled Neiman Marcus to increase sales in its existing stores. Recognizing that upscale retailing requires outstanding customer service, the company has intensified its training programs and swelled the overall number of sales associates within each store. To measure the effectiveness of its relationships with customers, Neiman Marcus conducts ongoing surveys that monitor customer satisfaction. Moreover, the firm employs an outside shopping service to shop each store, as well as the competition, regularly. Sales associates are rated on a broad range of customer service categories.

Emmanuelle Khanh Paris for Private Eyes in Accessories.

find yourself at neiman marcus. spring already has. *Neiman Marcus*

Neiman Marcus strives to create excitement through effective merchandising, promotion, and communication with customers. One way it does so is through its world-famous Neiman Marcus Christmas catalog. A monthly "magalogue," which is known as "The Bash" and is mailed to 500,000 Neiman Marcus customers, also promotes products as well as featuring designer profiles and fashion trends. The Neiman Marcus Holiday Express Train, which for several years carried fine quality merchandise to ten U.S. cities from San Antonio, Texas, to Cleveland, Ohio, not only generated nationwide media coverage but also represented a unique way to reach customers and markets too small to support a Neiman Marcus store. Instore events—more than 3,000 a year, from trunk shows spotlighting specific designers to fashion show luncheons to special tie-ins with charitable organizations—also bring customers into stores. These and many other merchandising activities help Neiman Marcus position itself as a specialty retailer and develop long-term relationships with customers.[1]

545

Careful implementation of its strategy has enabled Neiman Marcus to achieve its objectives. In Chapter 22 we examined strategic market planning, which is one dimension of managing marketing strategies. Even the best strategic marketing plan will fail if it is poorly implemented. This chapter therefore concentrates on other dimensions of managing marketing strategies, including organization, implementation, and control. First, we explore several issues regarding the implementation of marketing strategies. We then focus on the marketing unit's position in the organization and the ways the unit itself can be organized. Next we consider the basic components of the process of control and discuss the use of cost and sales analyses to evaluate the effectiveness of marketing strategies and measure the firm's performance. Finally, we describe a marketing audit.

The Marketing Implementation Process

*A*s indicated in Chapter 22, marketing implementation is the "how?" of marketing strategy; it involves activities directed at putting marketing strategies into action. Although implementation is often neglected in favor of strategic planning, the implementation process itself can determine whether a marketing strategy is successful. In short, good marketing strategy combined with bad marketing implementation is a guaranteed recipe for failure. In Figure 23.1, Timken discusses its strategy implementation in helping customers increase their overall productivity.

An important aspect of the implementation process is understanding that marketing strategies almost always turn out differently than expected. In essence, all organizations have two types of strategy: intended strategy and realized strategy.[2] **Intended strategy** is the strategy that the organization decided on during the planning phase and wants to use, whereas **realized strategy** is the strategy that actually takes place. Realized strategy comes about during the process of implementing the intended strategy. The realized strategy is not necessarily any better or worse than the intended strategy, though it is often worse.

Intended strategy
Strategy the company decides on during the planning phase

Realized strategy
Strategy that actually takes place

■ *Problems in Implementing Marketing Activities*

Why do marketing strategies sometimes turn out differently than expected? The most common reason is that managers fail to realize that marketing implementation is just as important as marketing strategy. The relationship between strategic planning and imple-

Figure 23.1
Marketing Implementation
Timken links strategic implementation to customer productivity and business success.

mentation creates a number of problems for managers when they plan implementation activities. Three of the most important problems are as follows:[3]

- *Marketing strategy and implementation are related.* Companies that experience this problem typically assume that strategic planning always comes first, followed by implementation. In reality, marketing strategies and implementation activities should be developed simultaneously. The content of the marketing strategy determines how it will be implemented. Likewise, implementation activities may require that changes be made in the marketing strategy. Thus it is important for marketing managers to understand that strategy and implementation are really two sides of the same coin.

- *Marketing strategy and implementation are constantly evolving.* This second problem refers to how strategy and implementation are both affected by the marketing environment. Since the environment is constantly changing, both marketing strategy and implementation must remain flexible enough to adapt. The relationship between strategy and implementation is never fixed; it is always evolving to accommodate changes in customer needs, government regulation, or competition. For example, when ValuJet began service from Atlanta, competitors such as Delta and Northwest moved to match ValuJet's discount fares to the same destination cities.

- *The responsibility for marketing strategy and implementation is separated.* This problem is often the biggest obstacle in implementing marketing strategies. Typically, marketing strategies are developed by the top managers in an organization. However, the responsibility for implementing those strategies rests at the frontline of the organization. This separation, shown in Figure 23.2, can impair implementation in two ways. First, because top managers are separated from the frontline, where the company interacts daily with customers, they may not grasp the unique problems associated with implementing marketing activities. Second, as noted in Chapter 22, people, not organizations, implement strategies. Frontline managers and employees are often responsible for implementing strategies, even though they had no voice in developing them. Consequently, these frontline employees may lack motivation and commitment.[4] We will discuss the importance of employee motivation later in this chapter.

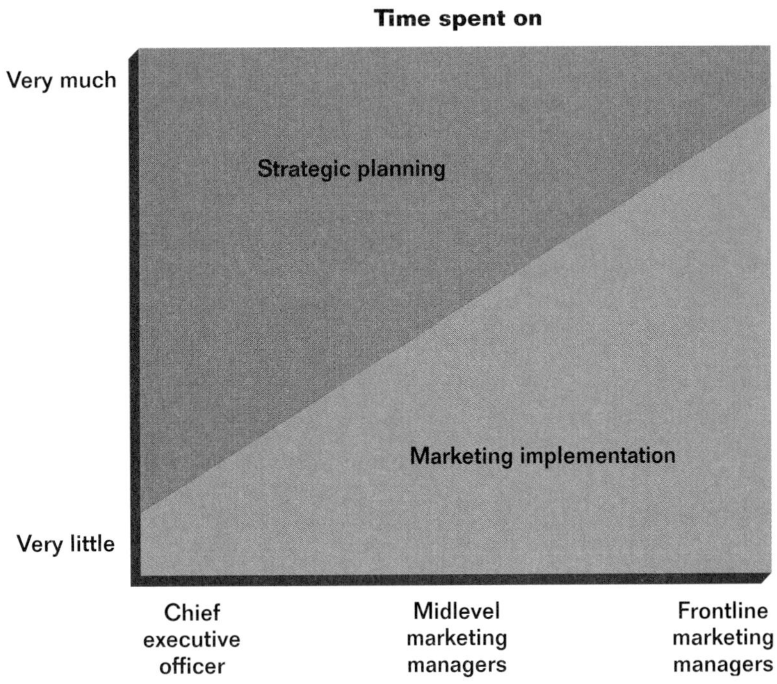

547

Figure 23.2
The Separation of Strategic Planning and Marketing Implementation

Source: Reproduced from O. C. Ferrell, George H. Lucas, and David J. Luck, *Strategic Marketing Management: Text and Cases,* with permission of South-Western Publishing Co. Copyright © 1994 by South-Western Publishing Co. All rights reserved.

Figure 23.3
Elements of Marketing Implementation
Source: From Lawrence R. Jauch and William F. Glueck, *Strategic Management and Business Policy*,
3/e. Copyright © 1988. Reproduced with permission of the McGraw-Hill Companies.

▆ *Components of Marketing Implementation*

The marketing implementation process has several components, all of which must mesh if the implementation is to succeed. These components are shown in Figure 23.3, and we have already discussed three of them: organizational resources, marketing strategy, and marketing structure. Of the others, systems refer to work processes, procedures, and the way that information is structured—elements ensuring that the organization's day-to-day activities are carried out. Typical organizational systems include marketing information systems, strategic planning systems, budgeting and accounting systems, manufacturing and quality control systems, and performance measurement systems.

The people component in Figure 23.3 refers to the importance of employees in the implementation process. It includes such factors as the quality, diversity, and skills of the work force within the organization and covers the human resources function as well. Figure 23.4 illustrates Hyatt's positive attitude toward diversity and its role in corporate success. Issues like employee recruitment, selection, and training have great bearing on the implementation of marketing activities.[5] Closely linked to the people component is leadership, or the art of managing people. It involves such issues as employee motivation, communication, and reward policies. We discuss these issues later in the chapter.

At the center of marketing implementation are shared goals; they draw the entire organization together into a single, functioning unit. These goals may be simple statements of the company's objectives. Northwest Airlines, for instance, has communicated to all levels of the organization the importance of on-time arrivals. On the other hand, the goals may be detailed mission statements, outlining corporate philosophy and direction. Shared goals appear in the center of Figure 23.3 because they hold all the other components together to ensure successful marketing implementation.[6] Without shared goals to hold the organization together, different parts of the organization might work toward different goals or objectives, thus limiting the success of the entire organization. Global Marketing describes how PepsiCo is implementing a new strategy to achieve its goal of outselling Coca-Cola.

Figure 23.4
Components of Marketing Implementation Hyatt values the diversity of its work force and credits its employees' input for the company's success.

It takes a lot of different points of view to come up with one grand vision.

Though values in the world and the work place may change over time, the values that Hyatt lives by have never waivered. We believe that regardless of background, we can always learn from each other. And we believe that, when you offer talented people unlimited respect and opportunities, your company's success and vision will be unlimited, too.

HYATT
HOTELS & RESORTS ®

To find out more about opportunities at Hyatt Hotels, contact a hotel near you, or write: Hyatt Hotels, 200 West Madison, Chicago, Illinois, 60606, Attn: Employment Office, Dept. LN 694. Proud to be an equal opportunity employer, M/F/D/V

PepsiCo Redesigns Its International Operations

PepsiCo sold $3.6 billion worth of Pepsi, Diet Pepsi, Pepsi Max, and other beverage products overseas in 1995, up 8 percent from the previous year, and its international beverage operations earned $226 million, up 16 percent from 1994. However, The Coca-Cola Co. continues to outsell PepsiCo nearly three cans to one outside the U.S., and it derives almost 80 percent of its earnings from overseas beverage sales, compared to PepsiCo's 6 percent. Pepsi also trails Coke in the United States. To gain market share and further differentiate itself from its archrival, PepsiCo plans to revamp its overseas marketing strategy with a complete redesign of the company's cans and bottles, a fresh advertising campaign, and a renovation of its overseas manufacturing and distribution systems. Projected cost of the overhaul? $300 to $500 million.

Code-named "Project Blue," PepsiCo's plans call for updating cans and bottles destined for overseas markets from the familiar red, white, and blue labels used at home to a royal blue design with a futuristic, three-dimensional graphic of the company's logo. According to PepsiCo officials, this is the first redesign of these products in five years, and

the change is more radical than earlier changes. PepsiCo also plans to launch a new advertising campaign with celebrity endorsers to tout Pepsi around the world. The firm already features tennis star Andre Agassi and supermodel Cindy Crawford in some overseas ads.

The purpose of Project Blue is to refocus PepsiCo's overseas image and make its marketing more consistent. These moves parallel a recent transformation in PepsiCo's overseas snacks division. For example, the firm's Doritos brand has been standardized globally in terms of shape, packaging, and positioning, although elements such as seasoning and thickness are still tailored for regional taste differences. These changes helped make Doritos the number one selling salty snack with $2 billion in sales in over twenty countries, including the United States. Executives hope Project Blue will have a similar effect on PepsiCo's international beverage division, giving Pepsi a boost in the global cola wars.

Sources: Lori Bongiorno, "The Pepsi Regeneration," *Business Week,* Mar. 11, 1996, pp. 70–73; Robert Frank, "PepsiCo to Revamp Beverage Line Outside the U.S.," *Wall Street Journal,* Mar. 15, 1996, p. B3; and "Marketplace Initiatives Fuel Growth in U.K., Korea, Turkey; Spain Launch in Late 1995 an Overwhelming Success," PRNewswire, Mar. 18, 1996, via America Online.

■ *Approaches to Marketing Implementation*

Once they grasp the problems and recognize the components of marketing implementation, marketing managers can decide on an approach for implementing marketing activities. Just as organizations can achieve their goals by using different marketing strategies, they can also implement their marketing strategies by using different approaches. In this section, we discuss two general approaches to marketing implementation: internal marketing and total quality management. Both approaches represent mindsets that marketing managers can adopt when organizing and planning marketing activities. These approaches are not mutually exclusive; indeed, many companies adopt both when designing marketing activities.

External customers
Individuals who patronize a business

Internal customers
A company's employees

Internal marketing
Coordinating internal exchanges between the firm and its employees to achieve successful external exchanges between the firm and its customers

Internal Marketing   **External customers** are the individuals who patronize a business—the familiar definition of customers—whereas **internal customers** are the employees who work for a company. For implementation to be successful, the needs of both groups of customers must be met. If the internal customers are not satisfied, then it is likely that the external customers will not be, either. Thus, in addition to marketing activities targeted at external customers, firms use internal marketing to attract, motivate, and retain qualified internal customers by designing internal products (jobs) that satisfy their wants and needs. **Internal marketing** is a management philosophy that coordinates internal exchanges between the organization and its employees to better achieve successful external exchanges between the organization and its customers.[7]

Figure 23.5
The Internal Marketing Framework

Source: Adapted from Nigel F. Piercy, *Market-Led Strategic Change*, Copyright © 1992, Butterworth-Heinemann Ltd., p. 371. Used with permission.

Generally speaking, internal marketing refers to the managerial actions necessary to make all members of the marketing organization understand and accept their respective roles in implementing the marketing strategy. This means that everyone, from the president of the company down to the hourly workers on the shop floor, must understand the role they play in carrying out their jobs and implementing the marketing strategy. Everyone must do his or her part to ensure that customers are satisfied. All personnel within the firm, both marketers and those who perform other functions, must recognize the tenet of customer orientation and service that underlies the marketing concept. Customer orientation is fostered by training and education and by keeping the lines of communication open throughout the firm.

Like external marketing activities, internal marketing may involve market segmentation, product development, research, distribution, and even public relations and sales promotion.[8] The internal marketing framework is shown in Figure 23.5. As in external marketing, the marketing mix in internal marketing is designed to satisfy the needs of employees. For example, an organization may sponsor sales contests to inspire sales personnel to boost their selling efforts. This helps the employees (and ultimately the company) to understand customers' needs and problems, teaches them valuable new skills, and heightens their enthusiasm for their regular jobs. In addition, many companies use planning sessions, workshops, letters, formal reports, and personal conversations as tools of internal distribution to ensure that employees comprehend the corporate mission, the organization's goals, and the marketing strategy. The ultimate results are more satisfied employees and improved customer relations.

Total Quality Management   Quality has become a major concern in many organizations, particularly in light of intense foreign competition, more demanding customers, and poorer profit performance owing to reduced market shares and higher costs. Over the last few years, several U.S. firms have lost the dominant, competitive positions they had held for decades. To regain a competitive edge, some firms are adopting a total quality management philosophy. **Total quality management (TQM)** is a philosophy that uniform commitment to quality in all areas of the organization will promote a culture that meets customers' perceptions of quality. It involves coordinating efforts directed at improving

Total quality management (TQM) A philosophy that uniform commitment to quality in all areas of an organization will promote a culture that meets customers' perceptions of quality

customer satisfaction, increasing employee participation and empowerment, forming and strengthening supplier partnerships, and facilitating an organizational culture of continuous quality improvement. BMW, in Figure 23.6, emphasizes its strong commitment to product quality. Customer satisfaction can be improved through higher-quality products and better customer service, such as reduced delivery times, faster responses to customer inquiries, and treatment of customers that shows caring on the company's part.

As a management philosophy, TQM relies heavily on the talents of employees to improve continually the quality of the organization's goods and services. TQM is founded on three basic principles:[9]

- *Continuous quality improvement.* Continuous improvement of an organization's goods and services is built around the notion that quality is free; by contrast, *not* having high quality goods and services can be very expensive, especially in terms of dissatisfied customers.[10] Continuous quality improvement also requires more than simple quality control, or the screening out of bad products during production. Rather, continuous improvement means building in quality from the very beginning—totally redesigning the product if necessary. It is a slow, long-term process of creating small improvements in quality. Companies that adopt TQM realize that the major advancements in quality occur because of an accumulation of these small improvements over time.

Benchmarking Comparing the quality of a firm's goods, services, or processes with that of the best-performing competitors

A primary tool of the continuous improvement process is **benchmarking,** the measuring and evaluating of the quality of an organization's goods, services, or processes as compared with the best-performing companies in the industry.[11] Benchmarking lets an organization know where it stands competitively in its industry, thus giving the company a goal to aim for over time. The design of the Ford Taurus attests to the value of benchmarking. By asking customers what they wanted in a car, Ford compiled a list of over four hundred desired features. Ford engineers then examined the best-selling cars in the industry, primarily foreign makes like the Honda Accord and Toyota Camry, to determine how the competition delivered each of these features. The result was an improved Taurus, which passed the Accord to become the best-selling car in America in the early 1990s.[12]

Empowerment Giving frontline employees authority and responsibility to make marketing decisions on their own

- *Empowered employees.* Ultimately, TQM succeeds or fails because of the efforts of the organization's employees. Thus employee recruitment, selection, and training are critical to the success of marketing implementation. **Empowerment** gives frontline employees the authority and responsibility to make marketing decisions without

Figure 23.6
Total Quality Management
BMW produces cars that excel in quality and performance.

seeking the approval of their supervisors.[13] Although employees at any level in an organization can be empowered to make decisions, empowerment is used most often at the frontline, where employees interact daily with customers.

One of the characteristics of empowerment is that employees can perform their jobs the way they see fit, as long as their methods and outcomes are consistent with the mission of the organization.[14] However, empowering employees is successful only if the organization is guided by an overall corporate vision, shared goals, and a culture that supports the TQM effort.[15] A great deal of time, effort, and patience is needed to develop and sustain a quality-oriented culture in an organization.

- *Quality-improvement teams.* The idea behind the team approach is to get the best and brightest people from a wide variety of perspectives working together on a quality-improvement issue. Team members are usually selected from a cross-section of jobs within the organization, as well as from among suppliers and customers. As we discussed in Chapter 16, suppliers can have a tremendous impact on the ability of a company to deliver quality products and services to its customers. Customers are included in quality-improvement teams because they are in the best position to know what they and other customers want from the company.

Total quality management can provide several benefits. Overall financial benefits include lower operating costs, higher returns on sales and investment, and an improved ability to use premium pricing rather than competitive pricing. For example, after Union Pacific upgraded the railroad's scheduling, maintenance, and customer service, it eliminated more than $700 million a year in lost revenue.[16] Additional benefits include faster development of innovations, improved access to global markets, higher levels of customer retention, and an enhanced reputation.[17]

Despite these advantages, only a handful of companies use the TQM approach. The reason is that putting the TQM philosophy into practice requires a substantial investment of time, effort, money, and patience on the part of the organization. However, companies that have the resources needed to implement TQM and the commitment of top management gain an effective means of achieving major competitive advantages in their respective industries.

Organizing Marketing Activities

The structure and relationships of a marketing unit, including lines of authority and responsibility that connect and coordinate individuals, strongly affect marketing activities. This section looks at the role of marketing within an organization and examines the major alternatives available for organizing a marketing unit.

■ *The Role of Marketing in an Organization's Structure*

As many industries become more competitive, both domestically and globally, marketing activities gain in importance. Firms that truly adopt the marketing concept develop a distinct organizational culture—a culture based on a shared set of beliefs that make the customer's needs the pivotal point of a firm's decisions about strategy and operations.[18] Instead of developing products in a vacuum and then trying to convince customers to make purchases, companies using the marketing concept begin with an orientation toward their customers' needs and desires. If the marketing concept serves as a guiding philosophy, the marketing unit will be closely coordinated with other functional areas, such as production, finance, and human resources.

Marketing must interact with functional departments in a number of key areas. It needs to work with manufacturing in determining the volume and variety of the company's products. Those in charge of production rely on marketers for accurate sales forecasts. Research and development departments depend heavily on information gathered by marketers about product features and benefits desired by consumers. Decisions made by the physical distribution department hinge on information about the urgency of delivery schedules and cost/service tradeoffs.

Figure 23.7
Meeting Customer Needs
Unisys promotes its focus
on the customer.

Marketing-oriented
organization   Tries to provide
what buyers want and to achieve
its own objectives in the process

A **marketing-oriented organization** concentrates on discovering what buyers want and providing it in such a way that it achieves its objectives. Such a company has an organizational culture that effectively and efficiently produces a sustainable competitive advantage. It focuses on customer analysis, competitor analysis, and the integration of the firm's resources to provide customer value and satisfaction, as well as long-term profits.[19] GTE, for example, visited General Electric, Land's End, and Fidelity Investments to learn how it could improve customer service. As a result of this analysis of companies with similar service-oriented operations, GTE has reduced the average time it takes to complete a customer order from three or four days to less than two hours.[20] Unisys is another example of a company that has a strong customer focus (see Figure 23.7).

A true marketing orientation means taking a completely different perspective on a firm's structure. Figure 23.8 contrasts the typical organizational hierarchy with the arrangement of a marketing-oriented company. In the traditional hierarchy, top management or the CEO represents the pinnacle of authority, and every level of the organization is under the authority of the levels above it. Frontline employees must answer to frontline

Figure 23.8
Traditional Versus
Marketing-Oriented
Organizations

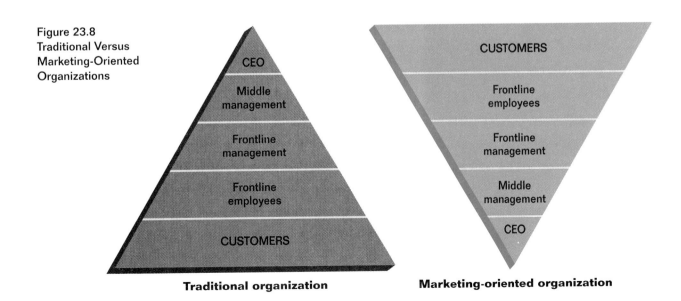

managers, frontline managers must answer to midlevel managers, and so on. The marketing-oriented approach, on the other hand, inverts this pyramid of authority, placing customers at the top. Every action within the organization is directed at serving customer needs.

In the marketing-oriented approach, too, each level must answer to the levels above it. But answering to the next level in this arrangement means taking actions necessary to ensure that each level performs its job well. For example, the role of the CEO in the marketing-oriented organization is to ensure that midlevel managers have everything they need to perform their jobs well. Likewise, the job of a frontline manager is to ensure that frontline employees are capable and able to service customers efficiently. The end result of the marketing-oriented approach is a complete focus on customer needs.

Both the links between marketing and other functional areas (such as production, finance, and human resources) and the importance of marketing to management evolve from the firm's basic orientation. Marketing encompasses the greatest number of business functions and occupies an important position when a firm is marketing-oriented; it has a limited role when the firm views the role of marketing as simply selling products that the company makes. However, a marketing orientation is not achieved simply by redrawing the organizational chart. Management must also adopt and use the marketing orientation as a management philosophy.

■ *Alternatives for Organizing the Marketing Unit*

How effectively a firm's marketing management can plan and implement marketing strategies also depends on how the marketing unit is organized. Effective organizational planning can give the firm a competitive advantage. The organizational structure of a marketing department establishes the authority relationships among marketing personnel and specifies who is responsible for making certain decisions and performing particular activities. This internal structure helps direct marketing activities.

One of the crucial decisions regarding structural authority is that of centralization versus decentralization. A **centralized organization** is one in which the top-level managers delegate very little authority to lower levels of the organization. In a **decentralized organization,** decision-making authority is delegated as far down the chain of command as possible. The decision to centralize or decentralize the organization directly affects marketing in the organization. For example, as indicated in Figure 23.8, most traditional organizations are highly centralized. In these organizations, most, if not all, marketing decisions are made at the top levels of the organization. However, as organizations become more marketing-oriented, centralized decision making proves to be somewhat ineffective. In these organizations, decentralized authority allows the organization to respond faster to customer needs.

In organizing a marketing unit, managers divide the work into specific activities and delegate responsibility and authority for those activities to persons in various positions within the unit. These positions include, for example, the sales manager, the research manager, and the advertising manager.

No single approach to organizing a marketing unit works equally well in all businesses. The best approach or approaches depend on the number and diversity of the firm's products, the characteristics and needs of the people in the target market, and many other factors. A marketing unit can be organized according to (1) functions, (2) products, (3) regions, or (4) types of customers. Firms often use some combination of organization by functions, products, regions, or customer types. Product features may dictate that the marketing unit be structured by products, whereas customers' characteristics require that it be organized by geographic region or by types of customers. By using more than one type of organization, a flexible marketing unit can develop and implement marketing plans to match customers' needs precisely.

Organizing by Functions   Some marketing departments are organized by general marketing functions, such as marketing research, product development, distribution, sales, advertising, and customer relations. The personnel who direct these functions report directly to the top-level marketing executive. This structure is fairly common

Centralized organization Top management delegates little authority to levels below it

Decentralized organization Decision-making authority delegated as far down the chain of command as possible

554

because it works well for some businesses with centralized marketing operations, such as Ford and General Motors. In more decentralized firms, such as grocery store chains, functional organization can cause serious coordination problems. But the functional approach may suit a large centralized company whose products and customers are neither numerous nor diverse.

Organizing by Products An organization that produces and markets diverse products may find the functional approach inadequate. The decisions and problems related to a single marketing function for one product may be quite different from those related to the same marketing function for another product. As a result, businesses that produce diverse products sometimes organize their marketing units according to product groups. Organizing by product groups gives a firm the flexibility to develop special marketing mixes for different products. Procter & Gamble, like many firms in the consumer packaged goods industry, is organized by product. One product manager oversees the Folger's coffee division, another the Tide detergent division, and so on. Each division develops its own product plans, implements them, monitors the results, and takes corrective action as necessary. The product manager may also draw on the resources of specialized staff in the company, such as the advertising, research, or distribution manager. Although organizing by products allows a company to remain flexible, this approach can be rather expensive because of the layers of management and employees that it creates.

Organizing by Regions A large company that markets products nationally (or internationally) may organize its marketing activities by geographic regions. Managers of marketing functions for each region report to their regional marketing manager; all the regional marketing managers report directly to the executive marketing manager. Frito Lay, for example, is organized into four regional divisions, allowing the company to get closer to its customers and to respond more quickly and efficiently to regional competitors. This form of organization is especially effective for a firm whose customers' characteristics and needs vary greatly from one region to another. Firms that try to penetrate the national market intensively may divide regions into subregions.

Organizing by Types of Customers Sometimes a company's marketing unit is organized according to types of customers. This form of internal organization works well for a firm that has several groups of customers whose needs and problems differ significantly. For example, Bic Corp. may sell pens to large retail stores, wholesalers, and institutions. Retailers may want more rapid delivery of small shipments and more personal selling by the producer than do either wholesalers or institutional buyers. Because the marketing decisions and activities required for these two groups of customers differ considerably, the company may find it efficient to organize its marketing unit by types of customers.

In an organization with a marketing department broken down by customer group, the marketing manager for each group reports to the top-level marketing executive and directs most marketing activities for that group. A marketing manager directs all activities needed to market products to a specific customer group.

Implementing Marketing Activities

*T*hrough planning and organizing, marketing managers provide purpose, direction, and structure for marketing activities. Likewise, understanding the problems and elements of marketing implementation, as well as selecting an overall approach, sets the stage for the implementation of specific marketing activities. As we have stated before, people are ultimately responsible for implementing marketing strategy. Therefore, the effective implementation of any and all marketing activities depends on motivating marketing personnel, effectively communicating within the marketing unit, coordinating all marketing activities, and establishing a timetable for the completion of each marketing activity.

555

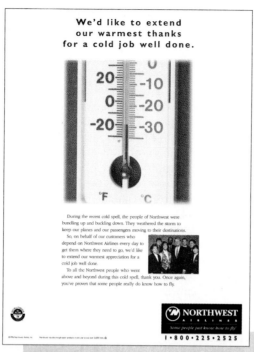

Figure 23.9
Motivating Employees   Some companies, such as Northwest Airlines, motivate their employees by acknowledging their employees' contributions. Other companies motivate their employees by offering rewards such as American Airlines flight certificates.

■ *Motivating Marketing Personnel*

People work to satisfy physical, psychological, and social needs. To motivate marketing personnel, managers must discover their employees' needs and then develop motivational methods that help employees satisfy those needs. It is crucial that the plan to motivate employees be fair, ethical, and well understood by employees. Additionally, rewards to employees must be tied to organizational goals. In general, to improve employee motivation, companies need to find out what workers think, how they feel, and what they want. Some of this information can be attained from an employee attitude survey. A firm can motivate its workers by directly linking pay with performance, informing workers how their performance affects department and corporate results, following through with appropriate compensation, promoting or implementing a flexible benefits program, and adopting a participative management approach.[21]

Besides tying rewards to organizational goals, managers must use different motivational tools to motivate individuals. Selecting effective motivational tools has become more complex because of greater differences among workers due to race, ethnicity, gender, and age. Indeed, one of the most common forms of diversity in today's organizations is that between generations of employees. Such differences, however, also broaden the range of individual value systems within an organization, which in turn calls for a more diverse set of motivational tools. For example, an employee might value autonomy or recognition more than a slight pay increase. Managers can reward employees with money, plus additional fringe benefits, prestige or recognition, or even offer such nonfinancial rewards as job autonomy, skill variety, task significance, and increased feedback (see Figure 23.9). It is crucial for management to show that it takes pride in its work force and to motivate employees to take pride in their company.

■ *Communicating Within the Marketing Unit*

With good communication, marketing managers can motivate personnel and coordinate their efforts. Marketing managers must be able to communicate with the firm's top management to ensure that marketing activities are consistent with the company's overall goals. Communication with top-level executives keeps marketing managers aware of the company's overall plans and achievements. It also guides the marketing unit's activities and indicates how they are to be integrated with those of other departments, such as finance, production, or human resources, with whose management the marketing manager must also communicate to coordinate marketing efforts. For example, marketing personnel must work with the production staff to help design products that customers want. To direct marketing activities, marketing managers must communicate with marketing personnel at the operations level, such as sales and advertising personnel, researchers, wholesalers, retailers, and package designers.

One of the most important types of communication in marketing is communication that flows upward from the frontline of the marketing unit to higher-level marketing managers. Customer-contact employees who work at the frontline interact daily with customers and thus are in a unique position to understand customers' wants and needs. By taking steps to encourage upward communication, marketing managers gain access to a rich source of information about what customers require, how well products are selling, whether marketing activities are working, and what problems are occurring in marketing implementation.[22] Upward communication also allows the marketing manager to understand the problems and needs of employees. This is an important aspect of the internal marketing approach that we discussed earlier in the chapter.

To facilitate communication, marketing managers should establish an information system within the marketing unit. The marketing information system (discussed in Chapter 5) should make it easy for marketing managers, sales managers, and sales personnel to communicate with each other. Marketers need an information system to support a variety of activities, such as planning, budgeting, sales analyses, performance evaluations, and the preparation of reports. An information system should also expedite communications with other departments in the organization and minimize destructive competition among departments for organizational resources.

■ *Coordinating Marketing Activities*

Because of job specialization and differences related to marketing activities, marketing managers must synchronize individuals' actions to achieve marketing objectives. In addition, they must work closely with managers in research and development, production, finance, accounting, and human resources to see that marketing activities mesh with other functions of the firm. Marketing managers must coordinate the activities of marketing staff within the firm and integrate those activities with the marketing efforts of external organizations—advertising agencies, resellers (wholesalers and retailers), researchers, and shippers, among others. Marketing managers can improve coordination by using internal marketing activities to make each employee aware of how his or her job relates to others and how his or her actions contribute to the achievement of marketing objectives. Technology in Marketing (on the next page) describes Deluxe Corp.'s efforts to integrate its diverse businesses, products, and activities.

■ *Establishing a Timetable for Implementation*

Successful marketing implementation requires that employees know the specific activities for which they are responsible and the timetable for completing each activity. One company that is very good at establishing implementation timetables is Domino's Pizza. Every activity in creating and delivering a pizza, from taking the phone order to handing the pizza to the customer, has an employee that is responsible for its implementation. In addition, all employees know the specified time frame for the completion of their activities.[23]

Establishing an implementation timetable involves several steps: (1) identifying the activities to be performed, (2) determining the time required to complete each activity, (3) separating the activities that must be performed in sequence from those that can be performed simultaneously, (4) organizing the activities in the proper order, and (5) assigning the responsibility for completing each activity to one or more employees, teams, or managers. Some activities must be performed before others, whereas others can be performed at the same time or later in the implementation process. This requires tight coordination

TECHNOLOGY IN MARKETING

Deluxe Corp. Adjusts to a Changing Environment

Deluxe Corp. faces a taxing problem: Americans are writing fewer checks—its core product—and transacting more business electronically through direct deposit, automated-teller machines, and even the Internet. The St. Paul–based firm has been printing and processing checks, deposit slips, and other financial documents for more than eighty years, and it dominates the industry with $1.5 billion in sales and a 51 percent market share. To survive in an increasingly electronic era, Deluxe has spent $650 million in recent years to diversify into everything from electronic-payment technology to greeting cards. But while these new businesses generate nearly half of the company's revenues, they contribute less than 10 percent to its profits. Deluxe also faces competition from companies that market checks directly to consumers, as well as from regional electronic funds transfer (EFT) networks and electronic-banking businesses.

To better coordinate Deluxe's marketing efforts, new CEO John A. "Gus" Blanchard III has implemented a cost-cutting program and restructured the organization. To slash $150 million in costs by the end of 1997, Blanchard plans to close twenty-six of forty-one check-printing plants, eliminating 1,200

jobs, the second round of layoffs in the company's history. He may lay off 30 to 50 percent of the company's officers. Blanchard also intends to cut capital spending by 30 percent. After realizing that Deluxe's check and electronic units were sometimes competing with each other, Blanchard folded the electronic businesses under the same management as checks for the first time. Blanchard says, "Everything seemed disconnected. There's a great opportunity for focus." Accordingly, Blanchard also proposes to sell off Deluxe's ink-manufacturing and financial-forms businesses and is even thinking about selling off the greeting card operation.

Blanchard hopes these cost-cutting and restructuring efforts will better focus Deluxe's marketing efforts on developing and marketing a variety of transaction services—check verification, home banking, ATM switching, and EFT settlement—for banks and EFT networks, its core customers. In the home banking area, for example, Blanchard wants to position Deluxe as an intermediary between banks and software giants such as Microsoft and Intuit Inc. by providing processing and customer database information.

Sources: *Hoover's Company Profile* database (Austin, Texas: Reference Press, 1995), via America Online; and Richard A. Melcher, "Deluxe Isn't Checking Out Yet," *Business Week*, Feb. 26, 1996, pp. 94, 96.

---

between departments—marketing, production, advertising, sales, and so on—to ensure that all implementation activities are completed on schedule. Pinpointing those implementation activities that can be performed simultaneously will greatly reduce the total amount of time needed to put a given marketing strategy into practice. Since scheduling is a complicated task, most organizations use sophisticated computer programs to plan the timing of marketing activities.

Controlling Marketing Activities

Marketing control process
Establishing performance standards and trying to match actual performance to those standards

*T*o achieve marketing as well as general organizational objectives, marketing managers must effectively control marketing efforts. The **marketing control process** consists of establishing performance standards, evaluating actual performance by comparing it with established standards, and reducing the differences between desired and actual performance.

Although the control function is a fundamental management activity, it has received little attention in marketing. There are both formal and informal control systems in organizations. The formal marketing control process, as mentioned before, involves performance standards, evaluation of actual performance, and corrective action to remedy

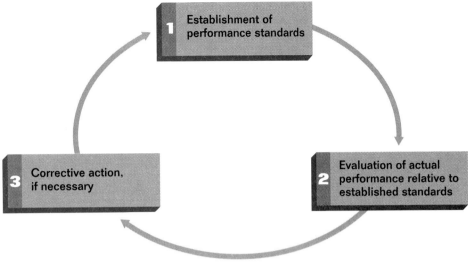

Figure 23.10
The Marketing Control Process

shortfalls (see Figure 23.10). The informal control process, however, involves self-control, social or group control, and cultural control through acceptance of a firm's value system. Which type of control system dominates depends on the environmental context of the firm.[24] We now discuss these steps in the control process and consider the major problems they involve.

■ *Establishing Performance Standards*

Planning and controlling are closely linked because plans include statements about what is to be accomplished. For purposes of control, these statements function as performance standards. A **performance standard** is an expected level of performance against which actual performance can be compared. Examples of performance standards might be the reduction of customers' complaints by 20 percent, a monthly sales quota of $150,000, or a 10 percent increase per month in new customer accounts. Performance standards are also given in the form of budget accounts; that is, marketers are expected to achieve a certain objective without spending more than a given amount of resources. As stated earlier, performance standards should be tied to organizational goals. Performance standards can also relate to products or service quality. Achieving performance standards is becoming increasingly difficult as a shortage of high-quality service employees grows more severe.[25]

■ *Evaluating Actual Performance*

To compare actual performance with performance standards, marketing managers must know what employees within the company are doing and have information about the activities of external organizations that provide the firm with marketing assistance. Cadillac, for example, evaluates its product and service level by how well it ranks on the J.D. Power & Associates Sales Satisfaction Survey. The automaker ranked number one among domestics and second only to Infiniti overall.[26] (We discuss specific methods for assessing actual performance later in this chapter.) Information is required about the activities of marketing personnel at the operations level and at various marketing management levels. Most businesses obtain marketing assistance from one or more external individuals or organizations, such as advertising agencies, intermediaries, marketing research firms, and consultants. To maximize benefits from external sources, a firm's marketing control process must monitor their activities. Although it may be difficult to obtain the necessary information, it is impossible to measure actual performance without it.

Records of actual performance are compared with performance standards to determine whether and how much of a discrepancy exists. For example, The Home Depot set a goal of opening 25 percent new stores but at year's end found it had exceeded that goal by opening 29 percent more stores.[27] Home Depot's situation illustrates that a discrepancy between performance standards and actual performance may be on the positive side; however, the effect of rapid expansion can place significant stress on an organization.

■ *Taking Corrective Action*

Marketing managers have several options for reducing a discrepancy between established performance standards and actual performance. They can take steps to improve actual performance, reduce or totally change the performance standard, or do both. Cellular phones provide an opportunity to improve sales force productivity (see Figure 23.11). Changes in actual performance may require the marketing manager to use better methods of motivating marketing personnel or find more effective techniques for coordinating marketing efforts. For example, when Blockbuster Video became a major shareholder in Discovery Zone, an indoor children's playground chain, it discovered many problems, including seventeen separate pricing systems nationwide and computer and accounting systems only recently adopted.[28]

Sometimes performance standards are unrealistic when they are written, and sometimes changes in the marketing environment make them unrealistic. For example, a company's annual sales goal may become unrealistic if several aggressive competitors enter the firm's market. In fact, changes in the marketing environment may dictate radical revisions in marketing strategy.

■ *Problems in Controlling Marketing Activities*

**Figure 23.11
Improving Sales Force
Productivity** Cellular
phones provide
assistance in improving
sales force productivity.

In their efforts to control marketing activities, marketing managers frequently run into several problems. Often the information required to control marketing activities is unavailable or is available only at a high cost. Even though marketing controls should be

flexible enough to allow for environmental changes, the frequency, intensity, and unpredictability of such changes may hamper control. In addition, the time lag between marketing activities and their results limits a marketing manager's ability to measure the effectiveness of specific marketing activities. This is especially true for all advertising activities.

Because marketing and other business activities overlap, marketing managers cannot determine the precise cost of marketing activities. Without an accurate measure of marketing costs, it is difficult to know if the outcome of marketing activities is worth the expense. Finally, marketing control may be difficult because it is very hard to develop exact performance standards for marketing personnel.

Methods of Evaluating Performance

*T*here are specific methods for assessing and improving the effectiveness of a marketing strategy. A marketer should state in the marketing plan what a marketing strategy is supposed to accomplish. These statements should set forth performance standards—usually in terms of profits, sales, costs, or communication standards—relating to such matters as brand recall. Actual performance must be measured in similar terms so that comparisons are possible. In this section we consider three general ways of evaluating the actual performance of marketing strategies: sales analysis, marketing cost analysis, and the marketing audit.

561

■ *Sales Analysis*

Sales analysis Use of sales figures to evaluate a firm's current performance

Sales analysis uses sales figures to evaluate a firm's current performance. It is probably the most common method of evaluation because sales data partially reflect the target market's reactions to a marketing mix and often are readily available, at least in aggregate form.

Marketers use current sales data to monitor the impact of current marketing efforts. However, that information alone is not enough. To provide useful analyses, current sales data must be compared with forecasted sales, industry sales, specific competitors' sales, or the costs incurred to achieve the sales volume. For example, knowing that a variety store attained a $600,000 sales volume this year does not tell management whether its marketing strategy has been successful. However, if managers know that expected sales were $550,000, then they are in a better position to determine the effectiveness of the firm's marketing efforts. In addition, if they know that the marketing costs needed to achieve the $600,000 volume were 12 percent less than budgeted, they are in an even better position to analyze their marketing strategy precisely.

Although sales may be measured in several ways, the basic unit of measurement is the sales transaction. A sales transaction results in a customer order for a specified quantity of an organization's product sold under specified terms by a particular salesperson or sales group on a certain date. Many organizations record these bits of information about their transactions. With such a record, a company can analyze sales in terms of dollar volume or market share.

Firms frequently use dollar volume sales analysis because the dollar is a common denominator of sales, costs, and profits. However, price increases and decreases affect total sales figures. This is especially true in the auto industry, where profit margins are being squeezed. Even though prices are increasing, customers are demanding rock bottom prices and low lease rates on everything but the hottest selling trucks.[29] If a company increased its prices by 10 percent this year and its sales volume is 10 percent greater than last year, it has not experienced any increase in unit sales. A marketing manager who uses dollar volume analysis should factor out the effects of price changes.

A firm's market share is the firm's sales of a product stated as a percentage of industry sales of that product. Market-share analysis lets a company compare its marketing strategy with competitors' strategies. The primary reason for using market-share analysis is to estimate whether sales changes have resulted from the firm's marketing strategy or from uncontrollable environmental forces. When a company's sales volume declines but its share of the market stays the same, the marketer can assume that industry sales declined (because of some uncontrollable factors) and that this decline was reflected in the firm's sales. However, if a company experiences a decline in both sales and market share, it should consider the possibility that its marketing strategy is not effective or was improperly implemented.

Even though market-share analysis can be helpful in evaluating the performance of a marketing strategy, the user must interpret results cautiously. When attributing a sales decline to uncontrollable factors, a marketer must keep in mind that such factors do not affect all firms in the industry equally. Not all firms in an industry have the same objectives, and some change objectives from one year to the next. Changes in the objectives of one company can affect the market shares of one or all companies in that industry. For instance, when UPS introduced same-day package delivery at a minimum price of $160, FedEx had to match the service and price to avoid losing market share. Within an industry, the entrance of new firms or the demise of established ones also affects a specific firm's market share, and market-share analysts should attempt to account for these effects. KFC, for example, had to reevaluate its marketing strategies when McDonald's introduced its own fried chicken product.

■ *Marketing Cost Analysis*

Marketing cost analysis Breaking down and classifying costs to determine which stem from specific marketing activities

Although sales analysis is critical for evaluating the effectiveness of a marketing strategy, it gives only part of the picture. A marketing strategy that successfully generates sales may also be extremely costly. To get a complete picture, a firm must know the marketing costs associated with using a given strategy to achieve a certain sales level. **Marketing cost analysis** breaks down and classifies costs to determine which are associated with specific marketing activities. By comparing costs of previous marketing activities with results generated, a marketer can better allocate the firm's marketing resources in the future. Marketing cost analysis lets a company evaluate the effectiveness of an ongoing or recent marketing strategy by comparing sales achieved and costs incurred. By pinpointing exactly where a company is experiencing high costs, this form of analysis can help isolate profitable or unprofitable customer segments, products, or geographic areas.

The task of determining marketing costs is often complex and difficult. Simply ascertaining the costs associated with marketing a product is rarely adequate. Marketers must usually determine the marketing costs of serving specific geographic areas, market segments, or even specific customers.

Fixed costs Costs based on how money was actually spent

Four broad categories are used in marketing cost analysis: fixed costs, variable costs, traceable common costs, and nontraceable common costs. **Fixed costs**—such as rent, salaries, office supplies, and utilities—are based on how the money was actually spent. However, fixed costs often do not explain what marketing functions were performed through the expenditure of those funds. It does little good, for example, to know that $80,000 is spent for rent each year. The analyst has no way of knowing whether the money

Variable costs Costs directly attributable to production and selling volume

is spent for the rental of production, storage, or sales facilities. **Variable costs** are directly attributable to production and selling volume. For example, sales force salaries might be allocated to the cost of selling a specific product item, selling in a specific geographic area, or selling to a particular customer. **Traceable common costs** can be allocated indirectly,

Traceable common costs Costs allocated indirectly to the functions that they support

using one or several criteria, to the functions that they support. For example, if the firm spends $80,000 annually to rent space for production, storage, and selling, the rental costs of storage could be determined on the basis of cost per square foot used for storage.

Nontraceable common costs Costs assignable only on an arbitrary basis

Nontraceable common costs cannot be assigned according to any logical criteria and thus are assignable only on an arbitrary basis. Interest, taxes, and the salaries of top management are nontraceable common costs.

Full-cost approach Including direct costs and both traceable and nontraceable common costs in the cost analysis

How these three categories of costs are dealt with depends on whether the analyst uses a full-cost or a direct-cost approach. When a **full-cost approach** is used, cost analysis includes variable costs, traceable common costs, and nontraceable common costs. Proponents of this approach claim that if an accurate profit picture is desired, all costs must be included in the analysis. However, opponents point out that full costing does not yield actual costs because nontraceable common costs are determined by arbitrary criteria. With different criteria, the full-costing approach yields different results. A cost-conscious operating unit can be discouraged if numerous costs are assigned to it arbitrarily. To eliminate such problems, the **direct-cost approach,** which includes variable costs

Direct-cost approach Including only direct costs and traceable common costs in the cost analysis

and traceable common costs but not nontraceable common costs, is used. However, critics of this approach say that it is not accurate because it omits one cost category.

■ *The Marketing Audit*

Marketing audit   A systematic examination of the marketing group's objectives, strategies, organization, and performance

A **marketing audit** is a systematic examination of the marketing group's objectives, strategies, organization, and performance. Its primary purpose is to identify weaknesses in ongoing marketing operations and plan the necessary improvements to correct these weaknesses. Like an accounting or financial audit, a marketing audit should be conducted regularly instead of just when performance evaluation mechanisms show that the system is out of control. The marketing audit is not a control process to be used only during a crisis, though, of course, it can help a business in trouble isolate problems and generate solutions. Marketing audits have also become more difficult as organizations merge and acquire other firms. To gain technology, world market share, new products, and distribution systems, many companies have even joined with competitors. Kimberly-Clark, for example, having acquired Scott Paper, is now the world's largest tissue marketer.[30]

A marketing audit may be specific and focus on one or a few marketing activities, or it may be comprehensive and encompass all of a company's marketing activities. Table 23.1 lists many possible dimensions of a marketing audit.

Customer-service audit Comparing the performance of specific customer-service activities with service goals and standards

An audit might deal with only a few of these areas, or it might include them all. For example, one specialized type of audit is the **customer-service audit,** in which specific customer-service activities are analyzed and service goals and standards are compared with actual performance.[31] Table 23.2 provides a typical outline for a customer-service audit. Specialized audits could also be performed for product development, pricing, sales, or advertising and other promotional activities. The scope of any audit depends on the costs involved, the target markets served, the structure of the marketing mix, and environmental conditions. The results of the audit can be used to reallocate marketing efforts and to reexamine marketing opportunities.

The marketing audit should aid evaluation by doing the following:

1. Describing current activities and results related to sales, costs, prices, profits, and other performance feedback

2. Gathering information about customers, competition, and environmental developments that may affect the marketing strategy

3. Exploring opportunities and alternatives for improving the marketing strategy

4. Providing an overall database to be used in evaluating the attainment of organizational goals and marketing objectives

Marketing audits can be performed internally or externally. An internal auditor may be a top-level marketing executive, a companywide auditing committee, or a manager from another office or of another function. Although it is more expensive, an audit by outside consultants is usually more effective because external auditors bring to the task more objectivity, more time for the audit, and greater experience.

There is no single set of procedures for all marketing audits. However, firms should adhere to several general guidelines. Audits are often based on a series of questionnaires administered to the firm's personnel. These questionnaires should be developed carefully to ensure that the audit focuses on the right issues. Auditors should develop and follow a step-by-step plan to guarantee that the audit is systematic. When interviewing company personnel, the auditors should strive to talk with a diverse group of people from many parts of the company.

Although the concept of auditing implies an official examination of marketing activities, many organizations audit their marketing activities informally. Any attempt to verify operating results and to compare them with standards can be considered an auditing activity. Many smaller firms probably would not use the word *audit,* but they do perform auditing activities.

Several problems may arise in an audit of marketing activities. Marketing audits can be expensive and time-consuming. Selecting the auditors may be difficult because objective, qualified personnel may not be available. Marketing audits can also be extremely disruptive because employees sometimes fear comprehensive evaluations, especially by outsiders.

Table 23.1 Dimensions of a Marketing Audit

Part I. The Marketing Environment Audit
Macroenvironment

A. Economic-demographic
1. What does the company expect in the way of inflation, material shortages, unemployment, and credit availability in the short run, intermediate run, and long run?
2. What effect will forecasted trends in the size, age distribution, and regional distribution of population have on the business?

B. Technological
1. What major changes are occurring in product technology? in process technology?
2. What are the major generic substitutes that might replace this product?

C. Political-legal
1. What laws are being proposed that may affect marketing strategy and tactics?
2. What federal, state, and local agency actions should be watched? What is happening with pollution control, equal employment opportunity, product safety, advertising, price control, etc., that is relevant to marketing planning?

D. Cultural
1. What attitude is the public taking toward business and the types of products produced by the company?
2. What changes in consumer lifestyles and values have a bearing on the company's target markets and marketing methods?

E. Ecological
1. Will the cost and availability of natural resources directly affect the company?
2. Are there public concerns about the company's role in pollution and conservation? If so, what is the company's reaction?

Task Environment

A. Markets
1. What is happening to market size, growth, geographical distribution, and profits?
2. What are the major market segments and their expected rates of growth? Which are high-opportunity and low-opportunity segments?

B. Customers
1. How do current customers and prospects rate the company and its competitors on reputation, product quality, service, sales force, and price?
2. How do different classes of customers make their buying decisions?
3. What evolving needs do the buyers in this market have, and what satisfactions are they seeking?

C. Competitors
1. Who are the major competitors? What are the objectives and strategy of each major competitor? What are their strengths and weaknesses? What are the sizes and trends in market shares?
2. What trends can be foreseen in future competition and substitutes for this product?

D. Distribution and dealers
1. What are the main trade channels bringing products to customers?
2. What are the efficiency levels and growth potentials of the different trade channels?

E. Suppliers
1. What is the outlook for the availability of key resources used in production?
2. What trends are occurring among suppliers in their patterns of selling?

F. Facilitators and marketing firms
1. What is the outlook for the cost and availability of transportation services? warehousing facilities? financial resources?
2. How effectively is the advertising agency performing? What trends are occurring in advertising agency services?

G. Publics
1. Where are the opportunity areas or problems for the company?
2. How effectively is the company dealing with its publics?

Part II. Marketing Strategy Audit

A. Business mission
1. Is the business mission clearly focused on customer satisfaction?
2. Is the business mission attainable?

B. Marketing objectives and goals
1. Are the corporate objectives clearly stated? Do they lead logically to the marketing objectives?
2. Are the marketing objectives stated clearly enough to guide marketing planning and subsequent performance measurement?
3. Are the marketing objectives appropriate, given the company's competitive position, resources, and opportunities?

Table 23.1 (continued)   Dimensions of a Marketing Audit

C. Strategy
1. What is the core marketing strategy for achieving the objectives? Is it sound?
2. Are the resources budgeted to accomplish the marketing objectives inadequate, adequate, or excessive?
3. Are the marketing resources allocated optimally to prime market segments, territories, and products?
4. Are the marketing resources allocated optimally to the major elements of the marketing mix, i.e., product quality, service, sales force, advertising, promotion, and distribution?

Part III. Marketing Organization Audit

A. Formal structure
1. Has the right balance been achieved between centralized and decentralized marketing authority? If employees have been empowered to make decisions, have adequate steps been taken to ensure a proper organizational culture?
2. Are the marketing responsibilities optimally structured along functional, product, end-user, and territorial lines?

B. Functional efficiency
1. Are there good communications and working relations between marketing and sales?
2. Is the product-management system working effectively? Are the product managers able to plan profits or only sales volume?
3. Are there any groups in marketing that need more training, motivation, supervision, or evaluation?

C. Interface efficiency
1. Are there any problems between marketing and manufacturing, R&D, purchasing, finance, accounting, and legal that need attention?

Part IV. Marketing Systems Audit

A. Marketing information system
1. Is the marketing intelligence system producing accurate, sufficient, and timely information about developments in the marketplace?
2. Is marketing research being adequately used by company decision makers?

B. Marketing planning system
1. Is the marketing planning system well conceived and effective?
2. Are sales forecasting and market-potential measurement soundly carried out?
3. Are sales quotas set on a proper basis?

C. Marketing control system
1. Are the control procedures (monthly, quarterly, etc.) adequate to ensure that the annual-plan objectives are being achieved?
2. Is provision made to analyze periodically the profitability of different products, markets, territories, and channels of distribution?
3. Is provision made to examine and validate periodically various marketing costs?

D. New-product development system
1. Is the company well organized to gather, generate, and screen new product ideas?
2. Does the company do adequate concept research and business analysis before investing heavily in a new idea?
3. Does the company carry out adequate product and market testing before launching a new product?

Part V. Marketing Productivity Audit

A. Profitability analysis
1. What is the profitability of the company's different products, served markets, territories, and channels of distribution?
2. Should the company enter, expand, contract, or withdraw from any business segments, and what would be the short- and long-run profit consequences?

B. Cost-effective analysis
1. Do any marketing activities seem to have excessive costs? Are these costs valid? Can cost-reducing steps be taken?

Part VI. Marketing Function Audits

A. Products
1. What are the product line objectives? Are these objectives sound? Is the current product line meeting these objectives?
2. Are there particular products that should be phased out?
3. Are there new products that are worth adding?
4. Are any products able to benefit from quality, feature, or style improvements?

565

Table 23.1 (continued) Dimensions of a Marketing Audit

B. Price
1. What are the pricing objectives, policies, strategies, and procedures? Are prices set on sound cost, demand, and competitive criteria?
2. Do the customers see the company's prices as being in or out of line with the perceived value of its products?
3. Does the company use price promotions effectively?

C. Distribution
1. What are the distribution objectives and strategies?
2. Is there adequate market coverage and service?
3. How effective are the following channel members: distributors, manufacturers' reps, brokers, agents, etc.?
4. Should the company consider changing its distribution channels?

D. Advertising, sales promotion, and publicity
1. What are the organization's advertising objectives? Are they sound?
2. Is the right amount being spent on advertising? How is the budget determined?
3. Are the ad themes and copy effective? What do customers and the public think about the advertising?
4. Are the advertising media well chosen?
5. Is the internal advertising staff adequate?
6. Is the sales promotion budget adequate? Is there effective and sufficient use of sales promotion tools, such as samples, coupons, displays, and sales contests?
7. Is the publicity budget adequate? Is the public relations staff competent and creative?

E. Sales force
1. What are the organization's sales force objectives?
2. Is the sales force large enough to accomplish the company's objectives?
3. Is the sales force organized along the proper principle(s) of specialization (territory, market, product)? Are there enough (or too many) sales managers to guide the field sales reps?
4. Does the sales compensation level and structure provide adequate incentive and reward?
5. Does the sales force show high morale, ability, and effort?
6. Are the procedures adequate for setting quotas and evaluating performance?
7. How does the company's sales force compare with the sales forces of competitors?

Source: Philip Kotler and Gary Armstrong, *Principles of Marketing*, 6th ed., © 1994, pp. 58–59. Adapted by permission of Prentice-Hall, Inc., Upper Saddle River, New Jersey

Table 23.2 Dimensions of a Customer-Service Audit

A. Identify Customer-Service Activities
1. What specific customer-service activities does the company currently provide?
   Product-related activities: repairs, maintenance, technical assistance
   Pricing-related activities: credit, financing, billing
   Distribution-related activities: delivery, installation, locations
   Promotion-related activities: customer-service phone lines, complaint handling
2. Are these customer services provided by our company or by outside contractors? If outside contractors provide these services, how are they performing?
3. What customer-service activities do customers want or need?

B. Review Standard Procedures for Each Activity
1. Do written procedures (manuals) exist for each activity? If so, are these procedures (manuals) up-to-date?
2. What oral or unwritten procedures exist for each activity? Should these procedures be included in the written procedures or should they be eliminated?
3. Do customer-service personnel regularly interact with other functions to establish standard procedures for each activity?

C. Identify Performance Goals by Customer-Service Activity
1. What specific, quantitative goals exist for each activity?
2. What qualitative goals exist for each activity?
3. How does each activity contribute to customer satisfaction within each marketing element (i.e., product, pricing, distribution, promotion)?
4. How does each activity contribute to the long-run success of the company?

D. Specify Performance Measures by Customer-Service Activity
1. What are the internal, profit-based measures for each activity?
2. What are the internal, time-based measures for each activity?
3. How is performance monitored and evaluated internally by management?
4. How is performance monitored and evaluated externally by customers?

Table 23.2 (continued) Dimensions of a Customer-Service Audit

E. Review and Evaluate Customer-Service Personnel

1. Are the company's current recruiting, selection, and retention efforts consistent with the customer-service requirements established by customers?
2. What is the nature and content of our employee training activities? Are these activities consistent with the customer-service requirements established by customers?
3. How are customer-service personnel supervised, evaluated, and rewarded? Are these procedures consistent with customer requirements?
4. What effect do employee evaluation and reward policies have on employee attitudes, satisfaction, and motivation?

F. Identify and Evaluate Customer-Service Support Systems

1. Are the quality and accuracy of our customer-service materials consistent with the image of our company and its products? (Examples: instruction manuals, brochures, form letters, etc.)
2. Are the quality and appearance of our physical facilities consistent with the image of our company and its products? (Examples: offices, furnishings, layout, etc.)
3. Are the quality and appearance of our customer-service equipment consistent with the image of our company and its products? (Examples: repair tools, telephones, computers, delivery vehicles, etc.)
4. Are our record-keeping systems accurate? Is the information always readily available when it is needed? What technology could be acquired to enhance our record-keeping abilities (i.e., bar code scanners, portable computers)?

Source: Reprinted from Christopher H. Lovelock, *Services Marketing*, Second Edition. Copyright © 1991 Prentice-Hall, a division of Simon & Schuster, Inc. Used with permission.

567

SUMMARY

Marketing implementation is an important part of the marketing management process. To help ensure effective implementation, marketing managers must consider why the intended marketing strategies do not always turn out as expected. Realized marketing strategies often differ from the intended strategies because of the three problems of implementation: that marketing strategy and implementation are related and are constantly evolving and that the responsibility for them is separated. Marketing managers must also consider other vital components of implementation—resources, systems, people, leadership, and shared goals—to ensure the proper implementation of marketing strategies.

Organizations follow two major approaches to marketing implementation: internal marketing and total quality management (TQM). Internal marketing is a management philosophy that refers to the coordination of internal exchanges between the organization and its employees to better achieve successful external exchanges between the organization and its customers. In this approach, all employees have both external and internal customers. For implementation to be successful, employees must serve the needs of both customer groups. The TQM approach relies heavily on the talents of employees to continually improve the quality of the organization's goods and services. The three essentials of the TQM philosophy are continuous quality improvement, empowered employees, and the use of quality improvement teams. One of TQM's primary tools is benchmarking, or measuring and evaluating the quality of an organization's goods, services, or processes in relation to the best-performing companies in the industry.

The organization of marketing activities involves the development of an internal structure for the marketing unit. The internal structure is the key to directing marketing activities. In a marketing-oriented organization, the focus is on finding out what buyers want and providing it in a way that lets the organization achieve its objectives. A centralized organization is one in which the top-level managers delegate very little authority to lower levels of the firm, while decision-making authority is delegated as far down the chain of command as possible in a decentralized organization. The marketing unit can be organized by (1) functions, (2) products, (3) regions, or (4) types of customers. An organization may use only one approach or a combination.

Proper implementation of a marketing plan depends on the motivation of personnel who perform marketing activities, effective communication within the marketing unit, the coordination of marketing activities, and establishment of a timetable for implementation. To motivate marketing personnel, managers must discover their employees' needs and then develop motivational methods that help employees satisfy those needs. A company's communication system must allow the marketing manager to communicate with high-level management, with managers of other functional areas in the firm, and with personnel involved in marketing activities both inside and outside the organization. Marketing managers must coordinate the activities of marketing personnel and integrate these activities with those in other areas of the company and with the marketing efforts of personnel in external organizations. Finally, successful marketing implementation requires that employees know the specific activities for which they are responsible and the timetable for completing each activity.

The marketing control process consists of establishing performance standards, evaluating actual performance by comparing it with established standards, and reducing the difference between desired and actual performance. Performance standards, which are established in the planning process, are expected levels of performance with which actual performance can be compared. In evaluating actual performance, marketing managers must know what employees within the firm are doing and must have information about the activities of external organizations that provide the firm with marketing assistance. Then actual performance is compared with performance standards. Marketers must determine whether a discrepancy exists and, if so, whether it requires corrective action, such as changing the performance standards or improving actual performance.

To maintain effective marketing control, an organization needs to develop a comprehensive control process that evaluates its marketing operations at a given time. The control of marketing activities is not a simple task. Problems encountered include environmental changes, time lags between marketing activities and their effects, and difficulty in determining the costs of marketing activities. In addition, it may be hard to develop performance standards.

Control of marketing strategy can be achieved through sales and cost analyses. For the purpose of analysis, sales are usually measured in terms of either dollar volume or market share. For a sales analysis to be effective, it must compare current sales performance with forecasted company sales, industry sales, specific competitors' sales, or the costs incurred to generate the current sales volume.

Marketing cost analysis involves an examination of accounting records and fixed costs, variable costs, and traceable and nontraceable common costs. Such an analysis is often difficult because there may be no logical, clear-cut way to allocate fixed costs into functional accounts. The analyst may choose either direct costing or full costing.

To control marketing strategies, it is sometimes necessary to audit marketing activities. A marketing audit is a systematic examination of the marketing group's objectives, strategies, organization, and performance. A marketing audit attempts to identify what a marketing unit is doing, to evaluate the effectiveness of these activities, and to recommend future marketing activities. The scope of a marketing audit can be very broad or very narrow. Some companies use specialized audits, such as a customer-service audit, to address problems within specific marketing functions.

IMPORTANT TERMS

Intended strategy	Benchmarking	Marketing control process	Nontraceable common costs
Realized strategy	Empowerment	Performance standard	
External customers	Marketing-oriented organization	Sales analysis	Full-cost approach
Internal customers	Marketing cost analysis	Direct-cost approach
Internal marketing	Centralized organization	Fixed costs	Marketing audit
Total quality management (TQM)	Decentralized organization	Variable costs	Customer-service audit
		Traceable common costs	

DISCUSSION AND REVIEW QUESTIONS

1. Why does an organization's intended strategy often differ from its realized strategy?
2. Discuss the three problems associated with implementing marketing activities. How are these problems related to the differences between intended and realized marketing strategies?
3. What is internal marketing? Why is it important in implementing marketing strategies?
4. How does the total quality management approach relate to marketing implementation? For what types of marketing strategies might TQM be best suited?
5. What determines the place of marketing within an organization? Which type of organization is best suited to the marketing concept? Why?
6. What factors can be used to organize the decision-making authority of a marketing unit? Discuss the benefits of each type of organization.

7. Why might an organization use multiple bases for organizing its marketing unit?
8. Why is the motivation of marketing personnel important in implementing marketing plans?
9. How does communication help in implementing marketing plans?
10. What are the major steps of the marketing control process?
11. Discuss the major problems in controlling marketing activities.
12. What is a sales analysis? What makes it an effective control tool?
13. Identify and contrast two cost analysis methods.
14. How is the marketing audit used to control marketing program performance?

APPLICATION QUESTIONS

1. IBM has decentralized its product development and marketing operations in order to be more responsive to its customers. Explain to what degree and how you would decentralize the following types of businesses. Would you empower the frontline employees?
   a. full-service restaurant
   b. fine-clothing store
   c. automobile dealership

2. Marketing units may be organized according to functions, products, regions, or types of customers. Describe how you would organize the marketing units for the following products:
   a. toothpaste with whitener; toothpaste with extra-strong nicotine cleaners; and toothpaste with bubble-gum flavor
   b. national line offering all types of winter and summer sports clothing for men and women
   c. life insurance company that provides life, health, and disability insurance

3. Why would it be important to implement both an internal and external marketing strategy for the following companies?
   a. McDonald's
   b. Ford Motor Co.
   c. Hoover Vacuum

4. The Ford Taurus is primarily the result of benchmarking, a total quality management tool. However, many U.S. businesses have not implemented TQM successfully. Give possible reasons for TQM's limited adoption.

5. Assume that you are the marketing manager for a small printing company in your city. Convince the owner of the company of the need for a customer-service audit, and explain briefly what will be involved in conducting the audit. What benefits would you expect? How often would you suggest conducting the audit?

Case 23.1   Marketing Casual Clothes at Work: Dressing Down, Productivity Up

Although the suit and tie remain the workday norm for many American employees, especially management and marketing personnel, many companies are beginning to relax their dress codes for one or two days a week, and some firms are easing them all week long. Even staid IBM, which once prescribed blue pinstripe suits and wingtip shoes for its sales force, has loosened its dress code for many employees. In fact, more than 70 percent of major U.S. companies have at least one day when employees can dress for comfort rather than success. The business suit, which first appeared in Britain in the late nineteenth century, may finally be going the way of the typewriter.

Employees say that being able to dress casually at work makes them feel more comfortable, and comfort in turn increases productivity, boosts morale, and improves camaraderie. Kathy Compton, director of public affairs at the Society for Human Resource Management (SHRM), reports, "I haven't found a company yet whose employees didn't love casual days." Employers also view casual days as a way to encourage creativity, reduce status distinctions on the job, and serve as an added benefit by saving employees money on clothing and dry cleaning.

Casual days have become a '90s benefit that companies can offer for little financial cost, although they may still need to set some basic rules for when and what casual dress is appropriate. Michael Losey, president of the SHRM, observes, "What we're seeing is a low-cost, low-risk way for companies to boost morale through a new kind of employee benefit. When it's introduced appropriately—where everyone understands the protocol—most companies that institute casual dress don't turn back."

Appropriateness is a big issue with casual dress codes. Are blue jeans OK, for example? What about athletic shoes? Different companies have different ideas about casual dress. Some firms still require public-contact personnel to wear suits while letting behind-the-scenes personnel dress down. Some permit jeans on once-a-month casual days, while others prohibit jeans outright. At Harrah's Entertainment headquarters in Memphis, Tennessee, Kathy Callahan, manager of executive communications, says, "Our guidelines are nothing ratty, revealing, or recreational." Some companies tie casual days to holidays, pay days, or bad weather days. American Express Travelers Cheque Group does not specify when employees can dress casually but simply asks employees to consider the following questions: "If I have a client meeting, am I dressed appropriately? If I have a staff meeting, am I dressed professionally?"

To help employees understand what clothing is acceptable on casual days, business magazines are running fashion portfolios, companies are holding fashion shows, and clothing manufacturers are offering toll-free telephone numbers and videos. Chrysler Financial, for example, held a fashion show to demonstrate its casual dress code to employees.

"Apparel retailers and manufacturers are responding by realigning their products, presentations, and marketing strategies," says Mark Manoff, a retail industry analyst. To capitalize on the market opportunity presented by the casual trend, several clothing companies have created new product lines. Haggar Clothing Co., for example, has introduced a line of City Casuals mix-and-match shirts, pants, vests, and jackets. It also set up a toll-free number for companies to request a free kit on designing, implementing, and controlling casual dress codes. Hartmarx, the nation's largest tailored clothing maker, has modified its strategy to emphasize casual collections, which now comprise more than 50 percent of its sales. Talbots, which has always marketed conservative red, navy, and white classics, hasn't had to modify its strategy much, but its sales have increased at an average of 10 percent a year as employees looking for workplace-appropriate casual dress learn to appreciate its casual but classic lines.

Levi Strauss & Co., maker of Levi's jeans and Docker's casual wear, has made the dress-down trend a linchpin of its marketing strategy. Through research, Levi Strauss has shown that employees allowed to dress more casually in the workplace are more productive. The company is working hard to promote this message and take advantage of the casual-dress trend with workplace-appropriate products, such as its Docker's brand casual wear for men and women. It has put together a "How to Put Casual Businesswear To Work" kit for companies, which includes surveys, case studies, helpful suggestions for implementing casual-day poli-

cies, and clothing suggestions. The company also offers a toll-free consultation number, provides a video on businesswear, and conducts fashion shows for interested companies. Over 15,000 companies, representing one-third of all U.S. companies that employ more than 5,000, have requested casual businesswear services from Levi. Levi Strauss believes these services are important because visual images, not written words, best illustrate casual style standards, and they reinforce clear standards even in the face of new employees, changing fashions, and human nature.

Although the business suit is not likely to disappear altogether—sartorial dress is still the norm for overseas negotiations because other countries are more conservative in terms of business garb—it will take its place beside khakis, jeans, and other casual wear in many U.S. closets. As employees learn to dress more casually professional, their increased comfort level contributes to greater productivity and more satisfying marketing exchanges.[32]

Questions for Discussion

1. How can casual-dress days help companies implement marketing strategies?
2. How is Levi Strauss & Co. taking advantage of the trend to dress down in the workplace?
3. How can dress-down policies contribute to more satisfying exchanges for both internal and external customers?

Case 23.2 Implementing a New Culture at Denny's

Based in Spartanburg, South Carolina, Flagstar Cos. is one of the largest food-service companies in the United States. Its operations include Denny's, Canteen, El Pollo Loco, Hardee's, and Quincy's Family Steakhouse restaurants. Since 1993, the company has had to develop and implement new plans to salvage its reputation after several racial discrimination lawsuits.

The problems surfaced on March 24, 1993, in San Jose, California, when thirty-two African-Americans filed suit against Denny's—a nationwide chain of 1,460 restaurants known for around-the-clock service and reasonably priced meals—alleging a pattern of racial discrimination in Denny's 330 California restaurants. They cited as evidence such practices as black customers being required to pay a cover charge to enter Denny's restaurants, having to pay for meals in advance, and being charged for items and services usually given free to white customers, such as birthday meals and dinner rolls. Additionally, the suit alleged that Denny's managers had made derogatory, sometimes threatening, racial remarks toward black patrons, as well as having them forcibly removed from the

restaurants. Finally, "racial coding" was allegedly employed by the company's managers to indicate situations in which too large a proportion of customers in a given restaurant were black. (This alleged racial coding resembled charges brought against Shoney's—Denny's chief competitor—in 1992, which had been accused of engaging in discriminatory hiring practices. The Shoney's case resulted in a $105 million settlement.)

In response to a Justice Department investigation that substantiated the allegations of bias against blacks cited in the San Jose suit, Denny's agreed to take measures to ensure the fair treatment of all customers, regardless of their race. Spokespersons for the company denied a pattern of discrimination in California, but admitted that the company had identified isolated areas of concern. They stated that these situations had developed from late-night security measures enacted in response to customers leaving without paying for their meals. Denny's assured all parties involved in the dispute that any time that racially motivated discriminatory activity is brought to the attention of management, it is dealt with harshly.

A day after the California suit was filed, Denny's signed a consent decree with the Justice Department in an effort to settle the dispute. Denny's agreed to take corrective action to, among other solutions, provide diversity training to restaurant employees, include nondiscrimination statements in all newspaper and television advertisements, and hire a "civil rights monitor" to oversee operations and ensure against racial discrimination for a four-year period, during which time "spot testing" of Denny's restaurants would occur. Denny's management also pointed out that the firm had already implemented a program in 1992 with goals of improving minority hiring and employee promotions, as well as increasing the number of black franchisees in the Denny's system.

However, in May 1993, a Denny's manager in Annapolis, Maryland, was fired for failing to report complaints lodged against the restaurant by a group of six black Secret Service agents. Just hours before the firing, the group had filed a racial discrimination suit in U.S. District Court in Baltimore. The new charges alleged that the group had entered the restaurant with a group of white Secret Service agents for breakfast, and that although the white agents were served within ten minutes of ordering, the black agents had to wait some forty-five minutes before their food arrived, too late for them to have time to eat. Ironically, this incident took place on the very day—April 1—that Denny's settled the original suit brought against it in California.

Eventually, both noted civil rights leader Reverend Jesse Jackson and the National Association for the Advancement of Colored People (NAACP) became involved in negotiations with Denny's. In June, the company hired Norman J. Hill to head human resource operations for Flagstar Companies. Hill, an African-American and the former vice president of human resources for competitor Perkins Family Restaurants, vowed to bring a different perspective and greater sensitivity to the situation.

In addition, Denny's announced a new advertising campaign addressing its racial problems. A sixty-second commercial featured then-Chairman Jerome Richardson and Denny's employees of various races assuring viewers that although mistakes were made, they were isolated and not indicative of the Denny's chain as a whole. The ad pledged that Denny's would provide fair and equal treatment of all customers. However, even before Denny's executives got a chance to view the finished commercial, the company landed in court again. Five current and former black employees in Cleveland, Ohio, filed a lawsuit charging the restaurant chain with racial bias and harassment. Flagstar ultimately paid $54 million in 1994 to settle these civil rights actions.

Apparently, the changes had not gone far enough. To combat the allegations of racial discrimination and bring boycotting customers back into Denny's restaurants, Flagstar launched a sweeping reformation, starting with the hiring of James B. Adamson, a former Burger King Corp. CEO, as chairman and CEO in 1995. Recognizing that change begins at the top, Adamson has carefully set a new tone for Flagstar and its restaurants.

Adamson has implemented sweeping changes from the boardroom to the kitchen. He centralized authority for restaurant operations to bring consistency to restaurant management, set strict rules, and warned employees and franchisees alike: "If you discriminate, you're history." Eight of Flagstar's twelve top executives—all white males—left the company, and the management committee now includes a Hispanic male, two white women, and a black woman in a newly created position responsible for diversity initiatives. Regional and district managers have been replaced with one layer of 300 managing partners who oversee company-owned restaurants and twenty-two franchise managers. A percentage of store managers' pay is now linked to diversity goals in hiring and promotion. At the store level, kitchens and dining rooms have been re-engineered. Any evidence of bigotry results in termination. A monitor continues to oversee operations to ensure against racial discrimination. All restaurants have a complaint number posted for customers.

The results of these changes are beginning to show. Blacks now comprise 17 percent of Flagstar's management, and 27 of the chain's 600 franchised restaurants are black-owned (three years ago, there was just one minority Denny's franchisee). However, that figure is much higher at McDonald's and Burger King. Minority purchasing contracts have surpassed $50 million, four years ahead of the NAACP goal.

Whether the sweeping changes Adamson has implemented will bring back the customers Denny's lost remains to be seen. Proactive leadership has set a positive tone for the whole organization to follow. Flagstar only recently began tracking demographic trends, but already Denny's same-store sales are up 0.9 percent during a period in which its rivals struggled. Reforming an entire organizational culture cannot be accomplished overnight, but Flagstar's Adamson has developed and implemented a plan to transform Denny's into a marketer that focuses on satisfying customers, whatever their race.[33]

Questions for Discussion

1. How did Denny's realized marketing strategy differ from its intended marketing strategy in serving racially diverse customers?
2. Were there problems in implementing the marketing strategy based on the separation of top-level and mid-level marketing managers and front-line managers? Explain.
3. Explain how Denny's could use total quality management and internal marketing to improve its service to all customers.

571

STRATEGIC CASE 7

Apple Computers

Apple Computer Inc. is truly the stuff of entrepreneurial legend. Founded in a garage in 1976 by two college dropouts, Steven Jobs and Stephen Wozniak, the company grew to worldwide revenues of $11.1 billion in 1995. However, the company earned just $424 million on those phenomenal sales, and it lost $69 million in the last quarter of the year, the crucial Christmas season. Although Apple customers tend to be vehement in their support of the company's products, Apple's share of the world computer market has been falling, reaching 7.1 percent in the fourth quarter of 1995, down from 8.2 percent the previous year. In 1996, Apple announced it would take a $125 million restructuring charge and lay off 1,300 employees. To many outsiders, it appears that Apple has lost its technological edge, and its future as an independent entity looks doubtful. To understand how the company found itself in this bleak predicament, we need to consider the firm's history, culture, and marketing strategy changes.

Birth of an Icon

Stephen Wozniak developed Apple's first product, the Apple I computer, which he and Steven Jobs built in Jobs's garage and sold without a monitor, keyboard, or casing. The Apple I's success helped Jobs recognize a demand for small, "user-friendly" computers. Wozniak therefore added a keyboard, color monitor, and eight slots for peripheral devices, giving the firm's next product, the Apple II, greater versatility and encouraging other firms to develop add-on devices and software. It worked: Jobs and Wozniak sold more than 13,000 Apple IIs by 1980, and revenues climbed from $7.8 million in 1978 to $117 million in 1980. The next ventures, the Apple III and Lisa computers, flopped, but Apple scored a huge success with the Macintosh, introduced in 1984. The Mac, which incorporated an easy-to-use graphical interface, was billed as the computer "For the Rest of Us." The Mac's rapid popularity soon established Apple as a leader in the expanding computer industry. Apple moved into the office market in 1986 with the Mac Plus and the LaserWriter printer. Wozniak left in 1983, and Jobs brought in John Sculley, a former PepsiCo executive, to manage the growing firm.

From Apple's garage-bound birth, Jobs and Wozniak, iconoclasts themselves, so engraved their personalities on Apple Computer's culture that it survived long after their departures. Their do-your-own-thing, ignore-the-Establishment philosophy gave Apple a unique culture of rebels, right down to the pirate flag flying over headquarters. Scorning dress codes, formal meetings, and other traditional business trappings, Apple's creative, defiant culture nurtured the development of the groundbreaking Macintosh computer and operating system, as well as numerous other successful products, and propelled Apple to the top of the computer industry.

Cultural Conflict

The do-it-your-way culture also created strife within the company, pitting the inventive "gearheads" and "wizards"—the engineers and programmers who developed products—against the managers Jobs imported to bring order and good business practices to the firm. Jobs, in fact, left the firm in 1985 in a power struggle with Sculley, largely over the future of the Macintosh platform. When Sculley took over the reins, he realized that Apple's employees would resent the big-business systems he wanted to implement. He also recognized that he had to retain Apple's technical wizards if the firm was to succeed. He therefore decided not to tinker with Apple's unique culture. However, glorifying Apple's technical personnel made them very tough to supervise. Combined with Sculley's feel-good approach to management, the result was a company run largely by consensus, and decisions were rarely final. One joke on the Apple grapevine was that "a vote can be 15,000 to 1 and still be a tie."

The Revolving Door

Apple's culture contributed to frequent power struggles and a seemingly revolving door on management offices. In 1995 alone, 14 of 45 vice presidents left or were dismissed. Major management upheavals occurred in 1981, 1985, 1990, 1993, and 1996, with numerous minor ones in between. Several of these disturbances led to the removal of chief executives. Sculley, for example, was dethroned in 1993 after an 84 percent drop in earnings. His replacement, Michael "Diesel" Spindler, brought a focus on business basics to the firm and quickly worked to address Apple's problems: overpriced products, inflated costs, and sluggish product development. He laid off 2,500 workers, cut R&D costs by more than $100 million a year, and launched a new product line based on the PowerPC microprocessor (which Apple developed with IBM and Motorola). Spindler's back-to-the-basics approach helped Apple rebound, but Spindler soon stumbled under Apple's consensus culture. An insider close to Spindler says, "It was fine for a while. But the system converts people. People don't convert the system."

Spindler was ousted in 1996 and replaced by Gilbert F. Amerlio as president and CEO. Each of these management upheavals brought restructurings and changes in strategy.

Frequent Strategy Changes

These frequent strategy changes may be the biggest source of Apple's disappointing performance in recent years. Over the years, Jobs, Sculley, then Spindler reversed, delayed, or evaded outright key decisions while trying to push their own agendas. For example, in April 1995, Spindler implemented a major reorganization of Apple but was forced to recant that decision six months later under fiscal pressures. A late 1995 decision to launch an all-out bid for market share failed after executives misread the market. The result was a storehouse of low-end computers, at a time when consumers wanted expensive powerhouse machines, and an $80 million inventory write-off. Meanwhile, savvy rivals IBM, Hewlett-Packard, and Compaq raked in the bucks and made further inroads into Apple's market share.

In fact, Apple has been consistent only in its inconsistency over the years. For example, Apple has traditionally relied on high-priced products to fund development and marketing of new technology. However, in a desperate bid to boost market share and improve efficiency, the firm has occasionally deviated from this strategy by introducing lower-priced Apple machines. But management has never given the latter strategy time to work, and it failed to implement other tactics that might have generated the same results.

One of the most significant examples of this inconsistency and wavering was the issue of whether to license the Mac operating system to other computer makers in order to create a "clone" industry that would increase market share for the Mac platform, much as IBM had done with its personal computer. The clone decision was debated as early as 1985, but until 1994, every time top management came close to making the licensing decision, it was stymied by lack of consensus. As one former Apple executive says, "I've never understood why somebody didn't just say: 'I'm the leader. This is the way it's going to be. Thanks for the discussion, but if you don't want to do it, leave.'"

When Spindler finally made the decision to license the technology in 1994, the rising popularity of Microsoft's Windows operating environment for the IBM-PC platform made the clone decision too late. Apple executives asserted that they could raise the Mac's share of the global market to 20 percent in five years, adding 1 percent each year, with the clones bringing in the rest. However, even though Apple executives said they would "aggressively" pursue licensees, thus far, Apple has licensed the Mac design only to Pioneer, Power Computing, Unmax, and Daystar.

Together, these firms sold about 200,000 Mac clones in 1995, a drop in the bucket compared with the 4.5 million shipped by Apple. In a last-ditch attempt to revive Mac software's faltering market share, Apple in 1996 gave Motorola the rights to use its current and future operating systems, as well as the right to sublicense the operating system to other computer makers likely to produce Apple clones. With Apple's global market share falling, securing additional licenses will be a hard sell. If Apple had made the licensing decision earlier, it might be in a far different position today.

Another delayed decision may be more risky for Apple—whether to merge with or sell the company to another firm. During his tenure, Michael Spindler held serious talks with IBM starting in 1994. IBM seemed like a perfect match: the two firms had collaborated with Motorola on the PowerPC chip, which both were committed to using in their products, and they shared two software joint ventures—Kaleida Labs and Taligent (both now defunct). Negotiations between Spindler and IBM's Louis Gerstner even generated a proposed marketing strategy for the merged firm, with IBM bringing out a new line of PCs based on the PowerPC chip already used in Power Macs, and the two firms using Apple's software, beefed up with IBM's OS/2 for the merged PowerPC line. However, with Spindler making many demands, negotiations deteriorated, and the merger talks broke down. A second attempt at negotiating a merger with IBM in 1995 also failed. Attempts to find another partner or suitor have failed thus far, though Apple is reportedly holding talks with Sun.

Another major issue for Apple has been the thorn of Microsoft's Windows. Windows, with its graphical interface, makes PCs work much like the Macintosh. When the first successful version of Windows appeared in 1990, Apple executives dismissed the threat, although they filed a lawsuit against Microsoft and Hewlett-Packard, claiming copyright protection for the "look and feel" of the Macintosh user interface. Apple lost the suit in 1992. Macintosh users continue to be passionate in their insistence that the Macintosh is a better machine than a Windows-based PC, but Apple has failed to capitalize on their fervor. At the same time, Microsoft has been very aggressive in upgrading Windows to the point where buyers just entering the market fail to see significant differences between a PC and a Mac beyond the fact that the Apple machine costs more. A new Mac operating system tentatively called Copland, the one project that could have countered the Windows 95 onslaught, is several years behind schedule.

Current Marketing Strategies

In the meantime, Apple is narrowing its focus to market segments in which it already has a solid presence, a strategy that may mean forever abandoning the possibility of regaining the position of industry leader. And,

573

like apparently everyone else inside and outside the computer industry, Apple is turning to the Internet. "Any project that doesn't have the word Internet in it doesn't get approved anymore," says one Apple manager. Apple may have an edge in the Internet arena: its Web servers sell for $3,000–$2,000 less than the cheapest models from Sun. The firm's expertise in media and entertainment, where many content providers are moving to the Web, may enhance its edge. Says one industry executive, "This whole Internet explosion is a real opportunity for Apple. It's not so much an advantage for them, but it takes away some of their disadvantages." Before he was removed in 1996, Spindler announced plans to use Apple's Newton and Pippin—a multimedia Mac player for the TV—as Internet devices.

To capitalize on these opportunities, Apple must develop new products and market them astutely and consistently. Shareholders and staunch Apple customers both hope new chief Amerlio will bring to Apple much-needed focus, consistency, and the strength to make sound decisions in the face of the firm's long tradition of consensus decision making. Whether Apple remains a viable independent firm depends on the strength of its new chief executive to overcome its problems or else guide Apple through the process of merging with a stronger firm so that it may continue to satisfy devout Macintosh customers.

Questions for Discussion

1. Describe how Apple's unique culture has contributed to its present situation. If you were the new chief executive, how would you deal with this culture?
2. How have Apple's frequent strategy changes brought it to where it is today? What do you see as the single most costly error made by executives?
3. Describe Apple's current strategy.
4. Propose a strategy to take Apple Computer into the twenty-first century, keeping in mind such factors as Microsoft Windows and the Internet. Describe how you would implement your strategy.

Sources: Peter Burrows, "An Insanely Great Paycheck," *Business Week,* Feb. 26, 1996, p. 42; Kathy Rebello and Peter Burrows, "The Fall of an American Icon," *Business Week,* Feb. 5, 1996, pp. 34–42; *Hoover's Company Profile* database (Austin, Texas: Reference Press, 1996), via America Online.

Chapter 24

Marketing and the Internet

The Internet is changing the way marketers do their jobs. This powerful technology provides marketers with faster, more efficient, and much more powerful methods of designing, promoting, and distributing products, conducting research, and gathering market information. Chapter 24 explores how marketers are using the Internet in their strategies, their relationships with customers, and their day-to-day work.

Because the technology changes almost daily, any printed matter on this subject can be out-of-date in a matter of days. With this concern in mind, Chapter 24 is actually located *on the Internet*, where we can update it as we learn more about the capabilities of this technology and its impact on marketing theory.

Chapter 24 is located on the Internet in the Pride/Ferrell Marketing Learning Center—a one-stop guide to the world of online marketing. This unique site serves as a forum for marketers and students of marketing to discuss how the Internet is changing the marketing paradigm. In addition to Chapter 24, the Marketing Learning Center also contains **Internet Exercises** for Chapters 1-23; a **Research Center**, with links to marketing organizations, publications, and other information sources; and the **Idea Exchange**, inviting you to share your perspectives on marketing and the Internet.

By using the dialogue created through the Marketing Learning Center, we hope to help track the evolution of online marketing and practice *as it is happening.*

http://www.hmco.com/college/PridFerr/home.html

Careers in Marketing

Some General Issues

As we noted in Chapter 1, between one-fourth and one-third of the civilian work force in the United States is employed in marketing-related jobs. Although the field offers a multitude of diverse career opportunities, the number of positions in each area varies. For example, millions of workers are employed in many facets of sales, but relatively few people work in public relations and marketing research.

Many nonbusiness organizations now recognize that they do, in fact, perform marketing activities. For that reason, the number of marketing positions is increasing in government agencies, hospitals, charitable and religious groups, educational institutions, and similar organizations. In fact, during the early 1990s, nonprofit organizations became more competitive and better managed, with job-growth rates often exceeding those of the private-sector firms.[1] Look for new opportunities in the emerging areas, such as the environmental industry. A surprising number of majors and backgrounds are appropriate, including marketing, for this growing industry needs far more than just technical and engineering talent to run smoothly. Indeed, many industries that have fallen on hard times recently are now turning to environmental projects to boost their businesses. Construction companies might turn to toxic waste cleanup, asbestos removal, and closing military bases. These opportunities are likely to increase during the next few years. However, do not expect salaries to compete with those in other industries at the outset.[2] Another emerging area ripe with opportunities is the Internet's World Wide Web. With so many businesses setting up home pages, demand will rise for people who have the skills to develop and design marketing-related materials for the Web.

When searching for a job, you might want to consider the many alternatives outside the traditional large corporation. Within the last five years, companies with more than 500 employees have shed over 5 million jobs through downsizing, reorganizations, and mergers. However, the job losses in larger companies have been more than offset by gains in smaller businesses employing fewer than 500 employees. In recent years, in fact, two-thirds of new jobs were created by new companies with fewer than twenty-five workers, and most were in firms employing fewer than ten.[3]

Many of the workers outplaced from large corporations are choosing an entrepreneurial path, creating even more new opportunities for first-time job seekers. Even those who have successful positions are leaving the corporation and heading to smaller companies, toward greater responsibility and autonomy. The traditional career path used to be graduation from college, then a job with a large corporation, and a climb up the ladder to management. This pattern began to shift in the 1970s, however, and people today are more likely to experience a career path of sideways "gigs" rather than sequential steps up a corporate ladder.[4]

The idea of entrepreneurship is becoming very appealing to a large percentage of Americans; 96 percent of people aged 25 to 44 say they are interested in owning their own business, while 57 percent of those aged 18 to 24 say they are likewise interested.[5] Entrepreneurship seems especially attractive to women, whose companies are expanding into industries traditionally dominated by men. From 1991 to 1994, companies owned by women increased 13 percent in the manufacturing industry, compared to a loss of 2 percent for all firms of that type. In transportation and communications, women-owned businesses increased 18 percent, compared to 5 percent for all firms in that industry.[6]

Table A.1 Top Salary Ranges for Middle Managers in Marketing

Position	Salary Range
National sales manager	$60,000–$100,000
Corporate strategic market planner	55,000– 75,000
International sales manager	50,000– 75,000
Advertising account supervisor	40,000– 70,000
Distribution manager	40,000– 60,000
Sales promotion manager	40,000– 55,000
Product/brand manager	35,000– 60,000
Purchasing manager	35,000– 55,000
Media manager	30,000– 55,000
Retail manager	25,000– 45,000

Also consider the potential job market beyond the United States. With increasing global and domestic competition and more complex products, students with marketing degrees will find excellent job prospects overseas.

Regardless of the area of marketing that you prefer, you are still likely to be better off financially when you have your college degree. College graduates, on average, still earn more than those who lack a degree. According to a recent study, the median salary for a high school graduate was $21,241 annually, whereas the median salary for all college graduates (including those with advanced degrees) was $37,359.[7]

Even though financial reward is not the sole criterion for selecting a career, it is only practical to consider how much you might earn in a marketing job. Table A.1 illustrates the top ten salary positions for middle managers in marketing. Note that all these careers relate directly to marketing. A national sales manager may earn $60,000 to $100,000 or an even higher salary. Brand managers make $35,000 to $60,000. A media manager could earn $30,000 to $55,000. Generally, entry-level marketing personnel earn more than their counterparts in economics and liberal arts but not as much as people who enter accounting, chemistry, or engineering positions. Average starting salaries for marketing graduates are approaching $25,000. Marketers who advance to higher-level positions often earn high salaries, and a significant proportion of corporate executives held marketing jobs before attaining top-level positions.

Many business recruiters recognize that students are unrealistic about the salaries, responsibilities, and perks that they demand, especially in today's "employer's market." Besides knowing the comparable salaries for a given position, students should adopt an attitude of "what can I do for the company in return for this salary?" Focusing on team spirit and commitment to the success of the company will help greatly in an interview. Successful job hunting requires not only realistic expectations on the part of job seekers about their own and the company's responsibilities, but also careful attention to the manner in which those expectations are expressed. In short, appropriate behavior during the interview process is important. What was acceptable on campus may prove inadequate in the corporate world. A person's dress and behavior could be the decisive factor in choosing one candidate over another in a competitive environment. According to a nationwide survey of company recruiters and hiring managers, current college graduates are sorely lacking in proper behavior and etiquette.[8]

"Mind your manners" is a credo by which job-seeking students should abide, and they should show good manners to all people they meet in a company. Students may also be judged on the way they introduce themselves—for instance, whether they look people in the eye and have a firm handshake. Their table manners, too, may be scrutinized, if lunch is on the interview agenda. And interviewers will usually be looking for an appropriate degree of enthusiasm. All of these characteristics are considered in addition to the student's academic performance and ability, and all job seekers should cultivate them. Furthermore, competing effectively in today's market requires the student to be innovative and persistent. However, careful attention should be paid to the manner and extent of that innovativeness. Hoping to be remembered, some students have attempted gimmickry to impress their interviewers, but recent surveys suggest that professional attitudes and behavior are more relevant for job seekers.[9] Students who will become job seekers would benefit from a trip to the school or public library, where there are many books on proper interviewing techniques, dress, and behavior.

When developing a plan for your job search, it is important to focus on your specific needs and skills. Target a marketplace or industry and do your homework to uncover the personnel needs in this particular area.[10] Follow the business news in weekly and monthly publications as well as daily newspapers. Keep a file on the marketplace, industry, or company you have targeted, and check to see if there are trade or professional societies in that industry, and if meetings are held in your area. Get some work experience in your selected industry if possible. Internships and temporary jobs are an excellent way to develop experience, as well as help you decide whether or not a particular field is for you.[11]

In addition to the services offered at your local college placement office, consider using one of the newest methods of job searching—the Internet. If you are willing to relocate to other areas of the country, you may want to check out the jobs available through the many new online listings. America Online's Help Wanted-USA service lists 12,000 to 15,000 new ads a week; E-Span offers 1,000 to 1,200. The Online Career Center has a World Wide Web page at http://www.occ.com/occ. And six of the nation's largest newspapers have joined forces to offer Careerpath.com in both print and on the World Wide Web; this service carries 40,000 to 50,000 help wanted ads at http://www.careerpath.com. Job hunters may even be able to meet with prospective employers for an online interview in the near future as companies increase efforts to streamline costs and expedite decision making. There is a down side to the online job search, however; although the job postings are many, so are the job seekers. And while they are rare, some suspicious "get-rich-quick" schemes and questionable "service" jobs have appeared.[12]

Also, consider whether you can enjoy the work associated with a particular career. Because you will spend almost 40 percent of your waking hours on the job, you should not allow such factors as economic conditions or status to override your personal goals as you select a lifelong career. Too often people do not weigh these factors realistically. You should give a good deal of thought to your choice of a career, and you should adopt a well-considered plan for finding a position that meets your personal and career objectives. One example of such a plan is the seven-step approach. The steps are as follows: (1) exploring yourself (getting to know who you are); (2) defining objectives; (3) documenting your abilities; (4) gathering information (about organizations and people); (5) getting interviews; (6) turning interviews into job offers; and (7) negotiating terms.[13]

After determining your objectives, you should identify the organizations that are likely to offer desirable opportunities. Learn as much as possible about these organizations before setting up employment interviews; job recruiters are impressed with applicants who have done their homework.

When making initial contact with potential employers by mail, enclose a brief, clearly written letter of introduction. After an initial interview, you should send a brief letter of thanks to the interviewer. The job of getting the right job is important, and you owe it to yourself to take this process seriously.

The Résumé

The résumé is one of the keys to being considered for a good job. Because it states your qualifications, experiences, education, and career goals, the résumé is a chance for a potential employer to assess your compatibility with the job requirements. For both the employer's and the individual's benefit, the résumé should be accurate and current.

In preparing a résumé, it helps to think of it as an advertisement. Envision yourself as a product, and the company you are interested in working for, particularly the person or persons doing the hiring, as your target market. To interest the customer in buying the product—hiring you—your résumé must communicate information about yourself and show how you can help that company achieve its objectives. It should convey enough information to persuade the organization to take a closer look at you by calling you in for an interview.

To be effective, the résumé should be targeted at a specific position, as Figure A.1 shows. This document is only one example of an acceptable résumé. The job target section is specific and leads directly to the applicant's qualifications for the job. The qualifications section details capabilities—what the applicant can do—and also shows that the person has an understanding of the job's requirements. Skills and strengths should be highlighted as to how they relate to the specific job. The achievement section ("Experiences" in Figure A.1) indicates success at accomplishing tasks or goals within the job market and at school. The work experience section includes an unusual listing, which might pique the interest of an interviewer: "helped operate relative's blueberry farm in Michigan for three summers." That is something that could help launch an interview discussion. It tends to incite rather than satisfy curiosity, thus inviting further inquiry. The solo cross-Canada canoe trek elicited many highly favorable comments from interviewers. The listing is exceedingly brief, but interviewers never failed to bring it up.[14]

LORRAINE MILLER
2212 WEST WILLOW
PHOENIX, AZ 12345
(416) 862-9169

EDUCATION: B.A. Arizona State University, 1997, Marketing, achieved a 3.4 on a 4.0 scale throughout college

POSITION DESIRED: Product manager with an international firm providing future career development at the executive level

QUALIFICATIONS:

- Communicates well with individuals to achieve a common goal
- Handles tasks efficiently and in a timely manner
- Understands advertising sales, management, marketing research, packaging, pricing, distribution, and warehousing
- Coordinates many activities at one time
- Receives and carries out assigned tasks or directives
- Writes complete status or research reports

EXPERIENCES:

- Assistant Editor of college newspaper
- Treasurer of the American Marketing Association (student chapter)
- Internship with 3-Cs Advertising, Berkeley, CA
- Student Assistantship with Dr. Steve Green, Professor of Marketing, Arizona State University
- Solo cross-Canada canoe trek, summer 1996

WORK RECORD:

1995–Present	Blythe and Co., Inc.	
	–Junior Advertising Account Executive	
1994–Present	Assistantship with Dr. Steve Green	
	–Research Assistant	
1992–1993	The Men	
	–Retail sales and consumer relations	
1990–1992	Farmer	
	–Helped operate relative's blueberry farm in Michigan for three summers	

Figure A.1
A Résumé Targeted at a Specific Position

Another type of résumé is the chronological résumé, which lists your work and educational history in order by date. This type of résumé is good for those entering the job market because it helps to highlight education and work experience. In some cases, education is more important than unrelated work experience because it indicates the career direction you desire, despite the work experience you have thus far.[15]

Common suggestions for improving résumés include deleting useless information, improving organization, using professional printing and typing, listing duties (not accomplishments), maintaining grammatical perfection, and avoiding an overly elaborate or fancy format.[16] Keep in mind that the person who will be looking at your résumé may have to look through hundreds in the course of his or her day, in addition to handling other duties. Consequently, it is important to keep your résumé short (one page is best, never more than two), concise, and neat. Moreover, you want your résumé to be distinctive so that it will stand out from all the others. The biggest problems in résumés are distortions and lies; 36 percent of the personnel experts surveyed thought that this was a major problem.[17] Applicants lie most often about previous salaries and tasks performed in former jobs.

In addition to the format and content of a résumé, the type styles and paper selection also warrant careful attention. Résumés that are easy to read are usually best. It is also best to use only one or two fonts and plain, white paper. When a résumé is sent to a large company, several copies are made and distributed. Textured, gray, or colored paper may make a good impression on the first person who sees the résumé, but it will not reproduce well for the others, who will see only a poor copy. You should also proofread your résumé with care. Typos and misspellings will grab attention—the wrong kind.

Along with the résumé itself, always be sure to submit a cover letter. In a letter you can convey something more than what is included in your résumé and can send a message that you personally are interested in the company.[18]

After the Interview

The search for the right candidate does not end with the résumé or the interview. Attention to common courtesy is important as a follow-up to your interview. A brief and sincere note of thanks should be sent to the interviewer, and it should receive as much care as the résumé. A short, typewritten letter is preferred to a handwritten note or card. Avoid not only typos, but also arrogant and overconfident statements, such as "I look forward to helping you lead Universal Industries into the twenty-first century."[19] Even in the thank-you letter, it is important to show team spirit and professionalism, as well as to convey proper enthusiasm. Everything that is said and done reflects the candidate.

After the Hire

Clearly, performing well in a job has always been a crucial factor in keeping a position. In a tight economy and job market, however, a person's attitude, as well as his or her performance, counts greatly. Students hired for their first job can commit costly political blunders and mistakes in sensitivity to their environment. Politics in the corporate world includes how you react to your boss, how you react to your coworkers, and your attitude in general. Here are a few of the rules to live by:

1. *Don't bypass your boss.* One of the major blunders an employee can make is to go over the boss's head to resolve a problem. This is even more hazardous in a bureaucratic organization. Employees should become aware of the generally accepted chain of command with regard to responsibility, and when problems occur, follow that protocol, beginning with their immediate superior. No boss likes to look incompetent, and making him or her appear so is sure to crush or hamper a budding career. However, there may be exceptions to this rule in emergency situations. It would be advantageous for an employee to discuss proper behavior in emergency situations with his or her supervisor before an emergency occurs.[20]

2. *Don't criticize your boss.* Adhering to the old adage "praise in public and criticize in private" will prevent you from being in the line of retaliatory fire. A more sensible and productive alternative is to present the critical commentary to your boss in a diplomatic way during a private session.

3. *Don't show disloyalty.* If dissatisfied with the position, a new employee may start a fresh job search, within or outside the organization. But it is not advisable to begin a publicized search within the company for another position unless you have held your current job for some time. Careful attention to the political climate in the organization should help you determine how soon to start a new job campaign and how public it may be. In any case, it is not a good idea to publicize that you are looking outside the company for a new position.

4. *Don't be a naysayer.* Employees are expected to become part of the organization team and work together with others. Behaviors to avoid—especially if you are a new employee—include being critical of others, refusing to support others' projects, always playing devil's advocate, refusing to help others when a crisis occurs, and complaining all the time, even about such matters as the poor quality of the food in the cafeteria, the crowded parking lot, or the temperature in the office.

5. *Learn to correct mistakes appropriately.* No one likes to admit having made a mistake, but one of the most important political skills you can acquire is how to minimize the impact of a blunder. It is usually advantageous to correct the damage as soon as possible to avoid further problems. Some suggestions: be the first to break the bad news to your boss; avoid being defensive; stay poised and don't panic; and have answers ready for fixing the blunder.[21]

Types of Marketing Careers

In considering marketing as a career, the first step is to evaluate broad categories of career opportunities in the areas of marketing research, sales, public relations, industrial buying, distribution management, product management, advertising, retail management, and direct marketing. Keep in mind that the categories described here are not all-inclusive and that each encompasses hundreds of marketing jobs.

Marketing Research

Clearly, marketing research and information systems are vital aspects of marketing decision making. Marketing researchers survey consumers to determine their habits, preferences, and aspirations. The information about buyers and environmental forces that research and information systems provide improves a marketer's ability to understand the dynamics of the marketplace and make effective decisions.

Marketing research firms are usually employed by a client organization, which could be a provider of goods or services, a nonbusiness organization, a government, a research consulting firm, or an advertising agency. The activities performed include concept testing, product testing, package testing, advertising testing, test-market research, and new-product research.

Marketing researchers gather and analyze data relating to specific problems. A researcher may be involved in one or several stages of research, depending on the size of the project, the organization of the research unit, and the researcher's experience. Marketing research trainees in large organizations usually perform a considerable amount of clerical work, such as compiling secondary data from a firm's accounting and sales records and periodicals, government publications, syndicated data services, and unpublished sources. A junior analyst may edit and code questionnaires or tabulate survey results. Trainees also may participate in primary data gathering by learning to conduct mail and telephone surveys, conducting personal interviews, and using observational methods of primary data collection. As a marketing researcher gains experience, the researcher may become involved in defining problems and developing hypotheses; designing research procedures; and analyzing, interpreting, and reporting findings. Exceptional personnel may assume responsibility for entire research projects.

Although most employers consider a bachelor's degree sufficient qualification for a marketing research trainee, many specialized positions require a graduate degree in business administration, statistics, or other related fields. Today trainees are more likely to have a marketing or statistics degree than a liberal arts degree. Courses in statistics, data processing, psychology, sociology, communications, economics, and English composition are valuable preparations for a career in marketing research.

The U.S. Bureau of Labor Statistics indicates that marketing research provides abundant employment opportunity, especially for applicants with graduate training in marketing research, statistics, economics, and the social sciences. Generally, the value of information gathered by marketing information and research systems will become more important as competition increases, thus expanding the opportunities for prospective marketing research personnel.

The three major career paths in marketing research are with independent marketing research agencies/data suppliers, advertising agency marketing research departments, and marketing research departments in businesses. In a company in which marketing research plays a key role, the researcher is often a member of the marketing strategy team. Surveying or interviewing consumers is the heart of the marketing research firm's activities. A statistician selects the sample to be surveyed, analysts design the questionnaire and synthesize the gathered data into a final report, data processors tabulate the data, and the research director controls and coordinates all these activities so that each project is completed to the client's satisfaction (the clients being consumer and industrial product manufacturers).[22] In marketing research agencies, a researcher deals with many clients, products, and problems. Advertising agencies use research as an ingredient in developing and refining campaigns for existing or potential clients.[23]

Salaries in marketing research depend on the type, size, and location of the firm, as well as the nature of the positions. Overall, the salaries of marketing researchers have increased slightly during the last few years. However, the specific position within the marketing research field determines the percentage of fluctuation.[24] Generally, starting salaries are somewhat higher and promotions somewhat slower than in other occupations requiring similar training. Typical starting salaries are $21,000 to $25,000 per year. Salaries range from $18,000 for a junior analyst to $35,000 or more for a senior analyst, and research directors often earn salaries of more than $60,000. Furthermore, marketing is playing a greater role in overall corporate planning as companies seek marketing information for strategic planning purposes. Marketing research directors are reporting to higher levels of management than ever before, and the number of corporate vice presidents who receive marketing research as regular input for decision making has doubled in recent years.

Sales

Millions of people earn a living through personal selling. Chapter 19 defined personal selling as personal, paid communication that attempts to inform customers and persuade them to purchase products in an exchange situation. Although this definition describes the general nature of many sales positions, individual selling jobs vary enormously with respect to the type of businesses and products involved, the educational background and skills required, and the specific activities sales personnel perform. Because the work is so varied, sales occupations offer numerous career opportunities for people with a wide range of qualifications, interests, and goals. A sales career offers the greatest potential compensation. The sales careers opportunities discussed in this section are business-to-business sales types. The following two sections describe what is involved in wholesale and manufacturer sales.

Wholesale Sales Wholesalers perform activities to expedite transactions in which purchases are intended for resale or for use in making other products. Wholesalers thus provide services to both retailers and producers. They can help match producers' products to retailers' needs and provide services that save producers time, money, and resources. Some activities associated with wholesaling include planning and negotiating transactions; assisting customers with sales, advertising, sales promotion, and publicity; handling transportation and storage activities; providing customers with inventory control and data processing assistance; establishing prices; and giving customers technical, management, and merchandising assistance.

The background needed by wholesale personnel depends on the nature of the product handled. A drug wholesaler, for example, needs extensive technical training and product knowledge and may have a degree in chemistry, biology, or pharmacology. A wholesaler of standard office supplies, on the other hand, may find it more important to be familiar with various brands, suppliers, and prices than to have technical knowledge about the products. A new wholesale representative may begin a career as a sales trainee or hold a nonselling job that provides experience with inventory, prices, discounts, and the firm's customers. A college graduate usually enters the sales force directly out of school. Competent salespersons also transfer from manufacturer and retail sales positions.

The number of wholesale sales positions is expected to grow about as fast as the average for all occupations. Earnings for wholesale personnel vary widely because commissions often make up a large proportion of their incomes.

Manufacturer Sales Manufacturer sales personnel sell a firm's products to wholesalers, retailers, and industrial buyers; they thus perform many of the same activities as wholesale salespersons. As in wholesaling, the educational requirements for manufacturer sales depend largely on the type and complexity of the products and markets. Manufacturers of nontechnical products usually hire college graduates who have a liberal arts or business degree and give them training and information about the firm's products, prices, and customers. Manufacturers of highly technical products generally prefer applicants who have degrees in fields associated with the particular industry and market.

More and more sophisticated marketing skills are being utilized in industrial sales. Industrial marketing originally followed the commodity approach to complete a sale, whereby the right product is in the right place at the right time and for the right price. Today industrial sales use the same marketing concepts and strategies as do marketers selling to consumers.

Employment opportunities in manufacturer sales are expected to increase at an average rate. Manufacturer sales personnel are well compensated and earn above-average salaries; most are paid a combination of salaries and commissions. The highest salaries are paid by manufacturers of electrical equipment, food products, and rubber goods. Commissions vary according to the salesperson's efforts, abilities, and sales territory and the type of products sold.

Industrial Buying

Industrial buyers, or purchasing agents, are responsible for maintaining an adequate supply of the goods and services that an organization requires for its operations. In general, industrial buyers purchase all items needed for direct use in producing other products and for use in the day-to-day operations. Industrial buyers in large firms often specialize in purchasing a single, specific class of products—for example, all petroleum-based lubricants. In smaller organizations, buyers may be responsible for many different categories of purchases, including raw materials, component parts, office supplies, and operating services.

An industrial buyer's main job is selecting suppliers that offer the best quality, service, and price. When the products to be purchased are standardized, buyers may compare suppliers by examining catalogs and trade journals, making purchases on the basis of description. Buyers who purchase highly homogeneous products often meet with salespeople to examine samples and observe demonstrations. Sometimes, buyers must inspect the actual product before purchasing; in other cases, they invite suppliers to bid on large orders. Buyers who purchase specialized equipment often deal directly with manufacturers to obtain specially designed items made to specifications. After choosing a supplier and placing an order, an industrial buyer usually must trace the shipment to ensure on-time delivery. Finally, the buyer sometimes is responsible for receiving and inspecting an order and authorizing payment to the shipper.

Training requirements for a career in industrial buying relate to the needs of the firm and the types of products purchased. A manufacturer of heavy machinery may prefer an applicant who has a background in engineering; a service company, on the other hand, may recruit liberal arts majors. Although it is not generally required, a college degree is becoming increasingly important for buyers who wish to advance to management positions. Entry-level positions are in the $20,000 to $25,000 range.

Employment prospects for industrial buyers are expected to increase faster than the average through the 1990s. Opportunities will be excellent for individuals with a master's degree in business administration or a bachelor's degree in engineering, science, or business administration. In addition, companies that manufacture heavy equipment, computer equipment, and communications equipment will need buyers with technical backgrounds.

Public Relations

Public relations encompasses a broad set of communication activities designed to create and maintain favorable relations between the organization and its publics—customers, employees, stockholders, government officials, and society in general. Public relations specialists help clients create the image, issue, or message they wish to present and communicate it to the appropriate audience. According to the Public Relations Society of America, 120,000 persons work in public relations in the United States. Half the billings found in the 4,000 public relations agencies and firms come from Chicago and New York. The highest starting salaries can also be found there. Communication is basic to all public relations programs. To communicate effectively, public relations practitioners first must gather data about the firm's client publics to assess their needs, identify problems, formulate recommendations, implement new plans, and evaluate current activities.

Public relations personnel disseminate large amounts of information to the organization's client publics. Written communication is the most versatile tool of public relations, and good writing ability is essential. Public relations practitioners must be adept at writing for a variety of media and audiences. It is not unusual for a person in public relations to prepare reports, news releases, speeches, broadcast scripts, technical manuals, employee publications, shareholder reports, and other communications aimed at both organizational personnel and external groups. In addition, a public relations practitioner needs a thorough knowledge of the production techniques used in preparing various communications. Public relations personnel also establish distribution channels for the organization's publicity. They must have a thorough understanding of the various media, their areas of specialization, the characteristics of their target audiences, and their policies regarding publicity. Anyone who hopes to succeed in public relations must develop close working relationships with numerous media personnel to enlist their interest in disseminating an organization's communications.

A college education combined with writing or media-related experience is the best preparation for a career in public relations. Most beginners have a college degree in journalism, communications, or public relations, but some employers prefer a business background. Courses in journalism, business administration, marketing, creative writing, psychology, sociology, political science, economics, advertising, English, and public speaking are recommended. Some employers ask applicants to present a portfolio of published articles, television or radio programs, slide presentations, and other work samples. Other agencies require written tests that include activities such as writing sample press releases. Manufacturing firms, public utilities, transportation and insurance companies, and trade and professional associations are the largest employers of public relations personnel. In addition, sizable numbers of public relations personnel work for health-related organizations, government agencies, educational institutions, museums, and religious and service groups.

Although some larger companies provide extensive formal training for new personnel, most new public relations employees learn on the job. Beginners usually perform routine tasks, such as maintaining files about company activities and searching secondary data sources for information that can be used in publicity materials. More experienced employees write press releases, speeches, and articles and help plan public relations campaigns.

Employment opportunities in public relations are expected to increase faster than the average for all occupations through the 1990s. One caveat is in order, however: competition for beginning jobs is keen. The prospects are best for applicants who have solid academic preparation and some media experience. Abilities that differentiate candidates, such as a basic understanding of computers, are becoming increasingly important. Annual earnings for salaried public relations specialists range from $15,000, for entry-level positions, to $52,000 for the top 10 percent. Median earnings are close to $30,000. In public relations positions with the federal government, salaries are typically higher, beginning with $21,000 for persons with a bachelor's degree.[25]

Distribution Management

A distribution (or traffic) manager arranges for the transportation of goods within firms and through marketing channels. Transportation is an essential distribution activity that permits a firm to create time and place utility for its products. It is the distribution manager's job to analyze various transportation modes and select the combination that minimizes cost and transit time while providing acceptable levels of reliability, capability, accessibility, and security.

To accomplish this task, a distribution manager performs many activities. First, the individual must choose one or a combination of transportation modes from the five major modes available: railroads, trucks, waterways, airways, and pipelines. Then the distribution manager must select the specific routes that the goods will travel and the particular carriers to be used, weighing such factors as freight classifications and regulations, freight charges, time schedules, shipment sizes, and loss and damage ratios. In addition, this person may be responsible for preparing shipping documents, tracing shipments, handling loss and damage claims, keeping records of freight rates, and monitoring changes in government regulations and transportation technology.

Distribution management employs relatively few people and is expected to grow about as fast as the average for all occupations in the near future. Manufacturing firms are the largest employers of distribution managers, although some traffic managers work for wholesalers, retail stores, and consulting firms. Salaries of experienced distribution managers vary but generally are much higher than the average for all nonsupervisory personnel.

Entry-level positions for distribution management pay between $20,000 and $25,000 per year. Starting jobs are diverse, ranging from inventory control and traffic scheduling to operations or distribution management. Inventory management is an area of great opportunity because of increasing global competition, especially from low-cost Japanese firms.

Most employers prefer graduates of technical programs or seek people who have completed courses in transportation, logistics, distribution management, economics, statistics, computer science, management, marketing, and commercial law. A successful distribution manager must be adept at handling technical data and be able to interpret and communicate highly technical information.

Product Management

The product manager occupies a staff position and is responsible for the success or failure of a product line. Product managers coordinate most of the marketing activities required to market a product; however, because they hold a staff position, they have relatively little actual authority over marketing personnel. Even so, they take on a large amount of responsibility and typically are paid quite well relative to other marketing employees. Being a product manager can be rewarding both financially and psychologically, but it can also be frustrating because of the disparity between responsibility and authority.

A product manager should have a general knowledge of advertising, transportation modes, inventory control, selling and sales management, sales promotion, marketing research, packaging, pricing, and warehousing. The individual must be knowledgeable enough to communicate effectively with personnel in these functional areas and to make suggestions and help assess alternatives when major decisions are being made.

Product managers usually need college training in an area of business administration. A master's degree is helpful, although a person usually does not become a product manager directly out of school. Frequently, several years of selling and sales management are prerequisites for a product management position, which often is a major step in the career path of top-level marketing executives. The average salary for an experienced product manager is $35,000 to $60,000.

Advertising

Advertising pervades our daily lives. Business and nonbusiness organizations use advertising in many ways and for many reasons. Advertising clearly needs individuals with diverse skills to fill a variety of jobs. Creativity, imagination, artistic talent, and expertise in expression and persuasion are important for copywriters, artists, and account executives. Sales and managerial ability are vital to the success of advertising managers, media buyers, and production managers. Research directors must have a solid understanding of research techniques and human behavior. A related occupation is advertising salesperson —one who sells newspaper, retail, radio, or classified advertising directly to clients or to advertising agencies.[26]

Advertising professionals disagree on the most beneficial educational background for a career in advertising. Most employers prefer college graduates. Some employers seek individuals with degrees in advertising, journalism, or business; others prefer graduates with broad liberal arts backgrounds. Still other employers rank relevant work experience above educational background.

"Advertisers look for generalists," says Kate Preston, a staff executive of the American Association of Advertising Agencies, "thus there are just as many economics or general liberal arts majors as M.B.A.s." Common entry-level positions in an advertising agency are found in the traffic department, account service (account coordinator), or in the media department (media assistant). Starting salaries in these positions are often quite low, but to gain experience in the advertising industry, employees must work their way up in the system. The entry-level salaries of media assistants and account coordinators are often $15,000 or less.[27]

A variety of organizations employ advertising personnel. Although advertising agencies are perhaps the most visible and glamorous of employers, many manufacturing firms, retail stores, banks, utility companies, and professional and trade associations maintain advertising departments. Advertising jobs can also be found with television and radio stations, newspapers, and magazines. Other businesses that employ advertising personnel include printers, art studios, letter shops, and package-design firms. Specific advertising jobs include advertising manager, account executive, research director, copywriter, media specialist, and production manager.

Employment opportunities for advertising personnel are expected to decrease as agency acquisitions and mergers continue. General economic conditions, however, strongly influence the size of advertising budgets and, hence, employment opportunities.

Retail Management

Although a career in retailing may begin in sales, there is more to retailing than simply selling. Many retail personnel occupy management positions. Besides managing the sales force, they focus on selecting and ordering merchandise, promotional activities, inventory control, customer credit operations, accounting, personnel, and store security.

How retail stores are organized varies. In many large department stores, retail management personnel rarely engage in the actual selling to customers; these duties are performed by retail salespeople. However, other types of retail organizations may require management personnel to perform selling activities from time to time.

Large retail stores offer a variety of management positions besides those at the very top, including assistant buyers, buyers, department managers, section managers, store managers, division managers, regional managers, and vice president of merchandising. The following list describes the general duties of four of these positions; the precise nature of these duties may vary from one retail organization to another.

A *section manager* coordinates inventory and promotions and interacts with buyers, salespeople, and ultimate consumers. The manager performs merchandising, labor relations, and managerial activities and can rarely expect to get away with as little as a forty-hour workweek.

The buyer's task is more focused. In this fast-paced occupation, there is much travel and pressure and the need to be open-minded with respect to new and potentially successful items.

The regional manager coordinates the activities of several stores within a given area. Sales, promotions, and procedures in general are monitored and supported.

The vice president of merchandising has a broad scope of managerial responsibility and reports to the president at the top of the organization.

Traditionally, retail managers began their careers as salesclerks. Today many large retailers hire college-educated people, put them through management training programs, and then place them directly in management positions. They frequently hire candidates with backgrounds in liberal arts or business administration. Sales and retailing are the greatest employment opportunities for marketing students.

Retail management positions can be exciting and challenging. Competent, ambitious individuals often assume a great deal of responsibility very quickly and advance rapidly. However, a retail manager's job is physically demanding and sometimes entails long working hours. In addition, managers employed by large chain stores may be required to move frequently during their early years with the company. Nonetheless, often positions in retail management offer the chance to excel and gain promotion. Growth in retailing, which is expected to accompany the growth in population, is likely to create substantial opportunities during the next ten years.[28] Although compensation programs for entry-level positions (management trainees) have historically been below average, this situation is changing rapidly, with major specialty, department, and discount stores offering entry salaries in the $20,000 to $25,000 range.

Direct Marketing

One of the most dynamic areas in marketing is direct marketing, in which the seller uses one or more direct media (telephone, mail, print, or television) to solicit a response. For example, Shell Oil uses its credit card billings (direct mail) to sell a variety of consumer products.

The telephone is a major vehicle for selling many consumer products. Telemarketing is direct selling to customers using a variety of technological improvements in telephone services. According to the American Telemarketing Association (Glenview, Illinois), $73 billion of the industry's sales come from business-to-business marketing, not from selling to consumers at home. In addition, the telemarketing industry has been growing at an average of 30 percent per year.

The use of direct mail catalogs appeals to market segments such as working women or people who find going to retail stores difficult or inconvenient. Newspapers and magazines offer great opportunity, particularly in special market segments. *Golf Digest,* for example is obviously a good medium for selling golfing equipment. Cable television provides many new opportunities for selling directly to consumers. Home shopping channels, for instance, have been very successful. Interactive cable will offer a new method to expand direct marketing by developing timely exchange opportunities for consumers.

The most important asset in direct marketing is experience. Employers often look to other industries to locate experienced professionals. This preference means that if you can get an entry-level position in direct marketing, you will have an advantage in developing a career.

Jobs in direct marketing include buyers, such as department store buyers, who select goods for catalog, telephone, or direct mail sales. Catalog managers develop marketing strategies for each new catalog that goes into the mail. Research/mail-list management involves developing lists of products that will sell in direct marketing and lists of names of consumers who are likely to respond to a direct mail effort. Order fulfillment managers direct the shipment of products once they are sold. Direct marketing's effectiveness is enhanced by periodic analysis of advertising and communications at all phases of contact with the consumer. Direct marketing involves all aspects of the marketing decision. It is becoming a more professional career area that provides great opportunity.

Financial Analysis in Marketing*

Our discussion in this book focuses more on fundamental concepts and decisions in marketing than on financial details. However, marketers must understand the basic components of selected financial analyses if they are to explain and defend their decisions. In fact, they must be familiar with certain financial analyses if they are to reach good decisions in the first place. Therefore, we examine three areas of financial analysis: cost-profit aspects of the income statement, selected performance ratios, and price calculations. To control and evaluate marketing activities, marketers must understand the income statement and what it says about the operations of their organization. They also need to be acquainted with performance ratios, which compare current operating results with past results and with results in the industry at large. In the last part of this appendix, we discuss price calculations as the basis of price adjustments. Marketers are likely to use all these areas of financial analysis at various times to support their decisions and to make necessary adjustments in their operations.

The Income Statement

The income, or operating, statement presents the financial results of an organization's operations over a period of time. The statement summarizes revenues earned and expenses incurred by a profit center, whether it is a department, brand, product line, division, or entire firm. The income statement presents the firm's net profit or net loss for a month, quarter, or year.

Table B.1 is a simplified income statement for a fictitious retail store. The owners of the store, Rose Costa and Nick Schultz, see that net sales of $250,000 are decreased by the cost of goods sold and by other business expenses to yield a net income of $83,000. Of course, these figures are only highlights of the complete income statement, which appears in Table B.2.

The income statement can be used in several ways to improve the management of a business. First, it enables an owner or manager to compare actual results with budgets for various parts of the statement. For example, Rose and Nick see that the total amount of

Table B.1 Simplified Income Statement for a Retailer	
Stoneham Auto Supplies **Income Statement for the Year Ended December 31, 1996**	
Net Sales	$250,000
Cost of Goods Sold	45,000
Gross Margin	$205,000
Expenses	122,000
Net Income$	83,000

*We gratefully acknowledge the assistance of Jim L. Grimm, Professor of Marketing, Illinois State University, in writing this appendix.

Table B.2 Income Statement for a Retailer

Stoneham Auto Supplies
Income Statement for the Year Ended December 31, 1996

Gross Sales			**$260,000**
Less: Sales returns and allowances			10,000
Net Sales			**$250,000**
Cost of Goods Sold			
Inventory, January 1, 1996 (at cost)		$48,000	
Purchases	$51,000		
Less: Purchase discounts	4,000		
Net purchases	$47,000		
Plus: Freight-in	2,000		
Net cost of delivered purchases		$49,000	
Cost of goods available for sale		$97,000	
Less: Inventory, December 31, 1996 (at cost)		52,000	
Cost of goods sold			$ 45,000
Gross Margin			**$205,000**
Expenses			
Selling expenses			
Sales salaries and commissions	$32,000		
Advertising	16,000		
Sales promotions	3,000		
Delivery	2,000		
Total selling expenses		$53,000	
Administrative expenses			
Administrative salaries	$20,000		
Office salaries	20,000		
Office supplies	2,000		
Miscellaneous	1,000		
Total administrative expenses		$43,000	
General expenses			
Rent	$14,000		
Utilities	7,000		
Bad debts	1,000		
Miscellaneous (local taxes, insurance, interest, depreciation)	4,000		
Total general expenses		$26,000	
Total expenses			$122,000
Net Income			**$ 83,000**

merchandise sold (gross sales) is $260,000. Customers returned merchandise or received allowances (price reductions) totaling $10,000. Suppose that the budgeted amount was only $9,000. By checking the tickets for sales returns and allowances, the owners can determine why these events occurred and whether the $10,000 figure could be lowered by adjusting the marketing mix.

After subtracting returns and allowances from gross sales, Rose and Nick can determine net sales from the statement. They are pleased with this figure because it is higher than their sales target of $240,000. Net sales is the amount the firm has available to pay its expenses.

A major expense for most companies that sell goods (as opposed to services) is the cost of goods sold. For Stoneham Auto Supplies, it amounts to 18 percent of net sales. Other expenses are treated in various ways by different companies. In our example, they are broken down into standard categories of selling expenses, administrative expenses, and general expenses.

The income statement shows that the cost of goods Stoneham Auto Supplies sold during fiscal year 1996 was $45,000. This figure was derived in the following way. First, the statement shows that merchandise in the amount of $51,000 was purchased during the year. In paying the invoices associated with these inventory additions, purchase (cash) discounts of $4,000 were earned, resulting in net purchases of $47,000. Special requests for selected merchandise throughout the year resulted in $2,000 of freight charges, which increased the net cost of delivered purchases to $49,000. When this amount is added to the beginning inventory of $48,000, the cost of goods available for sale during 1996 totals $97,000. However, the records indicate that the value of inventory at the end of the year was $52,000. Because this amount was not sold, the cost of goods that were sold during the year was $45,000.

Rose and Nick observe that the total value of their inventory increased by 8.3 percent during the year:

$$\frac{\$52,000 - \$48,000}{\$48,000} = \frac{\$4,000}{\$48,000} = \frac{1}{12} = .0825 \text{ or } 8.3\%$$

Further analysis is needed to determine whether this increase is desirable or undesirable. (Note that the income statement provides no details concerning the composition of the inventory held on December 31; other records supply this information.) If Nick and Rose determine that inventory on December 31 is excessive, they can implement appropriate marketing action.

Gross margin is the difference between net sales and cost of goods sold. Gross margin reflects the markup on products and is the amount available to pay all other expenses and provide a return to the owners. Stoneham Auto Supplies had a gross margin of $205,000:

Net Sales	$250,000
Cost of Goods Sold	− 45,000
Gross Margin	$205,000

Stoneham's expenses (other than cost of goods sold) during 1996 totaled $122,000. Observe that $53,000, or slightly more than 43 percent of the total, constituted direct selling expenses:

$$\frac{\$53,000 \text{ selling expenses}}{\$122,000 \text{ total expenses}} = .434 \text{ or } 43\%$$

The business employs three salespersons (one full-time) and pays competitive wages for the area. All selling expenses are similar to dollar amounts for fiscal year 1995, but Nick and Rose wonder whether more advertising is necessary because inventory increased by more than 8 percent during the year.

The administrative and general expenses are also essential for operating the business. A comparison of these expenses with trade statistics for similar businesses indicates that the figures are in line with industry amounts.

Net income, or net profit, is the amount of gross margin remaining after deducting expenses. Stoneham Auto Supplies earned a net profit of $83,000 for the fiscal year ending December 31, 1996. Note that net income on this statement is figured before payment of state and federal income taxes.

Income statements for intermediaries and for businesses that provide services follow the same general format as that shown for Stoneham Auto Supplies in Table B.2. The income statement for a manufacturer, however, is somewhat different in that the "purchases" portion is replaced by "cost of goods manufactured." Table B.3 shows the entire Cost of Goods Sold section for a manufacturer, including cost of goods manufactured. In other respects, income statements for retailers and manufacturers are similar.

Selected Performance Ratios

Rose and Nick's assessment of how well their business did during fiscal year 1996 can be improved through selective use of analytical ratios. These ratios enable a manager to compare the results for the current year with data from previous years and industry statistics. However, comparisons of the current income statement with income statements and

Table B.3 Cost of Goods Sold for a Manufacturer

ABC Manufacturing
Income Statement for the Year Ended December 31, 1996

Cost of Goods Sold			$ 50,000
Finished goods inventory January 1, 1996			
Cost of goods manufactured			
Work-in-process inventory, January 1, 1996		$20,000	
Raw materials inventory, January 1, 1996	$ 40,000		
Net cost of delivered purchases	240,000		
Cost of goods available for use	$280,000		
Less: Raw materials inventory, December 31, 1996	42,000		
Cost of goods placed in production		$238,000	
Direct labor		32,200	
Manufacturing overhead			
Indirect labor	$ 12,000		
Supervisory salaries	10,000		
Operating supplies	6,000		
Depreciation	12,000		
Utilities	10,000		
Total manufacturing overhead		$ 50,000	
Total manufacturing costs		$320,000	
Total work-in-process		$340,000	
Less: Work-in-process inventory, December 31, 1996		22,000	
Cost of goods manufactured			$318,000
			$368,000
Cost of goods available for sale			
Less: Finished goods inventory, December 31, 1996			48,000
Cost of Goods Sold			**$320,000**

industry statistics from other years are not very meaningful because factors such as inflation are not accounted for when comparing dollar amounts. More meaningful comparisons can be made by converting these figures to a percentage of net sales, as this section shows.

The first analytical ratios we discuss, the operating ratios, are based on the net sales figure from the income statement.

Operating Ratios

Operating ratios express items on the income, or operating, statement as percentages of net sales. The first step is to convert the income statement into percentages of net sales, as illustrated in Table B.4.

After making this conversion, the manager looks at several key operating ratios: two profitability ratios (the gross margin ratio and the net income ratio) and the operating expense ratio.

Table B.4 Income Statement Components as Percentages of Net Sales

Stoneham Auto Supplies
Income Statement as a Percentage of Net Sales for the Year Ended
December 31, 1996

		Percentage of net sales
Gross Sales		103.8%
Less: Sales returns and allowances		3.8
Net Sales		100.0%
Cost of Goods Sold		
Inventory, January 1, 1996 (at cost)		19.2%
Purchases	20.4%	
Less: Purchase discounts	1.6	
Net purchases	18.8%	
Plus: Freight-in	0.8	
Net cost of delivered purchases		19.6
Cost of goods available for sale		38.8%
Less: Inventory, December 31, 1996 (at cost)		20.8
Cost of goods sold		18.0
Gross Margin		82.0%
Expenses		
Selling expenses		
Sales salaries and commissions	12.8%	
Advertising	6.4	
Sales promotions	1.2	
Delivery	0.8	
Total selling expenses		21.2%
Administrative expenses		
Administrative salaries	8.0%	
Office salaries	8.0	
Office supplies	0.8	
Miscellaneous	0.4	
Total administrative expenses		17.2%
General expenses		
Rent	5.6%	
Utilities	2.8	
Bad debts	0.4	
Miscellaneous	1.6	
Total general expenses		10.4%
Total expenses		48.8
Net Income		33.2%

For Stoneham Auto Supplies, these ratios are determined as follows (see Tables B.2 and B.4 for supporting data):

$$\text{Gross margin ratio} = \frac{\text{gross margin}}{\text{net sales}} = \frac{\$205,000}{\$250,000} = 82\%$$

$$\text{Net income ratio} = \frac{\text{net income}}{\text{net sales}} = \frac{\$83,000}{\$250,000} = 33.2\%$$

$$\text{Operating expense ratio} = \frac{\text{total expense}}{\text{net sales}} = \frac{\$122,000}{\$250,000} = 48.8\%$$

The gross margin ratio indicates the percentage of each sales dollar available to cover operating expenses and achieve profit objectives. The net income ratio indicates the percentage of each sales dollar that is classified as earnings (profit) before payment of income taxes. The operating expense ratio indicates the percentage of each dollar needed to cover operating expenses.

If Nick and Rose feel that the operating expense ratio is higher than historical data and industry standards, they can analyze each operating expense ratio in Table B.4 to determine which expenses are too high and can take corrective action.

After reviewing several key operating ratios, in fact, managers will probably want to analyze all the items on the income statement. For instance, by doing so, Nick and Rose can determine whether the 8 percent increase in inventory was necessary.

Inventory Turnover

The inventory turnover rate, or stockturn rate, is an analytical ratio that can be used to answer the question, "Is the inventory level appropriate for this business?" The inventory turnover rate indicates the number of times that an inventory is sold (turns over) during one year. To be useful, this figure is then compared with historical turnover rates and industry rates.

The inventory turnover rate can be computed on cost as follows:

$$\text{Inventory turnover} = \frac{\text{cost of goods sold}}{\text{average inventory at cost}}$$

Rose and Nick would calculate the turnover rate from Table B.2 as follows:

$$\frac{\text{Cost of goods sold}}{\text{Average inventory at cost}} = \frac{\$45,000}{\$50,000} = 0.9 \text{ time}$$

They find that inventory turnover is less than once per year (0.9 time). Industry averages for competitive firms are 2.8 times. This figure convinces Rose and Nick that their investment in inventory is too large and that they need to reduce their inventory.

Return on Investment

Return on investment (ROI) is a ratio that indicates management's efficiency in generating sales and profits from the total amount invested in the firm. For example, for Stoneham Auto Supplies the ROI is 41.5 percent, which compares well with competing businesses.

We use figures from two different financial statements to arrive at ROI. The income statement, already discussed, gives us net income. The balance sheet, which states the firm's assets and liabilities at a given point in time, provides the figure for total assets (or investment) in the firm.

The basic formula for ROI is

$$\text{ROI} = \frac{\text{net income}}{\text{total investment}}$$

For Stoneham Auto Supplies, net income for fiscal year 1996 is $83,000 (see Table B.2). If total investment (taken from the balance sheet for December 31, 1996) is $200,000, then

$$\text{ROI} = \frac{\$83,000}{\$200,000} = 0.415 \text{ or } 41.5\%$$

The ROI formula can be expanded to isolate the impact of capital turnover and the operating income ratio separately. Capital turnover is a measure of net sales per dollar of investment; the ratio is figured by dividing net sales by total investment. For Stoneham Auto Supplies,

$$\text{Capital turnover} = \frac{\text{net sales}}{\text{total investment}} = \frac{\$250,000}{\$200,000} = 1.25$$

ROI is equal to capital turnover times the net income ratio. The expanded formula for Stoneham Auto Supplies is

$$\text{ROI} = \frac{\text{net sales}}{\text{total investment}} \times \frac{\text{net income}}{\text{net sales}}$$

$$= \frac{\$250,000}{\$200,000} \times \frac{\$83,000}{\$250,000}$$

$$= (1.25)(33.2\%) = 41.5\%$$

Price Calculations

An important step in setting prices is selecting a pricing method, as indicated in Chapter 21. The systematic use of markups, markdowns, and various conversion formulas helps in calculating the selling price and evaluating the effects of various prices. The following sections provide more detailed information about price calculations.

Markups

As indicated in the text, markup is the difference between the selling price and the cost of the item. That is, selling price equals cost plus markup. The markup must cover cost and contribute to profit; thus markup is similar to gross margin on the income statement.

Markup can be calculated on either cost or selling price as follows:

$$\frac{\text{Markup as percentage}}{\text{of cost}} = \frac{\text{amount added to cost}}{\text{cost}} = \frac{\text{dollar markup}}{\text{cost}}$$

$$\frac{\text{Markup as percentage}}{\text{of selling price}} = \frac{\text{amount added to cost}}{\text{selling price}} = \frac{\text{dollar markup}}{\text{selling price}}$$

Retailers tend to calculate the markup percentage on selling price.

Examples of Markup

To review the use of these markup formulas, assume that an item costs $10 and the markup is $5.

$$\text{Selling price} = \text{cost} + \text{markup}$$

$$\$15 = \$10 + \$5$$

Thus

$$\text{Markup percentage on cost} = \frac{\$5}{\$10} = 50\%$$

$$\text{Markup percentage on selling price} = \frac{\$5}{\$15} = 33\tfrac{1}{3}\%$$

It is necessary to know the base (cost or selling price) to use markup pricing effectively. Markup percentage on cost will always exceed markup percentage on price, given the same dollar markup, so long as selling price exceeds cost.

On occasion, we may need to convert markup on cost to markup on selling price, or vice versa. The conversion formulas are

$$\frac{\text{Markup percentage}}{\text{on selling price}} = \frac{\text{markup percentage on cost}}{100\% + \text{markup percentage on cost}}$$

$$\frac{\text{Markup percentage}}{\text{on cost}} = \frac{\text{markup percentage on selling price}}{100\% - \text{markup percentage on selling price}}$$

For example, if the markup percentage on cost is 33⅓ percent, then the markup percentage on selling price is

$$\frac{33\tfrac{1}{3}\%}{100\% + 33\tfrac{1}{3}\%} = \frac{33\tfrac{1}{3}\%}{133\tfrac{1}{3}\%} = 25\%$$

If the markup percentage on selling price is 40 percent, then the corresponding percentage on cost would be as follows:

$$\frac{40\%}{100\% - 40\%} = \frac{40\%}{60\%} = 66\tfrac{2}{3}\%$$

Finally, we can show how to determine selling price if we know the cost of the item and the markup percentage on selling price. Assume that an item costs $36 and the usual markup percentage on selling price is 40 percent. Remember that selling price equals markup plus cost. Thus if

$$100\% = 40\% \text{ of selling price} + \text{cost}$$

then

$$60\% \text{ of selling price} = \text{cost}$$

In our example, cost equals $36. Then

$$0.6X = \$36$$

$$X = \frac{\$36}{0.6}$$

$$\text{Selling price} = \$60$$

Alternatively, the markup percentage could be converted to a cost basis as follows:

$$\frac{40\%}{100\% - 40\%} = 66\tfrac{2}{3}\%$$

Then the computed selling price would be as follows:

$$\text{Selling price} = 66\tfrac{2}{3}\%(\text{cost}) + \text{cost}$$

$$= 66\tfrac{2}{3}\%(\$36) + \$36$$

$$= \$24 + \$36 = \$60$$

By remembering the basic formula—selling price equals cost plus markup—you will find these calculations straightforward.

Markdowns

Markdowns are price reductions a retailer makes on merchandise. Markdowns may be useful on items that are damaged, priced too high, or selected for a special sales event. The income statement does not express markdowns directly because the change in price is made before the sale takes place. Therefore, separate records of markdowns would be needed to evaluate the performance of various buyers and departments.

The markdown ratio (percentage) is calculated as follows:

$$\text{Markdown percentage} = \frac{\text{dollar markdowns}}{\text{net sales in dollars}}$$

In analyzing their inventory, Nick and Rose discover three special automobile jacks that have gone unsold for several months. They decide to reduce the price of each item from $25 to $20. Subsequently, these items are sold. The markdown percentage for these three items is

$$\text{Markdown percentage} = \frac{3(\$5)}{3(\$20)} = \frac{\$15}{\$60} = 25\%$$

Net sales, however, include all units of this product sold during the period, not just those marked down. If ten of these items have already been sold at $25 each, in addition to the three items sold at $20, then the overall markdown percentage would be

$$\text{Markdown percentage} = \frac{3(\$5)}{10(\$25) + 3(\$20)}$$

$$= \frac{\$15}{\$250 + \$60} = \frac{\$15}{\$310} = 4.8\%$$

Sales allowances are also a reduction in price. Thus the markdown percentage should include any sales allowances. It would be computed as follows:

$$\text{Markdown percentage} = \frac{\text{dollar markdowns} + \text{dollar allowances}}{\text{net sales in dollars}}$$

DISCUSSION AND REVIEW QUESTIONS

1. How does a manufacturer's income statement differ from a retailer's income statement?
2. Use the following information to answer questions a through c:

   TEA Company
   Fiscal year ended June 30, 1997

Net Sales	$500,000
Cost of Goods Sold	300,000
Net Income	50,000
Average Inventory at Cost	100,000
Total Assets (total investment)	200,000

   a. What is the inventory turnover rate for TEA Company? From what sources will the marketing manager determine the significance of the inventory turnover rate?
   b. What is the capital turnover ratio for fiscal year 1997? What is the net income ratio? What is the return on investment (ROI)?
   c. How many dollars of sales did each dollar of investment produce for TEA Company in fiscal year 1997?
3. Product A has a markup percentage on cost of 40 percent. What is the markup percentage on selling price?
4. Product B has a markup percentage on selling price of 30 percent. What is the markup percentage on cost?
5. Product C has a cost of $60 and a usual markup percentage of 25 percent on selling price. What price should be placed on this item?
6. Apex Appliance Company sells twenty units of product Q for $100 each and ten units for $80 each. What is the markdown percentage for product Q?

Sample Marketing Plan

NOTE: *This is a sample marketing plan for a hypothetical company that illustrates the marketing planning process described in Chapter 22. This plan lets you see how the planning concepts might be implemented. If you are asked to create a marketing plan, you may find it helpful to use this model for guidance, along with the concepts presented in Chapter 22. The preparation date for this sample marketing plan is March 1, 1997 as Star Software, Inc., plans for the next fiscal year, which begins on April 1.*

Star Software, Inc.: Marketing Plan

I. EXECUTIVE SUMMARY

Star Software, Inc. is a small, family-owned corporation in the first year of a transition from first-generation to second-generation leadership. Star Software provides computer software for a custom calendar program that supports particular products or manufacturers' promotional events to a customer base of approximately 400. Its staff of eighteen employees faces scheduling challenges, as Star's business is highly seasonal, with its greatest demand during October, November, and December. In other months, the equipment and staff are sometimes idle. A major challenge facing Star Software is how to increase profits and make better use of its resources during the off-season.

An evaluation of the company's internal strengths and weaknesses and external opportunities and threats served as the foundation for this strategic analysis and marketing plan. The plan focuses on the company's growth strategy, suggesting ways in which it can build on existing customer relationships and on the development of new products and/or services targeted to specific customer niches. Since Star Software, Inc. markets a product that is used primarily as a promotional tool by its clients, it currently is considered a business-to-business marketer.

II. ENVIRONMENTAL ANALYSIS

In business for over twenty years, Star Software, Inc., was founded as a commercial printing company and has evolved into a marketer of high-quality, custom-made calendar software and related business-to-business specialty items. In the mid-1960s, Bob McLemore purchased the company and, through his full-time commitment, turned it into a very successful family run operation. On April 1, 1997, Bob McLemore's 37-year-old son, Jonathan, will take over as Star Software's president to allow the elder McLemore to scale back his involvement.

A. The Marketing Environment

1. Competitive forces. The competition in the specialty advertising industry is very strong on a local and regional basis but somewhat weak nationally. Sales figures for the industry as a whole are very difficult to obtain since very little business is conducted on a national scale.

The competition within the calendar industry is very strong in the paper segment and very weak in the software-based segment. Currently, paper calendars hold a dominant market share of approximately 90 percent; however, the software-based segment is growing rapidly. The 10 percent market share held by software-based calendars is divided among many different firms. Star Software, which holds 30 percent of the software-based calendar market, is the only company that markets a software-based calendar product on a national basis. As software-based calendars become more popular, additional competition is expected to enter the market.

2. Economic forces. Nationwide, many companies have reduced their overall promotion budgets as they are faced with the need to cut expenses. However, most of these reductions have occurred in the budgets for mass media advertising (television, magazines, newspapers). While overall promotion budgets are shrinking, many companies are diverting a larger percentage of their budgets to sales promotion and specialty advertising. This trend is expected to continue as a weak, slow-growth economy forces most companies to become more interested in the "value" they receive from their promotion dollar. Specialty advertising, such as a software-based calendar, provides this value.

3. Political forces. There are no expected political influences or events that could affect the operations of Star Software.

4. Legal and regulatory forces. In recent years, more attention has been paid to "junk mail" in the advertising industry. A large percentage of specialty advertising products are distributed by mail, and some of these products are considered "junk." While this label is attached to the type of products that Star Software makes, the problem of junk mail falls on the clients of Star Software and not on the company itself. While legislation may be introduced to curb the tide of advertising delivered through the mail, the fact that more companies are diverting their promotion dollars to specialty advertising indicates that most companies do not fear the potential for increased legislation.

5. Technological forces. A major emerging technological trend deals with personal information managers (PIM) or personal digital assistants (PDA). A PDA is a handheld device, similar in size to a large calculator, that can store a wide variety of information ranging from personal notes, a calendar, and/or a rolodex. Some PDAs even have the ability to fax letters via microwave communication. As this trend continues, current software-based calendar products may have to be adapted to match the new technology.

6. Sociocultural forces. In today's society, consumers have less time for work or leisure. The hallmark characteristics for today's successful products are convenience and ease-of-use. In short, if the product does not save time and is not easy to use, consumers will simply ignore it.

Software-based calendars fit this consumer need quite well. A software-based calendar also fits in with other societal trends: a move to a paperless society, the need to automate repetitive tasks, and the growing dependence on computers, for example.

B. Target Market(s)

Star Software has effectively implemented a niche differentiation strategy in a somewhat diverse marketplace, focusing on commitment to service and quality. Its ability to differentiate its product has contributed to superior annual returns. Star's target market includes manufacturers or manufacturing divisions of large corporations that move their products through dealers, distributors, or brokers. Its most profitable product is a software program for a PC-based calendar, which can be tailored to meet client specifications by means of artwork, logos, and text. Clients use this calendar software as a promotional tool, providing a disk to their customers as an advertising premium. The calendar software is not produced for resale.

The calendar software initially was begun as an ancillary product to Star's commercial printing business. However, due to the proliferation of PCs and the growth in technology, the computer calendar soon overshadowed wall and desktop paper calendars in popularity. This shift in popularity was instrumental in the sale of the commercial printing plant and equipment to former employees. Star Software has maintained a long-term relationship with the former employees, who have added capabilities to reproduce computer disks and whose company serves as Star's primary supplier of finished goods. Star's staff focuses on the further development and marketing of the software.

C. Current Marketing Objectives and Performance

Star Software sends personal sales representatives to call on potential clients and create a calendar concept, including template demonstration disks, for use in sales presentations. Once the sale has been finalized, Star completes the concept, including design, copywriting, and customization of the demonstration disk software. Specifications are then sent to the supplier, located approximately one thousand miles away, where the disks are produced. Perhaps what differentiates Star from its competitors is its high level of service. Disks can be shipped to individual business locations for each manufacturer. Since product development and customization of this type can require significant amounts of time and effort, particularly during the product's first year, Star deliberately pursues a strategy of steady, managed growth.

Star Software markets its products on a company-specific basis, with an approximate 90 percent reorder rate annually and an average customer reorder relationship of about eight years. The first year in dealing with a new customer is the most stressful and time-consuming for Star's salespeople and product developers. The subsequent years are faster and significantly more profitable.

Although the company is currently debt-free except for the mortgage on its facility, about 80 percent of its accounts receivable are billed during the last three months of the calendar year. The seasonality of account billings, along with the added travel of its sales staff during this period, provides a special challenge to the company. The enormous need for cash to facilitate operations in the meantime causes the company to borrow significant amounts of money to cover the period until customer billing occurs.

As the fiscal year comes to an end on March 31, 1997, Star Software expects to see the best year in its history, with increases in both revenues and profits of approximately 10 percent over the previous year. Revenues are expected to exceed $4 million, and profits are expected to reach $1.3 million.

III. STRENGTHS AND WEAKNESSES

A. Strengths

1. Star Software maintains a product differentiation strategy resulting from a strong market orientation, commitment to high quality, and customization of products and support services.

2. There is little turnover among well-compensated employees who are liked by customers. The relatively small size of the staff promotes camaraderie with fellow employees and clients and fosters communication and quick response to clients' needs.

3. A long-term relationship with the primary supplier results in shared knowledge of the product's requirements, adherence to quality standards, and a common vision throughout the development and production process.

4. The high percentage of reorder business suggests a satisfied customer base as well as positive word of mouth, which generates some 30 percent of new business each year.

B. Weaknesses

1. The highly centralized management (the McLemores) hierarchy and lack of managerial backup may impede creativity and growth. Too much knowledge is held by too few people.

2. Despite the long-term successful working relationship with the supplier, the geographic distance could cause communication and logistical difficulties. Single-sourcing also can make Star Software vulnerable in the event of a natural disaster, strike, or dissolution of the current supplier. Contingency plans for suppliers should be considered.

3. The seasonality of the product line creates bottlenecks in productivity and cash flow, places excessive stress on personnel, and strains the facilities.

4. Both the product line and the client base lack diversification. Dependence on current reorder rates could breed complacency, invite competition, or create a false sense of customer satisfaction. The development of a product that would make the software calendar obsolete would probably put Star out of business.

5. While the size of the staff fosters camaraderie, it also impedes growth and new business development.

6. Star Software is reactive rather than assertive in its marketing efforts because of its heavy reliance on positive word of mouth for obtaining new business.

7. Star's current facilities are crowded. There is little room for additional employees or new equipment.

IV. OPPORTUNITIES AND THREATS

A. Opportunities

1. Advertising expenditures in the United States alone exceed $132 billion annually. More than $25 billion of this is spent on direct mail advertising and another $20 billion on specialty advertising. The potential for Star Software's growth is significant in this market.

2. Technological advances have freed up time for Americans and brought greater efficiency but also have increased the amount of stress in their fast-paced lives. Personal computers have become commonplace in the business office and in the home. In addition, there is a general trend toward a paperless society as laptop computers and personal information managers gain popularity.

3. As American companies look for ways to develop customer relationships rather than just close sales, reminders of this relationship could come in the form of acceptable premiums or gifts that are useful to the customer.

4. Computer-based calendars are easily distributed nationally and globally. The globalization of business creates an opportunity to establish new client relationships in foreign markets.

B. Threats

1. Reengineering, right-sizing, and outsourcing trends in management may alter traditional channel relationships with brokers, dealers, and distributors or eliminate them altogether.

2. Calendars are basically a generic product. The technology, knowledge, and equipment required to produce such an item, even a computer-based one, are minimal. The possible entry of new competitors is a significant threat.

3. Theft of trade secrets and software piracy through unauthorized copying are difficult to control.

4. Specialty advertising through promotional items relies on gadgetry and ideas that are new and different. As a result, product life cycles may be quite short.

5. Single-sourcing can be detrimental or even fatal to a company if the buyer-supplier relationship is damaged or if the supplying company has financial difficulty.

6. Competition from traditional paper calendars and other promotional items is strong.

C. Matching Strengths to Opportunities/Converting Weaknesses and Threats

1. The acceptance of technological advances and the desire to control time create a potential need for a computer-based calendar.

2. Star Software has more opportunity for business growth during its peak season than it can presently handle because of resource (human and capital) constraints.

3. Star Software must modify its management hierarchy, empowering its employees through a more decentralized marketing organization.

4. Star Software should discuss future growth strategies with its supplier and develop possible contingency plans in the event of unforeseen events. Possible satellite facilities in other geographic locations should be explored.

5. Star Software should consider diversifying its product line to satisfy new market niches, as well as developing products that are nonseasonal.

6. Star Software should consider surveying its current customers and its customers' clients to better understand their needs and changing desires.

V. MARKETING OBJECTIVES

Star Software, Inc., is in the business of helping other companies market their products and/or services. Besides formulating a market-oriented and customer-focused mission statement, Star Software should establish an objective to achieve cumulative growth in net profit of at least 50 percent over the next five year period. At least half of this 50 percent growth should come from new, nonmanufacturing customers and from products that are nonseasonal or are generally delivered in the off-peak period of the calendar cycle.

To accomplish its marketing objectives, Star Software should develop benchmarks to measure progress. Regular reviews of these objectives will provide feedback and possible corrective actions on a timely basis. The major marketing objective is to gain a better understanding of the needs and satisfaction of current customers. Since Star Software is benefitting from a 90 percent reorder rate, it must be satisfying its current customers. Star could use the knowledge of its successes with current clients to market to new customers. To capitalize on its success with current clients, benchmarks should be established to learn how it can improve the products it now offers through knowledge of its clients' needs and specific opportunities for new product offerings. These benchmarks should be determined through marketing research and Star's marketing information system.

Another objective should be to analyze the billing cycle Star now uses, in case there are ways to bill accounts receivable in a more evenly distributed manner throughout the year. Alternatively, repeat customers might be willing to place orders at off-peak cycles in return for discounts or added customer services.

Star Software also should create new products that can utilize its current equipment, technology, and knowledge base. It should conduct simple research and analyses of similar products or product lines with an eye toward developing specialty advertising products that are software based, but not necessarily calendar related.

VI. MARKETING STRATEGIES

A. Target Market(s)

Target market 1: Large manufacturers or stand-alone manufacturing divisions of large corporations with extensive broker, dealer, or distributor networks

For example, an agricultural chemical producer, such as Dow Chemical, distributes its products to numerous rural "feed and seed" dealers. Customizing calendars with Chicago Board of Trade futures or USDA agricultural report dates would be beneficial to these potential clients.

Target market 2: Nonmanufacturing, nonindustrial segments of the business-to-business market with extensive customer networks such as banks, medical services, or financial planners

For example, various sporting good manufacturers distribute to specialty shop dealers. Calendars could be customized to the particular sport, such as golf (with PGA, Virginia Slims, or other tour dates), running (with various national marathon dates), or bowling (with national tour dates).

Target market 3: Direct consumer markets for brands with successful licensing arrangements for consumer products, such as Coca-Cola

For example, products with major brand recognition and fan club membership, such as Harley-Davidson motorcycles or the Bloomington Gold Corvette Association, could provide additional markets for customized computer calendars. Brands with licensing agreements for consumer products could provide a market for consumer-direct computer calendars, in addition to the specialty advertising product, which would be marketed to the manufacturer/dealer relationship.

Target market 4: Industry associations that regularly hold or sponsor trade shows, meetings, conferences, or conventions

For example, national associations, such as the National Dairy Association or the American Marketing Association, frequently host meetings or annual conventions. Customized calendars could be developed for any of these groups.

B. Marketing Mix

1. Products. Star Software not only markets calendar software, but also the service of specialty advertising to its clients. Intangible attributes of Star's products are its ability to meet or exceed customer expectations consistently, its speed in response to customers' demands, and its anticipation of new customer needs. Intangible attributes are difficult for competitors to copy, thereby giving Star Software a competitive advantage.

2. Price. Star Software provides a high-quality specialty advertising product customized to its clients' needs. The value of this product and service is reflected in its premium price. Star should be sensitive to the price elasticity of its product and its overall consumer demand.

3. Distribution. Star Software uses direct marketing. Since its product is compact, lightweight, and nonperishable, it can be shipped from a central location direct to the client via United Parcel Service, Federal Express, or the U.S. Postal Service. The fact that Star can ship to multiple locations for each customer is an asset in selling its products.

4. Promotion. Since 90 percent of Star's customers reorder each year, the bulk of promotional expenditures should focus on new product offerings through direct-mail advertising and trade journals or specialty publications. Any remaining promotional dollars could be directed to personal selling (in the form of sales performance bonuses) for current and new products.

VII. MARKETING IMPLEMENTATION

A. Marketing Organization

Because Star's current and future products require extensive customization to match clients' needs, it is necessary to organize the marketing function by customer groups. This will allow Star to focus its marketing efforts exclusively on the needs and specifications of each target customer segment. Star's marketing efforts will be organized around the following customer groups: (1) manufacturing group, (2) nonmanufacturing, business-to-business group, (3) consumer product licensing group, and (4) industry associations group. Each group will be headed by a sales manager who will report to the marketing director (these positions must be created). Each group is responsible for the marketing of Star's products within that customer segment. In addition, each group will have full decision making authority. This represents a shift from the current highly centralized management hierarchy. Frontline salespeople will be empowered to make decisions that will better satisfy Star's clients.

These changes in marketing organization enable Star Software to be more creative and flexible in meeting customers' needs. Likewise, these changes overcome the current lack of diversification in Star's product lines and client base. Finally, this new marketing organization will give Star a better opportunity to monitor the activities of competitors.

B. Activities, Responsibility, and Timetables for Completion

All implementation activities are to begin along with the next fiscal year on April 1, 1997. Unless specified, all activities are the responsibility of Star Software's president, Jonathan McLemore.

- On April 1, create four sales manager positions along with the new position of marketing director. The marketing director will serve as project leader for a new business analysis team, to be composed of nine employees from a variety of positions within the company.
- By April 15, assign three members of the analysis team to each of the following projects: (1) research potential new product offerings and clients, (2) analyze the current billing cycle and billing practices, and (3) design a customer survey project. The marketing director is responsible.
- By June 30, the three project groups will report the results of their analyses. The full business analysis team will review all recommendations.
- By July 31, develop a marketing information system to monitor client reorder patterns and customer satisfaction.
- By July 31, implement any changes in billing practices as recommended by the business analysis team.
- By July 31, make initial contact with new potential clients for the current product line. Each sales manager is responsible.
- By August 31, develop a plan for one new product offering along with an analysis of its potential customers. The business analysis team is responsible.
- By August 31, finalize a customer satisfaction survey for current clients. In addition, the company will contact those customers who did not reorder for the 1998 product year to discuss their concerns. The marketing director is responsible.
- By January 1998, implement the customer satisfaction survey with a random sample of 20 percent of current clients who reordered for the 1998 product year. The marketing director is responsible.
- By February 1998, implement a new product offering, advertising to current customers and to a sample of potential clients. The business analysis team is responsible.
- By March 1998, analyze and report the results of all customer satisfaction surveys and evaluate the new product offering. The marketing director is responsible.
- Reestablish the objectives of the business analysis team for the next fiscal year. The marketing director is responsible.

VIII. EVALUATION AND CONTROL

A. Performance Standards and Financial Controls

A comparison of the financial expenditures with the plan goals will be included in the project report. The following performance standards and financial controls are suggested:

- The total budget for the billing analysis, new product research, and the customer survey will be equal to 60 percent of the annual promotional budget for the coming year.
- The breakdown of the budget within the project will be a 20 percent allocation to the billing cycle study, a 30 percent allocation to the customer survey and marketing information system development, and a 50 percent allocation to new business development and new product implementation.
- Each project team is responsible for reporting all financial expenditures, including personnel salaries and direct expenses, for their segment of the project. A standardized reporting form will be developed and provided by the marketing director.
- The marketing director is responsible for adherence to the project budget and will report overages to the company president on a weekly basis. The marketing director

also is responsible for any redirection of budget dollars, as required for each project of the business analysis team.

- Any new product offering will be evaluated on a quarterly basis to determine its profitability. Product development expenses will be distributed over a two year period, by calendar quarters, and will be compared with gross income generated during the same time period.

B. Monitoring Procedures

To analyze the effectiveness of Star Software's marketing plan, it is necessary to compare its actual performance with plan objectives. To facilitate this analysis, monitoring procedures should be developed for the various activities required to bring the marketing plan to fruition. These procedures include, but are not limited to, the following:

- A project management concept will be used to evaluate the implementation of the market plan by establishing time requirements, human resource needs, and financial or budgetary expenditures.

- A perpetual comparison of actual and planned activities will be conducted on a monthly basis for the first year and on a quarterly basis after the initial implementation phase. The business analysis team, including the marketing director, will report their comparison of actual and planned outcomes directly to the company president.

- Each project team is responsible for determining what changes must be made in procedures, product focus, or operations as a result of the studies conducted in its area.

Glossary

Accessory equipment Equipment used in production or office activities; does not become a part of the final physical product. (9)

Advertising A paid form of nonpersonal communication about an organization and/or its products that is transmitted to a target audience through a mass medium. (18)

Advertising appropriation The total amount of money that a marketer allocates for advertising for a specific time period. (18)

Advertising campaign The creation and execution of a series of advertisements to communicate with a particular target audience. (18)

Advertising platform The basic issues or selling points that an advertiser wishes to include in the advertising campaign. (18)

Advocacy advertising A form of advertising promoting a company's position on a public issue. (18)

Aesthetic modification Modification directed at changing the sensory appeal of a product by altering its taste, texture, sound, smell, or visual characteristics. (10)

Agents Functional middlemen representing buyers or sellers on a permanent basis. (14)

Aided recall test A posttest method of evaluating the effectiveness of advertising in which subjects are asked to identify advertisements they have seen recently; they are shown a list of products, brands, company names, or trademarks to jog their memory. (18)

Allowance Concession in price to achieve a desired goal; for example, industrial equipment manufacturers give trade-in allowances on used industrial equipment to enable customers to purchase new equipment. (20)

Approach The manner in which a salesperson contacts a potential customer. (19)

Arbitrary approach A method for determining the advertising appropriation in which a high-level executive in the firm states how much to spend on advertising for a certain time period. (18)

Area sampling A variation of stratified sampling, with geographic areas serving as the segments, or primary units, used in random sampling. (5)

Artwork The illustration in an advertisement and the layout of the components of an advertisement. (18)

Atmospherics The physical elements in a store's design that appeal to consumers' emotions and that encourage buying. (15)

Attitude An individual's enduring evaluation, feelings, and behavioral tendencies toward an object or idea. (6)

Attitude scale An instrument that can be used to measure consumer attitudes. It usually consists of a series of adjectives, phrases, or sentences about an object; subjects are asked to indicate the intensity of their feelings toward the object by reacting to the statements in a certain way. (6)

Automatic vending The use of machines to dispense products selected by customers when money is inserted. (15)

Average fixed cost The fixed cost per unit produced; it is calculated by dividing the fixed costs by the number of units produced. (21)

Average total cost The sum of the average fixed cost and the average variable cost. (21)

Average variable cost The variable cost per unit produced; it is calculated by dividing the variable cost by the number of units produced. (21)

Barter The trading of products. (20)

Base-point pricing A geographic pricing policy that includes the price at the factory, plus freight charges from the base point nearest the buyer. (20)

Benchmarking The measurement and evaluation of the quality of an organization's goods, services, or processes as compared with the best-performing companies in the industry. (23)

Benefit segmentation The division of a market according to benefits that customers want from the product. (8)

Better Business Bureau A local, nongovernmental regulatory agency, supported by local businesses, that aids in settling problems between specific business firms and customers. (2)

Bonded storage A storage service provided by many public warehouses, whereby the goods are not released until U.S. custom duties, federal or state taxes, or other fees are paid. (16)

Brand A name, term, symbol, design, or combination of these that identifies a seller's products and differentiates them from competitors' products. (11)

Brand equity The marketing and financial value associated with a brand's strength in the market, including actual proprietary brand assets, brand name awareness, brand loyalty, perceived brand quality, and brand associations. (11)

Brand-extension branding A type of branding in which a firm uses one of its existing brand names as part of a brand for an improved or new product that is usually in the same product category as the existing brand. (11)

Brand insistence The strongest degree of brand loyalty in which a customer prefers a specific brand so strongly that he or she will accept no substitute. (11)

Brand loyalty A customer's favorable attitude toward a brand and likelihood of consistent purchase. (11)

Brand manager A type of product manager responsible for a single brand. (9)

Brand mark The element of a brand, such as a symbol or design, that cannot be spoken. (11)

Brand name The part of a brand that can be spoken— including letters, words, and numbers. (11)

Brand preference A degree of customer loyalty in which a customer prefers one brand to competitive offerings and will purchase the brand if it is available but will accept substitutes if it is not. (11)

Brand recognition A customer's awareness that a brand exists and view that it is a purchase alternative. (11)

Breakdown approach A general approach for measuring company sales potential based on a general economic forecast and the market sales potential derived from it; the company sales potential is based on the general economic forecast and the estimated market sales potential. (8)

Breakeven point The point at which the costs of producing a product equal the revenue made from selling the product. (21)

Brokers Functional middlemen that bring buyers and sellers together temporarily and help negotiate exchanges. (14)

Buildup approach A general approach to measuring company sales potential in which the analyst initially estimates how much the average purchaser of a product will buy in a specified time period and then multiplies that amount by the number of potential buyers; estimates are calculated by individual geographic areas. (8)

Business analysis An analysis providing a tentative sketch of a product's compatibility in the marketplace, including its probable profitability. (10)

Business-to-business buying behavior *See* Organizational buying behavior.

Business-to-business market A market consisting of individuals, groups, or organizations that purchase specific kinds of products for resale, for direct use in producing other products, or for use in day-to-day operations; also called organizational market. (20)

Buy-back allowance A sum of money given to a reseller for each unit bought after an initial deal is over. (19)

Buying allowance A temporary price reduction to resellers for purchasing specified quantities of a product. (19)

Buying center The group of people within an organization who make organizational purchase decisions; these people take part in the purchase decision process as users, influencers, buyers, deciders, and gatekeepers. (7)

Buying power Resources such as money, goods, and services that can be traded in an exchange situation. (2)

Buying power index A weighted index consisting of population, effective buying income, and retail sales data. (2)

Captioned photograph A photograph with a brief description that explains the picture's content. (18)

Cash-and-carry wholesalers Limited-service wholesalers whose customers pay cash and furnish transportation. (14)

Cash discount A price reduction to the buyer for prompt payment or cash payment. (20)

Catalog marketing A type of marketing in which an organization provides a catalog from which customers make selections and place orders by mail or telephone. (15)

Catalog showrooms A form of warehouse showroom in which consumers shop from a catalog and buy at a warehouse where all products are stored out of buyers' reach. (15)

Category killer A large specialty store that concentrates on a single product line and competes on the basis of low prices and product availability. (15)

Causal studies Studies in which it is assumed that a particular variable X causes a variable Y. (5)

Centralized organization An organization in which the top-level managers delegate very little authority to lower levels of the organization. (23)

Cents-off offer Sales promotion device for established products whereby buyers receive a certain amount off the regular price shown on the label or package. (19).

Chain store A retail outlet that is part of a multiple outlet organization. (15)

Channel capacity The limit on the volume of information that a communication channel can handle effectively. (17)

Channel conflict Friction between marketing channel members, often resulting from role deviance or malfunction. (13)

Channel cooperation A helping relationship among channel members that enhances the welfare and survival of all necessary channel members. (13)

Channel leadership The guidance that a channel member with one or more sources of power gives to other channel members to help achieve channel objectives. (13)

Channel of distribution *See* Marketing channel.

Channel power The ability of one channel member to influence another channel member's goal achievement. (13)

Clayton Act A law passed in 1914 that prohibits specific practices, such as price discrimination, exclusive dealer arrangements, and stock acquisitions, that may decrease competition and tend to create a monopoly. (2)

Client-based relationships Satisfied customers who repeatedly use a service over time. (12)

Client publics The direct consumers of the product of a nonbusiness organization; for example, the client public of a university is its student body. (12)

Closing The part of the selling process in which the salesperson asks the prospect to buy the product. (19)

Codes of conduct Formalized rules and standards that describe what a company expects of its employees. (3)

Coding process The process by which a meaning is placed into a series of signs that represents ideas; also called encoding. (17)

Cognitive dissonance Doubts that may occur shortly after the purchase of a product when the buyer questions whether or not he or she made the right decision in purchasing the product. (6)

Combination compensation plan A plan by which salespeople are paid a fixed salary and a commission based on sales volume. (19)

Commercialization A phase of new-product development in which plans for full-scale manufacturing and marketing must be refined and settled and budgets for the product must be prepared. (10)

Commission merchants Agents that receive goods on consignment and negotiate sales in large markets. (14)

Communication A sharing of meaning through the transmission of information. (17)

Community shopping centers Shopping centers that include one or two department stores and some specialty stores, as well as convenience stores, which serve several neighborhoods and draw consumers who are not able to find desired products in neighborhood shopping centers. (15)

Company sales forecast The amount of a product that a firm actually expects to sell during a specific period at a specified level of company marketing activities. (8)

Company sales potential The maximum percentage of market potential that an individual firm within an industry can expect to obtain for a specific product. (8)

Comparative advertising Advertising that compares two or more identified brands in the same general product class; the comparison is made in terms of one or more specific product characteristics. (18)

Competition Organizations marketing products that are similar to or can be substituted for a marketer's products in the same geographic area. (2)

Competition-matching approach A method of ascertaining the advertising appropriation in which an advertiser tries to match a major competitor's appropriations in absolute dollars or in using the same percentage of sales for advertising. (18)

Competition-oriented pricing A pricing method in which an organization considers costs and revenues secondary to competitors' prices. (21)

Competitive advantage When a company matches its distinctive competency to the opportunities it has discovered in the market. (22)

Competitive advertising Advertising that points out a brand's uses, features, and advantages that benefit consumers but may not be available in competing brands. (18)

Component parts Finished items ready for assembly or products that need little processing before assembly and that become a part of the physical product. (9)

Concentrated targeting strategy A market segmentation strategy in which an organization directs its marketing efforts toward a single market segment through one marketing mix. (8)

Concept testing The stage in the product development process in which initial buying intentions and attitudes regarding a product are determined by presenting a written or oral description of the product to a sample of potential buyers and obtaining their responses. (10)

Consistency of quality The ability of a product to provide the same level of quality over time. (9)

Consumable supplies Items that facilitate an organization's production and operations, but do not become part of the finished product. (9)

Consumer buying behavior The decision processes and acts of ultimate consumers involved in buying and using products. (6)

Consumer buying decision process A five-stage purchase decision process that includes problem recognition, information search, evaluation of alternatives, purchase, and postpurchase evaluation. (6)

Consumer contests Sales promotion devices for established products based on the analytical or creative skill of contestants. (19)

Consumer jury A panel used to pretest advertisements; it consists of a number of actual or potential buyers of the product to be advertised. (18)

Consumer market Purchasers and/or household members who intend to consume or benefit from the purchased products and who do not buy products for the main purpose of making profits. (6)

Consumer movement Organized efforts by individuals, groups, and organizations seeking to protect consumers' rights. (2)

Consumer products Products purchased for the ultimate satisfaction of personal and family needs. (9)

Consumer protection legislation Laws enacted to protect consumers' safety, to enhance the amount of information available, and to warn of deceptive marketing techniques. (2)

Consumer sales promotion methods A category of sales promotion techniques that encourages or stimulates customers to patronize a specific retail store or to try and/or purchase a particular product. (19)

Consumer socialization The process through which a person acquires the knowledge and skills to function as a consumer. (6)

Consumer sweepstakes A sales promotion device for established products in which entrants submit their names for inclusion in a drawing for prizes. (19)

Containerization The consolidation of many items into a single container that is sealed at the point of origin and opened at the destination. (16)

Convenience products Relatively inexpensive, frequently purchased items for which buyers want to exert only minimal effort to obtain. (9)

Cooperative advertising An arrangement in which a manufacturer agrees to pay a certain amount of a retailer's media costs for advertising the manufacturer's products. (19)

Copy The verbal portion of advertisements; includes headlines, subheadlines, body copy, and signature. (18)

Corporate culture *See* Organizational culture.

Corporate strategy The strategy that determines the means for utilizing resources in the areas of production, finance, research and development, human resources, and marketing to reach the organization's goals. (22)

Cost comparison indicator Allows an advertiser to compare the costs of several vehicles within a specific medium relative to the number of persons reached by each vehicle. (18)

Cost-oriented pricing A pricing policy in which a firm determines price by adding a dollar amount or percentage to the cost of a product. (21)

Cost-plus pricing A form of cost-oriented pricing in which first the seller's costs are determined and then a specified dollar amount or percentage of the cost is added to the seller's cost to set the price. (21)

Count-and-recount A sales promotion method based on the payment of a specific amount of money for each product unit moved from a reseller's warehouse in a given period of time. (19)

Coupons New-product sales promotion technique used to reduce a product's price and prompt trial of a new or improved product, to increase sales volume quickly, to attract repeat purchasers, or to introduce new package sizes or features. (19)

Credence qualities Qualities of services that cannot be assessed even after purchase and consumption; for example, few customers are knowledgeable enough to assess the quality of an appendix operation, even after it has been performed. (12)

Culture The accumulation of values, knowledge, beliefs, customs, objects, and concepts that a society uses to cope with its environment and that it passes on to future generations. (6)

Cumulative discount A quantity discount that is aggregated over a stated period of time. (20)

Customary pricing A type of psychological pricing in which certain goods are priced primarily on the basis of tradition. (21).

Customer contact The necessary interaction between service provider and customer in order for the service to be delivered. (12)

Customer forecasting survey The technique of asking customers what types and quantities of products they intend to buy during a specific period in order to predict the sales level for that period. (8)

Customer service audit A specialized audit in which specific consumer service activities are analyzed and service goals and standards are compared to actual performance. (23)

Customer services Anything a company provides in addition to the product that adds value and builds relationships with customers. (9)

Customer service standards The level and quality of service a firm's management aims to provide for its customers. (16)

Cycle analysis A method of predicting sales by analyzing sales figures for a period of three to five years to ascertain whether sales fluctuate in a consistent, periodic manner. (8)

Cycle time The time it takes to complete a process. (16)

Database A collection of information arranged for easy access and retrieval. (5)

Dealer brand *See* Private distributor brand.

Dealer listing An advertisement that promotes a product and identifies the names of participating retailers that sell the product. (19)

Dealer loader A gift, often part of a display, that is given to a retailer for the purchase of a specified quantity of merchandise. (19)

Decentralized organization An organization in which decision-making authority is delegated as far down the chain of command as possible. (23)

Decline stage The stage in a product's life cycle in which sales fall rapidly. (9)

Decoding process The stage in the communication process in which signs are converted into concepts and ideas. (17).

Delphi technique A procedure in which experts create initial forecasts, submit them to the company for averaging, and have the results returned to them so that they can make individual refined forecasts. (8)

Demand curve A graph showing the relationship between price and quantity demanded. (21)

Demand-oriented pricing A pricing policy based on the level of demand for the product—resulting in a higher price for the product when demand is strong and a lower price when demand is weak. (21)

Demographic factors Individual characteristics such as age, sex, race, ethnicity, nationality, income, family, life cycle stage, and occupation. (6)

Demonstrations Sales promotion method manufacturers use temporarily to encourage trial use and purchase of the product or to show how the product works. (19)

Department stores Large retail organizations characterized by wide product mixes and organized into separate departments to facilitate marketing efforts and internal management. (15)

Depression A stage of the business cycle during which unemployment is extremely high, wages are very low, total disposable income is at a minimum, and consumers lack confidence in the economy. (2)

Depth interview A personal interview used to study motives. It has an open, informal atmosphere and may take several hours. (6)

Depth of product mix The average number of different products offered to buyers in a firm's product line. (9)

Derived demand A characteristic of industrial demand that arises because industrial demand stems from the demand for consumer products. (7)

Descriptive studies Research undertaken when marketers need to understand the characteristics of certain phenomena to solve a particular problem. (5)

Differentiated targeting strategy A targeting strategy in which an organization directs its marketing efforts at two or more segments by developing a marketing mix for each segment. (8)

Direct cost approach An approach to determining marketing costs in which cost analysis includes variable costs and traceable common costs but not nontraceable common costs. (23)

Direct marketing The use of the telephone and nonpersonal media to introduce products to consumers, who can then purchase them by mail or telephone. (15)

Direct ownership A situation in which a company owns subsidiaries or other facilities overseas. (4)

Direct-response marketing A type of marketing that occurs when a retailer advertises a product and makes it available through mail or telephone orders. (15)

Direct selling The marketing of products to ultimate consumers through face-to-face sales presentations at home or in the workplace. (15)

Discount stores Self-service, general merchandise stores offering brand name and private brand products at low prices. (15)

Discretionary income Disposable income that is available for spending and saving after an individual has purchased the basic necessities of food, clothing, and shelter. (2)

Disposable income After-tax income. (2)

Distinctive competency Something that an organization does extremely well, sometimes so well that it gives the company an advantage over its competition. (22)

Distribution The activities that make products available to customers when and where they want to purchase them. (13)

Distribution centers Large, centralized warehouses that receive goods from factories and suppliers, regroup the goods into orders, and ship the orders to customers quickly, with the focus on movement of goods rather than storage. (16)

Distribution variable The marketing mix variable in which marketing management attempts to make products available in the quantities desired, with adequate service, to a target market and to keep the total inventory, transportation, and storage costs as low as possible. (1)

Diversified growth A type of growth that occurs when new products are developed to be sold in new markets. (22)

Drop shippers Limited-service wholesalers that take title to products and negotiate sales but never actually take possession of products; also known as desk jobbers. (14)

Dual distribution The use of two or more channels to distribute the same product to the same target market. (13)

Dumping Selling products at unfairly low prices. (4)

Early adopters Individuals who choose new products carefully and are viewed by persons in the early majority, late majority, and laggard categories as being "the people to check with." (10)

Early majority Individuals who adopt a new product just prior to the average person; they are deliberate and cautious in trying new products. (10)

Economic forces Forces that determine the strength of a firm's competitive atmosphere and affect the impact of marketing activities because they determine the size and strength of demand for products. (2)

Economic order quantity (EOQ) The order size that minimizes the total cost of ordering and carrying inventory. (16)

Effective buying income (EBI) Income similar to disposable income consisting of salaries, wages, dividends, interest, profits, and rents, less federal, state, and local taxes. (2)

Electronic data interchange (EDI) A means of integrating order processing with production, inventory, accounting, and transportation. (16)

Empowerment Giving front-line employees the authority and responsibility to make marketing decisions without seeking the approval of their supervisors. (23)

Encoding *See* Coding process.

Environmental analysis The process of assessing and interpreting the information gathered through environmental scanning. (2)

Environmental scanning The process of collecting information about the forces in the marketing environment. (2)

Ethical issue An identifiable problem, situation, or opportunity requiring an individual or organization to choose from among several actions that must be evaluated as right or wrong, ethical or unethical. (3)

Evaluative criteria Objective and subjective characteristics that are important to a buyer and used to evaluate an evoked set. (6)

Evoked set A group of products that a buyer views as possible alternatives to purchase in a specific product category (6).

Exchange The provision or transfer of goods, services, or ideas in return for something of value. (1)

Exclusive dealing A situation in which a manufacturer forbids an intermediary to carry products of competing manufacturers. (13)

Exclusive distribution Using a single outlet in a fairly large geographic area to distribute a product. (13)

Executive judgment A sales forecasting method based on the intuition of one or more executives. (8)

Experience curve pricing A pricing approach in which a company fixes a low price that high-cost competitors cannot match and thus expands its market share; this approach is possible when a firm gains cumulative production experience and is able to reduce its manufacturing costs to a predictable rate through improved methods, materials, skills, and machinery. (21)

Experience qualities Qualities of services that can be assessed only after purchase and consumption (taste, satisfaction, courtesy, and the like). (12)

Expert forecasting survey Preparation of the sales forecast by experts, such as economists, management consultants, advertising executives, college professors, or other persons outside the firm. (8)

Exploratory studies Research conducted when more information is needed about a problem and the tentative hypothesis needs to be made more specific. (5)

Extended problem solving A type of consumer problem solving process used when unfamiliar, expensive, or infrequently bought products are purchased. (6)

External customers The individuals who patronize a business. (23)

External search The process of seeking information from sources other than one's memory. (6)

Facilitating agencies Organizations engaging in activities that support channel functions, such as transportation companies and financial institutions. (14)

Family branding A policy of branding all of a firm's products with the same name or at least part of the name. (11)

Family packaging A policy in an organization that all packages are to be similar or are to include one common element of the design. (11)

Feature article A form of publicity, up to three thousand words long, that is usually prepared for a specific publication. (18)

Federal Trade Commission (FTC) A government agency that regulates a variety of business practices and that curbs false advertising, misleading pricing, and deceptive packaging and labeling. (2)

Federal Trade Commission Act A 1914 law that established the Federal Trade Commission, which currently regulates the greatest number of marketing practices. (2)

Feedback The receiver's response to a decoded message. (17)

Field public warehouses Warehouses established by a public warehouse at the owner's inventory location. (16)

Fixed costs Costs that do not vary with changes in the number of units produced or sold; costs allocated on the basis of how money was actually spent, such as rent, salaries, office supplies, and utilities. (21) (23)

Fixed-order interval system An approach to inventory control in which products are ordered at predetermined intervals. (16)

F.O.B. (free-on-board) destination Part of a price quotation used to indicate who must pay shipping

charges. F.O.B. destination price means that the producer absorbs the costs of shipping the merchandise to the customer. (20)

F.O.B. (free-on-board) factory Part of a price quotation used to indicate who must pay shipping charges. F.O.B. factory price indicates the price of the merchandise at the factory, before it is loaded onto the carrier vehicle; the buyer must pay for shipping. (20)

Food brokers Intermediaries selling food and some general merchandise to merchant wholesalers, grocery chains, industrial buyers, and food processors. (14)

Franchise store A store owned by a franchisee who has contracted with the parent company to market specific products under conditions specified by the franchiser. (15)

Franchising An arrangement in which a supplier (franchiser) grants a dealer (franchisee) the right to sell products in exchange for some type of consideration. (15)

Free merchandise A sales promotion method aimed at retailers whereby free merchandise is offered to resellers that purchase a stated quantity of product. (19)

Free samples A new-product sales promotion technique that marketers use to stimulate trial of a product, to increase sales volume in early stages of the product's life cycle, or to obtain desirable distribution. (19)

Freight absorption pricing Pricing for a particular customer or geographical area whereby the seller absorbs all or part of the actual freight costs. (20)

Freight forwarders Businesses that consolidate shipments from several organizations into efficient lot sizes. (16)

Full-cost approach An approach to determining marketing costs in which cost analysis includes variable, traceable common costs, and nontraceable common costs. (23)

Full-service wholesalers Marketing intermediaries providing the widest range of wholesaling functions. (14)

Functional discount *See* Trade, or function, discount.

Functional middlemen Intermediaries that negotiate purchases and expedite sales for a fee but do not take title to products. (14)

Functional modification A change that affects a product's versatility, effectiveness, convenience, or safety, usually requiring the redesigning of one or more parts of the product. (10)

GATT *See* General Agreement on Tariffs and Trade.

General Agreement on Tariffs and Trade (GATT) International marketing negotiations to reduce worldwide tariffs and increase trade. (4)

General merchandise retailer A retail establishment that offers a variety of product lines that are stocked in depth. (15)

General merchandise wholesalers Full-service wholesalers with a wide product mix but limited depth within product lines. (14)

General publics The indirect consumers of the product of a nonbusiness organization; for instance, the general public of a university includes alumni, trustees, parents of students, and other groups. (12)

Generic brands Brands that indicate only the product category (such as *aluminum foil*), not the company name and other identifying terms. (11)

Geodemographic segmentation A method of market segmentation that divides people into Zip Code areas and smaller neighborhood units based on lifestyle information. (8)

Geographic pricing A form of pricing that involves reductions for transportation costs or other costs associated with the physical distance between the buyer and the seller. (20)

Globalization The development of marketing strategies as though the entire world (or regions of it) were a single entity. (4)

Good A tangible item. (9)

Government markets Markets made up of federal, state, county, and local governments, spending billions of dollars annually for goods and services to support their internal operations and to provide such products as defense, energy, and education. (7)

Green marketing Development, pricing, promotion, and distribution of products that do not harm the environment. (3)

Gross domestic product (GDP) Overall measure of a nation's economic standing in terms of the market value of the total output of goods and services produced in that nation for a given period of time. (4)

Group interview A method of uncovering people's motives relating to some issue, such as product usage, with an interviewer generating discussion on one or several topics among the six to twelve people in the group. (6)

Growth stage The product life cycle stage in which sales rise rapidly; profits reach a peak and then start to decline. (9)

Heterogeneity A condition resulting from the fact that services are typically performed by people; there may be variation from one service to another or variation in the service provided by a single individual from day to day and from customer to customer. (12)

Heterogeneous market A market made up of individuals with diverse product needs for products in a specific product class. (8)

Homogeneous market A type of market in which a large proportion of customers have similar needs for a product. (8)

Horizontal channel integration Combining institutions at the same level of operation under one management. (13)

Hypermarkets Stores that combine supermarket and discount store shopping in one location. (15)

Hypothesis An informed guess or assumption about a certain problem or set of circumstances. (5)

Ideas Concepts, philosophies, images, or issues. (9)

Idea generation The search by businesses and other organizations for product ideas that help them achieve their objectives. (10)

Illustrations Photographs, drawings, graphs, charts, and tables used to encourage an audience to read or watch an advertisement. (18)

Impulse buying An unplanned buying behavior that involves a powerful, persistent urge to buy something immediately. (6)

Income The amount of money received through wages, rents, investments, pensions, and subsidy payments for a given period. (2)

Independent store A single retail outlet owned by an individual, partnership, or corporation. (15)

Individual branding A branding policy in which each product is named differently. (11)

Industrial distributor An independent business organization that takes title to industrial products and carries inventories. (13)

Inelastic demand A type of demand in which a price increase or decrease will not significantly affect the quantity demanded. (7)

Information inputs Sensations received through sense organs. (6)

Innovators The first consumers to adopt a new product; they enjoy trying new products and tend to be venturesome. (10)

Input-output data A type of information, sometimes used in conjunction with the Standard Industrial Classification system, that is based on the assumption that the output or sales of one industry are the input or purchases of other industries. (7)

Inseparability A condition in which the consumer frequently is directly involved in the production process because services normally are produced at the same time that they are consumed. (12)

Institutional advertising A form of advertising promoting organizational images, ideas, and political issues. (18)

Institutional markets Markets that consist of organizations with charitable, educational, community, or other nonbusiness goals. (7)

Intangibility A characteristic of services; because services are performances, they cannot be seen, touched, tasted, or smelled, nor can they be possessed. (12)

Integrated marketing communication The coordination of promotional elements and other marketing efforts. (17)

Intended strategy In implementing marketing strategies, the strategy that the organization decided on during the planning phase and wants to use. (23)

Intensive distribution Using all available outlets to distribute a product. (13)

Intensive growth The type of growth that can occur when current products and current markets have the potential for increasing sales. (22)

Intermodal transportation Combining and coordinating two or more modes of transportation. (16)

Internal customers The employees who work for a company. (23)

Internal marketing A management philosophy that coordinates internal exchanges between the organization and its employees to better achieve successful external exchanges between the organization and its customers. (23)

Internal search An aspect of an information search in which buyers first search their memory for information about products that might solve their problem. (6)

International marketing Developing and performing marketing activities across national boundaries. (4)

Introduction stage The stage in a product's life cycle beginning at a product's first appearance in the marketplace, when sales are zero and profits are negative. (9)

Joint demand A characteristic of industrial demand that occurs when two or more items are used in combination to produce a product. (7)

Joint venture A partnership between a domestic firm and a foreign firm and/or government. (4)

Just-in-time (JIT) Making products and materials arrive just as they are needed for use in production or for resale. (16)

Kinesic communication Commonly known as body language, this type of interpersonal communication occurs in face-to-face selling situations when the salesperson and customers move their heads, eyes, arms, hands, legs, and torsos. (17)

Labeling Providing identifying, promotional, or other information on package labels. (11)

Laggards The last consumers to adopt a new product; they are oriented toward the past and suspicious of new products. (10)

Late majority People who are quite skeptical of new products; they eventually adopt new products because of economic necessity or social pressure. (10)

Layout The physical arrangement of the illustration, headline, subheadline, body copy, and signature of an advertisement. (18)

Learning A change in an individual's behavior caused by information and experience. (6)

Legal forces Forces that arise from the legislation and interpretation of laws; these laws, enacted by government units, restrain and control marketing decisions and activities. (2)

Level of involvement The intensity of interest and importance placed on a product by an individual. (6)

Level of quality The amount of quality a product possesses. (9)

Licensing An alternative to direct investment that requires a licensee to pay commissions or royalties on sales or supplies used in manufacturing. (4)

Lifestyle An individual's pattern of living expressed through activities, interests, and opinions. (6)

Limited-line wholesalers Full-service wholesalers that carry only a few product lines but offer an extensive assortment of products within those lines. (14)

Limited problem solving A type of consumer problem-solving process employed when buying products occasionally and when information about an unfamiliar brand in a familiar product category is needed. (6)

Limited-service wholesalers Intermediaries that provide some services and specialize in a few functions. (14)

Line extension A product that is closely related to existing products in the line but meets different customer needs. (10)

Line family branding A branding policy in which an organization uses family branding only for products within a line, not for all its products. (11)

Long-range plans Plans that cover more than five years. (22)

Mail-order wholesalers Limited-service wholesalers that sell products through catalogs. (14)

Mail surveys Questionnaires sent to respondents who are encouraged to complete and return them. (5)

Major equipment A category of industrial products that includes large tools and machines used for production purposes. (9)

Manufacturer brands Brands initiated by a producer; make it possible for a producer to be identified with its product at the point of purchase. (11)

Manufacturers' agents Independent middlemen who represent more than one seller and offer complete product lines. (14)

Marginal cost (MC) The cost associated with producing one more unit of a product. (21)

Marginal revenue (MR) The change in total revenue that occurs after an additional unit of a product is sold. (21)

Market An aggregate of individuals and/or organizations that have needs for products in a product class and have the ability, willingness, and authority to purchase such products. (6) (8)

Market density The number of potential customers within a unit of land area, such as a square mile. (8)

Marketing The process of creating, distributing, promoting, and pricing goods, services, and ideas to facilitate satisfying exchange relationships in a dynamic environment. (1)

Marketing audit A systematic examination of the marketing group's objectives, strategies, organization, and performance. (23)

Marketing channel A group of individuals and organizations that directs the flow of products to customers; also called channel of distribution or distribution channel. (13)

Marketing concept A managerial philosophy that an organization should try to satisfy customers' needs through a coordinated set of activities that also allows the organization to achieve its goals. (1)

Marketing control process A process that consists of establishing performance standards, evaluating actual performance by comparing it with established standards, and reducing the differences between desired and actual performance. (23)

Marketing cost analysis Breaking down and classifying costs to determine which are associated with specific marketing activities. (23)

Marketing environment The competitive, economic, political, legal and regulatory, technological, and sociocultural forces that surround the buyer and affect the marketing mix. (1)

Marketing ethics Principles that define acceptable conduct in marketing. (3)

Marketing implementation The process of putting marketing strategies into action. (22)

Marketing information system (MIS) A framework for the management and structuring of information gathered regularly from sources inside and outside an organization. (5)

Marketing intermediary A middleman linking producers to other middlemen or ultimate consumers through contractual arrangements or through the purchase and resale of products. (13)

Marketing management The process of planning, organizing, implementing, and controlling marketing activities to facilitate exchanges effectively and efficiently. (1)

Marketing mix Four marketing activities—production, distribution, promotion, and pricing—that a firm can control to meet the needs of customers within its target market. (1)

Marketing objective A statement of what is to be accomplished through marketing activities. (22)

Marketing-oriented organization An organization that concentrates on discovering what buyers want and providing it in such a way that the organization achieves its objectives. (23)

Marketing plan A written document that specifies an organization's resources, objectives, marketing strategy, and implementation and control efforts planned for use in marketing a specific product or product group. (1)

Marketing planning A systematic process of assessing marketing opportunities and resources, determining marketing objectives, defining marketing strategies, and establishing guidelines for implementation and control of the marketing program. (22)

Marketing planning cycle A circular process using feedback to coordinate and synchronize all stages of the marketing planning process. (22)

Marketing program A set of marketing strategies that are implemented and used at the same time. (22)

Marketing research The systematic design, collection, interpretation, and reporting of information to help marketers solve specific marketing problems or take advantage of marketing opportunities. (5)

Marketing strategy A plan of action for developing, distributing, promoting, and pricing products that meet the needs of specific customers. (1)

Market manager A person responsible for the marketing activities that are necessary to serve a particular group or class of customers. (9)

Market opportunity A combination of circumstances and timing that permits an organization to take action to reach a particular target market. (1)

Market orientation The organizationwide generation of market intelligence pertaining to current and future customer needs, dissemination of the intelligence across departments, and organizationwide responsiveness to it. (1)

Market potential The total amount of a product for all firms in an industry that customers will purchase within a specified period at a specific level of industry-wide marketing activity. (8)

Market requirements Relate to customers' needs or desired benefits. (22)

Market segment A group of individuals, groups, or organizations sharing one or more similar characteristics that make them have relatively similar product needs. (8)

Market segmentation The process of dividing a total market into groups of people or organizations with relatively similar product needs, to enable marketers to design a marketing mix that more precisely matches the needs of consumers in a selected segment. (8)

Market share A firm's sales in relation to total industry sales, expressed as a decimal or percentage. (20)

Market test A stage of new-product development that involves making a product available to buyers in one or more test areas and measuring purchases and consumer responses to promotion, price, and distribution efforts. (8)

Markup pricing A pricing method where the price is derived by adding a predetermined percentage of the cost to the cost of the product. (21)

Materials handling Physical handling of products. (16)

Maturity stage A stage in the product life cycle in which the sales curve peaks and starts to decline as profits continue to decline. (9)

Media plan A plan that sets forth the exact media vehicles to be used for advertisements and the dates and times that the advertisements are to appear. (18)

Medium of transmission That which carries the coded message from the source to the receiver or audience; examples include ink on paper and air wave vibrations produced by vocal cords. (17)

Medium-range plans Plans that encompass two to five years. (22)

Megacarriers Freight transportation companies providing several methods of shipment. (16)

Merchandise allowance A sales promotion method aimed at retailers; it consists of a manufacturer's agreement to pay resellers certain amounts of money for providing special promotional efforts, such as setting up and maintaining a display. (19)

Merchant wholesalers Independently owned businesses that take title to goods, assume ownership risks, and buy and resell products to industrial or retail customers. (14)

Micromarketing An approach to market segmentation in which organizations focus precise marketing efforts on very small geographic markets. (8)

Missionary salesperson A support salesperson, usually employed by a manufacturer, who assists the producer's customers in selling to their own customers. (19)

Mission statement A long-term view, or vision, of what the organization wants to become. (22)

Modified rebuy purchase A type of industrial purchase in which a new-task purchase is changed the second or third time, or the requirements associated with a straight-rebuy purchase are modified. (7)

Money refunds Sales promotion techniques in which the producer mails a consumer a specific amount of money when proof of purchase is established. (19)

Monopolistic competition A market structure in which a firm has many potential competitors and, in order to compete, the firm tries to develop a differential marketing strategy to establish its own market share. (2)

Monopoly A market structure in which an organization offers a product that has no close substitutes, making the organization the sole source of supply. (2)

Motive An internal energizing force that directs a person's behavior toward satisfying needs or achieving goals. (6)

MRO items An alternative term for supplies; supplies can be divided into Maintenance, Repair, and Operating (or overhaul) items. (9)

Multinational enterprise A company with operations or subsidiaries in many countries. (4)

Multiple sourcing An organization's decision to use several suppliers. (7)

NAFTA *See* North American Free Trade Agreement.

National Advertising Review Board (NARB) A self-regulatory unit that considers cases in which an advertiser challenges issues raised by the National Advertising Division (an arm of the Council of Better Business Bureaus) about an advertisement. (2)

Neighborhood shopping centers Shopping centers that usually consist of several small convenience and specialty stores and serve consumers living within ten minutes' driving time from the center. (15)

New product Any product that a given firm has not marketed previously. (10)

New-product development process A process consisting of seven phases: idea generation, screening, concept testing, business analysis, product development, test-marketing, and commercialization. (10)

News release A form of publicity that is usually a single page of typewritten copy containing fewer than three hundred words. (18)

New-task purchase A type of industrial purchase in which an organization is making an initial purchase of an item to be used to perform a new job or to solve a new problem. (7)

Noise Anything that reduces the clarity and accuracy of communication. (17)

Noncumulative discount A one-time price reduction based on the number of units purchased, the size of the order, or the product combination purchased. (20)

Nonprice competition A policy in which a seller elects not to focus on price and instead emphasizes distinctive product features, service, product quality, promotion, packaging, or other factors to distinguish its product from competing brands. (20)

Nonprofit marketing Marketing activities conducted by individuals and organizations to achieve some goal other than ordinary business goals such as profit, market share, or return on investment. (12)

Nonstore retailing The selling of products outside the confines of a retail facility. (15)

Nontraceable common costs Costs that cannot be assigned to any specific function according to any logical criteria and thus are assignable only on an arbitrary basis. (23)

North American Free Trade Agreement (NAFTA) An alliance that merges Canada, the United States, and Mexico into a single market. (4)

Objective-and-task approach An approach to determining the advertising appropriation: marketers determine the objectives a campaign is to achieve and then ascertain the tasks required to accomplish those objectives; the costs of all tasks are added to ascertain the total appropriation. (18)

Observation methods Research methods in which researchers record respondents' overt behavior, taking note of physical conditions and events. (5)

Odd-even pricing A type of psychological pricing that assumes that more of a product will be sold at $99.99 than at $100.00, indicating that an odd price is more appealing than an even price to customers. (21)

Off-peak demand The time when consumers do not want to use the service. (12)

Off-price retailers Stores that buy manufacturers' seconds, overruns, returns, and off-season merchandise for resale to consumers at deep discounts. (15)

Oligopoly A competitive structure in which a few sellers control the supply of a large proportion of a product. (2)

Online retailing Makes products available between buyers and sellers through computer connections. (15)

Opinion leader The member of a reference group who provides information about a specific sphere of interest to reference group participants seeking information. (6)

Opportunities Favorable conditions in the environment that could produce rewards for the organization if acted upon properly. (22)

Opportunity cost The value of the benefit that is given up by selecting one alternative rather than another. (12)

Order getter A type of salesperson who increases the firm's sales by selling to new customers and by increasing sales to present customers. (19)

Order lead time The average time lapse between placing an order and receiving it. (16)

Order processing The receipt and transmission of sales order information in the physical distribution process. (16)

Order taker A type of salesperson who primarily seeks repeat sales. (19)

Organizational buying behavior The purchase behavior of producers, government units, institutions, and resellers; also called industrial buying behavior. (7)

Organizational, or **corporate, culture** A set of values, beliefs, goals, norms, and rituals that members or employees of an organization share. (3)

Organizational, or **industrial, market** Individuals or groups that purchase a specific kind of product for one of three purposes: resale, direct use in producing other products, or use in general daily operations. (7)

Organizational products Products bought to use in a firm's operations, to resell, or to make other products. (9)

Organizational services Intangible products that an organization uses in its operations, such as financial products or legal services. (9)

Patronage motives Motives that influence where a person purchases products on a regular basis. (6)

Peak demand A point in time when consumers want to maximize the use of service activities. (12)

Penetration pricing A lowering of prices designed to penetrate the market and thus quickly produce a larger unit sales volume. (21)

Percent-of-sales approach A method for establishing the advertising appropriation whereby marketers simply multiply a firm's past sales, forecasted sales, or a combination of the two by a standard percentage based on both what the firm traditionally has spent on advertising and what the industry averages. (18)

Perception The process by which an individual selects, organizes, and interprets information inputs to create a meaningful picture of the world. (6)

Performance standard An expected level of performance against which actual performance can be compared. (23)

Perishability A condition where, because of simultaneous production and consumption, unused capacity to produce services in one time period cannot be stockpiled or inventoried for future time periods. (12)

Personal factors Factors influencing the consumer buying decision process that are unique to a particular individual. (6)

Personal interview survey A face-to-face interview that allows in-depth interviewing, probing, follow-up questions, or psychological tests. (5)

Personality A set of internal traits and distinctive behavioral tendencies that result in consistent patterns of behavior in certain situations. (6)

Personal selling Personal, paid communication that attempts to inform customers and persuade them to purchase products in an exchange situation. (19)

Physical distribution The activities used to move products from producers to consumers and other end users. (16)

Pioneer advertising A type of advertising that stimulates demand for a product by informing people about the product's features, uses, and benefits. (18)

Pioneer promotion A type of promotion that informs potential customers about a product, what it is, what it does, how it can be used, and where it can be purchased. (17)

Point-of-purchase (P-O-P) materials A sales promotion method that uses such items as outside signs, window displays, and display racks to attract attention, to inform customers, and to encourage retailers to carry particular products. (19)

Political forces Forces that strongly influence the economic and political stability of a country not only through decisions that affect domestic matters but through their authority to negotiate trade agreements and to determine foreign policy. (2)

Population All elements, units, or individuals that are of interest to researchers for a specific study. (5)

Portfolio retailing A situation in which one company operates multiple chains of stores. (15)

Posttest An evaluation of advertising effectiveness after the campaign. (18)

Premium, or **push, money** Extra compensation to salespeople for pushing a line of goods. (19)

Premiums Items that are offered free or at a minimum cost as a bonus for purchasing a product. (19)

Press conference A meeting used to announce major news events. (18)

Prestige pricing Setting prices at a high level to facilitate a prestige or quality image. (21)

Prestige-sensitive A characteristic of buyers who purchase products that signify prominence and status. (20)

Pretest Evaluation of an advertisement before it is actually used. (18)

Price The value that is exchanged for products in a marketing transaction. (20)

Price competition A policy whereby a marketer emphasizes price as an issue and matches or beats the prices of competitors. (20)

Price-conscious A characteristic of buyers who strive to pay low prices. (20)

Price differentiation A demand-oriented pricing method whereby a firm uses more than one price in the marketing of a specific product; differentiation of prices can be based on several dimensions, such as type of customers, type of distribution used, or the time of the purchase. (21)

Price discrimination A policy of charging some buyers lower prices than other buyers, which gives those paying less a competitive advantage. (20)

Price elasticity of demand A measure of the sensitivity of demand to changes in price. (21)

Price leaders Products sold at less than cost to increase sales of regular merchandise. (21)

Price lining A form of psychological pricing in which an organization sets a limited number of prices for selected lines of products. (21)

Price skimming Charging the highest possible price that buyers who most desire the product will pay. (21)

Price variable A marketing mix variable that relates to decisions and actions associated with establishing pricing objectives and policies and determining product prices. (1)

Pricing method A mechanical procedure for setting prices on a regular basis. (21)

Pricing objectives Overall goals that describe the role of price in an organization's long-range plans. (20)

Pricing policy A guiding philosophy or course of action designed to influence and determine pricing decisions. (21)

Primary data Data observed and recorded or collected directly from respondents. (5)

Primary demand Demand for a product category rather than for a specific brand of product. (17)

Private brand *See* Private distributor brand.

Private distributor brand A brand that is initiated and owned by a reseller; also called private brand, store brand, or dealer brand. (11)

Private warehouses Facilities operated by companies for storing and shipping their own products. (16)

Problem definition The first step in the research process toward finding a solution or launching a research study; the researcher thinks about the best ways to discover the nature and boundaries of a problem or opportunity. (5)

Process materials Materials used directly in the production of other products; unlike component parts, they are not readily identifiable. (9)

Procompetitive legislation Laws enacted to preserve competition. (2)

Producer markets Markets consisting of individuals and business organizations that purchase products for the purpose of making a profit by using them in their operations. (7)

Product A good, service, and/or idea received in an exchange. It is a complexity of tangible and intangible attributes, including functional, social, and psychological utilities or benefits. (1) (9)

Product adoption process The five-stage process of buyer acceptance of a product: awareness, interest, evaluation, trial, and adoption. (10)

Product advertising Advertising that promotes the uses, features, and benefits of products. (18)

Product design How a product is conceived, planned, and produced. (9)

Product development The phase in which the firm finds out if producing the product is feasible and cost-effective. (10)

Product differentiation The process of creating and designing products so that consumers perceive them as different from competing products. (9)

Product elimination The process of deleting a product from the product mix when it no longer satisfies a sufficient number of customers. (10)

Product features Specific design characteristics allowing a product to perform certain tasks. (9)

Product item A specific version of a product that can be designated as a distinct offering among an organization's products. (9)

Product life cycle The course of product development, consisting of four major stages: introduction, growth, maturity, and decline. As a product moves through these stages, the strategies relating to competition, pricing, promotion, distribution, and market information must be evaluated and possibly changed. (9)

Product line A group of closely related products that are considered a unit because of marketing, technical, or end-use considerations. (9)

Product manager A person who holds a staff position in a multiproduct company and is responsible for a product, a product line, or several distinct products that are considered an interrelated group. (9)

Product mix The composite of products that an organization makes available to customers. (9)

Product mix depth *See* Depth (of product mix).

Product mix width *See* Width (of product mix).

Product modification The changing of one or more of a product's characteristics. (10)

Product-portfolio analysis A strategic planning approach based on the philosophy that a product's market growth rate and its relative market share are important considerations in determining its marketing strategy. (22)

Product positioning The decisions and activities that are directed toward trying to create and maintain the firm's intended product concept in customers' minds. (9)

Product variable That aspect of the marketing mix dealing with researching customers' product wants and planning the product to achieve the desired product characteristics. (1)

Professional pricing Pricing used by persons who have great skills or experience in a particular field or activity, indicating that a price should not relate directly to the time and involvement in a specific case; rather, a standard fee is charged regardless of the problems involved in performing the job. (21)

Projective techniques Tests in which subjects are asked to perform specific tasks for particular purposes while in fact they are being evaluated for other purposes; assumes that subjects will unconsciously "project" their motives as they perform the tasks. (6)

Promotion The communication with individuals, groups, or organizations to directly or indirectly facilitate exchanges by influencing audience members to accept an organization's products. (17)

Promotion mix The specific combination of promotional methods that an organization uses for a particular product. (17)

Promotion variable A marketing mix variable used to inform individuals or groups about an organization and its products. (1)

Prospecting Developing a list of potential customers for personal selling purposes. (19)

Prosperity A stage of the business cycle characterized by low unemployment and relatively high total income, which together cause buying power to be high (provided the inflation rate stays low). (2)

Proxemic communication A subtle form of interpersonal communication used in face-to-face interactions when either party varies the physical distance that separates them. (17)

Psychological factors Factors that operate within individuals to partially determine their general behavior and thus influence their behavior as consumers. (6)

Psychological pricing A pricing method designed to encourage purchases that are based on emotional reactions rather than rational responses. (21)

Publicity Nonpersonal communication in news story form, regarding an organization and/or its products, that is transmitted through a mass medium at no charge. (18)

Public relations A broad set of communication activities used to create and maintain favorable relations between the organization and its public, such as customers, employees, stockholders, government officials, and society in general. (18)

Public warehouses Organizations that rent storage and related physical distribution facilities. (16)

Pull policy Promotion of a product directly to consumers with the intention of developing strong consumer demand. (17)

Purchasing power *See* Buying power.

Pure competition A market structure characterized by an extremely large number of sellers, none of them strong enough to significantly influence price or supply. (2)

Push policy The promotion of a product only to the next institution down the marketing channel. (17)

Quality The overall characteristics of a product that allow it to perform as expected in satisfying customer needs. (9)

Quality modification A change that relates to a product's dependability and durability and is generally executed by alterations in the materials or production process used. (10)

Quantity discount Deductions from list price that reflect the economies of purchasing in large quantities. (20)

Quota sampling Nonprobability sampling in which the final choice of respondents is left to the interviewers. (5)

Rack jobbers Full service specialty-line wholesalers that own and maintain display racks in stores. (14)

Random factor analysis A method of predicting sales whereby an attempt is made to attribute erratic sales variations to random, nonrecurrent events, such as a regional power failure or a natural disaster. (8)

Random sampling A type of sampling in which all the units in a population have an equal chance of appearing in the sample. (5)

Raw materials Basic materials that become part of a physical product; obtained from mines, farms, forests, oceans, and recycled solid wastes. (9)

Realized strategy In implementing marketing strategies, the strategy that actually takes place. (23)

Rebates Sales promotion techniques in which the producer mails a consumer a specified amount of money for making a single purchase. (19)

Receiver The individual, group, or organization that decodes a coded message. (17)

Recession A stage of the business cycle during which unemployment rises and total buying power declines, stifling both consumer and business spending. (2)

Reciprocity A practice unique to organizational sales in which two organizations agree to buy from each other. (7)

Recognition test A posttest method of evaluating the effectiveness of advertising; individual respondents are shown the actual advertisement and asked whether they recognize it. (18)

Recovery A stage of the business cycle during which the economy moves from recession toward prosperity. (2)

Recruiting A process by which the sales manager develops a list of applicants for sales positions. (19)

Reference group Any group that positively or negatively affects a person's values, attitudes, or behavior. (6)

Regional issues Versions of a magazine that differ across geographic regions and in which a publisher can vary the advertisements and editorial content. (18)

Regional shopping centers A type of shopping center that usually has the largest department stores, the widest product mix, and the deepest product lines of all shopping centers in an area. (15)

Regression analysis A method of predicting sales whereby a forecaster attempts to find a relationship between past sales and one or more independent variables, such as population or income. (8)

Regulatory forces Forces arising from regulatory units at all levels of government; these units create and enforce numerous regulations that affect marketing decisions. (2)

Reinforcement advertising An advertisement attempting to assure current users that they have made the right choice and telling them how to get the most satisfaction from the product. (18)

Relationship marketing Establishing long-term, mutually satisfying buyer–seller relationships. (1)

Reliability A condition existing when use of a research technique produces almost identical results in successive repeated trials. (5)

Reminder advertising Advertising used to remind consumers that an established brand is still around and that it has certain uses, characteristics, and benefits. (18)

Reorder point The inventory level that signals the need to place a new order. (16)

Reseller markets Markets consisting of intermediaries, such as wholesalers and retailers, that buy finished goods for profit. (7)

Retailer An organization that purchases products for the purpose of reselling them to ultimate consumers. (15)

Retailing Transactions in which the buyer intends to consume the product through personal, family, or household use. (15)

Retail positioning Identifying an unserved or underserved market niche, or segment, and serving it through a strategy that distinguishes the retailer from others in the minds of persons in that segment. (15)

Reverse marketing A process through which an organizational buyer develops a relationship with a supplier that shapes the products, services, operations, and capabilities of the supplier to better satisfy the buyer's requirements. (7)

Robinson-Patman Act A 1936 law prohibiting price discrimination that decreases competition and also prohibiting provision of services or facilities to purchasers on terms not offered equally to all purchasers. (2)

Role A set of actions and activities that a person in a particular position is supposed to perform, based on the expectations of both the individual and the persons surrounding the individual. (6)

Routinized response behavior A type of consumer problem solving process used when buying frequently purchased, low-cost items that require very little search and decision effort. (6)

Safety stock The amount of extra stock a firm keeps to guard against stockouts. (16)

Sales analysis The use of sales figures to evaluate a firm's current performance. (23)

Sales branches Manufacturer-owned middlemen selling products and providing support services to the manufacturer's sales force. (14)

Sales contest A sales promotion method used to motivate distributors, retailers, and sales personnel through the recognition of outstanding achievements. (19)

Sales-force forecasting survey Estimation by members of a firm's sales force of the anticipated sales in their territories for a specified period. (8)

Sales forecast The amount of a product a company expects to sell during a specific period at a specified level of marketing activities. (8)

Sales offices Manufacturer-owned operations that provide services normally associated with agents. (14)

Sales promotion An activity and/or material that acts as a direct inducement to resellers, salespersons, or consumers; it offers added value or incentive to buy or sell the product. (19)

Sample A limited number of units that represents the characteristics of a total population. (5)

Sampling Selecting representative units from a total population. (5)

Scan-back allowance Reward given by manufacturers to retailers based on the number of pieces scanned. (19)

Scrambled merchandising The addition of unrelated products and product lines to an existing product mix, particularly fast-moving items that can be sold in large volume. (15)

Screening A stage in the product development process in which the ideas that do not match organizational objectives are rejected and those with the greatest potential are selected for further development. (10)

Search qualities Tangible attributes that can be viewed prior to purchase. (12)

Seasonal analysis A method of predicting sales whereby an analyst studies daily, weekly, or monthly sales figures to evaluate the degree to which seasonal factors, such as climate and holiday activities, influence sales. (8)

Seasonal discount A price reduction that sellers give buyers who purchase goods or services out of season; these discounts allow the seller to maintain steadier production during the year. (20)

Secondary data Data compiled inside or outside the organization for some purpose other than the current investigation. (5)

Segmentation variables Dimensions or characteristics of individuals, groups, or organizations that are used to divide a market into segments. (8)

Selective demand Demand for a specific brand. (17)

Selective distortion The changing or twisting of currently received information that occurs when a person receives information inconsistent with his or her feelings or beliefs. (6)

Selective distribution Using only some available outlets to distribute a product. (13)

Selective exposure The process of selecting some inputs to be exposed to our awareness while ignoring many others. (6)

Selective retention Remembering information inputs that support personal feelings and beliefs and forgetting inputs that do not. (6)

Self-concept One's own perception or view of oneself. (6)

Selling agents Middlemen marketing a whole product line or a manufacturer's entire output. (14)

Service An intangible result of the application of human and mechanical efforts to people or objects. (9) (12)

Service heterogeneity *See* Heterogeneity.

Service inseparability *See* Inseparability.

Service intangibility *See* Intangibility.

Service perishability *See* Perishability.

Service quality Customers' perceptions of how well a service meets or exceeds their expectations. (12)

Sherman Antitrust Act Legislation passed in 1890 to prevent businesses from restraining trade and monopolizing markets. (2)

Shopping products Items for which buyers are willing to put forth considerable effort in planning and making the purchase. (9)

Short-range plans Plans that cover a period of one year or less. (22)

Significant others Superiors, peers, and subordinates in an organization who influence the ethical decision-making process. (3)

Single-source data Information provided by a single firm on household demographics, purchases, television viewing behavior, and responses to promotions like coupons and free samples. (5)

Situational factors Influences resulting from circumstances, time, and location that affect the consumer buying decision process. (6)

Social class An open aggregate of people with similar social ranking. (6)

Social factors The forces that other people exert on one's buying behavior. (6)

Social responsibility An organization's obligation to maximize its positive impact and minimize its negative impact on society. (3)

Sociocultural forces The influences in a society and its culture(s) that change people's attitudes, beliefs, norms, customs, and lifestyles. (2)

Socioeconomic factors *See* Demographic factors.

Sole sourcing An organization's decision to use only one supplier. (7)

Source A person, group, or organization with a meaning that it intends and attempts to share with a receiver or an audience. (17)

Special-event pricing Advertised sales or price cutting to increase revenue or lower costs. (21)

Specialty-line wholesalers Full-service wholesalers that carry only a single product line or a few items within a product line. (14)

Specialty products Items that possess one or more unique characteristics that a significant group of buyers is willing to expend considerable purchasing efforts to obtain. (9)

Standard Industrial Classification (SIC) System A system developed by the federal government for classifying industrial organizations, based on what the firm primarily produces; also classifies selected economic characteristics of commercial, financial, and service organizations; uses code numbers to classify firms in different industries. (7)

Statistical interpretation An interpretation that focuses on what is typical or what deviates from the average, and so indicates how widely respondents vary and how they are distributed in relation to the variable being measured. (5)

Stockout A shortage of a product resulting from carrying too few products in inventory. (16)

Store brand *See* Private distributor brand.

Storyboard A blueprint used by technical personnel to produce a television commercial; combines the copy with the visual material to show the sequence of major scenes in the commercial. (18)

Straight commission compensation plan A plan according to which a salesperson's compensation is determined solely by the amount of his or her sales for a given time period. (19)

Straight rebuy purchase A type of industrial purchase in which a buyer purchases the same products routinely under approximately the same terms of sale. (7)

Straight salary compensation plan A plan according to which salespeople are paid a specified amount per time period. (19)

Strategic alliances Partnerships formed to create competitive advantage on a worldwide basis. (4)

Strategic business unit (SBU) A division, product line, or other profit center within a parent company that sells a distinct set of products and/or services to an identifiable group of customers and competes against a well-defined set of competitors. (22)

Strategic channel alliance A marketing channel that distributes the products of one organization through the marketing channels of another organization. (13)

Strategic market plan An outline of the methods and resources required to achieve an organization's goals within a specific target market. (22)

Strategic market planning A process that yields a marketing strategy that is the framework for a marketing plan. (22)

Strategic windows Temporary periods of optimum fit between the key requirements of a market and the particular capabilities of a firm competing in that market. (22)

Stratified sampling A type of sampling in which the population of interest is divided into groups according to a common characteristic or attribute; then a probability sample is conducted within each group. (5)

Strengths Competitive advantages or distinctive competencies that give the firm an advantage in meeting the needs of its target markets. (22)

Styling The physical appearance of the product. (9)

Subculture A group of individuals who have similar values and behavior patterns within the group and differ from people in other groups; usually based on geographic regions or human characteristics, such as age or ethnic background. (6)

Suboptimization A situation in which managers or individual distribution functions take cost-reducing actions that increase the costs of other distribution functions. (16)

Superficial discounting A deceptive markdown sometimes called "was-is pricing" (the firm never intended to sell at the higher price); this is fictitious comparative pricing. (21)

Supermarkets Large, self-service stores that carry complete lines of food products, and some nonfood products. (15)

Superstores Giant retail outlets that carry food and nonfood products found in supermarkets, as well as most routinely purchased consumer products. (15)

Supplies *See* Consumable supplies.

Supply chain management Long-term partnerships among marketing channel members working together to reduce inefficiencies, costs, and redundancies in order to satisfy customers. (13)

Support personnel Members of the sales staff who facilitate selling but usually are not involved only with making sales. (19)

Survey methods Data-gathering methods that include interviews by mail, telephone, E-mail, and personal interviews. (5)

Sustainable competitive advantage A competitive advantage that cannot be copied by the competition. (22)

Tactile communication Interpersonal communication through touching. (17)

Target audience The group of people at which advertisements are aimed. (18)

Target market A specific group of buyers on whose needs and wants a company focuses its marketing efforts. (1)

Target public A group of people who have an interest in or a concern about an organization, a product, or a social cause. (12)

Technical salespersons Support salespersons who direct efforts toward the organization's current customers by providing technical assistance in system design, product application, product characteristics, or installation. (19)

Technological forces Forces that influence marketing decisions and activities because they affect people's lifestyles and standards of living, influence their desire for products and their reaction to marketing mixes, and have a direct impact on maintaining a marketing mix by influencing all its variables. (2)

Technology The application of knowledge and tools to solve problems and perform tasks more efficiently. (2)

Technology assessment A procedure for anticipating the effects of new products and processes on a firm's operation, other business organizations, and society. (2)

Telemarketing The performance of marketing-related activities by telephone. (15)

Telephone surveys The soliciting of respondents' answers to a questionnaire over the telephone, with the answers being written down by the interviewer. (5)

Television home shopping A form of selling in which products are presented to television viewers who buy products by calling a toll-free number and pay with credit cards. (15)

Test marketing A limited introduction of a product in areas chosen to represent the intended market to determine probable buyers' reactions to various parts of a marketing mix. (10)

Threats Conditions or barriers that may prevent a firm from reaching its marketing plan objectives. (22)

Time series analysis A forecasting method that uses the firm's historical sales data to discover patterns in the firm's sales volume over time. (8)

Total cost The sum of average fixed and average variable costs times the quantity produced. (21)

Total quality management (TQM) A philosophy that uniform commitment to quality in all areas of the organization will promote a culture that meets customers' perceptions of quality. (23)

Traceable common costs Costs that can be allocated indirectly, using one or several criteria, to the functions that they support. (23)

Trade, or **function, discount** A reduction off the list price a producer gives to an intermediary for performing certain functions. (20)

Trademark A legal designation indicating that the owner has exclusive use of a brand or part of a brand and that others are prohibited by law from using it. (11)

Trade marts Facilities that firms rent to exhibit products year-round. (14)

Trade name The legal name of an organization rather than the name of a specific product. (11)

Trade salesperson A type of salesperson not strictly classified as support personnel because he or she takes orders as well. (19)

Trade sales promotion methods A category of sales promotion techniques that stimulate wholesalers and retailers to carry a producer's products and to market these products more aggressively. (19)

Trade shows Industry exhibitions offering both selling and nonselling benefits. (14)

Trading company A company that links buyers and sellers in different countries. (4)

Traditional specialty retailers Stores that carry a narrow product mix with deep product lines. (15)

Transfer pricing The type of pricing used when one unit in a company sells a product to another unit; the price is determined by one of the following methods: actual full cost, standard full cost, cost plus investment, or market-based cost. (20)

Transportation Moving a product from where it is made to where it is purchased and used, thus adding time and place utility to the product. (16)

Transportation modes The means of moving goods from one location to another. (16)

Trend analysis An analysis that focuses on aggregate sales data, such as the company's annual sales figures, over a period of many years to determine whether annual sales are generally rising, falling, or staying about the same. (8)

Truck wholesalers Limited-service wholesalers that transport products directly to customers for inspection and selection; also known as truck jobbers or wagon jobbers. (14)

Tying agreement A practice requiring a channel member to buy other products from a supplier besides the one it wants. (13)

Unaided recall test A posttest method of evaluating the effectiveness of advertising; subjects are asked to identify advertisements that they have seen recently but are not shown any clues to help them remember. (18)

Undifferentiated targeting strategy A targeting strategy in which an organization defines an entire market for a particular product as its target market and designs a single marketing mix and directs it at that market. (8)

Uniform geographic pricing A type of pricing, sometimes called "postage-stamp price," that results in fixed average transportation; used to avoid the problems involved in charging different prices to each customer. (20)

Unit loading Grouping one or more boxes on a pallet or skid. (16)

Universal product code (UPC) A series of thick and thin lines that can be read by an electronic scanner to identify the product and provide inventory and pricing information. (11)

Unsought products Products purchased because of a sudden need that must be solved (e.g., emergency automobile repairs), products of which customers are unaware, and products that people do not necessarily think of purchasing. (9)

Usage rate The rate at which a product's inventory is used or sold during a specific time period. (16)

Validity A condition existing when a research method measures what it is supposed to measure, not something else. (5)

Value analysis An evaluation of each component of a potential purchase, including quality, design, or materials, to acquire the most cost-effective product. (7)

Value conscious Concern about price and quality aspects of a product. (20)

Variable costs Costs directly attributable to production and selling volume; costs that vary directly with changes in the number of units produced or sold. (21) (23)

Vendor analysis A formal, systematic evaluation of current and potential vendors. (7)

Vending *See* Automatic vending.

Venture team An organizational unit established to create entirely new products that may be aimed at new markets. (9)

Vertical channel integration Combining two or more stages of the marketing channel under one management. (13)

Vertical marketing system (VMS) A marketing channel in which channel activities are coordinated or managed by a single channel member to achieve efficient, low-cost distribution aimed at satisfying target market customers. (13)

Warehouse clubs Large-scale, members-only establishments that combine features of cash-and-carry wholesaling with discount retailing. (15)

Warehouse showrooms Retail facilities in large, low-cost buildings with large on-premise inventories and minimal services. (15)

Warehousing Designing and operating facilities for storing and moving goods. (16)

Warranty Document that specifies what the producer will do if the product malfunctions. (10)

Weaknesses Any limitations that a company might face in marketing strategy development or implementation. (22)

Wealth The accumulation of past income, natural resources, and financial resources. (2)

Wheeler-Lea Act Legislation enacted in 1938 to outlaw unfair and deceptive acts or practices, regardless of whether they injure competition. (2)

Wheel of retailing A hypothesis that holds that new types of retailers usually enter the market as low-status, low-margin, low-price operators but eventually evolve into high-cost, high-price merchants. (15)

Wholesaler An individual or organization that facilitates and expedites wholesale transactions. (14)

Wholesaling All transactions in which products are bought for resale, for making other products, or for general business use. (14)

Width of product mix The number of product lines a company offers. (9)

Willingness to spend An inclination to buy because of expected satisfaction from a product, the ability to buy, and numerous psychological and social forces. (2)

Zone pricing Regional prices that vary for major geographic zones, as the transportation costs increase. (20)

Notes

Chapter 1

1. Based on information from Greg Kable, "Easy on the Eyes: The First Looks at Two Upcoming German Roadsters Trigger a Pavlovian Salivation," *Autoweek*, June 26, 1995, pp. 18+; Dyan Machan, "Salvation in Stuttgart," *Forbes*, Sept. 11, 1995, pp. 154+; Neiman Marcus press release, Sept. 14, 1995, obtained from America Online; and Peter Robinson, material on Z3 from American Online.

2. Philip Kotler, *Marketing Management: Analysis, Planning, Implementation, and Control*, 8th ed. (Englewood Cliffs, N.J.: Prentice-Hall, 1994), p. 7.

3. "Dave Thomas: Building a Better Burger," *Sales & Marketing Management*, May 1993, pp. 52–53.

4. Karen Benezra, "Taco Bell Takes Bold Step Into Light," *Brandweek*, Feb. 6, 1995, p. 5.

5. Jagdish N. Sheth and Rajendras Sisodia, "More Than Ever Before, Marketing Is Under Fire to Account for What It Spends," *Marketing Management*, Fall 1995, pp. 13–14.

6. Joan G. Rigdon, "Netscape Is Putting a Price on the Head of any Big Bug Found in the Web Browser," *Wall Street Journal*, Oct. 11, 1995, p. B8.

7. Dottie Enrico, "M&M's Candies Singing the Blues," *USA Today*, Sept. 5, 1995, p. B1.

8. Ajay K. Kohli and Bernard J. Jaworski, "Market Orientation: The Construct, Research Propositions and Managerial Implications," *Journal of Marketing*, Apr. 1990.

9. Stanley F. Slater and John C. Narver, "Does Competitive Environment Moderate the Market Orientation-Performance Relationship?" *Journal of Marketing*, Jan. 1994, p. 46.

10. Robert Frank, "Fruity Teas and Mystical Sodas Are Boring Consumers," *Wall Street Journal*, Oct. 9, 1995, pp. B1, B2.

11. Alan Grant and Leonard Schlesinger, "Realize Your Customers' Full Profit Potential," *Harvard Business Review*, Sept./Oct. 1995, p. 59.

12. Ibid.

13. Kathy Rebello, "After Win95, What Do You Do for an Encore?" *Business Week*, Oct. 16, 1995, pp. 68–73.

14. Susan Greco, "The Road to One-to-One Marketing," *Inc.*, Oct. 1995, p. 63.

15. David Fischer, "The New Meal Deals," *U.S. News & World Report*, Oct. 30, 1995, p. 66.

16. Mary Kuntz, "Burma Shave Signs on the I-Way," *Business Week*, Apr. 17, 1995, p. 102.

17. Robert J. Dolan, "How Do You Know When the Price Is Right?" *Harvard Business Review*, Sept./Oct. 1995, p. 174.

18. Robert P. Bush, "Marketing Research in the 90s: Up Close and Personal," *Business Perspectives*, Spring 1995, p. 4.

19. "The AutoZone Success Story," corporate video; "Widening the Gap," 1995 AutoZone *Annual Report*; Rebecca Walters, "Nationwide Automotive Crafts Turn Around Plan," *Business First-Columbus*, June 5, 1995, p. 1; "AutoZone Removes Confusion 'WITT' Technology," *Discount Store News*, May 15, 1995, p. 77; Jerry Minkoff, "AutoZone on the Move," *Discount Merchandiser*, Jan. 1995, pp. 74–76; 1993 AutoZone *Annual Report*; 1992 AutoZone *Annual Report*; Patrick Spain, Alta Campbell, and Alan Chai, eds., *Hoover's Handbook of Emerging Companies, 1993–94* (Austin, Texas: Reference Press, Inc., 1993); Shelley Neumeierm, "Companies to Watch," *Fortune*, Dec. 2, 1991, p. 110; Lehman Brothers, Goldman, Sachs and Co., AutoZone Common Stock Prospectus, October 3, 1991; Shearman Lehman Brothers, AutoZone Stock Report, April 29, 1991.

20. Sources: Amy Cortese, with Kathy Rebello, "Windows 95: Can Microsoft's New Software Live up to Expectations?" *Business Week*, July 10, 1995, pp. 94–106; Mary Kathleen Flynn, with Libusha Kelly, "Beyond the Hype," *U.S. News & World Report*, Aug. 7, 1995, pp. 52–56; "For Microsoft, Nothing Succeeds Like Excess," *Wall Street Journal*, Aug. 25, 1995, pp. B1, B4; Katie Hafner, "Should You Do Windows?" *Newsweek*, Aug. 21, 1995, pp. 38–41; Kathy Rebello, "Start Me Up—Just Try," *Business Week*, Sept. 25, 1995, p. 114; and Kathy Rebello, with Mary Kuntz, "Feel the Buzz," *Business Week*, Aug. 8, 1995, p. 31.

Chapter 2

1. Based on information from Hoover's Handbook Database (Austin, Tex.: Reference Press, 1995), via America Online; Betsy Spethmann, "C-Jack, Free of Fat, Fans MLB Angst," *Brandweek*, Feb. 27, 1995, p. 4; Betsy Spethmann and Pam Weisz, "Nabisco Readies Reduced-Fat Planters; Ups Kid Promo Ante," *Brandweek*, Feb. 20, 1995, p. 4; and U.S. Bureau of the Census, *Statistical Abstract of the United States*, 114th ed. (Washington D.C.: U.S. Government Printing Office, 1994), pp. 144, 146.

2. Ram Subramanian, Kamalesh Kumar, and Charles Yauger, "The Scanning of Task Environments in Hospitals: An Empirical Study," *Journal of Applied Business Research*, Fall 1994, pp. 104–115.

3. P. Varadarajan, Terry Clark, and William M. Pride, "Controlling the Uncontrollable: Managing Your Market Environment," *Sloan Management Review*, Winter 1992, pp. 39–47.

4. John W. Verity, "Everyone's Rushing the Net," *Business Week*, June 5, 1995, pp. 116–118.

5. Wroe Alderson, *Dynamic Marketing Behavior* (Homewood, Ill.: Irwin, 1965), pp. 195–197.

6. George S. Day, "The Capabilities of Market-Driven Organizations," *Journal of Marketing*, Oct. 1994, pp. 37–52.

7. U.S. Bureau of the Census, *Statistical Abstract of the United States, 1994*, 114th ed. (Washington, D.C.: U.S. Government Printing Office, 1994), p. 471.

8. Cheryl Russell and Thomas A. Exter, "Mad Money," *American Demographics*, July 1993, pp. 26–32.

9. *Sales & Marketing Management, Survey of Buying Power,* Aug. 30, 1993.

10. Linda Himelstein and Ronald Grover, "Will Ticketmaster Get Scalped?" *Business Week,* June 26, 1995, pp. 64–70.

11. Mary Lou Steptoe, "Sherman Tank," *Journal of Business Strategy,* Jan./Feb. 1994, p. 12.

12. Frederick Cooper, III, "A Matter of Antitrust," *Computer Reseller News,* Apr. 25, 1994, pp. 79, 86.

13. Gene Koprowski, *Forbes,* Aug. 29, 1994, pp. 57–59.

14. Roy H. Campbell, "This Time, Calvin Klein's Provocative Ads 'Backfire'," *Philadelphia Inquirer,* Sept. 19, 1995, p. 1.

15. Thomas C. Willcox, "Beyond the Pale of the Sherman and Clayton Acts: The Federal Trade Commission's 'Invitation to Collude' Doctrine As a Deterrent to Violations of the Antitrust Laws," *Antitrust Bulletin,* Fall 1994, pp. 623–651.

16. Anne G. Perkins, "Advertising: The Costs of Deception," *Harvard Business Review,* May/June 1994, pp. 10–11.

17. Larry D. Compeau, Dhruv Grewal, and Diana S. Grewal, "Adjudicating Claims of Deceptive Advertised Reference Prices: The Use of Empirical Evidence," *Journal of Public Policy & Marketing,* Fall 1994.

18. Jeff Jensen, "Yamaha Balks at NAD Inquiry into Engine Ad," *Advertising Age,* Apr. 19, 1993, pp. 16–17.

19. "Productivity to the Rescue," *Business Week,* Oct. 9, 1995, p. 134.

20. "AT&T Stays Home," *USA Today,* Sept. 15, 1995, p. B1.

21. Leslie Miller, "Cyberspace Scares Many PC Novices," *USA Today,* Oct. 16, 1995, p. D1.

22. Amy Cortese, with John Verity, Russell Mitchell, and Richard Brandt, "Cyberspace: Crafting Software That Will Let You Build a Business Out There," *Business Week,* Feb. 27, 1995, pp. 78–86.

23. James Kim, "Despite Array of Products, There Is No Winner—Yet," *USA Today,* Nov. 13, 1995, p. E1; and "Who's on the Web?" *Newsweek,* Nov. 13, 1995, p. 14.

24. G. Pascal Zachary, "Restaurant Computers Speed Up Soup to Nuts," *Wall Street Journal,* Oct. 25, 1995, p. B1.

25. Joseph L. Bower and M. Clayton, "Disruptive Technologies: Catching the Wave," *Harvard Business Review,* Jan./Feb. 1995, pp. 43–53.

26. Mary George Beggs, "Seniors at Work," *Commercial Appeal,* Oct. 17, 1995, p. C1.

27. U.S. Bureau of the Census, *Statistical Abstract of the United States, 1994,* 114th ed. (Washington, D.C.: Government Printing Office, 1994), pp. 55, 60.

28. Susan Mitchell, "The Next Baby Boom," *American Demographics,* Oct. 1995, p. 24.

29. U.S. Bureau of the Census, *Statistical Abstract of the United States, 1994,* 114th ed. (Washington, D.C.: Government Printing Office, 1994), p. 13.

30. Leah Rickard and Jeanne Whalen, "Retail Trails Ethnic Changes," *Advertising Age,* May 1, 1995, pp. 1, 41.

31. Norvel D. Glenn, "What Does Family Mean?" *American Demographics,* June 1992, pp. 30–37.

32. "Better Child-Resistant Packages on the Way," *Consumer Reports,* Sept. 1995, p. 567.

33. Sources: Faye Rice, "Who Scores Best on the Environment," *Fortune,* July 26, 1993, p. 114; Gary Hoover, Alta Campbell, and Patrick J. Spain, eds., *Hoover's Handbook of American Business 1993* (Austin, Tex.: Reference Press, Inc., 1993), p. 116; American Telephone and Telegraph Company, *A Safe and Green Tomorrow,* internal corporate video documentary, 1992.

34. Sources: John Bovard, "Corporate Welfare Fueled by Political Contributions: Archer Daniels Midland's Ethanol Program," *Business and Society Review,* June 22, 1995, p. 22; Greg Burns and Richard A. Melcher, "A Grain of Activism at Archer Daniels Midland," *Business Week,* Nov. 6, 1995, p. 44; Dan Carney, "Dwayne's World: Archer Daniels Midland CEO Dwayne Orville Andreas," *Mother Jones,* July 1995, p. 44; Major Garrett, "The Supermarket to the World Pols: Clinton, Dole Helped Campaign Contributor ADM, Now Probed for Price Fixing," *Washington Times,* Sept. 5, 1995, p. A1; Ronald Henkoff, "So Who Is This Mark Whitacre, and Why Is He Saying These Things About ADM?" *Fortune,* Sept. 4, 1995, pp. 64–68; Hoover's Handbook Database (Austin, Texas: Reference Press, 1995), via America Online; David C. Korten, *When Corporations Rule the World* (West Hartford, Conn.: Kumarian Press, 1995), pp. 75, 224; Joann S. Lublin, "Is ADM's Board Too Big, Cozy, and Well-Paid?" *Wall Street Journal,* Oct. 17, 1995, p. B1; Richard A. Melcher and Greg Burns, "Archer Daniels' Cleanup: Don't Stop Now," *Business Week,* Jan. 29, 1996, p. 37; Robyn Meredith, "Archer Daniels Investors Launch Revolt," Oct. 20, 1995, pp. B1, B2; "10 Little Piggies: Corporations That Receive Government Benefits," *Mother Jones,* July 1995, p. 48; and Mark Whitacre and Ronald Henkoff, "My Life as a Corporate Mole for the FBI," *Fortune,* Sept. 4, 1995, pp. 52–62.

Chapter 3

1. Gregory Jaynes, "Where the Torts Blossom," *Time* (via America Online: tiafpt38); Eric Schine, "McDonald's Hot Coffee Gets Her Cool Cash," *Business Week,* Sept. 5, 1994; and Cindy Webb, "Boiling Mad," *Business Week,* Aug. 21, 1995, p. 32.

2. Andrew Stark, "What's the Matter with Business Ethics?" *Harvard Business Review,* May-June 1993, p. 38.

3. Neal Gross, Dori Jones Yang, and Julia Flynn, "Seasick in Cyberspace," *Business Week,* July 10, 1995, p. 110.

4. *Business Ethics,* Jan./Feb. 1995, p. 13.

5. Peggy H. Cunningham and O. C. Ferrell, "The Influence of Role Stress on Unethical Behavior by Personnel Involved in the Marketing Research Process," working paper, Queens University, 1995, p. 35.

6. Louis M. Brown and Anne O. Kandel, *The Legal Audit: Corporate Internal Investigation* (Deerfield, Ill.: Clark, Boardman, Callaghan, 1995), pp. 1–2.

7. Tony Mauro, *USA Today,* Oct. 11, 1995, p. 4A.

8. O. C. Ferrell and John Fraedrich, *Business Ethics* (Boston: Houghton Mifflin, 1994), p. 52.

9. F. Neil Brady, *Ethical Managing: Rules and Results* (New York: Macmillan, 1990), pp. 4–6.

10. O. C. Ferrell and Larry G. Gresham, "A Contingency Framework for Understanding Ethical Decision Making in Marketing," *Journal of Marketing,* Summer 1985, p. 90.

11. John Fraedrich and O. C. Ferrell, "Cognitive Consistency of Marketing Managers in Ethical Situations," *Journal of the Academy of Marketing Science* 1992: 245–252.

12. Joseph W. Weiss, *Business Ethics: A Managerial, Stakeholder Approach* (Belmont, Calif.: Wadsworth, 1994), p. 13.

13. O. C. Ferrell, Larry G. Gresham, and John Fraedrich, "A Synthesis of Ethical Decision Models for Marketing," *Journal of Macromarketing,* Fall 1989, pp. 58–59.

14. "Good Guys Finish First," *Business Ethics,* Mar./Apr. 1995, p. 13.

15. O. C. Ferrell, Larry G. Gresham, and John Fraedrich, "A Synthesis of Ethical Decision Models for Marketing," *Journal of Macromarketing,* Fall 1989, pp. 58–59.

16. Scott McCartney, "Compaq Suit Claims Packard Bell Sells New Computers Containing Used Parts," *Wall Street Journal*, April 11, 1995, p. A2.

17. Paul Raeburn, "Magazines Spread Tobacco Views to Kids, Study Says," *Commercial Appeal*, Nov. 1, 1995, p. B6.

18. Mark Maremont, "Eyeway Robbery," *Business Week*, Feb. 27, 1995, p. 48.

19. Linda K. Trevino and Stuart Youngblood, "Bad Apples in Bad Barrels: A Causal Analysis of Ethical Decision Making Behavior," *Journal of Applied Psychology* 75, no. 4, 1990, pp. 378–385.

20. Ibid.

21. Gene R. Laczniak and Patrick E. Murphy, *Ethical Marketing Decisions: The Higher Road* (Boston: Allyn and Bacon, 1993), p. 14.

22. Tom Rusk and D. Patrick Miller, *The Power of Ethical Persuasion: From Conflict to Partnership at Work and in Private Life* (New York: Viking, 1993).

23. Win Swenson, "The Organizational Guidelines Carrot and Stick Philosophy and Their Focus on Effective Compliance," in *Corporate Crime in America: Strengthening the Good Citizen Corporation* (Washington D.C.: United States Sentencing Commission, 1993), p. 17.

24. Patrick E. Murphy, "Improving Your Ethics Code," *Business Ethics*, Mar./Apr. 1994, p. 23.

25. Survey of *Forbes 500* Ethical Compliance Programs, The University of Memphis, Jan. 1995.

26. Judith Kamm, "Ethics: Easier Said than Done," Summer 1993, Josephson Institute.

27. Susan Gaines, "Handing Out Halos," *Business Ethics*, Mar./Apr. 1994, p. 21.

28. Ibid.

29. Margaret A. Stroup, Ralph L. Newbert, and Jerry W. Anderson, Jr., "Doing Good, Doing Better: Two Views of Social Responsibility," *Business Horizons*, Mar.–Apr. 1987, p. 23.

30. "Good Guys Finish First," *Business Ethics*, Mar./Apr. 1995, p. 13.

31. Dale Kurschner, "The 1995 Business Ethics Award," *Business Ethics*, Nov./Dec. 1995, p. 30.

32. Ron Trujillo, "Good Ethics Pay Off," *USA Today*, Oct. 23, 1995, p. 2B.

33. Ibid.

34. Dan Callahan and Mary Ellen Egan, "Target Coaches Teens to Reach Beyond the Checkout Lane," *Business Ethics*, Jan./Feb. 1995, p. 41.

35. Christy Fisher, "Seal of Green Planned: Environmental Group to Give Product Approvals," *Advertising Age*, Nov. 20, 1989, p. 3.

36. Paul Hawken and William McDonough, "Seven Steps to Doing Good Business," *Inc.*, Nov. 1993, pp. 79–90.

37. Bill Wagner, "A Recycling Approach Worth Copying," *Business Ethics*, May–June 1993, p. 17.

38. "Lasting Value Levi Strauss," *Business Ethics*, Nov.–Dec. 1993, p. 28.

39. Trujillo, p. 2B.

40. Sir Adrian Cadbury, "Ethical Managers Make Their Own Rules," *Harvard Business Review*, Sept.–Oct. 1987, p. 33.

41. Sources: Hoover's Company Profile Database, 1996 (Austin, Texas: Reference Press, 1996) via America Online; "Chocolate Aside, Hershey Keeps a Close Eye on Gifts," *Ethikos*, May/June 1991, pp. 4–6; "Key Corporate Policies," Hershey Foods Corporation booklet; "Guidelines for Ethical Business Practices," Hershey Foods Corporation booklet; "The Business Week 1,000," *Business Week*, 1992 Special Bonus Issue, p. 128; "Hershey Foods Philosophy and Values," Hershey Foods Corporation video, 1990; "A Tradition of Excellence," Hershey Foods Corporation, August 1990; Hershey Foods Corporation, *1990 Annual Report;* and Steven S. Ross, "Green Groceries," *Mother Jones*, Feb./Mar. 1989, pp. 48–49.

42. Sources: Geoffrey Cowley, "The Culture of Prozac," *Newsweek*, Feb. 7, 1994, pp. 41–42; Hoover's Handbook Database (Austin, Texas: Reference Press, 1995), via America Online; Dale Kurschner, "Interview: Randall Tobias," *Business Ethics*, July/Aug. 1995, pp. 31–34; Lawrence Mondi, "Did Prozac Make Him Do It?" *Time*, Nov. 28, 1994, p. 66; and Chris O'Malley," *Indianapolis Star,* September 22, 1995, via America Online.

Chapter 4

1. Based on information from Douglas Harbrecht, Geri Smith, and Gail DeGeorge, "Ripping Down Walls Across the Americas," *Business Week*, Dec. 26, 1994, pp. 78–79; Hoover's Handbook Database (Austin, Texas: Reference Press, 1995), via America Online; Ian Katz, "It's Carnival Time for Investors," *Business Week*, Mar. 13, 1995, p. 53; and Procter & Gamble, *1995 Annual Report.*

2. "Wal-Mart Will Open as Many as 232 Stores Next Year," *Commercial Appeal*, Oct. 11, 1995, p. B9.

3. Geraldine Fabrikant, "Blockbuster Grows in Overseas Markets," *Commercial Appeal*, Oct. 24, 1995, p. B5.

4. Amy Barrett, "It's a Small (Business) World," *Business Week*, Apr. 17, 1995, pp. 96–101.

5. "The Big Picture: Blind Overseas," *U.S. News & World Report*, Nov. 13, 1995, p. 6.

6. James Aley, "New Lift for the U.S. Export Boom," *Fortune*, Nov. 13, 1995, pp. 74, 76.

7. Theodore Levitt, "The Globalization of Markets," *Harvard Business Review*, May/June 1983, p. 92.

8. Terry Clark, "International Marketing and National Character: A Review and Proposal for an Integrative Theory," *Journal of Marketing*, Oct. 1990, pp. 66–79.

9. Joseph Pereira, "Unknown Fruit Takes on Unfamiliar Markets," *Wall Street Journal*, Nov. 9, 1995, p. B1.

10. Brian Bremner, with Edith Hill Updike, "'Made in America' Isn't the Kiss of Death Anymore," *Business Week*, Nov. 13, 1995, p. 62.

11. Nigel G. G. Campbell, John L. Graham, Alain Jolibert, and Hans Gunther Meissner, "Marketing Negotiations in France, Germany, the United Kingdom, and the United States," *Journal of Marketing*, Apr. 1988, pp. 49–62.

12. Brian Mark Hawrysh and Judith Lynne Zaichkowsky, "Cultural Approaches to Negotiations: Understanding the Japanese," *International Marketing Review*, 7, no. 2, 1990, pp. 28–42.

13. "In India, Beef-Free Mickey D," *Business Week*, Apr. 17, 1995, p. 52.

14. Laurel Wentz, "Local Laws Keep International Marketers Hopping," *Advertising Age*, July 11, 1985, p. 20.

15. James Cox, "USA Wants China to Curb Copyright Piracy," *USA Today*, Jan. 3, 1995, p. 2B.

16. Ekkehard Brose, Betsy Wittleder, Hans Sturm, eds., "Spotlight on German-American Economic Relations and the Global Economy," Washington, D.C.: Germany Embassy Press Department, Sept. 1995, p. 1.

17. Earl Naumann and Douglas J. Lincoln, "Non-Tariff Barriers and Entry Strategy Alternatives: Strategic Marketing

Implications," *Journal of Small Business Management,* Apr. 1991, pp. 60–70.

18. Barbara Rudolph, with Gavin Scott, "Northern Exposure," *Time,* Jan. 30, 1995 (via America Online: tiab9sq4).

19. William C. Symonds, "Meanwhile, to the North, NAFTA Is a Smash," *Business Week,* Feb. 27, 1995, p. 66.

20. David Hage, Robert F. Black, and David Fischer, et al., "Caught in the Undertow," *U.S. News & World Report,* Mar. 20, 1995, p. 47.

21. Geri Smith, Stanley Reed, and Elisabeth Malkin, "Mexico: A Rough Road Back," *Business Week,* Nov. 13, 1995, pp. 104–107.

22. Kerry Luft, "Chile on Hold for NAFTA Entry; Negotiations Stalled by Mexico Crisis, U.S. '96 Election," *Chicago Tribune,* Nov. 8, 1995.

23. Eric G. Friberg, "1992: Moves Europeans Are Making," *Harvard Business Review,* May/June 1989, p. 89.

24. Mark Memmott, "Jobs at the Heart of U.S./Japan Trade Talks," *USA Today,* Feb. 11, 1994, p. B1.

25. Mark Memmott, "U.S.: Japan Must Ease Import Rules," *USA Today,* Feb. 20, 1995, p. B1.

26. Martha T. Moore, "Latest Japan-U.S. Rift," *USA Today,* Nov. 6, 1995, p. 1B.

27. Aley, "New Lift for the U.S. Export Boom," p. 74.

28. Bremner and Updike, "'Made in America' Isn't the Kiss of Death Anymore."

29. Louis Kraar, "The Risks Are Rising in China," *Fortune,* Mar. 6, 1995, p. 179.

30. Ibid.

31. Amy Borrus, Pete Engardio, and Dexter Roberts, "The New Trade Superpower," *Business Week,* Oct. 16, 1995, pp. 56–57.

32. Ibid.

33. Louis Kraar, "Asia's Rising Export Powers," *Fortune,* Special Pacific Rim 1989 issue, pp. 43–50.

34. Mark Memmott, "Transitions Are Like Night and Day," *USA Today,* Feb. 24, 1994, p. B2.

35. "GATT Costs," *USA Today,* Feb. 24, 1994, p. B1.

36. Douglas Harbrecht, Owen Ullmon, Bill Javetski, and Geri Smith, "Finally, GATT May Fly," *Business Week,* Dec. 20, 1993, pp. 36–37.

37. John Benjamin Harris, "Export Strategies for the 1990s: A Strategic Plan for Minority Firms' Participation in Global Markets," Virginia State University, Aug. 31, 1991, pp. 40–42.

38. Andrew Kupfer, "How to Be a Global Manager," *Fortune,* Mar. 14, 1988, pp. 52–58.

39. Kathryn Rudie Harrigan, "Joint Ventures and Competitive Advantage," *Strategic Management Journal,* May 1988, pp. 141–158.

40. "More Companies Prefer Liaisons to Marriage," *The Wall Street Journal,* Apr. 12, 1988, p. 35.

41. Thomas Gross and John Neuman, "Strategic Alliances Vital in Global Marketing," *Marketing News,* June 1989, pp. 1–2.

42. Ghazi M. Habib and John J. Burnett, "An Assessment of Channel Behavior in an Alternative Structural Arrangement: The International Joint Venture," *International Marketing Review* 6, no. 3, 1989, pp. 7–21.

43. Margaret H. Cunningham, "Marketing's New Frontier: International Strategic Alliances," working paper, Queens University (Ontario), 1992.

44. Sources: Joyce Barnathan, Douglas Harbrecht, Ann Theresa Palmer, and William J. Holstein, "A Tidal Wave of Chinese Goods," *Business Week,* Dec. 12, 1994, p. 56; Ken Berzof, "Buying Stocks as Gifts for Children Can Help Draw Their Interest," *Courier-Journal,* June 12, 1995, p. 1C; Seth Faison, "Kou Qiu, Jordan! Slam Dunk! Pee-ow Liang!" *New York Times,* Mar. 3, 1996, section 4, p. 2; David P. Hamilton, "PC Makers Find China as a Chaotic Market Despite Its Potential," *Wall Street Journal,* Apr. 8, 1996, p. A1; *Hoover's Handbook* (Austin, Texas: Reference Press, 1994), pp. 814–815; Richard Tomlinson, "Physical Fitness Craze Sweeps China," *International Herald Tribune,* Feb. 20, 1995; and "20 Years of Innovation: There Is No Finish Line," Nike videotape.

45. Hoover's Handbook Database (Austin, Texas: Reference Press, 1995), via America Online; "KLM Denies Plan for Takeover of NWA," *Commercial Appeal,* Nov. 14, 1995, p. B8; and Stewart Toy, with Susan Chandler, Robert Neff, and Margaret Dawson, "Flying High," *Business Week,* Feb. 27, 1995, pp. 90–91.

Chapter 5

1. Based on information from Laurie Freeman, "Brands in Demand," *Advertising Age,* Feb. 27, 1995, pp. 21–22; Skip Hollandsworth, "Hot Potatoes," *Texas Monthly,* Jan. 1996, pp. 104–108, 112–114; and "Taking the Low-Fat Route to Fat City," *Fortune,* Feb. 20, 1995, pp. 18–19.

2. Robert P. Bush, "Up Close and Personal," *Business Perspectives,* Spring 1995, p. 2.

3. Reprinted from *Dictionary of Marketing Terms,* Peter D. Bennett, ed., 1988, pp. 117–118, published by the American Marketing Association. Used by permission.

4. Jim Masterson, "Research Adds Value to Products," *Marketing News,* Aug. 16, 1993, p. A6.

5. Keith L. Alexander, "For Fliers, First Class No Longer Means Prestige," *USA Today,* Nov. 24, 1995, p. 1B.

6. R. Douglas Shute, "Connecting to the Source," *Inc.,* Nov. 14, 1995, p. 27.

7. Christel Beard and Betsy Wiesendanger, "The Marketers' Guide to Online Databases," *Sales & Marketing Management,* Jan. 1993, p. 49.

8. Laurence N. Goal, "High Technology Data Collection for Measurement and Testing," *Marketing Research,* Mar. 1992, pp. 29–38.

9. "Sales Automation: Tracking Sales Leads Online," *Inc.,* Jan. 1993, p. 31.

10. Richard S. Teilelbaum, "*Reader's Digest:* Are Times Tough?: Here's an Answer," *Fortune,* Dec. 2, 1991, pp. 101–102.

11. Kyle Pope, "To Whom It May Concern: Electronic Bulletin Boards Are Helping Firms Swap Information and More with Customers and Staff," *Wall Street Journal,* Nov. 15, 1993, p. R22.

12. Pope, "To Whom It May Concern."

13. Ibid.

14. Commercenet Consortium/Nielsen Media Research, in "Who's on the Web?" *Newsweek,* Nov. 13, 1995, p. 14.

15. James Kim, "Businesses Bet on the Future," *USA Today,* Nov. 13, 1995, p. 1E.

16. Ellen Neuborne, "Shoppers Can Get Holiday Jollies on the 'Net," *USA Today,* Nov. 13, 1995, p. 4E.

17. Alison L. Sprout, "The Internet Inside Your Company," *Fortune,* Nov. 27, 1995, pp. 161–168.

18. Sprout, "The Internet Inside Your Company."

19. Bush, "Up Close and Personal," p. 3.

20. Lynne G. Coleman, "Researchers Say Non-Response Is the Single Biggest Problem," *Marketing News,* Jan. 7, 1991, p. 32.

21. Ibid.

22. Martha Farnsworth Riche, "Who Says Yes?" *American Demographics,* Feb. 1987, p. 8.

23. Diane K. Bowers, "Telephone Legislation," *Marketing Research*, Mar. 1989, p. 47.

24. Peter S. Tuckel and Harry W. O'Neill, "Call Waiting," *Marketing Research*, Spring 1995, p. 8.

25. Shute, "Connecting to the Source."

26. Martin Oppermann, "E-mail Surveys—Potentials and Pitfalls," *Marketing Research*, Summer 1995, p. 32.

27. Oppermann, "E-mail Surveys," p. 29.

28. Cynthia Webster, "Consumers' Attitudes Toward Data Collection Methods," Robert L. King, ed., *Marketing: Toward the 21st Century*, Proceedings of the Southern Marketing Association, Atlanta, Ga., Nov. 1991, p. 221.

29. James B. Treece and Wendy Zellner, with Walecia Konrad, "Detroit Tries to Rev Up," *Business Week*, June 12, 1989, p. 82.

30. *Practices, Trends and Expectations for the Market Research Industry 1987*, Market Facts, Inc., Apr. 29, 1987.

31. Jagdip Singh, Roy D. Howell, and Gary K. Rhoads, "Adaptive Designs for Likert-Type Data: An Approach for Implementing Marketing Surveys," *Journal of Marketing Research*, Aug. 1990, pp. 304–321.

32. Michael J. Olivette, "Marketing Research in the Electric Utility Industry," *Marketing News*, Jan. 2, 1987, p. 13.

33. Jerry Stafford and Neil Ubmeyer, "Product Shortages Hamper Research in the Soviet Union," *Marketing News*, Sept. 3, 1990, p. 6.

34. Cynthia Crossen, "Margin of Error," *Wall Street Journal*, Nov. 14, 1991, p. A7.

35. Christine Mormon, Gerald Zaltman, and Rohit Deshpande, "Relationships Between Providers and Users of Market Research: The Dynamics of Trust Within and Between Organizations," *Journal of Marketing Research*, Aug. 1992, pp. 314–328.

36. O. C. Ferrell and Steven J. Skinner, "Ethical Behavior and Bureaucratic Structure in Marketing Research Organizations," *Journal of Marketing Research*, Feb. 1988, pp. 103–104.

37. "Good-bye Guesswork: How Research Guides Today's Advertising," *Advertising Education Foundation*.

38. "The *Business Week* 1000" *Business Week*, Mar. 27, 1995, p. 106; Chrysler Corporation, "Reinventing Chrysler," internal corporate video documentary, 1992; "Detroit's Exports Take Off," *Fortune*, Nov. 1, 1993, p. 12; Therese Eiben, "U.S. Exporters Keep on Rolling," *Fortune*, June 14, 1993, p. 130; Kathleen Kerwin, "Detroit's Big Chance," *Business Week*, June 29, 1992, p. 82; Patricia Sellers, "The Best Way to Reach Your Buyers," *Fortune*, Autumn/Winter 1993, p. 14; Bill Vlasic, "That Daring Old Company and Its Jaunty Jalopy," *Business Week*, Jan. 15, 1996, p. 31; David Woodruff, "An Embarrassment of Glitches Galvanizes Chrysler," *Business Week*, Apr. 17, 1995, pp. 76–77; and Wilton Woods, "The World's Top Automakers Change Lanes," *Fortune*, Oct. 4, 1993, p. 73.

Chapter 6

1. Based on information from Todd Hyten, "Food Trends in Search of the Next Boston Chicken," *Boston Business Journal*, Mar. 17, 1995, p. 8; James Fink, "New Chicken Restaurants Seek Room in Crowded Pecking Order," *Business First—Buffalo*, Apr. 10, 1995, p. 8; Theresa Howard, "Boston Chicken Chain Targets New Market," *Nation's Restaurant News*, Feb. 27, 1995, pp. 1, 90; Karen Benezra, "Boston Market Carves New Niche," *Brandweek*, May 1, 1995, p. 4; and Bill Saporito, "What's for Dinner: The Battle for Stomach Share," *Fortune*, May 15, 1995, pp. 50–52, 56, 58, 64.

2. James F. Engel, Roger D. Blackwell, and Paul W. Miniard, *Consumer Behavior*, 8th ed. (Hinsdale, Ill.: Dryden Press, 1995), p. 4.

3. Paul M. Herr, Frank R. Kardes, and John Kim, "Effects of Word-of-Mouth and Product-Attribute Information on Persuasion: An Accessibility-Diagnosticity Perspective," *Journal of Consumer Research*, Mar. 1991, pp. 454–462.

4. Michael J. Houston, Terry L. Childers, and Susan E. Heckler, "Picture-Word Consistency and the Elaborative Processing of Advertisements," *Journal of Marketing Research*, Nov. 1987, pp. 359–369.

5. "A Child Shall Lead the Way: Marketing to Youths," *Credit Union Executive*, May–June 1993, pp. 6–8.

6. Alison M. Torrillo, "Dens Are Men's Territories," *American Demographics*, Jan. 1995, pp. 11, 38.

7. Katie Smith, "Trends Recorded in New Product Offerings," *Restaurant Hospitality*, Apr. 1993, p. 26.

8. Russell W. Belk, "Situational Variables and Consumer Behavior," *Journal of Consumer Research*, Dec. 1975, pp. 157–164.

9. Betsy Spethman, "So Long, Smucker!" *Brandweek*, July 10, 1995, p. 24.

10. "A Marker for Ethnic Pride," *Success*, Sept. 1992, p. 21.

11. David Aaker and Douglas Stayman, "Implementing the Concept of Transformational Advertising," *Psychology and Marketing*, May–June 1992, pp. 237–253.

12. Akshay R. Rao and Kent B. Monroe, "The Moderating Effect of Prior Knowledge on Cue Utilization in Product Evaluations," *Journal of Consumer Research*, Sept. 1988, pp. 253–264.

13. Cecile Lamalle, "Ethnic Accents," *Restaurant Hospitality*, Jan. 1993, pp. 94–105.

14. Kelley Damore, "Beta Users Praise GRASP for Its Scripting Language," *Infoworld*, Jan. 18, 1993, p. 19.

15. Fara Warner, "Chrysler Treads Off-Road Media," *Brandweek*, Mar. 22, 1993, p. 4.

16. Marcia Mogelonsy, "Snap, Crackle, Profits," *American Demographics*, Jan. 1995, p. 10.

17. Rebecca Piirto, "Clothes with Attitude," *American Demographics*, Oct. 1990, pp. 10, 52, 54.

18. MariaLisa Calta, "Pitching the Prune," *Eating Well*, Sept.–Oct. 1992, p. 18.

19. Chip Walker, "Meet the New Vegetarian," *American Demographics*, Jan. 1995, pp. 9–11.

20. Raj Mehta and Russell W. Belk, "Artifacts, Identity, and Transition: Favorite Possessions of Indians and Indian Immigrants to the United States," *Journal of Consumer Research*, Mar. 1991, pp. 393–411.

21. "Marketing the Mainline to Manilla," *American Demographics*, July 1995, p. 15.

22. Sources: Yumiko Ono, "Land of the Rising Fun," *Wall Street Journal*, Oct. 2, 1992, pp. A1, A10; Merry White, "Home Truths: Woman and Social Change in Japan," *Daedalus*, Fall 1992, pp. 61–82; Gayle Hanson, "Japan at Play," *Insight*, Apr. 27, 1992, pp. 6–13, 34–37; Gale Eisenstodt, "Value for Yen," *Forbes*, April 27, 1992, pp. 78–79; David Kilburn, "Dentsu Survey Tells What Japan Yens For," *Adweek*, Jan. 30, 1995, p. 16; Nancy Nottingham, "Camping Worldwide," *Billings (Montana) Gazette*, Jan. 15, 1995, p. D1; Kenichi Ohmae, "Letter From Japan," *Harvard Business Review*, May/June 1995, pp. 154–158; Jack Russell, "Working Women Give Japan Culture Shock," *Advertising Age*, Jan. 16, 1995, p. I24; and JETRO video, *The Newest Wave of Japanese Consumers*.

23. Sources: Diane Mastrull, "Campbell and Pace Recipe: A Mixing of Disparate Cultures," *Philadelphia Business*

Journal, Feb. 17, 1995, p. A1; Nancy Rotenier, "M-m! M-m! Better," *Forbes*, Mar. 27, 1995, p. 138; Tara Parker-Pope and Susan Carey, "Grand Metropolitan to Buy Pet Inc.," *Wall Street Journal*, Jan. 10, 1995, p. A3; Keven Lowery, "Campbell Spices Up Its Home Cookin' Soup Line with Four New Varieties," *PR Newswire*, Nov. 8, 1994; Joseph Weber, Gail Schares, Stephen Hutcheon, Ian Katz, and Pete Engardio, "Campbell: Now It's M-M-Global," *Business Week*, Mar. 15, 1993, pp. 52–54; Jonathan Karp, "Soup for the Masses," *Far Eastern Economic Review*, Oct. 29, 1992, p. 80; Richard L. Holman, "Campbell Soup Varieties in China," *Wall Street Journal*, Nov. 13, 1992, p. A10; "New Mainstream: Hot Dogs, Apple Pie, and Salsa," *Supermarket Business*, May 1992, pp. 92, 94; Bickley Townsend, "Market Research That Matters," *American Demographics*, Aug. 1992, pp. 58–60; and Geoffrey Lee Martin, "Aussies Worry About Lost Brands," *Advertising Age*, Oct. 26, 1992, p. 21.

Chapter 7

1. Based on information from Gary Hoover, Alta Campbell, and Patrick J. Spain, *Hoover's Handbook of American Business* (Austin, Texas: Reference Press, 1995), pp. 474–475; Norton Paley, "An Electrifying Competitor," *Sales & Marketing Management*, Sept. 1995, pp. 28–29; Sipko Huismans and Nadrew Campbell, "The Parent Trap," *Chief Executive*, Apr. 1995, pp. 46–49; Flannery William, "Sales Take Off, Profit Jumps for Emerson," *St. Louis Post-Dispatch*, Feb. 8, 1995, p. C5; and Dan Moreau and Joan Goldwasser, "37 Years of Higher Profits: How Emerson Does It," *Kiplinger's Personal Finance Magazine*, Jan. 1995, p. 30.

2. *Statistical Abstract of the United States*, 1995. p. 550.

3. Ibid.

4. "The Customers with Clout," *Fortune*, Oct. 2, 1995, p. 100.

5. *Statistical Abstract of the United States*, 1994, p. 352.

6. Ibid., pp. 550, 782.

7. Brooke Southall, "Maple Donuts Ad Gimmicks Fatten Sales," *Central Penn Business Journal*, Apr. 14, 1995, p. 1.

8. Gerry Blackwell, "There's No Question Apple's on a Roll," *Computing Canada*, May 1993, pp. 2–3.

9. Todd Spangler, Jan Jaben, and Priscilla Brown, "The Business Marketing 100," *Business Marketing*, Oct. 1992, pp. 144–146.

10. Lisa Coleman, "Overnight Isn't Fast Enough," *Brandweek*, July 31, 1995, pp. 26–27.

11. William Keenan, Jr., "Managing Phone Sales: There is a Difference," *Sales & Marketing Management*, June 1995, pp. 39–40.

12. J. Carlos Jarillo and Howard H. Stevenson, "Cooperative Strategies: The Payoffs and the Pitfalls," *Long Range Planning*, Feb. 1991, pp. 64–70.

13. Louis J. DeRose, "Meet Today's Buying Influence with Value Selling," *Industrial Marketing Management*, May 1991, pp. 87–90.

14. Larry Armstrong, "Beyond May I Help You," *Business Week*, Oct. 25, 1991, p. 102.

15. Weld F. Royal, "Cashing In On Complaints," *Sales & Marketing Management*, May 1995, pp. 88–89.

16. Michiel Leenders and David L. Blenkhorn, *Reverse Marketing: The New Buyer-Supplier Relationship* (New York: Free Press, 1988); and David L. Blenkhorn and Peter Banting, "How Reverse Marketing Changes Buyer Seller Roles," *Industrial Marketing Management*, Aug. 1991, pp. 185–190.

17. Frederick E. Webster, Jr., and Yoram Wind, *Organizational Buying Behavior* (Englewood Cliffs, N.J.: Prentice-Hall, 1972), pp. 78–80.

18. Robert D. McWilliams, Earl Naumann, and Stan Scott, "Determining Buying Center Size," *Industrial Marketing Management* 21, 1992, pp. 43–49.

19. Jarillo and Stevenson, pp. 64–70.

20. 1987 *Standard Industrial Classification Manual*, U.S. Office of Management and Budget, Washington, D.C.

21. Sources: "The Business Marketing 100," *Business Marketing*, Oct. 1992, p. 48; Kate Bertrand, "Chip Wars," *Business Marketing*, Feb. 1992, pp. 16–18, 20; Richard Brandt, "For Intel, One Good Friend Isn't Enough," *Business Week*, Mar. 1, 1993, pp. 86–87; Richard Brandt, "Intel: What a Tease—And What a Strategy," *Business Week*, Feb. 22, 1993, p. 40; Ani Handijan, "Andy Grove: How Intel Makes Spending Pay Off," *Fortune*, Feb. 22, 1993, pp. 56–61; Stratford Sherman, "The Secret to Intel's Success," *Fortune*, Feb. 8, 1993, p. 14; Jaikumar Vijayan, "Pentium Turnaround," *Computerworld*, Apr. 24, 1995, p. 16; Brad Morgan, "A Tale of Two Crises, or Lessons of Brand Management vs. Engineering," *Brandweek*, Mar. 13, 1995, p. 18; Scott McCartney, "Technology & Health: Compaq Will Use Pentium-Class Chip From Intel Competitor NexGen Inc.," *Wall Street Journal*, Mar. 31, 1995, p. 8; Intel, *Logo Usage Guidelines;* and Intel video, *Intel Inside Market Development Program.*

22. Sources: Bob Howard, "A Growth Industry for Our Time: Demand Mushrooms for Recycling and Related Environmental Services," *Orange County Business Journal*, Feb. 27, 1995, p. 22; Jeff Bailey, "WMX, Making a Move Into New York, To Buy Stake in Trash-Handling Plant," *Wall Street Journal*, Feb. 27, 1995, p. D7; Jeff Bailey, "WMX Slashes Its 1995 Spending Plans, Releases Improved 4th-Quarter Results," *Wall Street Journal*, Feb. 7, 1995, p. A5; Jeff Bailey and Warren Getler, "Inside Track: Browning Ferris Insiders Raise Bets; WMX's Pass," *Wall Street Journal*, Jan. 25, 1995, p. C1; Gary Hoover, Alta Campbell, and Patrick J. Spain, *Hoover's Handbook of American Business* (Austin, Texas: Reference Press, 1995), pp. 1126–1127; Julia Flynn, "The Ugly Mess At Waste Management," *Business Week*, Apr. 13, 1992, pp. 76–77; James A. Weber, "Waste Management Combines Telecom and Computers to Strategically Respond to Customer Needs," *Networking Management*, June 1992, p. 12; Jeanne Trombly, "Commercial Waste Processing," *BioCycle*, Jan. 1992, pp. 49–51; Leland Montgomery, "Down in the Dumps," *Financial World*, June 23, 1992, pp. 30, 32, 34; "Waste Management: Change With The Market Or Die," *Fortune*, Jan. 13, 1992, pp. 62–63; and Jeff Bailey, "Two Major Garbage Rivals Find Their Profits Trashed," *Wall Street Journal*, Mar. 4, 1993.

Chapter 8

1. Based on information from Rebecca Piirto, "Cable TV," *American Demographics*, June 1995, pp. 40–46; Jeffrey D. Zbar, "Wire Turns Hot for Cable Adding Hispanic Homes," *Advertising Age*, Jan. 23, 1995, pp. 36–37; and Kara Fitzsimmons, "Cable Operators Unfazed by New Competition," *Rochester Business Journal*, Feb. 3, 1995, p. 1.

2. "The Demographics of Death," *American Demographics*, May 1995, pp. 20–22.

3. *Discount Store News*, Mar. 15, 1993, p. 1.

4. Personal interview with James U. McNeal, Ph.D., Texas A&M University, Oct. 5, 1995.

5. *Statistical Abstract of the United States*, 1994, p. 234.

6. Yuri Radzievsky, "Untapped Markets: Ethnics in the U.S.," *Advertising Age*, June 21, 1993.

7. U.S. Bureau of the Census, *Current Population Survey*, 1970–1990.

8. G. Scott Thomas, "America's Most Educated Places," *American Demographics*, Oct. 1995, p. 56.

9. Gregory A. Patterson, "Different Strokes: Target 'Micromarkets' Its Way to Success," *Wall Street Journal,* May 31, 1995, p. A1.

10. John L. Lastovika and Erich A. Joachimsthaler, "Improving the Detection of Personality-Behavior Relationships in Consumer Research," *Journal of Consumer Research,* Mar. 1988, pp. 583–587.

11. Joseph T. Plummer, "The Concept and Application of Life Style Segmentation," *Journal of Marketing,* Jan. 1974, p. 33.

12. Calvin Sims, "Toy Maker Meets the Inner Child, Ages 21 and Up," *New York Times,* Dec. 27, 1992, p. E12.

13. Philip Kotler, *Marketing Management: Analysis, Planning, Implementation, and Control,* 6th ed. (Englewood Cliffs, N.J.: Prentice-Hall, 1994), p. 246.

14. David Hurwood, Elliot S. Grossman, and Earl Bailey, *Sales Forecasting* (New York: Conference Board, 1978); p. 2.

15. Sources: Paula Lerner and Woodfin Camp, "Soleful Endeavor," *People,* Dec. 12, 1994, pp. 69–70; Glenn Rifkin, "Mix and Match: A Shoe For Women, A Survivor's Tale," *New York Times,* July 3, 1994, p. 5; Carrie Conn, "L.A. Gear Announces Acquisition of Ryka," Ryka news release, Jan. 30, 1995; Mark Maremont, "Social Conscience For Sale?" *Business Week,* Mar. 20, 1995, p. 38; Chris Reidy, "Ryka Inc. Runs Short of Cash," *Boston Globe,* Apr. 7, 1995, p. 53; Sue Reinert, "Ryka's Support for Foundation Angers Company Shareholders," Quincy, Mass. *The Patriot Ledger,* Mar. 8, 1995, p. 29; phone interview with Ryka administrative assistant, Oct. 18, 1995; and Ryka Shoes, Inc., sales training video.

16. Sources: Rosanna Tamburri, "*Sports Illustrated* Sets Canadian Edition, but Magazine Publishers There Call Foul," *Wall Street Journal,* June 9, 1992, p. B5; Scott Donaton, "As Kids Speak, Magazine Read 'Tween Lines," *Advertising Age,* Feb. 1, 1992, pp. S4, S16; S. K. List, "The Right Place to Find Children," *American Demographics,* Feb. 1992, pp. 44–47; Dennis Chase, "Magazines Boost Circulation with Videos, Reader Clubs," *Advertising Age,* Oct. 26, 1992, p. 50; phone interview with Jane Wolf, editor for *Sports Illustrated,* Apr. 5, 1993; Shari Sanders, "Kids & Teens Show Who's Boss in Purchasing Power," *Discount Store News,* Apr. 3, 1995; Peter Jasco, "The CD-ROMization of Magazines," *Link-Up,* Mar./Apr. 1995, pp. 14–15; and Keith J. Kelly, "Magazine of the Year," *Advertising Age,* Mar. 6, 1995, pp. S1–S5.

Chapter 9

1. Based on information from Elaine Underwood, "Wal-Mart Gets Simmons Cookie Line," *Brandweek,* June 26, 1995, p. 61; Betsy Spethmann, "SnackWell's Keeps Rolling With Yogurt Intro," *Brandweek,* June 19, 1995, p. 3; Eleena de Lisser, "Pepsico Unit to Invest $225 Million To Expand Low-Fat Nonfat Snacks," *Wall Street Journal,* Jan. 18, 1995, p. B1; Betsy Spethmann, "Nabisco Leverage: SnackWell's Push," *Brandweek,* Mar. 27, 1995, pp. 1, 6; and Betsy Spethmann and Karen Benezra, "Get 'Well's Wish," *Brandweek,* June 19, 1995, pp. 1, 6.

2. Theodore Levitt, "Marketing Intangible Products and Product Intangibles," *Harvard Business Review,* May–June 1981, pp. 94–102.

3. Robert W. Haas, *Industrial Marketing Management,* 3rd ed. (Boston: Kent, 1986), pp. 15–25.

4. "L. L. Bean Launches Kids' Clothes," *Marketing News,* June 7, 1993, p. 11.

5. Donald Lichtenstein, Nancy Ridgway, and Richard G. Netemeyer, "Price Perceptions and Consumer Shopping Behavior: A Field Study," *Journal of Marketing Research,* May 1993, pp. 234–245.

6. Cyndee Miller, "Cosmetics Firms Finally Discover Ethnic Market," *Marketing News,* Aug. 30, 1993, p. 2.

7. Gerry Khermouch, "The Multifunctional Marketing Mystery," *Brandweek,* Sept. 25, 1995, pp. 26, 28–29.

8. Faye Rice, "How to Deal with Tougher Customers," *Fortune,* Dec. 3, 1990, pp. 39–48.

9. James Taylor, "As Government Spurns Safety Net Role, Marketers Become Players in Society," *Brandweek,* June 5, 1995, p. 16.

10. Shelly M. Reese, "Suitcase Savy," *American Demographics,* June 1995, p. 58.

11. Adapted from Michael Levy and Barton A. Weitz, *Retailing Management* (Homewood, Ill.: Irwin, 1995), p. 495.

12. Steve Gelsi, "Nike Plans to Export 800 Telephone Service," *Brandweek,* Sept. 25, 1995, p. 8.

13. Norton Paley, "Back from the Dead," *Sales & Marketing Management,* July 1995, pp. 30–31.

14. Calvin L. Hodock, "Strategies Behind the Winners and Losers," *Journal of Business Strategy,* Sept.–Oct. 1990, pp. 4–7.

15. Dick R. Wittink, "Who's to Blame When New Products Fail?" *Marketing News,* Aug. 30, 1993, p. 4.

16. Sources: Houghton Mifflin Company, *The American Heritage Dictionary,* 3rd ed., press kit; Joy Fleishhacker, "Book Review/Reference," *School Library Journal,* May 1994, p. 138; Houghton Mifflin Company, "World of Words," Jan./Feb. 1995; Richard A. Shaffer, "Can a PC Make You a Sharper Manager?" *Forbes,* Jan. 30, 1995, p. 110; Internet, Houghton Mifflin home page, www.hmco.com., Aug. 1995; and Houghton Mifflin, "The American Heritage Dictionary," video.

17. Sources: Patrick McGeehan, "Biking Icon Wants to Lose Training Wheels," *USA Today,* Aug. 8, 1995, pp. 1B–2B; Jan Larson, "The Bicycle Market," *American Demographics,* Mar. 1995, pp. 42–43, 46–48, 50; Laura Loro, "Schwinn Aims To Be a Big Wheel Again," *Advertising Age,* Jan. 2, 1995, p. 4; and John Beauge, "New Process Used to Make Bicycles," *Evening News* (Harrisburg, Penn.), June 5, 1995, p. 3.

Chapter 10

1. Based on information from Nora FitzGerald, "Attention, Civilians!" *Adweek,* June 26, 1995, p. 4; John T. Adams, III, "Turning Warfare Into Hardware," *HRMagazine,* Apr. 1995, p. 8; Brian O'Reilly, "What's a Hummer? Aah! Thought You'd Never Ask," *Fortune,* Oct. 2, 1995, pp. 146–150; Stephenie Overman, "Efforts That Save Jobs: Labor and Management Retool Defense Jobs," *HRMagazine,* Apr. 1995, pp. 46–51; and Stuart F. Brown, "Quest for the Boojum," *Popular Science,* July 1995, pp. 77–81.

2. Beth G. Fogurty, "A Nestea For People 'Who Know and Love Tea' and Another One That's Customized To Taste," *Beverage World,* May 31, 1995, pp. 1, 17.

3. Kim B. Clark and Takahiro Fujimoto, "The Power of Product Integrity," *Harvard Business Review,* Nov./Dec. 1990, pp. 108–118.

4. Pam Weisz, "1994's New Products Winners and Sinners, a la Consumer Panels," *Brandweek,* Dec. 12, 1994, pp. 22–24.

5. "Eddie Bauer to Offer Men's Cologne," *Marketing News,* Sept. 27, 1993, p. 2.

6. Peter F. Drucker, "The Discipline of Innovation," *Harvard Business Review,* May–June 1985, pp. 67–68.

7. Terence P. Paré, "How to Find Out What They Want," *Fortune,* Autumn–Winter 1993, p. 39.

8. Alison Fahey, "Thirsting for Something New," *Superbrands,* 1992, p. 54.

9. Christopher Power, "A Smithsonian for Stinkers," *Business Week,* Aug. 16, 1993, p. 82.

10. "Frito-Lay to Distribute Taco Bell Products," *Marketing News,* Mar. 15, 1993, p. 15.

11. Fara Warner, "Clorox Dumps Its Detergents and Sticks to Core Brands," *Adweek's Marketing Week,* May 27, 1991, p. 6.

12. Leslie Brennan, "Meeting the Test," *Sales & Marketing Management,* Mar. 1990, pp. 57–60.

13. Cyndee Miller, "Little Relief Seen for New Product Failure Rate," *Marketing News,* June 21, 1993, p. 5.

14. Adapted from Everett M. Rogers, *Diffusion of Innovations* (New York: Macmillan, 1962), pp. 81–86.

15. Ibid., pp. 247–250.

16. Tucker Comstock, "How One Company Sustained Its Lift," *Nation's Business,* Apr. 1995, p. 6.

17. Sources: Moody's Investor Service, Inc., "Moody's Company Data Report: Outboard Marine Corp.," 1995; Barnaby J. Feder, "Outboard Marine Gets New Chief," *New York Times,* Feb. 2, 1995, p. D5; Scott Kilman, "Outsider Picked to Be Outboard Marine's CEO," *Wall Street Journal,* Feb. 21, 1995, p. B4; Jeff Borden, "Outboard Marine Eyes Expansion as Ballast During Industry Cycles," *Crains Chicago Business,* Jan. 29, 1996, p. 10; Gary Samuels, "After the Storm," *Forbes,* July 3, 1995, pp. 65–66; and "Outboard Marine Corp.," video, April 4, 1996.

18. Sources: Karen Benezra, "Diet Cola Daze," *Brandweek,* Apr. 17, 1995, pp. 32–33; Eleena De Lisser, "PepsiCo Takes Aim at Dairy Market with 'Smoothies'," *Wall Street Journal,* June 1, 1995, p. B6; Glenn Collins, "Pepsi, In Search of More Share, To Test Another Low-Sugar Cola," *New York Times,* Mar. 25, 1995, pp. C1–C2; Gerry Khermouch, "Pepsi Lipton Push Slams Snapple," *Brandweek,* May 22, 1995, p. 4; Karen Benezra, "Cola Grail," *Brandweek,* Jan. 30, 1995, pp. 1, 6; Karen Benezra, "Pepsi Tests 'Revitalizing' Berry Soda," *Brandweek,* June 12, 1995, p. 6; and Laurie M. Grossman, "Marketing and Media: Pepsi to Uncork Ultimate No-Calorie, No-Caffeine Drink," *Wall Street Journal,* Dec. 2, 1994, p. B5.

Chapter 11

1. Based on information from Glenn Collins, "Pepsico Pushes a Star Performer," *New York Times,* Nov. 3, 1994, pp. D1, D16; Rose DeWolf, "Round Chips: Comfort Food," *Philadelphia Daily News,* Nov. 7, 1994, p. 51; Bob Garfield, "No Megabuck Bobbles in Ad Super Bowl," *Advertising Age,* Jan. 30, 1995, pp. 1, 3; Pam Weisz, "Repackaging," *Brandweek,* Feb. 27, 1995, pp. 25–27; and Frito-Lay press kit.

2. Peter D. Bennett, ed., *Dictionary of Marketing Terms* (Chicago: American Marketing Association, 1988), p. 18.

3. "Patent and Trademark Office Review," U.S. Patent and Trademark Office, 1995, p. 72.

4. Holly Heline, "Brand Loyalty Isn't Dead—But You're Not off the Hook," *Brandweek,* June 7, 1993, p. 14.

5. David A. Aaker, *Managing Brand Equity: Capitalizing On the Value of a Brand Name* (New York: Free Press, 1991), pp. 16–17.

6. Kurt Badenhausen, "Brands: The Management Factor," *Financial World,* Aug. 1, 1995, pp. 50–69.

7. Chip Walker, "What's in a Name?" *American Demographics,* Feb. 1991, pp. 54–57.

8. Emily DeNitto, "Back to Focus," *Brandweek,* May 29, 1995, p. 24.

9. Allyson Stewart, "U.S. Food, Drink Marketers Can Gain an Advantage via Europe," *Marketing News,* July 5, 1993, p. 8.

10. DeNitto, p. 24.

11. "Patent and Trademark Office Review," p. 72.

12. Robert Kerr, "Name Lab's Case File on How GEO Became GEO," *Commercial Appeal,* Nov. 17, 1993, p. C1.

13. Leonard L. Berry, Edwin E. Leikowith, and Terry Clark, "In Services, What's in a Name?" *Harvard Business Review,* Sept.–Oct. 1988, pp. 2–4.

14. Ibid.

15. Dorothy Cohen, "Trademark Strategy," *Journal of Marketing,* Jan. 1986, p. 63.

16. Robert Kerr, "Brand Naming Takes Science to a Level of Art," *Commercial Appeal,* Nov. 17, 1993, p. C3.

17. "Trademark Stylesheet," U.S. Trademark Association, no. 1A.

18. Dorothy Cohen, "Trademark Strategy Revisited," *Journal of Marketing,* July 1991, pp. 46–59.

19. Allan J. Magrath, "A Brand by Any Other Name," *Sales & Marketing Management,* June 1993, pp. 26–27.

20. Ibid.

21. Sam Bradley, "Licensing By the Numbers," *Brandweek,* June 19, 1995, p. 44.

22. Jeff Jansen, "Marvel Jolts Comics Industry Into New Era," *Advertising Age,* Apr. 3, 1995, p. 4.

23. "Freeze-Dried Pizza Said to Last 7 Years." *Marketing News,* Mar. 29, 1993. p. 9.

24. Ronald Grover, "Old Rockers Never Die—They Just Switch to CDs." *Business Week,* Aug. 17, 1992, p. 54.

25. James U. McNeal, *Consumer Behavior: An Integrative Approach* (Boston: Little, Brown, 1982), pp. 221–222.

26. Cyndee Miller, "Trendy Marketers Want Consumers to See Right Through Their Products," *Marketing News,* Feb. 1, 1993, pp. 1–2.

27. Louella Miles, "An Innovation Impasse?" *Marketing,* Mar. 30, 1995, pp. 27–29.

28. Sources: "Most Safety Labeling on Meat Is Postponed," *New York Times,* Oct. 10, 1993, p. 14 (N), p. 25 (L); Marian Burros, "Agricultural Department Unveils Cooking Labels for Meat," *New York Times,* Aug. 12, 1993, p. A8 (N), p. A18 (L); Joanne Silberner, "Back to the Meat Counter," *U.S. News and World Report,* May 4, 1992, p. 79; Anastasia Toufexis, "Playing Politics with Our Food," *Time,* July 15, 1991, p. 57; and National Livestock and Meat Board, *The Meat Consumer 1992,* video documentary, 1992.

29. Sources: "Evian Natural Spring Water Carves Out Bold New Look," press release, Oct. 1995; Greg W. Prince, "In Hot Water," *Beverage World,* Mar. 1995, pp. 90–95; "Bottled Water Sales Gush," *Discount Store News,* Apr. 3, 1995, p. F17; James Scarpa, "Tapping a Trend," *Restaurant Business,* May 1, 1995, p. 120; Greg W. Prince, "Sophisticated, Educated Proponents of the Planet," *Beverage World,* June 1995, p. 36; David Pringel, "Evian: How Did They Do That?" *Packaging Week,* Mar. 2, 1995, p. 21; Greg W. Prince, "Five Is Alive," *Beverage World,* June 1995, p. 35; and Greg W. Prince, "Driver's Seat," *Beverage World,* June 1995, pp. 32–38.

Chapter 12

1. Based on information from Dottie Enrico, "On-line Services Turn Up the Heat," *USA Today,* Aug. 9, 1995, p. B1; Cathy Taylor, "On-Line Big Four Face Image Crisis," *Brandweek,* Apr. 17, 1995, p. 9; David Kirkpatrick, "As the Internet Sizzles, Online Services Battle for Stakes," *Fortune,* May 1, 1995, pp. 86–89, 91–93; Tara Buckley, "The Internet Shuffle," *Brandweek,* Mar. 20, 1995, pp. 34, 36–37; and Melanie Wells, "On-line Competitors Crank Up Ad Campaigns," *USA Today,* May 31, 1995, p. B1.

2. Leonard L. Berry and A. Parasuraman, *Marketing Services: Competing Through Quality* (New York: Free Press, 1991), p. 5.

3. Michael Levy and Barton A. Weitz, *Retailing Management* (Homewood, Ill.: Irwin, 1992), p. 601.

4. Louise I. Driben, "The Service Edge," *Sales & Marketing Management*, June 1993, pp. 80–84.

5. *Statistical Abstract of the United States*, 1994, pp. 447, 783.

6. "1995 Staffing Industry Forecast," *Staffing Industry Report*, 1995.

7. "Services," *Business Week*, Jan. 9, 1995, pp. 84–91.

8. The material in this section has been adapted from Christopher H. Lovelock, *Services Marketing*, 3rd ed. (Englewood Cliffs, N.J.: Prentice-Hall, 1996), pp. 15–19; J. Paul Peter and James H. Donnelly, Jr., *A Preface to Marketing Management*, 6th ed. (Homewood, Ill.: Irwin, 1994), pp. 217–240; and Valarie A. Zeithaml, A. Parasuraman, and Leonard L. Berry, *Delivering Quality Service: Balancing Customer Perceptions and Expectations* (New York: Free Press, 1990).

9. Mary Jo Bitner, "Evaluating Service Encounters: The Effects of Physical Surroundings and Employee Responses," *Journal of Marketing*, Apr. 1990, pp. 69–82.

10. Michael D. Hartline and O. C. Ferrell, "Service Quality Implementation: The Effects of Organizational Socialization and Managerial Actions of Customer-Contact Employee Behavior," *Marketing Science Institute Working Paper Series*, Report no. 93-122 (Cambridge, Mass.: Marketing Science Institute, 1993).

11. Leonard L. Berry, *On Great Service: A Framework for Action* (New York: Free Press, 1995), pp. 53–54.

12. Peter and Donnelly, *A Preface to Marketing Management*, p. 225.

13. Hartline and Ferrell, "Service Quality Implementation," p. 27.

14. Ibid., p. 36.

15. Peter and Donnelly, *A Preface to Marketing Management*, p. 231.

16. Tom Paulu, "When the Rub Hits the Road," *Daily News (Longview, Wash.)*, June 7, 1995.

17. Zeithaml, Parasuraman, and Berry, *Delivering Quality Service*.

18. Valarie A. Zeithaml, "How Consumer Evaluation Processes Differ Between Goods and Services," in *Marketing of Services*, ed. James H. Donnelly and William R. George (Chicago: American Marketing Association, 1981), pp. 186–190.

19. A. Parasuraman, Leonard L. Berry, and Valarie A. Zeithaml, "An Empirical Examination of Relationships in an Extended Service Quality Model," *Marketing Science Institute Working Paper Series*, Report no. 90-122 (Cambridge, Mass.: Marketing Science Institute, 1990), p. 29.

20. Rahul Jacob, "How to Retread Customers," *Fortune Special Issue: The Tough New Consumer*, Autumn/Winter 1993, pp. 23–24.

21. Valarie A. Zeithaml, Leonard L. Berry, and A. Parasuraman, "Communication and Control Processes in the Delivery of Service Quality," *Journal of Marketing*, Apr. 1988, pp. 35–48.

22. Valarie A. Zeithaml, Leonard L. Berry, and A. Parasuraman, "The Nature and Determinants of Customer Expectations of Service," *Journal of the Academy of Marketing Science*, Winter 1993, pp. 1–12.

23. Hartline and Ferrell, "Service Quality Implementation," p. 36.

24. Bitner, "Evaluating Service Encounters," p. 70.

25. Hartline and Ferrell, "Service Quality Implementation," pp. 17–19.

26. Myron Glassman and Bruce McAfee, "Integrating the Personnel and Marketing Functions: The Challenge of the 1990s." *Business Horizons*, May–June 1992, pp. 52–59.

27. Philip Kotler, *Marketing for Nonprofit Organizations*, 2nd ed. (Englewood Cliffs, N.J.: Prentice-Hall, 1982), p. 37.

28. Ibid.

29. Sources: Laurie Niles, "Fireworks Sky Dance Is No Hurry-Up Job," *Omaha World-Herald*, June 30, 1995, p. B13; Glenn Jochum, "Sky's No Limit for Felix Grucci," *LI Business News*, Mar. 20, 1995, p. 23; Fireworks by Grucci, press kit; and Fireworks by Grucci, company video.

30. Sources: Takia Mahmood and Stephen P. Bradley, "The Promus Companies," Harvard Business School Publishing, Feb. 28, 1995; Pauline Yoshihashi, "Promus to Split Into Casino, Hotel Firms," *Wall Street Journal*, Jan. 31, 1995, p. A3; Martha Brannigan, "Promus Casino In New Orleans Begins Poorly," *Wall Street Journal*, June 12, 1995, p. A4; Harrah's Survey of Casino Entertainment 1995; Harrah's Entertainment Co., *Annual Report*, 1994; Promus Companies Corporate Fact Sheet; Harrah's Casino's Fact Sheet; and Elaine Underwood, "Casino Gambling's New Deal," *Brandweek*, Apr. 10, 1995, pp. 21–25.

Chapter 13

1. Based on information from Laurie Joan Aron, "Delivery Speed Keeps Electronics Boutique at the Top of Its Game," *Inbound Logistics*, Jan. 1996, pp. 31–36+.

2. Terry Lefton, "Nintendo's Game Plan," *Brandweek*, Feb. 8, 1993, pp. 23–24.

3. Sumit K. Majumdar and Venkatram Ramaswamy, "Going Direct to Market: The Influence of Exchange Conditions," *Strategic Management Journal*, June 1995, pp. 353–372.

4. Steven Burke, "Intel Seeks Closer Ties to Channel Elite," *Computer Reseller News*, May 15, 1995, p. 1.

5. James D. Hlavacek and Tommy J. McCuistion. "Industrial Distributors: When, Who, and How?" *Harvard Business Review*, Mar.–Apr. 1983, p. 97.

6. Kelly Shermach, "Retail Catalogs Designed to Boost Instore Sales," *Marketing News*, July 3, 1995, pp. 1, 3.

7. Rajiv Dant, Patrick Kaufmann, and Audhesh Paswan, "Ownership Redirection in Franchised Channels," *Journal of Public Policy and Marketing*, Spring 1992, pp. 33–34.

8. Leo Aspinwall, "The Marketing Characteristics of Goods," in *Four Marketing Theories* (Boulder: University of Colorado Press, 1961), pp. 27–32.

9. Allan J. Magrath, "Differentiating Yourself via Distribution," *Sales & Marketing Management*, Mar. 1991, pp. 50–57.

10. Lisa Harrington, "How to Join the Supply Chain Revolution," *Inbound Logistics*, Nov. 1995, p. 21.

11. Ibid.

12. Deborah C. Ruriani, "Logistics: Where Do We Go from Here?" *Inbound Logistics*, Aug. 1995, pp. 31–32.

13. Laurie Joan Aron, "Home Depot Finds Logistic Strength in Numbers," *Inbound Logistics*, Nov. 1994, p. 29.

14. James D. Martin, "Intermodal Needs Supply Chain Partnerships," *Inbound Logistics*, Apr. 1995, p. 16.

15. Phillip W. Seely, "Using Technology to Meet Customer Needs," *Inbound Logistics*, July 1995, p. 46.

16. Harrington, p. 20.

17. Elizabeth Jensen, "'What's Up, Doc?' Vertical Integration," *Wall Street Journal*, Oct. 16, 1995, p. B1.

18. Jordan D. Lewis, "Using Alliances to Build Market Power," *Planning Review*, Sept.–Oct. 1990, pp. 1–9, 48.

19. Robert D. Buzzell and Gwen Ortmeyer, "Channel Partnerships Streamline Distribution," *Sloan Management Review*, Spring 1995, p. 85.

20. Buzzell and Ortmeyer, "Channel Partnerships Streamline Distribution."

21. Ibid., p. 90.

22. Wroe Alderson, *Dynamic Marketing Behavior* (Homewood, Ill.: Irwin, 1965), p. 239.

23. Ibid., p. 85.

24. James C. Anderson and James A. Narus, "A Model of Distributor Firm and Manufacturer Firm Working Partnerships," *Journal of Marketing*, Jan. 1990, pp. 42–58.

25. Steven J. Skinner, Julie B. Gassenheimer, and Scott W. Kelley, "Cooperation in Supplier-Dealer Relations," *Journal of Retailing*, Summer 1992, pp. 174–193.

26. Ibid.

27. Jakki Mohr and John R. Nevin, "Communication Strategies in Marketing Channels: A Theoretical Perspective," *Journal of Marketing*, Oct. 1990, pp. 36–51.

28. Erle Norton, "Last of the U.S. Tire Makers Ride Out Foreign Invasion," *Wall Street Journal*, Feb. 4, 1993, p. 86.

29. Adel I. El-Ansary, "Perspectives on Channel System Performance," in *Contemporary Issues in Marketing Channels*, ed. Robert F. Lusch and Paul H. Zinszer (Norman: University of Oklahoma Press, 1979), p. 50.

30. Kenneth G. Hardy and Allan J. Magrath, "Ten Ways for Manufacturers to Improve Distribution Management," *Business Horizons*. Nov.–Dec. 1988, p. 68.

31. Janet E. Keith, Donald W. Jackson, and Lawrence A. Crosby, "Effect of Alternative Types of Influence Strategies Under Different Dependence Structures," *Journal of Marketing*, July 1990, pp. 30–41.

32. Zachary Schiller, David Woodruff, Kevin Kelly, and Michael Schroeder, "GM Tightens the Screws," *Business Week*, June 22, 1992, pp. 30–31.

33. Hardy and Magrath. *Ten Ways*, p. 68.

34. John F. Gaski and John R. Nevin, "The Differential Effects of Exercised and Unexercised Power Sources in a Marketing Channel," *Journal of Marketing Research*, July 1985, p. 139.

35. Gregory T. Gundlach and Ernest R. Cadotte, "Exchange Interdependence and Interfirm Interaction: Research in a Simulated Channel Setting," *Journal of Marketing Research*, Nov. 1994, pp. 516–532.

36. Sandra Skrovan, "Partnering with Vendors: The Ties That Bind," *Chain Store Age Executive*, Jan. 1994, p. 6MH.

37. Bert Rosenbloom, *Marketing Channels: A Management View* (Hinsdale, Ill.: Dryden, 1991), p. 208.

38. Rosenbloom, *Marketing Channels*, p. 103.

39. Ibid., p. 104.

40. Ibid., pp. 108–109.

41. Sources: Keith Anderson, "Reader Can Replace Her CUTCO Knives: Firm Still Guarantees Product," *Denver Post*, June 17, 1995, p. E4; Susan Burns, "The Amway Army," *Sarasota Magazine*, Jan. 1996, p. 48; Pamela Davis-Diaz, "No More Waiting for the Avon Lady," *St. Petersburg Times*, Mar. 13, 1995, p. 8; David W. Cravens, "The Changing Role of the Sales Force: Now It's Urgent," *Marketing Management*, Fall 1995, p. 49; Paul Johnson, "Vector Suspends Recruiting," *Wisconsin State Journal*, Apr. 21, 1994, p. 1F; Stratford Sherman, "Will the Information Superhighway Be the Death of Retailing?" *Fortune*, Apr. 18, 1994, p. 98; Debby Garbato Stankevich, "Henckels Sets Biggest Ad Push For Twinstar," *HFN: The Weekly Newspaper for the Home Furniture Network*, Sept. 11, 1995, p. 33; Debby Garbato Stankevich, "Pitching Upscale Cutlery: Vendors Boost In-Store Support," *HFN: The Weekly Newspaper for the Home Furniture Network*, Dec. 25, 1995, p. 33; Laurel Touby, "Direct Selling: Behind the Hype," *Executive Female*, Mar. 1994, p. 19.

42. Sources: "DealerNet Links Auto Buyers, Sellers Nationwide," *Marketing News*, July 31, 1995, p. 30; Mike McKesson, "'96 Promises to Transform Used Car Industry," *Marketing News*, Feb. 12, 1996, p. 7; and Keith Naughton, with Kathleen Kerwin, Bill Vlasic, Lori Bongiorno, and David Leonhardt, "Revolution in the Showroom," *Business Week*, Feb. 19, 1996, pp. 70–76.

Chapter 14

1. Based on information from "The Frieda's of the Future," *On the Cutting Edge*, Mar.–Apr. 1992; Robert Johnson, "Thorny Question: Will the Prickly Pear Be Kiwi of the '90s?" *Wall Street Journal*, Jan. 26, 1993; Frieda's Finest, press kit, 1993; and Robert Maynard, "Finding Ways to Talk with Customers," *Nation's Business*, Mar. 1995, p. 12.

2. Hoover's Handbook Database (Austin, Texas: Reference Press, 1995), accessed via America Online on Dec. 29, 1995.

3. *Statistical Abstract of the United States: 1995*, 115th ed., p. 550.

4. David E. Gumpert, "They Can Get It for You Wholesale," *Working Woman*, Aug. 1990, pp. 33–36, 94.

5. Harry G. Miller, "Micro-Enterprise Development: The Role of Wholesaling in Developing Countries," *International Journal of Technology Management* 9, no. 1 (1994): 113–120.

6. Chandrasekhar Das and Rajesh Tyagi, "Wholesaler: A Decision Support System for Wholesale Procurement and Distribution," *International Journal of Physical Distribution and Logistics Management* 24, no. 10 (1994): 4–12.

7. Hoover's Handbook Database, via America Online.

8. Ibid.

9. Richard A. Melcher, "The Middlemen Stay on the March," *Business Week*, Jan. 9, 1995, p. 87.

10. Bert Rosenbloom, *Marketing Channels: A Management View* (Hinsdale, Ill.: Dryden, 1991), p. 450.

11. Donald J. Bowersox and M. Bixby Cooper, *Strategic Marketing Channel Management* (New York: McGraw-Hill, 1992), pp. 41–42.

12. Hoover's Handbook Database, via America Online.

13. "The Broker's Role," *Progressive Grocer*, Dec. 1994, p. SS9.

14. Rosenbloom, *Marketing Channels*, p. 6.

15. Rosenbloom, p. 66.

16. Ibid.

17. Thomas V. Bonoma, "Get More Out of Your Trade Shows," *Harvard Business Review*, Jan.–Feb. 1983, pp. 75–83.

18. Rosenbloom, p. 450.

19. Rosenbloom, pp. 387–388.

20. Helen Berman, "The Advertising/Trade Show Partnership," *Folio: The Magazine for Magazine Management*, May 1, 1995, pp. 44–47.

21. Berman, "The Advertising/Trade Show Partnership."

22. Meg Whittemore, "Trade Shows' Direct Appeal," *Nation's Business*, Aug. 1993, pp. 48–49.

23. Kate Bertrand, "Trade Shows Can Be Global Gateways," *Advertising Age's Business Marketing*, Mar. 1995, pp. 19–20.

24. Melcher, "The Middlemen Stay on the March,"; and Mike McNamee, with Richard A. Melcher, Elisabeth Malkin, and Wendy Zellner, "Industry Outlook," *Business Week,* Jan. 8, 1996, p. 73.

25. Melcher, "Middlemen."

26. Ronald D. Michman, "Managing Structural Changes in Marketing Channels," *Journal of Consumer Marketing,* Fall 1990, pp. 33–42.

27. Christine Forbes, "Keeping the Gears in Sync," *Industrial Distribution,* Feb. 1993, pp. 24–26.

28. Rebecca Rolfes, "Wholesaling Without Borders," *Medical Marketing & Media,* Feb. 1991, pp. 74–76.

29. Hoover's Handbook Database, via America Online.

30. Joseph Weber, "On a Fast Boat to Anywhere," *Business Week,* Jan. 11, 1993, p. 94.

31. Rolfes, "Wholesaling Without Borders," pp. 74–76.

32. Sources: Elliot Zweibach, *Supermarket News,* Mar. 15, 1993, p. 4; *Supermarket News,* Apr. 4, 1993, p. 3; *PR Newswire,* July 7, 1993, p. 1; *Chain Store Age Executive Edition,* July 1993, p. 53; Robette Ledbetter, "At Fleming, Service Is Up and Film Is In," *Inform,* Jan. 1992, pp. 34–35; Michael Sansolo, "Niche Picking," *Progressive Grocer,* Sept. 1992, pp. 52–54; Fleming Companies, Inc., *Overview,* video, 1993; and "The Business Week 1000," *Business Week,* Mar. 27, 1995, p. 148.

33. Sources: Nanette Byrnes, "A Sleeping Giant Stirs Itself," *FW,* May 25, 1993, pp. 48–50; McKesson Corporation, information sheet, 1993; Milt Freudenheim, "Market Place: At Last, McKesson Finds Itself in the Pharmaceutical Spotlight," *New York Times,* Aug. 9, 1993, p. D8; Gary Forger, "Better Data Cuts Handling Time at McKesson," *Modern Materials Handling,* Aug. 1992, pp. 38–40; *McKesson Today,* July 1993; "The Business Week 1000," *Business Week,* Mar. 27, 1995, p. 303; and *Hoover's Handbook Database* (Austin, Texas: Reference Press, 1995), via America Online.

Chapter 15

1. Based on information from Elaine Underwood, "Talbots Broadens to Babies, Shoes, Maybe Home Furnishings," *Brandweek,* Aug. 24, 1995, p. 10; Talbots news release, Aug. 31, 1995, via America Online.

2. *Statistical Abstract of the United States: 1995,* 115th ed., p. 550.

3. Alexa Bell, "Eye on the Prize," *Restaurant Business,* Sept. 1, 1993, pp. 46–47.

4. *Communication News,* Apr. 1995, p. 53.

5. *Chain Store Age Executive,* May 1995, pp. 78–80.

6. *Chain Store Age Executive,* Feb. 1995, p. 102.

7. Laura Liebeck, *Discount Store News,* Feb. 6, 1995, pp. 23–24.

8. Gretchen Morgenson, "Back to Basics," *Forbes,* May 10, 1993, pp. 56–57.

9. Hattie Powell, "Grocers' Frills Fail to Thrill," *Business Week,* Aug. 14, 1995, p. 8.

10. Betsy Spethman, "Vons Opens Hybrid Megamarkets," *Brandweek,* June 28, 1993, p. 4.

11. Emily DeNitto, "Hypermarkets Seem to Be Big Flop in U.S.," *Advertising Age,* Oct. 4, 1993, p. 20.

12. J. Barry Mason, Morris L. Mayer, and Hazel F. Ezell, *Retailing* (Homewood, Ill.: Irwin, 1994), pp. 3–4.

13. Kirsten A. Conover, "Join the Club, Buy in Bulk," *Christian Science Monitor,* Jan. 28, 1993, p. 11.

14. Julie Liesse, "Welcome to the Club," *Advertising Age,* Feb. 1, 1993, p. 3.

15. Howard Schlossberg, "Warehouse Club Owners Hope to Sign Up Everybody Eventually," *Marketing News,* Sept. 13, 1993, p. 1.

16. Bob Ortega, "Warehouse-Club War Leaves Few Standing, and They Are Bruised," *Wall Street Journal,* Nov. 18, 1993, pp. A1, A6.

17. Barry Berman and Joel Evans, *Retail Management: A Strategic Approach* (New York: Macmillan, 1992), pp. 104–105.

18. R. Michelle Breyer, "When the Shoe Fits," *Austin American-Statesman,* Sept. 3, 1995, pp. D1, D3.

19. Stephanie Anderson Forest, "I Can Get It for You Retail," *Business Week,* Sept. 18, 1995.

20. Erick Schonfeld, "Spawn of Kmart Goes on Killing Spree," *Fortune,* Oct. 16, 1995, p. 241.

21. Kelly Shermach, "Retail Catalogs Designed to Boost In-store Sales," *Marketing News,* July 3, 1995, p. 1.

22. Laurel Campbell, "Fewer Catalogs in the Mail This Year," *Commercial Appeal,* Oct. 19, 1995, pp. B4, B7.

23. Ibid.

24. Elaine Underwood, "Why I'm a Home Shopper," *Brandweek,* Apr. 19, 1993, pp. 23–28.

25. Laurel Campbell, "Retailers Advised to Get New Customers Online," *Commercial Appeal,* Jan. 16, 1996, p. B10.

26. "Land's End on Internet," *Marketing News,* Aug. 14, 1995, p. 1.

27. "Franchising Fellowship," *Marketing Management,* Fall 1995, p. 4.

28. "Franchising Fellowship," p. 5.

29. "The Minnesota Mallers," *U.S. News & World Report,* June 26, 1989, p. 12.

30. *Chain Store Age Executive,* Dec. 1994, pp. 114–115.

31. George H. Lucas, Jr., and Larry G. Gresham, "How to Position for Retail Success," *Business,* Apr.–June 1988, pp. 3–13.

32. Nicholas Hirst, "How to Succeed in U.S. Retailing," *Canadian Business,* Oct. 1991, pp. 77–84.

33. Julie Baker, Dhruv Grewal, and A. Parasuraman, "The Influence of Store Environment on Quality Inferences and Store Image," *Journal of the Academy of Marketing Science,* Fall 1994, p. 328.

34. Stephen Brown, "The Wheel of Retailing: Past and Future," *Journal of Retailing,* Summer 1990, pp. 143–149.

35. Laurel Campbell, "Retail Forecast for First Half of '96: Slow," *Commercial Appeal,* Jan. 6, 1996, p. B8.

36. Ibid.

37. Sources: "Hot Shots: HFD Profiles 25 of the Industry's Most Influential Retail Buyers," *HFD,* July 20, 1992, pp. 47–48; Michael Hartnett, "Container Store Enjoys Steady Growth." *SCT Retailing Today,* Nov. 1992, pp. 67–68; Kathy Cornish, "Storing Up for Success," *Shopping Center World,* Nov. 1992, pp. 66, 68; Bob Weinstein, "Box Boys: The Container Store," *Entrepreneur,* June 1992, pp. 122–126: "Growth Plans for The Container Store," *Stores,* May 1992, p. 74; The Container Store, press kit; and *The Container Store,* video.

38. Gail DeGeorge, "A Theme Park You Can Live In," *Business Week,* Sept. 25, 1995, p. 57; "Disney Park Planned in Tokyo," *Wall Street Journal,* Nov. 8, 1995, p. A18; June Fletcher, "Dream-Builder Disney Offers Dream Homes," *Wall Street Journal,* Oct. 20, 1995, p. 13B; Rick Johnson, "A Strategy for Style," *Journal of Business Strategy,* Sept./Oct. 1991, pp. 38–43; Gareth R. Jones, "Michael Eisner's Disney Company," in Charles W. L. Hill and Gareth R. Jones, *Strategic Management: An Integrated Approach* (Boston: Houghton

Mifflin, 1991), pp. 784–805; Jeanne C. Meister, "Disney Approach Typifies Quality Service," *Marketing News*, Jan. 1990, p. 38; and Michael Oneal, with Stephen Baker and Ronald Grover, "Disney's Kingdom," *Business Week*, Aug. 14, 1995, pp. 30–34.

Chapter 16

1. Based on information from Lisa Harrington, "Weight Watchers: Transforming Spaghetti Plate Distribution into an Integrated Supply Chain," *Inbound Logistics*, Nov. 19, 1995, pp. 22–23; Keith L. Alexander, "A Health Kick at Weight Watchers," *Business Week*, Jan. 16, 1995, p. 36; and *Hoover's Company Profile* database (Austin, Texas: Reference Press, 1995), via America Online.

2. Tom Richman, "How 20 Best-Practice Companies Do It," *Harvard Business Review*, Sept./Oct. 1995, pp. 11–12.

3. Anne G. Perkins, "Manufacturing: Maximizing Service, Minimizing Inventory," *Harvard Business Review*, Mar./Apr. 1994, pp. 13–14.

4. John T. Mentzer, Roger Gomes, and Robert E. Krapfel, Jr., "Physical Distribution Service: A Fundamental Marketing Concept?" *Journal of the Academy of Marketing Science*, Winter 1989, p. 59.

5. Laurie Joan Aron, "Speeding the Plow," *Inbound Logistics*, Dec. 1995, p. 28.

6. Lloyd M. Rinehart, M. Bixby Cooper, and George D. Wagenheim, "Furthering the Intregation of Marketing and Logistics Through Customer Service in the Channel," *Journal of the Academy of Marketing Science*, Winter 1989, p. 67.

7. James Wetherbe, "Principles of Cycle Time Reduction," *Cycle Time Research* 1, no. 1 (1995): iv.

8. Michael Clements, "UPS, FedEx Race to Offer Same-Day Service," *USA Today*, Apr. 12, 1995, p. B1.

9. Getahn M. Ward, "Firms Tell Suppliers to Trash Paper, Take Orders by Computer," *Commercial Appeal*, July 16, 1995, p. C1.

10. Getahn M. Ward, "How to Start A System for Electronic Data Interchange," *Commercial Appeal*, July 16, 1995, p. C1.

11. Tom Andel, "Superhighway or Unbeaten Path?" *Transportation & Distribution*, Sept. 1994, p. 83.

12. The EOQ formula for the optimal order quantity is EOQ = $\sqrt{2DR/1}$, where EOQ = optimum average order size, D = total demand, R = cost of processing an order, and 1 = cost of maintaining one unit of inventory per year.

13. Gary Forger, "Jeep Puts JIT in High Gear," *Modern Materials Handling*, Jan. 1993, pp. 42–45.

14. Jeffrey H. Dyer, "Dedicated Assets: Japan's Manufacturing Edge," *Harvard Business Review*, Nov./Dec. 1994, pp. 174–178.

15. Douglas M. Lambert and James R. Stock, *Strategic Logistics Management* (Homewood, Ill.: Irwin, 1993), p. 265.

16. Adapted from John F. Magee, *Physical Distribution Systems* (New York: McGraw-Hill, 1967).

17. Cindy Muroff, "Private Warehouses Take a Tumble," *Distribution*, July 1993, pp. 72–74.

18. Ibid.

19. Carl M. Guelzo, *Introduction to Logistics Management* (Englewood Cliffs, N.J.: Prentice-Hall, 1986), p. 102.

20. Amy Zuckerman, "Logistics Lights Up Philips," *Inbound Logistics*, Sept. 1995, p. 26.

21. Peter D. Bennett, ed., *Dictionary of Marketing Terms* (Chicago: American Marketing Association, 1988), p. 204.

22. Walter L. Weart, "Railroads Get Back on Track," *Inbound Logistics*, May 1990, pp. 24–27.

23. *Jane's All the World's Aircraft 1991–92*, 82nd ed. (Alexandria, Va.: Jane's Information Group, 1991).

24. Lambert and Stock, *Strategic Logistics Management*, p. 174.

25. Lambert and Stock, *Strategic Logistics Management*, p. 175.

26. Wal-Mart Stores, Inc., *1993 Annual Report*, p. 2.

27. Thomas Dillon, "Containerization: An Idea That Made Sense," *Inbound Logistics*, Apr. 1991, pp. 25–28; and Allen R. Wastler, "Intermodal Leaders Ponder Riddle of Winning More Freight," *Traffic World*, June 19, 1989, pp. 14–15.

28. "Satisfying Customers Worldwide," *Inbound Logistics*, Nov. 1994, pp. 32–35.

29. Sources: Airborne Express, *Delivering Satisfaction Worldwide*, video, May 6, 1993; Alexandra Biesada, "Truck Soup," *Financial World*, Aug. 4, 1992, pp. 22–23; Agis Salpukas, "Federal Express Cuts Rates," *New York Times*, May 7, 1992, pp. D1, D8; Daniel Pearl, "Airborne Express Rushed to Keep Pace with Its Rivals," *Wall Street Journal*, July 13, 1992, p. D3; Peter Bradley, "Buyers Take All in Package Slugfest," *Purchasing*, Oct. 22, 1992, pp. 48–49, 51; and *Hoover's Company Profile* database (Austin, Texas: Reference Press, 1995), via America Online.

30. Laurie Joan Aron, "Home Depot Finds Logistics Strength in Numbers," *Inbound Logistics*, Nov. 1995, pp. 28–31; "The Business Week 1000," *Business Week*, Mar. 25, 1996, pp. 108–109; The Home Depot, *1994 Annual Report*; and Hoover's Handbook database (Austin, Texas: Reference Press, 1995), via America Online.

Chapter 17

1. Based on information from Columbia Sportswear Company, corporate information packet; Janet Bamford, "The Working Woman 50: America's Top Women Business Owners," *Working Women*, May 1995, pp. 43–44; Emily Mitchell, "Do What Mother Says," *Time*, Feb. 6, 1995; "The Best of 1994," *Business Week*, Jan. 9, 1995, pp. 101–107; Mike Sheridan, "Mother's Nature," *Sky*, Jan. 1995, pp. 54–58, 60–63; and Jamie Goldman, "Columbia Sportswear," *Advertising Age*, June 26, 1995, p. S32.

2. Jeffrey D. Zbar, "Wildlife Takes Center Stage as Cause-Related Marketing Becomes a $250 Million Show for Companies," *Advertising Age*, June 28, 1993, pp. 551–556.

3. In case you do not read Chinese, this says, "In the factory we make cosmetics, and in the store we sell hope." Prepared by Chih Kans Wang.

4. Terence A. Shimp, *Promotion Management and Marketing Communication* (Fort Worth, Tex.: Dryden, 1993), p. 35.

5. John S. McClenahen, "How Can You Possibly Say That?" *Industry Week*, July 17, 1995, pp. 17–19.

6. Mark Lacek, "Loyalty Marketing No Ad Budget Threat," *Advertising Age*, Oct. 23, 1995, p. 20.

7. John J. Burnett, *Promotion Management* (Boston: Houghton Mifflin, 1993), p. 7.

8. Chip Walker, "Word of Mouth," *American Demographics*, July 1995, pp. 38–40.

9. George E. Belch and Michael A. Belch, *Introduction to Advertising and Promotion* (Homewood, Ill.: Irwin, 1995), p. 9.

10. James M. Stearns and Shaheen Borna, "The Ethics of Lottery Advertising: Issues and Evidence," *Journal of Business Ethics*, Jan. 1995, pp. 43–51.

11. Weld F. Royal, "Scapegoat or Scoundrel?" *Sales & Marketing Management*, Jan. 1995, pp. 62–69.

12. Susan Edelman, "Sweepstakes Lawsuit Goes To Trial," *Record*, Mar. 12, 1995, p. A3.

13. A. II. Maslow, *Motivation and Personality* (New York: Harper and Row, 1954).

14. "Ban the Butts, Survey Says," *Incentive*, May 1995, p. 16.

15. Ira Teinowitz and Keith J. Kelly, "PM Fires Up Warning over Tobacco Ad Limits," *Advertising Age*, Nov. 20, 1995, pp. 3, 23.

16. Sources: James Scarpa, ed., "Pork Around the Clock," *Restaurant Business*, suppl., 1995, pp. 4, 34; Scott Hume, "That's All Folks," *Adweek*, May 9, 1994, pp. 1–2; Karen Straus, "Profitable, Popular Pork," *Restaurants & Institutions*, Nov. 11, 1992, pp. 81–90; Rod Smith, "NTF to Copy NPPC Strategy, Be Provocateur for Turkey," *Foodstuffs*, Jan. 25, 1993, pp. 3, 6; Julie Mettenburg, "Stealing More Than Attention," *Drovers Journal*, Mar. 1993, pp. 22–23; National Pork Producer's Council, *The Future of America's Plate*, 1993; Alan Bell, "Uncovering Links in the Quality Chain," *Pork*, May 1993, p. 54; and National Pork Producer's Council video, "The Retail Battle of '93," Apr. 23, 1993.

17. Sources: Robert Emproto and Greg Prince, "College Binge Drinking Data Shows Anti-Abuse Effort Has Miles To Go," *Beverage World*, Jan. 31, 1995, pp. 1, 3; Chris Reidy, "Questions Arise on Liquor Marketing," *Boston Globe*, Apr. 6, 1995, p. 69; Fara Warner, "Liquor Industry Tackles Teenage Drinking," *Wall Street Journal*, June 30, 1995, p. B4; and Anheuser-Busch Company, press kit, 1995.

Chapter 18

1. Based on information from The Blaze Company, The Beverly Hills Hotel press kit; The Blaze Company, The Beverly Hills Hotel case history; Ajay Sahgal, "The Pink Palace," *Los Angeles Times* magazine, May 21, 1995, pp. 19–22; Irene Lacher, "Always on Stage," *Los Angeles Times*, June 4, 1994, pp. E1–E3; Pat Steger, "Pink Palace Back From Rehab," *San Francisco Chronicle*, June 5, 1995, pp. E1–E2; "Hoteliers Spending Billions to Spruce Up," *USA Today*, May 23, 1995; Larry Lipson, "Now As Before, It's Pretty in Pink," *Los Angeles Daily News*, June 4, 1995, pp. 12, 14; Bernard Weinraub, "A Grand Hotel, Still Pink, Still Posh," *New York Times*, June 1, 1995, pp. B1, B4; and Pauline Yoshihashi, "A Grand Hotel Reopens: Will Stars Return?" *Wall Street Journal*, June 2, 1995, p. B9.

2. "100 Leading National Advertisers by Rank," *Advertising Age*, Sept. 27, 1995, p. 3.

3. C. Samuel Craig and Arijit Ghosh, "Using Household-Level Viewing Data to Maximize Effective Reach," *Journal of Advertising Research*, Jan.–Feb. 1993, pp. 38–47.

4. "A Big Fish in a Little Pond," *Sales & Marketing Management*, Nov. 1995, p. 18.

5. Diane Cyr, "Getting More Direct," *Brandweek*, Oct. 9, 1995, pp. 29, 32, 34, 36.

6. Jonathan J. Ward, "Quality in Print," *Sales & Marketing Management*, July 1993, pp. 28–31.

7. Cyndee Miller, "Demonstrating Your Point," *Marketing News*, Sept. 13, 1993, p. 2.

8. Dean M. Krugman, Leonard N. Reid, S. Watson Dunn, and Arnold M. Barban, *Advertising: Its Role in Modern Marketing*, 8th ed. (Fort Worth, Tex.: Dryden Press, 1993), p. 371.

9. Laureen Miles, "Coke's New Campaign: Message Is the Media," *Mediaweek*, Feb. 15, 1993, pp. 1–3.

10. M. Louise Ripley, "What Kind of Companies Take Their Advertising In-House," *Journal of Advertising Research*, Oct.–Nov. 1991, pp. 73–77.

11. George E. Belch and Michael A. Belch, *Introduction to Advertising and Publicity* (Chicago: Irwin, 1995), p. 518.

12. Kate Fitzgerald, "Sega 'Screams' Its Way to the Top," *Advertising Age*, Mar. 26, 1995, p. S2.

13. Belch and Belch, p. 530.

14. Sources: Advertising Council, *1992 Annual Report;* "Ad Council Targets Racism In Wake of L.A. Rioting," *Advertising Age*, May 11, 1992, pp. 1, 76; "Fifth Estater: Ruth Ann Wooden," *Broadcasting*, Nov. 2, 1992, p. 79; Jane Hodges and Susen Taras, "Born in War, Ad Council Still Thrives," *Advertising Age*, July 31, 1995, p. 30; Advertising Council video, "Advertising Council Campaigns Make a Difference"; "The Ad Council Commits to a New Focus: America's Youth," Advertising Council press release, May 15, 1995; and Advertising Council press kit, 1995.

15. Sources: Oscar Suris, "Oh! A Tangled Web: Spider-Man's Fans Rush to His Rescue," *Wall Street Journal*, Feb. 12, 1996, pp. A1, A6; Marvel Entertainment Group, Inc., *1994 Annual Report;* Karen Benezra, "Marketers of the Year Youth Marketing: Jerry Calabrese & Joel Erlich," *Brandweek*, Oct. 9, 1995, pp. 112–113; Jeff Jensen, "Marvel Jolts Comics Industry Into New Era," *Advertising Age*, Apr. 3, 1995, p. 4; Robert La Franco, "A Riff and a Rating," *Forbes*, Mar. 27, 1995, p. 18; "What's Hot In Games," *Discount Store News*, Sept. 4, 1995, p. 51; Sharon Holle, "Marvel Interactive Battle Pack Featuring First-Ever Touch-Tone Card Game," *PR Newswire*, Aug. 3, 1995; and Marvel Entertainment Group, Inc., press kit.

Chapter 19

1. Based on information from Laurie Hays, "IBM Chief Unveils Top-Level Shake-Up, Consolidating Sales Arm, Software Line," *Wall Street Journal*, Jan. 10, 1995, p. B6; Craig Stedman, "Users Laud IBM Reorganization—For Now," *Computerworld*, Jan. 30, 1995, p. 57; "Reengineering: Is There a Doctor in the House?" *Sales & Marketing Management*, Apr. 1995, p. S17; Chuck Paustian, "Icons Michael Jordan, IBM Journey the Comeback Trail," *Business Marketing*, Apr. 1995, p. 8; James Kaczman, "Just Fix It, Your Sales Process, That Is," *Sales & Marketing Management*, Sept. 1995, pp. 39–44; and Ira Sager, "The Few, the True, the Blue," *Business Week*, May 30, 1994, pp. 124–126.

2. Ted Pollock, "How Well Do You Know Your Competition?" *American Salesman*, Sept. 1993, pp. 25–30.

3. Allison Lucas, "The Thrill of Victory," *Sales & Marketing Management*, Nov. 1995, p. 92.

4. Mike Ryan, Jr., "Ask and You Shall Receive," *Cellular Business*, Aug. 1993, p. 44.

5. Gordon MacPherson, "Automation Is Not the Enemy," *Catalog Age*, May 1993, pp. 112–113.

6. Patricia Sellers, "Keeping the Buyers You Already Have," *Fortune* (special issue), Autumn/Winter 1993, pp. 56–58.

7. Sandra Hile Hart, William C. Moncrief, and A. Parasuraman, "An Empirical Investigation of Salespeople's Performance, Effort and Selling Method During a Sales Contest," *Journal of the Academy of Marketing Science*, Winter 1989, pp. 29–39.

8. Thomas A. Wotruba, John S. Moncrief, and Jerome A. Colleti, "Effective Sales Force Recognition Programs," *Industrial Marketing Management* 20 (1991): 9–15.

9. Seema Nayyar, "Aramis Shifts from Gifts to Sampling," *Brandweek*, Jan. 18, 1993, p. 5.

10. George E. Belch and Michael A. Belch, *Introduction to Advertising and Promotion* (Homewood, Ill.: Irwin, 1995), pp. 478–481.

11. Donnelley Marketing, Inc., "The 17th Annual Survey of Promotional Practices," 1995, p. 18.

12. Ibid., p. 26.

13. Laura Bird, "Coupon-Clipping Craze Seems to Be Waning," *Wall Street Journal*, Feb. 4, 1994, p. B1.

14. "Businesses Up in the Air over Frequent Flyers," *Purchasing,* July 15, 1993, pp. 21–22.

15. "High-Tech, Schmi-Tech, the Old Ways Are Booming," *Brandweek,* Oct. 18, 1993, p. 38.

16. Judith Springer Riddle, "L'Oreal Studio Care Line Due," *Brandweek,* June 28, 1993, p. 3.

17. "The 17th Annual Survey of Promotional Practices," pp. 22, 40.

18. Magid M. Abraham and Leonard Lodish, "Getting the Most out of Advertising and Promotion," *Harvard Business Review,* May–June 1990, pp. 50–60.

19. Sources: Brinker International, Inc., "Chili's Grill & Bar Suggestive Selling Training Guide"; Brinker International, Inc., "Creating the Sizzle Experience," Brinker International Sizzle Service Training Guide; Marilyn Alva, "The World According to Norman," *Restaurant Business,* July 1, 1995, pp. 52–62; Michael Sanson, "Fired Up!" *Restaurant Hospitality,* Feb. 1995, pp. 53–64; and Brinker International, Inc., video, "Suggestive Selling."

20. Sources: World Wide Web, http://www.nintendo, Jan. 30, 1996; Terry Lefton, "NBC, Nintendo Set Fall Blockbuster," *Brandweek,* May 22, 1995, p. 6; Joe Mandese and Kate Fitzgerald, "'Virtual' Promotion," *Advertising Age,* May 22, 1995, p. 40; Kate Fitzgerald, "Just Playing Along," *Advertising Age,* July 17, 1995, p. 24; Kate Fitzgerald, "Videogame Struggle Is Mortal Combat," *Advertising Age,* Oct. 10, 1995, p. 46; Terry Lefton, "Nintendo Flanks Competitors with Title Loyalty Program," *Brandweek,* Mar. 6, 1995, p. 13; Erin Flynn, "Kellogg, Nintendo Re-Tie Promo Knot," *Brandweek,* Jan. 21, 1995, p. 19; Geoffrey Smith, "Scary Stuff," *Financial World,* Feb. 21, 1995, p. 8; Judith Abrams, "Next-generation Hardware," *Dealerscope Merchandising,* May 1995, p. 20; and Kathleen Morris, "Nightmare in the Funhouse," *Financial World,* Feb. 21, 1995, pp. 32–35.

Chapter 20

1. Based on information from Tony Kennedy, "General Mills Blasts 2 Seeking Cereal Probe," *Minneapolis Star Tribune,* Mar. 8, 1995, p. 3; Laura B. Benko, "Lawmakers Call Cereal Prices Unfair," *Los Angeles Tribune,* Mar. 8, 1995, p. D2; Laurie Freeman, "Malt-O-Meal Stirring Up the Competition," *Advertising Age,* July 17, 1995, p. 4; Julie Ralston, "General Mills Hikes Prices, Cites Costs," *Advertising Age,* July 17, 1995, p. 2; Greg Burns, "A Froot Loop by Any Other Name," *Business Week,* June 26, 1995, pp. 72–76; and Richard Gibson, "Quaker Oats Co. Will Begin Marketing Value-Priced Cereals Under Its Brand," *Wall Street Journal,* Jan. 23, 1995, p. A4.

2. Donald Lichtenstein, Nancy M. Ridgway, and Richard G. Netemeyer, "Price Perceptions and Consumer Shopping Behavior: A Field Study," *Journal of Marketing Research,* May 1993, pp. 234–245.

3. "A New Vision at Mobile," *National Petroleum News,* June 1995, p. 62.

4. Bradley T. Gale, "Quality Comes First When Hatching Power Brands," *Planning Review,* July–Aug. 1992, pp. 4–10.

5. Jason Vogel, "Carriage Trade Coffee," *Financial World,* Apr. 25, 1995, pp. 62–65.

6. Gale, pp. 4–10.

7. Doug Carroll, "Price Wars Make Airline Giants Shrink," *USA Today,* Nov. 24, 1993, p. 1B.

8. Lichtenstein, Ridgway, and Netemeyer, "Price Perceptions," pp. 234–245.

9. Hollee Actman, "Little Editions," *Sporting Goods Business,* May 5, 1995, pp. 48–50.

10. Valerie A. Zeithaml, "Consumer Perceptions of Price, Quality and Value: A Means-End Model and Synthesis of Evidence," *Journal of Marketing,* July 1988, pp. 2–22.

11. Lichtenstein, Ridgway, and Netemeyer, "Price Perceptions," pp. 234–245.

12. Allan J. MaGrath, "Ten Timeless Truths About Pricing," *Journal of Consumer Marketing,* Winter 1991, pp. 5–13.

13. Sources: "Southwest Airlines' Herb Kelleher: Unorthodoxy at Work," *Management Review,* Jan. 1995, pp. 9–12; Bridget O'Brian, "Southwest Air Says First-Half Results Are Likely to be Hurt by Competition," *Wall Street Journal,* Feb. 13, 1995, p. A2; "Southwest Air's Pilots Ratify Unusual Pact With Stock Options," *Wall Street Journal,* Jan. 16, 1995, p. A4; Bridget O'Brian, "Fare Wars Hurt Two Airlines' Quarterly Data," *Wall Street Journal,* Jan. 27, 1995, p. B4; Susan Chandler and Eric Schine, "Not Bad, For a Dumb Idea," *Business Week,* Feb. 20, 1995, p. 40; Gary Hoover, Alta Campbell, and Patrick J. Spain, eds., *Hoover's Handbook of American Business 1995* (Austin, Texas: Reference Press, 1995), p. 972; Robert Levering and Milton Moskowitz, *The 100 Best Companies to Work for in America* (New York: Plume, 1994), pp. 412–417, 507; and *The Lone Star Flying Society Good Time Family Band,* internal corporate video documentary.

14. Sources: Ron Ruggless, "Family Value: Going Home Again," *Nation's Restaurant News,* Feb. 27, 1995, pp. 45–46; Carole Clancy, "Denny's Goes Retro," *Tampa Bay Business Journal,* June 30, 1995, p. A1; Mark Hamstra, "Family Chains Cultivate Distinct Personas in Quests for Guests," *Nation's Restaurant News,* Aug. 7, 1995, pp. 124–128; Denny's press release, Jan. 9, 1996; Mark Hamstra, "Family Chains Heed Casual-Theme Rivals, Adopt New Service, Ambience Upgrades," *Nation's Restaurant News,* July 24, 1995, pp. 45–48; and Sally Goll Beatty, "Denny's Bites Back With Lower Prices," *Wall Street Journal,* Jan. 8, 1996, pp. B1, B5.

Chapter 21

1. Based on information from T. L. Stanley, "Lamborghini Eyes More Accessible Car Image," *Brandweek,* Oct. 9, 1995, p. 5; Paul Dillon, "Lamborghini Starts Marketing," *Business Journal—Jacksonville,* June 23, 1995, p. A1; Faye Rice, "Lamborghini's Sales Drive," *Fortune,* June 12, 1995, p. 13; Raymond Serafin, "Even Lamborghini Must Think Marketing," *Advertising Age,* May 1, 1995, p. 4; Keith Naughton, "Lamborghini Bounces Back," *Detroit News,* Jan. 6, 1995, p. E3; Rebecca Walters, "Nelson Auto Group Adds Lamborghini To Its Lineup," *Business First—Columbus,* June 5, 1995, p. 3; and Andrew McIntosh, "Drive to Despair: Lamborghini Sued After Distribution Contract Terminated," *Gazette* (*Montana*), Jan. 28, 1995, p. D1.

2. Gary Strauss, "Savvy Buying More Than a Passing Fad," *USA Today,* Nov. 23, 1993, pp. B1, B2; Michael D. Hartline, "Lowering Intangible Prices: A Key to Delivering Retail Value in the 90s," working paper, University of Arkansas at Little Rock, 1993; and Nanette Byrnes, "The Brains Behind Brands," *Financial World,* Sept. 1, 1993, p. 54.

3. Reprinted from *Dictionary of Marketing Terms,* ed. Peter D. Bennett, 1988, p. 54, published by the American Marketing Association. Used by permission.

4. Martha T. Moore, "Extra Value Pays Off," *USA Today,* Nov. 24, 1993, p. B2.

5. *Dictionary of Marketing Terms,* p. 150.

6. James Cox, "Frugal Public Forces Firms to Hold Line," *USA Today,* Nov. 22, 1993, pp. B1, B2.

7. Jim Fox, "Category Killers Mount Major Canadian Invasion," *Discount Store News,* July 17, 1995, p. 44.

8. Herman Simon, "Pricing Opportunities—And How to Exploit Them," *Sloan Management Review,* Winter 1992, pp. 55–65.

9. Phillip D. White, "Fundamental Pricing Strategies for Credit Unions," *Credit Union Executive,* Nov.–Dec. 1992, pp. 21–23.

10. Robert M. Schindler and Alan R. Wiman, "Effects of Odd Pricing on Price Recall," *Journal of Business Research,* Nov. 1989, pp. 165–177.

11. John C. Groth and Stephen W. McDaniel, "The Exclusive Value Principle: The Basis for Prestige Pricing," *Journal of Consumer Marketing* 10, no. 1 (1993): 10–16.

12. Elaine Underwood, "A Shuttle Run Where Price Is No Object," *Brandweek,* Aug. 21, 1995, p. 38.

13. Sources: Megan Winzeler, "Steinway Strikes A Chord," *Sales & Marketing Management,* Aug. 1995, p. 16; Marla Matzer, "Play It Again," *Forbes,* Feb. 27, 1995, pp. 138–139; "Steinway & Sons Owner Agrees To Sell Company," *Wall Street Journal,* April 19, 1995, p. B9; Bruce A. Stevens, "Sales of Pianos Haven't Missed a Beat," *St. Louis Post Dispatch,* July 22, 1995, p. 15B; segment from "All Things Considered," radio program, National Public Radio, May 25, 1995; Steinway and Sons, correspondence with Advertising and Public Relations Director Leo Spellman, May 1993; and Steinway and Sons, *It's a Steinway,* corporate video documentary, Jan. 1990.

14. Sources: Back Yard Burgers, *1994 Annual Report;* Peter Romeo, "Top 50 Growth Chains," *Restaurant Business,* July 20, 1995, pp. 61, 112; "Financial Digest," *Nation's Restaurant News,* Mar. 27, 1995, p. 14; Catherine Pritchard, "New Attraction Planned for Haymount," *Fayetteville Observer-Times,* Feb. 18, 1995, p. 6; and "Back Yard Adds 51st Location," *Commercial Appeal,* Jan. 6, 1994, p. B5.

Chapter 22

1. Based on information from John Cypher, *Bob Kleberg and the King Ranch: A Worldwide Sea of Grass* (Austin, Texas: University of Texas Press, 1995); Dan McGraw, "A Fistful of Dollars: The King Ranch of Texas Rides into a Profitable New Business Era," *U.S. News & World Report,* July 24, 1995, pp. 36–38; and "Now Chairman Tenderfoot Takes Over," *Fortune,* Aug. 1, 1988, p. 217.

2. O. C. Ferrell, George H. Lucas, and David J. Luck, *Strategic Marketing Management: Text and Cases* (Cincinnati: South-Western, 1994), p. 142.

3. P. Rajan Varadarajan, Terry Clark, and William Pride, "Controlling the Uncontrollable: Managing the Market Environment," *Sloan Management Review,* Winter 1992, p. 97.

4. J. Paul Peter and James H. Donnelly, Jr., *A Preface to Marketing Management,* 5th ed. (Homewood, Ill.: Irwin, 1991), p. 9.

5. Adapted from Peter and Donnelly, *A Preface to Marketing Management,* pp. 8–12.

6. Ibid., p. 10.

7. Maggie Malone and John Leland, "Of Walls and Wanting," *Newsweek,* Jan. 8, 1996, pp. 54–55.

8. Phil West, "Saturn Corp. Rings Up First Profitable Month," *Commercial Appeal,* June 11, 1993, p. B2.

9. David M. Georgaff and Robert G. Mundick, "Managers' Guide to Forecasting," *Harvard Business Review,* Jan.–Feb. 1986, p. 120.

10. Alex Taylor III, "Why Electric Cars Make No Sense," *Fortune,* July 26, 1993, pp. 126–127.

11. Ibid.

12. Gerard J. Tellis and Peter N. Golder, "Pioneer Advantage: Marketing Logic or Marketing Legend," *USC Business,* Fall/Winter 1995, pp. 49–53.

13. Vic Sussman, with Kenan Pollack, "Gold Rush in Cyberspace," *U.S. News & World Report,* Nov. 13, 1995, pp. 72–80.

14. Derek F. Abell, "Strategic Windows," *Journal of Marketing,* July 1978, p. 21.

15. Julie Bell, "New Products: Predicting Flops and Fliers," *USA Today,* Dec. 26, 1995, p. 4B.

16. John Huey and Andrew Kupfer, "What That Merger Means for You," *Fortune,* Nov. 15, 1993, pp. 82–90.

17. Dennis W. Rook, "Growing and Keeping Brand Equity," *USC Business,* Fall/Winter 1995, p. 45.

18. Peter and Donnelly, *A Preface to Marketing Management,* p. 9.

19. Joseph P. Guiltinan and Gordon W. Paul, *Marketing Management: Strategies and Programs* (New York: McGraw-Hill, 1991), p. 43.

20. George S. Day, "Diagnosing the Product Portfolio," *Journal of Marketing,* Apr. 1977, pp. 30–31.

21. Andrew Campbell, Michael Goold, and Marcus Alexander, "Corporate Strategy: The Quest for Parenting Advantage," *Harvard Business Review,* Mar./Apr. 1995, pp. 120–132.

22. Roger A. Kerin, Vijay Majahan, and P. Rajan Varadarajan, *Contemporary Perspectives on Strategic Marketing Planning* (Boston: Allyn & Bacon, 1990).

23. Based on information from Bill Saporito, "The High Cost of Second Best," *Fortune,* July 26, 1993, pp. 99–102.

24. Dennis W. Rook, "Growing and Keeping Brand Equity," *USC Business,* Fall/Winter 1995, pp. 44–45.

25. Martha Brannigan, "Rocky Road: Alamo Maps a Turnaround," *Wall Street Journal,* Aug. 14, 1995, pp. B1, B4.

26. Cyndee Miller, "X Marks the Lucrative Spot, But Some Advertisers Can't Hit Target," *Marketing News,* Aug. 2, 1993, pp. 1, 14.

27. Ibid.

28. "Cheerios Adds X's to O's." *Marketing News,* July 19, 1993, p. 1.

29. "Busch Taps Japanese Beer Market," *Marketing News,* Oct. 11, 1993, p. 1.

30. Robert J. Dolan, "How Do You Know When the Price Is Right?" *Harvard Business Review,* Sept./Oct. 1995, pp. 174–183.

31. Ronald D. Michman, "Linking Futuristics with Marketing Planning, Forecasting, and Strategy," *Journal of Consumer Marketing,* Summer 1984, pp. 17, 23.

32. Ferrell, Lucas, and Luck, *Strategic Marketing Management,* p. 145.

33. Ibid., p. 43.

34. "Some Logos Hurt Brands," *Marketing News,* Nov. 8, 1993, p. 1.

35. Ferrell, Lucas, and Luck, *Strategic Marketing Management,* p. 44.

36. Douglas Bowman and Hubert Gatignon, "Determinants of Competitor Response Time to a New Product Introduction," *Journal of Marketing Research,* Feb. 1995, pp. 42–53.

37. Martha Brannigan and Eleena de Lisser, "A Slimmer Delta Still Loves to Fly, But Does It Show?" *Wall Street Journal,* Jan. 26, 1996, p. B3.

38. Michael Levy and Barton A. Weitz, *Retailing Management* (Homewood: Ill.: Irwin, 1992), p. 208.

39. Sources: "The Business Week 1000," *Business Week,* Mar. 25, 1996, p. 130; Christie Brown, "Pooper-Scooper Dooper," *Forbes,* Feb. 13, 1995, pp. 78–81; Hoover's Handbook of Emerging Companies 1995; Julie Liesse, "Superstores Add Bite to Pet Market's Bark," *Advertising Age,* Apr. 25, 1994, p. 42; Ryan Mathews, "Pet Projects," *Progressive Grocer,* July 1995, pp. 69–70; Jerry Minkoff, "Perking up Pet Supplies," *Discount Merchandiser,* July 1995, pp. 30–32; Marcia Mogelonsky, "Reigning Cats and Dogs," *American Demographics,* Apr. 1995, p. 10; "Pet Consolidation in Offing," *Discount Store News,* Mar. 21, 1994, pp. 3, 46; PETsMART Video; Marguerite Smith, "The New World of Health Care for Your Pet," *Money,* Apr. 1994, pp. 144–158; R. Lee Sullivan, "Puppy Love," *Forbes,* Dec. 20, 1993, pp. 138–142; and Tim Triplett, "Superstores Tap into Bond between Owners and Pets," *Marketing News,* Apr. 25, 1994, pp. 1–2.

40. Sources: *Hoover's Company Profile* database (Austin, Texas: Reference Press, 1995), via America Online; and Richard A. Melcher, with Greg Burns, "How Eagle Became Extinct," *Business Week,* Mar. 4, 1996, pp. 68–69.

Chapter 23

1. Based on information from Harcourt General, *1995 Annual Report;* and *Hoover's Company Profile* database (Austin, Texas: Reference Press, 1995), via America Online.

2. Based on Orville C. Walker, Jr., and Robert W. Ruekert, "Marketing's Role in the Implementation of Business Strategies: A Critical Review and Conceptual Framework," *Journal of Marketing,* July 1987, pp. 15–33.

3. Robert Howard, "Values Make the Company: An Interview with Robert Haas," *Harvard Business Review,* Sept.–Oct. 1990, pp. 132–144.

4. O. C. Ferrell, George H. Lucas, and David J. Luck, *Strategic Marketing Management: Text and Cases* (Cincinnati: South-Western, 1994), pp. 199–200.

5. Myron Glassman and Bruce McAfee, "Integrating the Personnel and Marketing Functions: The Challenge of the 1990s," *Business Horizons,* May–June 1992, pp. 52–59.

6. Ferrell, Lucas, and Luck, *Strategic Marketing Management,* pp. 190–200.

7. Adapted from Nigel F. Piercy, *Market-Led Strategic Change* (Newton, Mass.: Butterworth-Heinemann, 1992), pp. 374–385.

8. Sybil F. Stershic, "Internal Marketing Campaign Reinforces Service Goals," *Marketing News,* July 31, 1989, p. 11.

9. Adapted from Joseph R. Jablonski, *Implementing Total Quality Management* (Albuquerque, N.M.: Technical Management Consortium, 1990).

10. Philip B. Crosby, *Quality Is Free—The Art of Making Quality Certain* (New York: McGraw-Hill, 1979), pp. 9–10.

11. Piercy, *Market-Led Strategic Change.*

12. Jeremy Main, "How to Steal the Best Ideas Around," *Fortune,* Oct. 19, 1992, pp. 102–106.

13. Kenneth W. Thomas and Betty A. Velthouse, "Cognitive Elements of Empowerment: An 'Interpretive' Model of Intrinsic Task Motivation," *Academy of Management Review,* Oct. 1990, pp. 666–681.

14. Ferrell, Lucas, and Luck, *Strategic Marketing Management,* pp. 193–194.

15. Michael D. Hartline and O. C. Ferrell, "Service Quality Implementation: The Effects of Organizational Socialization and Managerial Actions on the Behaviors of Customer-Contact Employees," *Marketing Science Institute Working Paper Series,* Report no. 93–122 (Cambridge, Mass.: Marketing Science Institute, 1993), pp. 36–40.

16. "Consultants Never Mind the Buzzwords: Roll up Your Sleeves," *Business Week,* Jan. 26, 1996, via America Online.

17. Fred Steingraber, "Total Quality Management: A New Look at a Basic Issue," *Vital Speeches of the Day,* May 1990, pp. 415–416.

18. Rohit Deshpande and Frederick E. Webster, Jr., "Organizational Culture and Marketing: Defining the Research Agenda," *Journal of Marketing,* Jan. 1989, pp. 3–15.

19. Ajay K. Kohli and Bernard J. Jaworski, "Marketing Orientation: The Construct, Research Propositions, and Managerial Implications," *Journal of Marketing,* Apr. 1990, pp. 1–18.

20. John A. Byrne, "Everyone Seems to Be Studying U.S. Corporate Stars," *Business Week,* Sept. 18, 1995, via America Online.

21. David C. Jones, "Motivation the Catalyst in Profit Formula," *National Underwriter,* July 13, 1987, pp. 10, 13.

22. Hartline and Ferrell, "Service Quality Implementation," pp. 36–48.

23. John P. Cortez, "New Directions for Domino's," *Advertising Age,* Jan. 4, 1993, pp. 3, 33–34.

24. Bernard J. Jaworski, "Toward a Theory of Marketing Control: Environmental Context, Control Types, and Consequences." *Journal of Marketing,* July 1988, pp. 23–39.

25. Richard A. Melcher, "Industry Outlook 1996: Business Services," *Business Week,* Jan. 8, 1996, p. 107.

26. John O. Grettenberger (General Manager, Cadillac Motor Car Division), "Has Caddy Turned the Corner?" (editorial), *Business Week,* Jan. 8, 1996, via America Online.

27. Wendy Zellner, "Go-Go Goliaths," *Business Week,* Feb. 13, 1995, via America Online.

28. Richard A. Melcher and Elizabeth Roberts, "Are We Having Fun Yet?" *Business Week,* Oct. 9, 1995, via America Online.

29. Kathleen Kerwin and Keith Naughton, "Cruise Control?" *Business Week,* Jan. 8, 1996, pp. 82–83.

30. Michael J. Mandel, Christoper Ferrell, and Catherine Yang, "Land of the Giants," *Business Week,* Sept. 11, 1995, via America Online.

31. Christopher H. Lovelock, *Services Marketing,* 2nd ed. (Englewood Cliffs, N.J.: Prentice-Hall, 1991), p. 270.

32. Sources: Laurel Campbell, "Relax: Apparel Companies Riding the Dress-Down Trend," *Commercial Appeal,* Oct. 22, 1995, p. C3; "Casual Clothing in the Workplace," Levi Strauss & Co. newsletter, Jan. 1995, pp. 1–6; Cyndee Miller, "A Casual Affair," *Marketing News,* Mar. 13, 1995, pp. 1, 2; William Nabors, "The New Corporate Uniforms," *Fortune,* Nov. 13, 1995, pp. 132–152; "The New Professionalism: A Guide to Casual Businesswear," Levi Strauss & Co. newsletter, June 1995; Ellen Neuborne, "Managers Take 'Casual Days' Seriously," *USA Today,* Mar. 27, 1995, p. 6B; and "Sweatsuit," *Brandweek,* Feb. 20, 1995, pp. 24–26, 28.

33. Sources: Laura Bird, "Denny's TV Ad Seeks to Mend Bias Image," *Wall Street Journal,* June 21, 1993, p. B4; Laurie Campbell, "New Denny's Exec Relishes Challenge: Facing Firestorm," *Commercial Appeal,* June 20, 1993, p. C1; "Denny's to Settle Federal Bias Charge," *Commercial Appeal,* Mar. 27, 1993, p. B2; "Denny's Fires Annapolis Manager," *Commercial Appeal,* May 15, 1993, p. B1. James Harney, Civil Rights Leaders Divided Over Denny's," *USA Today,* June 4, 1993, p. 2A; Nicole Harris, "A New Denny's Diner by Diner," *Business Week,* Mar. 25, 1996, pp. 166, 168; Benjamin A. Holden, "TW Holdings' Denny's Restaurants Unit Signs Consent Decree in U.S. Bias Case," *Wall Street Journal,* Mar. 26, 1993, p. A6; Julia Lawlor, "Denny's Vows to

Fix Unequal Treatment," *USA Today*, Mar. 26, 1993, p. 2B; Andrew E. Serwer, "What to Do When Race Charges Fly," *Fortune*, July 12, 1993, pp. 95–96; and Amy Stevens, "Denny's Agrees to Alter Practices in Bias Settlement," *Wall Street Journal*, Mar. 30, 1993, p. B9.

Appendix A

1. Ingrid Johnson and Dennis Baylor, "Hey Business Majors, Nonprofits Need You," *Wall Street Journal's Managing Your Career*, Spring/Summer 1993, p. 11.

2. Robert D. Beard, "Making the World a Better Place," *Wall Street Journal's Managing Your Career*, Spring/Summer 1993, pp. 26, 29.

3. Jean Koretz, "Where the New Jobs Are," *Business Week*, Mar. 20, 1995, p. 24.

4. Darryl Estrine, "Planning a Career in a World Without Managers," *Fortune*, Mar. 20, 1995, pp. 72–77.

5. Anne R. Carey and Suzy Parker, "Would-Be Entrepreneurs," *USA Today*, May 11, 1995, p. B1.

6. Anne R. Carey and Web Bryant, "Women-Owned Business Growth," *USA Today*, Apr. 16, 1995, p. B1.

7. Carol Kleiman, "College Degree Still Boosts Salary," *Orlando Sentinel*, June 18, 1995, p. D1.

8. Jan Yager, "Mind Your Manners," *Wall Street Journal's Managing Your Career*, Fall 1993, pp. 4–5.

9. Barbara J. Mende, "No Flowers, Candy, Nuts or Strange Paper," *Wall Street Journal's Managing Your Career*, Fall 1993, pp. 18–19, 23.

10. Janis F. Kirk, "Focus on a Specific Job Market in Launching Your New Career," *Toronto Star*, July 8, 1995, p. C9.

11. Lyric W. Winik, "How to Find Your First Job," *Parade Magazine*, June 18, 1995, pp. 6–7.

12. Sana Siwolop, "Job Seekers Turning to Cyberspace as Nationwide Postings Proliferate," *Commercial Appeal*, Jan. 21, 1996, p. C3.

13. Geraldine Henze, *Winning Career Moves: A Complete Job Search Program for Managers and Professionals* (Homewood, Ill.: Business One Irwin, 1992), pp. 10–13.

14. Donald Asher, "Use Your Resume to Show Versatility," *Wall Street Journal's Managing Your Career*, Spring 1992, pp. 20, 23.

15. Donna J. Yena, *Career Directions*, 2nd ed. (Homewood, Ill.: Irwin Career Education Division, 1993), pp. 51–52.

16. Sal Divita, "Resume Writing Requires Proper Strategy," *Marketing News*, July 3, 1995, p. 6.

17. Burke Marketing Research for Robert Hall Inc., reported in *USA Today*, Oct. 2, 1987, p. B1.

18. Divita, "Resume Writing Requires Proper Strategy."

19. Mende, "No Flowers," p. 23.

20. Andrew J. DuBrin, "Deadly Political Sins," *Wall Street Journal's Managing Your Career*, Fall 1993, pp. 11–13.

21. Ibid.

22. Judith George, "Market Researcher," *Business Week Careers*, Oct. 1987, p. 10.

23. "What It's Like to Work in Marketing Research Depends on Where You Work—Supplier, Ad Agency, Manufacturer," *Collegiate Edition Marketing News*, Dec. 1985, pp. 1, 3.

24. Cyndee Miller, "Marketing Research Salaries Up a Bit, But Layoffs Take Toll," *Marketing News*, June 19, 1995, p. 1.

25. Michael Vermeulen, "What People Earn," *Parade Magazine*, June 18, 1995, p. 4.

26. Annette Selden, ed., *VGM's Handbook of Business & Management Careers* (Lincolnwood, Ill.: VGM Career Horizons, 1993), p. 11.

27. Vincent Daddiego, "Making It in Advertising," *Business Week Careers*, Feb. 1988, p. 42.

28. Selden, *VGM's Handbook*, pp. 82, 83.

Credits (continued from page iv)

Chapter 2

Page 24: Fat Free Cracker Jack. *Page 26:* Courtesy of Ford Motor Company. *Page 28:* Courtesy of Princeton Instruments. *Page 32:* © 1996 A.T. Cross Company. *Page 39:* Courtesy of SGS International Certification Services, Inc. *Page 40:* Advertisement from Newsweek 1996. © Newsweek, Inc. All rights reserved. Reprinted by permission. Photos (top to bottom): Andrea Renault/Globe Photos; Najlah Feanni/SABA; Steve McCurry/ Magnum. *Page 41:* Courtesy of IBM, Corp. *Page 44 (left and right):* Courtesy of Phillips Petroleum Company.

Chapter 3

Page 52: © Carol Lundeen. *Page 55 (left and right):* Courtesy of Liberty Mutual. *Page 57 (left):* Courtesy of The Dreiford Group. *Page 57 (right):* Courtesy of Consultants for Management Development. Photo courtesy Patrick's Photo & Media Services, Manitou Springs, CO. *Page 58:* Courtesy of The Body Shop, Inc. Page 61: Courtesy of *Business Ethics* Magazine. *Page 68 (left and right):* Friends of the Chicago River. *Page 70:* Consolidated Edison Company of New York, Inc.

Chapter 4

Page 78: © The Procter & Gamble Company. Used by permission. *Page 79:* Courtesy of Sprint Communications Company L.P. *Page 82:* Courtesy of Komatsu. *Page 86:* Photo courtesy of NTT. *Page 87:* Courtesy of CarDan & Associates, Inc. Permission granted by Amistad Industries, Inc. *Page 93:* Courtesy of Delta Airlines, Inc. *Page 94 (left and right):* Courtesy of Federal Express Corporation.

Chapter 5

Page 105: © Carol Lundeen. *Page 107 (left):* Courtesy of Maritz Marketing Research Inc., St. Louis. *Page 107 (right):* Reprinted with the permission of LEXIS-NEXIS, Copyright 1995 LEXIS-NEXIS, a division of Reed Elsevier Inc. All rights reserved. *Page 111: American Demographics* Magazine, © 1995. Reprinted with permission. *Page 119 (left):* Courtesy of Quality Controlled Services, St. Louis. *Page 119 (right):* Reprinted with permission of JRP Marketing Research Services, Inc. Ad was designed by Thomas J. Paul, Inc. of Jenkintown, PA. *Page 122:* Courtesy of Red Brick Systems, Inc., Michael Friedland & Associates, Agency. *Page 123:* Courtesy of SPSS.

Chapter 6

Page 131: Courtesy of Boston Chicken, Inc. *Page 133:* © Carol Lundeen. *Page 135:* Courtesy of Austin Gym. *Page 137:* Courtesy of Friendship Hospital for Animals, Inc. *Page 139:* © 1996 M.C. Escher / Cordon Art - Baarn - Holland. All rights reserved. *Page 143:* Reprinted with permission of Harley-Davidson Motor Company. Photo © John Mason. *Page 144:* Rick Dublin/Dublin Productions.

Chapter 7

Page 154: © Photo courtesy of Emerson Electric Co. *Page 157:* Courtesy of Federal Express Corporation. *Page 158:* Advertisement courtesy of Pella Corporation. *Page 160 (left):* Courtesy of National Gypsum Company. *Page 160 (right):* Courtesy of Ingram Library Services. *Page 163:* Courtesy of Malden Mills. *Page 167 (top)* Courtesy of 3M. *Page 167 (bottom):* Courtesy of IBM, Corp.

Chapter 8

Page 176: © Carol Lundeen. *Page 180:* © 1996 A.T. Cross Company. *Page 181 (left and right):* Courtesy of The Martin Agency. *Page 182 (left):* Courtesy of OshKosh. *Page 182 (right):* Courtesy of CIGNA. *Page 184 (left and right):* Courtesy of Oscar Mayer Foods, Madison, Wisconsin. *Page 187:* Courtesy of Chrysler Corporation. *Page 193:* Saatchi & Saatchi for British Airways.

Chapter 9

Page 205: SNACKWELL'S® is a registered trademark of Nabisco Brands Company. Used with permission. *Page 206 (left):* Courtesy of RE Max. *Page 206 (right):* Reproduced with permission of Clarity Coverdale Fury, Minneapolis, Minnesota. Courtesy of MADD, Minneapolis, Minnesota. *Page 209:* Ad compliments of Hammermill Papers. All rights reserved. *Page 210:* Reprinted with permission of Klein & Solin Advertising, Courtesy of Classico. *Page 212:* Courtesy of Seiko Corporation of America. *Page 216 (left):* Reprinted with permission of Mita Copystar of America, Inc. All rights reserved. *Page 216 (right):* Dremel, Racine, WI 53406. *Page 218:* Courtesy of SmithKline Beecham.

Chapter 10

Page 226: Photo courtesy of AM General Corp. *Page 228 (left and right):* Courtesy of Maple Leaf Meats. *Page 230 (left):* Courtesy of Delco Electronics. *Page 230 (right):* Courtesy of Precise International. *Page 233:* Courtesy of CNS, Inc. *Page 238:* L'eggs Products, a division of Sara Lee Corporation. *Page 240 (left):* KRAFT, MAXWELL HOUSE and GOOD TO THE LAST DROP and Design are registered trademarks of Kraft Foods, Inc. Used with permission. *Page 240 (right):* Courtesy of Campbell Soup Company.

Chapter 11

Page 249: © Carol Lundeen. *Page 251 (left):* Courtesy of CITGO Petroleum Corporation. *Page 251 (right):* KRAFT, MAXWELL HOUSE and GOOD TO THE LAST DROP ad Design are registered trademarks of Kraft Foods, Inc. Used with permission. *Page 252:* Besnier USA, Inc., Frierson & Mee, Inc. Agency. *Page 253:* Advertisement courtesy of Nestlé Food Company. *Page 257:* © The Procter & Gamble Company. Used by permission. *Page 258:* Courtesy of Wallace Chuch Associates, Inc. *Page 262:* Courtesy of American Plastics Council. *Page 265 (left):* Courtesy of The Dannon Company, Inc. *Page 265 (right):* Reproduced courtesy of Chesebrough Pond's, Inc.

Chapter 12

Page 273: © Carol Lundeen. *Page 276:* Courtesy of Transamerica Corporation. *Page 281:* Courtesy of Daniel Freeman Hospitals. *Page 282 (left & right):* Courtesy of Catholic Big Brothers, For Boys and Girls. *Page 287:* Courtesy of United Airlines. *Page 288:* Courtesy of American Museum of Natural History. *Page 289:* Courtesy of The Leith Agency. Reproduced with permission of The Health Education Board of Scotland.

Chapter 13

Page 299: Courtesy of Electronics Boutique, Inc. *Page 302:* Reprinted with permission Bayer Corporation. Photo © Peggy Barnett. *Page 305:* Courtesy of FORD Motor Company. *Page 308:* Image used by permission of Porsche Cars N.A., Inc. *Page 309:* Courtesy of Computer Associates. *Page 312:* Reprinted with permission of Meyer Tomatoes; Design, Jeff Knubis; Copy, Jeff Knubis; Photo, Nino Mascardi/The Image Bank. *Page 315:* Reprinted with permission from Louis Vuitton, NA, Inc.

Chapter 14

Page 322: © Robert Holmgren. *Page 325:* Photo courtesy of Fleming. *Page 327:* Photo courtesy of Supervalue. *Page 329:* Courtesy of W.W. Grainger, Inc. *Page 333:* Courtesy of Campbell Soup Company. *Page 334 (left):* Courtesy of Camp Dressor & McKee, Inc. *Page 334 (right):* Courtesy of GE Information Services.

Chapter 15

Page 343: © Carol Lundeen. *Page 346:* Courtesy of NORDSTROM. *Page 347:* Courtesy of Kroger Company. *Page 350:* © Carol Lundeen. *Page 353 (left):* Courtesy of Speigel, Inc.; Art Director, Randy Price; Photographer, Michael Mundy; Copy Director, Bernard Thurmond; Producer, Independent Artists. *Page 353 (right):* Courtesy William Sonoma, Inc. *Page 358:* Courtesy of Urban Retail Properties. *Page 359 (top):* Courtesy of Gallerina, Edina, Minnesota; Clarity Coverdate Fury, Minneapolis. *Page 359 (bottom):* Courtesy of Century 21.

Chapter 16

Page 368: © Carol Lundeen. *Page 369:* CF MotorFreight offers full less-than-truckload service throughout the United States, Canada, Mexico, Europe, Asia, The Caribbean and Latin America. *Page 371:* Courtesy of Ryder. *Page 372:* Courtesy of Graybar Services, Inc. *Page 375:* Courtesy of Lykes Bros. Steamship Co. *Page 376:* Courtesy of McKesson Corp. *Page 380:* Reprinted courtesy of Norfolk Southern Corporation. *Page 382:* Reprinted with permission from United Postal Service; courtesy of Bear Creek Corporation.

Chapter 17

Page 393: Courtesy of Columbia Sportswear. *Page 394:* Healthwise Creative Resource Group, Inc. *Page 399:* Courtesy of California Milk Processor Board. *Page 403:* Courtesy of *Animals* Magazine, MSPCA/AHES. *Page 406 (top):* Courtesy of Del Laboratories. *Page 406 (bottom):* Courtesy of Turner Broadcasting System, Inc. *Page 408:* Courtesy of FORD Motor Company.

Chapter 18

Page 415: © Jim Tunnell/Shooting Star. *Page 417 (top):* Courtesy of Timberland Company. *Page 417 (bottom):* Courtesy of Con Agra Foods. *Page 419:* Courtesy of American Museum of Natural History. *Page 423 (left and right):* Courtesy of Campbell Soup Company. *Page 427:* Reprinted with permission of Wonderlic Personnel Test, Inc. *Page 429:* Courtesy of Little Caesar Enterprises. *Page 432:* Reprinted with permission of Marvel Entertainment Group, Inc. *Page 433:* Reproduced with permission from UNISYS.

Chapter 19

Page 442: Courtesy of IBM, Corp. *Page 445 (left):* Reprinted with permission of Inquiry Handling service, Inc., San Fernando, CA. *Page 445 (right):* Courtesy of American Business Information. *Page 446:* Reprinted with permission from Eastman Kodak Company. *Page 451:* Reprinted with permission from Learning International. *Page 453 (left):* Courtesy Speigel, Inc. *Page 453 (right):* Copyright 1993 Tiffany and Company. *Page 457:* Courtesy of ACTMEDIA. *Page 459:* Courtesy of Publisher's Clearing House.

Chapter 20

Page 471: Reprinted with permission of Malt-O-Meal. *Page 474:* Courtesy of Daffy's. *Page 477 (left):* Courtesy of Binney & Smith,

Inc. *Page 477 (right):* © CANON U.S.A., Inc. *Page 481 (left):* Courtesy of A T & T. *Page 481(right):* Courtesy of MCI. *Page 483:* Courtesy of Chase Development Center.

Chapter 21

Page 490: Automobile Lamborghini USA. *Page 492:* Reproduced with permission of North Carolina Zoo; Loeffler Ketchum Mountjoy Advertising. *Page 494 (left):* Courtesy of Harry Winston. *Page 494 (right):* Courtesy of The Kohler Company. *Page 503 (bottom):* Courtesy of Denny's. Published February 1996 in *Ebony* Magazine. *Page 506:* Courtesy of Marriott Hotels, Resorts & Suites. *Page 508 (left):* Compliments of General Motors Parts. *Page 508 (right):* Reproduced with permission of Earle Palmer Brown. Courtesy of US Air.

Chapter 22

Page 517: Courtesy of The King Ranch Saddle Shop. *Page 521:* Courtesy of Lockheed Martin. *Page 524:* Courtesy of FORD Motor Cars. *Page 528 (left and right):* Reprinted with permission from Eastman Kodak Company. *Page 530 (left):* PLANTERS® is a registered trademark of Nabisco Brands Company. Trademarks and Planters advertisement used with permission. *Page 530 (right):* Courtesy of M & M * MARS, a division of MARS, Incorporated. *Page 535:* Reprinted with permission of NIKE, Inc. *Page 537:* Courtesy of A T & T.

Chapter 23

Page 545: Courtesy of Neiman Marcus. Illustration © 1996 Edwin Fotheringham; Photography © 1996 Kurt Lindsay. *Page 546:* Courtesy of The TIMKEN Company. *Page 548 (bottom):* Courtesy of HYATT Hotels Corporation. *Page 551:* © BMW of North America, Inc.; Ritta & Associates Agency. *Page 553:* Reproduced with permission from UNISYS. *Page 556 (left):* Courtesy Northwest Airlines. *Page 556 (right):* Ad reproduced with permission from American Airlines, Inc. Photo courtesy Lynn Sugarman © 1996. *Page 560 (left and right):* Courtesy of OKI Telecom.

Name Index

Aaker, David A., N627, N630
AAMCO, 355
ABC, 176, 365, 366
Abell, Derek F., N637
ABI/INFORM, 109(table)
Abraham, Magid M., N636
Abrams, Judith, N636
A.C. Nielsen Company, 234
Academy of Motion Picture Arts and
    Sciences, 415
Accord automobiles, 551
ACOG (Atlanta Committee for the
    Olympic Games), 15
Acorn data services, 186
Action Snacks, 262
Active Strips flexible bandages,
    229(table)
Actman, Hollee, N636
Acumax data management system, 341
Adams, John T., III, N629
Adamson, James B., 571
Adidas, 81, 90
ADM (Archer Daniels Midland
    Company), 49–50, 80(table)
Advanced Micro Devices, 172
Adventure Island, 542
Advertising Age magazine, 112(table),
    183, 200, 432
Advertising Council, 438
Advil, 219
A&E cable channel, 365
Aerosmith band, 439
Aetna Life & Casualty, 357
Agassi, Andre, 402, 549
Aikenhead home improvement store,
    387
Airborne Express, 159, 381, 386–387
Air Jordan shoes, 96
Air Littoral, 97
Air Southwest Company, 486
Ajax dishwashing liquid, 257
Ajinomoto, 49, 50
Alagem, Beny, 529
Alamo Rent-A-Car, Inc., 530
Albertson's, 341, 346(table)
Alcas Corporation, 318
Alcoa, 173–174
Alderson, Wroe, N623, N632
Alert Cab, 413
Alexander, Keith L., N626, N634
Alexander, Marcus, N637
Aley, James, N625, N626
Alliance for Social Responsibility, 69
All Sport, 246

Allstate Insurance Company, 207, 353,
    394
All Things Automotive Directory, 480
ALM Antillean Airlines, 97
Almond Joy candy bar, 73
Alva, Marilyn, N636
Amana refrigerators, 45
Ambassador greeting cards, 313
American Airlines, 30(table), 98, 478,
    556(illus.)
American Association of Advertising
    Agencies, 587
American Dairy Association, 466
American Demographics magazine, 114
American Express Company, 69, 353,
    402, 422, 490, 514, 535, 569
American Family Association, 60
American Family Publishers, 408
American Floral Marketing Council, 398
American Heart Association, 438
*The American Heritage College
    Dictionary*, 223
The American Heritage Dictionary,
    222–223
American Honda Motor Co., 320
American Marketing Association, 63,
    64(table), 106, 112(table), 603
American Museum of Natural History,
    288, 288(illus.), 419(illus.)
American Standard Inc., 332
American Stock Exchange, 109(table)
American Telemarketing Association,
    588
American Telephone & Telegraph
    Company (AT&T), 15, 47–49, 89,
    128, 148, 420(table), 444, 481(illus.),
    506, 520, 537, 537(illus.)
America Online (AOL), 27, 110, 111, 273,
    354, 422, 579
America's Cup sailboat race, 393
America's Cut, 412
Amerlio, Gilbert F., 573–574
AM General, 226–227
Amistad, 87, 87(illus.)
Amoco service stations, 14
Amway, 318, 352
Andel, Tom, N634
Anderson, James C., N632
Anderson, Jerry W., Jr., N625
Anderson, Keith, N632
Andreas, Dwayne, 49, 50
Andreas, Michael, 50
Angel Cups cake mix, 523
Anheuser, Aberhard, 542

Anheuser-Busch Inc., 15, 264(table),
    412–413, 532, 542–543
Animals magazine, 403(illus.)
Ann Taylor, 343
Aoki, 151
AOL (America Online), 27, 110, 111, 273,
    354, 422, 579
Aoyama, 151
A & P (Great Atlantic & Pacific Tea Co.),
    347
Apollo 13 (movie), 398
Apollo airline reservation system, 97
Apollo XIV Lunar Landing Module, 389
Apparel Mart, 335
Applebee's restaurants, 487
Apple Computer, Inc., 21, 69, 88, 89, 158,
    214, 256, 325, 387, 572–574
Apple Jacks cereal, 465
Aquafina bottled water, 247
Aquatred tires, 389–390
Archer Daniels Midland Company
    (ADM), 49–50, 80(table)
Architectural Digest magazine, 511
Arizona brand, 256
AriZona Iced Tea, 229(table)
Armani suits, 151, 490
Arm & Hammer, 239, 240(table),
    250(table), 260, 527
Armor All, 340
Armour, 13
Armstrong, Larry, N628
Arnotts Ltd., 152
Aron, Laurie Joan, N631, N634
Arriva tires, 389
ARTHUR D. LITTLE/ONLINE, 109(table)
Asher, Donald, N639
Aspinwall, Leo, N631
A.T. Cross pens, 32, 32(illus.), 180,
    180(illus.), 479
Atlanta Committee for the Olympic
    Games (ACOG), 15
AT&T (American Telephone & Telegraph
    Company), 15, 47–49, 89, 128, 148,
    420(table), 444, 481(illus.), 506, 520,
    537, 537(illus.)
AT&T Interchange online service, 273
Austin Gym, 134, 135(illus.)
AutoAdvantage, 479, 480
Auto-By-Tel, 320, 480
AutoMall, 479, 480
Auto Nation, 320
Auto Shack, 19, 259
Auto Todo, 337
AutoZone, 19–20, 259, 372

Corona beer, 543
Corsa CT tires, 389
Cortese, Amy, N623, N624
Cortez, John P., N638
Corvette automobiles, 3
Cosmo Cosmetics, 229(table)
Cosmopolitan magazine, 183
Council of American Survey Research Organizations (CASRO), 116
Council of Better Business Bureaus, 39, 40
County Business Patterns, 169
Courage Ltd., 543
Cover Girl makeup, 78
Covia Partnership, 97
Cowley, Geoffrey, N625
Cox, James, N625, N636
CPC International, Inc., 147, 152
CPSC (Consumer Product Safety Commission), 37(table)
Cracker Jacks snack food, 21, 24
Craftsman tools, 201, 214
Craig, C. Samuel, N635
Crane Co., 332
Crate and Barrel, 353
Cravens, David W., N632
Crawford, Cindy, 402, 549
Cray, 304
Crayola Tempera, 476, 477(illus.)
Creative Artists Agency, 429
Cremora coffee creamer, 518
Crest toothpaste, 78, 188, 217, 423
Crosby, Lawrence A., N632
Crosby, Philip B., N638
Crossen, Cynthia, N627
Cross pens, 32, 32(illus.), 180, 180(illus.), 479
Crossroads beer, 543
CrossRoads stores, 387
Cross Trainer shoes, 96
Cruiser bicycles, 223
Crystal Pepsi, 246
CSpan cable channel, 176
CSX, 383
Cunningham, Margaret H., N624, N626
Cuomo, Mario, 249
CUTCO Cutlery Corporation, 318–319
Cypher, John, N637
Cypress Gardens, 542
Cyr, Diane, N635
Cyrus, Billy Ray, 467

Daddiego, Vincent, N639
Daewoo, 89
Daffy's specialty store, 474(illus.)
Daimaru department stores, 79
Dairy Queen, 355
Dakin, 261
Dallas Market Center, 335
Dallas Trade Mart, 335
Damore, Kelley, N627
Daniel Starch research organization, 430
Dannon yogurt, 265(illus.)
Dant, Rajiv, N631
Dark Horse Comics, 440
Dartmouth University, 293
Das, Chandrasekhar, N632
Dash laundry detergent, 210

Data Map software, 112
Davis-Diaz, Pamela, N632
Dawson, Margaret, N626
Day, George S., N623, N637
Daystar computers, 573
Dayton Hudson Corporation, 345
Dayton (Ohio) Power and Light, 27(table)
Dayton's, 345
D&B-DONNELLY DEMOGRAPHICS, 109(table)
D&B-DUN'S ELECTRONIC BUSINESS DIRECTORY, 109(table)
DC Comics, 439–440
DealerNet, 320
Dearden, William, 74
De Beers diamonds, 255
Decca Recording Co., 237(table)
Decker, Alonzo G., 201
Decorative Center, 335
DeGeorge, Gail, N625, N633
Delco, 230(illus.)
Delights Fruitastic fruit bars and cookies, 205
de Lisser, Eleena, N629, N630, N637
Dell Computer, 172, 529
Del-Monte, 174, 264, 306
Delphi, 110, 273
Delta Airlines, 93, 93(illus.), 478, 536, 547
Deluxe Corp., 557, 558
Del Webb Development Co., 42
DeNitto, Emily, N630, N633
Denny's restaurants, 278, 487–488, 503(illus.), 570–571
Departures magazine, 490
DeRose, Louis J., N628
Deshpande, Rohit, N627, N638
Devil's Food Cookie Cakes, 205
DeWalt power tools, 202, 217
DeWolf, Rose, N630
Dexus Laboratories, 229(table)
DHL, 159, 381
DIALOG, 108, 109(table), 110
Diet Coke soft drink, 466
Diet Pepsi soft drink, 246, 247, 549
Digital Equipment, 172
Dillard's, 345, 354(table)
Dillon, Paul, N636
Dillon, Thomas, N634
Dior, Christian, 294
DiPilli, Liz, 120
Direct Tire Sales, 285
Discount Tire, 312, 389
Discovery cable channel, 176
Discovery Zone, 560
Disklavier piano, 511
Disney cable channel, 365
Disneyland, 250(table), 365
Disney-MGM Studios Theme Park, 365
The Disney Store, 349, 350(illus.)
Disney University, 365
Disney World, 43, 250(table), 397
Distilled Spirits Council, 413
Divita, Sal, N639
Dobbs International, 372
Docker's casual wear, 570
Dodge automobiles, 128, 230, 257
Dolan, Robert J., N623, N637

Dole, 322
Dole, Bob, 49
Domino's Pizza, 99, 191, 557
Donahue television show, 183, 236
Donaton, Scott, N629
Donkey Kong Country II videogame, 465
Donnelley Marketing Information Services, 186
Donnelly, James H., Jr., N631, N637
Doritos, 213, 249–250, 549
DOS computer operating system, 20, 21, 259
007 lipstick, 398
Dougherty, Janice, 541
Dougherty, Jim, 541
Dow Chemical, 602
Dow Corning, 38
Dow Jones News Retrieval, 108, 109(table)
Dremel power tools, 216, 216(illus.)
Dreyer's, 147
Driben, Louise I., N631
Driver's Mart, 320
Dr Pepper soft drink, 240(table), 255, 259, 355
Drucker, Peter F., N629
DuBrin, Andrew J., N639
Dun & Bradstreet, 169, 286
Duncan Hines, 523
Dunn, S. Watson, N635
Du Pont (E.I. du Pont de Nemours & Co.), 80(table), 173–174, 396
Dustbuster, 201
Dyer, Jeffrey H., N634

Eagle automobiles, 128, 129, 320, 404
Eagle Snacks Inc., 542–543
Eagle tires, 389
Eastern Oregon Correctional Institute, 236
Easter Seal Society, 69
Eastman Kodak, 69, 250(table), 255(table), 258, 260, 432, 527, 528(illus.)
Easy Ball track ball, 13
Econolink computerized order entry system, 340
Eddie Bauer, 89, 229–230
Edelman, Susan, N634
Edwards, Anthony, 21
Egan, Mary Ellen, N625
Egghead software, 21, 354(table)
Egg McMuffin sandwich, 79
E.I. du Pont de Nemours & Co., 80(table), 173–174, 396
Eiben, Therese, N627
Eisner, Michael, 366
El-Ansary, Adel I., N632
Electronics Boutique, 299–300
Elfa wire drawers and shelves, 365
Eli Lilly and Co., 75–76, 328, 336, 341
Elizabeth Arden cosmetics, 75
Elk Mountain beer, 543
El Pollo Loco, 570
Elsenstodt, Gale, N627
Embassy Suites, 422
Emerson Electric Company, 154–155
EMF Industries, 223

Subject Index